C++ Primer

Third Edition

Stanley B. Lippman
Josée Lajoie

ADDISON–WESLEY

An Imprint of Addison Wesley Longman, Inc.
Reading, Massachusetts • Harlow, England • Menlo Park, California
Berkeley, California • Don Mills, Ontario • Sydney
Bonn • Amsterdam • Tokyo • Mexico City

The publisher offers discounts on this book when ordered in quantity for special sales. For more information please contact:

Corporate, Government, and Special Sales
Addison Wesley Longman, Inc.
One Jacob Way
Reading, Massachusetts 01867

Library of Congress Cataloging-in-Publication Data

Lippman, Stanley B.
    C++ Primer / Stanley B. Lippman, Josée Lajoie. — 3rd ed.
       p. cm.
    Includes bibliographical references and index.
    ISBN 0-201-82470-1
    1. C++ (Computer program language) I. Lajoie, Josée. II. Title.
QA76.73.C15L57 1998
005. 13'3—dc21   98–9464
                                                  CIP

Cover photograph © 1997 Barbara Hricko Wait

Text printed on recycled and acid-free paper.

ISBN 0201824701

4 5 6 7 8 9   CRS 02 01 00 99

4th Printing November 1999

To Beth,
who makes this,
and all things,
possible

—

To Daniel and Anna,
who contain
virtually
all possibilities

– SBL

To Mark and Mom,
for their
unconditional love and support.

– JL

Contents

Preface

Quite a few changes have occurred between the second and third editions of *C++ Primer*. Most notably, C++ has undergone international standardization, which has not only added new features to the language, such as exception handling, run-time type identification, namespaces, a built-in Boolean data type, and a new cast notation, but has also extensively modified and extended existing features, such as templates, the class mechanism in support of both object-oriented and object-based programming, nested types, and overload function resolution. Perhaps of even more significance, an extensive library is now part of Standard C++, including what was previously referred to as the Standard Template Library, or STL. A new string type, a set of sequence and associative container types — such as vector, list, map, and set — and an extensible collection of generic algorithms to operate on those types are all features of this new standard library. There's not only quite a lot of new material to cover but also new ways to think about how we program in C++. In short, not only has C++ been, in effect, newly invented, but so has the *C++ Primer* for this, its third edition.

Not only has the treatment of the language changed fundamentally in this third edition, but so has the authorship: in the first place, we've doubled ourselves! Moreover, we've internationalized in the process, although we're firmly rooted in the North American continent: Stan is American; Josée is Canadian. Finally, the twin authorship reflects the twin primary activities of the C++ community: Stan is currently involved in the efficient workplace application of C++ at Walt Disney Feature Animation for 3D computer graphics and animation, while Josée is involved in the definition and implementation of C++, both as chair of the Core Language subcommittee of the standards effort and as a member of the C++ compiler team at the IBM Canada Laboratory.

Stan was one of the original members of the Bell Laboratories team working with Bjarne Stroustrup, the inventor of C++, and has been involved with C++ since 1984. Stan worked on the various implementations of cfront, the original C++ implementation, from Release 1.1 in 1986 through Release 3.0, leading the development team for the 2.1 and 3.0 releases. After that, he worked under Stroustrup on what was known as the Foundation Research Project on the Object Model component of a programming development environment.

Josée has been a member of the C++ compiler team at the IBM Canada Laboratory for eight years. She has been a member of the Standards committee since 1990. She was vice-chair of the committee for three years and has been the chair of the Core Language subcommittee for four years.

C++ Primer, Third Edition, represents an extensive revision of the text to reflect not only the changes and extensions to the language but also changes to the authors' insights and experience.

Structure of This Book

C++ Primer provides a comprehensive introduction to the International Standard on C++. It is a primer in the sense that it provides a consciously tutorial approach to describing the C++ language. (It is *not* a primer in the sense of providing a simplistic or "gentle" description of the language.) Programming aspects of the language, such as exception handling, the container types, object-oriented programming, and so on, are presented in the context of solving a particular problem or programming task. Language rules, such as the resolution of an overloaded function call or the type conversions supported under object-oriented programming, are given extensive treatment that may initially seem out of place in a primer. We believe that the coverage is necessary to a practical understanding of the language, and we view the material as something one goes back to rather than digests at one sitting. If you find it initially overwhelming or simply too dry, put this material aside until later — we identify such sections with the following convention: ◗

Knowledge of the C language is not assumed, although familiarity with some modern, block structured language will make the going easier. The book is intended as a first book on C++; it is not intended as a first book on programming! To be sure, we all start with a common vocabulary; however, the initial chapters cover some basic concepts, such as looping statements and variables, that some readers might find too introductory. Not to worry: the depth of coverage picks up quickly.

Much of the power of C++ comes from its support for new ways of programming and thinking about programming problems. Learning to use C++ effectively, therefore, requires more than simply learning a new set of syntax and semantics. To facilitate this larger learning, the book is organized around a series of extended examples. These examples are used both to introduce the details of various language features and to motivate them. When we learn language features in the context of a full example, it becomes clear why such features are useful, providing a sense of when and how we would use them for real-world problem solving. Additionally, this focus on examples allows early use of concepts that will be explained more fully as the reader's knowledge base is built up. Early examples contain simple uses of fundamental C++ concepts, giving a flavor for the kinds of programming one can do in C++ without requiring complete understanding of the details of design and implementation.

Chapters 1 and 2 form a self-contained introduction and overview to the entire C++ language. Part I is intended to get us up to speed on the concepts and language facilities supported by C++ — and the fundamentals on writing and executing a program. Upon finishing this part of the text, you should have a feel for the language support C++ provides *and a sense of not really understanding it at all*. That's ok: that's what the rest of the text is for!

Chapter 1 introduces us to the basic elements of the language: the built-in data types, variables, expressions, statements, and functions. It looks at a minimum legal C++ program, briefly discusses the process of compiling our programs, walks through what is spoken of as the *preprocessor*, and takes a first look at support for input and output. It presents a number of simple but complete C++ programs that the reader is encouraged to compile and execute. Chapter 2 introduces the support C++ provides for object-based and object-oriented programming through the class mechanism, illustrating both through the evolution of an array abstraction. In addition, it briefly introduces templates, namespaces, exception handling, and the standard library support for general container types and generic programming. This chapter is rather fast-paced, and some readers may find it somewhat overwhelming. If that is the case, we suggest you skim through it and return to it later.

Fundamental to C++ are the various facilities that allow the user to extend the language itself by defining new data types that then can be used with the flexibility and simplicity of the built-in data types. The first step to mastery is to understand the base language itself. Chapters 3 through 6 (Part II) introduce the language at this level.

Chapter 3 introduces the built-in and compound data types predefined by the language together with the string, complex, and vector class data types provided by the C++ standard library. These types form the basic building blocks of all our programs. Chapter 4 provides a detailed discussion of the expressions supported by the language, such as the arithmetic, relational, and assignment expressions. Statements, which form the smallest independent unit within a C++ program, are the topic of Chapter 5. The container types provided by the standard C++ library are the focus of Chapter 6. Rather than provide a simple listing of the available operations, we have walked through the implementation of a text query system to illustrate their design and use.

Chapters 7 through 12 (Part III) focus on the procedural-based programming support provided by C++. Chapter 7 introduces the C++ function mechanism. Functions encapsulate a set of operations that generally form a single task, such as print(). (The empty parentheses following a name indicate that it represents a function.) The notions of program scope and lifetime of variables, together with a discussion of the namespace facility, are the topics of Chapter 8. Chapter 9 extends the discussion of functions introduced in Chapter 7 to introduce function overloading. Function overloading allows multiple function instances that provide a common operation (but require differing implementations) to share a common name. For example, we can define a collection of print() functions to output different types of data. Chapter 10 introduces and illustrates the use of function templates. A function template provides a prescription for the automatic generation of a potentially infinite set of function instances varying by type but whose implementations remain invariant.

C++ supports an exception handling facility. An exception represents unexpected program behavior, such as the exhaustion of all available program memory. The portion of the program within which the exception occurs *throws* an exception — that is, makes it available to the rest of the program. Some function within the program must then *catch* the exception and do whatever is necessary. The treatment of exception handling is split across two chapters. In Chapter 11, the basic syntax and use of exception handling are introduced using a simple example of catching and throwing an exception of class type. Because the actual exceptions handled in our programs are usually class objects of an object-oriented class hierarchy, the discussion of how to throw and handle exceptions continues in Chapter 19, after the introduction of object-oriented programming.

Chapter 12 introduces the extensive collection of generic algorithms provided by the standard library and examines how they interact with the container types of Chapter 6 as well as with the built-in array type. The chapter begins by walking through a program design using the generic algorithms. Iterators, introduced in Chapter 6, are discussed further in Chapter 12 because they provide the glue that binds the generic algorithms to the actual containers. The concept of a function object is also introduced and illustrated. Function objects allow us to provide alternative semantics for operators used with the generic algorithms, such as the equality or the less-than operator. The algorithms themselves are detailed, with an illustration of their use, in the Appendix.

Chapters 13 through 16 (Part IV) focus on *object-based* programming — that is, the definition and use of the class facility to create independent abstract data types. By creating new types to describe the problem domain, C++ allows the programmer to write applications with much less concern for the various bookkeeping aspects that make programming tedious. The types fundamental to the application can be implemented once and reused, allowing the programmer to concentrate on the problem rather than the details of the implementation. Facilities for encapsulating the data can dramatically simplify subsequent maintenance and evolution of our applications.

Chapter 13 focuses on the general class mechanism: how to define a class, the concept of *information hiding* — that is, of separating the public class interface from the private implementation — and how to define and manipulate object instances of a class, as well as a discussion of class scope, nested classes, and classes as namespace members.

Chapter 14 details the special support C++ provides for the initialization, destruction, and assignment of class objects using special member functions spoken of, respectively, as a *constructor*, *destructor*, and *copy assignment operator*. We also look at the issue of memberwise initialization and copy, in which one class object is initialized or assigned with another object of its class, and the special *named return value* optimization for the efficient support of memberwise initialization and copy.

Chapter 15 looks at class-specific operator overloading, first presenting general concepts and design considerations and then looking at specific operators, such as the assignment, subscript, call, and class-specific new and delete operators. The notion of a friend to a class with special access permission and why friends are sometimes need-ed is also presented. User-defined conversions are then discussed, including the under-lying concepts and an extensive example of their use. The rules for function overload resolution are also discussed in this chapter in some detail, with extensive illustration by code examples.

Class templates are the topic of Chapter 16. A class template is a prescription for creating a class in which one or more types or values are parameterized. A vector class, for example, may parameterize the type of element it contains. A buffer class may pa-rameterize not only the type of element it holds but also the size of its buffer. In a more sophisticated usage, such as in distributed computing, the IPC interface, addressing interface, and synchronization interface might all be parameterized. This chapter in-cludes discussions on how to define a class template, how to create specific type in-stances of a class template, how to define the members of a class template (member functions, static members, and nested types), and how to organize our programs using class templates. It concludes with an extended class template example.

Object-oriented programming and the facilities in C++ that support it are the topic of Chapters 17, 18, 19, and 20 (Part IV). Chapter 17 introduces the C++ facilities that sup-port the primary elements of object-oriented programming: inheritance and dynamic binding. In object-oriented programming, parent/child relationships (spoken of as type/subtype relationships) are defined between classes that share common behavior. Rather than reimplement shared characteristics, a class inherits the data and operations of its parent class. The child class, or subtype, programs only its differences with its par-ent class. For example, we may define a parent Employee class type and two children: TemporaryEmpl and Manager. These subtypes inherit all the behavior of an Employee. They implement the behavior that is unique to each of their respective types.

A second aspect of inheritance, spoken of as *polymorphism*, is the ability of a parent type to refer to any of the subtypes that are inherited from it. An Employee, for example, can address its own type or that of TemporaryEmpl or Manager. Dynamic binding is the ability to resolve at run-time which operation to execute based on the actual type of the polymorphic object. In C++, this is handled through the virtual function mechanism.

Chapter 17 introduces the basic features of object-oriented programming. It walks through the design and implementation of a Query class hierarchy in support of the text query system we began implementing in Chapter 6.

Chapter 18 introduces the more-complicated inheritance hierarchies that are made possible through multiple and virtual inheritance. It extends the template class example of Chapter 16 into a three-level class template hierarchy using multiple and virtual inheritance.

Chapter 19 introduces the run-time type identification (RTTI) facility. RTTI allows our programs to query a polymorphic class object as to its type during execution of the program. For example, we can ask an Employee object whether it actually addresses a

Manager type. In addition, Chapter 19 revisits exception handling to discuss the standard library exception class hierarchy and illustrate defining and handling our own exception class hierarchies. It also provides an in-depth look at the support of overload function resolution in the presence of inheritance.

Chapter 20 illustrates in detail how to use the C++ *iostream* input/output library. It provides explanation and examples of the general input and output of data, of defining class-specific instances of the input and output operators, of how to recognize and set condition states, and of how to format data. The iostream library is a class hierarchy implemented using both virtual and multiple inheritance.

The *C++ Primer* concludes with an Appendix that provides a discussion and program example of each generic algorithm in alphabetical order for easy reference.

Finally, whenever one writes a book, what one chooses to leave out is often as important as what one covers. Certain aspects of the language — such as a detailed discussion of how constructors work, under what conditions internal temporary objects are created by the compiler, or general concerns about efficiency — do not fit well into a tutorial introduction to the language, although they are of general importance to programming real-world applications. Prior to embarking on a third edition of *C++ Primer*, Stan wrote *Inside the C++ Object Model* (see [LIPPMAN96a] in the Bibliography at the end of this Preface) to cover much of this companion material. Often, the text refers to a discussion within the Object Model when readers may wish to have the more detailed explanation, particularly for the treatment of object-based and object-oriented programming.

Certain portions of the C++ standard library have been intentionally left out, such as the support for locales and the numerical library. The C++ standard library is very extensive, and presenting all its aspects is beyond the scope of this primer. Some of the books in the Bibliography discuss the library in more detail (see [MUSSER96] and [STROUSTRUP97]). We believe that many books on various aspects of the C++ standard library will follow the publication of this book.

Changes to the Third Edition

The changes to the third edition fall into four general categories:

1. Coverage of new features added to the language: exception handling, runtime type identification, namespaces, the built-in bool type, and new-style cast notation.

2. Coverage of the new C++ standard library, including the complex and string types, auto_ptr and pair types, the sequence and associative container types (primarily the list, vector, map, and set containers), and generic algorithms.

3. Adjustments in the existing text to reflect refinements, changes, and extensions to existing language features in Standard C++. An example of a refinement is

the ability to forward declare a nested type, previously disallowed by the language. An example of a language change is the ability of a derived class instance of a virtual function to return a type publicly derived from the return type of the base class instance. This change supports a form of class operation spoken of as a *clone* or *factory* method (a `clone()` virtual function is illustrated in Section 17.5.7). An example of an extension to an existing feature is the ability to explicitly specify one or more of the template arguments to a function template. (Actually, templates have been greatly extended, almost to the point of being a new feature!)

4. Improvements in the treatment and organization of a majority of the advanced language features — in particular, templates, classes, and the treatment of object-oriented programming. A side effect of Stan having moved from the relatively small C++ provider community into the general C++ user community is, he believes, a deeper insight into the problems otherwise intelligent programmers have in using the C++ language intelligently. Accordingly, in this third edition, we've shifted the focus in many cases to better illustrate the concepts underlying a feature and how best to use it, pointing out potential pitfalls to avoid when appropriate.

The Future of C++

At the time of the publication of this book, the ISO/ANSI C++ Standards committee has completed its technical work for the first International Standard on C++. The Standard will be published by ISO in the summer of 1998.

C++ implementations supporting Standard C++ will be available soon after the publication of the Standard. With the publication of the Standard, the evolution of the C++ language will stabilize. This stability will allow for the development of sophisticated libraries, written in Standard C++, to address industry-specific problems. Thus, the major growth in the C++ world is expected to be in the area of libraries.

Once a Standard is published, the Standards committee nonetheless continues its work, albeit at a slower pace, to address the requests for interpretation provided by the users of the Standard. This will lead to minor clarifications and corrections to the C++ Standard. If need be, an International Standard is revised every five years to take into account the changes in the technology and in the needs of the industry.

What will be done five years after the publication of the C++ Standard is still unknown. It is possible that new library components that are in wide use in the industry will be added to the set of components of the C++ standard library. But for now, with the work of the C++ Standards committee complete, the fate of C++ rests solely in the hands of its users.

Acknowledgments

Special thanks, as always, go to Bjarne Stroustrup both for the wonderful language he has given us and for the consideration he has shown us throughout the years. Special thanks also go to the members of the C++ Standards committee for their dedication and hard work (often freely donated) and for the important contribution they have made with Standard C++.

The following individuals provided many helpful comments on various drafts of the manuscript: Paul Abrahams, Michael Ball, Stephen Edwards, Cay Horstmann, Brian Kernighan, Tom Lyons, Robert Murray, Ed Scheibel, Roy Turner, and Jon Wada. We'd like to particularly thank Michael Ball for his thoughtful comments and encouragement. We are especially grateful to Clovis Tondo and Bruce Leung for their in-depth review of the text.

Stan would like to extend a special warm thanks to Shyh-Chyuan Huang and Jinko Gotoh for their help and support on Firebird, to Jon Wada, and, of course, to Josée.

Josée would like to thank Gabby Silberman, Karen Bennet, and the team at the Centre for Advanced Studies for their support while writing this book. And a big thank you goes to Stan for taking her along on this great adventure.

Finally, we'd both like to thank the wonderful editorial staff for their hard work and vast patience: Debbie Lafferty, who has been with the Primer, gosh, since its very beginning; Mike Hendrickson; and John Fuller. The Big Purple Company did a wonderful job of typesetting. The illustration in Section 6.1 is by Elena Driskill. Many thanks to Elena for allowing us to reprint it.

Acknowledgments to the Second Edition

This book is the result of many invisible hands helping to keep its author on course. My most heartfelt thanks go to Barbara Moo. Her encouragement, advice, and close reading of innumerable drafts of the manuscript have been invaluable. Special thanks go to Bjarne Stroustrup for his continued help and encouragement, and for the wonderful language he has given us; to Stephen Dewhurst, who provided much early support as I was first learning C++; and to Nancy Wilkinson, another swashbuckling cfront coder and supplier of Gummi Bears.

Dag Brück, Martin Carroll, William Hopkins, Brian Kernighan, Andrew Koenig, Alexis Layton, and Barbara Moo provided especially detailed and perceptive comments. Their reviews have improved this book considerably. Andy Baily, Phil Brown, James Coplien, Elizabeth Flanagan, David Jordan, Don Kretsch, Craig Rubin, Jonathan Shopiro, Judy Ward, Nancy Wilkinson, and Clay Wilson reviewed various drafts of the manuscript and provided many helpful comments. David Prosser clarified many ANSI C questions. Jerry Schwarz, who implemented the iostream package, provided the original documentation on which Appendix A is based [now Chapter 20 in the third edition!]. His detailed and thoughtful review of that appendix is much appreciated. Grateful thanks go to the other members of the Release 3.0 development team: Laura Eaves, George Logothetis, Judy Ward, and Nancy Wilkinson.

The following provided reviews of the manuscript for Addison-Wesley: James Adcock, Steven Bellovin, Jon Forrest, Maurice Herlihy, Norman Kerth, Darrell Long, Victor Milenkovic, and Justin Smith.

The following have pointed out errors in various printings of the first edition: David Beckedorff, Dag Brück, John Eldridge, Jim Humelsine, Dave Jordan, Ami Kleinman, Andrew Koenig, Tim O'Konski, Clovis Tondo, and Steve Vinoski.

I am deeply appreciative of Brian Kernighan and Andrew Koenig for making available a number of typesetting tools.

Bibliography

The following texts either represent material that influenced the writing of this book or else represent significant material on C++ that is recommended.

[BOOCH94] Booch, Grady, *Object-Oriented Analysis and Design*, Benjamin/Cummings, Redwood City, CA (1994) ISBN 0-8053-5340-2.

[GAMMA95] Gamma, Erich, Richard Helm, Ralph Johnson, and John Vlissides, *Design Patterns*, Addison Wesley Longman, Inc., Reading, MA (1995) ISBN 0-201-63361-2.

[GHEZZI97] Ghezzi, Carlo, and Mehdi Jazayeri, *Programming Language Concepts, 3rd Edition*, John Wiley and Sons, New York, NY (1997) ISBN 0-471-10426-4.

[HARBISON88] Samuel P. Harbison and Guy L. Steele, Jr, *C: A Reference Manual, 3rd Edition*, Prentice-Hall, Englewood Cliffs, NJ (1988) ISBN 0-13-110933-2.

[ISO-C++97] Draft Proposed International Standard for Information Systems — Programming Language C++ - Final Draft (FDIS) 14882.

[KERNIGHAN88] Kernighan, Brian W., and Dennis M. Ritchie, *The C Programming Language*, Prentice-Hall, Englewood Cliffs, NJ (1988) ISBN 0-13-110362-8.

[KOENIG97] Koenig, Andrew, and Barbara Moo, *Ruminations on C++*, Addison Wesley Longman, Inc., Reading, MA (1997) ISBN 0-201-42339-1.

[LIPPMAN91] Lippman, Stanley, *C++ Primer, 2nd Edition*, Addison Wesley Longman, Inc., Reading, MA (1991) ISBN 0-201-54848-8.

[LIPPMAN96a] Lippman, Stanley, *Inside the C++ Object Model*, Addison Wesley Longman, Inc., Reading, MA (1996) ISBN 0-201-83454-5.

[LIPPMAN96b] Lippman, Stanley, Editor, *C++ Gems*, a SIGS Books imprint, Cambridge University Press, Cambridge, England (1996) ISBN 0-13570581-9.

[MEYERS98] Meyers, Scott, *Effective C++, 2nd Edition*, Addison Wesley Longman, Inc., Reading, MA (1998) ISBN 0-201-92488-9.

[MEYERS96] Meyers, Scott, *More Effective C++*, Addison Wesley Longman, Inc., Reading, MA (1996) ISBN 0-201-63371-X.

[MURRAY93] Murray, Robert B., *C++ Strategies and Tactics*, Addison Wesley Longman, Inc., Reading, MA (1993) ISBN 0-201-56382-7.

[MUSSER96] Musser, David R., and Atul Saini, *STL Tutorial and Reference Guide*, Addison Wesley Longman, Inc., Reading, MA (1996) ISBN 0-201-63398-1.

[NACKMAN94] Barton, John J., and Lee R. Nackman, *Scientific and Engineering C++, An Introduction with Advanced Techniques and Examples*, Addison Wesley Longman, Inc., Reading, MA (1994) ISBN 0-201-53393-6.

[NEIDER93] Neider, Jackie, Tom Davis, and Mason Woo, *OpenGL Programming Guide*, Addison Wesley, Inc., Reading, MA (1993) ISBN 0-201-63274-8.

[PERSON68] Person, Russell V., *Essentials of Mathematics, 2nd Edition*, John Wiley & Sons, Inc., New York, NY (1968) ISBN 0-132-84191-6.

[PLAUGER92] Plauger, P.J., *The Standard C Library*, Prentice-Hall, Englewood Cliffs, NJ (1992) ISBN 0-13-131509-9.

[SEDGEWICK88] Sedgewick, Robert, *Algorithms, 2nd Edition*, Addison Wesley Longman, Inc., Reading, MA (1988) ISBN 0-201-06673-4.

[SHAMPINE97] Shampine, L.F., R.C. Allen, Jr., and S. Pruess, *Fundamentals of Numerical Computing*, John Wiley & Sons, Inc., New York, NY (1997) ISBN 0-471-16363-5.

[STROUSTRUP94] Stroustrup, Bjarne, *The Design and Evolution of C++*, Addison Wesley Longman, Inc., Reading, MA (1994) ISBN 0-201-54330-3.

[STROUSTRUP97] Stroustrup, Bjarne, *The C++ Programming Language, 3rd Edition*, Addison Wesley Longman, Inc., Reading, MA (1997) ISBN 0-201-88954-4.

[UPSTILL90] Upstill, Steve, *The RenderMan Companion*, Addison Wesley Longman, Inc., Reading, MA (1990) ISBN 0-201-50868-0.

[WERNECKE94] Wernecke, Josie, *The Inventor Mentor*, Addison Wesley Longman, Inc., Reading, MA (1994) ISBN 0-201-62495-8.

[YOUNG95] Young, Douglas A., *Object-Oriented Programming with C++ and OSF/ Motif, 2nd Edition*, Prentice-Hall, Englewood Cliffs, NJ (1995) ISBN 0-132-09255-7.

Part I

C++, *An Overview*

There are two primary aspects to the programs we write

1. A collection of *algorithms* (that is, the programmed instructions to solve a particular task)
2. A collection of *data* against which the algorithms are run to provide each unique solution

These two primary program aspects, algorithms and data, have remained invariant throughout the short history of computing. What has evolved is the relationship between them. This relationship is spoken of as a *programming paradigm*.

In the procedural programming paradigm, a problem is directly modeled by a set of algorithms. A check-out/check-in system for loan materials of a public library, such as books, videos, and so on, is represented as a series of procedures, the two central procedures being the checking-out and checking-in of library materials. The data is stored separately, accessed either at a global location or by being passed into the procedures. Three prominent procedural languages are FORTRAN, C, and Pascal. C++ also supports procedural programming. Individual procedures, such as check_in(), check_out(), overdue(), fine(), and so on, are referred to as functions. Part III, Procedural-Based Programming, focuses on the support C++ provides for the procedural programming paradigm, with an emphasis on functions, function templates, and generic algorithms.

In the 1970s, the focus of program design shifted from the procedural paradigm to that of *abstract data types* (now generally referred to as *object-based* programming). In this paradigm, a problem is modeled by a set of data abstractions. In C++ we refer to these abstractions as *classes*. Our library check-out system, for example, under this paradigm is represented as the interaction between object instances of classes such as Book, Borrower, DueDate (an aspect of Time), and the inevitable Fine (an aspect of Money), representing the library abstractions. The algorithms associated with each class are referred to as the class's *public interface*. The data is privately stored within each object; access of the data is hidden from the general program. Three programming languages that support the abstract data type paradigm are CLU, Ada, and Mod-

1

ula-2. Part IV, Object-Based Programming, illustrates and discusses the support C++ provides for the abstract data type programming paradigm.

Object-oriented programming extends abstract data types through the mechanisms of *inheritance* (a "reuse" of an existing implementation) and *dynamic binding* (a reuse of an existing public interface). Special type/subtype relationships between previously independent types are now provided. A book, videotape, recording, and children's puppet are each *a kind of* library material, although each has its own check-out and check-in policy. The shared public interface and private data are placed in an abstract LibraryMaterial class. Each specific library material class *inherits* the shared behavior from the LibraryMaterial abstract class and need provide only the algorithms and data that support its behavior. Three prominent languages supporting the object-oriented paradigm are Simula, Smalltalk, and Java. Part V, Object-Oriented Programming, focuses on the support C++ provides for the object-oriented programming paradigm.

C++ is a multiparadigm language. Although we think of it primarily as an object-oriented language, it also provides support for procedural and object-based programming. The benefit is that we are able to provide a solution best suited to the problem — in practice, no one paradigm represents a best solution to every problem. The drawback is that it makes for a larger and more complicated language.

In Part I, we present a quick tour of the entire C++ language. One reason for this is to provide a first introduction to the language features so that we can more freely reference aspects of the language before we fully treat them. For example, we don't look at classes in detail until Chapter 13, but if we waited until then to mention classes we would end up presenting a great many unrepresentative and largely irrelevant program examples.

A second reason for providing a breadth-first tour of the language is aesthetic. Unless you are exposed to the beauty and complexity of a Beethoven sonata or the exhilaration of a Scott Joplin rag, it is easy to become alternately impatient and bored with the apparent irrelevant detail of sharps, flats, octaves, and chords; but until those details are mastered, making music remains largely beyond our means. Much the same holds true with programming. Stepping through the maze of operator precedence or rules governing the standard arithmetic conversions is a necessary but necessarily tedious foundation to mastering programming in C++.

Chapter 1 provides a first introduction to the basic elements of the language: the built-in data types, variables, expressions, statements, and functions. It looks at a minimum legal C++ program, discusses the process of compiling our programs, briefly walks through the preprocessor, and takes a first look at support for input and output. It presents a number of simple but complete C++ programs that the reader is encouraged to compile and execute.

In Chapter 2, we walk through a procedural program, an object-based program, and then an object-oriented program implementation of an array — that is, a numbered collection of elements of the same type. We then compare our array abstraction with the C++ standard library vector class and take a first look at the standard library generic algorithms. Along the way, we motivate and take a first peek at C++'s support for exception handling, templates, and namespaces. In effect, the entire language is introduced, although many of the details are deferred until later in the text.

Some readers may find portions of Chapter 2 rough going. Material is presented without the full explanation normally expected of a primer (the explanation is provided in subsequent chapters). If you should find yourself feeling overwhelmed or impatient at the level of detail, we recommend that you skim through or skip that portion, returning to it later when the material is more familiar. In Chapter 3, we begin the more traditional narrative pace, and the reader uncomfortable with Chapter 2 is recommended to start there.

1

Getting Started

This chapter introduces the basic elements of the language: the built-in data types, the definition of named objects, expressions, and statements, and the definition and use of named functions. It looks at a minimum legal C++ program, briefly discusses the process of compiling our programs, walks through the preprocessor, and takes a first look at support for input and output. It presents a number of simple but complete C++ programs.

1.1 Problem Solving

Programs often are written in response to some problem or task to be solved. Let's look at an example. A bookstore enters into a file the title and publisher of each book it sells. The information is entered in the order the books are sold. Every two weeks the owner computes by hand the number of copies of each title sold and the number sold from each publisher. The list is alphabetized by publisher and used for purposes of reordering. We have been asked to supply a program to do this work.

One method of solving a big problem is to break it down into a number of smaller problems. Ideally, these smaller problems are easier to solve and, taken together, solve our big problem. If our newly divided smaller problems are still too big to solve, we in turn break these problems into still smaller problems, continuing the process until, hopefully, we have a solution to each subdivided problem. This strategy is spoken of, variously, as *divide and conquer* and *stepwise refinement*. Our bookstore problem divides nicely into four subproblems, or tasks:

1. Read the sales file.
2. Count the sales by title and by publisher.
3. Sort the titles by publisher.
4. Write the results.

Items 1, 2, and 4 represent problems we know how to solve; they do not need to be broken down further. Item 3, however, is still a little more than we know how to do. So we reapply our method to this item:

3a. Sort the sales by publisher.

3b. Within each publisher, sort the sales by title.

3c. Compare adjacent titles within each publisher group. For each matching pair, increment an occurrence count of the first and delete the second.

Items 3a, 3b, and 3c also now represent problems that we know how to solve. Because we can solve all the subproblems that we have identified, we have in effect solved the original, bigger problem. Moreover, we see that the original order of tasks was incorrect. The sequence of actions required is the following:

1. Read the sales file.

2. Sort the sales file — first by publisher and then by title within publisher.

3. Compact duplicate titles.

4. Write the results into a new file.

The resulting sequence of actions is referred to as an *algorithm*. The next step is to translate our algorithm into a particular programming language — in this case, C++.

1.2 The C++ Program

In C++, an action is referred to as an *expression*. An expression terminated by a semicolon is referred to as a *statement*. The smallest independent unit in a C++ program is a statement. In a natural language, an analogous construct is the sentence. The following, for example, are statements in C++:

```
int book_count = 0;
book_count = books_on_shelf + books_on_order;
cout << "the value of book_count: " << book_count;
```

The first statement is a *declaration* statement. book_count is variously called an *identifier*, a *symbolic variable* (or *variable* for short), or an *object*. It defines an area of computer memory associated with the name book_count that holds integer values. 0 is a *literal constant*. book_count is *initialized* to a first value of zero.

The second statement is an *assignment* statement. It places in the area of computer memory associated with book_count the result of adding together books_on_shelf and books_on_order. Presumably, these are also integer variables defined and assigned values in earlier portions of the program.

The third statement is an *output* statement. cout is the output destination associated with the user's terminal. << is the output operator. The statement writes to cout — that is, the user's terminal — first the *string literal* enclosed within quotation marks and then the value stored in the area of computer memory associated with the name book_count. The output of this statement is

```
the value of book_count: 11273
```

presuming that the value of book_count at this point is 11,273.

Statements are logically grouped into named units referred to as *functions*. For example, all the statements necessary to read the sales file are organized into a function called readIn(). Similarly, we organize sort(), compact(), and print() functions.

In C++, every program must contain a function called main(), supplied by the programmer, before the program can be run. Here is how main() might be defined for the preceding algorithm:

```
int main()
{
    readIn();
    sort();
    compact();
    print();
    return 0;
}
```

A C++ program begins execution with the first statement of main(). In this case, the program begins by executing the function readIn(). Program execution continues by sequentially executing the statements within main(). The program terminates normally following execution of the last statement in main().

A function consists of four parts: a return type, the function name, a parameter list, and the function body. The first three parts are collectively referred to as the *function prototype*.

The parameter list, enclosed within parentheses, contains a comma-separated list of zero or more parameters. The function body is enclosed within a pair of curly braces. It consists of a sequence of program statements.

In this instance, the body of main() *invokes* the functions readIn(), sort(), compact(), and print(). When they have completed, the statement

```
return 0;
```

is executed. return, a predefined C++ statement, provides a method of terminating the execution of a function. When supplied with a value such as 0, that value becomes the *return value* of the function. In this case, a return value of 0 indicates the successful completion of main(). (In Standard C++, main() returns a value of 0 by default if an explicit return statement is not provided.)

Let's turn now to how the program is made ready for execution. First, we must provide definitions of readIn(), sort(), compact(), and print(). At this point, the following dummy instances are good enough:

```
void readIn()  { cout << "readIn()\n";  }
void sort()    { cout << "sort()\n";    }
```

```
void compact() { cout << "compact()\n";  }
void print()   { cout << "print()\n";     }
```

void is used to specify a function that does not provide a return value. As defined, each function will simply announce its presence on the user's terminal when invoked by main(). Later, we can replace these dummy instances with the actual functions as they are implemented.

This incremental method of building programs provides a useful measure of control over the programming errors we inevitably make. Trying to get a program to work all at once is simply too complicated and confusing.

A program source file's name generally consists of two parts: a file name — for example, bookstore — and a file suffix. The file suffix, by convention, serves to identify the contents of the file. The file

```
bookstore.h
```

by convention is interpreted to be a *header* file within either the C or C++ language. (The standard C++ header files, however, have no suffix — they represent the proverbial exception to the rule.)

The file

```
bookstore.c
```

by convention is interpreted to be a C program text file, whereas, under the UNIX operating system, the file

```
bookstore.C
```

by convention is interpreted to be a C++ program text file. The suffix for C++ program files varies among the different implementations of C++, particularly since, under DOS, the lowercase and uppercase C cannot be distinguished. Other suffix conventions to distinguish C++ program text files include

```
bookstore.cxx
bookstore.cpp
```

Similarly, the suffix for header files also varies among the different C++ implementations (this is one of the reasons that the standard C++ header files do not specify a file suffix). Check with your compiler's User's Guide for the appropriate suffix for your platform.

Using some text editor, enter the following complete program into a C++ source file.

```
#include <iostream>
using namespace std;

void read()    { cout << "read()\n";     }
void sort()    { cout << "sort()\n";     }
void compact() { cout << "compact()\n"; }
void write()   { cout << "write()\n";    }
```

```
int main() {
    read();
    sort();
    compact();
    write();

    return 0;
}
```

iostream is the iostream library standard header file (note that it has no suffix). It contains information about cout that is necessary to our program. #include is a *preprocessor directive*. It causes the contents of iostream to be read into our text file. (Section 1.3 discusses preprocessor directives.)

The names defined in the C++ standard library, such as the name cout, cannot be used in our program unless we follow the

```
#include <iostream>
```

preprocessor directive with the statement

```
using namespace std;
```

This statement is called a *using directive*. The names in the C++ standard library are declared in a namespace called namespace std and are not visible in our program text file unless we explicitly make them visible. The using directive tells the compiler to use the library names declared in namespace std. (We have more to say on namespaces and using directives in Sections 2.7 and 8.5.)[1]

Once the program has been entered into a file, say, prog1.C, the next step is to compile it. This is done as follows under the UNIX operating system ($ represents the system prompt):

```
$ CC prog1.C
```

The command name used to invoke the C++ compiler varies across implementations. (Under Windows, the command is usually invoked through clicking on a menu item.) CC is the command name for the C++ compiler we use on our UNIX workstations. Check the reference manual or ask your system administrator for the C++ command name on your system.

Part of the compiler's job is to analyze the program text for correctness. A compiler cannot detect whether the meaning of a program is correct, but it can detect errors in the *form* of the program. Two common forms of program error are the following:

1. Syntax errors. The programmer has made a "grammatical" error in the C++ language. For example:

---

1.   At the time of this writing, not all C++ implementations support namespaces. If your implementation does not support namespaces, the using directive must be omitted. Because many of the examples in this book were compiled with implementations not supporting namespaces, using directives have been omitted from most code examples.

```
int main ( {    // error: missing ')'
    readln():   // error: illegal character ':'
    sort();
    compact();
    print();

    return 0    // error: missing ';'
}
```

2. Type errors. Each item of data in C++ has an associated type. The value 10, for example, is an integer. The word "hello" surrounded by double quotation marks is a string. If a function expecting an integer argument is given a string, a type error is signaled by the compiler.

An error message contains a line number and a brief description of what the compiler believes we have done wrong. It is a good practice to correct errors in the sequence they are reported. Often a single error can have a cascading effect and cause a compiler to report more errors than actually are present. Once the error has been corrected, the program should be recompiled. This cycle is often referred to as *edit-compile-debug*.

A second part of the compiler's job is to translate formally correct program text. This translation, referred to as *code generation*, typically generates object or assembly instruction text understood by the computer on which the program is run.

The result of a successful compilation is an executable file. When run, our program generates the following output:

```
readln()
sort()
compact()
print()
```

C++ defines a built-in set of primitive data types: integer and floating point numeric types, a character type, and a Boolean type holding a value of either true or false. Each type is associated with a language *keyword*. Each object within our program is associated with a specific type. For example,

```
int    age = 10;
double price = 19.99;
char   delimiter = ' ';
bool   found = false;
```

defines four objects — age, price, delimiter, and found, respectively — of types integer, double precision floating point, character, and Boolean. Each type is provided with a literal constant initial value: the integer 10, the floating point 19.99, the blank character, and the Boolean false.

Type *conversions* take place implicitly between the built-in types. For example, when we assign age, which is of type int, a literal constant value of type double, as in

```
age = 33.333;
```

the value actually assigned to age is the truncated integer value 33. (These *standard conversions*, as well as type conversions in general, are discussed in detail in Section 4.14.)

An extended set of basic data types is provided within the C++ standard library, including, among others, string, complex number, vector, and list. For example:

```
// necessary header file to use a string object
#include <string>
string current_chapter = "Getting Started";

// necessary header to use a vector object
#include <vector>
vector<string> chapter_titles( 20 );
```

current_chapter is a string object initialized with the string literal "Getting Started". chapter_titles is a vector of 20 elements of the string type. The peculiar syntax of

```
vector<string>
```

directs the compiler to create a vector type capable of holding string elements. To define a vector object able to hold 20 integer elements, we would write

```
vector<int> ivec( 20 );
```

(We'll have much more to say about vectors throughout the text.)

Neither a language nor its standard library can in practice provide us with every data type our programming environment requires. Rather, modern languages provide a type definition facility that allows us to introduce new types into the language that can be used more or less as easily as the built-in types. In C++, this facility is the class mechanism. The string, complex, vector, and list standard library types are all classes programmed in C++. So too, in fact, is the iostream library.

The class facility is perhaps the most important component of C++, and in Chapter 2 we provide an extensive tour of the entire class mechanism.

1.2.1   Program Flow of Control

By default, statements are executed in a straight-line sequence. For example, in our earlier program, reproduced below, read() is always executed first, followed by sort(), compact(), and then write().

```
int main()
{
    read();
    sort();
    compact();
    write();

    return 0;
}
```

However, if there have been particularly slow sales, such as zero or one item, it is hardly worth either sorting or compacting, although we still need to write that one entry out or indicate that no sales occurred. We can do this through the conditional *if* statement (this presumes that we've rewritten read() to return the number of entries read):

```cpp
// read() returns the number of entries read
// its return value is of type int
int read() { ... }

// ...

int main()
{
    int count = read();

    // if number of entries read is greater than 1
    // then sort() and compact()

    if ( count > 1 ) {
        sort();
        compact();
    }

    if ( count == 0 )
        cout << "no sales for this month\n";
    else write();

    return 0;
}
```

The first if statement provides conditional execution based on the truth condition of the expression within parentheses. In this revised program, sort() and compact() are invoked only if count is greater than 1. In the second if statement, there are two execution branches. If the condition is true — in this case, if count is equal to 0 — we simply write that no sales occurred; otherwise, whenever count is not equal to 0, we invoke write(). The if statement is discussed in detail in Section 5.3.

A second common form of nonsequential statement execution is the iterative, or *loop*, statement. A loop repeats one or more statements while some condition remains true. For example:

```cpp
int main()
{
    int iterations = 0;
    bool continue_loop = true;
```

```
while ( continue_loop != false )
{
    iterations++;

    cout << "the while loop has executed "
         << iterations << " times\n";

    if ( iterations == 5 )
         continue_loop = false;
}

return 0;
}
```

In this somewhat contrived example, the *while* loop executes five times, until it-erations equals 5 and continue_loop is assigned the value false. The statement

```
iterations++;
```

increments iterations by 1. We'll look at a more realistic example of the while loop in Section 1.5 and look at looping statements in detail in Chapter 5.

1.3   Preprocessor Directives

Header files are made a part of our program by the *preprocessor include directive*. Pre-processor directives are specified by placing a pound sign (#) in the very first column of a line in our program. The program that handles directives is referred to as the *pre-processor* (it is now usually bundled into the compiler itself).

The #include directive reads in the contents of the named file. It takes one of two forms:

```
#include <some_file.h>
#include "my_file.h"
```

If the file name is enclosed by angle brackets (<,>) the file is presumed to be a project or standard header file. The search to find it will examine a predefined set of locations, which can be modified by setting a searchpath environment variable or through a command line option. (The methods of doing this vary significantly across platforms, and we recommend you ask a colleague or consult your compiler's *User's Guide* for further information.) If the file name is enclosed by a pair of quotation marks, the file is presumed to be a user-supplied header file. The search to find it begins in the directory in which the including file is located.

The included file may itself contain a #include directive. Because of nested include files, a header file may sometimes be included multiple times for a single source file. Con-ditional directives guard against the multiple processing of a header file. For example:

```
#ifndef BOOKSTORE_H
#define BOOKSTORE_H
    /* Bookstore.h contents go here */
#endif
```

The conditional directive

```
#ifndef
```

tests whether BOOKSTORE_H has not been defined previously. BOOKSTORE_H is a preprocessor constant. (It is a convention that preprocessor constants are written in all uppercase letters.) If BOOKSTORE_H has not been previously defined, the conditional directive evaluates as true and all the lines following #ifndef until the #endif is found are included and processed. Conversely, if the #ifndef directive evaluates as false, the lines between it and the #endif directive are ignored.

To guarantee that the header file is processed only once, we put the #define directive

```
#define BOOKSTORE_H
```

following the #ifndef. In this way, BOOKSTORE_H is defined the first time that the content of the header file is processed, preventing the #ifndef directive from evaluating as true in further evaluations in the program text file.

This strategy works well provided that no two header files necessary for inclusion test on a preprocessor constant of the same name.

The #ifdef directive is most frequently used to conditionally include program code depending on whether a preprocessor constant is defined. For example:

```
int main()
{
#ifdef DEBUG
    cout << "Beginning execution of main()\n";
#endif

    string word;
    vector< string > text;

    while ( cin >> word )
    {
#ifdef DEBUG
        cout << "word read: " << word << "\n";
#endif
        text.push_back( word );
    }

    // ...
}
```

In this example, if DEBUG is not defined, the program code actually compiled is

```
int main()
{
    string word;
    vector< string > text;

    while ( cin >> word )
    {
            text.push_back( word );
    }

    // ...
}
```

Otherwise, if DEBUG is defined, the program code passed to the compiler is as follows:

```
int main()
{
    cout << "Beginning execution of main()\n";

    string word;
    vector< string > text;

    while ( cin >> word )
    {
       cout << "word read: " << word << "\n";
       text.push_back( word );
    }

    // ...
}
```

We can define a preprocessor constant on the command line as we compile our program using the -D option followed by the name of the preprocessor constant:[2]

```
$ CC -DDEBUG main.C
```

or inside our program using the #define directive.

The preprocessor name __cplusplus (two underscores) is automatically defined when compiling C++, so we can conditionally include code based on whether we are compiling C++. For example:

```
#ifdef __cplusplus
    // ok: we're compiling C++
    // we'll explain extern "C" in Chapter 7!
    extern "C"
#endif
    int min( int, int );
```

---

2. This is true for UNIX systems. Windows programmers should check the compiler's User's Guide.

The name __STDC__ is defined when compiling Standard C. Of course, __cplusplus and __STDC__ are never defined at the same time.

Two other useful predefined names are __LINE__ and __FILE__. __LINE__ holds the current line number of the file being compiled. __FILE__ contains the name of the current file being compiled. They might be used as follows:

```
if ( element_count == 0 )
    cerr << "Error: " << __FILE__
         << " : line " << __LINE__
         << "element_count must be non-zero.\n";
```

Two additional predefined names hold, respectively, the compilation time (__TIME__) and date (__DATE__) of the file currently being compiled. The time format is hh:mm:ss, so that, for example, a file compiled at 17 minutes after eight in the morning would be represented as 08:17:05. If it were compiled on October 31, 1996, which is a Thursday, the date would be represented as

```
Oct  31  1996
```

The values of the __LINE__ and __FILE__ names are updated as, respectively, the line and file being processed change. The other four predefined names, however, remain constant during the compilation. These values cannot be modified.

assert() is a generally useful preprocessor macro provided in the C language Standard Library. We make frequent use of it within the text to assert a necessary precondition for the correct execution of our program. For example, if we need to read in a text file and sort the words, the necessary preconditions are that the file name is supplied to us and that we are able to open the file. To use assert(), we must include its associated header file.

```
#include <assert.h>
```

Here is a simple example of its use:

```
assert( filename != 0 );
```

Our assert() tests the truth condition that filename does not equal 0. This represents our assertion of a necessary precondition for the correct execution of the program code that follows the assertion. If the condition should evaluate as false — that is, filename is equal to 0 — the assertion fails: a diagnostic message is printed and the program terminates.

assert.h is the C name for a C library header file. A C++ program can refer to a C library header file using either its C or its C++ name. The C++ name for this header file is cassert. The C++ name of a C library header file is always the C name prefixed with the letter c and in which the .h file suffix has been dropped (as explained earlier, standard C++ header files do not specify a file suffix because the suffix for header files varies among C++ implementations).

A `#include` preprocessor directive for a C header file does not have the same effect depending on whether the C name or the C++ name is used. The following `#include` preprocessor directive

```
#include <cassert>
```

causes the contents of `cassert` to be read into our text file. But because all C++ library names are declared in namespace `std`, the name `assert()` is not visible in our program text file unless we explicitly make it visible with the following using directive:

```
using namespace std;
```

With a `#include` preprocessor directive that uses the C header file name,

```
#include <assert.h>
```

the name `assert()` can be used in our program text file directly without the need to use the using directive.[3] (Namespaces are used by library vendors to control the global namespace pollution problem caused by their library in the user's program namespace. Section 8.5 discusses this in greater detail.)

1.4   A Word About Comments

Comments serve as an aid to the human readers of our programs; they are a form of engineering etiquette. They may summarize a function's algorithm, identify the purpose of a variable, or clarify an otherwise obscure segment of code. Comments do not increase the size of the executable program. They are stripped from the program by the compiler before code generation.

There are two comment delimiters in C++. The comment pair (/*,*/) is the same comment delimiter used in the C language. The beginning of a comment is indicated by a /*. The compiler will treat everything that falls between the /* and a matching */ as part of the comment. A comment pair can be placed anywhere a tab, space, or newline is permitted and can span multiple lines of a program. For example:

```
/*
 * This is a first look at a C++ class definition.
 * Classes are used both in object-based and
 * object-oriented programming.  An implementation
 * of the Screen class is presented in Chapter 13.
 */
```

---

3. At the time of this writing, not all C++ implementations support the C++ names for C library header files. Because many of the examples in this book were compiled with implementations not supporting the C++ header file names, the examples refer to the C library header files sometimes with the C names and sometimes with the C++ names.

```
class Screen {
    /* This is referred to as the class body */
public:
    void home();    /* move cursor to 0,0 */
    void refresh();/* redraw Screen      */
private:
    /* Classes support "information hiding".    */
    /* Information hiding restricts a program's */
    /* access to the internal representation of */
    /* a class (its data).  This is done through */
    /* use of the "private:" label              */
    int height, width;
};
```

Too many comments intermixed with the program code can obscure the code. Surrounded as it is by comments, for example, the declaration of width and height is very nearly hidden. In general, it is preferable to place a comment block above the text that it is explaining. As with any software documentation, to be effective, comments must be updated as the software evolves. Too often, comments and the code they provide commentary on drift apart over time.

Comment pairs do not nest — that is, one comment pair cannot occur within a second pair. Try compiling the following program on your system. It completely befuddles most compilers.

```
#include <iostream>

/*
 * comment pairs /* */ do not nest.
 * "do not nest" is considered source code,
 * as are both these lines and the next.
 */

int main() {
    cout << "hello, world\n";
}
```

One way to fix the problem of the nested comment pairs is to put a space between the asterisk and the slash:

```
/* * /
```

The asterisk-slash sequence is treated as a comment delimiter only if the two characters are not separated by white space.

The second comment delimiter, indicated by a double slash (//), serves to delimit a single-line comment. Everything on the program line to the right of the delimiter is treated as a comment and ignored by the compiler. For example, here is our Screen class using the two comment delimiters:

```
/*
 * This is a first look at a C++ class definition.
 * Classes are used both in object-based and
 * object-oriented programming.  An implementation
 * of the Screen class is presented in Chapter 13.
 */

class Screen {
    // This is referred to as the class body
public:
    void home();// move cursor to 0,0
    void refresh();// redraw Screen
private:
    /* Classes support "information hiding".    */
    /* Information hiding restricts a program's */
    /* access to the internal representation of */
    /* a class (its data).  This is done through */
    /* use of the "private:" label              */

    // private data goes here ...
};
```

Programs typically contain a mixture of both comment forms. Multiline explanations are generally set off between comment pairs. Half-line and single-line remarks are more often delineated by the double slash.

1.5   A First Look at Input/Output

In C++, input and output is provided by the iostream library, an object-oriented class hierarchy implemented in C++ and provided as part of the standard library.

Input from our terminal, spoken of as *standard input*, is "tied" to the predefined iostream object cin (pronounced "see-in"). Output directed to our terminal, referred to as *standard output*, is tied to the predefined iostream object cout (pronounced "see-out"). A third predefined iostream object, cerr (pronounced "see-err"), referred to as *standard error*, is also "tied" to our terminal. cerr is typically used to generate warning and error messages to users of our programs.

Any program wishing to make use of the iostream library must include its associated system header file:

```
#include <iostream>
```

The output operator (<<) is used to direct a value to standard output or standard error. For example:

```
int v1, v2;
// ...
cout << "The sum of v1 + v2 = ";
cout << v1 + v2;
cout << '\n';
```

The two-character sequence \n represents the newline character. When written, the newline character terminates a line and causes the ensuing output to be directed to the next line. Rather than explicitly write the newline character, we can apply the predefined iostream *manipulator* endl.

A manipulator performs an operation on the iostream rather than simply providing data. endl, for example, inserts a newline character into the output stream and then flushes the output buffer. Rather than write

```
cout << '\n';
```

we write

```
cout << endl;
```

(The predefined iostream manipulators are discussed in Chapter 20.)

Successive occurrences of the output operator can be concatenated. For example:

```
cout << "The sum of v1 + v2 = " << v1 + v2 << endl;
```

Each successive output operator is applied in turn to cout. For readability, the concatenated output statement may span several lines. The following three lines make up a single output statement:

```
cout << "The sum of "
     << v1 << " + "
     << v2 << " = " << v1 + v2 << endl;
```

Similarly, the input operator (>>) is used to read a value from standard input. For example:

```
string file_name;
// ...
cout << "Please enter the file to be opened: ";
cin >> file_name;
```

Successive occurrences of the input operator can also be concatenated. For example:

```
string ifile, ofile;
// ...
cout << "Please enter input and output file names: ";
cin >> ifile >> ofile;
```

How might we read an unknown number of input values? At the end of Section 1.2, we did just that. The code sequence

```
string word;
while ( cin >> word )
        // ...
```

reads one string from standard input with each iteration of the while loop until all the strings are read. The condition

```
( cin >> word )
```

evaluates to false when the end-of-file is reached (how this occurs is explained in Chapter 20). Here is a simple program that uses the code sequence:

```
#include <iostream>
#include <string>

int main()
{
   string word;

   while ( cin >> word )
           cout << "word read is: " << word << '\n';

   cout << "ok: no more words to read: bye!\n";
   return 0;
}
```

The following are the first five words of James Joyce's novel *Finnegans Wake*:

```
riverrun, past Eve and Adam's
```

When these words are entered at the keyboard, the output of the program is as follows:

```
word read is: riverrun,
word read is: past
word read is: Eve
word read is: and
word read is: Adam's
word read is: ok: no more words to read: bye!
```

(In Chapter 6 we'll look at how we can remove the punctuation from the various input strings.)

1.5.1   File Input and Output

The iostream library also supports file input and output. All the operators that can be applied to standard input and output can also be applied to files that are opened for input or output (or both). To open a file for either input or output, in addition to the iostream header file we must include the header file

```
#include <fstream>
```

To open a file for output, we declare an object of type ofstream:

```
ofstream outfile( "name-of-file" );
```

To test whether the file is successfully opened, we can write

```
// evaluates to false if file failed to open
if ( ! outfile )
    cerr << "Sorry! We were unable to open the file!\n";
```

Similarly, to open a file for input, we declare an object of type ifstream:

```
ifstream infile( "name of file" );
if ( ! infile )
    cerr << "Sorry! We were unable to open the file!\n";
```

Here is a small program that reads an input text file, named in_file, and writes each word to an output file, named out_file, separating each word with a space in the output file.

```
#include <iostream>
#include <fstream>
#include <string>
int main()
{
    ofstream outfile( "out_file" );
    ifstream infile( "in_file" );

    if ( ! infile ) {
        cerr << "error: unable to open input file!\n";
        return -1;
    }

    if ( ! outfile ) {
        cerr << "error: unable to open output file!\n";
        return -2;
    }

    string word;
    while ( infile >> word )
            outfile << word << ' ';

    return 0;
}
```

Chapter 20 provides a full discussion of the iostream library, including file input and output. Now that we have a general sense of what the language provides for us, we next look at introducing new types into the language through the use of the class and template facilities.

2

A Tour of C++

The chapter begins with a look at the support C++ provides for an array type — that is, a sequential collection of elements of one type, such as an array of integer values, perhaps representing test scores, or an array of strings, perhaps representing the individual words contained within a text file such as this chapter. We then look at the weaknesses of the built-in array type and improve on it by providing an object-based Array type class and then extend that to an object-oriented hierarchy of specialized Array subtypes. Finally, we compare our Array class type with the C++ standard library vector class and take a first look at the generic algorithms. Along the way, we motivate and take a first peek at C++'s support for exception handling, templates, and namespaces.

2.1 The Built-In Array Data Type

As we've seen in Chapter 1, C++ provides built-in support for primitive arithmetic data types such as integer:

```
// declares an integer object, ival
// initialized to a first value of 1024
int ival = 1024;
```

It also supports double precision and single precision floating point data types:

```
// declares a double precision floating point object, dval
// initialized to a first value of 3.14159
double dval = 3.14159;

// declares a single precision floating point object, fval
// also initialized to a first value of 3.14159
float fval = 3.14159;
```

C++ also supports a Boolean data type as well as a character type to hold individual elements of the character set.

The arithmetic data types provide built-in support for assignment and for the usual arithmetic operations, such as addition, subtraction, multiplication, and division, as well as the relational operations, such as equality, inequality, greater than, less than, and so on. For example:

```
int ival2 = ival + 4096;    // addition
int ival3 = ival2 - ival;   // subtraction

dval = fval * ival; // multiplication
ival = ival3 / 2;   // division

bool result = ival2 == ival3;   // equality
result = ival2 + ival != ival3; // inequality
result = fval + ival2 < dval;   // less-than
result = ival > ival2;          // greater-than
```

In addition, the standard library provides support for a collection of basic class abstractions, such as string and complex number. (Until Section 2.7, we're going to conveniently forget all about the standard library vector class.)

Between the built-in data types and the standard library class types fall the *compound* types — in particular, the pointer and array types. (We'll look at the pointer type in Section 2.2.)

An *array* is an ordered container of elements of a single type. For example, the sequence

```
0 1 1 2 3 5 8 13 21
```

represents the first nine elements of the Fibonacci sequence. (Given the first two elements, each subsequent element is generated by adding together the previous two.)

To define and initialize an array to hold these elements, we write

```
int fibon[ 9 ] = { 0, 1, 1, 2, 3, 5, 8, 13, 21 };
```

The name of the array object is fibon. It is an integer array with a *dimension* of nine elements. The first element is 0, and the last element is 21. We access the elements by *indexing* into the array using the *subscript* operator. For example, to read the first element, we might write

```
int first_elem = fibon[ 1 ]; // not quite right
```

Unfortunately, this is incorrect, although it is not itself a language error.

One unintuitive aspect of array subscripting under C++ is that the element positions begin at 0 and not 1. The element at position 1 is really the second element. Similarly, the element at position 0 is really the first element. To access the last element of an array, we always index the dimension -1 element.

```
fibon[ 0 ]; // first element
fibon[ 1 ]; // second element
...
fibon[ 8 ]; // last element
fibon[ 9 ]; // oops ...
```

The element indexed by 9 is not an element of the array. The nine elements of fibon are indexed at positions 0–8. A common beginner error is to instead index positions 1–9. It's so common, in fact, that it has its own name: the *off-by-one* error.

Typically, we step through the elements of an array using a for loop. For example, the following program initializes an array of ten elements to the values 0 through 9 and then prints them in descending order to standard output:

```
int main()
{
    int ia[ 10 ];
    int index;

    for ( index = 0; index < 10; ++index )
        // ia[0] = 0, ia[1] = 1, and so on
        ia[ index ] = index;

    for ( index = 9; index >= 0; --index )
    cout  << ia[ index ] << " ";

    cout << endl;
}
```

Both loops iterate ten times. The three statements in parentheses following the keyword for do all the control work of the loop. The first statement assigns 0 to index,

```
index = 0;
```

It is executed once before the actual work of the loop begins. The second statement,

```
index < 10;
```

represents the *stopping condition* of the loop. It begins the actual loop sequence. If it evaluates to true, the statement (or statements) associated with the for loop are executed; if it evaluates to false, the loop terminates. In our example, each time that index evaluates to a value less than 10, the statement

```
ia[ index ] = index;
```

is executed. The third statement,

```
++index
```

is a shorthand notation for incrementing an arithmetic object by 1. It is equivalent to

```
index = index + 1;
```

It is executed after the statement associated with the for loop (the assignment of the element subscripted by index with the value of index). Its execution completes one iteration of the for loop. The sequence repeats itself by once again testing the condition. When the condition evaluates to false, the loop terminates. (We look at the for loop in detail in Chapter 5.) The second for loop operates in reverse order in printing the values.

Although C++ provides built-in support for an array type, that support is limited to the mechanics required to read and write individual elements. C++ does not support the *abstraction* of an array; there is no support for the operations one might wish to perform on an array, such as the assignment of one array to another, the comparison of two arrays for equality, or asking an array its size. Given two arrays, we cannot, for example, copy one to another as a unit using the assignment operator:

```
int array0[ 10 ], array1[ 10 ];
...
// error: cannot directly assign one array to another
array0 = array1;
```

If we wish to assign one array to another, we must program that ourselves, copying each element in turn:

```
for ( int index = 0; index < 10; ++index )
    array0[ index ] = array1[ index ];
```

Moreover, the array type has no self-knowledge. As we said, it does not know its size, so we must keep track of that independently of the array itself. This becomes troublesome when we wish to pass arrays as general arguments to functions. In C++, we say that an array, unlike the integer and floating point types, is not a *first-class* citizen of the language. It is inherited from the C language and reflects the separation of data and the algorithms that operate on that data that are characteristic of the procedural paradigm. In the rest of the chapter, we look at different strategies for giving the array the additional status powers of citizenry.

Exercise 2.1

Why do you think the built-in array does not support the assignment of one array with another? What information is required to support this operation?

Exercise 2.2

What operations should a first class array support?

2.2 Dynamic Memory Allocation and Pointers

Before we can move forward to our object-based design, we need to step back into a short digression on C++ program memory allocation. The reason is that we cannot realistically implement our designs (and therefore show realistic C++ code) without first introducing how to acquire and access memory during program execution. That is the purpose of this short section.

Under C++, objects can be allocated either statically — that is, by the compiler as it processes our program source code — or dynamically — that is, by a run-time library invoked during program execution. The primary trade-off between the two methods of memory allocation is efficiency versus flexibility: static memory allocation is considerably more efficient to allocate because it is done prior to program start-up. It is less flexible, however, because it requires that we know prior to the execution of the program the amount and type of memory that we need. We cannot, for example, easily process and store the words of an arbitrary text file using a statically allocated string array. In general, the storage of an unknown number of elements requires the flexibility of dynamic memory allocation.

Until now, all our memory allocation has been static. For example, the definition

```
int ival = 1024;
```

instructs the compiler to allocate sufficient storage to hold any value of type int, associate the name ival with that storage, and then place an initial value of 1024 in that storage. This is all done prior to program execution.

There are two values associated with the object ival: the value it contains — in this case, 1024 — and the address at which that value is stored. In C++, it is possible to access either value. When we write

```
int ival2 = ival + 1;
```

we are accessing the value that ival contains, adding 1 to it, and initializing ival2 with that new value. In our example, ival2 has an initial value of 1025. How do we access and store the memory address?

C++ supports a pointer type to hold the memory address values of objects. For example, to declare a pointer type capable of holding ival's address value, we write

```
// a pointer to an object to type int
int *pint;
```

C++ predefines a special *address-of* operator (&) that, when applied to an object, returns that object's address value. Thus, to assign pint to ival's memory address, we write

```
int *pint;
pint = &ival; // assign pint address of ival
```

To access the actual object pint addresses, we must first *dereference* pint using the *dereference* operator (*). For example, here is how we would indirectly add 1 to ival through pint:

```
// indirectly adding 1 to ival through pint
*pint = *pint + 1;
```

This is exactly equivalent to the following direct manipulation of ival:

```
// directly adding 1 to ival
ival = ival + 1;
```

In this example, there is no real benefit in using the indirect pointer manipulation of ival: it is both less efficient and more easily misprogrammed than the direct manipulation of ival. We presented it to provide a simple first look at pointers. One of the primary uses of pointers in C++ is the management and manipulation of dynamically allocated memory.

The two primary differences between static and dynamic memory allocation are as follows.

1. Static objects are named variables that we manipulate directly, whereas dynamic objects are unnamed variables we manipulate indirectly through pointers. We'll see an example of this in a moment.

2. The allocation and deallocation of static objects is handled automatically by the compiler; the programmer needs to understand it but need not do anything about it. The allocation and deallocation of dynamic objects, in contrast, must be managed explicitly by the programmer and, in practice, is considerably more error-prone. It is accomplished through the use of the new and delete expressions.

Objects are allocated dynamically through one of two versions of the *new expression*. The first instance allocates a single object of a specific type. For example,

```
int *pint = new int( 1024 );
```

allocates an unnamed object of type int, initializes that object to a first value of 1024, and then returns the address of the object in memory. The address is then used to initialize our pointer object, pint. For dynamically allocated memory, our only access is an indirect access through a pointer.

A second version of the new expression allocates an array of elements of a specified type and dimension. For example,

```
int *pia = new int[ 4 ];
```

allocates an array of four integer elements. Unfortunately, there is no way to specify an explicit initial value for the individual elements of a dynamically allocated array.

A sometimes confusing aspect of allocating a dynamic array is that the value returned is simply a pointer, the same type that is returned for the allocation of a single dynamic object. For example, the difference between pint and pia is that pia holds the address of the first element of the four-element array, whereas pint simply holds the address of the single object.

When we are finished using a dynamically allocated object or array of objects, we must explicitly deallocate the memory using one of two *delete expressions*. The deallocated memory can then be reused by the program. The single-object form of the delete expression is the following:

```
// delete a single object
delete pint;
```

The array form of the delete expression is as follows:

```
// delete an array of objects
delete [] pia;
```

What if we forget to delete our dynamically allocated memory? We end up with a *memory leak*. A memory leak is a chunk of dynamically allocated memory that we no longer have a pointer to, and thus we cannot return it to the program for later reuse. (Most systems now provide tools that can identify memory leaks within a program. Check with your system administrator.)

This admittedly rather whirlwind tour of the pointer data type and dynamic memory allocation is as likely to raise questions as to provide answers. Dynamic memory allocation and pointer manipulation, however, is a fundamental aspect of real-world programming in C++, and we didn't want to delay introducing it. We'll look at its use in our implementation of our object-based and object-oriented Array class implementations in the sections that follow. Section 8.4 looks at dynamic memory allocation and the use of the new and delete expressions in detail.

Exercise 2.3

Explain the difference between the four objects defined below.

```
(a) int ival = 1024;   (c) int *pi2 = new int( 1024 );
(b) int *pi = &ival;   (d) int *pi3 = new int[ 1024 ];
```

Exercise 2.4

What does the following code fragment do? What is its significant error? (Note that the use of the subscript operator with the pointer pia, below, is correct; the reason we can do this is explained in Section 3.9.2.)

```
int *pi = new int( 10 );
int *pia = new int[ 10 ];

while ( *pi < 10 ) {
        pia[ *pi ] = *pi;
        *pi = *pi + 1;
}

delete pi;
delete [] pia;
```

2.3   An Object-Based Design

In this section, we design and implement an array abstraction using the C++ class mechanism. Our initial implementation supports only an integer array. Later, using the template mechanism, we extend the abstraction to support an unlimited number of data types.

Our first step is to determine which operations to provide for our array class. Although we may wish to provide everything, we cannot provide everything all at once. The following is a first iteration of a set of supported operations.

1.   Our array class is to have some self-knowledge built into its implementation. As a first step, it will know its size.

2.   Our array class is to support the assignment of one array with another and the comparison of two arrays for both equality and inequality.

3.   Our array class is to support the following queries as to the values contained within it. What is the minimum value contained within the array? What is the maximum value? Does a specific value occur within the array, and, if so, what is the index of its first position?

4.   Our array class is to support the ability to sort itself. For argument's sake, let's assert that one set of potential users spoke of the importance of supporting arrays that are sorted. Others expressed no strong opinion either way.

In addition to supporting array operations, we must support the mechanics of an array. These include the following.

5.   The ability to specify a size with which to create the array. (We will not require that this value be known at compile-time.)

6.   The ability to initialize the array to a set of values.

7.   The ability to provide access via an index to the individual elements of the array. For argument's sake, let's assert that our users expressed a strong desire to use the subscript operator to accomplish this.

8.   The ability to intercept and flag bad index values. For argument's sake, let's presume that we feel very strongly about this ability and have not asked our users how they feel about it. We have decided that it is a necessary aspect of a well-designed array implementation.

Our discussions with potential users have created a great deal of enthusiasm. Now we need to deliver the actual implementation. But how do we translate the design into C++ code? The general form of a class supporting an object-based design looks like this:

```
class classname {
public:
    // the public set of operations
```

```
private:
   // the private implementation
};
```

Here, class, public, and private represent language keywords, and classname is a user-specified identifier used to name the class for subsequent reference. We'll name our class IntArray until we generalize the data types that it can support; at that point we'll rename our class Array.

A class name represents a new data type. We can use it to define objects of our class type in the same way we use the built-in types to define those objects. For example:

```
// a single IntArray class object
IntArray myArray;

// a pointer to a single IntArray class object
IntArray *pArray = new IntArray;
```

A class definition consists of two parts: the *class head*, composed of the keyword class and an associated class name, and the *class body*, enclosed by braces and terminated with a semicolon. The class head, by itself, serves as a declaration of the class. For example:

```
// declares the IntArray class to the program
// but does not provide a definition
class IntArray;
```

The class body contains the member definitions and access labels such as public and private. The class members consist of the operations the class can perform and the data necessary to represent the class abstraction. The operations are spoken of as *member functions*, or *methods*. For our IntArray class, they consist of the following:

```
class IntArray {
public:
   // equality and inequality operations: #2b
   bool operator==( const IntArray& ) const;
   bool operator!=( const IntArray& ) const;

   // assignment operator: #2a
   IntArray& operator=( const IntArray& );

   int  size() const; // #1
   void sort();       // #4

   int  min()  const; // #3a
   int  max()  const; // #3b

   // if the value is found within the array,
   // return the index of its first occurrence
   // otherwise, return -1
```

```
int find( int value ) const; // #3c

private:
    // the private implementation
};
```

The numbers to the right of the member functions refer to the item listing in our earlier specification. Right now, we're not going to explain the const modifier either within or following the argument list. It is an unnecessary detail at this point, but it is necessary for code expected to be used in real-world programs.

A named member function, such as min(), is invoked using one of two *member access operators*. There are actually two operators: a dot operator (.) for class objects and an arrow operator (->) for pointers to class objects. For example, to find the minimum value within our myArray class object, we write

```
// initialize min_val with the smallest element within myArray
int min_val = myArray.min();
```

To find the maximum value within our dynamically allocated IntArray object, we write

```
int max_val = pArray->max();
```

(Yes, we haven't yet introduced how we initialize our IntArray class objects with a size and set of values. There is a special *constructor* class member function to accomplish that. We'll introduce it shortly.)

Operators are applied to class objects in exactly the same way as for the built-in data types. Given two IntArray objects,

```
IntArray myArray0, myArray1;
```

the assignment operator is applied as follows:

```
// invokes the copy assignment member function:
// myArray0.operator=( myArray1 )
myArray0 = myArray1;
```

The invocation of the equality operator looks like this:

```
// invokes the equality member function:
// myArray0.operator==( myArray1 )
if ( myArray0 == myArray1 )
    cout << "!!our assignment operator works!\n";
```

The private and public keywords control access to the class members. Members that occur in a public section of the class body can be accessed from anywhere within the general program. Members that occur in the private section can be accessed only by the member functions (and friends) of the class (we're not going to explain friends until Section 15.2).

Generally, the public members provide the class *public interface* — that is, the set of operations that implement the behavior of the class. This consists of all or a subset of the member functions of the class. The private members provide the *private implementation* — that is, the data within which information is stored.

This division between the public interface and private implementation of a class is referred to as *information hiding*. Information hiding is an important software engineering concept that we look at in more detail in the later chapters of this text. Briefly, it provides two primary benefits for our programs.

1. If the private implementation of the class needs to be modified or extended, only the relatively small number of member functions requiring access to that implementation needs to be modified; the many user programs making use of our class generally do not need to be modified, although they may require recompiliation (we illustrate this in Section 6.18).
2. If there is an error in the state of the private class implementation, the amount of program code we need to examine in general is localized to the relatively small number of member functions requiring access to that implementation; the entire program need not be examined.

What are the data members necessary to represent our IntArray class? When declaring an IntArray object, the user will specify a size. We'll need to store that; we'll define a data member to do just that. In addition, we'll need to actually allocate and store the underlying array. This will be accomplished using the new expression; we'll define a pointer data member to store the address value the new expression returns:

```cpp
class IntArray {
public:
    // ...
    int size() const { return _size; }
private:
    //  internal data representation
    int _size;
    int *ia;
};
```

Because we have placed the _size data member within the private section of the class, we need to declare a public member function to provide users access to its value. Because C++ does not allow a data member and member function to share the same name, our general convention in these cases is to append an underscore to the data member. So we have the public access function, size(), and the private _size data member. In earlier editions of this text, we appended *get* and *set* to the access functions, but in practice this proved unwieldy.

Although this use of a public access function allows the user read access to the value, there seems to be something fundamentally wrong with this implementation, at least at first glance. Do you see what it is? Consider that both

```
IntArray array;
int array_size = array.size();
```

and

```
// presuming that _size were public
int array_size = array._size;
```

initialize array_size to the dimension of the array. The first instance, however, appears to require a function call, whereas the second involves only a direct memory access. Generally, a function call is significantly more expensive than a direct memory access. So does information hiding impose a significant expense — perhaps a prohibitive expense — on the run-time efficiency of a program? Happily, in general, the answer is no.

The solution provided by the language is the *inline function* mechanism. An inline function is expanded in place at its point of call. In general, that is, an inline function does not involve any function call at all.[1] For example, the call of size() within the condition clause of the for loop

```
for ( int index = 0; index < array.size(); ++index )
    // ...
```

is not actually invoked _size times but instead is inline-expanded during compilation into the following general form:

```
// general inline expansion of array.size()
for ( int index = 0; index < array._size; ++index )
    // ...
```

A member function defined within the class definition, such as size(), is automatically treated as an inline function. Alternatively, the inline keyword can be used to request that a function be treated as inline (we'll have more to say about inline functions in Section 7.6).

So far, we've provided for the operations required by the IntArray class (items 1–4 above) but not for the mechanics of initialization and the access of individual elements of the array (items 5-8).

One of the most common program errors is to use an object without having first properly initialized it. This is so common an error, in fact, that C++ provides an automatic initialization mechanism for user-defined classes: the class *constructor*.

---

1.   This is not always true, however. An inline function is a request to the compiler and not a guarantee. See Section 7.6 for a discussion.

A constructor is a special class member function used for initialization. If defined, it is automatically applied to each object of its class prior to a first use of that object. Who defines the constructor? The provider of the class — that is, we do. Identifying the necessary constructors for a class is an integral part of the class design.

A constructor is defined by giving it the same name as the class. In addition, no return type can be specified for a constructor. It is possible to define multiple constructors for a class even though they all use the same name — provided that the compiler can distinguish between them based on their parameter lists.

More generally, C++ supports a facility known as *function overloading*. Function overloading allows the same name to be used for two or more functions — with the constraint that each must have a unique parameter list, either by the number or the types of the parameters. (The unique parameter list allows the compiler to determine which instance of the overloaded functions to select for a particular invocation.) For example, the following is a valid set of min() overloaded functions (these could also be class member functions):

```
// an overloaded set of min() functions
// each must have a unique parameter list
#include <string>;

int    min( const int *pia, int size );
int    min( int, int );
int    min( const char *str );
char   min( string );
string min( string, string );
```

The run-time behavior of an overloaded function is the same as that of a nonoverloaded function. The primary overhead is the time during compilation to determine which of the multiple instances to invoke. Without support for function overloading, we would be required to provide a unique name for each function in our program. (Function overloading is examined in detail in Chapter 9.)

We've identified the following three constructors for our IntArray class:

```
class IntArray {
public:
   explicit IntArray( int sz = DefaultArraySize );
   IntArray( int *array, int array_size  );
   IntArray( const IntArray &rhs );
   // ...

private:
   static const int DefaultArraySize = 12;
     //  ...
};
```

The constructor

```
IntArray( int sz = DefaultArraySize );
```

is referred to as a *default constructor* because it does not require an argument to be supplied by the user. (We are not going to explain the keyword explicit present in the declaration of the default constructor at this time. We show it simply for completeness.) If the programmer does supply an argument, that is the value passed to the constructor. For example,

```
IntArray array1( 1024 );
```

passes an argument of 1024 to the constructor. On the other hand, if the user does not care to specify a size, the DefaultArraySize value is used instead. For example,

```
IntArray array2;
```

causes the default constructor to be invoked with the DefaultArraySize value. (A data member declared static is a special shared data member that occurs only once within the program regardless of the number of class objects that have been defined. It is a way of sharing data among all objects of the class — see Section 13.5 for a full discussion.)

Here is a slightly simplified implementation of our default constructor — simplified in that our version does not concern itself with the possibility of things going wrong. (What could possibly go wrong? Two things in this example: first, the dynamic memory available to our program is not infinite; it is possible for the new expression to fail. (In Section 2.6 we look at how we might handle that.) Second, the sz argument might be passed an invalid value, such as a negative or zero value or a value too large to store in a variable of type int.)

```
IntArray::
IntArray( int sz )
{
    // set the data members
    _size = sz;
    ia = new int[ _size ];

    // initialize the memory
    for ( int ix=0; ix < _size; ++ix )
        ia[ ix ] = 0;
}
```

This is the first time we've defined a class member function outside the body of the class. The only syntactic difference is the need to identify which class the member function belongs to. This is accomplished by using the *class scope operator*:

```
IntArray::
```

The double colon (::) operator is referred to as the *scope operator*. When attached to a class name, as above, it becomes a class scope operator. Scope can be informally thought of as a window of visibility. An object with global scope is visible to the end of the file in which it is defined. An object defined within a function is said to have *local scope*; it is visible only within the body of the function in which it is defined. Each class maintains a scope outside of which its members are not visible. The class scope operator alerts the compiler that the identifier that follows is to be found within the scope of the class. In our case,

```
IntArray::
IntArray( int sz )
```

tells the compiler that the IntArray() function being defined is a member of the IntArray class. (Although program scope is not something we need to focus on at this point, it is something we'll eventually need to understand. We return to program scope in detail in Chapter 8. Class scope in particular is discussed in Section 13.9.)

The second constructor for the IntArray class initializes the new IntArray class object with a built-in integer array. It requires two arguments: the actual array and a second argument indicating the size of the array. For example:

```
int ia[10] = {0,1,2,3,4,5,6,7,8,9};
IntArray iA3(ia,10);
```

The implementation of this constructor is almost identical to that of the first constructor. (Once again, at this point we do not protect our code from the things that can go wrong.)

```
IntArray::
IntArray( int *array, int sz )
{
    // set the data members
    _size = sz;
    ia = new int[ _size ];

    // copy the data members
    for ( int ix=0; ix < _size; ++ix )
        ia[ ix ] = array[ ix ];
}
```

The final IntArray constructor handles initialization of one IntArray object with another. It is invoked automatically whenever a definition of either of the following two forms occurs:

```
IntArray array;

// equivalent initializations
IntArray ia1 = array;
IntArray ia2( array );
```

This constructor is referred to as the class *copy constructor*, and we shall see a great deal more of it in later chapters. Here is our implementation, once again ignoring possible run-time program anomalies:

```
IntArray::
IntArray( const IntArray &rhs )
{ // copy constructor
   _size = rhs._size;
   ia = new int[ _size ];

   for ( int ix=0; ix < _size; ++ix )
        ia[ ix ] = rhs.ia[ ix ];
}
```

This example introduces a new compound type, that of a *reference* (IntArray &rhs). A reference is a kind of pointer without the special pointer syntax. (Thus, we write rhs._size and not rhs->_size.) Like a pointer, a reference provides indirect access to an object. (We have more to say about references and pointers in Section 3.6.)

Notice that all three constructors are implemented in similar ways. In general, when two or more functions duplicate the same general code, it makes sense to factor the code into a separate function that can be shared between them. Later, if a change in the implementation is required, it need be made only once. Moreover, the shared nature of the implementation is easier for the human reader to grasp.

How might we factor our constructors' code into an independent, shared function? Here is one possible implementation:

```
class IntArray {
public:
   // ...
private:
   void init( int sz, int *array );
   // ...
};

void
IntArray::
init( int sz, int *array )
{
   _size = sz;
   ia = new int[ _size ];

   for ( int ix=0; ix < _size; ++ix )
        if ( ! array )
             ia[ ix ] = 0;
        else ia[ ix ] = array[ ix ];
}
```

Our three rewritten constructors are as follows:

```
IntArray::IntArray( int sz ){ init( sz, 0 ); }
IntArray::IntArray( int *array, int sz )
      { init( sz, array ); }
```

```
IntArray::IntArray( const IntArray &rhs )
     { init( rhs.size, rhs.ia ); }
```

The class mechanism also supports a special *destructor* member function. A destructor is automatically invoked on each class object after the final use of the object in our program. We identify a destructor by giving it the name of the class preceded by a tilde (~). The destructor in general frees resources acquired during the construction and use of the class object. In the IntArray destructor, for example, the memory allocated during construction is deleted. Here is our implementation (constructors and destructors are discussed in detail in Chapter 14):

```
class IntArray {
public:
    // constructors
    explicit IntArray( int size = DefaultArraySize );
    IntArray( int *array, int array_size  );
    IntArray( const IntArray &rhs );

    // destructor
    ~IntArray() { delete [] ia; }

    // ...

private:
    //  ...
};
```

The array class will not be of much practical interest unless users can easily index into a class object to access individual elements. For example, our class needs to support the following general usage:

```
IntArray array;
int last_pos = array.size()-1;

int temp = array[ 0 ];
array[ 0 ] = array[ last_pos ];
array[ last_pos ] = temp;
```

We support indexing into an IntArray class object by providing a class-specific instance of the subscript operator. Here is our implementation supporting the required usage.

```
#include <cassert>
int&
IntArray::
operator[]( int index )
{
    assert( index >= 0 && index < size );
    return ia[ index ];
}
```

In general, the language supports *operator overloading* in which a new instance of an operator can be defined for a particular class type. Typically, a class provides one or more instances of the assignment operator, the equality operator, perhaps one or more relational operators, and an iostream input and output operator. (We provide additional illustrations of overloaded operators in Section 3.15. In Chapter 15, we discuss operator overloading in detail.)

Typically, the class definition and any associated constant values or typedef names are stored in a header file. The header file is named with the class name. So, for example, we would create an `IntArray.h` and `Matrix.h` pair of header files. All programs wishing to use either the IntArray or Matrix class include the associated header file.

Similarly, the member functions of a class not defined within the class definition are typically stored in a program text file having the same name as the class. For example, we would create an `IntArray.C` and `Matrix.C` pair of program text files in which to store the associated class member functions. (Remember that the suffix used to indicate a program text file varies across compilation systems; you should check for the convention followed under your system.) Rather than require that these functions be recompiled with each program wishing to use their associated classes, the member functions are precompiled and stored in a class library. The iostream library is one such example.

Exercise 2.5

The key feature of a C++ class is the separation of interface and implementation. The interface is the set of operations that users can apply to objects of the class. It consists of three parts: the name of the operations, their return values, and their parameter lists. Generally, that is all the user of the class is required to know. The private implementation consists of the algorithms and data necessary to support the public interface. Ideally, even though the class interface may grow, it does not change in ways incompatible with earlier versions during the lifetime of the class. The implementation, on the other hand, is free to evolve over the lifetime of the class. Choose one of the following abstractions and write the public interface for that class:

```
(a) Matrix    (c) Person    (e) Pointer
(b) Boolean   (d) Date      (f) Point
```

Exercise 2.6

The words *constructor* and *destructor* are somewhat misleading in that these programmer-supplied functions neither construct nor destroy the objects of the class to which they are applied by the compiler automatically. When we write

```
int main() {
   IntArray myArray( 1024 );
   // ...
   return 0;
}
```

the memory necessary to maintain the data members of myArray is allocated prior to application of the constructor. The compiler, in effect, internally transforms our program as follows (note that this is not legal C++ code[2]):

```
int main() {
   IntArray myArray;

   // Pseudo C++ Code -- apply constructor
   myArray.IntArray::IntArray( 1024 );
   // ...
   // Pseudo C++ Code -- apply destructor
   myArray.IntArray::~IntArray();

   return 0;
}
```

The constructors of a class serve primarily to initialize the data members of the class object. The destructor primarily frees any resources acquired by the class object during its lifetime. Define the set of constructors needed by the class you chose in Exercise 2.5. Does your class require a destructor?

Exercise 2.7

In Exercises 2.5 and 2.6, you have specified nearly the complete public interface necessary for use of the class. (We may still need to define a copy assignment operator, but we'll ignore that fact for now — C++ provides default support for the assignment of one class object with another. The problem is that this default behavior is often inadequate. See Section 14.6 for a discussion.) Write a program to exercise the public interface of the class you defined in the two previous exercises. Is it easy or awkward to use? Do you wish to revise the specification? Can you do that and maintain compatibility?

2.4   An Object-Oriented Design

Our implementations of min() and max() make no special assumptions about the storage of the array elements and therefore require that we examine each element. Had we required the elements to be sorted, the implementation of both operations would become a simple index into, respectively, the first and last element. Moreover, a search

---

2. For those interested, this material is covered in our companion volume, *Inside the C++ Object Model*.

for the presence of an element is considerably more efficient if the elements are known to be sorted. Supporting the elements in sorted order, however, adds to the complexity of the Array class implementation. Have we made a mistake in our design?

We haven't made a mistake so much as we've made a choice. A sorted array is a specialized implementation: when it is necessary, it is absolutely necessary; otherwise, the overhead of its support is a burden. Our implementation is more general and, in most circumstances, adequate; it supports a wider range of users. Unfortunately, if the user absolutely needs the behavior of a sorted array, our implementation cannot support that. There is no way for the user to override the more general implementations of min(), max(), and find(). In effect, we have chosen a generally useful implementation that is inappropriate under special circumstances.

On the other hand, for another category of user our implementation is too specialized: range-checking of the index adds overhead to each access of an element. We discounted the cost of this in our design (see item 8 in Section 2.3) with the assumption that being fast is of little value if we are incorrect. This assumption, however, does not hold true for at least one of our major users: a real-time virtual-immersion or virtual-reality provider. The arrays, in this case, represent shared vertices of complex 3D geometry. The scene flies by too quickly for an occasional error to be generally visible, but if the general access is too slow, the immersion effect breaks down. Our implementation, although considerably safer than a non-range-checking array class, is impractical for this application domain.

How might we support the needs of these three sets of users? The solutions are already present in the code, more or less. For example, our range-checking is localized within the subscript operator. Remove the invocation of check_range(), rename the array, and we now have two implementations: one with and one without range-checking. Copy more of the code, modify it to treat the array as sorted, and we now have support for a sorted array:

```
// Unsorted, with no bounds-checking
class IntArray{ ... };

// Unsorted, with bounds-checking
class IntArrayRC{ ... };

// Sorted, without bounds-checking
class IntSortedArray{ ... };
```

What are the drawbacks with this solution?

1.   We must maintain three array implementations containing considerable duplicated code. We'd prefer to have a single copy of the common code shared by three array classes, as well as any other array classes we later chose to support (perhaps a sorted array with bounds-checking).

2. Because the three array implementations are distinct types, we must write separate functions to operate on them, although the general operations within the functions may be identical. For example:

```
void process_array( IntArray& );
void process_array( IntArrayRC& );
void process_array( IntSortedArray& );
```

We'd prefer to write a single function that accepts not only all our existing array classes but also any future array classes provided that the same set of operations are applied to each class.

The object-oriented paradigm provides us with exactly these abilities. Item 1 is provided by the *inheritance* mechanism. When an IntArrayRC class (that is, an IntArray class with range-checking) inherits from an IntArray class, it has access to the data members and member functions of IntArray without requiring that we maintain two copies of the code. The new class need provide only the data members and member functions necessary to implement its additional semantics.

In C++, the class being inherited from, IntArray in this case, is spoken of as a *base class*. The new class is said to be *derived* from the base class. We call it the *derived class*, or the *subtype,* of the base class. We say that IntArrayRC is a kind of IntArray with specialized behavior to support range-checking of the index value. A subtype shares a *common interface* with its base class — that is, a common set of public operations. This sharing of a common interface allows the base class and subtype to be used interchangeably within a program without concern for the actual type of the object. In a sense, the common interface encapsulates the type-specific details of the individual subtypes. The type/subtype relationship between classes forms an *inheritance* or *derivation hierarchy.* For example, here is the implementation of a nonmember swap() function taking as its primary argument a reference to a base class IntArray object. The function swaps the two elements indexed by i and j.

```
#include <IntArray.h>

void swap( IntArray &ia, int i, int j )
{
   int tmp = ia[ i ];
   ia[ i ] = ia[ j ];
   ia[ j ] = tmp;
}
```

Here are three legal invocations of swap():

```
IntArray        ia;
IntArrayRC      iarc;
IntSortedArray  ias;
```

```
// ok: ia is an IntArray
swap( ia, 0, 10 );

// ok: iarc is a subtype of IntArray
swap( iarc, 0, 10 );

// ok: ias is also a subtype of IntArray
swap( ias, 0, 10 );

// error: string is not a subtype ...
string str( "not an IntArray!" );
swap( str, 0, 10 );
```

Each of the three array classes provides its own implementation of a subscript operator. What we require, of course, is that when

```
swap( iarc, 0, 10 );
```

is invoked, the IntArrayRC subscript operator is invoked; when

```
swap( ias, 0, 10 );
```

is invoked, the IntSortedArray subscript operator is invoked, and so on. The subscript operator to be invoked by swap() must potentially change with each invocation and must be determined by the actual type of the array whose elements are being exchanged. This is accomplished automatically under C++ through the *virtual function* mechanism.

The syntactic changes necessary to prepare our IntArray class for inheritance are minimal: we must (optionally) reduce the level of encapsulation to allow the derived classes access to the nonpublic implementation, and we must explicitly identify which functions we wish to be resolved through the virtual mechanism. The significant change is in our way of designing a class intended to serve as a base class.

In an object-based design, there is generally one provider and many users of a class. The provider designs and usually implements the class. The users exercise the public interface made available by the provider. This separation of activity is reflected in the division of the class into private and public access levels.

Under inheritance, there are now multiple class providers: one providing the base class implementation (and possibly some number of derived classes), and one or others providing derived classes throughout the lifetime of the inheritance hierarchy. This activity is also an implementation activity; the provider of the subtype often (but not always) needs access to the base class implementation. To provide that, while still preventing general access to the implementation, an additional access level, protected, is provided. The data members and member functions of a protected section of a class, while still unavailable to the general program, are available to the derived class. (Anything placed within a private section of the base class is available only to the class itself and not to any of the derived classes.) Here is our revised IntArray class:

```
class IntArray {
public:
   // constructors
   explicit IntArray( int size = DefaultArraySize );
   IntArray( int *array, int array_size  );
   IntArray( const IntArray &rhs );

   // virtual destructor!
   virtual ~IntArray() { delete [] ia; }

   // equality and inequality operations:
   bool operator==( const IntArray& ) const;
   bool operator!=( const IntArray& ) const;

   IntArray& operator=( const IntArray& );
   int size() const { return _size; }

   // we've removed the check on the index ...
   virtual int& operator[](int index) { return ia[index]; }
   virtual void sort();

   virtual int min() const;
   virtual int max() const;
   virtual int find( int value ) const;

protected:
   // see Section 13.5 for an explanation
   static const int DefaultArraySize = 12;
   void init( int sz, int *array );

   int _size;
   int *ia;
};
```

The criteria for designating a member public to a class do not change between an object-based and an object-oriented design. Our redesigned IntArray class intended to serve as a base class still declares its constructors, destructor, subscript operator, min(), max(), and so on, as public members. These members continue to provide the public interface, but now the interface serves not only the IntArray class but also the inheritance hierarchy derived from it.

The new design criterion is whether to declare the nonpublic members as either protected or private class members. A member is made private to a base class if we wish to prevent subsequently derived classes from having direct access to that member. A member is made protected if we believe it provides an operation or data storage to which a subsequently derived class requires direct access in order for that derived class to be effectively implemented. For our IntArray class, we have made all our data members protected, in effect allowing subsequent derivations access to the implementation details of IntArray.

The second design consideration for a class intended to serve as a base class is the identification of type-dependent member functions. We label these functions as *virtual*.

A type-dependent member function is one whose algorithm is determined by the implementation or behavior of a particular base or derived class. The implementation of the subscript operator, for example, is unique to each of our array types. Therefore, we declare it to be virtual.

The implementations of the two equality operators and the `size()` member function are independent of the array type against which they are being applied. Therefore, we do not declare them as virtual.

For a call to a nonvirtual function, the compiler selects the function that will be invoked at compile-time. The resolution of a virtual function call is delayed until runtime. At each call point within the executing program, the virtual function instance is selected based on the actual base or derived class type through which the function is being invoked. For example, consider the following:

```
void init( IntArray &ia )
{
    for ( int ix = 0; ix < ia.size(); ++ix )
        ia[ ix ] = ix;
}
```

The formal parameter ia may reference an IntSortedArray, an IntArrayRC, or an IntArray class object (we'll introduce our class derivations shortly). size(), being a nonvirtual function, is resolved and inline-expanded by the compiler. The subscript operator, however, cannot in general be resolved until each iteration of the for loop is executed because during compilation the actual array type ia addresses is not known.

(We look at virtual functions in considerable detail in Chapter 17, including the issue of virtual destructors and the potential inefficiency of designs using virtual functions. [LIPPMAN96a] looks at implementation and performance issues in detail.)

Once we have decided on our design, its implementation within C++ is straightforward. For example, here is our complete IntArrayRC derived class definition. It is placed in an independent header file, `IntArrayRC.h`, and includes the `IntArray.h` header file containing the IntArray class definition:

```
#ifndef IntArrayRC_H
#define IntArrayRC_H

#include "IntArray.h"

class IntArrayRC : public IntArray {
public:
    IntArrayRC( int sz = DefaultArraySize );
    IntArrayRC( int *array, int array_size );
    IntArrayRC( const IntArrayRC &rhs );
```

```
    virtual int& operator[]( int );

private:
    void check_range( int );
};
```

```
#endif
```

IntArrayRC needs to define only those aspects of its implementation that are different or in addition to the implementation of IntArray.

1. It must provide its own instance of the subscript operator, one that provides range-checking.
2. It must provide an operation to do the actual range-checking. (Because it is not part of the public interface, we declare it to be private.)
3. It must provide its own set of automatic initialization functions — that is, its own set of constructors.

The data members and member functions of IntArray are all available to IntArrayRC as if IntArrayRC had explicitly defined them itself. This is the meaning of

```
class IntArrayRC : public IntArray
```

The colon defines IntArrayRC to be derived from IntArray. (The public keyword indicates that the derived class shares the base class public interface. An object of type IntArrayRC can be used in any situation programmed to use objects of the base class type, as in our swap() example. This is explained in detail in Chapter 18.) IntArrayRC can be thought of as extending the IntArray class by providing the additional feature of subscript range-checking. Here is an implementation of the subscript operator:

```
inline int&
IntArrayRC::operator[]( int index )
{
    check_range( index );
    return ia[ index ];
}
```

Here, check_range() is implemented as an inline member function invoking the assert() macro (see Section 1.3 for a discussion of the assert() macro):

```
#include <cassert>

inline void
IntArrayRC::check_range( int index )
{
    assert( index >= 0 && index < size );
}
```

(We provide check_range() as a separate function to illustrate a private member function and to encapsulate the handling of range-checking in case we later want to change how bound errors are handled, perhaps by substituting assert() with support for exception handling.)

A derived class object actually consists of multiple parts; each base class is a class *subobject* with a separate part for the newly defined derived class portion. The initialization of a derived class object is carried out by the automatic invocation of each base class constructor to initialize the associated base class subobject followed by execution of the derived class constructor. From a design standpoint, the constructor for the derived class should initialize only those data members defined within the derived class itself and not those of its base class.

Although we introduce a class-specific version of the subscript operator and a private check_range() helping function, we introduce no additional data members requiring initialization. Therefore, we might reasonably assume that inheriting the base class constructors is sufficient and that we do not need to provide IntArrayRC constructors — after all, there is nothing for them to do!

In fact, however, we need to provide the IntArrayRC constructors, because base class constructors are never inherited by the derived class (nor is the destructor or the copy assignment operator), and because we need some interface by which to pass the necessary arguments to the base IntArray class constructors.

For example, suppose we define an IntArrayRC object as follows:

```
int ia[] = { 0, 1, 1, 2, 3, 5, 8, 13 };
IntArrayRC iarc( ia, 8 );
```

How can we pass ia and 8 to the IntArray base class constructor? (Admittedly, if the IntArray constructor were inherited, we would not have this problem. Actually, we would have other, more severe problems, but we haven't the space here to convince you of that.) In any case, the syntax of the derived class constructor provides the interface for passing arguments to the base class constructor. For example, here are our two necessary IntArrayRC constructors (we say a great deal more about constructors in Chapters 14 and 17, including an explanation of why we do not need to provide an IntArrayRC copy constructor):

```
inline IntArrayRC::IntArrayRC( int sz)
    : IntArray( sz ) {}

inline IntArrayRC::IntArrayRC( const int *iar, int sz )
    : IntArray( iar, sz ) {}
```

The portion of the constructor marked off by the colon is referred to as a *member initialization list*. It provides the mechanism by which the IntArray constructor is passed its argument. The bodies of both IntArrayRC constructors are null, because the job of the constructors is only to pass their arguments to the associated IntArray constructor. We do not provide an explicit IntArrayRC destructor, because the derived class does not introduce any data members requiring destruction. The inherited IntArray class members requiring destruction are handled by the IntArray class destructor. The base class destructor is automatically applied to the base class subobject within a derived class object whether or not the derived class itself defines a destructor.

The `IntArrayRC.h` header file holds the IntArrayRC two-class definition and the definition of all inline member functions defined outside the class definition. Had we defined any non-inline member functions, we would place them in an associated program text file, `IntArrayRC.C`.

Here is a small program that exercises our IntArray and IntArrayRC two-class hierarchy:

```
#include <iostream>
#include <IntArray.h>
#include <IntArrayRC.h>

extern void swap(IntArray&,int,int);

int main()
{
   int array[ 4 ] = { 0, 1, 2, 3 };
   IntArray ia1( array, 4 );
   IntArrayRC ia2( array, 4 );

   // error: off-by-one: should be size-1
   // not caught by IntArray object
   cout << "swap() with IntArray ia1\n";
   swap( ia1, 1, ia1.size() );

   // ok: caught by IntArrayRC object
   cout << "swap() with IntArrayRC ia2\n";
   swap( ia2, 1, ia2.size() );

   return 0;
}
```

When compiled and executed, the program generates the following results:

```
swap() with IntArray ia1
swap() with IntArrayRC ia2
Assertion failed:  index >= 0 && index < size
```

C++ supports two additional forms of inheritance: multiple inheritance, in which a class is derived from two or more base classes, and virtual inheritance, in which a single instance of a base class is shared among multiple derived classes. We defer this discussion until Chapter 18. A further aspect of object-oriented programming is the ability to query a base class reference or pointer as to the actual type it refers to at any point within the execution of our program. This is provided by the run-time type identification (RTTI) facility. RTTI is discussed in Section 19.1.

Exercise 2.8

A type/subtype inheritance relationship in general reflects an *is-a* relationship: a range-checking ArrayRC is a kind of Array, a Book is a kind of LibraryRentalMaterial, an AudioBook is a kind of Book, and so on. Which of the following pairs reflect an is-a relationship?

```
(a) member function isA_kindOf function
(b) member function isA_kindOf class
(c) constructor isA_kindOf member function
(d) airplane isA_kindOf vehicle
(e) motor isA_kindOf truck
(f) circle isA_kindOf geometry
(g) square isA_kindOf rectangle
(h) automobile isA_kindOf airplane
(i) borrower isA_kindOf library
```

Exercise 2.9

Identify which of the following operations are likely to be type-dependent and therefore candidates to be made virtual functions, and which can either be shared among all classes or are likely unique to a single base or derived class.

```
(a) rotate(); (b) print();
(c) size();    (d) dateBorrowed();
(e) rewind(); (f) borrower();
(g) is_late();(h) is_on_loan();
```

Exercise 2.10

There has been some controversy as to the use of the protected access level. Some people argue that the use of the protected access level to allow derived classes direct access to base class members violates the notion of encapsulation and therefore that all base class implementation details should be private. Others argue that without direct access to the base class members, the implementation of the derived class cannot be made sufficiently efficient to be of use and that without the protected keyword the class designer would be forced to make the base class members public. What do you think?

Exercise 2.11

A second controversy has to do with the need to explicitly declare a member function virtual. Some people argue that this means that if a class designer fails to recognize a function as needing to be virtual, the derived class designer is helpless to override the necessary function. They recommend making all member functions virtual. On the other hand, virtual functions are less efficient than nonvirtual functions.[3] Because they cannot be inlined (inlining occurs at compile-time, and virtual functions are resolved at run-time), they can be a source of run-time program inefficiency, particularly for small, frequently invoked type-independent functions such as the size of our Array. Again, what do you think?

Exercise 2.12

Each of the following abstractions implicitly consists of a family of abstract subtypes. For example, a LibraryRentalMaterial abstraction implicitly contains Books, Puppets, Videos, and so on. Choose one of the following and identify a hierarchy of subtypes for that abstraction; specify a small public interface for that hierarchy, including constructors; identify which, if any, functions are virtual; and write a small pseudocode program to exercise the public interface.

```
(a) Points       (b) Employees
(c) Shapes       (d) TelephoneNumbers
(e) BankAccounts (f) CourseOfferings
```

2.5   A Generic Design

Our IntArray class provides a useful alternative to the predefined integer array type. But what about users wishing to use an Array class of type `double` or `string`? The difference between the implementation of an Array class of type `double` and the IntArray class is simply the type of the elements it needs to contain; the code itself remains invariant.

The C++ template facility provides a facility for *parameterizing* types and values used within a class or function definition (we defer discussion of value parameters until Section 10.1). These parameters serve as placeholders in otherwise invariant code; later, the parameters are bound to actual types, either the built-in or user-defined types. For example, in an Array class template, we parameterize the type of elements contained within the Array. Later, we *instantiate* type-specific instances, such as an Array of `int`, `double`, and `string`. We can use these three instances within our program the same as if we had explicitly hand-coded them. Let's look at how to turn our IntArray class into the Array class template. Here is its definition:

```
template < class elemType >
class Array {
public:
    // parameterize element type
    explicit Array( int size = DefaultArraySize );
    Array( elemType *array, int array_size  );
    Array( const Array &rhs );
```

---

3. See [LIPPMAN96a] for a detailed discussion of virtual function performance issues.

```
        virtual ~Array() { delete [] ia; }

        bool operator==( const Array& ) const;
        bool operator!=( const Array& ) const;

        Array& operator=( const Array& );
        int size() const { return _size; }

        virtual elemType& operator[](int index){ return ia[index]; }
        virtual void sort();

        virtual elemType min() const;
        virtual elemType max() const;
        virtual int        find( const elemType &value ) const;
protected:
        static const int DefaultArraySize = 12;

        int _size;
        elemType *ia;
    };
```

The template keyword introduces the template. The parameters are enclosed within an angle-bracket pair (<,>) — in this case, the one parameter, elemType. The class
keyword indicates that the parameter represents a type. The identifier elemType serves
as the actual parameter name. Its seven occurrences within our Array class definition
serve as placeholders for the actual type.

With each instantiation of the Array class, either to int, double, string, and so on,
the actual type of the instantiation is substituted for the elemType parameter. Here is an
example of how the Array class template might be used:

```
    #include <iostream>
    #include "Array.h"

    int main()
    {
        const int array_size = 4;

        // elemType becomes int
        Array<int> ia(array_size);

        // elemType becomes double
        Array<double> da(array_size);

        // elemType becomes char
        Array<char> ca(array_size);

         int ix;
```

```
        for ( ix = 0; ix < array_size; ++ix ) {
                ia[ix] = ix;
                da[ix] = ix * 1.75;
                ca[ix] = ix + 'a';
        }

        for ( ix = 0; ix < array_size; ++ix )
                cout << "[ " << ix << " ]   ia: "   << ia[ix]
                        << "\tca: " << ca[ix]
                        << "\tda: " << da[ix] << endl;

        return 0;
}
```

In this example, we define three individual instances of the Array class template:

```
Array<int>    ia(array_size);
Array<double> da(array_size);
Array<char>   ca(array_size);
```

These instances are declared by following the class template name by a list of the actual types enclosed in angle brackets. What happens when we define a class template object such as ia, da, or ca? The compiler must allocate memory for the associated object. In order to do that, the formal template parameters are bound to the actual argument types specified. For ia, the instantiation of the Array class template yields the following class data members, with elemType bound to type int:

```
// Array<int> ia(array_size);
int _size;
int *ia;
```

The result is a class equivalent to our previously hand-implemented IntArray class. For da, the members become

```
// Array<double> da(array_size);
int _size;
double *ia;
```

with elemType bound to type double. Similarly, for ca, the members become

```
// Array<char> ca(array_size);
int _size;
char *ia;
```

with elemType bound to type char.

What about the member functions of the class template? Not all of them are automatically instantiated with the instantiation of the class template. Rather, only the member functions actually used by the program are instantiated, and this generally occurs in a separate phase of building a program. (We discuss this in detail in Section 16.8.)

When compiled and executed, the program produces the following output:

```
[ 0 ]   ia: 0 ca: a   da: 0
[ 1 ]   ia: 1 ca: b   da: 1.75
[ 2 ]   ia: 2 ca: c   da: 3.5
[ 3 ]   ia: 3 ca: d   da: 5.25
```

The template mechanism also supports object-oriented programming. A class template can serve as both a base and a derived class. Here is the definition of a template range-checking Array class:

```
#include <cassert>
#include "Array.h"

template <class elemType>
class ArrayRC : public Array<elemType> {
public:
    ArrayRC( int sz = Array<elemType>::DefaultArraySize )
            : Array< elemType >( sz ){};

    ArrayRC( elemType *ia, int sz )
            : Array< elemType >( ia, sz ) {}

    ArrayRC( const ArrayRC &rhs )
            : Array< elemType >( rhs ) {}

    virtual elemType&
    operator[]( int index )
    {
            assert( index >= 0 && index < Array<elemType>::size() );
            return ia[ index ];
    }

private:
    // ...
};
```

Each instantiation of the ArrayRC class instantiates the associated Array class template instance. For example, the definition

```
ArrayRC<int> ia_rc( 10 );
```

causes an int instance of both an Array class and an ArrayRC class to be instantiated. ia_rc behaves exactly the same as our nontemplate instance in the previous section. To illustrate this, let's rewrite the earlier program to exercise the Array and ArrayRC class template types. First, to support the statement

```
// swap() now must also be a template
swap( ia1, 1, ia1.size() );
```

we must define swap() to be a function template. For example:

```
#include "Array.h"
```

```
template <class elemType>
void swap( Array<elemType> &array, int i, int j )
{
   elemType tmp = array[ i ];
   array[ i ] = array[ j ];
   array[ j ] = tmp;
}
```

Each call of swap() generates the appropriate instance depending on the type of array. Here is the rewritten instance of main() using the Array and ArrayRC class templates:

```
#include <iostream>

#include "Array.h"
#include "ArrayRC.h"

template <class elemType>
inline void
swap( Array<elemType> &array, int i, int j )
{
   elemType tmp = array[ i ];
   array[ i ] = array[ j ];
   array[ j ] = tmp;
}

int main()
{
   Array<int>   ia1;
   ArrayRC<int> ia2;

   cout << "swap() with Array<int> ia1\n";
   int size = ia1.size();
   swap( ia1, 1, size );

   cout << "swap() with ArrayRC<int> ia2\n";
   size = ia2.size();
   swap( ia2, 1, size );

   return 0;
}
```

The results of this program are the same as for the nontemplate IntArray class implementation.

Exercise 2.13

Given the following type declarations

```
template <class elemType> class Array;
enum Status { ... };
typedef string *Pstring;
```

which, if any, of the following object definitions are in error?

```
(a) Array< int*& > pri( 1024 );
(b) Array< Array<int> > aai( 1024 );
(c) Array< complex< double > > acd( 1024 );
(d) Array< Status > as( 1024 );
(e) Array< Pstring > aps( 1024 );
```

Exercise 2.14

Rewrite the following class definition to make it a class template:

```
class example1 {
public:
    example1( double min, double max );
    example1( const double *array, int size );

    double& operator[]( int index );
    bool operator==( const example1& ) const;

    bool insert( const double*, int );
    bool insert( double );

    double min() const { return _min; };
    double max() const { return _max; };

    void min( double );
    void max( double );

    int count( double value ) const;

private:
    int size;
    double *parray;
    double _min;
    double _max;
};
```

Exercise 2.15

Given the following class template

```
template <class elemType>
class Example2 {
public:
    explicit Example2( elemType val = 0 )
                : _val( val ){}

    bool min( elemType value )     { return _val < value; }
    void value( elemType new_val ) { _val = new_val;      }
    void print( ostream &os )      { os << _val;          }
```

```
        private:
           elemType _val;
        };

        template<class elemType>
        ostream& operator<<( ostream &os, const Example2<elemType> &ex )
                   { ex.print( os ); return os; }
```

what happens when we write the following?

```
        (a) Example2< Array<int>* > ex1;
        (b) ex1.min( &ex1 );
        (c) Example2< int > sa( 1024 ), sb;
        (d) sa = sb;
        (e) Example2< string > exs( "Walden" );
        (f) cout << "exs: " << exs << endl;
```

Exercise 2.16

In our definition of Example2, we write

```
        explicit Example2( elemType val = 0 )
                   : _val( val ){}
```

The intention is to specify a default value so that a user can write either

```
        Example2< Type > ex1( value );
        Example2< Type > ex2;
```

However, our implementation constrains Type to be the subset of types that can legally be initialized with a value of 0. (For example, initializing a string object with a value of 0 is an error.)[4] In a similar manner, if Type does not support the output operator, an invocation of print() (and therefore of the Example2 output operator) fails. If Type does not support the less-than operator, an invocation of min() fails.

The language provides no means of indicating implicit constraints on the Type that a template can be instantiated with. The programmer discovers these constraints, in the worst case, when a program fails to compile. Do you think the language should support a Type-constraint syntax? If you do, indicate the syntax, and rewrite the Example2 definition to use it. If you do not, explain why.

Exercise 2.17

In the previous exercise, we say that if Type does not support either the output or the less-than operator, an attempt to invoke either print() or min() generates an error. In Standard C++, the errors are generated not when the class template is created but rather

---

4. The general program idiom to solve this problem is the following:
    Example2(elemType nval = elemType()) : _val(nval){}

when (and therefore if) the `print()` or `min()` function is invoked. Do you think this is the correct language semantics? Should the error be flagged at the point of template definition? Why or why not?

2.6   An Exception-Based Design

Exceptions are run-time program anomalies such as an out-of-bounds array index, the inability to open a specified file, the exhaustion of available program dynamic memory, and so on. Programmers generally develop their own styles for handling exceptions, leading to diverse coding practices that are potentially difficult to integrate into a single application.

Exception handling provides a standard language-level facility for responding to run-time program anomalies. It supports a uniform syntax and style that supports fine-tuning by individual programmers. The exception handling facility can significantly reduce the size and complexity of program code by eliminating the need to everywhere explicitly test for anomalous states and by factoring the code to test for anomalous states into specific, explicitly labeled portions of code.

The primary components of the exception handling facility are the following:

1.   The point within the program where the exception occurs. Recognition of the program anomaly results in the *raising* of an exception. When an exception is raised, normal program execution is suspended until the exception is *handled*. In C++, the raising of an exception is carried out by a `throw` expression. For example, in the following program fragment, an exception of type string is thrown in response to the failure to open a file:

```
if ( ! infile ) {
    string errMsg( "unable to open file: " );
    errMsg += fileName;
    throw errMsg;
}
```

2.   The point within the program where the exception is handled. Typically, program exceptions are raised and handled in separate function or member function invocations. Finding a handler often involves unwinding what is referred to as the *program call stack*. Once the exception is handled, normal program execution resumes. The resumption begins not where the exception occurred but where it is handled. In C++, the handling of an exception is carried out by a `catch` clause. For example, the following catch clause handles the exception thrown in item 1:

```
catch( string exceptionMsg ) {
    log_message( exceptionMsg );
    return false;
}
```

catch clauses are associated with try blocks. A try block groups one or more program statements with one or more catch clauses. For example, here is a function stats():

```
int*
stats( const int *ia, int size )
{
    int *pstats = new int[ 4 ];
    try {
            pstats[ 0 ] = sum_it(  ia, size );
            pstats[ 1 ] = min_val( ia, size );
            pstats[ 2 ] = max_val( ia, size );
    }
    catch( string exceptionMsg )
        { /* code to handle exception */ }

    catch( const statsException &statsExcp )
        { /* code to handle exception */  }

    pstats[ 3 ] = pstats[ 0 ]/size;
    do_something( pstats );

    return pstats;
}
```

There are four statements within stats() that are outside the try block. Of these, an exception can potentially be raised before completion of two of the statements:

```
(1) int *pstats = new int[ 4 ];
(2) do_something( pstats );
```

In statement (1), the new expression may fail. If this happens, the standard library raises the bad_alloc standard exception. Because bad_alloc is raised outside a try block, no attempt is made to handle it within stats(). Rather, the function terminates: pstats is never initialized, and the subsequent program statements within stats() are never executed. The exception mechanism assumes control and remains in control until the exception is handled.

In statement (2), a statement within do_something() or within a function invoked within do_something() or one invoked within a function invoked within do_something(), and so on, may raise an exception. That exception may or may not be caught prior to percolating back up the chain of function calls begun by the call of do_something(). If the exception is handled, stats() continues as if nothing had happened. If the exception is not handled prior to termination of do_something(), stats() in turn is terminated because the exception occurs outside a try block.

(Notice that if size is equal to 0,

```
pstats[ 3 ] = pstats[ 0 ]/size;
```

results in a division by zero. Although this results in undefined data being assigned to pstats[3], there is no standard exception raised for a division by zero.)

What about the three statements within the try block? The difference in behavior is the following: if a raised exception is active within stats() following termination of sum_it(), min_val(), or max_val(), rather than simply terminate stats() the associated catch clauses of the try block are examined in turn in an attempt to handle the raised exception. Let's say sum_it() raised the following exception:

```
throw string( "internal error: adump27832" );
```

pstats[0] is never initialized, nor are the subsequent two statements within the try block executed. Rather, the exception mechanism recognizes that sum_it() was invoked within a try block and examines the two associated catch clauses.

A catch clause is selected based on a matching of the type of the exception with the type associated with the catch clause. In our case, the exception is of type string and matches the catch clause.

```
catch( string exceptionMsg )
        { /* code to handle exception */ }
```

Control passes to the body of the selected catch clause, and the statements within it are executed in turn. That done, unless if the exception is rethrown within the catch clause the exception is considered handled, and control passes back to the program at this point. For example, if we had written

```
catch( string exceptionMsg )
{
    cerr << "stats(): exception occurred: "
         << exceptionMsg << endl;
    pstats[0] = pstats[1] = pstats[2] = 0;
}
```

then, on completion of the catch clause, program control would pass to the next executable statement following the set of catch clauses. In our case, the statement

```
pstats[ 3 ] = pstats[ 0 ]/size;
```

is executed, followed by the invocation of do_something() and the return of pstats. The function invoking stats() is unaware an exception was ever raised.

A preferred handling of the exception is probably the following:

```
catch( string exceptionMsg )
{
    cerr  << "stats(): exception occurred: "
          << exceptionMsg
          << " unable to stat array "
          << endl;
```

```
            delete [] pstats;
            return 0;
    }
```

In this case, the `catch` clause returns us to the invoking function, which we hope tests the return value of `stats()` against zero before attempting to index into it.

If the exception raised within the active `try` block is one not handled by its associated `catch` clauses, the function is terminated, and the exception mechanism next seeks a handler in the function that invoked `stats()`.

If the exception mechanism rolls the sequence of function invocations all the way back to `main()` and no handler is found, the standard library `terminate()` function is invoked. By default, `terminate()` ends the program.

A special `catch` clause capable of handling raised exceptions of all types is the following:

```
    catch( ... )
    {
        // handles all exceptions, although it cannot
        // directly access the exception object
    }
```

We can think of it as a kind of catch-all.

Exception handling provides a language-level facility for the uniform handling of program anomalies. It is discussed in detail in Chapters 11 and 19. Our companion text, *Inside the C++ Object Model* ([LIPPMAN96a]), discusses implementation issues and performance, as does the article "Exception Handling: Behind the Scenes", by Josée Lajoie in [LIPPMAN96b]. A good discussion of potential pitfalls in the use of exception handling is "Exception Handling: A False Sense of Security" by Tom Cargill, also in [LIPPMAN96b].

Exercise 2.18

The following function provides absolutely no checking of either possible bad data or the possible failure of an operation. Identify all the things that might possibly go wrong within the function (in this exercise, we don't yet want to worry about possible exceptions raised).

```
        int *alloc_and_init( string file_name )
        {
            ifstream infile( file_name );
            int elem_cnt;
            infile >> elem_cnt;
```

```
int *pi = allocate_array( elem_cnt );

int elem;
int index = 0;
while ( cin >> elem )
        pi[ index++ ] = elem;

sort_array( pi, elem_cnt );
register_data( pi );

return pi;
}
```

Exercise 2.19

The following functions invoked in `alloc_and_init()` raise the following exception types if they should fail:

```
allocate_array()  noMem
sort_array()      int
register_data()   string
```

Insert one or more `try` blocks and associated `catch` clauses where appropriate to handle these exceptions. Simply print the occurrence of the error within the `catch` clause.

Exercise 2.20

Go through the set of conditions identified as potential program failures within `alloc_and_init()` in Exercise 2.18, identifying those serious enough to warrant throwing an exception. Revise the function (either the Exercise 2.18 version or preferably the Exercise 2.19 version if you did that one) to throw the identified exceptions (throwing literal strings for now is good enough).

2.7   An Array by Any Other Name

One of the difficulties of distributing our code to sites other than those in which we program is that we cannot know what effect, if any, our global names may have. For example, if someone at Intel has written

```
class Array { ... };
```

then that site cannot use both that Array class and the one we've implemented in the same program. The visibility of the names makes the two implementations mutually exclusive.

The conventional way of solving this problem before Standard C++ was to prefix the globally visible names with some lexically unique string. For example, we might release our Array as

```
class Cplusplus_Primer_Third_Edition_Array { ... };
```

Although that name is certainly likely to be unique (we cannot guarantee that, however), it is also something of a handful to write. The Standard C++ namespace mechanism is a language-level solution to this problem.

The namespace mechanism allows us to encapsulate names that otherwise *pollute the global namespace*. In general, we use namespaces only when we expect our code to be used in external software sites. For example, here is how we might encapsulate our Array class:

```
namespace Cplusplus_Primer_3E {
    template <class elemType>
      class Array { ... };
    // ...
}
```

The name following the namespace keyword identifies a namespace separate from the global namespace within which we can place entities we wish to declare outside a function or class. The namespace does not change the meaning of the declarations within it; it changes only their visibility. Before continuing, let's extend our set of available namespaces:

```
namespace IBM_Canada_Laboratory {
    template <class elemType>
      class Array { ... };
    class Matrix { ... };
    // ...
}

namespace Disney_Feature_Animation {
    class Point { ... };
    template <class elemType, int size>
      class Array { ... };

    // ...
}
```

If the declarations within a namespace are not immediately visible to the program, how do we access them? We use a *qualified name notation* of the form

```
namespace_identifier::entity_name;
```

as in

```
Cplusplus_Primer_3E::Array<string> text;
IBM_Canada_Laboratory::Matrix mat;
Disney_Feature_Animation::Point origin( 5000, 5000 );
```

Although `Disney_Feature_Animation`, `IBM_Canada_Laboratory`, and `Cplusplus_Primer_3E` uniquely identify each respective namespace, they are somewhat cumbersome to use often within our programs. Using namespace identifiers such as `P3E`, `DFA`, or `IBM_CL` is more convenient, but it conveys considerably less information and increases the possibility of name collision. To provide for both meaningful namespace identifiers and programmer convenience in accessing the entities declared within the namespace, an alias facility is provided.

A *namespace alias* allows us to associate an alternative, shorter or generic name with an existing namespace. For example:

```
// provide a generic alias
namespace LIB = IBM_Canada_Laboratory;

// simply provide a shorter alias
namespace DFA = Disney_Feature_Animation;
```

This alias can then be used as a synonym to the original namespace. For example:

```
#include "IBM_Canada.h"
namespace LIB = IBM_Canada_Laboratory;

int main()
{
    LIB::Array<int> ia(1024);
    // ...
}
```

Potentially, an alias can also serve to encapsulate the actual namespace being used. In this scenario, for example, by changing the namespace assigned to the alias, we change the set of declarations we use without having to change the actual code accessing those declarations through the alias. For example:

```
namespace LIB = Cplusplus_Primer_3E;

int main()
{
    // in this case, this declaration need not change
    LIB::Array<int> ia(1024);
    // ...
}
```

For this technique to work in practice, however, the declarations within the two namespaces must provide the exact interface. For example, the following does not work because the Disney Array class wants both a type and a size parameter for its Array class:

```
namespace LIB = Disney_Feature_Animation;

int main()
```

```
    {
         // no longer a valid declaration
         LIB::Array<int> ia(1024);
         // ...
    }
```

More often, programmers would prefer unqualified access to the names declared within a namespace. Even with the ability to provide a shorter alias for a namespace identifier, it can often prove cumbersome to qualify every access of every name declared within a namespace. The *using directive* makes the declarations within a namespace visible so that they can be referred to without qualification. For example:

```
    #include "IBM_Canada_Laboratory.h"

    // makes all names visible
    using namespace IBM_Canada_Laboratory;

    int main()
    {
         // ok: IBM_Canada_Laboratory::Matrix
         Matrix mat( 4,4 );

         // ok: IBM_Canada_Laboratory::Array
         Array<int> ia( 1024 );
         // ...
    }
```

Both `using` and `namespace` are keywords. The namespace referred to must already have been declared, or a compile-time error results.

The *using declaration* provides a more selective name visibility mechanism. It allows for a single declaration within a namespace to be made visible. For example:

```
    #include "IBM_Canada_Laboratory.h"

    // only makes Matrix visible
    using IBM_Canada_Laboratory::Matrix;

    int main()
    {
         // ok: IBM_Canada_Laboratory::Matrix
         Matrix mat(4,4);

         // error: IBM_Canada_Laboratory::Array not visible
         Array<int> ia( 1024 );
         // ...
    }
```

To prevent the components of the C++ standard library from polluting the global namespace of users' programs, all the components of the C++ standard library are declared within a namespace called namespace std. As we mentioned in Chapter 1, even though we include a C++ library header file in a program text file, the components declared within that header file are not automatically visible in the text file. For example, under Standard C++, the following code sample does not compile properly:

```
#include <string>
// error: string is not visible
string current_chapter = "A Tour of C++";
```

All the declarations in the <string> header file are enclosed in namespace std. As mentioned in Chapter 1, we can use a using directive following the #include preprocessor directive to make the components of namespace std declared in the C++ header file <string> visible in the text file:

```
#include <string>
 using namespace std;

// ok: string is visible
string current_chapter = "A Tour of C++";
```

A using directive is usually seen as a poor choice for making the names declared in namespace std visible in our programs. In the example, the using directive makes all the components of namespace std declared in the header file <string> visible in the program text file. This brings back the global namespace pollution problem that namespace std tries to avoid in the first place and increases the chance that names of the C++ standard library components will collide with some of the global names declared in our program.

Now that we have seen a little bit more about the namespace mechanism, we know that two other mechanisms can be used instead of a using directive to refer to the name string hidden in namespace std. We can use the qualified name, as follows:

```
#include <string>
// ok: use qualified name
std::string current_chapter = "A Tour of C++";
```

Or we can use a using declaration as follows:

```
#include <string>
 using std::string;

// ok: using declaration makes string visible
string current_chapter = "A Tour of C++";
```

To use names declared in namespace std, we recommend the use of the more selective using declarations instead of using directives. This is another reason that no using directives appear in the code examples of this book. Ideally, a code example should have a using declaration for each library component it uses. To limit the size of the examples and also because many of the examples in this book were compiled with implementations not supporting namespaces, the using declarations are not shown. Section 8.6 discusses further how using declarations are used for the components of the C++ standard library.

In the following four chapters, we walk through the design of four additional classes. Chapter 3 concludes with the design and implementation of a String class, Chapter 4 with the design of an integer Stack class, Chapter 5 with a List class, and Chapter 6 with a redesign of the Stack class defined in Chapter 4. The namespace mechanism allows us to place each class in its own header file but still encapsulate their names in our single Cplusplus_Primer_3E namespace. We look at that technique and much more about namespaces in Chapter 8.

Exercise 2.21

Given the following namespace definition

```
namespace Exercise {
    template <class elemType>
        class Array { ... };

    template <class Etype>
        void print( Array< Etype > );

    class String { ... };
    template <class listType>
        class List { ... };
}
```

and the following program

```
int main() {
    const int size = 1024;
    Array< String > as( size );
    List< int > il( size );

    // ...

    Array< String > *pas = new Array<String>(as);
    List <int> *pil = new List<int>(il);

    print( *pas );
}
```

the current program implementation fails to compile because the type names are all encapsulated within the namespace. Modify the program to

  a. Use the qualified name notation to access the type definitions within the Exercise namespace.

  b. Use the using declaration to access the type definitions.

c. Use the namespace alias mechanism.

d. Use the using directive.

2.8   The Standard Array Is a Vector

Although the built-in array supports the mechanics of a container, as we've seen, it does not support the semantics of the container abstraction. In order to program at that level, prior to Standard C++, we had to either acquire or implement the class ourselves. With Standard C++, an array class is now part of the C++ standard library. It's not called an array; it is called a vector.

The vector, of course, is a class template. So we write

```
vector<int>    ivec( 10 );
vector<string> svec( 10 );
```

to define, respectively, a vector of ten integer objects and a vector of ten string objects.

There are two primary differences between our Array class templates implementation and that of the vector class template. The first difference is that the vector class template supports the notion both of assignment to an existing array element and of insertion of additional elements — that is, the vector's array grows dynamically at run-time if the programmer wishes to make use of that feature. The second difference is more sweeping and represents a significant shift of design paradigm. Rather than provide a large set of member operations that can be applied to a vector, such as sort(), min(), max(), find(), and so on, the vector class provides a minimal set: operations such as the equality and less-than operators, size(), and empty(). The general operations such as sort(), min(), max(), find(), and so on are instead provided as independent *generic algorithms*.

To define a vector, we must include its associated header file:

```
#include < vector >
```

The following are all valid definitions of vector objects:

```
#include < vector >

// ways of creating a vector object
vector<int> vec0;    // empty vector

const int size  = 8;
const int value = 1024;

// vector of size 8,
// each element initialized to 0
vector<int> vec1( size );

// vector of size 8,
// each element initialized to value 1024
vector<int> vec2( size, value );
```

```
// vec3 is of size 4
// initialized to the four values of ia
int ia[4] = { 0, 1, 1, 2 };
vector<int> vec3( ia, ia+4 );

// vec4 is a copy of vec2
vector<int> vec4( vec2 );
```

Now that we have defined our vectors, we need to traverse the elements within it. As with our Array class template, the standard vector class template supports the use of the subscript operator. For example:

```
#include <vector>
extern int getSize();

void mumble()
{
        int size = getSize();
        vector< int > vec( size );

        for ( int ix = 0; ix < size; ++ix )
                vec[ ix ] = ix;

        // ...
}
```

An alternative traversal idiom is the use of an *iterator pair* to mark the beginning and end of the vector. An iterator is a class object supporting the abstraction of a pointer type. The vector class template provides a begin() and end() pair of operations returning an iterator to, respectively, the beginning of the vector and 1 past the end of the vector. Together, the iterator pair marks the range of elements to traverse. For example, here is an equivalent implementation of the previous code fragment:

```
#include < vector >
extern int getSize();

void mumble()
{
        int size = getSize();
        vector< int > vec( size );

        vector< int >::iterator iter = vec.begin();

        for ( int ix = 0; iter != vec.end(); ++iter, ++ix )
                *iter = ix;

        // ...
}
```

The definition of `iter`

```
vector< int >::iterator iter = vec.begin();
```

initializes it to address the first element of `vec`. `iterator` is a typedef defined inside the vector class template holding elements of type `int`. The following advances the iterator to the next element of the vector:

```
++iter
```

This code dereferences the iterator to access the actual element:

```
*iter
```

The operations we are able to perform on a vector are surprisingly varied. They are not, however, provided as member functions of the vector class template but instead as an independent set of generic algorithms provided by the standard library. The following is a sampling of the generic algorithms available:

- *Search* algorithms: `find()`, `find_if()`, `search()`, `binary_search()`, `count()`, and `count_if()`.

- *Sorting* and general *ordering* algorithms: `sort()`, `partial_sort()`, `merge()`, `partition()`, `rotate()`, `reverse()`, and `random_shuffle()`.

- *Deletion* algorithms: `unique()` and `remove()`.

- *Numeric* algorithms: `accumulate()`, `partial_sum()`, `inner_product()`, and `adjacent_difference()`.

- *Generation* and *mutation* algorithms: `generate()`, `fill()`, `transform()`, `copy()`, and `for_each()`.

- *Relational* algorithms: `equal()`, `min()`, and `max()`.

The generic algorithms accept a pair of iterators that mark a range of elements over which to traverse. For example, to `sort()` all the elements of `ivec`, a vector of some size holding elements of some type, we need simply write the following:

```
sort( ivec.begin(), ivec.end() );
```

To `sort()` only the first half, we write

```
sort( ivec.begin(), ivec.begin()+ivec.size()/2 );
```

The generic algorithms also accept a pair of pointers into a built-in array. For example, given the array

```
int ia[7] = { 10, 7, 9, 5, 3, 7, 1 };
```

we can `sort()` the entire array as follows:

```
sort( ia, ia+7 );
```

We sort only the first four elements as follows:

```
sort( ia, ia+4 );
```

To use the algorithms, we must include their associated header file:

```
#include <algorithm>
```

Here is how we might apply a variety of the generic algorithms to a vector class object:

```
#include <vector>
#include <algorithm>
#include <iostream>

int ia[ 10 ] = {
     51, 23, 7, 88, 41, 98, 12, 103, 37, 6 };

int main()
{
     vector< int > vec( ia, ia+10 );

     // sort the array
     sort( vec.begin(), vec.end() );

     // grab value to search for
     int search_value;
     cin >> search_value;

     // search for an element
     vector<int>::iterator found;
     found = find( vec.begin(), vec.end(), search_value );
     if ( found != vec.end() )
          cout << "search_value found!\n";
     else cout << "search_value not found!\n";

     // reverse the array
     reverse( vec.begin(), vec.end() );

     // ...
}
```

The standard library also provides support for a *map* associative array — that is, an array of elements that can be indexed by something other than integer values. For example, a telephone directory might be supported as an array of telephone numbers indexed by the name of the person to whom the telephone belongs:

```
#include <map>
#include <string>
#include "TelephoneNumber.h"

map< string, telephoneNum > telephone_directory;
```

We look at vectors, maps, and the other container types supported by the C++ standard library in Chapter 6, walking through the implementation of a text query system by way of illustrating the use of these types. Chapter 12 looks at the generic algorithms, and the Appendix provides an alphabetical illustration of how each algorithm might be used.

This chapter has walked through, admittedly at a brisk pace, the primary support C++ provides for data abstraction (object-based programming), object-oriented programming, generic programming (templates, the container types, and generic algorithms), and programming in the large (exception handling and namespaces). In the remainder of this book, we revisit in more detail and at a slower pace the basic and the advanced features of C++.

Exercise 2.22

Explain the results of each vector definition:

```
string pals[] = {
       "pooh", "tigger", "piglet", "eeyore", "kanga" };

(a) vector<string> svec1( pals, pals+5 );
(b) vector<int>    ivec1( 10 );
(c) vector<int>    ivec2( 10, 10 );
(d) vector<string> svec2( svec1 );
(e) vector<double> dvec;
```

Exercise 2.23

Given the following function declaration, implement the body of min() to find and return the smallest element of vec using a for loop indexing into vec and then a for loop using an iterator to traverse vec:

```
template <class elemType>
elemType
    min( const vector<elemType> &vec );
```

Part II

The Basic Language

The program text we write and the program data we manipulate are stored as a sequence of bits in the memory of the computer. A *bit* is a single cell that holds a value of 0 or 1. In physical terms this value is an electrical charge that is either "off" or "on." A typical segment of computer memory might look like this:

00011011011100010110010000111011 . . .

This collection of bits at this level is without structure. It is difficult to speak of this bit sequence in any meaningful way. Occasionally, however, it is necessary or convenient to program on the level of individual or aggregate groupings of bits (particularly when we are accessing actual machine hardware). The C++ language provides a set of bitwise operators to support bit manipulation and a bitset container type with which to declare objects holding collections of bits (these operators and the bitset container types are discussed in Chapter 4).

Structure is imposed on the bit sequence by considering the bits in aggregates referred to as *bytes* and *words*. Generally, a byte is composed of 8 bits. A word is typically composed of 32 bits, or 4 bytes (workstation operating systems, however, are currently making a transition to 64-bit systems). Word sizes vary from one computer to the next. We speak of these values as being *machine-dependent*. The figure below illustrates our bit stream organized into four addressable byte rows.

1024	0	0	0	1	1	0	1	1
1032	0	1	1	1	0	0	0	1
1040	0	1	1	0	0	1	0	0
1048	0	0	1	1	1	0	1	1

Addressable Machine Memory

The organization of memory allows us to refer to a particular collection of bits. Thus, it is possible to speak of the word at address 1024 or the byte at address 1040, allowing us to say, for example, that the byte at address 1032 is not equal to the byte at address 1048.

It is still not possible, however, to speak meaningfully of the content of the byte at address 1032. Why? Because we do not know how to interpret its bit sequence. To speak of the meaning of the byte at address 1032, we must know the type of the value being represented.

Type abstraction allows for a meaningful interpretation of fixed-length bit sequences. C++ provides a predefined set of data types, such as characters, integers, and floating point numbers, and a set of fundamental data abstractions, such as string, vector, and complex numbers. It also provides a set of operators, such as the addition, subtraction, equality, and less-than operators, to manipulate these types, and a small set of statements for program flow control, such as the while loop and if statement. These elements form an alphabet with which many large, complex, real-world systems have been written. The first step in mastering C++ is understanding these basic components, which form the topic of Part II of C++ *Primer*.

Chapter 3 surveys the predefined and extended data types and looks at the mechanisms for constructing new types, primarily the class mechanism introduced in Section 2.3. Chapter 4 focuses on support for expressions, looking at the predefined operators together with the issues of type conversion, operator precedence, and associativity. The smallest independent unit of our programs is a statement. Program statements are the topic of Chapter 5. Chapter 6 introduces the standard library container types, such as vector and map, illustrating their use through the implementation of a text query system.

3

The C++ Data Types

This chapter surveys the *built-in*, or *primitive*, data types predefined within C++. It begins with a look at *literal constants*, such as 3.14159 and "pi", and then introduces the concept of a *symbolic variable*, or *object*. An object within a C++ program must be defined to be of a specific type. The remainder of the chapter walks through the different types for which an object may be declared. In addition, we contrast the built-in C++ support for strings and arrays with the class abstractions provided by the C++ standard library. Although the library abstractions are not primitive types, they are fundamental types to real-world C++ programs, and we wish to introduce them as early as possible to encourage and illustrate their use. We like to refer to these types as making up an *extended basic language* of primitive built-in and primitive class abstraction types.

3.1   Literal Constant

C++ predefines a set of numeric data types, which allow the representation of integers, floating point numbers, and individual characters and predefines a character array to represent a string.

- The type `char` is typically used to represent individual characters and small integers. It is represented in a single machine byte.

- The types `short`, `int`, and `long` represent integer values of different sizes. Typically, `short`s are represented in half a machine word, `int`s in a machine word, and `long`s in either one or two machine words (on 32-bit machines, `int`s and `long`s are usually the same size).

- The types `float`, `double`, and `long double` represent floating point single, double, and extended precision values. Typically, `float`s are represented in one word; `double`s in two words, and `long double` in either three or four words.

char, short, int, and long are collectively referred to as the *integral types*. Integral types may be either signed or unsigned. In a signed type, the left-most bit serves as the *sign bit*, and the remaining bits represent the value. In an unsigned type, all the bits represent the value. If the sign bit is set to 1, the value is interpreted as negative; if 0, positive. An 8-bit signed char may represent the values –128 through 127; an unsigned char, 0 through 255.

When a value such as 1 occurs in a program, it is referred to as a *literal constant*: literal because we can speak of it only in terms of its value; constant because its value cannot be changed. Every literal has an associated type. 0, for example, is of type int. 3.14159 is a literal constant of type double. We refer to a literal constant as *nonaddressable*; although its value is stored somewhere in the computer's memory, we have no means of accessing that address.

Literal integer constants can be written in decimal, octal, or hexadecimal notation. (This does not change the bit representation of the value.) The value 20, for example, can be written in any of the following three ways:

```
20      // decimal
024     // octal
0x14    // hexadecimal
```

Appending a 0 (zero) to a literal integer constant causes it to be interpreted as octal. Appending either 0x or 0X will cause a literal integer constant to be interpreted as hexadecimal. (Chapter 20, The iostream Library, discusses printing values in octal or hexadecimal notation.)

By default, literal integer constants are treated as signed values of type int. A literal integer constant can be specified as being of type long by following its value with either L or l (the letter "ell" in either uppercase or lowercase). Using the lowercase letter in general should be avoided, because it is easily mistaken for the number 1. In a similar manner, a literal integer constant can be specified as being unsigned by following its value with either U or u. An unsigned long literal constant can also be specified. For example:

```
128u  1024UL    1L     8Lu
```

A floating point literal constant can be written in either scientific or common decimal notation. Using scientific notation, the exponent can be written as either E or e. By default, literal floating point constants are treated as type double. A single precision literal constant is indicated by following the value with either F or f. Similarly, extended precision is indicated by following the value with either L or l (again, use of the lowercase instance is discouraged). (Note, too, that the F, f, L, and l suffixes can be applied only when the common decimal notation is used.) For example:

```
3.14159F 0.1f   12.345L  0.0
3e1      1.0E-3 2.       1.0L
```

The words `true` and `false` are literals of type `bool`. One can write, For example:

```
true    false
```

A printable literal character constant can be written by enclosing the character within single quotation marks. For example:

```
'a'         '2'         ','         ' ' (blank)
```

Selected nonprintable characters, the single and double quotation marks, and the backslash can be represented by the following *escape sequences* (an escape sequence begins with a backslash):

```
newline          \n
horizontal tab   \t
vertical tab     \v
backspace        \b
carriage return  \r
formfeed         \f
alert (bell)     \a
backslash        \\
question mark    \?
single quote     \'
double quote     \"
```

A generalized escape sequence takes the form

```
\ooo
```

where ooo represents a sequence of as many as three octal digits. The value of the octal digits represents the numerical value of the character in the machine's character set. The following examples are representations of literal constants using the ASCII character set:

```
\7 (bell)   \14 (newline)
\0 (null)   \062 ('2')
```

Additionally, a character literal can be preceded by L, as in

```
L'a'
```

This is spoken of as a *wide-character literal* and has type `wchar_t`. Wide-character literals support language character sets, such as Chinese and Japanese, in which some of the character values cannot be represented within a single `char`.

A string literal constant is composed of zero or more characters enclosed in double quotation marks. Nonprintable characters can be represented by their underlying escape sequence. A string literal can extend across multiple lines. A backslash as the last character on a line indicates that the string literal is continued on the next line. For example:

```
"" (null string)
"a"
"\nCC\toptions\tfile.[cC]\n"
"a multi-line \
```

```
string literal signals its \
continuation with a backslash"
```

A string literal is of type *array of const characters*. It consists of both the string literal and a terminating null character added by the compiler. For example, whereas

```
'A'
```

represents the single character A, the following represents the single character A followed by the null character.

```
"A"
```

The null character is the C and C++ language convention to signal the end of the string.

Just as there is a wide-character literal, such as

```
L'a'
```

there is a wide string literal, again preceded by L, such as

```
L"a wide string literal"
```

A wide string literal is of type *array of const wide characters*. It is also terminated by an equivalent wide null character.

Two string or wide string literals, if adjacent within the program, are concatenated and then suffixed with a trailing null. For example,

```
"two" "some"
```

is printed as *twosome*. What happens if you attempt to concatenate a string literal and a wide string literal? For example:

```
// this is not a good idea
"two" L"some"
```

The result is *undefined*—that is, there is no standard behavior defined for concatenating the two different types. Programs that use undefined behavior are said to be *nonportable*. Although the program may execute correctly for the current compiler, there is no guarantee that the same program, compiled under a different compiler or a subsequent release of the current compiler, will continue to run correctly. Tracking down these sorts of problems in previously working programs is, mildly put, a profoundly unpleasant task. We recommend not knowingly making use of undefined program idioms. When appropriate, we point out such idioms.

Exercise 3.1

Explain the difference between the following sets of literal constants:

```
(a) 'a', L'a', "a", L"a"
(b) 10, 10u, 10L, 10uL, 012, 0xC
(c) 3.14, 3.14f, 3.14L
```

Exercise 3.2

Which, if any, of the following are illegal?

```
(a) "Who goes with F\144rgus?\014"
(b) 3.14e1L
(c) "two" L"some"
(d) 1024f
(e) 3.14UL
(f) "multiple line
    comment"
```

3.2 Variables

Imagine that we are given the problem of computing 2 to the power of 10. Our first attempt might look like this:

```
#include <iostream>

int main() {
    // a first solution
    cout << "2 raised to the power of 10: ";
    cout << 2 * 2 * 2 * 2 * 2 * 2 * 2 * 2 * 2 * 2;
    cout << endl;
    return 0;
}
```

This solves the problem, although we might double- or triple-check to make sure that exactly 10 literal instances of 2 are being multiplied. Otherwise, we're satisfied. Our program correctly generates the answer 1,024.

We're next asked to compute 2 raised to the power of 17 and then to the power of 23. Changing our program each time is a nuisance. Worse, it proves to be remarkably error-prone. Too often, the modified program produces an answer with one too few or too many instances of 2. Finally, we are asked to produce a table listing the powers of 2 from 0 through 15. Using literal constants requires 32 lines of the general form

```
cout << "2 raised to the power of X\t";
cout << 2 * ... * 2;
```

where X increases by 1 with each pair of statements.

On the one hand, this gets the job done; our employer is unlikely to delve too deeply into how we accomplish our task provided that our results are correct and timely. In many production environments, in fact, the primary measure of success is the final output, and any discussion of process is likely to be dismissed as academic and impractical.

Although brute force solutions work, the process is often unpleasant and tinged with an aura of crisis. The attractiveness of such solutions is their simplicity; we understand exactly what needs to be done, although often it is not fun. Technologically sophisticated solutions in general require considerably more start-up time, when it often feels as if nothing is being accomplished. And because the process is automated, there is a greater potential for things to go wrong.

And things inevitably seem to go wrong. The benefit is that, amidst the inevitable errors and missteps, not only are things accomplished faster, but also the limits of the conceivable are extended. Sometimes, oddly enough, the process even becomes fun.

In our example, the alternative to the explicit brute force power of 2 computation is twofold: the use of named objects to read and write stepwise computations, and the introduction of flow-of-control constructs to provide for the repeated execution of a sequence of program statements while some truth condition holds. Here, then, is our alternative "technologically advanced" computation of 2 raised to the power of 10:

```cpp
#include <iostream>

int main()
{
    // objects of type int
    int value = 2;
    int pow = 10;

    cout << value << " raised to the power of "
         << pow << ": \t";

    int res = 1; // holds result

    // loop control statement: repeat calculation of res
    // until cnt is greater than pow
    for ( int cnt=1; cnt <= pow; ++cnt)
        res = res * value;

    cout << res << endl;
}
```

value, pow, res, and cnt are variables that allow for the storage, modification, and retrieval of values. The for loop allows for the repeated execution of our calculation until it's been executed pow times.

Although this level of generalization makes for a more flexible program, it is not yet a reusable program. A further level of generalization is necessary: to factor out the portion of the program that computes the exponential value and define it as a stand-alone function that others can invoke. For example:

```cpp
int
pow( int val, int exp )
{
    for ( int res = 1; exp > 0; --exp )
        res = res * val;
```

```
        return res;
    }
```

Now, each of our programs that requires computing an exponential value can use this instance of pow() rather than reimplement it. Generating a table of the powers of 2 can be done as follows:

```
#include <iostream>
extern int pow(int,int);

int main()
{
    int val = 2;
    int exp = 15;

    cout << "The Powers of 2\n";
    for ( int cnt=0; cnt <= exp; ++cnt )
        cout << cnt << ": "
                << pow(val,cnt) << endl;

    return 0;
}
```

In practice, our implementation of pow() is neither robust nor general enough. What if the exponent is negative, for example, or if it is 1,000,000? For a negative exponent, our function always returns 1. For a very large exponent, our int res variable is too small to hold the resulting value. Instead, an arbitrary and incorrect value is returned for a very large exponent. (The best solution in this case is to modify our implementation to return a value of type double.) In terms of generality, our function should be able to handle integer and floating point values and exponents, and so on. As you can see, writing a robust and general function for an unknown set of users is much more complicated than implementing a specific algorithm to meet our own immediate needs. (To see a real-world implementation of pow(), see [PLAUGER92].)

3.2.1   What Is a Variable?

A variable provides us with named memory storage that we can write to, retrieve, and manipulate throughout the course of our program. Each symbolic variable in C++ is associated with a specific data type, which determines the size and layout of its associated memory, the range of values that can be stored within that memory, and the set of operations that can be applied to it. We speak of a variable, alternatively, as an *object*. For example, here are the definitions of five objects of five differing types (we'll look at the details of the definition in a subsequent section):

```
int     student_count;
double  salary;
bool    on_loan;
```

```
string street_address;
char   delimiter;
```

Both a variable and a literal constant maintain storage and have an associated type. The difference is that a variable is *addressable*. There are two values associated with a variable:

1. Its data value, stored at some memory address. This is sometimes referred to as an object's *rvalue* (pronounced "are-value"). You might think of rvalue as meaning *read value*. Both a literal constant and a variable can serve as an rvalue.

2. Its address value — that is, its address in memory within which its data value is stored. This is sometimes referred to as a variable's *lvalue* (pronounced "ell-value"). You might think of lvalue as meaning *location value*. A literal constant cannot serve as an lvalue.

In the expression

```
ch = ch - '0';
```

the variable ch appears on both the right- and left-hand sides of the assignment operator. The right-hand instance is read. Its associated data value is fetched from its address in memory. The left-hand occurrence is written. The result of the subtraction operation is stored at the location value of ch; its previous value is overwritten. On the right-hand side of the expression, ch and the literal character constant serve as rvalues. On the left-hand side of the expression, ch serves as an lvalue.

In general, the left-hand side of an assignment operator always requires an lvalue. It is a compiler-time error, for example, to write either of the following:

```
// compile-time errors: left-hand side is not lvalue

// error: literal constant is not an lvalue
0 = 1;

// error: arithmetic expression is not an lvalue
salary + salary * 0.10 = new_salary;
```

In the course of the text, we'll see a number of situations in which the use of an rvalue or lvalue impacts the semantic behavior and performance of our programs — in particular in the passing in and return of values from a function.

The definition of a variable causes its associated memory storage to be allocated. Because an object can have only a single location, there can be only a single definition of each object within our program. This can be a problem if an object is defined in one file but needs to be accessed within another. For example:

```
// file module0.C
// defines fileName object
string fileName;
```

```
// ... assign fileName a value

// file module1.C
// needs to use fileName object

// oops: fails to compile:
// fileName undefined within module1.C
ifstream input_file( fileName );
```

In C++, an object must first be made known to the program before it is used. This is necessary in order for the compiler to guarantee the type correctness of the object's use. Referring to an unknown object results in a compile-time program error. In our example, the compilation of module1.C fails because fileName is undefined within it.

To compile module1.C, we must make fileName known to the program but without introducing a second definition. We do this by *declaring* the variable:

```
// file module1.C
// needs to use fileName object

// declares fileName, that is, makes it known to the
// program but without introducing a 2nd definition
extern string fileName;

ifstream input_file( fileName );
```

The *declaration* of an object makes known the type and name of the object to the program. It consists of the object's name and its type preceded by the keyword extern. (For a full discussion of extern, see Section 8.2.) A declaration is not a definition and does not result in an allocation of storage. In effect, it is an assertion that a definition of the variable exists elsewhere in the program.

Although a program can contain only one definition of an object, it can contain any number of object declarations. Rather than provide a separate declaration within each file in which an object is used, it is preferable to declare the object in a header file and include that header file whenever that declaration is needed. In this way, if the declaration needs to be modified we modify it only once and maintain a consistent declaration across the multiple files that use that declaration. (We'll have more to say about header files in Section 8.2.)

3.2.2   The Name of a Variable

The name of a variable, its *identifier*, can be composed of letters, digits, and the underscore character. It must begin with either a letter or an underscore. Upper- and lower-case letters are distinct. There is no language-imposed limit on the permissible length of a name, but out of consideration for our users, it should not be too long, such as gosh_this_is_an_impossibly_long_name_to_type.

C++ reserves a set of words for use within the language as keywords. The keyword identifiers may not be reused as program identifiers. We've already seen a number of language keywords. Table 3.1 lists the complete set of C++ keywords.

Table 3.1 C++ Keywords

asm	auto	bool	break	case
catch	char	class	const	const_cast
continue	default	delete	do	double
dynamic_cast	else	enum	explicit	export
extern	false	float	for	friend
goto	if	inline	int	long
mutable	namespace	new	operator	private
protected	public	register	reinterpret_cast	return
short	signed	sizeof	static	static_cast
struct	switch	template	this	throw
true	try	typedef	typeid	typename
union	unsigned	using	virtual	void
volatile	wchar_t	while		

There are a number of generally accepted conventions for naming objects, primarily concerning the readability of programs.

- The name of an object is normally written in lowercase letters. For example, one writes `index` and not `Index` or `INDEX`. (`Index` is presumed to be a type name, and `INDEX` is generally presumed to be a constant value, usually one defined by a preprocessor `#define` directive.)

- An identifier is provided with a *mnemonic* name — that is, a name that gives some indication of its use in a program, such as `on_loan` or `salary`. However, whether one writes `table` or `tbl` is more a question of style than of correctness.

- A multiword identifier traditionally either contains an underscore between each word or capitalizes the first letter of each embedded word. For example, one generally writes `student_loan` or `studentLoan` and not `studentloan` (although Stan, at least, has been known to write all three). In general, people with an ObjectOrientedBackground prefer capitalization, and those with a C_or_procedural_background favor the underscore. (Again, whether one writes `is_a`, `isA`, or `isa` is more a question of style than of correctness.)

3.2.3   The Definition of an Object

A simple definition consists of a type specifier followed by a name. The definition is terminated by a semicolon. For example:

```
double salary;
double wage;
int month;
int day;
int year;
unsigned long distance;
```

When more than one identifier of the same type is being defined, a comma-separated list of identifiers may follow the type specifier. The list may span multiple lines. It is terminated by a semicolon. For example, the preceding definitions can be rewritten as follows:

```
double salary, wage;
int month,
    day, year;
unsigned long distance;
```

A simple definition specifies the type and identifier of a variable. It does not provide a first, or initial, value. If the variable is defined at global scope, it is guaranteed to be provided with an initial value of zero. In our example, salary, wage, month, day, year, and distance are all initialized to zero because they are defined within the global scope. If the variable is defined at local scope or allocated dynamically through use of the new expression, an initial first value of zero is not provided. These objects are spoken of as *uninitialized*. An uninitialized object is not without a value; rather, its value is *undefined*. (Literally, its associated memory contains a random bit pattern of the memory's previous use.)

Because the use of an uninitialized object is a common program error and often difficult to uncover, we generally recommend that an initial value be provided for each defined object. (In some instances this is unnecessary; however, until you are able to recognize those instances, providing an initial value is the safer practice.) The class mechanism provides automatic initialization of class objects through what is referred to as a *default constructor* (this was introduced in Section 2.3). We'll see this in our discussion later in this chapter of the standard library string and complex number class types (Sections 3.11 and 3.15). For now, notice that in the following

```
int main() {
    // uninitialized local object
    int ival;

    // initialized with default string constructor
    string project;

    // ...
}
```

ival is an uninitialized local variable, but project is an initialized class object — initialized automatically with the default string class constructor.

An initial first value can be specified in the definition of an object. An object with a declared first value is spoken of as *initialized*. C++ supports two forms of variable initialization. The first form is an explicit syntax using the assignment operator:

```
int ival = 1024;
string project = "Fantasia 2000";
```

In the implicit form, the first value is placed within parentheses:

```
int ival( 1024 );
string project( "Fantasia 2000" );
```

In both cases, ival is initialized with a first value of 1,024 and project with "Fantasia 2000".

A comma-separated list of identifiers can also provide an explicit initial value for each object. The syntax is as follows:

```
double salary = 9999.99, wage = salary + 0.01;
int month = 08,
        day = 07, year = 1955;
```

The name of an object becomes visible immediately following the identifier in its definition, and thus it is legal, if not wise, to initialize an object to itself. For example:

```
// legal, but not wise
int bizarre = bizarre;
```

In addition, each built-in data type supports a special *constructor* syntax to initialize its object to zero. For example:

```
// sets ival to 0, dval to 0.0
int ival = int();
double dval = double();
```

In the following definition,

```
// int() applied to each of the 10 elements
vector< int > ivec( 10 );
```

int() is automatically applied to each of the ten elements contained within ivec. (Section 2.8 introduced vectors. Section 3.10 and Chapter 6 discuss them in more detail.)

An object can be initialized with an arbitrarily complex expression, including the return value of a function. For example:

```
#include <cmath>
#include <string>

double price = 109.99, discount = 0.16;
double sale_price( price * discount );
```

```
string pet( "wrinkles" );

extern int get_value();
int val =  get_value();

unsigned abs_val = abs( val );
```

abs(), a predefined function from the standard C math library, returns the absolute value of its argument. get_value() is a user-defined function that returns a random integer value.

Exercise 3.3

Which, if any, of the following are illegal definitions? Correct any that are identified as illegal.

```
(a) int car = 1024, auto = 2048;
(b) int ival = ival;
(c) int ival( int() );
(d) double salary = wage = 9999.99;
(e) cin >> int input_value;
```

Exercise 3.4

Distinguish between an lvalue and rvalue. Provide examples of both.

Exercise 3.5

Explain the difference between the following two instances of students and name:

```
(a) extern string name;
    string name( "exercise 3.5a" );

(b) extern vector<string> students;
    vector<string> students;
```

Exercise 3.6

Which, if any, of the following names are invalid? Correct each identified invalid name.

```
(a) int double = 3.14159;  (b) vector< int > _;
(c) string namespace;      (d) string catch-22;
(e) char 1_or_2 = '1';     (f) float Float = 3.14f;
```

Exercise 3.7

What are the differences, if any, between the following global and local object definitions?

```
string global_class;
int global_int;
```

```
int main() {
    int local_int;
    string local_class;

    // ...
}
```

3.3   Pointer Types

We briefly introduced pointers and dynamic memory allocation in Section 2.2. A pointer holds the address of another object, allowing for the indirect manipulation of that object. Typical uses of pointers are the creation of linked data structures such as trees and lists, the management of objects dynamically allocated during program execution, and as a function parameter type primarily for passing in arrays and large class objects.

Every pointer has an associated type. The difference between pointers of different data types is neither in the representation of the pointer nor in the values (addresses) the pointers may hold — these are generally the same for all data pointers.[1] The difference, rather, is in the type of the object being addressed. The type of a pointer instructs the compiler how to interpret the memory found at a particular address as well as how much memory that interpretation should span.

- An `int` pointer addressing memory location 1000 on a 32-bit machine spans the address space 1000–1003.

- A `double` pointer addressing memory location 1000 on a 32-bit machine spans the address space 1000–1007.

Here are some examples of pointer definitions:

```
int             *ip1, *ip2;
complex<double> *cp;
string          *pstring;
vector<int>     *pvec;
double          *dp;
```

A pointer is defined by prefixing the identifier with the dereference operator (*). In a comma-separated definition list, the dereference operator must precede each identifier intended to serve as a pointer. In the following example, `lp` is interpreted as a pointer to an object of type `long`, and `lp2` is interpreted as a data object of type `long` and not as a pointer:

```
long *lp, lp2;
```

---

1. This is not actually true for function pointers, which address the program text segment. Function pointers and data pointers are different. Pointers to functions are addressed in Section 7.9.

In this next example, fp is interpreted as a data object of type float and fp2 is interpreted as a pointer to a float:

```
float fp, *fp2;
```

For clarity, it is preferable to write

```
string *ps;
```

rather than

```
string* ps;
```

The possibility is that a programmer, later wishing to define a second string pointer, may incorrectly modify this definition as follows:

```
// oops: ps2 is not a string pointer
string* ps, ps2;
```

A pointer can hold a value of 0, indicating that it points to no object, or the address of a data object of the same type. Given the definition of ival

```
int ival = 1024;
```

the following definitions and assignments of the two pointers — pi and pi2 — are all legal.

```
// pi initialized to address no object
int *pi = 0;

// pi2 initialized to address ival
int *pi2 = &ival;

// ok: pi and pi2 now both address ival
pi = pi2;

// pi2 now addresses no object
pi2 = 0;
```

A pointer cannot hold a nonaddress value. For example, the following assignment results in a compile-time error:

```
// error: pi assigned int value of ival
pi = ival;
```

Nor can a pointer be initialized or assigned the address value of an object of another type. For example, given the following definitions

```
double dval;
double *pd = &dval;
```

both of the following result in a compile-time error:

```
// both are compile-time errors
// invalid type assignment: int* <== double*
pi = pd;
pi = &dval;
```

It is not that pi cannot physically hold the memory address associated with dval: it can. It is disallowed because pi and pd, although capable of holding the same address value, interpret the layout and extent of that memory very differently.

Of course, if all we wish to do is to hold the address value (and possibly compare the address value to a second address value), then the actual type of the pointer does not matter. A special pointer type is provided to support just that: the void* pointer can be assigned the address value of any data pointer type (a function pointer cannot be assigned to it).

```
// ok: void* can hold the
// address value of any pointer type
void *pv = pi;
pv = pd;
```

The void* indicates that the associated value is an address but that the type of the object at that address is unknown. We cannot operate on the object addressed by a void* pointer. We can only transport that address value or compare it to another address value. (We look at the void* pointer in more detail in Section 4.14.)

Given an int pointer object, pi, writing pi

```
// evaluates to the address contained within pi
// type: int*
pi;
```

evaluates to the address value that pi currently holds. Writing &pi

```
// evaluates to the actual address of pi
// type: int**
&pi;
```

evaluates to the address at which the pointer object pi is stored. How do we access the object pi addresses?

By default there is no way to access the actual object addressed by pi either to read or write to the object. To access an object addressed by a pointer, we must dereference the pointer. A special *dereference operator* (*) is provided to achieve indirect read and write access of the object addressed. For example, given the following definitions

```
int ival = 1024, ival2 = 2048;
int *pi = &ival;
```

here is how we might dereference pi to indirectly access ival:

```
// dereference pi, and assign the object it addresses,
// ival, in this case, the rvalue of ival2
*pi = ival2;

// the right-hand instance reads the value of the
// object addressed by pi; the left-hand instance
// writes the right-hand expression to the object
```

```
*pi = abs( *pi ); // ival = abs(ival);
*pi = *pi + 1;    // ival = ival + 1;
```

We know that when we take the address of an object of type int,

```
int *pi = &ival;
```

the result is int* — that is, a pointer to int. When we take the address of type pointer to int:

```
int **ppi = &pi;
```

the result is int** — that is, a pointer to a pointer to int. When we dereference ppi,

```
int *pi2 = *ppi;
```

we retrieve the address value held by the pointer ppi — in this case, the value held by pi, which is the address of ival. To actually access ival, we need to dereference ppi twice. For example:

```
cout << "The value of ival\n"
     << "direct value: " << ival << "\n"
     << "indirect value: " << *pi << "\n"
     << "doubly indirect value: " << **ppi
     << endl;
```

The following two assignment statements behave very differently, although both are legal. The first statement increases the value of the data object that pi addresses; the second increases the value of the address that the pointer pi contains.

```
int i, j, k;
int *pi = &i;

// add two to i (i = i + 2)
*pi = *pi + 2;

// add to the address pi contains
pi = pi + 2;
```

A pointer may have its address value added to or subtracted by an integral value. This sort of pointer manipulation, referred to as *pointer arithmetic*, may at first appear slightly nonintuitive until we realize that the addition is of data objects and not of discrete decimal values. The addition of 2 to a pointer increases the value of the address it contains by the size of two objects of its type. For example, allowing that a char is 1 byte, an int is 4 bytes, and a double is 8, the addition of 2 to a pointer increases its address value by 2, 8, or 16 depending on whether the pointer is of type char, int, or double.

In practice, pointer arithmetic is guaranteed to be well behaved only if the pointer addresses an array element. In the preceding example, it is not guaranteed that the three integer variables are stored contiguously in memory; ip+2, therefore, may or may not yield a valid address, depending on what is actually stored at that location. The typical idiom for pointer arithmetic is to iterate through an array. For example:

```
int ia[ 10 ];
int *iter = &ia[0];
int *iter_end = &ia[10];

while ( iter != iter_end ) {
    do_something_with_value( *iter );
    ++iter; // iter now addresses next item
}
```

Exercise 3.8

Given the following definitions

```
int ival = 1024, ival2 = 2048;
int *pi1 = &ival, *pi2 = &ival2, **pi3 = 0;
```

explain what is occurring in the following assignments. Identify which, if any, are in error.

```
(a)  ival = *pi3;    (e)  pi1 = *pi3;
(b)  *pi2 = *pi3;    (f)  ival = *pi1;
(c)  ival = pi2;     (g)  pi1 = ival;
(d)  pi2 = *pi1;     (h)  pi3 = &pi2;
```

Exercise 3.9

Pointers are an important aspect of C and C++ programming and yet are a common source of program error. For example,

```
pi = &ival2;
pi = pi + 1024;
```

is almost guaranteed to leave pi addressing a random area of memory. What is the assignment doing, and when would it not be an error?

Exercise 3.10

Similarly, the behavior of the following small program is undefined and likely to fail at run-time:

```
int foobar( int *pi ) {
    *pi = 1024;
    return *pi;
}

int main()
{
```

```
        int *pi2 = 0;
        int ival = foobar( pi2 );
        return 0;
    }
```

What is going on here that is a problem? How might you fix it?

Exercise 3.11

In the previous two exercises, errors occur because of an absence of run-time checking of the use of a pointer. If pointers play such a prominent part in C++ programming, why do you think there is not more safety built into the use of pointers? Can you think of any general guidelines for making the use of pointers safer?

3.4   String Types

C++ provides two string representations: the C-style character string and the string class type introduced with Standard C++. In general we recommend use of the string class, but in practice there are still many program situations in which it is either useful or necessary both to understand and use the older C-style character string. One example that we'll see later in Chapter 7 is the handling of command line options passed in through main() as an array of C-style character strings.

3.4.1   The C-Style Character String

The C-style character string originated within the C language and continues to be supported within C++. (In fact, until Standard C++, it was the only string support available apart from third-party string library classes.)

The string is stored within a character array and is generally manipulated through a char* pointer. The Standard C library provides a set of functions providing for the manipulation of C-style strings, such as the following:

```
        // returns the length of the string
        int strlen( const char* );

        // compares two strings for equality
        int strcmp( const char*, const char* );

        // copies the second string into the first
        char* strcpy(char*, const char* );
```

(The Standard C library is included as part of Standard C++.) To use these functions, we must include the associated C header file,

```
        #include <cstring>
```

The character pointer addressing a C-style string always refers to an associated character array. Even when we write a string literal, such as

```
const char *st = "The expense of spirit\n";
```

internally, the system stores the string literal within a character array. st then addresses the first element of that array. How might we manipulate st as a string?

Generally, we traverse a C-style string using pointer arithmetic, incrementing the pointer by 1 each time until we reach the terminating null character. For example:

```
while ( *st++ ) { ... }
```

The char* pointer st is dereferenced, and the character addressed is tested for its true or false value. A true value is any character other than that of the null character. The ++ is the increment operator and advances st to address the next character in the array.

In general, it is always necessary when using a pointer to test that it addresses some object before dereferencing it. Otherwise, the program is likely to fail. For example:

```
int
string_length( const char *st )
{
    int cnt = 0;
    if ( st )
        while ( *st++ )
                ++cnt;
    return cnt;
}
```

A C-style character string can be of zero length (and therefore treated as empty) in one of two ways: the character pointer can be set to zero and therefore point to no object; alternatively, the pointer can be set, but the array it refers to contains only the null character. For example:

```
// pc1 addresses no array object
char *pc1 = 0;

// pc2 addresses the null character
const char *pc2 = "";
```

C-style strings generally prove error-prone with the novice C or C++ programmer because of the low-level nature of its representation. In the following program sequence, we iterate through a number of typical beginner errors. The task of the program is straightforward: compute the length of st. Unfortunately, our first attempt is incorrect. Do you see the error?

```
#include <iostream>
const char *st = "The expense of spirit\n";
```

```
int main() {
    int len = 0;
    while ( st++ ) ++len;

    cout << len << ": " << st;
    return 0;
}
```

This program fails because `st` is not dereferenced — that is,

```
st++
```

tests whether or not the address `st` is 0 and not whether the character that it addresses is null. The condition will always evaluate as true, because each iteration of the loop adds 1 to the address in `st`. The program will execute forever or until the system stops it. A loop such as this is referred to as an *infinite loop*.

Our second version of the program corrects this mistake. It runs to completion. Unfortunately, its output is in error. Can you see the mistake we've made this time?

```
#include <iostream>
const char *st = "The expense of spirit\n";

int main()
{
    int len = 0;
    while ( *st++ ) ++len;

    cout << len << ": " << st << endl;
    return 0;
}
```

The mistake in this case is that `st` no longer addresses the string literal constant. It has been advanced one character beyond the terminating null character. (The output of the program depends on the contents of the addressed memory.) Here is one possible solution:

```
st = st - len;
cout << len << ": " << st;
```

The program is compiled and executed. Its output, however, is still incorrect. It now generates the following:

```
22: he expense of spirit
```

This reflects something of the nature of programming. Can you see the mistake we've made this time?

The terminating null character of the string is not taken into account when calculating the length of a string. `st` must be repositioned the length of the string *plus 1*. The following line is correct:

```
st = st - len - 1;
```

When compiled and executed, the program generates the following, finally correct output:

```
22: The expense of spirit
```

The program is now correct. In terms of program style, however, it is still something less than elegant. The statement

```
st = st - len - 1;
```

has been added to correct the error introduced by directly incrementing st. The reassignment of st does not fit into the original logic of the program, however, and the program is now somewhat more difficult to understand.

A program correction such as this is often referred to as a *patch* — something stretched over a hole in an existing program. We patched our program by compensating for a logic error in the original design. A better solution is to correct the original design flaw. One solution is to define a second character pointer and initialize it with st. For example:

```
const char *p = st;
```

p can now be used in our computation of the length of st, and st is left unchanged:

```
while ( *p++ )
```

3.4.2   string Type

As we have seen, use of a character pointer to represent a string is easy to get wrong because of its low-level representation. To shield programmers from the many common pitfalls associated with using C-style strings, it was not uncommon to find every project, department, or company site providing its own string class — in fact, the first two editions of this text did just that! The problem is that if everyone provides his or her own string implementation, portability and compatibility of our programs become, well, considerably more difficult. The C++ standard library provides a common implementation of a string class abstraction.

What are the sorts of operations that you would expect from a string class? What constitutes a minimal set of essential behavior?

1.   Support to initialize a string object both with a sequence of characters and with a second string object. With the C-style character string, the initialization of one string with another is not supported.

2.   Support to copy one string to another. With the C-style character string, this is achieved through the strcpy() library function.

3.   Support to access the individual characters to read and write. With the C-style character string, individual character access is achieved either through use of the subscript operator or by direct pointer dereferencing.

4.   Support to compare two strings for equality. With the C-style character string, string comparison is achieved through the strcmp() library function.

5. Support to append two strings, either concatenating one string to another or combining two strings to form a third. With the C-style character string, concatenation is achieved through the `strcat()` library function. Combining two strings to make a third is accomplished by first copying one string to a new instance using `strcpy()` and then concatenating the second string to the new instance using `strcat()`.

6. Support to know how many characters are contained in the string. With the C-style character string, the length of a string is returned by the `strlen()` library function.

7. Support to know whether a string is empty. With the C-style character string, this is accomplished in the following two-step conditional test:

```
char *str = 0;
//...
if ( ! str || ! *str )
     return;
```

The standard C++ library provides a string class type that supports these operations (and a great deal more, as we'll see in Chapter 6). In this section, we look at how the string type supports these operations.

To use the string type, you must include its associated header file:

```
#include <string>
```

For example, here is our character array of the previous section redefined as a string:

```
#include <string>
string st( "The expense of spirit\n" );
```

The length of `st` is returned by its `size()` operation (it does not include the terminating null character):

```
cout << "The size of "
     << st
     << " is " << st.size()
     << " characters, including the newline\n";
```

A second form of string construction defines an empty string. For example:

```
string st2; // empty string
```

How can we be sure it's empty? One way, of course, would be to test `size()` against 0:

```
if ( ! st.size() )
     // ok: empty
```

A more direct method is the `empty()` operation:

```
if ( st.empty() )
     // ok: empty
```

`empty()` returns the `bool` constant `true` if the string contains no characters; otherwise, it returns `false`.

A third form of string construction initializes one string object to a second. For example,

```
string st3( st );
```

initializes `st3` to be a copy of `st`. How can we check that? The equality operator compares two strings for equality, returning `true` if they are equal:

```
if ( st == st3 )
    // the initialization worked
```

How can we copy one string to another? The simplest method uses the assignment operator. For example,

```
st2 = st3; // copy st3 to st2
```

first deletes the storage containing the characters associated with st2, allocates the storage needed to contain the characters associated with st3, and then copies the characters associated with st3.

It is also possible to concatenate two or more strings through the use of either the plus operator (+) or the somewhat strange-looking compound assignment operator (+=). For example, given the two strings

```
string s1( "hello, " );
string s2( "world\n" );
```

we can concatenate the two strings to create a third string as follows:

```
string s3 = s1 + s2;
```

If, rather, we wanted to append s2 to s1 directly, then we would use the += operator:

```
s1 += s2;
```

Our initialization of `s1` and `s2` is made somewhat awkward by our including a blank space, a comma, and the newline. Their presence limits the reusability of these string objects, although it serves our immediate need. An alternative is to mix string objects and C-style character strings as follows:

```
const char *pc = ", ";
string s1( "hello" );
string s2( "world" );

string s3 = s1 + pc + s2 + "\n";
```

This concatenation strategy is preferable because it leaves `s1` and `s2` in more generally reusable form. It works because the string type is capable of automatically converting a C-style character string into a string object. This allows us, for example, to assign a C-style character string to a string object:

```
string s1;
const char *pc = "a character array";

s1 = pc; // ok
```

The reverse conversion, however, is not carried out automatically. There is no support for implicitly converting a string object into a C-style character string. For example, the following attempt to initialize str with s1 fails at compile-time:

```
char *str = s1; // compile-time type error
```

In order to effect this conversion, we must explicitly invoke the oddly named c_str() operation:

```
char *str = s1.c_str(); // almost ok, but not quite
```

The name c_str() is a reference to the relationship of the string type to the C-style character string representation. Literally, it says, get me the C-style string representation — that is, a character pointer to the beginning of the character array.

The initialization still fails, however, but for a different reason now: c_str() returns a pointer to constant array in order to prevent the array from being directly manipulated by the program (the next section examines the const modifier):

```
const char*
```

str is defined to be a nonconstant pointer, so the assignment is flagged as a type violation. The correct initialization is the following:

```
const char *str = s1.c_str(); //ok
```

The string type supports access of individual characters through the subscript operator. For example, in the following code fragment, all periods within a string are replaced with an underscore:

```
string str( "fa.disney.com" );

int size = str.size();
for ( int ix = 0; ix < size; ++ix )
    if ( str[ ix ] == '.' )
        str[ ix ] = '_';
```

This concludes all we wish to say about strings at this point, although there is a great deal more to say. For example, an alternative implementation of the preceding code fragment is as follows:

```
replace( str.begin(), str.end(), '.', '_' );
```

replace() is one of the generic algorithms we briefly introduced in Section 2.8 (and which we look at in detail in Chapter 12 — the Appendix provides an alphabetical listing of each algorithm together with an example of its use).

The begin() and end() operations return iterators to the beginning and end of the string. An iterator is a class abstraction of a pointer provided by the standard library (we looked at iterators briefly in Section 2.8 and look at them in detail in both Chapter 6 and Chapter 12).

replace() iterates across the characters spanning the range between begin() and end(). For each character equal to a period, the period is replaced by the underscore.

Exercise 3.12

Which, if any, of the following are in error?

```
(a) char ch = "The long, winding road";
(b) int ival = &ch;
(c) char *pc = &ival;
(d) string st( &ch );

(e) pc = 0;        (i) pc = '0';
(f) st = pc;       (j) st = &ival;
(g) ch = pc[0];    (k) ch = *pc;
(h) pc = st;       (l) *pc = ival;
```

Exercise 3.13

Explain the difference between the following two while loops:

```
while ( st++ )
        ++cnt;

while ( *st++ )
        ++cnt;
```

Exercise 3.14

Consider the following two semantically equivalent programs, one using C-style character strings and the other using the string type.

```
// ***** C-style character string implementation *****

#include <iostream>
#include <cstring>

int main()
{
    int errors = 0;
    const char *pc = "a very long literal string";

    for ( int ix = 0; ix < 1000000; ++ix )
    {
        int len = strlen( pc );
        char *pc2 = new char[ len + 1 ];
        strcpy( pc2, pc );
```

```
                    if ( strcmp( pc2, pc ))
                          ++errors;

                    delete [] pc2;
            }
        cout << "C-style character strings: "
              << errors << " errors occurred.\n";
    }

// ***** string implementation *****

#include <iostream>
#include <string>

int main()
{
    int errors = 0;
    string str( "a very long literal string" );

    for ( int ix = 0; ix < 1000000; ++ix )
    {
            int len = str.size();
            string str2 = str;
            if ( str != str2 )
                  ++errors;
    }
    cout << "string class: "
          << errors << " errors occurred.\n";
}
```

(a) Explain what the programs do.

(b) As it happens, on average, the string class implementation executes twice as fast as the C-style string class. The relative average execution times under the UNIX timex command are as follows:

```
user        0.96    # string class
user        1.98    # C-style character string
```

Did you expect that? How would you account for it?

Exercise 3.15

The C++ string type is an example of an object-based class abstraction. Is there anything you would change about its use or set of operations as presented in this section? Are there any additional operations you believe necessary? Useful? Explain.

3.5   const Qualifier

There are two problems with the following for loop, both concerning the use of 512 as an upper bound.

```
for ( int index = 0; index < 512; ++index )
    ... ;
```

The first problem is readability. What does it mean to test index against 512? What is the loop doing — that is, what makes 512 matter? (In this example, 512 is referred to as a *magic number*, one whose significance is not evident within the context of its use. It is as if the number had been plucked from thin air.)

The second problem is maintainability. Imagine that the program is 10,000 lines. The use of the value 512 occurs in 4% of the code. Of the 400 occurrences, 80% must be converted to 1024. To do that, we must understand which ones are to be converted and which are not. Getting even one instance wrong breaks the program and requires us to go back and reexamine each use.

The solution to both problems is the use of an object initialized to 512. By choosing a mnemonic name, perhaps bufSize, we make the program more readable. The test is now against the object rather than the literal constant:

```
index < bufSize
```

The 320 occurrences no longer need to be found and converted in case bufSize is changed. Rather, only the one line that initializes bufSize requires change. Not only does this approach require significantly less work, but also the likelihood of making an error is reduced significantly. The cost of the solution is one additional variable. The value 512 is now said to be *localized*.

```
int bufSize = 512; // input buffer size
// ...

for ( int index = 0; index < bufSize; ++index )
    // ...
```

The problem with this solution is that bufSize is an lvalue. It is possible for bufSize to be accidentally changed from within the program. For example, here is a common programmer error:

```
// accidentally changes the value of bufSize
if ( bufSize = 1 )
    // ...
```

In C++, "=" is the assignment operator and "==" is the equality operator. The programmer has accidentally changed bufSize's value to 1, and that results in a difficult-to-trace program error. (Such an error is difficult to find because the programmer gen-

erally does not *see* the code as being wrong, and that is why many compilers issue a
warning for this kind of assignment expression.)

The const type qualifier provides a solution. It transforms an object into a *constant*.
For example,

```
const int bufSize = 512; // input buffer size
```

defines bufSize to be a constant initialized with the value 512. Any attempt to change
that value from within the program results in a compile-time error. For this reason, it
is referred to as *read-only*. For example:

```
// error: attempt to write to const object
if ( bufsize = 0 ) ...
```

Because a constant cannot be modified after it is defined, it must be initialized. The
definition of an uninitialized constant results in a compile-time error.

```
const double pi; // error: uninitialized const
```

Once a constant is defined, we cannot change the value associated with a const object. Can we, on the other hand, assign its address to a pointer? For example, should
the following be allowed?

```
const double minWage = 9.60;

// ok? error?
double *ptr = &minWage;
```

Should this be allowed? minWage is a const object, so it is guaranteed not to be written over with a new value. ptr, however, is an ordinary pointer, and there is nothing
to stop us from subsequently writing

```
*ptr += 1.40; // modified minWage!
```

A compiler in general cannot keep track of which object a pointer addresses at any
point within the program (such bookkeeping requires *data flow analysis*, usually performed by a separate *optimizer* component). It is not feasible for the compiler to allow
a pointer to a nonconstant object to address a constant object and flag as an error only
an attempt to change the object indirectly through that pointer. Rather, any attempt to
have a pointer to a nonconstant object address a constant object results in a compile-
time error.

This does not mean that we cannot indirectly address a constant object; it means only
that we must do it by declaring a pointer that addresses a constant object. For example:

```
const double *cptr;
```

cptr is a pointer to a const object of type double. (We can read its definition from right
to left as "cptr is a pointer to an object of type double defined as const.") A subtle
point is that cptr is not itself a constant; we can reassign cptr to address a different
object but cannot modify the object cptr addresses. For example:

```
const double *pc = 0;
const double minWage = 9.60;

// ok: can't change minWage through pc
pc = &minWage;

double dval = 3.14;

// ok: can't change dval through pc
// although dval itself is not constant
pc = &dval; // ok

dval = 3.14159; // ok
*pc = 3.14159;   // error
```

The address of a constant object can be assigned only to a pointer to a constant object, such as pc. A pointer to a constant object, however, can also be assigned the address of a nonconstant object, such as

```
pc = &dval;
```

Although dval is not a constant, an attempt to modify its value through pc still results in a compile-time error (again because the compiler cannot in practice determine the actual object the pointer addresses at each point in the running program).

In real-world programs, a pointer to a constant object is most often used as the formal parameter of a function. It serves as a contract guaranteeing that the actual object being passed into the function is not being modified within that function. For example:

```
// in real-world programs, pointers to constants
// are most often used as parameters to functions
int strcmp( const char *str1, const char *str2 );
```

(We'll have a lot more to say about pointers to constant objects in our discussion of functions in Chapter 7.)

We can also define a constant pointer either to a constant or a nonconstant object. For example:

```
int errNumb = 0;
int *const curErr = &errNumb;
```

curErr is a constant pointer to a nonconstant object. (We can read its definition from right to left as "curErr is a constant pointer to an object of type int.") This means that we cannot assign curErr another address value, but we can modify the value curErr addresses. Here is how we might use curErr:

```
do_something();

if ( *curErr ) {
```

```
        errorHandler();
        *curErr = 0; // ok: reset object being addressed
    }
```

An attempt to assign to a constant pointer is flagged as an error during compilation:

```
    curErr = &myErrNumb; // error
```

A constant pointer to a constant object is defined by combining the two previous definitions. For example:

```
    const double pi = 3.14159;
    const double *const pi_ptr = &pi;
```

In this case, neither the value of the object addressed by pi_ptr nor the address itself can be changed. (We can read its definition from right to left as "pi_ptr is a constant pointer to an object of type double defined as const.")

Exercise 3.16

Explain the meaning of the following five definitions. Identify any illegal definitions.

```
    (a) int i;           (d) int *const cpi;
    (b) const int ic;    (e) const int *const cpic;
    (c) const int *pic;
```

Exercise 3.17

Which of the following initializations are legal? Explain why.

```
    (a) int i = -1;
    (b) const int ic = i;
    (c) const int *pic = &ic;
    (d) int *const cpi = &ic;
    (e) const int *const cpic = &ic;
```

Exercise 3.18

Based on the definitions in the previous exercise, which of the following assignments are legal? Explain why.

```
    (a) i = ic;        (d) pic = cpic;
    (b) pic = &ic;     (e) cpic = &ic;
    (c) cpi = pic;     (f) ic = *cpic;
```

3.6 Reference Types

A reference, sometimes referred to as an *alias,* serves as an alternative name for an object. A reference allows for the indirect manipulation of an object in a manner similar to the use of a pointer but without requiring use of pointer syntax. In real-world programs, references are primarily used as formal parameters to a function — usually to pass class objects into a function. In this presentation, however, we introduce and illustrate their use as independent objects.

A reference type is defined by following the type specifier with the address-of operator. A reference must be initialized. For example:

```
int ival = 1024;

// ok: refVal is a reference to ival
int &refVal = ival;

// error: a reference must be initialized to an object
int &refVal2;
```

Although a reference serves as a kind of pointer, it is not correct to initialize it to the address of an object, as we would a pointer. We can, however, define a pointer reference. For example:

```
int ival = 1024;

// error: refVal is of type int, not int*
int &refVal = &ival;

int *pi = &ival;

// ok: refPtr is a reference to a pointer
int *&ptrVal2 = pi;
```

Once defined, a reference cannot be made to refer to another object (this is why it must be initialized). For example, the following assignment does not cause refVal to now refer to min_val. Rather, it sets ival, the object referred to by refVal, to the value of min_val.

```
int min_val = 0;

// ival is set to the value of min_val
// refVal is not set to refer to min_val
refVal = min_val;
```

All operations on the reference are actually applied to the object to which the reference refers, including the address-of operator. For example:

```
refVal += 2;
```

adds 2 to ival, the object referred to by refVal. Similarly,

```
int ii = refVal;
```

assigns ii the value currently associated with ival, whereas

```
int *pi = &refVal;
```

initializes pi with the address of ival.

Each definition of a reference must be preceded by the address-of operator. (This is the same issue we discussed earlier with pointers.) For example:

```
// defines two objects of type int
int ival = 1024, ival2 = 2048;

// defines one reference and one object
int &rval = ival, rval2 = ival2;

// defines one object, one pointer, one reference
int ival3 = 1024, *pi = &ival3, &ri = ival3;

// defines two references
int &rval3 = ival3, &rval4 = ival2;
```

A const reference can be initialized to an object of a different type (provided there is a conversion from the one type to the other) as well as to nonaddressable values, such as literal constants. For example:

```
double dval = 3.14159;

// legal for const references only
const int &ir = 1024;
const int &ir2 = dval;
const double &dr = dval + 1.0;
```

The same initializations are not legal for non-const references. Rather, they result in compile-time errors. The reason is somewhat subtle and warrants a short explanation.

Internally, a reference maintains the address of the object for which it is an alias. In the case of nonaddressable values, such as a literal constant, and objects of a different type, to accomplish this the compiler must generate a temporary object that the reference actually addresses but that the user has no access to. For example, when we write

```
double dval = 1024;
const int &ri = dval;
```

the compiler transforms it into something like this:

```
int temp = dval;
const int &ri = temp;
```

If we were to assign ri a new value, we would not change dval but would instead change temp. To the user, it is as if the change simply did not work (and it doesn't for all the good it does the user).

const references don't exhibit this problem because they are read-only. Disallowing non-const references to objects or values requiring temporaries in general seems a better solution than to allow the reference to be defined but seem not to work.

Here is an example that is difficult to declare correctly the first time. We wish to initialize a reference to the address of a `const` object. A non-`const` reference definition is illegal and is flagged as a compile-time error:

```
const int ival = 1024;

// error: requires a const reference
int *&pi_ref = &ival;
```

Our first attempt to correct the definition of `pi_ref` might be the following, but it does not work — do you see why?

```
const int ival = 1024;

// still an error
const int *&pi_ref = &ival;
```

If we read this definition from right to left, we discover that `pi_ref` is a reference to a pointer to an object of type `int` defined to be `const`. Our reference isn't to a constant but rather to a nonconstant pointer that addresses a constant object. The correct definition is as follows:

```
const int ival = 1024;

// ok: this is accepted
const int *const &pi_ref = &ival;
```

Two primary differences between a reference and pointer are that a reference must always refer to an object and that the assignment of one reference with another changes the object being referenced and not the reference itself. Let's look at an example. When we write

```
int *pi = 0;
```

we initialize `pi` to 0 — that is, `pi` currently addresses no object. However, when we write

```
const int &ri = 0;
```

internally, recall that the following transformation takes place:

```
int temp = 0;
const int &ri = temp;
```

The assignment of one reference with another is a second difference. When, given the following,

```
int ival = 1024, ival2 = 2048;
int *pi = &ival, *pi2 = &ival2;
```

we write

```
pi = pi2;
```

ival, the object addressed by pi, remains unchanged. pi, rather, is assigned the object that pi2 addresses — ival2 in this case. What is significant is that pi and pi2 now both address the same object. (This can be a significant source of program error if we copy one class object with another in which one or more class members are pointers. We'll look at this problem in detail in Chapter 14.)

When, however, given the following

```
int &ri = ival, &ri2 = ival2;
```

we write

```
ri = ri2;
```

it is ival, the value referenced by ri, that is changed, and not the reference. After the assignment, the two references still refer to their original objects.

Real-world C++ programs rarely use stand-alone objects of type reference. Rather, references are primarily used as the formal parameters of a functions. For example:

```
// real-world example of how references are used

// return status of access. Place value in parameter
bool get_next_value( int &next_value );

// overloaded addition operator
Matrix operator+( const Matrix&, const Matrix& );
```

How does this use of a reference relate to our discussion of stand-alone objects of type reference? In an invocation such as

```
int ival;
while ( get_next_value( ival )) ...
```

the binding of the actual argument, in this case ival, with the formal parameter next_value is equivalent to the following stand-alone definition:

```
int &next_value = ival;
```

(The use of references as function parameters is discussed in detail in Chapter 7.)

Exercise 3.19

Which of the following definitions, if any, are invalid? Why? How would you correct them?

```
(a) int ival = 1.01;        (b) int &rval1 = 1.01;
(c) int &rval2 = ival;       (d) int &rval3 = &ival;
(e) int *pi = &ival;         (f) int &rval4 = pi;
(g) int &rval5 = *pi;        (h) int &*prval1 = pi;
(i) const int &ival2 = 1;    (j) const int &*prval2 = &ival;
```

Exercise 3.20

Given the definitions above, which, if any, of the following assignments are invalid?

```
(a) rval1 = 3.14159;
(b) prval1 = prval2;
(c) prval2 = rval1;
(d) *prval2 = ival2;
```

Exercise 3.21

What are the differences among the definitions in (a) and between the assignments in (b)? Which, if any, are illegal?

```
(a) int ival = 0;
    const int *pi = 0;
    const int &ri = 0;

(b) pi = &ival;
    ri = &ival;
    pi = &rval;
```

3.7   The bool Type

A bool object can be assigned the literal values true and false. For example:

```
// initialize a string to hold a word to search for
string search_word = get_word();

// initialize a bool variable to false
bool found = false;

string next_word;
while ( cin >> next_word )
   if ( next_word == search_word )
        found = true;
// ...

// shorthand notation for: if ( found == true )
if ( found )
      cout << "ok, we found the word\n";
  else cout << "nope, the word was not present.\n";
```

Although a bool object is considered to be one of the integral types, it cannot be declared to be either signed, unsigned, short, or long. The following, for example, is illegal:

```
// error: cannot specify bool as short
short bool found = false;
```

Both a `bool` object, such as `found`, and the `bool` literals are implicitly promoted to type `int` when an arithmetic value is necessary (such as in the following example): `false` becomes 0, and `true` becomes 1. For example:

```
bool found = false;
int occurrence_count = 0;

while ( /* mumble  */ )
{
   found = look_for( /* something */ );

   // found's value promoted to either 0 or 1
   occurrence_count += found;
}
```

Just as the literals `false` and `true` are automatically promoted to the integer values 0 and 1, if necessary, arithmetic and pointer values are implicitly converted to a value of type `bool`. A zero value or a null pointer value is converted to `false`; all other values are converted to `true`. For example:

```
// returns count of occurrences
extern int find( const string& );
bool found = false;
if ( found = find( "rosebud" ))
      // ok: found == true

// returns pointer to item if present
extern int* find( int value );

if ( found = find( 1024 ))
      // ok: found == true
```

3.8   Enumeration Types

Often when we program we need to define a set of alternative attributes to associate with an object. A file, for example, might be open in one of three states: input, output, and append.

Typically, we keep track of these state values and attributes by associating a unique constant number to each. Thus, we might write the following

```
const int input = 1;
const int output = 2;
const int append = 3;
```

and use these constants as follows:

```
bool open_file( string file_name, int open_mode);

// ...
open_file( "Phoenix_and_the_Crane", append );
```

Although this works, there are a number of weaknesses with it. The primary one is that there is no way to constrain the range of values being passed in to those of input, output, and append.

Enumerations provide an alternative method of not only defining but also grouping sets of integral constants. For example:

```
enum open_modes{ input = 1, output, append };
```

open_modes is an enumeration type. Each named enumeration defines a unique type and can be used as a type specifier. For example:

```
void open_file( string file_name, open_modes om );
```

input, output, and append are *enumerators*. They represent the complete set of values that objects of open_modes can be initialized with or assigned. For example:

```
open_file( "Phoenix and the Crane", append );
```

If we try to pass any value to open_file() other than one of input, output, or append, a compile-time error occurs. Moreover, if we pass it an equivalent integer value, as in the following, the compiler still flags it as an error.

```
// error: 1 is not an enumerator of open_modes ...
open_file( "Jonah", 1 );
```

In addition, we can declare objects of the enumeration type, such as

```
open_modes om = input;
// ...
om = append;
```

and use om in place of an enumerator:

```
open_file( "TailTell", om );
```

One thing that we cannot do with an enumerator is to print the actual enumerator names. When we write

```
cout << input << " " << om << endl;
```

it prints

```
1 3
```

One solution is to define an array of strings indexed by the value of the enumerator. Thus, we might write

```
cout << open_modes_table[ input ] << " "
     << open_modes_table[ om ]    << endl;
```

and generate

```
input append
```

A second thing we cannot do is to iterate over the values using the enumerators, as in

```
// not supported
for ( open_modes iter = input; iter != append; ++iter )
    // ...
```

There is no support for moving backward or forward from one enumerator value to a succeeding or preceding one.

An enumeration is defined with the enum keyword, an optional enumeration name, and a comma-separated list of enumerators enclosed in braces. By default, the first enumerator is assigned the value 0. Each subsequent enumerator is assigned a value 1 greater than the value of the enumerator that immediately precedes it. In our example, we assign input a value of 1. output is automatically assigned 2, and append, 3. The following enumeration associates shape with 0, sphere with 1, cylinder with 2, and polygon with 3.

```
// shape == 0, sphere == 1, cylinder == 2, polygon == 3
enum Forms{ shape, sphere, cylinder, polygon };
```

A value can be explicitly assigned to an enumerator. This value need not be unique. In the following example, point2d is assigned 2, point2w by default is bumped up by 1 to 3, point3d is explicitly assigned 3, and point3w, again by default, is bumped 1 to 4.

```
// point2d == 2, point2w == 3, point3d == 3, point3w == 4
enum Points { point2d = 2, point2w, point3d = 3, point3w };
```

Objects of an enumeration type can be defined, can participate in expressions, and can be passed as arguments to functions. An object of enumeration type can be initialized and assigned only with another object of the same enumeration type or with one of its set of enumerators. For example, although 3 is a legal value associated with Points, it cannot be explicitly assigned to a Points object:

```
void mumble() {
    Points pt3d = point3d; // ok: pt3d == 3

    // error: pt2w initialized with int
    Points pt2w = 3;

    // error: polygon is not a Points enumerator
    pt2w = polygon;

    // ok: both are objects of Points enum type
    pt2w = pt3d;
}
```

When necessary, however, an enumeration type is automatically promoted to an arithmetic type. For example:

```
const int array_size = 1024;

// ok: pt2w promoted to int
int chunk_size = array_size * pt2w;
```

3.9   Array Types

As we saw in Section 2.1, an array is a collection of objects of a single data type. The individual objects are not named; rather, each one is accessed by its position in the array. This form of access is referred to as *indexing* or *subscripting*. For example:

```
int ival;
```

declares a single integer object, whereas

```
int ia[ 10 ];
```

declares an array of ten integer objects. Each object is referred to as an *element* of ia. Thus

```
ival = ia[ 2 ];
```

assigns ival the value stored in the element of ia indexed by 2. Similarly,

```
ia[ 7 ] = ival;
```

assigns the element of ia indexed by 7 the value of ival.

An array definition consists of a type specifier, an identifier, and a dimension. The dimension, which specifies the number of elements contained in the array, is enclosed in a bracket pair. An array must be given a dimension size greater than or equal to 1. The dimension value must be a constant expression — that is, it must be possible to evaluate the value of the dimension at compile-time. This means that a non-const variable cannot be used to specify the dimension of an array. The following are examples of both legal and illegal array definitions:

```
extern int get_size();

// both buf_size and max_files are const
const int buf_size = 512, max_files = 20;
int staff_size = 27;

// ok: const variable
char input_buffer[ buf_size ];

// ok: constant expression: 20 - 3
char *fileTable[ max_files - 3 ];

// error: non-const variable
double salaries[ staff_size ];

// error: non-const expression
int test_scores[ get_size() ];
```

Although `staff_size` is initialized with a literal constant, `staff_size` itself is a non-const object. Access to its value can only be accomplished at run-time, so it is illegal as an array dimension. On the other hand, the expression

```
max_files - 3
```

is a constant expression because `max_files` is a `const` variable initialized with a value of 20. This evaluates at compile-time to a value of 17.

As we saw in Section 2.1, the elements of an array are numbered beginning with 0. For an array of ten elements, the correct index values are 0 through 9, not 1 through 10. In the following example, a for loop steps through the ten elements of an array, initializing each to the value of its index:

```
int main()
{
    const int array_size = 10;
    int ia[ array_size ];

    for ( int ix = 0; ix < array_size; ++ix )
        ia[ ix ] = ix;
}
```

An array can be explicitly initialized by specifying a comma-separated list of values enclosed in braces. For example:

```
const int array_size = 3;
int ia[ array_size ] = { 0, 1, 2 };
```

An explicitly initialized array need not specify a dimension value. The compiler will determine the array size by the number of elements listed:

```
// an array of dimension 3
int ia[] = { 0, 1, 2 };
```

If the dimension size is specified, the number of elements provided must not exceed that size. Otherwise, a compile-time error results. If the dimension size is greater than the number of listed elements, the array elements not explicitly initialized are set to 0.

```
// ia ==> { 0, 1, 2, 0, 0 }
const int array_size = 5;
int ia[ array_size ] = { 0, 1, 2 };
```

A character array can be initialized with either a list of comma-separated character literals enclosed in braces or a string literal. Note, however, that the two forms are not equivalent. The string constant contains the additional terminating null character. For example:

```
const char ca1[] = { 'C', '+', '+' };
const char ca2[] = "C++";
```

ca1 is of dimension 3; ca2 is of dimension 4. The following declaration will be flagged as an error:

```
// error: "Daniel" is 7 elements
const char ch3[ 6 ] = "Daniel";
```

An array cannot be initialized with another array, nor can one array be assigned to another. Additionally, it is not permitted to declare an array of references.

```
const int array_size = 3;
int ix, jx, kx;

// ok: array of pointers of type int*
int *iap [] = { &ix, &jx, &kx };

// error: array of references not allowed
int &iar[] = { ix, jx, kx };

// error: cannot initialize one array with another
int ia2[] = ia; // error

int main()
{
    int ia3[ array_size ]; // ok

    // error: cannot assign one array to another
    ia3 = ia;
    return 0;
}
```

To copy one array into another, each element must be copied in turn. For example:

```
const int array_size = 7;
int ia1[] = { 0, 1, 2, 3, 4, 5, 6 };

int main()
{
    int ia2[ array_size ];

    for ( int ix = 0; ix < array_size; ++ix )
            ia2[ ix ] = ia1[ ix ];

    return 0;
}
```

Any expression that results in an integral value can be used to index into an array. For example:

```
int someVal, get_index();
ia2[ get_index() ] = someVal;
```

Users should be aware, however, that the language provides no compile- or run-time range-checking of the index. Nothing stops a programmer from stepping across an array boundary except his or her attention to detail and a thorough testing of his or her code. It is not inconceivable for a program to compile and execute and still be fatally wrong.

Exercise 3.22

Which of the following array definitions are illegal? Explain why.

```
int get_size();
int buf_size = 1024;
```

```
(a) int ia[ buf_size ];        (d) int ia[ 2 * 7 - 14 ];
(b) int ia[ get_size() ];      (e) char st[ 11 ] = "fundamental";
(c) int ia[ 4 * 7 - 14 ];
```

Exercise 3.23

This code fragment intends to initialize each array element with the value of its index. It contains a number of indexing errors. Identify them.

```
int main() {
    const int array_size = 10;
    int ia[ array_size ];

    for ( int ix = 1; ix <= array_size; ++ix )
        ia[ ix ] = ix;

    // ...
}
```

3.9.1   Multidimensional Arrays

Multidimensional arrays can also be defined. Each dimension is specified with its own bracket pair. For example:

```
int ia[ 4 ][ 3 ];
```

defines a two-dimensional array. The first dimension is referred to as the *row* dimension; the second, the *column* dimension. ia is a two-dimensional array of four rows of three elements each. Multidimensional arrays can also be initialized.

```
int ia[ 4 ][ 3 ] = {
    { 0, 1, 2 },
    { 3, 4, 5 },
    { 6, 7, 8 },
    { 9, 10, 11 }
};
```

The nested braces, which indicate the intended row, are optional. The following initialization is equivalent although considerably less clear.

```
int ia[4][3] = { 0,1,2,3,4,5,6,7,8,9,10,11 };
```

The following definition initializes the first element of each row. The remaining elements are initialized to 0.

```
int ia[ 4 ][ 3 ] = { {0}, {3}, {6}, {9} };
```

Were the nested braces omitted, the results would be very different. The following definition

```
int ia[ 4 ][ 3 ] = { 0, 3, 6, 9 };
```

initializes the first three elements of the first row and the first element of the second row. The remaining elements are initialized to 0. Indexing into a multidimensional array requires a bracket pair for each dimension. For example, the following pair of nested for loops initializes a two-dimensional array.

```
int main()
{
    const int rowSize = 4;
    const int colSize = 3;
    int ia[ rowSize ][ colSize ];

    for ( int i = 0; i < rowSize; ++i )
        for ( int j = 0; j < colSize; ++j )
            ia[ i ][ j ] = i + j;
}
```

Although the expression

```
ia[ 1, 2 ]
```

is a legal construct in C++, its meaning is unlikely to be that intended by the programmer: `ia[1,2]` is equivalent to `ia[2]` because `1,2` is evaluated as a comma expression that yields the single value 2 (the comma expression is discussed in Section 4.10). This accesses the first element of the third row of `ia`. The programmer probably intended `ia[1][2]`.

In C++, multidimensional indexing requires a separate bracket pair for each index the programmer wishes to access.

3.9.2   Relationship of Array and Pointer Types

Given the following array definition,

```
int ia[] = { 0, 1, 1, 2, 3, 5, 8, 13, 21 };
```

what does it mean to simply write

```
ia;
```

The array identifier evaluates to the address of the first element contained within it. Its type is that of pointer to the type of the element the array contains. In the case of ia, its type is int*. So the following two forms are exactly equivalent, returning the address value of the first element of the array.

```
ia;
&ia[0];
```

Similarly, to access the value, we can write either of the following:

```
// both yield the value of the first element
*ia;
ia[0];
```

We know how to access the address of the second element using the subscript operator:

```
&ia[1];
```

It follows, then, that

```
ia+1;
```

also yields the address of the second element, and so on. Similarly, both of the following access the value of the second element:

```
*(ia+1);
ia[1];
```

Writing

```
*ia+1;
```

is quite different from writing

```
*(ia+1);
```

The dereference operator has a higher precedence than the addition operator (we discuss precedence in Section 4.13) and so is applied first. Dereferencing ia returns the value of the first element of the array. 1 is then added to it. By placing the parentheses around the expression, 1 is first added to ia, and then that new address value is dereferenced. Adding 1 to ia increments ia by the size of the underlying element type; ia+1 addresses the next element of the array.

The traversal of an array, then, can be accomplished either through subscripting, as we've done throughout the text so far, or through direct pointer manipulation. For example:

```
#include <iostream>
int main()
{
    int ia[9] = { 0, 1, 1, 2, 3, 5, 8, 13, 21 };
    int *pbegin = ia;
    int *pend = ia + 9;
```

```
        while ( pbegin != pend ) {
                cout << *pbegin << ' ';
                ++pbegin;
        }
}
```

pbegin is initialized to address the first element of the array. It is incremented with each iteration of the while loop to address the next element. The hard part is determining when to stop. In our example, we initialize pend to address 1 past the last element of the array. When pbegin equals pend, we know that we have iterated across the entire array.

If we factor the pair of pointers addressing the beginning and 1 past the end of the array into a separate function, then we now have the facility to iterate across an array without knowing its actual size (although the programmer invoking the function must know it). For example:

```
#include <iostream>

void ia_print( int *pbegin, int *pend )
{
    while ( pbegin != pend ) {
            cout << *pbegin << ' ';
            ++pbegin;
    }
}

int main()
{
    int ia[9] = { 0, 1, 1, 2, 3, 5, 8, 13, 21 };
    ia_print( ia, ia + 9 );
}
```

This is still restrictive, of course; it is constrained to support only pointers to arrays containing elements of type int. We can lift this constraint by turning ia_print() into a template function (we briefly introduced templates in Section 2.5). For example:

```
#include <iostream>

template <class elemType>
void print( elemType *pbegin, elemType *pend )
{
    while ( pbegin != pend ) {
            cout << *pbegin << ' ';
            ++pbegin;
    }
}
```

Now we can pass our generic print() function a pair of pointers into an array of any type for which the output operator is defined. For example:

```
int main()
{
    int ia[9] = { 0, 1, 1, 2, 3, 5, 8, 13, 21 };
    double da[4] = { 3.14, 6.28, 12.56, 25.12 };
    string sa[3] = { "piglet", "eeyore", "pooh" };

    print( ia, ia+9 );
    print( da, da+4 );
    print( sa, sa+3 );
}
```

This form of programming is referred to as *generic programming*. The standard library provides a collection of generic algorithms (we saw them briefly in Section 2.8 and at the end of Section 3.4) that accept a pair of begin/end pointers marking a range of elements over which to traverse. For example, the generic sort() algorithm can be invoked as follows:

```
#include <algorithm>
int main()
{
    int ia[6] = { 107, 28, 3, 47, 104, 76 };
    string sa[3] = { "piglet", "eeyore", "pooh" };

    sort( ia, ia+6 );
    sort( sa, sa+3 );
}
```

The generic algorithms are discussed in detail in Chapter 12. In the Appendix, they are listed in alphabetical order, with an example of the use of each.

More generally, the standard library provides a set of classes that encapsulate the abstractions of containers and pointers. We briefly introduced both in Section 2.8. In the next section, we look at the vector container type, which provides an object-based alternative to the built-in array.

3.10   The vector Container Type

The vector class provides an alternative representation to the built-in array (we briefly introduced the vector class in Section 2.8), and in general we recommend its usage. (There are still many program situations in which the use of a built-in array is necessary, such as the handling of command line options — we look at that in Section 7.8). The vector class, like the string class, is part of the standard library introduced with Standard C++.

To use a vector, we must include its associated header file:

```
#include <vector>
```

There are two very different forms of using a vector, what we call the *array idiom* and the *STL idiom*. In the array idiom, we mimic the use of the built-in array: we define a vector of a given size.

```
vector< int > ivec( 10 );
```

This is analogous to defining a built-in array of ten elements, as follows:

```
int ia[ 10 ];
```

The subscript operator can be used to access the elements of a vector in the same way that we would access the elements of a built-in array. For example:

```
void simple_example()
{
    const int elem_size = 10;
    vector< int > ivec( elem_size );
    int ia[ elem_size ];

    for ( int ix = 0; ix < elem_size; ++ix )
        ia[ ix ] = ivec[ ix ];

    // ...
}
```

We can query a vector as to its size() or test whether it is empty(). For example:

```
void print_vector( vector<int> ivec )
{
    if ( ivec.empty() )
        return;

    for ( int ix = 0; ix < ivec.size(); ++ix )
        cout << ivec[ ix ] << ' ';
}
```

The elements of a vector are initialized to the associated default value of the element type. The default value of the arithmetic and pointer types is 0. For a class type, the default value is obtained by calling the default constructor (see Section 2.3 for an introduction of the default constructor). Alternatively, we can provide an explicit initial value for each element. For example:

```
vector< int > ivec( 10, -1 );
```

defines ivec to contain ten elements of type int each initialized to –1.

With a built-in array, we can explicitly initialize the elements of the array to a set of constant values. For example:

```
int ia[ 6 ] = { -2, -1, 0, 1, 2, 1024 };
```

We cannot explicitly initialize a vector object in the same way. However, we can initialize it to all or a portion of an existing array by specifying the address of the beginning and *one past* the last element of the array we wish to have the vector initialized with. For example:

```
// copies the 6 elements of ia into ivec
vector< int > ivec( ia, ia+6 );
```

The two pointers passed to ivec mark the range of values with which to initialize the object. The second pointer always points one past the last element to be copied. The range of elements marked can also represent a subset of the array. For example:

```
// copies 3 elements: ia[2], ia[3], ia[4]
vector< int > ivec( &ia[ 2 ], &ia[ 5 ] );
```

Unlike a built-in array, a vector can be initialized with or assigned to another vector. For example:

```
vector< string > svec;

void init_and_assign()
{
        // initializing one vector with another
        vector< string > user_names( svec );
        // ...

        // copying one vector into another
        svec = user_names;
}
```

In the STL idiom,[2] a vector is used very differently. Rather than define it with a given size, we define an empty vector:

```
vector< string > text;
```

Rather than index and assign to an element, we instead insert an element into the vector. The push_back() operation, for example, inserts an element at the back of a vector. The following while loop reads a sequence of strings from standard input, inserting them one at a time into the vector:

```
string word;
while ( cin >> word ) {
        text.push_back( word );
        // ...
}
```

Although we can iterate across the elements using the subscript operator,

```
cout << "words read are: \n";
for ( int ix = 0; ix < text.size(); ++ix )
        cout << text[ ix ] << ' ';
cout << endl;
```

---

2. STL stands for Standard Template Library. Prior to inclusion within Standard C++, the vector class, together with the generic algorithms, was part of stand-alone library known as the STL ([see MUSSER96]).

more typically we use the iterator pair returned by the `begin()` and `end()` set of vector operations:

```
cout << "words read are: \n";
for ( vector<string>::iterator it = text.begin();
        it != text.end(); ++it )
            cout << *it << ' ';
cout << endl;
```

An iterator is a standard library class that represents the functionality of a pointer.

```
*it;
```

dereferences the iterator, accessing the actual object addressed.

```
++it;
```

advances the iterator to address the next element. (We look at iterators, vectors, and the general STL idiom in considerable detail in Chapter 6.)

One caution is to not mix the two usage idioms. For example, the definition

```
vector<int> ivec;
```

defines an empty vector. Writing

```
ivec[0] = 1024;
```

is an error, because there is as yet no first element. We can index only elements that are present within the vector. The `size()` operation returns the number of elements a vector contains.

Similarly, when we define a vector of a given size, as in

```
vector<int> ia( 10 );
```

any insertions add to the size of the vector rather than write over the existing elements. That may seem obvious; however, the following is not an uncommon beginner mistake:

```
const int size = 7;
int ia[ size ] = { 0, 1, 1, 2, 3, 5, 8 };
vector< int > ivec( size );
for ( int ix = 0; ix < size; ++ix )
        ivec.push_back( ia[ ix ]);
```

The programmer ends up with `ivec` containing 14 elements, with the elements of `ia` inserted beginning with the eighth element.

In addition, under the STL idiom, one or more elements of the vector can be removed. (Again, we look at all this and illustrate its use in Chapter 6.)

Exercise 3.24

Which, if any, of the following vector definitions are in error?

```
int ia[ 7 ] = { 0, 1, 1, 2, 3, 5, 8 };
```

```
(a) vector< vector< int > > ivec;
(b) vector< int >    ivec = { 0, 1, 1, 2, 3, 5, 8 };
(c) vector< int >    ivec( ia, ia+7 );
(d) vector< string > svec = ivec;
(e) vector< string > svec( 10, string( "null" ));
```

Exercise 3.25

Given the following function declaration

```
bool is_equal( const int*ia, int ia_size,
               const vector<int> &ivec );
```

implement the following behavior: if the two containers are of different sizes, compare only the elements of the size common to both. As soon as an element is not equal, return false. If all the elements compared are equal, then, of course, return true. Iterate across the vector using an iterator — follow the example in this section as a model. Write a main() function to exercise is_equal().

3.11   complex Number Types

The complex number class is part of the standard library. To use it, we must include its associated header file:

```
#include <complex>
```

A complex number has two parts: a real number part and an imaginary number part. An imaginary number represents the square root of a negative number. The term originated with Descartes. The general notation for a complex number is

```
2 + 3i
```

where 2 represents the real part and 3i represents the imaginary part. The two parts represent a single number.

The definition of a complex object takes one of the following general forms:

```
// a pure imaginary number: 0 + 7i
complex< double > purei( 0, 7 );

// imaginary defaults to zero: 3 + 0i
complex< float > real_num( 3 );

// real and imaginary default to zero: 0 + 0i
complex< long double > zero;

// initialize one complex object with another
complex< double > purei2( purei );
```

Here, the complex object has a `float`, `double`, or `long double` representation. An array of complex number objects can also be declared:

```
complex< double > conjugate[ 2 ] = {
                complex< double >( 2,  3 ),
                complex< double >( 2, -3 )
};
```

We can also declare a pointer or reference:

```
complex< double > *ptr = &conjugate[0];
complex< double > &ref = *ptr;
```

Complex numbers support addition, subtraction, multiplication, division, and the test for equality. In addition, there is support for accessing both the real and the imaginary parts. These operations are looked at in detail in Section 4.6.

3.12 Typedef Names

The `typedef` mechanism provides a general facility for introducing a mnemonic synonym for a built-in or user-defined data type. For example:

```
typedef double      wages;
typedef vector<int> vec_int;
typedef vec_int     test_scores;
typedef bool        in_attendance;
typedef int         *Pint;
```

These `typedef` names can serve as type specifiers within the program:

```
// double hourly, weekly;
wages hourly, weekly;

// vector<int> vec1( 10 );
vec_int vec1( 10 );

// vector<int> test0( class_size );
const int class_size = 34;
test_scores test0( class_size );

// vector< bool > attendance;
vector< in_attendance > attendance( class_size );

// int *table[ 10 ];
Pint table[ 10 ];
```

A typedef definition begins with the keyword `typedef`, followed by the data type and identifier. The identifier, or typedef name, does not introduce a new type but rather a synonym for the existing data type. A typedef name can appear anywhere in a program that a type name can appear.

A typedef name can serve as a program documentation aid. It can also reduce the notational complexity of a declaration. Typedef names, for example, are typically used to improve the readability of definitions of complex template declarations (see Section 3.14 for an example), pointers to functions (discussed in Section 7.9), and pointers to class member functions (discussed in Section 13.6).

Here is a question almost everyone answers incorrectly once. The mistake is in conceptualizing the typedef as a textual macro expansion. Given the following typedef,

```
typedef char *cstring;
```

what is the type of cstr in the following declaration?

```
extern const cstring cstr;
```

The first answer is almost always

```
const char *cstr
```

That is, a pointer to a constant character. But that is incorrect. The const modifies the type of cstr. cstr is a pointer, and therefore the definition declares cstr to be a const pointer to char (see Section 3.5 for a discussion of const pointer types):

```
char *const cstr;
```

3.13   volatile Qualifier

An object is declared volatile when its value can possibly be changed in ways outside either the control or detection of the compiler — for example, a variable updated by the system clock. Certain optimizations ordinarily performed by a compiler should therefore not be applied to objects the programmer specifies as volatile.

The volatile qualifier is used in much the same way as is the const qualifier — as an additional modifier to a type. For example:

```
volatile int display_register;
volatile Task *curr_task;
volatile int ixa[ max_size ];
volatile Screen bitmap_buf;
```

display_register is a volatile object of type int. curr_task is a pointer to a volatile Task class object. ixa is a volatile array of integers. Each element of the array is considered to be volatile. bitmap_buf is a volatile Screen class object. Each of its data members is considered to be volatile.

The essential purpose of the volatile qualifier is to notify the compiler that the object can change in ways undetectable by the compiler. The compiler, therefore, should not aggressively optimize code referring to the object.

3.14 The pair Type

The pair class, part of the standard library, allows us to associate two values of either the same or different types within a single object. To use the pair class, we must include the following header file:

```
#include <utility>
```

For example:

```
pair< string, string > author( "James", "Joyce" );
```

creates a pair object author consisting of two string objects initialized to "James" and "Joyce".

The individual elements of the pair can be accessed as first and second using the *member access notation*. For example:

```
string firstBook;

if ( author.first == "James" &&
     author.second == "Joyce" )
    firstBook = "Stephen Hero";
```

If we wish to define a number of objects of the same pair type, it is convenient to use a typedef, as follows:

```
typedef pair< string, string > Authors;

Authors proust( "marcel", "proust" );
Authors joyce( "james", "joyce" );
Authors musil( "robert", "musil" );
```

Here is a second pair. One holds the name of an object, and the other holds a pointer to its symbol table entry:

```
// forward declarations
class EntrySlot;
extern EntrySlot* look_up( string );

typedef pair< string, EntrySlot* > SymbolEntry;

SymbolEntry current_entry( "author", look_up( "author" ));
// ...

if ( EntrySlot *it = look_up( "editor" ))
{
    current_entry.first = "editor";
    current_entry.second = it;
}
```

We'll encounter the pair type again in our discussion of the standard library container types in Chapter 6 and the standard library generic algorithms in Chapter 12.

3.15 Class Types

The class mechanism supports the design of new types, such as the object-based string, vector, complex, and pair class types discussed in this chapter, as well as the object-oriented iostream class hierarchy introduced in Chapter 1. In Chapter 2, we walked through the underlying concepts and mechanisms supporting object-based and object-oriented class design through the implementation and evolution of an Array class abstraction. In this section, we briefly walk through the design and implementation of a simple object-based String class abstraction. This should be of comparative interest given our earlier discussion of both the C-style character string and the standard library string type. Our implementation in particular illustrates the support C++ provides for *operator overloading*, briefly introduced in Section 2.3. (Classes are introduced in detail in Chapters 13 through 15. Introducing some aspects of classes early in the book allows us to provide more interesting examples that use classes before we reach Chapter 13. The first-time reader may wish to skim this section now and wait for the more thorough presentation of classes in the later chapters.)

We should have a pretty good idea at this point of what our String class needs to do: we need to support both the initialization and assignment of a String object with either a string literal, a C-style character string, or another String object. We'll accomplish this with the special constructor class initialization function and class-specific instances of the assignment operator.

We need to support indexing to access the individual characters of the String in the same manner as the C-style character string and standard library string type. We'll accomplish this by providing a class-specific instance of the subscript operator.

In addition, we'd like to support operations to determine the size() of the String, compare two String objects for equality, or compare a String and a C-style character string, and read and write a String object. We'll accomplish these last two operations by providing class-specific instances of the equality, iostream input, and iostream output operators. Finally, we'll need access to the underlying C-style character string.

The definition of a class consists of the keyword class followed by an identifier that serves as the type specifier of the class, such as complex, vector, Array, and so on. In general, a class consists of a public section of operations and a private section of data. These operations are variously referred to as the *member functions* or *methods* of the class. They define the class *public interface* — that is, the set of operations a user can perform on objects of the class. The private data of our String class consists of _string, of type char* addressing a dynamically allocated character array; and _size, of type int, holding the size of the String. Here is our class definition:

```
#include <iostream>

class String;
istream& operator>>( istream&, String& );
ostream& operator<<( ostream&, const String& );

class String {
public:
        // overloaded set of constructors
        // provide automatic initialization
        // String str1;             // String()
        // String str2( "literal" ); // String( const  char* );
        // String str3( str2 );      // String( const String& );

        String();
        String( const char* );
        String( const String& );

        // destructor: automatic destruction
        ~String();

        // overloaded set of assignment operators
        // str1 = str2
        // str3 = "a string literal"

        String& operator=( const String& );
        String& operator=( const char* );

        // overloaded set of equality operators
        // str1 == str2;
        // str3 == "a string literal";

        bool operator==( const String& );
        bool operator==( const char* );

        // overloaded subscript operator
        // str1[ 0 ] = str2[ 0 ];

        char& operator[]( int );

        // member access functions
        int   size() { return _size;   }
        char* c_str() { return _string; }

private:
        int   _size;
        char *_string;

};
```

Our String class defines three constructors. As we discussed briefly in Section 2.3, the overload function mechanism allows the same function name or operator to refer to multiple instances provided that each instance can be distinguished by its parameter list. Our set of three constructors forms a valid set of overloaded functions distinguished first by the number and then by the type of their parameter. The first,

```
String();
```

is called the *default constructor* because it does not require an explicit initial value. When we write

```
String str1;
```

the default constructor is applied to str1.

Each of our other two String constructors takes a single argument. When we write

```
String str2( "a string literal" );
```

the constructor

```
String( const char* );
```

is applied to str2 based on the argument type. Similarly, when we write

```
String str3( str2 );
```

the constructor

```
String( const String& );
```

is applied to str3 — again, this is determined by the type of the argument being passed to the constructor. This constructor is called a *copy constructor* because it initializes one class object with a copy of a second. When we write,

```
String str4( 1024 );
```

the type of the actual argument does not match any of the parameter types expected by the set of constructors, so the definition of str4 results in a compile-time error.

An overloaded operator takes the general form

```
return_type operator op ( parameter_list );
```

where operator is a keyword, and op is one of the predefined operators, such as +, =, ==, [], and so on (the exact rules are covered in Chapter 15). The declaration

```
char& operator[]( int );
```

declares an overloaded instance of the subscript operator taking a single argument of type int and returning a reference to char. An overloaded operator can itself be overloaded provided that the parameter list of the separate instances can be distinguished. For example, we provide two distinct instances of the assignment and equality operators for our String class.

A named member function is invoked using the member access notation. For example, given the following String definitions

```
String object( "Danny" );
String *ptr = new String( "Anna" );
String array[2];
```

the member function size() can be invoked as follows, returning, respectively, values of size 5, 4, and 0 (we'll look at the implementation of our String class in a moment).

```
vector<int> sizes( 3 );

// member access dot notation for objects;
// object has a size of 5
sizes[ 0 ] = object.size();

// member access arrow notation for pointers
// ptr has a size of 4
sizes[ 1 ] = ptr->size();

// member access dot notation again
// array[0] has a size of 0
sizes[ 2 ] = array[0].size();
```

The overloaded operators are applied directly to the class objects. For example:

```
String name1( "Yadie" );
String name2( "Yodie" );

// applies: bool operator==(const String&)
if ( name1 == name2 )
    return;
else
// applies: String& operator=( const String& )
    name1 = name2;
```

The member functions of a class can be defined either within or outside the class definition. (Both size() and c_str(), for example, are defined within our String class definition.) Those member functions defined outside the class definition must inform the compiler not only of their name, return type, and parameter list but also which class they belong to. The member function definition should be placed in a program text file — for example, String.C — and needs to include the header file containing the class definition — in our example, String.h. For example:

```
// this is placed in a program text file: String.C

// include the String class definition
#include "String.h"

// include the strcmp() function declaration
// cstring is the Standard C library header
#include <cstring>
```

```
bool                    // return type
String::                // class it is a member of
operator==              // name of function: equality operator
(const String &rhs)// parameter list
{
    if ( _size != rhs._size )
        return false;
    return strcmp( _string, rhs._string ) ? false : true;
}
```

strcmp(), recall, is the C standard library function. It compares two C-style character strings. It returns 0 if they are equal, nonzero otherwise. The *conditional operator* (?:) tests the condition before the question mark. If it is true, the expression between the question mark and the colon is selected; if it is false, the expression after the colon is selected. In our example, the conditional operator returns false if strcmp() returns a nonzero value; otherwise, it returns true. (Section 4.7 discusses the conditional operator in detail.)

Because the equality operator is a small function likely to be frequently invoked, it is a good idea to declare it as an inline function. An inline function has its source expanded into the program at each invocation point, thereby eliminating the overhead associated with a function call. An inline function can provide a significant performance gain provided that the function is invoked sufficiently many times. (Inline functions are described in detail in Section 7.6.) A member function defined within the class definition, such as size(), is made inline by default. A member function defined outside the class must explicitly declare itself to be inline:

```
inline bool
String::operator==(const String &rhs)
{
        // as before
}
```

An inline member function defined outside the class body should be included within the header file containing the class definition. In our redefinition of the equality operator, we should move its definition from String.C to String.h.

Here is our equality operator comparing a String object to a C-style character string (it is also defined as inline and is placed within the String.h header file).

```
inline bool
String::operator==(const char *s)
{
    return strcmp( _string, s ) ? false : true;
}
```

The constructor is provided with the same name as the class. It must not specify a return value either in its declaration or in the constructor body. Either or all of the instances can be declared as inline.

```cpp
#include <cstring>

// default constructor
inline String::String()
{
    _size = 0;
    _string = 0;
}

inline String::String( const char *str )
{
     if ( ! str ) {
          _size = 0; _string = 0;
     }
     else {
          _size = strlen( str );
          _string = new char[ _size + 1 ];
          strcpy( _string, str );
     }
}

// copy constructor
inline String::String( const String &rhs )
{
     _size = rhs._size;
     if ( ! rhs._string )
          _string = 0;
     else {
          _string = new char[ _size + 1 ];
          strcpy( _string, rhs._string );
     }
}
```

Because we allocate memory dynamically using the new expression to hold the character string, we must deallocate that memory using the delete expression when the String object is no longer needed. This can be achieved automatically by defining a class destructor and placing the delete expression within it. A class destructor, if present, is automatically invoked on each class object following the end of the object's lifetime (Chapter 8 illustrates the three possible lifetimes of an object). A destructor is identified by giving it the name of the class preceded by a tilde (~). Here is our definition of the String class destructor:

```cpp
inline String::~String() { delete [] _string; }
```

The two overloaded assignment operators reference the special keyword this.

When we write

```
String name1( "orville" ), name2( "wilbur" );
name1 = "Orville Wright";
```

this points to name1 within our assignment operator.

More generally, the this pointer is automatically set within a class member function to address the left-hand class object through which the member function is invoked. When we write

```
ptr->size();
obj[ 1024 ];
```

within size(), the this pointer addresses ptr; within the subscript operator, the this pointer addresses obj. When we write *this we are accessing the actual object addressed by this (Section 13.4 discusses the this pointer in detail).

```
inline String&
String::operator=( const char *s )
{
    if ( ! s ) {
        _size = 0;
        delete [] _string;
        _string = 0;
    }
    else {
        _size = strlen( s );
        delete [] _string;
        _string = new char[ _size + 1 ];
        strcpy( _string, s );
    }
    return *this;
}
```

One common pitfall when copying one class object with another is to forget to first test that the two class objects are not actually the same. This error most typically occurs in a program when one or both objects are dereferences of a pointer. The this pointer again comes into play to support the test. For example:

```
inline String&
String::operator=( const String &rhs )
{
    // in expression
    // name1 = *pointer_to_string
    // this addresses name1,
    // rhs represents *pointer_to_string.
    if ( this != &rhs ) {
```

Here is the full implementation:

```
inline String&
String::operator=( const String &rhs )
{
    if ( this != &rhs )
    {
        delete [] _string;
        _size = rhs._size;

        if ( ! rhs._string )
                _string = 0;
        else {
                _string = new char[ _size + 1 ];
                strcpy( _string, rhs._string );
        }
    }
    return *this;
}
```

The subscript operator is nearly identical to the one we implemented for our Array class of Section 2.3:

```
#include <cassert>

inline char&
String::operator[]( int elem )
{
    assert( elem >= 0 && elem < _size );
    return _string[ elem ];
}
```

The input and output operators are implemented as nonmember functions. (The reasons for this are discussed in Section 15.2. Sections 20.4 and 20.5 provide a detailed discussion of overloading the iostream output and input operators.) Our input operator reads in a maximum of 4,095 characters. setw() is a predefined iostream manipulator. It reads a maximum of 1 less than the value passed to it, thereby guaranteeing that we don't overflow our inBuf character array. To use it, we must include the iomanip header file. (Chapter 20 discusses setw() in detail.)

```
#include <iomanip>

inline istream&
operator>>( istream &io, String &s )
{
    // artificial limit of 4096 characters read
    const int limit_string_size = 4096;
    char inBuf[ limit_string_size ];
```

```
    // setw() is part of iostream library
    // limits characters read to limit_string_size-1
    io >> setw( limit_string_size ) >> inBuf;

    s = inBuf; // String::operator=( const char* );
    return io;
}
```

The output operator requires access to the underlying char* representation in order to display the String. However, because it is not a member function of the class, it has no access privilege to _string. There are two possible solutions: one is to grant special access permission to the output operator (this is done by declaring it to be a *friend* of the class — we'll look at that in Section 15.2). The second is to provide an inline access function — in this case, c_str(), modeled on the solution provided by the standard library string class. Here is our implementation:

```
inline ostream&
operator<<( ostream& os, String &s )
{
    return os << s.c_str();
}
```

The following small program exercises our String class implementation. It reads a sequence of Strings from standard input and then steps through each String in turn, keeping track of the vowels present.

```
#include <iostream>
#include "String.h"
int main()
{
    int aCnt = 0, eCnt = 0, iCnt = 0, oCnt = 0, uCnt = 0,
        theCnt = 0, itCnt = 0, wdCnt = 0, notVowel = 0;

    // we don't define The( "The" ) and It( "It" )
    // in order to use operator==( const char* )
    String buf, the( "the" ), it( "it" );

    // invokes operator>>( ostream&, String& )
    while ( cin >> buf ) {
        ++wdCnt;

        // invokes operator<<( ostream&, const String& )
        cout << buf << ' ';

        if ( wdCnt % 12 == 0 )
            cout << endl;

        // invokes String::operator==(const String&) and
        //          String::operator==( const char* );
```

```
        if ( buf == the || buf == "The" )
                ++theCnt;
        else
        if ( buf == it || buf == "It" )
                ++itCnt;

        // invokes String::size()
        for ( int ix = 0; ix < buf.size(); ++ix )
        {
            // invokes String::operator[](int)
            switch( buf[ ix ] )
            {
                    case 'a': case 'A': ++aCnt; break;
                    case 'e': case 'E': ++eCnt; break;
                    case 'i': case 'I': ++iCnt; break;
                    case 'o': case 'O': ++oCnt; break;
                    case 'u': case 'U': ++uCnt; break;
                    default: ++notVowel; break;
            }
        }
    }

    // invokes operator<<( ostream&, const String& )
    cout << "\n\n"
         << "Words read: " << wdCnt   << "\n\n"
         << "the/The: "     << theCnt << '\n'
         << "it/It: "       << itCnt  << "\n\n"
         << "non-vowels read: " << notVowel << "\n\n"
         << "a: " << aCnt << '\n'
         << "e: " << eCnt << '\n'
         << "i: " << iCnt << '\n'
         << "o: " << oCnt << '\n'
         << "u: " << uCnt << endl;
}
```

The input to the program is a paragraph of a children's story Stan has written (we'll see it again in Chapter 6). When compiled and executed, our program generates the following output:

```
Alice Emma has long flowing red hair. Her Daddy says when the
wind blows through her hair, it looks almost alive, like a fiery
bird in flight. A beautiful fiery bird, he tells her, magical but
untamed. "Daddy, shush, there is no such thing," she tells him, at
the same time wanting him to tell her more. Shyly, she asks,
"I mean, Daddy, is there?"

Words read: 65

the/The: 2
it/It: 1
```

```
non-vowels read: 190

a: 22
e: 30
i: 24
o: 10
u: 7
```

Exercise 3.26

There is a great deal of duplicated code in the implementation of the constructors and assignment operators of the String class. Using the model presented in Section 2.3, try to factor the common code into a separate private member function. Reimplement the constructors and assignment operators to make use of it. Rerun the program to make sure it still works.

Exercise 3.27

Modify the program to count the consonants b, d, f, s, and t as well.

Exercise 3.28

Implement a member function to count the occurrence of a character in a String. Its declaration is as follows:

```
class String {
public:
    // ...
    int count( char ch ) const;
    // ...
};
```

Exercise 3.29

Implement a member operator function to concatenate one String with another, returning a new String. Its declaration is as follows:

```
class String {
public:
    // ...
    String operator+( const String &rhs ) const;
    // ...
};
```

4

Expressions

In Chapter 3, we looked at the built-in data types and those supported by the standard library. In this chapter we look at the predefined operators, such as addition, subtraction, assignment, the test for equality, and so on, that are used to manipulate that data. That done, we discuss the precedence of operator evaluation. For example, given the expression 3+4*5, the result is always 23 and not 35 because of the higher precedence of the multiplication operator and subsequent order of evaluation. Finally, we look at the issue of both implicit and explicit type conversion of objects. For example, in the expression 3+0.7, the integer value 3 is always promoted to a floating point number before the addition is carried out.

4.1   What Is an Expression?

An expression is composed of one or more *operands*. The simplest form of an expression consists of a single literal constant or object. The result, in general, is the operand's rvalue. For example, here are three simple expressions:

```
void mumble()
{
    3.14159;
    "melancholia";
    upperBound;
}
```

The result of 3.14159 is 3.14159. Its type is double. The result of "melancholia" is the address in memory of the first element of the string. Its type is const char*. The result of upperBound is its associated value. Its type is determined by its definition.

More generally, an expression consists of one or more operands and an operation to be applied to them. For example, the following are all expressions (we've left out the object definitions; the appropriate operation is applied automatically based on the type of the operand(s)):

```
salary + raise
ivec[ size/2 ] * delta
first_name + " " + last_name
```

The operations applied to the operands are represented by *operators*. For example, in the first expression, the floating point addition operator is applied to the operands `salary` and `raise`. In the second expression, the operand `size` is divided by 2. The result is used to index into the integer array `ivec`. Its value is multiplied by the operand `delta`. In the third expression, two string operands and a string literal are concatenated to form a new string using the instance of the addition operator defined by the standard library string class.

Operators that act on one operand are *unary* operators, such as the address-of (&) and dereference (*) operators, whereas operators that act on two operands, such as the addition and subtraction operators, are *binary* operators. Some operators represent both a unary and a binary operation (more exactly, the same symbol is used to represent two different operators). For example,

```
*ptr
```

represents the unary dereference operator. It returns the value stored in the object that `ptr` addresses. However,

```
var1 * var2
```

represents the binary multiplication operator. It computes the product of its two operands: `var1` and `var2`.

The evaluation of an expression performs one or more operations, yielding a result. Except when noted otherwise, the result of an expression is an rvalue. The data type of the result of an arithmetic expression is determined by the data type of the operand(s). When more than one data type is present, type conversions take place following a predefined set of type conversion rules. (We look at type conversions in detail in Section 4.14.)

When two or more operators are combined, the expression is referred to as a *compound expression*. For example, the purpose of the following expression is to determine whether the pointer `ptr` addresses an object (it addresses an object if its value is not zero) and whether the object addressed has a value other than zero:[1]

```
ptr != 0 && *ptr != 0
```

The full expression is composed of three subexpressions: the inequality test of `ptr` against zero, the dereference of `ptr`, and the inequality test against zero of the value resulting from the dereference. If `ptr` is defined as follows

```
int ival = 1024;
```

---

1. The explicit test against zero is optional. The following expression is equivalent and is the preferred real-world C++ program idiom: `ptr && *ptr`

```
int *ptr = &ival;
```

the result of the dereference subexpression is 1,024, and the results of the two subexpression tests for inequality to zero are both `true`. The result of the full expression is also `true`: ptr is not set to zero, and the object it addresses is not set to zero. (The `&&` operator is referred to as the *AND* operator: it evaluates to true if both its left- and right-hand subexpressions evaluate to true; otherwise, it evaluates to false.)

If we look at our compound expression closely, we will notice that its successful evaluation is dependent on the order of subexpression evaluation. For example, if the second half of the expression is evaluated first — that is, if ptr is dereferenced before it is confirmed not to equal zero — the program is likely to fail or be corrupted at runtime whenever ptr in fact is set to 0. In the case of the AND operator, the order of subexpression evaluation is strictly defined: If the left subexpression evaluates as false, the right subexpression is not evaluated; the program error cannot occur.

The order of subexpression evaluation in practice is a frequent source of program error for the beginning C and C++ programmer. It is difficult to uncover, because a visual inspection of our program does not reveal the error unless we understand the rules of subexpression evaluation. In general, the order of subexpression evaluation is determined by the *precedence* and *associativity* of its operators. We'll look at this in some detail in Section 4.13 after we look at the set of operators supported by C++. The following sections discuss the predefined C++ operators in their order of familiarity.

4.2   Arithmetic Operators

Table 4.1   Arithmetic Operators.

Operator	Function	Use
*	multiplication	expr * expr
/	division	expr / expr
%	remainder	expr % expr
+	addition	expr + expr
-	subtraction	expr - expr

Division between integers results in an integer. If the quotient contains a fractional part, it is truncated. For example:

```
int ival1 = 21 / 6;
int ival2 = 21 / 7;
```

result in both `ival1` and `ival2` being initialized with a value of 3.

The % operator computes the remainder of division between two values; the first value is divided by the second. This operator can be applied only to operands of the integral types (char, short, int, and long). When both operands are positive, the result is positive. If either (or both) operand is negative, however, the sign of the remainder is machine-dependent; portability, therefore, is not guaranteed. The % operator is alternatively spoken of as the *modulus,* or the *remainder,* operator.

```
3.14 % 3; // compile-time error: floating point operand
21 % 6;   // ok: result is 3
21 % 7;   // ok: result is 0
21 % -5;  // machine-dependent: result is -1 or 1

int ival = 1024;
double dval = 3.14159;

ival % 12;   // ok: returns a value between 0 and 11
ival % dval; // compile-time error: floating point operand
```

In certain instances, the evaluation of an arithmetic expression will result in an incorrect or undefined value. These occurrences are referred to as *arithmetic exceptions* (but do not result in an actual exception being thrown). An arithmetic exception may be due to the nature of mathematics — such as division by zero — or due to the nature of computers — such as *overflow* (in which the value is larger than the size of the type of the object being assigned). For example, a char of 8 bits, depending on whether it is signed or unsigned, may contain a maximum value of either 127 or 255. The following multiplication assigns a char the value 256, resulting in an overflow:

```
#include <iostream>

int main() {
    char byte_value = 32;
    int ival = 8;

    // overflow of byte_value's available memory
    byte_value = ival * byte_value;

    cout << "byte_value: " << static_cast<int>(byte_value) << endl;
}
```

To represent 256, 9 bits are required. The assignment of 256 to byte_value results in an overflow of its associated memory. The actual value byte_value contains is undefined and is likely to cause problems when executed. On an SGI workstation, for example, byte_value is set to a value of 0. When we first attempted to print it, using the expression

```
cout << "byte_value: " << byte_value << endl;
```

the output of the program looked like this:

```
byte_value:
```

After a few moments of puzzlement, we realized that the value 0, in the ASCII character set, represents the null character and prints literally as not being there. The peculiar expression

```
static_cast<int>(byte_value)
```

is referred to as an *explicit type conversion*, or *cast*. A cast instructs the compiler to convert an object (or expression) from its current type into a type specified by the programmer. In our case, we are converting `byte_value` to an object of type `int`. The program now outputs

```
byte_value: 0
```

In our case, what has changed is not the value associated with `byte_value` but rather how it is interpreted by the output operator. When printing `byte_value`, the form of its output is determined by its associated type. When treated as a `char`, its value is mapped to an associated ASCII representation (for example, 12 represents the newline character, 97 represents the lowercase *a*, 0 represents the null character, and so on); it is this representation, and not the value, that is printed. When treated as an `int`, on the other hand, its value is printed directly. (Type conversions are discussed in Section 4.14.)

Our narrative interruption, with the discussion of type conversion and the failure of `byte_value` to print as we expected, in a sense mimics what happens when our programs behave unexpectedly and we are required to put aside our programming task to track down what has gone wrong. Seemingly obscure or uninteresting language issues, such as the size of a data type, in practice sometimes affect the programs we write. An overflow such as the one that occurs with `byte_value` is not caught by the language, because it would involve a run-time check of each computation, and that is impractical from a performance standpoint. We simply must be alert to the possibility.

The Standard C++ header file `limits` provides information about an implementation's representation of the built-in types, such as the minimum and maximum value that a type can represent. In addition, the Standard C header files `climits` and `cfloat`, also available within a C++ compilation system, define preprocessor macros that provide similar information. For a discussion of how one might use these headers to avoid overflow and underflow, see Chapters 4 and 5 of [PLAUGER92].

Floating point arithmetic presents the additional problem of accuracy: only a fixed number of digits are available to represent values within the computer. Floating point *roundoff* occurs when a value is modified to fit within the `float`, `double`, or `long double` type intended to represent it. The resulting accuracy of addition, multiplication, and subtraction of floating point numbers is affected by the fixed precision of the underlying data type. (For a detailed discussion of roundoff error in numerical computation, see [SHAMPINE97].)

Exercise 4.1

What is the primary difference between the following two division expressions?

```
double dval1 = 10.0, dval2 = 3.0;
int ival1 = 10, ival2 = 3;

dval1 / dval2;
ival1 / ival2;
```

Exercise 4.2

Given an integral object, what operator might we use to determine whether it is even or odd? Write the expression.

Exercise 4.3

Locate and examine the Standard C++ header file `limits` and the Standard C header files `climits` and `cfloat` on your system.

4.3   Equality, Relational, and Logical Operators

Table 4.2 Equality, Relational, and Logical Operators.

Operator	Function	Use
!	logical NOT	!expr
<	less than	expr < expr
<=	less than or equal	expr <= expr
>	greater than	expr > expr
>=	greater than or equal	expr >= expr
==	equality	expr == expr
!=	inequality	expr != expr
&&	logical AND	expr && expr
||	logical OR	expr || expr
Note: The result of these operators is type bool.		

The equality, relational, and logical operators evaluate to either of the `bool` constants `true` or `false`. If such an operator is used within a context requiring an integer value, the result is promoted to a value of either 1 (`true`) or 0 (`false`). For example, in the following code fragment, we wish to count all the elements of a vector less than a user-specified value. To accomplish this, we add the result of the less-than operator to a count of the elements. (The += operator is a shorthand notation; it means that we are adding the right-hand expression to the current value of the left-hand operand. We discuss the compound assignment operators in Section 4.4.)

```
int elem_cnt = 0;

vector<int>::iterator iter = ivec.begin();
while ( iter != ivec.end() )
{
    // same as: elem_cnt = elem_cnt + (*iter < some_value)
    // true/false value of *iter < some_value
    //      is promoted to either 1 or 0
    elem_cnt += *iter < some_value;
    ++iter;
}
```

The logical AND (&&) operator evaluates to true only if both its operands evaluate to true. The logical OR (||) operator evaluates to true if either of its operands evaluates to true. The operands are guaranteed to be evaluated from left to right. Evaluation stops as soon as the truth or falsity of the expression is determined. Given the forms

```
expr1 && expr2
expr1 || expr2
```

expr2 is guaranteed not to be evaluated if either of the following is true:

- In a logical AND expression, expr1 evaluates to false.

- In a logical OR expression, expr1 evaluates to true.

A valuable use of the logical AND operator is to have expr1 evaluate to false in the presence of some boundary condition that would make the evaluation of expr2 dangerous. For example:

```
while ( ptr != 0 &&
        ptr->value < upperBound &&
        ptr->value >= 0 &&
        notFound( ia[ ptr->value ] ))
{ ... }
```

A pointer with a value of 0 is not addressing an object. Applying the member access operator to a 0-valued pointer is always troublesome. The first logical AND operator guards against that happening. Equally troublesome is an out-of-bounds array index. The second and third operands guard against that possibility. The last operand is safe to evaluate only when the first three operands evaluate as true.

The logical NOT operator (!) evaluates to true if its operand has a value of false or zero; otherwise, it evaluates to false. For example:

```
bool found = false;
```

```
// while the item has not been found
// and ptr still addresses an object
while ( ! found && ptr ) {
    found = lookup( *ptr );
    ++ptr;
}
```

The subexpression

```
! found
```

evaluates to `true` as long as `found` is equal to `false`. It is a shorthand notation for the explicit test:

```
// meaning of !found
found == false
```

Similarly, the test

```
if ( found )
```

is a shorthand notation for the explicit test:

```
if ( found == true )
```

Although use of the binary relational operators, such as the less-than or inequality operator, is straightforward, there is one potential pitfall we must be aware of: The order of evaluation of the left and right operands is deliberately left undefined by both the C and the C++ Standards and must therefore not contain order dependencies. For example, in the following

```
// oops! language does not define order of evaluation
if ( ia[ index++ ] < ia[ index ] )
    // swap elements
```

the programmer presumes that the left operand is evaluated first and that therefore `ia[0]` is compared to be less than `ia[1]`. The language, however, does not guarantee a left-to-right evaluation order; an implementation may in fact evaluate the right-hand operand first, in which case `ia[0]` is compared to itself and `ia[1]` is never evaluated. One safe and portable reimplementation looks like this:

```
if ( ia[ index ] < ia[ index+1 ] )
            // swap elements
++index;
```

A second potential pitfall is the following. Our intention is to determine whether `ival`, `jval`, and `kval` are each unique values. Do you see what's wrong?

```
// oops! this does not determine if the 3 values are unequal
if ( ival != jval != kval )
    // do something ...
```

As we've implemented it, the associated values 0, 1, and 0 cause the expression to evaluate as `true`. The reason is that the left operand of the second inequality expression is the `true`/`false` result of the first — that is, `kval` is tested for inequality against the promoted integer values of 0 or 1. To accomplish our test, we might rewrite the expression as follows:

```
if ( ival != jval && ival != kval && jval != kval )
    // do something ...
```

Exercise 4.4

Which, if any, of the following are likely to be incorrect or not portable? Why? How might each be corrected? (Note that the type of the object(s) is not significant in these examples.)

```
(a) ptr->ival != 0              (b) ival != jval < kval
(c) ptr != 0 && *ptr++          (d) ival++ && ival
(e) vec[ ival++ ] <= vec[ ival ];
```

Exercise 4.5

The order of evaluation of the binary operators is left undefined to permit the compiler freedom to provide an optimal implementation. The trade-off is between an efficient implementation and a potential pitfall in the use of the language by the programmer. Do you consider that an acceptable trade-off? Why or why not?

4.4   Assignment Operators

An initialization provides an object with a first value. For example:

```
int ival = 1024;
int *pi = 0;
```

An assignment, in contrast, overwrites an object's current value with a new value. For example:

```
ival = 2048;
pi = &ival;
```

Initialization and assignment are sometimes confused because both of them use the same operator (=). An object can be initialized only once: at the time of its definition. An object can be assigned multiple times throughout the program.

What happens when the type of the expression being assigned is not the same as the type of the object being assigned to? For example:

```
ival = 3.14159; // ok?
```

The rule is that the right-hand expression's type must exactly match the type of the object being assigned to. In this case, `ival` is of type `int`, and the literal constant 3.14159 is of type `double`. Is the assignment an error? No. The compiler attempts to implicitly convert the type of the right operand to the type of the object being assigned to. If a type conversion is possible, the compiler silently carries it out (if a loss of precision is involved, such as the conversion of a double to int, a warning is generally issued). In our example, 3.14159 is converted to a literal constant 3 of type int. This is the value assigned to ival.

If an implicit type conversion is not possible, the assignment is flagged as an error at compile-time. For example, the following assignment results in a compile-time error because there is no implicit conversion of a value of type int to that of type int*:

```
pi = ival; // error
```

(The set of implicit type conversions recognized by the language is discussed in Section 4.14.)

The left operand of the assignment operator must be an lvalue — that is, it must have an associated writable address value. An obvious example of an illegal non-lvalue assignment is the following:

```
1024 = ival; // error
```

Here is one possible solution:

```
int value = 1024;
value = ival; // ok
```

However, in some cases, having an lvalue in itself is not sufficient. For example, given the following object definitions

```
const int array_size = 8;
int ia[ array_size ] = { 0, 1, 2, 2, 3, 5, 8, 13 };
int *pia = ia;
```

the assignment

```
array_size = 512; // error
```

is illegal even though array_size is an lvalue; the const definition of array_size makes its address value not writable. Similarly, the assignment

```
ia = pia; // error
```

is illegal. Although ia is an lvalue, an array object itself cannot be assigned to; only the elements it contains can be assigned to.

The assignment

```
pia + 2 = 1; // error
```

is also illegal. Although pia+2 yields the address of ia[2], the result is not a writable address value. However, if the dereference operator is applied to the address value, as in

```
*(pia + 2) = 1; // ok
```

the assignment is ok: the dereference operator indicates that the assignment is to the object to which pia+2 refers.

The result of an assignment is the value actually placed in the left operand's associated storage. For example, the result of

```
ival = 0;
```

is 0, whereas the result of

```
ival = 3.14159;
```

is 3, both of type int. Because of this, an assignment can appear as a subexpression. For example, the following while loop

```
extern char next_char();
int main()
{
    char ch = next_char();

    while ( ch != '\n' ) {
            // do something ...
            ch = next_char();
    }

    // ...
}
```

can be rewritten as follows:

```
extern char next_char();
int main()
{
    char ch;

    while (( ch = next_char() ) != '\n' ) {
            // do something ...
    }

    // ...
}
```

The additional parentheses are necessary because of the lower precedence of the assignment operator to that of inequality. Precedence determines the order of evaluation within an expression, with higher operators being evaluated first. Without parentheses, the inequality test

```
next_char() != '\n'
```

is evaluated first, and ch is then assigned the true or false value of whether the result of next_char() is equal to the newline character — clearly not what we intended! (We look at precedence in detail in Section 4.13.)

Similarly, assignment operators can be concatenated provided that each of the operands being assigned is of the same general data type. For example, in the following

```
int main()
{
    int ival, jval;
    ival = jval = 0; // ok: each assigned 0
    // ...
}
```

`ival` and `jval` are each assigned 0. However, the following is illegal, because `ival` and `pval` are objects of different types, although 0 is a valid value that can be assigned to either:

```
int main()
{
    int ival; int *pval;
    ival = pval = 0; // error: not the same types
    // ...
}
```

The following may or may not be legal; however, it does not serve as a definition of both `ival` and `jval`:

```
int main()
{
    // ...
    int ival = jval = 0; // may or may not be legal
    // ...
}
```

The example is legal only if `jval` has been previously defined and is of the appropriate type to be assigned zero. In that case, `ival` is initialized to the result of assigning `jval` a value of 0, which itself is 0. In order for it to define both objects, it must be rewritten as follows:

```
int main()
{
    // ok: defines ival and jval...
    int ival = 0, jval = 0;
    // ...
}
```

We often apply an operator to an object and then reassign the result to the object, as in

```
int arraySum( int ia[], int sz )
{
    int sum = 0;
    for ( int i = 0; i < sz; ++i )
        sum = sum + ia[ i ];
    return sum;
}
```

For that reason, a set of compound assignment operators is provided. For example, the preceding function can be rewritten using the compound assignment-plus operator:

```
int arraySum( int ia[], int sz )
{
    int sum = 0;
    for ( int i = 0; i < sz; ++i )
            // equivalent of: sum = sum + ia[ i ];
            sum += ia[ i ];
    return sum;
}
```

The general syntactic form of the compound assignment operator is

```
a op= b;
```

where op= may be one of the following ten operators:

```
+=      -=    *=   /=   %=
<<=     >>=   &=   ^=   |=
```

Each compound operator is equivalent to the following "longhand" assignment:

```
a = a op b;
```

The longhand notation for summing a vector, for example, is

```
sum = sum + ia[ i ];
```

Exercise 4.6

The following is illegal. Why? How would you correct it?

```
int main() {
    float fval;
    int    ival;
    int   *pi;

    fval = ival = pi = 0;
}
```

Exercise 4.7

Although the following are not illegal, they do not behave as the programmer expects. Why? How would you reimplement them to reflect the programmer's likely intention?

```
(a) if ( ptr = retrieve_pointer() != 0 )
(b) if ( ival = 1024 )
(c) ival += ival + 1;
```

4.5 Increment and Decrement Operators

The increment (++) and decrement (--) operators provide a convenient notational shorthand for adding or subtracting 1 from an object. They are used most commonly to bump up or down by 1 the value of an index, iterator, or pointer into a collection. For example:

```cpp
#include <vector>
#include <cassert>

int main()
{
    int ia[10] = {0,1,2,3,4,5,6,7,8,9};
    vector< int > ivec( 10 );

    int ix_vec = 0, ix_ia = 9;
    while ( ix_vec < 10 )
            ivec[ ix_vec++ ] = ia[ ix_ia-- ];

    int *pia = &ia[9];
    vector<int>::iterator iter = ivec.begin();

    while ( iter != ivec.end() )
            assert( *iter++ == *pia-- );
}
```

The expression

```cpp
ix_vec++
```

is the *postfix* form of the increment operator. It increments ix_vec *after* the current value of ix_vec is used as the index into ivec. For example, for the first iteration of the while loop, ix_vec is evaluated to contain the value 0. That value serves as the index into ivec. ix_vec is incremented by 1 to the value 1, but this new value is not actually used until the next iteration of the loop. The postfix form of the decrement operator works in the same way. The current value of ix_ia is used to index into ia; ix_ia is then decremented by 1.

A *prefix* version of the two operators is also supported. In the prefix form, the current value is first either incremented or decremented and then its value is used. Thus, if we write

```cpp
// incorrect: off by one on both ends
int ix_vec = 0, ix_ia = 9;
while ( ix_vec < 10 )
        ivec[ ++ix_vec ] = ia[ --ix_ia ];
```

ix_vec is incremented by 1 to a value of 1 prior to its use as an index into ivec. Similarly, ix_ia is decremented by 1 to a value of 8 prior to its use as an index into ia. For our loop to behave correctly, we must set the initial value of the two indexes 1 less-than and 1 greater-than the values we actually wish to access.

```
// ok: corrected on both ends
int ix_vec = -1, ix_ia = 10;
while ( ix_vec < 10 )
        ivec[ ++ix_vec ] = ia[ --ix_ia ];
```

As a final example, consider the design of a stack. A stack is a fundamental computer science data abstraction allowing for the nesting and retrieval of values in *LIFO* sequence — that is, last in, first out. The two fundamental operations on a stack are *push* a new value onto the stack and *pop* the last value pushed onto the stack. For argument's sake, let's assume that the stack is implemented as a vector.

Our stack maintains an object top that indicates the next available slot into which to push a value. To implement the push semantics, we must assign the value to the slot indicated by top and then increment top by 1. Which instance of the increment operator does this require? We want to use the current value and then increment that value by 1. This is the behavior of the postfix form:

```
stack[ top++ ] = value;
```

To implement the pop semantics, we must first decrement top by 1 and then return the value of the slot indexed by the newly decremented value of top. This is the behavior of the prefix form:

```
int value = stack[ --top ];
```

(An implementation of our stack class is provided at the end of this chapter. The standard library stack class is discussed in Section 6.16.)

Exercise 4.8

Why do you think C++ wasn't named ++C?

4.6   Complex Number Operations

The complex number class provided by the standard library is an excellent model of an object-based class abstraction. Through its use of operator overloading, objects of the complex class type can be used nearly as easily as the simpler built-in arithmetic types. As we'll see in this section, not only are the usual arithmetic operators — such as addition, subtraction, multiplication, and division — supported, but also complex number objects can generally be intermixed with the built-in arithmetic types. For the programmer, the complex numbers are a part of the basic language even if their implementation is within the standard library. (Note that this section treats only the use of the complex number class; for an introduction to the mathematics of complex numbers, see [PERSON68] or any elementary book on mathematics.) One can write, for example:

```
#include <complex>

complex< double > a;
complex< double > b;

// ... assign to a and b ...

complex< double > c = a * b + a / b;
```

The complex and arithmetic data types can be intermixed in expressions, such as

```
complex< double > complex_obj = a + 3.14159;
```

Similarly, a complex number can be initialized with or assigned a value of an arithmetic data type, such as

```
double dval = 3.14159;
complex_obj = dval;
```

or

```
int ival = 3;
complex_obj = ival;
```

The reverse, however, is not automatically supported — that is, an arithmetic data type cannot be directly initialized or assigned with a complex number class object. For example, the following results in a compile-time error:

```
// error: no implicit conversion of a complex number
// to a built-in arithmetic data type

double dval = complex_obj;
```

To do this, we must explicitly indicate which component of the complex object we wish to assign. The complex number class supports a pair of operations for reading either the real or the imaginary part. For example, we can either use the *member access syntax*

```
double re = complex_obj.real();
double im = complex_obj.imag();
```

or the equivalent nonmember syntax:

```
// equivalent to the member syntax, above
double re = real( complex_obj );
double im = imag( complex_obj );
```

The complex number class supports four compound assignment operators: those of addition (+=), subtraction (-=), multiplication (*=), and division (/=). Thus, we can write, for example:

```
complex_obj += second_complex_obj;
```

Both the input and the output of a complex number are supported. The output of a complex number is an ordered pair separated by a comma and surrounded by parentheses. The first value is the real part, and the second value is the imaginary part. For example,

```
complex< double > complex0( 3.14159, -2.171 );
complex< double > complex1( complex0.real() );

cout << complex0 << " " << complex1 << endl;
```

yields the following:

```
( 3.14159, -2.171 ) ( 3.14159, 0.0 )
```

Any of the following forms of numeric representation can be read as a complex number:

```
// valid input forms of a complex number
// 3.14159         ==> complex( 3.14159 );
// ( 3.14159 )     ==> complex( 3.14159 );
// ( 3.14, -1.0 ) ==> complex( 3.14, -1.0 );

// could be read in as
// cin >> a >> b >> c
// where a, b, c are complex numbers

3.14159  ( 3.14159 )  ( 3.14, -1.0 )
```

Additional operations supported by the complex number class include sqrt(), abs(), polar(), sin(), cos(), tan(), exp(), log(), log10(), and pow().

Exercise 4.9

In the Rogue Wave implementation of the standard library available to us at the time of this writing, the four compound assignment operators support only a right-hand operand of type complex. For example, an attempt to write

```
complex_obj += 1;
```

results in a compile-time error, although Standard C++ specifies that the assignment is legal. (It is not uncommon to find implementations at this point still lagging behind the Standard.) We can fix this lapse by providing our own instance of the compound operators. For example, here is a nontemplate instance of compound addition assignment operator for complex<double>:

```
#include <complex>
inline complex<double>&
operator+=( complex<double> &cval, double dval )
{
    return cval += complex<double>( dval );
}
```

When we include this instance in our program, the compound assignment of 1, above, executes correctly. (This is an example of providing an overloaded operator for a class type. Operator overloading is discussed in detail in Chapter 15.)

Using the preceding definition as a model, provide implementations of the other three compound operators for complex<double>. Add them to the following small program and execute it.

```
#include <iostream>
#include <complex>

// compound operator definitions go here

int main()
{
    complex< double > cval( 4.0, 1.0 );

    cout << cval << endl;
    cval += 1;
    cout << cval << endl;
    cval -= 1;
    cout << cval << endl;
    cval *= 2;
    cout << cval << endl;
    cout /= 2;
    cout << cval << endl;
}
```

Exercise 4.10

The Standard C++ complex number type does not provide an increment operator, although its absence is not intrinsic to the nature of complex numbers — after all,

```
cval += 1;
```

in effect increments cval's real part by 1. Provide a definition of the increment operator, add it to the following program, and then compile and execute:

```
#include <iostream>
#include <complex>

// increment operator definitions go here

int main()
{
    complex< double > cval( 4.0, 1.0 );

    cout << cval << 'endl';
    ++cval;
    cout << cval << endl;
}
```

4.7   The Conditional Operator

The conditional operator provides a convenient notational alternative to simple if-else statements. For example, rather than write

```
bool is_equal = false;
if ( !strcmp( str1, str2 ))
    is_equal = true;
```

one can write

```
bool is_equal = !strcmp( str1, str2 ) ? true : false;
```

The conditional operator has the following syntactic form:

```
expr1 ? expr2 : expr3;
```

expr1 is always evaluated and results in either true or false. If it evaluates to true, expr2 is evaluated; otherwise, expr3 is evaluated. For example, the following

```
int min( int ia, int ib )
        { return ( ia < ib ) ? ia : ib; }
```

is a shorthand equivalent of

```
int min( int ia, int ib ) {
    if ( ia < ib )
            return ia;
    return ib;
}
```

The following program illustrates how the conditional operator might be used.

```
#include <iostream>

int main()
{
    int i = 10, j = 20, k = 30;

    cout << "The larger value of "
         << i << " and " << j << " is "
         << ( i > j ? i : j ) << endl;

    cout << "The value of " << i << " is"
         << ( i % 2  ? " odd." : " even." )
         << endl;

    /* the conditional operator can be nested,
     * but a deep nesting is difficult to read
     * in this example,
     * max is set to the largest of 3 variables
     */
```

```
int max = ( (i > j)
    ? (( i > k) ? i : k)
    : ( j > k ) ? j : k);

cout << "The larger value of "
     << i << ", " << j << " and " << k
     << " is " << max << endl;
}
```

When compiled and executed, the program generates the following output:

```
The larger value of 10 and 20 is 20
The value of 10 is even
The larger value of 10, 20 and 30 is 30
```

4.8   The sizeof Operator

The sizeof operator returns the size, in bytes, of an object or type name. It takes the following forms:

```
sizeof (type name );
sizeof ( object );
sizeof object;
```

The value returned is of type size_t, a machine-specific typedef found in the cst-ddef header file. Here is an example of how both forms of the sizeof operator are used:

```
#include <cstddef>

int ia[] = { 0, 1, 2 };

// sizeof returns size of the entire array
size_t array_size = sizeof ia;

// sizeof returns size of type int
size_t element_size = array_size / sizeof( int );
```

When sizeof is applied to an array, such as ia in the preceding example, it returns the size, in bytes, of the entire array, and not the size of simply its first element nor the number of elements that ia contains. For example, on a machine in which an int is 4 bytes long, sizeof indicates that the size of ia is 12 bytes. Similarly, when we write

```
int *pi = new int[ 3 ];
size_t pointer_size = sizeof ( pi );
```

the value returned by sizeof(pi) is the size in bytes of a pointer to type int and not of the array pi addresses.

Here is small function that exercises the sizeof() operator:

```
#include <string>
#include <iostream>
#include <cstddef>

int main()
{
    size_t ia;

    ia = sizeof( ia ); // ok
    ia = sizeof ia;    // ok

    // ia = sizeof int; // error
    ia = sizeof( int ); // ok

    int *pi = new int[ 12 ];

    cout << "pi: " << sizeof( pi )
         << " *pi: " << sizeof( *pi )
         << endl;

    // a string's size is independent of
    // the length of the string it addresses
    string st1( "foobar" );
    string st2( "a mighty oak" );

    string *ps = &st1;

    cout << "st1: "  << sizeof( st1 )
         << " st2: " << sizeof( st2 )
         << " ps: "  << sizeof( ps )
         << " *ps: " << sizeof( *ps )
         << endl;

    cout << "short :\t"    << sizeof(short)    << endl;
    cout << "short* :\t"   << sizeof(short*)   << endl;
    cout << "short& :\t"   << sizeof(short&)   << endl;
    cout << "short[3] :\t" << sizeof(short[3]) << endl;
}
```

When compiled and executed, the program generates the following output:

```
pi: 4 *pi: 4
st1: 12 st2: 12 ps: 4 *ps: 12
short : 2
short* : 4
short& : 2
short[3] : 6
```

As the program example shows, application of the `sizeof` operator on a pointer type returns the size of the memory necessary to contain an address of that type. Application of the `sizeof` operator on a reference type, however, returns the size of the memory necessary to contain the referenced object.

When `sizeof` is applied to type `char`, the result is guaranteed to be 1 under all C++ implementations.

```
// guaranteed to evaluate to 1 under all implementations
size_t char_size = sizeof( char );
```

The `sizeof` operator is evaluated at compile-time and so is considered a constant expression. As such, it can be used wherever a constant expression is required, such as the dimension of an array or as the nontype parameter of a template. For example:

```
// ok: compile-time constant expression
int array[ sizeof( some_type_T )];
```

4.9   The new and delete Expressions

Every program is provided with a pool of available memory it can use during program execution. This pool of available memory is referred to as the program's *free store* or *heap*. The allocation of memory at run-time is referred to as *dynamic memory allocation*. As we saw in Chapter 1, this is accomplished by applying the new expression to a type specifier, either that of a built-in type or a user-defined class type. The new expression returns a pointer to the newly allocated object. For example:

```
int *pi = new int;
```

allocates one object of type `int` from the free store, initializing `pi` with its address. The object actually allocated on the free store is uninitialized. We can specify an initial value as follows:

```
int *pi = new int( 1024 );
```

This not only allocates the object but also initializes it with a value of 1,024.

To dynamically allocate an array of objects, we write

```
int *pia = new int[ 10 ];
```

This allocates an array of ten objects of type `int` from the free store, initializing `pia` with its address. The elements of the array, however, are uninitialized. There is no syntax for specifying an explicit set of initial values for the elements of a dynamically allocated array. (In the case of an array of class objects, the default constructor, if defined, is applied to each element in turn.) For example:

```
string *ps = new string;
```

allocates one string class object from the free store, initializing `ps` with its address and then invoking the default string class constructor on that object. Similarly,

```
string *psa = new string[ 10 ];
```

allocates an array of ten string class objects from the free store, initializing psa with its address and then invoking the default string class constructor on each element of the array in turn.

One aspect of free store memory is that the objects allocated from it are unnamed. The new expression does not return the actual allocated object but rather returns the address of the allocated object. All manipulation of the object is done indirectly through that address.

When our use of the object is complete, we must explicitly return the object's memory to the free store. We do this by applying the delete expression to the pointer that addresses the object originally allocated through the new expression. (The delete expression should not be applied to a pointer that addresses memory that has not been allocated by the new expression.) For example:

```
delete pi;
```

deallocates the int object addressed by pi, returning it to the free store. Similarly,

```
delete ps;
```

deallocates the string class object addressed by ps after first applying the string destructor to it and then returning it back to the free store. Finally,

```
delete [] pia;
```

deallocates the array of ten int objects addressed by pia, returning the associated memory to the free store. The empty bracket pair between the delete keyword and the pointer to the array represents the special delete expression syntax for deallocating an array allocated through the new expression.

Chapter 8 looks at dynamic memory allocation and the use of the new and delete expressions in detail.

Exercise 4.11

Which of the following, if any, are illegal or in error?

```
(a) vector<string> svec( 10 );
(b) vector<string> *pvec1 = new vector<string>(10);
(c) vector<string> **pvec2 = new vector<string>[10];
(d) vector<string> *pv1 = &svec;
(e) vector<string> *pv2 = pvec1;

(f) delete svec;
(g) delete pvec1;
(h) delete [] pvec2;
(i) delete pv1;
(j) delete pv2;
```

4.10   Comma Operator

A comma expression is a series of expressions separated by commas. These expressions are evaluated from left to right. The result of a comma expression is the value of the rightmost expression. In the following example, each side of the conditional operator is a comma expression. The value of the first comma expression is ix; the value of the second is 0.

```
int main()
{
    // examples of a comma expression
    // ia, sz, and index are defined elsewhere ...
    int ival = (ia != 0)
                ? ix=get_value(), ia[index]=ix
                : ia=new int[sz], ia[index ]=0;
    // ...
}
```

4.11   The Bitwise Operators

Table 4.3   Bitwise Operators.

Operator	Function	Use
~	bitwise NOT	~expr
<<	left shift	expr1 << expr2
>>	right shift	expr1 >> expr2
&	bitwise AND	expr1 & expr2
^	bitwise XOR	expr1 ^ expr2
|	bitwise OR	expr1 | expr2
&=	bitwise AND assign	expr1 &= expr2
^=	bitwise XOR assign	expr1 ^= expr2
|=	bitwise OR assign	expr1 |= expr2

A bitwise operator interprets its operand(s) as an ordered collection of bits, either individually or grouped as fields. Each bit can contain either a 0 (off) or a 1 (on) value. A bitwise operator allows the programmer to test and set individual bits or bit-fields. An object utilized as a discrete collection of single bits is referred to as a *bitvector*. Bitvectors are a compact method of keeping yes/no information (sometimes spoken of as *flags*) on a set of items or conditions. In compilers, for example, the qualifiers to a type declaration, such as const and volatile, are sometimes stored within a bitvector.

The iostream library uses bitvectors to represent its format state, such as whether the integral output should be displayed in decimal, hexadecimal, or octal.

Just as there are two approaches in Standard C++ to the support of strings (the string class type and the C-style character array) and the ordered collections of elements (the template vector class and the built-in array type), there are two approaches to the support of bitvectors. In pre-Standard C++ and the C language, a bitvector is represented using a built-in integral type, typically an unsigned int. The object provides the bit container; the programmer manages the semantics using the bitwise operators discussed in this section. The standard library provides a bitset class that supports the bitvector class abstraction. A bitset object encapsulates the semantics of a bitvector; it answers queries such as, Are any of your bits set? How many of your bits are set? and provides a set of operations to manage the setting, resetting, and testing of bits.

In general, we recommend the use of the standard library class abstractions — in this case, the use of the bitset class over that of direct bitwise manipulation of integral data types. In our opinion, however, knowledge of both representations is still necessary because of the likely need to read and perhaps modify existing code. For completeness, we illustrate both approaches. In the rest of this section, we look at the use of the built-in integral types as bitvectors and the use of the bitwise operators. In the following section, we look at the bitset class.

When we are using an integral type as a bitvector, the type can be either signed or unsigned; an unsigned type is strongly recommended. How the "sign bit" is handled in a number of the bitwise operations is undefined and is therefore likely to differ across implementations; programs that work under one implementation may fail under another.

The bitwise NOT operator (~) flips the bits of its operand. Each 1 bit is set to 0; each 0 bit is set to 1.

The bitwise shift operators (<<, >>) shift the bits of the left operand some number of positions either left or right. The operand's excess bits are discarded. The left shift operator (<<) inserts 0-valued bits in from the right. The right shift operator (>>) inserts 0-valued bits in from the left if the operand is unsigned. If the operand is signed, it can either insert copies of the sign bit or insert 0-valued bits; again, this behavior is implementation defined.

The bitwise AND operator (&) takes two integral operands. For each bit position, the result is 1 if both operands contain 1; otherwise, the result is 0. (This operator should not be confused with the logical AND operator (&&); unfortunately, it seems that everyone has at one time or another done just that.)

The bitwise XOR (exclusive or) operator (^) takes two integral operands. For each bit position, the result is 1 if either but not both operands contain 1; otherwise, the result is 0.

The bitwise OR (inclusive or) operator (|) takes two integral operands. For each bit position, the result is 1 if either or both operands contain 1; otherwise, the result is 0. (This operator should not be confused with the logical OR operator (||).)

Let's look at a simple example. A teacher has 30 students in a class. Each week the class is given a pass/fail quiz. A bitvector will be used to track the results of each quiz. (Note that bits are numbered beginning with 0. Thus, bit 1 actually represents the second bit. In our example, we are wasting the first bit in order to speak of bit 1 as the first bit and so on. After all, our teacher is not a student of computer science.)

```
unsigned int quiz1 = 0;
```

The teacher must be able to turn on and off and to test individual bits. For example, student 27 has taken a makeup quiz and passed. The teacher must turn bit 27 on. The first step is to set the 27th bit of an integer to 1, while all the other bits remain 0. This can be done with the left shift operator and the integer constant 1:

```
1 << 27;
```

If this value is bitwise ORed with `quiz1`, all except the 27th bit will remain unchanged. The 27th bit is turned on:

```
quiz1 |= 1<<27;
```

Imagine that the teacher reexamined the quiz and discovered that student 27 actually had failed the makeup. The teacher must now turn off bit 27. This time the integer must have all the bits except the 27th turned on. Notice that this is the inverse of the previous integer. Applying the bitwise NOT to the previous integer will turn on every bit except the 27th:

```
~( 1<<27 );
```

If this value is bitwise ANDed with `quiz1`, all except the 27th bit will remain unchanged. The 27th bit is turned off:

```
quiz1 &= ~(1<<27);
```

Here is how the teacher can determine the on or off status of a bit. Consider student 27 again (actually, her name is Anna). The first step is to set the 27th bit of an integer to 1. The bitwise AND of this value with `quiz1` evaluates to `true` if bit 27 of `quiz1` is also on; otherwise, it evaluates to `false`:

```
bool hasPassed = quiz1 & (1<<27);
```

Because the bitwise operators are error-prone due to their low-level bit manipulations, typically they are encapsulated either in preprocessor macros or inline functions. For example:

```
inline bool bit_on( unsigned int ui, int pos )
{
    return ui & (1 << pos );
}
```

This might then be invoked as follows:

```
enum students { Danny = 1, Jeffrey, Ethan, Zev, Ebie, // ...
                AnnaP = 26, AnnaL = 27 };
const int student_size = 27;

//deliberately starts at 1
bool has_passed_quiz[ student_size+1 ];
for ( int index = 1; index <= student_size; ++index )
     has_passed_quiz[ index ] = bit_on( quiz1, index );
```

Of course, once we begin encapsulating the direct use of the bitwise operators, the next logical step is to provide an encapsulation of the whole notion of bitvectors — in the case of the standard library, the bitset class abstraction. As it happens, this is the very topic of the next section.

Exercise 4.12

Assume the following two definitions:

```
unsigned int ui1 = 3, ui2 = 7;
```

What is the result of each of the following expressions?

(a)   ui1 & ui2   (c)   ui1 | ui2
(b)   ui1 && ui2   (d)   ui1 || ui2

Exercise 4.13

Using the model of the bit_on() inline function, provide a bit_turn_on() (turns on a specified bit), a bit_turn_off() (turns off a specified bit), a flip_bit() (reverses the value of a specified bit), and a bit_off() (tests whether the specified bit is off) collection of inline functions operating on a bitvector represented as an unsigned int. Then write a small program to exercise the functions.

Exercise 4.14

What is the weakness of explicitly coding the functions of Exercise 4.13 to operate on an unsigned int? One alternative is the use of a typedef. A second alternative is the use of the template mechanism introduced in Section 2.5. Rewrite the bit_on() inline function defined above using a typedef and then using the function template mechanism.

4.12   bitset Operations

Table 4.4   bitset Operations

Operation	Function	Use
test(pos)	is pos bit on?	a.test(4)
any()	is any bit on?	a.any()
none()	are no bits on?	a.none()
count()	number of bits on	a.count()
size()	number of bit elems	a.size()
[pos]	access pos bit	a[4]
flip()	reverse all bits	a.flip()
flip(pos)	reverse pos bit	a.flip(4)
set()	turn on all bits	a.set()
set(pos)	turn on pos bit	a.set(4)
reset()	turn off all bits	a.reset()
reset(pos)	turn off pos bit	a.reset(4)

The problem of representing bitvectors with integral types is the low-level complexity of the expressions that use the bitwise operators to set, reset, and test the individual bits. For example, to turn on the 27th bit using our integral type, we write the following:

```
quiz1 |= 1<<27;
```

To do that with a bitset, we program either

```
quiz1[ 27 ] = 1;
```

or

```
quiz1.set( 27 );
```

(As noted in the previous section, the numbering of bits begins with zero: in practice, bit 27 refers to the 28th bit. In our example, we are wasting the first bit so that references to our bits begin with 1.)

To use the bitset class, we must include its associated header file:

```
#include <bitset>
```

A bitset can be declared in one of three ways. In its default definition, we simply indicate how large a bitvector we wish. For example:

```
bitset< 32 > bitvec;
```

declares a bitset object containing 32 bits numbered from 0 to 31. By default, all the bits are initialized to zero. To test whether a bitset object has any of its bits set, we use the any() operation; any() returns true if one or more bits of the bitset object are turned on. For bitvec, the test

```
bool is_set = bitvec.any();
```

evaluates, of course, to false. Conversely, the operation none() returns true if all the bits of the bitset object are set to zero. For bitvec, the test

```
bool is_not_set = bitvec.none();
```

evaluates to true. Alternatively, the count() operation returns the number of bits that are set:

```
int bits_set = bitvec.count();
```

There are two ways to set an individual bit. Either the set() operation or the subscript operator can be used. For example, the following for loop turns on each even-numbered bit:

```
for ( int index = 0; index < 32; ++index )
    if ( index % 2 == 0 )
        bitvec[ index ] = 1;
```

Similarly, there are two ways to test whether an individual bit is turned on. The test() operation takes the bit position as an argument and returns either true or false. For example:

```
if ( bitvec.test( 0 ))
    // our bitvec[ 0 ] worked!;
```

Again, alternatively, the subscript operator can be used:

```
cout << "bitvec: positions turned on:\n\t";
for ( int index = 0; index < 32; ++index )
    if ( bitvec[ index ] )
        cout << index << " ";
cout << endl;
```

To turn off an individual bit, we can use either the reset() or the subscript operator. Both of the following operations turn off bitvec's first bit:

```
// equivalent; turn off first bit
bitvec.reset( 0 );
bitvec[ 0 ] = 0;
```

set() and reset() can also be used to, respectively, turn on or turn off the entire bitset object. This is accomplished by invoking the desired operation without passing it a particular position. For example:

```
// reset all the bits to 0.
bitvec.reset();
if ( bitvec.none() != true )
```

```
        // oops! something is wrong

    // set all the bits to 1
    bitvec.set();
    if ( bitvec.any() != true )
        // oops! again, something is wrong
```

The `flip()` operation reverses the value of either an individual bit or the entire bitset object:

```
    bitvec.flip( 0 ); // reverses value of first bit
    bitvec[0].flip(); // also reverses the first bit!

    bitvec.flip();    // reverses value of all bits
```

There are two additional ways to construct a bitset object. Both provide a way to initialize individual bit positions to 1. One method is to provide an explicit unsigned value as an argument to the constructor. The first N bit positions of the bitset object are initialized to the corresponding bit values of the argument. For example,

```
    bitset< 32 > bitvec2( 0xffff );
```

has the effect of setting the lower 16 bits of `bitvec2` to 1:

```
    00000000000000001111111111111111
```

The following definition of `bitvec3`

```
    bitset< 32 > bitvec3( 012 );
```

sets bit positions 1 and 3 to 1 (presuming we count the bit positions beginning with 0):

```
    00000000000000000000000000001010
```

Alternatively, we can construct a bitset object by passing in a string argument representing a collection of zeros and ones, as in the following:

```
    // equivalent initialization as bitvec3
    string bitval( "1010" );
    bitset< 32 > bitvec4( bitval );
```

Both `bitvec4` and `bitvec3` have bit positions 1 and 3 set to 1 while the remaining bit positions are set to 0.

Alternatively, one can mark a range of the string elements with which to initialize the bitset. For example, in the following

```
    // start at position 6, for a length of 4: 1010
    string bitval( "1111110101100011010101" );
    bitset< 32 > bitvec5( bitval, 6, 4 );
```

`bitvec5` is initialized with bit positions 1 and 3 set to 1 while its remaining bit positions are set to 0, the same as `bitvec3` and `bitvec4`. If we leave off the third parameter indicating the length of characters with which to mark the range, the range consists of the indicated position to the end of the string. For example:

```
// start at position 6, continuing to end of string: 1010101
string bitval( "111111010110001101010101" );
bitset< 32 > bitvec6( bitval, 6 );
```

The bitset class supports two member functions that can convert a bitset object into another type. In the one case, we can convert any bitset object into a string representation using the to_string() operation:

```
string bitval( bitvec3.to_string() );
```

In the second case, we can convert any bitset object into an integral representation of type unsigned long using the to_ulong() operation, provided that the underlying representation of the bitset can be represented in an unsigned long. This is particularly useful if we need to pass a bitset into a C or pre-Standard C++ program.

The bitset class supports use of the bitwise operators. For example:

```
bitset<32> bitvec7 = bitvec2 & bitvec3;
```

initializes bitvec7 to the bitwise AND of the two bitvectors, whereas

```
bitset<32> bitvec8 = bitvec2 | bitvec3;
```

initializes bitvec8 to the bitwise OR. The bitwise compound assignment operators and bitwise shift operators are also supported (these are illustrated in the previous section).

Exercise 4.15

Which of the following declarations of a bitset object, if any, are in error?

```
(a) bitset<64> bitvec(32);
(b) bitset<32> bv( 1010101 );
(c) string bstr; cin >> bstr; bitset<8>bv( bstr );
(d) bitset<32> bv; bitset<16> bv16( bv );
```

Exercise 4.16

Which, if any, of the following uses of a bitset object are in error?

```
extern void bitstring(const char*);
bool bit_on(unsigned long, int );
bitset<32> bitvec;

(a) bitstring( bitvec.to_string().c_str() );
(b) if ( bit_on( bitvec.to_long(), 64 )) ...
(c) bitvec.flip( bitvec.count() );
```

Exercise 4.17

Consider the sequence 1,2,3,5,8,13,21. How might we initialize a bitset<32> to represent this sequence? Alternatively, given an empty bitset, write a small program to turn on each of the appropriate bits.

4.13   Precedence

Operator precedence is the order in which operators are evaluated in a compound expression. For example, what is the result finally assigned to ival?

```
int ival = 6 + 3 * 4 / 2 + 2;
```

A purely left-to-right evaluation yields a value of 20. Other possible results include 9, 14, and 36. Which one is ival actually assigned? 14.

In C++, multiplication and division have a higher precedence than addition. This means that they are evaluated first. Multiplication and division have the same precedence, however, so that they are evaluated from left to right. The order of expression evaluation, therefore, is the following:

```
1.  3 * 4 => 12
2.  12 / 2 => 6
3.  6 + 6 => 12
4.  12 + 2 => 14
```

The following condition test of the while loop behaves very differently from the intention of the programmer because of the lower precedence of the assignment operator compared with that of the inequality operator:

```
while ( ch = nextChar() != '\n' )
```

The programmer's intention is to assign ch the next character and then test that character to see whether it is null. The behavior of the expression, however, is to test the next character to see whether it is null. ch is then assigned the true or false value of the test. The next character is never assigned.

Precedence can be overridden by the use of parentheses, which mark subexpressions. In the evaluation of a compound expression, the first action is to evaluate all parenthetical subexpressions. Each subexpression is replaced by its result; evaluation continues. Innermost parentheses are evaluated before outer pairs. For example:

```
4 * 5 + 7 * 2 ==> 34
4 * ( 5 + 7 * 2 ) ==> 76
4 * ( (5 + 7) * 2 ) ==> 96
```

Here is our while loop expression properly parenthesized to reflect the programmer's intentions:

```
while ( (ch = nextChar()) != '\n' )
```

Operators have both a precedence and associativity. For example, the assignment operator is right-associative. The concatenated assignment expression

```
ival = jval = kval = lval // right associative
```

first assigns lval to kval, then the result of that to jval, and finally the result of that to ival. The arithmetic operators, on the other hand, are left-associative. The expression

```
    ival + jval + kval + lval // left associative
```
adds ival and jval, then kval, and finally lval.

Table 4.5 presents the full set of C++ operators in order of precedence. Each operator within a segment of the table shares the same precedence as the other operators within the segment. All the operators in one segment have a higher precedence than all the operators in segments occurring below. For example, the multiply and divide operators share the same precedence. They both have a greater precedence than any of the relational operators.

Exercise 4.18

Using Table 4.5, identify the order of evaluation of the following compound expressions:

```
    (a)   ! ptr == ptr->next
    (b)   ~ uc ^ 0377 & ui << 4
    (c)   ch = buf[ bp++ ] != '\n'
```

Exercise 4.19

The three expressions in Exercise 4.18 all evaluate in an order contrary to the intentions of the programmer. Parenthesize them to evaluate in an order you imagine to be the intention of the programmer.

Exercise 4.20

The following two expressions fail to compile due to operator precedence. Explain why using Table 4.5. How would you fix them?

```
    (a) int i = doSomething(), 0;
    (b) cout << ival % 2 ? "odd" : "even";
```

Table 4.5 Operator Precedence

Operator	Function	Use
::	global scope	::name
::	class scope	class::name
::	namespace scope	namespace::name
.	member selectors	object.member
->	member selectors	pointer->member
[]	subscript	variable[expr]
()	function call	name(expr_list)
()	type construction	type(expr_list)
		Continued

Table 4.5   Operator Precedence (Continued)

Operator	Function	Use
++	postfix increment	lvalue++
--	postfix decrement	lvalue--
typeid	type ID	typeid(type)
typeid	run-time type ID	typeid(expr)
const_cast	type conversion	const_cast<type>(expr)
dynamic_cast	type conversion	dynamic_cast<type>(expr)
reinterpret_cast	type conversion	reinterpret_cast<type>(expr)
static_cast	type conversion	static_cast<type>(expr)
sizeof	size of object	sizeof expr
sizeof	size of type	sizeof(type)
++	prefix increment	++lvalue
--	prefix decrement	--lvalue
~	bitwise NOT	~expr
!	logical NOT	!expr
-	unary minus	-expr
+	unary plus	+expr
*	dereference	*expr
&	address-of	&expr
()	type conversion	(type) expr
new	allocate object	new type
new	allocate/init object	new type(expr_list)
new	alloc/place object	new (expr_list) type(expr_list)
new	allocate array	all forms
delete	deallocate object	all forms
delete	deallocate array	all forms
->*	ptr to member select	pointer->*pointer_to_member
.*	ptr to member select	object.*pointer_to_member
*	multiply	expr * expr
/	divide	expr / expr
%	modulo (remainder)	expr % expr
+	add	expr + expr

Continued

Table 4.5 Operator Precedence (Continued)

Operator	Function	Use
-	subtract	expr - expr
<<	bitwise shift left	expr << expr
>>	bitwise shift right	expr >> expr
<	less than	expr < expr
<=	less than or equal	expr <= expr
>	greater than	expr > expr
>=	greater than or equal	expr >= expr
==	equality	expr == expr
!=	inequality	expr != expr
&	bitwise AND	expr & expr
^	bitwise XOR	expr ^ expr
|	bitwise OR	expr | expr
&&	logical AND	expr && expr
||	logical OR	expr || expr
?:	conditional expr	expr ? expr : expr
=	assignment	lvalue = expr
=,*=,/=, %=,+=,-=,<<=, >>=,&=,|=,^=	compound assign	lvalue += expr, etc.
throw	throw exception	throw expr
,	comma	expr , expr

4.14   Type Conversions

Consider the following assignment:

```
int ival = 0;

// typically compiles with a warning
ival = 3.541 + 3;
```

The final result is to assign ival the value of 6. The actual steps in accomplishing that are the following. We are adding values of two different types: 3.541 is a literal of type double, and 3 is a literal of type int. Rather than attempt to add values of the two different types, C++ provides a set of *arithmetic conversions* to transform the operands to a common type before performing the arithmetic. The rule is always to promote the smaller type to that of the larger type, thereby preventing any loss of precision. In this case, the integer value 3 is promoted to type `double` prior to carrying out the addition. These conversions are carried out automatically by the compiler without programmer intervention (and sometimes without programmer knowledge). For that reason, they are referred to as *implicit type conversions*.

The addition and result are both of type `double`. The value is 6.541. The next step is to assign the result to `ival`. If the left- and right-hand types of an assignment are not of the same type, the right-hand side, if possible, is converted to the type of the left-hand side. In this case, `ival` is of type `int`. The conversion of a `double` to `int` is accomplished automatically by truncation and not rounding; the decimal portion is simply discarded. 6.541 becomes 6, which is the value assigned to `ival`. Because the conversion of a `double` to `int` may result in a loss of precision, most compilers typically issue a warning.

Because type conversion from a `double` to `int` does not support rounding, we need to program that ourselves. For example:

```
double dval = 8.6;
int ival = 5;

ival += dval + 0.5; // ensure rounding
```

If we wish to, we can suppress the standard arithmetic conversions by specifying an *explicit type conversion*:

```
// instruct compiler to cast double to int
ival = static_cast< int >( 3.541 ) + 3;
```

In this example, we explicitly instruct the compiler to convert the value of type `double` to type `int` rather than follow the standard C++ arithmetic conversions.

In this section, we look in detail at the issue of both implicit type conversion (carried out automatically by the compiler without programmer intervention, as in the first example above) and explicit type conversion (the programmer instructs the compiler to convert an existing type to a specified second type through application of a *cast*, as in the second example above).

4.14.1 Implicit Type Conversions

The language defines a set of standard conversions between objects of the built-in types that are applied implicitly by the compiler when necessary. Implicit type conversions take place in the following general program situations:

- In an arithmetic expression of mixed types. In this case, the widest data type present becomes the target conversion type. These are spoken of as the *arithmetic conversions*. For example:

```
int    ival = 3;
double dval = 3.14159;

// ival is promoted to double: 3.0
```

```
ival + dval;
```

- In an assignment of an expression of one type to an object of a second type. In this case, the target conversion type is the type of the object assigned to. For example, in the first assignment, the literal 0, which is of type int, is converted to a pointer of type int* representing a null address value. In the second assignment, a value of type double is truncated to a value of type int.

```
// 0 is converted to the null pointer value of type int*
int *pi = 0;

// dval is truncated to int: 3
ival = dval;
```

- In passing an expression to an invocation of a function in which the type of the expression differs from the type of the formal parameter. In this case, the target conversion type is the parameter type. For example:

```
extern double sqrt( double );

// 2 is promoted to double: 2.0
cout << "The square root of 2 is "
     << sqrt( 2 ) << endl;
```

- In returning an expression from a function in which the type of the expression differs from the return type. In this case, the target conversion type is the function return type. For example:

```
double difference( int ival1, int ival2 )
{
   // result value is promoted to double
   return ival1 - ival2;
}
```

4.14.2 The Arithmetic Conversions

The arithmetic conversions ensure that the two operands of a binary operator, such as addition or multiplication, are promoted to a common type, which then represents the result type. The two general guidelines are the following:

1. Types are always promoted, if necessary, to a wider type in order to prevent any loss of precision.
2. All arithmetic expressions involving integral types smaller than an integer are promoted to an integer before evaluation.

The rules are defined as follows, defining a hierarchy of type conversions. (We begin with the widest type, that of long double.)

If one operand is of type long double, then the other is converted to type long double regardless of what the second type is. For example, in the following expression, the character constant lowercase 'a' is promoted to a long double (its ASCII value is 97) and then added to the long double literal.

```
3.14159L + 'a';
```

Otherwise, if neither is of type long double and if one operand is of type double, the other is converted to type double. For example:

```
int    ival;
float  fval;
double dval;

// fval and ival converted to double prior to addition
dval + fval + ival;
```

Similarly, if neither is of type double and if one operand is of type float, then the other is converted to type float. For example:

```
char cval;
int ival;
float fval;

// ival and cval converted to float prior to addition
cval + fval + ival;
```

Otherwise, because neither of the operands is of either of the three floating point types, they must both be of some integral type. Prior to determining the common target promotion type, a process spoken of as *integral promotion* is applied to all integral types smaller than an int.

Under integral promotion, types char, signed char, unsigned char, and short int are promoted to type int. unsigned short int is converted to type int if the int type on the machine is large enough to represent all the values of the unsigned short (usually this happens if the short is represented as a half word and the int as a word); otherwise, it is promoted to type unsigned int.

The types wchar_t and an enumeration type are promoted to the smallest integer type that can represent all the values of its *underlying type*. For example, given the following enumeration

```
enum status { bad, ok };
```

the associated values are 0 and 1. Both these values can be, but do not need to be, stored in a char representation. When the values are actually stored as chars, char represents the underlying type of the enumeration. Integral promotion of status, then, based on its underlying type, is to type int.

In the following expressions

```
char cval;
bool found;
enum mumble { m1, m2, m3 } mval;

unsigned long ulong;

cval + ulong; ulong + found; mval + ulong;
```

prior to determining the common type to which to promote both operands, cval, found, and mval are promoted to type int.

Once the integral promotions are performed, the comparison of types begins again. If one operand is of type unsigned long, then the second is converted to type unsigned long. In our example, all three objects being added to ulong are promoted to type unsigned long.

Otherwise, if neither is of type unsigned long and if one operand is of type long, the other is converted to type long. For example:

```
char cval;
long lval;

// cval and 1024 are promoted to long before addition
cval + 1024 + lval;
```

There is one exception to the general conversion to type long: if one operand is of type long and the other is of type unsigned int, then the unsigned int is promoted to type long only if type long on the machine is large enough to represent all the values of the unsigned int (usually this is not true on a 32-bit operating system in which long and int are both represented as a word size); otherwise, both are promoted to type unsigned long.

Otherwise, if neither is of type long and if one operand is of type unsigned int, the other is converted to type unsigned int. Otherwise, both operands must be of type int.

Although this presentation of the arithmetic conversions may have left you more bemused than edified, the general idea is to preserve the precision of the values involved in a multitype expression. This is achieved by promoting the differing types to that of the widest type present.

4.14.3 Explicit Conversions

An explicit conversion is spoken of as a *cast* and is supported by the following set of named cast operators: static_cast, dynamic_cast, const_cast, and reinterpret_cast. Although necessary at times, casts are a potential source of program error: by using them, the programmer turns off or dampens the language's type-checking facility. Before we look at how we can cast values from one type to another, let's first look at when we might need to do so.

A pointer of any non-const data type can be assigned to a pointer of type void*. A void* pointer is used whenever the exact type of an object is either unknown or will vary under particular circumstances. A void* pointer is sometimes referred to as a *generic* pointer because of its ability to address objects of any data types. For example:

```
int ival;
int *pi = 0;
char *pc = 0;
void *pv;

pv = pi; // ok: implicit conversion
pv = pc; // ok: implicit conversion

const int *pci = &ival;
pv = pci; // error: pv is not a const void*;
const void *pcv = pci; // ok
```

However, a void* pointer cannot be dereferenced directly. There is no type information to guide the compiler in interpreting the underlying bit pattern. Rather, a void* pointer must first be converted to a pointer to a particular type. However, in C++ there is no automatic conversion of a void* pointer to a pointer to a particular type. For example, consider the following:

```
#include <cstring>

int ival = 1024;
void *pv;
int *pi = &ival;
const char *pc = "a casting call";

void mumble()
{
    pv = pi; // ok: pv addresses ival
    pc = pv; // error: no standard conversion

    char *pstr = new char[ strlen( pc )+1 ];
    strcpy( pstr, pc );
}
```

The programmer is clearly mistaken in attempting to assign pv to pc in this case, because pv is addressing an integer and not a character array. When pc is subsequently passed to strlen(), which expects a null-terminated string, the program is badly in error, and by the time strcpy() is executed, the best we can hope for is for the program to abort. What makes this error difficult to fix is that it is easy to overlook. This is why C++ requires an explicit cast to assign a void* pointer to any explicit type:

```
void mumble()
{
```

```
                    // ok: still wrong, but now it compiles!
                    // explicit cast calls attention to the assignment.
                    // when program fails, casts should be among first
                    // constructs to examine ...

                    pc = static_cast< char* >( pv );

                    // still a disaster
                    char *pstr = new char[ strlen( pc )+1 ];
                    strcpy( pstr, pc );
          }
```

A second reason to perform an explicit cast is to override the usual standard conversions. The following compound assignment, for example, first promotes ival to double to add it to dval and then truncates the result to int to perform the assignment:

```
          double dval;
          int ival;

          ival += dval;
```

We can eliminate the unnecessary promotion of ival to double by explicitly casting dval to int:

```
          ival += static_cast< int >( dval );
```

A third reason for an explicit cast is to disambiguate a situation in which more than one conversion is possible. We will look at this case more closely in Chapter 9 in our discussion of overloading function names.

The general form for the explicit cast notation is the following:

```
          cast-name< type >( expression );
```

Here cast-name is one of static_cast, const_cast, dynamic_cast, or reinterpret_cast, type is the target type of the conversion, and expression is the value to be cast.

The four explicit cast notations attempt to categorize the kinds of casts to be performed. const_cast, as its name implies, casts away the const-ness of its expression (and also the volatility of a volatile object). For example:

```
          extern char *string_copy( char* );
          const  char *pc_str;

          char *pc = string_copy( const_cast< char* >( pc_str ));
```

An attempt to cast away const-ness using either of the other three forms results in a compile-time error. Similarly, it is a compile-time error to use the const_cast notation to perform a general type conversion.

Any type conversions that the compiler performs implicitly can be made explicit through use of a static_cast. For example:

```
double d = 97.0;
char  ch = static_cast< char >( d );
```

Why might we want to do this? An assignment of a larger arithmetic type to a smaller type almost always results in a compiler-generated warning alerting us to a potential loss of precision. When we provide the explicit cast, the warning message is turned off. The cast informs both the compiler and the reader of the program that we are aware of and are not concerned with the potential loss of precision.

Less-well-behaved static casts — that is, those that are potentially dangerous — are those of casting a void* pointer to some explicit pointer type, casting an arithmetic value into that of an enum, or casting a base class to that of a derived class (or pointer or reference to such classes). (Conversions between a base and a derived class are discussed in Chapter 19.)

These casts are potentially dangerous, because their correctness depends on the value that happens to be contained within the object at the point at which the conversion takes place. For example, given the following declarations

```
enum mumble { first = 1, second, third };

extern int ival;
mumble mums_the_word = static_cast< mumble >( ival );
```

the conversion of ival to a type mumble is correct only when the value contained within ival is either 1, 2, or 3.

A reinterpret_cast generally performs a low-level reinterpretation of the bit pattern of its operands, and its correctness in large part depends on the active management of the programmer. For example, in the following cast

```
complex<double> *pcom;
char *pc = reinterpret_cast< char* >( pcom );
```

the programmer must never lose sight of the actual object addressed by pc. Passing it to a string object, for example, such as

```
string str( pc );
```

is likely to result in bizarre run-time behavior of str.

This is a good example of how the explicit cast is dangerous. The initialization of pc with the address of a complex object occurs with no error or warning from the compiler due to the explicit reinterpret_cast. All subsequent use of pc treats it as a char* object, and thus the initialization of str with pc is absolutely correct. However, when we write

```
string str( pc );
```

the program's run-time behavior is now undefined.

Tracking down the cause of this sort of problem can prove extremely difficult, in particular if the cast of pcom to pc occurs in a file separate from the one in which str.size() is invoked (the expected trailing null is absent).

In a sense, this illustrates a fundamental paradox of the language. The strong type-checking is intended to prevent just such an error. An explicit cast, however, allows us to momentarily suspend type-checking. At the point where we initialize str with pc, type-checking is back on; pc is indeed the correct type: a char*. But it isn't, of course. Because of the explicit cast, the compiler does not know that.

Standard C++ introduced the named cast operators to highlight this paradox, given the practical infeasibility of disallowing explicit casts themselves. Prior to the introduction of named cast operators, an explicit cast was performed by a pair of parentheses (Standard C++ still supports this old-style cast):

```
char *pc = (char*) pcom;
```

The effect is the same as using the reinterpret_cast notation, but the visibility of the cast is considerably less, making it even more difficult to track down the rogue cast.

The language provides categories of the explicit cast notation, rather than a single notation, such as, for example:

```
// not part of C++
char *pc = explicit_cast< char* >( pcom );
```

As a result, the programmer (as well as readers and tools operating on the program) can clearly identify the potential risk level of each explicit cast in code.

Whenever we are faced with inexplicable run-time program behavior, the likely culprit is a dysfunctional pointer. One cause is an invalid explicit cast; it is therefore useful to use the reinterpret_cast operator to carry out and identify all explicit pointer casts. (A second common cause of a rogue pointer is that the memory being addressed becomes invalid. This can happen when we accidentally delete a pointer that is still being used or return the address of a local object. This issue is addressed in Section 8.4 when we look at dynamic memory allocation in detail.)

The dynamic_cast supports the run-time identification of class objects addressed either by a pointer or reference. Discussion of it is deferred until Section 19.1 when run-time type identification is introduced.

4.14.4 Old-Style Casts

The cast notation syntax just presented is sometimes referred to as the new-style cast notation; it was introduced with Standard C++. Prior to that, explicit casts were carried out with a considerably more general cast notation spoken of now as the old-style cast notation. Although the old-style cast notation continues to be supported within Standard C++, we recommend its usage only when writing code to be compiled either under the C language or pre-Standard C++.

The old-style cast notation takes one of the following two forms:

```
// C++ function cast notation
type (expr);

// C-language cast notation
(type) expr;
```

Old-style casts can be used in place of a static_cast, const_cast, or reinterpret_cast in Standard C++. In pre-Standard C++, only the old-style casts can be used. In code intended to be compiled under both C++ and the C language, only the C-language cast notation can be used.

Here are some examples of using the old-style cast notation:

```
const char *pc = (const char*) pcom;
int ival = (int) 3.14159;

extern char *rewrite_str( char* );
char *pc2 = rewrite_str( (char*) pc );
int addr_value = int( &ival );
```

The old-style cast notation remains supported for backward compatibility with programs written under pre-Standard C++ and to provide a compatible notation with the C language.

Exercise 4.21

Given the following set of definitions

```
char cval;   int ival;
float fval; double dval;
unsigned int ui;
```

identify the implicit type conversions, if any, taking place:

```
(a) cval = 'a' + 3;
(b) fval = ui - ival * 1.0;
(c) dval = ui * fval;
(d) cval = ival + fval + dval;
```

Exercise 4.22

Given the following set of definitions

```
void *pv;        int ival;
char *pc;        double dval;
const string *ps;
```

rewrite each of the following using a named cast notation:

```
(a) pv = (void*)ps;
(b) ival = int( *pc );
(c) pv = &dval;
(d) pc = (char*) pv;
```

4.15   A Stack Class Example

At the end of our discussion of the increment and decrement operators, we introduced the abstraction of a stack to illustrate the use of the postfix and prefix forms of these operators. We conclude this chapter with a brief walk-through of the design and implementation of an iStack class — that is, a Stack that supports only elements of type int.

A stack is a fundamental data abstraction of computer science allowing for the nesting and retrieval of values in LIFO sequence — that is, last in, first out. The two fundamental operations on a stack are *push* a new value onto the stack and *pop* (retrieve) the last value pushed onto the stack. Other operations support user queries as to whether the stack is full() or empty() and to determine the size() of that stack — that is, how many elements it contains. Our initial implementation supports only elements of type int. Here is the declaration of its public interface:

```
#include <vector>

class iStack {
public:
    iStack( int capacity )
              : _stack( capacity ), _top( 0 ) {}

    bool pop( int &value );
    bool push( int value );

    bool full();
    bool empty();
    void display();

    int size();

private:
    int _top;
    vector< int > _stack;
};
```

We've chosen a fixed-sized implementation for our iStack class to illustrate the use of the prefix and postfix instances of the increment and decrement operators (we'll modify it to grow dynamically at the end of Chapter 6). We store the elements in a vector of elements of type int named _stack. _top holds the value of the next available slot into which to push() a value. The current value of _top reflects the element count of the stack. size(), therefore, simply needs to return _top:

```
inline int iStack::size() { return _top; };
```

empty() returns true if _top is equal to 0, and full() returns true if _top is equal to
_stack.size():

```
inline bool iStack::empty() {
                return _top ? false : true; }

inline bool iStack::full()  {
                return _top < _stack.size()-1 ? false : true;
}
```

Here is our implementation of pop() and push(). We added a print function to
trace the execution of each:

```
bool iStack::pop( int &top_value )
{
    if ( empty() )
        return false;

    top_value = _stack[ --_top ];
    cout << "iStack::pop(): " << top_value << endl;

    return true;
}

bool iStack::push( int value )
{

    cout << "iStack::push( " << value << " )\n";

    if ( full() )
        return false;

    _stack[ _top++ ] = value;
    return true;
}
```

Before we exercise our Stack class, let's add a display() function allowing us to
view the contents. Given an empty stack, it outputs the following:

```
( 0 )
```

For a stack of the four elements 0, 1, 2, and 3, it generates

```
( 4 )( bot: 0 1 2 3 :top )
```

Here is our implementation:

```
void iStack::display()
{
    if ( !size() )
        { cout << "( 0 )\n"; return; }
    cout << "( " << size() << " )( bot: ";
```

```
        for ( int ix = 0; ix < _top; ++ix )
                cout << _stack[ ix ] << " ";
        cout << " :top )\n";
    }
```

The following small program exercises our class. A for loop iterates 50 times. It pushes each even value: 2, 4, 6, 8, and so on. Whenever the value is a multiple of 5, such as 5, 10, 15, and so on, it displays the contents of the stack. Whenever the value is a multiple of 10, such as 10, 20, 30, and so on, it pops the last two items from the stack and then displays the contents of the stack again.

```
        #include <iostream>
        #include "iStack.h"

        int main() {
            iStack stack( 32 );

            stack.display();
            for ( int ix = 1; ix < 51; ++ix )
            {
                if ( ix%2 == 0 )
                    stack.push( ix );

                if ( ix%5 == 0 )
                    stack.display();

                if ( ix%10  == 0) {
                    int dummy;
                    stack.pop( dummy ); stack.pop( dummy );
                    stack.display();
                }
            }
        }
```

When compiled and executed, it generates the following output:

```
        ( 0 )( bot:   :top )
        iStack::push( 2 )
        iStack::push( 4 )
        ( 2 )( bot: 2 4   :top )
        iStack::push( 6 )
        iStack::push( 8 )
        iStack::push( 10 )
        ( 5 )( bot: 2 4 6 8 10   :top )
        iStack::pop(): 10
        iStack::pop(): 8
        ( 3 )( bot: 2 4 6   :top )
        iStack::push( 12 )
        iStack::push( 14 )
        ( 5 )( bot: 2 4 6 12 14   :top )
```

```
iStack::push( 16 )
iStack::push( 18 )
iStack::push( 20 )
( 8 )( bot: 2 4 6 12 14 16 18 20   :top )
iStack::pop(): 20
iStack::pop(): 18
( 6 )( bot: 2 4 6 12 14 16   :top )
iStack::push( 22 )
iStack::push( 24 )
( 8 )( bot: 2 4 6 12 14 16 22 24   :top )
iStack::push( 26 )
iStack::push( 28 )
iStack::push( 30 )
( 11 )( bot: 2 4 6 12 14 16 22 24 26 28 30   :top )
iStack::pop(): 30
iStack::pop(): 28
( 9 )( bot: 2 4 6 12 14 16 22 24 26   :top )
iStack::push( 32 )
iStack::push( 34 )
( 11 )( bot: 2 4 6 12 14 16 22 24 26 32 34   :top )
iStack::push( 36 )
iStack::push( 38 )
iStack::push( 40 )
( 14 )( bot: 2 4 6 12 14 16 22 24 26 32 34 36 38 40   :top )
iStack::pop(): 40
iStack::pop(): 38
( 12 )( bot: 2 4 6 12 14 16 22 24 26 32 34 36   :top )
iStack::push( 42 )
iStack::push( 44 )
( 14 )( bot: 2 4 6 12 14 16 22 24 26 32 34 36 42 44   :top )
iStack::push( 46 )
iStack::push( 48 )
iStack::push( 50 )
( 17 )( bot: 2 4 6 12 14 16 22 24 26 32 34 36 42 44 46 48 50 :top )
iStack::pop(): 50
iStack::pop(): 48
( 15 )( bot: 2 4 6 12 14 16 22 24 26 32 34 36 42 44 46   :top )
```

Exercise 4.23

Some of our users have requested a peek() operation. peek() reads the top value without removing it from the stack, provided that the stack is not empty, of course. Provide an implementation of peek() and then augment our main() program to exercise it.

Exercise 4.24

What are the two primary weaknesses of our iStack design? How might they be corrected?

5

Statements

The smallest independent unit in a C++ program is a *statement*. In a natural language, an analogous construct is the sentence. In general, just as sentences are terminated with a period, statements are terminated with a semicolon. Thus, an expression, such as `ival+5`, becomes a *simple statement* by terminating it with a semicolon. A *compound statement* is a sequence of simple statements surrounded by a pair of curly braces. By default, statements are executed in the sequential order in which they occur. Except in the simplest programs, however, sequential program execution is inadequate to the problems we must solve. Special *flow-of-control* program statements allow for the conditional or repeated execution of a simple or compound statement based on the true or false evaluation of an expression. Conditional execution is supported by the *if*, *if-else*, and *switch* statements. Repeated execution is supported by the *while*, *do-while*, and *for* statements. These latter statements are often referred to as *loops*. This chapter looks in detail at the types of program statements supported by C++.

5.1 Simple and Compound Statements

The simplest form of program statement is the empty, or null, statement. It takes the following form (a single semicolon):

```
; // null statement
```

A null statement is useful when the syntax of the language requires the presence of a statement but the logic of the program does not. For example, in the following `while` statement, all the processing necessary to copy one C-style string to another is accomplished within what is spoken of as the *condition* portion of the statement (that part within parentheses). The form of the while loop, however, requires that a statement follow the condition. Because no additional work is required, we fulfill the syntactic requirement with a null statement:

```
while ( *string++ = *inBuf++ )
        ; // null statement
```

The accidental presence of a superfluous null statement does not generate a compile-time error. For example, the following

```
ival = dval + sval;; // ok: superfluous null statement
```

is composed of two statements: the expression statement assigning to `ival` and the null statement.

A simple statement consists of a single statement. For example:

```
// simple statements

int ival = 1024;  // declaration statement
ival;             // expression statement
ival + 5;         // another expression statement
ival = ival + 5;  // assignment statement
```

Conditional and looping statements syntactically permit only a single associated statement to be specified for execution; in practice, this is rarely sufficient. The logic of the program often requires that a sequence of two or more statements be executed. In these cases, a *compound statement* is used in place of a single statement. For example:

```
if ( ival0 > ival1 )
{
    // compound statement consisting of one
    // declaration and two assignment statements

    int temp = ival0;
    ival0 = ival1;
    ival1 = temp;
}
```

A compound statement is a sequence of statements enclosed by a pair of curly braces. The compound statement is treated as a single unit and can appear anywhere in the program that a single expression statement can appear. As an added syntactic convenience, a compound statement need not be terminated with a semicolon.

An empty compound statement is equivalent to a null statement and provides an alternative syntax to the use of a null statement, as in the following:

```
while ( *string++ = *inBuf++ )
        {} // equivalent of null statement
```

A compound statement containing one or more declaration statements, such as the preceding example, is also referred to as a *block*, or *statement block*. A block introduces a local scope within the program; identifiers declared within the block, such as `temp` in the example, are visible only within the block. Blocks, scope, and the lifetime of objects are considered in detail in Chapter 8.

5.2   Declaration Statement

In C++, the definition of an object, such as

```
int ival;
```

is treated as a statement of the language (spoken of as a *declaration statement*, although *definition* statement is more accurate in this case) and so can generally be placed anywhere within the program that a statement is allowed. Consider, for example, the following program (the declaration statements are numbered as //#n, where n is numbered consecutively beginning at 1):

```
#include <fstream>
#include <string>
#include <vector>

int main()
{
    string fileName; // #1

    cout << "Please enter name of file to open: ";
    cin >> fileName;

    if ( fileName.empty() ) {
        // yes, extreme: but we have a point to illustrate
        cerr << "fileName is empty(). bailing out. bye!\n";
        return -1;
    }

    ifstream inFile( fileName.c_str() ); // #2
    if ( ! inFile ) {
        cerr << "unable to open file. bailing out. bye!\n";
        return -2;
    }

    string inBuf;          // #3
    vector< string > text; // #4

    while ( inFile >> inBuf ) {
            for ( int ix = 0; ix < inBuf.size(); ++ix ) // #5
                // ch in this case is unnecessary,
                // but again illustrates a point
                if (( char ch = inBuf[ix] ) == '.' ) { // #6
                    ch = '_';
                    inBuf[ix] = ch;
                }
            text.push_back( inBuf );
    }
    if ( text.empty() )
            return 0;
```

```
// one declaration statement, two definitions
vector<string>::iterator iter = text.begin(), // #7
                         iend = text.end();

while ( iter != iend ) {
        cout << *iter << '\n';
        ++iter;
}

return 0;
}
```

The program contains seven declaration statements and eight object definitions. The declaration statements exhibit *locality of declaration* — that is, the declaration statements occur within the locality of the first use of the defined objects.

In the 1970s, computer program language design philosophy emphasized the virtue of defining all objects at the start of the program, function, or statement block prior to any program statements. (In C, for example, the definition of an object is not treated as a language statement, and all object definitions within a block must appear before any program statements. By necessity, C programmers habituate themselves to defining all objects at the top of each current block.) In part, this was a reaction to an error-prone idiom of object definition on-the-fly supported by FORTRAN.

Because the definition of an object is a statement of the language, object definitions in general can be placed anywhere that the other statements of the language can appear. Syntactically, this is what makes locality of declaration possible.

Is it necessary? For the built-in types, such as integers and floats, locality of declaration is primarily a matter of personal preference. The language encourages it by allowing declarations to occur within the condition part of the if, else-if, switch, while, and for loop (there are two examples in the preceding program). Those who favor locality of declaration believe that it makes for more easily understood programs.

Locality of declaration becomes necessary with the definition of class objects with associated constructors and a destructor. When we place these class objects at the beginning of a function or statement block, two things happen:

1. The associated constructors of all the class objects are invoked prior to doing anything within the function or statement block itself. Locality of declaration allows us to amortize the cost of initialization across the extent of the function or statement block.

2. Perhaps more important, a function or statement block often terminates prior to the execution of every program statement within it. Our earlier program, for example, exhibits two abnormal termination points: the failure to retrieve a file name and the failure to open the file specified by the user. Defining class

objects prior to successfully passing those termination points, such as `inBuf` and `text`, results in the execution of unnecessary constructor-destructor pairs. Given enough class objects or computationally expensive constructors and destructors, we unnecessarily impact the run-time efficiency of our programs. The outcome is still correct, but the performance at times becomes unacceptable. (This is why expert C programmers, with the habit of placing object definitions at the start of functions and statement blocks, may sometimes find their C++ programs performing with less efficiency than equivalent programs written in C.)

A declaration statement can consist of one or more object definitions. In our program, for example, we define two vector iterators in the same declaration statement:

```
// one declaration statement, two definitions
vector<string>::iterator iter = text.begin(),
                          iend = text.end();
```

The following pair of declaration statements are equivalent:

```
// equivalent two declaration statements
vector<string>::iterator iter = text.begin();
vector<string>::iterator iend = text.end();
```

Although choosing one or the other is primarily a question of personal preference, having multiple object definitions within a single declaration statement is more error-prone when we are mixing objects, pointers, and references. For example, in the following declaration statement, it is not clear whether the user intended to define one pointer and one object or simply incorrectly defined the second pointer as an object (the identifier names suggest that the second definition is in error):

```
// the intended programmer definitions?
string *ptr1, ptr2;
```

Separate declaration statements in this case leave little room for error:

```
string *ptr1;
string *ptr2;
```

In our own code, we tend to group definitions based on the intended usage of the objects involved. For example, in the following pair of declaration statements

```
int aCnt=0, eCnt=0, iCnt=0, oCnt=0, uCnt=0;
int charCnt=0, wordCnt=0;
```

those objects intended to maintain a count of the five English language vowels are grouped in one declaration statement; those intended to keep count of the total number of characters and words are grouped in a second. Although this approach seems perfectly sensible to us, we could not logically defend it as more correct or even preferable.

Exercise 5.1

Imagine that you have just been made lead of a small programming project and wish all the code to follow a uniform declaration policy. Clearly define and justify the declaration rules you wish the project to follow.

Exercise 5.2

Imagine that you have just been assigned to the project group of Exercise 5.1. You completely disagree not only with the stated declaration policy but also with any declaration policy at all. Clearly define and justify your reasons.

5.3   The if Statement

An if statement provides for the conditional execution of either a statement or statement block based on whether a specified expression is true. The syntactic form of the if statement is the following:

```
if ( condition )
    statement
```

The condition must be enclosed in parentheses. It can either be an expression, such as

```
if ( a + b > c ) { ... }
```

or an initialized declaration statement, such as

```
if ( int ival = compute_value() ) { ... }
```

The object defined within the condition is visible only within the associated statement or statement block. For example, the attempt to access ival following the if statement is a compile-time error:

```
if ( int ival = compute_value() )
{
    // ival visible only within
    // this if statement block
}

// error: ival not visible
if ( ! ival ) ...
```

To illustrate the use of the if statement, let's implement a function min() that returns the smallest value contained within a vector of elements of type int. In addition, a count of the occurrence of the minimum value within the vector is maintained. For each element in the vector, we need to do the following:

- Compare the element to the current minimum value.
- If it is less than the minimum value, assign this element the new minimum value and reset the counter to 1.
- If it is equal to the minimum value, increment the counter by 1.
- Otherwise, do nothing.
- After examining each element, return the value and the occurrence count to the user.

Two if statements are required:

```
if ( minVal > ivec[ i ]  ) ... // new minVal
if ( minVal == ivec[ i ] ) ... // another occurrence
```

A somewhat common programmer error in the use of the if statement is to fail to provide a compound statement when multiple statements must be executed upon a condition evaluating as true. Uncovering this can be very difficult, because the text of the program looks correct. For example:

```
if ( minVal > ivec[ i ] )
        minVal = ivec[ i ];
        occurs = 1; // not part of if statement
```

Contrary to the indentation and intention of the programmer,

```
occurs = 1;
```

is not treated as part of the if statement but rather is executed unconditionally following evaluation of the if statement. So the occurrence count is always set to 1. Here is the if statement written as the programmer intended (the exact placement of the left curly brace is a topic of endless debate!):

```
if ( minVal > ivec[ i ] )
{
        minVal = ivec[ i ];
        occurs = 1;
}
```

Our second if statement is as follows:

```
if ( minVal == ivec[ i ] )
        ++occurs;
```

Notice that the order of the if statements is significant. Our function will always be off by 1 if we place the statements in the following order:

```
if ( minVal > ivec[ i ] ) {
        minVal = ivec[ i ];
        occurs = 1;
}
```

```
// potential error if minVal
// has just been set to ivec[i]
if ( minVal == ivec[ i ] )
     ++occurs;
```

Not only is the execution of both if statements on the same value potentially dangerous, but it is also unnecessary. The same element cannot be both less than `minVal` and equal to it. If one condition is true, the other condition can be safely ignored. The if statement allows for this kind of either-or condition by providing an else clause.

The syntactic form of the if-else statement is the following:

```
if ( condition )
     statement1
else
     statement2
```

If `condition` evaluates to true, `statement1` is executed; otherwise, `statement2` is executed. For example:

```
if ( minVal == ivec[ i ] )
     ++occurs;
else
if ( minVal > ivec[ i ] ) {
     minVal = ivec[ i ];
     occurs = 1;
}
```

In this example, `statement2` is itself an if statement. If `minVal` is less than the element, no action is taken.

In the following example, one of the three statements is always executed:

```
if ( minVal < ivec[ i ] )
     {} // null statement
else
if ( minVal > ivec[ i ] ) {
     minVal = ivec[ i ];
     occurs = 1;
}
else // minVal == ivec[ i ]
     ++occurs;
```

The if-else statement introduces a source of potential ambiguity referred to as the *dangling-else* problem. This problem occurs when a statement contains more if clauses than else clauses. The question then arises, With which if does the additional else clause properly match up? For example:

```
if ( minVal <= ivec[ i ] )
     if ( minVal == ivec[ i ] )
          ++occurs;
```

```
else {
    minVal = ivec[ i ];
    occurs = 1;
}
```

The indentation indicates the programmer's belief that the else should match up with the outer if clause. In C++, however, the dangling-else ambiguity is resolved by matching the else with the last occurring unmatched if. In this case, the actual evaluation of the if-else statement is as follows:

```
if ( minVal <= ivec[ i ] ) {
    // effect of dangling-else resolution
    if ( minVal == ivec[ i ] )
        ++occurs;
    else { minVal = ivec[ i ]; occurs = 1; }
}
```

One method of overriding the default dangling-else matching is to place the last occurring if in a compound statement:

```
if ( minVal <= ivec[ i ] ) {
    if ( minVal == ivec[ i ] )
        ++occurs;
}
else { minVal = ivec[ i ]; occurs = 1; }
```

Some coding styles recommend always using compound statement braces to avoid possible confusion and error in later modifications of the code.

Here is a first iteration of our min() function. The second argument, occurs, will contain the occurrence count of the minimum value; we'll set this within the function as well as determine and return the actual minimum value. We use a for loop to iterate over the elements. (Unfortunately, our implementation contains a logic error — do you see it?)

```
#include <vector>

int min( const vector<int> &ivec, int &occurs )
{
    int minVal = 0;
    occurs = 0;

    int size = ivec.size();

    for ( int ix = 0; ix < size; ++ix ) {
        if ( minVal == ivec[ ix ] )
            ++occurs;
        else
        if ( minVal > ivec[ ix ] ) {
            minVal = ivec[ ix ];
            occurs = 1;
```

```
        }
    }

    return minVal;
}
```

In general, a function returns only a single value. Our requirement, however, is to return not only the minimum value contained within the vector but also a count of its occurrences within the vector. In our implementation, we add a reference parameter through which to pass a second value (see Section 7.3 for a discussion of reference parameters). Any assignment to occur within min() is reflected in the value of the object actually passed as the argument. For example:

```
int main()
{
    int occur_cnt = 0;
    vector< int > ivec;

    // ... fill ivec

    // occur_cnt holds count of occurrences set within min()
    int minval = min( ivec, occur_cnt );

    // ...
}
```

An alternative solution is to use a pair object (see Section 3.14 for a discussion of the pair type) that holds the two integer objects: the minimum value and occurrence count. The function then returns an instance of this pair object. For example:

```
// alternative implementation
// returning a pair object ...

#include <utility>
#include <vector>

typedef pair<int,int> min_val_pair;

min_val_pair
min( const vector<int> &ivec )
{
    int minVal = 0;
    int occurs = 0;

    // same until return ...

    return make_pair( minVal, occurs );
}
```

Unfortunately, under either solution our implementation of min() is incorrect. Do you see what the problem is? That's right: because we initialize minVal to 0, if the smallest array value is a value greater than 0, our implementation does not find it but rather returns 0, and occurs is set to 0.

A best first value for minVal is the first element of the array:

```
int minVal = ivec[0];
```

This guarantees that min() always returns the smallest value within the array. Although this corrects the bug in our program, it also introduces a small inefficiency. Here is the offending portion of the code. Do you see what the small efficiency cost is?

```
// revised beginning portion of min()
// introduces small inefficiency ...

int minVal = ivec[0];
occurs = 0;

int size = ivec.size();

for ( int ix = 0; ix < size; ++ix )
{
      if ( minVal == ivec[ ix ] )
            ++occurs;

      // ...
```

Because ix is initialized to 0, the first iteration of the loop always finds minVal equal to ivec[0], the value to which we've initialized minVal. By initializing ix to 1, we can avoid performing the unnecessary comparison and reassignment of minVal. This is an admittedly small improvement, and unfortunately, it introduces yet another bug into our program (maybe we should have just left things as they were!). Do you see what's wrong with our revised program?

```
// revised beginning portion of min()
// unfortunately, it introduces a program bug ...

int minVal = ivec[0];
occurs = 0;

int size = ivec.size();

for ( int ix = 1; ix < size; ++ix )
{
      if ( minVal == ivec[ ix ] )
            ++occurs;
      // ...
```

If `ivec[0]` turns out to be the minimum value, then occurs is never set to 1! The fix is easy, of course, but only after we first see that it's necessary:

```
int minVal = ivec[0];
occurs = 1;
```

Unfortunately, this still isn't quite right. What happens if the user, accidentally or otherwise, passes in an empty vector? Attempting to access the first element of an empty vector is incorrect, and is likely to result in a run-time program error. We must guard against this possibility, however improbable. One solution is the following: (alternative solutions include returning a bool value indicating whether the function succeeded):

```
int min( const vector< int > &ivec, int &occurs )
{
        int size = ivec.size();

        // handle anomaly of empty vector
        // occurs set to 0 indicates empty vector
        if ( ! size ) { occurs = 0; return 0; }

        // ok: vector contains at least one element
        int minVal = ivec[ 0 ]; occurs = 1;

        for ( int ix = 1; ix < size; ++ix )
        {
                if ( minVal == ivec[ ix ] )
                    ++occurs;
                else
                if ( minVal > ivec[ ix ] ){
                    minVal = ivec[ ix ];
                    occurs = 1;
                }
        }

        return minVal;
}
```

An alternative solution to the problem of an empty vector is to have `min()` return a bool value indicating success or failure, with the minimum value returned by reference:

```
// alternative solution to empty vector problem
bool min( const vector< int > &ivec, int &minVal, int &occurs );
```

Another design choice is to have `min()` throw an exception should an empty vector be passed to it. (See Chapter 11 for a discussion of exception handling.)

Unfortunately, errors such as these are not at all uncommon. As programmers, we are going to make mistakes at some point — at times even stupid mistakes. It happens.

The important thing is to accept that mistakes happen and to be on the alert for them, testing and reviewing our code as rigorously as circumstances permit.

The conditional operator can provide a convenient shorthand notation for a simple if-else test. For example, the following `min()` function template

```
template <class valueType>
inline const valueType&
min( valueType &val1, valueType &val2 )
{
    if ( val1 < val2 )
        return val1;
    return val2;
}
```

can alternatively be written as

```
template <class valueType>
inline const valueType&
min( valueType &val1, valueType &val2 )
{
    return ( val1 < val2 ) ? val1 : val2;
}
```

Long chains of if-else statements, such as the following, can often be difficult to read and prone to error when modifying:

```
if ( ch == 'a' ||
     ch == 'A' )
        ++aCnt;
else
if ( ch == 'e' ||
     ch == 'E' )
        ++eCnt;
else
if ( ch == 'i' ||
     ch == 'I' )
        ++iCnt;
else
if ( ch == 'o' ||
     ch == 'O' )
        ++oCnt;
else
if ( ch == 'u' ||
     ch == 'U' )
        ++uCnt;
```

An alternative construct to a chain of if-else statements is the switch statement, provided the values being tested against are constant expressions, such as the character constants tested above. The switch statement is the topic of the next section.

Exercise 5.3

Correct each of the following:

```
(a) if ( ival1 != ival2 )
        ival1 = ival2
    else ival1 = ival2 = 0;

(b) if ( ival < minval )
        minval = ival;
        occurs = 1;

(c) if ( int ival = get_value())
        cout << "ival = "
            << ival << endl;

    if ( ! ival )
        cout << "ival = 0\n";

(d) if ( ival = 0 )
        ival = get_value();

(e) if ( ival == 0 )
    else ival = 0;
```

Exercise 5.4

Change the declaration of occurs in the argument list of min() to be a nonreference argument type and rerun the program. How does the behavior of the program change?

5.4   The switch Statement

Deeply nested if-else statements can often be correct syntactically and yet not express the intended logic of the programmer. Unintended else-if matchings, for example, are more likely to pass unnoticed. Modifications to the statements are also much harder to get right. As an alternative method of choosing among a set of mutually exclusive choices, C++ provides the switch statement.

   To illustrate the use of the switch statement, let's consider the following problem: we have been asked to count the number of occurrences of each of the five vowels in random segments of text. (The conventional wisdom is that *e* is the most frequently occurring vowel in English.) Our program logic is as follows:

- Read each character in turn until there are no more characters to read.
- Compare each character to the set of vowels.
- If the character matches one of the vowels, add 1 to that vowel's count.
- Display the results.

The program was used to analyze a section of this text. Here is the output, which verifies the conventional wisdom regarding the frequency of the vowel *e*:

```
aCnt: 394
eCnt: 721
iCnt: 461
oCnt: 349
uCnt: 186
```

The switch statement consists of the following components:

1. The `switch` keyword, following by an expression in parentheses that is to be evaluated. In our case, the expression is the character read. For example:

    ```
    char ch;
    while ( cin >> ch )
            switch( ch )
    ```

2. A set of *case* labels consisting of the keyword `case` followed by a constant expression against which to compare the result of the `switch` expression, followed by a colon. In our case, each case label represents one of the five English vowels. For example:

    ```
    case 'a':
    case 'e':
    case 'i':
    case 'o':
    case 'u':
    ```

3. A sequence of program statements associated with one or a set of case labels. To accumulate a count of each vowel, for example, we would provide an assignment statement incrementing a vowel's count by 1.

4. An optional `default` label. The `default` label serves as a kind of `else` clause. If the `switch` expression does not match any of the `case` labels, the statements following the `default` label are evaluated. For example, if we wished to count the number of characters that were not vowels, we might add the following `default` label and statement:

    ```
    default: // everything not a vowel
        ++non_vowel_cnt;
    ```

The value following the `case` keyword must be a constant expression of an integral type. The following, for example, result in compile-time errors:

```
// illegal case label values
case 3.14: // noninteger
case ival: // nonconstant
```

In addition, no two case labels may have the same value; if they do, a compile-time error occurs.

The `switch` expression can be an arbitrarily complex expression, including the return of a function call. The result of the `switch` expression is compared against the value associated with each `case` label until either a match is successful or all labels have been examined. If the expression matches the value of a `case` label, execution begins with the first statement following that label. If no match is effected, execution begins with the first statement following the `default` label, if one is present; otherwise, the execution of the program continues with the first statement following the `switch` statement.

A common misunderstanding is that only the statements associated with the matched `case` label are executed. Rather, execution begins there but continues across `case` boundaries until the end of the `switch` statement is encountered. Getting this wrong is a good guarantee that we've also gotten our program wrong. For example, here is an incorrect implementation of our vowel-counting `switch` program:

```cpp
#include <iostream>
int main()
{
    char ch;
    int aCnt=0, eCnt=0, iCnt=0, oCnt=0, uCnt=0;

    while ( cin >> ch )
              // warning: deliberately incorrect!
              switch ( ch ) {
                  case 'a':
                      ++aCnt;
                  case 'e':
                      ++eCnt;
                  case 'i':
                      ++iCnt;
                  case 'o':
                      ++oCnt;
                  case 'u':
                      ++uCnt;
              }

    cout << "Number of vowel a: \t" << aCnt << '\n'
         << "Number of vowel e: \t" << eCnt << '\n'
         << "Number of vowel i: \t" << iCnt << '\n'
         << "Number of vowel o: \t" << oCnt << '\n'
         << "Number of vowel u: \t" << uCnt << '\n';
}
```

If ch is set to i, execution begins following `case` 'i'. iCnt is incremented. Execution, however, does not stop there but continues across `case` boundaries until the closing brace of the `switch` statement. Also, oCnt and uCnt are both incremented. If ch is next set to e, eCnt, iCnt, oCnt, and uCnt are all incremented.

The programmer must explicitly tell the compiler to stop statement execution within the switch statement. This is done by specifying a break statement after each execution unit within the switch statement. Under most conditions, the last statement of a case label is break.

When a break statement is encountered, the switch statement is terminated. Control shifts to the statement immediately following the closing brace of the switch. In our example, control is passed to the output statement. Our corrected switch statement is as follows:

```
switch ( ch ) {
    case 'a':
        ++aCnt;
        break;
    case 'e':
        ++eCnt;
        break;
    case 'i':
        ++iCnt;
        break;
    case 'o':
        ++oCnt;
        break;
    case 'u':
        ++uCnt;
        break;
}
```

A case label that deliberately omits a break statement should in most cases provide a comment stating that the omission is deliberate. Our programs are not only compiled and executed, but they are also read and reread, often by subsequent programmers charged with fixing or extending our original implementation. Code that is contrary to expected usage is particularly difficult to understand, because we're often not sure whether the deviation is deliberate and correct or an oversight and potential error. A comment documenting the programmer's intention in these cases significantly enhances the maintainability of the code.

When might the programmer wish to omit a break statement from a case label, allowing the program to *fall through* multiple case labels? One circumstance is when two or more values are to be handled by the same sequence of actions. This is necessary because only a single value can be associated with a case label. To indicate a range, therefore, we typically stack case labels following one another. For example, if we wished only to count vowels seen rather than count the individual vowels, we might write the following:

```
int vowelCnt = 0;
// ...
switch ( ch )
{
```

```
// any occurrence of a,e,i,o,u
// causes vowelCnt to be incremented
case 'a':
case 'e':
case 'i':
case 'o':
case 'u':
    ++vowelCnt;
    break;
}
```

Alternatively, some programmers prefer to bunch the `case` labels to emphasize that the cases represent a range of values to be matched against:

```
switch ( ch )
{
    // alternative legal syntax
    case 'a': case 'e':
    case 'i': case 'o': case 'u':
        ++vowelCnt;
        break;
}
```

There is one problem with our vowel-counting program as we've currently implemented it. For example, how does the program handle the following input?

```
UNIX
```

The capital *U* and the capital *I* are not recognized as vowels. Our program fails to count vowels occurring as uppercase characters. Here is our corrected `switch` statement, also making use of fall-through:

```
switch ( ch ) {
    case 'a': case 'A':
        ++aCnt;
        break;
    case 'e':  case 'E':
        ++eCnt;
        break;
    case 'i':  case 'I':
        ++iCnt;
        break;
    case 'o':  case 'O':
        ++oCnt;
        break;
    case 'u':  case 'U':
        ++uCnt;
        break;
}
```

The default label provides the equivalent of an unconditional else clause. If no case label matches the value of the switch expression and if the default label is present, the statements following the default label are executed. For example, let's add a default case to our switch statement to count the number of consonants:

```cpp
#include <iostream>
#include <ctype.h>
int main()
{
    char ch;
    int aCnt=0, eCnt=0, iCnt=0, oCnt=0, uCnt=0,
        consonantCnt = 0;

    while ( cin >> ch )
      switch ( ch )
      {
        case 'a': case 'A':
            ++aCnt;
            break;
        case 'e':  case 'E':
            ++eCnt;
            break;
        case 'i':  case 'I':
            ++iCnt;
            break;
        case 'o':  case 'O':
            ++oCnt;
            break;
        case 'u':  case 'U':
            ++uCnt;
            break;
        default:
            if ( isalpha( ch ))
                  ++consonantCnt;
            break;
      }

    cout << "Number of vowel a: \t" << aCnt << '\n'
         << "Number of vowel e: \t" << eCnt << '\n'
         << "Number of vowel i: \t" << iCnt << '\n'
         << "Number of vowel o: \t" << oCnt << '\n'
         << "Number of vowel u: \t" << uCnt << '\n'
         << "Number of consonants: \t" << consonantCnt << '\n';
}
```

isalpha() is a Standard C library routine; it evaluates to true if its argument is a letter of the alphabet. To use it, the programmer must include the system header file ctype.h. (We'll look at the ctype.h routines in more detail in Chapter 6.)

Although it is not strictly necessary to specify a break statement in the last label of a switch statement, the safest course is to always provide one. If an additional case label is added later to the bottom of the switch statement, the absence of the break statement in what now is no longer the last case label can result in the execution of both case labels.

A declaration statement can be placed within the condition of the switch statement, such as the following:

```
switch( int ival = get_response() )
```

ival is initialized, and that initial value becomes the value against which each case label is compared. ival is visible throughout the entire switch statement but not outside it.

Placement of a declaration statement associated with a case or default label is illegal unless it is placed within a statement block. For example, the following results in a compile-time error:

```
case illegal_definition:
    // error: declaration statement must
    // be placed within a statement block

    string file_name = get_file_name();
    // ...
    break;
```

Were the definition not enclosed within a statement block, it would be visible across case labels but initialized only if the case label within which it is defined is executed. Requiring a statement block ensures that the name is visible — and therefore can be used — only where it is guaranteed to have been initialized. To have our program compile, we must reimplement the case label, introducing a statement block, as follows:

```
case ok:
    {
        // ok: declaration statement within a statement block

        string file_name = get_file_name();
        // ...
        break;
    }
```

Exercise 5.5

Modify our vowel count program so that it also counts the number of blank spaces, tabs, and newlines read.

Exercise 5.6

Modify our vowel count program so that it counts the number of occurrences of the following two-character sequences: ff, fl, and fi.

Exercise 5.7

Each of the following exhibits a common programming error in the use of the switch statement. Identify and correct each error.

(a)
```
switch ( ival ) {
  case 'a': aCnt++;
  case 'e': eCnt++;
  default: iouCnt++;
}
```

(b)
```
switch (ival ) {
  case 1:
     int ix = get_value();
     ivec[ ix ] = ival;
     break;
  default:
     ix = ivec.size()-1;
     ivec[ ix ] = ival;
}
```

(c)
```
switch (ival ) {
  case 1, 3, 5, 7, 9:
     oddcnt++;
     break;
  case 2, 4, 6, 8, 10:
     evencnt++;
     break;
}
```

(d)
```
int ival=512 jval=1024, kval=4096;
int bufsize;
// ...
switch( swt ) {
  case ival:
     bufsize = ival * sizeof( int );
     break;
  case jval:
     bufsize = jval * sizeof( int );
     break;
```

```
        case kval:
            bufsize = kval * sizeof( int );
            break;
    }

(e)
    enum { illustrator = 1, photoshop, photostyler = 2 };
    switch (ival) {
      case illustrator:
        --illus_license;
        break;
      case photoshop:
        --pshop_license;
        break;
      case photostyler:
        --pstyler_license;
        break;
    }
```

5.5   The for Loop Statement

As we've seen, a great many program activities involve repeatedly executing a set of statements while some condition remains true; for example, while we have not reached the end-of-file, read and process the next element of the file; for each index value of a vector not equal to 1 past the last element of that vector, retrieve and process the vector element, and so on. The language provides three loop control statements to support the repeated execution of a single statement or statement block while a specified condition holds true. We have already seen numerous examples of both the for and the while loop.

The for and while loops begin with a test of their truth condition. This means that either loop can terminate without execution of the associated statement or statement block. A third loop structure, the do while loop, guarantees that the statement or statement block is executed at least once — the condition is tested after execution. In this section, we look at the for loop in detail. The while loop is the topic of Section 5.6, and the do while loop is examined in Section 5.7.

A for loop is used most commonly to step through a fixed-length data structure, such as an array or vector. For example:

```
#include <vector>
int main()
{
    int ia[10];

    for ( int ix = 0; ix < 10; ++ix )
            ia[ ix ] = ix;
```

```
vector<int> ivec( ia, ia+10 );
vector<int>::iterator iter = ivec.begin();

for ( ; iter != ivec.end(); ++iter )
    *iter *= 2;

return 0;
}
```

The syntactic form of the for loop is as follows:

```
for ( init-statement; condition; expression )
    statement
```

init-statement can be either a declaration statement or an expression. In general, it is used to initialize or assign a starting value that is incremented over the course of the loop. If an initialization is unnecessary or occurs elsewhere, the init-statement can be left off, as in the second for loop in the preceding example. However, the semicolon is necessary to announce the statement's absence (or rather provide for the null statement). The following are all legal instances of the init-statement:

```
// presumes index and iter are defined elsewhere
for ( index = 0; ...
for ( ; /* null init-statement */ ...
for ( iter = ivec.begin(); ...
for ( int lo = 0, hi = max; ...
for ( char *ptr = getStr(); ...
```

condition serves as the loop control. For as many iterations as condition evaluates as true, statement is executed. statement can be either a single or a compound statement. If the first evaluation of condition evaluates to false, statement is never executed. The following are all legal instances of condition:

```
(...; index < arraySize; ... )
(...; iter != ivec.end(); ... )
(...; *st1++ = *st2++; ... )
(...; char ch = getNextChar(); ... )
```

expression is evaluated after each iteration of the loop. It is generally used to modify the variables initialized in init-statement and tested in condition. If the first evaluation of the condition evaluates to false, expression is never executed. The following are all legal instances of expression:

```
( ...; ...; ++index )
( ...; ...; ptr = ptr->next )
( ...; ...; ++i, --j, ++cnt )
( ...; ...; ) // null instance
```

Given the following for loop,

```
const int sz = 24;
int ia[ sz ];
vector<int> ivec( sz );

for ( int ix = 0; ix < sz; ++ix ) {
    ivec[ ix ] = ix;
    ia[ ix ] = ix;
}
```

the order of evaluation is as follows:

1. init-statement is executed once at the start of the loop. In this example, ix is defined and initialized to 0.

2. condition is executed. If it evaluates to true, the compound statement is executed. In this example, as long as ix is less than sz, ix is assigned to ivec[ix] and ix is assigned to ia[ix]. A false condition terminates the loop. An initial false condition results in the compound statement never being executed.

3. expression is executed. Typically, this modifies the variable(s) initialized in init-statement and tested in condition. In the example, ix is incremented by 1.

These three steps represent one complete iteration of the for loop. Step 2 is now repeated, followed by step 3, until the condition evaluates to false; that is, ix is no longer less than sz.

Multiple objects can be defined in the init-statement; however, only one declaration statement may appear, so all the objects must be of the same general type. For example:

```
for ( int ival = 0, *pi = &ia, &ri = val;
      ival < size;
      ++ival, ++pi, ++ri )
            // ...
```

The definition of an object in the condition portion of the for loop is less easily managed: it must eventually evaluate to false, or the loop never terminates. Here is an example, slightly contrived:

```
#include <iostream>

int main()
{
    for ( int ix = 0;
          bool done = ix == 10;
          ++ix )
                cout << "ix: " << ix << endl;
}
```

The visibility of all objects defined within the condition of the for loop is limited to the body of the for loop. For example, the test of iter following the for loop is a compile-time error:[1]

```
int main()
{
    string word;
    vector< string > text;
    // ...
    for ( vector< string >::iterator
                    iter = text.begin(),
                    iter_end = text.end();
            iter != text.end(); ++iter )
    {
        if ( *iter == word )
            break;
        // ...
    }

    // error: iter and iter_end are not visible
    if ( iter != iter_end )
        // ...
}
```

Exercise 5.8

Which of the following for loop declarations, if any, are in error?

```
(a) for ( int *ptr = &ia, ix = 0;
        ix < size && ptr != ia+size;
        ++ix, ++ptr )
            // ...

(b) for ( ; ; ) {
        if ( some_condition )
            break;
        // ...
    }
```

---

1. The visibility of objects defined in the init-statement in pre-Standard C++ extended to the function or statement block enclosing the for loop itself. For example, given the following two for loops within the same statement block

```
{
    // legal: Standard C++
    // illegal: pre-Standard C++: ival defined twice
    for ( int ival = 0; ival < size; ++ival ) // ...
    for ( int ival = size-1; ival >= 0; --ival ) // ...
}
```

under pre-Standard C++, ival is flagged at compile-time as being multiply defined, whereas under Standard C++ both instances of ival are local to their respective for loops, and the program fragment is legal.

```
(c) for ( int ix = 0; ix < sz; ++ix )
        // ...

    if ( ix != sz )
        // ...

(d) int ix;
    for ( ix < sz; ++ix )
        // ...

(e) for ( int ix = 0; ix < sz; ++ix, ++ sz )
        // ...
```

Exercise 5.9

You have been asked to devise a style guide for the projectwide use of the for loop. Explain and illustrate usage rules, if any, for each of the three parts. If you believe strongly against usage rules — or at least with regard to the for loop — explain and illustrate why.

Exercise 5.10

Given the function declaration

```
bool is_equal( const vector<int> &v1,
               const vector<int> &v2 );
```

write the body of the function to determine whether the two vectors are equal. For vectors of unequal length, compare the number of elements of the smaller vector. For example, given the vectors (0,1,1,2) and (0,1,1,2,3,5,8), is_equal() returns true. v1.size() and v2.size() return the size of the vectors.

5.6   The while Statement

The syntactic form of the while loop is as follows:

```
while ( condition )
        statement
```

For as many iterations as the condition evaluates as true, the statement or statement block is executed. The sequence is as follows:

1. Evaluate the condition.
2. Execute the statement if the condition is true.

If the first evaluation of condition yields false, statement is never executed.

The condition of the while loop can be an expression, such as either of the following:

```
bool quit = false;
// ...
while ( ! quit ) {
        // ...
        quit = do_something();
}
string word;
while ( cin >> word ) { ... }
```

or it can be an initialized definition, such as

```
while ( symbol *ptr = search( name )) {
        // do something
}
```

In this latter case, ptr is visible only within the statement block associated with the while loop, the same as in the if, switch, and for statements.

Here is an example of a while loop iterating across a collection of elements addressed by a pair of pointers:

```
int sumit( int *parray_begin, int *parray_end )
{
    int sum = 0;

    if ( ! parray_begin || ! parray_end )
        return sum;

    while ( parray_begin != parray_end )
        // add value to sum
        // then increment pointer to next element
        sum += *parray_begin++;

    return sum;
}

int ia[6] = { 0, 1, 2, 3, 4, 5 };
int main()
{
    int sum = sumit( &ia[0], &ia[ 6 ] );
    // ...
}
```

For sumit() to execute correctly, both pointers must address elements within the *same* array (parray_end can safely address 1 past the last element of the array). If they do not, we say that the behavior of sumit() is *undefined*. (It will at best return a meaningless result value.) Unfortunately, there is no way within the language to guarantee that both pointers address the same array. As we'll see in Chapter 12, the standard library generic algorithms are implemented to accept a pointer to the first and last elements of a container.

Exercise 5.11

Which of the following `while` loop declarations, if any, are incorrect or in error?

```
(a) string bufString, word;
    while ( cin >> bufString >> word )
            // ...

(b) while ( vector<int>::iterator iter != ivec.end() )
            // ...

(c) while ( ptr = 0 )
              ptr = find_a_value();

(d) while ( bool status = find( word )) {
              word = get_next_word();
              if ( word.empty() )
                  break;
              // ...
    }

    if ( ! status )
            cout << "Did not find any words\n";
```

Exercise 5.12

The while loop is particularly good at executing while some condition holds; for example, while the end-of-file is not reached, read a next value. The for loop is generally thought of as a step loop: an index steps through a range of values in a collection. Write an idiomatic use of each loop and then rewrite each using the other loop construct. If you were able to program with only one loop, which construct would you choose? Why?

Exercise 5.13

Write a small function to read a sequence of strings from standard input until either the same word occurs in succession or all the words have been read. Use a while loop to read the text one word at a time. Use the break statement to terminate the loop if a word occurs in succession. Print the word if it occurs in succession, or else print a message saying that no word was repeated.

5.7 The do while Statement

Imagine that we have been asked to write an interactive program that converts miles into kilometers. The outline of the program looks like this:

```
int val;
bool more = true;   // dummy value to start loop

while ( more )
{
    val = getValue();
    val = convertValue(val);
    printValue(val);
    more = doMore();
}
```

The problem here is that the loop control is set up within the loop body. With the for and while loops, however, unless the loop control evaluates to true, the loop body is never executed. This means that we must provide a first value to start the loop going. Alternatively, we can use the do while loop. The do while loop guarantees that its statement is always executed at least once. The syntactic form of the do while loop is as follows:

```
do
            statement
while ( condition );
```

statement is executed before condition is evaluated. If condition evaluates as false, the loop terminates. Our program outline now looks like this:

```
do
{
    val = getValue();
    val = convertValue(val);
    printValue(val);
} while ( doMore() );
```

Unlike the other loop statements, the condition of the do while loop does not support an object definition — that is, we cannot write

```
// error: declaration statement within
// do loop condition is not supported

do {
    // ...
    mumble( foo );
} while ( int foo = get_foo() ) // error
```

because the condition is not evaluated until after the statement or statement block is initially executed.

Exercise 5.14

Which of the following do-while loops, if any, are in error?

```
(a) do
        string rsp;
        int val1, val2;
        cout << "please enter two values: ";
        cin  >> val1 >> val2;
        cout << "The sum of " << val1
             << " and " << val2
             << " = " << val1 + val2 << "\n\n"
             << "More? [yes][no] ";
        cin  >> rsp;
    while ( rsp[0] != 'n' );

(b) do {
        // ...
    } while ( int ival = get_response() );

(c) do {
        int ival = get_response();
        if ( ival == some_value() )
            break;
    } while ( ival );

    if ( !ival )
        // ...
```

Exercise 5.15

Write a small program that requests two strings from the user and reports which string is lexicographically less than the other (that is, comes before the other alphabetically). Continue to solicit the user until the user requests to quit. Use the string type, the string less-than operator, and the do while loop.

5.8   The break Statement

A break statement terminates the nearest enclosing while, do while, for, or switch statement. Execution resumes at the statement immediately following the terminated statement. For example, the following function searches an integer array for the first occurrence of a particular value. If it is found, the function returns its index; otherwise, the function returns –1. This is implemented as follows:

```
// val in ia? return index; otherwise, -1

int search( int *ia, int size, int value )
{
    // confirm ia != 0 and size > 0 ...

    int loc = -1;
```

```
for ( int ix = 0; ix < size; ++ix ) {
    if ( value == ia[ ix ] ) {
        // ok: found it!
        // set the location and leave
        loc = ix;
        break;
    }
} // end of for loop

// break to here ...
return loc;
}
```

In our example, break terminates the for loop. Execution resumes at the return statement immediately following the for loop. In this example, the break terminates the enclosing for loop and not the if statement within which it occurs. The presence of a break statement within an if statement not contained within a switch or loop statement is a compile-time error. For example:

```
// error: illegal presence of break statement
if ( ptr ) {
    if ( *ptr == "quit" )
        break;
    // ...
}
```

In general, a break statement can legally appear only somewhere within a loop or switch statement.

When a break occurs in a nested switch or loop statement, the enclosing loop or switch statement is unaffected by the termination of the inner switch or loop. For example:

```
while ( cin >> inBuf )
{
    switch( inBuf[ 0 ] ) {
    case '-':
        for ( int ix = 1; ix < inBuf.size(); ++ix ) {
            if ( inBuf[ ix ] == ' ' )
                break; // #1
            // ...
        }
        break; // #2
    case '+':
        // ...
    }
}
```

The break labeled //#1 terminates the for loop within the hyphen case label but does not terminate the enclosing switch statement. Similarly, the break labeled //#2 terminates the switch statement on the first character of inBuf but does not terminate the enclosing while loop, reading one string at a time from standard input.

5.9   The continue Statement

A continue statement causes the current iteration of the nearest enclosing loop statement to terminate. Execution resumes with the evaluation of the condition. Unlike the break statement, which terminates of the loop, the continue statement terminates only the current iteration. For example, the following program fragment reads a program text file one word at a time. Every word that begins with an underscore will be processed; otherwise, the current loop iteration is terminated:

```
while ( cin >> inBuf ) {
        if ( inBuf[0] != '_' )
            continue; // terminate iteration

        // still here? process string ...
}
```

The continue statement can legally appear only within a loop statement.

5.10   The goto Statement

The goto statement provides unconditional branching within a function from the goto statement to a label statement somewhere within the same function. Its use is deprecated in current thinking on good programming practice.

The syntactic form of the goto statement is

```
goto label;
```

where label is a user-supplied identifier. A label statement can be used only as the target of a goto and must be terminated by a colon. A label statement may not immediately precede a closing right brace. A null statement following the label statement is the typical method of handling this constraint. For example:

```
end: ; //null statement
    }
```

A goto statement may not jump forward over a declaration statement that is not enclosed within a statement block. The following, for example, results in a compile-time error:

```
int oops_in_error()
{
    // mumble ...
    goto end;
```

```
        // error: goto over declaration statement
        int ix = 10;
        // ... code using ix
    end: ;
    }
```

The correct implementation places the declaration statement and any statements making use of that declaration within a statement block. For example:

```
    int ok_its_fixed()
    {
        // mumble ...
        goto end;

        {
            // ok: declaration statement within statement block
            int ix = 10;
            // ... code using ix
        }
    end: ;
    }
```

The reasoning is the same as for declaration statements within a case label of a switch statement: the need of the compiler to insert invocations of constructor/destructor pairs for class objects. The statement block guarantees that both the constructor and the destructor are either executed or ignored and that the object is visible only where its initialization has been done.

A backward jump over an initialized object definition, however, is not illegal. Why? Jumping over the initialization of an object is a programming error; initializing an object multiple times, although inefficient, is still correct. For example:

```
    // backward jump over declaration statement ok

    void
    mumble( int max_size )
    {
      begin:
        int sz = get_size();
        if ( sz <= 0 ) {
            // issue warning ...
            goto end;
        }
        else
        if ( sz > max_size )
            // get a new size value
            goto begin;
```

```
    { // ok: entire block jumped over
        int *ia = new int[ sz ];
        doit( ia, sz ); // whatever that is ...
        delete [] ia;
    }

  end:
     ;
}
```

The goto statement is the most deprecated feature of modern programming languages. Use of the goto statement often renders a program's control flow difficult to understand or modify. Most uses can be replaced with a conditional or loop statement. If you do find yourself using a goto statement, we recommend that it not span a wide program sequence.

5.11   A Linked List Example

In each of Chapters 3 and 4, we have concluded with the design and implementation of a class to introduce and exercise the C++ class mechanism. Similarly, in this chapter, we conclude with the implementation of a singly linked list class. (In Chapter 6, we'll look at the doubly linked list container class provided by the standard library.) A first-time reader may wish to skip or skim this section, returning to it after having read Chapter 13. (The reader continuing through this section is presumed to have at least read either Section 2.3 or Section 3.15 and to therefore have some familiarity with the syntax and terminology of the class mechanism, such as what a constructor is and so on. If this is not the case, we recommend that you first read one or preferably both sections.)

A list is a sequence of items, each of which contains a value of some type and the address, perhaps null, of a next item on the list. A list may be empty; that is, there can be a list of no items. A list cannot be full, although the attempt to create a new list item can fail if the program's free store is exhausted.

What are the operations our list class must support? A user must be able to both *insert* and *remove* an item as well as search for — that is, *find* — an item. A user must be able to query the list as to its *size, display* it, and compare two lists for *equality*. In addition, we'll support *reversing* the elements of a list and *concatenating* two lists.

The simplest implementation of size() is to iterate across the list, returning a count of the elements traversed. A somewhat more complex implementation stores the size of the list as a data member. The second size() implementation becomes significantly more efficient: it simply returns the associated member. The additional complexity is the need to update the member with each element insertion and deletion.

We have chosen to update and store the count of elements in a _size data member. Our assumption is that user query of size() is likely to be frequent and must therefore necessarily be fast. (One of the benefits of separating the public interface from a private implementation is that if our assumption proves wrong, we can provide a new implementation without requiring changes in programs that use size() provided that we maintain the same return type and parameter list.)

Our general insert() operation takes two parameters: a pointer to an existing list element and a new value. The new value is inserted following the existing element. For example, given the list

```
1 1 2 3 8
```

the invocation of

```
mylist.insert( pointer_to_3, 5 );
```

modifies the list to

```
1 1 2 3 5 8
```

To support this, we need to provide the user with a way of gaining access to the address of a particular item, such as the element 3 in the preceding example. One method is through a find() operation. For example:

```
pointer_to_3 = mylist.find( 3 );
```

find() takes a value to search for as a required first argument. If the element is present, find() returns a pointer to that element; otherwise, find() returns 0.

There are two special cases of insert() we also wish to support: insertion at the front of the list and insertion at the end. These cases require the user to specify only the value to be inserted:

```
insert_front( value );
insert_end( value );
```

Removal supports the following set of operations: the removal of a single value, the removal of the front element, and the removal of all elements:

```
remove( value );
remove_front();
remove_all();
```

The display() operation provides a formatted output of both the size and the individual elements of the list. An empty list is displayed as

```
(0)( )
```

A list with seven elements looks like this:

```
(7)( 0 1 1 2 3 5 8 )
```

reverse() simply reverses the order of the elements. For example, after invoking

```
mylist.reverse();
```

the earlier list displays as follows:

```
(7)( 8 5 3 2 1 1 0 )
```

Concatenation appends a second list to the end of the first. For example, given the lists

```
(4)( 0 1 1 2 ) // list1
(4)( 2 3 5 8 ) // list2
```

the operation

```
list1.concat( list2 );
```

modifies list1 to

```
(8)( 0 1 1 2 2 3 5 8 )
```

To make list1 a true Fibonacci sequence, we can apply remove():

```
list1.remove( 2 );
```

Once we have defined the behavior of our list class, our next step is to proceed with its implementation. We have chosen to represent a *list* and *list_item* as separate class abstractions. (We are constraining our implementation at this point simply to hold values of type int. Our classes are therefore named ilist and ilist_item.)

Our list contains a member _at_front that addresses the front of the list, a member _at_end that addresses the end of the list, and a member _size that holds the current size of the list. When a list object is first defined, these three members must be initialized to zero. We guarantee this with a default constructor:

```
class ilist_item;

class ilist {
public:
    // default constructor
    ilist() : _at_front( 0 ),
              _at_end( 0 ), _size( 0 ) {}

    // ...
private:
    ilist_item *_at_front;
    ilist_item *_at_end;
    int _size;
};
```

This allows us to define ilist objects such as

```
ilist mylist;
```

but nothing else as yet. Let's add support for a query as to the size of the list. After declaring the member function size() in the public section of the class definition, we can define the member function as follows:

```
inline int ilist::size() { return _size; }
```

Now we can write

```
int size = mylist.size();
```

For the moment, we do not wish to permit one list object to be initialized or assigned to another (we'll change that later — the change won't require changes to user programs). To prevent both the initialization and the assignment, we declare the ilist copy constructor and copy assignment operator to be private members and do not provide a definition of either. Here is our revised ilist class definition:

```
class ilist {
public:
    // definitions not shown
    ilist();
    int size();
    // ...
private:
    // prohibiting assignment and initialization
    // of one ilist object with another
    ilist( const ilist& );
    ilist& operator=( const ilist& );

    // data members as before
};
```

Using this definition, both of the following result in compile-time errors because `main()` cannot access the private members of our ilist class:

```
int main()
{
    ilist yourlist( mylist ); // error
    mylist = mylist;          // error
}
```

Our next step is to support the insertion of an item. We've chosen to represent an item as an independent class abstraction containing a member _value holding the value and a member _next holding the address of the next item on the list, if any:

```
class ilist_item {
public:
    // ...
private:
    int          _value;
    ilist_item *_next;
};
```

The ilist constructor requires that a value be specified and optionally also allows a pointer to an ilist_item to be specified. If present, the pointer represents the ilist_item the new item is to follow on the list. For example, given the list

```
0 1 1 2 5
```

a constructor invocation

```
ilist ( 3, pointer_to_2 );
```

modifies the list to be

```
0 1 1 2 3 5
```

Here is our implementation. (Recall that the second argument, item, is optional; a default value of 0 is passed in if the user does not provide a value. The default value is specified in the declaration of a function and not in its definition; this is explained fully in Chapter 7.)

```
class ilist_item {
public:
    ilist_item( int value, ilist_item *item_to_link_to = 0 );
    // ...
};

inline
ilist_item::
ilist_item( int value, ilist_item *item )
            : _value( value )
{
    if ( !item )
        _next = 0;
    else {
        _next = item->_next;
        item->_next = this;
    }
}
```

The general ilist insert() operation takes a value to be inserted and a list_item pointer indicating the item after which the new item is to be inserted. Here is our first cut (there are two problems with it — can you spot them?):

```
inline void
ilist::
insert( ilist_item *ptr, int value )
{
    new ilist_item( value, ptr );
    ++_size;
}
```

The first problem is that the pointer is not verified to have a nonzero address. We must recognize and handle that case, because otherwise its occurrence is likely to cause our program to crash at run-time. How should we handle it? One possibility is to abort the program by invoking the C standard library abort() function (found in the cstdlib C header file):

```
#include <cstdlib>
// ...
if ( ! ptr )
    abort();
```

Alternatively, we can use the `assert()` macro. This also aborts our program but first announces the condition that triggered the assertion:

```
#include <cassert>

// ...
assert( ptr != 0 );
```

A third alternative is to throw an exception. For example:

```
if ( ! ptr )
    throw "Panic: ilist::insert(): ptr == 0";
```

In general, aborting a program is best avoided whenever possible. Aborting the program in effect leaves the user dead in the water while we or a support organization isolates and resolves the problem.

If we are unable to continue processing at the site of the error, throwing an exception is generally preferable to aborting the program. An exception transfers control to an earlier portion of the program, one possibly able to resolve the problem.

Our implementation recognizes and treats an empty pointer as a request for inserting the value at the front of the list:

```
if ( ! ptr )
    insert_front( value );
```

The second flaw in our implementation is more philosophical than dire. Our `_size` and `size()` implementation pair is a tentative design: although we believe that the storage and inline retrieval of the size of the list best meets our users' need, we may in practice need to replace it with a strategy in which the size is calculated on demand. Under a calculate-on-demand implementation, the `_size` member is eliminated. By writing

```
++_size;
```

we are tightly coupling the implementation of `insert()` with the current list class implementation. If our list class implementation changes, `insert()` is no longer correct and must also be changed, as must `insert_front()`, `insert_end()`, and the instances of remove. Rather than spread reliance of the implementation details of our list class across the multiple insert and remove operations, we have chosen to encapsulate the dependence within a pair of functions:

```
inline void ilist::bump_up_size()   { ++_size; }
inline void ilist::bump_down_size() { --_size; }
```

Because we have declared the pair inline, the efficiency of our implementation is not affected by our design. Here is our revised implementation:

```
inline void
ilist::
insert( ilist_item *ptr, int value )
{
```

```
          if ( !ptr )
              insert_front( value );
          else {
              bump_up_size();
              new ilist_item( value, ptr );
          }
      }
```

Implementing `insert_front()` and `insert_end()` is reasonably straightforward. Each must handle the special case of an empty list. Here are their implementations:

```
      inline void
      ilist::
      insert_front( int value )
      {
          ilist_item *ptr = new ilist_item( value );

          if ( !_at_front )
              _at_front = _at_end = ptr;
          else {
              ptr->next( _at_front );
              _at_front = ptr;
          }
          bump_up_size();
      }

      inline void
      ilist::
      insert_end( int value )
      {
          if ( !_at_end )
              _at_end = _at_front = new ilist_item( value );
          else   _at_end = new ilist_item( value, _at_end );

          bump_up_size();
      }
```

`find()` searches the list for a value. If it is present, `find()` returns a pointer to the value; otherwise, it returns 0. Here is its implementation:

```
      ilist_item*
      ilist::
      find( int value )
      {
          ilist_item *ptr = _at_front;
          while ( ptr )
          {
                  if ( ptr->value() == value )
                      break;
```

```
            ptr = ptr->next();
    }

    return ptr;
}
```

find() can be used as follows:

```
    ilist_item *ptr = mylist.find( 8 );
    mylist.insert( ptr, some_value );
```

or, more compactly, as

```
    mylist.insert( mylist.find( 8 ), some_value );
```

Before exercising our insert operations, we'll need our display() function so that we can see just how badly or not we've fouled up our implementation. display()'s algorithm is simple enough: beginning with the first element, we print each element in turn until we've printed them all. Do you see why the following for loop design fails?

```
    // oops! does not work correctly
    // intention: display all but last element of ilist

    for ( ilist_item *iter = _at_front;  // start at front of list
          iter != _at_end;               // terminate at end
          ++iter )                       // advance one item
            cout << iter->value() << ' ';

    // now display last element
    cout << iter->value();
```

The reason this fails is that the elements of a list are not stored contiguously in memory. The pointer arithmetic of

```
    ++iter;
```

does not advance iter to address the next element of the ilist. Rather, it adds the size in bytes of one ilist_item object to iter's address. We have no idea what object, if any, iter addresses after it is incremented or whether the loop ever terminates. To advance to the next ilist_item, iter must be explicitly reset after each iteration to the next item pointed to by the _next ilist_item data member:

```
    iter = iter->_next;
```

We've encapsulated access to the _value and _next members through a set of inline access functions. Here is our revised ilist_item class definition:

```
    class ilist_item {
    public:
        ilist_item( int value, ilist_item *item_to_link_to = 0 );
```

```
int         value() { return _value; }
ilist_item* next()  { return _next;  }


void next( ilist_item *link ) { _next = link;       }
void value( int new_value )   { _value = new_value; }
private:
    int         _value;
    ilist_item *_next;
};
```

Here is our `display()` implementation using the preceding ilist_item class definition:

```
#include <iostream>

class ilist {
public:
    void display( ostream &os = cout );
    // ...
};

void
ilist::
display( ostream &os )
{
    os << "\n( " << _size << " )( ";

    ilist_item *ptr = _at_front;
    while ( ptr ) {
            os << ptr->value() << " ";
            ptr = ptr->next();
    }

    os << ")\n";
}
```

Here is a small program exercising our ilist class as we've defined it so far.

```
#include <iostream>
#include "ilist.h"

int main()
{
    ilist mylist;

    for ( int ix = 0; ix < 10; ++ix ) {
            mylist.insert_front( ix );
            mylist.insert_end( ix );
    }
```

```
        cout << "Ok: after insert_front() and insert_end()\n";
        mylist.display();

        ilist_item *it = mylist.find( 8 );
        cout << "\n"
             << "Searching for the value 8: found it?"
             << ( it ? " yes!\n" : " no!\n" );

        mylist.insert( it, 1024 );
        cout << "\n"
             << "Inserting element 1024 following the value 8\n";

        mylist.display();

        int elem_cnt = mylist.remove( 8 );
        cout << "\n"
             << "Removed " << elem_cnt << " of the value 8\n";

        mylist.display();

        cout << "\n" << "Removed front element\n";
        mylist.remove_front(); mylist.display();

        cout << "\n" << "Removed all elements\n";
        mylist.remove_all(); mylist.display();
    }
```

It generates the following results when compiled and executed:

```
Ok: after insert_front() and insert_end()

( 20 )( 9 8 7 6 5 4 3 2 1 0 0 1 2 3 4 5 6 7 8 9 )

Searching for the value 8: found it? yes!

Inserting element 1024 following the value 8

( 21 )( 9 8 1024 7 6 5 4 3 2 1 0 0 1 2 3 4 5 6 7 8 9 )

Removed 2 of the value 8

( 19 )( 9 1024 7 6 5 4 3 2 1 0 0 1 2 3 4 5 6 7 9 )

Removed front element

( 18 )( 1024 7 6 5 4 3 2 1 0 0 1 2 3 4 5 6 7 9 )

Removed all elements

( 0 )( )
```

As well as inserting items into a list, users need to remove items from a list. We support three flavors of element removal:

```
void remove_front();
void remove_all();
int  remove( int value );
```

Here is our implementation of remove_front():

```
inline void
ilist::
remove_front()
{

    if ( _at_front ) {
        ilist_item *ptr = _at_front;
        _at_front = _at_front->next();

        bump_down_size();
        delete ptr;
    }
}
```

remove_all() repeatedly invokes remove_front() until the list is empty:

```
void
ilist::
remove_all()
{
    while ( _at_front )
            remove_front();

    _size = 0;
    _at_front = _at_end = 0;
}
```

The general remove() implementation also makes use of remove_front() for the special case of one or more instances of the item to be removed appearing at the front of the list. Otherwise, we iterate across the list with a previous and current pointer, removing the item and reconnecting the list with each instance we find. Here is its implementation:

```
int
ilist::
remove( int value )
{
    ilist_item *plist = _at_front;
    int elem_cnt = 0;

    while ( plist && plist->value() == value )
    {
```

```
            plist = plist->next();
            remove_front();
            ++elem_cnt;
        }

    if ( ! plist )
         return elem_cnt;

    ilist_item *prev = plist;
    plist = plist->next();

    while ( plist )
    {
        if ( plist->value() == value )
        {
            prev->next( plist->next() );
            delete plist;
            ++elem_cnt;
            bump_down_size();
            plist = prev->next();
            if ( ! plist )
            {
                _at_end = prev;
                return elem_cnt;
            }
        }
        else
        {
            prev = plist;
            plist = plist->next();
        }
    }

    return elem_cnt;
}
```

The following program exercises the set of remove operations, testing the following cases: (1) all items to be removed are located at the end of the list, (2) all items of the list are to be removed, (3) no items are present, and (4) items are located both at the front and back of the list.

```
#include <iostream>
#include "ilist.h"

int main()
{
    ilist mylist;
```

```
cout << "\n---------------------------------------------\n"
     << "test #1: items at end\n"
     << "---------------------------------------------\n";

mylist.insert_front( 1 ); mylist.insert_front( 1 );
mylist.insert_front( 1 );

mylist.insert_front( 2 ); mylist.insert_front( 3 );
mylist.insert_front( 4 );

mylist.display();

int elem_cnt = mylist.remove( 1 );
cout << "\n" << "Removed " << elem_cnt << " of the value 1\n";
mylist.display();

mylist.remove_all();

cout << "\n---------------------------------------------\n"
     << "test #2: items at front\n"
     << "---------------------------------------------\n";

mylist.insert_front( 1 ); mylist.insert_front( 1 );
mylist.insert_front( 1 );
mylist.display();

elem_cnt = mylist.remove( 1 );
cout << "\n" << "Removed " << elem_cnt << " of the value 1\n";
mylist.display();

mylist.remove_all();

cout << "\n---------------------------------------------\n"
     << "test #3: no items present\n"
     << "---------------------------------------------\n";

mylist.insert_front( 0 ); mylist.insert_front( 2 );
mylist.insert_front( 4 );
mylist.display();

elem_cnt = mylist.remove( 1 );
cout << "\n" << "Removed " << elem_cnt << " of the value 1\n";
mylist.display();

mylist.remove_all();

cout << "\n---------------------------------------------\n"
     << "test #4: items at front and end\n"
     << "---------------------------------------------\n";
```

```
        mylist.insert_front( 1 ); mylist.insert_front( 1 );
        mylist.insert_front( 1 );

        mylist.insert_front( 0 ); mylist.insert_front( 2 );
        mylist.insert_front( 4 );

        mylist.insert_front( 1 ); mylist.insert_front( 1 );
        mylist.insert_front( 1 );

        mylist.display();

        elem_cnt = mylist.remove( 1 );
        cout << "\n" << "Removed " << elem_cnt << " of the value 1\n";
        mylist.display();
    }
```

When compiled and executed, the program generates the following results:

```
--------------------------------------------------
test #1: items at end
--------------------------------------------------

( 6 )( 4 3 2 1 1 1 )

Removed 3 of the value 1

( 3 )( 4 3 2 )

--------------------------------------------------
test #2: items at front
--------------------------------------------------

( 3 )( 1 1 1 )

Removed 3 of the value 1

( 0 )( )

--------------------------------------------------
test #3: no items present
--------------------------------------------------

( 3 )( 4 2 0 )

Removed 0 of the value 1

( 3 )( 4 2 0 )
```

```
---------------------------------------------------
test #4: items at front and end
---------------------------------------------------

( 9 )( 1 1 1 4 2 0 1 1 1 )

Removed 6 of the value 1

( 3 )( 4 2 0 )
```

The last two operations we'd like to provide are concatenation (appending one list to the back of a second) and reversal (flipping the element order). Our first implementation of concat() is subtly incorrect. Do you see the problem?

```
void ilist::concat( const ilist &il )
{
    if ( ! _at_end )
            _at_front = il._at_front;
    else _at_end->next( il._at_front );
    _at_end = il._at_end;
}
```

The problem is that two ilist objects now point to the same sequence of items. Changes to one ilist, such as insert() or remove(), incorrectly also are reflected in the second ilist. The simplest solution to this problem is to copy each item. Our revised concat() uses insert_end():

```
void
ilist::
concat( const ilist &il )
{
        ilist_item *ptr = il._at_front;
        while ( ptr ) {
                insert_end( ptr->value() );
                ptr = ptr->next();
        }
}
```

Here is our implementation of reverse():

```
void
ilist::
reverse()
{
    ilist_item *ptr = _at_front;
    ilist_item *prev = 0;

    _at_front = _at_end;
    _at_end = ptr;

    while ( ptr != _at_front )
```

```
        {
            ilist_item *tmp = ptr->next();
            ptr->next( prev );
            prev = ptr;
            ptr = tmp;
        }

        _at_front->next( prev );
    }
```

The following small program exercises our implementation:

```
    #include <iostream>
    #include "ilist.h"

    int main()
    {
        ilist mylist;

        for ( int ix = 0; ix < 10; ++ix )
            { mylist.insert_front( ix ); }

        mylist.display();

        cout << "\n" << "reverse the list\n";
        mylist.reverse(); mylist.display();

        ilist mylist_too;
        mylist_too.insert_end( 0 ); mylist_too.insert_end( 1 );
        mylist_too.insert_end( 1 ); mylist_too.insert_end( 2 );
        mylist_too.insert_end( 3 ); mylist_too.insert_end( 5 );

        cout << "\n" << "mylist_too:\n";
        mylist_too.display();

        mylist.concat( mylist_too );
        cout << "\n" << "mylist after concat with mylist_too:\n";
        mylist.display();

    }
```

When compiled and executed, it generates the following output:

```
    ( 10 )( 9 8 7 6 5 4 3 2 1 0 )

    reverse the list

    ( 10 )( 0 1 2 3 4 5 6 7 8 9 )

    mylist_too:
```

```
( 6 )( 0 1 1 2 3 5 )
```

mylist after concat with mylist_too:

```
( 16 )( 0 1 2 3 4 5 6 7 8 9 0 1 1 2 3 5 )
```

On the one hand, our design and implementation are finished; we've not only implemented the operations we identified as necessary, but we've also tested them to confirm some level of correctness. The shortcomings are not in what we've provided but in what we have not provided.

The most serious deficiency of our ilist class is the inability of our users to iterate across the elements of the ilist. Our class as implemented simply does not support it, and, because we encapsulate the implementation, there is no way the user can directly provide it.

A second deficiency is that the class does not support the initialization or assignment of one ilist class object with another. Although this decision was deliberate on our part, that does not make it less of a nuisance for our users. Let's fix each deficiency in turn, beginning with that of initialization and copy.

To initialize one ilist object with another, we must define an ilist copy constructor. The reason we initially disallowed this is that the default behavior is all wrong for our list class (in general, it is wrong for any class that contains pointer members), and it is preferable to annoy a user by not providing some functionality than to provide the functionality incorrectly and clobber the user's program. (The reason the default behavior is incorrect is explained in Section 14.5.) The copy constructor implementation makes use of insert_end():

```
ilist::ilist( const ilist &rhs )
{
    ilist_item *pt = rhs._at_front;
    while ( pt ) {
        insert_end( pt->value() );
        pt = pt->next();
    }
}
```

The copy assignment operator must simply remove_all() the existing items and then insert_end() the values in turn of the second ilist object. Because the insertion code is the same in both cases, we can factor it into an insert_all() member:

```
void ilist::insert_all( const ilist &rhs )
{
    ilist_item *pt = rhs._at_front;
    while ( pt ) {
        insert_end( pt->value() );
        pt = pt->next();
    }
```

```
        }
```

We then implement the copy constructor and copy assignment operator as follows:

```
        inline ilist::ilist( const ilist &rhs )
            : _at_front( 0 ), _at_end( 0 )
            { insert_all( rhs ); }

        inline ilist& ilist::operator=( const ilist &rhs ) {
            if ( this != &rhs ) {
                remove_all();
                insert_all( rhs );
            }
            return *this;
        }
```

Finally, the user must be able to iterate across the individual elements of the ilist. One strategy to support this is simply to provide access to _at_front:

```
        ilist_item *ilist::front() { return _at_front(); }
```

The user is then able to implement the same general loop idiom as we did earlier:

```
        ilist_item *pt = mylist.front();
        while ( pt ) {
                do_something( pt->value() );
                pt = pt->next();
        }
```

Although this gets the job done, it is not our preferred solution. Rather, we prefer to support the more general concept of an iteration across elements of a container. In this section, we provide minimal support of the form

```
        for ( ilist_item *iter = mylist.init_iter(); iter;
              iter = mylist.next_iter() )
                    do_something( iter->value() );
```

(In Chapters 6 and 12 we look at the iterator types defined in support of the standard library container types and generic algorithms. (We briefly looked at iterators in Section 2.8.))

Our iterator is slightly more than a pointer, because it remembers the current item of the iteration, is able to return a next item, and is able to recognize the completion of an iteration. init_iter() by default initializes the iterator to _at_front. Optionally, the user can pass in an ilist_item pointer with which to start the iteration. next_iter() returns the next item in the list, or 0 if the iteration is complete. The implementation support includes an additional ilist_item pointer:

```
        class ilist {
        public:
            // ...
            init_iter( ilist_item *it = 0 );
```

```
private:
    // ...
    ilist_item *_current;
};
```

init_iter() looks like this:

```
inline ilist_item*
ilist::init_iter( ilist_item *it )
{
    return _current = it ? it : _at_front;
}
```

next_iter() advances _current to the next item, returning it unless the iteration is complete. If it is complete, next_iter() returns 0 until init_iter() resets _current. Here is our implementation:

```
inline ilist_item*
ilist::
next_iter()
{
    ilist_item *next = _current
                        ? _current = _current->next()
                        : _current;

    return next;
}
```

Our support for iteration could be problematic if the item pointed to by _current is removed. Our solution is to modify remove_front() and remove() to test whether _current addresses the item being removed. If it does, _current is advanced to address the next item (or no item if the item removed is the last on the list). If all the items are removed, then _current is set to point to no item. Here is our revised remove_front():

```
inline void
ilist::remove_front()
{
    if ( _at_front ) {
        ilist_item *ptr = _at_front;
        _at_front = _at_front->next();

        // don't want current to point to a deleted item
        if ( _current == ptr )
            _current = _at_front;

        bump_down_size();
        delete ptr;
    }
}
```

Here is the relevant portion of the revision of remove():

```
while ( plist )
    {
        if ( plist->value() == value )
        {
            prev->next( plist->next() );

            if ( _current == plist )
                _current = prev->next();
```

What if an item is inserted in front of the item _current addresses? In this case, we do not modify _current. To resynchronize the iteration, the user needs to invoke init_iter(). On the other hand, when we initialize or copy one ilist class object with another, _current is not copied but rather is reset to address no object.

Here is a small program to exercise our copy constructor and copy assignment operator as well as our support of iteration:

```
#include <iostream>
#include "ilist.h"

int main()
{
    ilist mylist;

    for ( int ix = 0; ix < 10; ++ix ) {
        mylist.insert_front( ix );
        mylist.insert_end( ix );
    }

    cout << "\n" << "Use of init_iter() and next_iter() "
         << "to iterate across each list item:\n";

    ilist_item *iter;
    for ( iter = mylist.init_iter();
          iter; iter = mylist.next_iter() )
        cout << iter->value() << " ";

    cout << "\n" << "Use of copy constructor\n";

    ilist mylist2( mylist );
    mylist.remove_all();

    for ( iter = mylist2.init_iter();
          iter; iter = mylist2.next_iter() )
        cout << iter->value() << " ";

    cout << "\n" << "Use of copy assignment operator\n";
```

```
        mylist = mylist2;

        for ( iter = mylist.init_iter();
              iter; iter = mylist.next_iter() )
            cout << iter->value() << " ";

        cout << "\n";

    }
```

When compiled and executed, this program generates the following output:

```
Use of init_iter() and next_iter() to iterate across each list item:
9 8 7 6 5 4 3 2 1 0 0 1 2 3 4 5 6 7 8 9
Use of copy constructor
9 8 7 6 5 4 3 2 1 0 0 1 2 3 4 5 6 7 8 9
Use of copy assignment operator
9 8 7 6 5 4 3 2 1 0 0 1 2 3 4 5 6 7 8 9
```

5.11.1   Providing a Generic List Class

Our ilist class is severely constrained in that it currently can hold elements only of type int. A more generally useful list type should provide support both for built-in and for class types. How might we transform our ilist class to support a wider variety of element types without either extensive reprogramming or code duplication? The class template mechanism provides a solution (it is discussed in detail in Chapter 16).

Through parameterization, the class template factors out type-dependent aspects of our class design — in our case, the underlying type of the element our list contains. Later, the user, wishing a particular kind of list, provides the actual type for the template parameter. For example:

```
    list< string > slist;
```

creates an instance of our list template class capable of holding string objects, whereas

```
    list< int > ilist;
```

creates an instance the equivalent of our original hand-coded ilist class. Using a class template definition, we can support an unlimited number of list element types with one class template implementation. Let's step through how we might do that, focusing on our list_item class.

The definition of a class template begins with the keyword template followed by a list of parameters marked by angle brackets. A type parameter consists of either typename or class, followed by an identifier. For example:

```
    template <class elemType>
    class list_item;
```

This declares list_item to be a class template with a single type parameter. `elemType` is an arbitrary identifier with which we chose to name our type parameter. The following is an equivalent declaration of our list_item class:

```
template <typename elemType>
class list_item;
```

The keywords `typename` and `class` are interchangeable. `typename` is new to Standard C++. It is more mnemonic but, as of this writing, less widely supported than the original `class` keyword. We predominantly use the `class` keyword for this reason and because old habits are difficult to change consistently. In any case, here is our definition of the list_item class template:

```
template <class elemType>
class list_item {
public:
    list_item( elemType value, list_item *item = 0 )
            : _value( value ) {
              if ( !item )
                    _next = 0;
              else {
                    _next = item->_next;
                    item->_next = this;
              }
    }

    elemType  value() { return _value; }
    list_item* next() { return _next;  }

    void next(  list_item *link    ) { _next = link;        }
    void value( elemType new_value ) { _value = new_value; }

private:
    elemType   _value;
    list_item *_next;
};
```

Each earlier occurrence of `int` in our ilist_item class definition is replaced with the `elemType` parameter in our list_item class template. When we write

```
list_item<double> *ptr = new list_item<double>( 3.14 );
```

the compiler automatically binds `elemType` to the actual type `double` and creates a list_item class capable of supporting elements of that type.

The transformation of ilist into the class template list is carried out in a similar fashion. Here is the class template definition:

```
template <class elemType>
class list {
public:
```

```
        list()
            : _at_front( 0 ), _at_end( 0 ), _current( 0 ),
              _size( 0 ) {}
        list( const list& );
        list& operator=( const list& );
        ~list() { remove_all(); }

        void insert( list_item<elemType> *ptr, elemType value );
        void insert_end( elemType value );
        void insert_front( elemType value );
        void insert_all( const list &rhs );

        int  remove( elemType value );
        void remove_front();
        void remove_all();

        list_item<elemType> *find( elemType value );
        list_item<elemType> *next_iter();
        list_item<elemType>* init_iter( list_item<elemType> *it );

        void display( ostream &os = cout );

        void concat( const list& );
        void reverse();
        int size() { return _size; }
    private:
        void bump_up_size()    { ++_size; }
        void bump_down_size() { --_size; }

        list_item<elemType> *_at_front;
        list_item<elemType> *_at_end;
        list_item<elemType> *_current;
        int _size;
    };
```

The class template objects can be used in exactly the same way as our explicitly coded ilist class objects. The primary advantage is our ability to support an unlimited number of list types with a single class template definition.

Templates make up a fundamental component of Standard C++ programming. In the Chapter 6, in fact, we look at the collection of template container class types provided by the standard library. Not surprisingly, this includes a class template list as well as the class template vector we've already looked at in Chapters 2 and 3.

The presence of the standard library list class introduces something of a dilemma. We've chosen to call our class "list" as well now rather than ilist. Unfortunately, that conflicts with the standard library list class. We cannot now use both classes in the same program. One solution, of course, is to rename our list class to remove the conflict. That works in this case because, after all, it's our code. In many instances that solution is not open to us.

The more general solution is the C++ namespace mechanism. Namespaces allow the library vendor to encapsulate otherwise global names in order to prevent name collisions. In addition, namespaces provide access notation to allow use of those names within our programs. The C++ standard library, for example, is packaged within the std namespace. Our third edition code might also be placed in a uniquely named namespace:

```
namespace Primer_Third_Edition
{
    template <typename elemType>
    class list_item{ ... };

    template <typename elemType>
    class list{ ... };

    // ...
}
```

A user wishing to exercise our list class might write the following:

```
// our list class header file
#include "list.h"

// make definitions visible to program
using namespace Primer_Third_Edition;

// ok: accesses our list class
list< int > ilist;

// ...
```

(Namespaces are discussed in detail in Sections 8.5 and 8.6.)

Exercise 5.16

We do not define an ilist_item destructor, although the class contains a pointer member. The reason is that the ilist_item class does not allocate the object addressed by _next, so it is not responsible for its deallocation. A common beginner error is to provide an ilist destructor defined as follows:

```
// a bad design choice
ilist_item::~ilist_item()
{
    delete _next;
}
```

Looking at remove_all() or remove_front(), explain why the presence of this destructor is a bad design choice.

Exercise 5.17

Our ilist class does not support either of these statements:

```
void ilist::remove_end();
void ilist::remove( ilist_item* );
```

Why do you think we excluded them? Sketch out an algorithm to support these two operations.

Exercise 5.18

Modify find() to take a second argument, an ilist_item*, which, if set, indicates where to begin searching for the item. If it is not set, the search should begin as before at the front of the list. (By providing this new parameter as the second argument and specifying a zero default argument, we preserve the original public interface. Code that uses the previous definition of find() does not need to be modified.)

```
class ilist {
public:
    // ...
    ilist_item* find( int value, ilist_item *start_at = 0 );
    // ...
};
```

Exercise 5.19

Using this new version of find(), implement count() , which returns a count of the occurrences of a value in an ilist. Write a small program to test your implementation.

Exercise 5.20

Revise insert(int value) to return the ilist_item pointer it has just inserted.

Exercise 5.21

Using the revised insert() function, implement

```
void ilist::
insert(ilist_item *begin, int *array_of_value, int elem_cnt );
```

in which array_of_value addresses an array of values to be inserted in the ilist, elem_cnt is the number of elements in the array, and begin indicates where to begin inserting the elements. For example, given an ilist of the values

```
(3)( 0 1 21 )
```

and an array such as the following

```
int ia[] = { 1, 2, 3, 5, 8, 13 };
```

the new insert operation might be called as follows:

```
ilist_item *it = mylist.find( 1 );
mylist.insert(it, ia, 6 );
```

It would modify mylist as follows:

```
(9)( 0 1 1 2 3 5 8 13 21 )
```

Exercise 5.22

One problem with concat() and reverse() is that both of them modify the original list. This is not always desirable. Provide an alternative pair of operations that returns a new ilist object:

```
ilist ilist::reverse_copy();
ilist ilist::concat_copy( const ilist &rhs );
```

6

Abstract Container Types

This chapter provides an extension of and completion to Chapters 3 and 4. We continue the discussion of types started in Chapter 3 by presenting more information on the string and vector types as well as presenting other container types provided by the C++ standard library. In addition, we continue the discussion of operators and expressions started in Chapter 4 by presenting the operations supported for objects of the container types.

A sequence container holds an ordered collection of elements of a single type. The two primary sequence containers are the vector and list types. (A third sequence container, deque — pronounced "deck" — provides the same behavior as a vector but is specialized to support efficient insertion and deletion of its first element. A deque is preferred over a vector, for example, in the implementation of a queue, an abstraction in which the first element is retrieved each time. In the remainder of the text, whenever we describe the operations supported by a vector, those operations are also supported by a deque.)

An associative container supports efficient query as to the presence and retrieval of an element. The two primary associative container types are the map and the set. A map is a key/value pair: the key is used for lookup, and the value contains the data we wish to use. A telephone directory, for example, is well supported by a map: the key is the individual's name, and the value is the associated phone number.

A set contains a single key value and supports the efficient query of whether it is present. For example, a text query system might build a set of words to exclude, such as *the, and, but,* and so on, when building a database of the words present within a text. The program would read each word of the text in turn, check whether it is in the set of excluded words, and either discard or enter the word within the database depending on the result of the query.

Both the map and the set can contain only a single occurrence of each key. A multimap and a multiset support multiple occurrences of the same key. Our telephone directory, for example, will probably need to support multiple listings for a single individual. One method of implementing that is with the use of a multimap.

In the sections that follow, we look at the container types in detail, motivating the discussion through a progressive implementation of a small text query program.

6.1   Our Text Query System

What does a text query system consist of?

1. An arbitrary text file indicated by the user.
2. A Boolean query facility in which the user can search for a word or sequence of adjacent words within the text.

If the word or sequence of adjacent words is found, the number of occurrences of each word and word sequence is displayed. If the user wishes, the sentence or sentences within which the word or word sequence occurs are also displayed. For example, if the user wished to find all references to either the Civil War or Civil Rights, the query might look like this[1]:

```
Civil && ( War || Rights )
```

The result of the query might look like this:

```
Civil: 12 occurrences
War:  48 occurrences
Rights: 1 occurrence

Civil && War: 1 occurrence
Civil && Rights: 1 occurrence

(8) Civility, of course, is not to be confused with
Civil Rights, nor should it lead to Civil War.
```

where (8) represents the sentence number of the text. Our system must be smart enough not to display the same sentence multiple times. Moreover, multiple sentences should be displayed in ascending order (that is, sentence 7 should always be displayed prior to sentence 9).

---

1. Note: To simplify our implementation, we require a space separating each word, including parentheses and the Boolean operators. So that

```
(War || Rights)
```

will not be understood by our program (a space is necessary before the W) nor

```
Civil&&(War||Rights)
```

Although this is unreasonable in a real-world system in which the user's convenience always overrides convenience for the implementers, we believe it is more than acceptable in a primarily introductory text such as this one.

What are the tasks that our program needs to support?

1.   It must allow the user to indicate the name of a text file to open and then must open and read the text.

2.   It must internally organize the text file so that it can identify the number of occurrences of each word in terms of the sentence it occurs in and its position within that sentence.

3.   It must support some form of Boolean query language. In our case, it will support the following:

&&   Both words are not only present but also adjacent within a line.

|| One or both words are present in a line.

!   The word is not present in a line.

()   A means of subgrouping a query.

Thus, one can write

```
Lincoln
```

to find all the sentences in which the word *Lincoln* occurs or write

```
! Lincoln
```

to find all the sentences in which the word *Lincoln* does not occur or write

```
( Abe || Abraham ) && Lincoln
```

to limit the sentences selected to those explicitly referring to Abe Lincoln or Abraham Lincoln.

We provide two implementations of our system. In this chapter, we provide an implementation solving the problem of retrieving and storing the text file as a map of word entries and their associated line and column locations. To exercise this solution, we provide a single-word query system. In Chapter 17, we provide an implementation of the full query system supporting the relational operators such as we discussed in the preceding paragraphs. We defer its implementation until then because the solution involves the use of an object-oriented Query class hierarchy.

For exposition within the text, we use the following six lines from an unpublished children's story Stan has written:[2]

---

2. Illustration by Elena Driskill, reprinted with permission.

Alice Emma has long flowing red hair. Her Daddy says
when the wind blows through her hair, it looks almost alive,
like a fiery bird in flight. A beautiful fiery bird, he tells her,
magical but untamed. "Daddy, shush, there is no such thing,"
she tells him, at the same time wanting him to tell her more.
Shyly, she asks, "I mean, Daddy, is there?"

11

At the end of our processing, the internal storage of the text to support individual
queries looks like this. (This involves reading the individual lines of text, separating

them into the individual words, stripping out punctuation, eliminating capitalization, providing some minimal support of suffixing, and eliminating semantically neutral words such as *and, a,* and *the*.)

```
alice ((0,0))
alive ((1,10))
almost ((1,9))
ask ((5,2))
beautiful ((2,7))
bird ((2,3),(2,9))
blow ((1,3))
daddy ((0,8),(3,3),(5,5))
emma ((0,1))
fiery ((2,2),(2,8))
flight ((2,5))
flowing ((0,4))
hair ((0,6),(1,6))
has ((0,2))
like ((2,0))
long ((0,3))
look ((1,8))
magical ((3,0))
mean ((5,4))
more ((4,12))
red ((0,5))
same ((4,5))
say ((0,9))
she ((4,0),(5,1))
shush ((3,4))
shyly ((5,0))
such ((3,8))
tell ((2,11),(4,1),(4,10))
there ((3,5),(5,7))
thing ((3,9))
through ((1,4))
time ((4,6))
untamed ((3,2))
wanting ((4,7))
wind ((1,2))
```

The following is a sample query session using the program implemented within this chapter (user entries are in italics):

```
please enter file name: alice_emma

enter a word against which to search the text.
to quit, enter a single character ==>  alice

alice occurs 1 time:
```

```
( line 1 ) Alice Emma has long flowing red hair. Her Daddy says
```

```
enter a word against which to search the text.
to quit, enter a single character ==>   daddy
```

```
daddy occurs 3 times:
```

```
( line 1 ) Alice Emma has long flowing red hair. Her Daddy says
( line 4 ) magical but untamed. "Daddy, shush, there is no such
thing,"
( line 6 ) Shyly, she asks, "I mean, Daddy, is there?"
```

```
enter a word against which to search the text.
to quit, enter a single character ==>   phoenix
```

```
Sorry. There are no entries for phoenix.
```

```
enter a word against which to search the text.
to quit, enter a single character ==>   .
Ok, bye!
```

To easily implement this program, we need to look in detail at the standard library container types as well as revisit the string class introduced in Chapter 3.

6.2   A vector or a list?

One of the first things our program must do is to store an unknown number of words from a text file. The words will be stored in turn as string objects. Our first question is, Should we store the words in a sequence or in an associative container?

At some point we will need to support the query as to the presence of a word and, if it is present, to retrieve its associated occurrences within the text. Because we are both searching for and retrieving a value, an associative map is the most appropriate container type to support this.

However, prior to that, we need to simply store the input text for processing — that is, to strip out punctuation, deal with suffixing, and so on. For this preliminary pass, a sequence, and not an associative container, is required. The question is, Should it be a vector or a list?

If you have programmed in C or in pre-Standard C++, your rule of thumb in choosing is probably something like this: if the number of elements to be stored is known at compile-time, use an array. If the number of elements to be stored is unknown or likely to vary widely, then use a list, dynamically allocating storage for each object and attaching that object to the list in turn.

This rule of thumb, however, does not hold for the sequence container types: the vector, deque, and list all grow dynamically. The criterion for choosing among these three is primarily concerned with the insertion characteristics and subsequent access requirements of the elements.

A vector represents a contiguous area of memory in which each element is stored in turn. Random access into a vector — that is, accessing element 5, then 15, then 7, and so on — is very efficient because each access is a fixed offset from the beginning of the vector. Insertion of an element at any position other than the back of the vector, however, is inefficient because it requires each element to the right of the inserted element to be copied. Similarly, a deletion of any element other than the last element of the vector is inefficient because each element to the right of the deleted element must be copied. This can be particularly expensive for large, complex class objects. (A deque also represents a contiguous area of memory; however, unlike a vector, it also supports the efficient insertion and deletion of elements at its front. It achieves this through a two-level array structure in which one level represents the actual container and a second level addresses the front and back of the container.)

A list represents noncontiguous memory doubly linked through a pair of pointers that address the elements to the front and back allowing for both forward and backward traversal. Insertion and deletion of elements at any position within the list is efficient: the pointers must be reassigned, but no elements need be moved by copying. Random access, on the other hand, is not well supported: accessing an element requires traversal of intervening elements. In addition, there is the space overhead of the two pointers per element.

Here are some criteria for choosing a sequence container type:

- If we require random access into a container, a vector is the clear choice over a list.
- If we know the number of elements we need to store, a vector is again to be preferred over a list.
- If we need to insert and delete elements other than at the two ends of the container, a list is the clear choice over a vector.
- Unless we need to insert or delete elements at the front of the container, a vector is preferable to a deque.

What if we need both to randomly access and to randomly insert and delete elements? The trade-off is between the cost of the random access versus that of copying contiguous elements to the right or left. In general, the predominant operation of the application (the search or insertion) should determine the choice of container type. (Making this decision may require profiling the performance of both container types.) If neither performance is satisfactory, it may be necessary to design a more complex data structure of our own.

How do we decide which container type to choose when we do not know the number of elements we need to store (that is, the container is going to grow dynamically) and when there is no need either for random access or insertion except at the back? Is a list or vector in this case significantly more efficient? (We'll postpone an answer to this question until the next section.)

A list grows in a straightforward manner: each time a new object is inserted into the list, the front pointer and back pointer of the two elements between which the new object is being inserted are reassigned to point to the new object. The front and back pointers of the new object, in turn, are initialized to address these two elements. The list holds only the storage necessary for the elements it contains. The overhead is two-fold: the two additional pointers associated with each value and the indirect access of the value through a pointer.

The representation and overhead of a dynamic vector are more complex. We look at that in the next section.

Exercise 6.1

Which is the most appropriate — a vector, a deque, or a list — for the following program tasks, or is neither preferred?

a. Read an unknown number of words from a file for the purpose of generating random English language sentences.

b. Read a fixed number of words, inserting them in the container alphabetically as they are entered.

c. Read an unknown number of words. Always insert new words at the back. Remove the next value from the front.

d. Read an unknown number of integers from a file. Sort the numbers and then print them to standard output.

6.3   How a vector Grows Itself

For a vector to grow dynamically, it must allocate the memory to hold the new sequence, copy the elements of the old sequence in turn, and deallocate the old memory. Moreover, if the elements are class objects, the copy and deallocation may require the invocation of the class copy constructor and destructor on each element in turn. Because a list simply links the new elements each time the container grows, there seems little question that a list is the more efficient of the two container types in its support of dynamic growth. But in practice this is not the case. Let's see why.

To be of even minimum efficiency, the vector cannot actually regrow itself with each individual insertion. Rather, when the vector needs to grow itself, it allocates additional storage capacity beyond its immediate need — it holds this storage in reserve. (The exact amount of additional capacity allocated is implementation-defined.) This strategy allows for a significantly more efficient regrowing of the container — so much so, in fact, that for small objects, a vector in practice turns out to grow more efficiently than a list. Let's look at some examples under the Rogue Wave implementation of the C++ standard library. But first, let's make clear the distinction between the capacity and size of a container.

Capacity is the total number of elements that can be added to a container before it needs to regrow itself. (Capacity is associated only with a container in which storage is contiguous: for example, a vector, deque, or string. A list does not require capacity.) To discover the capacity of a vector, we invoke its capacity() operation. Size, on the other hand, is the number of elements a container currently holds. To retrieve the current size of a container, we invoke its size() operation. For example:

```
#include <vector>
#include <iostream>

int main()
{
    vector< int > ivec;
    cout << "ivec: size: " << ivec.size()
         << " capacity: "  << ivec.capacity() << endl;

    for ( int ix = 0; ix < 24; ++ix ) {
        ivec.push_back( ix );
        cout << "ivec: size: " << ivec.size()
             << " capacity: "  << ivec.capacity() << endl;
    }
}
```

Under the Rogue Wave implementation, both the size and the capacity of ivec after its definition are 0. On inserting the first element, however, ivec's capacity is 256 and its size is 1. This means that 256 elements can be added to ivec before it needs to regrow itself. When we insert a 256th element, the vector regrows itself in the following way: it allocates double its current capacity, copies its current values into the new allocated memory, and deallocates its previous memory. As we'll see in a moment, the larger and more complex the data type, the less efficient the vector becomes compared with a list. Table 6.1 shows various data types, their sizes, and the initial capacity of their associated vector:

Table 6.1 Size, Capacity, and Various Data Types

Data Type	Size in Bytes	Capacity After Initial Insertion
int	4	256
double	8	128
simple class #1	12	85
string	12	85
large simple class	8,000	1
large complex class	8,000	1

As you can see, under the Rogue Wave implementation, a default capacity of elements near to or equal to 1,024 bytes is allocated with a first insertion; then it is doubled with each reallocation. For a large data type, with a small capacity, the reallocation and copying of the elements become the primary overhead in the use of the vector. (When we speak of a complex class, we mean a class that provides both a copy constructor and a copy assignment operator.) Table 6.2 shows the times, in seconds, for inserting tenmillion elements of the above types in both a list and vector. Table 6.3 shows the time to insert 10,000 elements (a larger element size was too slow).

Table 6.2   Time in Seconds to Insert 10,000,000 Elements

Data Type	List	Vector
int	10.38s	3.76s
double	10.72s	3.95s
simple class	12.31s	5.89s
string	14.42s	11.80s

Table 6.3   Time in Seconds to Insert 10,000 Elements

Data Type	List	Vector
large simple class	0.36s	2.23s
large complex class	2.37s	6.70s

As you can see, for small data types, a vector performs considerably better than a list, whereas for large data objects, the reverse is true: a list performs considerably better. This difference is due to the need to regrow and copy the elements of the vector. The size of the data type, however, is not the only criterion affecting the performance of the container. The complexity of the data type also affects the performance of element insertion. Why?

The insertion of an element, for either a list or a vector, requires invocation of the copy constructor for a class that defines one. (A copy constructor initializes one class object with another object of its type — see Section 2.2 for an initial discussion, and Section 14.5 for a detailed discussion.) This explains the difference in cost between the simple class and string class list insertion. The simple class objects and large simple class objects are inserted through a bitwise copy (the bits of the object are copied into the bits of the second object), whereas the string class objects and large complex class objects are inserted through an invocation of the string copy constructor.

In addition, however, the vector must invoke the copy constructor for each element with each reallocation of its memory. Moreover, the deallocation of the previous memory requires the invocation of the associated class destructor on each element (again, see Section 2.2 for an initial discussion of a destructor). The more frequently the vector is required to regrow itself, the costlier the element insertion becomes.

One solution, of course, is to switch from a vector to a list when the cost of the vector becomes prohibitive. An alternative, often preferable solution is to store large or complex class objects indirectly by pointer. For example, when we store the complex class object by pointer, the cost of inserting 10,000 elements within the vector dramatically goes down from 6.70s to 0.82s. Why? The capacity increases from 1 to 256, so the number of reallocations drops considerably. Second, the copy and deallocation of a pointer to a class object does not require the invocation of either the copy constructor or the destructor of the class.

The reserve() operation allows the programmer to set the container's capacity to an explicit value.[3] For example:

```
int main {
    vector< string > svec;
    svec.reserve( 32 ); // sets capacity to 32
    // ...
}
```

results in svec having a size of zero elements but a capacity of 32. What we found by experimentation, however, is that adjusting the capacity of a vector with a default capacity other than 1 seemed to always cause the performance to degrade. For example, with both the string and the double vectors, increasing the capacity through reserve()

---

3. Note that a deque does not support reserve().

resulted in a worse performance. On the other hand, increasing the capacity of a large, complex class provided significant performance improvement, as shown in Table 6.4.

Table 6.4   Time in Seconds to Insert 10,000 Elements with Adjustments to Capacity*

Capacity	Time in Seconds
default of 1	6.70
4,096	5.55
8,192	4.44
10,000	2.22
*Nonsimple class: 8,000 bytes with both a copy constructor and a destructor	

For our text query system, then, we'll use a vector to contain our string object with its default associated capacity. Although the vector grows dynamically as we insert an unknown number of strings within it, as our timings show, it still performs slightly better than a list. Before we get to our actual implementation, let's review how we can define a container object.

Exercise 6.2

Explain the difference between a vector's capacity and its size. Why is it necessary to support the notion of capacity in a container that stores elements contiguously but not, for example, in a list?

Exercise 6.3

Why is it more efficient to store a collection of a large, complex class objects by pointer but less efficient to store a collection of integer objects by pointer?

Exercise 6.4

In the following situations, which is the more appropriate container type, a list or a vector? In each case, an unknown number of elements are inserted. Explain your answer.

```
(a) Integer values
(b) Pointers to a large, complex class object
(c) Large, complex class objects
```

6.4   Defining a Sequence Container

To define a container object, we must first include its associated header file, which is one of these:

```
#include <vector>
#include <list>
```

```
#include <deque>
#include <map>
#include <set>
```

The definition of a container object begins with the name of the container type followed by the actual type of the elements to be contained.[3] For example:

```
vector< string > svec;
list< int >      ilist;
```

defines `svec` to be an empty vector of string objects and `ilist` to be an empty list of objects of type `int`. Both `svec` and `ilist` are empty. To confirm that, we can invoke the `empty()` operator. For example:

```
if ( svec.empty() != true )
     ; // oops, something wrong
```

The simplest method of element insertion is `push_back()`, which inserts the element to the back of the container. For example,

```
string text_word;
while ( cin >> text_word )
        svec.push_back( text_word );
```

reads one string at a time into `text_word` from standard input. `push_back()` then inserts a copy of the `text_word` string into `svec`. The list (and deque) containers also support `push_front()`, which inserts the new element at the front of the list. For example, suppose we have the following built-in array of type `int`:

```
int ia[ 4 ] = { 0, 1, 2, 3 };
```

The use of `push_back()`

```
for ( int ix = 0; ix < 4; ++ix )
     ilist.push_back( ia[ ix ] );
```

creates the sequence 0,1,2,3, whereas the use of `push_front()`

```
for ( int ix = 0; ix < 4; ++ix )
     ilist.push_front( ia[ ix ] );
```

---

3. Implementations that do not currently support default template parameters require a second argument specifying the *allocator*. Under these implementations, the above two definitions are declared as follows:

```
vector< string, allocator > svec;
list< int, allocator >      ilist;
```

The allocator class encapsulates the abstraction of allocating and deleting dynamic memory. It is predefined by the standard library and uses the new and delete operators. The use of an allocation class serves two purposes: by shielding the containers from the details of this or that memory allocation strategy, it simplifies the implementation of the container. Secondly, it is possible for the programmer to implement and/or specify alternative memory allocation strategies, such as the use of shared memory.

creates the sequence 3,2,1,0 within ilist.[4]

Alternatively, we may wish to specify an explicit size for the container. The size can be either a constant or nonconstant expression:

```
#include <list>
#include <vector>
#include <string>

extern int get_word_count( string file_name );
const int list_size = 64;

list< int > ilist( list_size );
vector< string > svec(get_word_count(string("Chimera")));
```

Each element within the container is initialized with the associated default value for its type. For an integer, a default value of 0 is used to initialize each element. For the string class, each element is initialized with the associated string default constructor.

Rather than initialize each element to its associated default value, we can specify a value with which to initialize each element. For example:

```
list< int > ilist( list_size, -1 );
vector< string > svec( 24, "pooh" );
```

In addition to providing an initial size, we can physically resize the container through the resize() operation. For example, when we write

```
svec.resize( 2 * svec.size() );
```

we double the current size of svec. Each new element is initialized with the default value associated with the underlying type of the element. If we wish to initialize each new element to some other value, we can specify that value as a second argument:

```
// initialize each new element to "piglet"
svec.resize( 2 * svec.size(), "piglet" );
```

By the way, what is the capacity of the original definition of svec? It has an initial size of 24 elements. What is its likely initial capacity? That's right — svec has a capacity of 24 as well. In general, the minimum capacity of a vector is its current size. When we double the size of a vector, in general we double its capacity.

We can also initialize a new container object with a copy of an existing container object. For example:

```
vector< string > svec2( svec );
list< int >      ilist2( ilist );
```

---

4. If element insertion at the front becomes the predominant container activity, a deque performs significantly more efficiently than a vector and should be preferred.

Each container supports a set of relational operators against which two containers can be compared: equality, inequality, less-than, greater-than, less-than-or-equal, and greater-than-or-equal. The comparison is based on a pairwise comparison of the elements of the two containers. If all the elements are equal and if both containers contain the same number of elements, the two containers are equal; otherwise, they are unequal. A comparison of the first unequal element determines the less-than or greater-than relationship of the two containers. For example, here is the output of a program comparing five vectors:

```
ivec1: 1 3 5 7 9 12
ivec2: 0 1 1 2 3 5 8 13
ivec3: 1 3 9
ivec4: 1 3 5 7
ivec5: 2 4

// first unequal element: 1, 0
// ivec1 greater than ivec2
ivec1 < ivec2 //false
ivec2 < ivec1 //true

// first unequal element 5, 9
ivec1 < ivec3 //true

// all elements equal but ivec4 has fewer elements
// so ivec4 is less than ivec1
ivec1 < ivec4 //false

// first unequal element: 1, 2
ivec1 < ivec5 //true

ivec1 == ivec1 //true
ivec1 == ivec4 //false
ivec1 != ivec4 //true

ivec1 > ivec2 //true
ivec3 > ivec1 //true
ivec5 > ivec2 //true
```

There are three constraints as to the types of containers that we can define (in practice, they pertain only to user-defined class types).

- The element type must support the equality operator.
- The element type must support the less-than operator (all the relational operators discussed earlier are implemented using these two operators).
- The element type must support a default value (again, for a class type, this is spoken of as a default constructor).

All the predefined data types, including pointers, meet these constraints, as do all the class types provided by the C++ standard library.

Exercise 6.5

Explain what the following program does:

```
#include <string>
#include <vector>
#include <iostream>

int main()
{
    vector<string> svec;
    svec.reserve( 1024 );

    string text_word;
    while ( cin >> text_word )
            svec.push_back( text_word );

    svec.resize( svec.size()+svec.size()/2 );
    // ...
}
```

Exercise 6.6

Can a container have a capacity less than its size? Is a capacity equal to its size desirable? Initially? After an element is inserted? Why or why not?

Exercise 6.7

In Exercise 6.5, if the program reads 256 words, what is its likely capacity after it is resized? If it reads 512? 1,000? 1,048?

Exercise 6.8

Given the following class definitions, which cannot be used for defining a vector?

```
(a) class cl1 {                    (b) class cl2 {
    public:                            public:
        cl1( int=0 );                      cl2( int=0 );
        bool operator==();                 bool operator!=();
        bool operator!=();                 bool operator<=();
        bool operator<=();                 // ...
        bool operator<();              };
        // ...
    };
```

```
(c) class cl3 {                  (d) class cl4 {
        public:                          public:
            int ival;                        cl4( int, int=0 );
    };                                       bool operator==();
                                             bool operator==();
                                             // ...
                                     };
```

6.5   Iterators

An iterator provides a general method of successively accessing each element within any of the sequential or associative container types. For example, let iter be an iterator into any container type. Then

```
++iter;
```

advances the iterator to address the next element of the container, and

```
*iter;
```

returns the value of the element addressed by the iterator.

Each container type provides both a begin() and an end() member function.

- begin() returns an iterator that addresses the first element of the container.

- end() returns an iterator that addresses 1 past the last element of the container.

To iterate over the elements of any container type, we write

```
for ( iter = container.begin();
      iter != container.end(); ++iter )
          do_something_with_element( *iter );
```

The definition of an iterator can look somewhat intimidating because of the template and nested class syntax. For example, here is the definition of a pair of iterators to a vector of string elements:

```
// vector<string> vec;
vector<string>::iterator iter = vec.begin();
vector<string>::iterator iter_end = vec.end();
```

iterator is a typedef defined within the vector class. The syntax

```
vector<string>::iterator
```

references the iterator typedef nested in the vector class holding elements of type string.

To print each string element to standard output, we write

```
for( ; iter != iter_end; ++iter )
        cout << *iter << '\n';
```

Where, of course, *iter evaluates to the actual string object.

In addition to the *iterator* type, each container defines a *const_iterator* type. The latter is necessary in order to traverse a `const` container. A const_iterator permits read-only access of the underlying elements of the container. For example:

```
#include <vector >
void even_odd( const vector<int> *pvec,
               vector<int> *pvec_even,
               vector<int> *pvec_odd )
{
    // must declare a const_iterator to traverse pvec
    vector<int>::const_iterator c_iter = pvec->begin();
    vector<int>::const_iterator c_iter_end = pvec->end();

    for ( ; c_iter != c_iter_end; ++c_iter )
         if ( *c_iter % 2 )
              pvec_odd->push_back( *c_iter );
         else pvec_even->push_back( *c_iter );
}
```

Finally, what if we wish to look at some subset of the elements — perhaps every other element or every third element — or to begin stepping through the elements starting from the middle? We can offset from an iterator's current position using scalar arithmetic. For example:

```
vector<int>::iterator iter = vec.begin()+vec.size()/2;
```

sets `iter` to address the middle element of vec, whereas

```
iter += 2;
```

advances `iter` two elements.

Iterator arithmetic works only with a vector and a deque and not with a list because the list elements are not stored contiguously in memory. For example,

```
ilist.begin() + 2;
```

is not correct because advancing two elements in a list requires following the internal *next* pointer twice. With a vector or deque, advancing two elements requires adding the size of two elements to the current address value (Section 3.3 provides a discussion of pointer arithmetic).

A container object can also be initialized with a pair of iterators marking the first and 1 past the last element to be copied. For example, suppose we have this:

```
#include <vector>
#include <string>
#include <iostream>

int main()
{
    vector<string> svec;
    string intext;
```

```
        while ( cin >> intext )
                svec.push_back( intext );

        // process svec ...
    }
```

We can define a new vector to copy all or a subset of the elements of svec:

```
    int main()
    {
       vector<string> svec;
       // ...

       // initialize svec2 with all of svec
       vector<string> svec2( svec.begin(), svec.end() );

       // initialize svec3 with first half of svec
       vector<string>::iterator it =
                     svec.begin() + svec.size()/2;
       vector<string>  svec3( svec.begin(), it );

       // process vectors ...

    }
```

Using the special istream_iterator type (discussed in detail in Section 12.4.3), we can more directly insert the text elements into svec:

```
    #include <vector>
    #include <string>
    #include < iterator >

    int main()
    {
       // input stream iterator tied to standard input
       istream_iterator<string> infile( cin );

       // input stream iterator marking end-of-stream
       istream_iterator<string> eos;

       // initialize svec with values entered through cin;
       vector<string> svec( infile, eos );

       // process svec
    }
```

In addition to a pair of iterators, two pointers into a built-in array can be used as element range markers. For example, suppose we have the following array of string objects:

```
#include <string>
string words[4] = {
        "stately", "plump", "buck", "mulligan"
};
```

We can initialize a vector of string by passing a pointer to the first element of the words array, and a second pointer *1 past* the last string element:

```
vector< string > vwords( words, words+4 );
```

The second pointer serves as a stopping condition; the object it addresses (usually 1 past the last object within a container or array) is not included in the elements to be copied or traversed.

Similarly, we can initialize a list of int elements as follows:

```
int ia[6] = { 0, 1, 2, 3, 4, 5 };
list< int > ilist( ia, ia+6 );
```

In Section 12.4, we revisit iterators in a bit more detail. For now, we've introduced iterators sufficiently to use them in our text query system implementation. But before we turn to that, we need to review some additional operations supported by the container types.

Exercise 6.9

Which, if any, of the following iterator uses are in error?

```
const vector< int > ivec;
vector< string >    svec;
list< int >         ilist;

(a) vector<int>::iterator     it = ivec.begin();
(b) list<int>::iterator       it = ilist.begin()+2;
(c) vector<string>::iterator it = &svec[0];
(d) for ( vector<string>::iterator
          it = svec.begin(); it != 0; ++it )
                // ...
```

Exercise 6.10

Which, if any, of the following iterator uses are in error?

```
int ia[7] = { 0, 1, 1, 2, 3, 5, 8 };
string sa[6] = {
    "Fort Sumter", "Manassas", "Perryville", "Vicksburg",
    "Meridian", "Chancellorsville" };

(a) vector<string> svec( sa, &sa[6] );
(b) list<int> ilist( ia+4, ia+6 );
(c) list<int> ilist2( ilist.begin(), ilist.begin()+2 );
(d) vector<int> ivec( &ia[0], ia+8 );
```

```
(e) list<string> slist( sa+6, sa );
(f) vector<string> svec2( sa, sa+6 );
```

6.6   Sequence Container Operations

The push_back() method provides a convenient shorthand notation for inserting a single element at the end of a sequence container. But what if we wish to insert an element at some other position within the container? Or if we wish to insert a sequence of elements at the end or at some other position within the container? In these cases, we would use the more general set of insertion methods.

For example, to insert an element at the beginning of a container, we would do the following:

```
vector< string > svec;
list< string > slist;
string spouse( "Beth" );

slist.insert( slist.begin(), spouse );
svec.insert(  svec.begin(), spouse  );
```

Here, the first argument to insert() is the position (an iterator addressing some position within the container), and the second argument to insert() is the value to be inserted. The value is inserted in front of the position addressed by the iterator. A more random insertion might be programmed as follows:

```
string son( "Danny" );

list<string>::iterator iter;
iter = find( slist.begin(), slist.end(), son );

slist.insert( iter, spouse );
```

Here, find() either returns the position within the container at which the element is found or else returns the end() iterator of the container to indicate that the search failed. (We'll come back to find() at the end of the next section.) As you might have guessed, the push_back() method is a shorthand notation for the following call:

```
// equivalent to: slist.push_back( value );
slist.insert( slist.end(), value );
```

A second form of the insert() method supports inserting a specified count of elements at some position. For example, if we wished to insert ten *Anna*s at the beginning of a vector, we would do the following:

```
vector<string> svec;
...
string anna( "Anna" );
svec.insert( svec.begin(), 10, anna );
```

The final form of the `insert()` method supports inserting a range of elements into the container. For example, given the following array of strings

```
string sarray[4] = { "quasi", "simba", "frollo", "scar" };
```

we can insert all or a subset of the array elements into our string vector:

```
svec.insert( svec.begin(), sarray, sarray+4 );
svec.insert( svec.begin() + svec.size()/2,
             sarray+2, sarray+4);
```

Alternatively, we can mark a range of values to insert through a pair of iterators, either of another vector of string elements:

```
// insert the elements contained within svec
// beginning in the middle of svec_two
svec_two.insert( svec_two.begin() + svec_two.size()/2,
                 svec.begin(), svec.end() );
```

or, more generally, any container of string objects: [6]

```
list< string > slist;

// ...

// insert the elements contained within svec
// in front of stringVal's location within slist
list< string >::iterator iter =
     find( slist.begin(), slist.end(), stringVal );
slist.insert( iter, svec.begin(), svec.end() );
```

6.6.1   Deletion

The general form of element deletion within a container is a pair of `erase()` methods: one to delete a single element and the second to delete a range of elements marked by a pair of iterators. A shorthand method of deleting the last element of a container is supported by the `pop_back()` method.

For example, to delete a specific element within the container, you simply invoke `erase()` with an iterator indicating its position. In the following code fragment, we use the generic `find()` algorithm to retrieve the iterator to the element we wish to delete and, if the element is present within the list, pass its position to `erase()`.

```
string searchValue( "Quasimodo" );
list< string >::iterator iter =
     find( slist.begin(), slist.end(), searchValue );
```

---

6. This last form requires that your compiler support template member functions. If your compiler does not as yet support this feature of Standard C++, then the two container objects must be of the same type, such as two vectors or two lists holding the same element type.

```
if ( iter != slist.end() )
    slist.erase( iter );
```

To delete all the elements in a container or a subset marked by a pair of iterators, we can do the following:

```
// delete all the elements within the container
slist.erase( slist.begin(), slist.end() );

// delete the range of elements marked by iterators
list< string >::iterator first, last;

first = find( slist.begin(), slist.end(), val1 );
last  = find( slist.begin(), slist.end(), val2 );

// ... check validity of first and last

slist.erase( first, last );
```

Finally, complementing the push_back() method that inserts an element at the end of a container, the pop_back() method deletes the last element of a container — it does not return the element, however; it simply removes it. For example:

```
vector< string >::iterator iter = buffer.begin();
for ( ; iter != buffer.end(); iter++ )
{
    slist.push_back( *iter );
    if ( ! do_something( slist ))
        slist.pop_back();
}
```

6.6.2   Assignment and Swap

What happens when we assign one container to another? The assignment operator copies the elements of the right-hand container object into the left-hand container in turn using the assignment operator of the element type of the container. What if the two containers are of unequal size? For example:

```
// slist1 contains 10 elements
// slist2 contains 24 elements
// after assignment, both hold 24 elements
slist1 = slist2;
```

The target of the assignment, slist1 in our example, now holds the same number of elements as the container from which the elements are copied (slist2 in our example). The previous ten elements contained within slist1 are erased. (In the case of slist1, the string destructor is applied to each of the ten string elements.)

swap() can be thought of as the complement to the assignment operator. When we write

```
slist1.swap( slist2 );
```

slist1 now contains 24 string elements that were copied using the string assignment operator the same as if we had written

```
slist1 = slist2;
```

The difference is that slist2 now contains a copy of the ten elements originally contained within slist1. Once again, if the sizes of the two containers are not the same, the container is resized to reflect the size of the container whose elements are being copied within it.

6.6.3   The Generic Algorithms

Those operations described in the previous sections are essentially all the operations a vector and deque container provide. Admittedly, that's a pretty thin interface, and it omits basic operations such as find(), sort(), merge(), and so on. Conceptually, the idea is to factor the operations common to all container types into a collection of generic algorithms that can be applied to all the container types as well as to the built-in array type. (The generic algorithms are discussed in detail in Chapter 12 and the Appendix.) The generic algorithms are bound to a particular container through an iterator pair. For example, here is how we invoke the generic find() algorithm on a list, vector, and array of differing types:

```
#include <list>
#include <vector>

int ia[ 6 ] = { 0, 1, 2, 3, 4, 5 };
vector<string> svec;
list<double> dlist;

// the associated header file
#include <algorithm>

vector<string>::iterator viter;
list<double>::iterator liter;
int *pia;

// find() returns an iterator to element, if found
// in case of array, returns a pointer ...
pia =   find( &ia[0], &ia[6], some_int_value );
liter = find( dlist.begin(), dlist.end(), some_double_value );
viter = find( svec.begin(),  svec.end(),  some_string_value );
```

The list container type provides additional operations, such as merge() and sort(), because it does not support random access into its elements. These are discussed in Section 12.6. Now let's turn to our text query system.

Exercise 6.11

Write a program that accepts the following definitions:

```
int ia[]  = { 1, 5, 34 };
int ia2[] = { 1, 2, 3 };
int ia3[] = { 6, 13, 21, 29, 38, 55, 67, 89 };
vector<int> ivec;
```

Using the various insertion operations and the appropriate values of ia2 and ia3, modify ivec to hold the sequence

```
{ 0, 1, 1, 2, 3, 5, 8, 13, 21, 55, 89 }
```

Exercise 6.12

Write a program that accepts the following definitions:

```
int ia[] = { 0, 1, 1, 2, 3, 5, 8, 13, 21, 55, 89 };
list<int> ilist( ia, ia+11 );
```

Using the single iterator form of erase(), remove all the odd-numbered elements in ilist.

6.7   Storing Lines of Text

Our first task is to read the text file against which our users wish to query. We'll need to retrieve the following information: each word, of course, but in addition the location of each word — that is, which line it is in and its position within that line. Moreover, we must preserve the text by line number in order to display the lines of text matching a query.

How will we retrieve each line of text? The standard library supports a getline() function declared as follows:

```
istream&
getline( istream &is, string str, char delimiter );
```

getline() reads the istream, inserting the characters, including white space, into the string object until either the delimiter is encountered, the end-of-file occurs, or the sequence of characters read equals the max_size() value of the string object, at which point the read operation fails.

Following each call of getline(), we'll insert str into the vector of strings representing the text. Here is the general implementation.[7] We've factored it into a function

---

7. It is compiled under an implementation that does not support default template parameter values, so we are required to explicitly provide an allocator:
```
vector< string, allocator > *lines_of_text;
```
In a fully compliant Standard C++ implementation, we need only specify the element type:
```
vector< string > *lines_of_text;
```

we've named `retrieve_text()`. To add to the information collected, we've defined a pair of values to store the line number and the length of the longest line. (The full program is listed in Section 6.14.)

```cpp
// return value is a pointer to our string vector
vector<string,allocator>*
retrieve_text()
{
    string file_name;

    cout << "please enter file name: ";
    cin  >> file_name;

    // open text file for input ...
    ifstream infile( file_name.c_str(), ios::in );
    if ( ! infile ) {
        cerr << "oops! unable to open file "
             << file_name << " -- bailing out!\n";
        exit( -1 );
    }
    else cout << '\n';

    vector<string, allocator> *lines_of_text =
                  new vector<string,allocator>;
    string textline;

    typedef pair<string::size_type, int> stats;
    stats maxline;
    int   linenum = 0;

    while ( getline( infile, textline, '\n' )) {
            cout << "line read: " << textline << '\n';

            if ( maxline.first < textline.size() ) {
                maxline.first = textline.size();
                maxline.second = linenum;
            }

            lines_of_text->push_back( textline );
            linenum++;
    }

    return lines_of_text;
}
```

The output of the program looks like this. (Unfortunately, the lines wrap around due to the size of the text page. We've manually indented the second line to improve readability.)

```
please enter file name: alice_emma

line read: Alice Emma has long flowing red hair. Her Daddy says
line read: when the wind blows through her hair, it looks almost
           alive,
line read: like a fiery bird in flight. A beautiful fiery bird, he
           tells her,
line read: magical but untamed. "Daddy, shush, there is no such
           thing,"
line read: she tells him, at the same time wanting him to tell her
           more.
line read: Shyly, she asks, "I mean, Daddy, is there?"

number of lines: 6
maximum length: 66
longest line: like a fiery bird in flight. A beautiful fiery bird,
              he tells her,
```

Now that each text line is stored as a string, we need to break each line into its individual words. For each word, we'll first strip out punctuation. For example, consider this line from the *Anna Livia Plurrabelle* section of *Finnegans Wake*.

```
"For every tale there's a telling,
and that's the he and she of it."
```

It yields the following individual strings with embedded punctuation:

```
"For
there's
telling,
that's
it."
```

These strings need to become

```
For
there
telling
that
it
```

One could argue that

```
there's
```

should become

```
there is
```

but in fact we're going in the other direction: we'll discard semantically neutral words such as *is, that, and, it, the,* and so on. So for our active word set against which to query, of our line from *Finnegans Wake*, only

```
tale
telling
```

are entered. (We'll implement this using a word exclusion set, which we discuss in detail in the later section on the set container type.)

In addition to removing punctuation, we'll need to strip out capitalization and provide some minimal handling of suffixing. Capitalization becomes a problem as in the following pair of text lines:

```
Home is where the heart is.
A home is where they have to let you in.
```

Clearly, a query on home needs to find both entries.

Suffixing solves the more complicated problem of recognizing, for example, that *dog* and *dogs* represent the same noun, and that *love, loves, loving,* and *loved* represent the same verb.

Our purpose in the following sections is to revisit the standard library string class, exercising its extensive collection of string manipulation operations. Along the way, we will further develop our text query system.

6.8   Finding a Substring

Our first task is to separate the string representing the line of text into its individual words. We'll do this by finding each embedded blank space. For example, given

```
Alice Emma has long flowing red hair.
```

by marking the six embedded blank spaces, we can identify the seven substrings representing the actual words of the line of text. To do this, we use one of the find() functions supported by the string class.

The string class provides a collection of search functions, each one named as a variant of *find*. find() is the most straightforward instance: given a string, it either returns the index position of the first character of the matching substring or returns the special value

```
string::npos
```

indicating no match. For example:

```
#include <string>
#include <iostream>

int main() {
    string name( "AnnaBelle" );
    int pos = name.find( "Anna" );
    if ( pos == string::npos )
        cout << "Anna not found!\n";
    else cout << "Anna found at pos: " << pos << endl;
}
```

Although the type of the index returned is almost always of type int, a more strictly portable and correct declaration uses

```
string::size_type
```

to hold the index value returned from find(). For example:

```
string::size_type pos = name.find( "Anna" );
```

find() does not provide us with the exact functionality we need; find_first_of(), however, provides it. find_first_of() returns the index position of the first character of the string that matches any character of a search string. For example, the following locates the first numeric value within a string:

```
#include <string>
#include <iostream>

int main() {
    string numerics( "0123456789" );
    string name( "r2d2" );

    string::size_type pos = name.find_first_of( numerics );
    cout << "found numeric at index: "
         << pos        << "\telement is "
         << name[pos] << endl;
}
```

In this example, pos is set to a value of 1 (the elements of a string, remember, are indexed beginning at 0).

However, this still does not do quite what we need. We need to find all occurrences in sequence and not just the first occurrence. We can do this by providing a second argument indicating the index position within the string to start our search. Here is a rewrite of our search of "r2d2". It is still not quite right, however. Do you see what is wrong?

```
#include <string>
#include <iostream>

int main() {
    string numerics( "0123456789" );
    string name( "r2d2" );

    string::size_type pos = 0;

    // something wrong with implementation!
    while (( pos = name.find_first_of( numerics, pos ))
              != string::npos )
           cout << "found numeric at index: "
                << pos        << "\telement is "
                << name[pos] << endl;
}
```

pos begins the loop initialized to 0. The string is searched beginning at position 0. A match occurs at index 1. pos is assigned that value. Because it is not equal to npos, the body of the loop is executed. A second find_first_of() executes with pos set to 1. Oops! Position 1 matches a second, third, and fourth time, and so on: we've programmed ourselves into an infinite loop. We need to increment pos 1 past the element found prior to each subsequent iteration of the loop:

```
// ok: corrected loop iteration
while (( pos = name.find_first_of( numerics, pos ))
              != string::npos )
{
        cout << "found numeric at index: "
             << pos        << "\telement is "
             << name[pos] << endl;

        // move 1 past element found
        ++pos;
}
```

To find the embedded white space within our line of text, we simply replace numerics with a string containing the possible white space characters we might encounter. However, if we are certain that only a blank space is used, we can explicitly supply a single character. For example:

```
// program fragment
while (( pos = textline.find_first_of( ' ', pos ))
           != string::npos )
        // ...
```

To mark the length of each word, we introduce a second positional object, as follows:

```
// program fragment

// pos: index 1 past word
// prev_pos: index beginning of word

string::size_type pos = 0, prev_pos = 0;

while (( pos = textline.find_first_of( ' ', pos ))
              != string::npos )
{
        // do something with string
        // now adjust positional markers
        prev_pos = ++pos;
}
```

For each iteration of our loop, prev_pos indexes the beginning of the word, and pos holds the index 1 *past* the end of the word (the position of the space). The length of each identified word, then, is marked by the expression

```
pos - prev_pos; // marks length of word
```

Now that we've identified the word, we need to copy it and then tuck it away in a string vector. One strategy for copying the word is to loop through `textline` from `prev_pos` to 1 less than `pos`, copying each character in turn, in effect extracting the substring marked by the two indexes. Rather than do that ourselves, however, the `substr()` string operation does it:

```
// program fragment
vector<string> words;

while (( pos = textline.find_first_of( ' ', pos ))
            != string::npos )
{
        words.push_back( textline.substr(
                            prev_pos, pos-prev_pos));
        prev_pos = ++pos;
}
```

The `substr()` operation generates a copy of a substring of an existing string object. Its first argument indicates the start position within the string. The optional second argument indicates the length of the substring (if we omit the second argument, the remainder of the string is copied).

There is one bug with our implementation: it fails to insert the last word of each line of text. Do you see why? Consider the line

```
seaspawn and seawrack
```

The first two words are marked by a blank space. The positions of the two blank spaces are returned in turn by the two invocations of `find_first_of()`. The third invocation, however, does not find a blank space; it sets `pos` to `string::npos`, terminating the loop. Processing of the final word, then, must follow termination of the loop.

Here is the full implementation, localized in a function we've named `separate_words()`. In addition to storing each word within a string vector, we've calculated the line and column position of each word. (We'll need this information later in support of positional text query.)

```
typedef pair<short,short> location;
typedef vector<location>  loc;
typedef vector<string>    text;
typedef pair<text*,loc*>  text_loc;

text_loc*
separate_words( const vector<string> *text_file )
{
    // words: holds the collection of individual words
    // locations: holds the associated line/col information
    vector<string>   *words = new vector<string>;
    vector<location> *locations = new vector<location>;
```

```
short line_pos = 0; // current line number

// iterate through each line of text
for ( ; line_pos < text_file->size(); ++line_pos )
{
    // textline: current line of text to process
    // word_pos: current column position within textline
    short  word_pos = 0;
    string textline = (*text_file)[ line_pos ];

    string::size_type pos = 0, prev_pos = 0;

    while (( pos = textline.find_first_of( ' ', pos ))
                != string::npos )
    {
        // store a copy of the current word substring
        words->push_back(
               textline.substr( prev_pos, pos - prev_pos ));

        // store the line/col info as a pair
        locations->push_back(
               make_pair( line_pos, word_pos ));

        // update position information for next iteration
        ++word_pos; prev_pos = ++pos;
    }

    // now handle last word of line
    words->push_back(
           textline.substr( prev_pos, pos - prev_pos ));

    locations->push_back(
               make_pair( line_pos, word_pos ));

}

    return new text_loc( words, locations );
}
```

The flow of control for our program thus far is as follows:

```
int main()
{
    vector<string> *text_file = retrieve_text();
    text_loc *text_locations  = separate_words( text_file );
    // ...
}
```

A partial trace of separate_words() on our input text_file looks like this:

```
textline: Alice Emma has long flowing red hair. Her Daddy says

eol: 52 pos: 5 line: 0 word: 0 substring: Alice
eol: 52 pos: 10 line: 0 word: 1 substring: Emma
eol: 52 pos: 14 line: 0 word: 2 substring: has
eol: 52 pos: 19 line: 0 word: 3 substring: long
eol: 52 pos: 27 line: 0 word: 4 substring: flowing
eol: 52 pos: 31 line: 0 word: 5 substring: red
eol: 52 pos: 37 line: 0 word: 6 substring: hair.
eol: 52 pos: 41 line: 0 word: 7 substring: Her
eol: 52 pos: 47 line: 0 word: 8 substring: Daddy
last word on line substring: says

    ...

textline: magical but untamed. "Daddy, shush, there is no such thing,"
eol: 60 pos: 7 line: 3 word: 0 substring: magical
eol: 60 pos: 11 line: 3 word: 1 substring: but
eol: 60 pos: 20 line: 3 word: 2 substring: untamed.
eol: 60 pos: 28 line: 3 word: 3 substring: "Daddy,
eol: 60 pos: 35 line: 3 word: 4 substring: shush,
eol: 60 pos: 41 line: 3 word: 5 substring: there
eol: 60 pos: 44 line: 3 word: 6 substring: is
eol: 60 pos: 47 line: 3 word: 7 substring: no
eol: 60 pos: 52 line: 3 word: 8 substring: such
last word on line substring: thing,"

    ...

textline: Shyly, she asks, "I mean, Daddy, is there?"
eol: 43 pos: 6 line: 5 word: 0 substring: Shyly,
eol: 43 pos: 10 line: 5 word: 1 substring: she
eol: 43 pos: 16 line: 5 word: 2 substring: asks,
eol: 43 pos: 19 line: 5 word: 3 substring: "I
eol: 43 pos: 25 line: 5 word: 4 substring: mean,
eol: 43 pos: 32 line: 5 word: 5 substring: Daddy,
eol: 43 pos: 35 line: 5 word: 6 substring: is
last word on line substring: there?"
```

Before we add to our set of text query routines, let's briefly cover the remaining search functions supported by the string class. In addition to find() and find_first_of(), the string class supports several other find operations: rfind() searches for the last — that is, rightmost — occurrence of the indicated substring. For example:

```
string river( "Mississippi" );

string::size_type first_pos = river.find( "is" );
string::size_type last_pos = river.rfind( "is" );
```

`find()` returns an index of 1, indicating the start of the first `"is"`, while `rfind()` returns an index of 4, indicating the start of the last occurrence of `"is"`.

`find_first_not_of()` searches for the first character of the string that does not match any element of the search string. For example, to find the first non-numeric character of a string, we can write

```
string elems( "0123456789" );
string dept_code( "03714p3" );

// returns index to the character 'p'
string::size_type pos = dept_code.find_first_not_of(elems);
```

`find_last_of()` searches for the last character of the string that matches any element of the search string. `find_last_not_of()` searches for the last character of the string that does not match any element of the search string. Each of these operations takes an optional second argument indicating the position within the string to begin searching.

Exercise 6.13

Write a program that, given the string
```
"ab2c3d7R4E6"
```
finds each numeric character and then each alphabet character first using `find_first_of()` and then `find_first_not_of()`.

Exercise 6.14

Write a program that, given the string
```
string line1 = "We were her pride of 10 she named us --";
string line2 = "Benjamin, Phoenix, the Prodigal";
string line3 = "and perspicacious pacific Suzanne";

string sentence = line1 + ' ' + line2 + ' ' + line3;
```
counts the number of words in the sentence and identifies the largest and smallest words. If more than one word is either the largest or smallest, keep track of all of them.

6.9   Handling Punctuation

Now that we've separated each line of text into individual words, we need to remove any punctuation that may have stuck to the word. For example, the following line
```
magical but untamed. "Daddy, shush, there is no such thing,"
```
separates as follows:
```
magical
but
untamed.
```

```
"Daddy,
shush,
there
is
no
such
thing,"
```

How can we remove the unwanted punctuation? First, we'll define a string with all the punctuation elements we wish to remove:

```
string filt_elems( "\",.;:!?)(\\/" );
```

(The \" and \\ sequences indicate that the quotation mark in the first sequence and the second backslash in the second sequence are to be treated as literal elements within the quoted string and not as the end of the string or as the continuation character to the next line.)

Next, we'll use the find_first_of() operation to find each matching element, if any, within our string:

```
while (( pos = word.find_first_of( filt_elems, pos ))
              != string::npos )
```

Finally, we need to erase() the punctuation character from the string:

```
word.erase(pos,1);
```

The first argument to this version of the erase() operation indicates the position within the string to begin removing characters. An optional second argument indicates the number of characters to delete. In our example, we are deleting the one character located at pos. If we omit the second argument, erase() removes all the characters from pos to the end of the string.

Here is the full listing of filter_text(). It takes two arguments: a pointer to our string vector containing the text, and a string object containing the elements to filter.

```
void
filter_text( vector<string> *words, string filter )
{
    vector<string>::iterator iter = words->begin();
    vector<string>::iterator iter_end = words->end();

    // if no filter is provided by user, default to a minimal set
    if ( ! filter.size() )
        filter.insert( 0, "\".," );

    while ( iter != iter_end ) {
            string::size_type pos = 0;

            // for each element found, erase it
            while (( pos = (*iter).find_first_of( filter, pos ))
```

```
                               != string::npos )
                        (*iter).erase(pos,1);
               iter++;
       }
   }
```

Do you see why we do not increment pos with each iteration of the loop? That is, do you see why the following is incorrect?

```
while (( pos = (*iter).find_first_of( filter, pos ))
              != string::npos )
{
        (*iter).erase(pos,1);
        ++pos; // not correct ...
}
```

pos represents a position within the string. For example, given the string

```
thing,"
```

the first iteration of the loop assigns pos the value 5, the position of the comma. After we remove the comma, the string becomes

```
thing"
```

Position 5 is now the double quotation mark. If we had incremented pos, we would have failed to identify and remove this punctuation character.

Here is how we invoke filter_text() within our main program:

```
string filt_elems( "\",.;:!?)(\\/" );
filter_text( text_locations->first, filt_elems );
```

And, finally, here is a sample trace of some of the strings within our text in which one or more filter elements are found:

```
filter_text: untamed.
found! : pos: 7.
after: untamed

filter_text: "Daddy,
found! : pos: 0"
after: Daddy,
found! : pos: 5,
after: Daddy

filter_text: thing,"
found! : pos: 5,
after: thing"
found! : pos: 5"
after: thing

filter_text: "I
```

```
        found! : pos: 0"
        after: I

        filter_text: Daddy,
        found! : pos: 5,
        after: Daddy

        filter_text: there?"
        found! : pos: 5?
        after: there"
        found! : pos: 5"
        after: there
```

Exercise 6.15

Write a program that, given the string

```
        "/.+(STL).*$1/"
```

erases all the characters except STL first using erase(pos,count) and then using erase(iter,iter).

Exercise 6.16

Write a program that accepts these definitions:

```
        string sentence( "kind of" );
        string s1( "whistle" );
        string s2( "pixie" );
```

Using the various insert string functions, provide sentence with the value

```
        "A whistling-dixie kind of walk."
```

6.10   A String by Any Other Format

One sort of nuisance detail of a text query system is the need to recognize the same word differing by tense, such as cry, cries, and cried, by number, such as baby and babies, and, more trivially, by capitalization, such as home and Home. The first two cases belong to the problem of word suffixing. Although the general problem of suffixing is outside the scope of this text, the following small sample solution provides a good exercise of the string class operations.

Before we turn to suffixing, however, let's first solve the simpler case of capitalization. Rather than try to be smart in recognizing special cases, we'll just replace all capital letters with their lowercase form. Our implementation looks like this:

```
        void
        strip_caps( vector<string,allocator> *words )
        {
```

```
vector<string,allocator>::iterator iter = words->begin();
vector<string,allocator>::iterator iter_end = words->end();

string caps( "ABCDEFGHIJKLMNOPQRSTUVWXYZ" );

while ( iter != iter_end ) {
        string::size_type pos = 0;
        while (( pos = (*iter).find_first_of( caps, pos ))
                    != string::npos )
            (*iter)[ pos ] = tolower( (*iter)[pos] );
        ++iter;
    }
}
```

The function

```
tolower( (*iter)[pos] );
```

is a Standard C library function that takes an uppercase character and returns its lowercase equivalent. To use it, we must include the header file

```
#include <ctype.h>
```

(This file includes declarations of other functions such as `isalpha()`, `isdigit()`, `ispunct()`, `isspace()`, `toupper()`, and others. To find a full listing and discussion, see [PLAUGER92]. The Standard C++ library defines a ctype class that encapsulates the Standard C library functionality as well as a set of nonmember functions such as `toupper()`, `tolower()`, and so on. To use them, we must include the Standard C++ header file

```
#include <locale>
```

As of this writing, however, an implementation of this support is not available to us, so we use the Standard C implementation.)

Suffixing is difficult to implement rigorously; however, even imperfect implementations yield significant improvements in the quality and size of our collection of words against which to query.

Our implementation handles only words that end in an `'s'`:

```
void
suffix_text( vector<string,allocator> *words )
{
    vector<string,allocator>::iterator
                        iter = words->begin(),
                        iter_end = words->end();

    while ( iter != iter_end ) {
            // if 3 or fewer characters, let it be
            if ( (*iter).size() <= 3 )
                { ++iter; continue; }
```

```
            if ( (*iter)[ (*iter).size()-1 ] == 's' )
                suffix_s( *iter );

            // additional suffix handling goes here such as
            // ed, ing, ly

            ++iter;
        }
    }
```

A simple heuristic is not to bother with words having fewer than four characters. This saves us from dealing with has, its, is, and so on but fails to catch, for example, tv and tvs as being the same word.

If the word ends in "ies", as in babies and cries, we need to replace the "ies" with 'y':

```
    string::size_type pos3 = word.size()-3;

    string ies( "ies" );
    if ( ! word.compare( pos3, 3, ies )) {
        word.replace( pos3, 3, 1, 'y' );
        return;
    }
```

compare() returns 0 if the two strings being compared are equal. pos3 identifies the position within word to begin the comparison. The second argument, 3 in this case, indicates the length of the substring beginning at pos3. The third argument is the actual string against which to compare. (There are actually six versions of compare(). We look at the other versions briefly in the next section.)

replace() substitutes one or more characters within a string with one or more alternative characters. In our example, we replace the three-character substring "ies" with a single repetition of the character 'y'. (There are ten overloaded instances of replace(). We'll revisit them briefly in the next section.)

Similarly, if the word ends in "ses", as in *promises* and *purposes*, we simply erase the ending "es":[8]

```
    string ses( "ses" );
    if ( ! word.compare( pos3, 3, ses )) {
        word.erase( pos3+1, 2 );
        return;
    }
```

If the word ends in "ous", as in oblivious, fulvous, and cretaceous, we do nothing. Similarly, if the word ends in "is", such as genesis, mimesis, and hepatitis, we do

---

8. There are exceptions, of course. *Crises*, for example, using our heuristic, becomes *cris*. Oops!

nothing. (This system is also not perfect, however. Kiwis, for example, requires that we drop the final 's'.) Also, if the word ends in "ius", as in genius, or in "ss", as in hiss, lateness, or less, we do nothing. To determine whether to do nothing, we use a second form of compare():

```
string::size_type spos = 0;
string::size_type pos3 = word.size()-3;

// "ous", "ss", "is", "ius"
string suffixes( "oussisius" );

if ( ! word.compare( pos3, 3, suffixes, spos, 3 ) ||      // ous
     ! word.compare( pos3, 3, suffixes, spos+6, 3 ) ||    // ius
     ! word.compare( pos3+1, 2, suffixes, spos+2, 2 ) ||  // ss
     ! word.compare( pos3+1, 2, suffixes, spos+4, 2 ))    // is
   return;
```

Otherwise, we simply drop the final 's':

```
// erase ending 's'
word.erase( pos3+2 );
```

Proper names, such as Pythagoras, Brahms, and the pre-Raphaelite painter Burne-Jones, fall outside the general rules. We'll handle them — well, we actually leave that as an exercise for the reader — when we introduce the set associative container type.

Before we turn to the map and set associative container types, we'll briefly cover some additional string operations in the next section.

Exercise 6.17

Our program does not handle suffixes ending in ed, as in surprised; ly, as in surprisingly; and ing, as in surprising. Add one of the following suffix handlers to the program: (a) suffix_ed(), (b) suffix_ly(), or (c) suffix_ing().

6.11   Additional String Operations

A second form of erase() takes a pair of iterators that mark the range of characters to be deleted. For example, given the string

```
string name( "AnnaLiviaPlurabelle" );
```

let's produce a string "Annabelle":

```
typedef string::size_type size_type;
size_type startPos = name.find( 'L' );
size_type endPos   = name.find_last_of( 'a' );

name.erase( name.begin()+startPos,
            name.begin()+endPos );
```

The character addressed by the second iterator is not part of the range of characters to be deleted. This means that we've produced Annaabelle, not Annabelle.

Finally, a third form takes an iterator that marks a character to be deleted. Let's pass it endPos to erase the second, stuttered 'a':

```
name.erase( endPos );
```

This leaves name with a string value of Annabelle.

The insert() operation supports the insertion of additional characters into the string at the indicated position. Its general form is

```
string_object.insert( position, new_string );
```

where position indicates the location within string_object in which to insert new_string. new_string can be a string, a C-style character string, or a single character. For example:

```
string string_object( "Missisippi" );
string::size_type pos = string_object.find( "isi" );
string_object.insert( pos+1, "s" );
```

The insert() operation supports marking a sub-portion of new_string. For example:

```
string new_string ( "AnnaBelle Lee" );
string_object += ' '; // append space

// find start and end position of new_string
pos = new_string.find( 'B' );
string::size_type posEnd = new_string.find( ' ' );

string_object.insert(
        string_object.size(),   // position within string_object
        new_string, pos,        // start position within new_string
        posEnd-pos              // number of characters to copy
)
```

string_object now contains the string "Mississippi Belle". If we wished to insert all of new_string starting at pos, we could omit the posEnd value.

Given the following two strings

```
string s1( "Mississippi" );
string s2( "Annabelle" );
```

From these we'd like to create a third string with the value "Miss Anna". How might we do that?

One method is to use the assign() and append() string operations. They allow us to, in turn, copy and concatenate a portion of one string object to another. For example:

```
string s3;

// copy first 4 characters of s1
s3.assign( s1, 0, 4 );
```

s3 now contains the value "Miss".

```
// concatenate a space
s3 += ' ';
```

s3 now contains the value "Miss ".

```
// concatenate the first 4 characters of s2
s3.append( s2, 0, 4 );
```

s3 now contains the value "Miss Anna". Alternatively, we can write it as

```
s3.assign( s1, 0, 4 ).append( ' ' ).append( s2, 0, 4 );
```

If we wish to extract a portion of the string that does not start at the beginning, we use an alternative form taking two integer values: a beginning position and a length. The position is counted beginning at 0. To extract "belle" from "Annabelle", for example, we specify a start position of 4 and a length of 5:

```
string beauty;

// assign "belle" to beauty
beauty.assign( s2, 4, 5 );
```

Alternatively, rather than provide a position and length, we can provide an iterator pair. For example:

```
// assign "belle" to beauty
beauty.assign( s2, s2.begin()+4, s2.end() );
```

In the following example, we have two strings representing a current and a pending task. We need to exchange them periodically as we move from one project to the other and back again. For example:

```
string current_project( "C++ Primer, 3rd Edition" );
string pending_project( "Fantasia 2000, Firebird segment" );
```

The swap() operation exchanges the values of the two strings. Each invocation of

```
current_project.swap( pending_project );
```

exchanges the string values of the two objects.

Given the string

```
string first_novel( "V" );
```

the subscript

```
char ch = first_novel[ 1 ];
```

returns an undefined character value, because the index is out of range: first_novel has a length of 1 indexed by the value 0. The subscript operator does not provide range-checking, nor do we want it to on well-behaved code, such as the following:

```
int
elem_count( const string &word, char elem )
{
    int occurs = 0;

    // well-behaved: no need to check for out-of-bounds
    for ( int ix=0; ix < word.size(); ++ix )
        if ( word[ ix ] == elem )
            ++occurs;
    return occurs;
}
```

For potentially ill-defined code, however, such as

```
void
mumble( const string &st, int index )
{
    // potential range error
    char ch = st[ index ];

    // ...
}
```

the alternative at() operation provides run-time range-checking of the index. If the index is valid, at() returns the associated character element in the same way that the subscript operator does. If the index is invalid, however, at() raises the out_of_range exception:

```
void
mumble( const string &st, int index )
{
    try {
      char ch = st.at(index);
      // ...
    }
    catch( std::out_of_range ) { ... }
    // ...
}
```

Any two strings that are not equal have a lexigraphical — that is, dictionary — ordering. For example, given the following two strings

```
string cobol_program_crash( "abend" );
string cplus_program_crash( "abort" );
```

the cobol_program_crash string object is lexigraphically less than the cplus_program_crash string object through a comparison of the first unequal character: e occurs before o in the English alphabet.

The compare() string operation provides for a lexigraphical comparison of two strings. Given

```
s1.compare( s2 );
```

`compare()` returns one of three possible values:

1. If s1 is greater than s2, `compare()` returns a positive value.
2. If s1 is less than s2, `compare()` returns a negative value.
3. If s1 is equal to s2, `compare()` returns 0.

For example:

```
cobol_program_crash.compare( cplus_program_crash );
```

returns a negative value, whereas

```
cplus_program_crash.compare( cobol_program_crash );
```

returns a positive value. The string relational operators (<,>,!=,==,<=,>=) provide an alternative shorthand notation for the `compare()` operation.

The overloaded set of six `compare()` operations allows us to mark a substring of either one or both strings for comparison. Examples are presented in the previous section in the discussion of suffixing.

`replace()` provides us with ten ways of replacing one or more existing characters within a string with one or more alternative characters (the numbers of existing and replacement characters do not need to be equal). The `replace()` operation has two primary formats, and a subset of variations is based on the method of marking the set of characters to be replaced. In one format, the first two arguments provide an index to the start position of the character set and a count of the number of characters to be replaced. In the second format, a pair of iterators is passed that marks the start position of the character set and 1 past the last character to be replaced. Here is an example of the first format:

```
string sentence(
    "An ADT provides both interface and implementation." );

string::size_type position = sentence.find_last_of( 'A' );
string::size_type length = 3;

// replace ADT with Abstract Data Type
sentence.replace( position, length, "Abstract Data Type" );
```

The first argument represents the start `position`, and the second argument represents the `length` of the string beginning with `position`; so a length of 3, and not 2, represents the string "ADT". The third argument represents the new string. There are a number of variants with which to specify the new string. For example, this variant takes a string object rather than a C-style string:

```
string new_str( "Abstract Data Type" );
sentence.replace( position, length, new_str );
```

The following variant, admittedly inefficient, inserts a subportion of the new string marked by a position and length.

```
#include <string>
typedef string::size_type size_type;

// get the position of the 3 words
size_type posA = new_str.find( 'A' );
size_type posD = new_str.find( 'D' );
size_type posT = new_str.find( 'T' );

// ok: replace T with "Type"
sentence.replace( position+2, 1, new_str, posT, 4 );

// ok: replace D with "Data "
sentence.replace( position+1, 1, new_str, posD, 5 );

// ok: replace A with "Abstract "
sentence.replace( position, 1, new_str, posA, 9 );
```

Another variant provides for the replacement of a substring with a single character repeated a specified number of times. For example:

```
string hmm( "Some celebrate Java as the successor to C++." );
string::size_type position = hmm.find( 'J' );

// ok: let's xxxx out Java
hmm.replace( position, 4, 4, 'x');
```

There is a final variant we'd like to illustrate in which we use a pointer into an array of characters and a length to mark the new string. For example:

```
const char *lang = "EiffelAda95JavaModula3";
int index[] = { 0, 6, 11, 15, 22 };

string ahhem(
        "C++ is the language for today's power programmers." );

ahhem.replace(0, 3, lang+index[1], index[2]-index[1]);
```

Here is an example of the second format in which an iterator pair is used to mark the substring targeted for replacement.

```
string sentence(
    "An ADT provides both interface and implementation." );

// points to the 'A' of ADT
string::iterator start = sentence.begin()+3;

// replace ADT with Abstract Data Type
sentence.replace( start, start+3, "Abstract Data Type" );
```

Four other variants allow the replacement string to be a string object, a character inserted N times, a pair of iterators, or a C-style string in which N characters are used as the replacement character set.

That is all we wish to say about the string operations. For more-detailed or complete information, see the C++ Standard definition [ISO-C++97]. (At the time of this writing, there is no preferred text on the Standard C++ library.)

Exercise 6.18

Write a program that accepts the following two strings:

```
string quote1( "When lilacs last in the dooryard bloom'd" );
string quote2( "The child is father of the man" );
```

Using the `assign()` and `append()` operations, create the string

```
string sentence( "The child is in the dooryard" );
```

Exercise 6.19

Write a program that, given the strings

```
string generic1( "Dear Ms Daisy:" );
string generic2( "MrsMsMissPeople" );
```

implements the function

```
string generate_salutation( string generic1,
                            string lastname,
                            string generic2,
                            string::size_type pos,
                            int length );
```

using the `replace()` operations, where `lastname` replaces `Daisy` and `pos` indexes into `generic2` of `length` characters replacing `Ms`. For example, the following

```
string lastName( "AnnaP" );
string greetings =
       generate_salutation( generic1, lastName, generic2, 5, 4 );
```

returns the string

```
Dear Miss AnnaP:
```

6.12   Building a Text Location Map

In this section, we build a collection of line and column locations for each unique word in our text to introduce and explore the map associative container type. (In the following section, we build a word exclusion set to introduce and explore the set associative container type.) In general, a set is most useful when we simply want to know whether or not a value has been seen, and a map is most useful when we wish to store (and possibly modify) an associated value. In both cases, the elements are stored in an ordered relationship to support efficient storage and retrieval.

In a map, also known as an *associative array*, we provide a key/value pair: the key serves as an index into the map, and the value serves as the data to be stored and retrieved. In our program example, each string object serves as a key, and the vector of line and column locations serves as the value. To access the location vector, we index into the map using the subscript operator. For example:

```
string query( "pickle" );
vector< location > *locat;

// returns vector<location>* associated with "pickle"
locat = text_map[ query ];
```

The map's key type — string, in our example — serves as the index. The associated location<vector>* value is returned.

To use a map, we must include its associated header file

```
#include <map>
```

The two primary activities in the use of a map (and set) are to populate it with elements and to query it as to the presence or absence of an element. In the next subsection, we look at how we define and insert key/value pairs. In the subsection after that, we look at how we discover whether an element is present and, if it is, how we retrieve its value.

6.12.1   Defining and Populating a Map

To define a map object, we must indicate, at a minimum, a key and value type. For example:

```
map<string,int> word_count;
```

defines a map object word_count that is indexed by a string and that holds an associated int value. Similarly,

```
class employee;
map<int,employee*> personnel;
```

defines a map object personnel that is indexed by an int (it represents a unique employee number) and that holds an associated pointer to an instance of class employee.

For our text query system, our map declaration is as follows:

```
typedef pair<short,short> location;
typedef vector<location>  loc;

map<string,loc*> text_map;
```

Because the compilers available to us at the time of this writing do not support default arguments for template parameters, in practice we must provide the following expanded definition:

```
map<string,loc*,    // key,value pair
    less<string>,   // relational operator for ordering
    allocator>      // default memory allocator
text_map;
```

By default, the associative container types are ordered using the less-than operator. We can always override that, however, indicating an alternative relational operator (see Section 12.3 on function objects).

Once the map is defined, the next step is to populate it with the key/value element pairs. Intuitively, what we'd like to write is the following:

```
#include <map>
#include <string>
map<string,int> word_count;

word_count[ string("Anna") ]  = 1;
word_count[ string("Danny") ] = 1;
word_count[ string("Beth") ]  = 1;

// and so on ...
```

When we write

```
word_count[ string("Anna") ] = 1;
```

the following steps take place:

1. An unnamed temporary string object initialized with "Anna" is constructed and passed to the subscript operator associated with the map class.
2. The word_count map is searched for the entry "Anna". The entry is not found.
3. A new key/value pair is inserted into word_count. The key, of course, is a string object holding the value "Anna". The value, however, is not 1, but 0.
4. The insertion done, the value is then assigned 1.

When a key is inserted into a map through the subscript operator, the associated value is initialized to the default value of the underlying element type. The default value of the built-in arithmetic types is 0.

In effect, using the subscript operator to initialize a map to a collection of elements causes each value to be initialized to a default value and then assigned the explicit value. If the elements are class objects for which the default initialization and assignment are computationally significant, the performance of our programs can be affected, although the program's correctness remains unaffected.

The preferred, if syntactically more intimidating, insertion method for a single element is the following:

```
// the preferred single element insertion method
word_count.insert(
   map<string,int>::
        value_type( string("Anna"), 1 )
);
```

The map defines a type value_type that represents its associated key/value pair. The effect of the lines

```
map< string,int >::
     value_type( string("Anna"), 1 )
```

is to create a pair object that is then directly inserted within the map. For readability, we can use a typedef:

```
typedef map<string,int>::value_type valType;
```

Using this, our insertion appears somewhat less complicated:

```
word_count.insert( valType( string("Anna"), 1 ));
```

To insert a range of key/value elements, we can use the insert() method, taking a pair of iterators. For example:

```
map< string, int > word_count;
// ... fill it up

map< string, int > word_count_two;

// insert a copy of all the key/value pairs
word_count_two.insert(word_count.begin(),word_count.end());
```

In this example, the same effect could be achieved by initializing the second map object to the first:

```
// initialize with a copy of all the key/value pairs
map< string, int > word_count_two( word_count );
```

Let's walk through how we might build our text map. separate_words(), discussed in Section 6.8, creates two vectors: a string vector of each word of the text and a location vector that holds a line and column pair of values. For each word element in the string vector, the equivalent element of the location vector provides the line and column information for that word. The string vector, that is, provides the collection of key values for our text map. The location vector provides the associated collection of values.

separate_words() returns these two vectors in a pair object that holds a pointer to each. The argument to our build_word_map() function is this pair object. The return value is the text location map — or, rather, a pointer to it:

```
// typedefs to make declarations easier
typedef pair< short,short >  location;
typedef vector< location >   loc;
typedef vector< string >     text;
typedef pair< text*,loc* >   text_loc;

extern map< string, loc* >*
          build_word_map( const text_loc *text_locations );
```

Our first prepatory steps are to allocate the empty map from the free store and to separate the string and location vectors from the pair argument passed in as the argument:

```
map<string,loc*> *word_map = new map< string, loc* >;

vector<string>   *text_words = text_locations->first;
vector<location> *text_locs  = text_locations->second;
```

Next, we need to iterate across the two vectors in parallel. There are two cases to consider:

1. The word does not yet exist within the map. In this case, we need to insert the key/value pair.
2. The word has already been inserted. In this case, we need to update the location vector of the entry with the additional line and column information.

Here is our implementation:

```
register int elem_cnt = text_words->size();
for ( int ix = 0; ix < elem_cnt; ++ix )
{
        string textword = ( *text_words )[ ix ];

        // exclusion strategies: do not enter in map
        // if fewer than 3 characters
        // or if present in the exclusion set
        if ( textword.size() < 3 ||
             exclusion_set.count( textword ))
                 continue;

        // determine whether the word is present
        // if count() returns 0, not present -- add it
        if ( ! word_map->count((*text_words)[ix] ))
        {
             loc *ploc = new vector<location>;
             ploc->push_back( (*text_locs)[ix] );
             word_map->insert( value_type( (*text_words)[ix], ploc ));
        }
        else
            // update the location vector of the entry
            (*word_map)[(*text_words)[ix]]->push_back((*text_locs)[ix]);
}
```

The syntactically complex expression

```
(*word_map)[(*text_words)[ix]]->push_back((*text_locs)[ix]);
```

is perhaps more easily understood if we decompose it into its individual components:

```
// get the word to update
string word = (*text_words)[ix];

// get the location vector
vector<location> *ploc = (*word_map)[ word ];

// get the line and column pair
location loc = (*text_locs)[ix];

// insert the new location pair
ploc->push_back(loc);
```

The remaining syntactic complexity is a result of our manipulating pointers to vectors rather than the vectors themselves. To directly apply the subscript operator, we cannot write

```
string word = text_words[ix]; // error
```

Instead, we must first dereference our pointer:

```
string word = (*text_words)[ix]; // ok
```

Finally, `build_word_map()` returns our built-in map:

```
return word_map;
```

Here is how we might invoke it within our `main()` function:

```
int main()
{
    // read in and separate the text
    vector<string,allocator> *text_file = retrieve_text();
    text_loc *text_locations = separate_words( text_file);

    // process the words
    // ...

    // build up the word/location map and invite query
    map<string,loc*,less<string>,allocator>
                *text_map = build_word_map( text_locations );

    // ...
}
```

6.12.2   Finding and Retrieving a Map Element

The subscript operator provides the simplest method of retrieving a value. For example:

```
// map<string,int> word_count;
int count = word_count[ "wrinkles" ];
```

This code behaves satisfactorily, however, only when there is an instance of the key present within the map. If the instance is not present, the use of the subscript operator causes an instance to be inserted. In this example, the key/value pair

```
string( "wrinkles" ), 0
```

is inserted into word_count and count is initialized to 0.

There are two map operations to discover whether the key element is present without its absence causing an instance to be inserted:

1. count(keyValue): count() returns the number of occurrences of keyValue within a map. (For a map, of course, the return value can be only 0 or 1.) If the return value is nonzero, we can safely use the subscript operator. For example:

    ```
    int count = 0;
    if ( word_count.count( "wrinkles" ))
        count = word_count[ "wrinkles" ];
    ```

2. find(keyValue): find() returns an iterator to the instance within the map if the instance is present or returns an iterator equal to end() if the instance is not present. For example:

    ```
    int count = 0;
    map<string,int>::iterator it = word_count.find( "wrinkles" );
    if ( it != word_count.end() )
        count = (*it).second;
    ```

The iterator to an element of a map addresses a pair object in which first holds the key and second holds the value (we'll look at this again in the next subsection).

6.12.3 Iterating across a Map

Now that we've built our map, we'd like to print its contents. We can do this by iterating across the elements marked by the begin() and end() pair of iterators. Here is our function, display_map_text(), that does just that.

```
void
display_map_text( map<string,loc*> *text_map )
{
    typedef map<string,loc*> tmap;
    tmap::iterator iter = text_map->begin(),
    iter_end = text_map->end();

    while ( iter != iter_end )
    {
            cout << "word: " << (*iter).first << " (";
```

```
                      int             loc_cnt    = 0;
                      loc             *text_locs = (*iter).second;
                      loc::iterator liter       = text_locs->begin(),
                                      liter_end = text_locs->end();

                      while ( liter != liter_end )
                      {
                              if ( loc_cnt )
                                  cout << ',';
                              else ++loc_cnt;

                              cout << '(' << (*liter).first
                                   << ',' << (*liter).second << ')';

                              ++liter;
                      }

                      cout << ")\n";
                      ++iter;
              }

          cout << endl;
      }
```

If the map is without elements, there is no point in bothering to invoke our display function. One method of discovering whether the map is empty is to invoke size():

```
      if ( text_map->size() )
          display_map_text( text_map );
```

But rather than unnecessarily counting all the elements, we can more directly invoke empty():

```
      if ( ! text_map->empty() )
          display_map_text( text_map );
```

6.12.4   A Word Transformation Map

Here is a small program to illustrate building, searching, and iterating across a map. We use two maps in our program. Our word transformation map holds two elements of type string. The key represents a word requiring special handling; the value represents the transformation we should apply whenever we encounter the word. For simplicity, we hard-code the pairs of map entries (as an exercise, you may wish to generalize the program to read pairs of word transformations from either standard input or a user-specified file). Our statistics map stores usage statistics of transformations performed. Here is our program.

```
#include <map>
#include <vector>
#include <iostream>
#include <string>

int main()
{
    map< string, string > trans_map;
    typedef map< string, string >::value_type valType;

    // a first expedient: hand-code the transformation map
    trans_map.insert( valType( "gratz", "grateful" ));
    trans_map.insert( valType( "'em",   "them"     ));
    trans_map.insert( valType( "cuz",   "because"  ));
    trans_map.insert( valType( "nah",   "no"       ));
    trans_map.insert( valType( "sez",   "says"     ));
    trans_map.insert( valType( "tanx",  "thanks"   ));
    trans_map.insert( valType( "wuz",   "was"      ));
    trans_map.insert( valType( "pos",   "suppose"  ));

    // ok: let's display it
    map< string,string >::iterator it;

    cout << "Here is our transformation map: \n\n";
    for ( it = trans_map.begin();
          it != trans_map.end(); ++it )
          cout << "key: "   << (*it).first << "\t"
               << "value: " << (*it).second << "\n";
    cout << "\n\n";

    // a second expedient: hand-code the text ...
    string textarray[14]={ "nah", "I", "sez", "tanx", "cuz", "I",
        "wuz", "pos", "to", "not", "cuz", "I", "wuz", "gratz" };

    vector< string > text( textarray, textarray+14 );
    vector< string >::iterator iter;

    // ok: let's display it
    cout << "Here is our original string vector:\n\n";
    int cnt = 1;
    for ( iter = text.begin(); iter != text.end(); ++iter, ++cnt )
        cout <<  *iter << ( cnt % 8 ? " " : "\n" );

    cout << "\n\n\n";

    // a map to hold statistics -- build up dynamically
    map< string,int > stats;
    typedef map< string,int >::value_type statsValType;
```

```
        // ok: the actual mapwork -- heart of the program
        for ( iter = text.begin(); iter != text.end(); ++iter )
            if (( it = trans_map.find( *iter )) != trans_map.end() )
            {
                    if ( stats.count( *iter ))
                        stats[ *iter ] += 1;
                    else stats.insert( statsValType( *iter, 1 ));
                    *iter = (*it).second;
            }

        // ok: display the transformed vector
        cout << "Here is our transformed string vector:\n\n";
        cnt = 1;
        for ( iter = text.begin(); iter != text.end(); ++iter, ++cnt )
            cout <<  *iter << ( cnt % 8 ? " " : "\n" );
        cout << "\n\n\n";

        // ok: now iterate over the statistics map
        cout << "Finally, here are our statistics:\n\n";
        map<string,int,less<string>,allocator>::iterator siter;

        for ( siter = stats.begin(); siter != stats.end(); ++siter )
            cout << (*siter).first      << " "
                << "was transformed "
                << (*siter).second
                << ((*siter).second == 1
                    ? " time\n" : " times\n" );
}
```

When executed, the program generates the following output:

```
Here is our transformation map:

key: 'em        value: them
key: cuz        value: because
key: gratz      value: grateful
key: nah        value: no
key: pos        value: suppose
key: sez        value: says
key: tanx       value: thanks
key: wuz        value: was


Here is our original string vector:

nah I sez tanx cuz I wuz pos
to not cuz I wuz gratz


Here is our transformed string vector:
```

```
no I says thanks because I was suppose
to not because I was grateful


Finally, here are our statistics:

cuz was transformed 2 times
gratz was transformed 1 time
nah was transformed 1 time
pos was transformed 1 time
sez was transformed 1 time
tanx was transformed 1 time
wuz was transformed 2 times
```

6.12.5   Erasing Elements from a Map

There are three variants of the erase() operation for removing elements from a map.
To erase a single element, we pass erase() either a key value or an iterator. To remove
a sequence of elements, we pass erase() an iterator pair. For example, if we wish to
allow our user to remove elements from text_map, we might do the following:

```
string removal_word;
cout << "type in word to remove: ";
cin  >> removal_word;

if ( text_map->erase( removal_word ))
    cout << "ok: " << removal_word << " removed\n";
else cout << "oops: " << removal_word << " not found!\n";
```

Alternatively, before we attempt to erase the word, we can check to see whether it
is present:

```
map<string,loc*>::iterator where;
where = text_map.find( removal_word );

if ( where == text_map->end() )
    cout << "oops: " << removal_word << " not found!\n";
else {
    text_map->erase( where );
    cout << "ok: " << removal_word << " removed!\n";
}
```

In our implementation of text_map, we store multiple locations associated with
each word. This arrangement complicates the storage and retrieval of the actual location values. An alternative implementation is to insert a word entry for each location.
A map, however, holds only a single instance of a key value. To provide multiple entries of the same key, we must use a multimap. Section 6.15 looks at the multimap associative container type.

Exercise 6.20

Define a map for which the index is the family surname and the key is a vector of the children's names. Populate the map with at least six entries. Test it by supporting user queries based on a surname, adding a child to one family and triplets to another, and printing out all the map entries.

Exercise 6.21

Extend the map of Exercise 6.20 by having the vector store a pair of strings: the child's name and birthday. Revise the Exercise 6.20 implementation to support the new pair vector. Test your modified test program to verify its correctness.

Exercise 6.22

List at least three possible applications in which the map type might be of use. Write the definition of each map and indicate how the elements are likely to be inserted and retrieved.

6.13   Building a Word Exclusion Set

A map consists of a key/value pair, such as an address and phone number keyed to an individual's name. In contrast, a set is simply a collection of key values. For example, a business might define a set `bad_checks` consisting of names of individuals who have issued bad checks to the company over the past two years. A set is most useful when we simply want to know whether or not a value is present. Before accepting our check, for example, that business may wish to query `bad_checks` to see whether either of our names are present.

For our text query system, we build a word exclusion set of semantically neutral words such as *the, and, into, with, but,* and so on. (Although this provides significant improvement in the quality of our word index, it does result in our inability to locate the first line of Hamlet's famous speech, "To be or not to be.") Prior to entering a word into our map, we check whether it is present within the word exclusion set. If it is, we do not enter it into the map.

6.13.1   Defining and Populating a Set

To define or use the set associative container type, we must include its associated header file.

```
#include <set>
```

Here is the definition of our word exclusion set object:

```
set<string> exclusion_set;
```

Individual elements are added to the set using the insert operation. For example:

```
exclusion_set.insert( "the" );
exclusion_set.insert( "and" );
```

Alternatively, we can insert a range of elements by providing a pair of iterators to insert(). For example, our text query system allows the user to specify a file of words to exclude from our map. If the user chooses not to supply a file, we fill the set with a default collection of words:

```
typedef set< string >::difference_type diff_type;
set< string > exclusion_set;

ifstream infile( "exclusion_set" );
if ( ! infile )
{
    static string default_excluded_words[25] = {
        "the","and","but","that","then","are","been",
        "can","can't","cannot","could","did","for",
        "had","have","him","his","her","its","into",
        "were","which","when","with","would"
    };

    cerr << "warning! unable to open word exclusion file! -- "
        << "using default set\n";

    copy( default_excluded_words, default_excluded_words+25,
        inserter( exclusion_set, exclusion_set.begin() ));
}
else {
    istream_iterator<string,diff_type> input_set(infile),eos;
    copy( input_set, eos, inserter( exclusion_set,
        exclusion_set.begin() ));
}
```

This code fragment introduces two elements that we have not yet seen: difference_type and the inserter class. difference_type is the type of the result of subtracting two iterators of our string set. The istream_iterator uses this as one of its parameters.

copy(), of course, is one of the generic algorithms (we discuss them in detail in Chapter 12 and the Appendix). Its first two arguments are either iterators or pointers that mark the range of elements to copy. The third argument is either an iterator or a pointer to the beginning of the container into which to copy the elements.

The problem is that copy() expects a container of a size equal to or greater than the number of elements to be copied. This is because copy() assigns each element in turn; it does not insert the elements. The associative containers, however, do not support the preassignment of a size. To copy the elements into our exclusion set, we must somehow have copy() insert rather than assign each element. The inserter class accomplishes just that. (It is discussed in detail in Section 12.4.)

6.13.2   Searching for an Element

The two operations to query a set object as to whether a value is present are find() and count(). find() returns an iterator addressing the element found, if the element is present, or returns an iterator equal to end() indicating that the element is not present. count() returns 1 if the element is found; it returns 0 if the element is not present. Within build_word_map(), we add a test of exclusion_set prior to entering the word within our map:

```
if ( exclusion_set.count( textword ))
    continue;
// ok: enter word into map
```

6.13.3   Iterating across a Set

To exercise our word/locations map, we implemented a small function to permit single word queries (support for the full query language is presented in Chapter 17). If the word is found, we wish to display each line within which the word occurs. A word, however, might occur multiple times within a single line, as in

```
tomorrow and tomorrow and tomorrow
```

and we want to make sure that we display this line only once.

One strategy for maintaining only one instance of each line is to use a set, as we do in the following code fragment:

```
// retrieve pointer to location vector
loc *ploc = (*text_map)[ query_text ];

// iterate across location entry pairs
// insert each line value into set
set< short > occurrence_lines;
loc::iterator liter = ploc->begin(),
              liter_end = ploc->end();

while ( liter != liter_end ) {
    occurrence_lines.insert( occurrence_lines.end(),
                             (*liter).first );
    ++liter;
}
```

A set can contain only a single instance of each key value. occurrence_lines, therefore, is guaranteed to contain one instance of each line within which the word occurs. To display these lines of text, we simply iterate across the set:

```
register int size = occurrence_lines.size();
cout << "\n" << query_text
     << " occurs " << size
     << (size == 1 ? " time:" : " times:")
     << "\n\n";

set< short >::iterator it=occurrence_lines.begin();
for ( ; it != occurrence_lines.end(); ++it ) {
     int line = *it;

     cout << "\t( line "
          << line + 1 << " ) "
          << (*text_file)[line] << endl;
}
```

(The full implementation of query_text() is presented in the following section.)

A set supports the operations size(), empty(), and erase() in the same way as does the map type described in the previous section. In addition, the generic algorithms provide a collection of set-specific functions such as set_union() and set_difference(). (We'll use these in Chapter 17 in support of our query language.)

Exercise 6.23

Add an exclusion set for recognizing words in which the trailing 's' should not be removed but for which there exists no general rule. For example, three words to place in this set are the proper names Pythagoras, Brahms, and Burne_Jones. Fold the use of this exclusion set into the suffix_s() function of Section 6.10.

Exercise 6.24

Define a vector of books you'd like to read within the next virtual six months, and a set of titles that you've read. Write a program that chooses a next book for you to read from the vector provided that you have not yet read it. When it returns the selected title to you, it should enter the title in the set of books read. If in fact you end up putting the book aside, provide support for removing the title from the set of books read. At the end of our virtual six months, print the set of books read and those books that were not read.

6.14   The Complete Program

This section presents the full working program developed within this chapter, with two modifications: rather than preserve the procedural organization of separate data structures and functions, we have introduced a TextQuery class to encapsulate both (we'll look at this use of a class in more detail in subsequent chapters), and we are presenting the text as it was modified to compile under the currently available implementations. The iostream library reflects a prestandard implementation, for example. Templates do not support default arguments for template parameters. To have the program run on your current system, you may need to modify this or that declaration.

```cpp
// standard library header files
#include <algorithm>
#include <string>
#include <vector>
#include <utility>
#include <map>
#include <set>

// prestandard iostream header file
#include <fstream.h>

// Standard C header files
#include <stddef.h>
#include <ctype.h>

// typedefs to make declarations easier
typedef pair<short,short>           location;
typedef vector<location,allocator>  loc;
typedef vector<string,allocator>    text;
typedef pair<text*,loc*>            text_loc;

class TextQuery {
public:
    TextQuery() { memset( this, 0, sizeof( TextQuery )); }

    static void
          filter_elements( string felems ) { filt_elems = felems; }

    void query_text();
    void display_map_text();
    void display_text_locations();
    void doit() {
        retrieve_text();
        separate_words();
        filter_text();
        suffix_text();
        strip_caps();
        build_word_map();
    }

private:

    void retrieve_text();
    void separate_words();
    void filter_text();
```

```cpp
      void strip_caps();
      void suffix_text();
      void suffix_s( string& );
      void build_word_map();

   private:
      vector<string,allocator>     *lines_of_text;
      text_loc                     *text_locations;
      map< string,loc*,
           less<string>,allocator> *word_map;
      static string                filt_elems;
};

string TextQuery::filt_elems( "\",.;:!?)(\\/" );

int main()
{
   TextQuery tq;
   tq.doit();
   tq.query_text();
   tq.display_map_text();
}

void
TextQuery::
retrieve_text()
{
   string file_name;

   cout << "please enter file name: ";
   cin  >> file_name;

   ifstream infile( file_name.c_str(), ios::in );
   if ( !infile ) {
        cerr << "oops! unable to open file "
             << file_name << " -- bailing out!\n";
        exit( -1 );
   }
   else cout << "\n";

   lines_of_text = new vector<string,allocator>;
   string textline;

   while ( getline( infile, textline, '\n' ))
          lines_of_text->push_back( textline );
}

void
TextQuery::
```

```
separate_words()
{
    vector<string,allocator> *words = new vector<string,allocator>;
    vector<location,allocator> *locations =
            new vector<location,allocator>;

    for ( short line_pos = 0; line_pos < lines_of_text->size();
          line_pos++ )
    {
            short   word_pos = 0;
            string textline = (*lines_of_text)[ line_pos ];

            string::size_type eol = textline.length();
            string::size_type pos = 0, prev_pos = 0;

            while (( pos = textline.find_first_of( ' ', pos ))
                        != string::npos )
            {
                    words->push_back(
                        textline.substr( prev_pos, pos - prev_pos ));
                    locations->push_back(
                        make_pair( line_pos, word_pos ));

                        word_pos++; pos++; prev_pos = pos;
            }

            words->push_back(
                textline.substr( prev_pos, pos - prev_pos ));

            locations->push_back(make_pair(line_pos,word_pos));
    }

    text_locations = new text_loc( words, locations );
}

void
TextQuery::
filter_text()
{
    if ( filt_elems.empty() )
        return;

    vector<string,allocator> *words = text_locations->first;

    vector<string,allocator>::iterator iter = words->begin();
    vector<string,allocator>::iterator iter_end = words->end();

    while ( iter != iter_end )
    {
```

```
                    string::size_type pos = 0;
                    while (( pos = (*iter).find_first_of( filt_elems, pos ))
                               != string::npos )
                               (*iter).erase(pos,1);
                    ++iter;
        }
}

void
TextQuery::
suffix_text()
{
    vector<string,allocator> *words = text_locations->first;

    vector<string,allocator>::iterator iter = words->begin();
    vector<string,allocator>::iterator iter_end = words->end();

    while ( iter != iter_end )
    {
        if ( (*iter).size() <= 3 )
              { iter++; continue; }

        if ( (*iter)[ (*iter).size()-1 ] == 's' )
              suffix_s( *iter );

        // additional suffix handling goes here ...

        iter++;
    }
}

void
TextQuery::
suffix_s( string &word )
{
    string::size_type spos = 0;
    string::size_type pos3 = word.size()-3;

    // "ous", "ss", "is", "ius"
    string suffixes( "oussisius" );

    if ( ! word.compare( pos3, 3, suffixes, spos, 3 ) ||
         ! word.compare( pos3, 3, suffixes, spos+6, 3 ) ||
         ! word.compare( pos3+1, 2, suffixes, spos+2, 2 ) ||
         ! word.compare( pos3+1, 2, suffixes, spos+4, 2 ))
               return;

    string ies( "ies" );
    if ( ! word.compare( pos3, 3, ies ))
```

```
    {
        word.replace( pos3, 3, 1, 'y' );
        return;
    }

    string ses( "ses" );
    if ( ! word.compare( pos3, 3, ses ))
    {
        word.erase( pos3+1, 2 );
        return;
    }

    // erase ending 's'
    word.erase( pos3+2 );

    // watch out for "'s"
    if ( word[ pos3+1 ] == '\'' )
        word.erase( pos3+1 );
}

void
TextQuery::
strip_caps()
{
    vector<string,allocator> *words = text_locations->first;

    vector<string,allocator>::iterator iter = words->begin();
    vector<string,allocator>::iterator iter_end = words->end();

    string caps( "ABCDEFGHIJKLMNOPQRSTUVWXYZ" );

    while ( iter != iter_end ) {
        string::size_type pos = 0;
        while (( pos = (*iter).find_first_of( caps, pos ))
                    != string::npos )
            (*iter)[ pos ] = tolower( (*iter)[pos] );
        ++iter;
    }
}


void
TextQuery::
build_word_map()
{
    word_map = new map< string, loc*, less<string>, allocator >;

    typedef map<string,loc*,less<string>,allocator>::value_type
            value_type;
```

```cpp
typedef set<string,less<string>,allocator>::difference_type
        diff_type;

set<string,less<string>,allocator> exclusion_set;

ifstream infile( "exclusion_set" );
if ( !infile )
{
   static string default_excluded_words[25] = {
     "the","and","but","that","then","are","been",
     "can","can't","cannot","could","did","for",
     "had","have","him","his","her","its","into",
     "were","which","when","with","would"
   };

   cerr << "warning! unable to open word exclusion file! -- "
        << "using default set\n";

   copy( default_excluded_words, default_excluded_words+25,
         inserter( exclusion_set, exclusion_set.begin() ));
}
else {
   istream_iterator< string, diff_type >
         input_set( infile ), eos;

   copy( input_set, eos,
         inserter( exclusion_set, exclusion_set.begin() ));
}

// iterate through the the words, entering the key/pair

vector<string,allocator> *text_words  = text_locations->first;
vector<location,allocator> *text_locs = text_locations->second;

register int elem_cnt = text_words->size();
for ( int ix = 0; ix < elem_cnt; ++ix )
{
   string textword = ( *text_words )[ ix ];

   if ( textword.size() < 3 ||
        exclusion_set.count( textword ))
             continue;

   if ( ! word_map->count((*text_words)[ix] ))
   { // not present, add it:
      loc *ploc = new vector<location,allocator>;
      ploc->push_back( (*text_locs)[ix] );
      word_map->insert( value_type( (*text_words)[ix], ploc ));
```

```
        }
        else (*word_map)[(*text_words)[ix]]->
                        push_back( (*text_locs)[ix] );
    }
}

void
TextQuery::
query_text()
{
    string query_text;

    do {
        cout << "enter a word against which to search the text.\n"
             << "to quit, enter a single character ==>   ";
        cin  >> query_text;

        if ( query_text.size() < 2 ) break;

        string caps( "ABCDEFGHIJKLMNOPQRSTUVWXYZ" );
        string::size_type pos = 0;
        while (( pos = query_text.find_first_of( caps, pos ))
                    != string::npos )
                query_text[ pos ] = tolower( query_text[pos] );

        // if we index into map, query_text is entered, if absent
        // not at all what we should wish for ...

        if ( !word_map->count( query_text )) {
            cout << "\nSorry. There are no entries for "
                 << query_text << ".\n\n";
            continue;
        }

        loc *ploc = (*word_map)[ query_text ];

        set<short,less<short>,allocator> occurrence_lines;
        loc::iterator liter = ploc->begin(),
                    liter_end = ploc->end();

        while ( liter != liter_end ) {
          occurrence_lines.insert(
            occurrence_lines.end(), (*liter).first);
          ++liter;
        }

        register int size = occurrence_lines.size();
        cout << "\n" << query_text
             << " occurs " << size
```

```
                   << (size == 1 ? " time:" : " times:")
                   << "\n\n";

        set<short,less<short>,allocator>::iterator
                   it=occurrence_lines.begin();
        for ( ; it != occurrence_lines.end(); ++it ) {
               int line = *it;

               cout << "\t( line "
                       // don't confound user with
                       // text lines starting at 0
                       << line + 1 << " ) "
                       << (*lines_of_text)[line] << endl;
        }

        cout << endl;
    }
    while ( ! query_text.empty() );
    cout << "Ok, bye!\n";
}

void
TextQuery::
display_map_text()
{
    typedef map<string,loc*,less<string>,allocator> map_text;
    map_text::iterator iter = word_map->begin(),
                       iter_end = word_map->end();

    while ( iter != iter_end ) {
       cout << "word: " << (*iter).first << " (";

       int            loc_cnt = 0;
       loc            *text_locs = (*iter).second;
       loc::iterator liter     = text_locs->begin(),
                     liter_end = text_locs->end();

       while ( liter != liter_end )
       {
          if ( loc_cnt )
               cout << ",";
          else ++loc_cnt;

          cout << "(" << (*liter).first
               << "," << (*liter).second << ")";

          ++liter;
       }
```

```
            cout << ")\n";
            ++iter;
        }

        cout << endl;
    }

void
TextQuery::
display_text_locations()
{
    vector<string,allocator>   *text_words  = text_locations->first;
    vector<location,allocator> *text_locs   = text_locations->second;

    register int elem_cnt = text_words->size();

    if ( elem_cnt != text_locs->size() )
    {
        cerr << "oops! internal error: word and position vectors "
             << "are of unequal size\n"
             << "words: " << elem_cnt << " "
             << "locs: "   << text_locs->size()
             << " -- bailing out!\n";
        exit( -2 );
    }

    for ( int ix = 0; ix < elem_cnt; ix++ )
    {
        cout << "word: " << (*text_words)[ ix ] << "\t"
             << "location: ("
             << (*text_locs)[ix].first  << ","
             << (*text_locs)[ix].second << ")"
             << "\n";
    }

    cout << endl;
}
```

Exercise 6.25

Explain why we need to use the special inserter iterator to populate the exclusion word set. (It is briefly explained in Section 6.13.1, and discussed in detail in Section 12.4.1.)

```
        set<string> exclusion_set;
        ifstream    infile( "exclusion_set" );

        // ...

        copy( default_excluded_words, default_excluded_words+25,
              inserter( exclusion_set, exclusion_set.begin() ));
```

Exercise 6.26

Our original implementation reflects a procedural solution — that is, a collection of global functions operating on an independent set of unencapsulated data structures. Our final program reflects an alternative solution in which we wrap the functions and data structures within a TextQuery class. Compare the two approaches. What are the drawbacks and strengths of each?

Exercise 6.27

In this version of the program, the user is prompted for the text file to be handled. A more convenient implementation would allow the user to specify the file on the program command line — we'll see how to support command line arguments to a program in Chapter 7. What other command line options should our program support?

6.15   Multimap and Multiset

Both a map and a set can contain only a single instance of each key. A multiset and a multimap allow for multiple occurrences of a key to be stored. In a phone directory, for example, someone might wish to provide a separate listing for each phone number associated with an individual. A listing of available texts by an author might provide a separate listing for each title, or a text might provide a separate location pair for each occurrence of a word within the text. To use a multimap or multiset, we need to include the associated map or set header file.

```
#include <map>
multimap< key_type, value_type > multimapName;

// indexed by string, holding list< string >
multimap< string, list< string > > synonyms;

#include <set>
multiset< type > multisetName;
```

For either a multimap or a multiset, one iteration strategy is to use a combination of the iterator returned by find() (it points to the first instance) and the value returned by count(). (This works because the instances are guaranteed to occur contiguously within the container.) For example:

```
#include <map>
#include <string>

void code_fragment()
{
    multimap< string, string > authors;
    string search_item( "Alain de Botton" );
```

```
      // ...
      int number = authors.count( search_item );
      multimap< string,string >::iterator iter;

      iter = authors.find( search_item );
      for ( int cnt = 0; cnt < number; ++cnt, ++iter )
          do_something( *iter );

      // ...
  }
```

An alternative, somewhat more elegant strategy is to use the pair of iterator values returned by the special multiset and multimap operation, equal_range(). If the value is present, the first iterator points to the first instance of the value and the second iterator points 1 past the last instance of the value. If the last instance is the last element of the multiset, the second iterator is set equal to end(). For example:

```
#include <map>
#include <string>
#include <utility>

void code_fragment()
{
   multimap< string, string > authors;
   // ...
   string search_item( "Haruki Murakami" );

   while ( cin && cin >> search_item )
      switch ( authors.count( search_item ))
      {
        // none present, go to the next item
        case 0:
          break;

        // single item. ordinary find()
        case 1: {
          multimap< string,string >::iterator iter;
          iter = authors.find( search_item );
          // do something with element
          break;
        }
        // multiple entries present ...
        default:
        {
            typedef multimap< string,string >::iterator iterator;
            pair< iterator, iterator > pos;

            // pos.first addresses first occurrence
            // pos.second addresses position in which
```

```
//      value no longer occurs
pos = authors.equal_range( search_item );
for ( ; pos.first != pos.second; pos.first++ )
        // do something with each element
        }
    }
}
```

Insertion and deletion are the same as for the simpler map and set associative container types. equal_range() is useful for providing the iterator pair necessary to mark the range of multiple elements to be erased. For example:

```
#include <multimap>
#include <string>

typedef multimap< string, string >::iterator iterator;
pair< iterator, iterator > pos;
string search_item( "Kazuo Ishiguro" );

// authors is a multimap<string,string>
// this is equivalent to
// authors.erase( search_item );
pos = authors.equal_range( search_item );
authors.erase( pos.first, pos.second );
```

Insertion adds an additional element each time. For example:

```
typedef multimap<string,string>::value_type valType;
multimap<string,string> authors;

// introduces a first key under Barth
authors.insert( valType(
  string( "Barth, John" ),
  string( "Sot-Weed Factor" )));

// introduces a second key under Barth
authors.insert( valType(
  string( "Barth, John" ),
  string( "Lost in the Funhouse" )));
```

One constraint on access of an element of a multimap is that the subscript operator is not supported. For example, the following

```
authors[ "Barth, John" ]; // error: multimap
```

results in a compile-time error.

Exercise 6.28

Reimplement the text query program of Section 6.14 to use a multimap in which each location is entered separately. What are the performance and design characteristics of the two solutions? Which do you feel is the preferred design solution? Why?

6.16   Stack

In Section 4.5 we illustrated the increment and decrement operators by implementing a stack abstraction. In general, stacks provide a powerful solution to the problem of maintaining a current state when multiple nesting states can occur dynamically during the course of program execution. Because a stack is an important data abstraction, the standard C++ library provides a class implementation. To use it, we must include its associated header file:

```
#include <stack>
```

The stack provided by the standard library is implemented slightly differently from ours in that the access and removal of the top element are separated into, respectively, a top() and pop() pair of operations. The full set of operations supported by the stack container are the following:

Table 6.5   Operations Supported by the Stack Container

Operation	Function
empty()	returns true if the stack is empty; false otherwise.
size()	returns a count of the number of elements on the stack.
pop()	removes, but does not return, the top element from the stack.
top()	returns, but does not remove, the top element on the stack.
push(item)	places a new top element on the stack.

The following program exercises this set of five stack operations:

```
#include <stack>
#include <iostream>

int main()
{
const int ia_size = 10;
int ia[ia_size ] = { 0, 1, 2, 3, 4, 5, 6, 7, 8, 9 };
```

```
// fill up the stack
int ix = 0;
stack< int > intStack;
for ( ; ix < ia_size; ++ix )
     intStack.push( ia[ ix ] );

int error_cnt = 0;
if ( intStack.size() != ia_size ) {
     cerr << "oops! invalid intStack size: "
          << intStack.size()
          << "\t expected: " << ia_size << endl;
     ++error_cnt;
}

int value;
while ( intStack.empty() == false )
{
     // read the top element of the stack
     value = intStack.top();

     if ( value != --ix ) {
        cerr << "oops! expected " << ix
             << " received " << value
             << endl;
        ++error_cnt;
     }

     // pop the top element, and repeat
     intStack.pop();
}

cout << "Our program ran with "
     << error_cnt << " errors!" << endl;
}
```

The declaration

```
stack< int > intStack;
```

declares intStack to be an empty stack of integer elements. The stack type is spoken of as a *container adapter* because it imposes the stack abstraction on an underlying container collection. By default, the stack is implemented using the deque container type, because a deque provides for the efficient insertion and deletion at the front of a container, and a vector does not support it. If we should wish to override the default, we can define a stack object that provides an explicit sequence container type as a second argument. For example:

```
stack< int, list<int> > intStack;
```

The elements of the stack are entered by value; each object is copied onto the underlying container. For large or complex class objects, this approach may prove overly expensive, particularly if we are only reading the elements. An alternative storage strategy is to define a stack of pointers. For example:

```
#include <stack>

class NurbSurface { /* mumble */ };
stack< NurbSurface* > surf_Stack;
```

Two stacks of the same type can be compared for equality, inequality, less-than, greater-than, less-than-equal, and greater-than-equal relationships provided that the underlying element type supports the equality and less-than operators. For these operations, the elements are compared in turn. The first pair of unequal elements determines the less-than or greater-than relationship.

We illustrate the program use of a stack in Section 17.7 in our support of complex user text queries such as

```
Civil && ( War || Rights )
```

6.17   Queue and Priority Queue

A queue abstraction exhibits a FIFO storage and retrieval policy — that is, first in, first out. Objects entering the queue are placed in the back. The next object retrieved is taken from the front of the queue. There are two flavors of queues provided by the standard library: the FIFO queue, which we will speak of simply as a queue, and a priority queue.

A priority queue allows the user to establish a priority among the items held within the queue. Rather than place a newly entered item at the back of the queue, the item is placed ahead of all those items with a lower priority. The user who defines the priority queue determines how that priority is to be decided. A real-world example of a priority queue is that of the line to check in luggage at an airport. Those whose flight is going to leave within the next 15 minutes are generally moved to the front of the line so that they can finish the check-in process before their plane takes off. A programming example of a priority queue is the scheduler of an operating system determining which, of a number of waiting processes, should execute next.

To use either a queue or priority_queue, the associated header file must be included:

```
#include <queue>
```

The full set of operations supported by the queue and priority_queue containers are shown in Table 6.6:

Table 6.6 Operations Supported by Queues and Priority Queues

Operations	Function
empty()	returns true if the queue is empty; false otherwise.
size()	returns a count of the number of elements on the queue.
pop()	removes, but does not return, the front element from the queue. In the case of the priority_queue, the front element represents the element with the highest priority.
front()	returns, but does not remove, the front element on the queue. This can only be applied to a queue.
back()	returns, but does not remove, the back element on the queue. This can only be applied to a queue.
top()	returns, but does not remove, the highest priority element of the priority_queue. This can only be applied to a priority_queue.
push(item)	places a new element at the end of the queue. In the case of a priority_queue, order the item based on its priority.

An ordering is imposed on the elements of a priority_queue so that the elements are arranged from largest to smallest, where largest is equivalent to having the highest priority. By default, the prioritization of the elements is carried out by the less-than operator associated with the underlying element type. If we should wish to override the default less-than operator, we can explicitly provide a function or function object to be used for ordering the priority_queue elements (Section 12.3 explains and illustrates this further).

6.18   Revisiting Our iStack Class

The iStack class presented in Section 4.15 is constrained in two regards:

1. It supports only a single type: type int. We'd prefer to support all element types. We can do this by transitioning our implementation to support a general Stack template class.
2. It has a fixed length. This is problematic in two regards: our stack can become full and therefore unusable, and to avoid having the stack become full, we end up allocating on average considerably too much space. The solution is to support a dynamically growing stack. We can do this by making direct use of the dynamic support provided by the underlying vector object.

Before we begin, here is our original iStack class definition:

```
#include <vector>

class iStack {
public:
    iStack( int capacity )
            : _stack( capacity ), _top( 0 ) {}

    bool pop( int &value );
    bool push( int value );

    bool full();
    bool empty();
    void display();

    int size();

private:
    int _top;
    vector< int > _stack;
};
```

Let's first transition the class to support dynamic allocation. Essentially, this means that we must insert and remove elements rather than index into a fixed-size vector. The data member _top is no longer necessary; the use of push_back() and pop_back() manages the top element automatically. Here is our revised implementation of pop() and push():

```
bool iStack::pop( int &top_value )
{
    if ( empty() )
        return false;
    top_value = _stack.back(); _stack.pop_back();
    return true;
}

bool iStack::push( int value )
{
    if ( full() )
        return false;
    _stack.push_back( value );
    return true;
}
```

empty(), size(), and full() must also be reimplemented — more tightly coupled in this version to the underlying vector:

```
inline bool iStack::empty(){ return _stack.empty(); }
inline int iStack::size() { return _stack.size();  }
```

```
inline bool iStack::full() {
        return _stack.max_size() == _stack.size();    }
```

display() requires a slight modification to remove its use of _top as an end condition to the for loop:

```
void iStack::display()
{
    cout << "( " << size() << " )( bot: ";
    for ( int ix = 0; ix < size(); ++ix )
            cout << _stack[ ix ] << " ";
    cout << " :top )\n";
}
```

Our only significant design decision has to do with our revised iStack constructor. Strictly speaking, our constructor no longer needs to do anything, and the following null constructor is sufficient for our reimplemented iStack class:

```
inline iStack::iStack() {}
```

However, it is not sufficient for our users. At this point, we have exactly preserved the original interface, so no existing user code needs to be rewritten. To be fully compatible with our original iStack interface, we must retain a single argument constructor, although we don't wish to require it as our original implementation did. Our modified interface accepts but does not require a single argument of type int:

```
class iStack {
public:
    iStack( int capacity = 0 );
    // ...
};
```

What do we do with the argument if it is present? We'll use it to set the vector's capacity:

```
inline iStack::iStack( int capacity )
{
    if ( capacity )
            _stack.reserve( capacity );
}
```

The transition from a nontemplate to a template class is even easier, in part because the underlying vector object already belongs to a class template. Here is our revised class declaration:

```
#include <vector>

template <class elemType>
class Stack {
public:
    Stack( int capacity=0 );
```

```
        bool pop( elemType &value );
        bool push( elemType value );

        bool full();
        bool empty();
        void display();

        int size();

    private:
        vector< elemType > _stack;
    };
```

To preserve compatibility with existing programs that use our earlier iStack class implementation, we provide the following typedef:

```
    typedef Stack<int> iStack;
```

We leave the revision of the member operations as an exercise.

Exercise 6.29

Reimplement the peek() function (Exercise 4.23 of Section 4.15) for our dynamic Stack class template.

Exercise 6.30

Provide the revised member operations for our Stack class template. Run the test program of Section 4.15 against the new implementation.

Exercise 6.31

Using the model of the List class in Section 5.11.1, encapsulate our Stack class template in the Primer_Third_Edition namespace.

Part III

Procedural-Based Programming

Part II introduced the basic components of the C++ programming language: the built-in data types (such as `int` and `double`), the class abstraction types (such as string and vector), and the operations that can be performed on these types. In Part III, we see how these basic program components can be grouped to form function definitions. Functions are used to implement the algorithms that perform the specific tasks of our programs.

For every C++ program we must define a function called `main()`, which is the first function invoked when a C++ program begins execution. `main()` invokes other functions to perform the program's required tasks. The functions within a program communicate, or exchange information, through values that the functions receive (called *parameters*) and through values that the functions return. Chapter 7 introduces the C++ function mechanism.

Functions are used to organize programs into smaller, independent units. Each function encapsulates an algorithm or a set of algorithms that apply to a specific set of data. We can declare objects and types so that they can be used throughout the entire duration of a program. But if these objects and types are used only in a subset of the program, it is preferable to limit where they can be accessed and associate their declarations with the functions that use them. Scope is the mechanism by which programmers can limit the visibility of declarations in their programs. In Chapter 8, we present the different scopes supported in C++; we also present how scope affects the visibility of declarations and the lifetime and run-time properties of C++ objects.

C++ provides many facilities to ease the use of functions in C++ programs. In Part III we review these facilities in turn. The first such facility is overloaded functions. Functions that provide a common operation but that operate on different data types and require differing implementations may share a common name. For example, functions for printing values of different types, such as integers, strings, and so on, can all be named `print()`. This capability eases the use of functions, because programmers do not have to remember different function names for a same operation. The compiler selects the appropriate function to call using the type of the function arguments. Chapter

9 discusses how overloaded functions are declared and used and how, given a function call, the compiler selects a function in a set of overloaded functions.

A second facility supported in C++ to ease the use of functions is function templates. A function template is a generic function definition that is used to automatically generate an infinite set of function definitions that vary by type but whose implementations remain invariant. Chapter 10 describes how function templates are defined and used to automatically generate, or instantiate, function definitions.

The functions within a program communicate by receiving values (or parameters) and by returning values. This mechanism may prove inadequate, however, when an extraordinary situation, or program anomaly, is encountered during the execution of a program. Such a situation, called a program *exception*, requires immediate attention and requires that a function quickly communicate to its calling functions that an exception has occurred. C++ provides an exception handling facility to allow communication between functions in these extraordinary circumstances. Exception handling is presented in Chapter 11.

Finally, the C++ standard library provides an extensive collection of often-used functions called generic algorithms. Chapter 12 describes the generic algorithms provided by the C++ standard library and examines how they interact with the container types of Chapter 6 as well as the built-in array type.

7

Functions

Now that we have seen how to declare variables (Chapter 3) and how to write expressions (Chapter 4) and statements (Chapter 5), this chapter looks at how to group these program components in function definitions to facilitate the reuse of these components within a program. This chapter describes how to declare and define functions as well as how to invoke them within our programs. This chapter presents the different kinds of function parameters that a function can receive and discusses the properties of each kind. It also presents the different kinds of values a function can return. We then examine four special kinds of functions: inline functions, recursive functions, non-C++ functions declared with linkage directives, and the function main(). We end this chapter with the introduction of a more advanced topic: function pointers.

7.1 Overview

A function can be thought of as a user-defined operation. In general, a function is represented by a name. The operands of a function, referred to as its *parameters*, are specified in a comma-separated *parameter list* enclosed in parentheses. The result of a function is referred to as its *return value*, and the type of the return value is called the function *return type*. A function that does not yield a value has a return type of void, meaning that it returns nothing. The actions a function performs are specified in the *body* of the function. The function body is enclosed in braces and is sometimes referred to as the *function block*. The function return type followed by the name of the function, the parameter list, and the function body compose the *function definition*. Here are some examples of function definitions:

```
inline int abs( int iobj )
{
    // return the absolute value of iobj
    return( iobj < 0 ? -iobj : iobj );
}
```

```
inline int min( int p1, int p2 )
{
   // return the smaller of two values
   return( p1 < p2 ? p1 : p2 );
}

int gcd( int v1, int v2 )
{
   // return the greatest common divisor
   while ( v2 )
   {
      int temp = v2;
      v2 = v1 % v2;
      v1 = temp;
   }
   return v1;
}
```

The function is evaluated whenever the function's name is followed by the call operator (()). If the function is defined to receive parameters, *arguments* for these parameters are provided when the function is called. These arguments are placed inside the call operator. Two adjacent arguments are separated by a comma. This arrangement is referred to as *passing arguments* to a function. In the following example, main() calls abs() twice and min() and gcd() once each. It is defined in the file main.C.

```
#include <iostream>

int main()
{
   // get values from standard input
   cout << "Enter first value: ";
   int i;
   cin >> i;
   if ( !cin ) {
      cerr << "!? Oops: input error - Bailing out!\n";
      return -1;
   }

   cout << "Enter second value: ";
   int j;
   cin >> j;
   if ( !cin ) {
      cerr << "!? Oops: input error - Bailing out!\n";
      return -2;
   }

   cout << "\nmin: " << min( i, j ) << endl;
   i = abs( i );
```

```
        j = abs( j );
        cout << "gcd: " << gcd( i, j ) << endl;
        return 0;
    }
```

A function call can cause one of two things to happen. If the function has been declared *inline*, the body of the function may be expanded at the point of its call during
compilation; if it is not declared inline, the function is invoked at run-time. A function
invocation causes program control to transfer to the function being invoked; execution
of the currently active function is suspended. When evaluation of the called function
is completed, the suspended function resumes execution at the point immediately following the call. The execution of a function completes following the execution of the
final statement within the function body or when a *return statement* is encountered in
the function body.

A function must be declared to the program before it is called; otherwise, a compile-time error results. The function definition, of course, serves as its declaration.
However, a function can be defined only once in a program. Typically, the definition
resides in its own program text file or in a text file containing it and the definitions of
other related functions. An additional mechanism for declaring a function is required
to allow the function to be used in files other than the one containing its definition.

The declaration of a function consists of the function return type, the name of the
function, and the parameter list. These three elements are referred to as the *function
declaration* or *function prototype*. A function can be declared multiple times in a file.

In our `main.C` example, if the functions `abs()`, `min()`, and `gcd()` were not defined
before `main()`, each of their calls within `main()` would generate a compile-time error.
However, for `main.C` to compile without errors, we are not required to define these
functions before `main()`; we could simply declare them as follows (a function declaration need not specify the names of the parameters, only the type of each parameter):

```
    int abs( int );
    int min( int, int );
    int gcd( int, int );
```

Function declarations (and the definitions of inline functions) are best placed within header files. These header files can then be included in every file where the functions
are called. In this way, all files share a common declaration; should that declaration
need to be modified, only that one instance need be changed. The header file for our
program might be defined as follows. Let's call it `localMath.h`:

```
    // definition in gcd.C
    int gcd( int, int );

    inline int abs(int i) {
        return( i<0 ? -i : i );
    }
```

```
inline int min(int v1,int v2) {
   return( v1<v2 ? v1 : v2 );
}
```

A function declaration describes the function's *interface*. It describes the kind of information the function must receive (the parameter list) and the kind of information it gives back, if anything (the return type). As a user of the function, we program to its interface; our code need not change regardless of how often the function body is modified provided that the function's interface remains the same. The mechanism by which we communicate to users the interface of our functions is to place declarations for our functions in header files, such as the header file `localMath.h`.

When our `main.C` program is compiled and executed, given the following input values from the user

```
Enter first value:   15
Enter second value:  123
```

the program produces the following results:

```
min:   15
gcd:   3
```

7.2   Function Prototype

A function prototype consists of the function return type, the name of the function, and the parameter list. A function prototype describes the interface of the function; it details the number and types of parameters that must be provided when the function is called and the type of the value that the function returns. In this section we examine the characteristics of function prototypes in greater detail.

7.2.1   Function Return Type

The return type of a function can be a predefined type, such as `int` or `double`, a compound type, such as `int&` or `double*`, a user-defined type, such as an enumeration or class, or `void`, meaning that the function does not return a value. The following are examples of possible function return types:

```
#include <string>
#include <vector>
class Date { /* definition */ };

bool look_up( int *, int );
double calc( double );
int count( const string &, char );
Date& calendar( const char* );
void sum( vector<int>&, int );
```

A function type and the built-in array type cannot be specified as a return type. The following, for example, is an error:

```
// illegal: array cannot be a return type
int[10] foo_bar();
```

Rather, we must return a pointer to the element type contained within the array:

```
// ok: pointer to first element of the array
int *foo_bar();
```

The pointer addresses the first element of the array being returned. (It is the responsibility of the user handling the return value to know the size of the array.)

Class types and the container types, in contrast, can be returned directly. For example:

```
// ok: return type is list of chars
list<char> foo_bar();
```

(This approach, however, is less efficient. See our discussion of returning by value in Section 7.4.)

A function must specify a return value; a declaration or definition without an explicit return value results in a compile-time error. For example:

```
// error: missing return type
const is_equal( vector<int> v1, vector<int> v2 );
```

In pre-Standard C++, in the absence of an explicit return type it was assumed that the return type was int. Under Standard C++, the return type of a function cannot be omitted. The correct declaration of is_equal() is

```
// ok: return type is specified
const bool is_equal( vector<int> v1, vector<int> v2 );
```

7.2.2 Function Parameter List

The parameter list of a function cannot be omitted. A function that does not have any parameters can be represented with either an empty parameter list or a parameter list containing the single keyword void. For example, the following declarations of fork() are equivalent:

```
int fork();        // implicit void parameter list
int fork( void ); // equivalent declaration
```

The parameter list consists of a comma-separated list of parameter types. A name can optionally follow each parameter type. The shorthand syntax for a comma-separated list of declarations is an error within a parameter list. For example:

```
int manip( int v1, v2 );     // error
int manip( int v1, int v2 ); // ok
```

No two parameter names appearing in a parameter list can be the same. A parameter name in the parameter list of a function definition allows the parameter to be accessed from within the body of the function. The parameter name is unnecessary in a function declaration. If it is present, its name should serve as a documentation aid. For example:

```
void print( int *array, int size );
```

There is no language-imposed penalty for specifying a different name for a parameter in the declaration(s) and definition of the same function. A reader of the program, however, may become confused.

In C++, it is possible to have two functions with the same name and different parameter lists; the functions are then called *overloaded functions*. The parameter list is referred to as the *signature* of a function, because it is used to distinguish one instance of a function from another. The name and signature of a function uniquely identify it. Chapter 9 discusses overloaded functions more fully.

7.2.3 Parameter Type-Checking

The function gcd() is declared as follows:

```
int gcd( int, int );
```

The declaration indicates that the function has two parameters of type int. The function's parameter list provides the compiler with the type information necessary for it to perform type-checking on the function arguments supplied when the function is called.

For example, what happens if the arguments are of type const char*? What could possibly be the result of the following call?

```
gcd( "hello", "world" );
```

Or what happens if gcd() is passed only one argument or more than two? What happens with the accidental concatenation of the values 24 and 312 in this call?

```
gcd( 24312 );
```

The only desirable result of attempting to compile either of the latter two calls of gcd() is a compile-time error; any attempt to execute these calls invites disaster. In C++, these two calls result in compile-time error messages of the following general form:

```
// gcd( "hello", "world" )
error: invalid argument types ( const char*, const char* ) --
        expecting ( int, int )

// gcd( 24312 )
error: missing value for second argument
```

What happens if the arguments are of type double? Should the call be flagged as an error?

```
gcd( 3.14, 6.29 );
```

As we saw in Section 4.14, a value of type `double` can be converted to a value of type `int`. Therefore, flagging the call as an error is too severe. Rather, the arguments are implicitly converted to `int` (through truncation), fulfilling the type requirements of the parameter list. Because it is a narrowing conversion, however, with a possible loss of precision, the compiler generally issues a warning. The call becomes

```
gcd( 3, 6 );
```

and returns a value of 3.

C++ is a *strongly typed* language. The arguments of every function call are *type-checked* during compilation. If there is a type mismatch between the type of an argument and the type of the corresponding function parameter, an implicit conversion is applied if possible, such as the conversion of `double` to `int` in the preceding example. If an implicit conversion is not possible or if the number of arguments is incorrect, a compile-time error is issued. This is why a function cannot be called until it has first been declared. The declaration is necessary for the compiler to perform type-checking on the arguments of the function call against the function parameter list.

Omitting an argument or passing an argument of the wrong type are common sources of serious run-time program errors in the pre-Standard C language. With the introduction of strong type-checking in C++, these interface errors are caught at compile-time.

Exercise 7.1

Which, if any, of the following function prototypes are invalid? Why?

```
(a) set( int *, int );
(b) void func();
(c) string error( int );
(d) arr[10] sum( int *, int );
```

Exercise 7.2

Write the prototypes for each of the following functions:

(a) A function named `compare` with two parameters that are references to a class named `matrix` and with a return value of type `bool`

(b) A function named `extract` with no parameters and returning a set of integers (where `set` is the container type defined in Section 6.13)

Exercise 7.3

Given the following declarations, which function calls, if any, are in error? Why?

```
double calc( double );
int count( const string &, char );
void sum( vector<int> &, int );
```

```
vector<int> vec( 10 );

(a) calc( 23.4, 55.1 );
(b) count( "abcda", 'a' );
(c) sum( vec, 43.8 );
(d) calc( 66 );
```

7.3   Argument Passing

Functions use allocated storage on the program's *run-time stack*. That storage remains associated with the function until the function terminates. At that point, the storage is automatically made available for reuse. The entire storage area of the function is referred to as the *activation record*.

Each function parameter is provided storage within the function activation record. The storage size of a parameter is determined by its type. Argument passing is the process of initializing the storage of the function parameters with the values of the function call arguments.

The default initialization method of argument passing in C++ is to copy the values of the arguments into the storage of the parameters. This is referred to as *pass-by-value*.

Under pass-by-value, the function never accesses the arguments of the call. The values that the function manipulates are its own local copies; they are stored on the run-time stack. Changes made to these values are not reflected in the values of the arguments. Once the function terminates and the function's activation record is popped off the run-time stack, these local values are lost.

Under pass-by-value, the contents of the arguments are not changed. This means that a programmer need not save and restore argument values when making a function call. Without a pass-by-value mechanism, each parameter not declared const would have to be considered potentially altered with each function call. Pass-by-value has the least potential for harm and requires the least work by the general user. Pass-by-value is a reasonable default mechanism for argument passing.

Pass-by-value, however, is not suitable for every situation. Situations under which pass-by-value is unsuitable include the following:

- When a large class object must be passed as an argument. The time and space costs to allocate and copy the class object onto the stack are often too high for real-world program applications.

- When the values of the arguments must be modified. In the function swap(), for example, the user wants to change the values of the arguments but cannot do so under pass-by-value.

```
// swap() does not swap the value of the arguments!
void swap( int v1, int v2 ) {
   int tmp = v2;
```

```
        v2 = v1;
        v1 = tmp;
    }
```

swap() exchanges the local copies of its arguments. The variables that represent swap()'s arguments are unchanged. This is illustrated in the following program, which calls swap():

```
        #include <iostream>
        void swap( int, int );

        int main() {
            int i = 10;
            int j = 20;

            cout << "Before swap():\ti: "
                 << i << "\tj: " << j << endl;

            swap( i, j );

            cout << "After swap():\ti: "
                 << i << "\tj: " << j << endl;
            return 0;
        }
```

Compiling and executing this program results in the following output:

```
        Before swap():    i: 10    j: 20
        After swap():     i: 10    j: 20
```

To obtain the desired behavior, two alternatives are available to the programmer. In one instance, the parameters are declared as pointers. swap(), for example, could be rewritten as follows:

```
        // pswap() swaps the values that v1 and v2 address
        void pswap( int *v1, int *v2 ) {
            int tmp = *v2;
            *v2 = *v1;
            *v1 = tmp;
        }
```

main() must be modified to call pswap(). The programmer must now pass the addresses of the two objects and not the objects themselves:

```
        pswap( &i, &j );
```

Compiling and executing this revised program shows the output to be correct:

```
        // use of pointers allows programmer to
        // access the arguments to the call

        Before swap():    i: 10    j: 20
        After swap():     i: 20    j: 10
```

The second alternative is to declare the parameters to be references. `swap()`, for example, could be rewritten as follows:

```
// rswap() swaps the values to which v1 and v2 refer
void rswap( int &v1, int &v2 ) {
    int tmp = v2;
    v2 = v1;
    v1 = tmp;
}
```

The call of `rswap()` in `main()` looks like the original call of `swap()`:

```
rswap( i, j );
```

Compiling and executing the program will show that the values of i and j are properly exchanged.

7.3.1   Reference Parameters

The declaration of a parameter as a reference overrides the default pass-by-value argument-passing mechanism. With pass-by-value, the function manipulates local copies of the arguments. When the parameters are references, the function receives the lvalue of the argument rather than a copy of its value. This means that the function knows where the argument resides in memory and can therefore change its value or take its address.

When is it appropriate to specify a parameter as a reference? It is appropriate in a case such as `swap()` when it would otherwise be necessary to change the parameters to be pointers to allow changing the values of the arguments. A second common use of reference parameters is to return additional results to the calling function. A third use is to pass large class objects to a function. Let's examine these last two situations in more detail.

As an example of a function that uses a reference parameter to return an additional result to the calling function, let's define a function named `look_up()` to search for a particular value in a vector of integers. If the value is found, `look_up()` returns an iterator referring to the vector element containing the value; otherwise, it returns an iterator referring to 1 past the last element of the vector to indicate that the value is not present. In the case of multiple occurrences, an iterator referring to the first occurrence of the value in the vector is returned. In addition, using the reference parameter occurs, `look_up()` returns a count of the number of occurrences.

```
#include <vector>

// the reference parameter 'occurs' may
// contain a second return value

vector<int>::const_iterator look_up(
    const vector<int> &vec,
```

```
      int value,     // is value in the vector?
      int &occurs ) // how many times?
{
    // res_iter initialized to one-past the last element
    vector<int>::const_iterator res_iter = vec.end();
    occurs = 0;

    for ( vector<int>::const_iterator iter = vec.begin();
          iter != vec.end();
          ++iter )
      if ( *iter == value )
      {
          if ( res_iter == vec.end() )
              res_iter = iter;
          ++occurs;
      }

    return res_iter;
}
```

A third circumstance under which it makes sense to declare a parameter as a reference is when we're passing large class objects to a function. Under pass-by-value, the entire object is copied with each call. Although pass-by-value is satisfactory for objects of built-in data types and small class objects, it is too inefficient for large class objects. With a reference parameter, the function has access to the class object specified as the argument and no local copy is made in the function activation record. For example:

```
class Huge { public: double stuff[1000]; };
extern int calc( const Huge & );

int main() {
   Huge table[ 1000 ];
   // ... initialize table

   int sum = 0;
   for ( int ix=0; ix < 1000; ++ix )
      // the function calc() will refer to the array
      // element of type Huge specified as an argument
      sum += calc( table[ix] );

   // ...
}
```

One may want to use a reference parameter to prevent copying a large class object used as an argument and, at the same time, prevent the function from modifying the value of the argument. Whenever a reference parameter is not intended to be modified within the function called, it is a good practice to declare the parameter as a reference to a const type. This approach allows the compiler to prevent unintentional changes from occurring. For example, the following program fragment violates the const-ness of foo()'s parameter xx. Because the parameter of foo_bar() is not a reference to a const type, there is no guarantee that foo_bar() does not change the value of its argument xx. This violates the const-ness of foo()'s parameter xx, and the program is flagged by the compiler as an error:

```
class X;
extern int foo_bar( X& );

int foo( const X& xx ) {
   // error: const passed to non-const
   return foo_bar( xx );
}
```

For this program to compile, we can change the type of foo_bar()'s parameter; either of the following declarations is acceptable:

```
extern int foo_bar( const X& );
extern int foo_bar( X ); // pass-by-value
```

Or we can pass an argument that is a copy of xx that foo_bar() is permitted to change:

```
int foo( const X &xx ) {
   // ...
   X x2 = xx; // copy values

   // when foo_bar() changes its reference parameter,
   // x2 is modified; xx remains unchanged
   return foo_bar( x2 ); // ok
}
```

A reference parameter to any built-in data type can be declared. For example, it is possible to declare a parameter that is a reference to a pointer should the programmer wish to modify the pointer itself rather than the object addressed by the pointer. For example, here is a function to swap two pointers:

```
void ptrswap( int *&v1, int *&v2 ) {
   int *tmp = v2;
   v2 = v1;
   v1 = tmp;
}
```

The declaration

```
int *&v1;
```

should be read from right to left: v1 is a reference to a pointer to an object of type int. Using the function main() to manipulate the function rswap(), we can modify its implementation to swap pointer values as follows:

```
#include <iostream>
void ptrswap( int *&v1, int *&v2 );
```

```
int main() {
   int i = 10;
   int j = 20;

   int *pi = &i;
   int *pj = &j;

   cout << "Before ptrswap():\tpi: "
        << *pi << "\tpj: " << *pj << endl;

   ptrswap( pi, pj );
   cout << "After ptrswap():\tpi: "
        << *pi << "\tpj: " << *pj << endl;
   return 0;
}
```

When compiled and executed, the program generates the following output:

```
 Before ptrswap():     pi: 10     pj: 20
 After ptrswap():      pi: 20     pj: 10
```

7.3.2   Relationship between Reference and Pointer Parameters

By now, you may wonder how to decide whether to declare a function parameter as a reference or as a pointer. After all, both kinds of parameters allow a function to modify the objects referred to by the function arguments. And both kinds of parameters allow for efficient passing of large class objects to a function. So how do we decide whether to declare a function parameter as a reference or as a pointer?

As mentioned in Section 3.6, a reference must be initialized to an object, and, once initialized, it can never be made to refer to another object. A pointer can address a sequence of different objects or address no object at all.

Because a pointer can either address an object or address no object at all, a function cannot safely dereference a pointer before it first confirms that the pointer actually addresses an object. For example:

```
class X;
void manip( X *px )
{
   // make sure it is nonzero before dereference
   if ( px != 0 )
      // dereference the pointer
}
```

With a reference parameter, on the other hand, the function does not need to guard against its referring to no object. A reference must refer to an object, even if we wish otherwise. For example:

```
class Type { };
void operate( const Type& p1, const Type& p2 );

int main() {
   Type obj1;
   // set obj1 to some value

   // error: argument for reference parameter cannot be 0
   Type obj2 = operate( obj1, 0 );
}
```

If a parameter may refer to different objects within a function or if the parameter may refer to no object at all, a pointer parameter must be used.

One important use of reference parameters is to allow us to implement overloaded operators efficiently while keeping their use intuitive. The full discussion of overloaded operators is in Chapter 15. To get us started, let's examine the following example, which uses a Matrix class type. We would like to support both the addition and assignment operations of two Matrix class objects and allow their use to be as "natural" as for the built-in types:

```
Matrix a, b, c;

c = a + b;
```

The addition and assignment operations for the Matrix class type are implemented using overloaded operators. An overloaded operator is a function with a funny name. In the case of our addition operator, the function name is operator+. Let's provide a definition for this overloaded operator:

```
Matrix        // addition returns a Matrix object
operator+(    // name of overloaded operator
   Matrix m1, // type of the left-hand operand
   Matrix m2 // type of the right-hand operand
)
{
   Matrix result;
   // do the computation in result
   return result;
}
```

This implementation supports the addition of two Matrix objects, such as

```
a + b;
```

but unfortunately it is unacceptably inefficient. Notice that the parameters of our operator+() are not references; this means that the arguments to operator+() are pass-by-value arguments. The contents of the two Matrix objects a and b are copied into the parameter area for the operator+() function. Because a Matrix class object is quite large, the time and space costs to allocate and copy such an object into the function parameter area are too high to be acceptable.

Let's pretend that, to improve the efficiency of our operator function, we decide to declare the parameters as pointers. Here is what the new implementation of operator+() looks like:

```
// new implementation with pointer parameters
Matrix operator+( Matrix *m1, Matrix *m2 )
{
    Matrix result;
    // do the computation in result
    return result;
}
```

However, this implementation has the following problem: although we have gained efficiency, it is at the expense of an intuitive use of the addition operator. The pointer parameters now require that we pass the arguments as addresses of the Matrix objects we want to add. Our addition operation must now be programmed as follows:

```
&a + &b; // not good, but also not impossible
```

Although this is ugly and is likely to result in some programmer complaints about not being user-friendly, attempting to add three objects in a compound expression becomes very difficult:

```
// oops: this doesn't work
// return type of &a + &b is a Matrix object
&a + &b + &c;
```

To make the addition of three objects well behaved under a pointer solution, the programmer must write the following:

```
// ok: this works, but ...
&( &a + &b ) + &c;
```

No one could be expected to write that, of course. Reference parameters provide the solution we need. When a parameter is a reference, the function receives the lvalue of the argument rather than a copy of its value. Because the function knows where the argument resides in memory, the argument value is not copied into the function parameter area. The argument for a reference parameter is the Matrix object itself; this allows us to use the operator as naturally as we use the addition operation for objects of built-in data types.

Here is our revised sketch of the overloaded addition operator for our Matrix class:

```
// new implementation with reference parameters
Matrix operator+( const Matrix &m1, const Matrix &m2 )
{
    Matrix result;
    // do the computation in result
```

```
    return result;
}
```

This implementation supports the addition of Matrix objects as follows:

```
a + b + c;
```

References were introduced into C++ explicitly for the support of class types —
in particular, to support an intuitive yet efficient mechanism to implement overloaded operators.

7.3.3   Array Parameters

Arrays in C++ are never passed by value. Rather, an array is passed as a pointer to its
first — that is, zeroth — element. For example,

```
void putValues( int[ 10 ] );
```

is treated by the compiler as having been declared as

```
void putValues( int* );
```

The array's size is not relevant to the declaration of the parameter. The following
three declarations are therefore equivalent:

```
// three equivalent declarations of putValues()
void putValues( int* );
void putValues( int[] );
void putValues( int[ 10 ] );
```

Because an array is passed as a pointer, this has two implications for programmers:

*   The changes to an array parameter within the called function are made to the
    array argument itself and not to a local copy. When the array that is the argu-
    ment of the call must remain unchanged, programmers will need to keep a
    copy of the original array. Alternatively, the function could indicate that it
    does not intend to change the array elements by declaring the elements in the
    parameter type as const:

    ```
    void putValues( const int[ 10 ] );
    ```

*   The size of an array is not part of its parameter type. The function being
    passed an array does not know its actual size, and neither does the compiler.
    When the compiler applies parameter type-checking on the argument type,
    there is no checking of the array sizes. For example:

    ```
    void putValues( int[ 10 ] ); // treated as int*
    int main() {
        int i, j[ 2 ];
        putValues( &i ); // ok: &i is int*; potential run-time error
    ```

```
           putValues( j );   // ok: j is converted to pointer to 0th
                             //      element; argument has type int*;
                             //      potential run-time error
           return 0;
    }
```

The extent of the parameter type-checking confirms that both calls of putValues()
provide an argument of type int*. Type-checking does not verify that the argument is
an array of ten elements.

By convention, C-style character strings are arrays of characters that encode their
termination point with a null character. All other array types, however, including
character arrays that wish to handle embedded null characters, must in some way
make their size known when passed as arguments to a function. One common mechanism is to provide an additional argument that contains the array's size. For example:

```
    void putValues( int[], int size );
    int main() {
       int i, j[ 2 ];
       putValues( &i, 1 );
       putValues( j, 2 );
       return 0;
    }
```

putValues() prints the values of an array in the following format:

```
    ( 10 )< 0, 1, 2, 3, 4, 5, 6, 7, 8, 9 >
```

where 10 represents the size of the array. Here is an implementation that uses the
additional parameter for the size of the array:

```
    #include <iostream>

    const lineLength = 12; // elements to a line
    void putValues( int *ia, int sz )
    {
       cout << "( " << sz << " )< ";
       for ( int i = 0; i < sz; ++i )
       {
          if ( i % lineLength == 0 && i )
             cout << "\n\t"; // line filled

          cout << ia[ i ];

          // separate all but last element
          if ( i % lineLength != lineLength-1 &&
                i != sz-1 )
             cout << ", ";
       }
       cout << " >\n";
    }
```

Another mechanism is to declare the parameter as a reference to an array. When the parameter is a reference to an array type, the array size becomes part of the parameter and argument types, and the compiler checks that the size of the array argument matches the one specified in the function parameter type.

```
// parameter is a reference to an array of 10 ints
void putValues( int (&arr)[10] );
int main() {
    int i, j[ 2 ];
    putValues( i ); // error: argument is not an array of 10 ints
    putValues( j ); // error: argument is not an array of 10 ints
    return 0;
}
```

Because the array size is now part of the parameter type, this version of putValues() accepts only arrays of ten ints. This limits the kind of arrays that can be passed as arguments to putValues(). However, it also allows its implementation to be greatly simplified:

```
#include <iostream>

void putValues( int (&ia)[10] )
{
    cout << "( 10 )< ";
    for ( int i = 0; i < 10; ++i ) {
        cout << ia[ i ];

        // separate all but last element
        if ( i != 9 )
            cout << ", ";
    }
    cout << " >\n";
}
```

Yet another mechanism is to use an abstract container type. (Abstract container types are introduced in Chapter 6.) This mechanism is examined further in the next subsection.

Although the previous two implementations of putValues() work, they have some severe limitations. The first implementation works only for arrays of ints. A second function is needed to handle an array of doubles, and a third for an array of longs, and so on. The second implementation works only for arrays of ten ints. Again, additional functions are needed to handle arrays of different sizes. A better implementation of putValues() is to define it as a function template. A function template is one whose code remains invariant across a wide set of different parameter types. Here is how our first implementation of putValues() could be rewritten as a function template to handle arrays of different types and sizes:

```
template <class Type>
    void putValues( Type *ia, int sz )
```

```
{
    // same as before
}
```

The template parameter is enclosed within an angle-bracket pair; in this case, the one template parameter is Type. The class keyword indicates that the template parameter represents a type. The identifier Type serves as the parameter name, and its occurrence within the parameter list of putValues() serves as a placeholder for the actual type with which the function template will be instantiated. With each instantiation, the actual type of the instantiation — int, double, string, and so on — is substituted for the Type parameter. We look further at function templates in Chapter 10.

A parameter can also be a multidimensional array. Such a parameter must specify the size of all its dimensions beyond that of its first. For example,

```
void putValues( int matrix[][10], int rowSize );
```

declares matrix to be a two-dimensional array. Each row consists of ten column elements. matrix can equivalently be declared as

```
int (*matrix)[10]
```

A multidimensional array is passed as a pointer to its zeroth element. In our example, the type of matrix is a pointer to an array of ten ints. As with array parameters that have only one dimension, the first dimension of a multidimensional array is not relevant to the type of the parameter. Type-checking for a parameter that is a multidimensional array otherwise verifies that the sizes of all the dimensions of the array parameter (except the first) are the same as those of the array argument.

Note that the parentheses around *matrix are necessary because of the higher precedence of the subscript operator. The following declaration

```
int *matrix[ 10 ];
```

declares matrix to be an array of ten pointers to ints.

7.3.4   Parameters of Abstract Container Types

The abstract container types introduced in Chapter 6 can also be used to declare function parameters. For example, we could have defined the putValues() function with a parameter of type vector<int> instead of using the built-in array type.

A container type is actually a class type and provides considerably more functionality than the built-in array data type. For example, a parameter of type vector<int> knows the number of elements it contains. We saw in the previous subsection that if the function has an array parameter, the first dimension of the array is unknown to the function and it may be necessary to define an additional parameter to convey the array's size to the function. Using a parameter of type vector<int> allows us to circumvent this limitation. For example, we could change the definition of our putValues() function as follows:

```
#include <iostream>
#include <vector>

const lineLength = 12; // elements to a line
void putValues( vector<int> vec )
{
    cout << "( " << vec.size() << " )< ";
    for ( int i = 0; i < vec.size(); ++i ) {

        if ( i % lineLength == 0 && i )
            cout << "\n\t"; // line filled

        cout << vec[ i ];

        // separate all but last element
        if ( i % lineLength != lineLength-1 &&
             i != vec.size()-1 )
            cout << ", ";
    }
    cout << " >\n";
}
```

The function main() invoking our new function putValues() looks like this:

```
void putValues( vector<int> );

int main() {
    int i, j[ 2 ];
    // assign to i and j some values

    vector<int> vec1(1); // create a vector of 1 element
    vec1[0] = i;
    putValues( vec1 );

    vector<int> vec2;      // create an empty vector
    // add elements to vec2
    for ( int ix = 0;
          ix < sizeof( j ) / sizeof( j[0] );
          ++ix )
        // vec2[ix] == j[ix]
        vec2.push_back( j[ix] );
    putValues( vec2 );

    return 0;
}
```

Notice that the parameter of putValues() is a pass-by-value parameter. When a parameter of container type is passed by value, the container and all its elements are copied into a local copy within the function called. Because this copying can be rather inefficient, it is better to declare parameters of container types as reference parameters.

How would you change the declaration of putValues()'s parameter?

Remember that when a function does not modify the value of its parameter, it is preferable to declare the parameter as a reference to a const type. The reference parameter of putValues() should therefore be declared as follows:

```
void putValues( const vector<int> & ) { ...
```

7.3.5   Default Arguments

A default argument is a value that, although not universally applicable, is judged to be an appropriate argument value for a parameter in a majority of cases. A default argument frees the programmer from having to attend to every small detail of the function's interface.

A function can specify a default argument for one or more of its parameters using initialization syntax within the parameter list. For example, a function to create and initialize a two-dimensional character array intended to simulate a terminal screen can provide default arguments for the height, width, and background character of the screen:

```
char *screenInit( int height = 24, int width = 80,
                  char background = ' ' );
```

A function that provides a default argument for a parameter can be invoked with or without an argument for this parameter. If an argument is provided, it overrides the default argument value; otherwise, the default argument is used. Each of the following calls of screenInit() is correct:

```
char *cursor;

// equivalent to screenInit(24,80,' ')
cursor = screenInit();

// equivalent to screenInit(66,80,' ')
cursor = screenInit(66);

// equivalent to screenInit(66,256,' ')
cursor = screenInit(66, 256);

cursor = screenInit(66, 256, '#');
```

Arguments to the call are resolved by position, and default arguments are used only to substitute the missing *trailing* arguments of a function call. For example, it is impossible to supply a character value as an argument for background without also supplying arguments for height and width.

```
// equivalent to screenInit('?',80,' ')
cursor = screenInit('?');

// error, not equivalent to screenInit(24,80,'?')
cursor = screenInit( , , '?');
```

Part of the work of designing a function with default arguments is the arrangement of the parameters within the parameter list so that those most likely to take a user-specified value occur first and those most likely to use the default arguments occur last. The design assumption within `screenInit()` (possibly arrived at through experimentation) is that `height` is the value most likely to be supplied by the user.

A function declaration can specify default arguments for all or only a subset of its parameters. The rightmost uninitialized parameter must be supplied with a default argument before any default argument for a parameter to its left can be supplied. Again, this is because arguments to a function call are resolved by position.

```
// error: width must have a default argument before
//        one is specified for height
char *screenInit( int height = 24, int width,
                  char background = ' ' );
```

A parameter can have its default argument specified only once in a file. The following, for example, is an error:

```
// ff.h
int ff( int = 0 );
```

```
// ff.C
#include "ff.h"
int ff( int i = 0 ) { ... } // error
```

By convention, the default argument is specified in the function declaration contained in the public header file (the one that describes the function's interface) and not in the function definition. If a default argument is provided in the parameter list of a function definition, the default argument is available only for function calls in the text file that contains the function definition.

Succeeding declarations of a function can specify additional default arguments — a useful method for customizing a general function for a specific application. The UNIX system library function `chmod()` changes the protection level of a file. Its function declaration is found in the system header file `<cstdlib>`. It is declared as follows:

```
int chmod( char *filePath, int protMode );
```

`protMode` represents a file-protection mode, and `filePath` represents the name and path location of the file. If a particular application is always changing a file's protection mode to *read-only*, rather than indicate this each time, `chmod()` can be redeclared to supply the value by default:

```
#include <cstdlib>
int chmod( char *filePath, int protMode=0444 );
```

Given the following function declaration declared in a header file

```
int ff( int a, int b, int c = 0 ); // ff.h
```

how can we redeclare ff() in our file to provide b with a default argument? The following is an error, because it respecifies c's default argument:

```
#include "ff.h"
int ff( int a, int b = 0, int c = 0 ); // error
```

The following also seems to be an error but in fact is the correct redeclaration:

```
#include "ff.h"
int ff( int a, int b = 0, int c ); // ok
```

At the point of this redeclaration of ff(), b is the rightmost argument without a default argument. Therefore, the rule that the default argument be assigned by position beginning with the rightmost argument has not been violated. In fact, we can now redeclare ff() a third time:

```
#include "ff.h"

int ff( int a, int b = 0, int c ); // ok
int ff( int a = 0, int b, int c ); // ok
```

A default argument does not have to be a constant expression. Any expression can be used. For example:

```
int aDefault();
int bDefault( int );
int cDefault( double = 7.8 );

int glob;

int ff( int a = aDefault() ,
        int b = bDefault( glob ) ,
        int c = cDefault() );
```

When the default argument is an expression, the expression is evaluated at the time the function is called. For example, cDefault() is called to obtain a value for c every time ff() is called without a third argument.

7.3.6   Ellipses

It is sometimes impossible to list the type and number of all the arguments that might be passed to a function. In these cases, ellipses (. . .) can be specified in the function parameter list.

Ellipses suspend type-checking. Their presence tells the compiler that, when the function is called, zero or more arguments may follow and that the types of the arguments are unknown. Ellipses may take either of two forms:

```
void foo( parm_list, ... );
void foo( ... );
```

The first form provides declarations for a certain number of function parameters. In this case, type-checking is performed when the function is called for the arguments that correspond to the parameters explicitly declared, whereas type-checking is suspended for the arguments that correspond to the ellipsis. In this first form, the comma following the parameter declarations is optional.

The standard C library output function `printf()` is an example in which an ellipsis is necessary. `printf()`'s first parameter is always a C-style character string.

```
int printf( const char* ... );
```

This requires that every call of `printf()` be passed a first argument of type `const char*`. In calls to `printf()`, whether other arguments follow the character string is determined by the first argument, referred to as a format string. Metacharacters in the format string, set off by %, indicate the presence of additional arguments. For example, the call

```
printf( "hello, world\n" );
```

has a single character string argument. However,

```
printf( "hello, %s\n", userName );
```

has two arguments. The % indicates the presence of a second argument; the s indicates that the type of the argument is a character string.

Most functions with an ellipsis use some information from a parameter that is explicitly declared to obtain the type and number of optional arguments provided in a function call. The first form of function declaration with ellipsis is therefore most commonly used.

Note that the following two declarations are not equivalent:

```
void f();
void f( ... );
```

In the first instance, f() is declared as a function that accepts no parameters; in the second, f() is declared as a function that can take zero or more arguments. The calls

```
f( someValue );
f( cnt, a, b, c );
```

are legal invocations of the second declaration only. The call

```
f();
```

can be used to invoke either the first or the second function.

Exercise 7.4

Which, if any, of the following declarations are errors? Why?

```
(a) void print( int arr[][], int size );
(b) int ff( int a, int b = 0, int c = 0 );
(c) void operate( int *matrix[] );
```

```
(d) char *screenInit( int height = 24, int width,
                          char background );
(e) void putValues( int (&ia)[] );
```

Exercise 7.5

The redeclaration of each of these functions is an error. Why?

```
(a) char *screenInit( int height, int width,
                         char background = ' ' );
    char *screenInit( int height = 24, int width,
                         char background );

(b) void print( int (*arr)[6], int size );
    void print( int (*arr)[5], int size );

(c) void manip( int *pi, int first, int end = 0 );
    void manip( int *pi, int first = 0, int end = 0 );
```

Exercise 7.6

Given the following function declarations, which ones, if any, of the following function calls are errors? Why?

```
// declarations
void print( int arr[][5], int size );
void operate(int *matrix[7]);
char *screenInit( int height = 24, int width = 80,
                  char background = ' ' );

(a) screenInit(); // function call

(b) int *matrix[5];
    operator( matrix ); // function call

(c) int arr[5][5];
    print( arr, 5 ); // function call
```

Exercise 7.7

Rewrite the putValues() function provided for vector<int> and presented in Subsection 7.3.4 to handle list<string> instead. Print one string per line so that a list of two strings would print as follows:

```
( 2 )
<
"first string"
"second string"
>
```

Write a function `main()` that invokes this new `putValues()` function for a list of strings containing the following values:

```
"put function declarations in header files"
"use abstract container types instead of built-in arrays"
"declare class parameters as references"
"use reference to const types for invariant parameters"
"use less than eight parameters"
```

Exercise 7.8

When would you use a parameter that is a pointer? When would you use a parameter that is a reference? Explain the advantages and disadvantages of each.

7.4 Returning a Value

A `return` statement is placed within the body of a function. This statement terminates the function that is currently executing. When a `return` statement is encountered during the execution of a program, the program control is returned to the function from which the now-terminated function was called. There are two forms of `return` statements:

```
return;
return expression;
```

The first form is used in a function that has a return type of `void`. A return statement is not strictly necessary in a function that has a return type of `void`. It is used primarily to cause a premature termination of the function. (This use of the `return` statement parallels the use of the `break` statement inside a loop. `break` statements are introduced in Section 5.8.) An implicit `return` takes place upon completion of a function's final statement. For example:

```
void d_copy( double *src, double *dst, int sz )
{
    /* copy "src" array into "dst"
     * simplifying assumption: arrays are same size
     */

    // if either pointer is 0, return
    if ( !src || !dst )
        return;

    // if the two parameters refer to the same array, return
    if ( src == dst )
        return;

    // nothing to copy
    if ( sz == 0 )
        return;
```

```
    // still here? then it's time to do some work
    for ( int ix = 0; ix < sz; ++ix )
        dst[ix] = src[ix];

    // no explicit return necessary
    // automatically returns to the calling function
}
```

The second form of the `return` statement provides the function result. The result can be an arbitrarily complex expression; it can itself contain a function call. An implementation of `factorial()`, for example, contains the following `return` statement (we will see an implementation of `factorial()` in the next section):

```
    return val * factorial(val-1);
```

A *value-returning* function — that is, a function not declared to have a return type of `void` — must return a value. The absence of a return value is a compile-time error. Although C++ cannot guarantee the correctness of a result, it at least guarantees that a result is provided for each value-returning function. The following program, for example, fails to compile because two of its exit points do not return a value.

```
    // definition of the Matrix class interface
    #include "Matrix.h"

    bool is_equal( const Matrix &m1, const Matrix &m2 )
    {
        /* if the content of two Matrix objects is the same,
         * return true;
         * otherwise, return false
         */

        // compare the number of columns
        if ( m1.colSize() != m2.colSize() )
            // program error: failure to return a value
            return;

        // compare the number of rows
        if ( m1.rowSize() != m2.rowSize() )
            // program error: failure to return a value
            return;

        // traverse each Matrix until either unequal
        // or all elements have been examined
        for ( int row = 0; row < m1.rowSize(); ++row )
            for ( int col = 0; col < m1.colSize(); ++col )
                if ( m1[row][col] != m2[row][col] )
                    return false;
```

```
// program error: failure to return a value
// when m1 == m2
}
```

If the type of the value returned does not exactly match the function return type, an implicit conversion, if possible, is applied. If no implicit conversion is possible, a compile-time error is generated. (Type conversions are discussed in Section 4.14.)

By default, the value returned by a function is *passed by value*. This means that the function to which control returns receives a copy of the value of the expression specified on the return statement. For example:

```
Matrix grow( Matrix* p ) {
    Matrix val;
    // ...
    return val;
}
```

grow() returns a copy of the value stored within val to the calling function. The calling function cannot modify val in any way.

This default behavior can be overridden. A function can be declared to return a pointer or a reference. When the function is returning a reference, the calling function receives the lvalue for val. The calling function can then modify val or take its address. grow() can be declared to return a reference as follows:

```
Matrix& grow( Matrix* p ) {
    Matrix *res;
    // allocate a larger Matrix in dynamic storage
    // res refers to this new Matrix
    // copy content of *p into *res
    return *res;
}
```

If the return value is a large class object, using a reference (or pointer) return type is more efficient than returning the class object by value. In some cases, the compiler can automatically transform a return by value to a return by reference. This optimization is called the *named return value optimization* and is described in Section 14.8.

The programmer should be aware of the following two potential pitfalls when declaring a function to return a reference:

1. Returning a reference to a local object. The lifetime of the local object terminates with the termination of the function. (The lifetime of local objects is discussed in Section 8.3.) The reference is left aliasing undefined memory after the function terminates. For example:

    ```
    // problem: returning a reference to a local object
    Matrix& add( Matrix &m1, Matrix &m2 )
    {
        Matrix result;
    ```

```
        if ( m1.isZero() )
            return m2;
        if ( m2.isZero() )
            return m1;

        // add the content of the two Matrix objects

        // oops: result refers to a questionable location after return
        return result;
    }
```

In this case, the return type should be declared as a nonreference. The local variable is then copied before the lifetime of the local object terminates:

```
    Matrix add( ...
```

2. The function returns an lvalue. Any modification of the value returned changes the actual object being returned. For example:

```
    #include <vector>

    int &get_val( vector<int> &vi, int ix ) {
        return vi[ix];
    }

    int ai[4] = { 0, 1, 2, 3 };
    vector<int> vec( ai, ai+4 ); // copy 4 elements of ai into vec

    int main() {
        // increments vec[0] to 1
        get_val( vec,0 )++;
        // ...
    }
```

To prevent the unintended modification of a reference return value, the return value should be declared as const:

```
    const int &get_val( ...
```

An example of returning an lvalue in order to modify the actual object being returned was presented in Section 2.3 in the discussion of the class IntArray overloaded subscript operator.

7.4.1   Parameters and Return Values versus Global Objects

The various functions of a program can communicate by two mechanisms. (By *communicate* we mean exchange values.) One method uses global program objects; the second method uses a function parameter list and return value.

A *global object* is defined outside a function definition. For example:

```
int glob;
int main() {
    // whatever
}
```

The object `glob` is a global object. (Chapter 8 further discusses global scope and global objects.) The general accessibility of a global object from anywhere within the program is both its main benefit and its most significant liability. The visibility of a global object makes it a convenient mechanism of communication between the parts of a program. The drawbacks of relying on global objects to communicate between functions are as follows:

- A function that uses the global object depends on the existence and type of that global object, making the reuse of that function in a different context much more difficult.

- If the program must be modified, global dependencies increase the likelihood of introducing bugs. Moreover, introducing local changes requires an understanding of the entire program.

- If a global object gets an incorrect value, the entire program must be searched to determine where the error occurs; there is no localization.

- Recursion is more difficult to get right when the function uses a global object. (Recursion occurs when a function calls itself. We look at recursion in Section 7.5.)

- In the presence of threads, special coding is required to synchronize the reading and writing of a global object among the various threads. A lack of synchronization is a common source of programming error when you're using threads. (See the article "Distributing Object Computing in C++" by Steve Vinoski and Doug Schmidt in [LIPPMAN96b] for an example of threads programming in C++.)

It is therefore recommended that the functions within a program communicate information through the use of their parameter lists and return values.

The likelihood of error in passing arguments to a function increases with the size of the parameter list. As a general rule, eight parameters should be the maximum. As an alternative to a large parameter list, the programmer might declare a parameter to be a class, an array, or one of the container types; such a parameter can be used to contain a group of parameter values.

Similarly, a function can return only one value. If the program's logic requires that multiple values be returned, the programmer might declare some of the function parameters to be references, in which case the function can directly modify the corresponding arguments and thus set the arguments to contain some additional "return" values, or the programmer might declare the function with a return type that is a class or one of the container types to contain a group of return values.

Exercise 7.9

What are the two forms of `return` statement? Explain when you would use each form.

Exercise 7.10

What potential run-time problem do you see with the following function definition?

```
vector<string> &readText( ) {
    vector<string> text;

    string word;
    while ( cin >> word ) {
        text.push_back( word );
        // ...
    }

    // ....
    return text;
}
```

Exercise 7.11

How would you return more than one value from a function? Describe the advantages and disadvantages of your approach.

7.5 Recursion

A function that calls itself, either directly or indirectly, is referred to as a *recursive function*. The following function `rgcd()` is a recursive function:

```
int rgcd( int v1, int v2 )
{
    if ( v2 != 0 )
        return rgcd( v2, v1%v2 );
    return v1;
}
```

A recursive function must always define a *stopping condition*; otherwise, the function will recurse "forever." This is sometimes called an *infinite recursion* error. In the case of `rgcd()`, the stopping condition is a remainder of 0.

The call

```
rgcd( 15, 123 );
```

evaluates to 3. Table 7.1 traces the execution.

Table 7.1   Trace of rgcd(15,123)

value1	value2	Return
15	123	rgcd(123, 15)
123	15	rgcd(15, 3)
15	3	rgcd(3, 0)
3	0	3

The last call,

```
rgcd(3,0);
```

satisfies the stopping condition. It returns the greatest common denominator, 3. This value successively becomes the return value of each prior call. The value is said to *percolate* upward until the execution returns to the function that called rgcd() in the first place.

A recursive function is likely to run slower than its nonrecursive (or *iterative*) counterpart because of the overhead associated with the invocation of a function. The recursive function, however, is likely to be smaller and more easily understood.

The factorial of a number n is the product of the counting sequence from 1 to n. The factorial of 5, for example, is 120.

```
1 x 2 x 3 x 4 x 5 = 120
```

Computing the factorial of a number lends itself to the implementation of a recursive function:

```
unsigned long
factorial( int val ) {
   if ( val > 1 )
      return val * factorial( val-1 );
   return 1;
}
```

The stopping condition in this case occurs when val contains a value of 1.

Exercise 7.12

Rewrite factorial() as an iterative function.

Exercise 7.13

What would happen if the stopping condition of factorial() were as follows?

```
if ( val != 0 )
```

7.6   Inline Functions

Consider the following `min()` function:

```
int min( int v1, int v2 )
{
    return( v1 < v2 ? v1 : v2 );
}
```

The benefits of defining a function for such a small operation include the following:

- It is generally easier to read a call of `min()` and interpret its meaning than to read an instance of the conditional operator and understand what the code is doing, especially when `v1` and `v2` are complex expressions.

- It is easier to change one localized implementation than 300 occurrences within an application. For example, if it is decided that the test should read

```
( v1 == v2 || v1 < v2 )
```

finding every coded occurrence would be tedious and prone to error.

- The semantics are uniform. Each test is guaranteed to be implemented in the same manner.

- The function can be reused rather than rewritten for other applications.

There is, however, one serious drawback to making `min()` a function: calling the function is slower than directly evaluating the conditional operator. The two arguments must be copied, machine registers must be saved, and the program must branch to a new location. The handwritten conditional operator is simply faster.

Inline functions provide a solution. A function specified as inline is expanded "in line" at each point in the program in which it is invoked. For example,

```
int minVal2 = min( i, j );
```

is expanded during compilation into

```
int minVal2 = i < j ? i : j;
```

The run-time overhead of making `min()` a function is thus removed.

`min()` is declared inline by specifying the `inline` keyword before the function's return type in the function declaration or definition:

```
inline int min( int v1, int v2 ) { /* ... */ }
```

Note, however, that the inline specification is only a recommendation to the compiler. The compiler may choose to ignore this recommendation, because the function declared inline is not a good candidate for expansion at the point of call. A recursive function, such as `rgcd()`, for example, cannot be completely expanded at the point of call (although its first invocation can). A 1,200-line function is also likely not to be expanded at the point of call. In general, the inline mechanism is meant to optimize small, straight-line, frequently called functions. It is of primary importance in the support of information hiding in the design of abstract data types, such as the IntArray class introduced in Section 2.3 with its `size()` inline member function.

An inline function definition must be visible for the compiler to be able to inline a function at the point of the call. Unlike a non-inline function, an inline function must be defined in every text file in which the inline function is called. Of course, the definitions of the inline function that appear in the different files that compose a program must be the same. For a program made of two files `compute.C` and `draw.C`, a programmer must not define the inline function `min()` to mean one thing in `compute.C` and something else in `draw.C`. If the two definitions are not the same, the program has undefined behavior: it is uncertain which of the many different definitions the compiler will use as the definition to call for non-inlined function calls, and the program may not behave as you expect.

The recommended way to ensure that this does not happen is to place the definition of the inline function in a header file and to include this header file in every text file in which the inline function is called. This approach guarantees that there is only one definition for the inline function and that programmers do not unnecessarily duplicate code, something that may lead to unintentional mismatch later on in the lifetime of the program.

Because `min()` is a common operation, an implementation of `min()` is provided by the C++ standard library. The `min()` operation is part of the generic algorithms described in Chapter 12 and its use is illustrated in the Appendix. The library defines `min()` as a function template, allowing the `min()` operation to be applied to operands of arithmetic types other than `int`. Function templates are discussed in Chapter 10.

7.7   Linkage Directives: extern "C" ◆

If the programmer wishes to call a function written in another programming language — in particular, C — the compiler must be told that different requirements apply when the function is called. For example, the function's name or the way the arguments are ordered when the function is called may be different whether the call is to a C++ function or to a function written in another programming language.

The programmer indicates to the compiler that a function is written in a different programming language using a *linkage directive*. A linkage directive can have one of two forms. It can be a *single statement* form or a *compound statement* form:

```
// single statement linkage directive
extern "C" void exit(int);

// compound statement linkage directive
extern "C" {
   int printf( const char* ... );
```

```
    int scanf( const char* ... );
}

// compound statement linkage directive
extern "C" {
#include <cmath>
}
```

The first form of linkage directive consists of the extern keyword followed by a string literal, followed by an "ordinary" function declaration. Although the function is written in another language, calls to it are still fully type-checked. For example, the compiler will check that the argument passed to the function exit() either has type int or can be implicitly converted to type int.

Multiple function declarations can be enclosed within the braces of a linkage directive compound statement, the second form of linkage directive. The braces serve as delimiters indicating to which declarations the linkage directive applies. The braces are otherwise ignored, and the names of functions declared within the braces are visible as if the functions were declared outside the compound statement. For example, the extern "C" compound statement in the preceding example indicates that the functions printf() and scanf() are functions written in the C programming language. The meaning of the declarations is otherwise the same as if printf() and scanf() were declared outside the extern "C" compound statement.

When a #include directive is enclosed within the braces of a compound statement linkage directive, all the function declarations within the header file are assumed to be functions written in the programming language of the linkage directive. In the preceding example, the functions declared within the header <cmath> are C functions.

A linkage directive cannot appear within a function body. The following code fragment is an error flagged at compile-time:

```
int main()
{
    // error: linkage directive cannot appear within a function
    extern "C" double sqrt( double );
    double getValue(); //ok

    double result = sqrt ( getValue() );
    //...
    return 0;
}
```

If we move the linkage directive outside the function body, the program compiles without errors:

```
extern "C" double sqrt( double );
```

```
int main()
{
    double getValue(); //ok

    double result = sqrt ( getValue() );
    //...
    return 0;
}
```

A linkage directive is more appropriately placed, however, within a header file, where the function declaration describing the function's interface belongs.

What if we wish to make a C++ function available to a C program? How can we do that? We also use the extern "C" linkage directive to make a C++ function available to a C program. For example:

```
// the calc() function can be called from C programs
extern "C" double calc( double dparm ) { /* ... */ }
```

If a function is declared more than once in the same file, the linkage directive can appear on every declaration. It can also appear only on the first declaration of the function, in which case the second and following declarations receive the linkage specified by the linkage directive on the first declaration. For example:

```
// ---- myMath.h ----
extern "C" double calc( double );

// ---- myMath.C ----
// declaration of calc() in myMath.h
#include "myMath.h"

// defines the extern "C" calc() function
// calc() can be called from C programs
double calc( double dparm ) { // ...
```

In this section, we saw examples only of the linkage specification for the C language; extern "C". extern "C" is the only linkage specification guaranteed to be supported by all C++ implementations. An implementation can provide other linkage specifications for languages commonly used in its environment. For example extern "Ada" can be used to declare functions written in the Ada language, extern "FORTRAN" for functions written in the FORTRAN language, and so on. Because the additional linkage specifications are implementation-specific, we recommend that you consult your implementation's user's guide for further information on the other linkage specifications it may provide.

This section introduces a first use of the keyword extern in C++. In Section 8.2, we will see other uses of extern with declarations of objects and functions.

Exercise 7.14

exit(), printf(), malloc(), strcpy(), and strlen() are C language library routines. Modify the following C program so that it compiles and links under C++.

```
const char *str = "hello";

void *malloc( int );
char *strcpy( char *, const char * );
int printf( const char *, ... );
int exit( int );
int strlen( const char * );

int main()
{   /* C language program */

    char* s = malloc( strlen(str)+1 );
    strcpy( s, str );
    printf( "%s, world\n", s );
    exit( 0 );
}
```

7.8   main(): Handling Command Line Options ◈

Often, when we execute our programs we pass command line options. For example, we might write

```
prog -d -o ofile data0
```

In effect, the command line options are arguments to main() and can be accessed within main() through an array of C-style character strings named argv. In this section, we illustrate how to support command line options.

Prior to this section, all our definitions of main() have declared an empty parameter list:

```
int main() { ... }
```

An expanded signature for main() allows us access to the options, if any, specified by the user on the command line:

```
int main( int argc, char *argv[] ) { ... }
```

argc holds a count of the command line options. argv holds the argc count of C-style character strings representing the white space separated command options. For example, given the command line

```
prog -d -o ofile data0
```

argc is set to 5, and argv is set to the following C-style character strings:

```
argv[ 0 ] = "prog";
argv[ 1 ] = "-d";
argv[ 2 ] = "-o";
```

```
argv[ 3 ] = "ofile";
argv[ 4 ] = "data0";
```

argv[0] is always set to the command being invoked. The indexes 1 through argc-1 represent the actual options passed to the command.

Let's look at how we might extract and evaluate the command line options stored in argv. In our example, we'll support the following usage:

```
program_name [-d] [-h] [-v]
             [-o output_file] [-l limit_value]
             file_name
             [ file_name [file_name [ ... ]]]
```

Anything in brackets is optional. Thus, for example, a minimal command line simply indicates a file to process:

```
prog chap1.doc
```

Alternative possible invocations include the following:

```
prog -l 1024 -o chap1-2.out chap1.doc chap2.doc
prog -d chap3.doc
prog -l 512 -d chap4.doc
```

The basic steps in handling the command line options are the following:

1. Extract each option in turn from argv. We'll use a for loop to do this, beginning our iteration at index 1 (thereby skipping the program name):

   ```
   for ( int ix = 1; ix < argc; ++ix ) {
      char *pchar = argv[ ix ];
      // ...
   }
   ```

2. Determine the type of option. If it begins with a hyphen, then we know it is one of { h, d, v, l, o }. Otherwise, it is either the actual limit value associated with -l, an output file name associated with -o, or the name of a file for the program to process. We'll use a switch statement to determine whether a hyphen is present:

   ```
   switch ( pchar[ 0 ] ) {
      case '-': {
         // recognize -h, -d, -v, -l, -o
      }

      default: {
         // handle limit value following -l
         //        output file following -o
         //        file names ...
      }
   }
   ```

3. Fill in the handling of the two cases of item 2.

If a hyphen is present, we then simply switch on the next character to determine the option specified by the user. Here is the general outline of that portion of our implementation:

```
case '-': {
    switch( pchar[ 1 ] )
    {
        case 'd':
            // handle debug
            break;

        case 'v':
            // handle version request
            break;

        case 'h':
            // handle help
            break;

        case 'o':
            // prepare to handle output_file
            break;

        case 'l':
            // prepare to handle limit_value
            break;

        default:
            // unrecognized option:
            // report it and exit
    }
}
```

The -d option turns on debugging. To handle that, we set an object

```
bool debug_on = false;
```

to true:

```
case 'd':
    debug_on = true;
    break;
```

Our program can contain code such as the following:

```
if ( debug_on )
    display_state_elements( obj );
```

The -v option displays the version number of the program and then exits:

```
case 'v':
    cout << program_name << "::"
```

```
         << program_version << endl;
    return 0;
```

The -h option generates the program's usage() message and then exits (the exit is done within usage()):

```
case 'h':
    // no break necessary: usage() exits
    usage();
```

The -o option indicates that a user-specified output file name follows. Similarly, the -l option indicates that a limit value follows. How should we handle that?

If the hyphen is not present, we know that we have one of either a limit value, a user-specified output file, or the name of a file to be processed. To distinguish between the three possibilities, we set objects that remember internal states to true

```
// if true, next argument is output file
bool ofile_on = false;

// if true, next argument is limit value
bool limit_on = false;
```

within the options handling portion of our implementation:

```
case 'l':
    limit_on = true;
    break;

case 'o':
    ofile_on = true;
    break;
```

When we encounter an argument that does not begin with a hyphen, we test the state objects to determine what the option represents:

```
// either a limit_value, output_file, or file_name
default: {
    // ofile_on set if -o seen
    if ( ofile_on ) {
        // handle output_file
        // turn off ofile_on
    }
    else
    if ( limit_on ) { // if -l seen
        // handle limit_value
        // turn off limit_on
    }
    else {
        // handle file_name
    }
}
```

If the argument is an output file, we reset ofile_on to false and tuck away the file's name:

```
if ( ofile_on ) {
    ofile_on = false;
    ofile = pchar;
}
```

If the argument is a limit value, we need to transform the C-style character string into a numeric representation. We do that using the atoi() standard library function; it takes a C-style character string as an argument and returns an int (there is also an atof() that returns a float value). To use atoi(), we include the ctype.h header file. We must also make sure that the limit value is non-negative and must reset limit_on to false:

```
// int limit;

else
if ( limit_on ) {
    limit_on = false;
    limit = atoi( pchar );
    if ( limit < 0 ) {
        cerr << program_name << "::"
             << program_version << " : error: "
             << "negative value for limit.\n\n";
        usage( -2 );
    }
}
```

Otherwise, if neither state object is true, we have a file to open for processing. We store its name in a string vector:

```
else
    file_names.push_back( string( pchar ));
```

When we're processing the command line, perhaps the most significant aspect of the design lies in the way we choose to handle invalid options. For example, we make specifying a negative limit value a fatal error. That may or may not be appropriate. Alternatively, we could have recognized it as out of bounds, alerted the user, and reset the value to 0 or some meaningful default value.

Two weaknesses in our implementation become apparent when our users foul up the spacing of our command options. For example, neither of the following is handled.

```
prog - d data01
prog -oout_file data01
```

(We leave both as exercises at the end of this section.)

Here is the full implementation of our program. (We've added print statements to illustrate the progress of its processing.)

```cpp
#include <iostream>

#include <string>
#include <vector>

#include <ctype.h>

const char *const program_name = "comline";
const char *const program_version = "version 0.01 (08/07/97)";

inline void usage( int exit_value = 0 )
{
    // prints out a formatted usage message,
    // and exits using the exit_value ...

    cerr << "usage:\n"
         << program_name << " "
         << "[-d] [-h] [-v] \n\t"
         << "[-o output_file] [-l limit] \n\t"
         << "file_name\n\t[file_name [file_name [ ... ]]]\n\n"
         << "where [] indicates optional option:\n\n\t"
         << "-h: help.\n\t\t"
         << "generates this message and exits\n\n\t"
         << "-v: version.\n\t\t"
         << "prints version information and exits\n\n\t"
         << "-d: debug.\n\t\tturns debugging on\n\n\t"
         << "-l limit\n\t\t"
         << "limit must be a non-negative integer\n\n\t"
         << "-o ofile\n\t\t"
         << "file within which to write out results\n\t\t"
         << "by default, results written to standard output\n\n"
         << "file_name\n\t\t"
         << "the name of the actual file to process\n\t\t"
         << "at least one file_name is required --\n\t\t"
         << "any number may be specified\n\n"
         << "examples:\n\t\t"
         << "$command chapter7.doc\n\t\t"
         << "$command -d -l 1024 -o test_7_8 "
         << "chapter7.doc chapter8.doc\n\n";

    exit( exit_value );
}

int main( int argc, char* argv[] )
{
    bool debug_on = false;
    bool ofile_on = false;
    bool limit_on = false;
    int limit = -1;
```

```cpp
string ofile;
vector<string, allocator> file_names;

cout << "illustration of handling command line arguments:\n"
     << "argc: " << argc << endl;

for ( int ix = 1; ix < argc; ++ix )
{
   cout << "argv[ " << ix << " ]: "
        << argv[ ix ] << endl;

   char *pchar = argv[ ix ];
   switch ( pchar[ 0 ] )
   {
      case '-':
      {
         cout << "case \'-\' found\n";
         switch( pchar[ 1 ] )
         {
            case 'd':
               cout << "-d found: "
                    << "debugging turned on\n";

               debug_on = true;
               break;

            case 'v':
               cout << "-v found: "
                    << "version info displayed\n";

               cout << program_name
                    << " :: "
                    << program_version
                    << endl;

               return 0;

            case 'h':
               cout << "-h found: "
                    << "help information\n";

               // no break necessary: usage() exits
               usage();

            case 'o':
               cout << "-o found: output file\n";
               ofile_on = true;
               break;
```

```
                case 'l':
                    cout << "-l found: "
                            << "resource limit\n";

                    limit_on = true;
                    break;

                default:
                    cerr << program_name
                            << " : error : "
                            << "unrecognized option: - "
                            << pchar << "\n\n";

                    // no break necessary: usage() exits
                    usage( -1 );
            }
            break;
        }

        default: // either a file name
            cout << "default nonhyphen argument: "
                    << pchar << endl;

            if ( ofile_on ) {
                ofile_on = false;
                ofile = pchar;
            }
            else
            if ( limit_on ) {
                limit_on = false;
                limit = atoi( pchar );
                if ( limit < 0 ) {
                    cerr << program_name
                            << " : error : "
                            << "negative value for limit.\n\n";

                    usage( -2 );
                }
            }
            else file_names.push_back( string( pchar ));
            break;
        }
    }

    if ( file_names.empty() ) {
        cerr << program_name
                << " : error : "
                << "no file specified for processing.\n\n";
```

```
            usage( -3 );
        }

    if ( limit != -1 )
        cout << "User-specifed limit: "
                << limit << endl;

    if ( ! ofile.empty() )
        cout << "User-specified output file: "
                << ofile << endl;

    cout << (file_names.size() == 1 ? "File " : "Files ")
            << "to be processed are the following:\n";

    for ( int inx = 0; inx < file_names.size(); ++inx )
        cout << "\t" << file_names[ inx ] << endl;
}
```

Here is an exercise of our program:

```
    a.out -d -1 1024 -o test_7_8 chapter7.doc chapter8.doc
```

Here is the trace of the processing of the command line options:

```
    illustration of handling command line arguments:
    argc: 8
    argv[ 1 ]: -d
    case '-' found
    -d found: debugging turned on
    argv[ 2 ]: -1
    case '-' found
    -1 found: resource limit
    argv[ 3 ]: 1024
    default nonhyphen argument: 1024
    argv[ 4 ]: -o
    case '-' found
    -o found: output file
    argv[ 5 ]: test_7_8
    default nonhyphen argument: test_7_8
    argv[ 6 ]: chapter7.doc
    default nonhyphen argument: chapter7.doc
    argv[ 7 ]: chapter8.doc
    default nonhyphen argument: chapter8.doc
    User-specifed limit: 1024
    User-specified output file: test_7_8
    Files to be processed are the following:
            chapter7.doc
            chapter8.doc
```

7.8.1   A Command Line Class

The details of processing the command line options are best encapsulated so that we don't clutter `main()`. One encapsulation strategy, of course, is to provide a function. For example:

```
extern int parse_options( int arg_count,
                          char **arg_vector );

int main( int argc, char *argv[] ) {
    // ...
    int option_status;
    option_status = parse_options( argc, argv );
    // ...
}
```

The design question is how to return the set of values passed by the user. Typically, these values are defined as global objects and are not passed into or back from the function. Alternatively, we can encapsulate the processing within a class.

The data members of the class are the objects representing the potential values to be set by the user. A set of public inline member functions provides access to these values. The constructor initializes these values to their default setting. A member function takes `argc` and `argv` as arguments and provides the handling of the options:

```
#include <vector>
#include <string>

class CommandOpt {
public:
    CommandOpt() : _limit( -1 ), _debug_on( false ) {}
    int parse_options( int argc, char *argv[] );

    string out_file() { return _out_file; }
    bool   debug_on() { return _debug_on; }
    int    files()    { return _file_names.size(); }

    // to access _file_names
    string& operator[]( int ix );

private:
    inline int usage( int exit_value = 0 );

    bool _debug_on;
    int _limit;
    string _out_file;
    vector<string, allocator> _file_names;

    static const char *const program_name;
    static const char *const program_version;
};
```

Here is our revised main():[1]

```
#include "CommandOpt.h"

int main( int argc, char *argv[] ) {
    // ...
    CommandOpt com_opt;
    int option_status;
    option_status = com_opt.parse_options(argc,argv);
    // ...
}
```

Exercise 7.15

Add handling for a -t option (which turns on a timer), and a -b option (which takes a bufsize argument). Be sure to update usage() as well. For example:

```
prog -t -b 512 data0
```

Exercise 7.16

Our implementation currently fails to handle the case of there being no space between the option and its associated value. Ideally, we would accept the option with or without the space. Modify our implementation to do this.

Exercise 7.17

Our implementation currently fails to handle the user error of adding a space between the hyphen and the option, as in

```
prog - d data0
```

Modify our implementation to recognize and explicitly flag this error.

Exercise 7.18

Our implementation currently fails to recognize multiple instances of the -l or -o option. Modify our implementation to do this. What should the policy be?

Exercise 7.19

Our implementation generates a fatal error if the user specifies an unknown option. Do you think this is reasonable? What else might we do?

Exercise 7.20

Add support for options beginning with a plus (+), providing handling for the options

---

1. The full implementation of the CommandOpt class is available at the Addison–Wesley Web site.

+s and +pt as well as +sp and +ps. Let's presume that +s turns strict handling on and that +p supports previous constructs that are now obsolete. For example:

```
prog +s +p -d -b 1024 data0
```

7.9   Pointers to Functions ◈

Let's assume that we have been asked to provide a sorting function to be called as follows:

```
sort( start, end, compare );
```

start and end are pointers to elements of an array of strings. The sort() function sorts the array elements between start and end. compare defines the comparison operation to be used when comparing two strings within the array.

What implementation should be used for compare? We may want to sort the strings within the array in lexicographic order — that is, in the same manner as words are sorted within a dictionary; or we may want to sort them by length so that the shorter strings are placed at the front of the array and the longer ones at the end. Some facility for specifying alternative comparison operations is needed.

(Note that Chapter 12 describes the sort() function and other general algorithms provided by the C++ standard library. In this section, to illustrate the use of function pointers, we write our own sort() function, which is a simplified version of the function in the C++ standard library.)

One strategy to resolve these requirements is to have the third argument compare be a function pointer specifying the comparison function to be used.

To simplify the use of the sort() function without restricting its flexibility, we may want to specify a default comparison operation to be used in the majority of cases. Let's assume that the most common case is to sort the strings in lexicographic order and that the default argument would specify a comparison operation that would use the compare() function for strings (this function is first introduced in Section 6.10).

This section considers how to implement our sort() function using function pointers.

7.9.1   The Type of a Pointer to Function

How can a pointer to function be declared? What will the parameter that takes a pointer to function as an argument look like? Here is the definition of the lexicoCompare() function used to compare two strings lexicographically:

```
#include <string>
int lexicoCompare( const string &s1, const string &s2 ) {
    return s1.compare(s2);
}
```

If all characters in the strings s1 and s2 are equal, then lexicoCompare() returns 0; otherwise, if the string represented by the first parameter is less than the string represented by the second parameter, a negative number is returned; if it is greater, a positive number is returned.

A function's name is not part of its type. A function's type is determined only by its return type and its parameter list. A pointer to `lexicoCompare()` must point to a function with the same type (with the same return type and the same parameter list) as `lexicoCompare()`. Let's try:

```
int *pf( const string &, const string & ); // oops: not quite
```

This is almost correct. The problem is that the compiler interprets the statement as the declaration of a function named `pf` taking two arguments and returning a pointer of type `int*`. The parameter list is correct, but the return type is not quite what we want. The dereference operator (*) is associated with the return type, in this case with the type specifier `int`, and not with `pf`. Parentheses are necessary to associate the dereference operator with `pf`:

```
int (*pf)( const string &, const string & ); //ok: this does it
```

This statement declares `pf` to be a pointer to a function that takes two parameters and has a return type of `int`; that is, a pointer to a function that has the same type as that of `lexicoCompare()`.

The following function shares the same type as `lexicoCompare()`, and each of them can be pointed to by `pf`:

```
int sizeCompare( const string &, const string & );
```

However, `calc()` and `gcd()` are functions that have a type different from the type of the preceding two functions and they cannot be pointed to by `pf`:

```
int calc( int , int );
int gcd( int , int );
```

A pointer that could point to either of these two functions can be defined as follows:

```
int (*pfi)( int, int );
```

An ellipsis is part of the function type. Two functions that have the same parameter list, except that one function has an additional ellipsis at the end of its parameter list, have different function types. Pointers to such functions will have different types.

```
int printf( const char*, ... );
int strlen( const char* );

int (*pfce)( const char*, ... ); // can point to printf()
int (*pfc)( const char* );       // can point to strlen()
```

There are as many distinct function types as there are distinct combinations of function return types and parameter lists.

7.9.2   Initialization and Assignment

Recall that an array name evaluates to a pointer to its first element when the array name is not modified by the subscript operator. A function name, when not modified by the call operator, evaluates as a pointer to a function of its type. For example, the expression

```
lexicoCompare;
```

evaluates to a pointer of type

```
int (*)( const string &, const string & );
```

Applying the address-of operator to the function name also yields a pointer to function of its function type. Thus, both lexicoCompare and &lexicoCompare have the same type. A pointer to function can be initialized as follows:

```
int (*pfi)( const string &, const string & ) = lexicoCompare;
int (*pfi2)( const string &, const string & ) = &lexicoCompare;
```

A pointer to function can also be assigned a value, as follows:

```
pfi = lexicoCompare;
pfi2 = pfi;
```

An initialization or assignment is legal only if the parameter list and return type of the pointer on the left-hand side of the assignment operator exactly match those of the function or pointer on the right-hand side. If there is a mismatch, a compile-time error message is issued; no implicit type conversion exists between one pointer to function type and another. For example:

```
int calc( int, int );
int (*pfi2s)( const string &, const string & ) = 0;
int (*pfi2i)( int, int ) = 0;

int main() {
    pfi2i = calc;  // ok
    pfi2s = calc;  // error: type mismatch
    pfi2s = pfi2i; // error: type mismatch
    return 0;
}
```

A function pointer can be initialized with or assigned the value zero, which indicates that the pointer does not point to any function.

7.9.3   Invocation

A pointer to a function can be used to call the function to which it refers. The dereference operator is not required in order to invoke the function. Both a direct call to the function using the function's name and an indirect call to the function using a pointer can be written the same way. For example:

```
#include <iostream>

int min( int*, int );
int (*pf)( int*, int ) = min;

const int iaSize = 5;
int ia[ iaSize ] = { 7, 4, 9, 2, 5 };

int main() {
   cout << "Direct call: min: "
        << min( ia, iaSize ) << endl;

   cout << "Indirect call: min: "
        << pf( ia, iaSize ) << endl;

   return 0;
}

int min( int* ia, int sz ) {
   int minVal = ia[ 0 ];
   for ( int ix = 1; ix < sz; ++ix )
     if ( minVal > ia[ ix ] )
         minVal = ia[ ix ];
   return minVal;
}
```

The call

```
pf( ia, iaSize );
```

can also be written using the longhand explicit pointer notation:

```
(*pf)( ia, iaSize );
```

The two forms yield the same result, although the second form makes it clearer to a reader that the call is performed through a function pointer.

Of course, if the pointer to function has a value of zero, either invocation results in a run-time error. Only pointers that have been initialized or assigned to refer to a function can be safely used to invoke a function.

7.9.4   Arrays of Pointers to Functions

It is possible to declare arrays of pointers to functions. For example,

```
int (*testCases[10])();
```

declares testCases to be an array of ten elements. Each element is a pointer to a function that takes no arguments and that has a return type of int.

Declarations such as the one for the array testCases are hard to read, because it is difficult to decipher with which piece of the declaration the function type is associated.

In these cases, the use of a typedef name can make declarations considerably easier to read. For example:

```
// typedefs make declarations easier to read
typedef int (*PFV)(); // typedef for pointer to function type

PFV testCases[10];
```

This declaration of testCases is equivalent to the previous one.

A call to a function referred to by one of the elements of testCases might look like this:

```
const int size = 10;
PFV testCases[size];
int testResults[size];

void runtests() {
   for ( int i = 0; i < size; ++i )
      // call to an array element
      testResults[ i ] = testCases[ i ]();
}
```

An array of pointers to functions can be initialized using an initializer list in which each initializer represents a function of the same type as the type of the array element. For example:

```
int lexicoCompare( const string &, const string & );
int sizeCompare( const string &, const string & );

typedef int ( *PFI2S )( const string &, const string & );
PFI2S compareFuncs[2] =
{
   lexicoCompare,
   sizeCompare
};
```

A pointer to compareFuncs can also be declared. Such a pointer is of the type "pointer to array of pointers to functions." The definition looks like this:

```
PFI2S (*pfCompare)[2] = &compareFuncs;
```

The declaration is decomposed as follows:

```
(*pfCompare)
```

The dereference operator declares pfCompare to be a pointer. The [2] that follows indicates that pfCompare is a pointer to an array of two elements:

```
(*pfCompare)[2]
```

The typedef PFI2S indicates the type of the array element, which is "pointer to a function returning int and taking two parameters of type const string &." The type of the array element is the same as the type of the expression &lexicoCompare. It is also the same as the type of the first element of compareFuncs, which can be obtained by writing either of the following:

```
compareFuncs[ 0 ];
(*pfCompare)[ 0 ];
```

To call lexicoCompare() through pfCompare, the programmer would write either of the following:

```
// equivalent invocations
pfCompare[ 0 ]( string1, string2 );      // shorthand
((*pfCompare)[ 0 ])( string1, string2 ); // explicit
```

7.9.5   Parameters and Return Types

To go back to the problem presented at the beginning of this section, where we were given the task of writing a sorting function, how can pointers to functions be used to write this function? Because a function parameter can be a pointer to function, we can pass a pointer to function as an argument to the sorting function to indicate which comparison operation to use:

```
int sort( string*, string*,
          int (*)( const string &, const string & ) );
```

Again, using a typedef name makes the declaration of sort() easier to read:

```
// typedef makes declaration of sort() easier to read
typedef int ( *PFI2S )( const string &, const string & );
int sort( string*, string*, PFI2S );
```

Because the function that will be used in most cases is lexicoCompare(), a default argument for the pointer to function parameter can be used:

```
// a default argument is provided for the 3rd parameter
int lexicoCompare( const string &, const string & );
int sort( string*, string*, PFI2S = lexicoCompare );
```

A definition of the sort() function might look like this:

```
1 void sort( string *s1, string *s2,
2            PFI2S compare = lexicoCompare )
3 {
4     // stopping condition for recursion
5     if ( s1 < s2 ) {
6         string elem = *s1;
7         string *low = s1;
8         string *high = s2 + 1;
9
10        for (;;) {
11            while ( compare( *++low, elem ) < 0 && low < s2) ;
12            while ( compare( elem, *--high ) < 0  && high > s1) ;
13
```

```
14              if ( low < high )
15                  low->swap(*high);
16              else break;
17          } // end, for(;;)
18
19          s1->swap(*high);
20          sort( s1, high - 1, compare );
21          sort( high + 1, s2, compare );
22      } // end, if ( s1 < s2 )
23 }
```

sort() is an implementation of C.A.R. Hoare's *quicksort* algorithm. Let's look at the function definition in detail. The function sorts the array elements between s1 and s2. sort() is a recursive function that applies itself to progressively smaller subarrays. The stopping condition is when s1 refers to the same element as s2 or refers to an element that is past the element referred to by s2 (line 5).

elem (line 6) is referred to as the *partition element*. All array elements that are lexicographically smaller than elem are moved to the left of elem; all elements greater are moved to the right. The array is now partitioned into two subarrays. sort() is recursively applied to each (lines 20–21).

The purpose of the for(;;) loop is to perform the partition (lines 10–17). At each iteration of the loop, low is advanced to index the first element of the array that is greater than or equal to elem (line 11). Similarly, high is decremented to index the rightmost element of the array equal to or less than elem (line 12). If low is no longer less than high, the elements have been partitioned and we break the loop; otherwise, the elements are swapped and the next loop iteration begins (lines 14–16). Although the array has been partitioned, elem is still the first element of the array. The swap() on line 19 places elem in its final position in the array before sort() is then applied to the two subarrays.

The comparison of the array elements is done by calling the function to which compare refers (lines 11–12). The swap() string operation is called to swap the strings to which the array elements refer. (The swap() string operation is introduced in Section 6.11.)

The following implementation of main() uses our sorting function:

```
#include <iostream>
#include <string>

// normally, these would be in a header file
int lexicoCompare( const string &, const string & );
int sizeCompare( const string &, const string & );
typedef int (*PFI)( const string &, const string & );
void sort( string *, string *, PFI=lexicoCompare );

string as[10] = { "a", "light", "drizzle", "was", "falling",
                  "when", "they", "left", "the", "museum" };
```

```
int main() {
   // call sort() which uses the default argument for compare
   sort( as, as + sizeof(as)/sizeof(as[0]) - 1 );

   // display the result of the sorted array
   for ( int i = 0; i < sizeof(as)/sizeof(as[0]); ++i )
      cout << as[ i ].c_str() << "\n\t";
}
```

When compiled and executed, the program produces the following output:

```
"a"
"drizzle"
"falling"
"left"
"light"
"museum"
"the"
"they"
"was"
"when"
```

A function parameter never has function type. Instead, a parameter of function type is automatically converted to the type pointer to function. For example:

```
// typedef represents a function type
typedef int functype( const string &, const string & );
void sort( string *, string *, functype );
```

sort() is treated by the compiler as having been declared as

```
void sort( string *, string *,
           int (*)( const string &, const string & ) );
```

The preceding two declarations of sort() are equivalent.

Note that, in addition to being used as a parameter type, a pointer to function can also be the type of a function's return value. For example:

```
int (*ff( int ))( int*, int );
```

This declaration declares ff() to be a function taking one parameter of type int. It returns a pointer to a function of type

```
int (*)( int*, int );
```

Again, the use of a typedef name can make declarations considerably easier to read. For example, the typedef PF makes it easier to decipher that ff() has a return type that is a pointer to function:

```
// typedefs make declarations easier to read
typedef int (*PF)( int*, int );

PF ff( int );
```

A function cannot be declared to return a function type. If it is, a compile-time error is generated. For example, the function ff() could not have been declared as follows:

```
// typedef represents a function type
typedef int func( int*, int );

func ff( int ); // error: ff() has a return type of function type
```

7.9.6   Pointers to extern "C" Functions

It is possible to declare pointers to functions to refer to functions written in other programming languages. This can be done using a linkage directive. For example, the pointer pf refers to a C function:

```
extern "C" void (*pf)(int);
```

When pf is used to call a function, the function called is a C function.

```
extern "C" void exit(int);

// pf refers to the C function exit()
extern "C" void (*pf)(int) = exit;

int main() {
   // ...
   // calls a C function, namely exit()
   (*pf)(99);
}
```

A pointer to a C function does not have the same type as a pointer to a C++ function. Remember that an initialization or assignment of a pointer to function is legal only if the type of the pointer assigned to matches exactly that of the function or pointer on the right-hand side of the assignment operator. Therefore, a pointer to a C function cannot be initialized or be assigned to point to a C++ function (and vice versa). When there is such a mismatch, a compile-time error message is issued. For example:

```
void (*pf1)(int);
extern "C" void (*pf2)(int);
int main() {
   pf1 = pf2; // error: pf1 and pf2 have different types
   // ...
}
```

Note that for some C++ implementations, the characteristics of a pointer to a C function are the same as the characteristics of a pointer to a C++ function. Some compilers may accept the preceding assignment as a language extension.

When a linkage directive applies to a declaration, all functions declared by the declaration are affected by the linkage directive. In the following example, the parameter pfParm is also a pointer to a C function. The linkage directive applies to the function to which this parameter refers.

```
// pfParm is a pointer to a C function
extern "C" void f1( void(*pfParm)(int) );
```

f1() is therefore a C function that has one parameter that is a pointer to a C function. And again, because a pointer to a C function does not have the same type as a pointer to a C++ function, the argument passed to f1() must be the name of a C function or a pointer to a C function. (Again, on implementations in which pointers to C functions and pointers to C++ functions have the same characteristics, the compiler may support a language extension that allows a pointer to a C++ function to be passed to f1() as an argument.)

Because a linkage directive applies to all the functions in a declaration, how could one declare a C++ function to have a parameter that is a pointer to a C function? The solution is to use a typedef. For example:

```
// FC represents the type:
// C function taking one int parameter and returning void
extern "C" typedef void FC( int );

// f2() is a C++ function with a parameter
// that is a pointer to a C function
void f2( FC *pfParm );
```

Exercise 7.21

Section 7.5 defines the function factorial(). Define a pointer to a function that can point to factorial(). Invoke the function through this pointer to generate the factorial of number 11.

Exercise 7.22

What are the types of the following declarations?

```
(a) int (*mpf)(vector<int>&);
(b) void (*apf[20])(double);
(c) void (*(*papf)[2])(int);
```

How would you use typedef names to make the declarations easier to read?

Exercise 7.23

The following functions are C library functions defined in the header <cmath>.

```
double abs(double);
double sin(double);
double cos(double);
double sqrt(double);
```

How would you declare an array of pointers to C functions and initialize this array to contain the four functions? Write a `main()` function that will call `sqrt()` through the array element with the argument 97.9.

Exercise 7.24

Let's go back to the `sort()` example. Provide the definition for the function

```
int sizeCompare( const string &, const string & );
```

so that if the two parameters refer to strings of the same size, then `sizeCompare()` returns 0; otherwise, if the string represented by the first parameter is shorter than the string represented by the second parameter, a negative number is returned; if it is greater, a positive number is returned. Remember that the string operation `size()` yields the size of a string. Change `main()` to call `sort()` with a third argument that is a pointer to `sizeCompare()`.

8

Scope and Lifetime

This chapter answers two important questions regarding declarations in C++: Where can the name introduced by a declaration be used? When is it safe for a program to use an object or invoke a function; that is, what is the lifetime of the run-time entity introduced by a declaration? To answer the first question, we present scopes and see how they delimit where names can be used in a program text file. The various C++ scopes are presented: global scope and local scopes as well as the more advanced topic of namespace scopes, presented at the end of the chapter. To answer the second question, we describe how declarations introduce global objects and functions (entities that last for the entire program duration), local objects (objects that last for a subset of the program duration) and dynamically allocated objects (objects whose lifetime is controlled by the programmer). We also examine the specific run-time properties associated with these objects and functions.

8.1 Scope

Every name in a C++ program must refer to a unique entity (an object, function, type, or template). This does not mean that a name can be used only once in a C++ program: a name can be reused to refer to different entities provided that there is some *context* by which the different meanings of the name can be distinguished. The general context used to distinguish the meanings of names is *scope*. C++ supports three forms of scope: *local* scope, *namespace* scope, and *class* scope.

A local scope is a portion of program text contained within a function definition (or function block). Each function represents a distinct local scope. Within a function, each compound statement (or block) also represents a distinct local scope.

A namespace scope is a portion of program text that is not contained within a function declaration, a function definition, or a class definition. The outermost namespace scope of a program is called *global scope* or *global namespace scope*. Objects, functions, types, and templates can be defined in global scope. A programmer can define *user-declared* namespaces nested within the global scope using *namespace definitions*. Each user-declared namespace is a different scope, and each is distinct from the global scope. As with the global scope, user-declared namespaces can contain declarations and definitions for objects, functions, types, and templates as well as other nested user-declared namespaces. User-declared namespaces are described in Sections 8.5 and 8.6.

Each class definition introduces a distinct *class scope*. Class definitions and class scopes are described in Chapter 13.

A name can refer to different entities in different scopes without penalty. In the following program fragment, for example, there are four entities named s1:

```
#include <iostream>
#include <string>

// compare s1 and s2 lexicographically
int lexicoCompare( const string &s1, const string &s2 )
   { ... }

// compare size of s1 and s2
int sizeCompare( const string &s1, const string &s2 )
   { ... }

typedef int (*PFI)( const string &, const string & );
// sort array of strings
void sort( string *s1, string *s2, PFI compare =lexicoCompare )
   { ... }

string s1[10] = { "a", "light", "drizzle", "was", "falling",
                  "when", "they", "left", "the", "school" };

int main()
{
    // call sort() -- use the default argument for compare
    // refers to global array s1
    sort( s1, s1 + sizeof(s1)/sizeof(s1[0]) - 1 );

    // display the sorted array
    for ( int i = 0; i < sizeof(s1) / sizeof(s1[0]); ++i )
       cout << s1[ i ].c_str() << "\n\t";
}
```

Because the definitions of the functions `lexicoCompare()`, `sizeCompare()`, and `sort()` are different scopes and because all are different from the global scope, each one of these scopes can define a variable named s1.

A name introduced by a declaration is potentially *visible* from its point of declaration to the end of the scope in which it is declared (including within nested scopes). Thus, the name of `lexicoCompare()`'s parameter s1 is visible until the end of its scope, that is, until the end of lexicoCompare()'s definition. The name of the global array s1 is visible from its point of declaration until the end of the file, including within nested scopes, such as within the definition of main().

In general, a name must be declared to refer to one single entity within a given scope. For example, if the following declaration is added to the preceding example, following the declaration for the array s1 in global scope, a compile-time error is generated:

```
void s1(); // error: redeclaration of the name s1
```

Overloaded functions are an exception to this rule: it is possible to define more than one function with the same name in the same scope, provided that each function has a different parameter list. Chapter 9 discusses overloaded functions.

In C++, a name must be declared before it can be used in expressions. If no declaration is found for s1 before its use in main(), a compiler error is generated. *Name resolution* is the process by which a name used in an expression is associated with a declaration. It is the process by which the name is given meaning. This process depends on how the name is used and on the scope in which the name is used. Throughout this book, we discuss name resolution in various contexts. Name resolution in local scope is discussed in the next subsection, name resolution in function template definitions is discussed in Section 10.9, name resolution in class scope is discussed at the end of Chapter 13, and name resolution in class template definitions is discussed in Section 16.12.

Scopes and name resolution are compile-time notions; they apply to some portion of program text. These notions give meaning to the program text in a source file. The compiler interprets the program text it reads according to the scope rules and name resolution rules.

8.1.1   Local Scope

A local scope is a portion of the program text contained within a function definition (or function block). Each function represents a distinct local scope. Within a function, each compound statement (or block) also represents its own local scope. Local block scopes can be nested. For example, the following function definition defines two levels of local scopes performing a binary search of a sorted vector of integers:

```
const int notFound = -1; // global scope

int binSearch( const vector<int> &vec, int val )
{ // local scope: level #1
    int low = 0;
    int high = vec.size() - 1;

    while ( low <= high )
    { // local scope: level #2
        int mid = ( low + high ) / 2;
        if ( val == vec[ mid ] ) return mid;
```

```
         if ( val < vec[ mid ] )
            high = mid - 1;
         else low = mid + 1;
      }
      return notFound; // local scope: level #1
   }
```

The first local scope is the scope of binSearch()'s function body. This first local scope declares the function parameters vec and val. It also declares the variables low and high. The while loop within binSearch() defines a nested local scope. This nested local scope declares one variable, the integer mid. This nested local scope uses the function parameters vec and val and the local variables high and low. The global scope encloses both local scopes. It declares one integer constant: notFound.

The names of the function parameters vec and val belong to the first local scope of the function body. These names cannot be redeclared within this first local scope. For example:

```
   int binSearch( const vector<int> &vec, int val )
   { // local scope: level #1
      int val; // error: invalid redeclaration of the name val
      // ...
```

The parameter names can be used within binSearch()'s function body as well as within the nested scope of the while loop. The function parameters vec and val cannot be referred to outside of binSearch()'s function body.

Name resolution in a local scope proceeds as follows: the immediate scope in which the name is used is searched. If a declaration is found, the name is resolved; if it is not found, the enclosing scope is searched. This process continues until either a declaration is found or the global scope has been searched. If the latter occurs and no declaration is found for the name, the use of the name is flagged as an error.

Because of the order in which scopes are searched during name resolution, a declaration in an enclosing scope is *hidden* by a declaration of the same name declared in a nested scope. In the earlier example, if a variable low were declared in global scope before the definition of binSearch(), the use of low in the nested local scope of the while loop would still refer to the local declaration of low; the global declaration would be hidden by the local declaration. For example:

```
   int low;

   int binSearch( const vector<int> &vec, int val )
   {
      // local declaration of low
      // hides declaration in global scope
      int low = 0;
      // ...
```

```
    // low is the local variable
    while ( low <= high )
    { // ...
    }
    // ...
}
```

Some statements allow a variable definition within their control structure. For example, a for loop permits the definition of a variable within its init-statement:

```
for ( int index = 0; index < vecSize; ++index )
{
    // index is visible only within here
    if ( vec[ index ] == someValue )
        break;
}
// error: index is not visible here
if ( index != vecSize ) // found element
```

Variables, such as index, defined within the for loop init-statement are visible only within the local scope of the for loop itself and local scopes nested within it (this is the case in Standard C++ but was different in pre-Standard C++), as if the for statement were written like this:

```
// Representation of compiler transformation
{ // invisible compound statement
    int index = 0;
    for ( ; index < vecSize; ++index )
    {
        // ...
    }
}
```

This prohibits the programmer from accessing the control variable outside the local scope of the loop. If the programmer wishes to test index to determine whether the value was found, the code fragment must be rewritten as follows:

```
int index = 0;
for ( ; index < vecSize; ++index )
{
    // ...
}
// ok: index is visible here
if ( index != vecSize ) // found element
```

Because a variable declared within the init-statement of the for loop is local to the loop itself, the variable name can be reused within the control structure of other for loops within the same local scope. For example:

```
void fooBar( int *ia, int sz )
{
   for (int i=0; i<sz; ++i) ... // ok
   for (int i=0; i<sz; ++i) ... // ok: different i
   for (int i=0; i<sz; ++i) ... // ok: different i
}
```

Similarly, a variable can be declared within the condition of an if or switch statement as well as within the condition of a while loop and for loop. For example:

```
if ( int *pi = getValue() )
{
   // pi != 0 -- it is OK to use *pi here
   int result = calc(*pi);
   // ...
}
else
{
   // pi visible here too
   // pi == 0
   cout << "error: getValue() failed" << endl;
}
```

Variables, such as pi, defined within the condition of an if statement are visible only within the if statement, its associated else statement, and the scopes nested within these statements. The value of the condition is that of the variable once it has been initialized. If pi is initialized with the value 0, the null pointer value, the condition is false and the else portion of the if statement is executed. If pi is initialized with any value other than the null pointer value, the condition is true and the if portion is executed. The if statement, switch statement, for loop statement, and while loop statement are discussed in Chapter 5.

Exercise 8.1

In the following code sample, identify the different scopes. Which of the following declarations of ix, if any, are errors? Explain why.

```
int ix = 1024;
int ix();

void func( int ix, int iy ) {
   int ix = 255;

   if ( int ix = 0 ) {
      int ix = 79;
      {
         int ix = 89;
      }
   }
}
```

```
    else {
       int ix = 99;
    }
}
```

Exercise 8.2

In the following code sample, to which declarations do the uses of ix and iy refer?

```
int ix = 1024;

void func( int ix, int iy ) {
   ix = 100;

   for( int iy = 0 ; iy < 400; iy += 100 ) {
      iy += 100;
      ix = 300;
   }
   iy = 400;
}
```

8.2   Global Objects and Functions

A function declaration in global scope introduces a *global function*. A variable declaration in global scope introduces a *global object*. A global object is a run-time entity that exists throughout the duration of the program. The *lifetime* of the storage in which a global object resides begins at program start-up and ends when the program terminates.

A global function that is called or that has its address taken must have a definition. Similarly, a global object that is used in a program must have a definition. Global objects and non-inline global functions must be defined only once in a program. Inline functions can be defined more than once in a program as long as the many definitions provided are exactly the same. This requirement that global objects and functions either have only one definition or have exactly the same definition many times in a program is called the *one definition rule* (ODR). In this section, we see how to declare and define global objects and functions in our programs to respect the ODR.

8.2.1   Declarations versus Definitions

As we have seen in Chapter 7, a function *declaration* specifies the function's name as well as the function's return type and parameter list. In addition to this information, a function *definition* provides a body for the function, which is a list of statements enclosed in curly braces. A function must be declared before it can be called. For example:

```
// declaration of function calc()
// definition is provided in another file
void calc(int);
```

```
int main()
{
    int loc1 = get(); // error: get() is not declared
    calc(loc1);       // ok: declaration for calc() is found
    // ...
}
```

An object definition has one of the following two forms:

```
type_specifier  object_name;
type_specifier  object_name  =  initializer;
```

For example, the following is a definition for obj1. In this definition, obj1 is initialized to 97:

```
int obj1 = 97;
```

The following is a definition for obj2 even though no initializer is specified:

```
int obj2;
```

An object defined in global scope without an explicit initializer is guaranteed to have its storage initialized to 0. Thus, in the following two definitions, both var1 and var2 have an initial value of 0:

```
int var1 = 0;
int var2;
```

There must be only one definition for a global object in a program. Because an object must be declared in a file before it can be used, it must be possible for a program composed of many files to simply declare an object in a file without defining it. How do we simply declare an object?

The keyword extern provides a method for declaring an object without defining it. Similar in effect to a function declaration, it promises that the object is defined elsewhere, either somewhere else in this text file or in another text file of the program. For example,

```
extern int i;
```

is a "pledge" to the program that elsewhere there exists a definition such as

```
int i;
```

The extern declaration does not cause storage to be allocated. It can appear multiple times within the same file or within different files of the same program. Typically, however, the declaration appears once in a public header file that is included when necessary in the files referring to the global object.

```
// header file
extern int obj1;
extern int obj2;
```

```
// text file
int obj1 = 97;
int obj2;
```

The declaration of a global object that specifies both the extern keyword and an explicit initializer is treated as a definition of that object. Storage is allocated, and any subsequent definitions of that object in the program are flagged as errors. For example:

```
extern const double pi = 3.1416; // definition
const double pi; // error: redefinition of pi
```

The extern keyword can also be specified with a function declaration. Its only effect is to make the implicit "defined elsewhere" nature of the declaration explicit. Such a declaration takes the following form:

```
extern void putValues( int*, int );
```

8.2.2   Interfile Declaration Matching

One of the occasional problems of declaring an object or function in multiple files is that the declarations in different files can differ or change over time. C++ provides some support that helps detect differences between function declarations in different files.

For example, in the file token.C, the function addToken() is defined as taking one parameter of type unsigned char. In the file lex.C, where it is called, addToken() is declared as taking one parameter of type char.

```
// ---- in file token.C ----
int addToken( unsigned char tok ) { /* ... */ }

// ---- in file lex.C ----
extern int addToken( char );
```

A call of addToken() in lex.C will cause the program to fail at the link phase. Were the preceding program to link successfully, the following scenario might occur. The compiled program tested on a Sun Sparc workstation executes correctly. The program is then sent to a field location using an IBM 390. The program compiles without a hitch. Unfortunately, the first time it is executed, it fails miserably. Not even the simplest test program works. What could have happened?

Here is part of the set of token declarations:

```
const unsigned char INLINE = 128;
const unsigned char VIRTUAL = 129;
```

The call of addToken() looks like this:

```
curTok = INLINE;
// ...
addToken( curTok );
```

chars are implemented as a signed type on the one machine and as an unsigned type on the other. The misdeclaration of addToken() causes each token with a value greater than 127 to overflow on the machine in which the char type is signed. If the code sample were allowed to compile and link, disastrous consequences would be likely at run-time.

In C++, there exists a mechanism by which the type and number of parameters of a function are encoded in the function name. This mechanism is called *type-safe linkage*. Type-safe linkage helps the implementation catch mismatches between function declarations in different files. In the preceding example, the parameter of type unsigned char and the parameter of type char have different types. Because of type-safe linkage, the addToken() function declared in lex.C will be flagged as an undefined function. The definition in token.C is seen as defining another function.

The type-safe linkage mechanism provides some measure of interfile type-checking for function calls. Type-safe linkage is also necessary to support overloaded functions. We discuss type-safe linkage further in the presentation of overloaded functions in Chapter 9.

Other kinds of type mismatches between declarations of the same object or function appearing in different files may not be caught at the compile or link phase. Because the compiler processes one file at a time, it cannot ordinarily detect type violations across files. These type violations can be a source of serious program errors. For example, erroneous interfile declarations of objects or of the return types of functions are not detected. Errors such as the following reveal themselves only in run-time exceptions or in the incorrect output of the program.

```
// in token.C
unsigned char lastTok = 0;
unsigned char peekTok() { /* ... */ }

// in lex.C
extern char lastTok;      // one token history
extern char peekTok();    // one token lookahead
```

The disciplined use of header files is fundamental to the prevention of this sort of interfile declaration mismatch error. This is the topic of our next subsection.

8.2.3   Some Words on Header Files

A header file provides a centralized location for all extern object declarations, function declarations, and inline function definitions; this is spoken of as *localization* of declarations. Files that must use or define an object or function *include* the header file(s).

Header files provide two safeguards. First, all files are guaranteed to contain the same declaration for a global object or function. Second, should a declaration require updating, only one change to the header file needs be made. Failing to update a declaration in a particular file is no longer a possibility. The addToken() example provides a token.h header file as follows:

```
// ----- token.h -----
typedef unsigned char uchar;
const uchar INLINE = 128;
// ...
const uchar LT = ...;
const uchar GT = ...;

extern uchar lastTok;
extern int addToken( uchar );
inline bool is_relational( uchar tok )
    { return (tok >= LT && tok <= GT); }

// ----- lex.C -----
#include "token.h"
// ...

// ----- token.C -----
#include "token.h"
// ...
```

Some care should be taken in designing header files. The declarations provided should logically belong together. A header file takes time to compile. If it is too large or filled with too many disparate elements, programmers may be reluctant to incur the compile-time cost of including it. To reduce the compile-time of header files, some C++ implementations provide support for *precompiled* header files. You should consult the reference manual of your C++ implementation to see how to create a precompiled header file from an ordinary C++ header file. If your application has large header files, using precompiled header files instead of ordinary header files can significantly reduce the compile-time of your application.

A second consideration is that a header file should never contain a definition for a non-inline function or an object. Each of the following, for example, represents such a definition and therefore should not appear in a header file:

```
extern int ival = 10;
double fica_rate;
extern void dummy() {}
```

Although ival is declared with extern, its explicit initialization makes it an actual definition. Similarly, although dummy() is explicitly declared as extern, the empty brace pair stands as the definition of that function. fica_rate, although not explicitly initialized, is also considered an actual definition in C++ because the extern keyword is absent. The inclusion of any of these definitions in two or more files of the same program will result in a linker error complaining about multiple definitions.

In the token.h header file presented above, both the constant INLINE and the inline function is_relational() appear to violate this rule. However, they do not. Although they are definitions, definitions for symbolic constants and inline functions are special kinds of definitions. Symbolic constants and inline functions can be defined many times.

When possible, the value of a symbolic constant replaces the occurrence of its name during the compilation of the program. This process of substitution is referred to as *constant folding*. For example, the compiler substitutes the value 128 for the name INLINE wherever INLINE is used in a file. For the compiler to be able to replace the name of a constant with its value, the definition of the constant (the value of its initializer) must be visible wherever the constant is used. For this reason, a symbolic constant can be defined in different files of the same program. Ideally, then, although an initialized constant can be included in many different files, constant folding will have made it unnecessary for even one definition to occur in the executable.

In some cases, however, constant folding of a symbolic constant is not possible. In such cases, it is preferable to move the initialization of the constant to a single program text file. This can be done by explicitly declaring the constant extern. For example:

```
// ----- header file -----
const int buf_chunk = 1024;
extern char *const bufp;

// ----- program text file -----
char *const bufp = new char[buf_chunk];
```

Although bufp is declared as const, its value cannot be computed at compile-time (its initializer is a new expression that requires the invocation of a library function). Were it initialized within the header file, bufp would be defined within each file that included its definition. Not only would this be waste of space, but also it would likely be counter to the intentions of the programmer.

A symbolic constant is any object of const type. Can you see why the following declaration, when placed inside a header file, causes a linker error when included in two separate files of the program?

```
// oops: shouldn't be in a header file
const char* msg = "?? oops: error: ";
```

The problem is that msg is not a constant; rather, it is a nonconstant pointer that refers to a constant value. The proper declaration of a constant pointer looks like this (see Chapter 3 for a full discussion of pointer declarations):

```
const char *const msg = "?? oops: error: ";
```

This definition of a constant pointer can appear in many files.

A similar situation to that of symbolic constants can occur with inline functions. For the compiler to be able to expand the function body "in line" at the point where it is invoked, it must see the definition of the inline function. (Inline functions are introduced in Section 7.6.) Therefore, an inline function that is of interest to more than a single file must be defined within a header file. The inline specification, however, is only a hint that the function must be inlined. Whether the compiler actually inlines the function — in general or at any particular call within the program — varies across implementations. If the compiler cannot inline a function at the point of invocation, the compiler generates a definition for the function in the executable. If a definition for the same function is generated in more than one file, an unnecessarily large executable may result for a program.

Most compilers will generate a warning if either of the following cases holds (generally, this requires turning on a warning mode of the compiler).

1. The definition of the function makes it inherently impossible to be inlined. For example, the compiler may complain that the function is too complex to inline. In this case, if possible, rewrite the function; otherwise, remove the inline specification and place the function definition within a program text file.

2. A particular call of the function cannot be inlined. For example, on the original C++ implementation from AT&T (cfront), a second call of an inline function within the same expression is not inlined. In this case, the expression can be rewritten to separate the two inline function calls.

Before you declare a function inline, you must analyze its run-time behavior. Making sure that the function is really inlined is a necessary part of writing programs. We recommend that an inherently uninlineable function not be declared inline and not be placed in a header file.

Exercise 8.3

Identify which ones of the following are declarations and which ones are definitions. Explain why they are declarations or definitions.

```
(a) extern int ix = 1024;
(b) int iy;
(c) extern void reset( void *p ) { /* ... */ }
(d) extern const int *pi;
(e) void print( const matrix & );
```

Exercise 8.4

Which one of the following declarations and definitions would you put in a header file? In a program text file? Explain why.

```
(a) int var;
(b) inline bool is_equal( const SmallInt &, const SmallInt & ) { }
(c) void putValues( int *arr, int size );
(d) const double pi = 3.1416;
(e) extern int total = 255;
```

8.3   Local Objects

A variable declaration in local scope introduces a *local object*. There are three kinds of local objects: *automatic objects, register objects,* and *local static objects*. What distinguishes these objects is the lifetime and properties of the storage in which the objects reside. The storage in which an automatic object resides lasts from the time the function in which it is declared is invoked to the time the function exits. A register object is an automatic object for which fast read and store of the object's value are supported. A local static object resides in storage that lasts for the entire duration of the program. In this section, we examine the properties of these three kinds of local objects.

8.3.1   Automatic Objects

An automatic object has its storage allocated at the time the function in which it is defined is invoked. Storage for an automatic object is allocated from the program's run-time stack and is part of the activation record of the function. Automatic objects are said to have *automatic storage duration*, or *automatic extent*. An uninitialized automatic object contains a random bit pattern left over from the previous use of that storage. Its value is spoken of as *unspecified*.

Upon termination of the function, its activation record is popped from the run-time stack. In effect, the storage associated with the automatic object is deallocated. The object's lifetime ends upon the termination of the function. Any value it contains is discarded.

Because the storage associated with automatic objects is deallocated upon termination of the function, the address of an automatic object should be used with caution. The address of an automatic object should never be the return value of a function, because, once the function exits, the address refers to invalid storage. For example:

```
#include "Matrix.h"

Matrix* trouble( Matrix *pm )
{
    Matrix res;

    // do something using pm
    // assign the result to res

    return &res; // bad!
}

int main()
{
    Matrix m1;
    // ...
```

```
        Matrix *mainResult = trouble( &m1 );
        // ...
    }
```

mainResult is set to the address of the automatic Matrix object res. Unfortunately, the
storage of res is deallocated on completion of trouble(). On the return to main(),
mainResult is addressing technically unallocated memory. (In this example, the
address may still remain valid because we have not yet invoked another function to
overlay some or all of the activation record allocated to support trouble(), making
such an error more difficult to detect.) Using mainResult later in main() will yield surprising results.

  However, passing the address of main()'s automatic object m1 to the function trou-
ble() is always safe. The storage for main() is guaranteed to remain on the stack for the
duration of the call to trouble(), and the memory for m1 remains accessible for the duration of the call to trouble().

  When the address of an automatic object is stored in a pointer with a lifetime longer than that of the automatic object, the pointer is said to be a *dangling pointer*. This is a
serious programmer error, because the contents of the addressed memory are unpredictable. If the bits at that address are somehow relevant (so that the program does not
generate a segment fault, for example), the program may run to completion but provide invalid results.

8.3.2   Register Automatic Objects

Automatic objects used heavily within a function can be declared with the keyword
register. If possible, the compiler will load the object into a machine register. If it cannot, the object remains in memory. Array indexes and pointers occurring within a
loop are good candidates for register objects.

```
        for ( register int ix = 0; ix < sz; ++ix ) // ...
        for ( register int *p = array ; p < arraySize; ++p ) // ...
```

  A parameter can also be declared as a register variable:

```
    bool find( register int *pm, int val ) {
        while ( *pm )
            if ( *pm++ == val ) return true;
        return false;
    }
```

  Register variables may increase the speed of a function if the variables selected are
used heavily.

  Using the keyword register is only a hint to the compiler. Some compilers may
ignore this hint and use register allocation algorithms to figure out the best candidates
to be placed within the available machine registers. Because the compiler is aware of

the machine architecture on which the program is run, it is often able to make a more informed decision when selecting the content of machine registers.

8.3.3   Static Local Objects

It is also possible to declare, within a function definition or within a compound statement of a function definition, a local object that will persist for the entire duration of the program. When the value of a local object must persist across invocations of the function, an ordinary automatic object cannot be used. The value of an automatic object is discarded each time the function exits.

The solution in this case is to declare the local object as static. A *static local object* has *static storage duration*, or *static extent*. Though its value persists across invocations of its function, the visibility of its name remains limited to its local scope. A static local object is initialized the first time the execution of the program passes through the object's declaration. For example, here is a version of gcd() that traces the depth of its recursion using a static local object:

```
#include <iostream>

int traceGcd( int v1, int v2 )
{
    static int depth = 1;
    cout << "depth #" << depth++ << endl;

    if ( v2 == 0 ) {
        depth = 1;
        return v1;
    }
    return traceGcd( v2, v1%v2 );
}
```

The value associated with the static local object depth persists across invocations of traceGcd(). The initialization is performed only once: when traceGcd() is first called. The following small program exercises traceGcd():

```
#include <iostream>
extern int traceGcd(int, int);

int main() {
    int rslt = traceGcd( 15, 123 );
    cout << "gcd of (15,123): " << rslt << endl;
    return 0;
}
```

When compiled and executed, the program generates the following results:

```
depth #1
depth #2
```

```
depth #3
depth #4
gcd of (15,123): 3
```

An uninitialized static local object is automatically initialized to 0 by the program. In contrast, automatic objects have arbitrary values unless they are explicitly initialized. The following program illustrates the difference between the default initialization of automatic and static local objects and the danger of not initializing automatic objects.

```cpp
#include <iostream>

const int iterations = 2;
void func() {
    int value1, value2; // uninitialized
    static int depth;    // implicitly initialized to 0

    if ( depth < iterations )
        { ++depth; func(); }
    else depth = 0;

    cout << "\nvalue1:\t" << value1;
    cout << "\tvalue2:\t" << value2;
    cout << "\tsum:\t" << value1 + value2;
}

int main() {
    for ( int ix = 0; ix < iterations; ++ix ) func();
    return 0;
}
```

The output of its execution is as follows:

```
value1: 0              value2:  74924        sum:  74924
value1: 0              value2:  68748        sum:  68748
value1: 0              value2:  68756        sum:  68756
value1: 148620         value2:  2350         sum:  150970
value1: 2147479844     value2:  671088640    sum:  -1476398812
value1: 0              value2:  68756        sum:  68756
```

Notice that value1 and value2 are uninitialized automatic objects. Their initial values, as shown in the output here, are completely random, and the result of their sum is unpredictable. However, even though depth is uninitialized, its initial value is guaranteed to be 0, ensuring that func() recursively invokes itself only twice.

8.4   Dynamically Allocated Objects

The lifetime of global objects and local objects is strictly defined. The programmer cannot change their lifetime in any way. However, it is sometimes necessary to create objects whose lifetime can be controlled by the programmer, whose allocation and deallocation can happen or be avoided depending on the results of the operations within the execution of the program. For example, one may want to allocate a string to contain the text of an error message only if the error is actually encountered during the execution of the program. If the program can generate more than one error message, the size of the string allocated will vary according to the size of the text for the error encountered. One does not know in advance the size of the string that should be allocated, because it depends on the kind of error encountered during the execution of the program.

A third kind of object allows the programmer to completely control when its allocation and deallocation take place. Such an object is called a *dynamically allocated object*. A dynamically allocated object is allocated on a pool of available memory referred to as the program's *free store*. A programmer creates a dynamically allocated object with a new *expression* and terminates the lifetime of such an object with a delete *expression*. A dynamically allocated object is either a single object or an array of objects. The size of an array allocated on the free store can be a value evaluated at run-time.

In this section on dynamically allocated objects, we will look at three forms of new expressions: one supporting the dynamic allocation of single objects, another supporting the dynamic allocation of arrays, and a third form, called the placement new expression. When the free store is exhausted, a new expression throws an exception; exceptions are examined further in Chapter 11. In Chapter 15, we discuss in detail the use of new and delete expressions with class types.

8.4.1   Dynamic Allocation and Deallocation of Single Objects

A new expression consists of the keyword new followed by a type specifier. This type specifier can refer to a built-in type or a class type. For example,

```
new int;
```

allocates one object of type int from the free store. Similarly,

```
new iStack;
```

allocates one iStack class object.

By itself, a new expression is not terribly useful. How can we actually use the allocated object? One aspect of free store memory is that the objects allocated from it are unnamed. The new expression does not return the actual allocated object but instead returns a pointer to the object. All manipulation of the object is done indirectly through pointers. For example:

```
int *pi = new int;
```

The new expression creates one object of type int, to which pi refers.

Allocating memory at run-time on the free store, such as through the preceding new expressions, is referred to as *dynamic memory allocation*. We say that the memory addressed by pi is allocated dynamically.

A second aspect of the free store is that the allocated memory is uninitialized. Free store memory contains random bit patterns left from previous uses of that memory prior to the execution of our program. The test

```
if ( *pi == 0 )
```

is always likely to fail, because the object addressed by pi contains random bits. We therefore recommend that objects created with a new expression be initialized. A programmer can initialize the object of type int in the preceding example as follows:

```
int *pi = new int( 0 );
```

The constant within the parentheses provides an initial value with which the object created by the new expression is initialized. pi therefore refers to an object of type int that has a value of 0. The expression within the parentheses is spoken of as the *initializer*. This initializer need not be a constant value. Any expression with a result that can be converted to type int is a valid initializer.

The sequence of operations in a new expression is as follows: the object is allocated from the free store, and then the object is initialized with the value within the parentheses. To allocate the object on the free store, the new expression calls the library operator new(). The preceding new expression is roughly equivalent to the following code sequence

```
int ival = 0;    // creates an int object initialized to 0
int *pi = &ival; // the pointer now addresses the object
```

except, of course, that the object pointed to by pi is allocated by the library operator new() and resides on the program's free store. Similarly,

```
iStack *ps = new iStack( 512 );
```

creates an object of type iStack with a size of 512 elements. In the case of a class object, the value or values in parentheses are passed to the associated constructor of the class, which is invoked following the successful allocation of the object. (Dynamic allocation of class objects is discussed in more detail in Section 15.8. The remainder of this section focuses on the built-in types.)

There is one problem with the new expressions presented thus far. The free store, unfortunately, represents a finite resource: at some point during program execution, we might in practice exhaust the free store, resulting in the failure of a new expression. If the operator new() called by the new expression cannot acquire the requested memory, in general it throws an exception called bad_alloc. (Exception handling in general is discussed in Chapter 11.)

The lifetime of the object to which `pi` refers ends when the memory in which the object resides is deallocated. The memory is deallocated when `pi` is the operand of a delete expression. For example,

```
delete pi;
```

deallocates the memory to which `pi` refers, ending the lifetime of the object of type `int`. The programmer controls when the lifetime of the object ends by deciding where to place the delete expression within the program. The delete expression calls the library operator `delete()` to return the memory to the free store. Because the free store is a finite resource, it is important to return allocated memory to the free store as soon as we no longer need it.

Looking at the preceding delete expression, you might ask, What happens if `pi` has for some reason been set to 0? Shouldn't the code look like this?

```
// is this necessary?
if ( pi != 0 )
    delete pi;
```

No. The language guarantees that operator `delete()` is not called by a delete expression if the pointer operand is set to 0. A test guarding against zero is always unnecessary. (In fact, under most implementations, if you add the explicit test of the pointer, the test will, in effect, be carried out twice.)

It is important here to discuss the distinction between the lifetime of `pi` and that of the object to which `pi` refers. The pointer `pi` itself is a global object declared in global scope. As a result, the storage for `pi` is allocated before the program starts and lasts until the program ends. This is different from the lifetime of the object addressed by `pi`, which is created when the new expression is encountered during the execution of the program. The memory to which `pi` refers is dynamically allocated, and the object held within this memory is a dynamically allocated object. `pi` is therefore a global pointer that refers to a dynamically allocated object of type `int`. When the delete expression is encountered during the execution of the program, the memory to which `pi` refers is deallocated. However, the memory for the pointer `pi` and its content are not themselves affected by the delete expression. After the delete expression, `pi` is called a dangling pointer, that is, a pointer that refers to invalid memory. A dangling pointer can be the source of program errors that are quite difficult to detect, and it is a good idea to set the pointer to 0 after the object it refers to has been deleted to make it clear that the pointer points to no object.

A delete expression must be applied only to a pointer that refers to memory that has been allocated on the free store by a new expression. Applying a delete expression to a pointer that does not refer to memory allocated on the free store is likely to result in undefined program behavior during execution of the program. However, as we saw earlier, there is no penalty for applying a delete expression to a pointer of value 0 —

that is, a pointer that does not refer to any object. The following are examples of safe and unsafe delete expressions:

```
void f() {
    int i;
    string str = "dwarves";
    int *pi = &i;
    short *ps = 0;
    double *pd = new double(33);

    delete str;  // bad: string "dwarves" is not a dynamic object
    delete pi;   // bad: pi refers to i, a local object
    delete ps;   // safe
    delete pd;   // safe
}
```

The following three common program errors are associated with dynamic memory allocation:

1. · Failing to apply a delete expression, thus preventing the memory from being returned to the free store. This is spoken of as a *memory leak*.

2. Applying a delete expression to the same memory location twice. This usually happens when two pointers somehow end up addressing the same dynamically allocated object. It can be a particularly nasty problem to track down. What happens is that the object is deleted through one of the multiple pointers that address the object. The object's memory is returned to the free store and then subsequently reused to hold some other object. Then the second pointer addressing the old object is deleted, and the new object is suddenly corrupted.

3. Reading or writing to the object after it has been deleted. This often happens because the pointer upon which a delete expression is applied is not reset to 0.

These kinds of errors in manipulating dynamically allocated memory are considerably easier to make than they are to track down and fix. To help the programmer better manage dynamically allocated memory, the C++ standard library provides support for the auto_ptr class type. This is the topic of the next subsection. Following that, we look at the dynamic allocation and deallocation of arrays using a second form of new and delete expressions.

8.4.2   auto_ptr ◆

auto_ptr is a class template provided by the C++ standard library that can help programmers automate the management of individual objects dynamically allocated through new expressions. (Unfortunately, there is no analogous support for managing arrays allocated through a new expression. You should not use auto_ptr to store arrays. If you should do so, the results are undefined.)

An auto_ptr object is initialized to point to a dynamically allocated object created by a new expression. When the lifetime of the auto_ptr object ends, the dynamically allocated object is automatically deallocated. In this subsection, we examine how to associate an auto_ptr object with an object created by a new expression.

Before the auto_ptr class template can be used, the following header file must be included:

```
#include <memory>
```

The definition of an auto_ptr object takes one of the following three general forms:

```
auto_ptr< type_pointed_to > identifier( ptr_allocated_by_new );
auto_ptr< type_pointed_to > identifier( auto_ptr_of_same_type );
auto_ptr< type_pointed_to > identifier;
```

type_pointed_to represents the type of the object created by the new expression. Let's look at each of the definitions in turn. In the most common case, we wish to directly initialize the auto_ptr object to the address of an object returned by a new expression. We can do this as follows:

```
auto_ptr< int > pi( new int( 1024 ) );
```

pi is initialized with the address of the object created by the new expression. This object is initialized to the value 1,024. We can check the value of the object referred to by the auto_ptr object in the same way that we would with an ordinary pointer:

```
if ( *pi != 1024 )
    // oops, something wrong
else *pi *= 2;
```

The object created by the new expression to which pi refers is deleted automatically when the lifetime of pi ends. If pi is a local object, the object to which pi refers is deleted at the end of the block in which pi is defined. If pi is a global object, the object to which pi refers is deleted at the end of the program.

What if we initialize the auto_ptr object to refer to an object of class type, such as the standard string type? For example:

```
auto_ptr< string >
    pstr_auto( new string( "Brontosaurus" ) );
```

Suppose that we now wish to access a string operation. With an ordinary string pointer, we'd do the following:

```
string *pstr_type = new string( "Brontosaurus" );
if ( pstr_type->empty() )
    // oops, something wrong
```

How would we access the string operation empty() using an auto_ptr object? We'd use exactly the same approach:

```
auto_ptr< string > pstr_auto( new string( "Brontosaurus" ) );
if ( pstr_auto->empty() )
   // oops, something wrong
```

The primary motive behind the auto_ptr class template is to support the same syntax as the one used with ordinary pointer types but additionally to provide for automatic management of the deletion of the object to which an auto_ptr object refers. Common sense might lead you to believe that this additional security comes at the cost of run-time efficiency, but this is not the case. Because support for these operations is inline (they are expanded at the point of call by the compiler), use of an auto_ptr object is not significantly more expensive than the direct use of a pointer.

What happens in the following case, in which we initialize pstr_auto2 with the value of pstr_auto, an auto_ptr to an underlying string object?

```
// who is responsible for deleting the string?
auto_ptr< string > pstr_auto2( pstr_auto );
```

Suppose we directly initialize one string pointer with another, as in

```
string *pstr_type2( pstr_type );
```

Both pointers hold the address of the string within the program free store, and we must be careful to apply delete to only one of the pointers. The auto_ptr class template, on the contrary, supports the notion of ownership.

When we define pstr_auto, it recognizes its ownership of the string with which we initialize it and recognizes that it is responsible for deleting the string. This is the responsibility that ownership confers upon an auto_ptr object.

The question is, What happens in terms of ownership when pstr_auto2 is initialized to point to the same object as pstr_auto? We don't want both auto_ptr objects to own the same underlying object — that gives rise to all the problems of multiple deletions that we wanted to prevent by using the auto_ptr type in the first place.

When one auto_ptr object is initialized with or assigned to a second auto_ptr object, the left-hand auto_ptr object being initialized or assigned to now holds the ownership for the underlying object on the free store. The right-hand auto_ptr object relinquishes all responsibility. In our example, then, it is pstr_auto2 now that deletes the string object, and not pstr_auto, and pstr_auto can no longer be used to refer to the string object.

Similar behavior happens with the assignment operator. Given the following two auto_ptr objects

```
auto_ptr< int > p1( new int( 1024 ) );
auto_ptr< int > p2( new int( 2048 ) );
```

the assignment operator can be used as follows to copy one auto_ptr object to another:

```
p1 = p2;
```

Prior to the assignment, the object referred to by p1 is deleted. After the assignment, p1 has ownership of the object of type `int` containing the value 2,048. p2 can no longer be used to refer to this object.

In the third form of auto_ptr definition, we create an auto_ptr object but do not initialize it with a pointer to an object on the free store. For example:

```
// does not currently refer to an object
auto_ptr< int > p_auto_int;
```

Because `p_auto_int` is not initialized to refer to an object, its internal pointer value is set to 0. This means that dereferencing it would result in the program having undefined behavior, as would happen if we directly dereferenced a pointer of value 0:

```
// oops: dereference of an auto_ptr pointing to no object
if ( *p_auto_int != 1024 )
    *p_auto_int = 1024;
```

With an ordinary pointer, one simply tests the pointer against 0. For example:

```
int *pi = 0;
if ( pi != 0 ) ...;
```

But how does one test an auto_ptr object to determine whether it refers to an underlying object? The `get()` operation returns the underlying pointer contained within the auto_ptr object. So, to determine whether the auto_ptr object refers to an object, we can program the following:

```
// revised test to guarantee p_auto_int refers to an object
if ( p_auto_int.get() != 0 &&
        *p_auto_int != 1024 )
        *p_auto_int = 1024;
```

If it refers to no object, how can we make it refer to one — that is, how can we set the underlying pointer of an auto_ptr object? We can do so through the application of the `reset()` operation. For example:

```
else
    // ok, let's set p_auto_int's underlying pointer
    p_auto_int.reset( new int( 1024 ) );
```

An auto_ptr object does not support the notion of being directly assigned the address of an object created by a new expression after it has been defined. One cannot write

```
void example()
{
    // by default, initialized with a value of 0
    auto_ptr< int > pi;
    {
        // not supported
        pi = new int( 5 );
    }
}
```

To reset an auto_ptr object, we must use the reset() function. reset() can be passed a pointer, or can be passed 0 if we wish to unset the auto_ptr object. If the auto_ptr currently refers to an object and the auto_ptr object has ownership of the object, then the object to which the current auto_ptr refers is deleted prior to resetting the underlying pointer. For example:

```
auto_ptr< string >
   pstr_auto( new string( "Brontosaurus" ) );

// deletes Brontosaurus object prior to resetting
pstr_auto.reset( new string( "Long-neck" ) );
```

In this case, it is more efficient to reassign the existing string object using the string assign() operation rather than delete the existing string object and reallocate a second one:

```
// more efficient form of resetting in this case

// use string's assign() to set new value
pstr_auto->assign( "Long-neck" );
```

One of the hard things about programming is that simply getting correct results is sometimes not enough. At times, we need not only to get the correct results but also to get them within a window of acceptable performance. A small thing such as deallocating and reallocating a string object when a call to assign() is sufficient is an example of the kind of minute detail that, under some cases, accumulates into a measurable performance bottleneck. These aren't details one should be fretting over while trying to provide an overall program solution, but eventually these kinds of details become part of the internal program checklist of experienced programmers.

The auto_ptr class template provides a great deal of safety and convenience for the handling of dynamically allocated memory. We still need to be careful, however, or else we can still get ourselves into trouble. What can we do wrong?

1. We must be careful not to initialize or assign the auto_ptr with a pointer that was not allocated through application of a new expression. If we do, the delete expression will be applied to a pointer not dynamically allocated, and this will result in undefined program behavior.

2. We must be careful not to have two auto_ptr objects hold ownership to the same object in the free store. One obvious way to make this mistake is to initialize or assign the same pointer to two objects. A more subtle way of mistakenly accomplishing this is through the use of the get() operation. For example:

```
auto_ptr< string >
   pstr_auto( new string( "Brontosaurus" ) );
```

```
// oops: now both point to the same object,
// and both have ownership of that object
auto_ptr< string > pstr_auto2( pstr_auto.get() );
```

The `release()` operation allows us to initialize or assign the underlying object of one auto_ptr object to a second one without having the two hold ownership to the same object. `release()` not only returns the address of the underlying object, as does the `get()` operation, but it also releases ownership of that object. The correct rewrite of the preceding code fragment is as follows:

```
// ok: both still point to the same object,
// but pstr_auto no longer has ownership
auto_ptr< string >
   pstr_auto2( pstr_auto.release() );
```

8.4.3 Dynamic Allocation and Deallocation of Arrays

A new expression can also allocate an array on the free store. In this case, the type specifier in the new expression must be followed with a bracket-enclosed dimension for the array size. The dimension can be an arbitrarily complex expression. The new expression returns a pointer to the first element of the array. For example:

```
// allocate a single object of type int
// with an initial value of 1024
int *pi = new int( 1024 );

// allocate an array of 1024 elements
// with uninitialized elements
int *pia = new int[ 1024 ];

// allocate a two-dimensional array of 4x1024 elements
int (*pia2)[ 1024 ] = new int[ 4 ][ 1024 ];
```

pi addresses a single object of type int initialized to a value of 1,024. pia addresses the first element of an array of 1,024 elements. pia2 addresses the first element of an array of four arrays of 1,024 elements — that is, pia2 addresses an array of 1,024 elements.

Generally, an array allocated on the free store cannot be given an initial set of values. (In Section 15.8, we will see how arrays of classes allocated on the free store can be initialized using the class default constructor.) It is not possible to specify an initializer in the preceding new expressions to initialize the elements of the arrays. An array of built-in type created on the free store must be initialized within a for loop in which the array elements are initialized one by one:

```
for ( int index = 0; index < 1024; ++index )
   pia[ index ] = 0;
```

The main benefit of a dynamically allocated array is that its first dimension does not need to be a constant value; that is, the dimension does not need to be known at compile-time, as does the dimension of an array introduced by a definition in local scope or global scope. This means that we can allocate the storage to be of a size that matches the current demand of the program.

For example, in real-world C++ programs, if a pointer potentially refers to many C-style strings during the execution of a program, the memory used to hold the C-style string to which the pointer refers is typically dynamically allocated during program execution based on the length of the string to be stored. This technique is considerably more efficient than allocating a fixed-size array capable of holding each string, because the fixed size of the array must be large enough to hold the largest possible string, although the majority of strings will likely be considerably smaller. Moreover, our program will fail if only one string instance is larger than the fixed size we decided on.

Here is how a new expression can be used to specify the first dimension of an array as a run-time value. Suppose we have the following C-style strings:

```
const char *noerr = "success";
// ...
const char *err189 = "Error: a function declaration must "
                     "specify a function return type!";
```

The dimension of the array to be allocated by the new expression can be specified by a value evaluated at run-time, as follows:

```
#include <cstring>

const char *errorTxt;

if (errorFound)
   errorTxt = err189;
else
   errorTxt = noerr;

int dimension = strlen( errorTxt ) + 1;
char *str1 = new char[ dimension ];

// actually copy the text for the error into str1
strcpy( str1, errorTxt );
```

dimension can be replaced by an expression evaluated at run-time:

```
// typical real-world program idiom, but
// sometimes confusing to beginning programmers
char *str1 = new char[ strlen( errorTxt ) + 1 ];
```

The addition of 1 to the return value of strlen() is necessary to accommodate the trailing null of C-style strings. Forgetting to allocate it is a common program error, and it's a headache to track down because it typically manifests itself indirectly as a read or write corruption of memory in some other portion of the program. Why? Most routines that handle arrays representing C-style strings traverse the array until encountering the trailing null. The absence of that null often results in serious program error, because the program is reading and possibly writing into raw memory. Avoiding these sorts of errors is one reason we recommend the use of the C++ standard library class string.

Note that only the first dimension of the array allocated by the new expression can be specified using an expression evaluated at run-time. The other dimensions must be constant values known at compile-time. For example:

```
int getDim();

// allocate a two-dimensional array
int (*pia3)[ 1024 ] = new int[ getDim() ][ 1024 ]; //ok

// error: the second dimension for the array is not a constant
int **pia4 = new int[ 4 ][ getDim() ];
```

The delete expression used to deallocate an array has the following form:

```
delete[] str1;
```

The empty bracket pair is necessary. It indicates to the compiler that the pointer addresses an array of elements on the free store and not simply a single object. Because str1 has type pointer to char, the compiler cannot tell without seeing the empty bracket pair that the storage to be deleted is an array.

What happens if you mistakenly omit the empty bracket pair? The compiler will not catch the error, and there is no guarantee that your program will behave correctly (this is particularly true with arrays of class types with destructors as illustrated in Section 14.4).

To avoid problems with the memory management of dynamically allocated arrays, we recommend in general that you use the standard library vector, list, or string container types. These types manage memory allocation automatically. The string type was introduced in Section 3.4, the vector type in Section 3.10. The container types are discussed in detail in Chapter 6.

8.4.4   Dynamic Allocation and Deallocation of const Objects

A programmer may want to create an object on the free store but prevent the program from changing the value of the object once it has been initialized. You can do this by creating the object on the free store as a const object. A programmer wanting to create a const object on the free store can use a new expression as follows:

```
const int *pci = new const int(1024);
```

A const object created on the free store has a few special properties. First, the const object must be initialized. If the parentheses containing the initializer are omitted, a compiler error is generated (except that, for an object of a class type with a default constructor, the initializer can be omitted). Second, the pointer initialized with the value returned from the new expression must be a pointer to const type. In the preceding example, pci is of type pointer to const int. The pointer refers to the const int object allocated by the new expression.

What does it mean for an object on the free store to be const? It means that once the object has been initialized, the value of the object cannot be changed. Although the value of the object cannot be modified, its lifetime is ended with a delete expression. For example:

```
delete pci;
```

Even though the operand of the delete expression is a pointer to const int, the delete expression is valid and causes the memory to which pci refers to be deallocated.

It is not possible to create a const array of elements of built-in type on the free store for the simple reason that it is not possible to initialize the elements of an array of built-in type created with a new expression. All objects created const on the free store must be initialized, and because a const array cannot be initialized (except for array of classes), attempting to create a const array of built-in type with a new expression results in a compile-time error:

```
const int *pci = new const int[100]; // error
```

8.4.5 Placement New Expressions ◆

There is a third form of new expression in which the programmer can request that the object be created in memory that is already allocated. This form of new expression is called a *placement new expression*. The programmer specifies the address of the memory where the object is to be created in the new expression. The form of this new expression is as follows:

```
new (place_address) type-specifier
```

place_address must be a pointer. To use this form of new expression, the header file <new> must be included. This facility allows the programmer to preallocate a large amount of memory that later will contain objects created by this form of new expression. For example:

```
#include <iostream>
#include <new>
const int chunk = 16;
class Foo {
public:
    int val()  { return _val; }
    Foo() { _val = 0; }
private:
    int _val;
};
```

```
// preallocate the memory, but no Foo objects
char *buf = new char[ sizeof(Foo) * chunk ];

int main() {
   // create a Foo object in buf
   Foo *pb = new (buf) Foo;

   // check that an object was placed in buf
   if ( pb->val() == 0 )
      cout << "new expression worked!" << endl;

   // cannot use pb here
   delete[] buf;

   return 0;
}
```

When compiled and executed, this program generates the following output:

```
new expression worked!
```

There is no delete expression to match a placement new expression. Such a delete expression is not needed, because placement new expressions do not allocate memory. In the preceding example, it is not the memory addressed by the pointer pb that must be deleted but rather the memory addressed by buf. This memory is deleted at the end of the program when the character buffer is no longer needed. Because buf refers to a character array, the delete expression has the form

```
delete[] buf;
```

When the character buffer is deleted, the lifetime of any object it contains ends. In our example, pb does not refer to a valid object of class type Foo anymore.

Exercise 8.5

Explain why the following new expressions are errors.

```
(a) const float *pf = new const float[100];
(b) double *pd = new double[10][getDim()];
(c) int (*pia2)[ 1024 ] = new int[ ][ 1024 ];
(d) const int *pci = new const int;
```

Exercise 8.6

Given the following new expression, how would you delete pa?

```
typedef int arr[10];
int *pa = new arr;
```

Exercise 8.7

Which ones of the following delete expressions, if any, are potential run-time errors? Why?

```
int globalObj;
char buf[1000];

void f() {
    int *pi = &globalObj;
    double *pd = 0;
    float *pf = new float(0);
    int *pa = new(buf)int[20];

    delete pi;    // (a)
    delete pd;    // (b)
    delete pf;    // (c)
    delete[] pa;  // (d)
}
```

Exercise 8.8

Which of the following auto_ptr declarations are illegal or likely to result in subsequent program error? Explain what the problem is with each one.

```
int ix = 1024;
int *pi = & ix;
int *pi2 = new int( 2048 );
```

(a) auto_ptr<int> p0(ix);   (b) auto_ptr<int> p1(pi);
(c) auto_ptr<int> p2(pi2);   (d) auto_ptr<int> p3(&ix);
(e) auto_ptr<int> p4(new int(2048));   (f) auto_ptr<int> p5(p2.get());
(g) auto_ptr<int> p6(p2.release());   (h) auto_ptr<int> p7(p2);

Exercise 8.9

Explain the difference between these two statements:

```
int *pi0 = p2.get();
int *pi1 = p2.release();
```

Under what conditions would each respective invocation be more appropriate?

Exercise 8.10

Suppose we have the following:

```
auto_ptr< string > ps( new string( "Daniel" ) );
```

What is the difference, if any, between the following two invocations of assign()? Which do you think is preferable? Why?

```
ps.get()->assign( "Danny" );
ps->assign( "Danny" );
```

8.5   Namespace Definitions ◈

By default, each object, function, type, or template declared in global scope, also
called *global namespace scope*, introduces a *global entity*. Every global entity introduced
in the global namespace scope must have a unique name. A function and an object,
for example, cannot have the same name, whether or not they are declared in the
same program text file.

This means that to use a library with our programs, we must ensure that the names
of the global entities in our programs do not collide with the names of the global entities from the library. This can be quite difficult to enforce if the program is made of libraries provided by many vendors and the various libraries introduce many names in
the global namespace scope. How can we be sure when combining libraries from these
different vendors that the names of the global entities in our programs won't clash
with the names of the global entities declared in the libraries? This name clashing problem is called the *global name space pollution* problem.

Programmers have been able to avoid these problems by making the names of
their global entities very long, often prefixing the names in their program with specific
character sequences. For example:

```
class cplusplus_primer_matrix { ... };
void inverse( cplusplus_primer_matrix & );
```

However, this solution is not ideal. A program written in C++ may have a potentially
large number of global classes, functions, and templates visible to the entire program.
It can be cumbersome for programmers to write programs that use such long names.

Namespaces allow us to better manage the global name space pollution problem.
The author of a library can define a namespace to hide the names in the library from
the global namespace. For example:

```
namespace cplusplus_primer {
   class matrix {  /* ... */  };
   void inverse ( matrix & );
}
```

The namespace cplusplus_primer is a *user-declared* namespace (in comparison to the
global namespace, which is implicitly declared and exists in every program).

Each user-declared namespace represents a distinct namespace scope. A user-declared
namespace scope can contain other nested namespace definitions as well as declarations
or definitions for functions, objects, templates, and types. The entities declared within a
namespace are called *namespace members*. Just as is the case for the global namespace scope,
each name in a user-declared namespace must refer to a unique entity within that

namespace. However, because different user-declared namespaces introduce different scopes, different user-declared namespaces may have members with the same name.

The name of a namespace member is automatically compounded or *qualified* by the name of its namespace. For example, the name of the matrix class declared in namespace cplusplus_primer is `cplusplus_primer::matrix`, and the name of the function is `cplusplus_primer::inverse()`.

The members of the namespace cplusplus_primer can be used in a program using their qualified names, as follows:

```
void func( cplusplus_primer::matrix &m )
{
    // ...
    cplusplus_primer::inverse(m);
    return m;
}
```

If another user-declared namespace (say, DisneyFeatureAnimation) also provides a matrix class and we want to use this class instead of the one defined in the namespace cplusplus_primer, then we need to modify func() as follows:

```
void func( DisneyFeatureAnimation::matrix &m )
{
    // ...
    DisneyFeatureAnimation::inverse(m);
    return m;
}
```

Of course, always referring to a namespace member using the qualified name notation

```
namespace_name::member_name
```

can be cumbersome. For this reason, some mechanisms, such as *namespace aliases*, *using declarations*, and *using directives* are provided to make it easier to use the namespace members in programs. We will present these mechanisms in Section 8.6.

8.5.1   Namespace Definitions

A user-declared namespace definition begins with the keyword namespace followed by the namespace name. This name must be a unique name in the scope in which the namespace is defined. It is an error if any other entity declared in the same scope as the namespace has the same name as the namespace. Of course, this means that the global name space pollution problem is not eliminated. However, the use of namespaces significantly reduces the problem.

Following the namespace name is a block of declarations delimited by curly braces ({ }). All declarations that can appear in the global namespace scope can also be placed into a user-declared namespace: classes, variables (with their initialization), functions (with their definition), and templates. Placing a declaration within a user-declared namespace does not change its meaning. The only difference is that the names introduced by the declarations in the user-declared namespace are compounded by the name of the namespace in which the declarations appear. For example:

```
namespace cplusplus_primer {
    class matrix { /* ... */ };
    void inverse ( matrix & );
    matrix operator+ ( const matrix &m1, const matrix &m2 )
        { /* ... */ }
    const double pi = 3.1416;
}
```

The name of the class declared in namespace cplusplus_primer is

```
cplusplus_primer::matrix
```

The name of the function is

```
cplusplus_primer::inverse()
```

The name of the constant is

```
cplusplus_primer::pi
```

The name of the class, function, or constant is qualified by the name of the namespace in which it is declared; these names are said to be *qualified names*.

The definition of a namespace does not have to be contiguous. For example, the preceding namespace could have been defined as follows:

```
namespace cplusplus_primer {
    class matrix { /* ... */ };
    const double pi = 3.1416;
}

namespace cplusplus_primer {
    void inverse ( matrix & );
    matrix operator+ ( const matrix &m1, const matrix &m2 )
        { /* ... */ }
}
```

The previous two examples are equivalent: both examples define the namespace cplusplus_primer to contain the class matrix, the function inverse(), the constant pi, and operator+(). A namespace definition is therefore cumulative.

The tokens

```
namespace namespace_name {
```

define a new namespace if namespace_name does not refer to a previously defined namespace, or, if it does, it reopens that namespace to add the new declarations.

The fact that namespace definitions can be discontiguous is of great help when we want to build a library. It allows us to easily organize the source code of the library into interface and implementation sections. For example:

```
// This portion of the namespace
// defines the library interface

namespace cplusplus_primer {
   class matrix { /* ... */ };
   const double pi = 3.1416;
   matrix operator+ ( const matrix &m1, const matrix &m2 );
   void inverse ( matrix & );
}

// This portion of the namespace defines
// the library implementation

namespace cplusplus_primer {
   void inverse ( matrix &m )
      { /* ... */ }
   matrix operator+ ( const matrix &m1, const matrix &m2 )
      { /* ... */ }
}
```

The first portion of the namespace provides the declarations and definitions that describe the library interface: type definitions, constant definitions, and function declarations. The second portion of the namespace provides the details of the library implementation — that is, the function definitions.

What helps us organize the source code of our library even more is that the definition for the same namespace can span different program text files. Namespace definitions in different program text files are also cumulative. Our library can then be organized as follows:

```
// ---- primer.h ----
namespace cplusplus_primer {
   class matrix { /* ... */ };
   const double pi = 3.1416;
   matrix operator+ ( const matrix &m1, const matrix &m2 );
   void inverse( matrix & );
}

// ---- primer.C ----
#include "primer.h"

namespace cplusplus_primer {
   void inverse( matrix &m )
      { /* ... */ }
   matrix operator+ ( const matrix &m1, const matrix &m2 )
      { /* ... */ }
}
```

A program using our library would look like this:

```
// ---- user.C ----
// defines the library interface
#include "primer.h"

void func( cplusplus_primer::matrix &m )
{
   // ...
   cplusplus_primer::inverse( m );

}
```

This program organization gives our library the modularity needed to hide the implementation from our users, while it allows the files primer.C and user.C to be compiled and linked into one program without causing any compile-time or link-time error.

8.5.2   The Scope Operator (::)

The name of a user-declared namespace member is automatically prefixed by the name of its namespace followed by the scope operator (::). A namespace member name is qualified by its namespace name.

Using a namespace member name, such as matrix, without qualifying it with the namespace name is an error. The compiler does not know to which declaration the name matrix refers:

```
// defines the library interface
#include "primer.h"

// error: cannot find a declaration for matrix
void func( matrix &m );
```

The declaration of a namespace member is hidden within its namespace. Unless we specify to the compiler in which namespace to search for a declaration, the compiler simply searches the current scope, and any scopes in which the current scope is nested, to find a declaration for the name. For example, if the preceding program is rewritten as

```
// defines the library interface
#include "primer.h"

class matrix { /* user definition */ };

// ok: finds the global matrix type
void func( matrix &m );
```

the definition for the class matrix in global scope is found and the program compiles properly. Because the declaration of the namespace member matrix is hidden within the namespace cplusplus_primer, the name of the namespace member does not collide with the class name declared in global scope. This is why we say that namespaces solve the global namespace pollution problem: the name of a namespace member is not found unless a user explicitly uses the scope operator prefixed by its namespace name. There are other mechanisms that can be used to make the declaration of a namespace member visible outside its namespace. These mechanisms are called *using declarations* and *using directives*. They will be introduced in the next section.

Note that the scope operator can also be used to refer to members of the global namespace. Because the global namespace does not have a name, the notation

```
::member_name
```

refers to a member of the global namespace. This can be quite useful for referring to members of the global namespace whose names have been hidden by names declared in nested local scopes.

In the following example, contrived to illustrate how the scope operator can be used to refer to a hidden global namespace member, the function computes a Fibonacci series. There are two definitions of the variable max. The global declaration indicates the maximum value for the series. The local declaration indicates the desired length of the series. (Recall that the parameters of a function are placed within the function's local scope.) Both declarations of max must be accessed within the function. Every unqualified use of max, however, refers to the local declaration. To access the global declaration, the scope operator must be used: ::max . Here is our implementation:

```
#include <iostream>
const int max = 65000;
const int lineLength = 12;

void fibonacci( int max )
{
   if ( max < 2 ) return;
   cout << "0 1 ";

   int v1 = 0, v2 = 1, cur;
   for ( int ix = 3; ix <= max; ++ix ) {
      cur = v1 + v2;
      if ( cur > ::max ) break;
      cout << cur << " ";
      v1 = v2;
      v2 = cur;
      if (ix % lineLength == 0) cout << endl;
   }
}
```

Here is an implementation of main() to exercise the function:

```
#include <iostream>
void fibonacci( int );
```

```
int main() {
    cout << "Fibonacci Series: 16\n";
    fibonacci( 16 );
    return 0;
}
```

Compiling and executing the program produces the following output:

```
Fibonacci Series: 16
0 1 1 2 3 5 8 13 21 34 55 89
144 233 377 610
```

8.5.3   Nested Namespaces

We mentioned earlier that a user-declared namespace can contain nested namespaces. We can use nested namespaces to further improve the organization of the code in our library. For example:

```
// ---- primer.h ----
namespace cplusplus_primer {
    // first nested namespace:
    // defines the matrix portion of the library
    namespace MatrixLib {
        class matrix {  /* ... */  };
        const double pi = 3.1416;
        matrix operator+ ( const matrix &m1, const matrix &m2 );
        void inverse( matrix & );
        // ...
    }
    // second nested namespace:
    // defines the zoology portion of the library
    namespace AnimalLib {
        class ZooAnimal { /* ... */ };
        class Bear : public ZooAnimal { /* ... */ };
        class Raccoon : public Bear { /* ... */ };
        // ...
    }
}
```

The namespace cplusplus_primer contains two nested namespaces: MatrixLib and AnimalLib.

The namespace cplusplus_primer is used to prevent names in the library from colliding with names in the global namespace of our users' programs. The library is also organized into smaller packages with nested namespaces to group related declarations and definitions. The namespace MatrixLib contains the matrix portion of the primer library, whereas AnimalLib contains the ZooAnimal portion of the library.

The declaration of a member of a nested namespace is hidden within the nested namespace. The name of such a member is automatically prefixed with the name of the outermost namespace and also with the name of the nested namespace. For example, the name of the class declared in the nested namespace MatrixLib is

```
cplusplus_primer::MatrixLib::matrix
```

and the name of the function is

```
cplusplus_primer::MatrixLib::inverse
```

A program can use the members of the nested namespace `cplusplus_primer::Matrix-Lib` as follows:

```
#include "primer.h"

// yes, this is horrible...
// we will soon introduce mechanisms to make namespace members
// easier to use!
void func( cplusplus_primer::MatrixLib::matrix &m )
{
   // ...
   cplusplus_primer::MatrixLib::inverse( m );

}
```

A nested namespace is a nested scope within the namespace that contains it. And during name resolution, nested namespaces behave similarly to nested blocks. For example, when a name is used in a namespace definition, the enclosing namespaces are searched for a declaration. In the following example, when a declaration is searched for Type, the declarations before the use of Type are considered. The declarations in the namespace MatrixLib are considered first; then the declarations in the namespace cplusplus_primer are considered, and finally the global scope declarations are considered.

```
typedef double Type;

namespace cplusplus_primer {
   typedef int Type; // hides ::Type

   namespace MatrixLib {
      int val;

      // Type: finds the declaration in cplusplus_primer
      int func(Type t) {
         double val; // hides MatrixLib::val
         val = ...;
      }
      // ...
   }
}
```

An entity declared in an enclosing namespace is hidden by an entity of the same name declared in a nested namespace. In the preceding example, the declaration for

Type in global scope is hidden by the declaration for Type in the namespace cplusplus_primer. When the name Type used in the namespace MatrixLib is resolved, the declaration in the namespace cplusplus_primer is found and func() is declared to have a parameter of type int.

Similarly, an entity declared in a namespace is hidden by an entity declared in local scope. In the preceding example, the declaration for val in the namespace MatrixLib is hidden by the declaration for val in the local scope of func(). When resolving the name val used in func(), the local scope declaration is found and the assignment in func() is to the local variable.

8.5.4   Namespace Member Definitions

We have seen that the definition of a namespace member can appear within the namespace definition itself. For example, the class matrix and the constant pi are defined within the definition of the nested namespace MatrixLib, whereas the definitions of the functions operator+() and inverse() are provided at some later point in the program:

```
// ---- primer.h ----
namespace cplusplus_primer {
   // first nested namespace:
   // defines the matrix portion of the library
   namespace MatrixLib {
      class matrix {  /* ... */  };
      const double pi = 3.1416;
      matrix operator+ ( const matrix &m1, const matrix &m2 );
      void inverse( matrix & );
      // ...
   }
}
```

It is also possible to define any namespace member outside its namespace definition. In such a case, the name of the namespace member must be qualified by the names of its enclosing namespaces. For example, the function operator+() can be defined in global scope as follows:

```
// ---- primer.C ----
#include "primer.h"

// global scope definition
cplusplus_primer::MatrixLib::matrix
   cplusplus_primer::MatrixLib::operator+
      ( const matrix& m1, const matrix &m2 )
         { /* ... */ }
```

In this definition, the name `operator+()` is qualified by the names of namespaces cplusplus_primer and MatrixLib. However, look at the use of the type matrix in the parameter list of `operator+()`. The name used is not qualified with the nested namespace name `cplusplus_primer::MatrixLib`. How can this be?

The definition of `operator+()` can use the names of the namespace members in their short form. This is because the definition of a namespace member is in the scope of its namespace. The members of namespace MatrixLib are considered when the names used in the definition of `operator+()` are resolved. Note, however, that the return type must still be qualified. This is because the return type is not in the scope of a function's definition. The namespace members can be used in their short forms only following the name of the member:

```
cplusplus_primer::MatrixLib::operator+
```

The definition of `operator+()` can use the namespace member names in their short form in any declaration or expression within the parameter list or the function body. For example, a local declaration within `operator+()` can create an object of class type matrix as follows:

```
// ---- primer.C ----
#include "primer.h"

cplusplus_primer::MatrixLib::matrix
   cplusplus_primer::MatrixLib::operator+
      ( const matrix &m1, const matrix &m2 )
{
   // declares a local variable of type:
   // cplusplus_primer::MatrixLib::matrix
   matrix res;

   // calculate the sum of two matrix objects
   return res;
}
```

Although a namespace member can be defined outside its namespace definition, there are restrictions on where this definition can appear. Only namespaces enclosing the member declaration can contain its definition. For example, `operator+()` can be defined in global scope, in the namespace cplusplus_primer, or in the namespace Matrix-Lib. These are the only three possibilities. A definition in namespace MatrixLib would look like this:

```
// ---- primer.C ----
#include "primer.h"

namespace cplusplus_primer {
   MatrixLib::matrix  MatrixLib::operator+
      ( const matrix &m1, const matrix &m2 ) { /* ... */ }
}
```

Note that a namespace member can be defined outside its namespace definition only if the member was previously declared within the namespace definition. The definition of operator+() just shown would be in error if it were not preceded by the following declaration that appears in primer.h:

```
namespace cplusplus_primer {
    namespace MatrixLib {
        class matrix {  /* ... */  };
        // the following declaration cannot be omitted
        matrix operator+ ( const matrix &m1, const matrix &m2 );
        // ...
    }
}
```

8.5.5   ODR and Namespace Members

As was mentioned earlier, a namespace definition can be discontiguous and can span many files. A namespace member can therefore be declared in many files. For example:

```
// primer.h
namespace cplusplus_primer {
    // ...
    void inverse( matrix & );
}
// use1.C
#include "primer.h"
// declares cplusplus_primer:: inverse() in use1.C

// use2.C
#include "primer.h"
// declares cplusplus_primer:: inverse() in use2.C
```

The member cplusplus::inverse() declared through the header file primer.h in use1.C refers to the same function as the member cplusplus::inverse() declared through the header file primer.h in use2.C.

Although the name of a namespace member is qualified, a namespace member is nonetheless a global entity. The ODR requirement (which was first discussed in Section 8.2) that non-inline functions and objects be defined only once in a program also applies to namespace members. To respect this requirement, a program using namespaces is generally organized as follows.

1. The declarations for the functions and objects that are members of the namespace are placed in a header file, which is to be included in the files where the namespace members are used.

```
// ---- primer.h ----
namespace cplusplus_primer {
    class matrix { /* ... */ };
```

```
      // function declarations
      extern matrix operator+ ( const matrix &m1, const matrix &m2 );
      extern void inverse( matrix & );

      // object declarations
      extern bool error_state;
}
```

2. The definitions for these members can appear in an implementation file.

```
// ---- primer.C ----
#include "primer.h"

namespace cplusplus_primer {
      // function definitions
      void inverse( matrix & )
          { /* ... */ }
      matrix operator+ ( const matrix &m1, const matrix &m2 )
          { /* ... */ }

      // object definitions
      bool error_state = false;
}
```

As with object declarations in global scope, the keyword `extern` must be used to specify that a namespace member is only declared and not defined. The keyword `extern` can also be used in declarations of namespace member functions; however, as for global functions, the use of the keyword `extern` is optional in this case.

8.5.6   Unnamed Namespaces

We may want to define an object, a function, a class type, or any other entity to be visible only to a small portion of the program. In this way, we reduce the problem of name space pollution even further. Because we know that this entity is used only in limited ways, we may not want to go to the effort to ensure that an entity has a unique name and does not collide with the names of other entities declared somewhere else in the program. When we declare an object within a function or within a nested block, the name introduced by the declaration is visible only within the block in which it is declared. But what if the programmer wants an entity to be available to multiple functions without making its name available to the entire program?

For example, suppose that we want to implement a set of sorting functions to sort the elements of a vector of type `double`:

```
// ----- SortLib.h -----
void quickSort( double *, double * );
void bubbleSort( double *, double * );
void mergeSort( double *, double * );
void heapSort( double *, double * );
```

All these functions use the same swap() function to swap the elements within the vector. However, we don't want swap() to be visible from within the entire program. We want to keep it localized to the file SortLib.C, because the four functions are the only functions invoking swap(). The following does not give us the results that we want. Can you see why?

```
// ----- SortLib.C -----
void swap( double *d1, double *d2 ) { /* ... */ }

// only the following sort functions use swap()
void quickSort( double *d1, double *d2 ) { /* ... */ }
void bubbleSort( double *d1, double *d2 ) { /* ... */ }
void mergeSort( double *d1, double *d2 ) { /* ... */ }
void heapSort( double *d1, double *d2 ) { /* ... */ }
```

Even though the function swap() is defined in SortLib.C and is not introduced in the header SortLib.h where the interface of the sort library is described, the function swap() is declared in global scope. It is therefore a global entity, and its name must not collide with the name of any other global entity.

In C++, one can use an *unnamed namespace* to declare an entity local to a file. An unnamed namespace definition begins with the keyword namespace. Because the namespace is unnamed, no name follows the namespace keyword. Following the namespace keyword is a block of declarations delimited by curly braces. For example:

```
// ----- SortLib.C -----
namespace {
   void swap( double *d1, double *d2 ) { /* ... */ }
}
// definitions of the sort functions as above
```

The function swap() is visible only within the file SortLib.C. If another file contains an unnamed namespace with the definition of a function swap(), the definition introduces a different function. The fact that there exist two definitions for the functions swap() is not an error, because the functions are different functions. Unnamed namespaces are not like other namespaces; the definition of an unnamed namespace is local to a particular file and never spans multiple text files.

The name swap() can be referred to in its short form in the file SortLib.C, following the definition of the unnamed namespace. It is not necessary to use the scope operator to refer to members of unnamed namespaces.

```
void quickSort( double *d1, double *d2 ) {
   // ...
   double* elem = d1;
   // ...
   // refers to unnamed namespace member swap()
   swap( d1, elem );
```

```
      // ...
    }
```

The members of an unnamed namespace are program entities. The function swap() can therefore be called throughout the duration of the program. However, the names of the members of an unnamed namespace are visible only within a specific file and are invisible to the other files that make up the program.

Prior to the introduction of namespaces in standard C++, the common solution to this localization of declaration problem was to use the static keyword inherited from C. A member of an unnamed namespace has properties that are similar to those of a global entity declared static. In C, a global entity declared static is invisible outside the file in which it is declared. For example, the declaration in SortLib.C can be rewritten in C as follows and will give swap() the same properties:

```
// SortLib.C
// swap() is invisible to other files of the program
static void swap( double *d1, double *d2 ) { /* ... */ }
// definitions of the sort functions as above
```

Many C++ implementations support global static declarations, although it is assumed that as namespaces become available on a wide range of C++ implementations, the use of global static declarations will be replaced with the use of unnamed namespace members.

Exercise 8.11

Why would you define your own namespace in your programs?

Exercise 8.12

Suppose we have the following declaration of the operator*() that is a member of the nested namespace cplusplus_primer::MatrixLib:

```
namespace cplusplus_primer {
    namespace MatrixLib {
        class matrix {  /* ... */  };
        matrix operator* ( const matrix &, const matrix & );
        // ...
    }
}
```

How would you define this operator in global scope? Provide only the prototype for the operator's definition.

Exercise 8.13

Explain why you would use an unnamed namespace in your programs.

8.6   Using Namespace Members ◆

Always referring to a namespace member using the qualified name notation
`namespace_name::member_name` is admittedly cumbersome, especially if the namespace
name is long. If we had to use qualified names all the time, we would want to create
namespaces with very short names not only because it is easier to read but also
because it is easier to type. However, the use of short namespace names increases the
risk of having the namespace name clash with other global names in our programs, so
it is preferable that we deliver our libraries with long namespace names.

Fortunately, there are mechanisms that ease the use of namespace members in our
programs. Namespace aliases, using declarations, and using directives are mechanisms that help us overcome the inconvenience of using very long namespace names.

8.6.1   Namespace Aliases

A *namespace alias* can be used to associate a shorter synonym with a namespace name.
For example, a long namespace name such as

```
namespace International_Business_Machines
   { /* ... */ }
```

can be associated with a shorter synonym as follows:

```
namespace IBM = International_Business_Machines;
```

A namespace alias declaration begins with the keyword `namespace`, followed by
the (shorter) name of the namespace alias, followed by the assignment operator, followed by the original namespace name. It is an error if the original namespace name
is not a name known to be a namespace name.

A namespace alias can also refer to a nested namespace. Remember the horrible
definition of `func()` introduced earlier:

```
#include "primer.h"

// hard to read!
void func( cplusplus_primer::MatrixLib::matrix &m )
{
   // ...
   cplusplus_primer:: MatrixLib::inverse( m );

}
```

A namespace alias can be defined to refer to the nested namespace
`cplusplus_primer::MatrixLib` and make the definition much easier to read:

```
#include "primer.h"
```

```
// shorter alias
namespace mlib = cplusplus_primer::MatrixLib;

// easier to read!
void func( mlib::matrix &m )
{
   // ...
   mlib::inverse( m );

}
```

A namespace can have many synonyms, or aliases. All the aliases and the original namespace name can be used interchangeably. For example, given that the alias name Lib refers to the namespace cplusplus_primer, the definition of func() can be written as follows while preserving the same meaning:

```
// alias refers to the namespace cplusplus_primer
namespace alias = Lib;

void func( Lib::matrix &m ) {
   // ...
   alias::inverse( m );

}
```

8.6.2   Using Declarations

It is possible to make the name of a namespace member visible so that the member can be referred to in a program using the unqualified form of its name, the one without the prefix namespace_name::. This is possible if the member is declared with a *using declaration.*

A using declaration begins with the keyword using, which is followed by the name of the namespace member. The member name in the using declaration must be the qualified name. For example:

```
namespace cplusplus_primer {
   namespace MatrixLib {
      class matrix { /* ... */ };
      // ...
   }
}

// using declaration for the namespace member matrix
using cplusplus_primer::MatrixLib::matrix;
```

A using declaration introduces a name in the scope in which the using declaration appears. For example, the preceding using declaration introduces the name matrix in global scope. After the using declaration has been encountered, a use of the name matrix in global scope or in scopes nested within global scope refers to the namespace member. For example, suppose the following declaration follows the using declaration.

```
void func( matrix &m );
```

This declaration declares the function func() to have a parameter type that is cplusplus_primer::MatrixLib::matrix.

A using declaration behaves like any other declaration: it has a scope, and the name it introduces is visible from the point of the using declaration to the end of the scope in which the declaration is found. A using declaration can appear in global scope as well as in any namespace scope. A using declaration can also appear in a local scope. As with any other declaration, a name introduced by a using declaration has these characteristics:

- It must be unique in its scope.

- It hides the same name introduced by a declaration in an enclosing scope.

- It is hidden by a declaration of the same name in a nested scope.

For example:

```
namespace blip {
    int bi = 16, bj = 15, bk = 23;
    // other declarations
}
int bj = 0;

void manip() {
    using blip::bi; // bi in function manip() refers to blip::bi
    ++bi;           // sets blip::bi to 17

    using blip::bj; // hides bj declared in global scope
                    // bj in function manip() refers to blip::bj
    ++bj;           // sets blip::bj to 16

    int bk;         // declaration in local scope of bk
    using blip::bk; // error: redeclaration of bk in manip()
}

int wrongInit = bk; // error: bk is not visible here
                    // should be blip::bk
```

The using declarations in the function manip() allow the function to refer to the members of the namespace blip in their short form. The using declarations are not visible outside the function manip(), and the user can use the short names only within the function manip(). Outside this function, the qualified names must be used.

Using declarations make namespace members easier to use. A using declaration introduces only one namespace member at a time. It allows us to be very specific regarding which names are used in our programs. A using declaration is introduced in a specific scope and allows us to specify exactly where in our program the names of namespace members are visible in their short form. In the next subsection, we see how all the member names of a namespace can be introduced into a scope all at once.

8.6.3   Using Directives

Namespaces were introduced with Standard C++. Prior C++ implementations did not support namespaces, and, as a consequence, pre-Standard libraries did not wrap their global declarations in namespaces. An important amount of C++ code and many applications were written before namespaces became available with various C++ implementations. By enclosing the content of a library in a namespace, we potentially break old applications using older versions of the library. If we wrap the content of the library in a namespace, all the names in the library become qualified, that is, prefixed with the name of the namespace followed by the scope operator. All applications using the names from the library in their short form no longer work.

We can use using declarations to make visible the library names that our programs use. For example, let's assume that the file primer.h contains a new version of the library in which the global declarations are wrapped into the namespace cplusplus_primer. We want to quickly make our program work with the new library. We can use two using declarations to make visible the names of the class matrix and the function inverse() from the namespace cplusplus_primer.

```
#include "primer.h"
using cplusplus_primer::matrix;
using cplusplus_primer::inverse;

// because of the using declarations
// the names matrix and inverse can be used without qualification
void func( matrix &m ) {
   // ...
   inverse( m );

}
```

If the library is quite large and if the application uses many of the library names, retrofitting a new version of the library that uses namespaces in old code may require many using declarations. Adding all the necessary using declarations just to allow the old code to compile and run as it did before can be tedious and error-prone. *Using directives* can be used to solve this problem and ease the migration to library versions that use namespaces for the first time.

A using directive begins with the keyword using, followed by the keyword namespace, followed by a namespace name. It is an error if the name does not refer to a previously defined namespace name. A using directive allows us to make all the names from a specific namespace visible in their short form. These members can then be used without the requirement that their names be qualified. For example, the preceding code example can be rewritten as follows:

```
#include "primer.h"
// using directive: all the members of cplusplus_primer become visible
using namespace cplusplus_primer;

// the names matrix and inverse can be used without qualification
void func( matrix &m ) {
    // ...
    inverse( m );

}
```

A using directive makes the namespace member names visible as if they were declared outside the namespace at the location where the namespace definition is located. For example, because of the using directive, it is as if the members of namespace cplusplus_primer were declared in global scope just before the definition of func(). A using directive does not declare local aliases for the namespace member names. Rather, it has the effect of lifting the namespace members into the scope containing the namespace definition. Code such as

```
namespace A {
    int i, j;
}
```

looks like

```
int i, j;
```

to code for which the following using declaration is in scope

```
using namespace A;
```

Let's look at an example to constrast the effect of a using declaration (which preserves the namespace scope but associates a local synonym with the member name) and a using directive (which has the effect of removing the namespace entirely):

```
namespace blip {
    int bi = 16, bj = 15, bk = 23;
    // other declarations
}
int bj = 0;

void manip() {
    using namespace blip; // using directive -
                          // clash between ::bj and blip::bj
                          // detected only when bj is used

    ++bi;                 // sets blip::bi to 17
    ++bj;                 // error: ambiguous
```

```
                           // global bj or blip::bj?
     ++::bj;               // ok: sets global bj to 1
     ++blip::bj;           // ok: sets blip::bj to 16

     int bk = 97;          // local bk hides blip::bk
     ++bk;                 // sets local bk to 98
}
```

The first thing that should be noted is that using directives are scoped. The using directive in manip() applies only within the block of the function manip(). To the function manip(), the members of namespace blip appear as if they were declared in global scope. Hence, the function manip() can refer to the names of these members using their short form. Code located outside the function manip() must use the qualified names.

The second thing to note is that ambiguity errors caused by using directives are detected when a name is used and not when the using directive is encountered. For example, the member bj appears to manip() as if it were declared outside the namespace blip, in global scope, at the location where the namespace definition is located. However, there is already a variable named bj in global scope. The use of the name bj within the function manip() is therefore ambiguous: the name refers both to the global variable and to the member of namespace blip. The using directive is not an error, however. Only when bj is used within manip() is the ambiguity error detected. If bj was never used within manip(), no error would be issued.

The third thing to note is that the use of qualified names is not affected by using directives. When manip() refers to ::bj, only the variable introduced in global scope is considered. When manip() refers to blip::bj, only the variable introduced in the namespace blip is considered.

The last thing to note is that, because the namespace members appear as if they were declared outside the namespace, *at the location where the namespace definition is located*, the members appear to the function manip() as if they were declared in global scope. This means that local declarations within manip() may hide some of the namespace member names. The local variable bk hides the namespace member blip::bk. Referring to bk within manip() is not ambiguous; it refers to the local variable bk.

Using directives are simple to use: with the use of a single using directive, all the member names are suddenly visible. Although this may seem a simple solution, overuse can introduce its own problem. If an application uses many libraries and if the names within these libraries are made visible with using directives, then we are back to square one, and the global name space pollution problem reappears. For example:

```
namespace cplusplus_primer {
    class matrix { };
    // other goodies ...
}
namespace DisneyFeatureAnimation {
    class matrix { };
```

```
     // here too ...
}
using namespace cplusplus_primer;
using namespace DisneyFeatureAnimation;

matrix m; // error, ambiguous:
// cplusplus_primer's or DisneyFeatureAnimation's?
```

Name ambiguity errors caused by multiple using directives are detected only at the point of use. In the preceding example, the ambiguity error is detected when the name matrix is used. This late detection can cause surprises to users. Errors can show up later even though the header files have not been changed and no new declarations have been added to the program. The errors show up when we suddenly decide to use new features in the library.

Using directives can be very useful in migrating applications to new library versions wrapped in namespaces. However, the use of many using directives can cause the global namespace pollution to reappear. This problem can be minimized by replacing the using directives with more-selective using declarations. Ambiguity errors caused by the more-specific using declarations are detected at the point of declaration. We therefore recommend that you use using declarations rather than using directives to better control the global name space pollution problem in your programs.

8.6.4   The Standard Namespace std

All the components of the C++ standard library are declared and defined within a namespace called namespace std. Every function, object, and class template declared in a standard header file, such as <vector> or <iostream>, is declared within namespace std.

If all the library components are declared in namespace std, what is wrong with the names of the library components used in the following example from Section 6.5?

```
#include <vector>
#include <string>
#include <iterator>

int main()
{
   // input stream iterator tied to standard input
   istream_iterator<string> infile( cin );

   // input stream iterator marking end-of-stream
   istream_iterator<string> eos;

   // initialize svec with values entered through cin;
   vector<string> svec( infile, eos );
```

```
    // process svec
}
```

That's right — the piece of code does not compile because the members of namespace std cannot be accessed without qualified names within the code sample. To fix this we can do one of the following things.

- Replace the names of the members of namespace std in the example with the appropriate qualified names.
- Use using declarations to make visible the members of namespace std used in the example.
- Use a using directive to make all the members from namespace std visible.

The members of namespace std used in the example are the following: the class template istream_iterator, the program's standard input cin, the class string, and the class template vector.

The simplest solution is to add a using directive following the #include directives, as follows:

```
using namespace std;
```

This using directive makes all the members of namespace std visible in our example. However, there are many things declared in namespace std. We prefer using declarations to reduce the chance of future name collisions as we add new global declarations to our program.

The using declarations needed to make the example compile without errors are the following:

```
using std::istream_iterator;
using std::string;
using std::cin;
using std::vector;
```

But where should we place these using declarations? If our program is composed of many files, it may be convenient to create a header file to contain all the using declarations for the members of namespace std that our application needs. This header file would be included following the C++ standard library header files in our program text files.

In this book, to keep the code examples short, and because many of the examples were compiled with implementations not supporting namespaces, we have not explicitly listed the using declarations needed to properly compile the examples. It is assumed that using declarations are provided for the members of namespace std used in the code examples.

Exercise 8.14

Explain the differences between using declarations and using directives.

Exercise 8.15

Given the full example in Section 6.14, write the using declarations necessary to make the member of namespace std visible in this example.

Exercise 8.16

Consider the following code sample:

```
namespace Exercise {
    int ivar = 0;
    double dvar = 0;
    const int limit = 1000;
}
int ivar = 0;

//1
void manip() {
    //2

    double dvar = 3.1416;

    int iobj = limit + 1;

    ++ivar;
    ++::ivar;
}
```

What are the effects of the declarations and expressions in this code sample if using declarations for all the members of namespace Exercise are located at //1? At //2 instead? Now answer the same question but replace the using declarations with a using directive for namespace Exercise.

9

Overloaded Functions

Now that we know how to declare and define functions and how to use functions in our programs, this chapter looks at a special kind of functions supported in C++: overloaded functions. Two functions are overloaded if they have the same name, are declared in the same scope, and have different parameter lists. In this chapter, we first look at how to declare a set of overloaded functions and why it is useful to do so. We then briefly look at how function overload resolution proceeds — that is, how a function call is resolved to one function in a set of overloaded functions. Function overload resolution is one of the most complex aspects of C++. For those of you who want to understand it in greater detail, two advanced sections are provided at the end of this chapter to describe argument type conversions and function overload resolution more fully.

9.1   Overloaded Function Declarations

Now that we know how to declare and define functions and how to use functions in our programs, we will look at a new aspect of functions supported within C++: *overloaded* functions. *Function overloading* allows multiple functions that provide a common operation on different parameter types to share a common name.

If you have written an arithmetic expression in a programming language, you have used a predefined overloaded function. For example, the expression

```
1 + 3
```

invokes the addition operation for integer operands, whereas the expression

```
1.0 + 3.0
```

invokes a different addition operation that handles floating point operands. The operation that is actually used is transparent to the user. The addition operation is overloaded to handle the different operand types. It is the responsibility of the compiler, and not of the programmer, to distinguish between the different operations and to apply the appropriate operation depending on the operands' types.

In this chapter, we see how to define our own overloaded functions.

9.1.1   Why Overload a Function Name

As is the case with the built-in addition operation, we may want to define a set of functions that perform the same general action but that apply to different parameter types. For example, suppose we want to define functions that return the largest of their parameters' values.

Without the ability to overload a function name, we must give each function its own unique name. For example, we could define a set of max() functions as follows:

```
int i_max( int, int );
int vi_max( const vector<int> & );
int matrix_max( const matrix & );
```

Each function, however, performs the same general action; each one returns the largest of its parameters' set of values. From a user's viewpoint, there is only one operation, that of determining a maximum value. The implementation details of how that is accomplished are of little interest to the users of the function.

This lexical complexity is not intrinsic to the problem of determining the largest of a set of values but rather reflects a limitation of the programming environment in which each name occurring at the same scope must refer to a unique entity (a unique object, function, class type, and so on). Such complexity presents a practical problem to the programmer, who must remember or look up each name. Function overloading relieves the programmer of this lexical complexity.

With function overloading, the programmer can simply write the following:

```
int ix = max( j, k );

vector<int> vec;
// ...
int iy = max( vec );
```

This technique gets the largest value in a variety of situations.

9.1.2   How to Overload a Function Name

In C++, two or more functions can be given the same name provided that each parameter list is unique in either the number or the types of the parameters. The following declarations are declarations for the overloaded function max():

```
int max( int, int );
int max( const vector<int> & );
int max( const matrix & );
```

A separate definition of max() is required for each overload declaration that has a unique set of parameters.

When a function name is declared more than once in a particular scope, the compiler interprets the second (and subsequent) declarations as follows.

- If the parameter lists of the two functions differ in either the number or type of their parameters, the two functions are considered to be overloaded. For example:

```
// overloaded functions
void print( const string & );
void print( vector<int> & );
```

- If both the return type and the parameter list of the two function declarations match exactly, the second declaration is treated as a redeclaration of the first. For example:

```
// declares the same function
void print( const string &str );
void print( const string & );
```

The parameter names are irrelevant when parameter lists are compared.

- If the parameter lists of the two functions match exactly but the return types differ, the second declaration is treated as an erroneous redeclaration of the first and is flagged at compile-time as an error. For example:

```
unsigned int max( int i1, int i2 );
int max( int , int ); // error: only return type is different
```

A function's return type is not enough to distinguish between two overloaded functions.

- If the parameter lists of the two functions differ only in their default arguments, the second declaration is treated as a redeclaration of the first. For example:

```
// declares the same function
int max( int *ia, int sz );
int max( int *, int = 10 );
```

A typedef name provides an alternative name for an existing data type; it does not create a new data type. Therefore, two function parameter lists that differ only in that one uses a typedef and the other uses the type to which the typedef corresponds are not different parameter lists. The following two function declarations of calc() are treated as having exactly the same parameter list. The second declaration results in a compile-time error, because, although it declares the same parameter list, it declares a different return type from the first declaration.

```
// typedef does not introduce a new type
typedef double DOLLAR;
```

```
// error: same parameter list, different return types
extern DOLLAR calc( DOLLAR );
extern int calc( double );
```

When a parameter type is const or volatile, the const or volatile qualifier is not taken into account when the declarations of different functions are identified. For example, the following two declarations declare the same function:

```
// declares the same function
void f( int );
void f( const int );
```

The fact that the parameter is const is relevant only within the definition of the function: it means that expressions in the function body cannot change the value of the parameter. However, for a pass-by-value argument, this is completely transparent to a user of the function: a user never sees the modifications applied by a function to a pass-by-value argument. (Pass-by-value arguments and other methods of argument passing are discussed in Section 7.3.) Declaring a parameter const when the argument is passed by value does not change in any way the kind of arguments that can be passed to the function. Any argument of type int can be used in a call to the function f(int) as well as the function f(const int). Because both functions accept the same set of arguments, the declarations just shown do not declare an overloaded function. The function f() can be defined as

```
void f( int i ) { }
```

or as

```
void f( const int i ) { }
```

Providing both of these definitions in the same program is an error, however, because these definitions define the same function twice.

However, if const or volatile applies to the type to which a pointer or reference parameter refers, then the const or volatile qualifier is taken into account when the declarations of different functions are identified.

```
// declares different functions
void f( int* );
void f( const int* );

// also declares different functions
void f( int& );
void f( const int& );
```

9.1.3   When Not to Overload a Function Name

When is it not beneficial to overload a function name? It is not beneficial whenever the different function names provide information that would make the program easier to understand. Here are some examples. The following set of functions operates on a common data abstraction. They may at first seem likely candidates for overloading:

```
void setDate( Date&, int, int, int );
Date &convertDate( const string & );
void printDate( const Date& );
```

These functions operate on the same data type — namely, the class Date — but do not share the same operation. In this case, the lexical complexity associated with the function names comes from a programmer convention that uses a set of operations and a common data type to name the functions. The C++ class mechanism makes this sort of convention unnecessary. Instead, these functions should be made member functions of the class Date, and, because each member function performs a different operation, the name of the member function should represent this operation. For example:

```
#include <string>
class Date {
public:
    set( int, int, int );
    Date &convert( const string & );
    void print();

    // ...
};
```

Here is another example. The following set of five member functions for a Screen class performs various move operations on the Screen's cursor. It might at first seem better to overload this set of functions under the name move():

```
Screen& moveHome();
Screen& moveAbs( int, int );
Screen& moveRel( int, int, char *direction );
Screen& moveX( int );
Screen& moveY( int );
```

The last two instances cannot both be overloaded, because their parameter lists are exactly the same. To provide a unique signature, we could compress the two functions into one as follows:

```
// combined function for moveX() and moveY()
Screen& move( int, char xy );
```

Each function now has a unique parameter list, allowing the set to be overloaded with the name move(). By our criterion, however, overloading these functions is a bad idea: the different function names provide information that would otherwise be lost, rendering the program more obscure. Although cursor movement is a general operation shared by all these functions, the specific nature of that movement is unique among certain of these functions. moveHome(), for example, represents a special instance of cursor movement. Which of the two calls is easier to understand for a reader of the program? Which of the two calls is easier to remember for a user of the Screen class?

```
// which is easier to understand?
myScreen.home(); // we think this one!
myScreen.move();
```

Overloading can be unnecessary at times, and different function definitions may not be required. In some cases, default arguments allow multiple function declarations to be compressed into a single function. For example, the two cursor functions

```
moveAbs(int,int);
moveAbs(int,int,char*);
```

are distinguished by the presence or absence of the char* third parameter. If the implementations of these two functions are very similar and if a default argument for the char* parameter can be found that, when passed to the function, has the meaning of no argument present, then these two functions can be merged. And there is just such a default argument in this case — a pointer of value 0:

```
move( int, int, char* = 0 );
```

Programmers are best served by not thinking of each language feature as the next mountain to climb. Use of a feature should follow from the logic of the application and not simply because it is there. Programmers should not force overloaded functions into their applications. Only where it feels natural to use them should they be implemented.

9.1.4   Overloading and Scope ◆

All the functions in a set of overloaded functions are declared in the same scope. A locally declared function, for example, hides rather than overloads a function declared at global scope. For example:

```
#include <string>
void print( const string & );
void print( double ); // overloads print()

void fooBar( int ival )
{
    // separate scope: hides both instances of print()
    extern void print( int );

    // error: print( const string & ) is hidden in this scope
    print( "Value: " );
```

```
      print( ival );  // ok: print( int ) is visible
}
```

A set of overloaded functions can also be declared within a class. Because each class maintains its own scope, the functions that are members of two distinct classes do not overload one another. Class member functions are described in Chapter 13. Overload resolution for class member functions is described in Chapter 15.

A set of overloaded functions can also be declared within a namespace. Each namespace also maintains its own scope, and the functions that are members of two distinct namespaces do not overload one another. For example:

```
#include <string>
namespace IBM {
   extern void print( const string & );
   extern void print( double ); // overloads print()
}
namespace Disney {
   // separate scope:
   // does not overload IBM's print() functions
   extern void print( int );
}
```

Using declarations and using directives are mechanisms by which namespace members can be made visible in other scopes. These mechanisms have some impact on the declarations of overloaded functions. Using declarations and using directives are introduced in Section 8.6.

How does a using declaration work for an overloaded function? Recall that a using declaration introduces an alias for a namespace member in the scope where the using declaration appears. What happens with the using declarations in the following program?

```
namespace libs_R_us {
   int max( int, int );
   int max( double, double );

   extern void print( int );
   extern void print( double );
}

// using declarations:
using libs_R_us::max;
using libs_R_us::print( double ); // error

void func()
{
   max( 87, 65 );     // calls libs_R_us::max( int, int )
   max( 35.5, 76.6 ); // calls libs_R_us::max( double, double )
}
```

The first using declaration introduces both functions libs_R_us::max() in global scope. It is then possible to call either max() function within func(). The types of the arguments on the function call determine which function is called. The second using declaration is an error. A user cannot specify a parameter list in a using declaration for a function. The only valid using declaration for libs_R_us::print() is

```
using libs_R_us::print;
```

A using declaration always declares aliases for *all* the functions in a set of overloaded functions. Why is this restriction necessary? This restriction ensures that the interface of the namespace libs_R_us is not violated. It is clear that, for a function call such as

```
print( 88 );
```

the author of the namespace expects the function libs_R_us::print(int) to be called. The author of the library provided different functions for a reason. Allowing users to selectively add to a scope one function in a set of overloaded functions but not all of the functions could lead to surprising program behavior.

What happens if a using declaration introduces a function in a scope in which a function of the same name already exists? Recall that a using declaration is a declaration. It is as if the functions introduced by the using declaration were declared where the using declaration appears. For this reason, the functions introduced by the using declaration overload the other declarations of the functions with the same name already present in the scope where the using declaration appears. For example:

```
#include <string>
namespace libs_R_us {
   extern void print( int );
   extern void print( double );
}

extern void print( const string & );

// libs_R_us::print( int ) and libs_R_us::print( double )
// overload print( const string & )
using libs_R_us::print;

void fooBar( int ival )
{
   print( "Value: " ); // calls global print( const string & )
   print( ival );      // calls libs_R_us::print( int )
}
```

The using declaration adds two declarations to global scope: one for print(int) and one for print(double). These declarations alias the functions in namespace libs_R_us. The declarations are added to the overload set for print(), of which the global function print(const string &) is already a member. When a function call is found in fooBar(), all the print() functions are considered.

If the using declaration introduces a function in a scope that already has a function of the same name with the same parameter list, then the using declaration is in error. A using declaration cannot declare the function print(int) to be an alias for the function in namespace libs_R_us if there already exists a function named print(int) in global scope. For example:

```
namespace libs_R_us {
   void print( int );
   void print( double );
}

void print( int );
using libs_R_us::print; // error: redeclaration of print(int)

void fooBar( int ival )
{
   print( ival );        // which print? ::print or libs_R_us::print?
}
```

Now that we have examined how a set of overloaded functions is affected by using declarations, let's see how it is affected by using directives. A using directive makes the namespace members appear as if they were declared outside the namespace. By removing the boundaries of the namespace, a using directive adds declarations to the scope in which the namespace was defined. If a function declared in this scope has the same name as a namespace member function, then the namespace member is added to the overload set. For example:

```
#include <string>
namespace libs_R_us {
   extern void print( int );
   extern void print( double );
}

extern void print( const string & );

// using directive:
// print(int), print(double) and print(const string &)
// are part of the same overload set
using namespace libs_R_us;

void fooBar( int ival )
{
   print( "Value: " ); // calls global print(const string &)
   print( ival );      // calls libs_R_us::print(int)
}
```

This is also true if many using directives are present. The member functions from different namespaces that have the same name are added to the same overload set. For example:

```
namespace IBM {
    int print(int);
}
namespace Disney {
    double print(double);
}

// using directives:
// form an overload set of functions from different namespaces
using namespace IBM;
using namespace Disney;

long double print(long double);

int main() {
    print(1);    // calls IBM::print(int)
    print(3.1);  // calls Disney::print(double)
    return 0;
}
```

The overload set for the function print() in global scope contains the functions print(int), print(double), and print(long double). These functions are all part of the overload set considered for the function calls in main(), even though these functions were originally declared in different namespace scopes.

Functions in an overloaded set are therefore declared in the same scope, even though these declarations may be introduced through using declarations and using directives, which make namespace members visible as if they were declared in other scopes.

9.1.5   extern "C" and Overloaded Functions ◈

As we have seen in Section 7.7, we can use the linkage directive extern "C" to specify that a function in our C++ program is written in the programming language C. How does the extern "C" linkage directive influence overloaded function declarations? Can some functions in the overloaded set be C++ functions while other functions are C functions?

A linkage directive can be specified for only one function in a set of overloaded functions. For example, a program that includes the following two declarations is not legal:

```
// error: two extern "C" functions in set of overloaded functions
extern "C" void print( const char* );
extern "C" void print( int );
```

The following overloading of calc() illustrates a typical use of the linkage directive in an overloaded set:

```
class SmallInt { /* ... */ };
class BigNum { /* ... */ };

// the C function can be called from C and C++ programs
// the C++ functions handle parameters that are C++ classes
extern "C" double calc( double );
extern SmallInt calc( const SmallInt& );
extern BigNum calc( const BigNum& );
```

The C language `calc()` function can be called from C programs and from C++ programs. The additional functions are C++ functions with class parameters that can be called only from C++ programs. The order of the declarations is not significant.

The linkage directive does not influence the function that is selected for a function call; only the types of the parameters are used to select the function called. The function chosen is the one that best matches the type of the function arguments. For example:

```
SmallInt si = 8;
int main() {
   calc( 34 ); // calls the C calc( double )
   calc( si ); // calls the C++ calc( const SmallInt & )
   // ...
   return 0;
}
```

9.1.6   Pointers to Overloaded Functions ◆

It is possible to declare a pointer to refer to a function in a set of overloaded functions. How can this be done? For example:

```
extern void ff( vector<double> );
extern void ff( unsigned int );

// which function does pf1 refer to?
void ( *pf1 )( unsigned int ) = &ff;
```

Because `ff()` is an overloaded function, the compiler does not know which function to select by just looking at the initializer expression: `&ff`. To select the function that initializes the pointer, the compiler searches for the function in the overload set that has the same return type and the same parameter list as the function type referred to by the pointer. In the preceding case, `ff(unsigned int)` is selected.

What if no function matches the pointer's type exactly? If no function matches exactly, the initialization results in a compile-time error. For example:

```
extern void ff( vector<double> );
extern void ff( unsigned int );

// error: no match: invalid parameter list
void ( *pf2 )( int ) = &ff;
```

```
// error: no match: invalid return type
double ( *pf3 )( vector<double> ) = &ff;
```

Assignments work in similar ways. If the address of an overloaded function is assigned to a pointer to function, the type of the pointer to function is used to select the function on the right-hand side of the assignment operator. And if the compiler does not find a function that exactly matches the type of the pointer, the assignment is in error; that is, there are no type conversions between two pointer to function types:

```
matrix calc( const matrix & );
int calc( int, int );

int ( *pc1 )( int, int ) = 0;
int ( *pc2 )( int, double ) = 0;

// ...
// ok: matches int calc( int, int );
pc1 = &calc;

// error: no match: invalid second parameter type
pc2 = &calc;
```

9.1.7   Type-Safe Linkage ◈

Overloading gives the appearance of permitting multiple occurrences of the same function name with different parameter lists. This is a lexical convenience that holds at the program source level. The downstream components of most compilation systems, however, require that each function be uniquely named. Most link editors resolve external references lexically. If the link editor sees two or more instances of the name print, it cannot analyze the types to distinguish between entities (by this point in the compilation, the type information is usually lost). Rather, the link editor flags print as multiply defined and quits.

To handle this problem, each function name with its associated parameter list is *encoded* as a unique internal name. The downstream components of the compilation system see only this encoded name. The exact details of the name transformation are unimportant; they are likely to vary across implementations. The general algorithm encodes the type and number of parameters and appends this encoding to the function name.

As we have seen in the section on global functions, Section 8.2, this special encoding also ensures that two declarations for functions with the same name and different parameter lists located in different files are not taken as declarations for the same function by the link editor. Because this encoding helps the link phase differentiate overloaded functions within the program, it is called *type-safe linkage*.

This special encoding is not applied to functions declared with the `extern "C"` linkage directive. This is why only one function in a set of overloaded functions can be declared `extern "C"`: two `extern "C"` functions with different parameter lists are seen as the same function by the link editors.

Exercise 9.1

Why would you declare overloaded functions?

Exercise 9.2

How should a set of overloaded functions for the following `error()` function be declared to handle the following calls?

```
int index;
int upperBound;
char selectVal;
// ...
error( "Array out of bounds: ", index, upperBound );
error( "Division by zero" );
error( "Invalid selection", selectVal );
```

Exercise 9.3

Explain the effect of the second declaration in each one of the following sets of declarations.

```
(a) int calc( int, int );
    int calc( const int, const int );

(b) int get();
    double get();

(c) int *reset( int * );
    double *reset( double * );

(d) extern "C" int compute( int *, int );
    extern "C" double compute( double *, double );
```

Exercise 9.4

Which ones of the following initializations, if any, are errors? Why?

```
(a) void reset( int * );
    void (*pf)( void * ) = reset;

(b) int calc( int, int );
    int (*pf1)( int, int ) = calc;

(c) extern "C" int compute( int *, int );
    int (*pf3)( int*, int ) = compute;
```

```
(d) void (*pf4)( const matrix & ) = 0;
```

9.2   The Three Steps of Overload Resolution

Function overload resolution is the process by which a function call is associated with *one* function in a set of overloaded functions. It is the process by which, in the presence of many functions with the same name, one function is selected for the arguments specified in the function call. Consider this example:

```
T t1, t2;
void f( int, int );
void f( float, float );

int main() {
   f( t1,t2 );
   return 0;
}
```

Here, function overload resolution will determine, given a type T, whether the call f(t1,t2) will call the function f(int,int) or the function f(float,float), whether the call is in error because none of these functions can be called with the arguments t1 and t2, or whether the call is *ambiguous* because the arguments specified in the call match both functions equally well.

Function overload resolution is one of the most complex aspects of the C++ programming language. Beginner C++ programmers may be overwhelmed at first trying to understand all of its details. For this reason, this section presents only an overview of how function overload resolution proceeds and gives you a feel for what happens. For those of you wanting to know more, the following two sections describe in greater detail the process of function overload resolution.

There are three steps in the process of function overload resolution. We will use the following example to illustrate these three steps:

```
void f();
void f( int );
void f( double, double = 3.4 );
void f( char*, char* );

int main() {
   f( 5.6 );
   return 0;
}
```

The steps of function overload resolution are the following:

1.   Identify the set of overloaded functions considered for the call and identify the properties of the argument list in the function call.

2. Select the functions from the set of overloaded functions that can be called with the arguments specified in the call, given the number of arguments and their types.

3. Select the function that best matches the call.

We will look at each step in turn.

The first step of function overload resolution identifies the set of overloaded functions considered for the call. The functions in this set are called *candidate functions*. A candidate function is a function with the same name as the function that is called and for which a declaration is visible at the point of the call. In the example, there are four candidate functions: `f()`, `f(int)`, `f(double, double)`, and `f(char*, char*)`.

The first step of function overload resolution also identifies the properties of the argument list in the function call, that is, the number of arguments and their types. In the example, the argument list consists of one argument of type `double`.

The second step of function overload resolution selects the functions from the set of candidate functions found in step 1 that can be called with the arguments specified in the call. The functions thus selected are called the *viable functions*. A viable function has the same number of parameters as there are arguments in the argument list in the call, or a viable function has more parameters than there are arguments in the argument list in the call and each additional parameter has an associated default argument. For a function to be viable, there must exist *conversions* that can convert each argument in the argument list to the type of its corresponding parameter in the function parameter list.

In the example, there are two viable functions that can be called with the argument list specified.

- `f(int)` is a viable function because it has only one parameter and because a conversion exists that can convert the argument of type `double` to the parameter of type `int`.

- `f(double, double)` is a viable function because a default argument is provided for the function's second parameter and its first parameter is of type `double`, which matches exactly the type of the argument.

If the second step of the function overload resolution process finds no viable function that can be called with the given argument list, then the function call is in error. There is no function that matches the call, and we say that it is a *no match* situation.

The third step of function overload resolution consists of selecting the function that matches the function call the best. This function is called the *best viable function* (also often called the *best match function*). To select this function, the conversions used to convert the arguments to the types of the corresponding viable function parameters are *ranked*. The best viable function is the function for which the following apply.

1. The conversions applied to the arguments are *no worse* than the conversions necessary to call any other viable function.
2. The conversions on some arguments are *better* than the conversions necessary for the same arguments when calling the other viable functions.

Type conversions and their ranking are examined in greater detail in Section 9.3. We will here briefly examine the ranking of the conversions in the example. When the viable function f(int) is considered, the conversion applied to the argument of type double to convert it to type int is a standard conversion. When the viable function f(double, double) is considered, the argument of type double is an exact match for the corresponding parameter. Because an exact match is better than a standard conversion — because not to do a conversion is better than to do any conversion — the best viable function selected for the call is f(double, double).

If the third step of function overload resolution finds no best viable function, then the function call is *ambiguous*; that is, the call does not match any viable function better than any other.

As indicated earlier, more details on the steps of function overload resolution can be found in Section 9.4. Function overload resolution also applies when an overloaded class member function is called or when an overloaded operator function is called. Section 15.10 discusses the rules for function overload resolution with class member functions. Section 15.11 discusses the rules for function overload resolution with overload operators. Function overload resolution must also take into account functions generated from function templates. Section 10.8 discusses how function templates influence function overload resolution.

Exercise 9.5

What happens during the last (third) step of the function overload resolution process?

9.3   Argument Type Conversions ◆

During the second step of function overload resolution, the compiler identifies and ranks the conversions that can apply to each argument in a function call to convert it to the type of the corresponding parameter in each viable function. There are three possible outcomes of this ranking:

1. An *exact match*. The argument matches the type of the function parameter exactly. For example, given the following three print() functions in the set of overloaded functions, each of the following three calls to print() results in an exact match:

    ```
    void print( unsigned int );
    void print( const char* );
    void print( char );
    ```

```
unsigned int a;

print( 'a' );    // matches print( char );
print( "a" );    // matches print( const char* );
print( a );      // matches print( unsigned int );
```

2. Match with a *type conversion*. The argument does not directly match the type of the parameter, but it can be converted to such a type:

```
void ff( char );

ff( 0 ); // argument converted from int to char
```

3. *No match*. The argument cannot be made to match a parameter of the declared functions, because no type conversions exist between the argument and the corresponding function parameter. Each of the arguments in the following two calls to print() results in a no match:

```
// print() declarations as above
int *ip;
class SmallInt { /* ... */ };
SmallInt si;

print( ip ); // error: no match
print( si ); // error: no match
```

For the argument to be an exact match, the argument need not exactly match the type of the parameter. There are some minor conversions that can be applied to the argument. The possible conversions in the exact match category are the following conversions:

1. Lvalue-to-rvalue conversion
2. Array-to-pointer conversion
3. Function-to-pointer conversion
4. Qualification conversions

We will examine these conversions in more detail later.

The category of a match with a type conversion is the most complex of the three categories. Several kinds of type conversions must be considered. The possible conversions can be grouped into three categories: *promotions*, *standard conversions*, and *user-defined conversions*. The promotions and standard conversions are examined later in this chapter. User-defined conversions will be presented later, after classes have been discussed in detail. A user-defined conversion is performed by a *conversion function*, a member function that allows a class to define its own set of "standard" conversions. Chapter 15 looks at conversion functions for classes and at function overload resolution involving user-defined conversions.

When selecting the best viable function for a function call, the compiler selects the function for which the type conversions on the arguments are the "best." Type conversions are ranked as follows: an exact match is better than a promotion, a promotion is better than a standard conversion, and a standard conversion is better than a user-defined conversion. We will examine the ranking of type conversions further in Section 9.4, but, as we describe the possible type conversions here, some of the examples in this section will show simple cases of how this ranking is used to select the best viable function.

9.3.1   Details of an Exact Match

The simplest case of exact match is when the arguments match the type of the function parameters exactly. For example, given the following two max() functions in the overload set, each of the following two calls to max() has arguments that exactly match the parameters of a particular function in the overload set:

```
int max( int, int );
double max( double, double );

int i1;

void calc( double d1 ) {
    max( 56, i1 );   // exactly matches max( int, int );
    max( d1, 66.9 ); // exactly matches max( double, double );
}
```

An enumeration type defines a unique type that matches exactly only the enumerators within the enumeration and the objects declared to be of the enumeration type. For example:

```
enum Tokens { INLINE = 128; VIRTUAL = 129; };
Tokens curTok = INLINE;

enum Stat { Fail, Pass };

extern void ff( Tokens );
extern void ff( Stat );
extern void ff( int );

int main() {
    ff( Pass );   // exactly matches ff( Stat )
    ff( 0 );      // exactly matches ff( int )
    ff( curTok ); // exactly matches ff( Tokens )
    // ...
}
```

As we mentioned earlier, an argument can be an exact match even though some minor type conversions must be applied to the argument to bring it to the type of the corresponding function parameter.

The first of these conversions is the lvalue-to-rvalue conversion. An lvalue represents an object that our program can address, an object from which a value can be fetched, and, unless the object is declared const, an object that can have its value modified. In contrast, an rvalue is an expression that denotes a value or is an expression that denotes a temporary object that the user cannot address and that cannot have its value modified. Here is a simple example:

```
int calc( int );

int main() {
    int lval, res;

    lval = 5; // lvalue: lval; rvalue: 5
    res = calc( lval );
                // lvalue: res;
                // rvalue: temporary to hold return value of calc()
    return 0;
}
```

In the first assignment expression, lval is the lvalue, and the literal constant 5 is the rvalue. In the second assignment expression, res is the lvalue, and the temporary that holds the return value of the function call to calc() is the rvalue.

In some situations an expression that is an lvalue is used when a value is expected. For example:

```
int obj1;
int obj2;

int main() {
    // ...
    int local = obj1 + obj2;
    return 0;
}
```

obj1 and obj2 are lvalue expressions. However, the addition in main() needs only the values stored in obj1 and obj2. Before the addition is performed, values are extracted from obj1 and obj2. This action of extracting a value from an object represented by an lvalue expression is an lvalue-to-rvalue conversion.

When a function expects a pass-by-value argument, an lvalue-to-rvalue conversion is performed when the argument is an lvalue. For example:

```
#include <string>
string color( "purple" );
void print( string );

int main() {
    print( color ); // exact match: lvalue-to-rvalue conversion
    return 0;
}
```

Because the argument in the call to print(color) is passed by value, an lvalue-to-rvalue conversion takes place to extract a value from color and pass it to print(string). Even though this lvalue-to-rvalue conversion takes place, the argument color is nonetheless an exact match for the call to print(string).

Not all function calls require that an lvalue-to-rvalue conversion take place on the arguments. A reference represents an lvalue; when a function has a reference parameter, the function that is called receives an lvalue. For this reason, there is no lvalue-to-rvalue conversion applied to an argument that has a corresponding reference parameter. For example, given the function

```
#include <list>
void print( list<int> & );
```

li in the following call is an lvalue representing the list<int> object passed to the function print().

```
list<int> li(20);

int main() {
    // ...
    print( li ); // exact match: no lvalue-to-rvalue conversion
    return 0;
}
```

Binding li to the reference parameter is an exact match.

The second conversion allowed in an exact match situation is the array-to-pointer conversion. As we mentioned in Section 7.3, a function parameter never has array type. Instead, the parameter is transformed to a pointer to the first element of the array. Similarly, an argument of type array of N T (where N is the number of array elements and T is the type of the array elements) is always converted to the type pointer to T. This conversion on the argument type is an array-to-pointer conversion. Even though this conversion takes place, the argument is nonetheless seen as an exact match for a parameter of type pointer to T. For example:

```
int ai[3];
void putValues(int *);

int main() {
    // ...
    putValues(ai); // exact match: array-to-pointer conversion
    return 0;
}
```

Before the function putValues() is called, an array-to-pointer conversion takes place that converts the argument ai from an array of three ints to a pointer to int. Even though putValues() has a pointer parameter and even though an array-to-pointer conversion takes place on the argument, the argument is nonetheless an exact match for the call to putValues().

The next conversion allowed in the exact match situation is the function-to-pointer conversion. This conversion was introduced briefly in Section 7.9. As with a parameter of array type, a parameter of function type is automatically transformed to a pointer to the function. An argument of function type is also automatically converted to the type pointer to function. This conversion on the argument type is called a function-to-pointer conversion. Even though this conversion takes place, the argument is nonetheless seen as an exact match for a parameter of type pointer to function. For example:

```
int lexicoCompare( const string &, const string & );

typedef int (*PFI)( const string &, const string & );
void sort( string *, string *, PFI );

string as[10];

int main()
{
    // ...
    sort( as,
          as + sizeof(as)/sizeof(as[0] - 1),
          lexicoCompare // exact match:
                        // function-to-pointer conversion
        );

    return 0;
}
```

Before the function sort() is called, a function-to-pointer conversion takes place that converts the argument lexicoCompare from a function type to a pointer to function type. Even though the function expects a pointer and the argument is a function name, and even though a function-to-pointer conversion takes place, the argument is an exact match for the third parameter of sort().

The last conversions listed under the exact match category are the qualification conversions. A qualification conversion affects only pointers. It is a conversion that adds const or volatile qualifiers (or both) to the type to which a pointer points. For example:

```
int a[5] = { 4454, 7864, 92, 421, 938 };
int *pi = a;
bool is_equal( const int * , const int * );

int func( int *parm ) {

    // exact match for pi and parm: qualification conversions
    if ( is_equal( pi, parm ) )
        // ...
```

```
        return 0;
    }
```

Before the function is_equal() is called, the arguments pi and parm are converted
from the type pointer to int to the type pointer to const int. This conversion, which
adds a const qualification to the type to which the pointer points, is a qualification
conversion. Even though the function expects two pointers to const int and the arguments are pointers to int, the arguments exactly match the parameters of is_equal().

A qualification conversion applies only to the type pointed to by a pointer. No type
conversion applies when a parameter is of const or volatile type and the argument is not:

```
    extern void takeCI( const int );

    int main() {
        int ii = ...;
        takeCI(ii); // no qualification conversion
        return 0;
    }
```

In the call to takeCI(), even though the parameter is of type const int, no qualification conversion is applied to the argument ii of type int. The argument exactly
matches the type of the function parameter.

This is also the case if the argument is a pointer and the const or volatile qualifier
applies to the pointer itself:

```
    extern void init( int *const );
    extern int *pi;

    int main() {
        // ...
        init(pi); // no qualification conversion
        return 0;
    }
```

The const qualifier on the parameter of init() applies to the pointer itself and not to
the type pointed to by the pointer. For this reason, the compiler does not take the
const qualifier into account when considering conversions to apply on the argument.
No qualification conversion is applied to the argument pi, and the argument exactly
matches the type of the function parameter.

The first three conversions in the exact match category (lvalue-to-rvalue, array-to-
pointer, and function-to-pointer conversions) are often referred to as *lvalue transformations*. As we will see in Section 9.4, even though lvalue transformations and qualification conversions are in the exact match category, an exact match in which only an
lvalue transformation is needed is ranked as better than an exact match requiring a
qualification conversion. We will see more detail on this in the next section.

An exact match can be forced by the use of an explicit cast. For example, given the set of overloaded functions

```
extern void ff(int);
extern void ff(void *);
```

the call

```
ff( 0xffbc ); // calls ff(int)
```

matches ff(int) exactly, because 0xffbc is a literal constant of type int written in hexadecimal notation. The programmer can force ff(void*) to be invoked by providing an explicit cast as follows:

```
ff( reinterpret_cast<void *>(0xffbc) ); // calls ff(void*)
```

When an explicit cast is applied to an argument, the type of the argument becomes the type that is the result of the cast. The use of explicit casts can help guide function overload resolution. For example, if the result of function overload resolution is ambiguous because the arguments match two or more viable functions equally well, explicit casts can be used to break the ambiguity and force a call to resolve to a particular viable function.

9.3.2   Details of a Promotion

A promotion is one of the following conversions.

- An argument of type char, unsigned char, or short is promoted to type int. An argument of type unsigned short is promoted to type int if the machine size of an int is larger than that of a short integer; otherwise, it is promoted to type unsigned int.

- An argument of type float is promoted to type double.

- An argument of an enumeration type is promoted to the first of the following type that can represent all the values of the enumeration constants: int, unsigned int, long, or unsigned long.

- An argument of type bool is promoted to type int.

A promotion is applied when the type of the argument is one of the source types just described and the function parameter type is the associated promoted type. For example:

```
extern void manip( int );

int main() {
    manip( 'a' ); // type char promotes to int
    return 0;
}
```

The character literal is of type char. Its promoted type is int. Because the promoted type matches the type of the parameter of function manip(), we say that the function call requires a promotion on its argument.

Suppose we have the following example:

```
extern void print( unsigned int );
extern void print( int );
extern void print( char );

unsigned char uc;
print( uc ); // print( int ): uc only requires a promotion
```

A machine on which the unsigned char type takes up one byte of storage and int types take up four bytes of storage, a promotion takes an argument of type unsigned char to the type int, because on this architecture the type int can represent all the values of the type unsigned char. Given the preceding overloaded function declarations, and given the architecture just described, the function that best matches an argument of type unsigned char is print(int). To match the other two functions would require the application of a standard conversion.

The following example illustrates the promotion of an argument of enumeration type:

```
enum Stat { Fail, Pass };

extern void ff( int );
extern void ff( char );

int main() {
    // ok: enumeration constant Pass promoted to int
    ff( Pass );  // ff( int )
    ff( 0 );     // ff( int )
    return 0;
}
```

Promotions of enumeration types can sometimes be surprising. Implementations often choose the representation of an enumeration type depending on the values of the enumeration constants. For example, suppose we have the architecture described earlier (char types are one byte, int types are four bytes) and the following enumeration type:

```
enum e1 { a1, b1, c1 };
```

Because there are only three enumeration constants — a1, b1, and c1 — with the values 0, 1, and 2 respectively, and because all the values of this enumeration type can be represented by the type char, an implementation will often choose the type char as the representation for e1. However, suppose we have another enumeration type e2 with a different set of enumeration constants:

```
enum e2 { a2, b2, c2=0x80000000 };
```

Because one of the enumeration constants has a value of 0x80000000, the implementation is obliged to choose a type for the representation of e2 that can represent the value 0x80000000. The representation chosen for e2 is unsigned int.

So even though both e1 and e2 are enumeration types, their representations differ. This causes e1 and e2 to promote to different types. For example:

```
#include <string>

string format( int );
string format( unsigned int );

int main() {
    format(e1);  // calls format( int )
    format(e2);  // calls format( unsigned int )
    return 0;
}
```

In the first call to format(), because the argument is of type e1 with a representation of type char, the argument promotes to type int and the function format(int) is selected for the call. In the second call to format(), because the argument is of type e2 with a representation of type unsigned int, the argument promotes to the type unsigned int. This causes the function format(unsigned int) to be selected for the second call. You should therefore be aware of the following: two enumeration types may behave quite differently during function overload resolution depending on the value of their enumeration constants, which determines the type to which they promote.

9.3.3   Details of a Standard Conversion

There are five kinds of conversions grouped in the category of standard conversion:

1. The integral conversions: the conversions from any integral type or enumeration type to any other integral type (excluding the conversions that were listed as promotions earlier).

2. The floating point conversions: the conversions from any floating point type to any other floating point type (excluding the conversions that were listed as promotions earlier).

3. The floating-integral conversions: the conversions from any floating point type to any integral type or from any integral type to any floating point type.

4. The pointer conversions: the conversion of the integer value zero to a pointer type and the conversion of a pointer of any type to the type void*.

5. The bool conversions: the conversions from any integral type, floating point type, enumeration type, or pointer type to the type bool.

Here are some examples:

```
extern void print( void* );
extern void print( double );

int main() {
   int i;
   print( i );   // matches print( double );
                 // i is converted by a standard conversion
                 // from int to double
   print( &i );  // matches print( void* );
                 // &i is converted by a standard conversion
                 // from int* to void*
   return 0;
}
```

The conversions that are grouped in categories 1, 2, and 3 are potentially dangerous conversions, because the target type of the conversion cannot represent all the values that the source type can represent. For example, the type `float` cannot represent with as much precision all the values that can be represented by the type `int`. This is why the conversions in these categories are standard conversions and not promotions.

```
int i;
void calc( float );
int main() {
   calc( i ); // floating-integral standard conversion
              // potentially dangerous depending on i's value
   return 0;
}
```

When the function `calc()` is called, a floating-integral standard conversion is applied to convert the argument from type `int` to type `float`. Depending on the value stored in `i`, it is possible that the value for `i` cannot be stored within a parameter of type `float` without a loss of precision.

All standard conversions are treated as requiring equal work. The conversion from `char` to `unsigned char`, for example, does not take precedence over the conversion from `char` to `double`. Closeness of type is not considered. If two viable functions require standard conversions on the argument to match the type of their parameter, the call is ambiguous and it is flagged at compile-time as an error. For example, given the following pair of overloaded functions

```
extern void manip( long );
extern void manip( float );
```

the following call is ambiguous:

```
int main() {
   manip( 3.14 ); // error: ambiguous;
                  // manip( float ) is not better
   return 0;
}
```

The literal constant 3.14 is of type double. A match is achieved with either function by means of a standard conversion. Because there are two standard conversions possible, the call is flagged as ambiguous. No one standard conversion is given precedence over another. The programmer can resolve the ambiguity either with an explicit cast, such as

```
manip( static_cast<long>( 3.14 ) ); // manip( long )
```

or through use of the float constant suffix:

```
manip( 3.14F ); // manip( float )
```

Here are more examples of function calls that are ambiguous and are flagged as errors because they match more than one function in an overloaded set:

```
extern void farith( unsigned int );
extern void farith( float );

int main() {
    // each call is ambiguous
    farith( 'a' );        // argument has type char
    farith( 0 );          // argument has type int
    farith( 2uL );        // argument has type unsigned long
    farith( 3.14159 );    // argument has type double
    farith( true );       // argument has type bool
    return 0;
}
```

The standard pointer conversions can at times seem counterintuitive. In particular, the value 0 can be converted to any pointer type: the pointer value thus created is called the *null pointer value*. This value 0 can be any constant expression of integer type. For example:

```
void set(int*);

int main() {
    // pointer conversion 0 to int* applies to both arguments
    set( 0L );
    set( 0x00 );
    return 0;
}
```

The constant expression 0L (the value 0 of type long int) and the constant expression 0x00 (the hexadecimal integer of value 0) have integer types and can therefore be converted to the null pointer value of type int*.

However, because enumeration types are not integer types, an enumeration value that evaluates to 0 cannot be converted to a pointer type. For example:

```
enum EN { zr = 0 };
set( zr ); // error: zr cannot be converted to int*
```

The call to set() is in error, because there is no conversion possible between the enumeration value zr and the parameter of type int* even if the enumeration value evaluates to zero.

Something else should be noticed: the constant expression 0 has type int. A standard conversion is necessary to bring this constant expression to a pointer type. If there is a function with a parameter of type int in the overload set, this function will be preferred for an argument that is 0. For example:

```
void print( int );
void print( void * );

void set( const char* );
void set( char* );

int main() {
   print( 0 ); // calls print( int )
   set( 0 );    // ambiguous
   return 0;
}
```

The argument is an exact match for the call to print(int). However, to call print(void*), a standard conversion is necessary to bring the value 0 to a pointer type. Because an exact match is better than a standard conversion, the function print(int) is selected for the call. The call to set() is ambiguous, because 0 matches the parameters of both functions set() through the application of a standard conversion. Because either function is equally good for the call, the call is ambiguous.

The last pointer conversion allows an argument of any pointer type to be converted to a parameter of type void*, because void* is a generic pointer to data type that can hold the value of any pointer to data type. Here are some examples:

```
#include <string>
extern void reset( void * );

int func( int *pi, string *ps ) {
   // ...
   reset( pi ); // pointer conversion: int* to void*
   // ...
   reset( ps ); // pointer conversion: string* to void*
   return 0;
}
```

Only pointers to data types can be converted to the type void* with a pointer standard conversion. Pointers to functions cannot be converted to the type void* with a standard conversion. For example:

```
typedef int (*PFV)();
extern PFV testCases[10]; // array of pointers to functions
```

```
extern void reset( void * );

int main() {
    // ...
    reset( testCases[0] ); // error: no standard conversion
                           // between int(*)() and void*
    return 0;
}
```

9.3.4   References

A function call argument or a function parameter can be a reference. How do references affect the rules on type conversions?

First, let's examine what happens if an argument is a reference. The type of the argument is never a reference type. When the argument is a reference, the argument is an lvalue whose type is the type of the object to which the reference refers. Consider this example:

```
int i;
int& ri = i;
void print( int );

int main() {
    print( i );  // lvalue argument of type int
    print( ri ); // same here
    return 0;
}
```

The argument in both function calls has type int. The fact that a reference is used as an argument in the second call has no effect on the type of the argument.

The standard conversions and promotions considered when an argument is a reference to type T are the same as those considered when the argument is an object of type T. For example:

```
int i;
int& ri = i;
void calc( double );

int main() {
    calc( i );  // floating-integral standard conversion
    calc( ri ); // same here
    return 0;
}
```

Now, how do reference parameters affect the conversions applied to an argument? The outcome of a match of an argument with a reference parameter is one of the following possibilities.

1. The argument is an appropriate initializer for the reference parameter. In this case, we say that the argument is an exact match for the parameter. For example:

```
void swap( int &, int & );

int manip( int i1, int i2 ) {
   // ...
   swap( i1, i2 ); // ok: calls swap( int &, int & )
   // ...
   return 0;
}
```

2. The argument cannot initialize the reference parameter. In this case, there is a no match situation and the argument cannot be used to call the function. For example:

```
int obj;
void frd( double & );
int main() {
   frd( obj ); // error: parameter must be: const double &
   return 0;
}
```

The call to frd() is in error. The argument is of type int and must be converted to type double to match the type of the reference parameter. The result of this conversion is a temporary value. Because the reference is not to a const type, a temporary cannot be used to initialize the reference.

Here is another example in which there is no match between the reference parameter and the argument.

```
class B;
void takeB( B& );
B giveB();

int main() {
   takeB( giveB() ); // error: parameter must be: const B &
   return 0;
}
```

The call to takeB() is in error. The argument is the return value from a function call; it is a temporary value that cannot be used to initialize a reference that is not to a const type.

In both of these cases, if the reference parameter is a reference to a const type, the argument is an exact match for the parameter.

We should note here that both an lvalue-to-rvalue conversion and a reference initialization are considered to be exact matches. Given the following code sample

```
void print( int );
void print( int& );

int iobj;
int &ri = iobj;

int main() {
    print( iobj ); // error: ambiguous
    print( ri );   // error: ambiguous
    print( 86 );   // ok: calls print( int )
    return 0;
}
```

the first function call is an error. The object iobj is an argument that is an exact match for both functions print(), causing the function call to be ambiguous. This is also true for the second function call. The reference ri refers to an object that is an exact match for both functions print(). The third call, however, is OK. The function print(int&) is not a viable function for this call. An integer constant is an rvalue and is not a valid initializer for a non-const reference parameter. The only function in the set of viable functions for the call print(86) is the function print(int). Because it is the only viable function, it is the function selected for the call.

In short, with a reference parameter, either the argument is an exact match if the argument is a valid initializer for the reference, or there is no match if the argument is not a valid initializer for the reference.

Exercise 9.6

Name two of the minor conversions allowed in an exact match.

Exercise 9.7

What is the rank of each conversion on the arguments in the following function calls?

```
(a) void print( int *, int );
    int arr[6];
    print( arr, 6 ); // function call

(b) void manip( int, int );
    manip( 'a', 'z' ); // function call

(c) int calc( int, int );
    double dobj;
    double = calc( 55.4, dobj ); // function call

(d) void set( const int * );
    int *pi;
    set( pi ); // function call
```

Exercise 9.8

Which ones of the following function calls, if any, are errors because no conversion exists between the type of the argument and the function parameter?

```
(a) enum Stat { Fail, Pass };
    void test( Stat );
    test( 0 ); // function call

(b) void reset( void * );
    reset( 0 ); // function call

(c) void set( void * );
    int *pi;
    set( pi ); // function call

(d) #include <list>
    list<int> oper();
    void print( list<int> & );
    print( oper() ); // function call

(e) void print( const int );
    int iobj;
    print( iobj ); // function call
```

9.4 Details of Function Overload Resolution ◆

As we explained in Section 9.2, there are three steps in the process of function overload resolution. These steps can be summarized as follows:

1. Identify the set of candidate functions considered for the call and identify the properties of the argument list in the function call.

2. Select the viable functions from the set of candidate functions; that is, choose the functions that can be called with the arguments specified in the call, given the number of arguments and their types.

3. Select the function that best matches the call by ranking the conversions applied to convert the arguments to the type of the viable function parameters.

We are now ready to examine these three steps in greater detail.

9.4.1 Candidate Functions

A candidate function is a function that has the same name as the function called. A candidate function will be found in one of the following two ways.

1. A declaration for the function is visible at the point of the call. Given the following example,

```
void f();
void f( int );
void f( double, double = 3.4 );
void f( char*, char* );

int main() {
    f( 5.6 ); // there are four candidate functions for this call
    return 0;
}
```

the four functions f() declared in global scope are visible at the point of the call. They are therefore part of the set of candidate functions.

2. If the type of a function argument is declared within a namespace, the namespace member functions that have the same name as the function called are added to the set of candidate functions. For example:

```
namespace NS {
    class C { /* ... */ };
    void takeC( C& );
}

// the type of cobj is class C declared in namespace NS
NS::C cobj;

int main() {
                    // no takeC() visible at the point of the call
    takeC( cobj ); // ok: calls NS::takeC( C& )
                    // because the argument is of type NS::C
                    // the function takeC() declared in
                    // namespace NS is considered
    return 0;
}
```

The candidate functions are therefore the union of the functions visible at the point of the call and the functions declared within the namespaces of the argument types.

When we are identifying the set of overloaded functions visible at the point of the call, the rules we have seen earlier on how to build a set of overloaded functions still apply.

A function declared in a nested scope hides rather than overloads a function having the same name in an enclosing scope. The candidate functions in such a situation are the functions declared in the nested scope, that is, the functions that are not hidden from the function call. In the following example, the candidate functions visible at the point of the call are format(double) and format(char*):

```
char* format( int );
void g() {
    char* format( double );
    char* format( char* );
```

```
        format(3); // calls format( double )
    }
```

Because the function format(int) declared in global scope is hidden, it is not included in the set of candidate functions.

The candidate functions can be introduced by using declarations that are visible at the point of the call. Consider the following example:

```
namespace libs_R_us {
    int max( int, int );
    double max( double, double );
}

char max( char, char );

void func()
{
    // namespace functions not visible
    // the three calls call global function max( char, char )
    max( 87, 65 );
    max( 35.5, 76.6);
    max( 'J', 'L' );
}
```

The functions max() defined in namespace libs_R_us are not visible at the point of the call. The only function visible is the function max() declared in global scope. This function is the only function in the set of candidate functions; it is the function called by all three calls located in func(). We can use a using declaration to make the functions max() declared in namespace libs_R_us visible. Where would we put the using declaration? If we place the using declaration in global scope,

```
char max( char, char );
using libs_R_us::max; // using declaration
```

the functions max() from namespace libs_R_us are added to the set of overloaded functions containing the function max() declared in global scope. All three functions are now visible within func() and become part of the set of candidate functions. With all three functions visible at the point of the call, the calls in func() are resolved as follows:

```
void func()
{
    max( 87, 65 );      // calls libs_R_us::max( int, int )
    max( 35.5, 76.6 ); // calls libs_R_us::max( double, double )
    max( 'J', 'L' );    // calls ::max( char, char )
}
```

But what if we had introduced the using declaration in the local scope of function func(), as follows?

```
void func()
{
    // using declaration
    using libs_R_us::max;

    // function calls as above
}
```

Which functions max() would be included in the set of candidate functions? Recall that using declarations nest. With the using declaration in local scope, the global function max(char, char) is hidden. The only visible functions at the point of the call are

```
libs_R_us::max( int, int )
libs_R_us::max( double, double )
```

These functions are the only two functions that are part of the set of candidate functions. The calls in func() then resolve as follows:

```
void func()
{
    // using declaration
    // global max( char, char ) hidden
    using libs_R_us::max;

    max( 87, 65 );      // calls libs_R_us::max( int, int )
    max( 35.5, 76.6 );  // calls libs_R_us::max( double, double )
    max( 'J', 'L' );    // calls libs_R_us::max( int, int )
}
```

Using directives also influence how we compose the set of candidate functions. Let's assume that we decide to use a using directive instead of a using declaration to make the functions max() for the namespace libs_R_us visible in func(). For example, with the following using directive in global scope, the set of candidate functions includes the global function max(char, char) and the functions max(int, int) and max(double, double) declared in namespace libs_R_us:

```
namespace libs_R_us {
    int max( int, int );
    double max( double, double );
}

char max( char, char );
using namespace libs_R_us; // using directive

void func()
{
    max( 87, 65 );      // calls libs_R_us::max( int, int )
    max( 35.5, 76.6 );  // calls libs_R_us::max( double, double )
    max( 'J', 'L' );    // calls ::max( char, char )
}
```

What happens if the using directive is placed instead in the local scope of func()
as follows?

```
void func()
{
   // using directive
   using namespace libs_R_us;

   // function calls as above
}
```

Which functions max() are part of the set of candidate functions? Recall that a using
directive makes the namespace members visible as if they were declared outside the
namespace, at the location where the namespace is defined. In our example, the members of namespace libs_R_us are visible to the local scope of func() as if the members
had been declared outside their namespace, in global scope. This implies that the set
of overloaded functions visible within func() is the same as earlier and includes the
following three functions:

```
max( char, char )
libs_R_us::max( int, int )
libs_R_us::max( double, double )
```

The resolution of the calls in func() is unaffected whether the using directive appears
in global scope or appears in func()'s local scope:

```
void func()
{
   using namespace libs_R_us;

   max( 87, 65 );       // calls libs_R_us::max( int, int )
   max( 35.5, 76.6 );   // calls libs_R_us::max( double, double )
   max( 'J', 'L' );     // calls ::max( char, char )
}
```

The candidate functions are therefore the union of the functions visible at the point
of the call — including the functions introduced by using declarations and using directives — and the member functions declared in the namespaces associated with the
types of the arguments. For example:

```
namespace basicLib {
   int print( int );
   double print( double );
}
namespace matrixLib {
   class matrix { /* ... */ };
   void print( const matrix & );
}
```

```
void display()
{
   using basicLib::print;

   matrixLib::matrix mObj;
   print( mObj ); // calls matrixLib::print( const matrix& )

   print( 87 );   // calls basicLib::print( int )
}
```

Which functions are the candidate functions for the call print(mObj)? The functions basicLib::print(int) and basicLib::print(double), introduced by the using declaration in the function display(), are candidate functions because they are visible at the point of the call. Because the function call argument is of type matrixLib::matrix, the function print() declared within the namespace matrixLib is also a candidate function. What are the candidate functions for the call print(87)? Only the functions basicLib::print(int) and basicLib::print(double) visible at the point of the call are candidate functions. Because the type of the argument is int, no additional namespace is examined to find additional candidate functions.

9.4.2   Viable Functions

A viable function is a function in the set of candidate functions. A viable function's parameter list will have the same number of parameters as there are arguments in the function call, or it will have more parameters. In this latter case, default arguments will be provided for the additional parameters so that the function can be called with the number of arguments specified in the argument list. A viable function is a function for which there exist conversions to convert each argument to the type of the corresponding parameter in the viable function parameter list. The conversions considered are those introduced in Section 9.3.

In the following example, there are two viable functions for the call f(5.6): they are f(int) and f(double).

```
void f();
void f( int );
void f( double );
void f( char*, char* );

int main() {
   f( 5.6 ); // 2 viable functions: f( int ) and f( double )
   return 0;
}
```

f(int) is a viable function because it has only one parameter. This matches the number of arguments in the function call. Also, there exists a standard conversion to convert the argument from type double to type int. f(double) is also a viable function.

This viable function has only one parameter, and the parameter is of type double, which is an exact match for the argument in the call. The candidate functions f() and f(char*,char*) are excluded from the set of viable functions because these functions cannot be called with one argument.

In the following example, the only viable function for the call format(3) is the function format(double). Although the candidate function format(char*) can be called with one argument, there exists no conversion between the argument of type int and the parameter type char*. Because no type conversion exists, this function is excluded from the set of viable functions.

```
char* format( int );
void g() {
   // global function format( int ) is hidden
   char* format( double );
   char* format( char* );
   format(3); // only one viable function: format( double )
}
```

In the following example, all three candidate functions are in the set of viable functions for the call to max() in func(). All three functions can be called with two arguments. Because the arguments are of type int, they are an exact match for the parameters of libs_R_us::max(int,int), they can be converted to the parameters of libs_R_us::max(double,double) with a floating-integral standard conversion, and they can be converted to the parameters of max(char,char) with a integral standard conversion.

```
namespace libs_R_us {
   int max( int, int );
   double max( double, double );
}

// using declaration
using libs_R_us::max;

char max( char, char );

void func()
{
   // the three max() functions are viable functions
   max( 87, 65 ); // calls libs_R_us::max( int, int )
}
```

Note that a candidate function with multiple parameters is excluded from the set of viable functions as soon as one of the arguments in the function call cannot be converted to its corresponding parameter in the candidate function parameter list. This is true even if there exists a conversion for all the other arguments. In the following example, the function min(char*,int) is excluded from the set of viable functions because there exists no conversion between the type of the first argument int and the type of the corresponding function parameter char*. Even though the second argument is an exact match for the function's second parameter, the function is nonetheless excluded:

```
extern double min( double, double );
extern int min( char*, int );

void func()
{
    // one candidate function min( double, double )
    min( 87, 65 ); // calls min( double, double )
}
```

If no viable functions exist after we eliminate the candidate functions with the wrong number of parameters or for which no appropriate type conversions exist, then the call results in a compile-time error. In this case, we say that no match is found.

```
void print( unsigned int );
void print( char* );
void print( char );

int *ip;
class SmallInt { /* ... */ };
SmallInt si;

int main() {
    print( ip ); // error: no viable function: no match
    print( si ); // error: no viable function: no match
    return 0;
}
```

9.4.3   Best Viable Function

The best viable function is the viable function that has the parameters that best match the types of the arguments. For each viable function, the type conversions on each argument are ranked to determine how well each argument matches its corresponding parameter. (Section 9.2 describes the supported type conversions). The best viable function is the viable function for which both of the following apply.

1. The conversions applied to the arguments are *no worse* than the conversions necessary to call any other viable function.
2. The conversions on some arguments are *better* than the conversions necessary for the same arguments when any of the other viable functions are called.

There may be more than one type conversion that is applied to convert an argument to the type of a corresponding function parameter. For example, in the following code sample

```
int arr[3];
void putValues(const int *);
```

```
int main() {
    putValues(arr); // 2 conversions in conversion sequence
                    // array-to-pointer + qualification conversion
    return 0;
}
```

a conversion sequence is applied to convert the argument arr from the type array of three ints to the type pointer to const int. This conversion sequence consists of the following conversions.

1. An array-to-pointer conversion converts the argument from an array of three ints to a pointer to int.
2. A qualification conversion converts the pointer to int to a pointer to const int.

It is therefore more appropriate to say that a *conversion sequence* is used to convert an argument to the type of a viable function parameter. Because a conversion sequence rather than a single conversion is applied to an argument to convert it to the type of a corresponding parameter, the third step of function overload resolution therefore ranks conversion sequences.

The rank of a conversion sequence is the rank of the worst conversion that makes up the sequence. As described in Section 9.2, the type conversions are ranked as follows: an exact match is better than a promotion, and a promotion is better than a standard conversion. In the preceding example, both conversions in the sequence have the rank of an exact match. The conversion sequence therefore has the rank of an exact match.

A conversion sequence is potentially composed of the following conversions, in the following order:

```
Lvalue Transformation ->
    Promotion or Standard Conversion ->
        Qualifications Conversion
```

The term *lvalue transformation* refers to the first three conversions described under the exact match category in Section 9.2: lvalue-to-rvalue transformation, array-to-pointer conversion, and function-to-pointer conversion. A conversion sequence is a sequence of zero or one lvalue transformation followed by zero or one promotion or zero or one standard conversion followed by zero or one qualification conversion. At most, one of each conversion is applied to convert an argument to the type of a corresponding parameter.

This conversion sequence is called a *standard* conversion sequence. There exists another kind of conversion sequence called a *user-defined* conversion sequence. A user-defined conversion sequence involves a class member conversion function. Class member conversion functions and user-defined conversion sequences are described in Chapter 15.

What are the conversion sequences on the arguments in the following example?

```
namespace libs_R_us {
   int max( int, int );
   double max( double, double );
}

// using declaration
using libs_R_us::max;

void func()
{
   char c1, c2;
   max( c1, c2 ); // calls libs_R_us::max( int, int )
}
```

The arguments in the call to max() are of type char. The conversion sequence on the arguments to call the function libs_R_us::max(int,int) is as follows:

1a. Because the arguments are passed by value, an lvalue-to-rvalue conversion extracts the value from the arguments c1 and c2.

2a. A promotion converts the arguments from char to int.

The conversion sequence on the arguments to call the function libs_R_us::max(double,double) is as follows:

1b. An lvalue-to-rvalue conversion extracts the value from the arguments c1 and c2.

2b. A floating-integral standard conversion converts the arguments from char to double.

The rank of the first conversion sequence is promotion (the worse conversion in the sequence), whereas the rank of the second conversion sequence is standard conversion. Because a promotion is better than a standard conversion, the function libs_R_us::max(int,int) is selected as the best viable function, or best match function, for the call.

If by ranking the conversion sequences on the arguments it is impossible to identify one viable function as matching the types of the arguments better than the other viable functions, the call is ambiguous. In the following example, both instances of calc() require the following conversion sequence:

1. An lvalue-to-rvalue conversion to extract the value from the arguments i and j.

2. A standard conversion to convert the arguments to the corresponding parameter.

Because each conversion sequence is as good as the other, the call is ambiguous:

```
int i, j;
extern long calc( long, long );
extern double calc( double, double );

void jj() {
```

```
        // error: ambiguous, no "best" match
        calc( i, j );
    }
```

A qualification conversion — a conversion that adds a const or volatile qualifier to the type to which a pointer points — has the rank of an exact match. However, if two conversion sequences are identical except that one has an additional qualification conversion at the end of its sequence, then the conversion sequence without the additional qualification conversion is the better conversion sequence. For example:

```
    void reset( int * );
    void reset( const int * );

    int* pi;

    int main() {
        reset( pi ); // sequence without qualification conversion
                     // better : reset( int * ) selected
        return 0;
    }
```

The standard conversion sequence applied on the argument to call the first candidate function reset(int*) is an exact match; it requires only an lvalue-to-rvalue conversion to extract the value of the argument. For the second candidate function reset(const int *), an lvalue-to-rvalue conversion is also applied, followed by a qualification conversion to convert the resulting value from a pointer to int to a pointer to const int. Both of these sequences are exact matches, but the preceding function call is not ambiguous. Because both conversion sequences are identical except for the additional qualification conversion at the end of the second conversion sequence, the sequence without the qualification conversion is considered a better match. Thus, the viable function reset(int*) is the best viable function.

Here is another example in which the qualification conversion influences which conversion sequence is selected:

```
    int extract( void * );
    int extract( const void * );

    int* pi;

    int main() {
        extract( pi ); // extract( void * ) selected
        return 0;
    }
```

There are two viable functions for the call: extract(void*) and extract(const void*). The conversion sequence applied to call the first viable function extract(void*) consists of an lvalue-to-rvalue conversion to extract the value of the argument, followed by a standard pointer conversion that converts this value from a pointer to `int` to a pointer to `void`. The conversion sequence applied to call the second viable function `extract(const void*)` is identical except for the additional qualification conversion that converts the result from a pointer to `void` to a pointer to `const void`. Because the two conversion sequences are identical except that the second conversion sequence has an additional qualification conversion at the end of its sequence, the first conversion sequence is selected as the better conversion sequence. The function `extract(void*)` is selected as the best viable function for the argument.

The `const` or `volatile` qualifiers also affect how the initialization of a reference parameter is ranked. As is the case for conversion sequences, if two reference initializations are identical except for the fact that one adds an additional `const` or `volatile` qualifier, the reference initialization without the additional qualification is a better reference initialization for the purpose of function overload resolution. For example:

```
#include <vector>
void manip( vector<int> & );
void manip( const vector<int> & );

vector<int> f();
extern vector<int> vec;

int main() {
    manip( vec ); // manip( vector<int> & ) is selected
    manip( f() ); // manip( const vector<int> & ) is selected
    return 0;
}
```

In the first call, the reference initialization to call either function is an exact match. But this call is not ambiguous. Because both reference initializations are identical except that the second one adds an additional `const` qualification, the initialization without the additional qualification is considered a better initialization. Hence the viable function `manip(vector<int>&)` is the best viable function for the first call.

In the second call, there is only one viable function for the call: `manip(const vector<int>&)`. Because the argument is a temporary that holds the return value of the function call `f()`, the argument is an rvalue that cannot be used to initialize the non-const reference parameter of `manip(vector<int>&)`. The best viable function for the second call is therefore the only viable function considered: `manip(const vector<int>&)`.

Of course, function calls can have more than one argument. The selection of the best viable function must take into account the ranking of the conversion sequences needed to convert all of the arguments. Let's examine an example:

```
extern int ff( char*, int );
extern int ff( int, int );

int main() {
```

```
        ff( 0, 'a' ); // ff( int, int )
        return 0;
    }
```

The function `ff()` taking two arguments of type `int` is selected as the best viable function because of the following reasons.

1. Its first argument is better. 0 is an exact match for a parameter of type `int`, whereas it requires a pointer standard conversion sequence to match a parameter of type `char*`.

2. Its second argument is equally good. The argument 'a' is of type `char` and requires a conversion sequence that has promotion rank to match the second parameter of both functions.

Here is another example:

```
        int compute( const int&, short );
        int compute( int&, double );

        extern int iobj;
        int main() {
            compute( iobj, 'c' ); // compute( int&, double )
            return 0;
        }
```

The two functions `compute(const int&, short)` and `compute(int&, double)` are viable functions. The second function is selected as the best viable function because of the following reasons.

1. Its first argument is better. The reference initialization for the first viable function is worse, because it adds a `const` qualification and the initialization for the second viable function does not.

2. Its second parameter is as good. The argument 'c' is of type `char` and requires a conversion sequence of standard conversion rank to match the second parameter of both functions.

9.4.4   Default Arguments

Default arguments can allow more functions into the set of viable functions. A viable function is a function that can be called with the argument list specified in the call. A viable function can have more parameters than there are arguments in the argument list in the function call if each additional parameter has an associated default argument:

```
        extern void ff( int );
        extern void ff( long, int = 0 );

        int main() {
            ff( 2L );    // matches ff( long, 0 );
```

```
        ff( 0, 0 ); // matches ff( long, int );
        ff( 0 );    // matches ff( int );
        ff( 3.14 ); // error: ambiguous
    }
```

For the first and third calls, even though the argument list only has one argument, the second function ff() is a viable function for both calls for the following reasons.

1. A default argument is provided for the function's second parameter.
2. Its first parameter is of type long, which matches the type of the argument of the first call exactly and the type of the argument of the third call with a conversion sequence that has standard conversion rank.

The last call is ambiguous, because both instances can match through the application of a standard conversion on the first argument. There is no preference given to ff(int), because it has exactly one argument.

Exercise 9.9

Explain what happens during function overload resolution for the call to compute() in main(). Which functions are candidate functions? Which functions are viable functions? What is the type conversion sequence applied to the argument to match the parameter in each viable function? Which function (if any) is the best viable function?

```
        namespace primerLib {
            void compute( );
            void compute( const void * );
        }

        using primerLib::compute;
        void compute( int );
        void compute( double, double = 3.4 );
        void compute( char*, char* = 0 );

        int main() {
            compute( 0 );
            return 0;
        }
```

What would happen if the using declaration were located in main(), before the call to compute()? Answer the same questions as before.

10

Function Templates

This chapter describes what a function template is and discusses how to define and use a function template. Using a function template is rather simple, and many beginner C++ programmers use function templates defined in libraries without even knowing that they are using function templates. Only advanced C++ users will define and use function templates as described in this chapter. The material in this chapter therefore serves to introduce material for a more advanced topic of C++. We begin the chapter by describing what a function template is and how to define one. We then illustrate simple uses of function templates. The chapter then moves on to more advanced topics. We first look at how to use function templates in more advanced ways: we look at template argument deduction in detail, and we look at how explicit template arguments can be specified when referring to a function template instantiation. We then look at how the compiler instantiates templates and the requirements this imposes on the organization of our programs, and we discuss how to define a specialization for a function template instantiation. The chapter then presents topics that are of interest to designers of function templates. We explain how function templates can be overloaded and how overload resolution involving function templates works. We also look at name resolution in function template definitions and explain how function templates can be defined in namespaces. The chapter ends with an example of the use of a function template.

10.1 Function Template Definition

A strongly typed language can sometimes seem an obstacle to implementing what are otherwise straightforward functions. For example, although the algorithm for the following function min() is trivial, strong typing requires that we implement an instance for each pair of types we wish to compare:

```
int min( int a, int b ) {
   return a < b ? a : b;
}

double min( double a, double b ) {
   return a < b ? a : b;
}
```

An attractive but subtly dangerous alternative to the explicit definition of each instance of min() is to use the macro expansion facility of the preprocessor. For example:

```
#define min(a,b) ((a) < (b) ? (a) : (b))
```

Although this definition works correctly for simple calls of min(), such as

```
min( 10, 20 );
min( 10.0, 20.0 );
```

it behaves unexpectedly under complex calls. That's because its mechanism does not behave like a function call but simply provides a text substitution of its arguments. As a result, the values of its two arguments are evaluated *twice*: once during the test of a and b and a second time during the evaluation of the value returned by the macro. For example:

```
#include <iostream>
#define min(a,b) ((a) < (b) ? (a) : (b))

const int size = 10;
int ia[size];

int main() {
   int elem_cnt = 0;
   int *p = &ia[0];

   // count the number of array elements
   while ( min(p++,&ia[size]) != &ia[size] )
      ++elem_cnt;

   cout << "elem_cnt : "    << elem_cnt
        << "\texpecting: " << size << endl;
   return 0;
}
```

This program provides an admittedly roundabout method of computing the number of elements of the integer array ia. The macro expansion of min() fails in this case, because the postfix increment operation applied to its pointer argument p is applied twice with each expansion. The outcome of executing this program is the following incorrect calculation:

```
elem_cnt : 5     expecting: 10
```

Function templates provide a mechanism by which we can preserve the semantics of function definitions and function calls (encapsulate a section of code in one program location and ensure that the arguments are evaluated only once prior to the invocation of the function) without having to bypass C++'s strong type-checking as is done with the macro solution.

A function template provides an algorithm that is used to automatically generate particular instances of a function varying by type. The programmer *parameterizes* all or a subset of the types in the interface (the parameter and return types) of a function whose body otherwise remains invariant. A function is a candidate to be made a template when its implementation remains invariant over a set of instances, each of which handles a unique data type, such as our function min().

For example, here is the function template definition of min():

```
template <class Type>
   Type min( Type a, Type b ) {
      return a < b ? a : b;
}

int main() {
   // ok: int min( int, int );
   min( 10, 20 );

   // ok: double min( double, double );
   min( 10.0, 20.0 );
   return 0;
}
```

If we substitute the function template for the preprocessor macro min() in the previous program, that program's output is now computed correctly:

```
elem_cnt : 10     expecting: 10
```

(The C++ standard library provides function templates for commonly used algorithms such as min() defined here. These algorithms are described in Chapter 12. To introduce function templates, we define our own simplified versions of some of the algorithms defined in the C++ standard library.)

The keyword template always begins both a definition and a declaration of a function template. The keyword is followed by a comma-separated list of template parameters bracketed by the less-than (<) and greater-than (>) tokens. This list is the *template parameter list*. It cannot be empty. A template parameter can be a *template type parameter* representing a type or a *template nontype parameter* representing a constant expression.

A template type parameter consists of the keyword class or the keyword typename followed by an identifier. In a function template parameter list, these keywords have the same meaning. They indicate that the parameter name that follows represents a potential built-in or user-defined type. The name of a template parameter is chosen by

the programmer. In our example, we decided to name `min()`'s template parameter `Type`
but we could have named it anything:

```
template <class Glorp>
    Glorp min( Glorp a, Glorp b ) {
        return a < b ? a : b;
    }
```

When the template is instantiated, an actual built-in or user-defined type is substituted for the template type parameter. Each of the types `int`, `double`, `char*`, `vec-
tor<int>`, or `list<double>*` are valid template argument types.

A template nontype parameter consists of an ordinary parameter declaration. A
template nontype parameter indicates that the parameter name represents a potential
value. This value represents a constant in the template definition. For example, `size` is
a template nontype parameter that is a constant value representing the size of the array
to which `arr` refers:

```
template <class Type, int size>
    Type min( Type (&arr) [size] );
```

When the function template `min()` is instantiated, the value for `size` will be replaced
by a constant value known at compile-time.

A function definition or declaration follows the template parameter list. Except for
the presence of the template parameters as type specifiers or as constant values, the
definition of a function template looks the same as that of a nontemplate function definition. Let's look at an example.

```
template <class Type, int size>
Type min( const Type (&r_array)[size] )
{
    /* parameterized function for finding
     * minimum value contained in array */

    Type min_val = r_array[0];
    for ( int i = 1; i < size; ++i )
        if ( r_array[i] < min_val )
            min_val = r_array[i];

    return min_val;
}
```

In our example, `Type` indicates the return type of `min()`, the type of its parameter
`r_array`, and the type of the local variable `min_val`; `size` indicates the size of the array
to which `r_array` refers. In the course of the program, `Type` will be substituted with
various built-in and user-defined types and `size` will be substituted with various constant values determined by the actual uses of `min()`. (Recall that the two uses of a
function are to invoke it and to take its address.) This process of type and value sub-

stitution is referred to as *template instantiation*. We look at template instantiation in the next section.

The function parameter list of our `min()` function template may look somewhat terse. As we discussed in Section 7.3, an array parameter is always passed as a pointer to the first element of the array, and the first dimension of an array argument is not known within a function definition. To alleviate this problem, we decided here to declare `min()`'s parameter as a reference to an array. This solves the problem of users having to pass a second argument to specify the size of the array, but its drawback is that its use with arrays of `int`s of different sizes generates, or instantiates, different instances of `min()`.

The name of a template parameter can be used after it has been declared as a template parameter and until the end of the template declaration or definition. A template type parameter serves as a type specifier for the remainder of the template definition; it can be used in exactly the same way as a built-in or user-defined type specifier, such as for variable declarations and casts. A template nontype parameter serves as a constant value for the remainder of the template definition; it can be used when constant values are required, perhaps to specify the size of an array in an array declaration or as the initial value of an enum constant.

```
// size specifies the size of the array parameter and
//       initializes a const int value
template <class Type, int size>
   Type min( const Type (&r_array)[size] )
{
   const int loc_size = size;
   Type loc_array[loc_size];
   // ...
}
```

If an object, function, or type having the same name as the template parameter is declared in global scope, the global scope name is hidden. In the following example, the type of `tmp` is not `double`, but it has the type of the template parameter `Type`:

```
typedef double Type;
template <class Type>
   Type min( Type a, Type b )
{
   // tmp has the type of the template parameter Type
   // not that of the global typedef
   Type tmp = a < b ? a : b;
   return tmp;
}
```

An object or type declared within the function template definition cannot have the same name as that of a template parameter:

```
template <class Type>
   Type min( Type a, Type b )
{
   // error: redeclares template parameter Type
   typedef double Type;
   Type tmp = a < b ? a : b;
   return tmp;
}
```

The name of a template type parameter can be used to specify the return type of the function template:

```
// ok: T1 represents the return type of min(),
//       T2 and T3 represent its parameter types
template <class T1, class T2, class T3>
   T1 min( T2, T3 );
```

The name of a template parameter can be used only once within the same template parameter list. The following, for example, is flagged at compile-time as an error:

```
// error: illegal reuse of template parameter name Type
template <class Type, class Type>
   Type min( Type, Type );
```

However, the name of a template parameter can be reused across function template declarations or definitions:

```
// ok: reuse of the name Type across templates
template <class Type>
   Type min( Type, Type );

template <class Type>
   Type max( Type, Type );
```

The names of the template parameters do not need to be the same across declarations and the definition of the template. The following three declarations of min(), for example, all refer to the same function template:

```
// all three declarations of min()
// refer to the same function template

// forward declarations of the template
template <class T> T min( T, T );
template <class U> U min( U, U );

// actual definition of the template
template <class Type>
   Type min( Type a, Type b ) { /* ... */ }
```

There is no constraint on how many times a template parameter can appear in the function parameter list. In the following example, `Type` is used to represent the type of two different function parameters:

```
#include <vector>
// ok: Type used many times in template parameter list
template <class Type>
   Type sum( const vector<Type> &, Type );
```

If a function template has more than one template type parameter, each template type parameter must be preceded by the keyword `class` or the keyword `typename`.

```
// ok: the keywords typename and class can be intermixed
template <typename T, class U>
   T minus( T*, U );

// error: must be <typename T, class U> or
//                 <typename T, typename U>
template <typename T, U>
   T sum( T*, U );
```

In a function template parameter list, the keywords `typename` and `class` have the same meaning and can be used interchangeably. Both of them can be used to declare different template type parameters of the same template parameter list (as is done for the preceding function template `minus()`). It seems more intuitive to use the keyword `typename` instead of the keyword `class` to designate a template type parameter; after all, the name of the keyword `typename` clearly indicates that the name that follows is a type name. However, the keyword `typename` was added to C++ more recently as part of Standard C++, and older programs are more likely to use the keyword `class` exclusively. (Not to mention that the keyword `class` is shorter to type than the keyword `typename`, and human beings being the way they are...)

The keyword `typename` was added to C++ to allow the parsing of template definitions. This topic is somewhat advanced, and we will only briefly explain here why the keyword `typename` is needed. For those of you wanting to know more, we recommend that you consult Stroustrup's book *Design and Evolution of C++*.

To parse a template definition, the compiler must distinguish between expressions that are types and those that are not. It is not always possible for the compiler to identify which expressions are types in a template definition. For example, if the compiler encounters the expression `Parm::name` in a template definition and if `Parm` is a template type parameter representing a class, does `name` refer to a type member of `Parm`?

```
template <class Parm, class U>
   Parm minus( Parm* array, U value )
{
   Parm::name * p; // Is this a pointer declaration or
                   // a multiplication? Multiplication.
}
```

The compiler does not know whether name is a type, because it cannot look for the definition of the class that Parm represents until the template is instantiated. To allow the template definition to be parsed on its own, users must indicate to the compiler which expressions are type expressions. The mechanism to tell the compiler that an expression is a type expression is to prefix the expression with the keyword typename. For example, if we wanted the expression Parm::name in the function template minus() to be a type name and hence make the entire expression a pointer declaration, we would modify it as follows:

```
template <class Parm, class U>
   Parm minus( Parm* array, U value )
{
   typename Parm::name * p; // ok: pointer declaration
}
```

The keyword typename can also be used in the template parameter list to indicate when a template parameter is a type.

A function template can be declared inline or extern in the same way as a nontemplate function. The specifier is placed following the template parameter list and not in front of the template keyword.

```
// ok: keyword follows template parameter list
template <typename Type>
   inline
   Type min( Type, Type );

// error: incorrect placement of inline specifier
inline
template <typename Type>
   Type min( Array<Type>, int );
```

Exercise 10.1

Identify which, if any, of the following function template definitions are illegal. Correct each one that you identify.

```
(a)   template <class T, U, class V>
         void foo( T, U, V );

(b)   template <class T>
         T foo( int *T );

(c)   template <class T1, typename T2, class T3>
         T1 foo( T2, T3 );

(d)   inline template <typename T>
         T foo( T, unsigned int* );
```

```
(e)  template <class myT, class myT>
        void foo( myT, myT );

(f)  template <class T>
        foo( T, T );

(g)  typedef char Ctype;
     template <class Ctype>
        Ctype foo( Ctype a, Ctype b );
```

Exercise 10.2

Which ones, if any, of the following template redeclarations are errors? Why?

```
(a)  template <class Type>
        Type bar( Type, Type );

     template <class Type>
        Type bar( Type, Type );

(b)  template <class T1, class T2>
        void bar( T1, T2 );

     template <typename C1, typename C2>
        void bar( C1, C2 );
```

Exercise 10.3

Rewrite the function putValues(), introduced in Section 7.3.3, as a function template. Parameterize the function template so that it has two template parameters (one for the type of the array element and one for the size of the array) and one function parameter that is a reference to an array. Provide the function template definition as well.

10.2   Function Template Instantiation

A function template specifies how individual functions can be constructed given a set of one or more actual types or values. This process of construction is referred to as *template instantiation*. It occurs implicitly as a side effect of either invoking a function template or taking the address of a function template. For example, in the following program, min() is instantiated twice: once for the type array of five ints and once for the type array of six doubles.

```
// definition of the function template min()
// with type parameter Type and nontype parameter size

template <typename Type, int size>
   Type min( Type (&r_array)[size] )
   {
```

```
         Type min_val = r_array[0];
         for ( int i = 1; i < size; ++i )
            if ( r_array[i] < min_val )
               min_val = r_array[i];

         return min_val;
      }

      // size not specified -- ok
      // size = number of values in initializer list
      int ia[] = { 10, 7, 14, 3, 25 };

      double da[6] = { 10.2, 7.1, 14.5, 3.2, 25.0, 16.8 };

      #include <iostream>
      int main()
      {
         // instantiation of min() for an array of 5 ints
         // with Type => int, size => 5
         int i = min( ia );
         if ( i != 3 )
            cout << "??oops: integer min() failed\n";
         else cout << "!!ok: integer min() worked\n";


         // instantiation of min() for an array of 6 doubles
         // with Type => double, size => 6
         double d = min( da );
         if ( d != 3.2 )
            cout << "??oops: double min() failed\n";
         else cout << "!!ok: double min() worked\n";
         return 0;
      }
```

The call

```
      int i = min( ia );
```

causes the instantiation of the following integer instance of min(), where Type is
replaced by int and size by 5:

```
      int min( int (&r_array)[5] )
      {
         int min_val = r_array[0];
         for ( int ix = 1; ix < 5; ++ix )
            if ( r_array[ix] < min_val )
               min_val = r_array[ix];
         return min_val;
      }
```

Similarly, the call

```
double d = min( da );
```
causes the instantiation of the instance of min() where Type is replaced by double and size by 6.

Both the type parameter Type and the nontype parameter size are used in the type of the function parameter. To determine the actual type and value to use as template arguments, the type of the function argument provided on the function call is examined. In our example, the type of ia (that is, array of five ints) and the type of da (that is, array of six doubles) are used to determine the template arguments for each instantiation. The process of determining the types and values of the template arguments from the type of the function arguments is called *template argument deduction*. We look in more detail at template argument deduction in the next section. (It is also possible not to rely on template argument deduction and instead to specify the template arguments explicitly. We look at how to do this in Section 10.4.)

A function template is instantiated either when it is invoked or when its address is taken. In the following example, the pointer pf is initialized with the address of a function template instantiation. The template arguments for the instantiation are determined by an examination of the parameter type of the function to which pf refers.

```
template <typename Type, int size>
    Type min( Type (&p_array)[size] ) { /* ... */ }

// pf points to int min( int (&)[10] )
int (*pf)(int (&)[10]) = &min;
```

The type of pf is pointer to function with a parameter of type int(&)[10]. The type of this parameter determines the type of the template argument for Type and the value of the template argument for size when min() is instantiated. The template argument for Type is int, and the template argument for size is 10. The function instantiated is min(int(&)[10]), and the pointer pf refers to this template instantiation.

When the address of a function template instantiation is taken, the context must be such that it allows a unique type or value to be determined for a template argument. If a unique type or value cannot be determined, a compile-time error is generated. For example:

```
template <typename Type, int size>
    Type min( Type (&r_array)[size] ) { /* ... */ }

typedef int (&rai)[10];
typedef double (&rad)[20];

void func( int (*)(rai) );
void func( double (*)(rad) );

int main() {
```

```
        // error: which instantiation of min()?
        func( &min );
    }
```

The function func() is overloaded, and it is not possible, by looking at the type of func()'s parameter, to determine a unique type for the template argument Type and a unique value for the template argument size. The call to func() could instantiate either one of the following functions:

```
        min( int (*)(int(&)[10]) )
        min( double (*)(double(&)[20]) )
```

Because it is not possible to identify a unique instantiation for the argument to func(), taking the address of a function template instantiation in this context causes a compile-time error.

This compile-time error can be eliminated if we use a cast to explicitly indicate the type of the argument:

```
        int main() {
            // ok: cast indicates the argument type
            func( static_cast< double(*)(rad) >(&min) );
        }
```

A better solution is to use explicit template arguments, as we will illustrate in Section 10.4.

10.3   Template Argument Deduction ◆

When a function template is called, the types and the values of the template arguments are determined by an examination of the types of the function arguments. This process is called *template argument deduction*.

The function parameter of the function template min() is a reference to an array of Type:

```
        template <class Type, int size>
            Type min( Type (&r_array)[size] ) { /* ... */ }
```

To match the function parameter, the function argument must also be an lvalue representing an array type. The following call is an error because pval is of type int* and not an lvalue of type array of ints.

```
        void f( int pval[9] ) {
            // error: Type (&)[] != int*
            int jval = min( pval );
        }
```

The return type of the function template instantiation is not considered when the types of the template arguments are determined during template argument deduction. For example, for a call to min() written as

```
double da[8] = { 10.3, 7.2, 14.0, 3.8, 25.7, 6.4, 5.5, 16.8 };
int i1 = min( da );
```

the instantiation of min() has a parameter of type pointer to array of eight doubles. The value returned by this instantiation is of type double. The return value is converted to int before i1 is initialized. Even though the result of calling min() is used to initialize an object of type int, this does not influence template argument deduction.

For template argument deduction to succeed, the type of a function argument need not exactly match the type of the corresponding function parameter. The following three kinds of type conversions are allowed: lvalue transformation, qualification conversion, and conversion to a base class instantiated from a class template. Let's look at each in turn.

Recall that an lvalue transformation is either an lvalue-to-rvalue conversion, an array-to-pointer conversion, or a function-to-pointer conversion. (These conversions are introduced in Section 9.3.) To illustrate how lvalue transformations affect template argument deduction, let's consider the function min2() with one template parameter named Type and two function parameters. min2()'s first function parameter is a pointer of type Type*. size is no longer a template parameter, as it was in the definition of min(); size has become a function parameter for which a value must be explicitly specified with a function argument when min2() is called:

```
template <class Type>
   // the first parameter is a Type*
   Type min2( Type* array, int size )
{
   Type min_val = array[0];
   for ( int i = 1; i < size; ++i )
      if ( array[i] < min_val )
         min_val = array[i];

   return min_val;
}
```

min2() can be called with a first argument of type array of four ints, as in the following example:

```
int ai[4] = { 12, 8, 73, 45 };

int main() {
   int size = sizeof (ai) / sizeof (ai[0]);

   // ok: array-to-pointer conversion
   min2( ai, size );
}
```

The function argument ai has type array of four ints and does not exactly match the type of the corresponding function parameter Type*. However, because the array-to-pointer conversion is allowed, the argument `ai` is converted to the type `int*` before the template argument `Type` is deduced. The template argument for `Type` is then deduced to be `int`, and the function template instantiated is `min2(int*,int)`.

A qualification conversion adds `const` or `volatile` qualifiers to pointers (qualification conversions are also introduced in Section 9.3). To illustrate how qualification conversions affect template argument deduction, let's consider the function `min3()` with a first function parameter of type `const Type*`:

```
template <class Type>
    // the first parameter is a const Type*
    Type min3( const Type* array, int size ) {
    // ...
}
```

`min3()` can be called with a first argument of type `int*`, as in the following example:

```
int *pi = &ai;
// ok: qualification conversion to const int*
int i = min3( pi, 4 );
```

The function argument `pi` has type pointer to `int` and does not exactly match the type of the corresponding function parameter `const Type*`. Because a qualification conversion is allowed, the function argument is converted to the type `const int*` before the template argument is deduced. The template argument for `Type` is then deduced to be `int`, and the function template instantiated is `min3(const int*,int)`.

Now let's look at conversion to a base class instantiated from a class template. Template argument deduction can proceed if the type of the function parameter is a class template and if the argument is a class that has a base class instantiated from the class template specified as the function parameter. To illustrate this conversion, let's consider a new function template named `min4()` with a parameter of type `Array<Type>&` (where `Array` is the class template defined in Section 2.5). (Chapter 16 presents a full discussion of class templates.)

```
template <class Type>
    class Array { /* ... */ };

template <class Type>
    Type min4( Array<Type>& array )
{
    Type min_val = array[0];
    for ( int i = 1; i < array.size(); ++i )
        if ( array[i] < min_val )
            min_val = array[i];

    return min_val;
}
```

min4() can be called with a first argument of type ArrayRC<int> as in the following example. (ArrayRC is a class template also defined in Chapter 2; class inheritance is discussed in detail in Chapters 17 and 18.)

```
template <class Type>
    class ArrayRC : public Array<Type> { /* ... */ };

int main() {
    ArrayRC<int> ia_rc( ia, sizeof(ia)/sizeof(int) );
    min4( ia_rc );
}
```

The function argument ia_rc is of type ArrayRC<int>. It does not exactly match the type of the corresponding function parameter Array<Type>&. Because the class ArrayRC<int> has Array<int> as one of its base classes, because Array<int> is a class instantiated from the class template specified as the function parameter, and because a function argument of derived class type can be used to deduce a template argument, the function argument ArrayRC<int> is converted to the type Array<int> before the template argument is deduced. The template argument for Type is then deduced to be int, and the function template instantiated is min4(Array<int>&).

More than one function argument can participate in template argument deduction for the same template argument. If a template parameter occurs multiple times in the function parameter list, each deduced type must exactly match the first type deduced for the template argument. For example:

```
template <class T> T min5( T, T ) { /* ... */ }
unsigned int ui;

int main() {
    // error: cannot instantiate min5( unsigned int, int )
    // must be: min( unsigned int, unsigned int ) or
    //          min( int, int )
    min5( ui, 1024 );
}
```

Both function arguments to min5() must have the same type — either both int or both unsigned int — because the template parameter T must be bound to a single type. The template argument for T deduced from the first function argument is int. The template argument for T deduced from the second function argument is unsigned int. Because the type of the template argument T is deduced to be a different type for both function arguments, the template argument deduction fails and the template instantiation is an error. (A way around this is to explicitly specify the template arguments when the function min5() is invoked. We will look at how do this in Section 10.4.)

The limitation of possible type conversions applies only to function arguments that participate in template argument deduction. For all other arguments, the full set of type conversions is allowed. The following function template `sum()` has two parameters. The argument for the first parameter, `op1`, participates in the deduction of the template argument `Type`. The argument for the second parameter, `op2`, does not.

```
template <class Type>
    Type sum( Type op1, int op2 ) { /* ... */ }
```

Because the second argument does not participate in template argument deduction, any type conversion can be applied to the second argument when an instantiation of the function template `sum()` is called. (The type conversions that can be applied to a function argument are described in Section 9.3.) For example:

```
int ai[] = { ... };
double dd;
int main() {
    // sum( int, int ) instantiated
    sum( ai[0], dd );
}
```

The type of the second function argument `dd` does not match the type of the corresponding function parameter `int`. However, this call to an instantiation of the function template `sum()` is not an error, because the type of the second argument is fixed and does not depend on a template parameter. The function `sum(int,int)` is instantiated for the call. The argument `dd` is converted to the type `int` using a floating-integral standard conversion.

The general algorithm for template argument deduction is therefore as follows.

1. Each function argument is examined in turn to identify the presence of a template parameter in the type of the corresponding function parameter.

2. If a template parameter is found, the corresponding template argument is deduced by an examination of the type of the function argument.

3. The function parameter type and function argument type do not have to match exactly. The following type conversions can be applied to the function argument to convert it to the type of the corresponding function parameter:

   • Lvalue transformations

   • Qualification conversions

   • Derived class to base class type conversion, given that the function parameter has the form `T<args>`, `T<args>&`, or `T<args>*`, where the parameter list `args` contains at least one of the template parameters.

4. If the same template parameter is found in more than one function parameter, the template argument deduced from each corresponding function argument must be the same.

Exercise 10.4

Name two type conversions allowed on function arguments involved in template argument deduction.

Exercise 10.5

Given the following template definitions

```
template <class Type>
    Type min3( const Type* array, int size ) { /* ... */ }
template <class Type>
    Type min5( Type p1,Type p2 ) { /* ... */ }
```

which ones of the following calls, if any, are errors? Why?

```
double dobj1, dobj2;
float fobj1, fobj2;
char cobj1, cobj2;
int ai[5] = { 511, 16, 8, 63, 34 };

(a) min5( cobj2, 'c' );
(b) min5( dobj1, fobj1 );
(c) min3( ai, cobj1 );
```

10.4   Explicit Template Arguments ◆

In some situations, it is not possible to deduce the type of the template arguments. As we saw in the previous section with the example of the function template min5(), if template argument deduction deduces two different types for the same template parameter, the compiler issues an error to indicate that template argument deduction failed.

In such situations, it is necessary to override the template argument deduction mechanism and *explicitly specify* the template arguments to be used. The template arguments are explicitly specified in a comma-separated list, bracketed by the less-than (<) and greater-than (>) tokens, following the name of the function template instantiation. For example, assuming that the template argument for T in our earlier use of min5() is intended to be unsigned int, the call to the function template instantiation min5() can be rewritten as follows:

```
// min5( unsigned int, unsigned int ) instantiated
min5< unsigned int >( ui, 1024 );
```

In this case, the template argument list <unsigned int> explicitly specifies the type of the template argument. Because the template argument is known, the function call is no longer an error.

Notice that in the call to the function min5(), the second function argument is 1024, which has type int. Because the type of the second function parameter is fixed to unsigned int by the explicit template argument, the second function argument is converted to the type unsigned int using an integral standard conversion.

We saw in the previous section that only a limited set of type conversions is allowed on function arguments used to deduce template arguments. The integral standard conversion int-to-unsigned int is not one of the conversions allowed. But when the template arguments are explicitly specified, there is no need to deduce the template arguments. The types of the function parameters are thus fixed. When the template arguments are explicitly specified, any implicit type conversion can be applied to convert a function argument to the type of the corresponding function parameter.

In addition to allowing type conversions on function arguments, explicit template arguments provide solutions to other programming problems. Consider the following problem. We wish to define a function template called sum() so that a function instantiated from this template would return a value of a type that is large enough to contain the sum of two values of any two types passed in any order. How can we do that? How should we specify sum()'s return type?

```
// T or U as the return type?
template <class T, class U>
    ??? sum( T, U );
```

In our case, the answer is to use neither parameter. Using either parameter is bound to fail at some point:

```
char ch; unsigned int ui;

// neither T nor U works as return type
sum( ch, ui ); // ok: U sum( T, U );
sum( ui, ch ); // ok: T sum( T, U );
```

A solution is to introduce a third template parameter simply to designate the function template return type.

```
// T1 does not appear in the function template parameter list
template <class T1, class T2, class T3>
    T1 sum( T2, T3 );
```

Because the return type might be a type different from the types of the function arguments, T1 is not mentioned in the function parameter list. This is a potential problem because the template argument for T1 cannot be deduced from the function arguments. However, if we provide explicit template arguments in a call to an instantiation of sum(), we will avoid the compiler error indicating that the template argument for T1 cannot be deduced. For example:

```
typedef unsigned int ui_type;
ui_type calc( char ch, ui_type ui ) {

    // ...
```

```
    // error: T1 cannot be deduced
    ui_type loc1 = sum( ch, ui );

    // ok: template arguments explicitly specified
    // T1 and T3 are unsigned int, T2 is char
    ui_type loc2  = sum< ui_type, char, ui_type >( ch, ui );
}
```

What we would really like is to specify an explicit template argument for T1 and omit the explicit template arguments for T2 and T3, because these template arguments can be deduced from the function arguments in the call.

In the explicit specification we need only list the template arguments that cannot be implicitly deduced, with the constraint that, as with default arguments, we can omit only trailing arguments. For example:

```
    // ok: T3 is unsigned int
    // T3 is deduced from the type of ui
    ui_type loc3 = sum< ui_type, char >( ch, ui );

    // ok: T2 is char and T3 is unsigned int
    // T2 and T3 are inferred from the type of pf
    ui_type (*pf)( char, ui_type ) = &sum< ui_type >;

    // error: only trailing arguments can be omitted
    ui_type loc4 = sum< ui_type, , ui_type >( ch, ui );
```

In other situations it is not possible to deduce the template arguments from the context where the function template instantiation is used. Without explicit template arguments, it is impossible to use function template instantiations in such contexts. It was the recognition and need to support these situations that led to the support of explicit template arguments in Standard C++. In the following example, the address of an instantiation of sum() is taken and passed as the argument to a call to the overloaded function manipulate(). As we saw in Section 10.2, it is not possible to select the instantiation of sum() passed as the argument by just looking at the parameter lists for the manipulate() functions. Two different instantiations of sum() could be instantiated and satisfy the call. The call to manipulate() is *ambiguous*. One solution to disambiguate the call is to provide an explicit cast. A better solution is the use of explicit template arguments. The explicit template arguments indicate which instantiation of function sum() is used and which manipulate() function is called. For example:

```
    template <class T1, class T2, class T3>
      T1 sum( T2 op1, T3 op2 ) { /* ... */ }

    void manipulate( int (*pf)( int,char ) );
    void manipulate( double (*pf)( float,float ) );
```

```
int main( )
{
   // error: which instantiation of sum?
   // int sum( int, char )  or
   // double sum( float, float )  ?
   manipulate( &sum );

   // takes the address of instantiation:
   // double sum( float, float )
   // calls: void manipulate( double (*pf)( float, float ) );
   manipulate( &sum< double, float, float > );
}
```

We must mention that explicit template arguments should be used only when they are absolutely necessary to resolve ambiguities or to use function template instantiations in contexts where the template arguments cannot be deduced. First, it is always easier to let the compiler determine the types and values of the template arguments. Second, if we modify the declarations in our programs so that the types of the function arguments in a call to a function template instantiation change, the compiler will automatically instantiate a function template with a different set of template arguments without our having to do anything. On the other hand, if we specified explicit template arguments, we must verify that the explicit template arguments are still appropriate for the new types of the function arguments. We therefore recommend that you omit explicit template arguments whenever possible.

Exercise 10.6

Name two situations in which the use of explicit template arguments is necessary.

Exercise 10.7

Given the following template definition for `sum()`

```
template <class T1, class T2, class T3>
   T1 sum( T2, T3 );
```

which ones of the following calls, if any, are errors? Why?

```
double dobj1, dobj2;
float fobj1, fobj2;
char cobj1, cobj2;

(a) sum( dobj1, dobj2 );
(b) sum<double,double,double>( fobj1, fobj2 );
(c) sum<int>( cobj1, cobj2 );
(d) sum<double, ,double>( fobj2, dobj2 );
```

10.5   Template Compilation Models ◈

The definition of a function template serves as a prescription for the definition of an infinite set of function instances. In itself, a template does not cause any function to be defined. For example, when the implementation sees the template definition

```
template <typename Type>
    Type min( Type t1, Type t2 )
{
    return t1 < t2 ? t1 : t2;
}
```

it stores an internal representation of `min()` but does not otherwise cause anything to happen. Later, when the implementation sees an actual use of `min()`, such as

```
int i, j;
double dobj = min( i, j );
```

it then instantiates an integer definition for `min()` from the template definition.

This brings up several questions. For the compiler to be able to instantiate a function template, must the definition of the template be visible when an instantiation is called? For example, must the definition of the function template `min()` appear before the integer instance of `min()` is used in the definition of `dobj`? Do we place function template definitions in header files (as we do with inline function definitions) to be included everywhere function template instantiations are used? Or can we provide function template declarations only in header files, placing the template definitions in text files (as we do with non-inline functions)?

To answer these questions, we must explain the C++ *template compilation model*, which specifies the requirements for the way programs that define and use templates must be organized. C++ supports two template compilation models: the inclusion model and the separation model. The rest of this section describes both models and explains how they are used.

10.5.1   Inclusion Compilation Model

Under the inclusion compilation model, we include the definition of the function template in every file in which a template is instantiated, usually by placing the definition within a header file as we do with inline functions. This is the model we have chosen to use in this book. For example;

```
// model1.h:
// inclusion model:
// template definitions are placed in a header file

template <typename Type>
    Type min( Type t1, Type t2 ) {
```

```
        return t1 < t2 ? t1 : t2;
    }
```

This header file is included in every file in which an instantiation of min() is used. For example:

```
// template definitions are included before
// template instantiations are used
#include "model1.h"

int i, j;
double dobj = min( i, j );
```

The header file can be included in many of our program text files. Does this imply that the compiler must instantiate the integer instance of min() in every file that calls the instantiation? No. The program must behave as if the integer instance of min() were instantiated only once. However, when and where the instantiation actually takes place is up to the implementation. For now, as far as we are concerned, we need to know only that the integer instance of min() is instantiated somewhere in our program. (As we will see at the end of this section, it is possible to specify when and where template instantiations take place using an explicit instantiation declaration. Such declarations must sometimes be used in the later stages of product development to improve the performance of our applications.)

There are some drawbacks in providing the function template definitions in a header file. The body of a function template describes implementation details that our users may want to ignore or that we may want to hide from our users. Indeed, if the definitions of our function templates are large, the level of detail present in the header file may be overwhelming. Moreover, compiling the same function template definitions across multiple files can unnecessarily add to the compile-time of our programs. The separation compilation model allows us to separate the declarations and definitions of our function templates. Let's see how we might use it.

10.5.2   Separation Compilation Model

Under the separation compilation model, the declarations of the function templates are placed in a header file and their definitions in a program text file. Under this model, the function template declarations and definitions are organized in the same way we organize the non-inline function declarations and definitions of our programs. For example:

```
// model2.h
// separation model:
// only the template declaration is provided
```

```
template <typename Type> Type min( Type t1, Type t2 );

// model2.C
// the template definition
export template <typename Type>
    Type min( Type t1, Type t2 ) { /* ...*/ }
```

A program that uses an instantiation of the function template `min()` need only include the header file before using the instantiation:

```
// user.C
#include "model2.h"

int i, j;
double d = min( i, j ); // ok: use that requires an instantiation
```

Even though the template definition for `min()` is not visible in the file `user.C`, the template instantiation `min(int,int)` can nonetheless be called within this file. However, to make this possible, the template `min()` had to be defined in a special way. Can you see how? If you look closely at the file `model2.C`, where the function template `min()` is defined, you will notice that the keyword `export` precedes the template definition. The template `min()` is defined to be an *exported* template. The `export` keyword indicates to the compiler that the template definition might be needed to generate function template instantiations used in other files. The compiler must then ensure that the template definition is available when these instantiations are generated.

We declare an exported function template by having the keyword `export` precede the `template` keyword in the definition of the template. When a function template is exported, we can use an instantiation of the template in any of the program text files; all we need do is to declare the template before we use it. If the `export` keyword were omitted from the definition of the template `min()`, the implementation might not instantiate the integer instance of the function template `min()` and we would not be able to link our program properly.

Note that some implementations may not require the keyword `export` to be present. Some implementations may support the following language extension: a non-exported function template definition may appear in only one of the program text files; instantiations used in other program text files are nonetheless properly instantiated. However, this behavior is an extension. Standard C++ requires that users mark the function template definitions as exported if only a declaration of the function template is visible in a program text file before the template is instantiated.

The `export` keyword does not need to appear on the template declaration located in the header file. The declaration of `min()` in `model2.h` does not specify the keyword `export`. The keyword could be present in this declaration, but it is not necessary.

A function template must be defined as an exported template only once in a program. Unfortunately, because the compiler processes one file at a time, it cannot ordinarily detect when a function template is defined as exported in more than one program text file. If such a situation happens, one of the following behaviors may follow:

1. A link-error may be generated to indicate that the function template is defined in more than one file.

2. The compiler may instantiate a function template more than once for the same set of template arguments, causing a link-error because of the duplicate definitions for the function template instantiation.

3. The implementation may instantiate the function template using one of the exported function template definitions and ignoring the other definitions.

It is therefore not certain that an error will be generated if more than one definition of an exported function template is provided in our program. We must be careful when organizing our programs to place our exported function template definitions in only one of the program text files.

The separation model allows us to nicely separate the interface of our function templates from their implementations, and it allows us to organize our programs so that the interfaces of our function templates are placed in header files and their implementations are placed in text files. However, not all compilers support the separation model, and those that support it do not always support it well. To support the separation model, more-sophisticated programming environments are needed, and they are not available on all C++ implementations. (Our companion text, *Inside the C++ Object Model*, describes the template instantiation mechanism supported by one C++ implementation: the Edison Design Group compiler.)

For the purpose of this book, because our template examples are fairly small and because we want the examples to be easy to compile on many C++ implementations, we will limit ourselves to the use of the inclusion model.

10.5.3 Explicit Instantiation Declarations

When we use the inclusion compilation model, we include the function template definitions in every program text file in which a template instantiation is used. We have seen that even though it is unknown exactly where and when the compiler instantiates a function template, the program must behave *as if* the template is instantiated for a particular set of template arguments *only once*. In reality, some compilers (especially older C++ compilers) instantiate a function template for a particular set of template arguments multiple times. Under this model, one of these instantiations is selected as *the* instantiation to be used by the program (when the program is linked or during some sort of prelink phase). The other instantiations are simply ignored.

Whether a function template is instantiated only once or multiple times, the program results are not affected, because, in the end, only one template instantiation is used by the program. However, the compile-time performance of our program might be greatly affected if function templates are instantiated multiple times. If the application is made of a large number of files and if a template is instantiated in all of these files, the time needed to compile the application can increase noticeably.

The instantiation problems of early compilers made the use of templates difficult. To help resolve this, Standard C++ provided *explicit instantiation declarations* to allow the programmer to take control over when template instantiations take place.

An explicit instantiation declaration is a declaration in which the `template` keyword is followed by the declaration for the function template instantiation in which the template arguments are explicitly specified. In the following example, an explicit instantiation declaration for `sum(int*,int)` is provided.

```
template <typename Type>
    Type sum( Type op1, int op2 ) { /* ... */ }

// explicit instantiation declaration
template int* sum< int* >( int*, int );
```

This explicit instantiation declaration is a request to instantiate the template `sum()` with the template argument `int*`. An explicit instantiation declaration for a given function template instantiation must appear only once in a program.

The definition for the function template must be provided in the file in which the explicit instantiation declaration appears. If this definition is not visible, the explicit instantiation declaration is an error. For example:

```
#include <vector>

template <typename Type>
    Type sum( Type op1, int op2 ); // declaration only

// define a typedef to refer to vector< int >
typedef vector< int > VI;

// error: sum() is not defined
template VI sum< VI >( VI , int );
```

When an explicit instantiation declaration appears in a program text file, what happens in the other files in which the function template instantiation is used? How do we tell the compiler that an explicit instantiation declaration appears in another program text file and that the function template must not be instantiated when it is used in the other files of the program?

Explicit instantiation declarations are used in combination with a compiler option that suppresses the implicit instantiation of templates in a program. The name of this option varies from compiler to compiler. For example, with the IBM compiler VisualAge for C++ for Windows, version 3.5, the option that suppresses implicit template instantiation is called `/ft-`. When we compile our application with this option, the compiler assumes that we will handle template instantiation with explicit instantiation declarations and it will not implicitly instantiate templates that are used in our application.

Of course, if we never provide an explicit instantiation declaration for a template instantiation and option /ft- is specified when the program is compiled, a link-error will be issued to say that the definition for the function template instantiation is missing. In such cases, the template is not instantiated implicitly.

Exercise 10.8

Name the two template compilation models supported in C++. Explain how programs with function template definitions are organized under each template compilation model.

Exercise 10.9

Given the following template definition for sum()

```
template <typename Type>
    Type sum( Type op1, char op2 );
```

how would you declare an explicit instantiation declaration for a template argument of type string?

10.6   Template Explicit Specialization ◆

It is not always possible to write a single function template that is best suited for every possible type with which the template may be instantiated. In some cases, we may be able to take advantage of some specific knowledge about a type to write a more efficient function than the one that is instantiated from the template. At other times, the general template definition is simply wrong for a type. For example, suppose we have this definition of the function template max():

```
// generic template definition
template <class T>
    T max( T t1, T t2 ) {
        return (t1 > t2 ? t1 : t2);
    }
```

If the function template is instantiated with a template argument of type const char*, the generic template definition does not give the right semantics if we intend each argument to be interpreted as a C-style character string and not as a pointer to a character. To get the right semantics, we must provide a specialized definition for the function template instantiation.

An *explicit specialization definition* is a definition in which the template keyword is followed by the less-than (<) and greater-than (>) tokens, followed by the definition of the function template specialization. This definition indicates the template name, the template arguments for which the template is specialized, the function parameter list, and the function body. In the following example, an explicit specialization is defined for max(const char*, const char*):

```
#include <cstring>

// const char* explicit specialization:
// overrides instantiation from the generic template definition

typedef const char *PCC;
template<> PCC max< PCC >( PCC s1, PCC s2 ) {
    return ( strcmp( s1, s2 ) > 0 ? s1 : s2 );
}
```

Because of this explicit specialization, the template is not instantiated with the type const char* when the function max(const char*, const char*) is called in the program. For all calls to max() with two arguments of type const char*, the specialized definition is invoked; for all others, an instantiation is instantiated from the generic template definition and then invoked. These functions might be invoked as follows:

```
#include <iostream>

// definition for function template max()
// and specialization for const char *
// appear here

int main() {
    // call to instantiation: int max< int >( int, int );
    int i = max( 10, 5 );

    // call to explicit specialization:
    // const char* max< const char* >( const char*, const char* );
    const char *p = max( "hello", "world" );

    cout << "i: " << i << " p: " << p << endl;
    return 0;
}
```

It is possible to declare a function template explicit specialization without defining it. For example, the explicit specialization for the function max(const char*, const char*) can be declared as follows:

```
// declaration of function template explicit specialization
template<> PCC max< PCC >( PCC, PCC );
```

When we are declaring or defining a function template explicit specialization, we must not omit the template keyword followed by the < > tokens from the specialization declaration. Similarly, the function parameter list cannot be omitted from the specialization declaration.

```
// error: invalid specialization declarations

// missing template<>
PCC max< PCC >( PCC , PCC );

// function parameter list missing
template<> PCC max< PCC >;
```

However, the explicit specification of the template arguments can be omitted from the explicit specialization declaration if the template arguments can be deduced from the function parameters.

```
// ok: template argument const char* deduced from parameter types
template<> PCC max( PCC , PCC );
```

In the following example, the function template sum() is explicitly specialized:

```
template <class T1, class T2, class T3>
   T1 sum( T2 op1, T3 op2 );

// explicit specialization declarations

// error: template argument for T1 cannot be deduced;
//        it must be explicitly specified
template<> double sum( float, float );

// ok: argument for T1 explicitly specified
// T2 and T3 are deduced to be float
template<> double sum<double>( float, float );

// ok: all template arguments explicitly specified
template<> int sum<int,char,char>( char , char );
```

Omitting the template<> portion of an explicit specialization declaration is not always an error. For example:

```
// generic template definition
template <class T>
   T max( T t1, T t2 ) { /* ... */ }

// OK: ordinary function declaration
const char* max( const char*, const char* );
```

However, this declaration of max() does not declare a function template specialization. Instead, it declares an ordinary function with a return type and a parameter list that match those of a template instantiation. Declaring an ordinary function that matches a template instantiation is not an error.

Why would we want to declare an ordinary function that matches a template instantiation instead of declaring an explicit specialization? As we have seen in Section 10.3, only a limited set of type conversions can be applied to convert an argument of a function template instantiation to the type of the corresponding function parameter if the argument participates in the deduction of a template argument. This is also the case if the function template is explicitly specialized: only the limited set of type conversions described in Section 10.3 is applied to the function arguments of a function template explicit specialization. Explicit specializations do not help us bypass the restrictions on type conversions. If we want to allow more than just the set of limited type conversions, we must define an ordinary function instead of a function template specialization. Section 10.8 examines this in greater detail and shows how function overload resolution proceeds for a call that matches both an ordinary function and a function template instantiation.

A function template explicit specialization can be declared even if the function template that it specializes is declared but not defined. In the preceding example, the function template sum() is only declared before the template is specialized. Even though the template definition is not needed, the template declaration is required. The name sum() must be known to be a template before it can be specialized.

The declaration of a function template explicit specialization must be seen before it is used in the source file. For example:

```
#include <iostream>
#include <cstring>

// generic template definition
template <class T>
  T max( T t1, T t2 ) { /* ... */ }

int main() {

    // instantiation of
    // const char* max<const char*>( const char*, const char* );
    // using the generic template definition
    const char *p = max( "hello", "world" );

    cout << " p: " << p << endl;
    return 0;
}

// invalid program: const char* explicit specialization:
// overrides generic template definition
typedef const char *PCC;
template<> PCC max< PCC >( PCC s1, PCC s2 ) { /* ... */ }
```

The preceding example uses the instantiation of max(const char*, const char*) before the explicit specialization is declared. Therefore, the compiler is entitled to assume that the function needs to be instantiated from the generic template definition. However, a program cannot have both an explicit specialization and an instantiation for the same template with the same set of template arguments. When the explicit specialization for `max(const char*,const char*)` is later encountered in the program text file, a compile-time error is issued.

If a program consists of more than one file, the declaration for a template explicit specialization must be visible in every file in which the specialization is used. A function template cannot be instantiated from the generic template definition in some files and be specialized for the same set of template arguments in other files. Consider the following example:

```
// ---- max.h ----
// generic template definition
template <class Type>
   Type max( Type t1, Type t2 ) { /* ... */ }

// ---- File1.C ----
#include <iostream>
#include "max.h"
void another();

int main() {

    // instantiation of
    // const char* max<const char*>( const char*, const char* );
    const char *p = max( "hello", "world" );

    cout << " p: " << p << endl;
    another();

    return 0;
}

// ---- File2.C ----
#include <iostream>
#include <cstring>
# include "max.h"

// template explicit specialization for const char*
typedef const char *PCC;
template<> PCC max< PCC >( PCC s1, PCC s2 ) { /*... */ }

void another() {

    // explicit specialization of
    // const char* max< const char* >( const char*, const char* );
    const char *p = max( "hi", "again" );

    cout << " p: " << p << endl;
```

```
    return 0;

}
```

The preceding program consists of two files. In File1.C, there is no declaration for the explicit specialization max(const char*,const char*). Instead, the function template is instantiated from the generic template definition. In File2.C, the explicit specialization is declared and the call max("hi","again") calls the explicit specialization. Because the same program instantiates the function template instantiation max(const char*,const char*) in one file and calls the explicit specialization in another file, this program is invalid. To remedy this problem, a declaration of the template explicit specialization must be provided before the call to max(const char*,const char*) in File1.C.

To help prevent such errors and ensure that the declaration for the template explicit specialization max(const char*,const char*) is included in every file that uses the function template max() with arguments of type const char*, the declaration for the explicit specialization should be placed in the header file "max.h" to be included in all the program text files that use the function template max():

```
// ---- max.h ----
// generic template definition
template <class Type>
    Type max( Type t1, Type t2 ) { /* ... */ }

// declaration of template explicit specialization for const char*
typedef const char *PCC;
template<> PCC max< PCC >( PCC s1, PCC s2 );

// ---- File1.C ----
#include <iostream>
#include "max.h"
void another();

int main() {

    // specialization of:
    // const char* max<const char*>( const char*, const char* );
    const char *p = max( "hello", "world" );

    //....
}
```

Exercise 10.10

Define a function template count() to count the number of occurrences of some value in an array. Write a program to call it. Pass it in turn an array of doubles, ints, and chars.

Introduce a specialized template instance of the count() function to handle strings. Re-run the program you wrote to call the function template instantiations.

10.7 Overloading Function Templates ◆

A function template can be overloaded. The following program, for example, provides three valid overloaded declarations for the function template min():

```
// definition of class template Array
// (introduced in Section 2.4)

template <typename Type>
   class Array{ /* ... */ };

// three function template declarations of min()

template <typename Type>
   Type min( const Array<Type>&, int ); // #1

template <typename Type>
   Type min( const Type*, int ); // #2

template <typename Type>
   Type min( Type, Type ); // #3
```

The following definition of main() illustrates how the three declarations of min() might be invoked.

```
#include <cmath>

int main()
{
   Array<int> iA(1024); // class instantiation
   int ia[1024];

   // Type == int; min( const Array<int>&, int )
   int ival0 = min( iA, 1024 );

   // Type == int; min( const int*, int )
   int ival1 = min( ia, 1024 );

   // Type == double; min( double, double )
   double dval0 = min( sqrt( iA[0] ), sqrt( ia[0] ) );

   return 0;
}
```

Of course, successfully declaring a set of overloaded function templates does not guarantee that they can be called successfully. Overloaded function templates may lead to ambiguities when a template instantiation is invoked. Here is an example of such an ambiguity. We saw earlier that, given the following template definition for min5()

```
template <typename T>
    int min5( T, T ) { /* ... */ }
```

a function is not instantiated from the template definition if min5() is called with arguments of different types; template argument deduction fails, and the call is in error because two different types are deduced for T from the function arguments.

```
int i;
unsigned int ui;

// ok: type deduced for T: int
min5( 1024, i );

// template argument deduction fails:
// two different types deduced for T
min5( i, ui );
```

To resolve the second call we could overload min5(), allowing for two different argument types:

```
template <typename T, typename U>
    int min5( T, U );
```

The following function call invokes an instantiation of this new function template:

```
// ok: int min5( int, unsigned int )
min5( i, ui );
```

Unfortunately, the earlier call is now ambiguous:

```
// error: ambiguous: two possible instantiations
//          from min5( T, T ) and min5( T, U )
min5( 1024, i );
```

The second declaration of min5() allows for function arguments of two different types. However, it does not require that they be different. T and U can both be of type int in this case. Both template declarations can be instantiated with a call in which the two function arguments have the same type. The only way to indicate which function template is preferred and to disambiguate the call is to explicitly specify the template arguments (see Section 10.4 for a discussion of explicit template arguments). For example:

```
// OK: instantiation from min5( T, U )
min5<int, int>( 1024, i );
```

However, in this case, we can do away with overloading the function template altogether. Because the set of calls handled by the min5(T,U) is a superset of those handled by min5(T,T), only the declaration min5(T,U) should be provided and min5(T,T) can be removed. Therefore, as we explained at the beginning of Chapter 9, even though overloading is possible, we must be careful when designing overloaded functions and make sure that the overloading is necessary. These design constraints also apply when we are defining overloaded function templates.

In some situations, even if two different function templates can be instantiated for a function call, the function call might still be unambiguous. Given the following two template definitions for sum(), here is a situation in which the first template definition is preferred even if an instantiation can be generated from either of these function templates.

```
template <typename Type>
   Type sum( Type*, int );

template <typename Type>
   Type sum( Type, int );

int ia[1024];

// Type == int ; sum<int>( int*, int );   or
// Type == int*; sum<int*>( int*, int );  ??
int ival1 = sum<int>( ia, 1024 );
```

Surprisingly enough, the preceding call is not ambiguous. The template is instantiated using the first template definition. The template definition that is the *most specialized* is chosen for the instantiation. The template argument for Type is therefore int and not int*.

For one template to be more specialized than another, both templates must have the same name, the same number of parameters, and, for the corresponding function parameters with different types, such as T* and T earlier, one of the parameters must be able to accept a superset of the arguments that the corresponding parameter in the other template can accept. For example, for the template sum(Type*,int), the first function parameter can match arguments only of pointer type. For the template sum(Type,int), the first function parameter can match arguments of pointer type as well as arguments of any other type. The second template accepts a superset of the types accepted by the first template. The template that accepts the more limited set of arguments is said to be more specialized. In our example, the template sum(Type*,int) is more specialized and is the template that is instantiated for the function call.

10.8 Overload Resolution with Instantiations ◆

As we saw in the previous section, a function template can be overloaded. A function template can also have the same name as an ordinary nontemplate function. For example:

```
// function template
template <class Type>
   Type sum( Type, int ) { /* ... */ }
```

```
// ordinary (nontemplate) function
double sum( double, double );
```

When a program calls sum(), the call can be resolved either to an instantiation of the function template or to the ordinary function. Which one is called depends on which one of these functions best matches the types of the function arguments. The function overload resolution process, which was introduced in Chapter 9, is used to determine which function best matches the arguments on the function call. For example, consider the following:

```
void calc( int ii, double dd ) {
    // does it call the template instantiation
    // or the ordinary function?
    sum( dd, ii );
}
```

Does sum(dd,ii) call a function instantiated from the template, or does it call the ordinary nontemplate function? To answer this question, let's step through the process of function overload resolution. The first step of function overload resolution consists of building the set of candidate functions that can be called. This set is made of functions that have the same name as the function that is called and for which a declaration is visible at the point of the call.

When a function template exists, an instantiation from that template is a candidate function if a function can be instantiated using the function call arguments. Whether a function can be instantiated depends on whether template argument deduction succeeds. (The process of template argument deduction is explained in Section 10.3.) In the preceding example, the function argument dd is used to deduce the template argument for Type. The template argument deduced is double and the template instantiation sum(double,int) is added to the set of candidate functions. Thus, there are two candidate functions for the call: the template instantiation sum(double,int) and the ordinary function sum(double,double).

Once the template instantiations have been added to the set of candidate functions, function overload resolution proceeds as usual.

The second step of function overload resolution selects the set of viable functions from the set of candidate functions. Recall that a viable function is a candidate function for which there exist type conversions that can convert each function argument to the type of the corresponding function parameter. (Section 9.3 presents the type conversions that can be applied to function arguments.) Type conversions exist both for the instantiation sum(double,int) and for the nontemplate function sum(double,double). Both of these functions are viable functions.

The third step of function overload resolution consists of ranking the type conversions applied to the arguments to select the best viable function. For our example, the ranking is as follows:

- For the function template instantiation `sum(double,int)`:

1. For the first argument, both the argument and the parameter have type `double`, and the conversion is an exact match.
2. For the second argument, both the argument and the parameter have type `int`, and the conversion is also an exact match.

- For the nontemplate function `sum(double,double)`:

1. For the first argument, both the argument and the parameter have type `double`, and the conversion is an exact match.
2. For the second argument, the argument has type `int` and the parameter has type `double`; the conversion applied is an floating-integral standard conversion.

Both functions are equally good when the first argument is considered. However, the function template instantiation is better for the second argument. Therefore, the function selected as the best viable function for the call is the instantiation `sum(double,int)`.

A function template instantiation is entered in the set of candidate functions only if template argument deduction succeeds. It is not an error if template argument deduction fails; in such cases, no function instantiation is added to the set of candidate functions. For example, suppose the function template `sum()` had been declared as follows:

```
// function template
template <class T>
    int sum( T*, int ) { .... }
```

Given the same function call as earlier, template argument deduction would fail because it is not possible for a function argument of type `double` to have a corresponding parameter of type `T*`. Because no function instantiation can be generated from the function template for this call, no instantiation is added to the set of candidate functions. The only function in the set of candidate functions is then the nontemplate function `sum(double,double)`. It is the function selected for the call, and the second argument is converted to type `double`.

What if template argument deduction succeeds but the template is explicitly specialized for the template arguments deduced? Then it is the explicit specialization that is entered in the set of candidate functions in the place of the function that would be instantiated from the generic template definition. For example:

```
// function template definition
template <class Type> Type sum( Type, int ) { /* ... */ }

// explicit specialization for Type == double
template<> double sum<double>( double,int );

// ordinary (nontemplate) function
double sum( double, double );
```

```
void manip( int ii, double dd ) {
   // calls template explicit specialization sum<double>()
   sum( dd, ii );
}
```

For the call to sum() in manip(), template argument deduction finds that the instantiation sum(double,int) generated from the generic template definition should be entered
into the set of candidate functions. However, an explicit specialization is provided for
sum(double,int), and it is this explicit specialization that is entered into the set of candidate functions. In fact, because this specialization is later found to be the best match
for the call, it is the function that is selected by function overload resolution.

Template explicit specializations are not automatically entered in the set of candidate functions. Only if template argument deduction succeeds is a template explicit
specialization considered for a function call. For example:

```
// function template definition
template <class Type>
   Type min( Type, Type ) { /* ... */ }

// explicit specialization for Type == double
template<> double min<double>( double,double );

void manip( int ii, double dd ) {
   // error: template argument deduction fails
   //         no candidate function for the call
   min( dd, ii );
}
```

The function template min() is specialized for the template argument double. However, this specialization is not entered in the set of candidate functions. Template
argument deduction fails for the call to min() in manip(), because the template argument deduced for Type from each function argument is different. For the first argument, the type double is deduced for Type. For the second argument, the type int is
deduced for Type. Because template argument deduction fails, no instantiation is
entered in the set of candidate functions and the specialization min(double,double) is
ignored. Because there is no other candidate function for the call, the call is in error.

As mentioned in Section 10.6, an ordinary function can have a return type and a
parameter list that match exactly those of a function that could be instantiated from a
template. In the following example, the function min(int,int) is an ordinary function
and not a specialization for the function template min() because, as you may remember, a specialization declaration must begin with the tokens template<>:

```
// function template declaration
template <class T>
  T min( T, T );

// ordinary function min( int, int )
int min( int, int ) { }
```

A function call could match equally well this ordinary function and a function instantiated from the function template. In the following example, both arguments in the call min(ai[0],99) have type int. There are two viable functions for this call: the ordinary function min(int,int) and a function with the same return type and parameter list instantiated from the function template.

```
int ai[4] = { 22, 33, 44, 55 };
int main() {
    // calls ordinary function min( int, int )
    min( ai[0], 99 );
}
```

However, such a call is not ambiguous. The nontemplate function, when present, is given precedence because it is explicitly implemented. Function overload resolution selects the ordinary function min(int,int) for the call.

Once function overload resolution resolves a call to an ordinary function, there is no going back later if the program does not contain a definition of this function. The function template is not instantiated to create a function body for the function if the function definition is not present. Instead, a link-time error will result. In the following example, the program calls but does not define the ordinary function min(int,int). This program generates a linker error:

```
// function template
template <class T>
  T min( T, T ) { .... }

// This ordinary function is not defined in this program
int min( int ,int );

int ai[4] = { 22, 33, 44, 55 };
int main() {
    // link error: min( int, int ) is called and not defined
    min( ai[0], 99 );
}
```

Why would it be useful to define an ordinary function with a return type and a parameter list that match those of a function instantiated from a template? Remember that when we're calling a function instantiated from a template, only a limited set of type conversions can be applied on a function argument that is used for template argument deduction. If we declare an ordinary function, all type conversions are considered to convert the arguments because the types of the ordinary function parameters are fixed. Let's look at an example that shows why we would want to declare an ordinary function.

Suppose that we want to define a function template specialization min <int>(int,int) and we want this function to be invoked when min() is called with arguments of any integer type, whether or not the arguments have the same type. Because of the restrictions on type conversions, calls with arguments of different integer types will not invoke the function template instantiation min<int>(int,int) directly. We could call the instantiation directly by specifying explicit template arguments. However, we would prefer a solution that does not require every call site to be modified. By defining an ordinary function, our program invokes our specialized version for min(int,int) whenever arguments of integer types are used, without the need for us to use explicit template arguments on every function call. For example:

```
// function template definition
template <class Type>
   Type min( Type t1, Type t2 ) { ... }

int ai[4] = { 22, 33, 44, 55 };
short ss = 88;

void call_instantiation() {
   // error: no candidate function for this call
   min( ai[0], ss );
}

// ordinary function
int min( int a1, int a2 ) {
   min<int>( a1, a2 );
}

int main() {
   call_instantiation();
   // calls the ordinary function
   min( ai[0], ss );
}
```

There are no candidate functions for the call min(ai[0],ss) in call_instantiation(). The attempt to generate a candidate function from the function template min() fails, because different template arguments are deduced for Type from the function arguments. The call is therefore in error. However, for the call to min(ai[0],ss) in main(), the declaration of the ordinary function min(int,int) is visible. This ordinary function is a viable function for the call: the type of the first argument is an exact match for the type of its corresponding parameter, and the second argument can be converted to the type of its corresponding parameter using a promotion. This ordinary function is the only function in the set of viable functions for the second call, and it is selected for the call.

Now that we have shown how function overload resolution proceeds when function template instantiations, function template specializations, and ordinary functions of the same name are involved, let's summarize the steps of function overload resolution for a call in which ordinary functions and function templates are considered:

1. Build the set of candidate functions.

   Function templates with the same name as the function called are considered. If template argument deduction succeeds with the function call arguments, a function template is instantiated, or if a template specialization exists for the template argument deduced, the template specialization is a candidate function.

2. Build the set of viable functions, as described in Section 9.3.

   From the set of candidate functions, keep only the functions that can be called with the function call arguments.

3. Rank the type conversions, as described in Section 9.3.

   a. If only one function is selected, call this function.

   b. If the call is ambiguous, remove the function template instantiations from the set of viable functions.

4. Perform overload resolution considering only the ordinary functions in the set of viable functions, as described in Section 9.3.

   a. If only one function is selected, call this function.

   b. Otherwise, the call is ambiguous.

Let's step through an example. Here are two declarations: a function template declaration and an ordinary function taking two arguments of type double.

```
template <class Type>
   Type max( Type, Type ) { .... }

// ordinary function
double max( double, double );
```

The following are three calls to max(). Can you tell which instance is invoked for each call?

```
int main() {
    int ival;
    double dval;
    float fd;

    // some values are assigned to ival, dval, and fd

    max( 0, ival );
    max( 0.25, dval );
    max( 0, fd );
}
```

Let's look at each call in turn.

- max(0,ival): The two arguments are both of type int. Two candidate functions exist for this call: the function template instantiation max(int,int) and the ordinary function max(double,double). The function template instantiation is an exact match for the function arguments. It is the function that is invoked.

- max(0.25,dval): The two arguments are both of type double. Two candidate functions exist for this call: the function template instantiation max(double,double) and the ordinary function max(double,double). The call is therefore ambiguous because it matches both functions exactly. Rule 3b indicates that the ordinary function is selected in this case.

- max(0,fd): The arguments are of type int and float, respectively. Only one candidate function exists for this call: the ordinary function max(double,double). Template argument deduction fails, because the template argument deduced for Type from the two function arguments is not a single type; no template instantiation is therefore entered in the set of candidate functions. The ordinary function is a viable function, because there exist type conversions that can convert the function arguments to the type of the corresponding function parameters. The ordinary function is selected. If the ordinary function were not declared, the call would be an error.

What if we had defined a second ordinary function for max()? For example:

```
template <class T> T max( T, T ) { .... }

// two ordinary functions
char max( char, char );
double max( double, double );
```

Is the resolution of the third call any different? Yes.

```
int main() {
    float fd;

    // resolved to which function?
    max( 0, fd );
}
```

Rule 3b states that, because the call is ambiguous, only the ordinary functions are considered. Neither of these functions is selected as the best viable function, because the type conversions on the arguments are equally bad for both functions: both arguments require a standard conversion to match the corresponding parameter in either of the viable functions. The call is therefore ambiguous and is flagged as an error by the compiler.

Exercise 10.11

Let's return to the example presented earlier:

```
template <class Type>
    Type max( Type, Type ) { .... }

double max( double, double );

int main() {
    int ival;
    double dval;
    float fd;

    max( 0, ival );
    max( 0.25, dval );
    max( 0, fd );
}
```

The following function template specialization is added to the set of declarations in global scope:

```
template <> char max<char>( char, char ) { .... }
```

Revisit the function calls in main() and list the candidate functions and list the viable functions for each calls.

Suppose that the following function call is added within main(). To which function does the call resolve? Why?

```
int main() {
    // ...
    max (0, 'J' );
}
```

Exercise 10.12

Suppose we have the following set of template definitions and specializations and variable and function declarations:

```
int i;            unsigned int ui;
char str[24];     int ia[24];

template <class T> T calc( T*, int );
template <class T> T calc( T, T );
template<> char calc( char*, int );
double calc( double, double );
```

Identify which, if any, template instantiation or function is invoked for each of the following calls. For each call, list the candidate functions, list the viable functions, and explain why the best viable function is selected.

```
(a) calc( str, 24 );   (d) calc( i, ui );
(b) calc( ia, 24 );    (e) calc( ia, ui );
(c) calc( ia[0], i );  (f) calc( &i, i );
```

10.9 Name Resolution in Template Definitions ◆

Inside a template definition, some constructs have a meaning that differs from one instantiation of the template to another, whereas other constructs have the same meaning for all instantiations of the template. This depends on whether or not the construct involves a template parameter. For example:

```
template<typename Type>
   Type min( Type* array, int size )
{
   Type min_val = array[0];
   for ( int i = 1; i < size; ++i )
      if ( array[i] < min_val )
         min_val = array[i];

   print( "Minimum value found: " );
   print( min_val );

   return min_val;
}
```

In min(), the types of array and of min_val depend on the actual type with which Type will be replaced when the template is instantiated, whereas the type of size, for example, remains int regardless of the type of the template parameter. The types of array and of min_val vary from one instantiation of the template to another. Because of this, we say that the types of these variables *depend on a template parameter*, whereas the type of size does not depend on a template parameter.

Because the type of min_val is unknown, it is also unknown which operation is used when min_val appears in an expression. For example, which print() function should be called by the function call print(min_val)? Should it be the print() function used for int types? Or should it be the function for float types? Is the call in error because there is no function print() that can be called with an argument of min_val's type? It is impossible to answer these questions until the template is instantiated and until we know what the type of min_val is. Because of this, we also say that the call print(min_val) depends on a template parameter.

There are no such questions with the constructs within min() that do not depend on a template parameter. For example, it is always known which function should be called for the call print("Minimum value found: "). It is the function used to print character strings. The print() function called does not vary from one instantiation of the template to another. Thus, we say that this call does not depend on a template parameter.

As we learned in Chapter 7, in C++, a function must be declared before it can be called. Must a function called in a template definition be declared before the template definition is seen? In the preceding example, must the function `print()` be declared before the call is seen in `min()`'s template definition? The answer depends on the kind of name to which we are referring. A construct that does not depend on a template parameter must be declared before it is used in a template definition. The definition for the function template `min()` as presented earlier is therefore incorrect. Because the call

```
print( "Minimum value found: " );
```

is not a call that depends on a template parameter, the function `print()` for character strings must be declared before it can be used in the template definition. To remedy this problem, a declaration for `print()` can be provided before the definition of `min()`, as follows:

```
// ---- primer.h ----

// this declaration is necessary:
// print( const char * ) is called in min()
void print( const char* );

template<typename Type>
   Type min( Type* array, int size ) {

   // ....

   print( "Minimum value found: " );
   print( min_val );

   return min_val;
}
```

On the other hand, the declaration for the `print()` function used by the call `print (min_val)` is not yet needed because we do not yet know which `print()` function to look for. It is not possible to know which `print()` function is called by `print(min_val)` until the type of `min_val` is known.

So when must the `print()` function invoked by the call `print(min_val)` be declared? It must be declared before the template is instantiated. For example:

```
#include <primer.h>
void print( int );

int ai[4] = { 12, 8, 73, 45 };

int main() {
   int size = sizeof(ai) / sizeof(int);
   // instantiation of min( int*, int )
   min( &ai[0], size );
}
```

The function main() calls the function template instantiation min(int*,int). In this instantiation of min(), Type is replaced by int and the type of the variable min_val is int. The function call print(min_val) therefore calls a function that can be invoked with an argument of type int. It is when min(int*,int) is instantiated that we know that the second call to the print() function has an argument of type int. It is at this time that a function print() that can be called with an argument of type int needs to be visible. In our example, the function that is selected is print(int). If the function print(int) had not been declared before the instantiation of min(int*,int) took place, the instantiation would result in a compile-time error.

Therefore, name resolution in a template definition happens in two steps: first, the names that do not depend on a template parameter are resolved when the template is defined; second, the names that depend on a template parameter are resolved when the template is instantiated. You may wonder why there are two steps. For example, why aren't all the names resolved when the template is instantiated?

If we are the designer of a function template, we would like to control how the names in the template definition are resolved. Let's assume that the function template min() is part of a library that defines other templates and functions. We want the instantiations of min() to use the other components of our library whenever possible. In the preceding example, the interface of our library is defined in the header <primer.h>. Both the declaration of the function print(const char*) and the definition for the function template min() are part of the interface of our library. We want the instantiations of min() to call the print() function provided with our library. The first step of name resolution guarantees that this will happen. When a name used in a template definition does not depend on a template parameter, it is guaranteed that the name will refer to another component defined in our library — that is, that it will refer to a declaration that we package with the function template definition in the <primer.h> header file.

In fact, the designer of a function template must make sure to provide declarations for all of the names used in a template definition that do not depend on a template parameter. If a name used in a template definition does not depend on a template parameter and if a declaration for this name is not found when the template is defined, the template definition is an error. The error is never reconsidered when the template is instantiated. For example:

```
// ---- primer.h ----
template<typename Type>
   Type min( Type* array, int size )
{
   Type min_val = array[0];
   // ...
   // error: print ( const char* ) not found
   print( "Minimum value found: " );
```

```
        // ok: depends on template parameter
        print( min_val );
        // ...
    }

    // ---- user.C ----
    #include <primer.h>

    // this declaration of print( const char* ) is ignored
    void print( const char* );
    void print( int );

    int ai[4] = { 12, 8, 73, 45 };

    int main() {
        int size = sizeof(ai) / sizeof(int);
        // instantiation of min( int*, int )
        min( &ai[0], size );
    }
```

The declaration for print(const char*) in user.C is not visible where the template definition appears. However, such a declaration is visible where the template min-(int*,int) is instantiated, but this declaration is not considered for the call print("Minimum value found: ") because the call does not depend on a template parameter. Unless a construct in a template definition depends on a template parameter, names are resolved in the context of the template definition and this resolution is never reconsidered in the context of the template instantiation. Therefore, it is the responsibility of the template designer to ensure that declarations for names used in the template definition are properly included with the template definition as part of the library interface.

Let's change hats now and assume that the library was written by somebody else and that we are instead a user of the library defined in the <primer.h> header file. There are situations in which we want the objects and functions defined in our program to be considered when our program instantiates a template from the library. For example, let's assume that our program defines a class type called SmallInt. We wish to instantiate the function min() from the library <primer.h> to obtain the minimum value within an array of objects of type SmallInt.

When the template min() is instantiated for an array of objects of type SmallInt, the template argument for Type is the class type SmallInt. This implies that min_val in the instantiation of min() has type SmallInt. To which print() function should the call print(min_val) in the instantiation of min() resolve?

```
        // ---- user.h ----
        class SmallInt { /* ... */ };
        void print( const SmallInt & );
```

```
// ---- user.C ----
#include <primer.h>
#include "user.h"
SmallInt asi[4];

int main() {
   // set the elements of asi

   // instantiation of min( SmallInt*, int )
   int size = sizeof(asi) / sizeof(SmallInt);
   min( &asi[0], size );
}
```

That's right — we want our function print(const SmallInt &) to be considered. Considering only the functions defined in the library <primer.h> is not good enough. The second step of name resolution guarantees that this will happen. When a name used in a template definition depends on a template parameter, the names declared in the instantiation context are considered. Therefore, we are certain that functions that can manipulate objects of type SmallInt will be considered for the operations in the function template if the template argument is of type SmallInt.

The location where a template is instantiated in the source code is called the template's *point of instantiation*. Knowing the location of a template's point of instantiation is important, because it determines which declarations are considered for the names that depend on a template parameter. A function template's point of instantiation is always in namespace scope, and it always follows the function that refers to the instantiation. For example, the point of instantiation for min(SmallInt*, int) is located immediately after the function main() in namespace scope:

```
// ...
int main() {
   // ...
   // use of min( SmallInt*, int )
   min( &asi[0], size );
}
// point of instantiation of min( SmallInt*, int )
// as if instantiation definition appeared as follows:
SmallInt min( SmallInt* array, int size )
   { /* ... */ }
```

But what if a template instantiation is used more than once in a source file? Where is the point of instantiation? Why does this matter? you will ask. In our SmallInt example, it matters because the declaration of our function print(const SmallInt &) must appear before the point of instantiation for min(SmallInt*, int). For example:

```
#include <primer.h>
void another();
```

```
SmallInt asi[4];

int main() {
    // set the elements of asi
    int size = sizeof(asi) / sizeof(SmallInt);
    min( &asi[0], size );

    another();
    // ...
}
// is point of instantiation here?

void another() {
    int size = sizeof(asi) / sizeof(SmallInt);
    min( &asi[0], size );
}
// Or here?
```

As it happens, there is a point of instantiation after every function definition that uses the instantiation. The compiler is free to choose any one of these points of instantiation to actually instantiate the function template. This implies that we must be careful when organizing our code to place all the declarations needed to resolve names dependent on the template parameter before the first point of instantiation of the template. It is therefore a good idea to make all the necessary declarations available in a header file to be included before any instantiation of the template is used. For example:

```
#include <primer.h>
// user.h contains the declarations needed by the instantiation
#include "user.h"
void another();

SmallInt asi[4];

int main() {
    // ...
}
// first point of instantiation for min( SmallInt*, int )

void another() {
    // ...
}
// second point of instantiation for min( SmallInt*, int )
```

What if the template instantiation is used in more than one file? For example, what if the function another() is in a different file from the function main()? Then there is a point of instantiation in every file in which the template instantiation is used. The compiler is free to choose any one of these files to instantiate the function template. We must then also be careful when organizing our code to place the header file "user.h" in every file in which the function template instantiation is used. This ensures that the instantiation of min(SmallInt*,int) refers to our function print(const SmallInt &) as we expect no matter which point of instantiation the compiler actually chooses.

Exercise 10.13

List the two steps of name resolution in template definitions. Explain how the first step addresses the concerns of library designers and how the second step provides the flexibility needed for template users.

Exercise 10.14

To which declarations do the names display and SIZE refer to in the instantiation of max(LongDouble*,SIZE)?

```
// ---- exercise.h ----
void display( const void* );
typedef unsigned int SIZE;

template<typename Type>
    Type max( Type* array, SIZE size )
{
    Type max_val = array[0];
    for ( SIZE i = 1; i < size; ++i )
        if ( array[i] > max_val )
            max_val = array[i];

    display( "Maximum value found: " );
    display( max_val );

    return max_val;
}
// ---- user.h ----
class LongDouble { /* ... */ };
void display( const LongDouble & );
void display( const char * );
typedef int SIZE;

// ---- user.C ----
#include <exercise.h>
#include "user.h"

LongDouble ad[7];

int main() {
    // set the elements of ad

    // instantiation of max( LongDouble*, SIZE )
    SIZE size = sizeof(ad) / sizeof(LongDouble);
```

```
        max( &ad[0], size );
    }
```

10.10 Namespaces and Function Templates ◆

As with any other global scope definitions, a function template definition can be placed in a namespace. (See Sections 8.5 and 8.6 for a discussion of namespaces). The meaning of such a template definition is the same as it is when the template is defined in global scope except that the name of the template is hidden within the namespace. The template name must be qualified by the namespace name when the template is used outside its namespace, or else a using declaration must be provided. For example:

```
    // ---- primer.h ----
    namespace cplusplus_primer {
        // template definition hidden in a namespace
        template<class Type>
            Type min( Type* array, int size ) { /* ... */ }
    }

    // ---- user.C ----
    #include <primer.h>
    int ai[4] = { 12, 8, 73, 45 };

    int main() {
        int size = sizeof(ai) / sizeof(ai[0]);

        // error: the function min() is not found
        min( &ai[0], size );

        using cplusplus_primer::min; // using declaration
        // ok: refers to min() in namespace cplusplus_primer
        min( &ai[0], size );
    }
```

What happens if our program uses a template that is defined in a namespace and we want to provide a specialization for it? (Template explicit specializations are introduced in Section 10.6.) For example, we want to use the template min() defined in namespace cplusplus_primer to find the minimum value in an array of objects of type SmallInt. However, we realize that the template definition provided in namespace cplusplus_primer does not quite work. The comparison in the template definition looks like this:

```
        if ( array[i] < min_val )
```

This statement compares two class objects of type SmallInt using the less-than (<) operator. This operator cannot apply to two class objects unless an overloaded operator<() is defined for the class SmallInt. (We will see how to define overloaded operators in Chapter 15.) Let's assume that we want to define a specialization for the `min()` function template so that it uses a function named `compareLess()` to find the minimum value in an array of SmallInt class objects. Here is a declaration of our `compareLess()` function:

```
// comparison function for SmallInt objects
// returns true if parm1 is less than parm2
bool compareLess( const SmallInt &parm1, const SmallInt &parm2 );
```

What would the definition of this function look like? To answer this, we need to look at the definition of our class SmallInt in more detail. Our SmallInt class allows us to define objects that can hold the same range of values as an 8-bit `unsigned char`; that is, 0–255. Its additional functionality is that it catches underflow and overflow errors. Except for that, we wish for it to behave in the same way as an `unsigned char`. The definition of the class SmallInt looks like this:

```
class SmallInt {
public:
   SmallInt( int ival ) : value( ival ) { }
   friend bool compareLess( const SmallInt &, const SmallInt & );
private:
   int value; // data member
};
```

There are a few things in this class definition that we should discuss. First, the class has one private data member, `value`. It is this data member that stores the value of an object of type SmallInt. The class also contains a constructor:

```
// constructor for class SmallInt
SmallInt( int ival ) : value( ival ) { }
```

This constructor has one parameter, `ival`. The only action it performs is to initialize the class data member `value` with the value of its parameter `ival`.

Now we can answer our earlier question. How is our function `compareLess()` defined? The function will compare the `value` data members of its two SmallInt parameters, as follows:

```
// returns true if parm1 is less than parm2
bool compareLess( const SmallInt &parm1, const SmallInt &parm2 ) {
   return parm1.value < parm2.value;
}
```

Notice, however, that the data member `value` is a private data member of the SmallInt class. How can this global function refer to the private data members without breaking the encapsulation of the class SmallInt and without causing a compile-time error? If you look at the definition of the SmallInt class, you will notice that the class definition declared the global function `compareLess()` as a friend. When a function is a friend of a class, it can refer to the class private members, as our function `compare-Less()` does. (Friends of classes are looked at further in Section 15.2.)

We are now ready to define our template specialization for `min()`. It uses the `compareLess()` function as follows:

```
// specialization of min() for arrays of SmallInt objects
template<> SmallInt min<SmallInt>( SmallInt* array, int size )
{
    SmallInt min_val = array[0];
    for ( int i = 1; i < size; ++i )
        // comparison uses our compareLess() function
        if ( compareLess( array[i], min_val ) )
            min_val = array[i];

    print( "Minimum value found: " );
    print( min_val );

    return min_val;
}
```

Where should we declare this specialization? How about this:

```
// ---- primer.h ----
namespace cplusplus_primer {
    // template definition hidden in a namespace
    template<class Type>
        Type min( Type* array, int size ) { /* ... */ }
}
// ---- user.h ----
class SmallInt { /* ... */ };
void print( const SmallInt & );
bool compareLess( const SmallInt &, const SmallInt & );

// ---- user.C ----
#include <primer.h>
#include "user.h"

// error: not a specialization for cplusplus_primer::min()
template<> SmallInt min<SmallInt>( SmallInt* array, int size )
    { /* ... */ }
// ...
```

Unfortunately, this code does not quite do it. An explicit specialization declaration for a function template must be declared in the namespace where the generic template is defined. We must then define the specialization for `min()` in the namespace cplusplus_primer. There are two ways of achieving this in our program.

Recall that namespace definitions can be discontiguous. We can reopen the definition of namespace cplusplus_primer to add the definition of the specialization as follows:

```
// ---- user.C ----
#include <primer.h>
#include "user.h"

namespace cplusplus_primer {
    // specialization for cplusplus_primer::min()
    template<> SmallInt min<SmallInt>( SmallInt* array, int size )
        { /* ... */ }
}
SmallInt asi[4];

int main() {
    // set the elements of asi using the set() member function

    using cplusplus_primer::min; // using declaration
    int size = sizeof(asi) / sizeof(SmallInt);
    // instantiation of min(SmallInt*,int)
    min( &asi[0], size );
}
```

Or we can define the specialization in the same way that we can define any namespace member outside its namespace definition: by qualifying the name of the namespace member by the name of its enclosing namespace.

```
// ---- user.C ----
#include <primer.h>
#include "user.h"

// specialization for cplusplus_primer::min()
// the name of the specialization is qualified
template<> SmallInt cplusplus_primer::
                    min<SmallInt>( SmallInt* array, int size )
    { /* ... */ }
// ...
```

Therefore, as the user of a library that contains template definitions, if we want to provide specializations for the templates in the library we must ensure that their definitions are properly placed within the namespace containing the original template definition.

Exercise 10.15

We now place the content of the header file <exercise.h> provided in Exercise 10.14 in namespace cplusplus_primer. How would you change the function main() so that it can instantiate the function template max() located in namespace cplusplus_primer?

Exercise 10.16

Again referring to Exercise 10.14, given that the content of the header file <exercise.h> is placed in namespace cplusplus_primer, we want to specialize the function template max() for arrays of objects of class LongDouble. We want the template specialization to use the function compareGreater() defined to compare two objects of class type LongDouble like this:

```
// comparison function for LongDouble objects
// returns true if parm1 is greater than parm2
bool compareGreater( const LongDouble &parm1,
                     const LongDouble &parm2 );
```

The definition of our class LongDouble looks as follows:

```
class LongDouble {
public:
    LongDouble(double dval) : value(dval) { }
    void set(double dval) { value = dval; }
    friend bool compareGreater( const LongDouble &,
                                const LongDouble & );
private:
    double value;
};
```

Provide the definition for the function compareGreater() and the definition for the specialization of max() that uses this function. Write a function main() that sets the elements of the array ad and then calls the specialization of max() to obtain the maximum value in ad; the values to initialize the elements of the array ad should be obtained by reading the values from the standard input cin.

10.11 Function Template Example

This section provides a program example of how function templates might be defined and used. The example defines a function template sort() that is used to sort the elements of an array. The array is itself represented by a class template, the Array class template introduced in Section 2.5. The function template sort() can thus be used to sort arrays of elements of any type.

We saw in Chapter 6 that the C++ standard library defines a container type called vector that behaves very much like the Array type defined in Section 2.5. Chapter 12 introduces the generic algorithms that can manipulate the container types described in Chapter 6. One of these algorithms is called sort() and can be used to sort the content of a vector. In this section, we will define our own "generic sort() algorithm" to manipulate our Array class. What we see in this section, then, is a much simplified version of what can be found in the C++ standard library.

The sort() function template for our Array class template is defined as follows:

```
#include "Array.h"

template <class elemType>
    void sort( Array<elemType> &array, int low, int high ) {
```

```
        if ( low < high ) {
            int lo = low;
            int hi = high + 1;
            elemType elem = array[lo];

            for (;;) {
                while ( min( array[++lo], elem ) != elem && lo < high ) ;
                while ( min( array[--hi], elem ) == elem && hi > low ) ;

                if (lo < hi)
                    swap( array, lo, hi );
                else break;
            }

            swap( array, low, hi );
            sort( array, low, hi-1 );
            sort( array, hi+1, high );
        }
    }
```

The function sort() uses two helping functions: min() and swap(). Both of these functions must be defined as function templates to handle all the argument types with which sort() will be instantiated. min() is defined as a function template so that we can find the minimum of two array elements of any type:

```
    template <class Type>
        Type min( Type a, Type b ) {
            return a < b ? a : b;
    }
```

swap() is defined as a function template so that we can swap two array elements of any type:

```
    #include "Array.h"

    template <class elemType>
        void swap( Array<elemType> &array, int i, int j )
    {
        elemType tmp = array[ i ];
        array[ i ] = array[ j ];
        array[ j ] = tmp;
    }
```

To be sure that our sort() function template actually works, we need to display the contents of the array after the array has been sorted. Because the display() function must be able to handle any array instantiated from our Array class template, we must also define the display() function as a function template:

```
#include <iostream>

template <class elemType>
    void display( Array<elemType> &array )
{ // display format: < 0 1 2 3 4 5 >

    cout << "< ";
    for ( int ix = 0; ix < array.size(); ++ix )
        cout << array[ix] << " ";
    cout << ">\n";
}
```

In this example, we use the inclusion compilation model and place all our function templates in the header file Array.h, following the definition of our Array class template.

The next step is to write a function that exercises these function templates. The function sort() is passed in turn an array of doubles, an array of ints, and an array of strings. Here is the program:

```
#include <iostream>
#include <string>
#include "Array.h"

double da[10] = {
    26.7, 5.7, 37.7, 1.7, 61.7, 11.7, 59.7,
    15.7, 48.7, 19.7 };

int ia[16] = {
    503, 87, 512, 61, 908, 170, 897, 275, 653,
    426, 154, 509, 612, 677, 765, 703 };

string sa[11] = {
    "a", "heavy", "snow", "was", "falling", "when",
    "they", "left", "the", "police", "station" };

int main() {

    // call the constructor to initialize arrd
    Array<double> arrd( da, sizeof(da)/sizeof(da[0]) );

    // call the constructor to initialize arri
    Array<int> arri( ia, sizeof(ia)/sizeof(ia[0]) );

    // call the constructor to initialize arrs
    Array<string> arrs( sa, sizeof(sa)/sizeof(sa[0]) );

    cout << "sort array of doubles (size == "
        << arrd.size() << ")" << endl;
    sort( arrd, 0, arrd.size()-1 );
    display(arrd);
```

```
    cout << "\sort array of ints (size == "
        << arri.size() << ")" << endl;
    sort( arri, 0, arri.size()-1 );
    display(arri);

    cout << "\sort array of strings (size == "
        << arrs.size() << ")" << endl;
    sort( arrs, 0, arrs.size()-1 );
    display(arrs);

    return 0;
}
```

When compiled and executed, this program generates the following output (the output of the array has been manually broken up to fit on the page):

```
sort array of doubles (size == 10)
< 1.7 5.7 11.7 14.9 15.7 19.7 26.7
  37.7 48.7 59.7 61.7 >

sort array of ints (size == 16)
< 61 87 154 170 275 426 503 509 512
  612 653 677 703 765 897 908 >

sort array of strings (size == 11)
< "a" "falling" "heavy" "left" "police" "snow"
  "station" "the" "they" "was" "when" >
```

Among the generic algorithms defined in C++ standard library (and in Chapter 12), you will also find a min() function and a swap() function. We find out in Chapter 12 how they can be used in our programs.

11

Exception Handling

Exception handling is a mechanism that allows two separately developed program components to communicate when a program anomaly, called an *exception*, is encountered during the execution of the program. In this chapter we first look at how to raise, or throw, an exception at the location where the program anomaly is encountered. We then look at how to associate handlers, or catch clauses, with a set of program statements using a try block, and we look at how exceptions are handled by catch clauses. We then introduce exception specifications, a mechanism that associates a list of exceptions with a function declaration and that guarantees that the function does not throw any other types of exceptions. We end the chapter with a discussion of design considerations for programs that use exceptions.

11.1 Throwing an Exception

Exceptions are run-time anomalies that a program may detect, such as division by 0, access to an array outside of its bounds, or the exhaustion of the free store memory. Such exceptions exist outside the normal functioning of the program and require immediate handling by the program. The C++ language provides built-in language features to raise and handle exceptions. These language features activate a run-time mechanism used to communicate exceptions between two unrelated (often separately developed) portions of a C++ program.

When an exception is encountered in a C++ program, the portion of the program that detects the exception can communicate that the exception has occurred by raising, or *throwing*, an exception. To see how exceptions are thrown in C++, let's reimplement the class iStack presented in Section 4.15 to use exceptions to indicate anomalies in the handling of the stack. The definition of the class iStack looks like this:

```
#include <vector>
```

```
class iStack {
public:
   iStack( int capacity )
         : _stack( capacity ), _top( 0 ) { }

   bool pop( int &top_value );
   bool push( int value );

   bool full();
   bool empty();
   void display();

   int size();

private:
   int _top;
   vector< int > _stack;
};
```

The stack is implemented using a vector of ints. When an iStack object is created, the constructor for iStack creates a vector of ints of the size specified with the initial value. This size is the maximum number of elements the iStack object can contain. The following, for example, creates an iStack object called myStack that can contain as many as 20 values of type int:

```
iStack myStack(20);
```

What can go wrong when we manipulate myStack? Here are two anomalies that may be encountered with our iStack class:

1. A pop() operation is requested and the stack is empty.
2. A push() operation is requested and the stack is full.

We decide that these anomalies should be communicated to the functions manipulating iStack objects using exceptions. So where do we start?

First, we must define the exceptions that can be thrown. In C++, exceptions are most often implemented using classes. Although classes are fully introduced in Chapter 13, we will define here two simple classes to use as exceptions with our iStack class, and we place these class definitions in the header stackExcp.h:

```
// stackExcp.h
class popOnEmpty { /* ... */ };
class pushOnFull { /* ... */ };
```

Chapter 19 discusses exceptions of class type in greater detail and discusses the exception class hierarchy provided by the C++ standard library.

We must then change the definition of the member functions pop() and push() to throw these newly defined exceptions. An exception is thrown using a *throw expression*. A throw expression looks a great deal like a return statement. A throw expression is composed of the keyword throw followed by an expression whose type is that of the exception thrown. What does the throw expression in pop() look like? Let's try this:

```
// oops, not quite right
throw popOnEmpty;
```

Unfortunately, this is not quite right. An exception is an object, and pop() must throw an object of class type. The expression in the throw expression cannot simply be a type. To create an object of class type, we need to call the class constructor. What does a throw expression that invokes a constructor look like? Here is the throw expression in pop():

```
// expression is a constructor call
throw popOnEmpty();
```

This throw expression creates an exception object of type popOnEmpty.

Recall that the member functions pop() and push() were defined to return a value of type bool: a true return value indicates that the operation succeeded, and a false return value indicates that it failed. Because exceptions are now used to indicate the failure of the pop() and push() operations, the return values from these functions are now unnecessary. We now define these member functions with a void return type. For example:

```
class iStack {
public:
   // ...

   // no longer return a value
   void pop( int &value );
   void push( int value );

private:
   // ...
};
```

The functions that use our iStack class will now assume that everything is fine unless an exception is thrown; they no longer need to test the return value of the member function pop() or push() to see whether the operation succeeds. We will see how to define a function to handle exceptions in the next two sections.

We are now ready to provide the new implementations of iStack's pop() and push() member functions:

```
#include "stackExcp.h"

void iStack::pop( int &top_value )
{
   if ( empty() )
      throw popOnEmpty();

   top_value = _stack[ --_top ];
```

```
       cout << "iStack::pop(): " << top_value << endl;
    }

    void iStack::push( int value )
    {
       cout << "iStack::push( " << value << " )\n";

       if ( full() )
          throw pushOnFull();

       _stack[ _top++ ] = value;
    }
```

Although exceptions are most often objects of class type, a throw expression can throw an object of any type. For example, although it's unusual, the function math-Func() in the following code sample throws an exception object of enumeration type. This code is valid C++ code:

```
    enum EHstate { noErr, zeroOp, negativeOp, severeError };

    int mathFunc( int i ) {
       if ( i == 0 )
          throw zeroOp; // exception of enumeration type

       // otherwise, normal processing continues
    }
```

Exercise 11.1

Which, if any, of the following throw expressions are errors? Why? For the valid throw expressions, indicate the type of the exception thrown.

```
    (a) class exceptionType { };
        throw exceptionType();
    (b) int excpObj;
        throw excpObj;
    (c) enum mathErr { overflow, underflow, zeroDivide };
        throw zeroDivide();
    (d) int *pi = &excpObj;
        throw pi;
```

Exercise 11.2

The IntArray class defined in Section 2.3 has a member operator function operator[]() that uses assert() to indicate that the index is outside the bounds of the array. Change the definition of operator[]() to instead throw an exception in this situation. Define an exception class to be used as the type of the exception thrown.

11.2   The Try Block

The following small program exercises our class iStack and the pop() and push() member functions defined in the previous section. The for loop in main() iterates 50 times. It pushes on the stack each value that is a multiple of 3 — 3, 6, 9, and so on. Whenever the value is a multiple of 4, such as 4, 8, 12, and so on, it displays the contents of the stack. Whenever the value is a multiple of 10, such as 10, 20, 30, and so on, it pops the last item from the stack and then displays the contents of the stack again. How do we change main() to handle the exceptions thrown by the iStack member functions?

```
#include <iostream>
#include "iStack.h"

int main() {
    iStack stack( 32 );

    stack.display();
    for ( int ix = 1; ix < 51; ++ix )
    {
        if ( ix % 3 == 0 )
            stack.push( ix );

        if ( ix % 4 == 0 )
            stack.display();

        if ( ix % 10  == 0) {
            int dummy;
            stack.pop( dummy );
            stack.display();
        }
    }
    return 0;
}
```

A *try block* must enclose the statements that can throw exceptions. A try block begins with the try keyword followed by a sequence of program statements enclosed in braces. Following the try block is a list of handlers called *catch clauses*. The try block groups a set of statements and associates with these statements a set of handlers to handle the exceptions that the statements can throw. Where should we place a try block or try blocks in the function main() to handle the exceptions popOnEmpty and pushOnFull? Let's try this:

```
for ( int ix = 1; ix < 51; ++ix ) {
    try { // try block for pushOnFull exceptions
        if ( ix % 3 == 0 )
            stack.push( ix );
    }
    catch  ( pushOnFull ) { ... }
```

```
        if ( ix % 4 == 0 )
            stack.display();

        try { // try block for popOnEmpty exceptions
            if ( ix % 10  == 0 ) {
                int dummy;
                stack.pop( dummy );
                stack.display();
            }
        }
        catch ( popOnEmpty ) { ... }
    }
```

The program as we have implemented it works correctly. Its organization, however, intermixes the handling of the exceptions with the normal processing of the program and thus is not ideal. After all, exceptions are program anomalies that occur
only in exceptional cases. We want to separate the code that handles the program
anomalies from the code that implements the normal manipulation of the stack. We
believe that this strategy makes the code easier to follow and easier to maintain. Here
is our preferred solution:

```
    try {
        for ( int ix = 1; ix < 51; ++ix )
        {
            if ( ix % 3 == 0 )
                stack.push( ix );

            if ( ix % 4 == 0 )
                stack.display();

            if ( ix % 10  == 0 ) {
                int dummy;
                stack.pop( dummy );
                stack.display();
            }
        }
    }
    catch ( pushOnFull ) { ... }
    catch ( popOnEmpty ) { ... }
```

Associated with the try block are two catch clauses that are capable of handling the
exceptions pushOnFull and popOnEmpty that may be thrown from the iStack member
functions push() and pop() called from within the try block. Each catch clause specifies
within parentheses the type of exception it handles. The code to handle the exception
is placed in the compound statement of the catch clause (between the curly braces). We
examine catch clauses in greater detail in the next section.

The program control flow in our example is one of the following.

1. If no exception occurs, the code within the try block is executed and the handlers associated with the try block are ignored. The function main() returns 0.

2. If the push() member function called within the first if statement of the for loop throws an exception, the second and third if statements of the for loop are ignored, the for loop and the try block are exited, and the handler for exceptions of type pushOnFull is executed.

3. If the pop() member function called within the third if statement of the for loop throws an exception, the call to display() is ignored, the for loop and the try block are exited, and the handler for exceptions of type popOnEmpty is executed.

When an exception is thrown, the statements following the statement that throws the exception are skipped. Program execution resumes in the catch clause handling the exception. If no catch clause capable of handling the exception exists, program execution resumes in the function terminate() defined in C++ standard library. We further discuss the function terminate() in the next section.

A try block can contain any C++ statement — expressions as well as declarations. A try block introduces a local scope, and variables declared within a try block cannot be referred to outside the try block, including within the catch clauses. For example, we could rewrite our function main() so that the declaration of the variable stack appears within the try block. In this case, it is not possible to refer to stack in the catch clauses:

```
int main() {
   try {
      iStack stack( 32 ); // ok: declaration in try block

      stack.display();
      for ( int ix = 1; ix < 51; ++ix )
      {
         // same as before
      }
   }
   catch ( pushOnFull ) {
      // cannot refer to stack here
   }
   catch ( popOnEmpty ) {
      // cannot refer to stack here
   }

   // cannot refer to stack here
   return 0;
}
```

It is possible to declare a function so that the entire body of the function is contained within the try block. In such a case, instead of placing the try block within the function definition we can enclose the function body within a *function try block*. This organization supports the cleanest separation between the code that supports the normal processing of the program and the code that supports the handling of the exceptions. For example:

```
int main()
try {
    iStack stack( 32 );

    stack.display();
    for ( int ix = 1; ix < 51; ++ix )
    {
        // same as before
    }

    return 0;
}
catch ( pushOnFull ) {
    // cannot refer to stack here
}
catch ( popOnEmpty ) {
    // cannot refer to stack here
}
```

Notice that the try keyword comes before the opening brace of the function body and the catch clauses are listed after the function body's closing brace. With this code organization, the code that supports the normal processing of main() is placed within the function body, clearly separated from the code that handles the exceptions in the catch clauses. However, variables declared within main()'s function body cannot be referred to within the catch clauses.

A function try block associates a group of catch clauses with a function body. If a statement within the function body throws an exception, the handlers that follow the function body are considered to handle the exception. Function try blocks are particularly useful with class constructors. We will reexamine function try blocks in this context in Chapter 19.

Exercise 11.3

Write a program that defines an IntArray object (where IntArray is the class type defined in Section 2.3) and performs the following actions. We have three files containing integer values.

1. Read the first file and assign the first, third, fifth, ..., nth value read (where n is an odd number) to the IntArray object; then display the content of the IntArray object.

2. Read the second file and assign the fifth, tenth, ..., nth value read (where n is a multiple of 5) to the IntArray object; then display the content of the IntArray object.

3. Read the third file and assign the second, fourth, sixth..., nth value read (where n is an even number) to the IntArray object; then display the content of the IntArray object.

Use the IntArray `operator[]()` defined in Exercise 11.2 to store values into and read values from the IntArray object. Because `operator[]()` may throw an exception, use one or more try blocks and catch clauses in your program to handle the possible exceptions thrown by `operator[]()`. Explain the reasoning behind where you located the try blocks in your program.

11.3   Catching an Exception

A C++ exception handler is a *catch clause*. When an exception is thrown from statements within a try block, the list of catch clauses that follows the try block is searched to find a catch clause that can handle the exception.

A catch clause consists of three parts: the keyword `catch`, the declaration of a single type or single object within parentheses (referred to as an *exception declaration*), and a set of statements within a compound statement. If the catch clause is selected to handle an exception, the compound statement is executed. Let's examine the catch clauses for the exceptions pushOnFull and popOnEmpty in the function `main()` in more detail.

```
catch ( pushOnFull ) {
   cerr << "trying to push a value on a full stack\n";
   return errorCode88;
}
catch ( popOnEmpty ) {
   cerr << "trying to pop a value on an empty stack\n";
   return errorCode89;
}
```

Both catch clauses have an exception declaration of class type; the first one is of type pushOnFull, and the second one is of type popOnEmpty. A handler is selected to handle an exception if the type of its exception declaration matches the type of the exception thrown. (We will see in Chapter 19 that the types do not have to match exactly: a handler for a base class can handle exceptions of a class type derived from the type of the handler's exception declaration.) For example, when the `pop()` member function of the class iStack throws a popOnEmpty exception, the second catch clause is entered. After an error message is issued to `cerr`, the function `main()` returns `errorCode89`.

If these catch clauses do not contain a return statement, where does the execution of the program continue? After a catch clause has completed its work, the execution of the program continues at the statement that follows the last catch clause in the list. In

our example, the execution of the program continues with the return statement in
main() and, after the catch clause for popOnEmpty generates an error message to cerr,
main() returns the value 0.

```
int main() {
    iStack stack( 32 );

    try {
        stack.display();
        for ( int ix = 1; ix < 51; ++ix )
        {
            // same as before
        }
    }
    catch ( pushOnFull ) {
        cerr << "trying to push a value on a full stack\n";
    }
    catch ( popOnEmpty ) {
        cerr << "trying to pop a value on an empty stack\n";
    }

    // execution of the program continues here
    return 0;
}
```

The C++ exception handling mechanism is said to be *nonresumptive*; once the exception has been handled, the execution of the program does not resume where the exception was originally thrown. In our example, once the exception has been handled,
the execution of the program does not continue in the pop() member function where
the exception was thrown.

11.3.1   Exception Objects

The exception declaration of a catch clause can be either a type declaration or an
object declaration. When should the exception declaration in a catch clause declare an
object? An object should be declared when it is necessary to obtain the value or
manipulate the exception object created by the throw expression. If we design our
exception classes to store information in the exception object when the exception is
thrown and if the exception declaration of the catch clause declares an object, the
statements within the catch clause can use this object to refer to the information stored
by the throw expression.

For example, let's change the design of the pushOnFull exception class. Let's store
within the exception object the value that cannot be pushed on the stack. The catch
clause is changed to display this value when the error message is generated to cerr. To
do this, we first need to change the definition of the pushOnFull class type. Here is our
new definition:

```
// new exception class:
// it stores the value that cannot be pushed on the stack
class pushOnFull {
public:
    pushOnFull( int i ) : _value( i ) { }
    int value() { return _value; }
private:
    int _value;
};
```

The new private data member _value holds the value that cannot be pushed on the stack. The constructor takes a value of type int and stores this value in the _value data member. Here is how the constructor can be invoked by the throw expression to store in the exception object the value that cannot be pushed on the stack:

```
void iStack::push( int value )
{
    if ( full() )
        // value stored in exception object
        throw pushOnFull( value );

    // ...
}
```

The class pushOnFull also has a new member function value() that can be used in the catch clause to display the value stored in the exception object. Here is how it can be used:

```
catch ( pushOnFull eObj ) {
    cerr << "trying to push the value " << eObj.value()
         << " on a full stack\n";
}
```

Notice that the catch clause's exception declaration declares the object eObj, which is used to invoke the member function value() of the class pushOnFull.

An exception object is always created at the throw point even though the throw expression is not a constructor call and even though it doesn't appear to be creating an exception object. For example:

```
enum EHstate { noErr, zeroOp, negativeOp, severeError };
enum EHstate state = noErr;

int mathFunc( int i ) {
    if ( i == 0 ) {
        state = zeroOp;
        throw state; // exception object created
    }
    // otherwise, normal processing continues
}
```

In this example, the object state is not used as the exception object. Instead, an exception object of type EHstate is created by the throw expression and initialized with the value of the global object state. How can a program tell that the exception object is distinct from the global object state? To answer this question we must first look at the catch clause exception declaration in more detail.

The exception declaration of a catch clause behaves very much like a parameter declaration. When a catch clause is entered, if the exception declaration declares an object, this object is initialized with a copy of the exception object. For example, the following function calculate() calls the function mathFunc() defined earlier. When the catch clause in calculate() is entered, the object eObj is initialized with a copy of the exception object created by the throw expression:

```
void calculate( int op ) {
   try {
      mathFunc( op );
   }
   catch ( EHstate eObj ) {
      // eObj is a copy of the exception object thrown
   }
}
```

The exception declaration in this example resembles a pass-by-value parameter. The object eObj is initialized with the value of the exception object in the same way that a pass-by-value function parameter is initialized with the value of the corresponding argument (pass-by-value parameters are discussed in Section 7.3).

As is the case for function parameters, the exception declaration of a catch clause can be changed to a reference declaration. The catch clause then directly refers to the exception object created by the throw expression instead of creating a local copy. For example:

```
void calculate( int op ) {
   try {
      mathFunc( op );
   }
   catch ( EHstate &eObj ) {
      // eObj refers to the exception object thrown
   }
}
```

For the same reasons that parameters of class type should be declared as references to prevent unnecessary copying of large class objects, it is also preferable if exception declarations for exceptions of class type are declared as references.

With an exception declaration of reference type, the catch clause is able to modify the exception object. However, any variable specified by the throw expression remains unaffected. For example, modifying eObj within the catch clause does not affect the global variable state specified by the throw expression:

```
void calculate( int op ) {
   try {
      mathFunc( op );
   }
   catch ( EHstate &eObj ) {
      // fix exception situation
      eObj = noErr; // global variable state is not modified
   }
}
```

The catch clause resets eObj to the value noErr after correcting the exception situation. Because eObj is a reference, we can expect this assignment to modify the global object state. However, the assignment modifies only the exception object created by the throw expression. And because the exception object is a distinct object from the global object state, state remains unchanged by the modification to eObj in the catch clause.

11.3.2   Stack Unwinding

The search for a catch clause to handle a thrown exception proceeds as follows: if the throw expression is located within a try block, the catch clauses associated with this try block are examined to see whether one of these clauses can handle the exception. If a catch clause is found, the exception is handled. If no catch clause is found, the search continues in the calling function. If the call to the function exiting with the thrown exception is located within a try block, the catch clauses associated with this try block are examined to see whether one can handle the exception. If a catch clause is found, the exception is handled. If no catch clause is found, the search continues in the calling function. This process continues up the chain of nested function calls until a catch clause for the exception is found. As soon as a catch clause that can handle the exception is encountered, the catch clause is entered and the execution of the program continues within this handler.

In our example, the first function that is searched for a catch clause is the pop() member function of the class iStack. Because the throw expression in pop() is not located within a try block, pop() exits with an exception. The next function examined is the function that calls the member function pop(), which is main() in our example. The call of pop() in main() is located within a try block. The catch clauses associated with this try block are considered to handle the exception. A catch clause for exceptions of type popOnEmpty is found and entered to handle the exception.

The process by which compound statements and function definitions exit because of a thrown exception in the search for a catch clause to handle the exception is called *stack unwinding*. As the stack is unwound, the lifetime of local objects declared in the compound statements and in function definitions that are exited ends. C++ guarantees that, as the stack is unwound, the destructors for local class objects are called even though their lifetime ends because of a thrown exception. We look into this in more detail in Chapter 19.

What if the program does not provide a catch clause for the exception that is thrown? An exception cannot remain unhandled. An exception is an important enough situation that the program cannot continue executing normally. If no handler is found, the program calls the `terminate()` function defined in the C++ standard library. The default behavior of `terminate()` is to call `abort()`, indicating the abnormal exit from the program. (In most situations, calling `abort()` is good enough. However, in some cases it is necessary to override the actions performed by `terminate()`. [STROUSTRUP97] shows how this can be done and discusses it in more detail.)

By now, you will probably have noticed many similarities between exception handling and function calls. A throw expression behaves somewhat like a function call, and the catch clause behaves somewhat like a function definition. The main difference between these two mechanisms is that all the information necessary to set up a function call is available at compile-time, and that is not true for the exception handling mechanism. C++ exception handling requires run-time support. For example, for an ordinary function call, the compiler knows at the point of the call which function will actually be called through the process of function overload resolution. For exception handling, the compiler does not know for a particular throw expression in which function the catch clause resides and where execution resumes after the exception has been handled. These decisions happen at run-time. The compiler cannot inform users when no handler exists for an exception. This is why the `terminate()` function exists: it is a run-time mechanism to tell users when no handler matches the exception thrown.

11.3.3   Rethrow

It is possible that a single catch clause cannot completely handle an exception. After some corrective actions, a catch clause may decide that the exception must be handled by a function further up the list of function calls. A catch clause can pass the exception to another catch clause further up the list of function calls by *rethrowing* the exception. A rethrow expression has this form:

```
throw;
```

A rethrow expression rethrows the exception object. A rethrow can appear only in the compound statement of a catch clause. For example:

```
catch ( exception eObj ) {
    if ( canHandle( eObj ) )
        // handle the exception
        return;
    else
        // rethrow it for another catch clause to handle
        throw;
}
```

The exception that is rethrown is the *original* exception object. This has some implications if the catch clause modifies the exception object before rethrowing it. The following does not modify the original exception object. Can you see why?

```
enum EHstate { noErr, zeroOp, negativeOp, severeError };

void calculate( int op ) {
   try {
      // exception thrown by mathFunc() has value zeroOp
      mathFunc( op );
   }
   catch ( EHstate eObj ) {
      // fix a few things

      // attempt to modify the exception object
      eObj = severeErr;

      // intends to rethrow an exception of value severeErr
      throw;
   }
}
```

Because `eObj` is not a reference, the catch clause receives a copy of the exception object, and any modifications to `eObj` within the handler modify the local copy. They do not affect the original exception object created by the throw expression. It is this original exception object that is rethrown by the rethrow expression. Because the original exception is not modified within the catch clause in our example, the object rethrown still has its initial `zeroOp` value.

To modify the original exception object, the exception declaration within the catch clause must declare a reference. For example:

```
catch ( EHstate &eObj ) {
   // modifies the exception object
   eObj = severeErr;

   // The value of the exception rethrown is severeErr
   throw;
}
```

`eObj` refers to the exception object created by the throw expression, and modifications to `eObj` in the catch clause affect the original exception object. These modifications are part of the exception object that is rethrown.

Therefore, another good reason to declare the exception declaration of the catch clause as a reference is to ensure that modifications applied to the exception object within the catch clause are reflected in the exception object that is rethrown. We will see another good reason why exception declarations for exceptions of class type should be references in Section 19.2, where we see how catch clauses can invoke the class virtual functions.

11.3.4   The Catch-All Handler

A function may want to perform some action before it exits with a thrown exception even though it cannot handle the exception that is thrown. For example, a function may acquire some resource, such as opening a file or allocating memory on the heap, and it may want to release this resource (close the file or release the memory) before it exits with the thrown exception. For example:

```
void manip() {
    resource res;
    res.lock();     // locks a resource

    // use res
    // some action that causes an exception to be thrown

    res.release(); // skipped if exception thrown
}
```

The release of the resource res is bypassed if an exception is thrown. To guarantee that the resource is released, rather than provide a specific catch clause for every possible exception and because we can't know all the exceptions that might be thrown, we can use a catch-all catch clause. This catch clause has an exception declaration of the form (...), where the three dots are referred to as an *ellipsis*. This catch clause is entered for any type of exception. For example:

```
// entered with any exception thrown
catch ( ... ) {
    // place our code here
}
```

A catch(...) is used in combination with a rethrow expression. The resource that has been locked is released within the compound statement of the catch clause before the exception is propagated further up the list of function calls with a rethrow expression:

```
void manip() {
    resource res;
    res.lock();
    try {
        // use res
        // some action that causes an exception to be thrown
    }
    catch (...) {
        res.release();
        throw;
    }
    res.release(); // skipped if exception thrown
}
```

To ensure that the resource is appropriately released if an exception is thrown and `manip()` exits with an exception, a `catch(...)` is used to release the resource before the exception is propagated to functions further up the list of function calls. We can also manage the acquisition and release of a resource by encapsulating the resource in a class, and having the class constructor acquire the resource and the class destructor release the resource automatically. We look at how to do this in Chapter 19.

A `catch(...)` clause can be used by itself or in combination with other catch clauses. If it is used in combination with other catch clauses, we must take some care when organizing the set of catch clauses associated with the try block.

Catch clauses are examined in turn, in the order in which they appear following the try block. Once a match is found, subsequent catch clauses are not examined. This implies that if a `catch(...)` is used in combination with other catch clauses, it must always be placed last in a list of exception handlers; otherwise, a compiler error is issued. For example:

```
try {
    stack.display();
    for ( int ix = 1; ix < 51; ++ix )
    {
        // same as before
    }
}
catch ( pushOnFull ) { }
catch ( popOnEmpty ) { }
catch (...) { } // must be last catch clause
```

Exercise 11.4

Explain why we say that the C++ exception handling model is nonresumptive.

Exercise 11.5

Given the following exception declarations, provide a throw expression that creates an exception object that can be caught by the following catch clauses.

```
(a) class exceptionType { };
    catch( exceptionType *pet ) { }
(b) catch(...) { }
(c) enum mathErr { overflow, underflow, zeroDivide };
    catch( mathErr &ref ) { }
(d) typedef int EXCPTYPE;
    catch( EXCPTYPE ) { }
```

Exercise 11.6

Explain what happens during stack unwinding.

Exercise 11.7

Give two reasons that the exception declaration of a catch clause should declare a reference.

Exercise 11.8

Using the code you developed for Exercise 11.3, modify the exception class you created so that the invalid index used with `operator[]()` is stored in the exception object when the exception is thrown and later displayed by the catch clause. Modify your program so that `operator[]()` throws an exception during the execution of the program.

11.4   Exception Specifications

It is not possible, looking at the declarations for the member functions `pop()` and `push()` of the class iStack, to determine that these functions may throw exceptions. One possible solution is to add a comment associated with the declaration of each member function. In this way, the class interface that appears in the header file also documents the exceptions the class member functions may throw:

```
class iStack {
public:
    // ...

    void pop( int &value ); // throw popOnEmpty
    void push( int value ); // throw pushOnFull

private:
    // ...
};
```

However, this is less than ideal. There is no guarantee that this documentation will remain up-to-date with later releases of our iStack class. Nor does it provide information to the compiler to guarantee that no other kinds of exceptions are thrown. An *exception specification* provides a solution that can be used to list the exceptions a function may throw with the function declaration. It guarantees that the function does not throw any other types of exceptions.

An exception specification follows the function parameter list. It is specified with the keyword `throw` followed by a list of exception types enclosed in parentheses. For example, the declarations of the member functions of the class iStack can be modified as follows to add the appropriate exception specifications:

```
class iStack {
public:
    // ...

    void pop( int &value ) throw(popOnEmpty);
```

```
        void push( int value ) throw(pushOnFull);

    private:
        // ...
    };
```

A call of pop() guarantees not to throw any exception other than an exception of type popOnEmpty. Similarly, a call of push() guarantees not to throw any exception other than an exception of type pushOnFull.

An exception declaration is part of the function's interface, and it must be specified on the function declarations that appear in header files. An exception specification is a contract between the function and the rest of the program. It is a guarantee that the function will not throw any exception not listed in its exception specification.

If a function declaration specifies an exception specification, a redeclaration of the same function must specify an exception specification with the same types. The exception specifications on different declarations of the same function are not cumulative. For example:

```
    // two declarations of the same function
    extern int foo( int = 0 ) throw(string);

    // error: exception specification omitted
    extern int foo( int parm ) { }
```

What happens if the function throws an exception that is not listed in its exception specification? Exceptions are thrown only if certain program anomalies are encountered, and it is not possible to know at compile-time whether a program encounters these exceptions at run-time. Therefore, violations of a function's exception specification can be detected only at run-time. If a function throws an exception not listed in its exception specification, the function unexpected(), defined in the C++ standard library, is invoked. The default behavior of unexpected() is to call terminate(). (In some situations, it may be necessary to override the actions performed by unexpected(). The C++ standard library provides a mechanism to override the default behavior of unexpected(). [STROUSTRUP97] discusses this in more detail.)

We should clarify that the function unexpected() is not called merely because a function throws an exception not listed in its exception specification. If the function handles the exception itself and if the exception is handled before it "escapes" outside the function, then all is fine. For example:

```
    void recoup( int op1, int op2 ) throw(ExceptionType)
    {
        try {
            // ...
            throw string("we're in control");
        }
```

```
   // handles the exception thrown
   catch ( string ) {
      // do whatever is needed
   }
} // OK, unexpected() is not called
```

Even though an exception of type string is thrown from within the function recoup()
and even though the function recoup() guarantees not to throw exceptions of a type
other than ExceptionType, because the exception is handled before it escapes from the
function recoup(), the function unexpected() is not called as a result of this exception
being thrown.

Violations of a function's exception specification are detected only at run-time. The
compiler does not generate compile-time errors if an expression can throw an exception of a type disallowed by the exception specification. If this expression is never executed or if it never throws the exception that is violating the exception specification,
the program runs as expected and the function exception specification is never violated. For example:

```
extern void doit( int, int ) throw(string, exceptionType);

void action (int op1, int op2 ) throw(string) {
   doit( op1, op2 ); // no compile-time error
   // ...
}
```

The function doit() can throw an exception of type exceptionType, which is not
allowed by the exception specification of the function action(). Even though this type
of exception is not allowed by the function action(), this function compiles successfully. Instead, the compiler generates code to ensure that if an exception violating the
exception specification is thrown, the run-time library function unexpected() is called.

An empty exception specification guarantees that the function does not throw any exception. For example, the function no_problem() guarantees not to throw an exception:

```
extern void no_problem() throw();
```

If a function declaration does not specify an exception specification, the function
can throw exceptions of any type.

No type conversion is allowed between the type of the exception thrown and a
type specified by the exception specification. For example:

```
int convert( int parm ) throw(string)
{
   // ...
   if ( somethingRather )
      // program error:
      // convert() does not allow exception of type const char*
      throw "help!";
}
```

The throw expression in the function convert() throws a C-style character string. The exception object created by this throw expression has type const char*. Usually, an expression of type const char* can be converted to the type string. However, an exception specification does not allow type conversions from the type of the exception thrown to the type specified by the exception specification. If convert() throws this exception, the function unexpected() is called. To correct this situation, the throw expression can be modified to explicitly convert the value of the expression to the type string as follows:

```
throw string( "help!" );
```

11.4.1   Exception Specifications and Pointers to Functions

An exception specification can also be provided in the declaration of a pointer to function. For example:

```
void (*pf)( int ) throw(string);
```

This declaration indicates that pf points to a function that can throw exceptions only of type string. As with function declarations, the exception specifications of different declarations for the same pointer to function are not cumulative, and all the declarations for the pointer pf must specify the same exception specification. For example:

```
extern void (*pf)( int ) throw(string);

// error: missing exception specification
void (*pf)( int );
```

When a pointer to function with an exception specification is initialized (or assigned to), there are restrictions on the type of the pointer used as the initializer (or used as the rvalue on the right-hand side of the assignment). The exception specifications of both pointers do not have to be identical. However, the exception specification of the pointer used as the initializer or rvalue must be either as restrictive as or more restrictive than the exception specification of the pointer that is initialized or assigned to. For example:

```
void recoup( int, int ) throw(exceptionType);
void no_problem() throw();
void doit( int, int ) throw(string, exceptionType);

// ok: recoup() is as restrictive as pf1
void (*pf1)( int, int ) throw(exceptionType) = &recoup;

// ok: no_problem() is more restrictive than pf2
void (*pf2)() throw(string) = &no_problem;

// error: doit() is less restrictive than pf3
void (*pf3)( int, int ) throw(string) = &doit;
```

The third initialization does not make sense. The pointer declaration guarantees that pf3 points to a function that will not throw any exceptions except those of type string. However, the function doit() may also throw an exception of type exception-Type. Because the function doit() does not satisfy the guarantee of the exception specification of pf3, the function doit() is not a valid initializer for pf3 and a compiler error is issued.

Exercise 11.9

Using the code you developed for Exercise 11.8, change the declaration of class IntArray operator[]() to add an appropriate exception specification to describe the exception this operator can throw. Modify your program so that operator[]() throws an exception not listed in its exception specification. What happens then?

Exercise 11.10

What exceptions can a function throw if it has an exception specification of the form throw()? If it has no exception specification?

Exercise 11.11

Which one, if any, of the following pointer assignments is in error? Why?

```
        void example() throw(string);
(a)  void (*pf1)() = example;

(b)  void (*pf2)() throw() = example;
```

11.5   Exceptions and Design Issues

There are some design issues associated with the use of exception handling in C++ programs. Although the support for exception handling is built into the language, not every C++ program should use exception handling. Exception handling should be used to communicate program anomalies between parts of the program that are developed independently, because throwing an exception is not as fast as a normal function call. For example, a library implementer may decide to communicate program anomalies to users of the library using exceptions. If a library function encounters an exceptional situation that it cannot handle locally, it may throw an exception to notify the program using the library.

In our example, our library defines the iStack class and its member functions. The function main() uses the library, and we should assume that the programmer writing main() is not the library implementer. The member functions of the class iStack are capable of detecting that a pop() operation is requested on an empty stack or that a push() operation is requested on a full stack, but the library implementer does not know the state of the program that caused the pop() or push() operations to be requested in the first place and cannot write pop() and push() to locally address this situation. Because these errors cannot be handled in the member functions, we decided to throw exceptions to notify the program using the library.

Even though C++ supports exception handling, C++ programs should use other error handling techniques (such as returning an error code) when appropriate. There is no clearcut answer to the question, "When should an error become an exception?" It is really up to the library implementer to decide what an "exceptional situation" is. Exceptions are part of a library's interface, and deciding which exceptions the library throws is an important phase of the library design. If the library is intended to be used within programs that cannot afford to crash, then the library must either handle the problem itself, or, if it can't, it must communicate program anomalies to the part of the program that uses the library and give the caller the choice as to which action should be taken when no meaningful action can be taken within the library code itself. Deciding what should be handled as an exception is a difficult part of the library design.

In our iStack example, it is debatable whether the push() member function should throw an exception if the stack is full. Another, some people would say better, implementation of push() is to handle this situation locally and grow the stack if it is full. After all, the only real limit is the memory available to our program. Our decision to throw an exception if the program attempts to push a value on a full stack may have been ill-considered. We can reimplement the member function push() to grow the stack if a request is made to push a value on a full stack:

```
void iStack::push( int value )
{
    // if full, grow the underlying vector
    if ( full() )
        _stack.resize( 2 * _stack.size() );

    _stack[ _top++ ] = value;
}
```

Similarly, should pop() throw an exception when a request is made to pop a value from an empty stack? One interesting observation is that the stack class of the C++ standard library (introduced in Chapter 6), does not throw an exception if a pop operation is requested and the stack is empty. Instead, the operation has undefined behavior: it is unknown what the program behavior is after such an operation has been requested. When the C++ standard library was designed, it was decided that an exception should not be thrown in this case. Allowing the program to continue running while an illegal state had been encountered was deemed appropriate in this situation. As we mentioned, different libraries will have different exceptions. There is no right answer to the question of what constitutes an exception.

Not all programs should worry about exceptions thrown by libraries. Although it is true that some systems cannot afford down time and should be built to handle exceptional situations, not every program has such requirements. Exception handling is primarily an aid to the implementation of fault-tolerant systems. Again, deciding whether our programs are to handle exceptions thrown from libraries or whether we should let the program terminate is a difficult part of the design process.

One last aspect of program design with exception handling is that the handling of exceptions in a program is usually layered. A program is usually built of components, and each component must decide which exceptions it will handle locally and which exceptions it will pass to higher levels of the program. What do we mean by component? For example, the text query system introduced in Chapter 6 can be broken into three components or layers. The first layer is the C++ standard library, which provides support for the basic operations on strings, maps, and so on. The second layer is the text query system itself, which defines functions, such as string_caps() and suffix_text(), that manipulate the text to be processed and uses the C++ standard library as a subcomponent. The third layer is the program that uses our text query system. Each component or layer is built independently, and each must decide which exceptional situation it will handle directly and which exceptions it will pass to higher levels of the program.

Not every function in a component or layer should be capable of dealing with exceptions. Usually, try blocks and associated catch clauses are used by functions that are the entry points into a program component. The catch clauses are designed to handle exceptions that the component does not want to let propagate to higher levels of the program. Exception specifications (discussed in Section 11.4) are also used with the functions that are the entry points into a component to guard against the escape of unwanted exceptions to higher levels of the program.

We look at other aspects of designing programs with exceptions in Chapter 19, after classes and class hierarchies have been introduced.

12

The Generic Algorithms

In our implementation of our Array class in Chapter 2, we provided member operations supporting `min()`, `max()`, `find()`, and `sort()`. The standard vector class, however, does not provide these apparently fundamental operations. To find the minimum or maximum value among the elements of a vector, we must instead invoke one of the *generic algorithms*: "algorithms" because they implement common operations such as `min()`, `max()`, `find()`, and `sort()`; "generic" because they operate across multiple container types — not only the vector and list types, for example, but also the built-in array type. The container is bound to the generic algorithm operating on it by an iterator pair (we discussed iterators briefly in Section 6.5) marking the elements to traverse. Special *function objects* allow us to override the default operator semantics of the generic algorithms. The generic algorithms, function objects, and a detailed look at iterators form the subject matter of this chapter.

12.1 Overview

Each generic algorithm is implemented independently of the individual container types. Because the type dependence of the algorithm has been removed, a single template instance can work across all the container types as well as the built-in array type. Consider the `find()` algorithm. Because it is independent of the container it is being applied to, the following general steps are required, presuming that the collection is unsorted:

1. Examine each element in turn.
2. If the element is equal to the value we are searching for, then return the element's position within the collection.
3. Otherwise, examine the next element, repeating step 2 until either the value is found or all the elements have been examined.
4. If we have reached the end of the collection and we have not found the value, return some value indicating that the value is not contained within the collection.

The algorithm, as we've stated it, is independent of the type of container it is applied to or the type of the value for which the search is being conducted. The requirements of the algorithm are the following:

1.   We need some way of traversing the collection. This includes the notions of advancing to a next element and recognizing when the next element represents the end of the collection. Typically, with the built-in array type (except for the C-style character string), we solve this problem by passing in two arguments: a pointer to the first element and a count of the number of elements to traverse. With a C-style character string, the element count is unnecessary; the end of string is indicated by a terminating null character.

2.   We need to be able to compare each container element to the value for which we are searching. Typically, this is solved either by using the equality operator associated with the value's underlying type or by passing in a pointer to a function to carry out the operation.

3.   We need a common type to represent both an element's position within the container and *no position* if the element is not found. Typically, we return the element's index, –1, or a pointer to the element, or 0.

The generic algorithms solve the first problem, container traversal, through the iterator abstraction. Iterators provide a generalization of a pointer. They minimally support an increment operator to access a next element, a dereference operator to access the actual element, and the equality and inequality operators to determine whether two iterators are equal. The range of elements over which the algorithm is to traverse is marked by a pair of iterators: a first iterator that addresses the first element to operate upon and a last iterator that marks 1 past the last element to operate upon. The element addressed by last is not itself operated upon; it serves as a *sentinel* to terminate the traversal. It also serves as the return value indicating no position. If the value is found, the iterator marking that position is returned.

The generic algorithms solve requirement 2, value comparison, by providing two versions of each algorithm: one that uses the equality operator of the underlying type of the element, and one that uses a function object or pointer to a function to implement the comparison (function objects are explained in Section 12.3). For example, here is the general implementation of find() in which the equality operator of the underlying type is used:

```
template < class ForwardIterator, class Type >
ForwardIterator
find( ForwardIterator first, ForwardIterator last, Type value )
{
    for ( ; first != last; ++first )
        if ( value == *first )
            return first;
    return last;
}
```

ForwardIterator is one of the five categories of iterators predefined by the standard library. A ForwardIterator supports both reading and writing of the element it addresses. (The five categories are presented in Section 12.4.)

The algorithms achieve type independence by never directly accessing the elements of the container; rather, all access and traversal of the elements is accomplished through the iterators. The actual container type (or whether it is a container type or built-in array) is unknown. To support the built-in array, ordinary pointers as well as iterators can be passed into the generic algorithms. For example, here is the use of find() with a built-in array of type int:

```
#include <algorithm>
#include <iostream>

int main()
{
    int search_value;
    int ia[ 6 ] = { 27, 210, 12, 47, 109, 83 };

    cout << "enter search value: ";
    cin  >> search_value;

    int *presult = find( &ia[0], &ia[6], search_value );

    cout << "The value " << search_value
         << ( presult == &ia[6]
              ? " is not present" : " is present" )
         << endl;
}
```

If the pointer returned is equal to the address of &ia[6] (that is, 1 past the elements of ia), then the search is unsuccessful; otherwise, the value is found.

Generally, when passing the address of array elements to a generic algorithm, we can write either

```
    int *presult = find( &ia[0], &ia[6], search_value );
```

or the less explicit

```
    int *presult = find( ia, ia+6, search_value );
```

If we wish to pass a subrange, we simply modify the indexes of the addresses being passed to the algorithm. For example, in this invocation of find(), only the second and third elements are searched (remember that elements are numbered beginning with zero):

```
    // only search elements ia[1] and ia[2]
    int *presult = find( &ia[1], &ia[3], search_value );
```

Here is a use of the vector container type with find():

```
#include <algorithm>
#include <vector>
#include <iostream>

int main()
{
    int search_value;
    int ia[ 6 ] = { 27, 210, 12, 47, 109, 83 };
    vector<int> vec( ia, ia+6 );

    cout << "enter search value: ";
    cin  >> search_value;

    vector<int>::iterator presult;
    presult = find( vec.begin(), vec.end(), search_value );

    cout << "The value " << search_value
         << ( presult == vec.end()
                ? " is not present" : " is present" )
         << endl;
}
```

Similarly, here is a use of the list container type with find():

```
#include <algorithm>
#include <list>
#include <iostream>

int main()
{
    int search_value;
    int ia[ 6 ] = { 27, 210, 12, 47, 109, 83 };
    list<int> ilist( ia, ia+6 );

    cout << "enter search value: ";
    cin >> search_value;

    list<int>::iterator presult;
    presult = find( ilist.begin(), ilist.end(), search_value );

    cout << "The value " << search_value
         << ( presult == ilist.end()
                ? " is not present" : " is present" )
         << endl;
}
```

In the next section, we walk through the design of a program that uses a variety of generic algorithms. In the section following that, we introduce function objects. Section 12.4 introduces some further details on iterators. We broadly introduce the generic algorithms in Section 12.5 — a detailed discussion and illustration of each algorithm is factored out into the Appendix. We end this chapter with a discussion of when use of the generic algorithms is not appropriate.

Exercise 12.1

One criticism of the generic algorithms is that their design, although elegant, places the burden of correctness on the programmer. For example, an invalid iterator or iterator pair marking an invalid range results in undefined run-time behavior. How valid is this criticism? Should use of the algorithms be limited to only the more-experienced programmers? In general, should programmers be protected against potentially error-prone constructs, such as the generic algorithms, pointers, and explicit casts?

12.2   Using the Generic Algorithms

Consider the following programming task. Let's say we are thinking of writing a children's illustrated book and wish to get a feel for the level of vocabulary appropriate to such books. Our idea is as follows: we'll read the text of some number of children's illustrated books, storing the text in individual string vectors (we already know how to do this — see Section 6.7). Here's what we'll do:

1. Make a copy of each vector.
2. Merge the five vectors into one large vector.
3. Sort the large vector in alphabetical order.
4. Remove all duplicate words.
5. Sort it again by word length.
6. Count the number of words longer than six characters (length is a presumable measure of complexity, at least in terms of vocabulary).
7. Remove any semantically neutral words (such as and, if, or, but, and so on).
8. Print the vector.

Hopefully, this sounds like a chapter-length task. Using the generic algorithms, however, we can reduce it to a short subsection of this chapter.

The argument to our function is a vector of vectors of strings. We accept it as a pointer and first test that it is non-null:

```
#include <vector>
#include <string>

typedef vector<string> textwords;
void process_vocab( vector<textwords>*pvec )
{
```

```
        if ( ! pvec ) {
            // issue warning message
            return;
        }

        // ...
    }
```

The first thing we wish to do is to create a single vector consisting of the elements of the individual vectors. We can accomplish that using the copy() generic algorithm as follows (we need to include the algorithm and iterator standard header files):

```
        #include <algorithm>
        #include <iterator>

        void process_vocab( vector< textwords >*pvec )
        {
            // ...
            vector< string > texts;

            vector<textwords>::iterator iter = pvec->begin();
            for ( ; iter != pvec->end(); ++iter )
                copy( (*iter).begin(), (*iter).end(),
                        back_inserter( texts ));

            // ...
        }
```

The copy() algorithm takes as its first two arguments a pair of iterators marking the range of elements to be copied. The third argument is an iterator marking where to begin placing the elements copied. back_inserter is spoken of as an *iterator adaptor*; it causes elements to be inserted at the back of the vector passed to it as an argument. (We look at iterator adaptors in detail in Section 12.4.)

unique() removes duplicate values from the container, but only those duplicate values that are adjacent. Given the sequence 01123211, the result is 012321 and not 0123. To achieve the latter result, we must first sort() the vector; that is, the sequence 01111223 becomes 0123. Well, almost. Actually, the result is 01231223.

unique() behaves somewhat unintuitively: the size of the container it acts upon is not changed. Rather, each unique element is assigned in turn to the next free slot beginning with the first. In our example, the physical result is 01231223; the sequence 1223 represents, so to speak, the *refuse* of the algorithm. unique() returns an iterator marking the beginning of this refuse. Typically, this iterator is then passed to the associated erase() container operation to delete the invalid elements. (Because the built-in array does not support an erase() operation, the family of unique() algorithms is less suited to the built-in array type.) Here is this portion of our function:

```
void process_vocab( vector< textwords >*pvec )
{
    // ...
    // sort the elements of texts
    sort( texts.begin(), texts.end() );

    // delete all duplicate elements
    vector<string>::iterator it;
    it = unique( texts.begin(), texts.end() );
    texts.erase( it, texts.end() );

    // ...
}
```

Here is a sample output of texts combining two small text files after sort() but prior to the invocation of unique():

```
a a a a alice alive almost
alternately ancient and and and and and and
and as asks at at beautiful becomes bird
bird blows blue bounded but by calling coat
daddy daddy daddy dark darkened darkening distant each
either emma eternity falls fear fiery fiery flight
flowing for grow hair hair has he heaven,
held her her her her him him home
houses i immeasurable immensity in in in in
inexpressibly is is is it it it its
journeying lands leave leave life like long looks
magical mean more night, no not not not
now now of of on one one one
passion puts quite red rises row same says
she she shush shyly sight sky so so
star star still stone such tell tells tells
that that the the the the the the
the there there thing through time to to
to to trees unravel untamed wanting watch what
when wind with with you you you you
your your
```

After application of unique() and the subsequent invocation of erase(), the texts vector looks like this:

```
a alice alive almost alternately ancient
and as asks at beautiful becomes bird blows
blue bounded but by calling coat daddy dark
darkened darkening distant each either emma eternity falls
fear fiery flight flowing for grow hair has
he heaven, held her him home houses i
immeasurable immensity in inexpressibly is it its journeying
lands leave life like long looks magical mean
more night, no not now of on one
```

```
passion puts quite red rises row same says
she shush shyly sight sky so star still
stone such tell tells that the there thing
through time to trees unravel untamed wanting watch
what when wind with you your
```

Our next task is to sort the strings by their length. To accomplish this, we'll use not the sort() but the stable_sort() algorithm. stable_sort() preserves the relative position of equivalent elements; within elements of the same length, the current alphabetical ordering is maintained. To accomplish the sorting by length, we provide our own less-than comparison operation. One way to accomplish this is the following:

```cpp
bool less_than( const string & s1, const string & s2 )
{
    return s1.size() < s2.size();
}

void process_vocab( vector< textwords >*pvec )
{
    // ...
    // sort the elements of texts by length
    // preserving the previous order of elements
    stable_sort( texts.begin(), texts.end(), less_than );

    // ...
}
```

Although this gets the job done, it is considerably less efficient than we might wish. less_than() is implemented as a single statement. Normally, it would be invoked as an inline function. By passing it in as a pointer to function, however, we prevent it from being inlined. An alternative strategy to preserve the inlineability of the operation is the use of a *function object*. For example:

```cpp
// a function object -- the operation is
// implemented as an instance of operator()
class LessThan {
public:
    bool operator()( const string & s1, const string & s2 )
                    { return s1.size() < s2.size(); }
};
```

A function object is a class in which the call operator (()) is overloaded. The body of the call operator implements the function case, the less-than comparison. The definition of a call operator looks bizarre at first because of the two occurrences of the parentheses. The sequence

```cpp
operator()
```

informs the compiler that we are overloading the call operator. The second pair of parentheses

```
( const string & s1, const string & s2 )
```

identifies the formal parameters being passed to the overloaded instance of the call operator. If we compare this definition with our earlier definition of less_than(), we notice that except for the replacement of operator() for less_than, the two are exactly the same.

An object of a function object is defined in the same way as an ordinary class object, although in this case we have not defined a constructor (there are no data members to initialize):

```
LessThan lt;
```

To invoke the member instance of the overloaded call operator, we simply apply the call operator to our class object, providing it with the required arguments. For example:

```
string st1( "shakespeare" );
string st2( "marlowe" );

// invokes lt.operator()( st1, st2 );
bool is_shakespeare_less = lt( st1, st2 );
```

Here is our reimplemention of process_vocab() in which we pass an unnamed LessThan function object to stable_sort():

```
void process_vocab( vector< textwords >*pvec )
{
    // ...
    stable_sort( texts.begin(), texts.end(), LessThan() );

    // ...
}
```

Within stable_sort(), the overloaded call operator is expanded inline. (stable_sort() is able to accept a third argument that is either a pointer to the function less_than() or an object of the class LessThan, because the argument is a type parameter of template mechanism. We look at function objects in more detail in Section 12.3.)

Here is the result of our stable_sort() of texts:

```
a i
as at by he in is it no
of on so to and but for has
her him its not now one red row
she sky the you asks bird blue coat
dark each emma fear grow hair held home
life like long mean more puts same says
star such tell that time what when wind
with your alice alive blows daddy falls fiery
lands leave looks quite rises shush shyly sight
```

```
still stone tells there thing trees watch almost
either flight houses night, ancient becomes bounded calling
distant flowing heaven, magical passion through unravel untamed
wanting darkened eternity beautiful darkening immensity journeying
alternately
immeasurable inexpressibly
```

Our next task is to count the number of words whose length is greater than six characters. We can accomplish this through the count_if() generic algorithm and a second function object, GreaterThan. It is a somewhat more complicated function object because we have generalized it to allow the user to provide an explicit size against which to test. We store the size in a class data member and initialize it with a class constructor. By default, it is initialized with a size of 6:

```cpp
#include <iostream>

class GreaterThan {
public:
    GreaterThan( int sz = 6 ) : _size( sz ){}
    int size() { return _size; }

    bool operator()( const string & s1 )
        { return s1.size() > _size;    }

private:
    int _size;
};
```

Here is how we might use it:

```cpp
void process_vocab( vector< textwords >*pvec )
{
    // ...
    // count number of strings greater than length 6
    int cnt = count_if( texts.begin(), texts.end(),
                        GreaterThan() );

    cout << "Number of words greater than length six are "
        << cnt << endl;

    // ...
}
```

Here is the output of this portion of our program:

```
Number of words greater than length six are 22
```

remove() behaves the same as unique() in that it does not actually alter the size of the container but rather separates the elements into those to be retained (copying them in turn to the front of the container) and those to be removed (which remain at the back). It returns an iterator marking the first element of those to be removed. Here is how we might use it to erase a collection of common words we do not wish to retain within the vector:

```
void process_vocab( vector< textwords >*pvec )
{
    // ...

    static string rw[] = { "and", "if", "or", "but", "the" };
    vector< string > remove_words( rw, rw+5 );

    vector<string>::iterator it2 = remove_words.begin();
    for ( ; it2 != remove_words.end(); ++it2 ) {
        // just to show another form of count()
        int cnt = count( texts.begin(), texts.end(), *it2 );
        cout << cnt << " instances removed:   "
             << (*it2) << endl;

        texts.erase(
            remove(texts.begin(),texts.end(),*it2 ),
            texts.end()
        );
    }

    // ...
}
```

Here is the result of `remove()` on `texts`:

```
1 instances removed:   and
0 instances removed:   if
0 instances removed:   or
1 instances removed:   but
1 instances removed:   the
```

Finally, we'd like to display the contents of the vector. One way to accomplish this is to iterate over the elements, displaying each one in turn, but because that makes no use of the generic algorithms, in this context that solution is inappropriate. Rather, we prefer to illustrate the use of the `for_each()` algorithm to output the elements of the vector. `for_each()` applies a pointer to function or function object to each element of a container marked by an iterator pair. In our case, our function object, PrintElem, prints the element to standard output:

```
class PrintElem {
public:
    PrintElem( int lineLen = 8 )
        : _line_length( lineLen ), _cnt( 0 )
    {}

    void operator()( const string &elem )
```

```
    {
        ++_cnt;
        if ( _cnt % _line_length == 0 )
            { cout << '\n'; }

        cout << elem << " ";
    }
private:
    int _line_length;
    int _cnt;
};

void process_vocab( vector< textwords >*pvec )
{
    // ...

    for_each( texts.begin(), texts.end(), PrintElem() );
}
```

That's it. We've completed our program, barely having done more than cobble together a sequence of generic algorithm invocations. For convenience, we've listed the complete program next, together with a main() function to drive it (it looks ahead to special iterator types, discussed in Section 12.4). We've listed the actual code executed, which is not fully Standard C++. In particular, the available implementations of the count() and count_if() algorithms represent older versions that do not return the result but rather require an additional argument to be passed within which the value is placed. In addition, the iostream library reflects a prestandard implementation requiring the use of an iostream.h header file.

```
#include <vector>
#include <string>
#include <algorithm>
#include <iterator>

// prestandard syntax for <iostream>
#include <iostream.h>

class GreaterThan {
public:
    GreaterThan( int sz = 6 ) : _size( sz ){}
    int size() { return _size; }

    bool operator()( const string &s1 )
                    { return s1.size() > _size; }
private:
    int _size;
};
```

```
class PrintElem {
public:

    PrintElem( int lineLen = 8 )
       : _line_length( lineLen ), _cnt( 0 )
    {}

    void operator()( const string &elem )
    {
       ++_cnt;
       if ( _cnt % _line_length == 0 )
          { cout << '\n'; }

       cout << elem << " ";
    }

private:
    int _line_length;
    int _cnt;
};

class LessThan {
public:
      bool operator()( const string & s1,
                       const string & s2 )
      {     return s1.size() < s2.size();   }
};

typedef vector<string, allocator> textwords;
void process_vocab( vector<textwords, allocator>*pvec )
{
    if ( ! pvec ) {
        // issue warning message
        return;
    }

    vector< string, allocator > texts;

    vector<textwords, allocator>::iterator iter;
    for ( iter = pvec->begin(); iter != pvec->end(); ++iter )
       copy( (*iter).begin(), (*iter).end(),
                back_inserter( texts ));

    // sort the elements of texts
    sort( texts.begin(), texts.end() );

    // ok, let's see what we have
    for_each( texts.begin(), texts.end(), PrintElem() );
```

```
cout << "\n\n"; // just to separate display output

// delete all duplicate elements
vector<string, allocator>::iterator it;
it = unique( texts.begin(), texts.end() );
texts.erase( it, texts.end() );

// ok, let's see what we have now
for_each( texts.begin(), texts.end(), PrintElem() );
cout << "\n\n";

// sort the elements based on default length of 6
// stable_sort() preserves ordering of equal elements …
stable_sort( texts.begin(), texts.end(), LessThan() );
for_each( texts.begin(), texts.end(), PrintElem() );

cout << "\n\n";

// count number of strings greater than length 6
int cnt = 0;

// obsolete form of count -- standard changes this
count_if( texts.begin(), texts.end(), GreaterThan(), cnt );

cout << "Number of words greater than length six are "
     << cnt << endl;

static string rw[] = { "and", "if", "or", "but", "the" };
vector<string,allocator> remove_words( rw, rw+5 );

vector<string, allocator>::iterator it2 =
      remove_words.begin();

for ( ; it2 != remove_words.end(); ++it2 )
{
   int cnt = 0;

   // obsolete form of count -- standard changes this
   count( texts.begin(), texts.end(), *it2, cnt );

   cout << cnt     << " instances removed:   "
        << (*it2) << endl;

   texts.erase(
      remove(texts.begin(),texts.end(),*it2),
      texts.end()
   );
}
```

```
        cout << "\n\n";
        for_each( texts.begin(), texts.end(), PrintElem() );
}

    // difference type is the type capable of holding the result
    // of subtracting two iterators of a container
    // -- in this case, of a string vector ...
    // ordinarily, this is handled by default ...

    typedef vector<string,allocator>::difference_type diff_type;

    // prestandard header syntax for <fstream>
    #include <fstream.h>

    main()
    {
        vector<textwords, allocator> sample;
        vector<string,allocator> t1, t2;
        string t1fn, t2fn;

        // request input files from user ...
        // should do some error checking in real-world program
        cout << "text file #1: "; cin >> t1fn;
        cout << "text file #2: "; cin >> t2fn;

        // open the files
        ifstream infile1( t1fn.c_str());
        ifstream infile2( t2fn.c_str());

        // special form of iterator
        // ordinarily, diff_type is provided by default ...
        istream_iterator< string, diff_type > input_set1( infile1 ),
                                              eos;
        istream_iterator< string, diff_type > input_set2( infile2 );

        // special form of iterator
        copy( input_set1, eos, back_inserter( t1 ));
        copy( input_set2, eos, back_inserter( t2 ));

        sample.push_back( t1 ); sample.push_back( t2 );
        process_vocab( &sample );
    }
```

Exercise 12.2

Word length is not the only nor possibly the best complexity measure of a piece of text. Another possible test is the length of a sentence. Write a program that reads in either a text file or text from standard input, builds a string vector for each sentence, and passes each vector to count(). Display the sentences in order of complexity. An interesting way to do that is to store each sentence as one large string in a second string vector and then pass that vector to sort() with a function object providing less-than semantics based on the smaller string. (To read a more detailed description of a particular generic algorithm or to see a further example of its use, refer to the Appendix, where the algorithms are listed in alphabetical order.)

Exercise 12.3

A more reliable test of the difficulty level of a piece of text is the structural complexity of its sentences. Let each comma count as 1 point, each semicolon or colon as 2 points, and each dash as 3 points. Modify the program of Exercise 12.2 to calculate the complexity of each sentence. Use count_if() to determine the presence of each punctuation character in the sentence vector. Display the sentences in order of complexity.

12.3 Function Objects

Our min() function is a good example of both the power and the limitation of the template mechanism.

```
template <typename Type>
const Type&
min( const Type *p, int size )
{
    int minIndex = 0;
    for ( int ix = 1; ix < size; ++ix )
        if ( p[ ix ] < p[ minIndex ] )
            minIndex = ix;
    return p[ minIndex ];
}
```

The power comes from the ability to define a single instance of min() that can be instantiated for an infinite number of types. The limitation is that although min() can be instantiated for an infinite number of types, it is not universally applicable to all types.

The constraint centers on the use of the less-than operator. In one case, the underlying type may not support the less-than operator. An Image class, for example, may not provide an implementation of a less-than operator, although we may be unaware of that and wish to discover the minimum frame number of the array of Image objects. An attempt to instantiate min() with an array of our Image class, however, results in a compile-time error:

```
error: invalid types applied to the < operator: Image < Image
```

In a second case, a less-than operator exists, but the provided semantics are inappropriate. For example, if we wish to discover a minimum string but wish to consider only letters of the alphabet and not be case-sensitive, then the less-than operator, although it is supported, supports the wrong semantics.

The traditional solution is to parameterize the comparison operator, in this case declaring a pointer to function taking two arguments and returning a value of type bool:

```
template < typename Type,
           bool (*Comp)(const Type&, const Type&)>
const Type&
min( const Type *p, int size, Comp comp )
{
    int minIndex = 0;
    for ( int ix = 1; ix < size; ++ix )
        if ( Comp( p[ ix ], p[ minIndex ] ))
            minIndex = ix;
    return p[ minIndex ];
}
```

This solution, together with our first implementation using the built-in less-than operator, provides general support for any type, including our Image class should we care to implement its semantics in terms of two Images. The primary performance drawback of a pointer to function is that its indirect invocation prevents it from being inlined.

An alternative parameterization strategy to that of a pointer to function is a function object (we saw a number of examples in the previous section). A function object is a class that overloads the function call operator (operator()). The operator encapsulates what normally would be implemented as a function. A function object is typically passed as an argument to a generic algorithm, although we can also define individual function objects. For example, if the class AddImages were defined as a function object to take two images, composite them (that is, add the two together) and then return a new image, we might declare an instance of it as follows:

```
AddImages AI;
```

To have the function object perform its operation, we apply the call operator, providing the necessary Image class operands. For example:

```
Image im1("foreground.tiff"), im2("background.tiff");
// ...

// invokes Image AddImages::operator()(const Image&,const Image&);
Image new_image = AI( im1, im2 );
```

The benefits of a function object over a pointer to function are twofold. First, if the overloaded call operator is an inline function, the compiler is able to perform the inlining, providing a possibly significant efficiency gain. Second, the function object can hold an arbitrary amount of additional data, either cached results or data to help in the current operation.

Here is our revised implementation of min() (note that a pointer to function can also be passed using this declaration, but without any checking of its prototype):

```
template < typename Type,
           typename Comp >
const Type&
min( const Type *p, int size, Comp comp )
{
      int minIndex = 0;
      for ( int ix = 1; ix < size; ++ix )
            if ( Comp( p[ ix ], p[ minIndex ] ))
                  minIndex = ix;
      return p[ minIndex ];
}
```

The generic algorithms in general support both forms of applying an operation: use of the built-in (or possibly overloaded) operator and use of a pointer to function or function object to perform the operation.

Where do function objects come from? In general, there are three sources of function objects.

- A set of arithmetic, relational, and logical function objects is predefined by the standard library.

- A set of predefined function adaptors allows us to specialize or extend the predefined function objects (or, for that matter, any function object).

- We can define our own function objects, to be passed to the generic algorithms and possibly against which to apply the function adaptors.

In this section, we look at each of these three function object sources in turn.

12.3.1 The Predefined Function Objects

The predefined function objects are divided into arithmetic, relational, and logical operations. Each object is a class template parameterized on the type of the operands. To use any of them, we must include the following header file:

```
#include <functional>
```

For example, the function object supporting addition is a class template named plus. To define an instance that can add two integers, we write

```
#include <functional>
plus< int > intAdd;
```

To invoke the addition operation, we apply the overloaded call operator to intAdd, just as we did in the previous section for our AddImage class:

```
int ival1 = 10, ival2 = 20;

// equivalent of int sum = ival1 + ival2;
int sum = intAdd( ival1, ival2 );
```

The class template plus implementation invokes the addition operator associated with the type of its parameter int. The primary use of this and the other predefined class function objects is as arguments to the generic algorithms, usually to override the default operation. For example, by default, sort() orders the elements of a container in ascending order using the less-than operator of the underlying element type. To sort the container in descending order, we pass the predefined class template greater, which invokes the greater-than operator of the underlying element type:

```
vector< string > svec;
// ...
sort( svec.begin(), svec.end(), greater<string>() );
```

The predefined function objects are listed in the following subsections broken into arithmetic, relational, and logical categories. Each one is illustrated both as a named object and as an unnamed object passed to a function. We use the following object definitions, including a simple class definition (operator overloading is discussed in detail in Chapter 15):

```
class Int {
public:
   Int( int ival = 0 ) : _val( ival ){}

   int operator-()         { return -_val;        }
   int operator%(int ival) { return _val % ival; }

   bool operator<(int ival){ return _val < ival; }
   bool operator!()        { return _val == 0;   }
private:
   int _val;
};

vector< string > svec;
string  sval1, sval2, sres;
complex cval1, cval2, cres;
int     ival1, ival2, ires;
Int     Ival1, Ival2, Ires;
double  dval1, dval2, dres;
```

In addition, we define the following two function templates into which we pass the various unnamed function objects:

```
template <class FuncObject, class Type>
    Type UnaryFunc( FuncObject fob, const Type &val )
        { return fob( val ); }
```

```
template <class FuncObject, class Type>
    Type BinaryFunc( FuncObject fob,
                          const Type &val1, const Type &val2 )
        { return fob( val1, val2 ); }
```

12.3.2 The Arithmetic Function Objects

The predefined arithmetic function objects support addition, subtraction, multiplication, division, modulus, and negation. The operator invoked is the instance associated with `Type`. For a class type providing overloaded instances of the operator, that instance is invoked.

- Addition: `plus<Type>`

```
plus<string> stringAdd;

// invokes string::operator+()
sres = stringAdd( sval1, sval2 );
dres = BinaryFunc( plus<double>(), dval1, dval2 );
```

- Subtraction: `minus<Type>`

```
minus<int> intSub;
ires = intSub( ival1, ival2 );
dres = BinaryFunc( minus<double>(), dval1, dval2 );
```

- Multiplication: `multiplies<Type>`

```
multiplies<complex> complexMultiplies;
cres = complexMultiplies( cval1, cval2 );
dres = BinaryFunc( multiplies<double>(), dval1, dval2 );
```

- Division: `divides<Type>`

```
divides<int> intDivides;
ires = intDivides( ival1, ival2 );
dres = BinaryFunc( divides<double>(), dval1, dval2 );
```

- Modulus: `modulus<Type>`

```
modulus<Int> IntModulus;
Ires = IntModulus( Ival1, Ival2 );
ires = BinaryFunc( modulus<int>(), ival2, ival1 );
```

- Negation: `negate<Type>`

```
negate<int> intNegate;
ires = intNegate( ires );
Ires = UnaryFunc( negate<Int>(), Ival1 );
```

12.3.3 The Relational Function Objects

The predefined relational function objects support equality, inequality, greater than, greater than or equal, less than, and less than or equal.

- Equality: equal_to<Type>

```
equal_to<string> stringEqual;
sres = stringEqual( sval1, sval2 );
ires = count_if( svec.begin(), svec.end(),
                 equal_to<string>(), sval1 );
```

- Inequality: not_equal_to<Type>

```
not_equal_to<complex> complexNotEqual;
cres = complexNotEqual( cval1, cval2 );
ires = count_if( svec.begin(), svec.end(),
                 not_equal_to<string>(), sval1 );
```

- Greater than: greater<Type>

```
greater<int> intGreater;
ires = intGreater( ival1, ival2 );
ires = count_if( svec.begin(), svec.end(),
                 greater<string>(), sval1 );
```

- Greater than or equal: greater_equal<Type>

```
greater_equal<double> doubleGreaterEqual;
dres = doubleGreaterEqual( dval1, dval2 );
ires = count_if( svec.begin(), svec.end(),
                 greater_equal<string>(), sval1 );
```

- Less than: less<Type>

```
less<Int> IntLess;
Ires = IntLess( Ival1, Ival2 );
ires = count_if( svec.begin(), svec.end(),
                 less<string>(), sval1 );
```

- Less than or equal: less_equal<Type>

```
less_equal<int> intLessEqual;
ires = intLessEqual( ival1, ival2 );
ires = count_if( svec.begin(), svec.end(),
                 less_equal<string>(), sval1 );
```

12.3.4 The Logical Function Objects

The predefined logical function objects support logical And (returns true if both of its operands evaluate as true — applies the && operator associated with Type), logical Or (returns true if either of its operands evaluate as true — applies the || operator associated with Type), and logical Not (returns true if its operand evaluates as false — applies the ! operator associated with Type).

- Logical And: logical_and<Type>

```
logical_and<int> intAnd;
ires = intAnd( ival1, ival2 );
dres = BinaryFunc( logical_and<double>(), dval1, dval2 );
```

- Logical Or: logical_or<Type>

```
logical_or<int> intSub;
ires = intSub( ival1, ival2 );
dres = BinaryFunc( logical_or<double>(), dval1, dval2 );
```

- Logical Not: logical_not<Type>

```
logical_not<Int> IntNot;
Ires = IntNot( Ival1, Ival2 );
dres = UnaryFunc( logical_not<double>(), dval1 );
```

12.3.5 Function Adaptors for Function Objects

The standard library also provides a set of function adaptors with which to specialize and extend both unary and binary function objects. The adaptors are special classes divided into the following two categories.

1. Binders: a binder is a function adaptor that converts a binary function object into a unary object by binding one of the arguments to a particular value. For example, to count all the elements within a container that are less than or equal to 10, we would pass count_if() a less_equal function object with one of its arguments bound to 10. In the following section we'll look at how we do that.

2. Negators: a negator is a function adaptor that reverses the truth value of a function object. For example, to count all the elements within a container that are greater than 10, we could pass count_if() the negator of our less_equal function object with one of its arguments bound to 10. Of course, in this case, it is considerably more straightforward to simply pass a binder of the greater function object with one of its arguments bound to 10.

There are two predefined binder adaptors provided by the standard library: bind1st and bind2nd. As you might expect, bind1st binds the value to the first argument of the binary function object, and bind2nd binds the value to the second. For example, to count all the elements within a container that are less than or equal to 10, we would pass count_if() the following:

```
count_if( vec.begin(), vec.end(),
          bind2nd( less_equal<int>(), 10 ));
```

There are two predefined negator adaptors provided by the standard library: not1 and not2. Again, as you might expect, not1 reverses the truth value of a unary predicate function object, and not2 reverses the truth value of a binary predicate function. To negate our binding of the less_equal function object, we would write the following:

```
count_if( vec.begin(), vec.end(),
          not1( bind2nd( less_equal<int>(), 10 )));
```

We'll see more examples of using both binders and negators in the Appendix, in which examples of using each generic algorithm are found.

12.3.6 Implementing a Function Object

We've already defined a number of function objects in support of our program implementation in Section 12.2. In this section, we walk through the steps and variations for defining class function objects. (Chapter 13 covers in detail the general definition of a class; Chapter 15 discusses operator overloading.)

The simplest form of a function object class definition consists of the overloaded function call operator. For example, here is a unary function object that determines whether a value is less than or equal to 10:

```
// simplest form of Function Object class
class less_equal_ten {
public:
    bool operator() ( int val )
        { return val <= 10;  }
};
```

We can now use this object in the same way that we use the predefined function objects. For example, here is a revised invocation of count_if() using our function object:

```
count_if( vec.begin(), vec.end(), less_equal_ten() );
```

This class is admittedly pretty limited. We can apply a negator to count all the elements within the container that are greater than 10:

```
count_if( vec.begin(), vec.end(),
          not1(less_equal_ten()));
```

Alternatively, we can expand our implementation by allowing the user to provide a value against which to compare each container element. One method of doing this is

to introduce a data member to store the value to be compared, along with a constructor
to initialize the member to the user-specified value:

```
class less_equal_value {
public:
   less_equal_value( int val ) : _val( val ){}
   bool operator() ( int val ) { return val <= _val; }

private:
   int _val;
};
```

We can now use this object to specify an arbitrary integer value. For example, the
following invocation counts the number of elements less than or equal to 25.

```
count_if( vec.begin(), vec.end(), less_equal_value( 25 ));
```

An alternative class implementation without the use of a constructor would be to
parameterize the class based on the value to be compared. For example:

```
template < int _val >
class less_equal_value {
public:
   bool operator() ( int val ){ return val <= _val; }
};
```

Here is how we would invoke this class to count the number of elements less than
or equal to 25.

```
count_if( vec.begin(), vec.end(), less_equal_value<25>());
```

We'll see more examples of defining our own function objects in the Appendix, in
which examples of using each generic algorithm are presented.

Exercise 12.4

Using the predefined function objects and function adaptors, create a function object
to do the following:

```
(a) Find all values that are greater than 1024.
(b) Find all strings that are not equal to "pooh".
(c) Multiply all values by 2.
```

Exercise 12.5

Define a function object to evaluate three objects and return the middle value. Define
a function to do the same operation. Show examples of using each object directly and
by passing each to a function. Compare and contrast the behavior of each.

12.4   Revisiting Iterators

The following function template implementation does not compile. Can you see why?

```
// this fails to compile as implemented
template < typename type >
int
count( const vector< type > &vec, type value )
{
    int count = 0;
    vector< type >::iterator iter = vec.begin();
    while ( iter != vec.end() ) {
            if ( *iter == value )
                ++count; ++iter; }
    return count;
}
```

The problem is that vec is a const reference, but we are attempting to bind a non-const iterator to it. Were this permitted, nothing would prevent us from subsequently modifying the elements of the vector through the iterator. To prevent that, the language requires that an iterator bound to the const vector be a const iterator. We do that as follows:

```
// ok: this compiles without error
vector< type >::const_iterator iter = vec.begin();
```

This requirement that a const container be bound only to a const iterator parallels the behavior of permitting a const pointer to address only a const array. In both cases, the language seeks to guarantee that the contents of the const container do not change.

Both the begin() and the end() operations are overloaded to return either a const or non-const iterator depending on the const-ness of the container. For example, given the following pair of declarations

```
vector< int > vec0;
const vector< int > vec1;
```

the begin() and end() invocations on vec0 return a non-const iterator, whereas those on vec1 return a const iterator:

```
vector< int >::iterator iter0 = vec0.begin();
vector< int >::const_iterator iter1 = vec1.begin();
```

Of course, it is always permissible to assign a non-const iterator to a const iterator. For example:

```
// ok: initializing a non-const iterator to a const
vector< int >::const_iterator iter2 = vec0.begin();
```

12.4.1 Insert Iterators

Here is another program fragment with a serious but subtle problem. Do you see the problem?

```
int ia[] = { 0, 1, 1, 2, 3, 5, 5, 8 };
vector< int > ivec( ia, ia+8 ), vres;
// ...

// results in undefined run-time behavior ...
unique_copy( ivec.begin(), ivec.end(), vres.begin() );
```

The problem here is that vres has been allocated no space to hold the eight integer values being copied into it from ivec. The unique_copy() algorithm uses assignment to copy each element value, but the assignment will fail because there is no space available within vres.

One strategy would be to provide two versions of the unique_copy() algorithm: one that assigns the elements and a second one that inserts them. The insertion instance would in turn need to support alternative instances for inserting the elements at the front or back or at some arbitrary position within the container.

An alternative strategy, and the one adopted by the standard library, is to define a set of three insert iterator adaptor functions that return special insert iterators:

- back_inserter(), which causes the container's push_back() insert operation to be invoked in place of the assignment operator. The argument to back _inserter() is the container itself. For example, we can correct our unique_copy() invocation by writing

  ```
  // ok: unique_copy() now inserts using vres.push_back() ...
  unique_copy( ivec.begin(), ivec.end(),
               back_inserter( vres ) );
  ```

- front_inserter(), which causes the container's push_front() insert operation to be invoked in place of the assignment operator. The argument to front_inserter() is also the container itself. Note, however, that the vector class does not support a push_front() operation, and the attempt to use it on a vector is an error:

  ```
  // oops, error:
  // vector does not support a push_front() operation
  // use either a deque or a list container
  unique_copy( ivec.begin(), ivec.end(),
               front_inserter( vres ) );
  ```

- inserter(), which causes the container's insert() insert operation to be invoked in place of the assignment operator. inserter() takes two arguments: the container itself and an iterator into the container indicating the position at which insertion should begin. For example:

  ```
  unique_copy( ivec.begin(), ivec.end(),
               inserter( vres, vres.begin() ) );
  ```

The iterator marking the position to begin insertion does not remain fixed but instead is incremented with each element that is inserted so that each element is inserted in turn. It is as if we had written

```
vector< int >::iterator iter = vres.begin(),
                iter2 = ivec.begin();

for ( ; iter2 != ivec.end(); ++iter, ++iter2 )
    vres.insert( iter, *iter2 );
```

12.4.2 Reverse Iterators

The begin() and end() operations return, respectively, an iterator to the first element of the container and an iterator to 1 past the last element of the container. It is also possible to return a reverse iterator: one that traverses the container from the last element to the first. The operations supporting that capability for all the container types are rbegin() and rend(). As with forward iterators, there are both a const and a non-const instance.

```
vector< int > vec0;
const vector< int > vec1;

vector< int >::reverse_iterator r_iter0 = vec0.rbegin();
vector< int >::const_reverse_iterator r_iter1 = vec1.rbegin();
```

A reverse iterator is traversed in the same manner as a forward iterator. The difference is in the implementation of the next (and previous) operators. For a forward iterator, ++ accesses the next element in the container; for a reverse iterator, it accesses the previous element. For example, to traverse a vector backward, one would write

```
// reverse iterator of vector from back to front
vector< type >::reverse_iterator r_iter;
for ( r_iter = vec0.rbegin(); // binds r_iter to last element
      r_iter != vec0.rend();   // not equal 1 past 1st element
      r_iter++ )               // decrements! iterator one element
{ /* ... */ }
```

Although it may seem confusing to have the meaning of the increment and decrement operators reversed, it lets the programmer transparently pass a pair of reverse iterators to an algorithm. For example, to sort our vector in descending order, we simply pass sort() a pair of reverse iterators, as follows:

```
// sorts vector in ascending order
sort( vec0.begin(), vec0.end() );

// sorts vector in descending order
sort( vec0.rbegin(), vec0.rend() );
```

12.4.3 iostream Iterators

The standard library provides support for both input and output iostream iterators to work in conjunction with the standard library container types and generic algorithms. The istream_iterator class supports iterator operations on an istream or one of its derived classes, such as an ifstream input file stream. Similarly, the ostream_iterator supports iterator operations on an ostream or one of its derived classes, such as an ofstream output file stream. To use either iterator, the iterator header file must be included:

```
#include <iterator>
```

For example, in the following program, we use an istream iterator to read a collection of integers from standard input into a vector and then use an ostream iterator as the target of the unique_copy() generic algorithm.

```
#include <iostream>
#include <iterator>
#include <algorithm>
#include <vector>
#include <functional>

/*
 * input:
 * 23 109 45 89 6 34 12 90 34 23 56 23 8 89 23
 *
 * output:
 * 109 90 89 56 45 34 23 12 8 6
 */

int main()
{
        istream_iterator< int > input( cin );
        istream_iterator< int > end_of_stream;

        vector<int> vec;
        copy ( input, end_of_stream, inserter( vec, vec.begin() ));

        sort( vec.begin(), vec.end(), greater<int>() );

        ostream_iterator< int > output( cout, " " );
        unique_copy( vec.begin(), vec.end(), output );
}
```

12.4.4 istream_iterator

An istream_iterator is declared using the following general form:[1]

```
istream_iterator<Type> identifier( istream& );
```

where Type represents any built-in or user-defined class type for which an input operator is defined. The argument to the constructor can be either an istream class object, such as cin, or any publicly derived istream subtype, such as ifstream. For example:

```
#include <iterator>
#include <fstream>
#include <string>
#include <complex>

// read a sequence of complex objects from standard input
istream_iterator< complex > is_complex( cin );

// read a sequence of strings from a named file
ifstream infile( "C++Primer" );
istream_iterator< string > is_string( infile );
```

Each application of the increment operator on an istream_iterator object reads the next element of the input stream using operator>>(). To read the input stream through an istream_iterator through a generic algorithm, we need to provide an iterator pair indicating the begin and end positions within the file. The istream_iterator initialized with an istream object, such as is_string, provides the beginning position. To define the ending position, we use the special istream_iterator default constructor:

```
// constructs an end-of-stream iterator to serve as
// the end marker of the iterator pair ...
istream_iterator< string > end_of_stream;

vector<string> text;

// ok: provide the iterator pair
copy( is_string, end_of_stream,
      inserter( text, text.begin() ));
```

---

1. If your compiler does not yet support default values for template parameters, then you will need to provide an explicit second argument to the istream_iterator constructor: the difference_type of the container into which the elements are to be placed. The difference_type is the type capable of holding the result of subtracting two iterators of a container. For example, in Section 12.2, in the presentation of the program run under a compiler not yet supporting default values for template parameters, we wrote

```
typedef vector<string,allocator>::difference_type diff_type;
istream_iterator< string, diff_type > input_set1( infile1 ), eos;
istream_iterator< string, diff_type > input_set2( infile2 );
```

Under a fully compliant Standard C++ compiler, we would simply write the following:

```
istream_iterator< string > input_set1( infile1 ), eos;
istream_iterator< string > input_set2( infile2 );
```

12.4.5 ostream_iterator

An ostream_iterator is declared using one of the following two general forms:

```
ostream_iterator<Type> identifier( ostream& )
ostream_iterator<Type> identifier( ostream&, char* delimiter )
```

where Type represents any built-in or user-defined class type for which an output operator (operator>>) is defined. The delimiter represents a C-style character string that is output to the file following each element. Because it is a C-style string, it must be null-terminated; otherwise, the behavior is undefined (it'll likely blow up at run-time). The ostream argument can be either an actual ostream class object, such as cout, or any publicly derived ostream subtype, such as an ofstream. For example:

```
#include <iterator>
#include <fstream>
#include <string>
#include <complex>

// write a sequence of complex objects to standard output
// separating each element by a space
ostream_iterator< complex > os_complex( cout, " " );

// write a sequence of strings to a named file
// placing each on a separate line
ofstream outfile( "dictionary" );
ostream_iterator< string > os_string( outfile, "\n" );
```

Here is a simple example of reading standard input and echoing it to standard output using unnamed stream iterator objects and the generic copy() algorithm.

```
#include <iterator>
#include <algorithm>
#include <iostream>

int main()
{
    copy( istream_iterator< int >( cin ),
          istream_iterator< int >(),
          ostream_iterator< int >( cout ));
}
```

Finally, here is a small program that opens a file specified by the user, echoing it to standard output, again using the copy() algorithm and an ostream_iterator:

```
#include <string>
#include <algorithm>
#include <fstream>
#include <iterator>
```

```
int main()
{
    string file_name;
    cout << "please enter a file to open: ";
    cin >> file_name;

    if ( file_name.empty() || !cin ) {
        cerr << "unable to read file name\n"; return -1;
    }

    ifstream infile( file_name.c_str());
    if ( ! infile ) {
        cerr << "unable to open " << file_name << endl;
        return -2;
    }

    istream_iterator< string > ins( infile ), eos;
    ostream_iterator< string > outs( cout, " " );

    copy( ins, eos, outs );
}
```

12.4.6 The Five Categories of Iterators

To support the full set of generic algorithms, the standard library defines five categories of iterators based on the set of operations they provide: InputIterators, OutputIterators, ForwardIterators, BidirectionalIterators, and RandomAccessIterators. The following is a brief discussion of their characteristics.

1. An InputIterator can be used to read the elements of a container but is not guaranteed to support writing into a container. An InputIterator must provide the following minimum support (iterators that provide additional support can also be used as InputIterators provided that they meet this minimum requirement set): the testing of two iterators for both equality and inequality, the forward incrementing of the iterator to address a next element using the prefix and postfix instances of operator (++), and the reading of an element through use of the dereference operator (*). Generic algorithms requiring this level of support include `find()`, `accumulate()`, and `equal()`. Any algorithm requiring the support of an InputIterator can also be passed any of the iterator categories listed in items 3, 4, and 5.

2. An OutputIterator can be thought of as having the opposite functionality of an InputIterator; that is, it can be used to write into the elements of a container but is not guaranteed to support the reading of a container. OutputIterators are generally used as a third argument to an algorithm and mark the position where writing should begin. `copy()`, for example, takes an OutputIterator as a

third argument. Again, any algorithm requiring the support of an OutputIterator can be passed any of the iterator categories listed in items 3, 4, and 5.

3. A ForwardIterator can be used to read from and write to a container in one direction of traversal (yes, the next category supports bidirectional traversal). Generic algorithms minimally requiring a ForwardIterator include `adjacent _find()`, `swap_range()`, and `replace()`. Of course, any algorithm requiring the support of a ForwardIterator can also be passed the iterator categories defined by items 4 and 5.

4. A BidirectionalIterator reads from and writes to a container in both directions. Generic algorithms minimally requiring a BidirectionalIterator include `in place_merge()`, `next_permutation()`, and `reverse()`.

5. A RandomAccessIterator, in addition to supporting all the functionality of a BidirectionalIterator, provides access to any position within the container in constant time. Generic algorithms requiring a RandomAccessIterator include `binary_search()`, `sort_heap()`, and `nth_element()`.

A map, a set, and a list maintain bidirectional iterators. This means, in effect, that they cannot be used with the generic algorithms requiring a RandomAccessIterator, such as `sort_heap()` and `nth_element()`; we'll look at alternative operations available to the list container in Section 12.6. A vector and a deque maintain random access iterators and can therefore be used with all the generic algorithms.

Exercise 12.6

Explain why each of the following is incorrect. Identify which errors are caught during compilation.

```
(a) const vector<string> file_names( sa, sa+6 );
    vector<string>::iterator it = file_names.begin()+2;

(b) const vector<int> ivec;
    fill( ivec.begin(), ivec.end(), ival );

(c) sort( ivec.begin(), ivec.rend() );

(d) list<int> ilist( ia, ia+6 );
    binary_search( ilist.begin(), ilist.end() );

(e) sort( ivec1.begin(), ivec2.end() );
```

Exercise 12.7

Write a program to read a sequence of integer numbers from standard input using an istream_iterator. Write the odd numbers into one file using an ostream_iterator. Each value should be separated by a space. Write the even numbers into a second file also using an ostream_iterator. Each of these values should be placed on a separate line.

12.5   The Generic Algorithms

The first two arguments to all the generic algorithms (with the necessary fistful of exceptions that make the rule) are a pair of iterators, generally referred to as first and last, marking the range of elements within the container or built-in array over which to operate. The element range notation (sometimes called a *left-inclusive interval*) is usually written as

```
// to be read as: includes first and
// each element up to but not including last
[ first, last )
```

indicating that the range begins with first and ends with but does not include last. When

```
first == last
```

the range is said to be empty.

A requirement of the iterator pair is that it must be possible to reach last beginning with first through repeated application of the increment operator. However, the compiler cannot itself enforce this; failure to meet this requirement results in undefined run-time behavior — usually an eventual core dump of the program.

Each algorithm's declaration indicates the minimum category of iterator support it requires (see Section 12.4 for a brief discussion of the five iterator categories). find(), for example — which implements a one-pass, read-only traversal over a container — minimally requires an InputIterator. It can also be passed a Forward-, Bidirectional-, or RandomAccessIterator. Passing it an OutputIterator results in an error. Errors in passing an invalid category of iterator to an algorithm are not guaranteed to be caught at compile-time, because the iterator categories are not actual types. Rather, they are type parameters passed to the function template.

Some algorithms support multiple versions; one uses a built-in operator, and a second accepts either a function object or a pointer to function providing an alternative implementation of that operator. unique(), for example, by default compares two adjacent elements using the equality operator of the underlying element type of the container. If, however, the underlying element type does not provide an equality operator or if we wish to define element equality differently, we can pass either a function object or pointer to a function that provides the intended semantics. Other algorithms, however, are separated into two uniquely named instances, the predicate instance in each case ending with the suffix _if, as in find_if(). For example, there is a replace() instance using the built-in equality operator and a replace_if() instance taking a predicate function object or a pointer to function.

For those algorithms that modify the container over which they operate, there are generally two versions: an in-place version that changes the container against which it is applied and a version that returns a copy of the container with the changes applied. There are, for example, both a `replace()` and a `replace_copy()` algorithm. The copy version always contains `_copy` in its name. Not every algorithm that transforms its associated container, however, is provided with a copy version. The `sort()` algorithms, for example, do not provide a copy instance. In this case, if we wish the algorithm to operate on a copy, we need to make and pass the copy ourselves.

To use any of the generic algorithms, we must include the associated header file:

```
#include <algorithm>
```

To use any of the four numeric algorithms — `adjacent_difference()`, `accumulate()`, `inner_product()`, and `partial_sum()` — we must include

```
#include <numeric>
```

The algorithms are listed under the following nine categories (the categories are for convenience in presenting the algorithms and have no formal connection with the standard library). The Appendix provides an alphabetical discussion and illustration of each algorithm in turn.

12.5.1 Search Algorithms

The 13 search algorithms provide various strategies for determining whether a value is present within a container. The three algorithms `equal_range()`, `lower_bound()`, and `upper_bound()` provide a form of binary search. They indicate where in the container a value can be inserted and still preserve the sorted ordering of the container.

```
adjacent_find(), binary_search(), count(), count_if(), equal_range(),
find(), find_end(), find_first_of(), find_if(), lower_bound(),
upper_bound(), search(), search_n()
```

12.5.2 Sorting and General Ordering Algorithms

The 14 sorting and general ordering algorithms provide various strategies for ordering the elements of a container. A partition divides the container into two groups. The first group consists of those elements that satisfy some condition; the second, those that do not. For example, we can partition a container based on whether the elements are odd or even or whether a word begins with a capital letter. A stable algorithm maintains the relative order of elements that either are of equal value or that equally meet some condition. For example, given the sequence

```
{ "pshew", "honey", "Tigger", "Pooh" }
```

a stable partition based on whether a word begins with a capital letter generates the sequence in which the relative order of the two word categories is maintained:

```
{ "Tigger", "Pooh", "pshew", "honey" }
```

This is not guaranteed with the unstable instance of the algorithm. (Note that the sort algorithms cannot be used with a list or the associative containers, such as a set or map.)

```
inplace_merge(), merge(), nth_element(), partial_sort(),
partial_sort_copy(), partition(), random_shuffle(), reverse(),
reverse_copy(), rotate(), rotate_copy(), sort(), stable_sort(),
stable_partition()
```

12.5.3   Deletion and Substitution Algorithms

The 15 delete and substitute algorithms provide various strategies to replace or remove one or a range of elements. `unique()` removes adjacent equal elements. `iter_swap()` exchanges the values of the elements addressed by the pair of iterators; it does not change the iterators themselves.

```
copy(), copy_backwards(), iter_swap(), remove(), remove_copy(),
remove_if(), remove_copy_if(), replace(), replace_copy(),
replace_if(), replace_copy_if(), swap(), swap_range(), unique(),
unique_copy()
```

12.5.4   Permutation Algorithms

Consider the following sequence of three characters: {a,b,c}. There are six possible permutations on this sequence: abc, acb, bac, bca, cab, and cba. Moreover, these permutations are lexicographically ordered based on the less-than operator. That is, abc is the first permutation. Why? It is because each element is less than the element that follows it. acb is the next permutation, because it is anchored by a, the smallest element in the sequence. Similarly, those permutations that are anchored by b, the second smallest element, come before those that are anchored by c. With the two permutations of bac and bca, bac comes before bca because the sequence ac is less than the sequence ca. Given the permutation bca, we can say that its previous permutation is bac and that its next permutation is cab. There is no previous permutation of the sequence abc, nor is there a next permutation of cba.

```
next_permutation(), prev_permutation()
```

12.5.5   Numeric Algorithms

The following four algorithms provide numeric operations on a container. To use them, we must include the <numeric> header file.

```
accumulate(), partial_sum(), inner_product(), adjacent_difference()
```

12.5.6 Generation and Mutation Algorithms

The six generation and mutation algorithms either fill a new sequence or replace an existing sequence with a collection of values.

    fill(), fill_n(),for_each(), generate(), generate_n(), transform().

12.5.7 Relational Algorithms

The seven relational algorithms provide a variety of strategies for comparing one container with another (min() and max() simply compare two elements). lexicographical_compare() provides a dictionary ordering (see the later discussion of permutations and the discussion in the Appendix).

        equal(), includes(), lexicographical_compare(), max(), max_element(),
        min(), min_element(), mismatch()

12.5.8 Set Algorithms

The four set algorithms provide general set operations on any container type. Union creates a sorted sequence of the elements within the two containers. Intersection creates a sorted sequence of elements present in both containers. Difference creates a sorted sequence of elements present in the first container but not in the second. Symmetric difference creates a sorted sequence of elements present in either container but not in both.

        set_union(), set_intersection(), set_difference(),
        set_symmetric_difference()

12.5.9 Heap Algorithms

A heap is a form of binary tree represented as an array. The standard library provides a max-heap representation in which the key value in each node is either larger than or equal to the key value of its children.

        make_heap(), pop_heap(), push_heap(), sort_heap()

12.6   When Not to Use the Generic Algorithms

The associative containers, such as maps or sets, internally maintain their elements in an ordered relationship to allow for fast lookup and retrieval. It is not permitted, therefore, to apply a reordering generic algorithm, such as sort() or partition(), to an associative container. If we should need to reorder the elements in an associative container, we must first copy them into a sequential container such as a vector or list.

The list container is a doubly linked list: in addition to the actual data, each element maintains two link members addressing, respectively, the next and previous list elements. The primary advantage of a list is the efficient insertion and deletion of an element or range of elements anywhere within the list. The primary disadvantage is the absence of random element access. For example, although we can write

```
vector<string>::iterator vec_iter = vec.begin() + 7;
```

to initialize vec_iter with the address of a vector's eighth element, it is illegal to write

```
// error: iterator arithmetic is not supported for list
list<string>::iterator list_iter = slist.begin() + 7;
```

because the elements of the list are noncontiguous. To reach the eighth element of a list, we must traverse the intervening links.

Because the list container does not support random access, the merge(), remove(), reverse(), sort(), and unique() generic algorithms are best not used with list objects, although none of these algorithms explicitly requires a RandomAccessIterator. Rather, the specific list member instances of each algorithm are provided (as is a list-specific splice() operation):

- list::merge() merges the sorted list with a second sorted list.
- list::remove() removes elements that equal some value.
- list::remove_if() removes elements that equal some condition.
- list::reverse() reverses the elements of the list.
- list::sort() sorts the elements of the list.
- list::splice() moves the elements of one list into this list.
- list::unique() deletes consecutive copies of an element.

12.6.1 list::merge()

```
void list::merge( list rhs );
template <class Compare>
    void list::merge( list rhs, Compare comp );
```

The elements of the two ordered lists are merged based either on the less-than operator of the underlying element type or a user-specified comparison operation. (Note that the elements of rhs are *moved* into the list object invoking merge(); following the operation, rhs is empty.) For example:

```
int array1[ 10 ] = { 34, 0, 8, 3, 1, 13, 2, 5, 21, 1 };
int array2[ 5 ] =  { 377, 89, 233, 55, 144 };

list< int > ilist1( array1, array1 + 10 );
list< int > ilist2( array2, array2+5 );

// merge requires that both lists be ordered
ilist1.sort(); ilist2.sort();
ilist1.merge( ilist2 );
```

After the `merge()` operation is applied, `ilist2` is empty; `ilist1` contains the first 15 elements of the Fibonacci sequence in ascending order.

12.6.2 list::remove()

```
void list::remove( const elemType &value );
```

The `remove()` operation deletes all instances of the specified value. For example:

```
ilist1.remove( 1 );
```

12.6.3 list::remove_if()

```
template < class Predicate >
    void list::remove_if( Predicate pred );
```

The `remove_if()` operation removes all elements for which the specified condition returns true. For example,

```
class Even {
public:
       bool operator()( int elem ) { return ! ( elem % 2 ); }
};

ilist1.remove_if( Even() );
```

removes all even elements in the list object defined in the discussion of `merge()`.

12.6.4 list::reverse()

```
void list::reverse();
```

The `reverse()` operation reverses the order of list elements.

```
ilist1.reverse();
```

12.6.5 list::sort()

```
void list::sort();
template <class Compare>
    void list::sort( Compare comp );
```

By default, the `sort()` operation places the elements of the list in ascending order based on the less-than operator of the underlying element type. An alternative comparison operator can be specified as an argument. For example,

```
list1.sort();
```

orders `list1` in ascending order, whereas

```
list1.sort( greater<int>() );
```

orders `list1` in descending order using the greater-than operator.

12.6.6 list::splice()

```
void list::splice( iterator pos, list rhs );
void list::splice( iterator pos, list rhs, iterator ix );
void list::splice( iterator pos, list rhs,
                   iterator first, iterator last );
```

The splice() operator moves one or a range of elements from one list to another. There are three forms: splice all the elements of one list onto another, splice a range of elements contained in one list onto another, and move a single element within one list onto another. In each form, an iterator is provided that indicates the location where the element or range of element is to be inserted. The elements are spliced immediately preceding the location. For example, given the following two lists

```
int array[ 10 ] = { 0, 1, 1, 2, 3, 5, 8, 13, 21, 34 };
list< int > ilist1( array, array + 10 );
list< int > ilist2( array, array+2 ); // contains 0, 1
```

the following use of splice() moves the first element of ilist1 into ilist2. ilist2 now contains the elements 0, 1, and 0, whereas ilist1 no longer contains 0:

```
// ilist2.end() indicates position to splice element
// the elements spliced precede that location
// ilist1 indicates the list from which element is to be moved
// ilist1.begin() indicates which element to move

ilist2.splice( ilist2.end(), ilist1, ilist1.begin() )
```

In the next use of splice(), two iterators are passed indicating a subrange of elements to move:

```
list< int >::iterator first, last;

first = ilist1.find( 2 );
last  = ilist1.find( 13 );
ilist2.splice( ilist2.begin(), ilist1, first, last );
```

In this case, the elements 2, 3, 5, and 8 are moved from ilist1 and spliced into the front of ilist2. ilist1 now contains the five elements 1, 1, 13, 21, and 34. To move these last elements into ilist2, we can use the final form of the splice() operator:

```
list< int >::iterator pos = ilist2.find( 5 );
ilist2.splice( pos, ilist1 );
```

ilist1 is now empty. The remaining five elements are spliced into ilist2 immediately preceding the position of the element value 5.

12.6.7 list::unique()

```
void list::unique();
template <class BinaryPredicate>
    void list::unique( BinaryPredicate pred );
```

The unique() operation removes duplicate adjacent copies. By default, it applies the equality operator of the underlying type. For example, given the values {0,2,4,6,4,2,0}, applying unique() results in exactly the same list of seven elements because there are no adjacent duplicate elements. If we first sort the list, yielding {0,0,2,2,4,4,6}, the result of applying unique() is the four unique values {0,2,4,6}.

```
ilist.unique();
```

A second form of unique() accepts an alternative comparison operator. For example,

```
class EvenPair {
public:
      bool operator()( int val1, int val2 )
          { return ! ( val2 % val1 );      }
};

ilist.unique( EvenPair() );
```

removes all adjacent elements in which the second element divides evenly into the first.

These member operations should be used in preference to their generic algorithm counterparts when applied to a list object. The other generic algorithms, such as find(), transform(), for_each(), and so on, execute equally efficiently on list objects (again, the individual generic algorithms are discussed in detail in the Appendix).

Exercise 12.8

Reimplement the program of Section 12.2 using a list instead of a vector.

Part IV

Object-Based Programming

Part 4 focuses on object-based programming — that is, the definition and use of the C++ class facility to define new types that can be manipulated as easily as built-in types. By creating new types to describe the problem domain, C++ allows the programmer to write applications that are easier to understand. The class facility allows the programmer to separate the details associated with the underlying implementation of the new type, about which only the implementor of the new type cares, from the definition of the interface and operations that are provided for users of the type. With this separation there is less concern for the various bookkeeping aspects that make programming tedious. Types fundamental to the application can be implemented once and reused. Facilities for encapsulating the data and functions supporting the implementation of the new type can simplify subsequent maintenance and evolution of our applications dramatically.

Chapter 13 focuses on the general class mechanism: how to define a class, the concept of *information hiding* (that is, of a public class interface and private implementation) and how to define and manipulate object instances of a class, as well as a discussion of class scope, nested classes, and classes as members of namespaces. Chapter 14 details the special support C++ provides for the initialization, destruction, and assignment of class objects using special member functions named the *constructor, destructor*, and *copy assignment operator*. We also look at the issue of memberwise initialization and copy, in which one class object is initialized or assigned the value of another object of its class type.

Chapter 15 looks at class-specific operator overloading. Operator overloading allows operands of class types to be used with the built-in operators described in Chapter 4. Operator overloading allows uses of objects of class types to be as intuitive as uses of objects of built-in types. Chapter 15 first presents the general concepts and design considerations of operator overloading, then looks at specific operators, such as the assignment, subscript, call, and the class-specific new and delete operators. It is sometimes necessary to declare an overloaded operator as a friend to a class, with special access permission. This chapter explains why friends are sometimes necessary. The chapter then presents another special kind of class member function, *conversion functions*, which allow the programmer to define a set of standard conversions for class types. These conversion functions are applied implicitly by the compiler when class objects are used as function arguments, or as operands to the built-in or overloaded operators. The chapter concludes with a presentation of the rules for function overload resolution involving class arguments, class member functions, and overloaded operators.

Class templates are the topic of Chapter 16. A class template is a prescription for creating a class in which one or more types or values are parameterized. A vector class, for example, may parameterize the type of the elements it contains. A buffer class may parameterize not only the type of the elements it holds, but the size of its buffer as well. This chapter discusses how to define a class template and how to create specific instances of a class template. The support for C++ classes is reviewed in the light of templates, thus member functions, friend declarations, and nested types are discussed. The chapter also revisits the template compilation model discussed in Chapter 10 to illustrate how it affects class templates.

13

Classes

The C++ class mechanism allows users to define their own data types. For this reason, classes are often called *user-defined types*. A class may add functionality to an already existing type — such as the IntArray class introduced in Chapter 2, which provides more functionality than the type array of ints. Classes can also be used to introduce altogether new types, such as a Screen class or an Account class. Classes are typically used to define abstractions that do not map naturally to the built-in data types.

In this chapter we see how to define class types and how to use class objects. We see how the class definition introduces both the class data members that define the internal representation of the class, and the class member functions that define the set of operations that may be applied to objects of class type. We show how *information hiding* is used within the class definition to declare the internal representation and implementation of a class as private, whereas the operations to be performed on class objects by the program are public. The private internal representation is said to be *encapsulated*, and the public portion of the class is referred to as the *class interface*.

The chapter then looks at a special kind of class members: *static members*. We then look at how pointers to members can be used to refer to class data members or member functions. We also introduce unions, which are a special kind of class type for overlaying objects of different types. The chapter concludes with a discussion on class scope and name resolution in class scope. These topics are reviewed for the different kinds of classes that can be defined: nested classes, classes as namespace members, and local classes.

13.1 Class Definition

A class definition has two parts: the *class head*, composed of the keyword class followed by the class name; and the *class body*, enclosed by a pair of curly braces. A class definition must be followed either by a semicolon or a list of declarations. For example:

```
class Screen { /* ... */ };
class Screen { /* ... */ } myScreen, yourScreen;
```

Within the class body, the class data members and member functions are declared, and the access levels of these class members are specified. The class body defines the *class member list*.

Each class definition introduces a different class type. Even if two class types have exactly the same member list, they are nonetheless different types. For example:

```
class First {
    int memi;
    double memd;
};

class Second {
    int memi;
    double memd;
};

class First obj1;
Second obj2 = obj1; // error: obj1 and obj2 have different types
```

A class body defines a scope. The declarations of the class members within the class body introduce the member names into the scope of their class. If two classes have members with the same name, the program is not in error and the members refer to different objects. We look at class scope in more detail in Section 13.9.

After a class type has been introduced, this class type can be referred to in two ways:

1. Specifying the keyword class followed by the class name. In the previous example, the declaration of obj1 refers to the class First in this way.
2. Only specifying the class name. In the previous example, the declaration of obj2 refers to the class Second in this way.

Both methods of referring to a class type are equivalent. The first method is borrowed from C and is also valid in C++ to refer to class types in declarations; the second method was introduced in C++ to make class types easier to use in declarations.

13.1.1 Data Members

The class data members are declared in the same way variables are declared. For example, the Screen class may have the following data members:

```
#include <string>
class Screen {
    string              _screen;    // string( _height * _width )
    string::size_type   _cursor;    // current Screen position
    short               _height;    // number of Screen rows
    short               _width;     // number of Screen columns
};
```

Because we have decided to use a string for the internal representation of a Screen class object, the data member _screen is of type string. _cursor is an index into the string data member and it refers to the current Screen position. Its type is

```
string::size_type
```

which is a portable type to hold the value of an index into a string (Section 6.8 introduces size_type).

As with variable declarations, it is not necessary to declare the two members of type short separately. The following definition is an equivalent definition for Screen:

```
class Screen {
/*
 * _screen addresses a string of size _height * _width;
 * _cursor points to current Screen position;
 * _height and _width refer to number of rows and columns.
 */
    string              _screen;
    string::size_type   _cursor;
    short               _height, _width;
};
```

A class data member can be of any type. For example:

```
class StackScreen {
    int topStack;
    void (*handler)();     // pointer to function
    vector<Screen> stack;  // vector of classes
};
```

The data members seen thus far in this subsection are *nonstatic* data members. A class can also have *static* data members. Static data members have special properties, which we examine in Section 13.5.

As we have seen, data member declarations look very much like variable declarations in block scope or in namespace scope. However, except for a minor exception with static data members, a data member cannot be initialized explicitly in the class body. For example:

```
class First {
    int    memi = 0;   // error
    double memd = 0.0; // error
};
```

Class data members are initialized using the class constructor. Class constructors were briefly introduced in Section 2.3. We discuss constructors and class initialization in detail in Chapter 14.

13.1.2   Member Functions

Users will want to perform a wide range of operations on objects of type Screen. A set of cursor movement operations is required. The ability to test and set portions of the screen must be provided. The user should be able to copy one Screen object to another. The user should also be able to set the actual dimensions of the screen at run-time. This set of operations can be implemented with class *member functions*.

The member functions of a class are declared inside the class body. A member function declaration consists of a declaration that looks just like a function declaration that appears in namespace scope. (Recall that the global scope is also a namespace scope. Section 8.2 discusses global functions. Section 8.5 discusses namespaces.) For example:

```
class Screen {
public:
    void home();
    void move( int, int );
    char get();
    char get( int, int );
    bool checkRange( int, int );
    // ...
};
```

The definition of a member function can also be placed inside the class body. For example:

```
class Screen {
public:
    // definitions for home() and get()
    void home() { _cursor = 0; }
    char get()  { return _screen[_cursor]; }
    // ...
};
```

The function home() positions the cursor at the top left-hand corner of the screen. The function get() returns the character value of the current cursor position.

Member functions are distinguished from ordinary functions by the following properties:

- Member functions are declared within the scope of their class. This means that the name of a member function is not visible outside the scope of its class. A member function is referred to using the dot or arrow member access operator as follows:

```
ptrScreen->home();
myScreen.home();
```
Section 13.9 considers class scope in detail.

* Member functions have full access privileges to both the public and private members of the class whereas, in general, ordinary functions have access only to the public members of the class. Of course, the member functions of one class, in general, have no access privileges to the members of another class.

A member function can be an overloaded function (Overloaded functions are presented in Chapter 9). However, a member function only overloads other member functions of its own class. A class member function is unrelated to, and therefore cannot overload, functions declared either in other classes or in namespace scope. The declaration of get(int,int), for example, only overloads the get() member function previously declared in class Screen:

```
class Screen {
public:
    // declarations of overloaded member function get()
    char get() { return _screen[_cursor]; }
    char get( int, int );
    // ...
};
```

We look at class member functions in more detail in Section 13.3.

13.1.3   Member Access

It often happens that the internal representation of a class type is modified subsequent to its initial use by various programs. For example, imagine that a study is conducted of users of our Screen class, and that it is determined that all the Screen class objects defined are of the dimension 80 x 24. In this case it may be desirable to implement a less flexible but more efficient representation for the Screen class, as follows:

```
class Screen {
public:
    // member functions
private:
    // static member initialization discussed in 13.5
    static const int _height = 24;
    static const int _width = 80;
    string            _screen;
    string::size_type _cursor;
};
```

The old implementation for the member functions — that is, how they manipulate the class data members — is not appropriate anymore. The member functions must be reimplemented. This change, however, does not require the interface of the class member functions (their parameter list and return type) to be changed.

If the data members were public and could be accessed by any function of the program, what would be the effect on users of class Screen of this change in the class internal representation?

- Every function that directly accesses the data members of the old Screen representation is broken. It is necessary to locate and rewrite all those portions of code before the program can be used again.

- Because the interface of the member functions has not changed, every function that manipulates the Screen objects only through the Screen member functions requires no change to its working code. However, because the member functions themselves were reimplemented, recompilation of the program is necessary.

Information hiding is a formal mechanism for preventing the functions of a program to access directly the internal representation of a class type. The access restriction to the class members is specified by the labeled *public*, *private*, and *protected* sections within the class body. The keywords `public`, `private`, and `protected` are called *access specifiers*. Members declared within a public section are public members; those declared within a private or protected section are private or protected members.

- A *public member* is accessible from anywhere within a program. A class that enforces information hiding limits its public members to the member functions that define the operations that can be used by the general program to manipulate objects of that class type.

- A *private member* can be accessed only by the member functions and *friends* of its class. A class that enforces information hiding declares its data members as private.

- A *protected member* behaves as a public member to a *derived class*, and behaves as a private member to the rest of the program. (We saw an instance of how protected members are used in the IntArray class in Chapter 2. A full discussion of protected members is deferred until Chapter 17, in which derived classes and the concept of *inheritance* are introduced.)

The following definition of Screen specifies its public and private sections:

```
class Screen {
public:
    void home(){ _cursor = 0; }
    char get() { return _screen[_cursor]; }
    char get( int, int );
    void move( int, int );
    // ...
```

```
private:
   string              _screen;
   string::size_type   _cursor;
   short               _height, _width;
};
```

By convention, the public members of a class are presented first. (For a discussion of why older C++ code presented private members first, and why that style still persists in some quarters, see [LIPPMAN96a].) The private members are listed at the bottom of the class body.

A class may contain multiple public, protected, or private labeled sections. Each section remains in effect until either another section label or the closing right brace of the class body is seen. If no access specifier is specified, by default the section immediately following the opening left brace of the class body is private.

13.1.4   Friends

In some cases it is convenient to allow certain functions to access the private members of a class without allowing access to the entire program. The *friend* mechanism allows a class to grant functions access to its nonpublic members.

A friend declaration begins with the keyword `friend`. It may appear only within a class definition. Since friends are not members of the class granting friendship, they are not affected by the public, private, or protected section in which they are declared within the class body. Here we choose to group all friend declarations immediately following the class head:

```
class Screen {
   friend istream&
      operator>>( istream&, Screen& );
   friend ostream&
      operator<<( ostream&, const Screen& );
public:
   // ... rest of the Screen class
};
```

The input and output operators can now refer directly to the private members of class Screen without error. A simple implementation of the output operator might be as follows:

```
#include <iostream>
ostream& operator<<( ostream& os, const Screen& s )
{
   // ok to refer to _height, _width, and _screen
   os << "<" << s._height
      << "," << s._width << ">";
```

```
    os << s._screen;

    return os;
}
```

A friend may be a namespace function, a member function of another previously defined class, or an entire class. In making one class a friend, all the member functions of the friend class are given access to the nonpublic members of the class granting friendship. (Section 15.2 provides a detailed discussion of friends.)

13.1.5 Class Declaration versus Class Definition

A class is said to be *defined* once the end of the class body (that is, the closing curly brace) has been encountered. Once the class is defined, all the class members are known. The size of the class is then known as well.

It is possible to declare a class without defining it. For example:

```
class Screen; // declaration of the Screen class
```

This declaration introduces the name Screen into the program, and indicates that Screen refers to a class type.

A class type that is declared but not defined can only be used in limited ways. One cannot define objects of a class type if the class is not defined, because the size of the class type is not known and the compiler does not know how much storage to reserve for an object of that class type.

However, a pointer or reference to that class type can be declared. Pointers and references are permitted because both have a fixed size that is independent of the size of the type to which they refer. However, because the size of the class and the class members are unknown, one cannot apply the dereference operator (*) to such a pointer, or use the pointer or reference to refer to a class member until the class is completely defined.

A data member can be declared to be of a class type only if the definition for the class has already been seen. Where the class definition has not yet been seen in the program text file, the data member can only be a pointer or a reference to that class type. For example, here is a definition of the class StackScreen with a data member that is a pointer to a class Screen that is declared but not defined:

```
class Screen; // declaration
class StackScreen {
    int topStack;
    // ok: pointer to a Screen object
    Screen *stack;
    void (*handler)();
};
```

Because a class is not considered defined until its class body is complete, a class cannot have data members of its own type. However, a class is considered declared as soon as its class head has been seen. A class can then have data members that are pointers and references to its own class type. For example:

```
class LinkScreen {
    Screen window;
    LinkScreen *next;
    LinkScreen *prev;
};
```

Exercise 13.1

Given a class named Person, with the following two data members

```
string _name;
string _address;
```

and the following member functions

```
Person( const string &n, const string &a )
       : _name( n ), _address( a ) { }
string name() { return _name; }
string address() { return _address; }
```

which members would you declare in the public section of the class and which members would you declare in the private section of the class? Explain your choice.

Exercise 13.2

Explain the difference between a class declaration and a class definition. When would you use a class declaration? A class definition?

13.2   Class Objects

The definition of a class, such as the class Screen, does not cause any storage to be allocated. Storage is only allocated when an object of class type is defined. For example, given the following implementation of the Screen class

```
class Screen {
public:
    // member functions
private:
    string             _screen;
    string::size_type  _cursor;
    short              _height;
    short              _width;
};
```

the definition

```
Screen myScreen;
```

allocates an area of storage sufficient to contain the four data members of the Screen class. The name myScreen refers to that area of storage. Each class object has its own copy of the class data members. Modifying the data members of myScreen does not change the data members of any other Screen object.

An object of class type has a scope determined by the location of the object's definition within the text file. An object of class type may be defined in a scope different from the scope in which the class type is defined. For example:

```
class Screen {
    // member list
};

int main()
{
    Screen mainScreen;
}
```

The class type Screen is declared in global scope, whereas the object mainScreen is declared in the local scope of main().

An object of class type also has a lifetime. Depending on whether the object is declared within a namespace scope or within a local scope, and depending on whether it is declared as static or not, the object may exist for the duration of the entire program or only for the duration of a particular function's invocation. Objects of class type behave very much like other objects when considering their scope and lifetime. The scope and lifetime of objects are introduced in Chapter 8.

Objects of the same class type can be initialized and assigned to one another. By default, copying a class object is equivalent to copying all of its data members. For example:

```
Screen bufScreen = myScreen;
// bufScreen._height = myScreen._height
// bufScreen._width  = myScreen._width
// bufScreen._cursor = myScreen._cursor
// bufScreen._screen = myScreen._screen
```

Pointers and references to class objects can also be declared. A pointer to a class type can be initialized or assigned the address of a class object of the same class type. Similarly, a reference to a class type can be initialized with the lvalue for an object of the same class type. (Object-oriented programming extends this to permit a pointer or reference of a base class to refer to an object of a derived class):

```
int main()
{
    Screen myScreen, bufScreen[10];
    Screen *ptr = new Screen;
    myScreen = *ptr;
    delete ptr;
    ptr = bufScreen;
```

```
        Screen &ref = *ptr;
        Screen &ref2 = bufScreen[6];
    }
```

By default, a class object is passed by value when specified as a function argument or as a function return value. It is possible to declare a function parameter or a return type as a pointer or as a reference to a class type. Section 7.3 presents parameters that are pointers or references to class types and explains when they should be used. Section 7.4 presents return types that are pointers or references to class types and explains when they should be used.

The member access operators must be used to access either the data members or the member functions of a class object. The dot member access operator (.) is used with a class object or reference; the arrow member access operator (->) is used with a pointer to a class object. For example:

```
    #include "Screen.h"

    bool isEqual( Screen& s1, Screen *s2 )
    { // return false if not equal, true if equal

        if ( s1.height() != s2->height() ||
             s1.width() != s2->width() )
                return false;

        for ( int ix = 0; ix < s1.height(); ++ix )
            for ( int jy = 0; jy < s2->width(); ++jy )
                if ( s1.get( ix, jy ) != s2->get( ix, jy ) )
                    return false;

        return true; // still here? equal.
    }
```

isEqual() is a nonmember function that compares two Screen objects for equality. isEqual() has no access privilege to the private data members of Screen and hence cannot refer to the data members of s1 and s2 directly. It must rely on the public member functions of the Screen class.

For isEqual() to obtain the value of the screen height and width, it must use the member functions height() and width(), referred to as access functions. These functions provide read-only access to the private data members of the class. Their implementation is straightforward:

```
    class Screen {
    public:
        int height() { return _height; }
        int width()  { return _width; }
        // ...
```

```
private:
    short _height, _width;
    // ...
};
```

Applying the arrow member access operator to a pointer to a class object is equivalent to applying the dereference operator (*) to the pointer to obtain the class object to which the pointer refers, and then applying the dot member access operator to access the desired class member. For example, the expression

```
s2->height()
```

can be rewritten as

```
(*s2).height()
```

and has exactly the same result.

13.3   Class Member Functions

Class member functions implement the set of operations that can be performed on a class object. The set of operations that can be performed on a Screen class object is defined by the member functions declared in our Screen class:

```
class Screen {
public:
    void home() { _cursor = 0; }
    void move( int, int );
    char get() { return _screen[_cursor]; }
    char get( int, int );
    bool checkRange( int, int );
    int height() { return _height; }
    int width() { return _width; }
    // ...
};
```

Although each class object has its own copy of the class data members, there exists only one copy of each class member function. For example:

```
Screen myScreen, groupScreen;
myScreen.home();
groupScreen.home();
```

When the function home() is called for the object myScreen, the data member _cursor accessed within home() is the data member of the object myScreen. When the function home() is called for the object groupScreen, the data member _cursor refers the object groupScreen's data member; however, the same member function home() is called. How can the same member function refer to the data members of two different class objects? This support is implemented through the this pointer, which is examined in the next section.

13.3.1   Inline versus Non-Inline Member Functions

Notice that the definitions for the functions home(), get(), height(), and width() are provided within the class body. These functions are said to be defined *inline* in the class definition. These functions are handled *automatically* as inline functions. Inline functions are introduced in Section 7.6.

These member functions could also be declared inline in the class body by explicitly specifying the keyword inline before the return types of the member function definitions as follows:

```
class Screen {
public:
    // Using the inline keyword
    // to declare inline member functions
    inline void home() { _cursor = 0; }
    inline char get() { return _screen[_cursor]; }
    // ...
};
```

The definitions of home() and get() in this example have exactly the same meaning as the definitions of home() and get() in the previous example, in which the keyword inline was omitted. Because it is redundant, our examples do not specify explicitly the keyword inline for member functions defined in their class body.

Member functions larger than one or two lines are best defined outside the class body. This requires a special declaration syntax to identify the function as a member of its class: The name of the member function must be *qualified* by the name of its class. For example, here is the definition of the function checkRange(), where the name of the function is qualified with Screen:::

```
#include <iostream>
#include "Screen.h"

// member function name is qualified with Screen::
bool Screen::checkRange( int row, int col )
{ // validate coordinates
    if ( row < 1 || row > _height ||
         col < 1 || col > _width ) {
      cerr << "Screen coordinates ( "
           << row << ", " << col
           << " ) out of bounds.\n";
      return false;
    }
    return true;
}
```

A member function must be first declared inside the body of its class and the class body must be visible before a member function can be defined outside its class body. For example, if the header Screen.h were not included before the definition of the function checkRange(), the previous program would be in error. The class body defines the complete list of class members. This list cannot be expanded once the class body is complete.

Usually, a member function defined outside its class body is not an inline function. However, such a function can be declared as an inline function either by using explicitly the inline keyword on the function declaration that appears in the class body, by using explicitly the inline keyword on the function definition that appears outside the class body, or both. For example, the following implementation defines move() to be an inline member function of Screen:

```
inline void Screen::move( int r, int c )
{ // move _cursor to absolute position
   if ( checkRange( r, c ) ) // valid screen position?
   {
      int row = (r-1) * _width; // row location
      _cursor = row + c - 1;
   }
}
```

The function get(int,int) can be declared inline by specifying the inline keyword as follows:

```
class Screen {
public:
   inline char get( int, int );
   // the other member function declarations are unchanged
};
```

Its function def.__ion follows the class definition. The inline keyword may be omitted from this definition:

```
char Screen::get( int r, int c )
{
   move( r, c ); // position _cursor
   return get(); // the other get() member function
}
```

Since inline functions must be defined in every text file in which they are called, an inline member function that is not defined within the class body must be placed in the header file in which the class definition appears. For example, the definitions for move() and get() presented earlier should be placed in the header file Screen.h, following the definition of the class Screen.

13.3.2   Access to Class Members

A member function definition is said to be in class scope regardless of whether the definition is located within or outside its class body. This has two implications:

1. The member function definition can refer to any of the class members, whether the member is private or public, without violating the class access restrictions.
2. The member function can access the members of its class without using the dot and arrow member access operators.

For example:

```
#include <string>

void Screen::copy( const Screen &sobj )
{
    // if this Screen object and sobj are the same object,
    // no copy necessary
    // we look at the 'this' pointer in Section 13.4
    if ( this != &sobj )
    {
        _height = sobj._height;
        _width = sobj._width;
        _cursor = 0;

        // creates a new string;
        // its content is the same as sobj._screen
        _screen = sobj._screen;
    }
}
```

Notice that even though the data members _screen, _height, _width, and _cursor are private members of class Screen, the member function copy() can refer to these private members without any error. If a data member such as _screen, _height, _width, and _cursor is used without a member access operator, the member function refers to the data member of the class object for which the member function is called. For example, if the function copy() is used as follows

```
#include "Screen.h"

int main()
{
    Screen s1;
    // Set the content of s1

    Screen s2;
    s2.copy(s1);

    // ...
}
```

within the definition of the member function copy(), the parameter sobj refers to the object s1 defined in main(). The object s2 mentioned before the dot member access operator is the object for which the member function copy() is called. For this call to copy(), the class members _screen, _height, _width, and _cursor that are referred to in the definition of copy() without a member access operator in fact refer to the data members of the object s2. In the next section we look at access to class members within member function definitions in more detail, and we look at how this is supported through the use of the this pointer.

13.3.3 Private versus Public Member Functions

A class member function can be declared within the public, protected, or private section of the class body. How does one decide where a member function should be declared? A public member function defines an operation that a user of the class will want to perform. The set of public member functions defines the *interface* of the class. For example, the class Screen member functions home(), move(), and get() define operations used by programs to manipulate objects of type Screen.

Because we hide the internal representation of the class from the users of the class by declaring the data members as private, we must provide public member functions to manipulate Screen objects. This is known as *information hiding*. Information hiding protects user code from changes to the class representation.

Equally important, the internal state of the class object is protected from random program modification. A small set of functions provides all modifications of the object. If an error occurs, the search space for the mistake is limited to this function set, greatly easing the problems of maintenance and program correctness.

So far we have only seen member functions supporting read access of the private data members. Here are two set() functions that allow a user to modify a Screen object. First, these two new member functions must be added to the class body:

```
class Screen {
public:
   void set( const string &s );
   void set( char ch );
   // other member function declarations remain unchanged
};
```

The definitions for these member functions are as follows:

```
void Screen::set( const string &s )
{ // write string beginning at current _cursor position

   int space = remainingSpace();
   int len = s.size();
   if ( space < len ) {
     cerr << "Screen: warning: truncation: "
          << "space: " << space
          << "string length: " << len << endl;
     len = space;
   }
```

```
   _screen.replace( _cursor, len, s );
   _cursor += len - 1;
}

void Screen::set( char ch )
{
   if ( ch == '\0' )
      cerr << "Screen: warning: "
           << "null character (ignored).\n";
   else _screen[_cursor] = ch;
}
```

An assumption of our Screen class implementation is that a Screen object does not contain embedded null characters. This is the reason that set() does not permit a null character to be written to the screen.

The functions presented are public member functions. They can be invoked from anywhere within the program. Private member functions, however, can only be invoked by other member functions (and friends) of the class. They cannot be invoked directly by the program. Private member functions provide support to other member functions in implementing the class abstraction. The function remainingSpace() used in the function set(const string&) is one of these functions. The member function remainingSpace() is a private member function of the class Screen:

```
class Screen {
public:
   // other member function declarations remain unchanged
private:
   inline int remainingSpace();
};
```

remainingSpace() returns the amount of space remaining on the screen:

```
inline int Screen::remainingSpace()
{ // current position is no longer remaining
   int sz = _width * _height;
   return( sz - _cursor );
}
```

A full discussion of protected member functions is deferred until Chapter 17.

The following is a small program written to exercise a portion of the member functions implemented thus far:

```
#include "Screen.h"
#include <iostream>

int main() {
   Screen sobj(3,3); // constructor defined in Section 13.3.4
   string init("abcdefghi");
```

```
            cout << "Screen Object ("
                 << sobj.height() << ", "
                 << sobj.width() << " )\n\n";

            // Set the content of the screen
            string::size_type initpos = 0;
            for ( int ix = 1; ix <= sobj.width(); ++ix )
               for ( int iy = 1; iy <= sobj.height(); ++iy )
               {
                  sobj.move( ix, iy );
                  sobj.set( init[ initpos++ ] );
               }

            // Print the content of the screen
            for ( int ix = 1; ix <= sobj.width(); ++ix )
            {
               for ( int iy = 1; iy <= sobj.height(); ++iy )
                  cout << sobj.get( ix, iy );
               cout << "\n";
            }

            return 0;
         }
```

When compiled and executed, the program generates the following output:

```
         Screen Object ( 3, 3 )

         abc
         def
         ghi
```

13.3.4   Special Member Functions

One set of special member functions manages class objects and handling activities such as initialization, assignment, memory management, type conversion, and destruction. These functions are usually invoked implicitly by the compiler.

An initialization member function is called a *constructor*. It is invoked implicitly each time a class object is defined or allocated by a new expression. A constructor is declared by giving it its class name. Here is a declaration for the Screen class constructor that provides a default argument value for the parameters hi, wid, and bkground:

```
         class Screen {
         public:
             Screen( int hi = 8, int wid = 40, char bkground = '#' );
             // other member function declarations remain unchanged
         };
```

Here is a definition for the Screen constructor:

```
Screen::Screen( int hi, int wid, char bk ) :
    _height( hi ),  // initializes _height with hi
    _width( wid ),  // initializes _width with wid
    _cursor ( 0 ),  // initializes _cursor to 0
    _screen( hi * wid, bk ) // size of _screen is hi * wid
                            // all positions initialized with
                            // character value of bk
{ // all the work is done with the member initialization list
  // Section 14.5 discusses member initialization list
}
```

Each declared Screen object is initialized automatically by the Screen constructor. For example:

```
Screen s1;                       // Screen(8,40,'#')
Screen *ps = new Screen( 20 );   // Screen(20,40,'#')

int main() {
    Screen s(24,80,'*');         // Screen(24,80,'*')
    // ...
}
```

Chapter 14 introduces constructors, destructors, and assignment operators in more detail. Chapter 15 introduces conversion functions and the memory management functions in more detail.

13.3.5   const and volatile Member Functions

Usually, any attempt to modify a const object from within a program is flagged as a compile-time error. For example:

```
const char blank = ' ';
blank = '\n'; // error
```

A class object, however, is not ordinarily modified directly by the program. Rather, the set of public member functions is invoked when a class object must be modified. To respect the const-ness of a class object, the compiler must distinguish between unsafe and safe member functions (that is, between the member functions that attempt to modify the class object from those that don't). For example:

```
const Screen blankScreen;
blankScreen.display();  // reads the class object
blankScreen.set( '*' ); // error: modifies the class object
```

The class designer indicates which member functions do not modify the class object by declaring them as const member functions. For example:

```
class Screen {
public:
    char get() const { return _screen[_cursor]; }
    // ...
};
```

Only member functions declared as const can be invoked for a class object that is const. The const keyword is placed between the parameter list and the body of the member function. A const member function defined outside the class body must specify the const keyword in both its declaration and its definition. For example:

```
class Screen {
public:
    bool isEqual( char ch ) const;
    // ...
private:
    string::size_type  _cursor;
    string             _screen;
    // ...
};

bool Screen::isEqual( char ch ) const
{
    return ch == _screen[_cursor];
}
```

It is illegal to declare as const a member function that modifies a class data member. In the following simplified Screen definition, for example

```
class Screen {
public:
    int ok() const { return _cursor; }
    void error( int ival ) const { _cursor = ival; }
    // ...
private:
    string::size_type _cursor;
    // ...
};
```

the definition of ok() is a valid const member function definition because it does not change the value of _cursor. The definition of error(), however, does modify the value of _cursor and therefore cannot be declared as a const member function. The function definition results in the following compiler error message:

```
error: cannot modify a data member within a const member function
```

In general, any class that is expected to be used extensively should declare the member functions that do not modify the class data members as const member functions. However, declaring a member function as const does not prevent all the modifications a programmer might expect. Declaring a member function const guarantees that the member function does not modify the class data members, but if the class contains pointers, the objects to which the pointers refer may be modified within a const member function. This modification is not detected as an error by the compiler. This often takes beginner C++ programmers by surprise. For example:

```
#include <cstring>

class Text {
public:
    void bad( const string &parm ) const;
private:
    char *_text;
};

void Text::bad( const string &parm ) const
{
    _text = parm.c_str(); // error: _text cannot be modified

    for ( int ix = 0; ix < parm.size(); ++ix )
        _text[ix] = parm[ix]; // bad style but not an error
}
```

Although _text cannot be modified, _text is of type char*, and the characters to which _text refers may be modified within a const member function of class Text. The member function bad() reflects a bad programming style. However, the compiler does not help detecting such situations and a programmer must remain vigilant because a const member function does not guarantee that everything to which the class object refers will remain invariant throughout the invocation of the member function.

A const member function can be overloaded with a non-const member function that has the same parameter list. For example:

```
class Screen {
public:
    char get(int x, int y);
    char get(int x, int y) const;
    // ...
};
```

In this case, the const-ness of the class object determines which of the two functions is invoked:

```
int main() {
    const Screen cs;
    Screen s;

    char ch = cs.get(0,0); // calls const member
    ch = s.get(0,0);       // calls non-const member
}
```

Constructors and destructors are exceptions in that, even though a constructor or destructor is never a const member function, they can be called for const class objects. The const-ness of a class object is established when the constructor ends its execution and the class object has been initialized. The const-ness disappears once the destructor is invoked. A const class object is therefore considered const from the time its construction completes to the time its destruction starts.

A member function can also be declared as volatile (the volatile qualifier was introduced in Section 3.13). A class object is declared volatile if its value can possibly be changed in ways outside either the control or detection of the compiler (for example, if it is a data structure that represents an I/O port). Similar to const class objects, only volatile member functions, constructors, and the destructor can be invoked for a volatile class object:

```
class Screen {
public:
    char poll() volatile;
    // ...
};
char Screen::poll() volatile { ... }
```

13.3.6 Mutable Data Members

There are problems, though, when we declare an object of our Screen class const. The behavior we expect is that once the const Screen object has been initialized, its content cannot be modified. But we should be able to inspect the content of the Screen object without problems. For example, given the following const Screen class object cs,

```
const Screen cs( 5, 5 );
```

we want to inspect the content of cs at the location (3, 4). We do this as follows:

```
// read Screen at position ( 3, 4 )
// oops: does not work!
cs.move( 3, 4 );
char ch = cs.get();
```

However, this does not work. Can you see why? move() is not a const member function and cannot be made a const member function easily. The definition of move() is as follows:

```
inline void Screen::move( int r, int c )
{
    if ( checkRange( r, c ) )
    {
        int row = (r-1) * _width;
        _cursor = row + c - 1; // modifies _cursor
    }
}
```

Notice that move() modifies the _cursor class data member, and for this reason cannot be declared a const member function without modification.

It may seem strange, however, that _cursor cannot be modified for a const object of class Screen. _cursor is just an index. By modifying _cursor, we do not modify the content of the Screen itself. We only attempt to remember the Screen position to be inspected. Modifying _cursor even though the Screen object is const should be allowed, since doing so is necessary to inspect the content of a Screen object and does not modify the content of the Screen itself.

To allow a class data member to be modified even though it is the data member of a const object, we can declare the data member as *mutable*. A mutable data member is a member that is never const, even when it is the data member of a const object. A mutable member can always be updated, even in a const member function. To declare a member as a mutable data member, the keyword mutable must precede the declaration of the data member in the class member list:

```
class Screen {
public:
    // member functions
private:
    string                  _screen;
    mutable string::size_type _cursor; // mutable member
    short                   _height;
    short                   _width;
};
```

Any const member function can now modify _cursor, and we can now declare the member function move() as a const member function. Even though move() modifies the _cursor data member, no compiler error is generated:

```
// move() is a const member function
inline void Screen::move( int r, int c ) const
{
    // ...

    // ok: const member function can modify mutable members
    _cursor = row + c - 1;
    // ...
}
```

The operations presented at the beginning of this subsection can now be performed to inspect the const Screen object cs without error.

Notice that only _cursor is declared as a mutable data member. _screen, _height, and _width are not because the values of these data members should never change in a Screen class object that is const.

Exercise 13.3

Explain the behavior of copy() in the following invocation:

```
Screen myScreen;
myScreen.copy( myScreen );
```

Exercise 13.4

Additional cursor movements might include moving forward or backward one character at a time. On reaching the bottom right corner or top left corner of the screen, the cursor wraps around. Implement the forward() and backward() functions.

Exercise 13.5

Another useful capability might include moving the cursor up or down one row of the screen. On reaching the top or bottom row of the screen, the cursor does not wrap around; it sounds a bell and remains where it is. Implement the up() and down() functions, knowing that writing the character '007' to cout will sound the bell.

Exercise 13.6

Revisit the Screen member functions introduced thus far and change the member functions to const member functions where appropriate. Explain your decision.

13.4   The Implicit this Pointer

Each class object maintains its own copy of the class data members. For example:

```
int main() {
    Screen myScreen( 3, 3 ), bufScreen;

    myScreen.clear();
    myScreen.move( 2, 2 );
    myScreen.set( '*' );
    myScreen.display();

    bufScreen.reSize( 5, 5 );
    bufScreen.display();
}
```

myScreen has its own _width, _height, _cursor, and _screen data members. bufScreen has its own separate set. However, there exists only one copy of each class member function. Both myScreen and bufScreen call the same copy of any particular member function.

We have seen in the previous section that a member function can refer to the members of its class without using the member access operators. The definition for the function move(), for example, is as follows:

```
inline void Screen::move( int r, int c )
{
   if ( checkRange( r, c ) ) // valid screen position?
   {
      int row = (r-1) * _width; // row location
      _cursor = row + c - 1;
   }
}
```

If the function move() is called for the object myScreen, the data members _width and _cursor accessed within move() are the data members of myScreen. If the function move() is called for the object bufScreen, the data members accessed are those of buf-Screen. How does the data member _cursor, manipulated by move(), become bound in turn to the data member belonging to myScreen and then to the one belonging to buf-Screen? The short answer is the this pointer.

Each class member function contains a pointer that addresses the object for which the member function is called. The pointer is called this. Its type in a non-const member function is a pointer to the class type, a pointer to a const class type in a const member function, and a pointer to a volatile class type in a volatile member function. For example, within the member function move() of class Screen, the this pointer is of the type Screen*. Within a non-const member function of the class List, the this pointer is of type List*.

Because the this pointer addresses the class object for which the member function is called, if the function move() is called for the object myScreen, the this pointer addresses the object myScreen. Similarly, if the function move() is called for the object buf-Screen, the this pointer addresses the object bufScreen. The data member _cursor, manipulated by move(), becomes bound in turn to the data member belonging to my-Screen and bufScreen.

One way of understanding this is to take a brief look at how a compiler implements the this pointer. There are two transformations that must be applied to support the this pointer:

1. Translate the definition of the class member function. Each class member function is defined with one additional parameter: the this pointer. For example:

    ```
    // pseudocode that illustrates the compiler expansion
    // of a member function definition --
    // not legal C++ code
    inline void move( Screen* this, int r, int c )
    {
       if ( checkRange( r, c ) )
       {
          int row = (r-1) * this->_width;
          this->_cursor = row + c - 1;
       }
    }
    ```

In the member function definition, the use of the `this` pointer to access the class data members `_width` and `_cursor` is made explicit.

2. Translate each invocation of the class member function to add an additional argument — the address of the object for which the member function is invoked. For example,

```
myScreen.move( 2, 2 )
```

is translated into

```
move( &myScreen, 2, 2 )
```

The programmer can refer to the `this` pointer explicitly in a member function definition. For example, it is legal although unnecessary to define the member function `home()` as follows:

```
inline void Screen::home()
{
    this->_cursor = 0;
}
```

There are circumstances, however, when the programmer does need to refer to the `this` pointer explicitly, as we saw with the Screen member function `copy()` defined earlier. The next subsection presents some examples.

13.4.1   When to Use the this Pointer

Our function `main()` calls the member functions of the class Screen on the objects `myScreen` and `bufScreen` such that each action is in a separate statement. We can define the Screen class member functions to allow the concatenation of member function calls when they apply to the same Screen object. For example, the calls in the function `main()` could be rewritten as

```
int main() {
    // ...
    myScreen.clear().move(2,2).set('*').display();
    bufScreen.reSize(5,5).display();
}
```

This seems to follow the instinctive way of manipulating Screen objects, where a sequence of actions is used: Clear the Screen object `myScreen`, move its cursor to the location (2,2), set this location to the character `'*'`, then display the result.

The member access operators dot and arrow are left-associative operators. When a sequence of these operators is found, the order of execution is left to right. For example, `myScreen.clear()` is invoked first, followed by the call to `myScreen.move()`, and so on. For `myScreen.move()` to be invoked following the call to `myScreen.clear()`, `clear()` must return the class object `myScreen`. The definition of the member function `clear()` must return the class object for which it is invoked. As we have seen, access to the class object within a class member function is through the this pointer. Here is the implementation for clear():

```
// the declaration for clear() is in the class body
// it specifies a default argument for bkground = '#'
Screen& Screen::clear( char bkground )
{ // reset the cursor and clear the screen

    _cursor = 0;
    _screen.assign(        // assign the string
       _screen.size(),     // with size() characters
       bkground            // of value bkground
    );

    // return the object for which the function was invoked
    return *this;
}
```

Notice that the return type of the member function is Screen&, which indicates that the member function returns a reference to an object of its own class type. To allow the concatenation of the Screen member functions within main(), the member functions move() and set() need to be revised. Their return type must be changed from void to Screen& and they must return *this from within their definitions.

Similarly, the Screen member function display() might be implemented as follows:

```
Screen& Screen::display()
{
    typedef string::size_type idx_type;

    for ( idx_type ix = 0; ix < _height; ++ix )
    { // for each row

        idx_type offset = _width * ix; // row position

        for ( idx_type iy = 0; iy < _width; ++iy )
           // for each column, write element
           cout << _screen[ offset + iy ];

        cout << endl;
    }
    return *this;
}
```

The Screen member function reSize() might be implemented as follows:

```
// the declaration for reSize() is in the class body
// it specifies a default argument for bkground = '#'
Screen& Screen::reSize( int h, int w, char bkground )
{ // resize a screen to height h and width w
```

```
    // remember the content of the screen
    string local(_screen);

    // replaces the string to which _screen refers
    _screen.assign(        // assign the string
        h * w,             // with h * w characters
        bkground           // of value bkground
    );

    typedef string::size_type idx_type;
    idx_type local_pos = 0;

    // copy content of old screen into the new one
    for ( idx_type ix = 0; ix < _height; ++ix )
    { // for each row

        idx_type offset = w * ix; // row position
        for ( idx_type iy = 0; iy < _width; ++iy )
            // for each column, assign the old value
            _screen[ offset + iy ] = local[ local_pos++ ];
    }

    _height = h;
    _width = w;
    // _cursor remains unchanged

    return *this;
}
```

Not all uses of the this pointer in member function definitions are to return the object to which the member function is applied. When we introduced the copy() member function in Section 13.3, we saw another use for the this pointer:

```
void Screen::copy( const Screen& sobj )
{
    // if this Screen object and sobj are the same object,
    // no copy necessary
    if ( this != &sobj )
    {
        // copy the value of sobj into *this
    }
}
```

The this pointer holds the address of the class object for which the member function is called. If the address of the object to which sobj refers is equal to the value of the this pointer, then both sobj and this refer to the same object, and the copy operation is not necessary. We look at this construct again when we look at the copy assignment operator in Section 14.7.

Exercise 13.7

The this pointer can be used to modify the class object to which it refers as well as to override the object with a new object of the same type. For example, here is the member function assign() of the class classType. Can you explain what it does?

```
classType& classType::assign( const classType &source )
{
   if ( this != &source )
   {
      this->~classType();
      new (this) classType( source );
   }
   return *this;
}
```

Recall that ~classType() is the name of the destructor. The new expression may look a little bit funny, but we have seen this new expression called placement new expression in Section 8.4.

What is your opinion of this kind of coding style? Do you believe this is a safe operation? Why or why not?

13.5   Static Class Members

It is sometimes necessary for all the objects of a particular class type to access a global object. Perhaps a count is needed of how many objects of a particular class type have been created at any one point in the program, or the global object may be a pointer to an error-handling routine for the class, or it may be a pointer to the free store memory for objects of this class type. In these cases it is simply more efficient to provide one global object used by all the objects of the particular class type than to have each class object maintain its own separate data member. Even though this object is a global object, it exists only for the purpose of supporting the implementation of this class abstraction.

In these cases, a class static data member provides a better solution. A static data member acts as a global object that belongs to its class type. Unlike other data members where each class object has its own copy, there is only one copy of a static data member per class type. A static data member is a single, shared object accessible to all objects of its class type.

There are two advantages of using a static data member over using a global object:

1.   A static member is not entered into the program's global namespace, thus removing the possibility of an accidental conflict of names with other global objects in our program.

2. Information hiding can be enforced. A static member can be a private member; a global object cannot.

A data member is made static by prefixing the data member declaration within the class body with the keyword static. Static data members obey the public/private/ protected access rules. For example, in the Account class defined here, _interestRate is declared as a private static member of type double.

```
class Account {
    Account( double amount, const string &owner );
    string owner() { return _owner; }
private:
    static double  _interestRate;
    double         _amount;
    string         _owner;
};
```

Why is _interestRate declared static while _amount and _owner are not? It is because each Account object has a different owner and contains a different amount of money, but the interest rate on all the Account objects is the same.

Because there is only one _interestRate data member shared by all Account objects in the entire program, declaring _interestRate as a static data member reduces the storage needed for each Account object.

Although the current value of _interestRate is the same for every Account object, its value may change over time. Therefore, we decided not to declare the static data member as const. Because _interestRate is static, it needs to be updated only once. We are assured that each Account object will then access the same updated value. Were each class object to maintain its own copy, each copy would have to be updated, leading to inefficiency and a greater potential for error.

In general, a static data member is initialized outside the class definition. Just as in the case of member functions defined outside the class definition, the name of the static member in such a definition must be qualified by its class name. For example, here is how we might initialize _interestRate:

```
// explicit initialization of a static class member

#include "account.h"
double Account::_interestRate = 0.0589;
```

As with any global object, only one definition of a static data member can be provided in a program. This means that static data member initializations should not be placed in header files, but rather in the files containing the definitions of the class non-inline member functions.

Static data members can be declared to be of any type. They can be const objects, arrays, class objects, and so forth. For example:

```
#include <string>
class Account {
  // ...
private:
  static const string name;
};

const string Account::name( "Savings Account" );
```

As a special case, a const static data member of integral type can be initialized within the class body with a constant value. For example, if we decided to use an array of characters instead of a string to store the name of the account, we could have specified the size of the array using a const data member of type int. For example:

```
// header file
class Account {
  // ...
private:
  static const int nameSize = 16;
  static const char name[nameSize];
};

// text file
const int Account::nameSize; // member definition needed
const char Account::name[nameSize] = "Savings Account";
```

There are a few interesting things to note about this special case. A const static data member of integral type initialized with a constant value is a *constant expression*. A class designer can declare such a static data member if there is a need to use a named constant value within the class body. For example, because the const static data member nameSize is a constant expression, the class designer uses it to specify the size of the array data member name.

When a const static data member is initialized within the class body, the data member must still be defined outside the class definition. However, because the initial value of the static data member is specified in the class body, the definition outside the class definition must not specify an initial value.

Because name is an array (and is not of integral type) it cannot be initialized within the class body. Any attempt to do so results in a compile-time error. For example:

```
class Account {
  // ...
private:
  static const int nameSize = 16; // ok: integral type
  static const char name[nameSize] =
                     "Savings Account"; // error
};
```

name must be initialized outside the class definition.

This example illustrates one last point. Notice that the member nameSize specifies the size of the array name in the definition that appears outside the class definition:

```
const char Account::name[nameSize] = "Savings Account";
```

nameSize is not qualified by the class name Account. And even though nameSize is a private member, the definition of name is not in error. How can this be? Just as the definition of a class member function can refer to the class private members, so can the definition of a static data member. The definition of the static data member name is in the scope of its class and can refer to the class Account's private data members after the qualified name Account::name has been seen. We see more on class scope in Section 13.9.

A class static data member can be accessed within a member function of its class without the use of the member access operator:

```
inline double Account::dailyReturn()
{
    return( _interestRate / 365 * _amount );
}
```

However, within a nonmember function, a static data member must be accessed in one of two ways. The member access operators can be used:

```
class Account {
    // ...
private:
    friend int compareRevenue( Account& , Account* );
    // the rest is unchanged
};

// reference and pointer parameters to
// illustrate object and pointer access
int compareRevenue( Account &ac1, Account *ac2 )
{
    double ret1, ret2;
    ret1 = ac1._interestRate * ac1._amount;
    ret2 = ac2->_interestRate * ac2->_amount;
    // ...
}
```

Both ac1._interestRate and ac2->_interestRate refer to the static member Account::_interestRate.

Because there is only one copy of a class static data member, it does not have to be accessed through an object or a pointer. The other way to access a static data member is to access it directly, using its name qualified by the name of its class:

```
// static member accessed with its qualified name
if ( Account::_interestRate < 0.05 )
```

When a static data member is not accessed through a class member access operator, the name of the class followed by the scope operator

```
Account::
```

must be specified because the static member is not a global object and cannot be found in global scope. The following definition of the friend function `compareRevenue()` is equivalent to the one just presented:

```
int compareRevenue( Account &ac1, Account *ac2 )
{
   double ret1, ret2;
   ret1 = Account::_interestRate * ac1._amount;
   ret2 = Account::_interestRate * ac2->_amount;
   // ...
}
```

The unique nature of the static data member — that a single instance exists independently of any object of the class — allows it to be used in ways that are illegal for nonstatic data members:

1. A static data member can be of the same class type as that of which it is a member. A nonstatic data member is restricted to being declared as a pointer or a reference to an object of its class. For example:

```
class Bar {
public:
   // ...
private:
   static Bar mem1; // ok
   Bar *mem2;       // ok
   Bar mem3;        // error
};
```

2. A static data member can appear as a default argument to a member function of the class, but a nonstatic member cannot. For example:

```
extern int var;

class Foo {
private:
   int var;
   static int stcvar;
public:
   // error: resolves to nonstatic Foo::var
   // there is no associated class object
   int mem1( int = var );

   // ok: resolves to static Foo::stcvar
   // an associated class object unnecessary
   int mem2( int = stcvar );
```

```
      // ok: global instance of int var
      int mem3( int = ::var );
};
```

13.5.1   Static Member Functions

The member functions raiseInterest() and interest() access the class static data
member _interestRate:

```
class Account {
public:
   void raiseInterest( double incr );
   double interest() { return _interestRate; }
private:
   static double _interestRate;
};

inline void Account::raiseInterest( double incr )
{
   _interestRate += incr;
}
```

The problem is that each member function must be called by applying a class
member access operator to a particular class object. Because the member functions do
not access any data member other than the static data member _interestRate, it is really irrelevant which object is used to call the functions. None of the object (nonstatic)
data members are ever accessed or modified as a result of such a call.

A better alternative is to declare such a member function as a static member function. This can be done as follows:

```
class Account {
public:
   static void raiseInterest( double incr );
   static double interest() { return _interestRate; }
private:
   static double _interestRate;
};

inline void Account::raiseInterest( double incr )
{
   _interestRate += incr;
}
```

The declaration of a static member function is the same as that of a nonstatic member
function except that the function declaration in the class body is preceded with the key-

word static and the function may not be declared as const or volatile. The function definition that appears outside of the class body must not specify the keyword static.

A static member function does not have a this pointer; therefore, referring either implicitly or explicitly to the this pointer within a static member function results in a compile-time error. Attempting to access a nonstatic class member refers implicitly to the this pointer and thus results in a compile-time error. For example, the member function dailyReturn() presented earlier could not be declared as a static member function because it accesses the nonstatic data member _amount.

A static member function may be invoked for a class object or a pointer to a class object using the member access operators dot and arrow. A static member function can also be accessed or invoked directly using a qualified name even if no class objects are ever declared. Here is a small program to illustrate the use of static class members:

```
#include <iostream>
#include "account.h"

bool limitTest( double limit )
{
    // no Account class objects defined yet
    // ok: call static member function
    return limit <= Account::interest() ;
}

int main() {
    double limit = 0.05;

    if ( limitTest( limit ) )
    {
        // pointer to static class member is
        // declared as ordinary pointer
        void (*psf)(double) = &Account::raiseInterest;
        psf( 0.0025 );
    }

    Account ac1( 5000, "Asterix" );
    Account ac2( 10000, "Obelix" );
    if ( compareRevenue( ac1, &ac2 ) > 0 )
        cout << ac1.owner()
             << " is richer than "
             << ac2.owner() << "\n";
    else
        cout << ac1.owner()
             << " is poorer than "
             << ac2.owner() << "\n";
    return 0;
}
```

Exercise 13.8

Given the following class Y, with two static data members and two static member functions,

```
class X {
public:
   X( int i ) { _val = i; }
   int val() { return _val; }
private:
   int _val;
};

class Y {
public:
   Y( int i );
   static X xval();
   static int callsXval();
private:
   static X _xval;
   static int _callsXval;
};
```

initialize _xval to 20 and _callsXval to 0.

Exercise 13.9

Using the classes in Exercise 13.8, implement the two static member access functions for class Y. callsXval() simply keeps count of how many times xval() is called.

Exercise 13.10

Which ones, if any, of the following static data member declarations and definitions are errors? Explain why.

```
// example.h
class Example {
public:
   static double rate = 6.5;

   static const int vecSize = 20;
   static vector<double> vec(vecSize);
};

// example.C
#include "example.h"
double Example::rate;
vector<double> Example::vec;
```

13.6   Pointer to Class Member

Let's assume that our class Screen defines four new member functions — forward(), back(), up(), and down() — that move the cursor one position to the right, left, up, or down the screen respectively. First we must declare these new member functions in the class body:

```
class Screen {
public:
    inline Screen& forward();
    inline Screen& back();
    inline Screen& end();
    inline Screen& up();
    inline Screen& down();
    // other member functions as before
private:
    inline int row();
    // other private members as before
};
```

The member functions forward() and back() move the cursor one character at a time. On reaching the bottom right-hand corner or top left-hand corner of the screen, the cursor wraps around.

```
inline Screen& Screen::forward()
{ // advance _cursor one screen element

    ++_cursor;

    // check for end of screen; wrap around
    if ( _cursor == _screen.size() )
        home();

    return *this;
}

inline Screen& Screen::back()
{ // move _cursor backward one screen element

    // check for top of screen; wrap around
    if ( _cursor == 0 )
        end();
    else
        --_cursor;

    return *this;
}
```

end() sets the cursor to the bottom right-hand corner of the screen. It complements the member function home() introduced earlier:

```
inline Screen& Screen::end()
{
    _cursor = _width * _height - 1;
    return *this;
}
```

up() and down() move the cursor up and down one row of the screen. On reaching the top or bottom row of the screen, the cursor does not wrap around, but rather sounds a bell and remains where it is:

```
const char BELL = '\007';

inline Screen& Screen::up()
{ // move _cursor up one row of screen
  // do not wrap around; rather, ring bell

    if ( row() == 1 ) // at top?
       cout << BELL << endl;
    else
       _cursor -= _width;

    return *this;
}

inline Screen& Screen::down()
{
    if ( row() == _height ) // at bottom?
       cout << BELL << endl;
    else
       _cursor += _width;

    return *this;
}
```

row() is a private member function that supports the implementation of up() and down() that returns the current row of the cursor position:

```
inline int Screen::row()
{ // return current row
    return ( _cursor + _width ) / _width;
}
```

Users of the Screen class have been asking for a function repeat() that performs some user-specified operation n times. A nongeneral implementation could be the following:

```
Screen &repeat( char op, int times )
{
```

```
       switch( op ) {
          case DOWN: // invoke Screen::down() n times
             break;
          case UP:   // invoke Screen::up() n times
             break;
          // ...
       }
    }
```

Although this implementation works, it has a number of drawbacks. One problem is that it relies on the member functions of Screen to remain unchanged. Each time a member function is added or removed, repeat() must be updated. A second problem is its size. By having to test for each possible member function, the full listing of repeat() is large and seems unnecessarily complex.

An alternate, more general implementation replaces op with a parameter of type pointer to Screen member function. repeat() no longer needs to determine the intended operation. The entire switch statement can be removed. The definition and use of pointers to class members are the topics of the following subsections.

13.6.1   The Type of a Class Member

A pointer to a function may not be assigned the address of a member function even when the return type and parameter list of the two match exactly. For example, pfi, which follows, is a pointer to a function that takes no parameters and has a return type of int:

```
    int (*pfi)();
```

Given two global functions, HeightIs() and WidthIs()

```
    int HeightIs();
    int WidthIs();
```

assignment of either or both of HeightIs() and WidthIs() to pfi is legal and correct:

```
    pfi = HeightIs;
    pfi = WidthIs;
```

The class Screen also defines two access functions — height() and width() — which also take no parameters and have a return type of int:

```
    inline int Screen::height() { return _height; }
    inline int Screen::width()  { return _width; }
```

The assignment of either the height() or width() member function to pfi, however, is a type violation, and a compile-time error is generated:

```
    // illegal assignment: type violation
    pfi = &Screen::height;
```

Why is there a type violation? A member function has an additional type attribute absent from a nonmember function — *its class*. A pointer to a member function must match the type of the function it is assigned, not in two but in three areas: (1) the type and number of parameters, (2) the return type, and (3) the class type of which it is a member.

The type mismatch between a pointer to member function and a pointer to function is due to the difference in representation between these two kinds of pointers. A pointer to function stores the address of a function and can be used directly to call that function. (Pointers to functions are discussed in Section 7.9.) A pointer to member function must first be bound to an object or a pointer to obtain a `this` pointer for the function invocation before the function to which it refers can be called. (In the next subsection we see how a pointer to member function is bound to an object or a pointer to call a member function.) Although both an ordinary pointer to function and a pointer to member function are called pointers, they are different beasts.

The declaration of a pointer to member function requires an expanded syntax that takes the class type into account. The same also holds true for pointers to class data members. Consider the type of the Screen class member `_height`. Its complete type is "member of class Screen of type `short`." Consequently, the complete type of a pointer to `_height` is "pointer to member of class Screen of type `short`." This is written as follows:

```
short Screen::*
```

A definition of a pointer to a member of class Screen of type `short` looks like this:

```
short Screen::*ps_Screen;
```

`ps_Screen` can be initialized with the address of `_height` as follows:

```
short Screen::*ps_Screen = &Screen::_height;
```

Similarly, it can be assigned the address of `_width` like this:

```
ps_Screen = &Screen::_width;
```

`ps_Screen` may be set to either `_width` or `_height` since both are Screen class data members of type `short`.

The type mismatch between a pointer to data member and an ordinary pointer is also due to the difference in representation between these two kinds of pointers. An ordinary pointer contains all the information needed to refer to an object. A pointer to data member must first be bound to an object or a pointer before it can be used to access the data member. (In the next subsection, we see how a pointer to data member is bound to an object or pointer.) (The companion text to C++ *Primer*, *Inside the C++ Object Model* ([LIPPMAN96a]), also discusses pointer to member representations.)

A pointer to member function is defined by specifying the function return type, parameter list, and class. For example, a pointer to a Screen member function capable of referring to the member functions `height()` and `width()` has the following type:

```
int (Screen::*)()
```

this type specifies a pointer to a member function of class Screen taking no parameters and returning a value of type int.

A pointer to a member function can be declared, initialized, and assigned, as follows:

```
// all pointers to class member may be assigned the value 0
int (Screen::*pmf1)() = 0;
int (Screen::*pmf2)() = &Screen::height;

pmf1 = pmf2;
pmf2 = &Screen::width;
```

The use of a typedef can make the pointer-to-member syntax easier to read. For example, the following typedef defines Action to be an alternative type name for the following type

```
Screen& (Screen::*)()
```

that is, a pointer to a member function of class Screen taking no parameters and returning a reference to a Screen class object.

```
typedef Screen& (Screen::*Action)();

Action default = &Screen::home;
Action next = &Screen::forward;
```

A pointer to member function type may be used to declare function parameters and function return types. A default argument may be specified for a parameter of type pointer to member function. For example:

```
Screen& action( Screen&, Action );
```

action() is declared as taking two parameters: a reference to a Screen class object and a pointer to a member function of class Screen taking no parameters and returning a reference to a Screen class object. action() can be invoked in any of the following ways:

```
Screen myScreen;
typedef Screen& (Screen::*Action)();
Action default = &Screen::home;

extern Screen& action( Screen&, Action = &Screen::display );

void ff()
{
    action( myScreen );
    action( myScreen, default );
    action( myScreen, &Screen::end );
}
```

The invocation and use of a pointer to class member is covered in the next subsection.

13.6.2   Using a Pointer to Class Member

Pointers to class members must always be accessed through a specific object or pointer
to an object of class type. We do this by using the two pointer to member operators (.*
for class objects and references, and ->* for pointers to class objects). For example, a
member function is invoked through a pointer to member function as follows:

```
int (Screen::*pmfi)() = &Screen::height;
Screen& (Screen::*pmfS)( const Screen& ) = &Screen::copy;

Screen myScreen, *bufScreen;

// direct invocation of member function
if ( myScreen.height() == bufScreen->height() )
   bufScreen->copy( myScreen );

// equivalent invocation through pointers to members
if ( (myScreen.*pmfi)() == (bufScreen->*pmfi)() )
   (bufScreen->*pmfS)( myScreen );
```

The calls

```
(myScreen.*pmfi)()
(bufScreen->*pmfi)()
```

require the parentheses because the precedence of the call operator — () — is higher
than the precedence of the pointer to member operators. Without the parentheses,

```
myScreen.*pmfi()
```

would be interpreted to mean

```
myScreen.*(pmfi())
```

It would invoke the function pmfi() and bind its return value to the pointer to
member object operator (.*). Of course, the type of pfmi does not support such a use
and a compile-time error would be generated.

Similarly, pointers to data members are accessed in the following manner:

```
typedef short Screen::*ps_Screen;
Screen myScreen, *tmpScreen = new Screen( 10, 10 );

ps_Screen pH = &Screen::_height;
ps_Screen pW = &Screen::_width;

tmpScreen->*pH = myScreen.*pH;
tmpScreen->*pW = myScreen.*pW;
```

Here is an implementation of the repeat() member function we discussed at the
beginning of this section, modified to take a pointer to member function:

```
typedef Screen& (Screen::*Action)();

Screen& Screen::repeat( Action op, int times )
{
    for ( int i = 0; i < times; ++i )
      (this->*op)();
    return *this;
}
```

The parameter op is a pointer to member function that refers to the member function that is to be called times number of times.

A declaration wishing to provide default arguments for the parameters of repeat() might look like this:

```
class Screen {
public:
    Screen &repeat( Action = &Screen::forward, int = 1 );
    // ...
};
```

Invocations of repeat() might look like this:

```
Screen myScreen;
myScreen.repeat(); // repeat( &Screen::forward, 1 );
myScreen.repeat( &Screen::down, 20 );
```

A table of pointers to member functions can also be defined. In the following example, Menu is a table of pointers to Screen member functions that provide for cursor movement. CursorMovements is an enumeration providing a set of indices into Menu.

```
Action Menu[] = {
    &Screen::home,
    &Screen::forward,
    &Screen::back,
    &Screen::up,
    &Screen::down,
    &Screen::end
};

enum CursorMovements {
    HOME, FORWARD, BACK, UP, DOWN, END
};
```

We can define an overloaded instance of move() that accepts a CursorMovements parameter and that uses the Menu table to call the selected member function. Here is its implementation:

```
Screen& Screen::move( CursorMovements cm )
{
    ( this->*Menu[ cm ] )();
```

```
    return *this;
}
```

The subscript operator ([]) has higher precedence than the pointer to member operator (->*). The first statement in move() first selects the member function to call by indexing the Menu table. It then calls the member function using the this pointer and the pointer to member operator. The member function move() might be utilized in an interactive program in which the user selects a cursor movement from a menu displayed on the screen.

13.6.3 Pointers to Static Class Members

There is a difference between pointers to nonstatic class members and pointers to static class members. The pointer to class member syntax is not used to refer to a class static member. Static class members are global objects and functions that belong to the class. Pointers to these are ordinary pointers. (Recall that a static member function does not have a this pointer).

The declaration of a pointer to a static class member looks the same as that of a pointer to a nonclass member. Dereferencing the pointer does not require a class object. For example, let's look at the Account class again:

```
class Account {
public:
    static void raiseInterest( double incr );
    static double interest() { return _interestRate; }
    double amount() { return _amount; }
private:
    static double _interestRate;
    double _amount;
    string _owner;
};

inline void Account::raiseInterest( double incr )
{
    _interestRate += incr;
}
```

The type of &_interestRate is double*; it is not

```
// incorrect type for &_interestRate
double Account::*
```

The definition of a pointer to _interestRate is as follows:

```
// OK:  double*  not  double Account::*
double *pd = &Account::_interestRate;
```

It is dereferenced the same way an ordinary pointer is dereferenced. It does not require an associated class object. For example:

```
Account unit;
// uses ordinary dereference operator
double daily = *pd /365 * unit._amount;
```

However, because both _interestRate and _amount are private members, we need to use the static member function interest() and the nonstatic member function amount() instead.

The type of a pointer to interest() is that of an ordinary pointer to function,

```
// correct
double (*)()
```

and not a pointer to member function of class Account:

```
// incorrect
double (Account::*)()
```

The pointer definition and indirect call to interest() are also handled in the same way as those of nonclass pointers:

```
// ok: double(*pf)()   not    double(Account::*pf)()
double (*pf)() = &Account::interest;

double daily = pf() / 365 * unit.amount();
```

Exercise 13.11

What is the type of the Screen class members _screen and _cursor?

Exercise 13.12

Define and initialize a pointer to member with the value of Screen::_screen. Define and assign a pointer to member the value of Screen::_cursor.

Exercise 13.13

Define a typedef for each distinct type of Screen member function.

Exercise 13.14

Pointers to members may also be declared as class data members. Modify the Screen class definition to contain a pointer to a Screen member function of the same type as home() and end().

Exercise 13.15

Modify the existing Screen constructor (or introduce a new constructor) to take a parameter of type pointer to Screen member function whose parameter list and return type are the same as those for the member functions home() and end(). Provide a default argument for this parameter. Use this parameter to initialize the data member introduced in Exercise 13.14. Provide a Screen member function to allow the user to set this member.

Exercise 13.16

Define an overloaded instance of repeat() that takes a parameter of type cursorMovements.

13.7 Union: A Space-Saving Class

A *union* is a special kind of class. The data members in a union are stored in memory in such a way that they overlap each other. Each member begins at the same memory address. The amount of storage allocated for a union is the amount necessary to contain its largest data member. Only one member at a time may be assigned a value.

Let's look at an example illustrating why and how a union is used. The lexical analyzer of a compiler separates the user's program into a sequence of tokens. The statement

```
int i = 0;
```

is converted into a sequence of five tokens:

1. The type keyword int
2. The identifier i
3. The operator =
4. The constant 0 of type int
5. The semicolon ;

These tokens are passed from the lexical analyzer to the parser. The first step of the parser is to identify the token sequence it receives. The information provided must allow the parser to recognize the token sequence as a declaration. For this reason, each token has associated information that allows the parser to recognize the previous sequence of tokens as the following:

```
Type ID Assign Constant Semicolon
```

Once the parser identifies the token sequence to be a declaration, it then analyzes the particular value of each token. In this case, it determines that

```
Type <==> int
ID <==> i
Constant <==> 0
```

It does not need any further information about Assign and Semicolon, since these two tokens only have one possible value: = and ; .

One representation of a token, therefore, might use two members — token and value. token is a unique code that identifies the token as one of the following: Type, ID, Assign, Constant, or Semicolon. For example, the unique code may be an integer value that represents ID by 85 and Semicolon by 72. value holds the particular value of the token. For example, for the ID token in the previous declaration, value will contain the character string i; for the Type token, value will contain a representation for the type int.

The representation of the data member value is problematic. Although it contains only one value for any given token, value can hold multiple data types. For the ID token, value refers to a character string; for the Constant token, it refers to an integer value.

One possible way of representing multiple data types, of course, is to use a class. The compiler writer can declare value to be of a class type that contains a member for each possible data type that value may represent.

Using a class as the representation for value solves the problem. However, for a given token, value has only one of the multiple possible data types, and only one of the multiple class members is used. The class type, however, carries the cumulative storage for all the data members that represent all the possible data types. Preferably, the class would maintain storage sufficient to hold only one of the multiple possible data types at a time, not storage to hold them all. A union permits just that. Here is a definition for a union representing the token data type:

```
union TokenValue {
    char _cval;
    int _ival;
    char *_sval;
    double _dval;
};
```

If the largest data type among the members of TokenValue is dval, the size of TokenValue is the size of an object of type double. The members of a union are public members by default. The name of a union can be used in a program wherever a class name can be used. For example:

```
// object of type TokenValue
TokenValue last_token;

// pointer to an object of type TokenValue
TokenValue *pt = new TokenValue;
```

The members of a union are accessed through the class member access operators (. and ->), just like class members, using a union object or a pointer to a union before the operator. For example:

```
last_token._ival = 97;
char ch = pt->_cval;
```

Union members can be declared as either public, protected, or private:

```
union TokenValue {
public:
    char _cval;
    // ...
```

```
private:
   int priv;
};

int main() {
   TokenValue tp;
   tp._cval = '\n'; // ok

   // error: main() cannot access private member
   //        TokenValue::priv
   tp.priv = 1024;
}
```

A union cannot have a static data member or a member that is a reference. A union cannot have a member of a class type that defines either a constructor, destructor, or copy assignment operator. For example:

```
union illegal_members {
   Screen s;        // error: has constructor
   Screen *ps;      // ok
   static int is;   // error: static member
   int &rfi;        // error: reference member
};
```

Member functions, including constructors and destructors, can be defined for a union.

```
union TokenValue {
public:
   TokenValue(int ix) : _ival(ix) { }
   TokenValue(char ch) : _cval(ch) { }
   // ...
   int ival() { return _ival; }
   char cval() { return _cval; }
private:
   int _ival;
   char _cval;
   // ...
};

int main() {
   TokenValue tp(10);
   int ix = tp.ival();
   // ...
}
```

Here is an example of how the union TokenValue might be used:

```
enum TokenKind { ID, Constant /* and other tokens */ };
```

```
class Token {
public:
   TokenKind tok;
   TokenValue val;
};
```

An object of type Token might be used as follows:

```
int lex() {
   Token curToken;
   char *curString;
   int curIval;

   // ...
   case ID: // identifier
      curToken.tok = ID;
      curToken.val._sval = curString;
      break;

   case Constant: // integer constant
      curToken.tok = Constant;
      curToken.val._ival = curIval;
      break;

   // ... etc.
}
```

The danger of using a union is the possibility of accidentally retrieving the value currently stored in the union through an inappropriate data member. For example, if the last assignment is to _ival, the programmer does not want to retrieve that value through the member _sval. Doing so will certainly lead to a program error.

To help safeguard against this kind of error, a programmer should define an additional object with a purpose of keeping track of the type of the value currently stored in the union. This additional object is referred to as the *discriminant* of the union. This is the role of the tok member within the class Token. For example:

```
char *idVal;
// verify value of discriminant before referring to sval
if ( curToken.tok == ID )
   idVal = curToken.val._sval;
```

A good practice when handling a union object that is a class member is to provide a set of access functions for each union data type. For example:

```
#include <cassert>
// access function to union member sval
string Token::sval() {
   assert( tok==ID );
   return val._sval;
}
```

When defining a union, the name of the union is optional. If the name of the union is not used as a type name in the program to declare other objects, there is no reason to provide a name when the union type is defined. For example, the following definition of Token is equivalent to its previous definition. The only difference is that the union is without a name:

```
class Token {
public:
    TokenKind tok;
    // name of union type omitted
    union {
        char _cval;
        int _ival;
        char *_sval;
        double _dval;
    } val;
};
```

There is a special instance of a union referred to as an *anonymous union*. An anonymous union is a union without a name that is *not* followed by an object definition. For example, here is a Token class definition containing an anonymous union:

```
class Token {
public:
    TokenKind tok;
    // anonymous union
    union {
        char _cval;
        int _ival;
        char *_sval;
        double _dval;
    };
};
```

The data members of an anonymous union can be accessed directly in the scope where the anonymous union is defined. For example, here is the lex() function recoded to use the Token class definition containing an anonymous union:

```
int lex() {
    Token curToken;
    char *curString;
    int curIval;

    // ... figure out what the token is
    // ... now set curToken
    case ID:
        curToken.tok = ID;
        curToken._sval = curString;
        break;
```

```
        case Constant: // integer constant
            curToken.tok = Constant;
            curToken._ival = curIval;
            break;
        // ... etc.
    }
```

An anonymous union removes one level of member access operator because the member names of the union are accessed as members of the Token class. An anonymous union cannot have private or protected members, nor can it define member functions. An anonymous union defined in global scope must be declared within an unnamed namespace (or be declared static).

13.8   Bit-field: A Space-Saving Member

A special class data member, referred to as a *bit-field*, can be declared to hold a specified number of bits. A bit-field must have an integral data type. It can be either signed or unsigned. For example:

```
class File {
    // ...
    unsigned int modified : 1; // bit-field
};
```

The bit-field identifier is followed by a colon, followed by a constant expression specifying the number of bits. modified, for example, is a bit-field consisting of a single bit.

Bit-fields defined in consecutive order within the class body are, if possible, packed within adjacent bits of the same integer, thereby providing for storage compaction. For example, in the following declaration, the five bit-fields are to be stored in the single unsigned int first associated with the bit-field mode.

```
    typedef unsigned int Bit;

    class File {
    public:
        Bit mode: 2;
        Bit modified: 1;
        Bit prot_owner: 3;
        Bit prot_group: 3;
        Bit prot_world: 3;
        // ...
    };
```

A bit-field is accessed in the same manner as the other data members of a class. For example, a bit-field that is a private member of its class can only be accessed from within the definitions of the member functions and friends of its class:

```
void File::write()
{
   modified = 1;
   // ...
}

void File::close()
{
   if ( modified )
      // ... save contents
}
```

Here is a simple example of how a bit-field larger than 1 bit might be used (Section 4.11 discusses the bitwise operators used in the example):

```
enum { READ = 01, WRITE = 02 }; // File modes

int main() {
   File myFile;

   myFile.mode |= READ;
   if ( myFile.mode & READ )
      cout << "myFile.mode is set to READ\n";
}
```

Typically, a set of inline member functions are defined to test the value of a member bit-field. For example, the class File might define the members isRead() and isWrite().

```
inline int File::isRead() { return mode & READ; }
inline int File::isWrite() { return mode & WRITE; }

if ( myFile.isRead() ) /* ... */
```

With these member functions, the bit-fields can now be declared as private members of class File.

The address-of operator (&) cannot be applied to a bit-field, and so there can be no pointers referring to class bit-fields. Nor can a bit-field be a static member of its class.

The C++ standard library provides a bitset class template that facilitates the manipulation of sets of bits. It should be used instead of bit-fields whenever possible. The bitset class template and its operations are presented in Section 4.12.

Exercise 13.17

Rewrite the examples in this section such that the class File uses the bitset class and its operators described in Section 4.12 instead of declaring and manipulating bit-field data members directly.

13.9   Class Scope ◆

A class body defines a scope. The declarations of the class members within the class body introduce the member names into the scope of their class.

   The member access operators (dot and arrow) and the scope resolution operator (::) can be used in programs to access the members declared in class scope. When the dot or arrow operator is used, the name before the operator denotes an object or a pointer to an object of class type, and the member name that follows the operator is looked up in the scope of the class. Similarly, when the scope resolution operator is used, the name of the member that follows the operator is looked up in the scope of the class with the name that appears before the operator. (In Chapters 17 and 18 we also see that a derived class can refer to members of its base classes.)

   It is not always necessary to refer to class members using the member access operators or the scope resolution operator. Certain portions of program text are in class scope, and the class members can be accessed directly within these portions of program text. The first portion of program text that is in class scope is the definition of the class itself. A class member name can be used in its class body following its declaration. For example:

```
class String {
public:
    typedef int index_type;

    // parameter type refers to String::index_type
    char& operator[]( index_type );
};
```

   The order in which the class members are declared within the class body is important. Members declared later in the class body cannot be used by the declarations of members declared earlier. For example, if the declaration of the member operator[]() appears before the declaration of the typedef index_type, the declaration of operator[]() is in error because it uses the undeclared name index_type:

```
class String {
public:
    // error: name index_type is not declared
    char& operator[]( index_type );

    typedef int index_type;
};
```

   There are two exceptions to the rule that names used in class definitions must be declared before their use. The first exception is for names used in the definition of inline member functions, the second exception is for names used as default arguments. Let's examine each situation in turn.

The resolution of names used in the definition of an inline member function takes place in two steps. First, the function declaration (that is, the function return type and the parameter list) is processed at the location where it appears in the class definition, then the function body is processed in the completed scope of the class — once all the declarations for the class members have been seen. Let's look at our example, defining the member operator[]() inline within the class body:

```
class String {
public:
    typedef int index_type;
    char& operator[]( index_type elem )
        { return _string[ elem ]; }
private:
    char *_string;
};
```

The first step of name resolution looks up the names used in the declaration of the member operator[](). The parameter type name index_type is looked up during this first step. Because this first step takes place when the member function definition is encountered in the class body, the name index_type must be declared before the definition of member operator[]().

Notice that the member _string is declared in the class body following the definition of member operator[](). This is okay and _string is not an undeclared name within the body of operator[](). Names in member function bodies are looked up during the second step of name resolution in inline member function definitions. This name resolution happens in the completed scope of the class. It is as if the member function bodies were processed last, just before the end of the class body. At that point all of the class members have been declared.

Default arguments are also resolved in the second step of name resolution — in the completed scope of the class. For example, the declaration of the member function clear() uses the name of the static member bkground defined later in the class definition:

```
class Screen {
public:
    // bkground refers to the static member
    // declared later in the class definition
    Screen& clear( char = bkground );
private:
    static const char bkground = '#';
};
```

Although default arguments in member function declarations are resolved in the completed scope of the class, a program is in error if a default argument refers to a nonstatic member. A nonstatic data member must be bound to an object of its class type or bound to a pointer to an object of its class type before its value can be used in a program. Using a nonstatic data member as a default argument violates this constraint. For example, if the previous example is rewritten as

```
class Screen {
public:
    // ...
    // error: bkground is a nonstatic member
    Screen& clear( char = bkground );
private:
    const char bkground;
};
```

the name of the default argument resolves to the nonstatic data member bkground and the default argument is in error.

The definitions of the class members that appear outside of the class body are other portions of program text (beside the class definition) that are in class scope. For these portions of program text, the names of class members are found even though these members are not accessed through the member access operators or the scope resolution operator. Let's look at how name resolution proceeds in these member definitions.

In general, if the definition of a class member appears outside the class body, the program text that follows the name of the member being defined is considered in class scope until the end of the member definition. For example, let's move the definition of operator[]() outside of class String:

```
class String {
public:
    typedef int index_type;
    char& operator[]( index_type );
private:
    char *_string;
};

// operator[]() accesses index_type and _string
inline char& String::operator[]( index_type elem )
{
    return _string[ elem ];
}
```

Notice that the parameter list refers directly to the member typedef index_type without qualifying its name with String::. The program text that follows the member name String::operator[] until the end of the member function definition is in class scope. The types declared in the scope of class String are considered to resolve type names used in the member function parameter list.

The definitions of static data members also appear outside the class definition. In these definitions, the program text that follows the name of the static member being defined is also considered in class scope until the end of the member definition. For example, the initializer for a static member can refer directly to class members without the need to use the dot, arrow, or scope resolution operators:

```
class Account {
   // ...
private:
   static double _interestRate;
   static double initInterest();
};

// refers to Account::initInterest()
double Account::_interestRate = initInterest();
```

The initializer for `_interestRate` invokes to the static member function `Account::init Interest()`, even though a qualified name is not used to refer to `initInterest()`.

Not only the initializer, but everything following the name of the static member `_interestRate` until the semicolon ending the static member definition is in the scope of class Account. The definition of the static member `name` can then refer to the class member `nameSize` as follows:

```
class Account {
   // ...
private:
   static const int nameSize = 16;
   static const char name[nameSize];
};

// nameSize is not qualified by Account
const char Account::name[nameSize] = "Savings Account";
```

Even though the member `nameSize` is not qualified by the class name Account, the definition of `name` is not in error. The definition of the static data member `name` is in the scope of its class and can refer to the class Account's members after the qualified name `Account::name` has been seen.

In the definition of a class member that appears outside the class body, the program text before the member name being defined is not in the scope of the class. If this program text must refer to a class member, the scope resolution operator must be used. For example, if the type of a static member is the member typedef `Money` of class Account, the name `Money` must be qualified when the static data member is defined outside the class body:

```
class Account {
   typedef double Money;
   // ...
private:
   static Money _interestRate;
   static Money initInterest();
};
```

```
        // Money must be qualified by Account::
        Account::Money Account::_interestRate = initInterest();
```

Every class maintains its own associated scope. Two different classes have two different class scopes. In general, the members of one class cannot be used directly in the member definitions of the other class, unless one class is a base class of the other. Inheritance and base classes are introduced in Chapter 17 and 18.

13.9.1   Name Resolution in Class Scope

Of course the names used in class scope do not always have to be class member names. Name resolution in class scope finds names declared in other scopes as well. During name resolution, if a name used in class scope does not resolve to a class member name, the scopes surrounding the class or member definition are searched to find a declaration for this name. In this subsection, we look at how names used in class scope are resolved.

A name used within a class definition (except in inline member function definitions and default arguments) is resolved as follows:

1. The declarations of the class members that appear before the use of the name are considered.
2. If the resolution in step 1 is not successful, the declarations that appear in namespace scope before the class definition are considered. (Recall that global scope is also a namespace scope.) (Namespaces are introduced in Section 8.5.)

    For example:

```
typedef double Money;
class Account {
    // ...
private:
    static Money _interestRate;
    static Money initInterest();
    // ...
};
```

The compiler first looks for a declaration of Money in the scope of the class Account. The compiler only considers the declarations for the members declared before the use of Money. Because no member declaration is found, the compiler then looks for a declaration of Money in global scope. Only the declarations located before the definition of the class Account are considered. The declaration for the global typedef Money is found and it is the type used in the declarations of _interestRate and initInterest().

A name used within the definition of a class member function is resolved as follows:

1. Declarations in the member function local scopes are considered first. (Local scopes and local declarations are introduced in Section 8.1.)

2. If the resolution in step 1 is not successful, the declarations for all the class members are considered.

3. If the resolution in step 2 is not successful, the declarations that appear in namespace scope before the member function definition are considered.

Let's examine how names used in an inline member function body are resolved:

```
int _height;

class Screen {
public:
    Screen( int _height ) {
        _height = 0; // which _height? The parameter
    }
private:
    short _height;
};
```

When looking for a declaration for the name _height used in the definition of Screen's constructor, the compiler first looks in the local scope of the constructor. A function parameter is declared in the local scope of its function. The name _height used in the constructor definition refers to this parameter declaration.

If the parameter declaration had not been found, the compiler would then have looked in class scope, considering all member declarations of Screen. This lookup would find the declaration of the member _height. The class member _height is said to be hidden by the constructor's parameter declaration. Even though the class member is hidden, it is still possible to use it in the constructor's body by qualifying the member's name with the name of its class or by using the this pointer explicitly. For example:

```
int _height;

class Screen {
public:
    Screen( long _height ) {
        this->_height = 0; // refers to Screen::_height
        // also valid:
        // Screen::_height = 0;
    }
private:
    short _height;
};
```

Assuming that the parameter declaration and the member declaration had not been found, the compiler would then have looked in the surrounding namespace scopes. In our example, declarations in global scope visible before the definition of the class Screen are considered. This lookup finds the declaration of the global object _height. The global object _height is said to be hidden by the class member declaration. Even though the global object is hidden, it is still possible to use it in the constructor body by qualifying the global name with the global scope resolution operator:

```
int _height;

class Screen {
public:
   Screen( long _height ) {
       ::_height = 0; // refer to global object
   }
private:
   short _height;
};
```

If the constructor is declared outside the class definition, the third step of name resolution not only considers the declarations in global scope that appear before the definition of class Screen, but also considers the global scope declarations that appear before the member function definition. For example:

```
class Screen {
public:
   // ...
   void setHeight( int );
private:
   short _height;
};

int verify(int);

void Screen::setHeight( int var ) {
   // var: refers to the parameter
   // _height: refers to the class member
   // verify: refers to the global function
   _height = verify( var );
}
```

Notice that the declaration of the global function verify() is not visible before the definition of the class Screen. However, the third step of name resolution considers the namespace scope declarations visible before the member definition, and the declaration for the global function verify() is found.

A name used within the definition of a class static member is resolved as follows:

1. The declarations for all class members are considered.
2. If the resolution in step 1 is not successful, the declarations that appear in namespace scope before the static member definition are considered.

During step 2, the compiler considers the namespace scope declarations that appear before the static data member definition, and not just those that appear before the class definition.

Exercise 13.18

Name the portions of program text that are considered in class scope.

Exercise 13.19

Name the portions of program text that are in class scope and for which the completed scope of the class is considered (that is, for which all the members declared in the class body are considered).

Exercise 13.20

To which declarations does the name Type refer when used in the body of class Exercise and in the definition of its member function setVal()? (Remember, different uses may refer to difference declarations.) To which declarations does the name initVal refer when used in the definition of the member function setVal()?

```
typedef int Type;
Type initVal();

class Exercise {
public:
    // ...
    typedef double Type;
    Type setVal( Type );
    Type initVal();
private:
    int val;
};

Type Exercise::setVal( Type parm ) {
    val = parm + initVal();
}
```

The definition of the member function setVal() is in error. Can you see why? Apply the necessary changes so that the class Exercise uses the global typedef Type and the global function initVal().

13.10 Nested Classes ◆Ⓐ

A class can be defined within another class. Such a class is called a *nested class*. A nested class is a member of its enclosing class. The definition of a nested class can occur within a public, protected, or private section of its enclosing class.

The name of a nested class is visible in its enclosing class scope, but not in other class scopes or in namespace scopes. This means that the name of a nested class does not collide with the same name declared in an enclosing scope. For example:

```
class Node { /* ... */ };

class Tree {
public:
    // Node is encapsulated within the scope of Tree
    // Within class scope Tree::Node hides ::Node
    class Node {...};

    // ok: resolves to nested class: Tree::Node
    Node *tree;
};

// Tree::Node is not visible at global scope
// Node resolves to global declaration of Node
Node *pnode;

class List {
public:
    // Node is encapsulated within the scope of List
    // Within class scope List::Node hides ::Node
    class Node {...};

    // ok: resolves to class: List::Node
    Node *list;
};
```

A nested class can have the same kinds of members as a nonnested class:

```
// Not ideal configuration: evolving class definition
class List {
public:
    class ListItem {
        friend class List;         // friend declaration
        ListItem( int val = 0 );   // constructor
        ListItem *next;            // pointer to its own class
        int value;
    };
    // ...
private:
    ListItem *list;
    ListItem *at_end;
};
```

A private member is a member that can be accessed only by the definitions of the members and friends of its class. An enclosing class has no access privileges to the private members of a nested class unless it is declared as a friend of the nested class. This is why ListItem declares List to be a friend, to allow the member definitions of List to access the private members of ListItem. Nor does the nested class have any special access privileges to the private members of its enclosing class. If we wanted to grant List-

Item access to the private members of class List, the enclosing class List would have to declare the nested class ListItem as a friend. In the previous example it is not a friend, and therefore ListItem cannot refer to the private members of List.

Declaring the class ListItem as a public member of class List means that the nested class can be used as a type within the entire program — outside the definitions of members and friends of class List. For example:

```
// ok: declaration in global scope
List::ListItem *headptr;
```

This is more permissive than we intended. The nested class ListItem supports the abstraction of our List class and we do not want the ListItem type to be accessible to the entire program. A better design, then, is to define the nested class ListItem as a private member of class List:

```
// Not ideal configuration: evolving class definition
class List {
public:
    // ...
private:
    class ListItem {
        // ...
    };
    ListItem *list;
    ListItem *at_end;
};
```

Now, only the definitions of the members and friends of List can access the type ListItem. There is no longer any harm in making all members of the class ListItem public. Because the class is a private member of List, only members and friends of the List class can access the members of ListItem. With this new design, the friend declaration is no longer needed. Here is our new definition for class List:

```
// Ok, now we got it!
class List {
public:
    // ...
private:
    // ListItem is now a private nested type
    class ListItem {
    // and its members are now public
    public:
        ListItem( int val = 0 );
        ListItem *next;
        int value;
    };
    ListItem *list;
    ListItem *at_end;
};
```

   The ListItem constructor is not defined inline within the definition of the class ListItem. It must be defined outside the class definition. Where can one define it? The constructor for ListItem is not a member of class List and therefore cannot be defined in the body of class List. The constructor for ListItem must be defined in global scope — the scope that contains the enclosing class definition. When a member function of a nested class is not defined inline in the nested class body, it must be defined outside the outermost enclosing class.

   Here is a possible definition for the ListItem constructor. However, the following syntax for the global scope definition is not correct:

```
class List {
public:
   // ...
private:
   class ListItem {
   public:
      ListItem( int val = 0 );
      // ...
   };
};

// error: ListItem not in scope
ListItem::ListItem( int val ) { ... }
```

   The problem is that the name ListItem is not visible in global scope. The use of ListItem in global scope must indicate that ListItem is a nested class within the scope of class List. This is done by qualifying the class name ListItem with the name of its enclosing class List. Here is the correct syntax:

```
// name of nested class qualified with name of enclosing class
List::ListItem::ListItem( int val ) {
   value = val;
   next = 0;
}
```

   Note that only the nested class name is qualified. The first qualifier List:: names the enclosing class. It qualifies the name that follows — that of the nested class List-Item. The second ListItem names the constructor, not the nested class. The member name in the following definition is not correct:

```
// error: the constructor name is ListItem not List::ListItem
List::ListItem::List::ListItem( int val ) {
   value = val;
   next = 0;
}
```

   If ListItem had declared a static member, its definition would also need to be defined in global scope. The static member name in such a definition could look like this:

```
int List::ListItem::static_mem = 1024;
```

Note that member functions and static data members do not have to be public members of the nested class to be defined outside the class definition. Private members of the class ListItem can also be defined in global scope.

A nested class can also be defined outside its enclosing class. For example, the definition of ListItem could be provided in global scope as follows:

```
class List {
public:
    // ...
private:
    // this declaration is required
    class ListItem;
    ListItem *list;
    ListItem *at_end;
};

// name of nested class qualified with name of enclosing class
class List::ListItem {
public:
    ListItem( int val = 0 );
    ListItem *next;
    int value;
};
```

In the global definition, the name of the nested class ListItem must be qualified by the name of its enclosing class List. Note that the declaration of ListItem in the body of class List cannot be omitted. A definition in global scope cannot be specified for a nested class if that class was not first declared as a member of its enclosing class. A nested class does not have to be a public member of its enclosing class to be defined in global scope.

Until the definition for the nested class has been seen, only pointers and references to the nested class can be declared. The declarations of List's data members list and at_end are still valid even though the class ListItem is defined in global scope because both of these members are pointers. If one of these members had been an object instead of a pointer, the member declaration in class List would cause a compiler error. For example:

```
class List {
public:
    // ...
private:
    // this declaration is required
    class ListItem;
    ListItem *list;
    ListItem at_end; // error: undefined nested class ListItem
};
```

Why would one want to define a nested class outside its class definition? Maybe the nested class supports implementation details for the enclosing class and we don't want the users of our List class to peek at the details of the class ListItem. For this reason, we don't want to put the definition of the nested class in the header file containing the interface of our List class. The definition of the nested class ListItem can then only be provided within the text files containing the implementation of the List class and its members.

A nested class can be first declared and then later defined in the body of the enclosing class. This allows for nested classes that have members that refer to one another. For example:

```
class List {
public:
    // ...
private:
    // declaration of List::ListItem
    class ListItem;
    class Ref {
        // pli is of type: List::ListItem*
        ListItem *pli;
    };
    // definition of List::ListItem
    class ListItem {
        // pref is of type: List::Ref*
        Ref *pref;
    };
};
```

If the class ListItem is not declared before the definition of class Ref, the declaration of the member pli is in error because the name ListItem is not declared.

A nested class may not access the nonstatic members of its enclosing class directly, even though these members are public. Any access to a nonstatic member of the enclosing class requires that it be done through a pointer, reference, or object of the enclosing class. For example:

```
class List {
public:
    int init( int );
private:
    class ListItem {
    public:
        ListItem( int val = 0 );
        void mf( const List & );
        int value;
        int memb;
    };
};
```

```
List::ListItem::ListItem( int val )
{
    // List::init() is a nonstatic member of class List
    // must be used through an object or pointer of type List
    value = init( val ); // error: illegal use of init
}
```

When nonstatic members of a class are used, the compiler must be able to identify the object to which the nonstatic member belongs. Within a member function of class ListItem, the this pointer is only applied implicitly to the members of the class List-Item, and not to members of enclosing classes. Because of the implicit this pointer, we know that the data member value refers to the object for which the constructor is called. The this pointer within the constructor of ListItem has type ListItem*. What is needed to access the member init() is an object of type List or a pointer of type List*.

The following member function mf() refers to init() through the reference parameter. We then know that the member function init() is called for the object specified as the function argument:

```
void List::ListItem::mf( const List &il ) {
    memb = il.init(); // ok: refers to init() through a reference
}
```

Although an object, pointer, or reference is needed to access the enclosing class nonstatic data members, the nested class may access the static members, type names, and enumerators of the enclosing class directly (given that these members are public). A type name is either a typedef name, the name of an enumeration, or the name of a class. For example:

```
class List {
public:
    typedef int (*pFunc)();
    enum ListStatus { Good, Empty, Corrupted };
    // ...
private:
    class ListItem {
    public:
        void check_status();
        ListStatus status; // ok
        pFunc action; // ok
        // ...
    };
    // ...
};
```

pFunc, ListStatus, and ListItem each are nested type names within the scope of the enclosing class List. All three names and the enumerators of ListStatus can be referred to within the scope of ListItem. These members can be referred to without being qualified:

```
void List::ListItem::check_status()
{
   ListStatus s = status;
   switch ( s ) {
      case Empty: ...
      case Corrupted: ...
      case Good: ...
   }
}
```

Outside the scope of ListItem and outside the scope of the enclosing List class, referring to the static members, type names, and enumerators of the enclosing class requires the scope resolution operator. For example:

```
List::pFunc myAction; // ok
List::ListStatus stat = List::Empty; // ok
```

When referring to an enumerator, we don't write

```
List::ListStatus::Empty
```

because the enumerators can be accessed directly in the scope where the enumeration is defined. Why? An enumeration definition does not maintain its own associated scope as does a class definition.

13.10.1   Name Resolution in Nested Class Scope

Let's now examine how name resolution proceeds in a nested class definition and in the definition of its members.

A name used within a nested class definition (except in inline member function definitions and default arguments) is resolved as follows:

1.   The declarations of the members of the nested class that appear before the use of the name are considered.

2.   If the resolution in step 1 is not successful, the declarations of the members of the enclosing class that appear before the use of the name are considered.

3.   If the resolution in step 2 is not successful, the declarations that appear in namespace scope before the nested class definition are considered.

For example:

```
enum ListStatus { Good, Empty, Corrupted };
class List {
public:
   // ...
private:
   class ListItem {
   public:
      // Look up:
      // 1) in List::ListItem
```

```
            // 2) in List
            // 3) in global scope
            ListStatus status; // refers to global enum
            // ...
        };
        // ...
    };
```

The compiler first looks for a declaration of ListStatus in the scope of the class List-tItem. Because no member declaration is found, the compiler then looks for a declaration of ListStatus in the scope of the class List. Because no declaration is found in class List either, the compiler then looks for a declaration of ListStatus in global scope. Only the declarations located before the use of ListStatus are considered for the lookup in these three scopes. The declaration for the global enum ListStatus is found and it is the type used in the declaration of status.

If the nested class ListItem is defined in global scope, outside the body of its enclosing class List, all the members of class List have been declared and all these declarations are considered:

```
    class List {
    private:
        class ListItem;
        // ...
    public:
        enum ListStatus { Good, Empty, Corrupted };
        // ...
    };

    class List::ListItem {
    public:
        // Look up:
        // 1) in List::ListItem
        // 2) in List
        // 3) in global scope
        ListStatus status; // List::ListStatus
        // ...
    };
```

The name resolution for ListStatus first looks in the scope of the class ListItem. Because no member declaration is found, the compiler then looks for a declaration of ListStatus in the scope of the class List. Because the complete definition of the class List has been seen, this lookup considers all of the members of List. This lookup finds the nested enum ListStatus within List even though it is declared after the declaration of ListItem. status is an enum object of List's ListStatus. If List did not have a member named ListStatus, name lookup would then search the global scope for declarations that appear before the definition of the nested class ListItem.

A name used within the definition of a member function of a nested class is resolved as follows:

1. Declarations in the member function local scopes are considered first.
2. If the resolution in step 1 is not successful, the declarations for all the nested class members are considered.
3. If the resolution in step 2 is not successful, the declarations for all the enclosing class members are considered.
4. If the resolution in step 3 is not successful, the declarations that appear in namespace scope before the member function definition are considered.

In the following code fragment, to which declaration does `list` refer in the definition of the member function `check_status()`?

```
class List {
public:
    enum ListStatus { Good, Empty, Corrupted };
    // ...
private:
    class ListItem {
    public:
        void check_status();
        ListStatus status; // ok
        // ...
    };
    ListItem *list;
    // ...
};

int list = 0;
void List::ListItem::check_status()
{
    int value = list; // which list?
}
```

It is very likely that the programmer intended `list` within `check_status()` to refer to the global object:

- `value` and the global object `list` are both of type `int`. The `List::list` member is a pointer type and cannot be assigned to `value` without an explicit reinterpret cast.
- `ListItem` is not permitted to access a private data member of its enclosing class, such as `list`.
- `list` is a nonstatic data member and it must be referred to in member functions of ListItem through an object, pointer, or reference.

However, given all that, the name `list` used in the member `check_status()` re-solves to the `list` data member of class List. Remember, if the name is not found within the scope of the nested class ListItem, the scope of its enclosing class is searched next before the global scope is searched. The member `list` of the enclosing class List hides the object in global scope. An error message is generated because the use of the pointer `list` in `check_status()` is not valid.

Access permission and type compatibility are checked only after a name is re-solved. If the use of the name is an error, name resolution does not look for a declaration that suits the use of the name better. Instead, an error message is generated.

To access the global object `list`, the global scope resolution operator must be used:

```
void List::ListItem:: check_status() {
    value = ::list; // ok
}
```

If the member function `check_status()` is instead defined inline in the body of class ListItem, this last modification causes the compiler to generate an error message saying that the name `list` in global scope is undeclared.

```
class List {
public:
    // ...
private:
    class ListItem {
    public:
        // error: no visible declaration for ::list
        void check_status() { int value = ::list; }
        // ...
    };
    ListItem *list;
    // ...
};

int list = 0;
```

The global object `list` is declared following the definition of the class List. For a member function defined inline in the class body, only the global declarations visible before the enclosing class definition are considered. If the definition of `check_status()` appears following the definition of List, the global declarations visible before the definition of `check_status()` are considered and the global declaration of the object `list` is found.

Exercise 13.21

Chapter 11 has a running example using the class iStack. Change this example to declare the exception classes pushOnFull and popOnEmpty as public nested classes of class iStack. Modify the definition of class iStack and the definitions of its member functions and the definition of main() presented in Chapter 11 to refer to these nested classes.

13.11 Classes as Namespace Members ◆

The classes in namespace scope presented thus far are classes defined in the global namespace scope. Classes can also be defined in user-declared namespaces. The name of a class defined in a user-declared namespace is only visible in the scope of that namespace and not in the global scope or in other namespaces. This means that the class name does not collide with other names declared in other namespaces. For example:

```
namespace cplusplus_primer {
   class Node { /* ... */ };
}
namespace DisneyFeatureAnimation {
   class Node { /* ... */ };
}
Node *pnode; // error: Node is not visible in global scope

// OK: declares nodeObj to be of type DisneyFeatureAnimation::Node
DisneyFeatureAnimation::Node nodeObj;

// using declaration: makes Node visible in global scope
using cplusplus_primer::Node;
Node another; // cplusplus_primer::Node
```

As illustrated in the previous two sections, a class member (that is, a member function, a static data member, or a nested class) may be defined outside the body of its class. As a library implementor, if we place our class definitions in a user-declared namespace, where can we place the definitions of the class members defined outside the body of their classes? These definitions can be placed either in the namespace containing the outermost class definition or in one of its enclosing namespaces. This allows us to organize the code of our library as follows:

```
// --- primer.h ---
namespace cplusplus_primer {
   class List {
   // ...
   private:
      class ListItem {
      public:
         void check_status();
         int action();
         // ...
      };
   };
}
```

```
// --- primer.C ---
#include "primer.h"

namespace cplusplus_primer {
    // ok: check_status() defined in same namespace as List
    void List::ListItem::check_status() { }
}

// ok: action() defined in global scope,
//      in a namespace enclosing the definition of class List
// The member name is qualified with the namespace name
int cplusplus_primer::List::ListItem::action() { }
```

The members of the nested class ListItem can be defined in the namespace cplusplus_primer, which contains the definition of the class List, or in global namespace scope, which encloses the definition of namespace cplusplus_primer. In either case, the member name in the definition must be properly qualified with the names of its enclosing classes, and the names of its enclosing user-declared namespaces outside of which it is declared.

How does name resolution proceed in a member definition that appears in a user-declared namespace? For example, how does name resolution proceed in the definition of action() to find a declaration for someVal?

```
int cplusplus_primer::List::ListItem::action() {
    int local = someVal;
    // ...
}
```

The local scopes within the member function definition are examined first, followed by a search in the completed scope of the class ListItem, followed by a search in the completed scope of the class List. So far, this follows name resolution described in Section 13.10. Then, the declarations from namespace cplusplus_primer are examined. Finally, the declarations in global scope are examined. When considering the declarations in namespace cplusplus_primer or in global scope, only the declarations located before the definition of the member function action() are considered. For example:

```
// --- primer.h ---
namespace cplusplus_primer {
    class List {
    // ...
    private:
        class ListItem {
        public:
            int action();
            // ...
        };
    };
```

```
        const int someVal = 365;
    }

    // --- primer.C ---
    #include "primer.h"

    namespace cplusplus_primer {

        int List::ListItem::action() {
            // ok: cplusplus_primer::someVal
            int local = someVal;

            // error: calc() is not declared yet
            double result = calc( local );
            // ...
        }

        double calc(int) { }
        // ...
    }
```

The definition of namespace cplusplus_primer is not contiguous. The definitions of class List and of the object someVal appear in the first section of the namespace definition placed in the header file primer.h. The definition of the function calc() appears in the namespace definition provided in the implementation file primer.C. The use of calc() in action() is in error because it is declared after it is used in the definition of action(). If calc() is part of the interface of namespace cplusplus_primer, it should be declared in the portion of the namespace that appears in the header file, as follows:

```
    // --- primer.h ---
    namespace cplusplus_primer {
        class List {
            // ...
        };
        const int someVal = 365;
        double calc(int);
    }
```

Otherwise, if calc() is only used in action() to help its implementation and is not part of the namespace interface, it must be declared before action() so that it can be referred to within the definition of action().

This is similar to the lookup for declarations in global scope that we saw in the previous sections: The declarations appearing before the member definition are considered, whereas the declarations following the member definition are ignored.

Here is a small trick to remember the order in which the scopes are examined when looking up a name that appears in a member definition located outside its class definition. The names by which the member name is qualified indicate the order in which the scopes are searched. For example, the name of the member action() in the previous example is qualified as follows:

```
cplusplus_primer::List::ListItem::action()
```

The qualifiers cplusplus_primer::List::ListItem:: indicate the reverse order in which the class scopes and namespace scopes are to be searched. The first class scope searched is that of the class ListItem. Then, the class scope of its enclosing class List is searched. The scope of the namespace cplusplus_primer is searched last before the scope containing the definition of action() is examined. During such a search, the lookup in any class scope always considers all class member declarations, whereas the lookup in any namespace scope only considers the declarations that have been seen before the member definition.

A class defined in namespace scope is potentially visible to the entire program. If the header file primer.h is included in more than one program text file, using the name cplusplus_primer::List in these different files refers to the same class. A class is a program entity for which more than one definition may be provided within a program. The definition of a class must be provided once in every text file in which the class or its members are either defined or used. The class definition, however, must be exactly the same in all the text files in which it appears. For this reason, a namespace class definition should be provided in a header file, such as primer.h. This header can then be included in every text file in which the class members are defined or used. This prevents any mismatch from happening if the text for the class definition is coded more than once.

The non-inline member functions and the static data members of a namespace class are also program entities. However, only one definition for these members must be provided in the entire program. For this reason, the definitions for these members are not placed with the class definition in the header file, but rather in a separate text file of their own, such as in the program text file primer.C.

Exercise 13.22

Using the class iStack defined in Exercise 13.21, now declare the exception classes push-OnFull and popOnEmpty as members of namespace LibException as follows,

```
namespace LibException {
    class pushOnFull{ };
    class popOnEmpty{ };
}
```

and declare the class iStack as a member of the namespace Container. Modify the definition of class iStack and the definitions of its member functions and the definition of main() to refer to these classes as namespace members.

13.12 Local Classes ◈

A class can also be defined inside a function body. Such a class is called a *local class*. A local class is only visible in the local scope in which it is defined. Unlike a nested class, there is no syntax to refer to the member of a local class outside the local scope in which the class is defined. For this reason, the member functions of a local class must be defined within the class definition. In practice this limits the complexity of the member functions of a local class to a few lines of code each. Beyond that, the code becomes difficult for the reader to understand.

Because there is no syntax to define the members of a local class in a namespace scope, a local class is not permitted to declare static data members.

A class nested within a local class can be defined outside its class definition. However, the definition must appear in the local scope that contains the definition of the enclosing local class. The name of the nested class in the local scope definition must be qualified by the name of the enclosing class. The declaration of the nested class in the enclosing class cannot be omitted. For example:

```
void foo( int val )
{
    class Bar {
    public:
        int barVal;
        class nested; // nested class declaration required
    };

    // definition of nested class
    class Bar::nested {
        // ...
    };
}
```

The enclosing function has no special access privileges to the private members of the local class. This can be modified, of course, by making the enclosing function a friend to the local class. However, private members hardly ever seem necessary in a local class. The portion of a program that can access a local class is very limited. A local class is encapsulated within its local scope. Further encapsulation through information hiding is likely overkill. There is hardly ever a reason in practice not to make all members of a local class public.

As with a nested class, the names from the enclosing scope that a local class can access are limited. A local class can only access type names, static variables, and enumerators defined within the enclosing local scopes. For example:

```
int a, val;
```

```
void foo( int val )
{
    static int si;
    enum Loc { a = 1024, b };
    class Bar {
    public:
        Loc locVal; // ok;
        int barVal;
        void fooBar( Loc l = a ) { // ok: Loc::a
            barVal = val;      // error: local object
            barVal = ::val;    // ok: global object
            barVal = si;       // ok: static local object
            locVal = b;        // ok: enumerator
        }
    };
    // ...
}
```

Name resolution within the body of a local class (excluding within member function definitions) is resolved lexically by searching the enclosing scopes for declarations that appear before the local class definition. The resolution of names used in the body of the member functions of a local class are first looked up in the complete scope of the class before the enclosing scopes are searched.

As always, if the first declaration found renders the use of the name invalid, no further declarations are considered. Even though the use of val in fooBar() is in error, the global variable val is not found unless the name val is prefixed with the global scope resolution operator.

14

Class Initialization, Assignment, and Destruction

This chapter looks in detail at the automatic initialization, assignment, and destruction of class objects during the course of our program. Initialization is supported by a *constructor*. A constructor is a possibly overloaded user-defined function supplied by the class designer that is applied automatically to each class object prior to the first use of that object within the program. A complementary user-defined member function, the *destructor*, is applied automatically to each class object following the last use of that object. The destructor is primarily used to free resources acquired either within a class constructor or during the lifetime of the class.

By default, both the initialization and assignment of one class object with another object of its class is supported by *default memberwise semantics*, in which each class data member is copied in turn. While this is sufficient in the general case, under certain circumstances, default memberwise semantics are inadequate for the safe and correct handling of the class. In these cases, special *copy constructor* and *copy assignment operator* definitions need to be provided by the class designer. Often, the most difficult aspect of supporting these special member functions is recognizing that we need to provide them.

14.1 Class Initialization

Consider the following class definition:

```
class Data {
public:
   int ival;
   char *ptr;
};
```

To use an object of this class safely, we must ensure that its two members are initialized correctly. What that means, however, varies from one class to another. For example, should `ival` be permitted to contain a negative value or zero? What are the correct initial values for its two members? We cannot say until we understand the abstraction the class is meant to represent. If it is meant to represent an employee of some company, then `ptr` is likely to be set to the employee's name and `ival` set to a unique employee number. A negative number or zero would be invalid. Alternatively, if the class represents the current temperature of a city or town, then either a negative, zero, or positive number is valid. Another possibility is that Data represents a *reference-counted string*: the value of `ival` is the current number of references to the string addressed by `ptr`. Under this abstraction, `ival` is initialized with a first value of 1. If that value drops to 0, the class object is deallocated.

Mnemonic names for the class and its two data members would, of course, make the intention of the class clearer to readers of the program, but would provide no additional information for the compiler. For the compiler to understand our intentions, we must provide one or an overloaded set of special *constructor* initialization functions. The appropriate constructor is selected based on the set of initial values specified in the definition of the object. For example, each of the following might represent a legal and unique initialization of a Data class object.

```
Data dat01( "Venus and the Graces", 107925 );
Data dat02( "about" );
Data dat03( 107925 );
Data dat04;
```

There are occasions in our programs (as with `dat04`) when we need a class object but do not as yet know what the initial values should be. Perhaps these values can only be determined later. Yet we still need to provide some initial value, if only to indicate that no value has as yet been selected. In a sense, it is sometimes necessary to initialize a class object to indicate that it is *not yet* initialized. Most classes provide a special *default constructor* that requires no initial values to be specified. Typically a default constructor initializes the class object such that we can subsequently recognize it as being uninitialized.

Is our Data class required to provide a constructor? As it happens, it is not because all its data members are public. A mechanism inherited from the C language supports an explicit initialization list similar to that used to initialize an array. For example:

```
int main()
{
        // local1.ival = 0; local1.ptr = 0
        Data local1 = { 0, 0 };

        // local2.ival = 1024;
        // local2.ptr = "Anna Livia Plurabelle"
```

```
                Data local2 = { 1024, "Anna Livia Plurabelle" };

            // ...
      }
```

The values are resolved positionally based on the declaration order of the data members. The following, for example, is a compile-time error because ival is declared before ptr:

```
      // error: ival = "Anna Livia Plurabelle"
      //         ptr  = 1024
      Data local2 = { "Anna Livia Plurabelle" , 1024 };
```

Two primary drawbacks to the explicit initialization list are that it can only be applied to class objects for which all the data members are public (that is, the explicit initialization list does not support the use of data encapsulation and abstract data types —these are absent in the C language, from which this form of initialization is derived) and that it requires the explicit intervention of the programmer, adding to the possibility of accident (forgetting to provide the initialization list) or error (somehow mixing up or missetting the order of initialization).

Given these drawbacks, can the use of an explicit initialization list in lieu of a constructor ever be justified? In practice, yes. For some applications it is more efficient to use an explicit initialization list to initialize large data structures with constant values. For example, perhaps we are building a color palette or dumping into program text large amounts of constant values such as the control vertices and knot values of a complex geometric model. In these cases the explicit initialization can be accomplished at load time, saving the start-up cost of a constructor, even one defined as inline, particularly for global objects.[1]

In general, however, the preferred class initialization mechanism is the constructor, which is guaranteed to be applied automatically by the compiler to each class object prior to the first use of that object. In the next section, we look at the class constructor in detail.

14.2   The Class Constructor

The constructor is identified by providing it with the same name as the class. To declare a default constructor, we write [2]

```
      class Account {
      public:
         // default constructor ...
```

---

1. See [LIPPMAN96a] for a more detailed discussion with examples and rough performance timings.
2. Normally we would declare _name to be of type string. We declare it to be a C-style character string to postpone considering initialization issues of class data members until Section 14.4.

```
    Account();
    // ...
private:
    char *_name;
    unsigned int _acct_nmbr;
    double _balance;
};
```

The only syntactic constraint on a constructor is that it must not specify a return type, even that of void. For example, both of the following declarations are errors:

```
// errors: constructor must not specify a return value
void     Account::Account() { ... }
Account* Account::Account( const char *pc ) { ... }
```

There is no constraint on the number of constructors we may declare for a class, provided the parameter list of each constructor is unique.

How can we know which or how many constructors to define? Minimally, we need to allow the user to provide an initial value for each data member that needs to be set. An account number, for example, may either be set or generated automatically to guarantee its uniqueness. For our purposes, let's say that it is generated automatically. This leaves us with the need to allow for the initialization of the two members _name and _balance:

```
Account( const char *name, double open_balance );
```

An Account object being initialized with this constructor can be defined as follows:

```
Account newAcct( "Mikey Metz", 0 );
```

Alternatively, if there are many accounts that begin with an opening balance of zero, a user may request only to specify a name, and to have the constructor initialize _balance to zero automatically. One solution is to provide a second constructor of the form

```
Account( const char *name );
```

An alternate solution is to provide a default value of zero to the two-parameter constructor:

```
Account( const char *name, double open_balance = 0.0 );
```

Both constructors provide the functionality requested by the user, and in that sense either solution is acceptable. Our preferred solution is the use of the default argument because it reduces the number of constructors associated with the class.

Should we also provide support for specifying an opening balance but no client name? As it happens, the class specification disallows this explicitly. Our two-parameter constructor with a default second argument provides a complete interface for accepting initial values for the data members of class Account that can be set by the user:

```
class Account {
public:
        // default constructor ...
        Account();

        // parameter names are not necessary in declaration
        Account( const char*, double=0.0 );

        const char* name() { return _name; }
        // ...
private:
        // ...
};
```

The following are both legal Account class object definitions passing one or two arguments to our constructor:

```
int main()
{
        // ok: both invoke two-parameter constructor
        Account acct( "Ethan Stern" );
        Account *pact = new Account( "Michael Lieberman", 5000 );

        if ( strcmp( acct.name(), pact->name() ))
                // ...
}
```

C++ requires that the constructor be applied to the defined class object prior to the first use of that object. This means that both acct and the object pointed to by pact must have the constructor applied prior to the condition test of the if statement.

Internally, the compiler rewrites our program, inserting an invocation of the constructor. Here is how the definition of acct in main() is likely to be augmented:

```
// Pseudo C++ code
// illustrating internal constructor insertion

int main()
{
   Account acct;
   acct.Account::Account("Ethan Stern", 0.0);

   // ...
}
```

Of course, if the constructor instance is defined as inline, it is expanded at its point of invocation.

The handling of the new expression is slightly more complicated. The constructor is invoked only if the new expression succeeds in acquiring memory. The augmentation of pact's definition is likely to look like this (this is somewhat simplified):

```
// Pseudo C++ code
// constructor insertion using new expression
int main()
{
        // ...

        Account *pacct;
        try {
                pact = _new( sizeof( Account ));
                pact->Account::Account(
                        "Michael Lieberman", 5000.0);

        }
        catch( std::bad_alloc ) {
                // operator new failed
                // constructor is never executed
        }
        // ...
}
```

There are three generally equivalent forms for specifying the arguments to a constructor:

```
// generally equivalent forms
Account acct1( "Anna Press" );
Account acct2 = Account( "Anna Press" );
Account acct3 = "Anna Press";
```

The acct3 form can only be used when specifying a single argument. For two or more arguments, only the acct1 and acct2 forms can be used. In general, we recommend using the acct1 form:

```
// recommended constructor form
Account acct1( "Anna Press" );
```

A common mistake of new users of the language is to declare an object initialized with the default constructor as follows:

```
// oops! this does not behave as intended
Account newAccount();
```

This compiles cleanly. However, when we try to use it, such as the following

```
// compile-time error
if ( ! newAccount.name() ) ...
```

the compiler complains that we cannot apply member access notation to a function! The definition

```
// defines a function newAccount,
// not an Account class object
Account newAccount();
```

is interpreted by the compiler to define a function taking no parameters and returning an object of type Account — hardly what we intended! The correct declaration of a class object initialized using the default constructor is to leave off the trailing, empty parentheses:

```
// ok: defines a class object ...
Account newAccount;
```

A class object can only be defined without specifying a set of arguments provided it either declares no constructors or it declares a default constructor. Once a class declares one or more constructors, a class object cannot be defined that does not invoke one of the constructor instances. In particular, if a class declares a constructor taking one or more parameters, but does not declare a default constructor, every class object definition must provide the required arguments. For example, someone in our project may argue that it makes no sense to define a default constructor for the Account class because every valid account must have a user name. A revised Account class might then remove the default constructor:

```
class Account {
public:
        // parameter names are not necessary in declaration
        Account( const char*, double=0.0 );

        const char* name() { return _name; }
        // ...
private:
        // ...
};
```

Now every Account class object *must* provide, at a minimum, a C-style character string argument to the class constructor for it to be a valid class object definition. Although this may adhere more strictly to the specification of the Account class abstraction, in practice this is likely to prove impractical. Why? The container classes (such as vector, for example) require their class elements to provide either a default constructor or no constructor at all. Similarly, allocation of a dynamic array of class objects also requires either a default constructor or no constructor at all. Our newly defined Account class, for example, fails should a user write the following:

```
// error: requires a default Account constructor
Account *pact = new Account[ new_client_cnt ];
```

In practice it is almost always necessary to provide a default constructor if other constructors are being defined as well.

What if there are no appropriate default values for a class? Our Account class, for example, requires a name to be specified for an Account class object to be valid. In this case, the best we can do is to initialize the object to indicate that it is not yet initialized with a valid set of values. For example:

```
// default Account constructor
inline Account::
Account() {
    _name = 0;
    _balance = 0.0;
    _acct_nmbr = 0;
}
```

We then need to program checks within the Account member functions to guarantee the integrity of the Account class object prior to its use.

There is an alternative syntax for the initialization of a class member: the *member initialization list*, a comma-separated list of a member name and its initial value. The default Account constructor, for example, can be rewritten as follows:

```
// default Account constructor using
// member initialization list
inline Account::
Account()
        : _name( 0 ),
          _balance( 0.0 ), _acct_nmbr( 0 )
{}
```

The member initialization list can only be specified within the constructor definition, not its declaration. The initialization list is placed between the parameter list and the body of the constructor. It is set off by a colon. Here is our two-parameter constructor, making partial use of the member initialization list:

```
inline Account::
Account( const char* name, double opening_bal )
        : _balance( opening_bal )
{
        _name = new char[ strlen(name)+1 ];
        strcpy( _name, name );

        _acct_nmbr = get_unique_acct_nmbr();
}
```

get_unique_acct_nmbr() is a nonpublic function that returns an account number guaranteed not to be in use.

A constructor may not be declared with either the const or volatile keyword (see Section 13.3.5 for a discussion). It is illegal, for example, to write either of the following:

```
class Account{
public:
    Account() const;    // error
    Account() volatile; // error
    // ...
};
```

Obviously, this can't mean that const or volatile class objects cannot be initialized with a constructor. Rather, the appropriate constructor is applied to a class object independent of whether it is const, non-const, or volatile. The const-ness of a class object is established when the constructor ends its execution and the class object has been initialized. The const-ness disappears once the destructor is invoked. A const class object is therefore considered const from the time its constructor completes to the time its destruction starts. The same holds true for a volatile class object.

Consider the following program fragment:

```
// in some header file
extern void print( const Account &acct );

// ...

int main()
{
   // converts "oops" into an Account object
   // using Account::Account( "oops", 0.0 )
   print( "oops" );

   // ...
}
```

By default, a single-parameter constructor (or a multiparameter constructor with default values for all but the first parameter) serves as a conversion operator. In the program fragment, the Account constructor is applied implicitly by the compiler to convert the literal string to an Account object in the invocation of print(), although the conversion is inappropriate in this situation.

Unintended implicit class conversions such as the conversion of "oops" into an Account object have proved a common source of difficult-to-trace program errors. The keyword explicit was introduced into Standard C++ to help us rein in this form of unwelcome compiler aid. The explicit modifier informs the compiler not to provide implicit conversions:

```
class Account{
public:
       explicit Account( const char*, double=0.0 );
       // ...
};
```

explicit can only be applied to a constructor. (Conversion operators and the explicit keyword are discussed in Section 15.9.2.)

14.2.1 The Default Constructor

A default constructor is a constructor that is able to be invoked without user-specified arguments. This does not mean that it cannot accept arguments. It means only that a default value is associated with each parameter of the constructor. For example, each of the following represents a default constructor:

```
// each is a default constructor
Account::Account() { ... }
iStack::iStack( int size = 0 ) { ... }
Complex::Complex(double re=0.0,double im=0.0) { ... }
```

When we write

```
int main()
{
    Account acct;
    // ...
}
```

the compiler first checks to see whether a default constructor for the Account class is defined. One of the following occurs:

1. The default constructor is defined. It is applied to acct.
2. The default constructor is defined, but it is nonpublic. The definition of acct is flagged at compile-time as an error: main() has no access privilege.
3. No default constructor is defined, but one or more constructors requiring arguments is defined. The definition of acct is flagged at compile-time as an error: too few constructor arguments.
4. No default constructor is defined, nor any other constructor. The definition is legal. acct is uninitialized and no constructor is invoked.

Items 1 and 3 should be reasonably well understood at this point (if not, glance back through this chapter from the beginning until this point — hopefully this does not result in an infinite reader loop!). Let's look a bit more closely at items 2 and 4.

If our Account class declares all its members public and declares no constructor, such as the following,

```
class Account{
public:
    char        *_name;
    unsigned int _acct_nmbr;
    double       _balance;
};
```

then the definition of each Account class object results in no class-specific initialization taking place. The initial values of the three members depend on the context of each object definition. Objects with static extent, such as the following,

```
// static extent
// each object's associated memory
// is zeroed out

Account global_scope_acct;
static Account file_scope_acct;

Account foo()
{
    static Account local_static_acct;
    // ...
}
```

are guaranteed to have their members "zeroed out" (the same holds true for non-class objects).

Objects defined either locally or allocated dynamically, however, are guaranteed to be filled initially with the random bits of the memory's previous use on the program's run-time stack. For example:

```
// local and heap objects are uninitialized
// until either is initialized or assigned

Account bar()
{
    Account local_acct;
    Account *heap_acct = new Account;
    // ...
}
```

New users often mistakenly believe that the compiler generates and applies a default constructor automatically if one is not present—initializing the class data members. For our Account class as we've defined it, this is simply not true. No default constructor is generated nor is one invoked. For more complex classes containing class data members or making use of inheritance, this is partially true: A default constructor may be generated, but it does not provide initial values for data members of the built-in or compound types, such as pointers and arrays.

If we want class data members of the built-in and compound types to be initialized, we must do so explicitly in one or a set of constructors. Without doing so, it is next to impossible to distinguish between a valid and uninitialized value associated with the data members of the built-in and compound types of local and dynamically allocated class objects.[3]

---

3. For those who previously programmed in C, this definition of Account behaves exactly as if, in C, we had written
```
    typedef struct {
        char        *_name;
        unsigned int _acct_nmbr;
        double       _balance;
    } Account;
```

14.2.2 Constraining Object Creation

The accessibility of a constructor is determined by the access section in which it is declared. We can limit or explicitly forbid certain forms of object creation by placing the associated constructor in a nonpublic access section. In this example, the default Account constructor is declared private, and the two-parameter constructor is declared public:

```
class Account {
    friend class vector< Account >;
public:
    explicit Account( const char*, double = 0.0 );
    // ...
private:
    Account();
    // ...
};
```

The general program can only define Account objects with an associated name or name and opening account balance. The member functions of Account and its friend vector class can define Account objects using either constructor interface.

The predominant uses of nonpublic constructors in real-world C++ programs are

1. to prevent the copying of one class object with another object of its class (discussed in the following subsection) and
2. to indicate that a constructor is intended to be invoked only when the class serves as a base class within an inheritance hierarchy and not as an object to be manipulated directly within the application (see our discussion of inheritance and object-oriented programming in Chapter 17).

14.2.3 The Copy Constructor

The initialization of one class object with another object of its class is referred to as *default memberwise initialization*. Conceptually, the copying of one class object with another is accomplished by copying each of the class nonstatic data members in turn. The class designer can override the default behavior by providing a special class *copy constructor*. If defined, it is invoked whenever one class object is initialized with another object of its class.

Often, default memberwise initialization is inappropriate for the correct behavior of our class. We override the default behavior by defining an explicit instance of the copy constructor. Our Account class requires we do this because otherwise two Account objects will have the same account number, which is expressly not permitted in the class specification.

The copy constructor takes a formal parameter of a reference to an object of the class (traditionally declared as const). Here is our implementation:

```
inline Account::
Account( const Accout &rhs )
          : _balance( rhs._balance )
{
      _name = new char[ strlen(rhs._name)+1 ];
      strcpy( _name, rhs._name );

      // must not copy rhs._acct_nmbr
      _acct_nmbr = get_unique_acct_nmbr();
}
```

When we write

```
Account acct2( acct1 );
```

the compiler determines if an explicit copy constructor for the Account class is declared. If it is declared and it is accessible, it is invoked. If it is declared but inaccessible, the definition of acct2 is a compile-time error. If an instance of the copy constructor is not declared, default memberwise initialization is carried out. If we subsequently introduce or remove a declaration of a copy constructor, user programs need not change. They do, however, need to be recompiled. (Section 14.6 looks at memberwise initialization in detail.)

Exercise 14.1

Which, if any, of the following statements are untrue? Why?

(a) A class must provide at least one constructor.

(b) A default constructor is a constructor with no parameters for its parameter list.

(c) If there are no meaningful default values for a class, the class should not provide a default constructor.

(d) If a class does not provide a default constructor explicitly, the compiler generates one automatically, initializing each data member to the default value of its associated type.

Exercise 14.2

Provide one or a set of constructors for the following set of data members. Explain your choices.

```
class NoName{
public:
    // constructor(s) go here ...
    // ...
protected:
```

```
    char  *pstring;
    int   ival;
    double dval;
};
```

Exercise 14.3

Choose one of the following abstractions (or choose your own). Determine what data (that can be set by users) is appropriate for the class. Provide an appropriate set of constructors. Explain your decisions.

(a) Book

(b) Date

(c) Employee

(d) Vehicle

(e) Object

(f) Tree

Exercise 14.4

Using the following Account class definition

```
class Account{
public:
    Account();
    explicit Account( const char*, double=0.0 );
    // ...
};
```

explain what happens with the following definitions:

```
(a) Account acct;
(b) Account acct2 = acct;
(c) Account acct3 = "Rena Stern";
(d) Account acct4( "Anna Engel", 400.00 );
(e) Account acct5 = Account( acct3 );
```

Exercise 14.5

The parameter of the copy constructor does not strictly need to be const, but it does strictly need to be a reference. Why is the following wrong?

```
Account::Account( const Account rhs );
```

14.3   The Class Destructor

One purpose of a constructor is to provide for the automatic acquisition of a resource. We saw an example of this in our Account class constructor in which a character array is allocated through application of the new expression, and a unique account number is secured. Alternatively, we might wish to set a mutual exclusion lock on an area of shared memory or a critical section of a thread. What's missing is a symmetric operation that provides for the automatic deallocation or return of a resource associated with a class object about to end its lifetime. A *destructor* is just such a special class member function. It serves as the complement to the constructors of the class.

A destructor is a special user-defined member function that is invoked automatically whenever an object of its class goes out of scope or whenever the delete expression is applied to a pointer to a class object. The destructor is given the name of the class prefixed with a tilde (~). It can neither return a value nor can it take any parameters. Because it cannot specify any parameters, it cannot be overloaded. Although we can define multiple class constructors, we can provide only a single destructor to be applied to all objects of our class. Here is our Account class destructor:

```
class Account {
public:
        Account();
        explicit Account( const char*, double=0.0 );
        Account( const Account& );
        ~Account();
        // ...
private:
        char         *_name;
        unsigned int _acct_nmbr;
        double       _balance;
};

inline
Account::~Account()
{
        delete [] _name;
        return_acct_nmbr( _acct_nmbr );
}
```

Notice that we did not implement our destructor to reset the values of our data members:

```
inline
Account::~Account()
{
        // necessary
        delete [] _name;
        return_acct_nmbr( _acct_nmbr );
```

```
          // unnecessary
          _name = 0;
          _balance = 0.0;
          _acct_nmbr = 0;
     }
```

Although doing so is not wrong, it is unnecessary because the memory associated with the members is about to be reclaimed. More generally, consider the following class:

```
class Point3d {
public:
     // ...
private:
     float x, y, z;
};
```

A constructor is necessary to allow users to initialize the three coordinate members. But is a destructor necessary? The destructor is not necessary in this case. There is no resource deallocation required for a Point3d class object. The memory of the three coordinate members is created and destroyed automatically by the compiler at the beginning and end of each object's lifetime.

In general, if the data members of a class are contained by value, as are our three coordinate members of the Point3d class, no destructor is necessary. Not every class requires a destructor, even if we have provided one or more constructors for that class. Destructors serve primarily to relinquish resources acquired either within the constructor or during the lifetime of the class object, again such as freeing a mutual exclusion lock or deleting memory allocated through operator new.

A destructor is not limited only to relinquishing resources. A destructor, in general, can perform any operation that the class designer wishes to have executed subsequent to the last use of an object of that class. For example, a common technique for program performance instrumentation is to define a Timer class. The Timer's constructor starts some form of program clock. Its destructor stops the clock and in some way displays the results. A Timer class object might then be defined conditionally within critical code segments we wish to time, such as the following:

```
     {
          // beginning of critical code segment
     #ifdef PROFILE
          Timer t;
     #endif
          // critical code segment
          // destruction of t automatically
          // displays accumulated time ...
     }
```

To be sure we understand the behavior of a destructor (and constructor, for that matter), let's walk through an example using the following program fragment:

```
(1)     #include "Account.h"
(2)     Account global( "James Joyce" );
(3)     int main()
(4)     {
(5)         Account local( "Anna Livia Plurabelle", 10000 );
(6)         Account &loc_ref = global;
(7)         Account *pact = 0;
(8)
(9)         {
(10)            Account local_too( "Stephen Hero" );
(11)            pact = new Account( "Stephen Dedalus" );
(12)        }
(13)
(14)        delete pact;
(15)    }
```

How many constructors are invoked? Four: one for the global object, global, on line (2); one each for the two local objects, local and local_too, on lines (5) and (10) respectively; and one for the heap object allocated on line (11). Neither the declaration of the reference to a class object, loc_ref, on line (6) nor that of the pointer to class object, pact, on line (7) results in a constructor being invoked. A reference serves as an alias for an already constructed object. In this case, loc_ref serves as an alias for global. A pointer, too, only addresses an object that has already been constructed (in this case, the object allocated on the heap on line (11)) or addresses no object at all (line (7)).

Similarly, there are four destructors invoked: one for the global object, global, declared on line (2); one each for the two local objects; and one for the heap object deleted on line (14). Unlike constructors, however, there is no associated source code statement to indicate the invocation of a destructor on a class object. Rather, the compiler simply inserts the invocation subsequent to the last use of the object but before termination of the associated scope.

Global class objects have their constructors and destructors applied during the initialization and cleanup phases of program execution. Although such global objects are well-behaved if used within the file in which they are defined, their safe and efficient use becomes a challenging design problem within C++ when referenced across separately compiled files.[4]

A destructor is not invoked when either a reference or a pointer to a class object goes out of scope (the object referred to has not terminated its lifetime).

---

4. See the article by Jerry Schwarz in [LIPPMAN96b] for the original discussion of the problem and the still most widespread solution.

The language guards internally against applying operator delete to a pointer addressing no object, and so we do not need to write code to guard against that:

```
// unnecessary -- carried out implicitly by compiler
if ( pact != 0 ) delete pact;
```

Whenever an individual heap object is deleted within a function, it is preferable to use an auto_ptr class object rather than an actual pointer (see Section 8.4 for a discussion of auto_ptr). This is particularly true with heap class objects when the failure to apply the delete expression, such as in the event of an exception being thrown, results not only in a memory leak but in the destructor not being called. For example, here is our program example rewritten to use an auto_ptr (it's modified slightly because an auto_ptr object doesn't support the notion of being explicitly reset to address another object, apart from assigning a second auto_ptr to it):

```
#include <memory>
#include "Account.h"
Account global( "James Joyce" );
int main()
{
    Account local( "Anna Livia Plurabelle", 10000 );
    Account &loc_ref = global;
    auto_ptr<Account> pact( new Account( "Stephen Dedalus" ));

    {
        Account local_too( "Stephen Hero" );
    }

    // auto_ptr object destroyed here
}
```

14.3.1 Explicit Destructor Invocation

In some program situations it is necessary to invoke the destructor explicitly on a particular class object. This comes up most often in conjunction with placement operator new (see Section 8.4 for a discussion). Let's look at an example. When we write

```
char *arena = new char[ sizeof Image ];
```

in effect we've allocated raw heap storage of a size equivalent to a class object of type Image. The associated memory is uninitialized and is filled with the random bit sequence of its previous use. When we write

```
Image *ptr = new (arena) Image( "Quasimodo" );
```

no new memory is allocated. Rather, `ptr` is assigned the address associated with arena. Through `ptr`, however, the memory is interpreted as an Image class object. Moreover, although no memory is allocated, the constructor is applied to the existing memory. In effect, placement operator new allows us to construct a class object at a specific, pre-allocated memory address.

When we finish with Quasimodo's image, we may wish to operate on an image of Esmerelda at the same memory location addressed by arena. On the one hand, we know exactly how to do that:

```
Image *ptr = new (arena) Image( "Esmerelda" );
```

The problem is that this overwrites our image of Quasimodo, which we've modified and wish to store on disk. Ordinarily, we accomplish this through the Image class destructor, but if we apply operator delete

```
// no good: deletes memory as well as invokes destructor
delete ptr;
```

then in addition to invoking the destructor, we delete the underlying heap memory as well, which is not what we wish. Rather, we may explicitly invoke the Image destructor

```
ptr->~Image();
```

leaving the underlying memory available to a subsequent invocation of placement operator new.

It is worth noting that although `ptr` and arena address the same heap memory, applying the delete operator to arena

```
// no destructor invoked
delete arena;
```

does not result in the Image destructor being invoked because arena is of type char* and, recall, the compiler only calls the destructor if the pointer in the delete expression points to a class type with a destructor.

14.3.2 Potential for Program Code Bloat

An inline destructor can be an unsuspected source of program code bloat because it is inserted at each exit point within a function for each active local class object. For example, in the following code fragment

```
Account acct( "Tina Lee" );
int swt;
// ...
switch( swt ) {
case 0:
  return;
```

```
case 1:
   // do something
   return;
case 2:
   // do something else
   return;
// and so on
}
```

the destructor must be expanded inline prior to each return statement. In the case of the Account class destructor, its size is small and the associated overhead of its multiple expansions is slight. If it does prove to be a problem, however, the solution is either to declare the destructor to be non-inline or to rewrite the program code. One possible rewrite is to replace the return statement in each case label with a break statement, and introduce a single return point following the switch:

```
// rewritten to provide a single return point
switch( swt ) {
case 0:
   break;
case 1:
   // do something
   break;
case 2:
   // do something else
   break;
// and so on
}

// single return point
return;
```

Exercise 14.6

Given the following set of class data members, in which pstring addresses a dynamic character array, write an appropriate destructor.

```
class NoName {
public:
      ~NoName();
      // ...
private:
      char  *pstring;
      int    ival;
      double dval;
};
```

Exercise 14.7

For the class chosen in Exercise 14.3 of Section 14.2, determine if a destructor is necessary. If not, explain why. Otherwise, provide its implementation.

Exercise 14.8

How many destructor invocations occur in the following code fragment?

```
void mumble( const char *name, double balance, char acct_type )
{
        Accout acct;

        if ( ! name )
            return;

        if ( balance <= 99 )
            return;

        switch( acct_type ) {
            case 'z': return;
            case 'a':
            case 'b': return;
        }

        // ...

}
```

14.4   Class Object Arrays and Vectors

An array of class objects is defined in the same way as an array of a built-in type. For example,

```
Account table[ 16 ];
```

defines an array of 16 Account objects. Each element in turn is initialized with the default Account constructor. If we wish, we can provide explicit arguments to the constructors within a brace-enclosed array initialization list. For example,

```
Account pooh_pals[] = { "Piglet", "Eeyore", "Tigger" };
```

defines an array of three elements initialized in turn with the constructors

```
Account( "Piglet", 0.0 );  // first element
Account( "Eeyore", 0.0 );  // second element
Account( "Tigger", 0.0 );  // third element
```

A single argument to a constructor can simply be specified explicitly, as in the previous example. If we wish to specify multiple arguments, we need to use the full constructor syntax. For example:

```
Account pooh_pals[] = {
    Account( "Piglet", 1000.0 ),
    Account( "Eeyore", 1000.0 ),
    Account( "Tigger", 1000.0 )
};
```

To specify the default constructor in an array initialization list, we use the full constructor syntax with an empty parameter list. For example:

```
Account pooh_pols[] = {
    Account( "Woozle", 10.0 ),
    Account( "Heffalump", 10.0 ),
    Account()
};
```

Alternatively, we can achieve an equivalent array of three elements by writing

```
Account pooh_pols[3] = {
    Account( "Woozle", 10.0 ),
    Account( "Heffalump", 10.0 )
};
```

That is, the array initialization list is applied in turn to each successive element of the array. Those elements without an explicit set of constructor arguments are initialized with the default constructor of the class. If the class does not define a default constructor, the initialization list must supply constructor arguments for each element of the array.

The individual elements of a class array are accessed using the subscript operator just as for an array of built-in types. So, for example,

```
pooh_pals[0];
```

accesses Piglet, whereas

```
pooh_pals[1];
```

accesses Eeyore, and so on. To access the class members of a particular array element, we compound the subscript and member access operators. For example:

```
pooh_pals[1]._name != pooh_pals[2]._name();
```

There is no way to provide a set of explicit values with which to initialize the array elements of an array of class objects allocated on the heap. A class must either provide a default constructor or provide no constructors if it wishes to support array allocation through invocation of the new expression. In practice, nearly all classes provide a default constructor.

The declaration

```
Account *pact = new Account[ 10 ];
```

creates an array of ten Account class objects allocated on the heap. Each is initialized with the Account class default constructor.

To deallocate the array addressed by pact, we must apply the delete expression. However, simply writing

```
// oops: not quite right
delete pact;
```

is insufficient because it doesn't identify pact as pointing to an array of class objects. The effect is to apply the Account destructor to the first element only, which is not at all what we want. To have the destructor applied to each of the array elements, we must include an empty pair of braces between the delete operator and the address of the object to be deleted:

```
// ok:
// indicates pact addresses an array
delete [] pact;
```

The empty bracket pair identifies pact as addressing an array. The compiler retrieves the count of elements within the array, and ensures that the destructor is applied to each.

14.4.1 Heap Array Initialization ◆

By default, then, the initialization of an array of class objects allocated on the heap requires two steps: (1) the actual allocation of the array, in which the default constructor, if defined, is applied to each element and (2) the subsequent assignment of each element to a specific value.

To provide a single initialization step, the programmer must herself intervene, supporting the following semantics: specifying initial values for all or a subset of the array elements and ensuring that the default constructor is applied to those elements not provided with an initial value. The following is one of many possible program solutions; it makes use of placement operator new.

```
#include <utility>
#include <vector>
#include <new>
#include <cstddef>
#include "Accounts.h"

typedef pair<char*,double> value_pair;

/* init_heap_array(),
 *      declared as a static member function,
 *      provides for allocation and initialization
 *      of heap array of class objects.
 *
```

```
 * init_values: initial value pairs for array elements
 * elem_count: number of elements in array
 *               if 0, array is size of init_values vector.
 */
Account*
Account::
init_heap_array(
        vector<value_pair> &init_values,
        vector<value_pair>::size_type elem_count = 0 )
{
    vector<value_pair>::size_type
        vec_size = init_values.size();

    if ( vec_size == 0 && elem_count == 0 )
        return 0;

    // size of array to allocate is either elem_count
    // or, if elem_count is 0, size of vector ...
    size_t elems = elem_count
                    ? elem_count : vec_size;

    // grab a chunk of raw memory to store array
    char *p = new char[sizeof(Account)*elems];

    // individually initialize each array element
    int offset = sizeof( Account );
    for ( int ix = 0; ix < elems; ++ix )
    {
        // offset to the ixth element.
        // if an initial value pair is provided,
        //      pass that pair to the constructor;
        // otherwise, invoke the default constructor

        if ( ix < vec_size )
            new( p+offset*ix ) Account( init_values[ix].first,
                                        init_values[ix].second );
        else new( p+offset*ix ) Account;
    }

    // ok: elements allocated and initialized;
    //      return pointer to first element
    return (Account*)p;
}
```

The trick here is to "preallocate" a chunk of memory sufficient to hold the requested class array. We allocate it as raw memory to avoid having the default constructor invoked for each array element. This is what the following statement does:

```
char *p = new char[sizeof(Account)*elems];
```

Next the program walks through the chunk, offsetting p to the address of the next Account element and invoking the two-parameter constructor if a pair of initial values has been provided, or else invoking the default constructor:

```
for ( int ix = 0; ix < elems; ++ix ) {
    if ( ix < vec_size )
        new( p+offset*ix ) Account( init_values[ix].first,
                                    init_values[ix].second );
    else new( p+offset*ix ) Account;
}
```

As we saw in Section 14.3, the placement new operator allows us to apply a class constructor to a preallocated area of memory. In this case we use placement operator new to apply the Account class constructor to each of the preallocated array elements in turn. Because we've overridden the ordinary allocation mechanism in generating our initialized heap array class, we must also provide support for its deallocation. Applying the conventional delete operator does not work:

```
delete [] ps;
```

Why? ps (we'll presume it has been initialized by a call of init_heap_array()) has not been allocated with the ordinary array operator new, and so the number of elements associated with ps is unknown. We must do the work ourselves:

```
void
Account::
dealloc_heap_array( Account *ps, size_t elems )
{
    for ( int ix = 0; ix < elems; ++ix )
        ps[ix].Account::~Account();

    delete [] reinterpret_cast<char*>(ps);
}
```

If you recall, within the initialization function we used pointer arithmetic to access each array element,

```
new( p+offset*ix ) Account;
```

whereas here we access each element by indexing into ps,

```
ps[ix].Account::~Account();
```

The difference is that although both ps and p address the same region of memory, ps is declared as a pointer to an object of class Account, whereas p is declared as a pointer to char. Indexing into p would yield the ixth byte of the array, not the ixth Account class object. Since the associated type is invalid with regard to p, we are required to program the pointer arithmetic ourselves.

We declare both functions as static members of the class:

```
typedef pair<char*,double> value_pair;
```

```
class Account {
public:
    // ...
    static Account* init_heap_array(
                    vector<value_pair> &init_values,
                    vector<value_pair>::size_type elem_count = 0 );
    static void dealloc_heap_array( Account*, size_t );
    // ...
};
```

14.4.2 vector of Class Objects

When we define a vector of five class objects, such as

```
vector< Point > vec( 5 );
```

the initialization of the elements occurs as follows[5]:

1.   A temporary object of the underlying class type is created. The default con-
     structor of the class is applied to create it.

2.   The copy constructor is applied to each element of the vector in turn, initializ-
     ing each class object with a copy of the temporary class object.

3.   The temporary class object is destroyed.

Although the final result is the same as for defining an array of five class objects,
such as

```
Point pa[ 5 ];
```

the cost of initializing the vector is greater: (1) the construction and destruction of the
temporary object, of course, and (2) copy constructors generally tend to be computationally more complex than default constructors.

As a general design rule, then, a vector of class objects is best suited for element
insertion only; that is, we define an empty vector. If we have precalculated the number
of elements to be inserted, or have a good guess as to the size, we reserve the associated
memory. We then proceed with element insertion. For example:

```
vector< Point > cvs; // empty
int cv_cnt = calc_control_vertices();

// reserve memory to hold cv_cnt Point objects
// cvs is still empty ...
cvs.reserve( cv_cnt );
```

---

5.   The signature of the associated constructor is as follows. The copy constructor applies a value to each element
in turn. By providing a class object as the second argument, the creation of the temporary object is unnecessary.

```
explicit vector( size_type n, const T& value=T(),const Allocator&=Allocator());
```

```
// open a file and prepare to iterate through it
ifstream infile( "spriteModel" );
istream_iterator<Point> cvfile( infile ),eos;

// ok, now insert the elements
copy( cvfile, eos, inserter( cvs, cvs.begin() ));
```

(copy(), the inserter class, and the istream_iterator are discussed in Chapter 12.) The definition of list and deque objects follows the same behavior as that of vector objects. The insertion of a class object into each of the container types is accomplished using the copy constructor.

Exercise 14.9

Which of the following, if any, are incorrect? Correct each instance that you identify as incorrect.

```
(a) Account *parray[10] = new Account[10];
(b) Account iA[1024] = {
       "Nhi", "Le", "Jon", "Mike", "Greg", "Brent", "Hank"
       "Roy", "Elena" };
(c) string *ps=string[5]("Tina","Tim","Chyuan","Mira","Mike");
(d) string as[] = *ps;
```

Exercise 14.10

In each of the following situations, which is the more appropriate, if any: a static array, such as Account pA[10]; a dynamic array; or a vector? Explain why.

(a) A collection of 256 elements are needed to store class Color objects within a function named Lut(). The values are constant.

(b) An unknown collection of Account elements is needed. Data for each account is stored in a file to be read.

(c) A collection of elem_size strings are to be generated and passed back to a text manager by the function gen_words(elem_size).

Exercise 14.11

A potential pitfall in the use of dynamic class arrays is to forget to place the bracket pair to indicate the pointer addresses an array; that is, to write

```
// oops: no check if parray addresses an array
delete parray;
```

rather than

```
// ok: retrieve size of array parray addresses
```

```
delete [] parray;
```

The presence of the bracket pair causes the compiler to retrieve the size of the array. The destructor is then applied `size` times to each element of the array in turn. Otherwise, a single element is destructed. The full space allocated is returned to the free store in either case.

In the original language design, extensive discussion took place on whether to require the bracket pair to initiate a search, on one hand, or whether to retain the original language requirement for the programmer to provide the explicit array size within the bracket pair:

```
// original language design required explicit size
delete [10] parray;
```

Why do you think the language was changed so as not to require the user to provide the explicit size of the array, requiring storage and retrieval of the size, but was not changed to omit the bracket pair on the delete expression, requiring that the implementation remember whether the pointer addresses a single object or an array? How would you have designed the language?

14.5 The Member Initialization List

Let's modify our Account class by redeclaring its _name member to be of type string:

```
#include <string>
class Account {
public:
        // ...
private:
        unsigned int _acct_nmbr;
        double       _balance;
        string       _name;
};
```

We'll need to modify our constructors as well. This involves two issues: (1) maintaining compatibility with the original interface while accommodating the new type and (2) initializing a member class object with an associated set of constructors.

The original two-parameter Account constructor

```
Account( const char*, double = 0.0 );
```

is insufficient for our new string class type. For example,

```
string new_client( "Steve Hall" );
Account new_acct( new_client, 25000 );
```

fails because there is no implicit conversion of a string object to char*. Writing

```
Account new_acct( new_client.c_str(), 25000 );
```

works, but is likely to prove confusing to users. One solution is simply to add a new constructor of the form

```
Account( string, double = 0.0 );
```

Now when we write

```
Account new_acct( new_client, 25000 );
```

this instance is invoked, whereas older code such as

```
Account *open_new_account( const char *nm )
{
        Account *pact = new Account( nm );
        // ...
        return pact;
}
```

continues to invoke the original two-parameter instance.

Because the string class provides for the conversion of char* into a string object (class conversions are discussed in the next chapter), we can also simply replace the original two-parameter constructor with the new instance taking a first parameter of type string. In this case, when we write

```
Account myAcct( "Tinkerbell" );
```

"Tinkerbell" is converted to a temporary string object. That object is then passed to the two-parameter constructor taking a first parameter of type string.

The design trade-off is between a proliferation of Account constructors versus a somewhat less efficient handling of char* arguments due to the creation of the string temporary. Our design choice is to provide two versions of the two-parameter constructor. Our revised set of Account constructors is the following:

```
#include <string>

class Account {
public:
        Account();
        Account( const char*, double=0.0 );
        Account( const string&, double=0.0 );
        Account( const Account& );
        // ...
private:
        // ...
};
```

The next issue is how to properly initialize a class data member that has an associated set of constructors. This breaks down into the following three subcategories:

1. How do we invoke its default constructor? We'll need to do this within the default Account constructor.

2. How do we invoke its copy constructor? We'll need to do this within the Account copy constructor and the two-parameter Account constructor taking a string as its first parameter.

3. More generally, how do we pass arguments to the constructor of a member class object? We'll need to do this within the two-parameter Account constructor taking char* as its first parameter.

The solution is the member initialization list (briefly introduced in Section 14.2). Class data members can be initialized explicitly through the member initialization list, a comma-separated list of member/name argument pairs. For example, here is our re-implementation of our two-parameter constructor using the member initialization list (_name, recall, is now a member class object of type string):

```
inline Account::
Account( const char* name, double opening_bal )
        : _name( name ), _balance( opening_bal )
{
        _acct_nmbr = get_unique_acct_nmbr();
}
```

The member initialization list follows the signature of the constructor and is set off by a colon. The member name is specified, followed by the initial values enclosed within parentheses, similar to the syntax of a function call. If the member is a class object, the initial values become the arguments that are passed to the appropriate constructor, which is then applied to the member class object. In our example, name is passed to the string constructor applied to _name. _balance is initialized with the parameter opening_bal.

Similarly, here is our other two-parameter Account constructor:

```
inline Account::
Account( const string& name, double opening_bal )
        : _name( name ), _balance( opening_bal )
{
        _acct_nmbr = get_unique_acct_nmbr();
}
```

In this case the string copy constructor is invoked, initializing the member class object _name to the string parameter name.

A common question of the programmer new to C++ concerns the difference between use of the initialization list and assignment of the data members within the body of the constructor. For example, what is the difference between

```
inline Account::
Account( const char *name, double opening_bal )
        : _name( name ), _balance( opening_bal )
{
```

```
                _acct_nmbr = get_unique_acct_nmbr();
        }
```

and

```
        inline Account::
        Account( const char *name, double opening_bal )
        {
                _name = name;
                _balance = opening_bal;
                _acct_nmbr = get_unique_acct_nmbr();
        }
```

The end result of both implementations is the same. At the end of both constructor invocations, the three members hold the same set of values. The difference is that only the member initialization list provides for the initialization of the class data members. Within the body of the constructor, the setting of a data member to a value is an assignment. The significance of this distinction depends on the type of the data member.

Conceptually, it is important to think of the execution of a constructor as consisting of two phases: (1) either an implicit or an explicit initialization phase and (2) a general computation phase. The computation phase consists of all the statements within the body of the constructor. Any setting of data members within the computation phase is treated as an assignment, not as an initialization. The failure to keep this distinction clear is a common source of program error and of program inefficiency.

The initialization phase can either be implicit or explicit, depending on whether or not the member initialization list is present. An implicit initialization phase invokes in the order of declaration all base class default constructors, then all member class object default constructors. (We consider base classes in Chapter 17 in our discussion of object-oriented programming.) For example, when we write

```
        inline Account::
        Account()
        {
                _name = "";
                _balance = 0.0;
                _acct_nmbr = 0;
        }
```

the initialization phase is implicit. Before the body of our constructor is executed, the default string constructor associated with _name is invoked. This means that our assignment of a null string to _name is unnecessary.

For class objects, the distinction between initialization and assignment is significant. A member class object should always be initialized in the member initialization list rather than assigned to within the body of the constructor. A more correct implementation of the default Account constructor is the following:

```
inline Account::
Account() : _name( string() )
{
        _balance = 0.0;
        _acct_nmbr = 0;
}
```

It is more correct that we have removed the unnecessary assignment of _name within the constructor body. The explicit invocation of a default constructor, however, is unnecessary. The following is a more compact but equivalent implementation:

```
inline Account::
Account()
{
        _balance = 0.0;
        _acct_nmbr = 0;
}
```

This still leaves us with a question regarding the initialization of the two data members declared to be of the built-in types. For example, is it equally as significant whether we initialize _balance within the member initialization list or within the body of the constructor? The answer is no. The initialization or assignment of a nonclass data member, with two exceptions, is equivalent both in its result and in its performance. That said, our preferred implementation is to use the member initialization list:

```
// preferred initialization style
inline Account::
Account() : _balance( 0.0 ), _acct_nmbr( 0 )
{}
```

The two exceptions are const and reference data members of any type. const and reference data members must always be initialized in the member initialization list; otherwise, a compile-time error results. For example, the following constructor implementation results in a compile-time error:

```
class ConstRef {
public:
    ConstRef( int ii );
private:
    int i;
    const int ci;
    int &ri;
};

ConstRef::
ConstRef( int ii )
```

```
{ // assignment
    i = ii;   // ok
    ci = ii;  // error: cannot assign to a const
    ri = i;   // error: ri is uninitialized
}
```

By the time the body of the constructor begins executing, the initialization of all const and reference class data members must have already taken place. This can be done only by specifying them in the member initialization list. A correct implementation is the following:

```
// ok: initialize reference and const
ConstRef::
ConstRef( int ii )
        : ci( ii ), ri( i )
{ i = ii; }
```

Each member may be named only once in the member initialization list. The order of initialization is determined not by the order of names in the initialization list but by the class declaration order of the members. For example, given the following declaration order of the Account data members,

```
class Account {
public:
      // ...
private:
      unsigned int _acct_nmbr;
      double       _balance;
      string       _name;
};
```

the order of initialization for the following default constructor implementation

```
inline Account::
Account() : _name( string() ), _balance( 0.0 ), _acct_nmbr( 0 )
{}
```

is _acct_nmbr, _balance, then _name. However, the members named in the initialization list (or in an implicitly initialized member class object) are always initialized prior to the assignment of members within the body of the constructor. For example, in the following constructor,

```
inline Account::
Account( const char *name, double bal )
        : _name( name ), _balance( bal )
{
        _acct_nmbr = get_unique_acct_nmbr();
}
```

the order of initialization is _balance, _name, then _acct_nmbr.

This apparent anomaly between the initialization order and the order within the initialization list can lead to the following difficult-to-uncover error when using one class member to initialize another:

```
class X {
    int i;
    int j;
public:
    // oops!  do you see the problem?
    X( int val )
        : j( val ), i( j )
        {}
    // ...
};
```

Although it looks as if j is initialized with val, prior to being used to initialize i, in fact i is initialized first and is therefore initialized with the as yet uninitialized j. Our recommendation is always to place the initialization of one member with another (if you really feel that it is necessary) within the body of the constructor, as follows:

```
// preferred idiom
X::X( int val ) : i( val ) { j = i; }
```

Exercise 14.12

What, if anything, is wrong with the following constructor definitions? How would you fix those identified as wrong?

```
(a) Word::Word( char *ps, int count = 1 )
        : _ps( new char[strlen(ps)+1] ),
          _count( count )
    {
        if ( ps )
            strcpy( _ps, ps );
        else {
            _ps = 0;
            _count = 0;
        }
    }

(b) class CL1 {
    public:
        CL1() { c.real(0.0); c.imag(0.0); s = "not set"; }
        // ...
    private:
        complex<double> c;
        string s;
    };
```

```
(c) class CL2 {
    public:
        CL2( map<string,location> *pmap, string key )
            : _text( key ), _loc( (*pmap)[key] ) {}
        // ...
    private:
        location _loc;
        string   _text;
    };
```

14.6   Memberwise Initialization ◆

The initialization of one class object by another object of its class, such as

```
Account oldAcct( "Anna Livia Plurabelle" );
Account newAcct( oldAcct );
```

is referred to as *default memberwise initialization. Default* because it occurs automatically whether or not we supply an explicit constructor. *Memberwise* because the unit of initialization is the individual nonstatic data member rather than a bitwise copy of the entire class object.

The most simple conceptual model of memberwise initialization is to think of the compiler generating a special class copy constructor internally. Within the copy constructor, each nonstatic data member in turn is initialized in the order of declaration. For example, given our first definition of the Account class

```
class Account {
public:
        // ...
private:
        char        *_name;
        unsigned int _acct_nmbr;
        double       _balance;
};
```

the default Account copy constructor can be thought of as being defined as follows:

```
inline Account::
Account( const Account &rhs )
{
        _name = rhs._name;
        _acct_nmbr = rhs._acct_nmbr;
        _balance = rhs._balance;
}
```

The initialization of a class object with another object of its class occurs in following program situations:

1.   The explicit initialization of one class object with another; for example:

```
Account newAcct( oldAcct );
```

2. The passing of a class object as an argument to a function; for example:

```
extern bool cash_on_hand( Account acct );

if ( cash_on_hand( oldAcct ))
    // ...
```

3. The passing of a class object as the return value of a function; for example:

```
extern Account
        consolidate_accts( const vector< Account >& )
{
    Account final_acct;
    // do the finances ...
    return final_acct;
}
```

4. The definition of a nonempty sequence container type; for example:

```
// five string copy constructors invoked
vector< string > svec( 5 );
```

(In this example, one temporary is created using the string default constructor and then this temporary is copied in turn into the five elements of the vector using the string copy constructor.)

5. The insertion of a class object into a container type; for example:

```
svec.push_back( string( "pooh" ));
```

For most real-world class definitions, default memberwise initialization is inadequate for the safe and correct usage of the class. This most commonly occurs when a data member of a class is a pointer addressing heap memory that is deleted by the class destructor, as is _name in our Account class.

After default memberwise initialization, both newAcct._name and oldAcct._name address the same C-style character string. If oldAcct goes out of scope and the Account destructor is applied to it, newAcct._name now addresses deleted memory. Alternatively, if newAcct modifies the string addressed by _name, it is modified for oldAcct as well. These kinds of addressing errors can be very difficult to track down.

One solution to the problem of pointer "aliasing" is to allocate a second copy of the string and initialize newAcct._name to address that. To accomplish this we must override the default memberwise initialization of our Account class. We do this by providing an explicit instance of the copy constructor implementing the correct class initialization semantics.

The internal semantics of a class may also invalidate default memberwise initialization. As we explained earlier, no two objects of our Account class must ever hold the same account number. To guarantee this we must override default memberwise initialization of our Account class. Here is our copy constructor that resolves both problems:

```
inline Account::
Account( const Account &rhs )
{
        // handle problem of pointer aliasing
        _name = new char[ strlen(rhs._name)+1 ];
        strcpy( _name, rhs._name );

        // handle problem of unique account number
        _acct_nmbr = get_unique_acct_nmbr();

        // ok: this memberwise copy works …
        _balance = rhs._balance;
}
```

In many cases the hardest part about the solution is simply recognizing that it's needed.

An alternative to providing a copy constructor is to disallow memberwise initialization altogether. This can be done with the following two steps:

1. Declare the copy constructor as private. This prevents memberwise initialization from occurring everywhere within the program except within the member functions and friends of the class.

2. Prevent memberwise initialization within the friends and member functions of the class by deliberately not providing a definition (we still need a declaration of step 1, however). The language doesn't allow us to prevent a member function or friend class from accessing any private class member. However, by not providing a definition, any attempt to invoke the copy constructor, although legal within the compilation system, generates a link-time error because there is no definition for which to resolve it.

For example, to disallow memberwise initialization of the Account class we would declare the class as follows:

```
class Account {
public:
        Account();
        Account( const char*, double=0.0 );

        // ...
private:
        Account( const Account& );
        // ...
};
```

14.6.1 Member Class Object Initialization

What happens when we replace our C-style character string declaration of _name with the declaration of _name as a string class type? How is the default memberwise initialization behavior affected? How does our explicit copy constructor need to change? We look at each of these questions in turn in this subsection.

Default memberwise initialization examines each member in turn. If the member is a built-in or compound data type, the member-to-member initialization proceeds directly. In our original Account class definition, for example, because _name is a pointer, it is initialized directly:

```
newAcct._name = oldAcct._name;
```

Member class objects, however, are handled differently. When we write

```
Account newAcct( oldAcct );
```

the two objects are recognized as Account class objects. If the Account class provides an explicit copy constructor, it is invoked to accomplish the initialization; otherwise, default memberwise initialization is applied.

Similarly, when a member class object is recognized, the same process is applied recursively. Does the class provide an explicit copy constructor? If it does, that instance is invoked to initialize the member class object. Otherwise, default memberwise initialization is applied to the member class object. If all the members of that class are built-in or compound data types, each is initialized in turn, thus completing the initialization of the member class object. Otherwise, if one or more of those members are themselves member class objects, the process is applied recursively until each built-in and compound data member is handled.

In our example, the string class provides an explicit copy constructor. _name is initialized through invocation of that instance. The default Account copy constructor can now be thought of as being defined as follows:

```
inline Account::
Account( const Account &rhs )
{
        _acct_nmbr = rhs._acct_nmbr;
        _balance = rhs._balance;

        // Pseudo C++ code
        // illustrate invoking copy constructor
        // of a class member object
        _name.string::string( rhs._name );
}
```

The default memberwise initialization of the Account class now handles the allocation and deallocation of _name correctly but still copies the account number incorrectly, and so we must still provide an explicit copy constructor. The following is a not quite right. Do you see why?

```
// not quite right ...
inline Account::
Account( const Account &rhs )
{
      _name = rhs._name;
      _balance = rhs._balance;
      _acct_nmbr = get_unique_acct_nmbr();
}
```

The implementation is not right because we fail to distinguish between initialization and assignment. As a result, rather than invoking the string copy constructor, we invoke the default string constructor in the implicit initialization phase and the string copy assignment operator within the body of the constructor. The fix is simple:

```
inline Account::
 Account( const Account &rhs )
        : _name( rhs._name )
{
   _balance = rhs._balance;
   _acct_nmbr = get_unique_acct_nmbr();
}
```

Once again, the real work is in recognizing that we need to apply a fix in the first place. (Both implementations result in _name holding the value of rhs._name. The first implementation simply requires twice the work.) A general rule of thumb is to initialize all member class objects within the member initialization list.

Exercise 14.13

Which class definition is likely to need a copy constructor?

(a) A Point3w representation containing four float members

(b) A matrix class in which the actual matrix is allocated dynamically within the constructor and is deleted within its destructor

(c) A payroll class in which each object is provided with a unique ID

(d) A word class containing a string object and vector object of line and column location pairs.

Exercise 14.14

Given the following classes, implement a copy constructor for each, as well as a default constructor, and a destructor.

```
(a) class BinStrTreeNode {
    public:
        // ...
    private:
        string _value;
        int    _count;
        BinStrTreeNode *_leftchild;
        BinStrTreeNode *_rightchild;
    };

(b) class BinStrTree {
    public:
        // ...
    private:
        BinStrTreeNode *_root;
    };

(c) class iMatrix {
    public:
        // ...
    private:
        int _rows;
        int _cols;
        int *_matrix;
    };

(d) class theBigMix {
    public:
        // ...
    private:
        BinStrTree    _bst;
        iMatrix       _im;
        string        _name;
        vector<float> *_pvec;
    };
```

Exercise 14.15

For the class chosen in Exercise 14.3 of Section 14.2, determine if a copy constructor is necessary. If not, explain why. Otherwise, provide its implementation.

Exercise 14.16

Identify each instance of memberwise initialization in this program fragment:

```
Point global;

Point foo_bar( Point arg )
{
```

```
        Point local = arg;
        Point *heap = new Point( global );
        *heap = local;
        Point pa[ 4 ] = { local, *heap };
        return *heap;
}
```

14.7   Memberwise Assignment ◆

The assignment of one class object with another object of its class is handled by *default memberwise assignment*. The mechanics are essentially the same as those of default memberwise initialization, but it makes use of an implicit copy assignment operator in place of the copy constructor. For example,

```
        newAcct = oldAcct;
```

by default assigns each nonstatic member of newAcct in turn with the value of the corresponding member of oldAcct. Once again, conceptually it's as if the compiler has generated the following copy assignment operator:

```
        inline Account&
        Account::
        operator=( const Account &rhs )
        {
                _name = rhs._name;
                _balance = rhs._balance;
                _acct_nmbr = rhs._acct_nmbr;
        }
```

In general, if default memberwise initialization is inappropriate for a class, default memberwise assignment is inappropriate as well. For the original Account class definition in which _name is declared to be of type char*, for example, the memberwise assignment of _name and _acct_nmbr are both inappropriate.

We override default memberwise assignment by providing an explicit instance of the copy assignment operator within which we implement the correct class copy semantics. The general form of the copy assignment operator is the following,

```
        // general form of copy assignment operator
        className&
        className::
        operator=( const className &rhs )
        {
                // guard against self-assignment
                if ( this != &rhs )
                {
                        // class copy semantics go here
                }
```

```
        // return the object assigned
        return *this;
    }
```

where the conditional test

```
    if ( this != &rhs )
```

prevents assigning a class object to itself. This is particularly inappropriate in a copy assignment operator that first frees a resource currently associated with the class in order to assign the resource associated with the class being copied. For example, consider the Account copy assignment operator:

```
    Account&
    Account::
    operator=( const Account &rhs )
    {
        // guard against self-assignment
        if ( this != &rhs )
        {
            delete [] _name;
            _name = new char[strlen(rhs._name)+1];
            strcpy( _name,rhs._name );
            _balance = rhs._balance;
            _acct_nmbr = rhs._acct_nmbr;
        }
        return *this;
    }
```

When one class object is assigned to another object of its class, such as

```
    newAcct = oldAcct;
```

the following steps take place:

1. The class is examined to determine whether an explicit copy assignment operator is provided.
2. If it is, its access level is checked to determine whether or not it may be invoked within this portion of the program.
3. If it is not accessible, a compile-time error message is generated; otherwise, it is invoked to carry out the assignment.
4. If an explicit instance is not provided, default memberwise assignment is carried out.
5. Under default memberwise assignment, each data member of a built-in or compound type is assigned the value of its corresponding member.
6. Each member class object has steps 1 through 6 applied to it recursively until all data members of the built-in and compound types are assigned.

For example, if we again modify the Account class definition to have _name be a member class object of type string, the default memberwise assignment of

```
newAcct = oldAcct;
```

is now carried out by the compiler as if it had generated the following copy assignment operator:

```
inline Account&
Account::
operator=( const Account &rhs )
{
        _balance = rhs._balance;
        _acct_nmbr = rhs._acct_nmbr;

        // this invocation is correct at the
        // programmer level as well.
        // same as shorthand: _name = rhs._name;
        _name.string::operator=( rhs._name );
}
```

Default memberwise assignment of an Account class object, however, is still inappropriate because of the memberwise copy of the _acct_nmbr member. We must still provide an explicit copy assignment operator, but now revise it to handle _name as a member class string object:

```
Account&
Account::
operator=( const Account &rhs )
{
        // guard against self-assignment
        if ( this != &rhs )
        {
                // invokes string::operator=(const string& )
                _name = rhs._name;
                _balance = rhs._balance;
        }
        return *this;
}
```

To prevent memberwise copy altogether, we do the same as we did to prevent memberwise initialization: declare the operator private and do not provide an actual definition of the operator.

In general, the copy constructor and copy assignment operator should be thought of as a unit. If we require one, we more than likely require the other. If we prohibit one, we should likely prohibit the other.

Exercise 14.17

Provide a copy assignment operator for each of the classes defined in Exercise 14.14 of Section 14.6.

Exercise 14.18

For the class chosen in Exercise 14.3 of Section 14.2, determine if a copy assignment operator is necessary. If it is, provide it. Otherwise, explain why it is unnecessary.

14.8   Efficiency Considerations ◆

In general, it is more efficient to pass a class object to a function either through a pointer or a reference than by value. For example, the function signature

```
bool sufficient_funds( Account acct, double );
```

requires that each invocation memberwise initialize the parameter acct with the actual Account object being passed. Either revised function signature

```
bool sufficient_funds( const Account *pacct, double );
bool sufficient_funds( const Account &acct, double );
```

simply requires that the address value of the Account object be copied. No class initialization need occur (see Section 7.3 for a discussion of the relationship between reference and pointer parameters).

Although it is also more efficient to return a pointer or a reference to a class object rather than return a class object by value, it is considerably more difficult to program correctly. For example, consider the following addition operator:

```
// does the job, but may be prohibitively inefficient
// for large matrix objects
Matrix
operator+( const Matrix& m1, const Matrix& m2 )
{
    Matrix result;
    // do the arithmetic ...
    return result;
}
```

The overloaded addition operator allows the user to write

```
Matrix a, b;
// ...

// both invoke operator+()
Matrix c = a + b;
a = b + c;
```

However, returning `result` by value, if Matrix is a large and complex class, may be unacceptably expensive — particularly if the operation is frequently carried out and discovered to be a performance bottleneck.

Although the following revised implementation improves our program's performance measurably,

```
// more efficient, but the address is invalid following the
// return -- likely to cause a run-time program failure
Matrix&
operator+( const Matrix& m1, const Matrix& m2 )
{
     Matrix result;
     // do the addition ...
     return result;
}
```

it also results in frequent run-time program failures: The address value of `result` is undefined following completion of the function within which it is defined. (In effect, we are returning a reference to a local object that formally no longer exists following completion of the function.)

The address value we return must remain valid following completion of the function. Although the following implementation provides a persistent address value,

```
// no way to guarantee the memory is not lost to the program.
// Because matrix can be large, this loss can be significant.
Matrix&
operator+( const Matrix& m1, const Matrix& m2 )
{
     Matrix *result = new Matrix;
     // do the addition ...
     return *result;
}
```

it also results in significant memory leakage: no portion of the program is responsible for applying the `delete` expression to the object after its last use. In practice, this is not acceptable.

A programmer's solution is to redefine the addition operator as a named function taking a third reference parameter within which to store the result:

```
// this provides the efficiency we require
// but is less intuitive for users ...
void
mat_add( Matrix &result,
         const Matrix& m1, const Matrix& m2 )
{
         // directly compute into result
}
```

This solves the performance problem, but the class can no longer be used with operator syntax and the general ability either to initialize objects

```
// no longer supported
Matrix c = a + b;
```

or to have them participate as subexpressions:

```
// also no longer supported
if ( a + b > c ) ...
```

The inability of the language to return a class object efficiently was considered a significant weakness of the language. One proposed solution was a language extension to name the function's returning class object. For example:

```
Matrix
operator+( const Matrix& m1, const Matrix& m2 )
name result
{
    Matrix result;
    //...
    return result;
}
```

The compiler would then rewrite the function internally to take a third reference parameter:

```
// internally rewritten function
// under proposed language extension
void
operator+( Matrix &result,
           const Matrix& m1, const Matrix& m2 )
{
    // directly compute into result
}
```

and transform all uses of the function to compute the result directly in the target class object. For example,

```
Matrix c = a + b;
```

becomes transformed internally into

```
Matrix c;
operator+( c, a, b );
```

This name return value extension never became part of the language — but the optimization did. It was realized that a compiler could recognize the return of the class object and provide the return value transformation without requiring an explicit language extension. Given a function of the general form

```
classType
functionName( paramList )
{
      classType namedResult;
      // do the work ...
      return namedResult;
}
```

the compiler transforms both the function and all its uses internally to the form

```
void
functionName( classType &namedResult, paramList )
{
      // directly compute into namedResult
}
```

eliminating both the return by value of the class object and the need to invoke the class copy constructor. To trigger it, the class object returned must be the same named object at each return point within the function.

One final point about C++ class object efficiency. The initialization of a class object such as

```
Matrix c = a + b;
```

is always more efficient than its assignment. For example, while the program results are exactly the same, writing

```
Matrix c;
c = a + b;
```

requires considerably more computation to reach those results. Similarly, it is more efficient to write

```
for ( int ix = 0; ix < size-2; ++ix ) {
      Matrix matSum = mat[ix] + mat[ix+1];
      // ...
}
```

than

```
Matrix matSum;
for ( int ix = 0; ix < size-2; ++ix ) {
      matSum = mat[ix] + mat[ix+1];
      // ...
}
```

The reason the assignment is always more expensive is that, in general, we cannot substitute directly the target of the assignment for the local object being returned. That is, whereas

```
Point3d p3 = operator+( p1, p2 );
```

can be safely transformed into

```
// Pseudo C++ code
Point3d p3;
operator+( p3, p1, p2 );
```

it is not safe to transform

```
Point3d p3;
p3 = operator+( p1, p2 );
```

into

```
// Pseudo C++ code
// not safe in case of an assignment
operator+( p3, p1, p2 );
```

The problem is that the transformed function requires the object passed to it to represent raw storage. Why? Because the first thing done to the object is to apply the constructor that had been applied to the named local object. If the object being passed in has already been constructed, then it is potentially semantically disastrous to construct it a second time.

An object being initialized is guaranteed to represent raw storage. An object being assigned, if the class declares associated constructors (and that is the case we are considering), is guaranteed not to represent raw storage and so cannot be directly passed safely to the function.

Instead, the compiler must create raw storage in the form of a temporary class object, pass that object to the function, then memberwise assign the temporary object to the target of the assignment. Finally, if the class has an associated destructor, it must apply the destructor to the temporary object. For example, a likely transformation of

```
Point3d p3;
p3 = operator+( p1, p2 );
```

is the following

```
// Pseudo C++ code
Point3d temp;
operator+( temp, p1, p2 );
p3.Point3d::operator=( temp );
temp.Point3d::~Point3d();
```

Michael Tiemann, author of the GNU C++ compiler, proposed the name *return value language extension*. His discussion of the issue can be found in [LIPPMAN96b]. Our companion text, *Inside the C++ Object Model* ([LIPPMAN96a]), provides a more advanced discussion of the topics introduced in this chapter.

15

Overloaded Operators and User-Defined Conversions

Chapter 15 looks at two special categories of functions: overloaded operators and conversion functions. These functions allow objects of class types to be used in expressions as intuitively as objects of built-in types. This chapter first presents the general concepts and design considerations of operator overloading. It then presents the notion of a friend to a class with special access permission, and discusses why friends are sometimes needed, especially when implementing overloaded operators. The chapter then looks at specific overloaded operators that require special attention when defined for a class type: the assignment, subscript, call, member access arrow, increment and decrement, and class-specific new and delete operators. The second special category of functions is the next focus of this chapter: the member conversion functions that define a set of "standard conversions" for a class type. These conversion functions are applied implicitly by the compiler when class objects are used as function arguments, or as operands to the built-in or overloaded operators. The chapter concludes with a more advanced presentation on the rules for function overload resolution involving class arguments, class member functions, and overloaded operators.

15.1 Operator Overloading

As we have seen in the examples in previous chapters, operator overloading allows the programmer to define versions of the predefined operators (as discussed in Chapter 4) for operands of class type. For example, the String class presented in Section 3.15 defines many overloaded operators. Here is the definition of our String class:

```
#include <iostream>

class String;
istream& operator>>( istream &, String & );
ostream& operator<<( ostream &, const String & );

class String {
public:
    // overloaded set of constructors
    // provide automatic initialization
    String( const char * = 0 );
    String( const String & );

    // destructor: automatic deinitialization
    ~String();

    // overloaded set of assignment operators
    String& operator=( const String & );
    String& operator=( const char * );

    // overloaded subscript operator
    char& operator[]( int ) const;

    // overloaded set of equality operators
    // str1 == str2;
    bool operator==( const char * ) const;
    bool operator==( const String & ) const;

    // member access functions
    int   size() { return _size;   }
    char* c_str() { return _string; }
private:
    int   _size;
    char *_string;
};
```

The class String has three sets of overloaded operators. The first set defines the assignment operators for class String:

```
// overloaded set of assignment operators
String& operator=( const String & );
String& operator=( const char * );
```

The first assignment operator is the copy assignment operator, which supports the assignment of one object of type String to another. Copy assignment operators are discussed in detail in Section 14.7. The second assignment operator supports the assignment of a C-style character string to an object of type String, as follows:

```
String name;
name = "Sherlock"; // use of operator=( char * )
```

We look at assignment operators that are not copy assignment operators in Section 15.3.

The second set of overloaded operators defines one operator — the subscript operator:

```
// overloaded subscript operator
char& operator[]( int ) const;
```

This operator allows programs to index into objects of class String the same way we index into an object of built-in array type:

```
if ( name[0] != 'S' )
    cout << "oops, something went wrong\n";
```

We look at the overloaded subscript operator in more detail in Section 15.4.

The third set of overloaded operators defines equality operators for objects of class String. A program can compare two objects of class String for equality, or can compare an object of class String with a C-style character string for equality.

```
// overloaded set of equality operators
// str1 == str2;
bool operator==( const String & ) const;
bool operator==( const char * ) const;
```

We look at this operator in more detail in the next subsection.

Overloaded operators allow objects of class type to be used with the operators defined in Chapter 4, allowing the manipulation of objects of class type to be as intuitive as that of objects of built-in types. For example, if we want to define an operation to support the concatenation of two objects of type String, we could decide to implement this new operation as a member function named concat(). But why choose the name concat() and not append(), for example? Although the name chosen is both logical and mnemonic, users may forget the exact name we chose. It is often easier to remember the name of an operation if we define it as an overloaded operator. Instead of concat(), for example, we prefer to name the new String operation operator+=(). This new operator can be used as follows:

```
#include "String.h"
int main() {
    String name1 = "Sherlock";
    String name2 = "Holmes";

    name1 += " ";
    name1 += name2;

    if ( ! ( name1 == "Sherlock Holmes" ) )
        cout << "concatenation did not work\n";
}
```

An overloaded operator is declared in the class body in the same way as an ordinary member function, except that its name consists of the keyword operator followed

by one of a large subset of the predefined C++ operators (see Table 15.1). operator+=()
might be declared as follows in class String,

```
class String {
public:
    // overloaded set of += operators
    String& operator+=( const String & );
    String& operator+=( const char * );
    // ...
private:
    // ...
};
```

and defined as follows:

```
#include <cstring>

inline String& String::operator+=( const String &rhs )
{
    // if the String referred to by rhs is not empty
    if ( rhs._string )
    {
        String tmp( *this );

        // create a storage area large enough
        // to contain the concatenated Strings
        _size += rhs._size;
        delete[] _string;
        _string = new char[ _size + 1 ];

        // first copy original String into new storage location
        // then append the String referred to by rhs
        strcpy( _string, tmp._string );
        strcpy( _string + tmp._size, rhs._string );
    }
    return *this;
}

inline String& String::operator+=( const char *s )
{
    // if s is not a null pointer
    if ( s )
    {
        String tmp( *this );

        // create a storage area large enough
        // to contain the result of the concatenation
        _size += strlen( s );
        delete[] _string;
        _string = new char[ _size + 1 ];
```

```
        // first copy original String into new storage location
        // then append the C-style string referred to by s
        strcpy( _string, tmp._string );
        strcpy( _string + tmp._size, s );
    }
    return *this;
}
```

15.1.1 Class Member versus Nonmember

Let's look at our String class equality operators in a little bit more detail. The first operator allows us to compare for equality two objects of class String, and the second operator allows us to compare an object of class String with a C-style character string. For example:

```
#include "String.h"

int main() {
    String flower;
    // set flower to something

    if ( flower == "lily" ) // ok
        // ...
    else
    if ( "tulip" == flower ) // error
        // ...
}
```

The first use of the equality operator in main() calls the String class overloaded operator==(const char *). However, the second use of the equality operator results in a compiler error. How can this be?

The problem is that an overloaded operator that is a class member is only considered when the operator is used with a *left* operand that is an object of class type. Because the left operand is not of class type, the compiler tries to find a built-in operator that can take a left operand that is a C-style character string and a right operand that is of class String. Of course, no such operator exists and the compiler issues an error message for the second use of the equality operator in main().

But, you will say, it is possible to create an object of class String from a C-style character string using the class constructor. Why doesn't the compiler implicitly do the following conversion:

```
        if ( String( "tulip" ) == flower ) // ok: calls member operator
```

The short answer is efficiency. Overloaded operators do not require that both operands be of the same type. A Text class, for example, could define the following equality operators as member functions

```
class Text {
public:
   Text( const char * = 0 );
   Text( const Text & );

   // overloaded set of equality operators
   bool operator==( const char * ) const;
   bool operator==( const String & ) const;
   bool operator==( const Text & ) const;

   // ....
};
```

and the expression in `main()` could be rewritten to the following just as well:

```
if ( Text( "tulip" ) == flower ) // call Text::operator==()
```

So, to find the equality operator for this comparison, the compiler would have to look at all the class definitions, to find all the constructors that can convert the left operand to a class type, and then find the associated overloaded equality operators for each of these class types to see if any can perform the equality operation. The compiler would then need to decide which combination of constructor and equality operator, if any, best matches the right-hand operand! If the compiler was required to do this, the time it would take to compile C++ programs would increase significantly. Instead, the compiler only considers the member overloaded operators defined in the class of the left operand (and the overloaded operators defined in its base classes, as we will see in Chapter 19).

However, it is possible to declare overloaded operators that are not class members. Overloaded operators that are not class members are considered for the erroneous comparison in `main()`. This comparison, in which the C-style character string is the left operand, can become valid if we replace the member equality operators in String with equality operators declared in namespace scope, as follows:

```
bool operator==( const String &, const String & );
bool operator==( const String &, const char * );
```

Notice that these global overloaded operators have one more parameter than the member overloaded operators. With a member operator, the implicit `this` pointer is used as an implicit first parameter. For example, with the member operators, the expression

```
flower == "lily"
```

is rewritten by the compiler as

```
flower.operator==( "lily" )
```

and `flower`, the left operand, is referred to within the definition of the member overloaded operator through the `this` pointer. (The `this` pointer is introduced in Section 13.4.). With a global overloaded operator, the parameter that represents the left operand must be specified explicitly.

With the global overloaded operators for class String, the expression

```
flower == "lily"
```

calls the operator:

```
bool operator==( const String &, const char * );
```

Which operator does the second use of the equality operator call?

```
"tulip" == flower
```

We did not define the following overloaded operator:

```
bool operator==( const char *, const String & );
```

Do we need to? We could, but we don't need to. When an overloaded operator is a namespace function, conversions are considered for both the first and the second parameters of the operator; that is, for both the left and the right operand of the equality operator. This means that the compiler interprets the second use of the equality operator as follows,

```
operator==( String("tulip") , flower );
```

and invokes the following overloaded operator to perform the comparison:

```
bool operator==( const String &, const String & );
```

Okay, so now you are probably wondering why we provided the second overloaded operator.

```
bool operator==( const String &, const char * );
```

The type conversion from C-style character string to class String can also be applied to the right operand. The function main() compiles without error if we simply define one namespace overloaded operator that accepts two operands of class String:

```
bool operator==( const String &, const String & );
```

Whether we provide only this one overloaded operator or whether we provide these additional two operators

```
bool operator==( const char *, const String & );
bool operator==( const String &, const char * );
```

will depend on the run-time costs of the type conversion from C-style string to String; that is, it will depend on the additional cost caused by the constructor call on programs using our String class. If we anticipate the equality operator to be used frequently for comparisons between C-style strings and objects of type String, it may be a good idea to provide all three instances of the namespace global operator. (We have more to say about performance in the section on friends that follows.)

We look at conversions to class type using constructors in more detail in Section 15.9. We also reexamine function overload resolution in the light of conversions to and from class types in Section 15.10, and examine function overload resolution involving overloaded operators in Section 15.12.

In general, then, how does one decide between making an operator a class member or a namespace member? In some cases, the programmer has no choice.

- When an overloaded operator is a class member, the class member operator is only invoked when the operator is used with a *left* operand that is an object of class type. If the operator must be used with a left operand of another type, then the overloaded operator *must* be a namespace member.

- The assignment ("="), subscript ("[]"), call ("()"), and member access arrow ("->") operators are required by the language to be defined as class member operators. The definition of any one of these operators as a namespace member is flagged at compile time as an error. For example:

```
// error: must be a class member
char& operator[]( String & ,int ix );
```

We look at the assignment operator in more detail in Section 15.3, at the subscript operator in Section 15.4, at the call operator in Section 15.5, and at the member access operator arrow -> in Section 15.6.

Otherwise, the choice is up to the class designer whether to declare the operator as either a class member or a namespace member. Symmetric operators, such as the equality operator, are best defined as namespace members if either operand can be of class type, as is the case with our String class.

Before completing this subsection, let's define the namespace equality operators for class String:

```
bool operator==( const String &str1, const String &str2 )
{
    if ( str1.size() != str2.size() )
        return false;
    return strcmp( str1.c_str(), str2.c_str() ) ? false : true;
}

inline bool operator==( const String &str, const char *s )
{
    return strcmp( str.c_str(), s ) ? false : true;
}
```

15.1.2   Overloaded Operator Names

Only the predefined set of C++ operators may be overloaded. Table 15.1 lists the operators that may be overloaded.

Table 15.1 Overloadable Operators

+	-	*	/	%	^	&	|	~
!	,	=	<	>	<=	>=	++	--
<<	>>	==	!=	&&	||	+=	-=	/=
%=	^=	&=	|=	*=	<<=	>>=	[]	()
->	->*	new	new[]	delete	delete[]			

The designer of a class may not declare an overloaded operator with a name not presented in this list. For example, if an overloaded operator** that provides an algorithm for exponentiation is declared, a compile-time error is generated.

The following four C++ operators cannot be overloaded:

```
// nonoverloadable operators
::  .*  .  ?:
```

The predefined meaning of an operator for the built-in types may not be changed. For example, the built-in integer addition operation cannot be replaced with an operation that checks for overflow.

```
// error: cannot redefine built-in operator for ints
int operator+( int, int );
```

Nor may additional operators be defined for the built-in data types. For example, an operator+ taking two operands of array types cannot be added to the set of built-in operations.

The programmer may only define overloaded operators for operands of class type or enumeration type. This is enforced by the requirement that an overloaded operator may be declared either as a member of a class, or as a namespace member and must take at least one parameter of class or enumeration type (either passed by value or passed by reference).

The predefined precedence of the operators (Section 4.13 discusses operator precedence) cannot be overridden. Regardless of the class type and of the operator implementation,

```
x == y + z;
```

always performs operator+ before operator==. As with the predefined operators, when using an overloaded operator, precedence can be overridden with the use of parentheses.

The predefined *arity* of the operator must be preserved. The unary logical NOT operator, for example, cannot be defined as a binary operator for two objects of class String. The following implementation is illegal and results in a compile-time error:

```
// illegal: ! is a unary operator
bool operator!( const String &s1, const String &s2 )
{
    return( strcmp( s1.c_str(), s2.c_str() ) != 0 );
}
```

For built-in types, four predefined operators ("+", "-", "*", and "&") serve as both unary and binary operators. Either or both arities of these operators can be overloaded.

Default arguments for overloaded operators are illegal, except for `operator()`.

15.1.3   Overloaded Operator Design

The assignment, address of, and comma operators have predefined meanings for operands of class types. These operators can also be overloaded for class operands. For any other operator to have meaning when applied to an operand of class type, the designer of the class must define it explicitly. The choice of which operators to provide is determined by the expected uses of the class.

Always begin by defining the public interface of the class. Which operations must the class provide for its users? These will be the minimum set of public member functions. Once this set is defined, it is possible to consider which operations should be defined as overloaded operators.

Once the public interface of the class is defined, look for a logical mapping between each operation and an operator:

- `isEmpty()` becomes the logical NOT operator, `operator!()`.
- `isEqual()` becomes the equality operator, `operator==()`.
- `copy()` becomes the assignment operator, `operator=()`.

Each operator has an associated meaning from its predefined use. Binary +, for example, is strongly identified with addition. Mapping binary + to an analogous operation within a class type can provide a convenient notational shorthand. For example, addition for the matrix type, which adds two objects of type matrix together, is an appropriate extension of binary +.

The worst abuse of operator overloading is not the obvious abuse of defining subtraction to be `operator+()`. No responsible programmer would do that. The worst abuse is an operator with an operation that is ambiguous to its users.

An operator with ambiguous meaning, in this sense, is one that supports equally well a number of different interpretations. A perfectly clear and well-reasoned explanation of `operator+()` is of very little comfort to the users of our String class who believe it to serve as a concatenation operator. When the meaning of an overloaded operator is not obvious, it is probably a good idea not to provide it.

The equivalence between the meaning of a compound operator and the meaning of the corresponding single operators for operands of built-in types (for example, the equivalence between + followed by = and the compound operator +=) must also be defined explicitly for a class. For example, if `operator+()` and `operator=()` are defined for our class String to support separate operations of concatenation and memberwise copy,

```
String s1( "C" );
String s2( "++" );

s1 = s1 + s2; // s1 == "C++"
```

these overloaded operators do *not* support implicitly the equivalent compound assignment operat ::

```
s1 += s2;
```

The compou   assignment operator must be defined explicitly. If it is defined, it should provide tne expected meaning.

Exercise 15.1

Why does the following *not* invoke the overloaded operator==(const String &, const String &)?

```
"cobble" == "stone"
```

Exercise 15.2

Provide overloaded inequality operators that can handle the following three cases:

```
String != String
String != C-style string
C-style string != String
```

Explain why you chose to implement one or multiple operators.

Exercise 15.3

Identify which member functions of the Screen class implemented in Chapter 13, in Sections 13.3, 13.4, and 13.6, are candidates for operator overloading.

Exercise 15.4

Explain why the overloaded input and output operators defined for class String in Section 3.15 are declared as global functions and not as member functions.

Exercise 15.5

Implement the overloaded input and output operators for the class Screen defined in Chapter 13.

15.2 Friends

Let's reexamine the definition of the overloaded equality operators for class String defined in namespace scope and introduced in the previous section. The equality operator for two String objects is as follows:

```
bool operator==( const String &str1, const String &str2 )
{
    if ( str1.size() != str2.size() )
        return false;
    return strcmp( str1.c_str(), str2.c_str() ) ? false : true;
}
```

Compare this definition with the definition of the operator when it is defined as a member function:

```
bool String::operator==( const String &rhs ) const
{
    if ( _size != rhs._size )
        return false;
    return strcmp( _string, rhs._string ) ? false : true;
}
```

Do you see the difference? Notice that we had to modify how the definition refers to the private data members of class String. Because the new equality operator is a global function, and not a class member function, it cannot refer to String's private data members directly. Instead, it uses the access member functions size() and c_str() to obtain the size of the String object and its underlying C-style character string.

Another possible implementation is to declare the global equality operators as *friends* of class String. By declaring a function or operator as a friend, a class grants this function or operator access to its nonpublic members.

A friend declaration begins with the keyword friend. It may appear only within a class definition. Since friends are not members of the class granting friendship, they are not affected by the public, private, or protected section in which they are declared within the class body. Here we choose to group all friend declarations immediately following the class head:

```
class String {
    friend bool operator==( const String &, const String & );
    friend bool operator==( const char *, const String & );
    friend bool operator==( const String &, const char * );
public:
    // ... rest of class String
};
```

The three friend declarations in class String declare the three overloaded comparison operators declared in global scope (and introduced in the previous section) as friends of class String.

Now that the equality operators have been declared as friends, their definition may refer to String's private members directly:

```
// friend operators: refer to String private members directly
bool operator==( const String &str1, const String &str2 )
{
   if ( str1._size != str2._size )
      return false;
   return strcmp( str1._string, str2._string ) ? false : true;
}

inline bool operator==( const String &str, const char *s )
{
   return strcmp( str._string, s ) ? false : true;
}
// etc.
```

One might successfully argue, in this case, that direct access of the _size and _string members is unnecessary since c_str() and size(), being inline, provide equivalent efficiency while preserving the member encapsulation. Use of an access function rather than direct member access does not always mean a less efficient implementation. Because of these access functions there is no need to declare the equality operators of our String class as friend functions.

How do we decide, then, whether an operator that is not a class member should be made a friend or whether it should use the access member functions? In general, a class implementor should try to minimize the number of namespace functions and operators that have access to the internal representation of a class. If access member functions are provided and they are equally efficient, then it is preferable to use them and isolate the namespace operators from the changes in the class representation, just as it is done with other namespace functions. If the class implementor decides not to provide access member functions for some of the class private members, and if the namespace operators need to refer to these private members to perform their operations, then the use of the friend mechanism becomes necessary.

The use of friend declarations is most common to allow nonmember overloaded operators to access the private members of a class of which it is a friend. The reason for this is that, except for having to provide symmetry to the left and right operands, an overloaded operator would otherwise be a member function with full access to the class private members.

While the predominant use of friend declarations is that of overloaded operators, there are occasions when a namespace function, a member function of another previously defined class, or an entire class must be declared as a friend. In making one class a friend to another class, the member functions of the friend class are given access to the nonpublic members of the class granting friendship. Here we examine in more detail friend declarations for functions other than operators.

A class must declare as a friend each function in a set of overloaded functions that it wishes to make a friend. For example:

```
extern ostream& storeOn( ostream &, Screen & );
extern BitMap& storeOn( BitMap &, Screen & );
// ...

class Screen
{
    friend ostream& storeOn( ostream &, Screen & );
    friend BitMap& storeOn( BitMap &, Screen & );
    // ...
};
```

If a function manipulates objects of two distinct class types, and the function needs to access the nonpublic members of both classes, the function may either be declared as a friend to both classes or made a member function of one class and a friend to the other. Let's look at how this might be done.

If we decide that a function must be made a friend to both classes, the friend declarations are as follows:

```
class Window; // declaration only
class Screen {
    friend bool is_equal( Screen &, Window & );
    // ...
};

class Window {
    friend bool is_equal( Screen &, Window & );
    // ...
};
```

If we decide that the function must be made a member function of one class and a friend to another class, the member function declaration and the friend declaration are as follows:

```
class Window;
class Screen {
public:
    // copy is a member of class Screen
    Screen& copy( Window & );
    // ...
};

class Window {
```

```
        // Screen::copy is a friend of class Window
        friend Screen& Screen::copy( Window & );
        // ...
    };

    Screen& Screen::copy( Window & ) { /* ... */ }
```

A member function of a class cannot be declared as a friend of another class until its class definition has been seen. This is not always possible. For example, what if the Screen class must declare the member functions of the Window class as friends and the Window class must declare the member functions of the Screen class as friends? In a case such as this, the entire Window class can be declared as a friend to the Screen class. For example:

```
    class Window;
    class Screen {
        friend class Window;
        // ...
    };
```

The nonpublic members of class Screen may now be accessed within each of the Window member functions.

Exercise 15.6

Reimplement the input and output operators defined for class Screen in Example 15.5 as friend functions and modify their definition to access the class private members directly. Which implementation is preferable? Explain why.

15.3   Operator =

The assignment of one class object with another object of its class type is performed using the copy assignment operator. This special assignment operator was described in Section 14.7.

Other assignment operators can be defined for a class type. If objects of a class type are to be assigned values of a type other than their own class type, assignment operators accepting a parameter of this other type can be defined. For example, to support the assignment of a C-style character string to an object of our String class, such as,

```
    String car ("Volks");
    car = "Studebaker";
```

we provide the following assignment operator that accepts a const char*. This operator has been declared earlier in our String class:

```
class String {
public:
   // assignment operator for char*
   String& operator=( const char * );
   // ....
private:
   int    _size;
   char *_string;
};
```

This assignment operator is implemented as follows. If the String object is assigned a null pointer value, the String object is reset to be empty; otherwise, the content of the String object is a copy of the C-style character string that it is assigned:

```
String& String::operator=( const char *sobj )
{
   // sobj is the null pointer,
   if ( ! sobj ) {
      _size = 0;
      delete[] _string;
      _string = 0;
   }
   else {
      _size = strlen( sobj );
      delete[] _string;
      _string = new char[ _size + 1 ];
      strcpy( _string, sobj );
   }
   return *this;
}
```

_string refers to a copy of the C-style character string to which the parameter sobj refers. Why a copy? We cannot assign sobj to _string directly:

```
_string = sobj; // error: type mismatch
```

sobj is a pointer to const. A pointer to const cannot be assigned to a pointer to non-const (as illustrated in Section 3.5). We could decide to define the assignment operator as follows

```
String& String::operator=( char *sobj ) { // ...
```

which now allows _string to refer directly to the C-style character string to which sobj refers. However, this creates other problems. Recall that a C-style character string has type const char*. Defining the parameter as a pointer to non-const prohibits the assignment expression we wanted to allow in the first place!

```
car = "Studebaker"; // not allowed with operator=( char * ) !
```

We have no choice. The parameter must be a const char* to allow C-style character strings to be assigned to String objects. There are other problems if _string is made to refer directly to the C-style character string to which `sobj` refers. We don't know to what `sobj` refers. It may refer to a character array that can be modified in ways unknown to the String object. For example:

```
char ia[] = { 'd', 'a', 'n', 'c', 'e', 'r' };
String trap = ia; // trap._string refers to ia
ia[3] = 'g';  // not what we want: changes ia and trap._string
```

If `trap._string` was made to refer to `ia` directly, the object `trap` would have very surprising behavior; its value could change without invoking any of the String member functions. We therefore believe that allocating memory to hold the value of the C-style character string to which `_string` refers gives us less surprising behavior for our String class objects.

Notice that our assignment operator uses a `delete` expression. `_string` refers to an array of characters allocated on the heap. To prevent a memory leak, the C-style character string to which `_string` refers is deallocated using a `delete` expression before `_string` is made to refer to the memory allocated to hold the new string value. Because `_string` refers to an array of character, the array version of the `delete` expression must be used. (Array `delete` expressions are discussed in Section 8.4.)

One last thing to note about our assignment operator: The return type of the assignment operator is a reference to the String class. Why would we declare this assignment operator to return a reference? For built-in types, assignment operators can be chained together as follows:

```
// chain of assignment operators
int iobj, jobj;
iobj = jobj = 63;
```

Assignment operators associate right to left. The order of the previous assignments is as follows:

```
iobj = (jobj = 63);
```

We would like to preserve this behavior for assignments to objects of our String class, such that the following, for example, is supported:

```
String verb, noun;
verb = noun = "count";
```

The first assignment in this chain calls the assignment operator for `const char*` defined earlier. The type of the result of this assignment must be such that it can be used as an argument for the String class copy assignment operator. For this reason, even though the parameter of the assignment operator is `const char*`, its return type is a reference to the String class.

Assignment operators can be overloaded. In our String class, the set of overloaded assignment operators is the following:

```
// overloaded set of assignment operators
String& operator=( const String & );
String& operator=( const char * );
```

There may be an assignment operator for every type that must be assigned to a String object. However, every assignment operator must be defined as a class member function.

15.4   Operator [ ]

A subscript operator, operator[](), can be defined for classes that represent a container abstraction and from which individual elements are retrieved. Our String class, the IntArray class presented in Chapter 2, or the vector class template defined in the C++ standard library are examples of container classes for which it makes sense to declare a subscript operator. A subscript operator must be defined as a class member function.

Users of our class String need to have both read and write access to the individual characters of the _string class member. We want to support the following use for String class objects:

```
String entry( "extravagant" );
String mycopy;

for ( int ix = 0; ix < entry.size(); ++ix )
    mycopy[ ix ] = entry[ ix ];
```

The subscript operator must be able to appear both on the right- and the left-hand side of an assignment operator. To appear on the left-hand side, its return value must be an lvalue. This is achieved by specifying the return type as a reference:

```
#include <cassert>

inline char&
String::operator[]( int elem ) const
{
    assert( elem >= 0 && elem < _size );
    return _string[ elem ];
}
```

The return value of the subscript operator is the lvalue of the indexed element. This is why it can appear on the left-hand side of an assignment. For example, the following assigns a character value to the zero element of color._string:

```
String color( "violet" );
color[0] = 'V';
```

Notice that the subscript operator is defined to perform bound checking on the index value it receives. Here we decided to use the C library function assert() to perform this check. We could instead throw an exception to indicate that elem has a negative value or a value greater than the size of the C-style character string to which _string refers. (Exception handling and throw expressions are discussed in Chapter 11.)

15.5   Operator ( )

The function call operator can be overloaded for objects of class type. We have already seen a use of this overloaded operator when we saw function objects in Section 12.3. If a class type is defined to represent an operation, the function call operator can be overloaded for this class type to invoke this operation. For example, the class absInt is defined to encapsulate the operation of setting a value of type int to its absolute value:

```
class absInt {
public:
    int operator()( int val ) {
        int result = val < 0 ? -val : val;
        return result;
    }
};
```

An overloaded operator() must be declared as a member function. Its parameter list may have any number of parameters. The parameters may have any of the types allowed for function parameters presented in Sections 7.2 and 7.3. The return value of the overloaded operator() may have any of the types allowed for function return values in Sections 7.2 and 7.4.

An overloaded operator() is invoked by applying an argument list to an object of its class type. We will examine how the overloaded operator() for our class absInt is used by one of the generic algorithms defined in Chapter 12. The following example calls the generic algorithm transform() to apply the operation defined by absInt to every element contained within the vector ivec; that is, to set each vector element to its absolute value.

```
#include <vector>
#include <algorithm>

int main() {
    int ia[] = { -0, 1, -1, -2, 3, 5, -5, 8 };
    vector< int > ivec( ia, ia+8 );

    // set each element of ivec to its absolute value
    transform( ivec.begin(), ivec.end(), ivec.begin(), absInt() );

    // ....
}
```

The first and second arguments of transform() indicate the range of elements to which the absInt operation is applied. The third argument refers to the beginning of the vector, where the result of the absInt operation is stored.

The fourth argument of `transform()` is a temporary object of class absInt created by invoking the default constructor of absInt. The instantiation of the generic algorithm `transform()` invoked by `main()` might look like this:

```
typedef vector<int>::iterator iter_type;

// instantiation of transform()
// applies the operation absInt
// to the element of a vector of ints

iter_type transform( iter_type iter, iter_type last,
                     iter_type result, absInt func )
{
   while ( iter != last )
      *result++ = func( *iter++ ); // invokes absInt::operator()

   return iter;
}
```

`func` is an object of class type with a type that represents the operation absInt, setting a value of type `int` to its absolute value. The object `func` is used to invoke the overloaded `operator()` of class absInt. The argument passed to this overloaded operator is `*iter`, which refers to the vector element for which we want to obtain the absolute value.

15.6 Operator ->

The member access operator arrow can be overloaded for objects of class type. It must be defined as a class member function. It is defined to give a class type a "pointer-like" behavior. It is most often used with a class type that represents a "smart pointer"; that is, a class that behaves very much like a built-in pointer type, but that supports some additional functionality.

For example, let's assume that we want to define a class type to represent a pointer to a Screen class object, where the Screen class is the one introduced in Chapter 13:

```
class ScreenPtr {
   // ...
private:
   Screen *ptr;
};
```

We want to define the class ScreenPtr such that an object of this type is always guaranteed to refer to a Screen object. It cannot refer to no object, as does a built-in pointer. Our applications can then use objects of type ScreenPtr without first testing whether they refer to a Screen object or not. To obtain this behavior, we define the class ScreenPtr with a constructor, but with no default constructor (constructors are discussed in detail in Section 14.2):

```
class ScreenPtr {
public:
    ScreenPtr( Screen &s ) : ptr( &s ) { }
    //....
};
```

A definition for an object of type ScreenPtr must provide an initializer, an object of type Screen, to which the ScreenPtr object is made to refer, otherwise the ScreenPtr object definition is in error:

```
ScreenPtr p1; // error: ScreenPtr has no default constructor

Screen myScreen( 4, 4 );
ScreenPtr ps( myScreen ); // ok
```

For the class ScreenPtr to behave like a built-in pointer, some overloaded operators must be defined. The two operators we define are the dereference operator (*) and the member access operator arrow:

```
// overloaded operators to support pointer behavior
class ScreenPtr {
public:
    Screen& operator*()  { return *ptr; }
    Screen* operator->() { return ptr; }
    //....
};
```

The member access operator arrow is overloaded as a unary operator; that is, it takes no parameter. When it is used in an expression, it is selected solely on the type of the left operand. For example, given the statement

```
point->action();
```

point is examined to determine its type. If point is a pointer of some class type, the statement uses the semantics of the built-in member access operator arrow. If point is an object or a reference of some class type, the class is examined for an overloaded member access operator arrow. If a member operator is not defined, the statement is in error since a class object or reference must ordinarily use the dot member access operator to refer to class members. If an overloaded member access operator arrow is defined, it is bound to point and invoked.

The return type of an overloaded member access operator arrow must either be a pointer to a class type or an object of a class for which the member access operator arrow is defined. If the return type is a pointer to class type, the semantics for the built-in member access operator arrow are then applied to the return value. If the return value is another class object or reference, the process is applied recursively until either a pointer type is returned or the statement is in error. For example, we can use the ScreenPtr object ps to access the members of class Screen as follows:

```
ps->move( 2, 3 );
```

Because the left-hand operand of the member access operator arrow is of class type ScreenPtr, the overloaded operator of this class is used. The operator returns a pointer to a Screen class object. The built-in member access operator arrow is in turn applied to this return value to call to the member function move() of class Screen.

The following is a small program that exercises our ScreenPtr class. The object of type ScreenPtr is used just like any object of type Screen*:

```cpp
#include <iostream>
#include <string>
#include "Screen.h"

void printScreen( ScreenPtr &ps )
{
    cout << "Screen Object ("
         << ps->height() << ", "
         << ps->width() << " )\n\n";

    for ( int ix = 1; ix <= ps->height(); ++ix )
    {
        for ( int iy = 1; iy <= ps->width(); ++iy )
            cout << ps->get( ix, iy );
        cout << "\n";
    }
}

int main() {
    Screen sobj( 2, 5 );
    string init( "HelloWorld" );
    ScreenPtr ps( sobj );

    // Set the content of the screen
    string::size_type initpos = 0;
    for ( int ix = 1; ix <= ps->height(); ++ix )
        for ( int iy = 1; iy <= ps->width(); ++iy )
        {
            ps->move( ix, iy );
            ps->set( init[ initpos++ ] );
        }

    // Print the content of the screen
    printScreen( ps );

    return 0;
}
```

Of course, this kind of manipulation of pointer to class objects is not as efficient as using the built-in pointer type. The smart pointer class must therefore provide additional functionality that is important to the design of our application to justify the additional cost of using it.

15.7   Operators ++ and --

To continue the implementation of the ScreenPtr class introduced in the previous section, there are two other operators supported for the built-in pointer types that we would like to define for this class: the increment (++) and decrement (--) operators. We would like to be able to use our ScreenPtr class to refer to the elements of an array of Screen objects. To do this we need to add some data members to our ScreenPtr class.

First we define a new data member called size that either contains the value zero (to indicate that the ScreenPtr object points to a single object) or contains the size of the array to which the ScreenPtr object refers. We also define a data member called offset to remember the offset within the array to which the ScreenPtr object refers:

```
class ScreenPtr {
public:
    // ...
private:
    int size;     // size of the array; zero if single object
    int offset;   // offset of ptr within the array
    Screen *ptr;
};
```

With this additional functionality and these new data members, we must modify the constructor of class ScreenPtr. The user of our ScreenPtr class must provide an additional argument to the constructor if the ScreenPtr object created refers to an array:

```
class ScreenPtr {
public:
    ScreenPtr( Screen &s , int arraySize = 0 )
            : ptr( &s ), size ( arraySize ), offset( 0 ) { }
private:
    int size;
    int offset;
    Screen *ptr;
};
```

The additional constructor argument indicates the size of the array. To preserve the previous functionality, a default argument is provided for the constructor's second parameter to set the value of size to zero if a second argument is not provided when a ScreenPtr object is created. In this case, it is assumed that the object refers to a single Screen object. Objects of our new ScreenPtr class can be defined as follows:

```
Screen myScreen( 4, 4 );
ScreenPtr pobj( myScreen ); // ok: refers to single object
```

```
const int arrSize = 10;
Screen *parray = new Screen[ arrSize ];
ScreenPtr parr( *parray, arrSize ); // ok: refers to array
```

We are now ready to define the overloaded increment and decrement operators for ScreenPtr. There is a small problem. There are two kinds of increment and decrement operators, the prefix version and the postfix version. Fortunately, both a prefix and postfix instance of the overloaded increment and decrement operators can be defined. The declarations for the prefix operators look as one might expect:

```
class ScreenPtr {
public:
    Screen& operator++();
    Screen& operator--();
    // ...
};
```

The prefix increment and decrement operators are defined as unary operator functions. For example, the prefix increment operator can be used as follows:

```
const int arrSize = 10;
Screen *parray = new Screen[ arrSize ];
ScreenPtr parr( *parray, arrSize );

for ( int ix = 0;
      ix < arrSize;
      ++ix, ++parr // equivalent to parr.operator++()
    )
      printScreen( parr );
```

These overloaded operators may be defined as follows:

```
Screen& ScreenPtr::operator++()
{
    if ( size == 0 ) {
        cerr << "cannot increment pointer to single object\n";
        return *ptr;
    }
    if ( offset >= size - 1 ) {
        cerr << "already at the end of the array\n";
        return *ptr;
    }

    ++offset;
    return *++ptr;
}

Screen& ScreenPtr::operator--()
{
    if ( size == 0 ) {
        cerr << "cannot decrement pointer to single object\n";
```

```
        return *ptr;
    }
    if ( offset <= 0 ) {
        cerr << "already at the beginning of the array\n";
        return *ptr;
    }

    --offset;
    return *--ptr;
}
```

To distinguish the declaration of the postfix operators from the declaration of the prefix operators, the declarations for the overloaded increment and decrement postfix operators have an extra parameter of type int. In the following example, pre- and postfix pairs of operators for the ScreenPtr class are declared.

```
class ScreenPtr {
public:
    Screen& operator++();      // prefix operators
    Screen& operator--();
    Screen& operator++(int); // postfix operators
    Screen& operator--(int);
    // ...
};
```

The postfix operators might be implemented as follows:

```
Screen& ScreenPtr::operator++(int)
{
    if ( size == 0 ) {
        cerr << "cannot increment pointer to single object\n";
        return *ptr;
    }
    if ( offset == size ) {
        cerr << "already one past the end of the array\n";
        return *ptr;
    }

    ++offset;
    return *ptr++;
}

Screen& ScreenPtr::operator--(int)
{
    if ( size == 0 ) {
        cerr << "cannot decrement pointer to single object\n";
        return *ptr;
    }
    if ( offset == -1 ) {
        cerr << "already one before the beginning of the array\n";
```

```
        return *ptr;
    }

    --offset;
    return *ptr--;
}
```

Note that the parameter need not be given a name because it is not used within the operator definition. The additional integer parameter is transparent to users of the postfix operator. The compiler provides a default value for it, which can be ignored. This is why the parameter is left unnamed. Here is an example of the use of the postfix operator:

```
const int arrSize = 10;
Screen *parray = new Screen[ arrSize ];
ScreenPtr parr( *parray, arrSize );

for ( int ix = 0; ix < arrSize; ++ix )
    printScreen( parr++ );
```

An explicit call to a postfix operator requires that an actual value for the integer second argument be specified. With our ScreenPtr class, the argument specified for this explicit call is ignored because it is not used within the definition of the overloaded operator:

```
parr.operator++(1024); // call postfix operator++
```

The overloaded increment and decrement operators can also be declared as friend functions. For example, we can change the definition of class ScreenPtr to declare these operators as friend functions as follows:

```
class ScreenPtr {
    // nonmember declarations
    friend Screen& operator++( ScreenPtr & );        //prefix
    friend Screen& operator--( ScreenPtr & );
    friend Screen& operator++( ScreenPtr &, int ); //postfix
    friend Screen& operator--( ScreenPtr &, int );
public:
    // member definitions
};
```

Exercise 15.7

Provide the definitions for the overloaded increment and decrement operators of class ScreenPtr when they are declared as friend functions.

Exercise 15.8

The class ScreenPtr can now represent a pointer that points to an array of Screen classes. Modify the overloaded operator*() and overloaded operator->() (defined in Section 15.6) to ensure that if the ScreenPtr object refers to an array element, the pointer does not refer to one before the beginning of the array or to one past the end of the array. Hint: These overloaded operators should use the new data members `size` and `offset`.

15.8   Operators new and delete

By default, the allocation and deallocation of a class object on the free store is performed by the global operator `new()` and operator `delete()` defined in the C++ standard library. (We introduced these operators in Section 8.4.) A class may assume its own memory management by providing class member operators called operator `new()` and operator `delete()`. If defined within a class, these member operators are invoked in place of the global operators to allocate and deallocate objects of their class type. As an example, let's define operator `new()` and operator `delete()` as members of our Screen class.

A class member operator `new()` must have a return type of `void*` and take a first parameter of type `size_t`, where `size_t` is a typedef defined in the system header file `<cstddef>`. Here is the declaration for the Screen class operator `new()`:

```
class Screen {
public:
   void *operator new( size_t );
   // ...
};
```

When a `new` expression creates an object of class type, the compiler looks to see if the class has a member operator `new()`. If it has, this operator is selected to allocate the memory for the class object; otherwise, the global operator `new()` is called. For example, the following `new` expression

```
Screen *ps = new Screen;
```

creates an object of class type Screen on the free store, and because class Screen has a member operator `new()`, the class member operator `new()` is called. The operator's `size_t` parameter is initialized automatically with a value that represents the size of class Screen in bytes.

Adding or removing a class operator `new()` does not require a change to user code. A `new` expression has the same form whether it calls a global operator `new()` or a class member operator `new()`. If the class Screen doesn't define its own operator `new()`, the `new` expression is still valid, but it calls instead the global operator `new()`.

The programmer can selectively invoke the global operator `new()` through the use of the global scope resolution operator. For example,

```
Screen *ps = ::new Screen;
```

invokes the global operator `new()` even if class Screen defines operator `new()` as a member.

The class member operator `delete()` must have a `void` return type and a first parameter of type `void*`. Here is the declaration of our Screen class operator `delete()`:

```
class Screen {
public:
   void operator delete( void * );
};
```

When the operand of a `delete` expression is a pointer to an object of class type, the compiler looks to see if the class has a member operator `delete()`. If it has, this operator is selected to deallocate the memory for the class object; otherwise, the global operator `delete()` is called. The following `delete` expression,

```
delete ps;
```

deallocates the memory for the object of class Screen to which `ps` refers. Because class Screen has a member operator `delete()`, the class member operator `delete()` is called. The operator's `void*` parameter is initialized automatically with the value of `ps`.

Adding or removing a class operator `delete()` does not require a change to user code. A `delete` expression has the same form whether it calls a global operator `delete()` or a class member operator `delete()`. If the class Screen doesn't define its own operator `delete()`, the `delete` expression above is still valid, but instead it calls the global operator `delete()`.

The programmer can selectively invoke the global operator `delete()` by using the global scope resolution operator. For example:

```
::delete ps;
```

invokes the operator `delete()` defined in global scope even if class Screen defines operator `delete()` as a member. In general, the operator `delete()` used should match the operator `new()` that is used to allocate the storage. For example, if `ps` refers to storage that was allocated with a `new` expression invoking the global operator `new()`, then the `delete` expression should also invoke the global operator `delete()`.

The operator `delete()` defined for a class type and called by a `delete` expression may have two parameters instead of one. The first parameter must still be of type `void*`. The second parameter must be of the predefined type `size_t` (remember to include the library header `<cstddef>`). For example:

```
class Screen {
public:
   // replaces:
   // void operator delete( void * );
   void operator delete( void *, size_t );
};
```

If present, the additional parameter is initialized automatically by the compiler with the size in bytes of the object addressed by the first parameter. (This parameter is essential in an object-oriented class hierarchy in which operator delete() may be inherited by a derived class. Chapter 17 discusses inheritance in detail.)

Let's examine in more detail the implementation of our Screen class member operator new() and operator delete(). Our memory allocation strategy is to manage a linked list of available Screen class objects addressed by a single freeStore pointer. Each call to the Screen member operator new() returns the next class object pointed to by freeStore. Each call to the member operator delete() returns the class object at the beginning of the list addressed by freeStore. If the linked list of class objects addressed by freeStore is empty, a call is made to the global operator new() to allocate a block of storage able to contain screenChunk Screen objects.

Both screenChunk and freeStore contain values that are of interest only to the Screen class. Therefore, we want to encapsulate them as private members of class Screen. Additionally, there must be only a single instance of these data members for all Screen class objects created. Therefore, these members are declared as static members. A third data member, next, is defined to maintain the linked list of Screen objects.

```
class Screen {
public:
    void *operator new( size_t );
    void operator delete( void *, size_t );
    // ...
private:
    Screen *next;
    static Screen *freeStore;
    static const int screenChunk;
};
```

Here is a possible implementation of the Screen member operator new():

```
#include "Screen.h"
#include <cstddef>

// static members are initialized within
// program text files, not header files
Screen *Screen::freeStore = 0;
const int Screen::screenChunk = 24;

void *Screen::operator new( size_t size )
{
    Screen *p;

    if ( !freeStore ) {
        // linked list empty: grab a chunk
        // this call is to the global new
        size_t chunk = screenChunk * size;
        freeStore = p =
            reinterpret_cast< Screen* >( new char[ chunk ] );
```

```
        // now thread the memory allocated
        for ( ;
                p != &freeStore[ screenChunk - 1 ];
                ++p )
            p->next = p+1;
        p->next = 0;
    }

    p = freeStore;
    freeStore = freeStore->next;
    return p;
}
```

Here is a possible implementation for the Screen member operator delete():

```
    void Screen::operator delete( void *p, size_t )
    {
        // insert the "deleted" object back
        // into the free list

        ( static_cast< Screen* >( p ) )->next = freeStore;
        freeStore = static_cast< Screen* >( p );
    }
```

It is possible to declare an operator new() for a class without declaring a corresponding operator delete(). In this case the class objects are deleted using the global operator delete(). It is also possible to declare an operator delete() without declaring a corresponding operator new(). In this case the class objects are created using the global operator new(). However, these operators usually come in pairs and, as is the case in this example, the class designer most often needs to provide both.

Operator new() and operator delete() are static members of their class, and they obey the usual constraints for static member functions. These operators are made static member functions without the need for the programmer to declare them static explicitly. In particular, recall that a static member function is without a this pointer and therefore can only access static data members of its class directly. (See Section 13.5 for a discussion of static member functions.) The reason for this is that these operators are invoked either before the class object is constructed (operator new()) or after it has been destroyed (operator delete()).

An allocation using operator new(), such as

```
    Screen *ptr = new Screen( 10, 20 );
```

is equivalent to the following two-statement sequence:

```
    // Pseudo C++ code
    ptr = Screen::operator new( sizeof( Screen ) );
    Screen::Screen( ptr, 10, 20 );
```

That is, the new expression first calls the class operator new() to allocate the storage and then calls the constructor to initialize the object. If operator new() fails, an exception of type bad_alloc is thrown and the constructor is never invoked.

A deallocation using operator delete(), such as

```
delete ptr;
```

is equivalent to the following two-statement sequence:

```
// Pseudo C++ code
Screen::~Screen( ptr );
Screen::operator delete( ptr, sizeof( *ptr ) );
```

That is, the delete expression first calls the object's destructor and then calls the class operator delete() to deallocate the storage. If ptr has a value of 0, the destructor and the operator delete() are never called.

15.8.1   Array Operator new[] and Operator delete[]

Our class operator new() defined in the previous subsection is invoked only for the allocation of single class objects. For example, the following new expression invokes the Screen operator new():

```
// invokes Screen::operator new()
Screen *ps = new Screen( 24, 80 );
```

whereas the following new expression invokes the global operator new[]() to handle the allocation of an array of Screen objects on the free store:

```
// invokes ::operator new[]()
Screen *psa = new Screen[10];
```

It is also possible to declare operator new[]() and operator delete[]() for arrays as class members.

A class member operator new[]() must have a return type of void* and take a first parameter of type size_t. Here is the declaration for our Screen class operator new[]():

```
class Screen {
public:
    void *operator new[]( size_t );
    // ...
};
```

When a new expression creates an array of objects of class type, the compiler looks to see if the class has a member operator new[](). If it does, this operator is selected to allocate the memory for the array; otherwise, the global operator new[]() is called. The following new expression creates an array of ten objects of class Screen on the free store:

```
Screen *ps = new Screen[10];
```

Because class Screen has a member operator new[] (), it is the operator called by the new expression. The operator's size_t parameter is initialized automatically with a value that represents the size of the storage required to store an array of ten Screen objects in bytes.

Even though class Screen has a member operator new[] (), the programmer can invoke the global operator new[] () to create an array of Screen objects through the use of the global scope resolution operator. For example, the following new expression invokes the operator new[] () defined in global scope:

```
Screen *ps = ::new Screen[10];
```

The member operator delete[] () must have a void return type and a first parameter of type void*. For example, here is the declaration for our Screen class operator delete[] ():

```
class Screen {
public:
   void operator delete[]( void* );
};
```

To delete an array of classes, the delete expression must use the array syntax:

```
delete[] ps;
```

When the operand of such a delete expression is a pointer to class type, the compiler looks to see if the class has a member operator delete[] (). If it does, this operator is selected to deallocate the memory for the array; otherwise, the global operator delete[] () is called. The operator's void* parameter is initialized automatically with a value that represents the beginning of the storage in which the array is stored.

Even though class Screen has a member operator delete[] (), the programmer can invoke the global operator delete[] () selectively by using the global scope resolution operator. For example,

```
::delete[] ps;
```

invokes the operator delete[] () defined in global scope.

Adding or removing a class operator new[] () or a class operator delete[] () does not require a change to user code. The new expressions and delete expressions have the same form whether a global operator or a class operator is called.

A new expression that creates an array first calls the class operator new[] () to allocate the storage and then calls the default constructor to initialize iteratively every element of the array. If the class has a constructor, but no default constructor, the new expression is an error. No syntax exists to specify initializers for the array elements or to specify arguments for a class constructor in a new expression for arrays.

A delete expression that deletes an array first calls the class destructor to destroy iteratively every element of the array, and then calls the class operator delete[] () to deallocate the storage. It is important that the delete expression for arrays use the array syntax. In the following statement

```
delete ps;
```

if ps refers to an array of class objects, the absence of [] is likely to cause the destructor only to be invoked on the first element of the array, although the correct amount of storage is likely to be deallocated.

The operator delete[]() for a class may also have two parameters instead of one, the second parameter being of the predefined type size_t. For example:

```
class Screen {
public:
    // replaces:
    // void operator delete( void* );
    void operator delete[]( void*, size_t );
};
```

If present, the additional parameter is initialized automatically by the compiler with the size in bytes of the storage required to store the array.

15.8.2   Placement Operator new() and Operator delete()

A class member operator new() can be overloaded, provided that each declaration has a unique parameter list. The first parameter of any class operator new() must always be a parameter of type size_t. For example:

```
class Screen {
public:
    void *operator new( size_t );
    void *operator new( size_t, Screen* );
    // ...
};
```

The additional parameters are initialized with the placement arguments specified in a new expression. For example:

```
void func( Screen *start ) {
    Screen *ps = new (start) Screen;
    // ...
}
```

The portion of the new expression following the keyword new and appearing between parentheses represents the placement arguments. The previous new expression calls the member operator new() that takes two parameters. The first parameter is initialized automatically with the value representing the size of the class Screen in bytes. The second parameter is initialized with the value of the placement argument start.

It is also possible to overload the class member operator delete(). However, such an operator is never invoked from a delete expression. An overloaded operator delete() is only called implicitly by the implementation if the constructor called by a new expression (yes, this is not a typo, we really mean a new expression) throws an exception. Let's examine in more detail when such an operator delete() is used.

The actions of the following new expression

```
Screen *ps = new ( start ) Screen;
```

are as follows:

1. It calls the class operator new(size_t, Screen*).
2. It then calls the default constructor for class Screen to initialize the object.
3. It then initializes ps with the address of the Screen object.

Let's assume that the class operator new(size_t, Screen*) allocates memory by calling the global operator new(). How does the class designer ensure that the memory allocated by this operator new() is deallocated properly if the Screen constructor called in step 2 throws an exception? How does the class designer protect the user's code against such a memory leak? The class designer can provide an overloaded operator delete() that is called in this situation (and in this situation only).

If the class designer provides an overloaded operator delete() with parameters with types that match the parameter types of operator new(), the implementation automatically calls this operator delete() to deallocate the storage. For example, given the following placement new expression,

```
Screen *ps = new (start) Screen;
```

if the default constructor for class Screen exits by throwing an exception, the implementation looks for an operator delete() in the scope of class Screen. For an operator delete() to be considered, it must have parameters with types that match those of the operator new() called. Because the first parameter of an operator new() is always of type size_t and the first parameter of an operator delete() is always of type void*, the first parameter of each function is not considered for this comparison. The implementation looks in class Screen for an operator delete() of the following form:

```
void operator delete( void*, Screen* );
```

If this operator delete() is found in class Screen, it is called to deallocate the storage if the constructor called by the new expression throws an exception. If this operator delete() is not found, then no operator delete() is called.

The class designer can then decide whether to provide an operator delete() that matches a specific operator new(), depending on whether the operator new() allocates storage or whether it reuses storage already allocated. If it allocates storage, then a placement operator delete() should be provided to deallocate the memory in case the constructor throws an exception when called from a new expression. If the placement operator new() does not allocate storage, then there is no need to provide a matching operator delete() to deallocate the memory.

It is also possible to overload a class placement operator new[]() and operator delete[]() for arrays:

```
class Screen {
public:
    void *operator new[]( size_t );
    void *operator new[]( size_t, Screen* );
    void operator delete[]( void*, size_t );
    void operator delete[]( void*, Screen* );
    // ...
};
```

The placement operator new[]() is used when a new expression allocating an array specifies matching placement arguments. For example,

```
void func( Screen *start ) {
    // calls Screen::operator new[]( size_t, Screen* )
    Screen *ps = new (start) Screen[10];
    // ...
}
```

If the constructor called by this new expression throws an exception, the matching overloaded operator delete[]() defined in class Screen is called automatically by the implementation.

Exercise 15.9

Explain which, if any, of the following initializations are errors. Explain why.

```
class iStack {
public:
    iStack( int capacity )
          : _stack( capacity ), _top( 0 ) {}
    // ...
private:
    int _top;
    vector< int > _stack;
};

(a) iStack *ps = new iStack(20);
(b) iStack *ps2 = new const iStack(15);
(c) iStack *ps3 = new iStack[ 100 ];
```

Exercise 15.10

Explain what happens in the following new and delete expressions:

```
class Exercise {
public:
    Exercise();
```

```
    ~Exercise();
};

Exercise *pe = new Exercise[20];
delete[] pe;
```

Change the new and delete expressions to call the global operators new() and delete().

Exercise 15.11

Explain why a class designer should provide a class placement operator delete().

15.9   User-Defined Conversions

We have already seen how type conversions are applied to operands of built-in types. In Section 4.14 we examined how type conversions apply to the operands of the built-in operators. In Section 9.3 we examined how type conversions apply to the arguments of a function call to bring them to the type of the function parameters. For example, type conversions are applied to the operands in the following six addition operations:

```
    char ch; short sh; int ival;

    /* one operand of each addition
     * requires a type conversion */

    ch + ival;          ival + ch;
    ch + sh;            sh + ch;
    ival + sh;          sh + ival;
```

The operands ch and sh are promoted to type int. The operation taking place is the addition of two values of type int. The promotions are handled implicitly by the compiler and are therefore transparent to the user.

In this section we consider how the designer of a class can provide a set of user-defined conversions for objects of class type. These user-defined conversions are also invoked implicitly by the compiler when necessary. To illustrate why user-defined conversions are needed, we reuse our class SmallInt introduced in Section 10.9.

Recall that this class allows us to define objects that can hold the same range of values as an 8-bit unsigned char — that is, 0 to 255. Additionally, it catches under- and overflow errors. Other than that, it behaves in the same way as an unsigned char.

We want to be able to add and subtract SmallInt objects both with other SmallInt objects and with objects of built-in arithmetic type. We can implement support for these operations by providing six SmallInt operator functions:

```
    class SmallInt {
        friend operator+( const SmallInt &, int );
        friend operator-( const SmallInt &, int );
```

```
   friend operator-( int, const SmallInt & );
   friend operator+( int, const SmallInt & );
public:
   SmallInt( int ival ) : value( ival ) { }
   operator+( const SmallInt & );
   operator-( const SmallInt & );
   // ...
private:
   int value;
};
```

The member operators allow us to add and subtract SmallInt objects with other SmallInt objects. The friend global operators allow us to add and subtract SmallInt objects with objects of built-in arithmetic types. Only six operators are necessary because any built-in arithmetic type can be converted to match a parameter of type int. For example, the expression

```
SmallInt si( 3 );
si + 3.14159
```

is resolved in two steps:

1.   The double literal constant 3.14159 is converted to the integer value 3.
2.   operator+(const SmallInt &,int) is invoked, returning a value of 6.

If we want to support the bitwise, logical, relational, and compound assignment operators as well, the number of required operators becomes — well, daunting. What we would prefer, instead of providing all the overloaded operators, is a way of automatically converting a SmallInt class object into an object of type int.

C++ provides a mechanism by which each class can define a set of conversions that can be applied to objects of its class type. For SmallInt, we define a conversion of a SmallInt object to that of type int. Here is the implementation:

```
class SmallInt {
public:
   SmallInt( int ival ) : value( ival ) { }

   // conversion operator:
   // SmallInt ==> int
   operator int() { return value; }

   // no overloaded operators provided

private:
   int value;
};
```

Operator int() is a *conversion function* that defines a *user-defined conversion*. A user-defined conversion is a conversion between a class type and the type specified in the conversion function; in this case, the type int. The definition of the conversion function defines what the conversion means and the actions the compiler must perform when the conversion is applied. The meaning of the conversion to int for an object of class SmallInt is to return the value of type int stored in the data member value.

A SmallInt class object can now be used anywhere an int object can be used. Given that the overloaded operators are no longer provided, and that the class SmallInt provides a conversion function to type int instead, the following addition,

```
SmallInt si( 3 );
si + 3.14159;
```

is now resolved in the following two steps:

1. The SmallInt conversion function is invoked, yielding the integer value 3.
2. The integer value 3 is promoted to 3.0 and added to the double literal constant 3.14159, yielding the double value 6.14159.

This behavior mimics more closely the behavior of operands of built-in types compared with the behavior of the overloaded operators we defined earlier. When a value of type int is added to a value of type double, the operation performed is the addition for operands of type double (the value of type int being converted to a value of type double) and the result of the addition yields a value of type double.

The following program illustrates the use of the SmallInt class:

```cpp
#include <iostream>
#include "SmallInt.h"
SmallInt si1, si2;

int main() {
   cout << "enter a SmallInt, please:  ";
   while ( cin >> si1 ) {
      cout << "The value read is "
           << si1 << "\nIt is ";

      // SmallInt::operator int() invoked twice
      cout << ( ( si1 > 127 )
               ? "greater than "
               : ( ( si1 < 127 )
                 ? "less than "
                 : "equal to ") ) << "127\n";

      cout << "\nenter a SmallInt, please \
              (ctrl-d to exit):  ";
   }
   cout << "bye now\n";
}
```

When compiled and executed, the program generates the following results:

```
enter a SmallInt, please:   127

The value read is 127
It is equal to 127

enter a SmallInt, please (ctrl-d to exit):   126

The value read is 126
It is less than 127

enter a SmallInt, please (ctrl-d to exit):   128

The value read is 128
It is greater than 127

enter a SmallInt, please (ctrl-d to exit):   256
***SmallInt range error: 256 ***
```

The code implementing the SmallInt class has been changed to add additional support and now is as follows:

```
#include <iostream>

class SmallInt {
   friend istream&
      operator>>( istream &is, SmallInt &s );
   friend ostream&
      operator<<( ostream &os, const SmallInt &s )
      { return os << s.value; }
public:
   SmallInt( int i=0 ) : value( rangeCheck( i ) ){}
   int operator=( int i )
      { return( value = rangeCheck( i ) ); }
   operator int() { return value; }
private:
   int rangeCheck( int );
   int value;
};
```

The definitions for the member functions defined outside the class body are as follows:

```
istream& operator>>( istream &is, SmallInt &si ) {
   int ix;
   is >> ix;
   si = ix; // SmallInt::operator=(int)
   return is;
}
```

```
int SmallInt::rangeCheck( int i )
{
/* if any bits are set other than the first 8
 * the value is too large: report, then exit */

    if ( i & ~0377 ) {
        cerr << "\en***SmallInt range error: "
             << i << " ***" << endl;
        exit( -1 );
    }
    return i;
}
```

15.9.1   Conversion Functions

A *conversion function* is a special kind of class member function. It defines a user-defined conversion to convert a class object into some other type. A conversion function is declared in the class body by specifying the keyword operator followed by the type that is the target type of the conversion.

The name that follows the keyword operator in the declaration of a conversion function does not have to be a built-in type name. The Token class, defined next, defines multiple conversion functions. One conversion function is defined using the typedef name tName. Another conversion function defines a conversion to the class type SmallInt:

```
#include "SmallInt.h"

typedef char *tName;
class Token {
public:
    Token( char*, int );
    operator SmallInt() { return val; }
    operator tName()    { return name; }
    operator int()      { return val; }
    // other public members
private:
    SmallInt val;
    char *name;
};
```

Notice that the definitions for the conversion functions to SmallInt and int are the same. The value of the member val is returned by the conversion function Token::operator int(). Because val has type SmallInt, the conversion function SmallInt::operator int() is applied implicitly to convert val to type int. Token::operator int() itself is applied implicitly by the compiler to convert an object of type Token to a value of type int. For example, the compiler uses this conversion function to convert implicitly the arguments t1 and t2 of type Token to type int, the type of print()'s parameter:

```
#include "Token.h"

void print( int i )
{
    cout << "print( int ) : " << i << endl;
}

Token t1( "integer constant", 127 );
Token t2( "friend", 255 );

int main()
{
    print( t1 ); // t1.operator int()
    print( t2 ); // t2.operator int()
    return 0;
}
```

When compiled and executed, this small program generates the following output:

```
print( int ) : 127
print( int ) : 255
```

A conversion function takes the general form

```
operator type();
```

where type is replaced by a built-in type, a class type, or a typedef name. Conversion functions in which type represents either an array or a function type are not allowed. A conversion function must be a member function. Its declaration must not specify a return type nor can a parameter list be specified. Each of the following declarations, for example, are errors:

```
operator int( SmallInt & );   // error: nonmember

class SmallInt {
public:
    int operator int();        // error: return type
    operator int( int = 0 );   // error: parameter list
    // ...
};
```

An explicit cast may cause a conversion function to be invoked. If the value converted is of a class type that has a conversion function and the type of the conversion function is that specified by the cast, then the class conversion function is called. For example:

```
#include "Token.h"
Token tok( "function", 78 );

// functional notation: invokes Token::operator SmallInt()
SmallInt tokVal = SmallInt( tok );
```

```
// static_cast: invokes Token::operator tName()
char *tokName = static_cast< char * >( tok );
```

The conversion function Token::operator char*() may have an undesired side effect. Can you see what it is? Attempting to access the private member Token::name directly is flagged by the compiler as an error:

```
char *tokName = tok.name; // error: Token::name is private
```

However, our conversion function provides the very access we sought to protect by allowing users to change Token::name directly. This may not be what we want. Here is an example of how such a modification could happen:

```
#include "Token.h"
Token tok( "function", 78 );

char *tokName = tok; // ok: implicit conversion
*tokName = 'P'; // oops: the token name is now Punction!
```

Our intention is to permit read-only access on the converted Token class object. To enforce this, the conversion operator must return a type const char*:

```
typedef const char *cchar;
class Token {
public:
   operator cchar() { return name; }
   // ...
};

// error: conversion char* to const char* not allowed
char *pn = tok;
const char *pn2 = tok; // ok
```

Another solution is to change the definition to Token to use the string type defined in the C++ standard library. For example:

```
class Token {
public:
   Token( string, int );
   operator SmallInt() { return val; }
   operator string()   { return name; }
   operator int()      { return val; }
   // other public members
private:
   SmallInt val;
   string name;
};
```

The semantics of Token::operator string() are to return the string that represents the name of the token by value. This prevents the program from unintentionally modifying the value of Token's private member name.

When using a conversion function, must the target type of the conversion match the type of the conversion function exactly? For example, will the following code invoke the conversion function `operator int()` defined in class Token?

```
extern void calc( double );
Token tok( "constant", 44 );

// is tok.operator int() invoked? yes.
// int --> double by standard conversion
calc( tok );
```

If the target of the conversion (in this case type `double`) does not match the type of the conversion function (in this case type `int`) exactly, a conversion function can still be invoked if the target type can be reached through a standard conversion sequence. (Standard conversion sequences are described in Section 9.3). To call the function `calc()`, `Token::operator int()` is invoked to convert tok from type Token to type `int`. A standard conversion is then applied to convert the result of the user-defined conversion from type `int` to type `double`.

Only standard conversion sequences are allowed following the user-defined conversion. If, to reach the target type, a second user-defined conversion must be applied, no conversion is applied implicitly by the compiler. For example, if Token did not define an `operator int()`, the following call would be illegal:

```
extern void calc( int );
Token tok( "pointer", 37 );

// without Token::operator int() defined,
// this call will generate a compile-time error
calc( tok );
```

Without `Token::operator int()` defined, the conversion of tok to type `int` would require the invocation of two user-defined conversion functions. The argument tok would first need to be converted from type Token to type SmallInt using the conversion function

```
Token::operator SmallInt()
```

and the result of this user-defined conversion would then need to be converted to type `int` using the conversion function

```
SmallInt::operator int()
```

If `Token::operator int()` is not defined, the call `calc(tok)` is flagged at compile-time as an error because no implicit conversion exists from the type Token to the type `int`.

If there is no logical mapping between the type of a conversion function and a class type, providing a conversion function may become ambiguous to the reader of the program. For example:

```
class Date {
public:
   // guess which member is returned!
   operator int();
private:
   int month, day, year;
};
```

What value should be returned by the conversion function operator int() of Date? Whatever choice is made for whatever good reason, the use of Date objects will be ambiguous to a reader of the program because there is no logical one-to-one mapping between an object of type Date and a value of type int. In this case it is better *not* to define the conversion function.

15.9.2   A Constructor as a Conversion Function

The collection of constructors for a class taking a single parameter, such as SmallInt's constructor SmallInt(int), defines a set of implicit conversions from values of the constructors' parameter types to values of type SmallInt. SmallInt(int), for example, converts values of type int into SmallInt values.

```
extern void calc( SmallInt );
int i;

// need to convert i into a SmallInt value
// SmallInt(int) accomplishes this
calc( i );
```

In the call calc(i), i is converted into a SmallInt value by invoking the constructor SmallInt(int). The constructor is called by the compiler to create a temporary object of type SmallInt. A copy of the value of this object is then passed to calc(). It is as if the previous function call is written as follows:

```
// Pseudo C++ code:
// a temporary SmallInt object is created
{
   SmallInt temp = SmallInt( i );
   calc( temp );
}
```

The braces in the example indicate the lifetime of the generated SmallInt temporary; that is, the temporary is destroyed at the end of the function call statement.

The type of a constructor parameter may be another class type. For example:

```
class Number {
public:
   // create a Number value from a SmallInt value
   Number( const SmallInt & );
```

```
   // ok: explicit cast
   long lval = static_cast< int >( num );
```

The conversion is then explicit, using the conversion function `Number::operator int()` followed by the standard conversion from `int` to `long`.

Ambiguity when selecting a user-defined conversion sequence for an implicit conversion may also arise when two classes define conversions to each other. For example:

```
class SmallInt {
public:
   SmallInt( const Number & );
   // ...
};

class Number {
public:
   operator SmallInt();
   // ...
};

extern void compute( SmallInt );
extern Number num;

compute( num ); // error: two conversions possible
```

The argument `num` can be converted to the type SmallInt in two different ways. The constructor `SmallInt::SmallInt(const Number&)` can be used or the conversion function `Number::operator SmallInt()` can be used. Because these two functions are equally good, the call is in error.

The programmer can call the conversion function of class Number explicitly to resolve the ambiguity:

```
   // ok: explicit invocation resolves ambiguity
   compute( num.operator SmallInt() );
```

However, the programmer cannot resolve the ambiguity by using an explicit cast because both the conversion function and the constructor are considered for a conversion specified by an explicit cast:

```
   compute( SmallInt( num ) ); // error: still ambiguous
```

As you can see, providing many conversion functions and constructors to perform implicit conversions may lead to surprising results. Conversion functions and constructors should be used judiciously. It is possible to limit the use of constructors for implicit conversions (and hence limit their surprising effects) by declaring the constructors to be explicit.

15.10.1   Function Overload Resolution — Revisited

Chapter 9 describes in detail how a call to an overloaded function is resolved. When the arguments to a function call are arguments of class type, pointers to class type, or pointers to members, a greater set of functions is considered as possible candidate functions for the call. Hence, using arguments of class type influences the first step of function overload resolution — selecting the set of candidate functions.

During the third step of the function overload resolution process, the best match function is selected. To perform this selection, the type conversions that can convert the arguments to the type of the corresponding function parameters are ranked. For arguments and parameters of class type, the set of possible conversions must include the user-defined conversion sequences we introduced in the previous section. The third step of the function overload resolution process must therefore rank user-defined conversion sequences.

In this section, we examine in detail how arguments and parameters of class type influence the set of candidate functions and how user-defined conversions influence the selection of the best match function.

15.10.2   Candidate Functions

A candidate function is a function that has the same name as the function called. For example, let's say that we have a function call that is as follows:

```
SmallInt si(15);
add( si, 566 );
```

A candidate function for the call must be named add. Which declarations for the function add() are considered?

As with any function call, the declarations of the function add() visible at the point of the call are candidate functions. For example, the two functions add() declared in global scope are candidate functions for the following call:

```
const matrix& add( const matrix &, int );
double add( double, double );

int main() {
   SmallInt si(15);
   add( si, 566 );
   // ...
}
```

Considering functions visible at the point of the call is not particular to function calls with arguments of class type. However, for such function calls, two other scopes are searched for functions declarations:

1. If an argument is an object of class type, a pointer to a class type, a reference to
    a class type, or a pointer to a member of a class, given that the class type is de-
    clared within a user-declared namespace, the functions declared in that
    namespace and that have the same name as the function called are added to
    the set of candidate functions. For example:

    ```
    namespace NS {
        class SmallInt { /* ... */ };
        class String { /* ... */ };
        String add( const String &, const String & );
    }

    int main() {
        // the type of si is class SmallInt:
        // the class is declared in namespace NS
        NS::SmallInt si(15);

        add( si, 566 ); // NS::add() is a candidate function
        return 0;
    }
    ```

    The argument si has type SmallInt, which is a class type declared in namespace
    NS. The function add(const String&, const String&) declared in namespace
    NS is added to the set of candidate functions.

2. If an argument is an object of class type, a pointer to a class type, a reference to
    a class type, or a pointer to a member of a class, and the class has friend func-
    tions with the same name as the function called, the friend functions are added
    to the set of candidate functions. For example:

    ```
    namespace NS {
        class SmallInt {
            friend SmallInt add( SmallInt, int ) { /* ... */ }
        };
    }

    int main() {
        NS::SmallInt si(15);

        add( si, 566 ); // the friend add() is a candidate function
        return 0;
    }
    ```

    The function argument si has type SmallInt. Its friend function add(SmallInt,
    int) is a member of namespace NS, even though it is never declared in
    namespace NS directly. A normal lookup in namespace NS does not find the

friend function. However, the call to the function add() with an argument of type SmallInt considers friend functions declared within the member list of class SmallInt and adds them to the set of candidate functions.

Hence, if a function call has an argument that is an object of class type, a pointer to a class type, a reference to a class type, or a pointer to a member of a class, the candidate functions are the union of the functions visible at the point of call, the functions declared within the namespace where the class type is defined, and the functions that are declared as friends within the class member list.

If we put all the pieces of the previous example together,

```
namespace NS {
    class SmallInt {
        friend SmallInt add( SmallInt, int ) { /* ... */ }
    };
    class String { /* ... */ };
    String add( const String &, const String & );
}

const matrix& add( const matrix &, int );
double add( double, double );

int main() {
    // the type of si is class SmallInt:
    // the class is declared in namespace NS
    NS::SmallInt si(15);

    add( si, 566 ); // calls the friend function
    return 0;
}
```

the candidate functions are

1. the global functions:

    ```
    add( const matrix &, int )
    add( double, double )
    ```

2. the namespace function:

    ```
    NS::add( const String &, const String & )
    ```

3. the friend function:

    ```
    NS::add( SmallInt, int )
    ```

Function overload resolution selects the class SmallInt's friend function NS::add(SmallInt,int) as the best match for the call because both arguments specified in the call match the friend function's parameters exactly.

Of course, a function call may have more than one argument of class type, pointer to a class type, reference to a class type, or pointer to a member of a class. The class type that corresponds to each of these arguments may be different. Each argument is examined in turn to find candidate functions from the namespace where the class is defined and from the class friend functions. Therefore, a set of candidate functions for a call with arguments of class type may contain functions from different namespaces and may contain friend functions declared in different classes.

15.10.3   Candidate Functions for Function Calls in Class Scope

When a function call of the form

```
calc(t)
```

appears in class scope (in a member function, for example), the first set of candidate functions described in the previous subsection (that is, the set containing the function declarations visible at the point of the call) may contain functions that are not member functions. Name resolution is used to find the set of candidate functions visible at the point of the call. Name resolution in class scope is discussed extensively in Section 13.9 on class scope, in Section 13.10 on nested classes, in Section 13.11 on classes as namespace members, and in Section 13.12 on local classes.

Let's examine an example:

```
namespace NS {
    struct myClass {
        void k( int );
        static void k( char* );
        void mf();
    };
    int k( double );
};

void h(char);

void NS::myClass::mf() {
    h('a'); // calls global h( char )
    k(4);   // calls myClass::k( int )
}
```

As mentioned in Section 13.11, the qualifiers NS::myClass:: are searched in the reverse order of the qualifiers, looking first in myClass and then in namespace NS, to find a visible declaration for a name used in the definition of the member function mf(). Let's first consider the call

```
h( 'a' );
```

Name resolution in the definition of the member function mf() first considers the member functions of myClass for the call to h(). Because no member function named h() is found in the scope of myClass, the namespace NS is then examined for candidate functions. Because no function named h() is found in the scope of the namespace NS, the global scope is then examined for candidate functions. The global function h(char) is found and is the only function in the set of candidate functions visible at the point of the call.

During this search, as soon as a function declaration is found, the search for the candidate functions visible at the point of the call ends. This set contains only the functions declared in the scope where name resolution succeeds. This can be seen with the set of candidate functions for the call

```
k( 4 );
```

The scope of the class myClass is first considered for candidate functions for this call. The two member functions k(int) and k(char*) are found. Because the set of candidate functions visible at the point of call only contains the functions declared in the scope where name resolution succeeds, the scope of namespace NS is not searched for candidate functions and the function k(double) is excluded from the set of candidate functions.

If overload resolution finds the call to be ambiguous because there is no best match function in the set of candidate functions, the function call is in error. Further enclosing scopes are not searched for other candidate functions that better match the function call arguments.

15.10.4 Ranking User-Defined Conversion Sequences

A function call argument can be converted implicitly to the type of a function parameter using a user-defined conversion sequence. How do user-defined conversion sequences influence function overload resolution? For example, given the following call to calc(), which function is called?

```
class SmallInt {
public
    SmallInt( int );
};

extern void calc( double );
extern void calc( SmallInt );
int ival;

int main() {
    calc( ival ); // call which calc()?
}
```

The function with parameters that best match the type of the function call arguments is selected. This function is called the best match or the best viable function. To select the best viable function, the implicit conversions on the function arguments are ranked. The best viable function is the function for which the conversions applied to the arguments are *no worse* than the conversions necessary to call any other viable function, and the conversions on some arguments are *better* than the conversions nec-essary for the same arguments when calling any other viable function.

A standard conversion sequence is always better than a user-defined conversion se-quence. For example, regarding the call to calc() in the previous example, both functions calc() are viable functions. calc(double) is a viable function because there exists a stan-dard conversion to convert the argument of type int to the type of the parameter double. calc(SmallInt) is also a viable function because there exists a user-defined conversion that can convert the argument of type int to the type of the function parameter SmallInt. This user-defined conversion uses the constructor SmallInt(int) to perform the conver-sion. Because a standard conversion sequence is better than a user-defined conversion se-quence, the viable function calc(double) is selected as the best viable function for the call.

But what if two user-defined conversion sequences are compared? If two user-defined conversion sequences use different conversion functions or use different con-structors, both conversion sequences are considered equally good. For example:

```
class Number {
public:
    operator SmallInt();
    operator int();
    // ...
};

extern void calc( int );
extern void calc( SmallInt );
extern Number num;

calc( num ); // error: ambiguous
```

Both calc(int) and calc(SmallInt) are viable functions. calc(int) is a viable function because the conversion function Number::operator int() can convert the ar-gument of type Number to the type of the parameter int. calc(SmallInt) is also a vi-able function because the conversion function Number::operator SmallInt() can convert the argument of type Number to the type of the function parameter SmallInt. Because user-defined conversions always have the same rank, the compiler cannot de-termine which user-defined conversion sequence is better. The previous function call is ambiguous, and the call is flagged as a compile-time error.

The programmer can resolve the ambiguity by making the conversion explicit. For example:

```
// explicit conversion resolves ambiguity
calc( static_cast< int >( num ) );
```

The explicit cast forces the compiler to convert the argument num to type int using the conversion function Number::operator int(). The argument then has type int, which is an exact match for the function calc(int) selected as the best viable function.

Let's assume that the class Number does not define the conversion function Number::operator int(). Would the call

```
// Only Number::operator SmallInt() defined
calc( num ); // still ambiguous?
```

still be ambiguous? Remember that the class SmallInt also defines a conversion
function that can convert a value of type SmallInt to a value of type int.

```
class SmallInt {
public:
    operator int();
    // ...
};
```

One could assume that the function calc(int) can still be called by first converting
the argument num from type Number to type SmallInt using the conversion function
Number::operator SmallInt() and then converting the result of that conversion to the
type int by using the conversion function SmallInt::operator int(). However, this is
not the case. Remember that only one user-defined conversion can be part of a user-
defined conversion sequence. Only standard conversions are considered following the
first user-defined conversion. If Number::operator int() is not defined, the function
calc(int) is not considered a viable function because there is no implicit conversion
that can convert the argument num to the type of the function parameter of type int.

Hence, if Number::operator int() is not defined, calc(SmallInt) is the only viable
function. It would be the function selected as the best viable function.

If two user-defined conversion sequences use the same conversion function, then
the rank of the standard conversion sequence that follows the conversion function is
used to select the best user-defined conversion sequence. For example:

```
class SmallInt {
public:
    operator int();
    // ...
};

void manip( int );
void manip( char );

SmallInt si ( 68 );

main() {
    manip( si ); // calls manip( int )
}
```

Both manip(int) and manip(char) are viable functions. manip(int) is a viable function because the conversion function SmallInt::operator int() can convert the argument of type SmallInt to the type of the parameter int. manip(char) is also a viable

function because the conversion function SmallInt::operator int() can convert the argument of type SmallInt to the type int, and then a standard conversion can convert the result of the conversion function to the type char. The user-defined sequences are then

```
manip(int) : operator int() -> exact match
manip(char): operator int() -> standard conversion
```

Because both user-defined conversion sequences use the same conversion function, the rank of the standard conversion sequence is used to determine the best sequence. Because an exact match is better than a standard conversion, the function manip(int) is chosen as the best viable function.

Note that the standard conversion sequences following the user-defined conversion are only used as a criterion of selection if the two user-defined conversion sequences use the same conversion function. This is somewhat different from the examples presented at the end of Section 15.9. In that section, we illustrate how the compiler selects a user-defined conversion to convert a value of a particular type to a given target type. In that case both the source and the target types are fixed, and the compiler selects between different user-defined conversions that can convert between these two types. Here, two different functions are considered, with different parameter types, and the target types vary. If two different parameter types require different user-defined conversions, it is not possible to select one parameter type as being better than another unless the user-defined conversions involve the same conversion function. In this case we can use the standard conversions that follow the user-defined conversions to select the best target type. For example:

```
class SmallInt {
public:
   operator int();
   operator float();
   // ...
};

void compute( float );
void compute( char );

SmallInt si ( 68 );

main() {
   compute( si ); // ambiguous
}
```

Both compute(float) and compute(char) are viable functions. compute(float) is a viable function because the conversion function SmallInt::operator float() can convert the argument of type SmallInt to the type of the function parameter float. compute(char) is also a viable function because the conversion function SmallInt::-

operator int() can convert the argument of type SmallInt to the type int, and then a standard conversion can convert the result of the conversion function to the type char. The user-defined sequences are then

```
compute(float): operator float() -> exact match
compute(char): operator int() -> standard conversion
```

Because both user-defined conversion sequences use different conversion functions, it is not possible to determine which function has the best parameter type for the call. The rank of the standard conversion sequence is not used to determine the best conversion sequence, and hence the best parameter type. The call is flagged by the compiler as ambiguous.

Exercise 15.12

There are no conversion functions defined for the classes in the C++ standard library, and many of the constructors taking one argument are declared to be explicit. However, many overloaded operators are defined for the classes in the C++ standard library. Why do you think this design decision was chosen?

Exercise 15.13

Why is the overloaded input operator for class SmallInt defined at the beginning of Section 15.9 not implemented in the following manner?

```
istream& operator>>( istream &is, SmallInt &si )
{
    return ( is >> si.value );
}
```

Exercise 15.14

Show the possible user-defined conversion sequences for each of the following initializations. What is the outcome of each initialization?

```
class LongDouble {
    operator double();
    operator float();
};

extern LongDouble ldObj;

(a) int ex1 = ldObj;
(b) float ex2 = ldObj;
```

Exercise 15.15

Name the three sets of candidate functions considered during function overload resolution if a function argument has class type.

Exercise 15.16

Which `calc()` function, if any, is selected as the best viable function for the following call? Show the conversion sequences needed to call each function and explain why the best viable function is selected.

```
class LongDouble {
public
   LongDouble( double );
   // ...
};

extern void calc( int );
extern void calc( LongDouble );
double dval;

int main() {
   calc( dval ); // which function?
}
```

15.11 Overload Resolution and Member Functions ◆

Member functions can also be overloaded. Function overload resolution is also used to select the best viable function for a member function call. Overload resolution for member functions is very similar to overload resolution for nonmember functions. The process is composed of the same three steps:

1. Select the candidate functions.
2. Select the viable functions.
3. Select the best match function.

There are some minor differences in how candidate functions and viable functions are selected for calls to member functions. We will examine these differences in this section.

15.11.1 Declarations of Overloaded Member Functions

Class member functions can be overloaded. For example:

```
class myClass {
public:
   void f( double );
```

```
        char f( char, char ); // overloads myClass::f( double )
        // ...
};
```

As with functions declared in namespace scope, member functions declared within a class can be given the same name provided that each parameter list is unique, in either the number or the types of their parameters. If two member function declarations with the same name differ only in their return type, the second declaration is treated as an erroneous declaration and is flagged as a compile-time error. For example:

```
class myClass {
public:
    void mf();
    double mf(); // error: not a valid overloaded function
    // ...
};
```

However, unlike namespace functions, member functions must be declared only once in the class member list. If both the return type and the parameter list of two member function declarations with the same name match exactly, the second declaration is flagged by the compiler as an invalid member function redeclaration. For example:

```
class myClass {
public:
    void mf();
    void mf(); // error: invalid redeclaration
    // ...
};
```

All the functions in a set of overloaded functions are declared within the same scope. Therefore, member functions never overload functions declared in namespace scope. Also, because each class maintains its own scope, the functions that are members of two distinct classes do not overload one another.

A set of overloaded member functions may contain both static and nonstatic member functions. For example:

```
class myClass {
public:
    void mcf( double );
    static void mcf( int* ); // overloads myClass::mcf( double )
    // ...
};
```

Whether the static or nonstatic member function is called depends on the result of function overload resolution. We look at function overload resolution, when both a static and a nonstatic member function are viable functions, in more detail in the next section.

15.11.2   Candidate Functions

For a member function call of one of the following forms,

```
mc.mf( arg );
pmc->mf( arg );
```

if `mc` is an expression of type myClass and `pmc` is an expression of type pointer to the type myClass, the set of candidate member functions for both of these calls is composed of functions found in the scope of class myClass when looking up declarations for `mf()`.

Similarly, for a function call of the form

```
myClass::mf( arg );
```

the set of candidate functions is composed of functions found when looking up declarations for `mf()` in the scope of class myClass. For example:

```
class myClass {
public:
   void mf( double );
   char mf( char, char = '\n' );
   static void mf( int* );
   // ...
};

int main() {
   myClass mc;
   int iobj;
   mc.mf( iobj );
}
```

The candidate functions for the function call in `main()` are the three member functions `mf()` declared in myClass:

```
void mf( double );
char mf( char, char = '\n' );
static void mf( int* );
```

If no member function named `mf()` exists in myClass, the set of candidate functions is empty. (Actually, functions in base classes may then be considered. How base class member functions are entered in the set of candidate functions is discussed in Section 19.3). If no candidate function exists for a function call, the call is flagged at compile-time as an error.

15.11.3   Viable Functions

A viable member function is a function from the set of candidate member functions
that can be called with the argument list specified on the call. It is a function for which
implicit type conversions exist between the type of the arguments and the type of the
function's parameters. For example:

```
class myClass {
public:
    void mf( double );
    char mf( char, char = '\n' );
    static void mf( int* );
    // ...
};

int main() {
    myClass mc;
    int iobj;
    mc.mf( iobj ); // which member function mf()? it is ambiguous
}
```

There are two viable member functions for the call to the member function mf()
in main():

```
void mf( double );
char mf( char, char = '\n' );
```

1. mf(double) is a viable member function because it has only one parameter and
    because a standard conversion exists that can convert the argument iobj of
    type int to the parameter type double.
2. mf(char, char) is a viable member function because a default argument is pro-
    vided for the function's second parameter and a standard conversion exists that
    can convert the argument iobj of type int to the type of the first parameter char.

When the best viable member function is selected, the type conversions on each argument are ranked. The best viable member function is the viable member function for
which the conversions applied to the arguments are *no worse* than the conversions necessary to call any other viable member function, and the conversions on some arguments are *better* than the conversions necessary for the same arguments when calling
any other viable function.

In the previous example, the conversion applied to the argument to match the parameters of either viable member function is a standard conversion. The function call
is then ambiguous because both member functions are equally good for the argument
specified on the function call.

Independent of the form of the function call, both static and nonstatic member
functions may be included in the set of viable functions. For example:

```
class myClass {
public:
   static void mf( int );
   char mf( char );
};

int main() {
   char cobj;
   myClass::mf( cobj );   // which member function?
}
```

Even though the member function mf() is called using the class name and the
scope resolution operator (myClass::mf()), and even though mf() is not called
through an object or pointer to an object using a class member access operator dot or
arrow, the nonstatic member function mf(char) is included in the set of viable functions for the call, along with the static member function mf(int).

Function overload resolution then proceeds to select the best viable function by
ranking the type conversions on the function's arguments. The argument cobj of type
char is an exact match for the parameter of mf(char). The argument can be converted
to the type of the parameter of mf(int) through a promotion. Looking at the ranks of
the conversions applied to the argument in this example, the member function
mf(char) is selected as the best viable function.

However, the member function selected is a nonstatic member function that cannot be called directly. It must be called through an object of, or pointer to an object of,
type myClass using one of the member access operators dot or arrow. What happens
then? If the best viable function selected is a nonstatic member function, and the call
cannot actually take place because no object is specified for the call (as is the case here),
the call is flagged as an error by the compiler.

Another aspect of member functions that must be taken into account when selecting the set of viable functions is the const or volatile attributes of nonstatic member
functions. (const and volatile member functions are introduced in Section 13.3). How
do these attributes influence function overload resolution? Given the following member functions for the class myClass,

```
class myClass {
public:
   static void mf( int* );
   void mf( double );
   void mf( int ) const;
   // ...
};
```

the static member function mf(int*), the const member function mf(int), and the non-const member function mf(double) are all included in the set of candidate functions for the following function call. Which member functions are included in the set of viable functions?

```
int main() {
    const myClass mc;
    double dobj;
    mc.mf( dobj ); // which member function mf()?
}
```

Examining the conversions that can be applied to the function argument, mf(double) and mf(int) are viable functions. The argument dobj of type double is an exact match for the parameter of mf(double). The argument dobj can be converted to the type of the parameter of mf(int) through a standard conversion.

When the member function call uses a dot or arrow member access operator, the type of the object or pointer through which the member function is called is taken into account when selecting the functions that are included in the set of viable functions.

mc is a const object. Only const nonstatic member functions can be called for const objects. Because non-const nonstatic member function mf(double) cannot be called, it is excluded from the set of viable functions. The only viable function for the call is the const member function mf(int), which is selected as the best viable function for the call.

What if the const object is used to call a static member function? Since static member functions cannot be declared const or volatile, can a static member function be called through a const object? For example:

```
class myClass {
public:
    static void mf( int );
    char mf( char );
};
int main() {
    const myClass mc;
    int iobj;
    mc.mf( iobj ); // can static member function be called?
}
```

Static member functions are generic to all objects of a particular class type. Static member functions can only access the class static members directly. The nonstatic members of the const object mc, for example, cannot be accessed by the static member function mf(int). For this reason it is always valid to call a static member function for a const object using the dot or arrow operator.

Hence, static member functions are never excluded from the set of viable functions because of the const or volatile qualifiers of the object or pointer through which the member function is called. Static member functions are seen as matching any object or pointer of their class type.

In the previous example, because `mc` is a `const` object, the member function `mf(char)` is excluded from the set of viable functions. However, the member function `mf(int)` is included in the set of viable functions because it is a static function. Because it is the only viable function for the call, `mf(int)` is selected as the best viable function.

15.12 Overload Resolution and Operators ◆

As we have seen in the previous sections, overloaded operators and conversion functions can be declared for class types. How does the compiler decide, on encountering an operator such as the addition operator in the following initialization,

```
SomeClass sc;
int iobj = sc + 3;
```

whether to use the overloaded addition operator for the class SomeClass or whether to use a conversion function to convert the operand sc to a built-in type and then use a built-in addition operator?

The answer depends on the set of overloaded operators and conversion functions defined for the class SomeClass. The process of function overload resolution is applied to select the operator to use to perform the addition. In this section we look at how overload resolution proceeds to select operators when they are used with operands of class types.

Overload resolution for overloaded operators follows the usual three-step process presented in Section 9.2:

1. Select the candidate functions.
2. Select the viable functions.
3. Select the best match function.

We examine these three steps in detail in this section.

Function overload resolution is never applied if an operator only has operands of built-in types. For such operands, a built-in operator is guaranteed to be used. (The use of operators with operands of built-in types is described in Chapter 4). For example:

```
class SmallInt {
public:
    SmallInt( int );
};

SmallInt operator+ ( const SmallInt &, const SmallInt & );
```

```
void func() {
    int i1, i2;
    int i3 = i1 + i2;
}
```

Because i1 and i2 are operands of type int and do not have class type, the built-in operator+ is used for the addition i1 + i2. The overloaded operator operator+(const SmallInt&, const SmallInt&) is ignored, even though the operands could be converted to the type SmallInt through a user-defined conversion invoking the constructor Small-Int(int). The overload resolution process described here is not used in such cases.

Also, the overload resolution process for operators described here only applies when the operator syntax is used. For example:

```
void func() {
    SmallInt si(98);
    int iobj = 65;
    int res = si + iobj; // operator syntax used
}
```

If the function call syntax is used instead, as in

```
int res = operator+( si , iobj ); // function call syntax used
```

then the overload resolution for namespace functions described in Section 15.10 applies. If the member function call syntax is used instead, as in

```
// member function call syntax used
int res = si.operator+( iobj );
```

then the overload resolution for class member functions described in Section 15.11 is used instead.

15.12.1 Candidate Operator Functions

A candidate operator function is a function that has the same name as the function called. For the use of the addition operator that follows,

```
SmallInt si(98);
int iobj = 65;
int res = si + iobj;
```

a candidate operator function is named operator+. Which declarations for operator+() are considered?

Potentially, *five* sets of candidate operator functions are built for the use of an operator using the operator syntax with an operand of class type. The first three sets are the same as those built for ordinary function calls with arguments of class types:

1. The set of operators visible at the point of the call. The declarations of operator+() visible when the operator is used are candidate operator functions. For example,

operator+() declared in global scope is a candidate function for the use of operator+() in main():

```
SmallInt operator+ ( const SmallInt &, const SmallInt & );

int main() {
   SmallInt si(98);
   int iobj = 65;
   int res = si + iobj; // ::operator+() is a candidate function
}
```

2. The set of operators declared within the namespace where the type of an operand is defined. If an operand has class type and the type is declared within a user-declared namespace, the operator functions declared in that namespace with the same name as the operator used are candidate operator functions. For example:

```
namespace NS {
   class SmallInt { /* ... */ };
   SmallInt operator+ ( const SmallInt&, double );
}

int main() {
   // the type of si is class SmallInt:
   // the class is declared in namespace NS
   NS::SmallInt si(15);

   // NS::operator+() is a candidate function
   int res = si + 566;
   return 0;
}
```

The operand si has type SmallInt, a class type declared in namespace NS. The overload operator operator+(const SmallInt&, double) declared in namespace NS is added to the set of candidate operator functions.

3. The set of operators that are declared as friends of an operand's class type. For operands of class type, if the class definition declares friend operator functions with the same name as the operator used, the friend operator functions are added to the set of candidate operator functions. For example:

```
namespace NS {
   class SmallInt {
      friend SmallInt operator+(const SmallInt&, int )
                                { /* ... */ }
   };
}
```

```
int main() {
    NS::SmallInt si(15);

    // the friend operator+() is a candidate
    int res = si + 566;
    return 0;
}
```

The operand si has type SmallInt. Its friend operator function opera-
tor+(const SmallInt&, int) is a member of namespace NS, even though it is
never declared in namespace NS directly. A normal lookup in namespace NS
does not find the friend operator function. However, the use of operator+()
with an argument of type SmallInt considers friend functions declared in the
scope of class SmallInt and adds them to the set of candidate functions.

The previous three sets of candidate operator functions are established in the same
way as the sets of candidate functions for function calls with arguments of class type.
However, for operators used with the operator syntax, two other sets of candidate operator functions are established, which makes five sets of candidate operator functions:

4.   The set of member operators declared in the class of the left-hand operand. If
     operator+() is used with a left operand of class type, the set of member oper-
     ator candidates is built by searching for declarations for the member opera-
     tor+() in the class of the left operand. For example:

```
class myFloat {
    myFloat( double );
};
class SmallInt {
public:
    SmallInt( int );
    SmallInt operator+ ( const myFloat & );
};

int main() {
    SmallInt si(15);

    int res = si + 5.66; // the member operator+() is a candidate
}
```

The member operator SmallInt::operator+(const myFloat &) defined in class
SmallInt is included in the set of candidate functions for the use of operator+()
in main().

5.   The set of built-in operators. Given the types that can be used with a built-in
     operator+(), the candidate operator functions for the built-in binary opera-
     tor+() are the following:

```
int operator+( int, int )
double operator+( double, double )
T* operator+( T*, I )
T* operator+( I, T* )
```

The first declaration represents the built-in operator used to add any two values of integral type. The second declaration represents the built-in operator used to add any two values of floating point type. The third and fourth declarations represent the built-in operator for pointer types, which is used to add values of integral type to pointer values. These declarations are only symbolic. They are used to describe the set of built-in operator candidates that the compiler considers for any addition operation.

When composing the first four sets of candidate operator functions, it is possible that the set of candidates will be empty. For example, if no member function named operator+() is found in class SmallInt, the set of member candidate operator functions (that is, the fourth set) is empty.

The set of candidate operator functions is the union of the five sets of candidate functions listed previously. For example:

```
namespace NS {
    class myFloat {
        myFloat( double );
    };
    class SmallInt {
        friend SmallInt operator+(const SmallInt &, int ) { /* ... */ }
    public:
        SmallInt( int );
        operator int();
        SmallInt operator+( const myFloat & );
        // ...
    };
    SmallInt operator+( const SmallInt &, double );
}

int main() {
    // the type of si is class SmallInt:
    // the class is declared in namespace NS
    NS::SmallInt si(15);

    int res = si + 5.66; // which operator+ ?
    return 0;
}
```

The five sets of candidate functions give seven candidate operator functions for the use of operator+() in main():

1. The first set of candidate functions is empty. There are no declarations for an overloaded operator+() visible in global scope where operator+() is used in main().

2. The second set of candidate functions contains the operators declared within the namespace NS where the class type SmallInt is defined. The following operator is defined in namespace NS:

    ```
    NS::SmallInt NS::operator+( const SmallInt &, double );
    ```

3. The third set of candidate functions contains the operators declared as friends of the class SmallInt. The following operator is a friend of class SmallInt:

    ```
    NS::SmallInt NS::operator+( const SmallInt &, int );
    ```

4. The fourth set of candidate functions contains the operators declared as members of class SmallInt. The following operator is a member of class SmallInt:

    ```
    NS::SmallInt NS::SmallInt::operator+( const myFloat & );
    ```

5. The fifth set of candidate functions contains the built-in binary operators:

    ```
    int operator+( int, int )
    double operator+( double, double )
    T* operator+( T*, I )
    T* operator+( I, T* )
    ```

Phew! Yes, establishing the list of candidate operator functions for an operator using the operator syntax can involve quite a bit of work. Once the set of candidate functions is established, the viable functions and the best viable function are found as before, by analyzing the conversions that can apply on the operands of the candidate operators.

15.12.2 Viable Functions

A set of viable operator functions is selected from the set of candidate operator functions by selecting only the operator functions that can be called with the operands specified when the operator is used. For example, which of the seven candidate functions in our example are viable functions? The use of the operator is as follows:

```
NS::SmallInt si(15);
si + 5.66;
```

The left operand is of type SmallInt and the right operand is of type double.

The first candidate function is a viable function for this use of operator+():

```
NS::SmallInt NS::operator+( const SmallInt &, double );
```

The left operand si of type SmallInt is an exact match as an initializer for the reference parameter of the overloaded operator. The right operand is a value of type double, which is also an exact match for the second parameter of the overloaded operator.

The second candidate function is also a viable function for this use of operator+():

```
NS::SmallInt NS::operator+( const SmallInt &, int );
```

The left operand si of type SmallInt is an exact match as an initializer for the reference parameter of the overloaded operator. The right operand is a value of type int that can be converted to the second parameter of the overloaded operator through a standard conversion.

The third candidate function is also a viable function for this use of `operator+()`:

```
NS::SmallInt NS::SmallInt::operator+( const myFloat & );
```

The left operand `si` is of type SmallInt, which is the class type in which the overloaded operator is defined as a member function. The right operand is a value of type `int`, which can be converted to the class type myFloat through a user-defined conversion sequence using the constructor `myFloat(double)`.

The fourth and fifth viable functions are the built-in operators:

```
int operator+( int, int )
double operator+( double, double )
```

The class SmallInt contains a conversion function that can convert a value of type SmallInt to a value of type `int`. With the first built-in operator, the conversion function is used to convert the left operand of type SmallInt to the type `int`. The second operand of type `double` is converted to type `int` with a standard conversion. With the second built-in operator, the conversion function is used to convert the left operand of type SmallInt to the type `int`, and the result of this conversion is then converted to a value of type `double` using a standard conversion. The second operand of type `double` is an exact match for the second parameter.

The best viable function in the set of five viable functions is the first viable function, the overloaded `operator+()` declared in namespace NS:

```
NS::SmallInt NS::operator+ ( const SmallInt &, double );
```

For this overloaded operator, both operands match the parameters exactly.

15.12.3   Ambiguity

Providing both conversion functions that perform implicit conversions to built-in types and overloaded operators for the same class type may lead to ambiguities between the overloaded operators and the built-in operators. For example, given a class String defined with the following comparison function,

```
class String {
    // ...
public:
    String( const char * = 0 );
    bool operator== ( const String & ) const;
    // no operator== ( const char * ) provided
};
```

and the following use of `operator==()`,

```
String flower( "tulip" );
```

```
void foo( const char *pf ) {
   // calls overloaded String::operator==()
   if ( flower == pf )
      cout << pf << " is a flower!\n";
   // ...
}
```

the comparison

```
flower == pf
```

invokes the String equality member operator

```
String::operator==( const String & ) const;
```

A user-defined conversion that calls the constructor

```
String( const char * )
```

is applied to convert the right operand pf from the type const char* to the type String, the type of the parameter of the member operator==().

If the conversion function operator const char*() is added to the definition of class String

```
class String {
   // ...
public:
   String( const char * = 0 );
   bool operator== ( const String & ) const;
   operator const char*(); // new conversion function
};
```

the earlier use of operator==() is now ambiguous

```
// equality test no longer compiles!
if ( flower == pf )
```

Because of the introduction of the conversion function operator const char*(), the built-in comparison operator

```
bool operator==( const char *, const char * )
```

is now also a viable function. The left operand flower of type String can be converted to the type const char* using the new user-defined conversion.

There are now two viable operator functions for the use of operator==() in foo(). The first viable function

```
String::operator==( const String & ) const;
```

requires a user-defined conversion to convert the right operand pf from type const char* to the type String. The second viable function:

```
bool operator==( const char * , const char * )
```

requires a user-defined conversion to convert the left operand flower of type String to the type const char*.

The first viable function is therefore better for the left operand, whereas the second viable function is better for the right operand. The call is then flagged as ambiguous because no best viable function can be found.

This is why one must be careful when designing the interface for a class, and when declaring overloaded operators, constructors, and conversion functions for a particular class type. User-defined conversions are applied implicitly by the compiler. This may cause built-in operators to become viable functions for the use of an operator with operands of class types. Conversion functions and nonexplicit constructors should therefore be used judiciously.

Exercise 15.17

Name the five sets of candidate functions considered during function overload resolution if an operator is used with an operand of class type.

Exercise 15.18

Which operator+(), if any, is selected as the best viable function for the addition operation in main()? List the candidate functions, the viable functions, and the type conversions on the arguments for each viable function.

```
namespace NS {
   class complex {
      complex( double );
      // ...
   };
   class LongDouble {
      friend LongDouble operator+( LongDouble &, int ) { /*...*/ }
   public:
      LongDouble( int );
      operator double();
      LongDouble operator+( const complex & );
      // ...
   };
   LongDouble operator+( const LongDouble &, double );
}

int main() {
   // the type of si is class SmallInt:
   // the class is declared in namespace NS
   NS:: LongDouble ld(16.08);

   double res = ld + 15.05; // which operator+ ?
   return 0;
}
```

16

Class Templates

This chapter describes class templates, and how to define and use them. A class template is a prescription for creating a class in which one or more types or values are parameterized. It is possible to use class templates as a beginner C++ programmer without understanding the mechanism behind template definitions and instantiations. In fact, throughout this book we have used the class templates defined in the C++ standard library (like vector, list, and so forth) without the need to describe the template mechanism in great detail. Only more advanced C++ programmers will define their own class templates and use the mechanisms described in this chapter. The material in this chapter is therefore introductory material for a more advanced topic of C++.

The chapter is split into introductory and advanced sections. The introductory sections show how class templates are defined, illustrate simple uses of class templates, and discuss how class templates are instantiated. The introductory sections also look at the different kinds of members that can be defined for class templates: member functions, static data members, and nested types. The advanced sections present material necessary for writing production-level applications. We first look at how the compiler instantiates templates and the requirements this imposes on the organization of our programs. We then present how to define specializations and partial specializations for a class template or for a member of a class template. The chapter then looks at two topics that are of interest to designers of class templates: how names in class template definitions are resolved and how class templates can be defined in namespaces. The chapter ends with a more extensive example of defining and using a class template.

16.1 Class Template Definition

Let's assume that we want to define a class to support the mechanism of a queue. A queue is a data structure for a collection of objects in which objects are added at one end, the back, and removed at the other end, the front. The behavior of a queue is spoken of as first in, first out, or *FIFO*. (The C++ standard library defines a queue type, and it is briefly described in Section 6.17. In this chapter, we define our own simple queue type to introduce class templates.)

We decide that our class Queue will support the following operations:

- Add an item to the back of the queue:

    ```
    void add( item );
    ```

- Remove an item from the front of the queue:

    ```
    item remove();
    ```

- Determine if the queue is empty:

    ```
    bool is_empty();
    ```

- Determine if the queue is full:

    ```
    bool is_full();
    ```

A definition for our class Queue might look like this:

```
class Queue {
public:
    Queue();
    ~Queue();

    Type& remove();
    void add( const Type & );
    bool is_empty();
    bool is_full();
private:
    // ....
};
```

The question is, what type should we use for Type? Let's assume we choose to implement our class Queue, replacing Type with int. The class Queue is then defined to handle collections of objects of type int. Were the programmer to assign one of these objects a value of another type, the value assigned is either converted to int or, if no conversion exists, the assignment is flagged at compile-time as an error. For example:

```
Queue qObj;
string str( "vivisection" );

qObj.add( 3.14159 ); // ok: item added to the queue == 3
qObj.add( str );     // error: no conversion from string to int
```

Because each object in the collection is an object of type int, the C++ type system guarantees that only values of type int, or values that can be converted to type int, can be assigned to an object of type Queue. This is good when the programmer wishes to use a queue of objects of type int, of course. This is not as good, however, when the programmer wishes to use the class Queue to represent a collection of doubles, chars, complex numbers, or strings.

One method of coping is simply to use brute force. The programmer copies the entire Queue class implementation, modifying it to work with doubles, then with complex numbers, then with strings, and so on. And, since class names cannot be overloaded, each implementation must be given a unique name: IntQueue, DoubleQueue, ComplexQueue, StringQueue. As each new class type is needed, the code is copied, changed, and renamed.

What are the problems with this method of class type duplication? There is the lexical complexity of each uniquely named Queue class. Then, too, there is the administrative complexity — imagine having to propagate a modification in the general implementation of the class IntQueue to each specific instance. In general, providing manually generated copies for individual types is a never-ending process and is endlessly complicated to maintain.

Fortunately, the C++ template facility provides for the automatic generation of class types. We can use a class template to generate a class Queue automatically for a queue of any particular type. The template definition for the Queue class might look like this:

```
template <class Type>
class Queue {
public:
   Queue();
   ~Queue();

   Type& remove();
   void add( const Type & );
   bool is_empty();
   bool is_full();
private:
   // ....
};
```

The programmer writes

```
Queue<int> qi;
Queue< complex<double> > qc;
Queue<string> qs;
```

to generate, in turn, a Queue class of ints, complex numbers, and strings.

The implementation of our Queue class is presented in the following sections to illustrate the definition and use of class templates. The implementation uses a pair of class template abstractions:

1. The class template Queue itself provides the public interface described earlier, and a pair of data members: `front` and `back`. The class template Queue is implemented as a linked list.
2. The class template QueueItem represents one node of a Queue's linked list. Each item entered into the queue is stored in a QueueItem object. A QueueItem object contains a pair of data members: `value` and `next`. The actual type of `value` varies with each instance of Queue. `next` is a link to the next QueueItem object in the queue.

Before we look at the implementations of these templates in more detail, let's examine further how to declare and define templates. Here is the declaration of the class template QueueItem:

```
template <class T>
    class QueueItem;
```

The `template` keyword always begins both a definition and a declaration of a class template. This keyword is followed by a comma-separated list of template parameters surrounded by the less than (<) and greater than (>) tokens. This list is referred to as the *template parameter list* of the class template. It cannot be empty. A template parameter may be a type parameter or a nontype parameter representing a constant expression.

A template *type parameter* consists of the keyword `class` or the keyword `typename` followed by an identifier. In a template parameter list, the keyword `class` and the keyword `typename` have the same meaning. (The keyword `typename` is not supported by pre-Standard C++ implementations. Section 10.1 discusses in more detail why this keyword was added to C++: because it must sometimes be used to guide the compiler in the interpretation of template definitions.) These keywords indicate that the parameter name that follows represents a built-in or a user-defined type. For example, in the forward declaration of the class template QueueItem presented earlier, there is one template type parameter named T. Any built-in or user-defined type such as `int`, `double`, `char*`, complex, or string is a valid argument for T.

A class template can have multiple type parameters:

```
template <class T1, class T2, class T3>
    class Container;
```

However, each template type parameter must be preceded by the keyword `class` or the keyword `typename`. The following template declaration, for example, is in error:

```
// error: must be <typename T, class U> or
//                 <typename T, typename U>
template <typename T, U>
    class collection;
```

Once declared, the type parameter serves as a type specifier for the remainder of the class template definition. It can be used in the class template definition in exactly the same way as a built-in or user-defined type is used in a nontemplate class definition. For example, a type parameter can be used to declare data members, member functions, members of nested classes, and so forth.

A template *nontype parameter* consists of an ordinary parameter declaration. A nontype parameter indicates that the parameter name represents a potential value. This value represents a constant in the class template definition. For example, a Buffer class template may have a type parameter to indicate the type of the elements it holds and an nontype parameter that is a constant value representing its size. For example:

```
template <class Type, int size>
    class Buffer;
```

A class definition or declaration follows the template parameter list. Except for the presence of the template parameters, the definition of a class template looks the same as that of a nontemplate class:

```
template <class Type>
class QueueItem {
public:
    // ...
private:
    // Type represents the type of a data member
    Type item;
    QueueItem *next;
};
```

In the example, Type is used to indicate the type of the data member item. In the course of the program, Type will be substituted with various built-in and user-defined types. This process of type substitution is called *template instantiation*.

The name of a template parameter can be used after it has been declared as a template parameter and until the end of the template declaration or definition. If a variable with the same name as the template parameter is declared in global scope, that name is hidden. In the following example, item is not of type double. Its type is that of the template parameter:

```
typedef double Type;

template <class Type>
class QueueItem {
public:
    // ...
private:
    // item is not of type double
    Type item;
    QueueItem *next;
};
```

The name of a template parameter cannot be used as the name for a class member declared within the class template definition:

```
template <class Type>
class QueueItem {
public:
   // ...
private:
   // error: member cannot have the same name as
   //          the template parameter Type
   typedef double Type;
   Type item;
   QueueItem *next;
};
```

The name of a template parameter can be introduced only once within the template parameter list. The following, for example, is flagged at compile-time as an error:

```
// error: illegal reuse of template parameter named Type
template <class Type, class Type>
   class container;
```

The name of a template parameter can be reused across class template declarations or definitions:

```
// ok: reuse of the name 'Type' across templates
template <class Type>
   class QueueItem;

template <class Type>
   class Queue;
```

The names of the template parameters do not need to be the same across forward declarations and the definition of the class template. The following three declarations of QueueItem, for example, all refer to the same class template:

```
// all three declarations of QueueItem
// refer to the same class template

// declarations of the template
template <class T> class QueueItem;
template <class U> class QueueItem;

// actual definition of the template
template <class Type>
   class QueueItem { ... };
```

The parameters of a class template can have default arguments. This is true whether the parameter is a type parameter or a nontype parameter. Just like default arguments for function parameters (introduced in Section 7.3), a default argument for a template parameter is a type or value that is used if no argument is specified when

the template is instantiated. The default argument should be a type or value that is
suitable for a majority of the class template instantiations. In the following example, if
the name of the template instantiation does not specify the size for `Buffer`, the `Buffer`
instantiated has a size of 1,024 items.

```
template <class Type, int size = 1024>
    class Buffer;
```

Subsequent declarations of the class template can provide additional default arguments for the template parameters. As it is the case with default arguments for function
parameters, the rightmost uninitialized parameter must be supplied with a default argument before any default argument for a parameter to its left may be supplied. For example:

```
template <class Type, int size = 1024>
    class Buffer;

// ok: default arguments from the two declarations are considered
template <class Type = string , int size>
    class Buffer;
```

(Note that default arguments for template parameters are not supported by pre-
Standard C++ implementations. Many examples in this book, in Chapter 12 for example, were written not to use default arguments for template parameters to compile on
a pre-Standard C++ implementation.)

Inside the class template definition, the name of the class template can be used as
a type specifier whenever a nontemplate class name can be used. For example, here is
a more complete version of the definition of the QueueItem class template:

```
template <class Type>
class QueueItem {
public:
    QueueItem( const Type & );
private:
    Type item;
    QueueItem *next;
};
```

Notice that each occurrence of the QueueItem class template name within the class
template definition is a shorthand notation for

```
QueueItem<Type>
```

This shorthand notation can only be used within the definition of the class template QueueItem itself (and the definitions of its members that appear outside the class
template definition, as we will see in the next sections). When QueueItem is used as a
type specifier in another template definition, the full template parameter list must be
specified. In the following example, the class template is used in the definition of the

function template display. In this case, the name of the class template QueueItem must be followed by the template parameters, as in QueueItem<Type>.

```
template <class Type>
void display( QueueItem<Type> &qi )
{
    QueueItem<Type> *pqi = &qi;
    // ...
}
```

16.1.1 Queue and QueueItem Class Template Definitions

Here is the definition of the class template Queue. It is placed in a header file named Queue.h together with the definition for the class template QueueItem.

```
#ifndef QUEUE_H
#define QUEUE_H

// declaration of QueueItem
template <class T> class QueueItem;

template <class Type>
class Queue {
public:
    Queue() : front( 0 ), back ( 0 ) { }
    ~Queue();

    Type& remove();
    void add( const Type & );
    bool is_empty() const {
        return front == 0;
    }
private:
    QueueItem<Type> *front;
    QueueItem<Type> *back;
};
#endif
```

Within the definition of the class template Queue, the use of the name Queue may omit the parameter list <Type>. However, the parameter list cannot be omitted when the definition of Queue refers to the class template QueueItem. The following declaration of front, for example, is an error:

```
template <class Type>
class Queue {
public:
    // ...
```

```
    private:
        // error: QueueItem is not a known Type
        QueueItem *front;
    };
```

Exercise 16.1

Identify which, if any, of the following template class declarations (or declaration pairs) are illegal.

```
(a) template <class Type>
      class Container1;

    template <class Type, int size>
      class Container1;

(b) template <class T, U, class V>
      class Container2;

(c) template <class C1, typename C2>
      class Container3 {};

(d) template <typename myT, class myT>
      class Container4 {};

(e) template <class Type, int *ptr>
      class Container5;

    template <class T, int *pi>
      class Container5;

(f) template <class Type, int val = 0>
      class Container6;
    template <class T = complex<double>, int v>
      class Container6;
```

Exercise 16.2

The following definition of List is incorrect. How would you fix it?

```
template <class elemenType>
class ListItem;

template <class elemType>
class List {
public:
    List<elemType>()
        : _at_front( 0 ), _at_end( 0 ), _current( 0 ), _size( 0 )
        {}
    List<elemType>( const List<elemType> & );
```

```
    List<elemType>& operator=( const List<elemType> & );

    ~List();

    void insert( ListItem *ptr, elemType value );
    int  remove( elemType value );

    ListItem *find( elemType value );

    void display( ostream &os = cout );
    int size() { return _size; }
private:
    ListItem *_at_front;
    ListItem *_at_end;
    ListItem *_current;
    int _size;
};
```

16.2   Class Template Instantiation

A class template definition specifies how individual classes can be constructed given
a set of one or more actual types or values. The class template definition for Queue
serves as a template for the automatic generation of type-specific instances of Queue
classes. For example, a Queue class for objects of type int is created automatically
from the generic class template definition when the programmer writes

```
    Queue<int> qi;
```

This generation of a class from the generic class template definition is called *template instantiation*. When a Queue class for objects of type int is instantiated, each occurrence of the template parameter Type within the class template definition is
replaced with type int. The Queue class for int literally becomes

```
    class Queue<int> {
    public:
        Queue<int>() : front( 0 ), back ( 0 ) { }
        ~Queue<int>();

        int& remove();
        void add( const int & );
        bool is_empty() const {
            return front == 0;
        }
    private:
        QueueItem<int> *front;
        QueueItem<int> *back;
    };
```

Similarly, to create a Queue class for objects of type string, the programmer writes

```
Queue<string> qs;
```

In this case, each occurrence of the template parameter Type within the class template
definition is replaced by the type string. The objects qi and qs are objects of class type.

There is no special relationship between the instantiations of a class template for
different types. Rather, each instantiation of a class template constitutes an independent class type. The Queue instantiation for the type int has no access permission, for
example, to the nonpublic members of the Queue instantiation for strings.

The name of the class template instantiation is Queue<int> or Queue<string>. The
<int> or <string> tokens that follow the class template name Queue are referred to as
the template arguments. The template arguments must be specified in a comma-separated list and bracketed by the less than (<) and greater than (>) tokens. The name of a
class template instantiation must always specify the template arguments explicitly.
Unlike template arguments for function template instantiations, the template arguments for class template instantiations are never deduced from the context in which a
class template instantiation is used:

```
Queue qs;   // error: which template instantiation?
```

An instantiation of the class template Queue can be used by the general program
wherever a nontemplate class type can be used:

```
// the return type and two parameters are instantiations of Queue
extern Queue< complex<double> >
    foo( Queue< complex<double> > &, Queue< complex<double> > & );

// pointer to member function of an instantiation of Queue
bool (Queue<double>::*pmf)() = 0;

// explicit cast of 0 to a pointer to an instantiation of Queue
Queue<char*> *pqc = static_cast< Queue<char*>* > ( 0 );
```

Objects of a class type that is an instantiation of the class template Queue are declared and used exactly the same as objects of a nontemplate class type:

```
extern Queue<double> eqd;
Queue<int> *pqi = new Queue<int>;
Queue<int> aqi[1024];

int main() {
   int ix;
   if ( ! pqi->is_empty() )
      ix = pqi->remove();
   // ...
   for ( ix = 0; ix < 1024; ++ix )
      eqd[ ix ].add( ix );
   // ...
}
```

A template declaration or definition can refer to a class template or to an instantiation of a class template:

```
// function template declaration
template <class Type>
void bar( Queue<Type> &,   // refers to generic template
          Queue<double> & // and to template instantiation
)
```

However, outside the context of a template definition, only class template instantiations can be used. For example, a nontemplate function must always specify which particular instantiation of the class template Queue it uses:

```
void foo( Queue<int> &qi )
{
   Queue<int> *pqi = &qi;
   // ...
}
```

A class template is instantiated only when the name of an instantiation is used in a context that requires a class definition to exist. Not all uses of a class require the class definition to be known. For example, it is not necessary to know the definition of a class before pointers and references to a class can be declared. For example:

```
class Matrix;
Matrix *pm; // ok: definition of class Matrix not needed

void inverse( Matrix & ); // ok too
```

Therefore, declaring pointers and references to a class template instantiation do not cause the class template to be instantiated. (We should mention here that some implementations supporting pre-Standard C++ instantiate a template the first time the name of an instantiation is encountered in the program text.) For example, the following function foo() declares a pointer and a reference to the class template instantiation Queue<int>. However, these declarations do not cause the template Queue to be instantiated:

```
// Queue<int> is not instantiated for its uses in foo()
void foo( Queue<int> &qi )
{
   Queue<int> *pqi = &qi;
   // ...
}
```

A class definition is needed when an object of this class type is defined. For example, the definition of obj1 in the following example is an error. This object definition requires that the size of Matrix be known for the compiler to allocate the right amount of storage for obj1:

```
class Matrix;
Matrix obj1; // error: class Matrix is not defined
```

```
class Matrix { ... };
Matrix obj2; // ok
```

A class template is therefore instantiated when an object is defined with a type that is a class template instantiation. In the following example, the definition of the object qi causes the template Queue<int> to be instantiated:

```
Queue<int> qi; // Queue<int> is instantiated
```

The definition of the class Queue<int> becomes known to the compiler at this point, called the *point of instantiation* of the class Queue<int>.

Similarly, if a pointer or reference refers to a class template instantiation, only when examining the object to which such a pointer or reference refers is the class template instantiated. In the function foo() defined earlier, Queue<int> is instantiated if the pointer pqi is dereferenced, if qi is used to obtain the value of the object to which it refers, or if either pqi or qi are used to access the data members or member functions of Queue<int>:

```
void foo( Queue<int> &qi )
{
    Queue<int> *pqi = &qi;

    // Queue<int> is instantiated because of member function call
    pqi->add( 255 );
    // ...
}
```

The definition of the class Queue<int> becomes known to the compiler before its member function add() is called in foo().

Remember that the definition of class template Queue refers to the class template QueueItem as follows:

```
template <class Type>
class Queue {
public:
    // ...
private:
    QueueItem<Type> *front;
    QueueItem<Type> *back;
};
```

When Queue is instantiated for the type int, the members front and back for the instantiation Queue<int> are pointers to QueueItem<int>. The instantiation of Queue<int> therefore refers to the instantiation of the class template QueueItem for the type int. However, because these members are pointers, the type QueueItem<int> is only instantiated when these members are dereferenced in the member functions of class Queue<int>.

We have decided that QueueItem is intended as an auxiliary class to help in the implementation of the class Queue. It is not intended to be used by the general program. Therefore, programs only manipulate Queue class objects. Instantiations of the class template QueueItem are only caused by the instantiation of the class template Queue and the instantiation of its members. In the following sections we look at the instantiation of class template members.

Depending on the types with which a class template is instantiated, some design considerations must be taken into account when defining a class template. For example, can you see why the following definition of the QueueItem constructor is likely to be unacceptable for a wide range of type instantiations?

```
template <class Type>
class QueueItem {
public:
    QueueItem( Type ); // bad design choice
    // ...
};
```

This definition of the QueueItem constructor implements the pass-by-value argument semantics. This performs adequately when QueueItem is instantiated with a built-in type (as in the instantiation of QueueItem<int>, for example). However, when QueueItem is instantiated with a large class type (such as Matrix, for example), the run-time impact of this choice is no longer acceptable. (Section 7.3 discusses the performance implications of declaring pass-by-value parameters as opposed to declaring reference parameters.) This is why the argument to the constructor is declared as a reference to a const type:

```
QueueItem( const Type & );
```

Another design consideration underlies the implementation of this constructor. The following constructor definition is acceptable if the type with which QueueItem is instantiated does not have an associated constructor:

```
template <class Type>
class QueueItem {
    // ...
public:
    // potentially inefficient
    QueueItem( const Type &t ) {
        item = t; next = 0;
    }
};
```

If the template argument is a class type with a constructor (string, for example), it results in item being initialized twice! The default constructor for string is invoked to initialize item prior to the execution of the body of the QueueItem constructor. item, newly constructed, is then memberwise assigned. Explicitly initializing item within

the constructor member initialization list in the definition of the QueueItem constructor resolves this problem:

```
template <class Type>
class QueueItem {
    // ...
public:
    // item initialized in constructor member initialization list
    QueueItem( const Type &t )
                : item(t) { next = 0; }
};
```

(Section 14.5 discusses member initialization lists, and when and how they should
be used.)

16.2.1   Template Arguments for Nontype Parameters

A class template parameter can be a nontype template parameter. There are some
restrictions on the kind of template argument that can be used with such a nontype
template parameter. We examine these restrictions here. The following example uses
the class Screen first introduced in Chapter 13. It is redefined here to be a template,
parameterized by its height and width:

```
template <int hi, int wid>
class Screen {
public:
    Screen() : _height( hi ), _width( wid ), _cursor ( 0 ),
                _screen( hi * wid, '#' )
            { }
    // ...
private:
    string          _screen;
    string::size_type _cursor;
    short           _height;
    short           _width;
};

typedef Screen<24,80> termScreen;
termScreen hp2621;

Screen<8,24> ancientScreen;
```

The expression to which a nontype parameter is bound must be a constant expression. That is, it must be possible to evaluate it at compile-time. In the previous example, the typedef termScreen refers to the template instantiation Screen<24,80>. The
template argument for hi is 24 and the argument for wid is 80. In both cases the template argument is a constant expression.

However, given the class template BufPtr defined here, its instantiation results in

a compiler error since the pointer value resulting from the invocation of operator new()
is not known until run-time:

```
template <int *ptr> class BufPtr { ... };

// error: template argument cannot be evaluated at compile-time
BufPtr< new int[24] > bp;
```

Similarly, the value of a non-const object is not a constant expression. It cannot be
used as a template argument for a nontype template parameter. However, the address
of any object of namespace scope (even if the object is not of const type) is a constant
expression (whereas the address of a local object is not). The address of an object of
namespace scope can therefore be used as the argument for a nontype template parameter. Similarly, the result of a sizeof expression is a constant expression that can be
used as the argument for a nontype template parameter:

```
template <int size> Buf{ ... };
template <int *ptr> class BufPtr { ... };

int size_val = 1024;
const int c_size_val = 1024;

Buf< 1024 > buf0; // ok
Buf< c_size_val > buf1; // ok
Buf< sizeof(size_val) > buf2; // ok: sizeof(int)
BufPtr< &size_val > bp0; // ok

// error: cannot be evaluated at compile-time
Buf< size_val > buf3;
```

Here is another example that illustrates how a nontype template parameter can be
used to represent a constant value in a class template definition, and how a template
argument is used to specify a value for this template parameter:

```
template <class Type, int size>
class Fixed_Array {
public:
   Fixed_Array( Type *ar) : count( size )
   {
      for ( int ix = 0; ix < size; ++ix )
         array[ ix ] = ar[ ix ];
   }
private:
   Type array[ size ];
   int count;
};

int ia[4] = { 0, 1, 2, 3 };
Fixed_Array< int, sizeof( ia ) / sizeof( int ) > iA( ia );
```

Expressions that evaluate to the same value are considered equivalent template arguments for a template nontype parameter. The following three Screen instances, for example, all refer to the same template instantiation Screen<24,80>:

```
const int width = 24;
const int height = 80;

// all: type Screen< 24, 80 >
Screen< 2*12, 40*2 > scr0;
Screen< 6+6+6+6, 20*2+40 > scr1;
Screen< width, height > scr2;
```

Some conversions are allowed between the type of a template argument and the type of a nontype template parameter. The set of conversions allowed is a subset of the conversions allowed on function arguments:

1. Lvalue transformations, including lvalue-to-rvalue conversion, array-to-pointer conversion, and function-to-pointer conversion; for example:

    ```
    template <int *ptr> class BufPtr { ... };

    int array[10];
    BufPtr< array > bpObj; // array-to-pointer conversion
    ```

2. Qualification conversions; for example:

    ```
    template <const int *ptr> class Ptr { ... };

    int iObj;
    Ptr< &iObj > pObj; // conversion from int* to const int*
    ```

3. Promotions; for example:

    ```
    template <int hi, int wid> class Screen { ... };

    const short shi = 40;
    const short swi = 132;
    Screen< shi, swi > bpObj2; // promotion from short to int
    ```

4. Integral conversions; for example:

    ```
    template <unsigned int size> Buf{ ... };

    Buf< 1024 > bObj; // conversion from int to unsigned int
    ```

(These conversions are further described in Section 9.3.)

For example, consider the following set of declarations:

```
extern void foo( char * );
extern void bar( void * );
typedef void (*PFV)( void * );
```

```
const unsigned int x = 1024;

template <class Type,
          unsigned int size,
          PFV handler> class Array { ... };

Array<int, 1024U, bar> a0; // ok: no conversion needed
Array<int, 1024U, foo> a1; // error: foo != PFV

Array<int, 1024, bar> a2; // ok: 1024 converted to unsigned int
Array<int, 1024, foo> a3; // error: foo != PFV

Array<int, x, bar> a4; // ok: no conversion needed
Array<int, x, foo> a5; // error: foo != PFV
```

The Array class objects a0 and a4 are correctly defined because the template arguments match the type of their corresponding template parameters exactly. The Array
class object a2 is correctly defined because the template argument 1024 of type int is
converted to the type of the nontype template parameter size (with the type unsigned
int) using an integral conversion. The declarations for the Array class objects a1, a3,
and a5 are in error because no conversions exist between any two function types.

The following conversion that converts the value 0 of integer type to a value of
pointer type is not allowed:

```
template <int *ptr>
class BufPtr { ... };

// error: 0 is of type int
// implicit conversion to the null pointer value using
// an implicit pointer conversion is not applied
BufPtr< 0 > nil;
```

Exercise 16.3

Identify which, if any, of the following uses of a template instantiation causes the template to be instantiated.

```
template < class Type >
   class Stack { };

void f1( Stack< char > ); // (a)

class Exercise {
   // ...
   Stack< double > &rsd; // (b)
   Stack< int >    si;   // (c)
};

int main() {
```

```
        Stack< char > *sc;      // (d)
        f1( *sc );              // (e)

        int iObj = sizeof( Stack< string > ); // (f)
    }
```

Exercise 16.4

Identify which, if any, of the following template instantiations are valid. Explain why.

```
        template < int *ptr > class Ptr { ... };
        template < class Type, int size > class Fixed_Array { ... };
        template < int hi, int wid > class Screen { ... };

        (a) const int size = 1024;
            Ptr< &size > bp1;

        (b) int arr[10];
            Ptr< arr > bp2;

        (c) Ptr < 0 > bp3;

        (d) const int hi = 40;
            const int wi = 80;
            Screen< hi, wi+32 > sObj;

        (e) const int size_val = 1024;
            Fixed_Array< string, size_val > fa1;

        (f) unsigned int fasize = 255;
            Fixed_Array< int, fasize > fa2;

        (g) const double db = 3.1415;
            Fixed_Array< double, db > fa3;
```

16.3   Member Functions of Class Templates

As with nontemplate classes, a member function of a class template can either be defined within the class template definition, in which case the member function is an inline member function, or the member function can be defined outside the class template definition. We have already seen examples of inline member functions when we introduced the class template Queue. For example, the constructor for Queue is defined inline within the class template definition.

```
        template <class Type>
        class Queue {
            // ...
        public:
```

```
       // inline constructor member function
       Queue() : front( 0 ), back ( 0 ) { }
       // ...
    };
```

A member function of a class template defined outside its class template definition must use a special syntax to indicate that it is a member of a class template. The definition of the member function must be preceded by the keyword template followed by the template parameters. For example, the Queue constructor could be defined outside the class template definition as follows:

```
    template <class Type>
    class Queue {
    public:
       Queue( );
    private:
       // ...
    };
    template <class Type>
    inline Queue<Type>::
       Queue( ) { front = back = 0; }
```

The first occurrence of Queue (the one preceding the scope operator : :) is followed by the template parameter list. This represents the class template to which the member function belongs. The second occurrence of Queue in the constructor definition (the one following the scope operator) represents the name of the constructor member function. Its name may but does not need to be followed by the template parameter list. Following the member function name is a function definition that looks very much like a nontemplate function definition. However, the definition of a member function of a class template can refer to the template parameter Type wherever a type name can be used in ordinary function definitions.

A member function of a class template is itself a template. Standard C++ requires that such a member function be instantiated only when it is called or its address is taken. (Some pre-Standard implementations instantiate the member functions of a class template when the class template is itself instantiated.) The type used to instantiate the member function is the type of the class object for which the member function is called. For example:

```
    Queue<string> qs;
```

The object qs is of type Queue<string>. When this class object is initialized, the constructor for the class Queue<string> is called. The template argument with which the constructor member function is instantiated in this case is string.

A member function of a class template is not instantiated automatically when the class template is itself instantiated. The member function is instantiated only if it is used by the program (a use of a function, recall, invokes the function or takes its address). Exactly when the member function of a class template is instantiated impacts how names are resolved in the definition of a class template member function (discussed further in Section 16.11) and when a member function specialization can be declared (discussed further in Section 16.9).

16.3.1   Queue and QueueItem Template Member Functions

To become a bit more familiar with how to define and use class template member functions, let's further examine the class template Queue and its member functions.

```
template <class Type>
class Queue {
public:
    Queue() : front( 0 ), back ( 0 ) { }
    ~Queue();

    Type remove();
    void add( const Type & );
    bool is_empty() const {
        return front == 0 ;
    }
private:
    QueueItem<Type> *front;
    QueueItem<Type> *back;
};
```

The destructor and the member functions remove() and add() are not defined in the class template definition. These member functions are defined outside the class template definition as shown in the following examples. The destructor for Queue empties the queue of items:

```
template <class Type>
Queue<Type>::~Queue()
{
    while ( ! is_empty() )
        remove();
}
```

The member function Queue<Type>::add() places a new item at the back of the queue. Here is its implementation:

```
template <class Type>
void Queue<Type>::add( const Type &val )
{
    // allocate a new QueueItem object
    QueueItem<Type> *pt =
        new QueueItem<Type>( val );
```

```
        if ( is_empty() )
           front = back = pt;
        else
        {
           back->next = pt;
           back = pt;
        }
    }
```

The member function `Queue<Type>::remove()` returns the value of the item at the front of the queue. The associated QueueItem object is deleted.

```
#include <iostream>
#include <cstdlib>

template <class Type>
Type Queue<Type>::remove()
{
    if ( is_empty() )
    {
        cerr << "remove() on empty queue\n";
        exit( -1 );
    }

    QueueItem<Type> *pt = front;
    front = front->next;

    Type retval = pt->item;
    delete pt;
    return retval;
}
```

We decided to add the member function definitions to the header `Queue.h`, and to include these definitions in every file where instantiations of the member functions are used. (We look at why we decided to do this, and at the more general question of template compilation model, in Section 16.8.)

The following program illustrates how the member functions of the Queue class template might be used and instantiated:

```
#include <iostream>
#include "Queue.h"

int main()
{
    // the class Queue<int> is instantiated
    // new expression requires that Queue<int> be defined
    Queue<int> *p_qi = new Queue<int>;

    int ival;
```

```
        for ( ival = 0; ival < 10; ++ival )
            // the member function add() is instantiated
            p_qi->add( ival );

        int err_cnt = 0;
        for ( ival = 0; ival < 10; ++ival ) {
            // the member function remove() is instantiated
            int qval = p_qi->remove();

            if ( ival != qval ) err_cnt++;
        }

        if ( !err_cnt )
            cout << "!! queue executed ok\n";
        else cerr << "?? queue errors: " << err_cnt << endl;
        return 0;
    }
```

When compiled and executed, this program generates the following output:

```
    !! queue executed ok
```

Exercise 16.5

Using the class template Screen defined in Section 16.2, reimplement the member functions of the class Screen implemented in Chapter 13, Sections 13.3, 13.4, and 13.6, as template member functions.

16.4   Friend Declarations in Class Templates

There are three kinds of friend declarations that may appear within a class template:

1. A nontemplate friend class or friend function. In the following example, the function foo(), the member function bar(), and the class foobar are friends to all instantiations of the class template QueueItem.

```
    class Foo {
        void bar();
    };

    template <class T>
    class QueueItem {
        friend class foobar;
        friend void foo();
        friend void Foo::bar();
        // ...
    };
```

The class foobar and the function foo() do not have to be declared or defined in global scope before the class template QueueItem declares them as friends.

However, the class Foo must be defined before the class QueueItem can declare one of its members as a friend. Recall that a class member can only be introduced by the definition of its class. QueueItem cannot refer to `Foo::bar()` before the class definition for Foo has been seen.

2.   A *bound* friend class template or function template. In the following example, a one-to-one mapping is defined between the instantiation of the class template QueueItem and its friends, also template instantiations. For each instantiation of the class template QueueItem, a single associated instantiation of `foobar`, `foo()`, and `Queue::bar()` are friends.

```
template <class Type>
   class foobar{ ... };

template <class Type>
   void foo( QueueItem<Type> );

template <class Type>
class Queue {
      void bar();
      // ...
};

template <class Type>
class QueueItem {
   friend class foobar<Type>;
   friend void foo<Type>( QueueItem<Type> );
   friend void Queue<Type>::bar();

   // ...
};
```

A declaration or definition must be provided for a template before it can be used in a friend declaration of a class template. In our example, the class templates foobar and Queue must be declared, and the function template foo() must be declared before the friend declarations in class QueueItem.

The syntax used with the friend declaration for foo() may seem surprising:

```
friend void foo<Type>( QueueItem<Type> );
```

The name of the function is followed by a list of explicit template arguments: foo<Type>. This syntax is used to specify that the friend declaration refers to an instantiation of the function template foo(). If the list of explicit template arguments were omitted as follows,

```
friend void foo( QueueItem<Type> );
```

then the friend declaration would be interpreted as referring to a nontemplate function with a parameter type that is an instance of the class template QueueItem. As mentioned in Section 10.6, a function template and a nontemplate function with the same name can coexist, and the presence of the function template declaration before the definition of class QueueItem does not force the friend declaration to refer to this template. The list of explicit template arguments must be specified for the friend declaration to refer to an instantiation of the function template.

3. An *unbound* friend class template or function template. In the following example, a one-to-many mapping is defined between the instantiation of the class template QueueItem and the friend. For each type instantiation of QueueItem, all instantiations of foobar, foo(), and Queue<T>::bar() are friends.

```
template <class Type>
class QueueItem {
    template <class T>
        friend class foobar;

    template <class T>
        friend void foo( QueueItem<T> );

    template <class T>
        friend void Queue<T>::bar();

    // ...
};
```

We should note that this kind of friend declaration in a class template is not supported by implementations that support pre-Standard C++.

16.4.1   Queue and QueueItem Friend Declarations

Because QueueItem is not intended to be used by the general program, the declaration of the QueueItem constructor is moved into a private section of the class template QueueItem. Queue must now be declared a friend of QueueItem to create and manipulate QueueItem class objects.

There are two methods of declaring a class template to be a friend. The first method is to declare all possible Queue instances to be friends of each QueueItem instantiation:

```
template <class Type>
class QueueItem {
    // all Queue instantiations are friends
    // to each QueueItem instantiation
    template <class T> friend class Queue;
};
```

This is not really the design intention, however. It makes no sense, for example, to have a Queue instantiated with the type string be a friend to a QueueItem instantiated with the type `complex<double>`. `Queue<string>` should be a friend only to the instantiation of the QueueItem for strings. That is, we want a one-to-one mapping between a Queue and QueueItem instance for every type instantiated. This is achieved by using the second kind of friend declaration:

```
template <class Type>
class QueueItem {
    // each QueueItem instantiation has the associated
    // Queue instantiation as its friend
    friend class Queue<Type>;

    // ...
};
```

This declaration specifies that for every instantiation of QueueItem with a particular type, the corresponding Queue instantiation is its friend. That is, a Queue instantiation for the type `int` is a friend to a QueueItem instantiation for the type `int`. It is not a friend of the QueueItem instantiations for the type `complex<double>` or for the type string.

At any given point, a user may need the ability to display the contents of a Queue object. One method of allowing this is to provide an overloaded instance of the output operator. This operator needs to be declared as a friend function of the Queue class template because it must access the class private members. What should the operator's signature look like?

```
// what form of Queue argument?
ostream& operator<<( ostream &, ??? );
```

Since Queue is a class template, the name of a template instantiation must specify the full argument list. For example:

```
ostream& operator<<( ostream &, const Queue<int> & );
```

This defines an output operator for the instantiation of the class template Queue for items of type `int`. However, what about a Queue of items of type string?

```
ostream& operator<<( ostream &, const Queue<string> & );
```

Rather than define each particular output operator explicitly as it is needed, let's define a general output operator that can handle all the instantiations of Queue. For example:

```
ostream& operator<<( ostream &, const Queue<Type> & );
```

For this to work, however, we must in turn make this overloaded output operator a function template:

```
template <class Type> ostream&
    operator<<( ostream &, const Queue<Type> & );
```

That done, each time a Queue instantiation is passed to an ostream, the function template is instantiated and invoked. Here is one possible implementation of the output operator as a function template:

```
template <class Type>
ostream& operator<<( ostream &os, const Queue<Type> &q )
{
    os << "< ";
    QueueItem<Type> *p;
    for ( p = q.front; p; p = p->next )
        os << *p << " ";
    os << " >";
    return os;
}
```

If a Queue of objects of type int contains the values 3, 5, 8, and 13, the output of this Queue displays as follows:

```
< 3 5 8 13 >
```

Notice that the output operator refers to Queue's private member front. The next thing we need to do is to declare the operator as a friend of Queue, as follows:

```
template <class Type>
class Queue {
    friend ostream&
        operator<<( ostream &, const Queue<Type> & );
    // ...
};
```

Notice that, in this case, as with the friend declaration within the class template Queue earlier in this section, this declaration creates a one-to-one mapping between an instantiation of Queue and its corresponding operator<<() instance.

The actual display of the Queue's elements relies on QueueItem's output operator<<():

```
os << *p;
```

The QueueItem output operator also needs to be implemented as a template function. This ensures that an appropriate operator<<() is instantiated automatically when needed:

```
template <class Type>
ostream& operator<<( ostream &os, const QueueItem<Type> &qi )
{
    os << qi.item;
    return os;
}
```

Because this operator accesses QueueItem's private member item, this operator must be declared as a friend of the class template QueueItem. This is done as follows:

```
template <class Type>
class QueueItem {
    friend class Queue<Type>;
    friend ostream&
        operator<<( ostream &, const QueueItem<Type> & );
    // ...
};
```

The QueueItem output operator`<<()` relies on item itself to handle the actual display:

```
os << qi.item;
```

This introduces a subtle type dependency on the instantiation of Queue. In effect, each user-defined class type bound to Queue that intends to display itself must provide an output operator. There is no language mechanism either to specify or enforce that dependency in the definition of the class template Queue itself. Rather, if the output operator is not defined for a type used to instantiate the template Queue, and an attempt is made to display the content of this instantiation, a compile-time error is issued at the point where the invalid output operator is used. Queue can be instantiated with a type that does not define an output operator — provided there is no attempt to display the Queue's contents.

The following program illustrates how the friend functions of the Queue class template and the friend functions of the QueueItem class template might be instantiated and used:

```
#include <iostream>
#include "Queue.h"

int main() {
    Queue<int> qi;
    // instantiates both instances:
    //    ostream& operator<<(ostream &os, const Queue<int> &)
    //    ostream& operator<<(ostream &os, const QueueItem<int> &)
    cout << qi << endl;

    int ival;
    for ( ival = 0; ival < 10; ++ival )
        qi.add( ival );
    cout << qi << endl;

    int err_cnt = 0;
    for ( ival = 0; ival < 10; ++ival ) {
        int qval = qi.remove();
        if ( ival != qval ) err_cnt++;
    }

    cout << qi << endl;
    if ( !err_cnt )
        cout << "!! queue executed ok\n";
```

```
        else cout << "?? queue errors: " << err_cnt << endl;
        return 0;
}
```

When compiled and executed, this program generates the following output:

```
<  >
< 0 1 2 3 4 5 6 7 8 9  >
<  >
!! queue executed ok
```

Exercise 16.6

Using the Screen class template defined in Exercise 16.5, reimplement the input and output operators defined for class Screen in Exercise 15.6 of Section 15.2 as templates. Explain your reason behind the kind of friend declarations you choose to add to the class template Screen.

16.5   Static Data Members of Class Templates

A class template can declare static data members. Each instantiation of the class template has its own set of static data members. To illustrate this, let's introduce operator new() and operator delete() for the class template QueueItem. To do this we will need to add two static data members to the class QueueItem:

```
        static QueueItem<Type> *free_list;
        static const unsigned QueueItem_chunk;
```

The modifications to the QueueItem class template definition look like this:

```
        #include <cstddef>

        template <class Type>
        class QueueItem {
           // ...
        private:
           void *operator new( size_t );
           void operator delete( void *, size_t );
           // ...
           static QueueItem *free_list;
           static const unsigned QueueItem_chunk;
           // ...
        };
```

Operator new() and operator delete() are declared as private to prevent the general program from creating objects of type QueueItem on the free store. Only members of QueueItem and friends (such as the template Queue) can create (and delete) objects of type QueueItem on the free store.

The definition of operator new() might be implemented as follows:

```
template <class Type> void*
   QueueItem<Type>::operator new( size_t size )
{
   QueueItem<Type> *p;
   if ( ! free_list )
   {
      size_t chunk = QueueItem_chunk * size;
      free_list = p =
         reinterpret_cast< QueueItem<Type>* >
                           ( new char[chunk] );

      for ( ; p != &free_list[ QueueItem_chunk - 1 ]; ++p )
         p->next = p + 1;
      p->next = 0;
   }

   p = free_list;
   free_list = free_list->next;
   return p;
}
```

Here is the template implementation of the operator delete():

```
template <class Type>
void QueueItem<Type>::
   operator delete( void *p, size_t )
{
   static_cast< QueueItem<Type>* >( p )->next = free_list;
   free_list = static_cast< QueueItem<Type>* > ( p );
}
```

All that remains to be done now is to initialize the static members free_list and QueueItem_chunk. The template form for the definition of a static data member is as follows:

```
/* for each QueueItem instantiation, generate the
 * associated free_list, initialize it to 0
 */
template <class T>
   QueueItem<T> *QueueItem<T>::free_list = 0;

/* for each QueueItem instantiation, generate the
 * associated QueueItem_chunk, initialize it to 24
 */
template <class T>
   const unsigned int
   QueueItem<T>::QueueItem_chunk = 24;
```

The template definition of a static data member must appear outside the class template definition. For this reason, the template definition starts with the keyword `template` followed by the class template parameter list `<class T>`. The name of the static data member is prefixed by `QueueItem<T>::`, which indicates that the member belongs to the class template QueueItem. The static data member definitions are added to the header file `Queue.h`. These definitions must be included in the files in which instantiations of the static data members are used. (We look at why we decided to do this, and at the related topic of template compilation model, in Section 16.8.)

A static data member is instantiated from the template definition only if it is used in a program. A static member of a class template is itself a template. The template definition for the static data member does not cause any memory to be allocated. Memory is only allocated for particular instantiations of the static data member. Each static data member instantiation corresponds to a class template instantiation. An instantiation of a static data member, then, is always referred to through a particular class template instantiation. For example:

```
// error: QueueItem is not an actual instantiation
int ival0 = QueueItem::QueueItem_chunk;

int ival1 = QueueItem<string>::QueueItem_chunk; // ok
int ival2 = QueueItem<int>::QueueItem_chunk;     // ok
```

Exercise 16.7

Using operator `new()`, operator `delete()`, and their associated static members `screenChunk` and `freeStore` defined in Section 15.8, implement these operators and static members for the class template Screen defined in Exercise 16.6.

16.6   Nested Types of Class Templates

The class template QueueItem is designed to serve only in the implementation of a Queue. To enforce this, QueueItem has a private constructor that allows the member functions of its friend class template Queue, but no other classes or functions (except its own member functions), to create objects of the type QueueItem. Although QueueItem is a class template visible to the entire program, the program is unable either to create QueueItem objects or to refer to any of QueueItem's members without calling Queue's member functions.

An alternative implementation strategy is to nest the definition of the class template QueueItem within the private section of the class template Queue. With QueueItem being a nested private type, it becomes inaccessible to the general program. And because it is a private nested type, only the class template Queue and the friends of Queue — the output operator — can access it. If we make the members of QueueItem public, it no longer becomes necessary to declare Queue as a friend to QueueItem.

This implementation preserves the semantics of our original implementation and models more elegantly the relationship between the QueueItem and the Queue class templates.

Because a Queue requires an associated QueueItem class for each type with which it is instantiated, the nested class is also a class template. Nested classes of class templates are automatically class templates, and the template parameter of the enclosing class template can be used within the nested class template. For example:

```
template <class Type>
class Queue {
   // ...
private:
   class QueueItem {
   public:
      QueueItem( Type val )
               : item( val ), next( 0 ) { ... }

      Type item;
      QueueItem *next;
   };
   // because QueueItem is a nested type,
   // and not a template defined outside of Queue,
   // the template argument <Type> can be omitted
   // after QueueItem
   QueueItem *front, *back;
   // ...
};
```

Each instantiation of Queue generates its own QueueItem class with the appropriate template argument for Type. The mapping between an instantiation for the QueueItem class template and an instantiation of the enclosing Queue class template is one to one.

A nested class of a class template is not instantiated automatically when the enclosing class template is instantiated. The nested class is only instantiated if it is itself used in a context that requires a complete class type. For example, we mention in Section 16.2 that if the class template Queue is instantiated for the type int, the type QueueItem<int> is not instantiated automatically. The members front and back are pointers to QueueItem<int> and it is not necessary to instantiate the type QueueItem<int> if only pointers to this class type are declared. Making QueueItem a nested class of the class template Queue does not change this. QueueItem<int> is still only instantiated when the members front and back are dereferenced in the member functions of class Queue<int>.

Enumerations and typedefs can also be declared within a class template. For example:

```
template <class Type, int size>
class Buffer {
public:
   enum Buf_vals { last = size-1, Buf_size };
   typedef Type BufType;
   BufType array[ size ];
   // ...
};
```

Rather than providing an explicit `Buf_size` data member, the Buffer class template declares an enumeration type with a pair of nested enumerators initialized with the value of a template parameter. For example, the declaration

```
Buffer<int, 512> small_buf;
```

sets its `Buf_size` to 512 and `last` to 511. Similarly, the declaration

```
Buffer<int, 1024> medium_buf;
```

sets its `Buf_size` to 1024 and `last` to 1023.

A public nested type can be used outside its class definition. However, for a public nested type (or an enumerator of a nested enumeration) of a class template, only an instantiation of the nested type can be referenced by the general program. In this case the name of the nested type must be prefixed with the name of the class template instantiation. For example:

```
// error: which instantiation of Buffer?
Buffer::Buf_vals bfv0;

Buffer<int,512>::Buf_vals bfv1; // ok
```

This rule also applies if the nested type does not use one of the enclosing class template parameters. For example:

```
template <class T> class Q {
public:
    enum QA { empty, full }; // invariant
    QA status;
    // ...
};

#include <iostream>

int main() {
    Q<double> qd;
    Q<int> qi;

    qd.status = Q::empty; // error: which instantiation of Q?
    qd.status = Q<double>::empty; // ok

    int val1 = Q<double>::empty;
    int val2 = Q<int>::empty;
    if ( val1 != val2 )
        cerr << "implementation error!" << endl;
    return 0;
}
```

Although `empty` has the same value in each instantiation of Q, code that refers to `empty` must specify to which particular instance of Q the enumerator belongs.

Exercise 16.8

Define the class List and its nested class ListItem defined in Section 13.10 as class templates. Also provide the template definitions for the associated class members.

16.7　Member Templates ◆

A function or class template can be a member of an ordinary class or a member of a class template. The definition of a member template looks like the definition of a template: The member definition is preceded by the keyword `template`, followed by a template parameter list. For example:

```
template <class T>
class Queue {
private:
   // class member template
   template <class Type>
      class CL
   {
      Type member;
      T mem;
   };
   // ...
public:
   // function member template
   template <class Iter>
      void assign( Iter first, Iter last )
   {
      while ( ! is_empty() )
         remove();   // calls Queue<T>::remove()

      for ( ; first != last; ++first )
         add( *first );   // calls Queue<T>::add( const T & )
   }
};
```

(Note that member templates are not supported by pre-Standard C++ implementations. This feature was added to C++ to support the implementation of the abstract container types presented in Chapter 6, as we explain in the following paragraphs.)

The declaration of a member template has template parameters of its own. For example, the class member template CL has its own template parameter named `Type`, and the function member template `assign()` has its own template parameter `Iter`. In addition, the definition of a member template can also use the template parameters of the enclosing class template. For example, the class member template CL has a data member with the type `T`, the template parameter of the enclosing class template Queue.

Declaring a member template within the class template Queue means that an instantiation of Queue contains a potentially infinite number of nested classes CL and a potentially infinite number of member functions assign(). For example, the instantiation Queue<int> may contain the following nested types:

```
Queue<int>::CL<char>
Queue<int>::CL<string>
```

Similarly, Queue<int> may contain the following member functions:

```
void Queue<int>::assign( int *, int * )
void Queue<int>::assign( vector<int>::iterator,
                         vector<int>::iterator )
```

A member template follows the same access rules as other class members. Because the class member template CL is a private member of the class template Queue, only member functions and friends of Queue can refer to instantiations of the class member template. Because the function member template assign() is a public member, it can be used by the entire program.

A member template is only instantiated when it is itself used in a program. For example, assign() is instantiated when used in main() as follows:

```
int main()
{
    // instantiation of Queue<int>
    Queue<int> qi;

    // instantiation of Queue<int>::assign( int *, int * )
    int ai[4] = { 0, 3, 6, 9 };
    qi.assign( ai, ai + 4 );

    // instantiation of Queue<int>::assign( vector<int>::iterator,
    //                                      vector<int>::iterator)
    vector<int> vi( ai, ai + 4 );
    qi.assign( vi.begin(), vi.end() );

}
```

The function member template assign() of the class template Queue is a good example of why member templates are needed to support container types. For example, given a queue of type Queue<int>, we would like to be able to add to the queue the content of any other container (the content of a list, a vector, or a simple array) with elements that are either of type int (the type of the elements in the queue) or of a type that can be converted to type int. The member template assign() allows us to do just that. Because any container type can be used, we program the interface of the function member template assign() to use iterators, and thus isolate its implementation from the actual container type to which the iterators refer.

In the function `main()`, the member template `assign()` is first instantiated with the type `int*`, which allows the content of an array of `int` to be assigned to `qi`. The member template is then instantiated with the type `vector<int>::iterator`, which allows the content of a vector of `int` to be assigned to `qi`. The container with elements that are assigned to the queue does not have to contain elements of type `int`. Any type that can be converted to `int` is also valid. To explain why, let's look at the definition of `assign()`:

```
template <class Iter>
   void assign( Iter first, Iter last )
{
   // remove items for the Queue

   for ( ; first != last; ++first )
      add( *first );
}
```

The function `add()` called by `assign()` is the member function `Queue<Type>::add()`. In an instantiation for Queue with the type `int`, this member function has the following prototype:

```
void Queue<int>::add( const int &val )
```

The argument `*first` must either be of type `int` or of a type that can initialize a parameter of type reference to `const int`. Type conversions are allowed. For example, to reuse the class SmallInt defined in Section 15.9, the content of a container of elements of type SmallInt can be assigned to a queue of type `Queue<int>` using the function member template `assign()`. This is possible because the class SmallInt contains a conversion function that can convert a value of type SmallInt to a value of type `int`:

```
class SmallInt {
public:
   SmallInt( int ival = 0 ) : value( ival ) { }

   // conversion function: SmallInt ==> int
   operator int() { return value; }

   // ...
private:
   int value;
};

int main()
{
   // instantiation of Queue<int>
   Queue<int> qi;

   vector<SmallInt> vsi;
   // set the content of the vector
```

```
        // instantiation of
        // Queue<int>::assign( vector<SmallInt>::iterator,
        //                         vector<SmallInt>::iterator )
        qi.assign( vsi.begin(), vsi.end() );

        list<int*> lpi;
        // set the content of the list

        // error when member template assign() is instantiated
        // no conversion from int* to int
        qi.assign( lpi.begin(), lpi.end() );
    }
```

The first instantiation of assign() is valid because there exists an implicit conversion from the type SmallInt to the type int, and the call to add() in the first instantiation of assign() is valid. The second instantiation is an error because an object of type int* cannot initialize a reference to the type const int. The call to add() in the second instantiation of assign() is an error.

The container types defined in the C++ standard library have a function member template called assign() that behaves exactly like the member template assign() of our class template Queue.

Any member function can be defined as a member template. A constructor, for example, can be defined as a member template. We can define such a constructor for our class template Queue as follows:

```
        template <class T>
        class Queue {
            // ...
        public:
            // constructor member template
            template <class Iter>
            Queue( Iter first, Iter last )
                : front( 0 ), back( 0 )
            {
                for ( ; first != last; ++first )
                    add( *first );
            }
        };
```

Such a constructor allows the initialization of a queue with the content of another container. The container types defined in the C++ standard library also have constructor member templates to allow their initialization with the content of any other container. In fact, the first definition for main() in this section uses the constructor member template for vector:

```
        vector<int> vi( ai, ai + 4 );
```

This definition instantiates the constructor member template of the container vector<int> with the type int*, to allow the vector to be initialized with the content of an array of elements of type int.

Like nontemplate members, a member template can be defined outside its enclosing class or class template definition. For example, the class member template CL or the member function template assign() can be defined outside the class template Queue as follows:

```
template <class T>
class Queue {
private:
    template <class Type> class CL;
    // ...
public:
    template <class Iter>
        void assign( Iter first, Iter last );
    // ...
};

template <class T> template <class Type>
    class Queue<T>::CL<Type>
{
    Type member;
    T mem;
};

template <class T> template <class Iter>
    void Queue<T>::assign( Iter first, Iter last )
{
    while ( ! is_empty() )
        remove();

    for ( ; first != last; ++first )
        add( *first );
}
```

The definition of a member template defined outside the class template definition must be preceded by the class template parameter list, followed by the member's own template parameter list. This is why the definition for the member function template assign() starts with

```
template <class T> template <class Iter>
```

The first template parameter list template<class T> is that of the class template Queue. The second template parameter list template<class Iter> is that of the member template assign(). The template parameters do not have to have the same name as those specified within the class template definition. For example, the following still defines the function member template assign() of the class template Queue:

```
template <class TT> template <class IterType>
```

```
void Queue<TT>::assign( IterType first, IterType last )
{ ... }
```

16.8   Class Templates and Compilation Model ◆

A class template definition serves only as a prescription for the definition of an infinite set of class types. In itself, the template definition does not define a class type. For example, when the compiler sees the class template definition

```
template <class Type>
    class Queue { ... };
```

it stores an internal representation of Queue. Later, when the compiler sees an actual use of an instantiation of this class template, such as

```
int main() {
    Queue<int> *p_qi = new Queue<int>;
}
```

it instantiates the class type Queue<int> using the stored internal representation of the template definition for Queue.

A class template is instantiated only if it is used in a context that requires a complete class definition. (This was discussed in greater detail in Section 16.2.) In the previous example, the class template instantiation Queue<int> is instantiated because the compiler must know the size of the class type Queue<int> to allocate the right amount of storage for the object created by the new expression.

The compiler can only instantiate a class template if the actual class template definition, and not just the declaration, has been seen. A class template definition must be provided before the template is used in a way that requires its instantiation:

```
// class template declaration
template <class Type>
    class Queue;

Queue<int>* global_pi = 0; // ok: class definition not needed

int main() {
    // error: instantiation needed
    //        the class template definition must be visible
    Queue<int> *p_qi = new Queue<int>;
}
```

A class template may be instantiated for the same type in more than one file. As is the case with class types, in which a class definition must be provided in every file in which the class members are used, the compiler instantiates a class template for a particular type in every file in which this instantiation is used in a context that requires a complete class definition. To ensure that the class template definition is available in every file in which it must be instantiated, class template definitions should be placed in header files.

Member functions, static data members, and nested types of class templates behave very much like templates themselves. The definitions for the members of a class template are used to generate the member instances for each particular class template instantiation. For example, when the compiler sees the member function definition

```
template <class Type>
void Queue<Type>::add( const Type &val )
    { ... }
```

it stores an internal representation of `Queue<Type>::add()`. Later, when the compiler sees an actual use of this member function, through an object of type `Queue<int>` for example, it instantiates `Queue<int>::add(const int &)` from the stored internal representation of the member function definition:

```
#include "Queue.h"

int main() {
    // instantiation of Queue<int>
    Queue<int> *p_qi = new Queue<int>;
    int ival;
    // ...
    // instantiation of Queue<int>::add( const int & )
    p_qi->add( ival );
    // ...
}
```

Instantiating the class template for a particular type does not cause the definitions of the class template members to be instantiated automatically for the same type. The members are instantiated only if they are themselves used in the program in a way that requires their definition to be known (that is, if a nested type is used in a way that requires a complete class type, if a member function is called, if the address of a member is taken, or if the value of a static data member is examined).

The instantiation of member functions and static data members of class templates brings up the same kinds of questions that we discussed for function templates in Section 10.5: For the compiler to be able to instantiate a member function or a static member of a class template, must the definition of the member be visible when one of their instantiations is used? For example, must the definition of the member function add() appear before its integer instance is called in `main()`? Do we place the definitions of member functions and static data members of class templates in header files (as we do with inline member function definitions) to be included everywhere one of their instantiations is used? Or is the instantiation of the class template definition enough to allow the use of these members, allowing the member definitions to be placed in text files (where we usually put the definitions for non-inline member functions and static data members of class types)?

To answer these questions, we must revisit the C++ *template compilation model*, which specifies the requirements on how programs that define and use templates must be organized. The two template compilation models described in Section 10.5 — the inclusion model and separation model — also apply to the definitions of member functions and static data members of class templates. The rest of this section describes both models and how they are used with these member definitions.

16.8.1   Inclusion Compilation Model

Under the inclusion compilation model, the definition of the member functions and static members of class templates must be included in every file in which they are instantiated. This happens automatically for inline member functions defined inline within the class template definition. However, if a member function is defined outside the class template definition, the definition should be placed within the header file that contains the class template definition. This is the model we have chosen to use in this book. For example, the definitions for the templates Queue and QueueItem, as well as the template definitions for their member functions and static data members, are placed in the header file `Queue.h`.

As was the case with function template definitions, there are some drawbacks in providing the definitions for the members of a class template in a header file. The member function definitions may be quite large and may describe implementation details that our users may want to ignore or that we may want to hide from our users. Moreover, compiling the same function template definitions across multiple files can add to the compile-time of our programs unnecessarily. The separation compilation model, if available, allows us to separate the class template interface (that is, the class template definition) from its implementation (that is, the definitions of its member functions and static data members). Let's see how we might use it.

16.8.2   Separation Compilation Model

With the separation compilation model, the class template definition and the definitions of its inline member functions are placed in a header file, whereas the definitions of the non-inline member functions and static data members are placed in a program text file. With this model, the definitions for a class template and its members are organized in the same way we organize the definitions of nontemplate classes and their members. For example:

```
// ----- Queue.h -----
// declares Queue to be an exported class template
```

```
export template <class Type>
class Queue {
   // ...
public:
   Type& remove();
   void add( const Type & );
   // ....
};

// ----- Queue.C -----
// exported definition of class template Queue in Queue.h
#include "Queue.h"

template <class Type>
   void Queue<Type>::add( const Type &val ) { ... }

template <class Type>
   Type& Queue<Type>::remove() { ... }
```

A program that uses a member function instantiation need only include the header file before using the instantiation:

```
// ----- User.C -----
#include "Queue.h"

int main() {
   // instantiation of Queue<int>
   Queue<int> *p_qi = new Queue<int>;
   int ival;
   // ...
   // ok: instantiation of Queue<int>::add( const int & )
   p_qi->add( ival );
   // ...
}
```

Even though the template definition for the member function add() is not visible in the file User.C, the template instantiation Queue<int>::add(const int &) can nonetheless be called within this file. However, to make this possible, the class template has to be declared in a special way — as an *exported* class template.

An exported class template is a template for which only the class template definition is required for the member function instantiations or the static data member instantiations to be used. The definitions for these members can be omitted from the files in which the instantiations are used.

An exported class template is declared by having the keyword export precede the keyword template in the definition or declaration of the class template.

```
export template <class Type>
   class Queue { ... };
```

In our example, the keyword export is applied to the class template Queue in the file Queue.h, and this header file is included in Queue.C, the file containing the definitions of the class template member functions. The definitions for the member functions add() and remove() are then declared automatically as exported. The definitions for these members do not need to be present in other files before instantiations of the member functions are used.

Note that even though the class template is declared as exported, the definition of the class template itself cannot be omitted from the file User.C. The instantiation for the class Queue<int> in User.C provides the class definition that declares the member functions Queue<int>::add() and Queue<int>::remove(). These declarations are necessary before the member functions can be called. So, even though the class template itself is declared as exported, the export keyword only affects the class template member functions and static date members.

It is also possible only to declare individual members of a class template as exported. In this case the keyword export is not specified on the class template itself. It is only specified on the specific member definitions to be exported. For example, if the author of the Queue class template only wants the member function Queue<Type>::add() to be exported (that is, only wants to remove this member function definition from the header file Queue.h), the keyword export can be specified on the definition of the member function add():

```
// ----- Queue.h -----
template <class Type>
class Queue {
    // ...
public:
    Type& remove();
    void add( const Type & );
};

// necessary since remove() is not exported
template <class Type>
    Type& Queue<Type>::remove() { ... }

// ----- Queue.C -----
#include "Queue.h"

// only the member function add() is exported
export template <class Type>
    void Queue<Type>::add( const Type &val ) { ... }
```

Notice that the template definition for the member function remove() is moved to the header Queue.h. This is necessary since remove() is no longer an exported template and hence its definition must be visible in the files in which instantiations of remove() are called.

The definition of a member function or static data member of a class template must be defined as exported only once in a program. Unfortunately, because the compiler processes one file at a time, it cannot ordinarily detect when these members are defined as exported in more than one program text file. If such a situation happens, one of the following behaviors may happen:

1. A link-error may be generated to indicate that more than one template definition is provided for the same member of a class template.

2. The compiler may instantiate the member more than once for the same set of template arguments, causing a link-error because of the duplicate definitions for the template instantiation.

3. The implementation may instantiate the member using one of the exported template definitions and ignoring the other definitions.

It is therefore not certain that an error will be generated if more than one definition of an exported member of a class template is provided in our program. We must be careful when organizing our programs to place these member definitions in only one of the program text files.

The separation model allows us to separate nicely the interface of our class templates from their implementations, it allows us to organize our programs such that the interface of our class templates is placed in header files and their implementations are placed in text files. However, not all compilers support the separation model or, if they do support it, they do not support it well. To support the separation model, more sophisticated programming environments are needed and these are not available on all C++ implementations.

For the purpose of this book, because our template examples are fairly small and because we want the examples to be easy to compile on many C++ implementations, we limit ourselves to the use of the inclusion compilation model.

16.8.3   Explicit Instantiation Declarations

When using the inclusion compilation model, the definition for a member of a class template is included in every program text file where one of its instantiations is used. It is unknown exactly where and when the compiler instantiates the definition of a member of a class template, and some compilers (especially older C++ compilers) may actually instantiate the member definition for a particular set of template arguments multiple times. One of these instantiations is then selected as *the* instantiation to be used by the program (when the program is linked or during some sort of prelink phase). The other instantiations are simply ignored.

Whether the member is instantiated only once or multiple times, the program results are not affected because, in the end, only one template instantiation is used by the program. However, the compile-time performance of our program might be greatly affected if templates are instantiated multiple times. If the application is made of a large number of files, and a template is instantiated in all of these files, the time needed to compile the application can increase noticeably.

The instantiation problems of early compilers made the use of templates difficult. To help resolve this, Standard C++ provided *explicit instantiation declarations* to allow the programmer to take control over when template instantiations take place.

An explicit instantiation declaration is a declaration in which the keyword template is followed by the keyword class and the name of the class template instantiation. In the following example, an explicit instantiation for the class Queue<int> is declared. This explicit instantiation declaration is a request to instantiate the class template Queue with the template argument int:

```
#include Queue.h

// explicit instantiation declaration
template class Queue<int>;
```

When a class template is instantiated explicitly, all of its members are also instantiated explicitly for the same template argument type. This implies that not only must the definition for the class template be provided in the file where the explicit instantiation declaration appears, but all the definitions for the class template members must be provided as well. If these definitions are not present, the explicit instantiation declaration is an error. For example:

```
template <class Type>
    class Queue;

// error: template Queue and its members are not defined
template class Queue<int>;
```

When an explicit instantiation declaration appears in a program text file, what happens in the other text files where the class template instantiation is used? How do we tell the compiler that an explicit instantiation declaration appears in another program text file and that the class template and its members must not be instantiated when it is used in the other text files of the program?

The solution in this case is the same as the one presented when we discussed function templates (in Section 10.5.3). A compiler option that suppresses the implicit instantiation of templates must be used. When we compile our application with this option, the compiler assumes that we will handle template instantiation with explicit instantiation declarations and it will not instantiate templates implicitly that are used in our application.

Exercise 16.9

Where would you place the definitions for the member functions and static data members of your class templates if the implementation you use supports the separation compilation model? Explain why.

Exercise 16.10

Given the class template Screen you developed in the exercises of the previous sections (in particular, the member functions you defined in Exercise 16.5 of Section 16.3, and the static members you defined in Exercise 16.7 of Section 16.5), organize these definitions to take advantage of the template separation compilation model.

16.9   Class Template Specializations ◆

Before we look at class template specializations and see why our programs might need to define them, let's add two new member functions to the class template Queue. The member functions min() and max() iterate through the items in the Queue to find the minimum value and the maximum value respectively (preferably, we could use the generic algorithms min() and max() presented in Chapter 12; however, to introduce template specializations, we define these functions as member functions of the class template Queue) :

```
template <class Type>
class Queue {
   // ...
public:
   Type min();
   Type max();
   // ...
};


// find minimum value in the Queue
template <class Type>
   Type Queue<Type>::min( )
{
   assert( ! is_empty() );
   Type min_val = front->item;
   for ( QueueItem *pq = front->next; pq != 0; pq = pq->next )
      if ( pq->item < min_val )
         min_val = pq->item;
   return min_val;
}
```

```
// find maximum value in the Queue
template <class Type>
   Type Queue<Type>::max( )
{
   assert( ! is_empty() );
   Type max_val = front->item;
   for ( QueueItem *pq = front->next; pq != 0; pq = pq->next )
      if ( pq->item > max_val )
         max_val = pq->item;
   return max_val;
}
```

The following statement in the member function `min()` compares two items in the Queue:

```
pq->item < min_val
```

This introduces a hidden requirement on the types with which the Queue class template is instantiated: A type used as a template argument must either be able to use the predefined less than operator defined for built-in types, or be a user-defined class type that defines its own `operator<()`. If `operator<()` is not defined for such a type, and an attempt is made to call `min()` on a Queue of items of this type, a compile-time error is issued at the point where the invalid comparison operator is used in `min()`. (A similar problem exists with the member function `max()` and its use of `operator>()`.)

Let's assume that we have the following type with which we would like to instantiate the class template Queue:

```
class LongDouble {
public:
   LongDouble( double dval ) : value( dval ) { }
   bool compareLess( const LongDouble & );
private:
   double value;
};
```

However, no `operator<()` exists to compare two values of type LongDouble, and the member functions `min()` and `max()` cannot be used with a Queue of type `Queue<Long-Double>`. One solution to this problem is to define global operators `operator<()` and `operator>()` that use the LongDouble member function `compareLess()` to compare two values of type `Queue<LongDouble>`. These global operators are then invoked automatically within `min()` and `max()` to compare the items in a Queue of type `Queue<LongDouble>`. However, to introduce class template specializations, we consider another solution. We do not want the generic member function definitions for the class template Queue to be used to instantiate the member functions `min()` and `max()` if the template argument is the class type LongDouble. Instead, we want to define instances for `Queue<LongDouble>::min()` and `Queue<LongDouble>::max()` that use the LongDouble member function `compareLess()`.

We can do this by providing a specialized definition for a member of a class template instantiation using an *explicit specialization definition*. An explicit specialization definition is a definition in which the keyword `template` is followed by the less than (<) and the greater than (>) tokens, followed by the definition of the specialization for the class member. In the following example, explicit specializations are defined for the member functions `min()` and `max()` of the class template instantiation `Queue<LongDouble>`:

```
// explicit specialization definitions
template<> LongDouble Queue<LongDouble>::min( )
{
    assert( ! is_empty() );
    LongDouble min_val = front->item;
    for ( QueueItem *pq = front->next; pq != 0; pq = pq->next )
        if ( pq->item.compareLess( min_val ) )
            min_val = pq->item;
    return min_val;
}

template<> LongDouble Queue<LongDouble>::max( )
{
    assert( ! is_empty() );
    LongDouble max_val = front->item;
    for ( QueueItem *pq = front->next; pq != 0; pq = pq->next )
        if ( max_val.compareLess( pq->item ) )
            max_val = pq->item;
    return max_val;
}
```

Even though the class type `Queue<LongDouble>` is instantiated from the generic class template definition, each object of type `Queue<LongDouble>` uses the specializations for the member functions `min()` and `max()` — these member functions are not instantiated from the generic member function definitions for the class template Queue.

Because the explicit specialization definitions for the member functions `min()` and `max()` are function definitions and not template definitions, (and because these definitions are not declared inline), they cannot be placed in a header file. They must be placed in a program text file. Fortunately, it is possible just to declare a function template explicit specialization without defining it. For example, the explicit specialization for the member functions `min()` and `max()` can be declared as follows

```
// declarations of function template explicit specialization
template<> LongDouble Queue<LongDouble>::min( );
template<> LongDouble Queue<LongDouble>::max( );
```

By placing these declarations in a header file, and the associated definitions in a program text file, we can then organize the code for the explicit specializations as we would with any other nontemplate class member definitions.

In some cases the entire class template definition may be inappropriate for use with a particular type. In this case the programmer can provide a definition to specialize the entire class template. For example, the programmer may choose to provide a complete definition of Queue<LongDouble>:

```
// QueueLD.h: defines class specialization Queue<LongDouble>
#include "Queue.h"

template<> class Queue<LongDouble> {
    Queue<LongDouble>();
    ~Queue<LongDouble>();

    LongDouble& remove();
    void add( const LongDouble & );
    bool is_empty() const;
    LongDouble min();
    LongDouble max();
private:
    // Some particular implementation
};
```

An explicit specialization for a class template can be defined only after the general class template has been declared (although the general template does not have to be defined). That is, the name must be known to be a class template name before the template can be specialized. In the previous example, if the header file Queue.h is not included before the definition of the template explicit specialization, a compiler error is generated to indicate that Queue is not a template name.

If we define a class template specialization, we must also define each member function or static data member associated with this specialization. The generic member definitions of the class template are never used to create the definitions for the members of an explicit specialization. This is because the class template specialization may have a completely different set of class members from the generic template. If we decide to provide an explicit specialization definition for the class type Queue<longDouble>, not only must we provide the definitions for the member functions min() and max(), but we must also provide the definitions for all of the other member functions as well.

If an entire class is specialized, the tokens template<> marking the specialization definition are only placed before the definition of the explicit specialization definition for the class template. The definitions of members of a class template specialization must not be preceded with the tokens template<>. For example:

```
#include "QueueLD.h"

// defines the member function min()
// of class template specialization
LongDouble Queue<LongDouble>::min( ) { }
```

A class template cannot be instantiated from the generic template definition in some files and be specialized in other files for the same set of template arguments. For example, given the specialization of the template QueueItem<LongDouble>, the specialization must be declared in every file where it is used:

```
// ---- File1.C ----
#include "Queue.h"

void ReadIn( Queue<LongDouble> *pq ) {
   // uses of pq->add()
   // cause the instantiation of QueueItem<LongDouble>
}

// ---- File2.C ----
#include "QueueLD.h"

void ReadIn( Queue<LongDouble> * );

int main() {
   // uses specialization definition for QueueItem<LongDouble>
   Queue<LongDouble> *qld = new Queue<LongDouble>;

   ReadIn( qld );
   // ...
}
```

The previous program is in error, although implementations most often do not diagnose such erroneous programs. To avoid such errors, the header QueueLD.h should be included in every file where Queue<LongDouble> is used and before it is first used in each file.

16.10 Class Template Partial Specializations ◆

If a class template has more than one template parameter, one might want to specialize the class template for a particular template argument or a set of template arguments without specializing the template for every template parameter. That is, one might want to provide a template that matches a generic template except that some of the template parameters have been replaced by actual types or values. This is possible using a class template *partial specialization*. A class template partial specialization might be needed to define a more appropriate or efficient implementation than the generic template definition for a particular set of template arguments.

For example, let's use the class template Screen introduced in Section 16.2. The partial specialization Screen<hi,80> provides a more efficient implementation for screens with 80 columns:

```
template <int hi, int wid>
class Screen {
    // ...
};

// partial specialization of class template Screen
template <int hi>
class Screen<hi, 80> {
public:
    Screen();
    // ...
private:
    string              _screen;
    string::size_type _cursor;
    short               _height;
    // Uses special algorithms for screens with 80 columns
};
```

A class template partial specialization is a template, and the definition of a partial specialization looks like a template definition. Such a definition begins with the keyword `template` followed by a template parameter list enclosed by the less than and greater than tokens. The parameter list of a class template partial specialization differs from the parameter list of the corresponding generic class template definition. The partial specialization for `Screen` only has one nontype template parameter named `hi`, because the template argument for `wid` is known to be 80. The template parameter list for the partial specialization only lists the parameters for which the template arguments are still unknown.

The partial specialization has the same name as the generic template to which it corresponds; namely, `Screen`. However, the name of a class template partial specialization is always followed by a template argument list. In the previous example, the template argument list is `<hi,80>`. Because the argument value for the first template parameter is unknown, the argument list uses the name of the template parameter `hi` as a place holder; the other argument is a value, the value 80 for which the template is partially specialized.

A class template partial specialization is instantiated implicitly when used in a program. In the following example, the class template partial specialization is instantiated with a template argument for `hi` that is 24.

```
Screen<24,80> hp2621;
```

Notice that the instantiation for `Screen<24,80>` could be instantiated from the generic class template definition as well as from the partial specialization. Why is it then that the partial specialization is chosen to instantiate the template? When class template partial specializations are declared, the compiler chooses the template definition that is the most specialized for the instantiation. When no partial specialization can be used, the generic template definition is used. For example, when Screen<40,132> must be instantiated, this instantiation does not match the partial specialization provided. The partial specialization is only used to instantiate Screen types with 80 columns.

The definition of a partial specialization is completely disjointed from the definition of the generic template. The partial specialization may have a completely different set of members from the generic class template. A class template partial specialization must have its own definitions for its member functions, static data members, and nested types. The generic definitions for the members of a class template are never used to instantiate the members of the class template partial specialization. For example, the constructor for the partial specialization Screen<hi,80> must be defined. Here is a possible definition:

```
// constructor for partial specialization Screen<hi,80>
template<int hi>
Screen<hi,80>::Screen() : _height( hi ), _cursor ( 0 ),
                          _screen( hi * 80, bk )
                   { }
```

If the template definition for the constructor of Screen<hi,80> is not provided and the partial specialization is used to instantiate a class type, the generic class template's constructor definition is not used to instantiate the member function.

16.11 Name Resolution in Class Templates ◆

In the discussion on name resolution in function templates in Section 10.9, we mention that this resolution proceeds in two steps. The same two steps apply to the resolution of names used in class template definitions and in the definition of their members. Each step applies to different kinds of names: the first step applies to names that have the same meaning in all instantiations of the class template, and the second step applies to names that have potentially different meanings from one template instantiation to another. Let's look at some examples using the member function remove() of the class template Queue:

```
// Queue.h:
#include <iostream>
#include <cstdlib>

// definition of class Queue

template <class Type>
Type Queue<Type>::remove() {
   if ( is_empty() ) {
      cerr << "remove() on empty queue\n";
      exit( -1 );
   }
```

```
        QueueItem<Type> *pt = front;
        front = front->next;
        Type retval = pt->item;
        delete pt;

        cout << "value removed: ";
        cout << retval << endl;

        return retval;
    }
```

In the expression:

```
    cout << retval << endl;
```

retval is of type Type, and its actual type is not known until the member function remove() is instantiated. The operator<<() chosen depends on the actual type of retval, that is, on the type with which the template parameter Type is replaced. It is therefore impossible to know which operator<<() is called until remove() is instantiated. Different instantiations of remove() will likely call a different operator<<(). Because of this, we say that the operator<<() selected *depends* on a template parameter.

However, the situation is different for the call to exit(). The function argument for the call to exit() is a literal, with a value that is the same in all instantiations of the member function remove(). Because the function call does not use arguments with types that depend on the template parameter Type, we are guaranteed that the call to exit() in all instantiations invokes the function exit() declared in the header cstdlib. Similarly, we know that for the expression

```
    cout << "value removed: ";
```

the global operator

```
    ostream& operator<<( ostream &, const char * );
```

is always called. The argument "value removed: " is a C-style character string with a type that does not depend on the template parameter Type. It is therefore guaranteed that this use of operator<<() has the same meaning in all instantiations of the member function remove(). A construct that has the same meaning in all instantiations of a template is a construct that does *not* depend on a template parameter.

The two steps of name resolution in the definitions of class templates or in the definition of members of class templates are therefore the following:

1. The names that do not depend on a template parameter are resolved when the template is defined.
2. The names that depend on a template parameter are resolved when the template is instantiated.

This two-step approach supports requirements from both the class template designer and the user of the class template. As a class template designer, we want to control as much as possible how the names in the template definition are resolved. If the class template is part of a library that defines other templates and functions, we want the instantiations of a class template and its members to use the other components of our library whenever possible. The first step of name resolution guarantees that this happens. When a name used in a template definition does not depend of a template parameter, the name is resolved only after considering the declarations visible in the header file before the template definition.

In fact, the designer of a class template must make sure to provide declarations for all of the names used in a template definition that do not depend on a template parameter. If a name used in a template definition does not depend on a template parameter, and a declaration for this name is not found when the template is defined, the template definition is an error. If the header files `iostream` and `cstdlib` were not included before the definition of the member function `remove()` of the class template Queue, the expression

```
cout << "value removed: ";
```

or the call to `exit()` would be in error.

The second step of name resolution is necessary if the functions and operators associated with the type with which the template is instantiated are to be considered. For example, if the class template Queue is instantiated with the class type LongDouble defined in the Section 16.9, we want the following expression in Queue's member function `remove()`:

```
cout << retval << endl;
```

to invoke the output `operator<<()` associated with the class LongDouble. For example:

```
#include "Queue.h"
#include "ldouble.h"
// contains:
// class LongDouble { ... };
// ostream& operator<<( ostream &, const LongDouble & );

int main() {
    // instantiation of Queue<LongDouble>
    Queue<LongDouble> *qld = new Queue<LongDouble>;

    // instantiation of Queue<LongDouble>::remove()
    // invokes output operator for LongDouble
    qld->remove();
    //...
}
```

The exact location where a template is instantiated is called the template's *point of instantiation*. Knowing where a template's point of instantiation is located is important because it determines which declarations are considered for the names that depend on a template parameter.

A class template point of instantiation is always in namespace scope and it always immediately precedes the declaration or definition that refers to the class template instantiation. The point of instantiation of a member function or a static data member of a class template always immediately follows the declaration or definition that refers to the instantiation of the member of the class template.

In the previous example, the point of instantiation of Queue<LongDouble> immediately precedes main(), and the compiler considers all the declarations before this point to resolve the names dependent on the template parameter that are used in the definition of template Queue. The point of instantiation of the member function remove() immediately follows main(), and the compiler considers all the declarations before this point to resolve the names dependent on the template parameter and used in the definition of the member function remove().

As mentioned in Section 16.2, a class template is instantiated if it is used in a context that requires a complete class definition. The members of a class template instantiation are not instantiated automatically when the class template is instantiated. Instead, the members are instantiated only when they themselves are used in the program. Because of this, the point of instantiation of a class template may be different from the point of instantiation of its members, and different members will have different points of instantiation. To prevent errors, declarations for names used in the definition of a class template and in the definitions of its members should be placed in header files, and included before the first instantiation of the class template and before the instantiation of any of its members.

16.12 Namespaces and Class Templates ◆

As with any other global scope definitions, a class template definition can be placed in a namespace. (See Sections 8.5 and 8.6 for a discussion of namespaces). The meaning of such a template definition is the same as when the template is defined in global scope, except that the name of the template is hidden within the namespace. The template name must either be qualified by the namespace name when the template is used outside its namespace, or a using declaration must be provided. For example:

```
#include <iostream>
#include <cstdlib>

namespace cplusplus_primer {

    template <class Type>
    class Queue { // ...
    };
```

```
            template <class Type>
            Type Queue<Type>::remove()
            {
                // ...
            }
        }
```

The class template name Queue must be qualified by the namespace name cplusplus_primer when it is used outside of the namespace, or be introduced through a using declaration. The class template Queue is otherwise used as described earlier in this chapter — it is instantiated in the same way, and it may have member functions, static data members, and nested types, and so forth. For example:

```
        int main() {
            using cplusplus_primer::Queue; // using declaration

            // refers to the namespace cplusplus_primer's class template
            Queue<int> *p_qi = new Queue<int>;
            // ...
            p_qi->remove();
        }
```

The template cplusplus_primer::Queue is instantiated because of its use by the new expression

```
            ... = new Queue<int>;
```

p_qi is a pointer to the class type cplusplus_primer::Queue<int>. When this pointer is used to refer to the member function remove(), it refers to the member function remove() of this template instantiation.

Declaring a class template within a namespace also impacts how specializations and partial specializations for the class template and its members are declared. (Specializations are discussed in Section 16.9 and partial specializations in Section 16.10). A specialization declaration for a class template or for a member of a class template must be declared in the namespace where the generic template is defined.

In the following example, specialization declarations for the class type Queue-<char*> and for the member function remove() of the class type Queue<double> are declared within the namespace cplusplus_primer.

```
        #include <iostream>
        #include <cstdlib>

        namespace cplusplus_primer {

            template <class Type>
            class Queue { ... };

            template <class Type>
```

```
      Type Queue<Type>::remove() { ... }

      // specialization declaration
      // for cplusplus_primer::Queue<char*>
      template<> class Queue<char*> { ... };

      // specialization declaration for
      // cplusplus_primer::Queue<double>::remove() member function
      template<> double Queue<double>::remove() { ... }
}
```

Although the specializations are members of the namespace cplusplus_primer, their definitions do not have to appear within the namespace cplusplus_primer per se. It is possible to define a template specialization outside its namespace's definition, provided that the definition appears in a namespace enclosing the namespace cplusplus_primer and provided that the name of the specialization is appropriately qualified with the namespace name. For example:

```
namespace cplusplus_primer
{
    // definition of Queue and its member functions

}

// specialization declaration
// for cplusplus_primer::Queue<char*>
template<> class cplusplus_primer::Queue<char*> { ... };

// specialization declaration for member function
// cplusplus_primer::Queue<double>::remove()
template<> double cplusplus_primer::Queue<double>::remove()
    { ... }
```

The specialization declarations for cplusplus_primer::Queue<char*> and for the member function remove() of the class type cplusplus_primer::Queue<double> are provided in global scope. Because the global scope encloses the namespace cplusplus_primer, and because the names of the specializations are qualified by the namespace name cplusplus_primer, these definitions are valid specialization definitions for the class template Queue defined in namespace cplusplus_primer.

16.13 A Template Array Class

In this section we complete the implementation of the Array class template introduced in Section 2.5 (this class template is extended through single inheritance in Section 18.3, and through multiple inheritance in Section 18.6). Here is the complete header file for the Array class template:

```
#ifndef ARRAY_H
#define ARRAY_H
#include <iostream>

template <class elemType> class Array;
template <class elemType> ostream&
    operator<<( ostream &, const Array<elemType> & );

template <class elemType>
class Array {
public:
    explicit Array( int sz = DefaultArraySize )
        { init( 0, sz ); }
    Array( const elemType *ar, int sz )
        { init( ar, sz ); }
    Array( const Array &iA )
        { init( iA._ia, iA._size ); }
    ~Array() { delete[] _ia; }

    Array & operator=( const Array & );
    int size() const { return _size; }

    elemType& operator[]( int ix ) const
        { return _ia[ix]; }

    ostream &print( ostream &os = cout ) const;
    void grow();

    void sort( int,int );
    int find( elemType );
    elemType min();
    elemType max();
private:
    void init( const elemType *, int );
    void swap( int, int );

    static const int DefaultArraySize = 12;

    int _size;
    elemType *_ia;
};

#endif
```

The code common to the implementation of the three constructors is factored out into an independent member function called init(). Since it is not intended to be invoked by users of the Array class template, it is made a private member.

```
template <class elemType>
   void Array<elemType>::init( const elemType *array, int sz )
{
   _size = sz;
   _ia = new elemType[ _size ];

   for ( int ix = 0; ix < _size; ++ix )
      if ( ! array )
         _ia[ ix ] = 0;
      else _ia[ ix ] = array[ ix ];
}
```

The implementation of the copy assignment operator is straightforward. As mentioned in Section 14.7, the implementation of this operator guards against an object being copied to itself:

```
template <class elemType> Array<elemType>&
   Array<elemType>::operator=( const Array<elemType> &iA )
{
   if ( this != &iA ) {
      delete[] _ia;
      init( iA._ia, iA._size );
   }
   return *this;
}
```

The member function print() handles the actual output of an object with a type that is an instantiation of the Array class template. Its output is perhaps more elaborate than necessary, but displays nicely on a page. Given an instantiation of type Array<int> containing the elements 3, 5, 8, 13, and 21, the output of the object looks like this:

```
(5) < 3, 5, 8, 13, 21 >
```

The ostream output operator simply invokes print(). Here is an implementation of both functions:

```
template <class elemType> ostream&
   operator<<( ostream &os, const Array<elemType> &ar )
{
   return ar.print( os );
}

template <class elemType>
   ostream & Array<elemType>::print( ostream &os ) const
{
   const int lineLength = 12;

   os << "( " << _size << " )< ";
   for ( int ix = 0; ix < _size; ++ix )
   {
```

```
        if ( ix % lineLength == 0 && ix )
            os << "\n\t";
        os << _ia[ ix ];

        // don't generate comma for last item on line
        // nor for the last element of the array
        if ( ix % lineLength != lineLength-1 &&
             ix != _size-1 )
            os << ", ";
    }
    os << " >\n";
    return os;
}
```

The statement in the member function print() that handles the actual display of the Array element value

```
        os << _ia[ ix ];
```

introduces a hidden requirement on the types with which the Array class template is instantiated: A type used as a template argument must be either a built-in type or a user-defined class type that defines its own output operator. If the output operator is not defined for such a type, and an attempt is made to display the content of the instantiation of Array with this type, a compile-time error is issued at the point where the invalid output operator is used.

The grow() member function increases the size of an Array object. In our example, it simply grows the Array object by half its current size:

```
        template <class elemType>
          void Array<elemType>::grow()
        {
            elemType *oldia = _ia;
            int oldSize = _size;

            _size = oldSize + oldSize/2 + 1;
            _ia = new elemType[_size];

            int ix;
            for ( ix = 0; ix < oldSize; ++ix)
                _ia[ix] = oldia[ix];

            for ( ; ix < _size; ++ix )
                _ia[ix] = elemType();
            delete[] oldia;
        }
```

The find(), min(), and max() member functions implement an iterative search through the internal array _ia. These member functions could be implemented much more efficiently, of course, were the array guaranteed to be sorted.

```
template <class elemType>
   elemType Array<elemType>::min( )
{
   assert( _ia != 0 );
   elemType min_val = _ia[0];
   for ( int ix = 1; ix < _size; ++ix )
      if ( _ia[ix] < min_val )
         min_val = _ia[ix];
   return min_val;
}

template <class elemType>
   elemType Array<elemType>::max()
{
   assert( _ia != 0 );
   elemType max_val = _ia[0];
   for ( int ix = 1; ix < _size; ++ix )
      if ( max_val < _ia[ix] )
         max_val = _ia[ix];
   return max_val;
}

template <class elemType>
   int Array<elemType>::find( elemType val )
{
   for ( int ix = 0; ix < _size; ++ix )
      if ( val == _ia[ix] ) return ix;
   return -1;
}
```

Finally, the Array class template provides a sort() member function. The implementation is that of the quicksort algorithm. The member function looks very similar to the nonmember function template implementation defined in Section 10.11. swap() is intended simply as a helping function to sort(). It is not part of the Array class template public interface, and is therefore made a private member:

```
template <class elemType>
   void Array<elemType>::swap( int i, int j )
{
   elemType tmp = _ia[i];
   _ia[i] = _ia[j];
   _ia[j] = tmp;
}

template <class elemType>
   void Array<elemType>::sort( int low, int high )
{
   if ( low >= high ) return;
   int lo = low;
```

```
        int hi = high + 1;
        elemType elem = _ia[low];

        for (;;) {
            while ( _ia[++lo] < elem && lo < high ) ;
            while ( _ia[--hi] > elem && hi > low ) ;
            if ( lo < hi )
                swap( lo, hi );
            else break;
        }

        swap( low, hi );
        sort( low, hi-1 );
        sort( hi+1, high );
    }
```

Implementing the code, of course, is no guarantee that the code actually works. try_array() is a template function intended to test our Array class template implementation. It looks like this:

```
    #include "Array.h"

    template <class elemType>
        void try_array( Array<elemType> &iA )
    {
        cout << "try_array: initial array values:\n";
        cout << iA << endl;

        elemType find_val = iA [ iA.size()-1 ];
        iA[ iA.size()-1 ] = iA.min();

        int mid = iA.size()/2;
        iA[0] = iA.max();
        iA[mid] = iA[0];
        cout << "try_array: after assignments:\n";
        cout << iA << endl;

        Array<elemType> iA2 = iA;
        iA2[mid/2] = iA2[mid];
        cout << "try_array: memberwise initialization\n";
        cout << iA << endl;

        iA = iA2;
        cout << "try_array: after memberwise copy\n";
        cout << iA << endl;

        iA.grow();
        cout << "try_array: after grow\n";
        cout << iA << endl;
```

```
        int index = iA.find( find_val );
        cout << "value to find: " << find_val;
        cout << "\tindex returned: " << index << endl;

        elemType value = iA[index];
        cout << "value found at index: ";
        cout << value << endl;
}
```

Let's take a look at our function template `try_array()`. The first step is to print out the initial Array. This confirms the instantiation of the template output operator and provides us with a snapshot of the initial Array against which to compare the success (or failure) of our subsequent modifications of the Array. `find_val` holds a value to later pass to `find()`.Were `try_array()` a nontemplate function, the value would have been a constant literal. However, because no one value serves every possible type instantiation, the value cannot be a constant literal. The elements of the Array are randomly assigned other elements of the Array, exercising `min()`, `max()`, `size()`, and, of course, the subscript operator.

`iA2` is memberwise initialized with `iA`, invoking the Array class template copy constructor. `iA2` then exercises its subscript operator with an assignment to element `mid/2`. (These two lines are of more interest when `iA` is actually a derived subtype of Array and the subscript operator is declared a virtual function. We'll look at this again in Chapter 18 in our discussion of inheritance.) `iA` is subsequently memberwise copied with the modified `iA2`, invoking the Array class assignment operator. Following that, both the `grow()` and `find()` member functions are exercised. The function deliberately fails to test the return value of `find()`. Recall that `find()` returns a value of -1 if the element for which it searches is not found. A -1 index into an Array will result in an underflow error. (In Chapter 18, a bounds-checking Array class template is derived from Array to catch this error.)

We'd like to confirm that our template implementation works over a variety of data types — for example, integers, floating point values, and strings. Here is a version of `main()` to exercise `try_array()` with each of these three data types:

```
#include "Array.C"
#include "try_array.C"
#include <string>

int main()
{
    static int ia[] = { 12,7,14,9,128,17,6,3,27,5 };
    static double da[] = {12.3,7.9,14.6,9.8,128.0 };
    static string sa[] = { "Eeyore", "Pooh", "Tigger",
                           "Piglet", "Owl", "Gopher", "Heffalump" };
```

```
    Array<int> iA( ia, sizeof(ia)/sizeof(int) );
    Array<double> dA( da, sizeof(da)/sizeof(double) );
    Array<string> sA( sa, sizeof(sa)/sizeof(string) );

    cout << "template Array<int> class\n" << endl;
    try_array(iA);

    cout << "template Array<double> class\n" << endl;
    try_array(dA);

    cout << "template Array<string> class\n" << endl;
    try_array(sA);

    return 0;
}
```

Here is the output when the instantiation of the Array class template is for the type double:

```
try_array: initial array values:
( 5 )< 12.3, 7.9, 14.6, 9.8, 128 >

try_array: after assignments:
( 5 )< 14.6, 7.9, 14.6, 9.8, 7.9 >

try_array: memberwise initialization
( 5 )< 14.6, 7.9, 14.6, 9.8, 7.9 >

try_array: after memberwise copy
( 5 )< 14.6, 14.6, 14.6, 9.8, 7.9 >

try_array: after grow
( 8 )< 14.6, 14.6, 14.6, 9.8, 7.9, 0
   0, 0 >

value to find: 128index returned: -1
value found at index: 3.35965e-322
```

The out-of-bounds index causes the last value returned by the program to be invalid. The same out-of-bounds index causes the string instantiation of the Array class template to crash during execution. Here is that output:

```
template Array<String> class

try_array: initial array values:
( 7 )< Eeyore, Pooh, Tigger, Piglet, Owl, Gopher
   Heffalump >

try_array: after assignments:
( 7 )< Tigger, Pooh, Tigger, Tigger, Owl, Gopher
   Eeyore >
```

```
try_array: memberwise initialization
( 7 )< Tigger, Pooh, Tigger, Tigger, Owl, Gopher
   Eeyore >

try_array: after memberwise copy
( 7 )< Tigger, Tigger, Tigger, Tigger, Owl, Gopher
   Eeyore >

try_array: after grow
( 11 )< Tigger, Tigger, Tigger, Tigger, Owl, Gopher
   Eeyore, <empty>, <empty>, <empty>, <empty> >

value to find: Heffalumpindex returned: -1
Memory fault(coredump)
```

Exercise 16.11

Change the Array class template defined in this section to remove the member functions sort(), find(), max(), min(), and swap(), and change the function template try_array() to use the generic algorithms (defined in Chapter 12) instead.

Part V

Object-Oriented Programming

Object-oriented programming extends object-based programming to provide for type/subtype relationships. This is achieved through a mechanism referred to as *inheritance*. Rather than reimplementing shared characteristics, a class inherits the data members and member functions of its parent class. In C++, inheritance is supported through a mechanism referred to as *class derivation*. The class that is being inherited from is spoken of as the *base class*. The new class is spoken of as the *derived class*. We speak of the set of base and derived class instances as the class inheritance *hierarchy*.

For example, in 3D computer graphics, both an OrthographicCamera and a PerspectiveCamera are generally derived from an abstract base class Camera. The set of operations and data common to all cameras is defined within the abstract Camera class. Each derived class implements only its differences from the abstract Camera, either through providing alternative implementations of inherited member functions or through the introduction of additional members.

If the base and derived classes share the same public interface, the derived class is said to be a *subtype* of its base class. A PerspectiveCamera, for example, is a subtype of Camera. In C++, a special type/subtype relationship exists in which a base class pointer or a reference can address any of its derived class subtypes without programmer intervention. (This ability to manipulate more than one type with a pointer or a reference to a base class is spoken of as *polymorphism*.) For example, given the function

```
void lookAt( const Camera *pcamera );
```

we implement lookAt() by programming the base class Camera interface independent of whether pcamera addresses a PerspectiveCamera, an OrthographicCamera, or some future derived Camera subtype as yet undefined.

Each individual invocation of lookAt() passes in the address of an object of one of the Camera subtypes. It is converted automatically by the compiler into the appropriate base class pointer. For example:

```
// ok: converted automatically to Camera*
OrthographicCamera ocam;
lookAt( &ocam );

// ...

// ok: converted automatically to Camera*
PerspectiveCamera *pcam = new PerspectiveCamera;
lookAt( pcam );
```

Our implementation of lookAt() is shielded from the actual Camera subtypes of our application. If we should later wish to add to or remove a subtype, our implementation of lookAt() need not change.

Subtype polymorphism allows us to write the kernel of our application independent of the individual types we wish to manipulate. Rather, we program the public interface of the base class of our abstraction through base class pointers and references. At run-time, the actual type being referenced is resolved and the appropriate instance of the public interface is invoked.

The run-time resolution of the appropriate function to invoke is termed *dynamic binding* (by default, functions are resolved *statically* at compile-time). In C++, dynamic binding is supported through a mechanism referred to as class *virtual functions*. Subtype polymorphism through inheritance and dynamic binding provide the foundation for object-oriented programming, the topic of the following chapters.

Chapter 17 covers the facilities within C++ supporting object-oriented programming, and examines how inheritance affects such class mechanisms as the constructor, destructor, and memberwise initialization and assignment. To enliven the discussion, a Query class hierarchy is developed in support of the text query system introduced in Chapter 6.

Chapter 18 examines the more complicated inheritance hierarchies possible through multiple and virtual inheritance. It extends the template class example of Chapter 16 into a three-level class template hierarchy using multiple and virtual inheritance.

Chapter 19 discusses Run-Time Type Identification (RTTI), as well as provides an in-depth look at the support of overload function resolution under inheritance. It also reexamines the exception handling facility to discuss the standard library exception class hierarchy, and illustrates how to define and handle our own exception classes.

Chapter 20 provides an in-depth discussion of the iostream library. The iostream library is a class hierarchy that supports both virtual and multiple inheritance.

17

Class Inheritance and Subtyping

In Chapter 6, to motivate and illustrate our discussion of the abstract container types, we walked through a partial implementation of a text query system, which in its final form we encapsulated within a TextQuery class. We left it without a front end, however, deferring support of the actual user query until we were prepared to cover object-oriented programming. In this chapter we implement the front-end query language as a single-inheritance Query class hierarchy to introduce and walk through object-oriented design and programming in C++. In addition, we modify and extend our TextQuery class of Chapter 6 to provide a fully integrated text query system.

The program to run our text query system is the following:

```
#include "TextQuery.h"

int main()
{
    TextQuery tq;

    tq.build_text_map();
    tq.query_text();
}
```

build_text_map() is a slightly modified form of the doit() member function of Chapter 6. Its primary task is to build a word location map indexed by each significant word within the text. (If you recall, we do not store semantically neutral words such as if, and, but, and so on. In addition, we remove capital letters and handle suffixing of plurals, such as transforming testifies into testify and marches into march.) Associated with each word is a location vector where each vector element stores the line and column of each occurrence of the word within the text.

query_text() solicits and transforms each user query into an internal object-oriented Query class hierarchy making use of single inheritance and dynamic binding. The internal query representation is evaluated against the word location map constructed by `build_text_map()`. The solution is a unique set of lines within the text file that satis-fies the criteria of the query. For example:

```
Enter a query-please separate each item by a space.
Terminate query (or session) with a dot( . ).

==> fiery && ( bird || shyly )

        fiery ( 1 ) lines match
        bird ( 1 ) lines match
        shyly ( 1 ) lines match
         ( bird || shyly )  ( 2 ) lines match
        fiery &&  ( bird || shyly )  ( 1 ) lines match

Requested query: fiery &&  ( bird || shyly )

( 3 ) like a fiery bird in flight. A beautiful fiery bird, he tells her,
```

The query facility we have chosen to support consists of the following elements:

1. A single word, such as `Alice` or `untamed`. All lines in which the word appears are displayed with the line number in parentheses. (The lines are displayed in ascending order.) For example:

```
==> daddy
    .

    daddy ( 3 ) lines match

Requested query: daddy

( 1 ) Alice Emma has long flowing red hair. Her Daddy says
( 4 ) magical but untamed. "Daddy, shush, there is no such thing,"
( 6 ) Shyly, she asks, "I mean, Daddy, is there?"
```

2. A Not Query, using the ! operator. All lines in which the name does not appear within the text are displayed. For example, here is the not-ing of item 1:

```
==> ! daddy
    .

        daddy ( 3 ) lines match
        ! daddy ( 3 ) lines match

Requested query:  ! daddy

( 2 ) when the wind blows through her hair, it looks almost alive,
( 3 ) like a fiery bird in flight. A beautiful fiery bird, he tells her,
( 5 ) she tells him, at the same time wanting him to tell her more.
```

3. An Or Query, using the || operator. All lines in which either of the two names appear within the text are displayed. For example:

```
==> fiery || untamed
    .
        fiery ( 1 ) lines match
        untamed ( 1 ) lines match
        fiery || untamed ( 2 ) lines match

Requested query: fiery || untamed

( 3 ) like a fiery bird in flight. A beautiful fiery bird, he tells her,
( 4 ) magical but untamed. "Daddy, shush, there is no such thing,"
```

4. An And Query, using the **&&** operator. All lines in which both words are not only present but adjacent within the text are displayed. This includes the last word of a line and the first word of the subsequent line. For example:

```
==> untamed && Daddy
    .
        untamed ( 1 ) lines match
        daddy ( 3 ) lines match
        untamed && daddy ( 1 ) lines match

Requested query: untamed && daddy

( 4 ) magical but untamed. "Daddy, shush, there is no such thing,"
```

These elements can be combined, as in

```
fiery && bird || shyly
```

However, the order of evaluation is left to right, with each element maintaining the same precedence level. And so the evaluation of the previous compound query matches fiery bird or shyly, not fiery bird or fiery shyly:

```
==> fiery && bird || shyly
    .
        fiery ( 1 ) lines match
        bird ( 1 ) lines match
        fiery && bird ( 1 ) lines match
        shyly ( 1 ) lines match
        fiery && bird || shyly ( 2 ) lines match

Requested query: fiery && bird || shyly

( 3 ) like a fiery bird in flight. A beautiful fiery bird, he tells her,
( 6 ) Shyly, she asks, "I mean, Daddy, is there?"
```

To allow subgrouping of a query, our query facility must also support parentheses. For example:

```
fiery && ( bird || shyly )
```

finds all references to either `fiery bird` or `fiery shyly`.[1] The result of the query is illustrated at the start of this section.

Our system must be smart enough not to display the same line multiple times.

17.1 Defining a Class Hierarchy

Our primary focus in this chapter is in building up the class hierarchy to represent the user query. Our initial design is to represent each query operation as an individual class:

```
NameQuery // Shakespeare
NotQuery  // !Shakespeare
OrQuery   // Shakespeare || Marlowe
AndQuery  // William && Shakespeare
```

Each class defines an `eval()` member function that solves the query for the operation each represents. The `eval()` member function for NameQuery, for example, simply returns the location vector of line and column numbers at which the word occurs (see Section 6.8). The OrQuery `eval()` member function, however, must build up a union of the location vectors of its two operands, and so on.

Thus the query

```
untamed || fiery
```

consists of an OrQuery class object containing two NameQuery objects as its operands. This supports simple queries, but presents a problem when handling compound queries such as the following:

```
Alice || Emma && Weeks
```

This query consists of two subqueries: the OrQuery object containing the Name-Query objects `Alice` and `Emma`, and the AndQuery object. The right operand of the AndQuery is the NameQuery `Weeks`.

```
AndQuery
    OrQuery
        NameQuery ("Alice")
        NameQuery ("Emma")
    NameQuery ("Weeks")
```

The left operand, however, is the OrQuery object that precedes it. It could as easily represent a NotQuery or another AndQuery object as well. How can we internally represent an operand when it can be one of four possible query class types? Our problem is twofold:

---

1. Recall that to simplify our implementation, we require a space separating each word, including parentheses and the query operators. While this is unreasonable in a real-world system, we believe it is acceptable in a primarily introductory text such as this.

1. We need to be able to declare the type of the operand within the OrQuery, AndQuery, and NotQuery classes such that each can hold each of the four different query class types.
2. We need to be able to invoke the class-specific instance of the eval() member function at run-time for each operand through whatever solution we come up with in item 1.

A non-object-oriented solution is to define the operand type to be a union, and to provide a *discriminant* to indicate the actual type of the operand:

```
// a non-object-oriented solution
union op_type {
        // union cannot contain class objects with
        // associated constructors
        NotQuery *nq;
        OrQuery  *oq;
        AndQuery *aq;
        string   *word;
};

enum opTypes {
        Not_query=1, Or_query, And_query, Name_query
};

class AndQuery {
public:
        // ...
private:
        /*
         * op_types contain the actual operands of the query
         * opTypes identify the type of each operand
         */

        op_type _lop, _rop;
        opTypes _lop_type, _rop_type;
};
```

Alternatively, we can do away with the union, and store the object through a void* pointer, as follows:

```
class AndQuery {
public:
        // ...
private:
        void *_lop, *_rop;
        opTypes _lop_type, _rop_type;
};
```

We still need the discriminant because we cannot use an object addressed by a void* pointer directly, and there is no way to query the pointer itself as to its actual type. (We do not recommend this solution under C++; it is, however, a common programming idiom of the C language.)

The primary drawback with either of these solutions is that the burden of type resolution rests with the programmer. For example, under the void* solution, the AndQuery eval() operation is likely to be implemented as follows:

```
void
AndQuery::
eval()
{
    // non-object-oriented solution
    // burden of type resolution rests with programmer

    // figure out the actual type of the left op
    switch( _lop_type ) {
      case And_query:
            AndQuery *paq = static_cast<AndQuery*>(_lop);
            paq->eval();
            break;
      case Or_query:
            OrQuery *poq = static_cast<OrQuery*>(_lop);
            poq->eval();
            break;
      case Not_query:
            NotQuery *pnotq = static_cast<NotQuery*>(_lop);
            pnotq->eval();
            break;
      case Name_query:
            NameQuery *pnmq = static_cast<NameQuery*>(_lop);
            pnmq->eval();
            break;
    }

    // same for right operand ...
}
```

The two primary disadvantages of explicit programmer management of type resolution are: the increased size and complexity of the code to handle each unique type directly and the difficulty of adding to or removing from the supported set of types without breaking existing code.

Object-oriented programming provides an alternative solution in which the burden of type resolution shifts from the programmer to the compiler. For example, here is the AndQuery eval() operation reimplemented under an object-oriented design (eval() is declared as a virtual function):

```
// object-oriented solution
// burden of type resolution shifts to the compiler

// note: _lop and _rop are now objects of class type
// their definitions are shown later

void
AndQuery::
eval()
{
    _lop->eval();
    _rop->eval();
}
```

If we should add to or delete from the types being supported, this portion of our code does not need to be either modified or recompiled.

17.1.1   An Object-Oriented Design

Of what does the object-oriented design of the four query types consist? How do we solve the two representational problems defined earlier?

Through *inheritance* we define a relationship between the four previously independent query class types. We achieve this by introducing an abstract Query class to serve as a *base class* from which the other classes are *derived* (or built from). An abstract class can be thought of as an incomplete class that is more or less finished with each subsequent class *derivation* — in our case, the four query class types: AndQuery, OrQuery, NotQuery, and NameQuery.

Our abstract Query base class defines the set of data and function members that are common to all the query types. Derivations from Query, such as AndQuery, attempt to define what is unique to each particular type of query. NameQuery, for example, is a particular instance of Query in which the operand is always a string. We refer to NameQuery as a *derived class*. We say that Query serves as its *base class*. (The same is true of the other query class types as well.) A derived class inherits the data members and the member functions of its base class and can use them directly as if they were members of the derived class.

The primary benefit of an inheritance hierarchy is that we can program to the public interface of the abstract base class rather than to the individual types that form its inheritance hierarchy, in this way shielding our code from changes in that hierarchy. We define eval(), for example, as a public virtual function of the abstract Query base class. By writing code such as

```
    _rop->eval();
```

user code is shielded from the variety and volatility of our query language. This not only allows for the addition, revision, or removal of types without requiring changes to user programs, but frees the provider of a new query type from having to recode behavior or actions common to all types in the hierarchy itself. This is supported by two special characteristics of inheritance: *polymorphism* and *dynamic binding*.

When we speak of polymorphism within C++, we primarily mean the ability of a pointer or a reference of a base class to address any of its derived classes. For example, if we define a nonmember function eval() as follows,

```
// pquery can address any of the classes derived from Query
void eval( const Query *pquery )
{
    pquery->eval();
}
```

we can invoke it legally, passing in the address of an object of any of the four query types:

```
int main()
{
    AndQuery aq;
    NotQuery notq;
    OrQuery *oq = new OrQuery;
    NameQuery nq( "Botticelli" );

    // ok: each is derived from Query
    // compiler converts to base class automatically

    eval( &aq );
    eval( &notq );
    eval( oq );
    eval( &nq );
}
```

whereas an attempt to invoke eval() with the address of an object not derived from Query results in a compile-time error:

```
int main()
{
        string name( "Scooby-Doo" );

        // error: string is not derived from Query
        eval( &name );
}
```

Within eval(), the execution of

```
pquery->eval();
```

must invoke the appropriate eval() virtual member function based on the actual class object pquery addresses. In the previous example, pquery in turn addresses an AndQuery object, a NotQuery object, an OrQuery object, and a NameQuery object. At each invocation point during the execution of our program, the actual class type addressed by pquery is determined, and the appropriate eval() instance is called.

Dynamic binding is the mechanism through which this is accomplished. (We'll look at the design and use of virtual functions in detail in Section 17.5.)

In the object-oriented paradigm, the programmer manipulates an unknown instance of a bound but infinite set of types. (The set of types is bound by its inheritance hierarchy. In theory, however, there is no limit to the depth and breadth of that hierarchy.) In C++ this is achieved through the manipulation of objects through base class pointers and references only. In the object-based paradigm, the programmer manipulates an instance of a fixed, singular type that is completely defined at the point of compilation.

Although the polymorphic manipulation of an object requires that the object be accessed either through a pointer or a reference, the manipulation of a pointer or a reference in C++ does not in itself necessarily result in polymorphism. For example, consider

```
// no polymorphism
int *pi;

// no language-supported polymorphism
void *pvi;

// ok: pquery may address any Query derivation
Query *pquery;
```

In C++, polymorphism exists only within individual class hierarchies. Pointers of type void* can be described as polymorphic, but they are without explicit language support — that is, they must be managed by the programmer through explicit casts and some form of discriminant that keeps track of the actual type being addressed. (One might say that they are not first-class polymorphic objects.)

The C++ language supports polymorphism in the following ways:

1. Through the implicit conversion of a derived class pointer, a reference to a pointer, or a reference of its public base type:

   ```
   Query *pquery = new NameQuery( "Glass" );
   ```

2. Through the virtual function mechanism:

   ```
   pquery->eval();
   ```

3. Through the dynamic_cast and typeid operators (these are discussed in detail in Section 19.1):

   ```
   if ( NameQuery *pnq =
         dynamic_cast< NameQuery* >( pquery )) ...
   ```

We solve our representational problem by defining each operand of the And-Query, NotQuery, and OrQuery class as a pointer of type Query*. For example:

```
class AndQuery {
public:
    // ...
```

```
private:
    Query *_lop;
    Query *_rop;
};
```

Both operands can now address any of the query class types derived from the abstract Query base class, either those defined now or in the future. The evaluation of each operand, which occurs during program execution, is independent of its actual type due to the virtual mechanism

```
_rop->eval();
```

Figure 17.1 illustrates the inheritance hierarchy of the abstract Query class and its four derived classes. How do we translate Figure 17.1 into C++ program code?

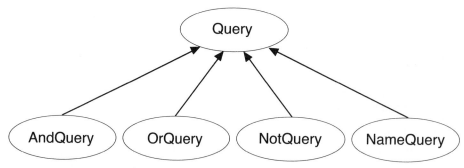

Figure 17.1   Query Class Hierarchy

In Section 2.4, we walked through the implementation of an IntArray class hierarchy. The syntactic outline of defining our Query class hierarchy pictured in Figure 17.1 is similar:

```
class Query { ... };
class AndQuery  : public Query { ... };
class OrQuery   : public Query { ... };
class NotQuery  : public Query { ... };
class NameQuery : public Query { ... };
```

Inheritance is specified through the *class derivation list*. Under single inheritance, it takes the general form

```
: access-level base-class
```

where access-level is one of public, protected, or private (the meaning of protected and private inheritance is discussed in Section 18.3) and base-class is the name of a previously defined class. Query, for example, serves as a public base class of the four query types.

The class specified in the derivation list must be defined prior to being specified as a base class. The following forward declaration of Query, for example, is not sufficient for it to serve as a base class:

```
// error: Query must be defined
class Query;
class NameQuery : public Query { ... };
```

The forward declaration of a derived class does not include its derivation list, but simply the class name — the same as if it were a nonderived class. For example, the following forward declaration of NameQuery results in a compile-time error:

```
// error: a forward declaration must not
// include the derivation list of the derived class
class NameQuery : public Query;
```

The correct forward declaration is as follows:

```
// forward declarations of both derived and
// nonderived classes simply list the class name
class Query;
class NameQuery;
```

The primary difference between the Query base class and the IntArray base class of Section 2.4 is that Query does not represent an actual object in our application domain. Users of the IntArray class hierarchy are likely to define and manipulate IntArray class objects directly. Users of the Query class hierarchy define Query pointers and references only. These are used for the indirect manipulation of objects of the class types derived from Query. Query is said to be an *abstract base class*; IntArray, a *concrete base class*. The predominant form of object-oriented design is the definition of an abstract base class, such as Query, and a single, public derivation.

Exercise 17.1

A library supports the following categories of lending materials, each with its own check-out and check-in policy. Organize these into an inheritance hierarchy:

```
book           audio book
record         children's puppet
video          sega video game
rental book    sony playstation video game
cdrom book     nintendo video game
```

Exercise 17.2

Choose one of the following general abstractions containing a family of types (or choose one of your own). Organize the types into an inheritance hierarchy:

```
(1) Graphical file formats (such as gif, tiff, jpeg, bmp)
(2) Geometric primitives (such as box, circle, sphere, cone)
(3) C++ language types (such as class, function, member function)
```

17.2   Identifying the Members of the Hierarchy

As we described in Section 2.4, in an object-based design, there is generally one provider and many users of a class. The provider designs and usually implements the class. The users exercise the public interface made available by the provider. This separation of activity is reflected in the division of the class into private and public access levels.

Under inheritance, there are now multiple class providers: one providing the base class implementation (and possibly some number of derived classes) and one or others providing derived classes throughout the lifetime of the inheritance hierarchy. This activity is also an implementation activity. The provider of the subtype often (but not always) needs access to the base class implementation. To provide that, while still preventing general access to the implementation, an additional access level, protected, is provided. The data members and member functions of a protected section of a class, although still unavailable to the general program, are available to the derived class. (Anything placed within a private section of the base class is only available to the class itself, and not to any of the derived classes.)

The criteria for designating a member public to a class does not change between an object-based and an object-oriented design. What does change is whether to declare the nonpublic members as either protected or private. A member is made private to a base class if we wish to prevent subsequently derived classes from having direct access to that member. A member is made protected if we believe it provides an operation or data storage a subsequently derived class requires direct access to in order for that derived class to be effectively implemented. An additional design consideration for a class intended to serve as a base class is the identification of type-dependent member functions. These are the virtual functions of the class hierarchy.

The next step in our design of the Query class hierarchy is to determine the following:

1.   What operations should the public interface of the Query class hierarchy provide?
2.   Of these, which should be declared as virtual?
3.   What additional operations, if any, do the individual derived class types require?
4.   What data members, if any, should be declared within our abstract Query class?
5.   What data members, if any, are required by the individual derived class types?

Unfortunately, there is no magic formula for answering these questions. Nor, once answered, for guaranteeing either their correctness or completeness. As we shall see, the process of object-oriented design is iterative, and requires both additions to and modifications of our evolving class hierarchy. In the remainder of this section we walk through an iterative evolution of the Query class hierarchy.

17.2.1   Defining the Base Class

The members of the Query class represent

1.   The set of operations supported by all the derived class query types. This includes both virtual operations overridden by the derived class types and non-virtual operations that are shared among the derived classes. We'll look at an example of each.

2.   The set of data members common to the derived classes. By factoring these members out of the derived classes into our abstract Query class, we are able to access the members independent of the actual type on which we are operating. Again, we'll look at two examples.

Given a query such as

```
fiery || untamed
```

the two primary operations are (1) to evaluate the query lines of text matching the query and (2) to display the matching lines to the user. We'll name these operations eval() and display(), respectively.

The computation of eval() is specific to each derived query class type and must therefore be declared as virtual within the Query class definition. Each derived class must provide its own implementation. The Query base class provides the public interface against which we will program.

The display() of the matching lines of text is independent of the actual derived class query type. The algorithm requires access to the representation of the text itself and a list of the lines matching the query. This algorithm is invariant whether the operation is an AndQuery, OrQuery, or so on. Rather than duplicate the operation and supporting data in each derived class, we define a single instance within Query that is inherited by each.

With this design we can invoke either operation without knowledge of the actual type of the object we are manipulating. For example:

```
void
doit( Query *pq )
{
    // virtual invocation
    pq->eval();

    // static invocation of Query::display()
    pq->display();
}
```

How should the matching lines of text be represented? For each word within the query, its presence is indicated by an associated location vector built up while we processed the text. A location, recall, is a line and column pair of short integers. The word location map constructed by build_text_map() contains all the location vectors of all the words recognized by our system. The map is indexed by a string representing the word. For example, given our input text

```
Alice Emma has long flowing red hair. Her Daddy says
when the wind blows through her hair, it looks almost alive,
like a fiery bird in flight. A beautiful fiery bird, he tells her,
magical but untamed. "Daddy, shush, there is no such thing,"
she tells him, at the same time wanting him to tell her more.
Shyly, she asks, "I mean, Daddy, is there?"
```

here are the text location map entries for some of the words with multiple entries (the word represents the key to the map; the value pairs in parentheses are the elements of the location vector — note the lines and columns are numbered beginning with 0):

```
bird ((2,3),(2,9))
daddy ((0,8),(3,3),(5,5))
fiery ((2,2),(2,8))
hair ((0,6),(1,6))
her ((0,7),(1,5),(2,12),(4,11))
him ((4,2),(4,8))
she ((4,0),(5,1))
tell ((2,11),(4,1),(4,10))
```

The location vector, however, does not necessarily represent the solution to the query. For example, fiery occurs in two locations, but represents only one actual line to display.

We need to calculate a unique set of lines represented by the location vector. One strategy is to create a vector of each line number within the location vector; pass the line vector to the unique() generic algorithm, erasing the duplicate elements (see the discussion and example of using unique() in the Appendix). The remaining lines should already be in ascending order. To be certain, we can apply the generic sort() algorithm to the line vector.

An alternative strategy that we have chosen is to build a set object of the line numbers within the location vector. A set object automatically holds a unique set of values in ascending order. We'll need a function to turn our location vector into a set of unique line numbers:

```
set<short>* Query::_vec2set( const vector< location >* );
```

We declare _vec2set() to be a protected Query member function. It is not public because it does not belong to the set of operations we wish users of the Query class hierarchy to invoke. It is not private because it is an auxiliary function that we wish to make available to the derived classes. (The underscore is meant to indicate that it is not part of the public interface of the Query class hierarchy.)

For example, the location vector for bird contains two entries for the same line. Its solution set, therefore, consists of a single entry: (2). The location vector for tell contains three entries, two for the same line. Its solution set, therefore, consists of two entries: (2,4). Here are the corresponding solution sets for the location vectors listed previously:

```
bird     (2)
daddy    (0,3,5)
fiery    (2)
hair     (0,1)
her      (0,1,2,4)
him      (4)
she      (4,5)
tell     (2,4)
```

A NameQuery is evaluated simply by retrieving the location vector associated with its name, turning that vector into a set of unique lines, then displaying the associated lines of text.

A NotQuery represents all the lines in which its operands do not occur. The query

```
! daddy
```

represents the set of lines (1,2,4). To evaluate this we need to know how many lines are contained within the text. (We never calculated this information because it was not apparent until now that we need it; however, it will soon become apparent that we need even more information!) To evaluate more easily the NotQuery operation, it is convenient that we generate a set of all the lines in the text (0,1,2,3,4,5). We can then solve this by taking the `set_difference()` of the two sets. (The NameQuery set for daddy is (0,3,5).)

An OrQuery represents the union of all lines in which each of its operands occurs. For example, given the query

```
fiery || her
```

the unique set of lines is (0,1,2,4). This is the union of the line (2) associated with `fiery` and the lines (0,1,2,4) associated with `her`. Our line solution set must not contain duplicates and must be in ascending order.

Until now, we have been able to evaluate each query simply by dealing with the set of unique line occurrences. The AndQuery, however, requires that we examine both the line and column values of each location pair. For example, the operands of the query

```
her && hair
```

occur on four separate lines. The AndQuery semantics, as we've defined them, require that a matching line contain the exact sequence `her hair`. The occurrence on the first line does not match, although the words are adjacent,

```
Alice Emma has long flowing red hair. Her Daddy says
```

whereas the occurrence of the two words on the second line match exactly:

```
when the wind blows through her hair, it looks almost alive,
```

The other two occurrences of `her` contain no adjacent occurrence of `hair` — they clearly do not match. The solution to the query, then, is the second line of the text: (1).

Were it not for the AndQuery operation, we would not need to maintain a location vector for each operation. However, because any derived query type can be an operand of an AndQuery, each must calculate and maintain not just the set of unique lines, but the line and column location pair. For example, consider either of the following two queries:

```
fiery && ( hair || bird || potato )
fiery && ( ! burr )
```

The possibility of a NotQuery being an operand to an AndQuery means that we must create not simply a vector containing an entry for each line number, but a vector holding a location pair for each line and column within the text. (We'll look at this again when we walk through the NotQuery eval() function in Section 17.5.)

One necessary data member, therefore, is the location vector associated with the evaluation of each operation. We have the choice of declaring it as a member of each derived class or of declaring it as a member of the abstract Query base class that each derived class inherits. The space required to represent the member is the same for both approaches. By placing it in the common Query base class, we localize its initialization and access support. This is what we have chosen to do.

Whether we choose to represent the set of unique line numbers (we'll call it the *line solution set*) as a data member or calculate it on-the-fly each time we need it is an implementation decision. We have chosen to calculate it on demand, then tuck its address away for later access. It, too, is declared as a member of the abstract Query base class.

To display the set of matching lines, we need both the line solution set and the actual text file in which the lines are stored. However, whereas each operation requires its own location vector, only a single, shared instance of the text file is necessary. Therefore, we define it as a static data member of Query. (The implementation of the display() function depends only on these two members.)

Here, then, is a first iteration of our Query abstract base class representation, but without declaring any constructors, destructor, or copy assignment operator as yet (we get to these in Section 17.4 and Section 17.6 respectively):

```
#include <vector>
#include <set>
#include <string>
#include <utility>

typedef pair< short, short > location;

class Query {
public:
    // constructors and destructor
    // are discussed in Section 17.4

    // copy constructor and copy assignment operator
```

```
        // are discussed in Section 17.6

        // operations supporting public interface
        virtual void eval() = 0;
        void display () const;

        // read access functions
        const set<short> *solution() const;
        const vector<location> *locations() const { return &_loc; }

        static const vector<string> *text_file() {return _text_file;}

    protected:
        set<short> *_vec2set( const vector<location>* );

        static vector<string> *_text_file;

        set<short>          *_solution;
        vector<location>   _loc;
};

inline const set<short>*
Query::
solution()
{
    return _solution
           ? _solution
           : _solution = _vec2set( &_loc );
}
```

The peculiar syntax

```
        virtual void eval() = 0;
```

indicates that no virtual definition is provided for the eval() function of the abstract base class Query. Why? Because there is no meaningful algorithm for it to define. This instance of eval() is called a *pure virtual function*. It serves as a placeholder in the public interface of the class hierarchy. It is not intended ever to be invoked within our program. Rather, each subsequent derived class provides an actual instance. (We look at virtual functions in detail in Section 17.5.)

17.2.2   Defining the Derived Classes

Each derived class inherits the data members and member functions of its base class. The derived class needs to program only those aspects that differ from or extend the behavior of the base class. NameQuery, for example, must define an instance of eval(). In addition, it needs to provide support for the name of a word. We'll represent the name with a string member class object. Finally, to retrieve the associated location vector, the word location map must be available. Because only a single instance shared by all the NameQuery class objects is needed, we declare it to be a static data member. Here is our initial NameQuery class definition (again noting that we are deferring consideration of constructors, the destructor, and copy assignment operator for now):

```
typedef vector<location> loc;

class NameQuery : public Query {
public:
    // ...

    // overrides virtual Query::eval() instance[2]
    void eval();

    // read access function
    string name() const { return _name; }

    static const map<string,loc*> *word_map() { return _word_map; }

protected:
    string _name;
    static map<string,loc*> *_word_map;
};
```

The NotQuery class, in addition to providing its instance of the eval() virtual function, must provide support for its single operand. Because the operand can be any of the derived query class types, we define it to be of type pointer to Query. The NotQuery solution, recall, must represent not just the lines of text in which its operand does not appear, but all the column locations within each line as well. For example, given the NotQuery

```
! daddy
```

its NameQuery operand contains the following location vector:

```
daddy ((0,8),(3,3),(5,5))
```

The NotQuery location vector must include every column of lines (1,2,4). In addition, it must include every column of line (0) except column (8), every column of line (3) except column (3), and every column of line (5) except column (5).

The simplest way to calculate this is to have a shared, single location vector that contains a line and column pair for every word occurrence in the text; we'll look at the implementation when we present the NotQuery eval() function in Section 17.5. In any case, we define this member as a static member of the NotQuery class.

---

2. The derived class instance of an inherited virtual function such as eval() does not need to but may specify the virtual keyword. The compiler recognizes the instance based on a comparison of the function's prototype.

Here is the initial NotQuery class definition (once again noting that we are deferring consideration of constructors, the destructor, and copy assignment operator for now):

```
class NotQuery : public Query {
public:
    // ...

    // alternative syntax: explicit virtual keyword
    // instance overrides that of Query::eval()
    virtual void eval();

    // read access functions
    const Query *op() const { return _op; }
    static const vector<location>*all_locs(){ return _all_locs; }

protected:
    Query *_op;
    static const vector< location > *_all_locs;
};
```

The AndQuery and OrQuery classes are both binary operations, and so must support a left and right operand. Both operands can be any of the derived query class types, and so we define both members to be of type pointer to Query. Each must also provide its respective instance of the eval() virtual function. Here is our initial OrQuery class definition:

```
class OrQuery : public Query {
public:
        // ...

        virtual void eval();

        const Query *rop() const { return _rop; }
        const Query *lop() const { return _lop; }

protected:
        Query *_lop;
        Query *_rop;
};
```

In addition, each AndQuery class object must have access to the number of words contained on each line. Otherwise, the AndQuery evaluation cannot find adjacent words spanning two lines. For example, given the query

```
tell && her && magical
```

the matching sequence spans the third and fourth lines:

```
like a fiery bird in flight. A beautiful fiery bird, he tells her,
magical but untamed. "Daddy, shush, there is no such thing,"
```

The associated location vectors for the three words are as follows:

```
her      ((0,7),(1,5),(2,12),(4,11))
magical  ((3,0))
tell     ((2,11),(4,1),(4,10))
```

Unless the AndQuery eval() function can determine that line (2) holds 12 words, it cannot determine that magical is adjacent to her. We'll make a single instance available through a static data member we've named _max_col. (The eval() implementation is detailed in Section 17.5.) Here, then, is our initial AndQuery class definition:

```
class AndQuery : public Query {
public:
        // constructors discussed in 17.4
        virtual void eval();

        const Query *rop() const { return _rop; }
        const Query *lop() const { return _lop; }

        static void max_col( const vector< int > *pcol )
                    { if ( !_max_col ) _max_col = pcol; }

protected:
        Query *_lop;
        Query *_rop;
        static const vector< int > *_max_col;
};
```

17.2.3   Summary

The public interface of each of our four derived classes consists of the inherited public members of Query and the public members of the individual derived classes. When we write

```
Query *pq = new NameQuery( "Monet" );
```

we may only access the public interface of Query through pq. When we write

```
pq->eval();
```

because eval() is declared to be a virtual function, the derived class eval() instance is invoked associated with the derived class object actually addressed by pq. In this case, the NameQuery instance is invoked. When we write

```
pq->display();
```

the nonvirtual Query display() function is always invoked. However, display() still reflects the solution set of the actual derived class object addressed by pq. Rather than relying on the virtual mechanism, we instead factored the shared operation and its supporting data into the common abstract Query base class. display() is an example of polymorphic programming supported not by virtual functions but inheritance alone. Here is our implementation (this is an interim solution, as we'll see in the last section):

```
void
Query::
display()
{
    if ( ! _solution->size() ) {
            cout << "\n\tSorry, "
                 << " no matching lines were found in text.\n"
                 << endl;
    }

    set<short>::const_iterator
            it = _solution->begin(),
            end_it = _solution->end();

    for ( ; it != end_it; ++it ) {
            int line = *it;

            // don't confound user with text lines starting at 0 ...
            cout << "( " << line+1 << " ) "
                 << (*_text_file)[line] << '\n';
    }

    cout << endl;
}
```

In this section we have provided a first definition of our Query class hierarchy. One question we have not yet considered is how we are to build the actual data structure using the class hierarchy to represent the user's query. In fact, our implementation in support of this will cause us to modify and extend the definition through which we've just worked. Before we turn to that, we need to look at the mechanism of inheritance under C++ in more detail.

Exercise 17.3

Consider the following members of the library class hierarchy of Exercise 17.1 at the end of Section 17.1. Identify which instances are likely virtual function candidates, and which, if any, are likely to be common among all library materials and therefore able to be fully represented within the base class. (Note: LibMember is the abstraction representing a member of the library able to borrow library materials. Date is a class representing a calendar day of a particular year.)

```
class Library {
public:
    bool check_out( LibMember* );
    bool check_in ( LibMember* );
```

```
        bool is_late( const Date& today );
        double apply_fine();
        ostream& print( ostream&=cout );

        Date* due_date() const;
        Date* date_borrowed() const;

        string title() const;
        const LibMember* member() const;
    };
```

Exercise 17.4

Identify the base and derived class members for the chosen class hierarchy of Exercise 17.2 at the end of Section 17.1. Identify virtual functions as well as public and protected members.

Exercise 17.5

Which of the following, if any, are incorrect?

```
            class Base { ... };

            (a) class Derived : public Derived { ... };
            (b) class Derived : Base { ... };
            (c) class Derived : private Base { ... };
            (d) class Derived : public Base;
            (e) class Derived inherits Base { ... };
```

17.3   Base Class Member Access

A derived class object actually consists of multiple parts. Each base class represents a *subobject* made up of the nonstatic data members of the base class. The derived class object is made up of its base class subobjects and a derived part consisting of the nonstatic data members of the derived class. Our NameQuery object, for example, consists of a Query subobject containing the inherited _loc and _solution data members, and the NameQuery class portion containing the data member _name.

Within the derived class, the inherited members of the base class subobject can be accessed directly as if they are members of the derived class. (The depth of the inheritance chain does not limit access to these members nor does it add to the cost of that access.) For example:

```
    void
    NameQuery::
    display_partial_solution( ostream &os )
    {
        os << _name
```

```
            << " is found in "
            << (_solution ? _solution->size() : 0)
            << " lines of text\n";
    }
```

The same is true of accessing the inherited member functions of the base class: We invoke them as if they are members of the derived class, either through an object of its class

```
    NameQuery nq( "Frost" );

    // invokes NameQuery::eval()
    nq.eval();

    // invokes Query::display()
    nq.display();
```

or directly within a member function

```
    void
    NameQuery::
    match_count()
    {
        if ( ! _solution )
            // invokes Query::_vec2set()
            _solution = _vec2set( &_loc );
        return _solution->size();
    }
```

There is one exception to the direct access of a base class member within the derived class — when the name of the base class member is reused within the derived class. For example:

```
    class Diffident {
    public: // ...
    protected:
        int _mumble;
        // ...
    };

    class Shy : public Diffident {
    public: // ...
    protected:
        // lexically hides visibility of Diffident::_mumble
        string _mumble;

        // ...
    };
```

Within the scope of Shy, the unqualified use of _mumble always resolves to the _mumble string member of class Shy, even if its use is illegal. For example:

```
void
Shy::
turn_eyes_down()
{
    // ...
    _mumble = "excuse me"; // ok

    // error: int Diffident::_mumble is hidden
    _mumble = -1;
}
```

It is not unusual to hear programmers mumbling about the stupidity of their compiler when the compiler flags a usage like this as a type error. Although we can see what the programmer means, the compiler needs a little help. To access a base class member with a name that has been reused within a derived class, we must qualify the base class member with its class scope operator. For example, here is a correct reimplementation of turn_eyes_down():

```
void
Shy::
turn_eyes_down()
{
    // ...
    _mumble = "excuse me"; // ok

    // ok: qualified to the base class instance
    Diffident::_mumble = -1;
}
```

A common misunderstanding of those new to the language is the expectation that base and derived class member functions make up a set of overloaded functions. For example:

```
class Diffident {
public:
    void mumble( int softness );
    // ...
};

class Shy : public Diffident {
public:
    // lexically hides visibility of Diffident::mumble
    // they do not form a pair of overloaded instances
    void mumble( string whatYaSay );
    void print( int soft, string words );
    // ...
};
```

An attempt to invoke the base class instance within the derived class, however, results in a compile-time error. For example:

```
Shy simon;

// ok: Shy::mumble( string )
simon.mumble( "pardon me" );

// error: expected first argument of type string
// Diffident::mumble( int ) is not visible
simon.mumble( 2 );
```

While the base class members can be accessed directly, they retain the scope of the base class in which they are defined. The overloaded candidate functions of a name must all occur in the same scope. If this were not the case, the following two instances of the nonvirtual member function turn_aside()

```
class Diffident {
public:
    void turn_aside();
    // ...
};

class Shy : public Diffident {
public:
    // lexically hides the visibility of
    // Diffident::turn_aside()
    void turn_aside();

    // ...
};
```

would result in a redefinition error because both instances have the same signature. They are not in error because each resides in the scope of the class in which they are defined.

What if we really wish to provide an overloaded set of instances of both the derived and base class members? Are we required to write small inline stub functions within the derived class invoking the base class instance? Although this accomplishes our goal,

```
class Shy : public Diffident {
public:
    // ok: one way to provide an overloaded set
    //     of base and derived class members

    void mumble( string whatYaSay );
    void mumble( int softness ) {
            Diffident::mumble( softness ); }
    // ...
};
```

it is unnecessary under Standard C++. We can achieve the same result with the *using declaration,* as follows:

```
class Shy : public Diffident {
public:
    // ok: under Standard C++, the using declaration
    //     creates an overloaded set of
    //     base and derived class members

    void mumble( string whatYaSay );
    using Diffident::mumble;

    // ...
};
```

In effect, the using declaration enters each named member of the base class into the scope of the derived class. The base class member is now entered into the set of overloaded instances associated with the name of the member function within the derived class. (The using declaration for a member function cannot specify the parameter list, only the member function name. This means that if the function is overloaded within the base class, all the overloaded instances are added to the scope of the derived class type. We cannot add only one instance of the set of overloaded base class members.)

Another common misunderstanding of new C++ programmers is the extent to which they may access the protected members of a base class. When we write

```
class Query {
public:
    const vector<location>* locations() const { return &_loc; }
    // ...
protected:
    vector<location> _loc;
    // ...
};
```

we are saying that a class derived from Query may directly access the _loc data member, while the rest of the program must use the public access function. What this means, however, is that the derived class has access to the protected _loc data member of *its* base class subobject. The derived class does not have access to the protected members of an independent base class object. For example:

```
bool
NameQuery::
compare( const Query *pquery )
{
    // ok: protected member of its Query subobject
    int myMatches = _loc.size();

    // error: has no direct access rights to the
```

```
        // protected member of an independent Query object
        int itsMatches = pquery->_loc.size();

        return myMatches == itsMatches;
    }
```

NameQuery has access to the protected members of only one Query class object: its own Query subobject. (These protected members are accessed within the derived class through the implicit this pointer [the this pointer is introduced in Section 13.4].) The immediate solution to the compile-time error is to rewrite the compare() function to make use of the public location() member function:

```
    bool
    NameQuery::
    compare( const Query *pquery )
    {
        // ok: protected member of its Query subobject
        int myMatches = _loc.size();

        // ok: use public access method
        int itsMatches = pquery->locations()->size();

        return myMatches == itsMatches;
    }
```

The real problem, however, is an incorrect design on our part. Because _loc is a member of the Query base class, compare() properly belongs as a member of the Query class, not to the derived NameQuery class. Often, member access problems between a derived and base class can be resolved by moving the operation to the class that contains the inaccessible member, as in this case.

This form of member access constraint does not apply within a class for other objects of its own class. For example:

```
    bool
    NameQuery::
    compare( const NameQuery *pname )
    {
        int myMatches = _loc.size(); // ok
        int itsMatches = pname->_loc.size(); // ok as well

        return myMatches == itsMatches;
    }
```

The derived class may access directly the protected base class members of other objects of its own class, as well as the protected and private members of other objects of its own class.

Consider the following initialization of a Query base class pointer with the address of a derived class NameQuery object:

```
Query *pb = new NameQuery( "sprite" );
```

If we invoke a virtual function defined within the Query base class, such as

```
pb->eval(); // invokes NameQuery::eval()
```

the derived NameQuery class instance is invoked. Except for a virtual function declared in the Query base class and overriden in the NameQuery derived class, there is no way to access a NameQuery member directly through pb:

1. If Query and NameQuery both declare a nonvirtual member function of the same name, the Query instance is always invoked through pb.

2. Similarly, if Query and NameQuery both declare a data member of the same name, the Query instance is always accessed through pb.

3. If NameQuery introduces a virtual function not present in Query, such as suffix(), for example, an attempt to invoke it through pb results in a compile-time error:

   ```
   // error: suffix() is not a member of Query
   pb->suffix();
   ```

4. Similarly, if we try to access a nonvirtual member function or a data member of NameQuery through pb, a compile-time error results:

   ```
   // error: _name is not a member of Query
   pb->_name;
   ```

   Qualification of the member to be accessed does not help in this case:

   ```
   // error: Query has no NameQuery base class
   pb->NameQuery::name();
   ```

In C++, a base class pointer can only access the data members and member functions, including virtual member functions, declared (or inherited) within its class regardless of the actual object it may address. Declaring a member function virtual only delays resolution of which instance to invoke based on the actual class type addressed by pb during execution of the program.

While this may seem inflexible, it provides two significant benefits:

1. The run-time execution of a virtual member function can never fail because an instance for the actual class type does not exist. If some appropriate instance does not exist, the program cannot be compiled.

2. The virtual mechanism can be optimized. A virtual function call often costs no more than an indirect invocation of a function through a pointer (see [LIPPMAN96a] for a full discussion). (We look at virtual functions in detail in Section 17.5.)

The Query base class defines a static data member _text_file:

```
static vector<string> *_text_file;
```

Does the derivation of NameQuery create a second instance of _text_file unique to the NameQuery class? No. All derived class objects refer to the same, single, shared static member. Regardless of the number of classes derived from Query, there exists a single instance of _text_file. If we wish, we may access it through a derived class object using the member access syntax:

```
nameQueryObject._text_file; // ok
```

Finally, if a derived class wishes to access the private members of its base class directly, the base class must declare the derived class explicitly to be a friend. For example:

```
class Query {
    friend class NameQuery;
public:
    // ...
};
```

NameQuery can now access the private members of not only its own base class subobject, but the private and protected members of all Query objects.

What if we were to derive a StringQuery class from NameQuery? A StringQuery supports a shorthand AndQuery notation, so that rather than having to write

```
beautiful && fiery && bird
```

the user can simply write

```
"beautiful fiery bird"
```

Does StringQuery inherit NameQuery's friendship with Query? No. Friendship is not inherited. The derived class does not become a friend of a class that granted friendship to one of its base classes. If the derived class requires one or more of the same friendships, each must be granted explicitly by the respective class. StringQuery, for example, has no special access privilege to Query. If it needs special access, Query must grant it explicitly.

Exercise 17.6

Given the following base and derived class definitions

```
class Base {
public:
    foo( int );
    // ...
protected:
    int _bar;
    double _foo_bar;
};

class Derived : public Base {
public:
    foo( string );
```

```
        bool bar( Base *pb );
        void foobar();
        // ...
    protected:
        string _bar;
    };
```

identify what is wrong with each of the following code fragments and how each might be fixed:

```
(a) Derived d; d.foo( 1024 );
(b) void Derived::foobar() { _bar = 1024; }
(c) bool Derived::bar( Base *pb )
          { return _foo_bar == pb->_foo_bar; }
```

17.4   Base and Derived Class Construction

A derived class, recall, consists of one or more base class subobjects and a derived class portion. NameQuery, for example, consists of a Query subobject and a string member class object. For the purposes of illustrating the behavior of a derived class constructor, let's introduce a built-in data member as well:

```
class NameQuery : public Query {
public:
    // ...
protected:
    bool    _present;
    string  _name;
};
```

_present, if set to false, indicates that _name is not present in the text.

Let's first consider the case in which we do not define a NameQuery class constructor. In this case, when we define a NameQuery object,

```
NameQuery nq;
```

first the default Query class constructor, then the default string class constructor (associated with the member class object _name) are invoked. _present is left uninitialized, which is a potential source of program error.

To initialize _present , we can define a default NameQuery constructor, as follows:

```
inline NameQuery::NameQuery(){ _present = false; }
```

Now, the definition of nq invokes three constructors: the default Query base class constructor, the string default constructor to initialize the data member _name, and the NameQuery default constructor.

What if we wish to pass an argument to the Query base class constructor? How might we do that? We can answer this through reason by analogy.

To pass one or more arguments to the constructor of a member class object, we do so through the member initialization list (we can also initialize nonclass data members using the member initialization list — see Section 14.5 for a discussion). For example:

```
inline NameQuery::
NameQuery( const string &name )
         : _name( name ), _present( false )
    {}
```

To pass one or more arguments to a base class constructor, we also use the member initialization list. In the following example we pass the string constructor the argument name, and the Query base class constructor the object addressed by ploc:

```
inline
NameQuery::
NameQuery( const string &name,
           vector<location> *ploc )
         : _name( name ), Query( *ploc ), _present( true )
         {}
```

Although Query is placed second in the member initialization list, it is always invoked prior to the string constructor associated with _name. The order of constructor invocation is always the following:

1. The base class constructor. If there is more than one base class, the constructors are invoked in the order the base classes appear in the class derivation list, not in the order in which they are listed in the member initialization list. (We look at multiple inheritance in Chapter 18.)

2. Member class object constructor. If there is more than one member class object, the constructors are invoked in the order in which the objects are declared within the class, not the order in which they are listed in the member initialization list (see Section 14.5 for a detailed discussion).

3. The derived class constructor.

As a general rule, the derived class constructor should never assign a value to a base class data member directly, but rather pass the value to the appropriate base class constructor. Otherwise, the implementations of the two classes become *tightly coupled*, and it can be more difficult to modify or extend the base class implementation correctly. (Our responsibility as the designer of the base class is to provide the appropriate set of base class constructors.)

In the remainder of this section, we step through, in turn, the design of the Query base class constructor, and the four derived class constructors. That done, we briefly consider an alternative Query hierarchy design to consider hierarchies deeper than two. We conclude this section with a look at class destructors.

17.4.1   The Base Class Constructor

Our Query class declares two nonstatic data members, _solution and _loc:

```
class Query {
public:
    // ...
protected:
    set<short> *_solution;
    vector<location> _loc;
    // ...
};
```

Our default Query class constructor only needs to initialize _solution explicitly. The default vector constructor is invoked automatically to initialize _loc. Here is its implementation:

```
inline Query::Query(): _solution( 0 ) {}
```

We also need to define a second Query class constructor. This one takes a reference to a location vector as follows:

```
inline
Query::
Query( const vector< location > &loc )
    : _solution( 0 ), _loc( loc )
{}
```

This second Query constructor is invoked only within a NameQuery constructor when the NameQuery object represents a word present in the text. In this case, the precalculated location vector associated with the word is passed in. The other three derived class types calculate their location vectors within their associated eval() member function. (We'll see an example of this in the next subsection. The eval() member function implementations are presented in Section 17.5 in our discussion of virtual functions.)

The question now is at what access level should we declare the constructors? We do not wish to declare them as public because a Query class object is only intended to exist in our program as a subobject within a class object of one of its derived subtypes. We indicate this by declaring the constructor to be protected rather than public:

```
class Query {
public:
    // ...
protected:
    Query();
    // ...
};
```

The second Query constructor is invoked under an even more restrictive condition: Not only should it only construct a Query subobject, but it should only construct a Query subobject of a NameQuery object. We can ensure this by declaring this second constructor private and declaring the NameQuery class a friend of class Query. (As we discussed in the previous section, a derived class can access only the public and protected members of its base class. Any attempt within the OrQuery, AndQuery, and NotQuery classes to invoke this second constructor now results in a compile-time error.)

```
class Query {
    friend class NameQuery;
public:
    // ...
protected:
    Query();
    // ...
private:
    explicit Query( const vector<location>& );
};
```

(One might argue against this second constructor instance, contending that it is more appropriate to fill _loc within the NameQuery eval() function. This two-constructor design, however, better serves our purpose in illustrating the uses of a base class constructor.)

17.4.2   The Derived Class Constructor

Our NameQuery class also defines two constructors. They are made public because actual NameQuery objects are expected to be defined within our application.

```
class NameQuery : public Query {
public:
    explicit NameQuery( const string& );
    NameQuery( const string&, vector<location>* );
    // ...
protected:
    // ...
};
```

The one-parameter constructor accepts a string parameter. This is passed to the string constructor invoked to initialize the string data member _name. The default Query base class constructor is invoked implicitly:

```
inline
NameQuery::
NameQuery( const string &name )
    // Query::Query() invoked implicitly
    : _name( name )
{}
```

The two-parameter constructor also accepts a string parameter. It also accepts a second parameter of type pointer to a location vector. This is passed to the private Query base class constructor. (Note, we are no longer considering _present as a data member of NameQuery):

```
inline
NameQuery::
NameQuery( const string &name, vector<location> *ploc )
          : _name( name ), Query( *ploc )
{}
```

Here is how they might be used:

```
string title( "Alice" );
NameQuery *pname;

// see if "Alice" occurs with the word text map
// if so, retrieve its associated location vector

if ( vector<location> *ploc = retrieve_location( title ))
     pname = new NameQuery( title, ploc );
else pname = new NameQuery( title );
```

The NotQuery, OrQuery, and AndQuery classes each define a single constructor, as follows, in which the default Query base class constructor is invoked implicitly:

```
inline NotQuery::
NotQuery( Query *op = 0 ) : _op( op ) {}

inline OrQuery::
OrQuery( Query *lop = 0, Query *rop = 0 )
        : _lop( lop ), _rop( rop )
{}

inline AndQuery::
AndQuery( Query *lop = 0, Query *rop = 0 )
          : _lop( lop ), _rop( rop )
{}
```

In Section 17.7, we build up our individual derived class objects to represent each user query.

17.4.3   An Alternative Class Hierarchy

While our Query class hierarchy is a sufficient design, it is not the only design possible. For example, because the AndQuery and OrQuery classes both support a binary operation, there is some duplication between the two classes. We can factor the data members and member functions common to the two classes into an abstract Binary-Query base class. The new subtree of our Query hierarchy is pictured in Figure 17.2.

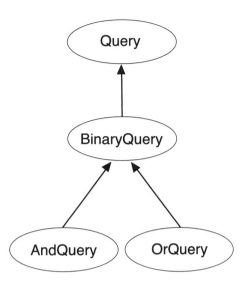

Figure 17.2   An Alternative Class Hierarchy

The BinaryQuery class is also an abstract base class — that is, actual objects of the class do not occur in our application. There is no meaningful implementation of eval(), and so we choose not to provide a definition overriding the pure virtual instance declared within our Query base class. Within the BinaryQuery class, the pure virtual instance of eval() is also active. (We look at pure virtual functions in detail in Section 17.5.)

The two access members lop() and rop(), common to both derived classes, are lifted up into the BinaryQuery class. They are defined as nonstatic inline member functions. Similarly, the two data members _lop and _rop declared by both derived classes are lifted up into the BinaryQuery class. They are declared as protected nonstatic data members. The public constructor of the two derived classes is combined into a single protected BinaryQuery constructor:

```
class BinaryQuery : public Query {
public:
    const Query *lop() { return _lop; }
    const Query *rop() { return _rop; }

protected:
    BinaryQuery( Query *lop, Query *rop )
               : _lop( lop ), _rop( rop )
    {}

    Query *_lop;
    Query *_rop;
};
```

It seems as if the two derived classes now only need to provide the appropriate eval() instance:

```
// oops: these class definitions are incorrect

class OrQuery : public BinaryQuery {
public:
        virtual void eval();
};

class AndQuery : public BinaryQuery {
public:
        virtual void eval();
};
```

As we have defined them, however, they are incomplete. Surprisingly, if we compile these two class definitions, they compile without error. If we attempt to define an actual class object, such as

```
// error: missing AndQuery class constructor
AndQuery proust( new NameQuery( "marcel" ),
                 new NameQuery( "proust " ));
```

the definition of proust is flagged as an error: The AndQuery class, we're told, is missing a constructor definition supporting the passing in of two arguments.

We had assumed that both AndQuery and OrQuery inherit the BinaryQuery constructor in the same way they both inherit the lop() and rop() member access functions. They do not, however. A derived class does not inherit the constructors of its base class. (The reasoning is that this could lead too easily to the introduction of uninitialized derived class member errors. For example, imagine if we subsequently add one or another nonclass data member to AndQuery. The inherited base class constructor is no longer adequate for the initialization of the AndQuery derived class. The programmer adding the new member, however, may not realize this. The error, however, reveals itself not in the construction of the AndQuery object, but in some subsequent use of the object. In practice, these sorts of errors prove difficult to trace. An overloaded instance of the base class new and delete operators are inherited and do sometimes result in just this sort of problem illustration.)

Each derived class must provide its own set of constructors. In the case of our AndQuery and OrQuery classes, the constructors serve no other purpose than to provide an interface by which to pass the two operands to the BinaryQuery constructor. Here is our corrected implementation:

```
// ok: these class definitions are correct

class OrQuery : public BinaryQuery {
public:
```

```
        OrQuery( Query *lop, Query *rop )
                : BinaryQuery( lop, rop ) {}

        virtual void eval();
};

class AndQuery : public BinaryQuery {
public:
        AndQuery( Query *lop, Query *rop )
                : BinaryQuery( lop, rop ) {}

        virtual void eval();
};
```

If we look at Figure 17.2 again, we see that BinaryQuery is the immediate base class of AndQuery and OrQuery. Query is the immediate base class of BinaryQuery. Query is a nonimmediate base class of AndQuery and OrQuery.

A derived class constructor can invoke legally only the constructor of its immediate base class (virtual inheritance provides an exception to this rule, as it does to so many others as well; see Section 18.5). For example, it is an error for AndQuery to invoke the Query constructor in its member initialization list.

The definition of an AndQuery or OrQuery class object now results in the following three constructor invocations: the Query nonimmediate base class constructor, the BinaryQuery immediate base class constructor, and the AndQuery or OrQuery derived class constructor. (The invocation order of base class constructors reflects a depth-first traversal of the inheritance hierarchy of the derived class.) The performance impact of the additional BinaryQuery class derivation is negligible, however, because we have defined it as inline.

Because the modified hierarchy preserves the public interface of the original design, the change is noninvasive to code already making use of the hierarchy. However, although source-level user code does not need to be modified, it does need to be recompiled using the new definition for our class hierarchy. This requirement to recompile an entire system, however, may deter some users from transitioning to the new design.

17.4.4   Lazy Error Detection

Programmers new to C++ are often surprised that the illegal definitions of the AndQuery and OrQuery classes (both were missing the necessary constructor declaration) compiles without error. Had we not attempted to define an actual AndQuery object, we might have delivered, to our mortification, the modified class hierarchy without having uncovered our error. What's going on? Consider the following:

1. If an error is flagged at the point of declaration, then we cannot continue to compile our application until the error is fixed. If, however, the conflicting declara-

tion is part of a library for which we do not have access to the source code, resolving the conflict may actually be nontrivial. Moreover, we may never have reason to trigger the error within our application, so that although the declaration represents a potential error, that error is never realized in our code.

2. On the other hand, if it is not flagged until a point of use, then our code potentially is filled with untriggered language errors an unwary programmer might set off at any time. Under this strategy, compiling our code successfully doesn't guarantee that it is free of language semantic errors, only that our program does not make use of code in violation of the semantic rules of the language.

Generating an error message at a use point is a form of *lazy evaluation*, a common design strategy to improve program performance. It is often applied to the allocation or initialization of a potentially expensive resource until it's actually needed. If it is never required, we save the expense of its unnecessary setup. If the resources are needed, but not all at once, we amortize our program's setup cost.

In C++, potential "combination" errors having to do with overloaded functions, templates, and class inheritance in general are flagged at a use point rather than the point of declaration. Whether or not you are convinced this is the right strategy (in practice, we believe it is; having to resolve every potential error when combining multiple components simply is not productive), it is the strategy in place. This means that we must test our own code conscientiously to uncover and resolve latent errors. Latent errors when combining two or more large components are marginally acceptable. Latent errors in a single component, such as the Query class hierarchy, generally are not.

17.4.5   Destructors

When the lifetime of a derived class object ends, the derived and base class destructors, if defined, are invoked automatically as well as the destructors of any member class objects. For example, given the following NameQuery class object,

```
NameQuery nq( "hyperion" );
```

the order of destructor invocations is the following: (1) the NameQuery class destructor, (2) the string destructor for the data member _name, and (3) the Query base class destructor. More generally, the order of destructor invocations for a derived class object is the reverse of its constructor order of invocation.

Here are our Query base and derived class destructors (these would all be declared as public members of the respective classes):

```
inline Query::
~Query(){ delete _solution; }

inline NotQuery::
~NotQuery(){ delete _op; }
```

```
inline OrQuery::
~OrQuery(){ delete _lop; delete _rop; }

inline AndQuery::
~AndQuery(){ delete _lop; delete _rop;  }
```

There are two things to note here: (1) We do not provide an explicit NameQuery destructor. Why? Because there is no program-level cleanup that we need to provide. Both the Query base class destructor and the _name string class destructor are invoked automatically. (2) Within the derived class destructors, the delete expression is applied to a Query* pointer. But it is not the Query destructor that we want invoked. Rather, we need to invoke the destructor of the class type of the object actually addressed by the pointer. To accomplish this, we must declare our Query base class destructor to be virtual. We look at virtual destructors and virtual functions in general in the next section.

There is one last item we should mention. An implicit assumption of our implementation is that the operands addressed within the NotQuery, OrQuery, and AndQuery class objects are allocated on the heap. This is why we apply the delete operator to each operand within the respective destructors. This is not an assumption enforceable at the language level, however. The language does not distinguish between heap and non-heap addresses. On one level, then, our implementation is unsafe.

As we'll see in Section 17.7, we've encapsulated the allocation and construction of the Query hierarchy in a UserQuery manager class. This provides us with sufficient confidence, at least for our *C++ Primer*, that our assumption is not violated. As a general-purpose library, however, further assurance is required. A program-level strategy of enforcement is to overload the new and delete operators for the classes of the hierarchy. One possible program-level strategy is the following: The new operators mark the objects as being allocated on the heap. They then allocate the object using the new expression. The delete operators check for the presence of the mark. If present, they apply the delete expression to the operand.

Exercise 17.7

Identify the base and derived class constructors and destructors for the chosen class hierarchy of Exercise 17.2 at the end of Section 17.1.

Exercise 17.8

Reimplement the OrQuery class to derive it from an abstract UnaryQuery class.

Exercise 17.9

What is wrong with the following class definition?

```
class Object {
public:
   virtual ~Object();
   virtual string isA();
protected:
   string _isA;
private:
   Object( string s ) : _isA( s ){}
};
```

Exercise 17.10

Given the following base class definition,

```
class ConcreteBase {
public:
   explicit ConcreteBase( int );
   virtual ostream& print( ostream& );
   virtual ~Base();

   static int object_count();
protected:
   int _id;
   static int _object_count;
};
```

What is wrong with the following?

```
(a) class C1 : public ConcreteBase {
    public:
      C1( int val )
        : _id( _object_count++ ){}
      // ...
    };
```

```
(b) class C2 : public C1 {
    public:
      C2( int val )
        : ConcreteBase( val ), C1( val ){}
      // ...
    };
```

```
(c) class C3 : public C2 {
    public:
      C3( int val )
        : C2( val ), _object_count( val ){}
      // ...
    };
```

```
(d) class C4 : public ConcreteBase {
    public:
```

```
            C4( int val )
              : ConcreteBase( _id+val ){}
            // ...
      };
```

Exercise 17.11

In the original definition of C++, the order of initialization within the member initialization list determined the order of constructor invocation. This was changed to the current language rule back around 1986. Why do you think the original language rule was changed?

17.5   Base and Derived Class Virtual Functions

By default, the member functions of a class are nonvirtual. When a member function is nonvirtual, the function invoked is the one defined in the static type of the class object (or pointer or reference) through which it is invoked. For example:

```
void Query::display( Query *pb )
{
    set<short> *ps = pb->solutions();
    // ...
    display();
}
```

The static type of pb is Query*. The function invoked for the nonvirtual solutions() is the Query member function. The nonvirtual function display() is invoked through the implicit this pointer. The static type of the this pointer is also Query*. The function invoked is the Query member function.

To declare a function virtual, we simply specify the keyword virtual:

```
class Query {
public:
    virtual ostream& print( ostream& = cout ) const;
    // ...
};
```

When a member function is virtual, the function invoked is the one defined in the dynamic type of the class object (or pointer or reference) through which it is invoked. As it happens, however, the static and dynamic type of a class object is the same. The virtual function mechanism works only as we expect when used with pointers and references.

Polymorphism, that is, is enabled only when a derived class subtype is addressed indirectly through either a base class reference or pointer. The use of a base class object does not preserve the type-identity of the derived class. For example, consider the following code fragment:

```
NameQuery nq( "lilacs" );

// ok: but nq 'sliced' to Query subobject
Query qobject = nq;
```

The inititialization of qobject with nq is perfectly legal: qobject is now equal to the Query base class subobject of nq. qobject, however, is not a NameQuery object. The NameQuery portion of nq is literally *sliced off* prior to the initialization of qobject. The NameQuery class portion doesn't fit into the memory directly allocated to hold the Query object. One of the ironies of object-oriented programming in C++ is that we must use pointers and references but not objects to support it. For example, in the following code fragment,

```
void print( Query object,
            const Query *pointer,
            const Query &reference )
{
    // cannot determine until run-time the
    // actual instance of print() invoked
    pointer->print();
    reference.print();

    // always invokes Query::print()
    object.print();
}

int main()
{
    NameQuery firebird( "firebird" );
    print( firebird, &firebird, firebird );
}
```

the two invocations through pointer and reference are resolved to their dynamic type. In this example, they both invoke NameQuery::print(). The invocation through object always invokes Query::print(). (We'll see a program code example of the effect of slicing in Section 18.6.2.)

In the following subsections, we illustrate the definition and use of virtual functions by walking through the implementation of a variety of instances. Each virtual member function illustrates a different aspect of object-oriented design.

17.5.1   Virtual Input/Output

The first virtual operation we'd like to provide is that of printing a query either to standard output or to a file:

```
ostream& print( ostream &os = cout ) const;
```

We must declare print() to be virtual because each implementation is type dependent, but must be able to be invoked through a Query* pointer. For example, for AndQuery, print() might look as follows:

```
ostream&
AndQuery::print( ostream &os ) const
{
    _lop->print( os );
    os << " && ";
    _rop->print( os );
}
```

We must declare print() to be a virtual function of the Query abstract base class. Otherwise, we cannot invoke print() through the Query* operand data members of the AndQuery, OrQuery, and NotQuery classes. But there is no meaningful implementation of print() for the Query base class. For the moment, we'll simply define it as a null function. (Later, we'll redefine it as a pure virtual function.)

```
class Query {
public:
    virtual ostream& print( ostream &os=cout ) const {}
    // ...
};
```

The base class first introducing a virtual function must specify the virtual keyword within the class declaration. If the definition is placed outside the class, the keyword virtual must not again be specified. For example, the following definition of print() results in a compile-time error:

```
// error: the keyword virtual can only appear
//         within the class definition
virtual ostream& Query::print( ostream& ) const { ... }
```

The correct definition must not include the keyword virtual.

The class introducing the virtual function must either define it or declare it as a pure virtual function (again, for the moment, we are defining it as a null function.) The derived class may either provide its own instance, which then becomes the active instance of that function for the derived class, or else it may inherit the active base class instance. The derived class instance, if defined, is said to *override* the inherited base class instance.

Before we walk through the four derived class implementations, we first need to consider the presence of parentheses within a query. For example, given the query

```
fiery && bird || shyly
```

the user is searching for any occurrence of the word pair

```
fiery bird
```

or of the single adverb

```
shyly
```

On the other hand, the query

```
fiery && ( bird || hair )
```

searches for any sequence of either the word pair

```
fiery bird
```

or

```
fiery hair
```

If our implementations of the print() instances do not reproduce the original parentheses, they'll be of small value to the user. To keep track of the necessary left and right parentheses to generate, we retrofit a pair of nonstatic data members into our abstract Query base class together with their supporting access functions (this kind of member retrofitting is a normal part of evolving a class hierarchy):

```
class Query {
public:
    // ...

    // set _lparen and _rparen
    void lparen( short lp ) { _lparen = lp; }
    void rparen( short rp ) { _rparen = rp; }

    // get the value of _lparen and _rparen
    short lparen() { return _lparen; }
    short rparen() { return _rparen; }

    // print the left and right parens
    void print_lparen( short cnt, ostream& os ) const;
    void print_rparen( short cnt, ostream& os ) const;

protected:

    // hold count of left and right parentheses
    short _lparen;
    short _rparen;
    // ...
};
```

_lparen represents the number of left parentheses a particular object should print; _rparen represents the number of right parentheses. (In Section 17.7, we'll see how these numbers are calculated and how the two members are assigned.) Here is an example of processing a highly "parenthesized" query:

```
==> ( untamed || ( fiery || ( shyly ) ) )
evaluate word: untamed
_lparen: 1
_rparen: 0
```

```
evaluate Or
_lparen: 0
_rparen: 0

evaluate word: fiery
_lparen: 1
_rparen: 0

evaluate Or
_lparen: 0
_rparen: 0

evaluate word: shyly
_lparen: 1
_rparen: 0

evaluate right parens:
_rparen: 3

( untamed ( 1 ) lines match
( fiery ( 1 ) lines match
( shyly ( 1 ) lines match
( fiery || ( shyly ( 2 ) lines match3
( untamed || ( fiery || ( shyly ))) ( 3 ) lines match

Requested query: ( untamed || ( fiery || ( shyly )))
( 3 ) like a fiery bird in flight. A beautiful fiery bird, he tells her,
( 4 ) magical but untamed. "Daddy, shush, there is no such thing,"
( 6 ) Shyly, she asks, "I mean, Daddy, is there?"
```

Here is our NameQuery implementation:

```
ostream&
NameQuery::
print( ostream &os ) const
{
    if ( _lparen )
        print_lparen( _lparen, os );

    os << _name;

    if ( _rparen )
        print_rparen( _rparen, os );

    return os;
}
```

---

3. Oops. The right parentheses are not recognized until after the OrQuery displays its partial solution.

Here is its declaration:

```
class NameQuery : public Query {
public:
        virtual ostream& print( ostream &os ) const;
        // ...
};
```

In order for a derived class instance of a virtual function to override the instance active in its base class, its prototype must match that of the base class exactly. For example, if we left off the const, or declared a second parameter, the NameQuery instance would not override the active base class instance. The return value must also be the same, with one exception: The return value of the derived instance can be a publicly derived class type of the type of the return value of the base instance. For example, if the base instance returned a Query*, the derived instance can return a NameQuery*. (We'll look at an example of why we might do this when we implement our clone() function.) Here is our NotQuery declaration and implementation of print():

```
class NotQuery : public Query {
public:
        virtual ostream& print( ostream &os ) const;
        // ...
};

ostream&
NotQuery::
print( ostream &os ) const
{
        os << " ! ";
        if ( _lparen )
            print_lparen( _lparen, os );

        _op->print( os );

        if ( _rparen )
            print_rparen( _rparen, os );
        return os;
}
```

The invocation of print() through _op is, of course, a virtual invocation.

The AndQuery and OrQuery declarations and implementations are essentially a duplicate of one another. We only show that of AndQuery:

```
class AndQuery : public Query {
public:
        virtual ostream& print( ostream &os ) const;
        // ...
};
```

```
ostream&
AndQuery::
print( ostream &os ) const
{
        if ( _lparen )
            print_lparen( _lparen, os );

        _lop->print( os );
        os << " && ";
        _rop->print( os );

        if ( _rparen )
                print_rparen( _rparen, os );

        return os;
}
```

This implementation of our virtual `print()` function allows us to output any Query subtype to an ostream or any stream derived from ostream. For example:

```
cout << "The query request is ";
Query *pq = retrieveQuery();
pq->print( cout );
```

Although this facility is useful, it is insufficient. In addition, we wish to be able to output any current or future class type derived from Query using the iostream output operator. For example:

```
Query *pq = retrieveQuery();
cout << "The query request "
     << *pq
     << " generated the following results:\n";
```

We cannot provide a virtual output operator directly since the output operators are already members of the ostream class. Instead, we must provide an indirect virtual function as follows:

```
inline ostream&
operator<<( ostream &os, const Query &q )
{
        // virtual invocation of print()
        return q.print( os );
}
```

When we write

```
AndQuery query;
// set query ...
cout << query << endl;
```

our ostream operator is invoked, in turn invoking

```
q.print( os )
```

with q bound to the AndQuery class object query and os bound to cout. If instead
we wrote

```
NameQuery query2( "Salinger" );
cout << query2 << endl;
```

the NameQuery instance of print() is invoked. The call

```
Query *pquery = retrieveQuery();
cout << *pquery << endl;
```

invokes the instance of print() associated with the object pquery addresses at that
point in the execution of our program.

17.5.2 Pure Virtual Functions

Our primary coding task to support a user query is the actual implementation of the
type-specific operations associated with each query operator. To implement this we
defined the four concrete class types: AndQuery, OrQuery, and so on. Our primary
design task, however, is to encapsulate the handling of each concrete query behind a
type-independent interface. This allows us to provide the kernel of our application in
code unaffected by the addition or removal of particular types.

To implement this, we defined our abstract Query class type. We do not program
the types of queries a user may specify, but the abstract actions that we apply to all
query types. For example:

```
void doit_and_bedone( vector< Query* > *pvec )
{
    vector<Query*>::iterator
        it = pvec->begin(),
        end_it = pvec->end();

    for ( ; it != end_it; ++it )
    {
        Query *pq = *it;
        cout << "processing " << *pq << endl;
        pq->eval();
        pq->display();
        delete pq;
    }
}
```

In theory, this supports the unlimited addition of future query types without having either to change or recompile our system kernel — provided, that is, our abstract
Query base class public interface is sufficient to support each new query type.

Our intention in providing the public interface of our Query class is to define a set
of operations sufficient to support all current and future query types. In practice, that's

a pretty tall order, and not one we can guarantee for all possible future types of query operations. Providing a common interface for those types about which we already know, on the other hand, is certainly do-able. Any claim that does beyond that is best viewed with some skepticism.

Because Query is an abstract class that does not actually occur in our application, there is no meaningful implementation we can provide for its virtual functions. They serve merely as placeholders to be overridden by subsequently derived subtypes. They are not intended ever to be invoked directly themselves.

The language provides us with a syntactic construct by which to signify that a virtual function is providing an interface for subsequent subtypes to override but must not itself be invoked through the virtual mechanism: a *pure virtual function*. A pure virtual function is declared as follows,

```
class Query {
public:
    // declares a pure virtual function
    virtual ostream& print( ostream&=cout ) const = 0;
    // ...
};
```

where the declaration of the function is followed by the assignment of 0.

A class containing (or inheriting) one or more pure virtual functions is recognized as an abstract base class by the compiler. An attempt to create an independent class object of an abstract base class results in a compile-time error. (Similarly, it is an error to invoke a pure virtual function through the virtual mechanism.) For example:

```
// Query declares one or more pure virtual functions
// The programmer, therefore, may not create
// independent Query class objects

// ok: Query subobject within NameQuery
Query *pq = new NameQuery( "Nostromo" );

// error: new expression allocates Query object
Query *pq2 = new Query;
```

An abstract base class can only occur as a subobject in subsequently derived classes. These are exactly the semantics we desire for the Query base class.

17.5.3   Static Invocation of a Virtual Function

When we invoke a virtual function using the class scope operator, we override the virtual mechanism, causing the virtual function to be resolved statically at compile-time. For example, presuming that we have defined an isA() virtual function for each of the base and derived classes of the Query hierarchy,

```
Query *pquery = new NameQuery( "dumbo" );

// invokes isA() dynamically through virtual mechanism
// the NameQuery::isA() instance is invoked
pquery->isA();

// invokes isA statically at compile-time
// the Query::isA instance is invoked
pquery->Query::isA();
```

the explicit invocation of `Query::isA()` is resolved at compile-time to the base class Query instance even though `pquery` happens to address a NameQuery object.

Why might we wish to override the virtual mechanism? Often, for efficiency. Within a derived class virtual function, it is sometimes necessary to invoke a base class instance to complete an operation that has been factored across the base and derived instances. A Camera virtual `display()` function, for example, is likely to display the information common to all Cameras. A PerspectiveCamera instance of the `display()` function displays the information unique to PerspectiveCamera. Rather than duplicate the Camera operations within PerspectiveCamera's implementation of `display()`, we invoke the Camera instance. We know exactly the instance we wish to invoke, so there is no need to go through the virtual mechanism if we can override it. Moreover, if Camera's instance is declared as `inline`, its compile-time invocation results in an inline expansion.

Here is another illustration of when we might wish to override the virtual mechanism. It also shows us another aspect of pure virtual functions, one that programmers new to C++ often find counterintuitive.

The AndQuery and OrQuery instances of `print()` are the same except for the literal string representing the operator. Rather than providing two instances, let's implement a single instance the two can share. To accomplish this, we'll again define an abstract BinaryQuery base class from which AndQuery and OrQuery are derived. BinaryQuery defines the two operands plus an additional string data member to hold the value of the operator. Because it is an abstract class, we declare `print()` to be a pure virtual function.

```
class BinaryQuery : public Query {
public:
        BinaryQuery( Query *lop, Query *rop, string oper )
                    : _lop(lop), _rop(rop), _oper(oper){}

        ~BinaryQuery() { delete _lop; delete _rop; }
        ostream &print( ostream& =cout ) const = 0;

protected:
        Query *_lop;
        Query *_rop;
        string _oper;
};
```

Here is our single BinaryQuery instance of print() to be invoked by both the AndQuery and OrQuery derived classes:

```
inline ostream&
BinaryQuery::
print( ostream &os ) const
{
        if ( _lparen )
            print_lparen( _lparen, os );

        _lop->print( os );
        os << ' ' << _oper << ' ';
        _rop->print( os );

        if ( _rparen )
            print_rparen( _rparen, os );

        return os;
}
```

Hmm. We seem to have backed ourselves into a paradox. On the one hand we feel it is necessary to declare this instance of print() as a pure virtual function to announce BinaryQuery as an abstract base class to the compiler. We're now guaranteed that independent objects of the BinaryQuery class cannot be defined within our application.

On the other hand it is necessary for us both to define the BinaryQuery virtual print() instance and to invoke it through objects of the AndQuery and OrQuery classes.

As is usual with an apparent paradox, we are missing information: A pure virtual function, although it may not be invoked through the virtual mechanism, can be invoked statically. For example:

```
inline ostream&
AndQuery::
print( ostream &os ) const
{
        // ok: suppress virtual mechanism
        // invoke BinaryQuery::print statically
        BinaryQuery::print( os );
}
```

17.5.4   Virtual Functions and Default Arguments

Consider the following simple class hierarchy:

```
#include <iostream>

class base {
public:
        virtual int foo( int ival = 1024 ) {
            cout << "base::foo() -- ival: " << ival << endl;
```

```
        return ival;
    }

    // ...
};

class derived : public base {
public:
    virtual int foo( int ival = 2048 ) {
        cout << "derived::foo() -- ival: " << ival << endl;
        return ival;
    }

    // ...
};
```

The intention of the class designer is that the base class instance of foo(), if invoked without an argument, should be passed a default argument of 1024. For example:

```
base b;
base *pb = &b;

// base::foo( int ) is invoked
// intention is that it should return 1024
pb->foo();
```

Similarly, the intention of the programmer is that the derived class instance of foo(), if invoked without an argument, should be passed a default argument of 2048. For example:

```
derived d;
base *pb = &d;

// derived::foo( int ) is invoked --
// intention is that it should return 2048
pb->foo();
```

As it happens, this is not the semantic behavior of the C++ virtual mechanism. For example, here is a small program exercising our class hierarchy:

```
int main()
{
    derived *pd = new derived;
    base *pb = pd;

    int val = pb->foo();
    cout << "main() : val through base: "
         << val << endl;

    val = pd->foo();
```

```
        cout << "main() : val through derived: "
             << val << endl;
}
```

When compiled and executed, the program generates the following output:

```
derived::foo() -- ival: 1024
main() : val through base: 1024
derived::foo() -- ival: 2048
main() : val through derived: 2048
```

In both invocations, the derived class instance of foo() is invoked correctly. This is because the actual instance of foo() invoked is determined at run-time based on the actual class type addressed by both pd and pb. The default argument to be passed to foo(), however, is not determined at run-time; rather, it is determined at compile-time and is based on the type of the object through which the function is being invoked. When foo() is invoked through pb, the default argument is determined by the declaration of base::foo(), which is 1024. When foo() is invoked through pd, the default argument is determined by the declaration of derived::foo(), which is 2048.

If a derived class instance, when invoked through a base class pointer or reference, is passed the default argument specified by the base class, then why specify a default argument in a derived class instance?

We may wish to have a different default argument based not on the specific subtype implementation of foo() that is invoked, but rather on the type of the pointer or reference through which the function is invoked. For example, the values 1024 and 2048 may represent image sizes. If we wish to produce a less detailed image, we invoke foo() through base. If we wish a finer resolution, we invoke foo() through derived.

But what if we really wish for the actual default argument passed to foo() to be based on the actual instance of the function invoked? Unfortunately, the virtual mechanism does not support this directly. One programming solution is to specify a default argument that can be recognized as indicating that no value has been passed by the user. The intended default argument is instead declared local to the function and is used if no explicit value is passed in. For example:

```
void
base::
foo( int ival = base_default_value )
{
   int real_default_value = 1024;

   if ( ival == base_default_value )
        ival =   real_defar lt_value;

   // ...
}
```

where `base_default_value` is an agreed-upon value for the entire hierarchy that, if present, indicates the user has not provided an explicit value. The derived class instance is implemented in a similar manner:

```
void
derived::
foo( int ival = base_default_value )
{
    int real_default_value = 2048;

    if ( ival == base_default_value )
        ival =  real_default_value;

    // ...
}
```

17.5.5   Virtual Destructors

In the following function we apply the `delete` expression as follows:

```
void doit_and_bedone ( vector< Query* > *pvec )
{
    // ...
    for ( ; it != end_it; ++it )
    {
        Query *pq = *it;
        // ...
        delete pq;
    }
}
```

In order for the function to execute correctly, the destructor of the dynamic type addressed by pq must be invoked when the `delete` expression is applied. In order for that to happen we must declare the Query class destructor as virtual:

```
class Query {
public:
    virtual ~Query() { delete _solution; }
    // ...
};
```

The destructor of each subsequently derived class is now treated automatically as virtual. `doit_and_bedone()` executes correctly.

The behavior of the destructor under inheritance is as follows: The destructor of the derived class is invoked first. In the case of pq, it is a virtual function call. On completion, the destructor of the immediate base class is invoked statically — inline expanded if declared as such. For example, if pq addresses an AndQuery object,

```
delete pq;
```

invokes the AndQuery destructor through the virtual mechanism. That done, the BinaryQuery destructor is invoked statically. Following that, the Query destructor is also statically invoked.

Given the following class hierarchy

```
class Query {
public: // ...
protected:
    virtual ~Query();
    // ...
};

class NotQuery : public Query {
public:
    ~NotQuery();
    // ...
};
```

the access level of the NotQuery destructor is public when invoked through a NotQuery object, but is protected when invoked through a Query pointer or reference. That is, the virtual function assumes the access level of the class type through which it is being invoked. Thus:

```
int main()
{
    Query *pq = new NotQuery;

    // illegal: destructor is protected
    delete pq;
}
```

As a general rule of thumb, we recommend that the root base class of a class hierarchy declaring one or more virtual functions declare its destructor virtual as well. However, unlike the base class constructor, the base class destructor, in general, should not be made protected.

17.5.6   The eval() Virtual Function

The heart of the query class hierarchy is the eval() virtual function (and yet it is actually the least interesting in terms of language features). Once again, there is no meaningful implementation for the abstract Query class, and so we declare it as a pure virtual instance:

```
class Query {
public:
    virtual void eval() = 0;
    // ...
};
```

The actual evaluation of a name occurs during the building of the word location map. If the word is present in the text, its location vector is present in the map. In our implementation, the location vector, if present, is passed to the NameQuery constructor along with the name of the word. There is nothing for the NameQuery eval() instance to do.

However, we cannot allow it to inherit the pure virtual instance declared with Query. Why? NameQuery is a concrete class representing actual objects in our application domain. Were it to inherit the pure virtual function of Query, NameQuery would be an abstract class and we would be prohibited from creating the NameQuery class object. Instead, we simply define eval() to be a null function:

```
class NameQuery : public Query {
public:
    virtual void eval() {}
    // ...
};
```

NotQuery finds each line of the text within which the operand is not found. All line and column pairs of these lines are entered into the NotQuery instance of _loc. Here is our implementation:

```
void NotQuery::eval()
{
    // make sure the operand is evaluated
    _op->eval();

    // _all_locs is a vector of all text location pairs
    // it is a static member of NotQuery:
    // static const vector<location>* _all_locs
    vector< location >::const_iterator
            iter = _all_locs->begin(),
            iter_end = _all_locs->end();

    // get the set of lines in which the operand occurs
    set<short> *ps = _vec2set( _op->locations() );

    // for each line the operand is not found
    // copy all the location pairs into _loc
    for ( ; iter != iter_end; ++iter )
    {
            if ( ! ps->count( (*iter).first ))
            _loc.push_back( *iter );
    }
}
```

Here is a trace of an evaluation of a Not query. The operand appears in lines 0, 3, and 5 of the text. (Internally, recall, we index the text within a string vector, and so begin our counting with zero; when we display the line numbers to the user, we begin our counting with one.) The NotQuery evaluation, therefore, creates a location vector in which all the line and column pairs of lines 1, 2, and 4 are entered. (We've edited the location vector to minimize the display.)

```
==> ! daddy
daddy ( 3 ) lines match
display_location vector:
        first: 0           second: 8
        first: 3           second: 3
        first: 5           second: 5
! daddy ( 3 ) lines match
display_location vector:
        first: 1           second: 0
        first: 1           second: 1
        first: 1           second: 2
        ...
        first: 1           second: 10
        first: 2           second: 0
        first: 2           second: 1
        ...
        first: 2           second: 12
        first: 4           second: 0
        first: 4           second: 1
        ...
        first: 4           second: 12
```

```
Requested query:  ! daddy
( 2 ) when the wind blows through her hair, it looks almost alive,
( 3 ) like a fiery bird in flight. A beautiful fiery bird, he tells her,
( 5 ) she tells him, at the same time wanting him to tell her more.
```

OrQuery merges the location vector of its two operands. It makes use of the generic merge() algorithm. In order for merge() to be able to order the line and column pairs, we define a function object to determine which of two line and column pairs is less than another. Here is our implementation:

```cpp
class less_than_pair {
public:
    bool operator()( location loc1, location loc2 )
    {
        return (( loc1.first < loc2.first ) ||
                ( loc1.first == loc2.first ) &&
                ( loc1.second < loc2.second ));
    }
};

void OrQuery::eval()
{
    // evaluate the left and right operands
    _lop->eval();
```

```
        _rop->eval();

        // prepare to merge the two location vectors
        vector< location, allocator >::const_iterator
                riter = _rop->locations()->begin(),
                liter = _lop->locations()->begin(),
                riter_end = _rop->locations()->end(),
                liter_end = _lop->locations()->end();

        merge( liter, liter_end, riter, riter_end,
                inserter( _loc, _loc.begin() ),
                less_than_pair() );
}
```

Here is a trace of an evaluation of an Or query in which we display the location vector of each of the OrQuery operands, and of the resulting merge(). (Again, recall that the line numbers displayed to the user begin at one, whereas internally they begin at zero.)

```
==> fiery || untamed
fiery ( 1 ) lines match
display_location vector:
        first: 2          second: 2
        first: 2          second: 8

untamed ( 1 ) lines match
display_location vector:
        first: 3          second: 2

fiery || untamed ( 2 ) lines match
display_location vector:
        first: 2          second: 2
        first: 2          second: 8
        first: 3          second: 2

Requested query: fiery || untamed
( 3 ) like a fiery bird in flight. A beautiful fiery bird, he tells her,
( 4 ) magical but untamed. "Daddy, shush, there is no such thing,"
```

The AndQuery implementation iterates across the location vector of its two operands looking for adjacent words. Each pair it finds is inserted in _loc. The primary work of its implementation is keeping the locations of its two operands in sync so that we can compare them for adjacency.

```
void AndQuery::eval()
{
        // evaluate the left and right operands
        _lop->eval();
        _rop->eval();
```

```
// grab the iterators
vector< location, allocator >::const_iterator
        riter = _rop->locations()->begin(),
        liter = _lop->locations()->begin(),
        riter_end = _rop->locations()->end(),
        liter_end = _lop->locations()->end();


 // loop through while both have elements to compare
while ( liter != liter_end && riter != riter_end )
{
    // while left line number is greater than right
    while ( (*liter).first > (*riter).first ) {
        ++riter;
        if ( riter == riter_end ) return;
    }

    // while left line number is less than right
    while ( (*liter).first < (*riter).first )
    {
        // if match is found with the last word on
        // one line and the first word of the next …
        // _max_col: identifies last word on line

        if ( (*liter).first == (*riter).first-1 &&
             (*riter).second == 0 &&
             (*liter).second == (*_max_col)[ (*liter).first ] )
        {
            _loc.push_back( *liter );
            _loc.push_back( *riter );
            ++riter;
            if ( riter == riter_end ) return;
        }

        ++liter;
        if ( liter == liter_end ) return;
    }

    // while both are on the same line
    while ( (*liter).first == (*riter).first )
    {
        if ( (*liter).second+1 == ((*riter).second) )
        { // ok: an adjacent match
          _loc.push_back( *liter ); ++liter;
          _loc.push_back( *riter ); ++riter;
        }
        else
        if ( (*liter).second <= (*riter).second )
          ++liter;
```

```
            else ++riter;

            if ( liter == liter_end || riter == riter_end )
                return;
        }
    }
}
```

Here is a trace of an evaluation of an And query in which we display the location vector of each of the AndQuery operands, and of the location vector of the final evaluation. (Again, recall that the line numbers displayed to the user begin at one, whereas internally they begin at zero.)

```
==> fiery && bird
fiery ( 1 ) lines match
display_location vector:
        first: 2            second: 2
        first: 2            second: 8
bird ( 1 ) lines match
display_location vector:
        first: 2            second: 3
        first: 2            second: 9
fiery && bird ( 1 ) lines match
display_location vector:
        first: 2            second: 2
        first: 2            second: 3
        first: 2            second: 8
        first: 2            second: 9

Requested query: fiery && bird
( 3 ) like a fiery bird in flight. A beautiful fiery bird, he tells her,
```

Finally, here is a trace of an evaluation of a compound And-Or query. The location vector of each intermediate result is displayed, as well as the location vector of the displayed result.

```
==> fiery && ( bird || untamed )
fiery ( 1 ) lines match
display_location vector:
        first: 2            second: 2
        first: 2            second: 8
bird ( 1 ) lines match
display_location vector:
        first: 2            second: 3
        first: 2            second: 9
untamed ( 1 ) lines match
display_location vector:
        first: 3            second: 2
( bird || untamed ) ( 2 ) lines match
display_location vector:
```

```
            first: 2          second: 3
            first: 2          second: 9
            first: 3          second: 2
fiery &&  ( bird || untamed )  ( 1 ) lines match
display_location vector:
            first: 2          second: 2
            first: 2          second: 3
            first: 2          second: 8
            first: 2          second: 9
```

```
Requested query: fiery &&  ( bird || untamed )
( 3 ) like a fiery bird in flight. A beautiful fiery bird, he tells her,
```

17.5.7   Virtually a Virtual new Operator

Given a pointer to one of the concrete query subtypes, it is trivial to allocate a duplicate object on the heap. For example:

```
NotQuery *pnq;
// set pnq ...

// the new expression invokes the
// NotQuery copy constructor ...
NotQuery *pnq2 = new NotQuery( *pnq );
```

If we are given a pointer to the abstract Query class, however, allocating a duplicate object is considerably less trivial. For example:

```
const Query *pq = pnq->op();
// how do we duplicate pq?
```

If we were able to declare a virtual instance of operator new, the problem would be solved. The correct instance of the new operator would be invoked automatically. Unfortunately, the new operator cannot be made virtual because it is a static member function applied to raw memory prior to the construction of the class object (see Section 15.8 for a discussion).

Although we cannot make the new operator virtual, we can provide a surrogate new operator to allocate and copy our objects onto the free store. This surrogate is generally named clone():

```
class Query {
public:
   virtual Query *clone() = 0;
   // ...
};
```

Here is one possible implementation of our NameQuery instance:

```
class NameQuery : public Query {
public:
   virtual Query *clone()
      // invokes the NameQuery copy constructor
      { return new NameQuery( *this ); }

   // ...
};
```

This works exactly right when the target pointer type is that of a Query*, such as the following:

```
Query *pq = new NameQuery( "Valery" );
Query *pq2 = pq->clone();
```

It works somewhat less well when the target pointer type is an actual NameQuery*. In this case we are required to provide a downcast of the returned Query* pointer back to that of a NameQuery*:

```
NameQuery *pnq = new NameQuery( "Rilke" );
NameQuery *pnq2 =
   static_cast<NameQuery*>( pnq->clone() );
```

(The reason the downcast is necessary is explained in Section 19.1.1)

Earlier we said there is one exception to the requirement that the return type of the derived class must match exactly that of the base class instance. The exception is to support this very case. If the base instance of a virtual function returns a class type (or a pointer or a reference to a class type), the derived instance may return a class publicly derived from the class returned by the base class instance (or a pointer or a reference to a class type).

```
class NameQuery : public Query {
public:
   virtual NameQuery *clone()
      { return new NameQuery( *this ); }

   // ...
};
```

Now, the initialization of both pq2 and pnq2 can be achieved without the need of an explicit cast:

```
// Query *pq = new NameQuery( "Broch" );
Query *pq2 = pq->clone(); // ok

// NameQuery *pnq = new NameQuery( "Rilke" );
NameQuery *pnq2 = pnq->clone(); // ok
```

Here is the NotQuery clone implementation:

```
class NotQuery : public Query {
public:
    virtual NotQuery *clone()
        { return new NotQuery( *this ); }

    // ...
};
```

The AndQuery and OrQuery instances are implemented in a similar manner. In order for these implementations of clone() to succeed, we must provide explicit NotQuery, AndQuery, and OrQuery copy constructor instances. We'll do just that in Section 17.6.

17.5.8   Virtual Functions, Constructors, and Destructors

As we saw in Section 17.4, the order of constructor invocations within a derived class object is to first invoke the base class constructor, then that of the derived class. For example, when we define a NameQuery class object, such as

```
NameQuery poet( "Orlen" );
```

the order of constructor invocation is first Query, then NameQuery.

While the Query base class constructor is executing, the NameQuery portion of poet is uninitialized. In effect, the poet is not yet a NameQuery; only its Query subobject has been constructed.

What should happen if within the base class constructor, a virtual function is invoked for which both a base and a derived class instance is defined? Which would be invoked? If it were possible for the derived class instance of the virtual function to be invoked, and should it access any of the derived class members, the result of the invocation is formally undefined. Informally, the program is likely to crash.

To prevent this, the virtual instance that is invoked within the base class constructor is always the virtual instance that is active within the base class. In effect, inside a base class constructor, the derived class object is an object of the base type.

The same holds true inside the base class destructor for the derived class object: The derived class portion is also undefined, but this time it is not because it has not been constructed, but because it has already been destroyed.

Exercise 17.12

Within the NameQuery object, the most straightforward internal representation of the location vector is a pointer initialized with the pointer stored within the text location map. This is also the most efficient because we'd be copying a single address rather than each location pair within the vector. The AndQuery, OrQuery, and NotQuery classes must construct their location vectors based on the evaluation of their operands. When the lifetime of one of these class objects ends, the associated location vector must be deleted. When the lifetime of a NameQuery object ends, the location vector must *not* be deleted. How might we store the location vector as a pointer within the Query base class, delete the instances associated with the AndQuery, OrQuery, and NotQuery class objects but not that of the NameQuery class objects? (Note that we are not permitted to add a flag to the Query class indicating whether or not to delete the pointer to the location vector!)

Exercise 17.13

What is wrong with the following class definition?

```
class AbstractObject {
public:
   ~AbstractObject();
   virtual void doit() = 0;
   // ...
};
```

Exercise 17.14

Why is it that, given

```
NameQuery nq( "Sneezy" );
Query q( nq );
Query *pq = &nq;
```

the invocation

```
pq->eval();
```

invokes the NameQuery instance of eval(), whereas

```
q.eval();
```

invokes the Query instance?

Exercise 17.15

Which virtual function redeclarations of the Derived class are in error?

```
(a) Base* Base::copy( Base* );
    Base* Derived::copy( Derived* );

(b) Base* Base::copy( Base* );
    Derived* Derived::copy( Base* );

(c) ostream& Base::print( int, ostream&=cout );
    ostream& Derived::print( int, ostream& );

(d) void Base::eval() const;
    void Derived::eval();
```

Exercise 17.16

In practice, our programs are unlikely to run correctly the first time we exercise them and the first time we exercise them against real data. It is often useful to incorporate a debugging strategy into the design of our classes. Implement a debug() virtual function for our Query class hierarchy that displays the data members of the respective classes. Support a level of detail control as (a) an argument to the debug() function and (b) as a class data member. (The latter allows individual class objects to turn on or turn off the display of debugging information.)

Exercise 17.17

What are likely errors in the following inheritance hierarchy?

```
class Object {
public:
   virtual void doit() = 0;
   // ...
protected:
   virtual ~Object();
};

class MyObject : public Object {
public:
   MyObject( string isA );
   string isA() const;
protected:
   string _isA;
};
```

17.6   Memberwise Initialization and Assignment ◆

One of our responsibilities in designing a class is to make sure the class behaves correctly and efficiently under memberwise initialization (introduced in Section 14.6) and memberwise assignment (introduced in Section 14.7). In this section we consider these operations under inheritance.

As of yet, we have not provided any explicit handling of memberwise initialization. Let's walk through what happens by default with our Query class hierarchy.

The abstract Query base class defines three nonstatic data members:

```
class Query {
public: // ...
protected:
   int _paren;
   set<short> *_solution;
   vector<location> _loc;
```

```
      // ...
   };
```

_solution, if set, addresses a set allocated on the free store by the _vec2set() member function. The Query destructor applies the delete expression to _solution.

The Query class needs to provide both an explicit copy constructor and explicit copy assignment operator. (If this is not apparent to you, please review Section 14.6). Before we provide these, however, let's first step through default memberwise copy in their absence.

The NameQuery derived class contains a string member class object and a Query base class subobject. Given the following NameQuery object, folk,

```
      NameQuery folk( "folk" );
```

the initialization of music with folk

```
      NameQuery music = folk;
```

causes the following steps to occur

1. The compiler checks to see if the NameQuery class defines an explicit instance of a copy constructor. It does not. Therefore, the compiler prepares to apply default memberwise initialization.

2. The compiler next checks to see if the NameQuery class contains any base class subobjects. Yes, it contains a Query base class subobject.

3. The compiler checks to see if the Query base class defines an explicit instance of a copy constructor. It does not. Therefore, the compiler prepares to apply default memberwise initialization.

4. The compiler checks to see if the Query class contains any base class subobjects. No, it does not.

5. The compiler examines each nonstatic member of the Query class in order of declaration. If the member is a nonclass object, such as _paren and _solution, it initializes the music object member with the value of folk's member. If the member is a class object, such as _loc, it applies step 1 recursively. Yes, the vector class defines an explicit instance of a copy constructor. The copy constructor is invoked to initialize music._loc with folk._loc.

6. The compiler next examines each nonstatic member of the NameQuery class in order of declaration. The string member class object is recognized as providing an explicit copy constructor. It is invoked to initialize music._name with folk._name.

The default initialization of music with folk is now complete. It is well behaved except for the default copy of _solution that, if permitted, is likely to cause our program to fail. We override the default handling by providing an explicit Query class copy constructor. One solution is to copy the entire solution set, such as the following:

```
Query::Query( const Query &rhs )
            : _loc( rhs._loc ), _paren(rhs._paren)
{
    if ( rhs._solution )
    {
        _solution = new set<short>;
        set<short>::iterator
                    it = rhs._solution->begin(),
                    end_it = rhs._solution->end();

        for ( ; it != end_it; ++it )
            _solution->insert( *it );
    }
    else _solution = 0;
}
```

However, because our implementation of the solution set is to have it calculated on demand, there is really no imperative to copy it now. The purpose of our copy constructor is to prevent its default copy. It's sufficient to initialize _solution to 0:

```
Query::Query( const Query &rhs )
            : _loc( rhs._loc ),
              _paren(rhs._paren), _solution( 0 )
{}
```

The initialization of music with folk follows the same steps 1 and 2. Step 3 now finds that Query defines an explicit copy constructor. The copy constructor is invoked. Steps 4 and 5 are no longer carried out. Step 6 is carried out as before.

Once again, the default memberwise initialization of music with folk is complete. It is well behaved. NameQuery has no need to provide an explicit copy constructor.

The NotQuery derived class contains a Query base class subobject and a Query* data member, _op, addressing its operand allocated on the free store. The NotQuery destructor applies the delete expression to the operand.

The NotQuery class cannot safely allow default memberwise initialization of its _op member, and so must provide an explicit copy constructor. Its implementation makes use of the virtual clone() function defined in the previous section.

```
inline NotQuery::
NotQuery( const NotQuery &rhs )
        // invokes Query::Query( const Query &rhs )
        : Query( rhs )
        { _op = rhs._op->clone(); }
```

The memberwise initialization of one NotQuery class object with another causes the following two steps to occur:

1. The compiler checks to see if the NotQuery class defines an explicit instance of the copy constructor. It does.

2. The NotQuery copy constructor is invoked to carry out the member-wise initialization.

That's it. It is the responsibility of the NotQuery copy constructor to carry out the correct initialization of both its base class subobject and nonstatic data members. The AndQuery and OrQuery instances are similar to NotQuery, and are left as an exercise for the reader.

Memberwise assignment is similar to memberwise initialization. If an explicit copy assignment operator is present, it is invoked to assign one class object with an-other. Otherwise, default memberwise assignment is applied.

If a base class is present, the base class subobject is memberwise assigned first. If the base class provides an explicit copy assignment operator, it is invoked. Otherwise, default memberwise assignment is applied recursively to the base classes and members of the base class subobject.

Each nonstatic data member is examined in turn in the order of declaration. If it is a nonclass type, the right-hand instance is copied to the left. If it is a class type and the class defines an explicit copy assignment operator, the operator is invoked. Otherwise, default memberwise assignment is applied recursively to the base classes and members of the member class object.

Here is our Query copy assignment operator. Once again, we don't need to copy the solution set at this point, but rather simply prevent its default copy:

```
Query&
Query::
operator=( const Query &rhs )
{
      // prevent self-assignment
      if ( &rhs != this )
      {
            _paren = rhs._paren;
            _loc = rhs._loc;
            delete _solution;
            _solution = 0;
      }

      return *this;
}
```

NameQuery does not require an explicit copy assignment operator. The assign-ment of one NameQuery object with another results in the following two steps:

1. The explicit Query copy assignment operator is invoked to assign the Query subobjects of the two NameQuery objects.

2. The explicit string copy assignment operator is invoked to assign the string
    member class objects of the two NameQuery objects.

We cannot do better with an explicit copy assignment operator for NameQuery.
The default memberwise assignment behavior is sufficient.

NotQuery, OrQuery, and AndQuery each require an explicit copy assignment operator to copy their respective operands safely. Here is the NotQuery instance:

```
inline NotQuery&
NotQuery::
operator=( const NotQuery &rhs )
{
    // prevent self-assignment
    if ( &rhs != this )
    {
        // invoke Query copy assignment operator
        this->Query::operator=( rhs );

        // copy the operand
        _op = rhs._op->clone();
    }

    return *this;
}
```

Unlike the copy constructor, there is no special portion of the copy assignment operator through which to invoke the base class copy assignment operator. There are two syntactic forms for invoking it: our explicit invocation illustrated earlier, and through an explicit cast as follows:

```
(*static_cast<Query*>(this)) = rhs;
```

The AndQuery and OrQuery copy assignment instances are similar and left as an exercise.

Here is a small test program to exercise our implementation — as a sanity check that it actually works. We simply create or copy an object, then print out its values.

```
#include "Query.h"

int
main()
{
    NameQuery nm( "alice" );
    NameQuery nm2( "emma" );

    NotQuery nq1( &nm );
    cout << "notQuery 1: " << nq1 << endl;

    NotQuery nq2( nq1 );
    cout << "notQuery 2: " << nq2 << endl;
```

```
        NotQuery nq3( &nm2 );
        cout << "notQuery 3: " << nq3 << endl;

        nq3 = nq2;
        cout << "notQuery 3 assigned nq2: " << nq3 << endl;

        AndQuery aq( &nq1, &nm2 );
        cout << "AndQuery : " << aq << endl;

        AndQuery aq2( aq );
        cout << "AndQuery 2: " << aq2 << endl;

        AndQuery aq3( &nm, &nm2 );
        cout << "AndQuery 3: " << aq3 << endl;

        aq2 = aq3;
        cout << "AndQuery 2 after assign: " << aq2 << endl;
    }
```

When compiled and executed, the program generates the following output:

```
notQuery 1:  ! alice
notQuery 2:  ! alice
notQuery 3:  ! emma
notQuery 3 assigned nq2:  ! alice
AndQuery :   ! alice && emma
AndQuery 2:  ! alice && emma
AndQuery 3: alice && emma
AndQuery 2 after assign: alice && emma
```

Exercise 17.18

Implement the AndQuery and OrQuery copy constructors.

Exercise 17.19

Implement the AndQuery and OrQuery copy assignment operators.

Exercise 17.20

What are the likely indications that a class requires an explicit instance of a copy constructor and copy assignment operator?

17.7 A UserQuery Manager Class

Given a query, such as

```
fiery && ( bird || potato )
```

our task is to build up the equivalent Query hierarchy:

```
AndQuery
    NameQuery( "fiery" )
    OrQuery
        NameQuery( "bird" )
        NameQuery( "potato" )
```

The question is, how can we best do this? The process of evaluating the query resembles a finite state machine. We begin with an empty state, and with each element of the query shift from one state to another until the entire query is evaluated. The heart of our implementation is a large switch statement within an operation we've named eval_query(). Each word of the query is read in turn from a string vector and is tested against each of the possible values the query might contain:

```
vector<string >::iterator
    it    = user_query->begin(),
    end_it = user_query->end();

for ( ; it != end_it; ++it )
    switch( evalQueryString( *it ))
    {
        case WORD:
            evalWord( *it );
            break;

        case AND:
            evalAnd();
            break;

        case OR:
            evalOr();
            break;

        case NOT:
            evalNot();
            break;

        case LPAREN:
            ++_paren;
            ++_lparenOn;
            break;

        case RPAREN:
            --_paren;
            ++_rparenOn
            evalRParen();
            break;
    }
```

The five eval operations (`evalWord()`, `evalAnd()`, `evalOr()`, `evalNot()`, and `evalR-Paren()`) do the actual building of the Query hierarchy. Before we look in detail at their implementation, let's first consider their organization.

One strategy is to define each as an individual function, as we did originally in Chapter 6 with our text query routines. The user query and derived Query subtypes represent independent data on which the functions operate. This represents a procedural programming model; one we choose not to pursue.

As we did in Section 6.14 in introducing a TextQuery class within which to encapsulate our Chapter 6 operations and data, we wish here to introduce a UserQuery class within which to encapsulate and manage these operations and data.

One data member is the string vector to contain the actual user query. A second data member is a pointer of type `Query*` to address the hierarchical representation of the query built up in `eval_query()`. Three additional members are defined to handle the processing of parentheses: `_paren`, to help us in altering the default precedence of operator evaluation (we'll give an example in a moment), and `_lparenOn` and `_rparenOn` to keep a count of the number and kind of parentheses associated with the current query node (we saw the use of these in Section 17.5.1 in the discussion of the virtual `print()` function).

In addition to these five members, we require two more. Consider the following query:

```
fiery || untamed
```

Our eventual goal is to represent this query as the following OrQuery object:

```
OrQuery
    NameQuery( "fiery" )
    NameQuery( "untamed" )
```

The order of processing the query, however, is somewhat problematic. First we define a NameQuery but we haven't as yet defined our OrQuery to which to add it. What we need is a place to store the NameQuery object momentarily for later retrieval.

The traditional data structure for "placing something somewhere for later retrieval" is a stack. We'll place our NameQuery object on a stack. When we next encounter the OrQuery operator, we'll retrieve our NameQuery object and pass it as the OrQuery's left operand.

That accomplished, what should we do with the OrQuery object? Our OrQuery object at this point is incomplete. It is missing its right operand. We need to put it aside until its right operand becomes available.

We can place it on the same stack as we place the NameQuery object. The OrQuery object, however, represents a different state of processing: It is an incomplete operator. Rather, we prefer to define two stacks: One stack to hold objects that are a complete operand of a compound query (This is where we place the NameQuery object and we name this stack the `_query_stack`.) and a second stack to hold incomplete operators with a missing right operand. We think of this stack as containing the current operation to complete, and so we name it _current_op. This is where we place the OrQuery object. When we define the second NameQuery object, we retrieve the OrQuery object from _current_op and add the NameQuery object as its second operand. The OrQuery object is now complete. We push it on _query_stack.

When processing of the user query is complete, if everything has gone well, _current_op is empty and _query_stack should contain one object. This object is the full representation of the user query. In our example, it is the OrQuery object.

To see how this works, let's walk through a few actual queries. Our first example is a simple NotQuery:

```
! daddy
```

The following is a trace of the actual processing of the query. The final object on _query_stack is the NotQuery object:

```
evalNot() : incomplete!
      push on _current_op (size == 1 )
evalWord() : daddy
      pop _current_op : NotQuery
      add operand: WordQuery : NotQuery complete!
      push NotQuery on _query stack
```

The indented text under the eval operation indicates the operation being performed. Our second example, a compound OrQuery, illustrates both conditions. It also illustrates pushing a complete operator onto _query_stack.

```
==> fiery || untamed || shyly

evalWord() : fiery
      push word on _query stack
evalOr() : incomplete!
      pop _query_stack : fiery
      add operand : WordQuery : OrQuery incomplete!
      push OrQuery on _current_op (size == 1 )
evalWord() : untamed
      pop _current_op : OrQuery
      add operand: WordQuery : OrQuery complete!
      push OrQuery on _query stack
evalOr() : incomplete!
      pop _query_stack : OrQuery
      add operand : OrQuery : OrQuery incomplete!
      push OrQuery on _current_op (size == 1 )
evalWord() : shyly
      pop _current_op : OrQuery
      add operand: WordQuery : OrQuery complete!
      push OrQuery on _query stack
```

Our last example illustrates both a compound query and the use of parentheses to alter the order of evaluation:

```
==> fiery && ( bird || untamed )

evalWord() : fiery
        push word on _query stack
evalAnd() : incomplete!
        pop _query_stack : fiery
        add operand : WordQuery : AndQuery incomplete!
        push AndQuery on _current_op (size == 1 )
evalWord() : bird
        _paren is set to 1
        push word on _query stack
evalOr() : incomplete!
        pop _query_stack : bird
        add operand : WordQuery : OrQuery incomplete!
        push OrQuery on _current_op (size == 2 )
evalWord() : untamed
        pop _current_op : OrQuery
        add operand: WordQuery : OrQuery complete!
        push OrQuery on _query stack
evalRParen() :
        _paren: 0 _curent_op.size(): 1
        pop _query_stack : OrQuery
        pop _current_op: AndQuery
        add operand : OrQuery : AndQuery complete!
        push AndQuery on _query_stack
```

The implementation of our text query system is composed of three components: (1) the object-based TextQuery class, which does the actual text processing (again, it's detailed in Section 6.14); (2) the object-oriented Query class hierarchy to represent and evaluate each user query; and (3) the object-based UserQuery class, which represents a form of finite-state machine to build up the Query hierarchy.

Up until now, we have implemented these three components largely independent of one another and without conflict. Unfortunately, that's no longer the case. Do you see the problem? The Query class hierarchy does not support the object construction requirements imposed on it by the UserQuery implementation through which we've just traced!

1. The AndQuery, OrQuery, and NotQuery classes currently require each of their respective operands to be present at the time of each object's definition. Our processing, however, requires that we define an incomplete object.

2. Our processing requires that we subsequently add an operand to the AndQuery, OrQuery, and NotQuery classes. Moreover, this must be a virtual operation. We must add the operand through the Query* pointer pushed onto _current_op. However, adding the operand is type-dependent based on whether it is a unary

operation (NotQuery) or a binary operation (OrQuery and AndQuery). As defined, our Query class hierarchy does not provide this operation.

What has happened is that the domain analysis yielded an interface at odds with the actual implementation of the design. It is not that the analysis was incorrect, but simply incomplete. This is more or less a problem to the degree that the phases of analysis, design, and implementation are separate and viewed as a sequential *waterfall* with no allowance for feedback and revision. Fundamentally, we must accept the fact that we cannot think of or anticipate everything. The difficulty is distinguishing — both in our minds and in those of our management — between the inevitable missteps of a complex process and the mistakes due to an individual's lack of thoroughness due either to inattention or lack of time.

In this case we must either ourselves go back and modify the Query class hierarchy or negotiate to have those changes made. In an ineffective organization, recriminations will delay implementation, and projects will become progressively less ambitious and more bureaucratic. In our case, as the authors of the text, we'll simply go in and twiddle the code, modifying the subtype constructors and adding a virtual add_op() member function to support adding operands to an operator after it has been defined (we'll see its use in a moment when we look at the evalRParen() and evalWord() operations).

17.7.1   Defining the UserQuery Class

A UserQuery object can either be initialized with a pointer to a string vector representing a user query, or subsequently passed the address of a user query through the query() member function. This permits a single query object to be used for multiple user queries. The actual building up of the Query class hierarchy is carried out by the eval_query() operation. For example:

```
// define an instance without an associated user query
UserQuery user_query;

string text;
vector<string> query_text;

// cycle through each user request
do {
        while( cin  >> text )
                query_text.push_back( text );

        // pass the query to UserQuery object
        user_query.query( &query_text );

        // evaluate the query and return
        // root of the Query* hierarchy …
```

```
            Query *query = user_query.eval_query();
      }
      while ( /* user-wishes-to-continue-querying-text */ );
```

Here is our definition of our UserQuery class:

```
      #ifndef USER_QUERY_H
      #define USER_QUERY_H

      #include <string>
      #include <vector>
      #include <map>
      #include <stack>

      typedef pair<short,short>          location;
      typedef vector<location,allocator>  loc;

      #include "Query.h"

      class UserQuery {
      public:
         UserQuery( vector< string,allocator > *pquery = 0 )
                 : _query( pquery ), _eval( 0 ), _paren( 0 ) {}

         Query *eval_query();      // builds the hierarchy
         void   query( vector< string,allocator > *pq );
         void   displayQuery();

         static void
                 word_map( map<string,loc*,less<string>,allocator> *pwm )
                         { if ( !_word_map ) _word_map = pwm; }

      private:
         enum QueryType { WORD = 1, AND, OR, NOT, RPAREN, LPAREN };

         QueryType evalQueryString( const string &query );
         void      evalWord( const string &query );
         void      evalAnd();
         void      evalOr();
         void      evalNot();
         void      evalRParen();
         bool      integrity_check();

         int             _paren;
         Query           *_eval;
         vector<string>  *_query;

         stack<Query*,vector<Query*> > _query_stack;
         stack<Query*,vector<Query*> > _current_op;
```

```
        static short _lparenOn, _rparenOn;
        static map<string,loc*,less<string>,allocator>
                *_word_map;
};

    #endif
```

Notice that we declared our two stacks to contain elements of type pointer to Query rather than the Query objects themselves. While both implementations support the correct application behavior, storing the objects directly is considerably less efficient: Each object (and its operands) must be memberwise copied onto the stack (each operand, recall, is memberwise copied by a virtual invocation of clone()), then subsequently destroyed. Unless we are actually modifying the class objects we place within a container, storing them by pointer is significantly more efficient.

Here are the various eval operations. We've defined each to be inline. The evalAnd() and evalOr() operations execute the following steps: Each pops _query_stack (this takes two operations with the standard library stack class, recall: top() to get the element and pop() to remove it from the stack. One or the other allocates either an AndQuery or an OrQuery object from the heap, passing it the object retrieved from _query_stack. Each passes the AndQuery or OrQuery object the count of any left and right parentheses the operator needs to output on displaying itself. Finally, each pushes the incomplete operator onto _current_op:

```
    inline void
    UserQuery::
    evalAnd()
    {
        Query *pop   = _query_stack.top(); _query_stack.pop();
        AndQuery *pq = new AndQuery( pop );

        if ( _lparenOn )
           {  pq->lparen( _lparenOn ); _lparenOn = 0; }

        if ( _rparenOn )
           {  pq->rparen( _rparenOn ); _rparenOn = 0; }

        _current_op.push( pq );
    }

    inline void
    UserQuery::
    evalOr()
    {
        Query *pop   = _query_stack.top(); _query_stack.pop();
        OrQuery *pq = new OrQuery( pop );

        if ( _lparenOn )
```

```
        { pq->lparen( _lparenOn ); _lparenOn = 0; }

    if ( _rparenOn )
        { pq->rparen( _rparenOn ); _rparenOn = 0; }

    _current_op.push( pq );
}
```

The steps of the evalNot() operation are as follows: It allocates a new NotQuery object from the heap. It passes the NotQuery object the count of any left and right parentheses the operator needs to output on displaying itself. Lastly, it pushes the incomplete operator onto _current_op:

```
inline void
UserQuery::
evalNot()
{
    NotQuery *pq = new NotQuery;

    if ( _lparenOn )
        { pq->lparen( _lparenOn ); _lparenOn = 0; }

    if ( _rparenOn )
        { pq->rparen( _rparenOn ); _rparenOn = 0; }

    _current_op.push( pq );
}
```

When a right closing parentheses is seen, the evalRParen() operation is invoked. If the number of active left parentheses is greater than the number of elements in _current_op, then the operation does nothing. Otherwise, it executes the following steps: It pops _query_stack to retrieve the current unassigned operand. It pops _current_op to retrieve the current incomplete operator. It invokes the virtual add_op() Query member function, passing the incomplete operator the unassigned operand. Lastly, it pushes the now complete operator onto _query_stack:

```
inline void
UserQuery::
evalRParen()
{
    if ( _paren < _current_op.size() )
    {
        Query *poperand = _query_stack.top();
        _query_stack.pop();

        Query *pop = _current_op.top();
        _current_op.pop();
```

```
        pop->add_op( poperand );
        _query_stack.push( pop );
    }
}
```

The evalWord() operation executes the following steps: It looks for the word within the associated _word_map of the text file. If the word is present, it retrieves the location vector and allocates a new NameQuery object on the heap, invoking the two-parameter NameQuery constructor. If the word is not present, it allocates a new NameQuery object on the heap, invoking the one-parameter NameQuery constructor. If the number of elements within _current_op is less than or equal to the number of parentheses seen, there is no incomplete operator waiting for the NameQuery operand. The NameQuery is therefore pushed onto _query_stack; otherwise, the incomplete operator on _current_op is retrieved. The virtual add_op() Query member function is invoked, passing the incomplete operator the NameQuery object, and the now-complete operator is pushed onto _query_stack:

```
inline void
UserQuery::
evalWord( const string &query )
{
    NameQuery *pq;
    loc        *ploc;

    if ( ! _word_map->count( query ))
        pq = new NameQuery( query );
    else {
        ploc = ( *_word_map )[ query ];
        pq = new NameQuery( query, *ploc );
    }

    if ( _current_op.size() <= _paren )
        _query_stack.push( pq );
    else {
        Query *pop = _current_op.top();
        _current_op.pop();
        pop->add_op( pq );
        _query_stack.push( pop );
    }
}
```

Exercise 17.21

Provide a destructor, copy constructor, and copy assignment operator for the User-Query class.

Exercise 17.22

Provide a `print()` function for UserQuery. Explain what you chose for it to display.

17.8 Putting It Together

The `main()` program of our query text application looks as follows:

```
#include "TextQuery.h"

int main()
{
    TextQuery tq;

    tq.build_text_map();
    tq.query_text();
}
```

The `build_text_map()` member function is the renamed `doit()` member function of Section 6.14:

```
inline void
TextQuery::
build_text_map()
{
    retrieve_text();
    separate_words();
    filter_text();
    suffix_text();
    strip_caps();
    build_word_map();
}
```

The `query_text()` member function is a replacement for the instance defined in Section 6.14. In our original `query_text()` implementation, it assumed the responsibility for soliciting the user query and for displaying the result of the evaluation. We've chosen to maintain those responsibilities within `query_text()` while reimplementing the actions it carries out:

```
void
TextQuery::query_text()
{
    /* local objects:
     *
     * text: holds each word of the query in turn
     * query_text: vector to hold user query
     * caps: filter to support turning caps to lower case
     *
     * user_query : UserQuery object to encapsulate
```

```
                    actual evaluation of user query
 */
string text;
string caps( "ABCDEFGHIJKLMNOPQRSTUVWXYZ" );
vector<string, allocator> query_text;
UserQuery user_query;

// initialize UserQuery static data members
NotQuery::all_locs( text_locations->second );
AndQuery::max_col( &line_cnt );
UserQuery::word_map( word_map );

do {
    // remove earlier query, if any
    query_text.clear();

    cout << "Enter a query - please separate each item "
         << "by a space.\n"
         << "Terminate query (or session) "
         << "with a dot( . ).\n\n"
         << "==> ";

    /*
     * grab query from standard input,
     * remove all capitalization, then
     * tuck away in query_text …
     *
     * note: should do all processing of user query
     *       that we do with text itself ...
     */
    while( cin  >> text )
    {
            if ( text == "." )
                break;

            string::size_type pos = 0;
            while (( pos = text.find_first_of( caps, pos ))
                    != string::npos )
                  text[pos] = tolower( text[pos] );

            query_text.push_back( text );
    }

    // ok: if we have a query, process it …
    if ( ! query_text.empty() )
    {
        // pass the query to UserQuery object
        user_query.query( &query_text );
```

```
                    // evaluate the UserQuery
                    // return Query* hierarchy …
                    // Section 17.7 describes this

                    // query is a Query* member of TextQuery
                    query = user_query.eval_query();

                    // evaluate the Query hierarchy
                    // see Section 17.5 for implementation
                    query->eval();

                    // ok: display solution
                    // a TextQuery member function
                    display_solution();

                    // give us an extra line on user terminal
                    cout << endl;
                }
            }
            while ( ! query_text.empty() ); cout << "Ok, bye!\n";
        }
```

The full text of the program can be found at the Addison-Wesley ftp site listed on the back cover. As a final exercise of our program, we've applied it against a number of online texts. The first query is made against Herman Melville's short story *Bartleby*. It illustrates a compound AndQuery in which an adjacent match against words on succeeding lines is found. (Note that words placed within slash marks are meant to be italicized.)

```
Enter a query – please separate each item by a space.
Terminate query (or session) with a dot( . ).
==> John && Jacob && Astor

        john ( 3 ) lines match
        jacob ( 3 ) lines match
        john && jacob ( 3 ) lines match
        astor ( 3 ) lines match
        john && jacob && astor ( 5 ) lines match

Requested query: john && jacob && astor
( 34 ) All who know me consider me an eminently /safe/ man. The late
John Jacob
( 35 ) Astor, a personage little given to poetic enthusiasm, had no hes-
itation in
( 38 ) my profession by the late John Jacob Astor, a name which, I admit,
I love to
( 40 ) bullion. I will freely add that I was not insensible to the late
John Jacob
( 41 ) Astor's good opinion.
```

This next query, exercising parentheses and compound operators, is made against *Heart of Darkness*, a novella by Joseph Conrad.

```
==> horror || ( absurd && mystery ) || ( North && Pole )

          horror ( 5 ) lines match
          absurd ( 8 ) lines match
          mystery ( 12 ) lines match
          ( absurd && mystery )  ( 1 ) lines match
          horror ||  ( absurd && mystery )  ( 6 ) lines match
          north ( 2 ) lines match
          pole ( 7 ) lines match
          ( north && pole )  ( 1 ) lines match
          horror ||  ( absurd && mystery )  ||  ( north && pole )
                   ( 7 ) lines match
```

```
Requested query: horror ||  ( absurd && mystery )  ||  ( north && pole )
( 257 ) up I will go there.' The North Pole was one of these
( 952 ) horrors. The heavy pole had skinned his poor nose.
( 3055 ) some lightless region of subtle horrors, where pure,
( 3673 ) " 'The horror! The horror!'
( 3913 ) the whispered cry, 'The horror! The horror! '
( 3957 ) absurd mysteries not fit for a human being to behold.
( 4088 ) wind. 'The horror! The horror!'
```

The final query is made against a portion of *Portrait of a Lady* by Henry James. It illustrates a compound query and represents a large text file.

```
==> clever && trick || devious

          clever ( 46 ) lines match
          trick ( 12 ) lines match
          clever && trick ( 2 ) lines match
          devious ( 1 ) lines match
          clever && trick || devious ( 3 ) lines match
```

```
Requested query: clever && trick || devious
( 13914 ) clever trick she had guessed. Isabel, as she herself grew old-
er,
( 13935 ) lost the desire to know this lady's clever trick. If she had
( 14974 ) desultory, so devious, so much the reverse of processional.
There were
```

Exercise 17.23

Our handling of the user query fails currently in that it does not apply the same preprocessing to each word as the front end does in building up the text; see Sections 6.9 and 6.10. Thus, for example, a user wishing to find maps discovers that only map is recognized in our representation of the text. Modify query_text() to provide equivalent preprocessing.

Exercise 17.24

The query system would be enhanced by a second InclusiveAndQuery, perhaps represented by a single &. It would evaluate as true if both words were on the same line, rather than having both words be adjacent. For example, given the line

```
We were her pride of ten, she named us
```

the InclusiveAndQuery

```
pride & ten
```

evaluates as true, whereas our original AndQuery

```
pride && ten
```

evaluates as false. Provide the necessary support for an InclusiveAndQuery.

Exercise 17.25

Our current implementation of display_solution(), included here, only prints to standard output. A more reasonable implementation would allow the user to indicate an ostream with which to direct the display. Modify display_solution() to allow a user-specified ostream object. What other changes are necessary within the UserQuery class definition?

```
void TextQuery::
display_solution()
{
    cout << "\n"
         << "Requested query: "
         << *query << "\n\n";

    const set<short> *solution = query->solution();
    if ( ! solution->size() ) {
        cout << "\n\tSorry, "
             << " no matching lines were found in text.\n"
             << endl;
        return;
    }

    set<short>::const_iterator
        it = solution->begin(),
        end_it = solution->end();

    for ( ; it != end_it; ++it ) {
        int line = *it;

        // don't confound user with text lines starting at 0 ...
        cout << "( " << line+1 << " ) "
             << (*lines_of_text)[line] << '\n';
    }
```

```
        cout << endl;
    }
```

Exercise 17.26

What our TextQuery class really needs is the ability to accept command line arguments from the user.

    (a) Identify a possible command line syntax for our text query system.

    (b) Indicate the additional data members and member functions that are necessary.

    (c) Sketch out a command line facility implementation (see Section 7.8 for an example).

Exercise 17.27

As a possible programming project, consider one of the following enhancements to the query system:

    (a) Introduce support for representing an AndQuery as a string, as in "Motion Picture Screen Cartoonists."

    (b) Introduce support for evaluating words based on their presence within the same sentence rather than the same line.

    (c) Introduce a history system in which the user can refer to a previous query by number, possibly adding to it or combining it with another.

    (d) Rather than display the count of matches and all the matching lines, allow the user to indicate a range of lines to display, both for intermediate query evaluation and the final query. For example:

```
==> John && Jacob && Astor

(1)         john ( 3 ) lines match
(2)         jacob ( 3 ) lines match
(3)         john && jacob ( 3 ) lines match
(4)         astor ( 3 ) lines match
(5)         john && jacob && astor ( 5 ) lines match

// New facility: let user choose which query to display
// user types in number
==> display?   3

// System then asks how many lines to display
// return displays all, else user can enter single line number or range
==> how many( return displays all, else enter single line or range) 1-3
```

18

Multiple and Virtual Inheritance

The predominant inheritance model in real-world C++ applications is that of public inheritance from a single base class. In general, we can expect the majority of our uses of inheritance to fall within this model as well. In some cases, however, single inheritance is an inadequate solution, because either (1) it fails to model a program domain abstraction or (2) the model it provides is unnecessarily complex and nonintuitive. In these cases, multiple inheritance, or a specialization of it — virtual inheritance — is the preferred solution. The support C++ provides for multiple and virtual inheritance is the primary focus of this chapter.

18.1 Setting the Stage

Before we look at the details of multiple and virtual inheritance, let's briefly motivate their use. Our first example is taken from 3D computer graphics. Before we can introduce the problem, however, we must first introduce the problem domain.

A scene is represented within the computer by a *scene graph*. A scene graph contains some geometry (the 3D models), one or more lights (without some light, the models are shrouded in darkness), a camera (without a camera, we cannot view the scene), and several transformation nodes with which to position the elements.

Rendering is the process of applying light and camera information to the geometry to yield a 2D image for display. The two primary concerns of a rendering algorithm are (1) the nature of the light sources illuminating the scene and (2) the material attributes of the geometric surfaces, such as color, roughness, transparency, and translucency. The feathers of a fairy's moon-white wing, for example, are illuminated quite differently from the diamond-shaped teardrops that fall from its eyes, although both are illuminated by the same honey-silver light.

Adding to, repositioning, and tweaking the attributes of both the lighting and geometry for each scene is one of the labor-intensive tasks of the computer artist. Our task is to provide interactive support for on-screen manipulation of the scene graph. In the current version of our tool, imagine that we have chosen to use the Open Inventor C++ framework (see [WERNECKE94]) to implement the underlying scene graph, which we extend through subtyping to provide our own necessary class abstractions. For example, Open Inventor provides the following three built-in light sources derived from an abstract SoLight base class:

```
class SoSpotLight : public SoLight { ... };
class SoPointLight : public SoLight { ... };
class SoDirectionalLight : public SoLight { ... };
```

where So is a lexical prefix used to provide a unique name to otherwise common graphic domain names (the framework was designed prior to the introduction of namespaces). A *point light* is a light source that radiates in all directions (think of the sun). A *directional light* radiates in one particular direction. A spotlight is a cone-shaped light such as that used in theatrical productions to light a portion of a stage.

By default, Open Inventor renders the scene graph to the screen using OpenGL (see [NEIDER93]). While this is sufficient for interactive display, nearly all images generated for use within the film industry render with Pixar's RenderMan (see [UPSTILL90]). As part of the task of adding support for rendering the scene graph using RenderMan, we need to provide our own specialized light subtypes:

```
class RiSpotLight : public SoSpotLight { ... };
class RiPointLight : public SoPointLight { ... };
class RiDirectionalLight : public SoDirectionalLight { ... };
```

This works as expected. Our new subtypes hold the additional information necessary for rendering through RenderMan. The Open Inventor base class still allows us to render simultaneously through OpenGL. Things go awry with the need to extend our support to shadows.

In RenderMan, a spotlight and a directional light support casting the shadows (we call these *shadow-capable light sources* [SCLS]); a point light does not. The general algorithm requires that we iterate through all the light sources within the scene and generate a *shadow map* for each SCLS that is turned on. The problem is that the lights are stored within the scene graph as polymorphic SoLight objects. Although we can encapsulate the common data and necessary operations in an SCLS class, it is not clear how to hook the class into the existing Open Inventor hierarchy.

There is no workable position within the Open Inventor SoLight subtree to derive the SCLS class singly so that both the SdRiSpotLight and the SdRiDirectionalLight can subsequently inherit from it. Without multiple inheritance, the best we can do is to compose each SCLS category light with an SCLS member class object and a method to invoke the appropriate operation:

```
SoLight *plight = next_scene_light();

if ( RiDirectionalLight *pdilite =
     dynamic_cast<RiDirectionalLight*>( plight ))
        pdilite->scls.cast_shadow_map();
else
if ( RiSpotLight *pslite =
     dynamic_cast<RiSpotLight*>( plight ))
        pslite->scls.cast_shadow_map();
// and so on ...
```

(The dynamic_cast operator is part of the Run-Time Type Identification (RTTI) mechanism. It supports the run-time query of a polymorphic pointer or reference as to actual type of the object it addresses [RTTI is discussed in Chapter 19].)

With multiple inheritance, we can encapsulate the SCLS subtypes, shielding our code from having to be modified with each addition or deletion of an SCLS category of light source. This is pictured in Figure 18.1.

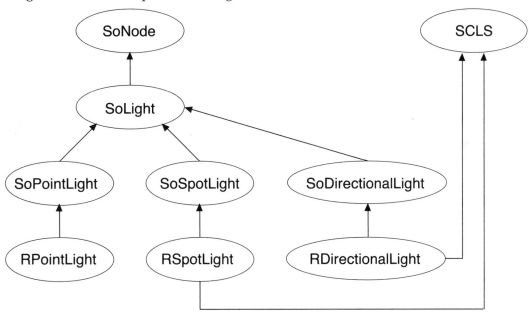

Figure 18.1 Multiple Inheritance Light Hierarchy

```
class RiDirectionalLight :
      public SoDirectionalLight, public SCLS { ... };

class RiSpotLight :
      public SoSpotLight, public SCLS { ... };

// ...
```

```
SoLight *plight = next_scene_light();
if ( SCLS *pscls = dynamic_cast<SCLS*>(plight))
      pscls->cast_shadow_map();
```

This is still a less-than-perfect solution. If we had access to the Open Inventor source code, we could have dispensed with multiple inheritance by adding an SCLS pointer member to SoLight together with support for the cast_shadow_map() operation:

```
class SoLight : public SoNode {
public:
   void cast_shadow_map()
         { if ( _scls ) _scls->cast_shadow_map(); }
   // ...
protected:
   SCLS *_scls;
};

// ...

SdSoLight *plight = next_scene_light();
plight->cast_shadow_map();
```

The most widely used real-world application using multiple (and virtual) inheritance is the Standard C++ input/output iostream library. The two primary user-visible iostream classes are the istream class (for input) and the ostream class (for output). Attributes common to both classes include

1. Format state information (is an integral value represented in decimal, octal, or hexadecimal notation; is a floating point value represented in fixed decimal or scientific notation, and so on)

2. Condition state information (is the stream object in a good or fail state, and so on)

3. Locale information (does the day or month come first in a display, such as 7/4/76, and so on)

4. The actual buffer used to hold the data to be read or to be written

These common attributes are factored into an abstract ios base class, from which both the istream and ostream classes are derived.

The iostream class is a second example of multiple inheritance. It provides support to read from and write to the same file. It inherits from both the istream and ostream classes. Unfortunately, by default, it also inherits two separate instances of the ios base class, which we neither need nor can manage easily.

Virtual inheritance provides a solution to the problem of inheriting multiple

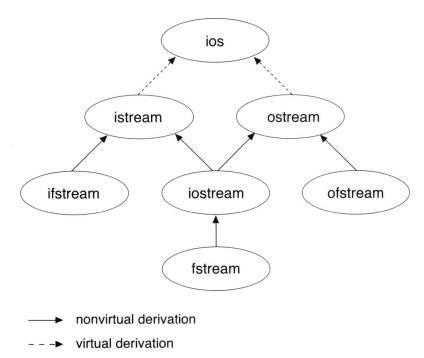

Figure 18.2 Virtual Inheritance iostream Hierarchy (Simplified)

instances of a base class when only a single, shared instance is required. A simplified iostream class hierarchy is pictured in Figure 18.2.

Support for distributed object computing is another real-world example of virtual and multiple inheritance. For a detailed discussion and illustration, see the set of articles on distributed object computing by Douglas Schmidt and Steve Vinoski in [LIPPMAN96b].

Multiple and virtual inheritance are the primary focus of this chapter. Our focus here is on the use and behavior of multiple and virtual inheritance. In our companion text, *Inside the C++ Object Model*, more advanced performance and design issues are examined.

In the following discussion, we have chosen a pedagogical (that is, teaching) example — that of a zoo animal hierarchy. Our zoo animals exist at different levels of abstraction. There are the individual animals, of course, such as Ling-ling, Mowgli, and Balou. Each animal belongs to a species; Ling-ling, for example, is a Giant Panda. Species in turn are members of families. A Giant Panda is a member of the Bear family, although as we'll see in Section 18.5, for a long time that relationship was the object of intense dispute within the specialized field of zoology. Each family in turn is a member of the animal kingdom — in this case, the more limited kingdom of a particular zoo.

Each level of abstraction contains data and operations that support a wider category of users. For example, the abstract ZooAnimal class holds information that is common to all the zoo animals and provides the public interface of all general queries that can be made. The Bear class contains information that is unique to the Bear family, and so on.

In addition to the actual zoo animal classes, there are auxiliary classes that encapsulate various abstractions such as endangered animals. In our implementation of a Panda class, for example, a Panda is multiply derived from Bear and Endangered.

18.2 Multiple Inheritance

To support multiple inheritance, the derivation list, as in

```
class Bear : public ZooAnimal { ... };
```

is extended to support a comma-separated list of base classes. For example:

```
class Panda : public Bear, public Endangered { ... };
```

Each listed base class must also specify its access level, one of `public`, `protected`, or `private`. As with single inheritance, a base class under multiple inheritance can be listed only if its definition has already been seen.

There is no language-imposed limit on the number of base classes from which a class can be derived. In practice, two base classes seems to be the most common, with one base class often representing a public abstract interface and the second base class providing a private implementation (although neither of our two previous examples illustrate this). Derived classes inheriting from three or more immediate base classes follow a *mixin-based* design style in which each base class represents a *facet* of the complete interface of the derived class.

Under multiple inheritance, a derived class contains a base class subobject for each of its base classes (see Section 17.3 for a discussion of the base class subobject of a derived class). For example, when we write

```
Panda ying_yang;
```

ying_yang is made up of a Bear class subobject (which itself contains a ZooAnimal base class subobject), an Endangered class subobject, and the nonstatic data members, if any, declared within the Panda class (see Figure 18.3).

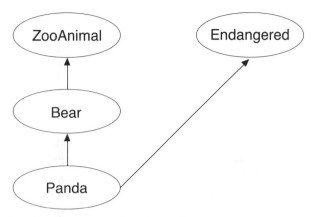

Figure 18.3 Multiple Inheritance Panda Hierarchy

The base class constructors are invoked in the declaration order within the class derivation list. For ying_yang, for example, the order of constructor invocation is the following: the Bear constructor (because Bear is derived from ZooAnimal; however, prior to the execution of the Bear constructor, the ZooAnimal constructor is invoked), the Endangered constructor, then the Panda constructor.

As we discussed in Section 17.4, the order of constructor invocation is *not* affected by either the presence of the base class within the member initialization list or the order in which they are listed. That is, were Bear's default constructor to be invoked implicitly and therefore not listed within the member initialization list, such as the following,

```
// Bear's default constructor is invoked prior to
// Endangered's two-argument constructor ...

Panda::Panda()
    : Endangered( Endangered::environment,
                  Endangered::critical )
{ ... }
```

Bear's default constructor is still invoked prior to the explicitly listed two-argument constructor of Endangered.

Similarly, the order of destructor invocation is always the reverse of the constructor order. In our example, the order of destructor invocation is the following: ~Panda(), ~Endangered(), ~Bear(), ~ZooAnimal().

Under single inheritance, as we saw in Section 17.3, the public and protected members of the base class can be accessed directly as if they were members of the derived class. The same holds true with multiple inheritance. Under multiple inheritance, however, there is the possibility of inheriting a member with the same name from two or more base classes. In this case, direct access is ambiguous and results in a compile-time error.

The compile-time error, however, is *not* triggered by the potential ambiguity of an unqualified access of the two members, but only by an actual attempt to access them (see the discussion in Section 17.4.4). For example, if both Bear and Endangered define a `print()` member function, then a statement such as the following,

```
ying_yang.print( cout );
```

results in a compile-time error, even if the two inherited member functions define different parameter types:

```
Error:  ying_yang.print( cout ) -- ambiguous, one of
            Bear::print( ostream& )
            Endangered::print( ostream&, int )
```

The reason for this is that the inherited member functions do not form a set of overloaded functions within the derived class (see Section 17.3 for a discussion). `print()`, therefore, is resolved only using name resolution on the name `print` rather than using overload resolution based on the actual argument types passed to `print()`. (We'll look at how this might be resolved in Section 18.4.)

Under single inheritance, a pointer, a reference, or an object of a derived class, if necessary, is converted automatically to a pointer, a reference, or an object of a publically derived base class. Again, the same holds true with multiple inheritance. A Panda pointer, reference, or object, for example, can be converted to a pointer, a reference, or an object of a ZooAnimal, Bear, or Endangered class. For example:

```
extern void display( const Bear& );
extern void highlight( const Endangered& );

Panda ying_yang;

display( ying_yang );   // ok
highlight( ying_yang ); // ok

extern ostream&
       operator<<( ostream&, const ZooAnimal& );

cout << ying_yang << endl; // ok
```

Once again, however, under multiple inheritance, the possibility of an ambiguous conversion is much greater. For example, consider the following two functions:

```
extern void display( const Bear& );
extern void display( const Endangered& );
```

An unqualified invocation of `display()` with a Panda object, such as

```
Panda ying_yang;
display( ying_yang ); // error: ambiguous
```

results in a compile-time error of the following general form:

```
Error:  display( ying_yang ) -- ambiguous, one of
            extern void display( const Bear& );
            extern void display( const Endangered& );
```

There is no way for the compiler to distinguish between the immediate base classes in terms of a derived class conversion. Each conversion is equally applicable. (We'll look at how this might be resolved in Section 18.4.1.)

To see how the virtual function mechanism is affected by multiple inheritance, let's define a set of virtual functions for each of Panda's immediate base classes. (Virtual functions were introduced in Section 17.2, and were discussed in detail in Section 17.5.)

```
class Bear : public ZooAnimal {
public:
      virtual ~Bear();
      virtual ostream& print( ostream& ) const;
      virtual string isA() const;
      // ...
};

class Endangered {
public:
      virtual ~Endangered();
      virtual ostream& print( ostream& ) const;
      virtual void highlight() const;
      // ...
};
```

Let's now define Panda to provide its own instance of print(), its own destructor, and to introduce a new virtual function, cuddle(), as follows:

```
class Panda : public Bear, public Endangered
{
public:
      virtual ~Panda();
      virtual ostream& print( ostream& ) const;
      virtual void cuddle();
      // ...
};
```

The set of virtual functions that can be invoked directly from a Panda object are the following:

Table 18.1 Active Panda Virtual Functions

Name of Virtual Function	Active Instance
destructor	Panda::~Panda()
print(ostream&) const	Panda::print(ostream&)
isA() const	Bear::isA()
highlight() const	Endangered::highlight()
cuddle()	Panda::cuddle()

When a Bear or ZooAnimal pointer or reference is initialized with or assigned the address of a Panda class object, both the Panda-specific and Endangered portions of the Panda interface are no longer accessible. For example:

```
Bear *pb = new Panda;

pb->print( cout );  // ok: Panda::print(ostream&)
pb->isA();          // ok: Bear::isA()
pb->cuddle();       // error: not part of Bear interface
pb->highlight();    // error: not part of Bear interface
delete pb;          // ok: Panda::~Panda()
```

(Note that if the Panda object had been assigned to a ZooAnimal pointer, the set of invocations illustrated earlier resolve exactly the same.)

Similarly, when an Endangered pointer or reference is initialized with or assigned the address of a Panda class object, both the Panda-specific and Bear portions of the Panda interface are no longer accessible. For example:

```
Endangered *pe = new Panda;

pe->print( cout );// ok: Panda::print(ostream&)

// error: not part of Endangered interface
pe->isA();

// error: not part of Endangered interface
pe->cuddle();

pe->highlight(); // ok: Endangered::highlight()
delete pe;       // ok: Panda::~Panda()
```

The handling of the virtual destructor is consistent regardless of the pointer type through which we delete the object. For example, given

```
// ZooAnimal *pz = new Panda;
delete pz;

// Bear *pb = new Panda;
delete pb;
```

```
// Panda *pp = new Panda;
delete pp;

// Endangered *pe = new Panda;
delete pe;
```

the exact same order of destructor invocations occurs. The order of destructor invocations is the reverse of the constructor order: The Panda destructor is invoked through
the virtual mechanism. Following execution of the Panda destructor, the Endangered,
Bear, then ZooAnimal destructors are invoked statically in turn.

The memberwise initialization and assignment of a multiply derived class behaves
the same as under single inheritance (see the discussion in Section 17.6). For example,
given our declaration of Panda,

```
class Panda : public Bear, public Endangered
{ ... };
```

the following memberwise initialization of ling_ling

```
Panda yin_yang;
Panda ling_ling = yin_yang;
```

invokes the Bear copy constructor (however, because Bear is derived from ZooAnimal, prior to execution of the Bear copy constructor, the ZooAnimal copy constructor
is invoked), then the Endangered copy constructor, prior to executing the body of the
Panda copy constructor. Memberwise assignment behaves similarly.

Exercise 18.1

Which, if any, of the following declarations are in error. Explain why.

```
(a) class CADVehicle : public CAD, Vehicle { ... };
(b) class DoublyLinkedList:
        public List, public List { ... };
(c) class iostream:
        private istream, private ostream { ... };
```

Exercise 18.2

Given the following class hierarchy, each class of which defines a default constructor,

```
class A { ... };
class B : public A { ... };
class C : public B { ... };
class X { ... };
class Y { ... };
class Z : public X, public Y { ... };
class MI : public C, public Z { ... };
```

what is the order of constructor execution for the following definition?

```
MI mi;
```

Exercise 18.3

Given the following class hierarchy, each class of which defines a default constructor,

```
class X { ... };
class A { ... };
class B : public A { ... };
class C : private B { ... };
class D : public X, public C { ... };
```

which, if any, of the following conversions are not permitted?

```
D *pd = new D;
```

```
(a) X *px = pd;  (c) B *pb = pd;
(b) A *pa = pd;  (d) C *pc = pd;
```

Exercise 18.4

Given the following class hierarchy, with the following collection of virtual functions,

```
class Base {
public:
   virtual ~Base();
   virtual ostream& print();
   virtual void log();
   virtual void debug();
   virtual void readOn();
   virtual void writeOn();
   // ...
};

class Derived1 : virtual public Base {
public:
   virtual ~Derived1();
   virtual void writeOn();
   // ...
};

class Derived2 : virtual public Base {
public:
   virtual ~Derived2();
   virtual void readOn();
   // ...
};

class MI : public Derived1, public Derived2 {
public:
```

```
            virtual ~MI();
            virtual ostream& print();
            virtual void debug();
            // ...
        };
```

which instance of each function is invoked for the following?

```
        Base *pb = new MI;
```

```
        (a) pb->print();   (c) pb->readOn();   (e) pb->log();
        (b) pb->debug();   (d) pb->writeOn();  (f) delete pb;
```

Exercise 18.5

Using the class hierarchy defined in Exercise 18.4, identify the virtual functions active when invoked through (a) pd1 and (b) d2:

```
        (a) Derived1 *pd1 = new MI;
        (b) MI obj;
            Derived2 d2 = obj;
```

18.3   Public, Private, and Protected Inheritance

A public derivation is referred to as *type inheritance*. The derived class is a subtype of the base class; it overrides the implementation of all type-specific member functions of the base class while inheriting those that are shared. The derived class in general reflects an *is-a* relationship; that is, it provides a specialization of its more general base class. A Bear is a kind of ZooAnimal. An AudioBook is a kind of LibBook; both are a kind of LibraryLendingMaterial. We say that a Bear is a subtype of ZooAnimal, as is Panda. Similarly, we say that AudioBook is a subtype of LibBook, and that both are subtypes of LibraryLendingMaterial. A subtype can be substituted transparently anywhere the program expects its public base type, and continues to execute correctly (provided, of course, the subtype is implemented correctly). All of our examples of inheritance up to now have reflected subtype inheritance.

A private derivation is referred to as *implementation inheritance*. The derived class does not support the public interface of the base class directly; rather, it wishes to reuse the implementation of the base class while providing its own public interface. To illustrate the issues involved, let's implement a PeekbackStack.

A PeekbackStack supports the peeking into the stack using the peekback() method,

```
        bool
        PeekbackStack::
        peekback( int index, type &value ) { ... }
```

where value holds the element at index if peekback() returns true. If peekback() returns false, the index is invalid and value is set to the top element of the stack.

There are two likely areas of error in our implementation of PeekbackStack:

1. The implementation of the PeekbackStack abstraction; that is, have we correctly implemented its behavior?
2. The implementation of the underlying representation; that is, have we correctly managed the allocation and deallocation of memory, the copying of stack objects, and so on?

A stack is generally implemented with either an array or linked list of elements (the standard library stack by default is composed of a deque, although we can specify a vector if we wish — see Chapter 6). What we'd like is a fully guaranteed (well, at least a tested and fully supported) implementation of either an array or list that we can just plug into our PeekbackStack. If we can do that, then we're free to concentrate on getting our stack behavior right.

As it happens, we have our IntArray class, which we implemented in Section 2.3 (yes, for the purposes of our discussion, we are ignoring both the standard library deque class and providing support for element types other than int). The question, then, is how the IntArray class might best be reused within our PeekbackStack implementation. Our first thought, of course, is inheritance. (Note that we will need to modify the IntArray class, changing its members from private to protected.) Here is our implementation:

```cpp
#include <IntArray.h>

class PeekbackStack : public IntArray {
private:
    const int static bos = -1;

public:
    explicit PeekbackStack( int size )
            : IntArray( size ), _top( bos ){}

    bool empty() const { return _top == bos; }
    bool full()  const { return _top == size()-1; }
    int  top()   const { return _top; }

    int pop() {
        if ( empty() )
            /* handle error condition */ ;
        return ia[ _top-- ];
    }

    void push( int value ) {
        if ( full() )
            /* handle error condition */ ;
        ia[ ++_top ] = value;
    }
```

```
        bool peekback( int index, int &value ) const;

    private:
        int _top;
    };

    inline bool
    PeekbackStack::
    peekback( int index, int &value ) const
    {
        if ( empty() )
            /* handle error condition */ ;

        if ( index < 0 || index > _top )
        {
            value = ia[ _top ];
            return false;
        }

        value = ia[ index ];
        return true;
    }
```

This achieves exactly what we wanted — and more. Program code using our new PeekbackStack class may also make inappropriate use of its IntArray base class public interface. For example:

```
    extern void swap( IntArray&, int, int );
    PeekbackStack is( 1024 );

    // oops: unexpected misuses of our PeekbackStack
    swap(is,i,j);
    is.sort();
    is[0] = is[512];
```

The PeekbackStack class abstraction should guarantee "last in, first out" behavior with regard to the access of the elements it contains. However, the availability of the additional IntArray interface seriously compromises any guarantee of that behavior.

The problem is that a public derivation defines an *is-a* relationship. A Peekback-Stack, however, is not a kind of IntArray. Rather, a PeekbackStack has an IntArray as part of its implementation. The public interface of an IntArray is not part of the Peek-backStack class public interface. The PeekbackStack class wishes to reuse the implementation of the IntArray class; however, a PeekbackStack is not an IntArray subtype.

A private base class reflects a form of inheritance that is not based on subtype relationships. The entire public interface of the base class becomes private in the derived class. Each of the preceding misuses of a PeekbackStack class instance is now illegal except within the friends and member functions of the derived class.

The only change required of our earlier PeekbackStack definition is to replace the
`public` keyword with `private` in the class derivation list. The other `public` and `private`
keywords within the class definition itself need not change.

```
class PeekbackStack : private IntArray { ... };
```

18.3.1   Inheritance versus Composition

The implementation of the PeekbackStack class as a private derivation of the IntArray
class works — but is it necessary? Is anything gained in this case by inheritance? In
this case, no.

Public inheritance is a powerful mechanism in support of an *is-a* subtype relationship. The PeekbackStack implementation, however, represents a *has-a* relationship
with regard to the IntArray class. The PeekbackStack class has an IntArray as part of
its implementation. A *has-a* relationship is in general best supported by *composition*
rather than by inheritance. Composition is implemented by making one class a member of the other class. In this case, an IntArray object is made a member of Peekback-
Stack. Here is our *has-a* IntArray instance implementation of PeekbackStack:

```
class PeekbackStack {
private:
    const int static bos = -1;

public:
    explicit PeekbackStack( int size ) :
    stack( size ), _top( bos ){}

    bool empty() const { return _top == bos; }
    bool full()  const { return _top == stack.size()-1; }
    int  top()   const { return _top; }

    int pop() {
        if ( empty() )
            /* handle error condition */ ;
        return stack[ _top-- ];
    }

    void push( int value ) {
        if ( full() )
            /* handle error condition */ ;
        stack[ ++_top ] = value;
    }
    bool peekback( int index, int &value ) const;

private:
    int _top;
    IntArray stack;
};
```

```
inline bool
PeekbackStack::
peekback( int index, int &value ) const
{
    if ( empty() )
        /* handle error condition */ ;

    if ( index < 0 || index > _top )
    {
        value = stack[ _top ];
        return false;
    }

    value = stack[ index ];
    return true;
}
```

The following represents a very broad guideline as to whether to use composition or private inheritance in a class design in which a *has-a* relationship exists:

- If we wish to override any of the virtual functions of a class, we must inherit from it privately.

- If we wish to allow the class to refer to one of a hierarchy of possible types, we must use composition by reference, we discuss this in detail in Section 18.3.4.

- If, as with our PeekbackStack class, we wish simply to reuse the implementation, composition by value is to be preferred over inheritance. If a lazy allocation of the object is desired, composition by reference (using a pointer) is the generally preferred design choice.

18.3.2   Exempting Individual Members

In our private PeekbackStack derivation of IntArray, all the protected and public members of the IntArray class are inherited as private members of the PeekbackStack class. However, it would still be useful if clients of this PeekbackStack implementation were able to query a PeekbackStack instance as to its size:

```
is.size();
```

The class designer can exempt individual members of a base class from the effects of the nonpublic derivation. The following, for example, exempts the size() member function of IntArray:

```
class PeekbackStack : private IntArray {
public:
    // maintain public access level
    using IntArray::size;
```

```
    // ...
};
```

Another reason to exempt individual members is to allow subsequent derivations access to the protected members of the private base class. For example, suppose users wanted a PeekbackStack subtype that grows dynamically. To provide that, a class derived from PeekbackStack needs access to the protected IntArray elements ia and _size:

```
template <class Type>
class PeekbackStack : private IntArray {
public:
    using IntArray::size;
    // ...

protected:
    using IntArray::_size;
    using IntArray::ia;
    // ...
};
```

The derived class can only restore the inherited member to its original access level. The access level cannot be made either more or less restrictive than the level originally specified within the base class.

A common pattern of multiple inheritance is to inherit the public interface of one class and the private implementation of a second class. For example, the Booch Components, a C++ class library, includes a growable Queue implemented as follows (see the article by Michael Vilot and Grady Booch in [LIPPMAN96b] for more details):

```
template < class item, class container >
class Unbounded_Queue:
        private Simple_List< item >,// implementation
        public  Queue< item >        // interface
{ ... };
```

18.3.3   Protected Inheritance

A third form of derivation is *protected inheritance*. Under protected inheritance, all the public members of the base class become protected members of the derived class. This means they can be accessed from classes subsequently derived from the class, but not from outside the class hierarchy. For example, if we wished to derive a PeekbackStack from Stack, the private derivation

```
// oops: this does not support a subsequent derivation
// of a PeekbackStack: all IntArray members are now private
class Stack : private IntArray { ... };
```

is too restrictive, because making the IntArray members within Stack private prohibits a subsequent derivation from accessing those members. To support

```
class PeekbackStack : public Stack { ... };
```

Stack must be a protected derivation of IntArray:

```
class Stack : protected IntArray { ... };
```

18.3.4   Object Composition

There are actually two forms of object composition:

1. *Composition by value*, in which an actual object of the class is declared to be a member, as illustrated two subsections ago by our revised PeekbackStack implementation
2. *Composition by reference*, in which the object is addressed indirectly through either a reference or a pointer member to the class object

Composition by value provides automatic management of the object's lifetime and copy semantics, and provides more efficient, direct access of the object itself. Under what circumstances is composition by reference to be preferred?

For example, let's say that we decide that Endangered is better represented by composition rather than by inheritance. Should we define an Endangered object directly within ZooAnimal or refer to it indirectly through a pointer or reference? Let's consider (1) if all ZooAnimals exhibit this characteristic and, if not, (2) if it changes over time; that is, if the characteristic may either be added to or removed over time.

If the answer to item 1 is that all ZooAnimal objects exhibit this characteristic, then composition by value is generally preferred. (By *generally* we mean that composition by value is not necessarily the most efficient representation strategy for large class objects, particularly if they are copied often. Composition by reference, in this case, can allow us to avoid unnecessary copying when used in conjunction with a strategy of reference counting and what is called *copy on write*. (The trade-off is an increase in the complexity of managing the object.) A discussion of this technique, however, is beyond the scope of a language primer. A fine explanation of the technique can be found in [KOENIG97], Chapters 6 and 7.)

If the answer to item 1 is that only some ZooAnimal objects exhibit this characteristic, then composition by reference is generally preferred (why should the unendangered objects have to lug around an Endangered class object?).

Because the Endangered class object may not be present, we must represent it by a pointer rather than a reference. (A pointer set to 0 is understood to refer to no object. A reference must always refer to an object. Section 3.6 explains this distinction in detail.)

If the answer to item 2 is yes, then we must provide run-time access functions to insert and remove an Endangered object.

In our example, being endangered is a characteristic of some minority of ZooAnimal subtypes. In addition, at least theoretically, it is a reversible condition and our Panda may one day no longer be threatened with extinction.

```
class ZooAnimal {
public:
    // ...
    const Endangered* Endangered() const;
    void addEndangered( Endangered* );
    void removeEndangered();
    // ...
protected:
    Endangered *_endangered;
    // ...
};
```

If our application is intended to run on multiple platforms, it is useful to encapsulate the platform-dependent information in an abstract class hierarchy. The application can then program a platform-independent abstract interface. For example, to display our ZooAnimal objects under both UNIX and PCs, we might define a Display-Manager class hierarchy:

```
class DisplayManager{ ... };
class DisplayUnix : public DisplayManager{ ... };
class DisplayPC : public DisplayManager{ ... };
```

Our ZooAnimal *is not a* kind of DisplayManager, but rather *has an* instance of a DisplayManager. ZooAnimal contains a DisplayManager object through composition rather than through inheritance. Our first question is whether it should be through composition by value or composition by reference?

Composition by value cannot represent a DisplayManager object through which we can address either an actual DisplayUnix or actual DisplayPC object. Only a DisplayManager reference or pointer ZooAnimal data member allows us to manipulate a DisplayManager subtype at run-time. That is, only composition by reference supports object-oriented programming (see [LIPPMAN96a] for a detailed explanation).

Our second question is how can we decide between declaring the ZooAnimal member to be a DisplayManager reference or pointer?

1. If the actual DisplayManager subtype is provided at the creation of the Zoo-Animal object, and does not change over the course of the program, only then may a DisplayManager reference member be declared.

2. If a *lazy allocation strategy* is adopted in which the actual DisplayManager subtype is not allocated until an actual attempt to display an object is made, then we must represent the DisplayManager member as a pointer and initialize it to 0.

3. If we wish to toggle the display mode during run-time, we must also represent the DisplayManager member as a pointer and initialize it to 0. By *toggle* we mean to allow the user either to determine or switch among the DisplayManager subtypes as the program executes.

In practice, of course, it is unlikely that each ZooAnimal subobject of our application requires its own DisplayManager subtype with which to display itself. A static ZooAnimal DisplayManager pointer is the most likely design choice in this case.

Exercise 18.6

Identify which of the following are type inheritance and which are implementation inheritance.

```
(a) Queue : List
(b) EncryptedString : String
(c) Gif : FileFormat
(d) Circle : Point
(e) Dqueue : Queue, List
(f) DrawableGeom : Geom, Canvas
```

Exercise 18.7

Replace our Array member of PeekbackStack in Section 18.3.1 with the standard library deque. Write a small program to exercise it.

Exercise 18.8

Contrast composition by value with composition by reference. Give an example of each use to illustrate your discussion.

18.4   Class Scope under Inheritance

Each class maintains its own scope, within which the names of its members and any nested types are defined (see Sections 13.9 and 13.10 for a detailed discussion). Under inheritance, the scope of the derived class is nested within the scope of its immediate base classes. If a name is unresolved within the scope of the derived class, the enclosing base class scope is searched for a definition of the name.

It is this hierarchical nesting of class scopes under inheritance that allows the members of the base class to be accessed directly as if they are members of the derived class. Let's walk through a few examples using single inheritance, then extend the discussion to consider multiple inheritance as well. Given the following simplified ZooAnimal class definition,

```
class ZooAnimal {
public:
    ostream &print( ostream& ) const;

    // public for exposition purposes only
    string is_a;
    int    ival;
```

```
private::
    double dval;
};
```

and the following simplified derived Bear class definition,

```
class Bear : public ZooAnimal {
public:
    ostream &print( ostream& ) const;
    int mumble( int );

    // public for exposition purposes only
    string name;
    int    ival;
};
```

when we write

```
Bear bear;
bear.is_a;
```

the actual process of name resolution is as follows:

1. bear is an object of the Bear class. The scope of the Bear class is searched for is_a first. It is not found.
2. Since Bear is derived from ZooAnimal, the ZooAnimal class scope is next examined to find a declaration of is_a. It is found to be a member of the ZooAnimal base class. The reference is resolved successfully.

Although a base class member can be accessed directly as if it were a member of the derived class, in practice it retains its base class membership. Normally we do not care which actual class contains the member. It becomes our concern when a base and derived class member share the same name. For example, when we write

```
bear.ival;
```

the ival instance accessed is the Bear member found using step 1 of the lookup process described earlier.

In effect, a derived class member with the same name as a member of the base class hides direct access of the base class member. To access the base class member, we must qualify it with the class scope operator:

```
bear.ZooAnimal::ival;
```

This directs the compiler to search within the ZooAnimal class scope for a declaration of ival.

Let's illustrate the use of the class scope operator with a slightly absurd example (by slightly absurd, we mean that you should never actually do this in production code!):

```
int ival;

int Bear::mumble( int ival )
```

```
    {
        return ival +         // parameter instance
               ::ival +       // global instance
               ZooAnimal::ival +
               Bear::ival;
    }
```

The unmodified reference to ival is resolved to the formal parameter instance. (If ival were not defined within mumble(), the Bear member instance of ival is accessed. If ival were also not defined within class Bear, the ZooAnimal member instance of ival is accessed. If ival were also not defined within class ZooAnimal, the global instance of ival is accessed.)

The resolution of a class member is always performed prior to determining whether the access is actually legal, which may at first seem counterintuitive. For example, consider this revised implementation of mumble():

```
    int dval;
    int Bear::mumble( int ival )
    {
        // error: resolves to private member ZooAnimal::dval
        return ival + dval;
    }
```

We might argue that the lookup algorithm should resolve to the first legally accessible identifier it finds, rather than the most immediate identifier, but it does not. In this example, the lookup algorithm executes as follows:

1. Is dval defined within the local scope of the Bear member function? No.
2. Is dval defined within the class Bear scope? No.
3. Is dval defined within the base class ZooAnimal scope? Yes. The reference is resolved to this instance.

Now that the instance is resolved, the compiler checks to see if access of that instance is legal. In this case, it is not: dval is a private data member, and may not be accessed directly within mumble(). A correct (and probably the intended) resolution requires an explicit scope operator:

```
    return ival + ::dval; // ok
```

The primary rationale governing resolving a member prior to considering its access level is to prevent possibly subtle changes in the program semantics based on a seemingly unrelated change in the access level of a member. For example, consider an invocation such as

```
    int dval;
    int Bear::mumble( int ival )
    {
        foo( dval );
        // ...
    }
```

Were foo() an overloaded function, moving ZooAnimal::dval from a private to a protected member might very well change the entire call sequence within mumble() — something the class designer was likely completely unaware of when changing the member's access level.

A member function with the same name and signature between the base and derived class behaves the same as a same-named data member: The derived class member hides the base class member lexically within the scope of the derived class. To invoke the base class member, the base class scope operator must be used. For example:

```cpp
ostream& Bear::print( ostream &os ) const
{
    // invokes ZooAnimal::print(os)
    ZooAnimal::print( os );

    os << name;
    return os;
}
```

18.4.1   Class Scope Under Multiple Inheritance

How does the introduction of multiple inheritance affect class scope lookup? All the immediate base classes are searched simultaneously, giving rise to the possibility of an ambiguous reference if a member with the same name is inherited from two or more base classes. Let's walk through a few examples to see how the ambiguity can arise and the different strategies for resolving it. First, consider the following set of classes:

```cpp
class Endangered {
public:
    ostream& print( ostream& ) const;
    void highlight();
    // ...
};

class ZooAnimal {
public:
    bool onExhibit() const;
    // ...
private:
    bool highlight( int zoo_location );
    // ...
};

class Bear : public ZooAnimal {
public:
    ostream& print( ostream& ) const;
    void dance( dance_type ) const;
    // ...
};
```

When we derived our Panda class using multiple inheritance,

```
class Panda : public Bear, public Endangered {
public:
    void cuddle() const;
    // ...
};
```

although there are two latent ambiguities in the inheritance of both the `print()` and `highlight()` functions from the Bear and Endangered base classes, no error message is issued until an ambiguous attempt to reference either of those functions occurs.

While the ambiguity of the two inherited `print()` members is reasonably obvious, the conflict between the two `highlight()` members might come as something of a surprise (admittedly, that's its purpose here). After all, the two instances have different access levels and different function prototypes. Moreover, the Endangered instance is a member of one of the two immediate base classes whereas the ZooAnimal instance is a member of the base class of the second immediate base class.

It doesn't matter (well, we'll see that actually it does matter, but only under virtual inheritance). Bear inherits the private ZooAnimal `highlight()` member; it is visible lexically even if it is not legal to invoke it either within Bear or Panda. Panda inherits two lexically visible members named `highlight`, and so any unqualified reference results in a compile-time error.

A lookup of an identifier begins with a search of the immediate scope in which the reference occurs. For example, if we write

```
int main()
{
    Panda yin_yang;
    yin_yang.dance( Bear::macarena );
}
```

the immediate scope is the class to which `yin_yang` belongs — Panda. If we write

```
void Panda::mumble()
{
    dance( Bear::macarena );
    // ...
}
```

the immediate scope is the local scope of the `mumble()` member function. If a declaration is found, of course, the identifier is resolved and lookup concludes. Otherwise, the enclosing scopes are searched.

Under multiple inheritance, the search simulates the simultaneous examination of each base class inheritance subtree — in our example, both the Endangered and the Bear/ZooAnimal subtrees. If a declaration is found in only one base class subtree, the identifier is resolved and the lookup algorithm concludes. This is what happens with the invocation of dance():

```
// ok: Bear::dance()
yin_yang.dance( Bear::macarena );
```

If a declaration is found in two or more base class subtrees, the reference is ambiguous, and a compile-time error message is generated. This is what happens with the unqualified invocation of print():

```
int main()
{
    // error: ambiguous: one of
    //    Bear::print( ostream& ) const
    //    Endangered::print( ostream& ) const
    Panda yin_yang;
    yin_yang.print( cout );
}
```

A program-level solution to the member ambiguity is to qualify explicitly the instance we wish to invoke using the class scope operator. For example:

```
int main()
{
    // ok: but not preferred
    Panda yin_yang;
    yin_yang.Bear::print( cout );
}
```

While this solves the problem, in general it is not a satisfactory solution. The reason is that the user has now been placed in the position of having to decide what the right behavior is for the Panda class. This burden of responsibility should never be placed on the user of a class. Rather, the class designer has to attend to these details. The preferred solution is for the Panda class itself to resolve any ambiguities intrinsic to its inheritance hierarchy. The simplest way to do this is to define a named instance within the derived class that provides the desired behavior. For example:

```
inline void Panda::highlight() {
    Endangered::highlight();
}

inline ostream&
Panda::print( ostream &os ) const
{
    Bear::print( os );
    Endangered::print( os );
    return os;
}
```

Because successfully compiling the declaration of a multiply derived class does not guarantee that there are no latent ambiguities, we strongly recommend that each of its methods, however trivial, be exercised during unit testing of the class.

Exercise 18.9

Given the following class hierarchy, with the following collection of data members,

```
class Base1 {
public:
    // ...
protected:
    int    ival;
    double dval;
    char   cval;
    // ...
private:
    int    *id;
    // ...
};

class Base2 {
public:
    // ...
protected:
    float  fval;
    // ...
private:
    double dval;
    // ...
};

class Derived : public Base1 {
public:
    // ...
protected:
    string sval;
    double dval;
    // ...
};

class MI : public Derived, public Base2 {
public:
    // ...
protected:
    int            *ival;
    complex<double> cval;
    // ...
};
```

and the following `MI::foo()` member function skeleton,

```
int ival;
double dval;

void MI::
foo( double dval )
{
    int id;
    //...
}
```

(a) Identify the set of members visible from within MI. Are there any visible from multiple base classes?

(b) Identify the set of members visible from within `MI::foo()`.

Exercise 18.10

Using the class hierarchy defined in Exercise 18.9, identify which of the assignments, if any, are in error within the `MI::bar()` member function:

```
void MI::
bar()
{
    int sval;
    // exercise questions occur here ...
}
```

```
(a) dval = 3.14159;  (d) fval = 0;
(b) cval = 'a';       (e) sval = *ival;
(c) id = 1;
```

Exercise 18.11

Using the class hierarchy defined in Exercise 18.9, and the following skeleton of the `MI::foobar()` member function,

```
int id;

void MI::
foobar( float cval )
{
    int dval;
    // exercise questions occur here ...
}
```

(a) Assign the local instance of `dval` the sum of the `dval` member of Base1 added to the `dval` member of Derived.

(b) Assign the real portion of the `cval` of MI to the `fval` member of Base2.

(c) Assign the cval member of Base1 to the first character of the sval member of Derived.

Exercise 18.12

Given the following class hierarchy, with the following collection of member functions named print(),

```
class Base {
public:
   void print( string ) const;
   // ...
};

class Derived1 : public Base {
public:
   void print( int ) const;
   // ...
};

class Derived2 : public Base {
public:
   void print( double ) const;
   // ...
};

class MI : public Derived1, public Derived2 {
public:
   void print( complex<double> )const;
   // ...
};
```

(a) Why does the following result in a compile-time error?

```
MI mi;
string dancer( "Nijinsky" );
mi.print( dancer );
```

(b) How can we revise the definition of MI to allow this to compile and execute correctly?

18.5   Virtual Inheritance ◆

By default, inheritance in C++ is a specialized form of composition by value. When we write

```
class Bear : public ZooAnimal { ... };
```

each Bear class object contains all the nonstatic data members of its ZooAnimal base class subobject together with the nonstatic data members declared within Bear. Similarly, when a derived class is itself an object of derivation, as in

```
class PolarBear : public Bear { ... };
```

each PolarBear class object contains all the nonstatic data members declared within PolarBear together with all the nonstatic data members of its Bear subobject and all the nonstatic data members of its ZooAnimal subobject.

Under single inheritance, the specialized form of composition by value supported by inheritance provides the most efficient and compact object representation. It becomes a problem only under multiple inheritance when a base class occurs multiple times within the derivation hierarchy. The most prominent real-world example of this is the iostream class hierarchy. Recall from Figure 18.2 that both the ostream and istream classes are derived from the abstract ios base class. The iostream class is subsequently derived from both ostream and istream:

```
class iostream :
     public istream, public ostream { ... };
```

By default, each iostream class object contains two ios subobjects: the instance contained within its istream subobject and the instance within its ostream subobject. Why is this bad? In terms of simple efficiency, storing two copies of the ios subobject wastes storage, because iostream needs only one instance. Moreover, the ios constructor is invoked twice, once for each subobject. A more serious problem is the ambiguity to which the two instances give rise. For example, any unqualified access to an ios member is a compile-time error: Which instance is intended? What if the ostream and istream classes initialize their ios subobjects slightly differently? How do we ensure a coherent pair of ios values by the iostream class? Under the default composition by value mechanism, there is really no good way of ensuring that.

The language solution is to provide an alternative composition by reference inheritance mechanism: *virtual inheritance*. Under virtual inheritance, only a single, shared base class subobject is inherited regardless of how many times the base class occurs within the derivation hierarchy. The shared base class subobject is called a *virtual base class*. Using virtual inheritance, the duplication of base class subobjects and the ambiguities to which the duplication gives rise are removed.

For the purposes of walking through the syntax and semantics of virtual inheritance, we have chosen to use the Panda class as a pedagogical example. Within zoological circles, for more than a 100 years there has been an occasionally fierce debate as to whether the Panda belongs to the Raccoon or the Bear family. Since software design is primarily a service industry, our most practical solution is to derive Panda from both:

```
class Panda : public Bear,
              public Raccoon, public Endangered { ... };
```

Our virtual inheritance Panda hierarchy is pictured in Figure 18.4, in which the
two dotted arrows indicate a virtual derivation of both Bear and Raccoon from Zoo-
Animal, and the three solid arrows indicate a nonvirtual derivation of Panda from
Bear, Raccoon, and, for good measure, our Endangered class from Section 18.2.

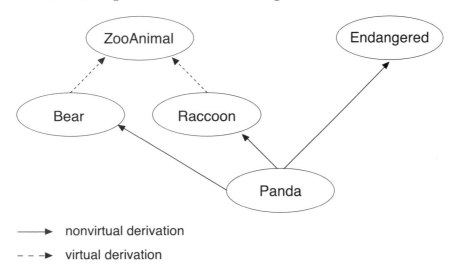

Figure 18.4 Virtual Inheritance Panda Hierarchy

If we examine Figure 18.4, we notice a nonintuitive aspect of virtual inheritance:
The virtual derivation (in our case, of Bear and Raccoon) has to be made prior to any
actual need for it to be present. Virtual inheritance becomes necessary only with the
declaration of Panda, but if Bear and Raccoon are not already virtually derived, the designer of the Panda class is out of luck.

Does this mean that we should derive our base classes virtually just in case some-
time down the hierarchical life cycle virtual inheritance may be needed? No. We
strongly recommend against that. The performance impact (and added complexity of
subsequent class derivations) can be significant; see [LIPPMAN96a] for performance
measurements and discussion.

Are we saying that we should never use virtual inheritance? Again, no. In practice,
however, in nearly all successful uses of virtual inheritance, the entire hierarchical subtree requiring virtual inheritance, such as the iostream library or our Panda subtree, is
designed at one time by either the same individual or the project design group.

In general, unless virtual inheritance provides a solution to an immediate design
problem, we recommend against its use. Of course, with that said, let's now look at
how we might use it.

18.5.1   Virtual Base Class Declaration

A base class is specified as being derived through virtual inheritance by modifying its declaration with the keyword virtual. For example, the following declarations make ZooAnimal a virtual base class of both Bear and Raccoon:

```
// the order of the keywords public and virtual
// is not significant

class Bear : public virtual ZooAnimal { ... };
class Raccoon : virtual public ZooAnimal { ... };
```

The virtual derivation is not an explicit aspect of the base class itself, but rather of its relationship to the derived class. As we stated earlier, virtual inheritance provides for composition by reference. That is, access of the subobject and its nonstatic members is carried out by indirection. This provides the necessary flexibility to combine the multiply inherited virtual base class subobjects into a single shared instance within the derived class. At the same time, an object of the derived class can be manipulated through a pointer or a reference to a base class type even though the base class is virtual. For example, all of the following Panda base class conversions execute correctly even though Panda is designed as a virtual inheritance hierarchy:

```
extern void dance( const Bear* );
extern void rummage( const Raccoon* );

extern ostream&
    operator<<( ostream&, const ZooAnimal& );

int main()
{
    Panda yin_yang;

    dance( &yin_yang );    // ok
    rummage( &yin_yang );  // ok
    cout << yin_yang;      // ok
    // ...
}
```

Any class that can be specified as a base class can be specified as a virtual base class as well, and may contain all the class elements supported by nonvirtual base classes. For example, here is our ZooAnimal class declaration:

```
#include <iostream>
#include <string>

class ZooAnimal;
extern ostream&
    operator<<( ostream&, const ZooAnimal& );
```

```
class ZooAnimal {
public:
    ZooAnimal( string name,
               bool onExhibit, string fam_name )
          : _name( name ),
            _onExhibit( onExhibit), _fam_name( fam_name )
    {}

    virtual ~ZooAnimal();
    virtual ostream& print( ostream& ) const;
    string name() const { return _name; };
    string family_name() const { return _fam_name; }
    // ...

protected:
    bool    _onExhibit;
    string _name;
    string _fam_name;
    // ...
};
```

The declaration and implementation of the immediate derived class instance is the same as under a nonvirtual derivation except for the use of the virtual keyword. For example, here is our Bear class declaration:

```
class Bear : public virtual ZooAnimal {
public:
    enum DanceType {
        two_left_feet, macarena, fandango, waltz };

    Bear( string name, bool onExhibit=true )
        : ZooAnimal( name, onExhibit, "Bear" ),
          _dance( two_left_feet )
    {}

    virtual ostream& print( ostream& ) const;
    void dance( DanceType );
    // ...

protected:
    DanceType _dance;
    // ...
};
```

Similarly, here is our Raccoon class declaration:

```
class Raccoon : public virtual ZooAnimal {
public:
    Raccoon( string name, bool onExhibit=true )
            : ZooAnimal( name, onExhibit, "Raccoon" ),
              _pettable( false )
```

```
        {}

        virtual ostream& print( ostream& ) const;

        bool pettable() const { return _pettable;   }
        void pettable( bool petval ) { _pettable = petval; }
        // ...

protected:
        bool _pettable;
        // ...
    };
```

18.5.2   Special Initialization Semantics

A derivation in which one or more virtual base classes are indirectly present requires special initialization semantics. Take a moment to look over the Bear and Raccoon class implementations in the previous section. Can you identify the initialization problem resulting from our Panda class derivation?

```
        class Panda : public Bear,
                      public Raccoon, public Endangered {
        public:
                Panda( string name, bool onExhibit=true );
                virtual ostream& print( ostream& ) const;

                bool sleeping() const { return _sleeping; }
                void sleeping( bool newval ) { _sleeping = newval; }
                // ...

        protected:
                bool _sleeping;
                // ...
            };
```

That's right. The problem is that both the Bear and the Raccoon base class constructors provide the ZooAnimal constructor with an explicit set of arguments. Even worse, in our example the arguments are not only different for the family name, they are invalid for our Panda class.

In a nonvirtual derivation, a derived class can initialize explicitly only its immediate base classes (see Section 17.4 for a discussion). In a nonvirtual derivation of Zoo-Animal, for example, Panda cannot directly invoke the ZooAnimal constructor in the Panda member initialization list. In a virtual derivation, however, only Panda may invoke directly the constructor of its ZooAnimal virtual base class.

The initialization of a virtual base class becomes the responsibility of the *most derived class* as determined by the declaration of each particular class object. For example: when we declare a Bear class object, as in

```
Bear winnie( "pooh" );
```

Bear is the most derived class of the winnie class object, and it is Bear's invocation of the ZooAnimal constructor that is executed. When we write

```
cout << winnie.family_name();
```

the output is

```
The family name for pooh is Bear.
```

Similarly, when we declare

```
Raccoon meeko( "meeko" );
```

Raccoon is the most derived class of the meeko class object, and it is Raccoon's invocation of the ZooAnimal constructor that is executed. When we write

```
cout << meeko.family_name();
```

the output is

```
The family name for meeko is Raccoon.
```

Now, when we declare a Panda class object, as in

```
Panda yolo( "yolo" );
```

Panda is the most derived class of the yolo class object, and so it becomes the responsibility of the Panda class to initialize ZooAnimal.

When a Panda object is initialized, (1) the explicit invocations of the ZooAnimal constructor within Raccoon and Bear are no longer executed during the execution of their respective constructors, and (2) the ZooAnimal constructor is invoked with the arguments specified for the ZooAnimal constructor in the initialization list of the Panda constructor. Here is our implementation:

```
Panda::Panda( string name, bool onExhibit=true )
            : ZooAnimal( name, onExhibit, "Panda" ),
              Bear( name, onExhibit ),
              Raccoon( name, onExhibit ),
              Endangered( Endangered::environment,
                          Endangered::critical )
              _sleeping( false )
    {}
```

If the Panda constructor does not specify arguments explicitly for the ZooAnimal constructor, one of two actions occurs: Either the ZooAnimal default constructor is called or, if there is no default constructor, the compiler issues an error message when the definition of Panda's constructor is compiled.

When we write

```
cout << yolo.family_name();
```

the output is

```
The family name for yolo is Panda.
```

Within Panda, both the Bear and Raccoon classes serve as intermediates rather than as the most derived class. As an intermediate derived class, direct invocations of all virtual base class constructors are suppressed automatically. Were Panda subsequently derived from, then Panda itself would become an intermediate class of the derived class object, and its invocation of the ZooAnimal constructor would be suppressed automatically.

You may perhaps have noticed that the two arguments being passed to both the Bear and Raccoon constructors are unnecessary when the classes serve as intermediate derived classes. A design solution to avoid the unnecessary argument passing is to provide an explicit constructor to be invoked when the class serves as an intermediate derived class. Our intermediate Bear class constructor, for example, might be modified as follows:

```
class Bear : public virtual ZooAnimal {
public:
    // when the most derived class
    Bear( string name, bool onExhibit=true )
        : ZooAnimal( name, onExhibit, "Bear" ),
          _dance( two_left_feet )
    {}

    // ... rest the same

protected:
    // when an intermediate derived class
    Bear() : _dance( two_left_feet ) {}

    // ... rest the same
};
```

We designate this instance of the constructor as protected because it is intended only to be invoked by subsequently derived classes. Presuming that we provide a similar default constructor for Raccoon, we can now revise our Panda constructor as follows:

```
Panda::Panda( string name, bool onExhibit = true )
        : ZooAnimal( name, onExhibit, "Panda" ),
          Endangered( Endangered::environment,
                      Endangered::critical )
          _sleeping( false )
    {}
```

18.5.3 Constructor and Destructor Order

Virtual base classes are always constructed prior to nonvirtual base classes regardless of where they appear in the inheritance hierarchy. For example, in the following admittedly whimsical TeddyBear derivation, there are two virtual base classes: the immediate ToyAnimal instance and the ZooAnimal instance from which Bear is derived:

```
class Character { ... };
class BookCharacter : public Character { ... };
class ToyAnimal { ... };

class TeddyBear : public BookCharacter,
                  public Bear, public virtual ToyAnimal
                  { ... };
```

The hierarchy is pictured in Figure 18.5, in which the virtual derivations are indicated with dashed arrows and the nonvirtual derivations are indicated with solid arrows.

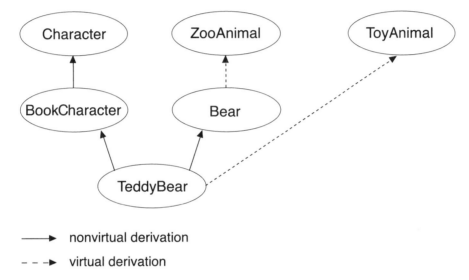

Figure 18.5 Virtual Inheritance TeddyBear Hierarchy

The immediate base classes are examined in the order of their declaration for the presence of virtual base classes. In our example, the inheritance subtree of BookCharacter is examined first, then that of Bear, and finally that of ToyAnimal. Each subtree is examined depth first; that is, the search begins with the root class and moves down. For the BookCharacter subtree, first Character, then BookCharacter are examined. For the Bear subtree, first ZooAnimal, then Bear are examined.

The order of virtual base class constructor invocations for TeddyBear, under this search algorithm, is ZooAnimal followed by ToyAnimal.

Once the virtual base class constructors are invoked, the nonvirtual base class constructors are invoked in the order of declaration: BookCharacter then Bear. Prior to execution of the BookCharacter constructor, its base class Character constructor is invoked.

Given the declaration

```
TeddyBear Paddington;
```

the order of base class constructors is as follows:

```
ZooAnimal();      // Bear's virtual base class
ToyAnimal();      // immediate virtual base class
Character();      // BookCharacter's nonvirtual base class
BookCharacter();// immediate nonvirtual base class
Bear();           // immediate nonvirtual base class
TeddyBear();      // most derived class
```

where the initialization of ZooAnimal and ToyAnimal are the responsibility of Teddy-Bear, the most derived class of the `Paddington` class object.

The order of copy constructor invocations under memberwise initialization (and of copy assignment operators under memberwise assignment) are the same. The order of base class destructor calls is guaranteed to be the reverse order of constructor invocation.

18.5.4 Visibility of Virtual Base Class Members

Let's redefine our Bear class to provide its own instance of the ZooAnimal `onExhibit()` member function:

```
bool Bear::onExhibit() { ... }
```

Referring to `onExhibit()` through a Bear class object now resolves to the Bear instance:

```
Bear winnie( "a lover of honey" );
winnie.onExhibit(); // Bear::onExhibit()
```

Referring to `onExhibit()` through a Raccoon class object still resolves to the inherited ZooAnimal member:

```
Raccoon meeko( "a lover of all foods" );
meeko.onExhibit(); // ZooAnimal::onExhibit()
```

The derived Panda class inherits the members of its two base classes. These fall into three categories:

1. The ZooAnimal virtual base class instances, such as `name()` and `family_name()`, which are not overridden by either the Bear or Raccoon derivations

2. The ZooAnimal virtual base class instance of `onExhibit()` inherited through Raccoon and the overriding instance Bear defines

3. The specialized Bear and Raccoon instances of the ZooAnimal `print()` function

Which of the inherited members can be accessed unambiguously and directly within the scope of the Panda class? Under a nonvirtual derivation, the answer is none. All unqualified references under a nonvirtual derivation are ambiguous. Under a virtual derivation, all of the members under items 1 and 2 can be accessed unambiguously and directly. For example, given the Panda class object

```
Panda spot( "Spottie" );
```

the call

```
spot.name();
```

invokes the shared ZooAnimal virtual base class name() member function. The call

```
spot.onExhibit();
```

invokes the derived Bear onExhibit() member function.

When two or more instances of a member are inherited through separate derivation paths (this applies not only to member functions, but data members and nested types as well) and if both represent the same virtual base class member, there is no ambiguity because a single instance of the member is shared (item 1); if one represents a virtual base class member and the other a subsequently derived instance, there is also no ambiguity (the specialized derived class instance is given precedence over the shared virtual base class instance [item 2]); but if both represent subsequently derived class instances, the direct access of the member is ambiguous. This is best resolved by providing an overriding instance in the derived class (item 3).

For example, under a nonvirtual derivation, an unqualified reference to onExhibit() through a Panda class object is ambiguous.

```
// error: ambiguous under nonvirtual derivation
Panda yolo( "a lover of bamboo" );
yolo.onExhibit();
```

Under a nonvirtual derivation, each inherited instance is given equal weight in resolving the reference, and so an unqualified reference results in a compile-time ambiguity error (see the discussion in Section 18.4.1).

Under a virtual derivation, the inheritance of a virtual base class member is given less weight than a subsequently redefined instance of that member. The inherited Bear instance of onExhibit() is given precedence over the ZooAnimal instance inherited through Raccoon:

```
// ok: unambiguous under virtual inheritance
// Bear::onExhibit() invoked
yolo.onExhibit();
```

If two or more base classes at the same derivation level redefine a virtual base class member, they are accorded equal precedence within the derived class. For example, if Raccoon also defined an onExhibit() member, Panda would need to qualify each access with the appropriate class scope operator.

```
bool Panda::onExhibit()
{
    return Bear::onExhibit() &&
        Raccoon::onExhibit() &&
        ! _sleeping;
}
```

Exercise 18.13

Given the following class hierarchy,

```
class Class { ... };
class Base : public Class { ... };
class Derived1 : virtual public Base { ... };
class Derived2 : virtual public Base { ... };
class MI : public Derived1,
           public Derived2 { ... };
class Final : public MI, public Class { ... };
```

(a) What is the order of constructor and destructor for the definition of a Final class object?

(b) How many Base subobjects does a Final class object contain? How many Class subobjects?

(c) Which of the following assignments is a compile-time error?

```
Base      *pb;
MI        *pmi;
Class     *pc;
Derived2 *pd2;

(i)  pb = new Class;   (iii) pmi = pb;
(ii) pc = new Final;   (iv)  pd2 = pmi;
```

Exercise 18.14

Given the following class hierarchy, with the following members,

```
class Base {
public:
    bar( int );
    // ...
protected:
    int ival;
    // ...
};

class Derived1 : virtual public Base {
public:
    bar( char );
    foo( char );
    // ...
protected:
    char cval;
    // ...
};

class Derived2 : virtual public Base {
```

```
public:
    foo( int );
    // ...
protected:
    int  ival;
    char cval;
    // ...
};
```

```
class VMI : public Derived1, public Derived2 {};
```

which inherited members can be accessed without qualification from within the VMI
class? Which require qualification?

Exercise 18.15

Given the following Base class with the following three constructors,

```
class Base {
public:
    Base();
    Base( string );
    Base( const Base& );
    // ...
protected:
    string _name;
};
```

define the associated three constructors for the following:

```
(a) one of either
    class Derived1 : virtual public Base{ ... };
    class Derived2 : virtual public Base{ ... };
(b) class VMI : public Derived1, public Derived2{ ... };
(c) class Final : public VMI{ ... };
```

18.6   A Multiple, Virtual Inheritance Example ◆

In this section we illustrate the definition and use of a multiple, virtual hierarchy by
implementing the Array class template hierarchy introduced in Section 2.4. We base
our implementation on the Array class template presented in Chapter 16, but modified to serve as a concrete base class. We preface our implementation with a brief
introductory discussion of using class templates with inheritance.

An instance of a class template can serve as an explicit base class, such as the following:

```
class IntStack : private Array<int> {};
```

Alternatively, a class template can be derived from a nontemplate base class, such
as the following,

```
class Base {};
template < class Type >
    class Derived : public Base {};
```

or serve as both a derived and base class of a derivation:

```
template < class Type >
    class Array_RC : public virtual Array<Type> {};
```

In the first example, the integer instantiation of the Array class template serves as a private base class of the nontemplate IntStack class. In the second example, the nontemplate Base class serves as the base class of each Derived class template instantiation. In the third example, each instantiation of the Array_RC class template has the associated Array class template instantiation as its base class. For example,

```
Array_RC<int> ia;
```

generates an integer instance of both the Array and Array_RC class templates.

In addition, the template parameter itself can serve as a base class. For example, [MURRAY93] illustrates this case,

```
template < typename Type >
    class Persistent : public Type{ ... };
```

which defines a derived persistent subtype for each instantiated type. As Murray notes, an implicit constraint on Type is that it be a class type. For example:

```
Persistent< int > pi; // oops, error
```

results in a compile-time error because the built-in types may not be the object of derivation.

When serving as a base class, a class template must be qualified with its full parameter list. Given the following class template definition, for example,

```
template < class T > class Base {};
```

one writes

```
template < class Type >
    class Derived : public Base<Type> {};
```

not

```
// error: Base is a template
// and template arguments must be specified
template < class Type >
    class Derived : public Base{};
```

In the next section, the Array class template defined in Chapter 16 serves as a virtual base class to (1) a range-checking Array subtype, (2) a sorted Array subtype, and (3) an Array subtype that is both sorted and supports range-checking. The original Array class template definition, however, is not suitable for derivation:

- All its data members and auxiliary functions are private, not protected.

- None of the type-dependent functions, such as the subscript operator, are specified as virtual.

Does this mean that our original implementation was wrong? No. It was correct insofar as we understood it. At the time of the original class template Array implementation, we hadn't realized the need for specialized Array subtypes. Now that we do, however, we need to revise the Array class template definition (the member function implementation remains the same). Here is our new Array class template definition:

```cpp
#ifndef ARRAY_H
#define ARRAY_H

#include <iostream>

// needed for the forward declaration of operator<<
template <class Type> class Array;

template <class Type> ostream&
    operator<<( ostream&, const Array<Type>& );

template <class Type>
class Array {
    static const int ArraySize = 12;
public:
    explicit Array( int sz = ArraySize ) { init( 0, sz ); }
    Array( const Type *ar, int sz )      { init( ar, sz); }
    Array( const Array &iA )    { init( iA.ia, iA.size()); }
    virtual ~Array()            { delete [] ia; }

    Array& operator=( const Array& );
    int size() { return _size; }
    virtual void grow();

    virtual void print( ostream& = cout );

    Type at( int ix ) const { return ia[ ix ]; }
    virtual Type& operator[]( int ix ) { return ia[ix]; }

    virtual void sort( int,int );
    virtual int find( Type );
    virtual Type min();
    virtual Type max();

protected:
    void swap( int,int );
    void init( const Type*, int );
```

```
        int _size;
        Type *ia;
};

#endif
```

One problem with this move toward polymorphism is that the general use of the subscript operator has gone from an inline memory access to a considerably more expensive virtual function call. For example, in the following function, whichever type to which ia actually refers, a simple inline read of the element is all that is necessary:

```
int find( const Array< int > &ia, int value )
{
    for ( int ix = 0; ix < ia.size(); ++ix )
            // now a virtual function call
            if ( ia[ ix ] == value )
                    return ix;
    return -1;
}
```

To accommodate performance concerns, we provide an inline at() member function providing a direct read of the element.

18.6.1   A Range-Checking Array Class Derivation

In the try_array() function of section 16.13 used to exercise our earlier implementation of the Array class template, there is the following two-statement sequence:

```
int index = iA.find( find_val );
Type value = iA[ index ];
```

find() returns the index of the first occurrence of find_val, or -1 if the value does not occur within the array. This code is incorrect because it does not test for a possible return value of -1. Since -1 falls outside the array boundary, each initialization of value is potentially invalid; each execution of our program is potentially in error. Let's define a range-checking Array subtype. We'll call it Array_RC and define it in a header file named Array_RC.h:

```
#ifndef ARRAY_RC_H
#define ARRAY_RC_H

#include "Array.h"

template <class Type>
class Array_RC : public virtual Array<Type> {
public:
    Array_RC( int sz = ArraySize )
            : Array<Type>( sz ) {}
```

```
        Array_RC( const Array_RC& r );
        Array_RC( const Type *ar, int sz );
        Type& operator[]( int ix );
};
```

```
#endif
```

Within the definition of the derived class, each reference to the template base class type specifier must be fully qualified with its formal parameter list. One writes

```
Array_RC( int sz = ArraySize )
        : Array<Type>( sz ) {}
```

not

```
// error: Array is not a type specifier
Array_RC( int sz = ArraySize ) : Array( sz ) {}
```

The only specialized behavior of the Array_RC class is the range-checking performed by its subscript operator. Otherwise, the Array class template implementation can be reused as is. However, because constructors are *not* inherited, recall, the Array_RC class defines a set of three constructors. The virtual derivation of Array_RC with Array anticipates the subsequent multiple derivation that we will look at later.

Here is the full Array_RC member function implementation placed in a file named Array_RC.C (the Array function definitions are placed in an Array.C header file because we use the inclusion model of template instantiation [see Section 16.8.1 for a discussion]):

```
#include "Array_RC.h"
#include "Array.C"
#include <assert.h>

template <class Type>
Array_RC<Type>::Array_RC( const Array_RC<Type> &r )
        : Array<Type>( r ) {}

template <class Type>
Array_RC<Type>::Array_RC( const Type *ar, int sz )
        : Array<Type>( ar, sz ) {}

template <class Type>
Type &Array_RC<Type>::operator[]( int ix ) {
        assert( ix >= 0 && ix < Array<Type>::_size );
        return ia[ ix ];
}
```

Why do we qualify the referenced members of the Array base class, such as the following qualification of _size?

```
Array<Type>::_size;
```

We must do so to prevent the Array base class from being examined until the template is instantiated. We do this by making the reference depend on the template parameter. That is, the names in the definition of Array_RC are resolved when the template is defined, except for the names that depend explicitly on a template parameter. When the unqualified name _size is used, the compiler must find a definition for _size unless the name depends explicitly on a template parameter. The name _size is made to depend on the template parameter by prefixing it with the base class name Array<Type>. The compiler then does not attempt to resolve name _size until the template is instantiated. (We'll see more examples of this in the class definition of Array_Sort.)

Each instantiation of Array_RC generates an associated Array class instance. For example,

```
Array_RC<string> sa;
```

generates both a string Array_RC and an associated String Array instance. The following program reruns try_array() (see Section 16.13 for the implementation), passing it objects of the Array_RC subtype. If our implementation is correct, the boundary violation will be caught.

```
#include "Array_RC.C"
#include "try_array.C"

main()
{
    static int ia[10] = { 12,7,14,9,128,17,6,3,27,5 };
    Array_RC<int> iA( ia,10 );

    cout << "class template instantiation Array_RC<int>\n";
    try_array( iA );

    return 0;
}
```

When compiled and executed, the program generates the following output:

```
class template instantiation Array_RC<int>

try_array: initial array values:
( 10 )< 12, 7, 14, 9, 128, 17
    6, 3, 27, 5 >

try_array: after assignments:
( 10 )< 128, 7, 14, 9, 128, 128
    6, 3, 27, 3 >

try_array: memberwise initialization
( 10 )< 128, 7, 14, 9, 128, 128
    6, 3, 27, 3 >
```

```
try_array: after memberwise copy
( 10 )< 128, 7, 128, 9, 128, 128
   6, 3, 27, 3 >

try_array: after grow
( 16 )< 128, 7, 128, 9, 128, 128
   6, 3, 27, 3, 0, 0
   0, 0, 0, 0 >

value to find: 5index returned: -1
Assertion failed: ix >= 0 && ix < _size
```

18.6.2   A Sorted Array Class Derivation

Here is our second Array specialization — a sorted Array subtype. We'll call it
Array_Sort and define it in a header file named Array_S.h:

```
#ifndef ARRAY_S_H
#define ARRAY_S_H

#include "Array.h"

template <class Type>
class Array_Sort : public virtual Array<Type> {
protected:
    void set_bit()   { dirty_bit = true; }
    void clear_bit() { dirty_bit = false; }
    void check_bit() {
      if ( dirty_bit ) {
          sort( 0, Array<Type>::_size-1 );
          clear_bit();
      }
    }

public:
    Array_Sort( const Array_Sort& );
    Array_Sort( int sz = Array<Type>::ArraySize )
        : Array<Type>( sz )
          { clear_bit();  }

    Array_Sort( const Type* arr, int sz )
        : Array<Type>( arr, sz )
          { sort( 0,Array<Type>::_size-1 ); clear_bit(); }

    Type& operator[]( int ix )
        { set_bit(); return ia[ ix ]; }

    void print( ostream& os = cout )
        { check_bit(); Array<Type>::print( os ); }
```

```
        Type min() { check_bit(); return ia[ 0 ]; }
        Type max() { check_bit(); return ia[ Array<Type>::_size-1 ]; }

        bool is_dirty() const { return dirty_bit; }
        int find( Type );
        void grow();

    protected:
        bool dirty_bit;
    };

    #endif
```

Array_Sort introduces an additional data member, dirty_bit. If dirty_bit is set, the array is no longer guaranteed to be in sorted order. A number of supporting access functions are also provided: is_dirty() returns the value of dirty_bit; set_bit() assigns dirty_bit a value of true; clear_bit() assigns dirty_bit a value of false; and check_bit() resorts the array if dirty_bit is set to true, then clears dirty_bit. Any operation that potentially places the array in a nonsorted order invokes set_bit().

Each reference to the base Array class template must specify the complete parameter list of the class.

```
        Array<Type>::print( os );
```

invokes the base class print() function for the associated Array class instance of each Array_Sort instantiation. For example,

```
        Array_Sort<string> sas;
```

instantiates both a string Array_Sort and a string Array class instance.

```
        cout << sas;
```

instantiates the string Array instance of the output operator, to which sas is passed. Within the operator, the call

```
        ar.print( os );
```

invokes the string Array_Sort virtual instance of print(). First, check_bit() is invoked. That done, the string Array instance of print() is invoked statically. (Invoked statically, you will recall, means that the function is resolved at compile-time and inline expanded if appropriate.) A virtual function is ordinarily invoked dynamically at run-time based on the actual object addressed ar. The virtual mechanism is overridden when a virtual function is invoked explicitly using the class scope operator, as in Array::print(). This is an important efficiency aid when we are invoking an explicit base class instance of a virtual function within the derived class instance of that function, as we do within Array_Sort's instance of print(). See Section 17.5 for a discussion.)

The member functions defined outside the class definition are placed in a file named Array_S.C. The declaration can look alarmingly complex due to the template syntax. However, except for the parameter lists, the declaration is the same as for a nontemplate class:

```
template <class Type>
Array_Sort<Type>::
Array_Sort( const Array_Sort<Type> &as )
        : Array<Type>( as )
{
        // note: as.check_bit() does not work!
        // -- see explanation below ...
        if ( as.is_dirty() )
                sort( 0, Array<Type>::_size-1 );
        clear_bit();
}
```

Each use of the template name as a type specifier must be qualified with its full parameter list. We write

```
template <class Type>
Array_Sort<Type>::
Array_Sort( const Array_Sort<Type> &as )
```

and not

```
template <class Type>
Array_Sort<Type>::
Array_Sort<Type>( // error: not a type specifier
```

because the second occurrence of Array_Sort serves as the name of the function and *not* as a type specifier.

The reason we write

```
if ( as.is_dirty() )
        sort( 0, _size );
```

rather than

```
as.check_bit();
```

is twofold. The first reason is type safety: check_bit() is a non-const member function — it modifies its associated class object. The argument as is passed as a reference to a constant object. A call of check_bit() on as violates its const-ness and is flagged as an error during compilation.

The second reason is that the copy constructor is not concerned with the array associated with as other than to determine if the newly created Array_Sort object needs to be sorted. The associated dirty_bit data member of the new Array_Sort object is not yet initialized, remember. When the body of the Array_Sort constructor begins, only the ia and _size members inherited from the Array class have as yet been initialized. The Array_Sort constructor must both initialize its additional data members (by calling

clear_bit()) and enforce any specialized behavior of its subtype (by calling sort()).
An alternative implementation of the Array_Sort constructor might be the following:

```
// an alternative implementation
template <class Type>
Array_Sort<Type>::
Array_Sort( const Array_Sort<Type> &as )
    : Array<Type>( as )
{
    dirty_bit = as.dirty_bit;
    check_bit();
}
```

Here is an implementation of the grow() member function.[1] The strategy is to reuse
the inherited Array class instance to allocate the additional memory, then resort the array elements and clear dirty_bit:

```
template <class Type>
void Array_Sort<Type>::grow()
{
    Array<Type>::grow();
    sort( 0, Array<Type>::_size-1 );
    clear_bit();
}
```

Here is a binary search implementation of the Array_Sort instance of find():

```
template <class Type>
int Array_Sort<Type>::find( Type val )
{
    int low = 0;
    int high = Array<Type>::_size-1;
    check_bit();

    while ( low <= high ) {
        int mid = ( low + high )/2;
        if ( val == ia[ mid ])
            return mid;
        if ( val < ia[ mid ] )
            high = mid-1;
        else low = mid+1;
    }
    return -1;
}
```

Let's try out the Array_Sort class implementation using the try_array() function. The

---

1. This has the potential danger of a dangling reference if the client has stored the address of an element returned
by reference from the original array before grow() copies to a new location. For a full discussion, see Tom Cargill's
article in [LIPPMAN96b].

following program tests both an integer and string instantiation of the Array_Sort class.

```
#include "Array_S.C"
#include "try_array.C"
#include <string>

main()
{
    static int ia[ 10 ] = { 12,7,14,9,128,17,6,3,27,5 };
    static string sa[ 7 ] = {
            "Eeyore", "Pooh", "Tigger",
            "Piglet", "Owl", "Gopher", "Heffalump"
    };

    Array_Sort<int> iA( ia,10 );
    Array_Sort<string> SA( sa,7 );

    cout << "class template instantiation Array_Sort<int>"
        << endl;
    try_array( iA );

    cout << "class template instantiation Array_Sort<string>"
        << endl;
    try_array( SA );

    return 0;
}
```

When the program is compiled and executed the string instance output looks as follows — note that it fails during execution when it attempts to display an element using an index with an out-of-bounds value of -1.

```
class template instantiation Array_Sort<string>

try_array: initial array values:
( 7 )< Eeyore, Gopher, Heffalump, Owl, Piglet, Pooh
   Tigger >

try_array: after assignments:
( 7 )< Eeyore, Gopher, Owl, Piglet, Pooh, Pooh
   Pooh >

try_array: memberwise initialization
( 7 )< Eeyore, Gopher, Owl, Piglet, Pooh, Pooh
   Pooh >

try_array: after memberwise copy
( 7 )< Eeyore, Piglet, Owl, Piglet, Pooh, Pooh
   Pooh >
```

```
try_array: after grow
( 11 )< <empty>, <empty>, <empty>, <empty>, Eeyore, Owl
     Piglet, Piglet, Pooh, Pooh, Pooh >

value to find: Tiggerindex returned: -1
Memory fault(coredump)
```

Notice that the display of the memberwise copied Array class string instance is *not* sorted. Why? Because the virtual function is invoked through an object of the class rather than a pointer or a reference. As we explain in Section 17.5, when called through a class object, the instance invoked reflects the active virtual function of the class type of that object, not the class type of the object that may have been assigned to it. Thus, the Sort instance through the Array class object is never invoked. (We include this simply as a demonstration. We would not do this in actual production code.)

18.6.3   A Multiply-Derived Array Class

Finally, let's define a sorted, range-checking array. It can be defined by inheriting from both Array_RC and Array_Sort. Here is the implementation (once again, our implementation is limited to three constructors and a subscript operator; the code is placed in a header file named Array_RC_S.h):

```cpp
#ifndef ARRAY_RC_S_H
#define ARRAY_RC_S_H

#include "Array_S.C"
#include "Array_RC.C"

template <class Type>
class Array_RC_S : public Array_RC<Type>,
                   public Array_Sort<Type>
{
public:
    Array_RC_S( int sz = Array<Type>::ArraySize )
        : Array<Type>( sz )
        { clear_bit(); }

    Array_RC_S( const Array_RC_S &rca )
      : Array<Type>( rca )
      { sort( 0,Array<Type>::_size-1 ); clear_bit(); }

    Array_RC_S( const Type* arr, int sz )
      : Array<Type>( arr, sz )
      { sort( 0,Array<Type>::_size-1 ); clear_bit(); }

    Type& operator[]( int index ) {
      set_bit();
      return Array_RC<Type>::operator[]( index );
```

```
    }
};
```

```
#endif
```

The class inherits two implementations of each Array class interface function: those of Array_Sort and those of the virtual Array base class inherited through Array_RC (except for the subscript operator, in which an overriding instance is inherited from both base classes). In a nonvirtual derivation, a call of find(), for example, is flagged as ambiguous — which inherited instance should be invoked? In a virtual derivation, however, the overriding Array_Sort set of instances is given precedence over the virtual base class instances inherited through Array_RC (this is discussed in detail in Section 18.5.4). Under virtual inheritance, an unqualified invocation of find() is resolved to the inherited Array_Sort class instance.

The subscript operator is redefined in both the Array_RC and Array_Sort base classes, and so are given equal precedence. Within Array_RC_Sort, an unqualified invocation of the subscript operator is ambiguous. The class must provide its own instance or else users of the class will not be able to apply the subscript operator directly to objects of the class. Semantically, what does it mean to invoke the subscript operator for the Array_RC_S class? To reflect the sorted nature of its derivation, it must set the inherited dirty_bit data member. To reflect the range-checking nature of its derivation, it must provide a test of the submitted index. That done, it can return the indexed element of the array. The latter two steps are provided by the inherited Array_RC subscript operator. The call

```
    return Array_RC::operator[]( index );
```

invokes this operator explicitly. Because it is an explicit invocation, the virtual mechanism is overridden. Because it is an inline function, its static resolution results in an inline expansion of its code.

Let's try out the implementation with an execution of the try_array() function, providing it in turn with an integer and string class instantiation of the Array_RC_S template class. Here is the program:

```
#include "Array_RC_S.h"
#include "try_array.C"
#include <string>

int main()
{
    static int ia[ 10 ] = { 12,7,14,9,128,17,6,3,27,5 };
    static string sa[ 7 ] = {
        "Eeyore", "Pooh", "Tigger",
        "Piglet", "Owl", "Gopher", "Heffalump"
    };
```

```
        Array_RC_S<int> iA( ia,10 );
        Array_RC_S<string> SA( sa,7 );

        cout << "class template instantiation Array_RC_S<int>"
            << endl;
        try_array( iA );

        cout << "class template instantiation Array_RC_S<string>"
            << endl;
        try_array( SA );

        return 0;
    }
```

Here is the output of the string instantiation of the template Array_RC_S class. The out-of-bound index error is now caught.

```
    class template instantiation Array_RC_S<string>

    try_array: initial array values:
    ( 7 )< Eeyore, Gopher, Heffalump, Owl, Piglet, Pooh
       Tigger >

    try_array: after assignments:
    ( 7 )< Eeyore, Gopher, Owl, Piglet, Pooh, Pooh
       Pooh >

    try_array: memberwise initialization
    ( 7 )< Eeyore, Gopher, Owl, Piglet, Pooh, Pooh
       Pooh >

    try_array: after memberwise copy
    ( 7 )< Eeyore, Piglet, Owl, Piglet, Pooh, Pooh
       Pooh >

    try_array: after grow
    ( 11 )< <empty>, <empty>, <empty>, <empty>, Eeyore, Owl
       Piglet, Piglet, Pooh, Pooh, Pooh >

    value to find: Tiggerindex returned: -1
    Assertion failed: ix >= 0 && ix < size
```

The presentation of our Array hierarchy is intended simply to illustrate the definition and use of both multiple and virtual inheritance. For an advanced discussion of array class design considerations see [NACKMAN94]. For most of our array needs, of course, the standard library vector class is sufficient.

Exercise 18.16

Add an additional member function to Array: spy(). If invoked, it remembers the operations applied to the class object: (a) number of index accesses, (b) number of times each member function is invoked, (c) the element value searched for, when find() is invoked, and (d) number of successful element searches. Explain your design. Modify the entire collection of Array subtypes so that spy() works for them as well.

Exercise 18.17

An associative array is another name for the standard library map due to its support of indexing based on a key value. Do you think an associative array makes a good candidate for subtyping our Array class? Why or why not?

Exercise 18.18

Reimplement our Array hierarchy using the standard library template container class and as many of the generic algorithms as possible.

19

Uses of Inheritance in C++

With inheritance, a pointer or a reference to a base class type can refer to an object of a derived class type. Our programs can then be written to manipulate these pointers or references, independent of the actual type of the objects to which they refer. This ability to manipulate more than one derived type with a base class pointer or reference is called *polymorphism*. In this chapter we look at three language features that provide special support for polymorphism. We first look at the Run-time Type Identification feature (also often called *RTTI*), which allows programs to retrieve the actual derived type of an object referred to through a pointer or a reference to a base class type. We then examine how exception handling is affected by class inheritance: how exceptions can be defined as class hierarchies and how handlers for a base class type can handle exceptions of a derived class type. Finally, we review the rules for function overload resolution to see how class inheritance influences the possible type conversions on a function argument and how it influences the selection of the best viable function.

19.1 Run-Time Type Identification

RTTI allows programs that manipulate objects as pointers or references to base classes to retrieve the actual derived types of the objects to which these pointers or references refer. Two operators are provided for the RTTI support in C++:

1. A `dynamic_cast` operator that allows for type conversions that are performed at run-time and that allows programs to navigate through a class hierarchy safely, converting a pointer to a base class to a pointer to a derived class or converting an lvalue referring to a base class to a reference to a derived class, only when the conversion is actually guaranteed to succeed

2. A `typeid` operator that indicates the actual derived type of the object referred to by a pointer or a reference

However, for the derived class type information to be retrieved, the operand of either the dynamic_cast operator or the typeid operator must be of a class type with one or more virtual functions. That is, the RTTI operators are run-time events for classes with virtual functions and compile-time events for all other types. In this section we look at the support provided by these two operators in more detail.

The use of RTTI in our programs is sometimes necessary when implementing applications such as debuggers or databases, in which the type of the objects manipulated by the application is only known at run-time, by inspecting the RTTI information stored with the objects' types. The use of the RTTI operators should, however, be minimized. The C++ static type system (that is, compile-time type checking) should be used whenever possible because it is safer and more efficient.

19.1.1   The dynamic_cast Operator

A dynamic_cast operator can be used to convert a pointer that refers to an object of class type to a pointer to a class in the same class hierarchy. A dynamic_cast operator can also be used to convert an lvalue for an object of class type to a reference to a class in the same class hierarchy. Unlike the other casts supported in C++, a dynamic_cast is a cast that is performed at run-time. If the pointer or lvalue operand cannot be cast to the target type of the conversion, the dynamic_cast fails. If a dynamic_cast to a pointer type fails, the result of the dynamic_cast is the value 0. If a dynamic_cast to a reference type fails, an exception is thrown. We show examples of failing dynamic_cast operations later.

Before we examine the behavior of the dynamic_cast in greater detail, let's examine why a user may need to use a dynamic_cast in a C++ program. Let's assume that our program uses a class library to represent the different kinds of employees in our company. The classes in the hierarchy support member functions to calculate our company's payroll. For example:

```
class employee {
public:
   virtual int salary();
};

class manager : public employee {
public:
   int salary();
};

class programmer : public employee {
public:
   int salary();
};
```

```
void company::payroll( employee *pe ) {
   // use of pe->salary()
}
```

Our company has different kinds of employees. The parameter to the company member function payroll() is a pointer to an employee class that may either refer to a manager type or a programmer type. Because payroll() calls the virtual member function salary(), the appropriate overriding function in either the manager or programmer class is called, depending on the kind of employee to which pe refers.

Let's assume that the employee class does not suit our needs any longer and we wish to modify it. We want to add an additional member function called bonus() to be used in addition to the member function salary() when calculating our company's payroll. We can do this by adding an additional virtual member function to the classes in the employee hierarchy. For example:

```
class employee {
public:
   virtual int salary();
   virtual int bonus();
};

class manager : public employee {
public:
   int salary();
};

class programmer : public employee {
public:
   int salary();
   int bonus();
};

void company::payroll( employee *pe )
{
   // use of pe->salary() and pe->bonus()
}
```

If payroll()'s parameter pe refers to an object of type manager, the virtual member function bonus() defined in the base class employee is called because the manager class does not override the virtual function bonus() defined in class employee. If payroll()'s parameter pe refers to an object of type programmer, the virtual member function bonus() defined in the class programmer is called.

When adding virtual functions to a class hierarchy, it becomes necessary to recompile all of the class member functions in the class hierarchy. We can add the virtual member function bonus() if we have access to the source code implementing the member functions of the classes employee, manager, and programmer. This is not always the case. If the previous class hierarchy is provided by a third-party library vendor, the vendor may have provided only the headers defining the interface of the classes in the library and the object files for the library. The source code for the class member functions may not be available. In this case, recompiling the member functions for the classes in the hierarchy is not possible.

If we wish to extend the class library, we cannot add virtual member functions. We may still want to add the functionality, in which case the use of the `dynamic_cast` becomes necessary.

The `dynamic_cast` operator is used to obtain a pointer to a derived class to use some detail of the derived class that is not otherwise available. For example, let's assume that we extend the library by adding the additional member function `bonus()` to the class programmer. We can add the declaration of this member function to the definition of the class programmer available in the header file, and define this new member function in one of our own program text files:

```
class employee {
public:
   virtual int salary();
};

class manager : public employee {
public:
   int salary();
};

class programmer : public employee {
public:
   int salary();
   int bonus();
};
```

Remember that our function `payroll()` receives a parameter that is a pointer to the base class employee. We can use the `dynamic_cast` operator to obtain a pointer to the derived class programmer and use this pointer to call the member function `bonus()`, as follows:

```
void company::payroll( employee *pe )
{
   programmer *pm = dynamic_cast< programmer* >( pe );

   // if pe refers to an object of type programmer,
   // the dynamic_cast is successful,
   // and pm refers to the start of the programmer object
   if ( pm ) {
      // use pm to call programmer::bonus()
   }
```

```
        // if pe does not refer to an object of type programmer,
        // the dynamic_cast fails,
        // and pm has the value 0
        else {
            // use of employee's member functions
        }
    }
```

The dynamic_cast

```
    dynamic_cast< programmer* >( pe )
```

converts its operand pe to the type programmer*. The cast is successful if pe refers to an object of type programmer, otherwise, the cast fails and the result of the dynamic_cast is the value 0.

The dynamic_cast operator therefore performs two operations at once. It verifies that the requested cast is indeed valid, and then only if it is valid does it perform the cast. The verification takes place at run-time. The dynamic_cast is safer than the other C++ cast operations because the other casts do not verify whether the cast can actually be performed.

In the previous example, if at run-time pe actually points to a programmer object, the dynamic_cast operation is successful and pm is initialized to point to a programmer object. Otherwise, the result of the dynamic_cast operation is 0 and pm is initialized with the value 0. By checking the value of pm, the function company::payroll() knows when pe refers to a programmer object. It can then use the member function programmer::bonus() to calculate a programmer's salary. If the dynamic_cast fails because pe refers to a manager object, the more general pay calculation that does not use the new member function programmer::bonus() is used instead.

The dynamic_cast is used for safe casting from a pointer to a base class to a pointer to a derived class, often referred to as safe *downcasting*. It is used when one must use the features of the derived class that are not present in the base class. Manipulating objects of derived class type with pointers to base class type is usually handled automatically through virtual functions. In some situations however, the use of virtual functions is not possible. The dynamic_cast offers an alternate mechanism for such situations, although this mechanism is more error prone than virtual member functions and should be used with caution.

One possible error is using the result of the dynamic_cast before appropriately testing that its result has the value 0. If it does, then this result cannot be used as if it refers to a class object. For example:

```
    void company::payroll( employee *pe ) {
        programmer *pm = dynamic_cast< programmer* >( pe );

        // potential error: uses pm before testing its value
        static int variablePay = 0;
```

```
        variablePay += pm->bonus();
        // ...
    }
```

The result of the dynamic_cast operator must always be tested to verify that the cast is successful before using the resulting pointer. A better definition for the company::payroll() function is as follows:

```
    void company::payroll( employee *pe )
    {
        // dynamic_cast and test in condition expression
        if ( programmer *pm = dynamic_cast< programmer* >( pe ) ) {
            // use pm to call programmer::bonus()
        }
        else {
            // use of employee's member functions
        }
    }
```

The result of the dynamic_cast operation is used to initialize the variable pm inside the condition expression of the if statement. This is possible because declarations in conditions yield values. The true path of the if statement is executed if pm is not zero; that is, if the dynamic_cast is successful because the pointer pe actually points to a programmer object, otherwise the declaration yields the value 0 and the else path is taken. Because the dynamic_cast operation and the test of its result are now in a single statement, it is not possible to insert code by mistake between the dynamic_cast and the test, and to use pm before it is tested appropriately.

In the previous example, a dynamic_cast operation converts a pointer to a base class to a pointer to a derived class. A dynamic_cast can also be used to convert an lvalue of a base class type to a reference to a derived class type. The syntax for such a dynamic_cast operation is the following,

```
        dynamic_cast< Type& >( lval )
```

where Type& is the target type of the conversion and lval is the lvalue of base class type. The dynamic_cast operation converts the operand lval to the desired type Type& only if lval actually refers to an object that is of a type that has a base class or a derived class that is of type Type.

Because there is no such thing as a null reference (see Section 3.6), it is not possible to verify the success of a reference dynamic_cast by comparing its result (the reference resulting from the dynamic_cast) with 0. If one wants to use references instead of pointers in the previous example, the condition

```
        if ( programmer *pm = dynamic_cast< programmer* >( pe ) )
```

cannot be rewritten as follows:

```
        if ( programmer &pm = dynamic_cast< programmer& >( pe ) )
```

An error situation is reported differently by the dynamic_cast operator when it is used to convert to a reference type. A reference dynamic_cast that fails, throws an exception.

The previous example must then be rewritten to use a dynamic_cast to a reference type as follows:

```
#include <typeinfo>
void company::payroll( employee &re )
{
    try {
        programmer &rm = dynamic_cast< programmer & >( re );
        // use re to call programmer::bonus()
    }
    catch ( std::bad_cast ) {
        // use of employee's member functions
    }
}
```

If a reference dynamic_cast fails, an exception of type bad_cast is thrown. The class type bad_cast is defined in the C++ standard library. To refer to this type in our program, as in the previous example, we must include the header <typeinfo>. (We look at the exceptions defined in the C++ standard library in the next section.)

When should a reference dynamic_cast be used instead of a pointer dynamic_cast? This is really a programmer's choice. With a reference dynamic_cast, it is not possible to ignore a cast that fails and use the result of the dynamic_cast without testing it properly for its result, as can be done with a pointer dynamic_cast. However, using exceptions adds an associated run-time cost to a program (as explained in Chapter 11) and some programmers may prefer using pointer dynamic_casts instead.

19.1.2   The typeid Operator

A second operator provided with the RTTI support is the typeid operator. The typeid operator allows a program to ask of an expression: What type are you? If the expression is of class type and the class contains one or more virtual member functions, then the answer may be different than the type of the expression itself. For example, if the expression is a reference to a base class, the typeid operator indicates the derived class type of the underlying object. For example:

```
#include <typeinfo>

programmer pobj;
employee &re = pobj;

// we look at name() in the subsection on type_info below
// name() returns the C-style string: "programmer"
cout << typeid( re ).name() << endl;
```

The operand of the `typeid` operator `re` is of the type employee. However, because `re` is a reference to a class type with virtual functions, the result of the `typeid` operator indicates the type of the underlying object to be that of programmer (and not employee, the type of the operand `re`). When using the `typeid` operator, a program text file must include the header <typeinfo> defined in the C++ standard library, as is done in this example.

What is the `typeid` operator used for? It is used for advanced system programming development, when building debuggers for example, or it is used to deal with persistent objects retrieved from a database. In such systems, when a program manipulates an object through a pointer or a reference to a base class, the program needs to find out the actual type of the object manipulated to list the properties of an object properly during a debugging session or to store and retrieve an object properly in a database. To find out the actual type of an object, the `typeid` operator can be used.

The `typeid` operator can be used with expressions and type names of any type. For example, expressions of built-in types as well as constants can be used as operands for the `typeid` operator. When the operand is not of class type, then the `typeid` operator indicates the type of the operand:

```
int iobj;

cout << typeid( iobj ).name() << endl; // prints: int
cout << typeid( 8.16 ).name() << endl; // prints: double
```

When the operand of the `typeid` operator is of class type, but not of a class type with virtual functions, then the `typeid` operator indicates the type of the operand as well, not the type of the underlying object:

```
class Base { /* no virtual function */ };
class Derived : public Base { /* no virtual function */ };

Derived dobj;
Base *pb = &dobj;

cout << typeid( *pb ).name() << endl; // prints: Base
```

The operand of the `typeid` operator has type Base, the type of the expression *pb. Because Base is not a class type with virtual functions, the result of the `typeid` operator indicates that the expression type is Base, even though the type of the underlying object to which pb refers has type Derived.

The result of the `typeid` operator can be compared. For example:

```
#include <typeinfo>

employee *pe = new manager;
employee& re = *pe;
```

```
if ( typeid( pe ) == typeid( employee* ) ) // true
    // do something
/*
if ( typeid( pe ) == typeid( manager* ) )  // false
if ( typeid( pe ) == typeid( employee ) )  // false
if ( typeid( pe ) == typeid( manager ) )   // false
*/
```

The condition of the if statement compares the result of using the `typeid` operator with an operand that is an expression with the result of using the `typeid` operator with an operand that is a type name. Notice that the comparison

```
typeid( pe ) == typeid( employee* )
```

yields true. This may seem surprising to users accustomed to writing:

```
// call to a virtual function
pe->salary();
```

which results in calling the function `salary()` of the manager derived class. `typeid(pe)` behaves differently from the virtual function call mechanism. This is because the operand `pe` is a pointer, not a class type. For the derived class type to be retrieved, the operand of `typeid` must be of class type (with virtual functions). The expression `typeid(pe)` indicates the type of `pe`; that is, pointer to employee. It compares equally to the typeid expression `typeid(employee*)`, whereas the results of the other comparisons are false.

It is when the expression `*pe` is used with `typeid` that the result indicates the type of the underlying object referred to by `pe`:

```
typeid( *pe ) == typeid( manager )  // true
typeid( *pe ) == typeid( employee ) // false
```

In these comparisons, because `*pe` is an expression of class type, and because the class has virtual functions, the result of `typeid` indicates the type of the underlying object to which the operand refers; that is, manager.

The `typeid` operator can also be used with references. For example:

```
typeid( re ) == typeid( manager )    // true
typeid( re ) == typeid( employee )   // false

typeid( &re ) == typeid( employee* ) // true
typeid( &re ) == typeid( manager* )  // false
```

In the first two comparisons, the operand `re` is of a class type with virtual functions. The result of the `typeid` operator thus indicates the type of the underlying object to which `re` refers. In the last two comparisons, the operand `&re` is of type pointer. The result of the `typeid` operator thus indicates the operand's type; that is, `employee*`.

The `typeid` operator actually returns a class object of type `type_info`. The class type `type_info` is defined in the header `<typeinfo>`. The class interface describes what can be done with the result of the `typeid` operator. We examine this interface in the next subsection.

19.1.3 The type_info Class

The exact definition of the type_info class is implementation-dependent, but certain features of this class are the same for every C++ program:

```cpp
class type_info {
    // Implementation-dependent representation
private:
    type_info( const type_info& );
    type_info& operator= ( const type_info& );
public:
    virtual ~type_info();

    int operator==( const type_info& ) const;
    int operator!=( const type_info& ) const;

    const char * name() const;
};
```

Because the copy constructor and the copy assignment operator of the class type_info are private members, users cannot define objects of type type_info in their program. For example:

```cpp
#include <typeinfo>

type_info t1; // error: no default constructor
              // error: private copy constructor
type_info t2 ( typeid( unsigned int ) );
```

The only way to create type_info objects in a program is to use the `typeid` operator.

The class also has overloaded comparison operators. These operators allow two type_info objects to be compared and hence allow the results obtained using the `typeid` operator to be compared, as we have seen in the previous subsection.

```cpp
typeid( re )  == typeid( manager )    // true
typeid( *pe ) != typeid( employee )   // false
```

The `name()` function returns a C-style character string for the name of the type represented by the type_info object. This function can be used in our programs as follows:

```cpp
#include <typeinfo>
int main() {
    employee *pe = new manager;

    // prints: "manager"
    cout << typeid( *pe ).name() << endl;
}
```

To use the member function name(), one must not forget to include the <typeinfo> header.

The type name is the only information guaranteed to be provided by all C++ implementations, through the type_info member function name(). As mentioned at the beginning of this section, the RTTI support is implementation dependent and some implementations may provide additional member functions for the class type_info that are not listed here. You should consult the reference manual for your compiler to identify the exact RTTI support provided. What additional support could be provided? Basically any information that a compiler can provide about a type can be added. For example:

1. a list of the class member functions
2. what the layout of an object of this class type looks like in storage; that is, how the member and base subobjects are mapped

One common technique that an implementation can choose to extend the RTTI support is to add the additional information in a class type derived from the class type_info. Because the class type_info contains a virtual destructor, the dynamic_cast operator can be used to determine if a particular kind of extended RTTI support is available. For example, let's say that an implementation provides additional support for RTTI through a class named extended_type_info, derived from the class type_info. Using a dynamic_cast, a program can find out whether the type_info object that the typeid operator returns is an extended_type_info type, and whether the additional RTTI support can be used in their program, as follows:

```
#include <typeinfo>

// typeinfo contains the definition of extended_type_info

typedef extended_type_info eti;

void func( employee* p )
{
   // downcast from type_info* to extended_type_info*
   if ( eti *eti_p = dynamic_cast<eti *>( &typeid( *p ) ) )
   {
      // if dynamic_cast succeeds
      // use extended_type_info information through eti_p
   }
   else
   {
      // if dynamic_cast fails
      // use standard type_info information
   }
}
```

If `dynamic_cast` succeeds, the `typeid` operator returns an object that is of extended_type_info type, meaning that the implementation supports additional RTTI support that the program can use. If the `dynamic_cast` fails, then only the basic RTTI support can be used by the program.

Exercise 19.1

Given the following class hierarchy, in which each class defines a default constructor and a virtual destructor,

```
class X { ... };
class A { ... };
class B : public A { ... };
class C : public B { ... };
class D : public X, public C { ... };
```

which, if any, of the following `dynamic_casts` fail?

```
(a) D *pd = new D;
    A *pa = dynamic_cast< A* >( pd );

(b) A *pa = new C;
    C *pc = dynamic_cast< C* >( pa );

(c) B *pb = new B;
    D *pd = dynamic_cast< D* >( pb );

(d) A *pa = new D;
    X *px = dynamic_cast< X* >( pa );
```

Exercise 19.2

Explain when you would use `dynamic_cast` instead of a virtual function.

Exercise 19.3

Using the class hierarchy defined in Exercise 19.1, rewrite the following piece of code to perform a reference `dynamic_cast` to convert the expression *pa to the type D&:

```
if ( D *pd = dynamic_cast< D* >( pa ) )
   // use D's members
}
else {
   // use A's members
}
```

Exercise 19.4

Given the following class hierarchy, in which each class defines a default constructor and a virtual destructor,

```
class X { ... };
class A { ... };
class B : public A { ... };
class C : public B { ... };
class D : public X, public C { ... };
```

which type name in each case is printed to standard output?

```
(a) A *pa = new D;
    cout << typeid( pa ).name() << endl;

(b) X *px = new D;
    cout << typeid( *px ).name() << endl;

(c) C cobj;
    A& ra = cobj;
    cout << typeid( &ra ).name() << endl;

(d) X *px = new D;
    A& ra = *px;
    cout << typeid( ra ).name() << endl;
```

19.2   Exceptions and Inheritance

Exception handling provides a standard language-level facility for responding to run-time program anomalies. C++ supports a uniform syntax and style for exception handling, and also supports fine-tuning of the exception handling facilities by individual programmers. Basic C++ support for exception handling is introduced in Chapter 11. Chapter 11 shows how a program may throw an exception; how, when an exception is thrown, program control transfers to an exception handler, if one exists for that exception; and how exception handlers are associated with try blocks.

The possibilities of exception handling become even more diverse when hierarchies of class types are used as exceptions. In this section we examine how to write our programs to throw and handle exceptions from such hierarchies.

19.2.1   Exceptions Defined as Class Hierarchies

In Chapter 11, we used two class types to describe the kinds of exceptions thrown by the member functions of our iStack class:

```
class popOnEmpty { ... };
class pushOnFull { ... };
```

In real-life C++ programs, the class types representing exceptions are most often organized into groups or hierarchies. What would the rest of the exception hierarchy for our two exception classes look like?

We can define a base class, called Excp, from which both of the exception classes are derived. This base class encapsulates the data members and member functions common to both derived classes:

```
class Excp { ... };
class popOnEmpty : public Excp { ... };
class pushOnFull : public Excp { ... };
```

One operation that the base class Excp can provide is a facility to print error messages. This facility is of use to both exception classes in the hierarchy:

```
class Excp {
public:
    // print error message
    static void print( string msg ) {
        cerr << msg << endl;
    }
};
```

The exception class hierarchy can be further refined. Other classes can be derived from the base class Excp to describe in a more detailed manner the possible exceptions that can be detected in our programs:

```
class Excp { ... };

class stackExcp : public Excp { ... };
    class popOnEmpty : public stackExcp { ... };
    class pushOnFull : public stackExcp { ... };

class mathExcp : public Excp { ... };
    class zeroOp : public mathExcp { ... };
    class divideByZero : public mathExcp { ... };
```

These further refinements allow for a more precise identification of the program anomalies that can happen in our program. The additional exception classes are organized into layers. As the hierarchy becomes deeper, every layer becomes a more specific exception. For example, the first and most general layer of our previous exception class hierarchy is represented by class Excp. The second layer specializes the class Excp into two different classes: stackExcp (for exceptions occurring when manipulating our iStack class) and mathExcp (for exceptions that happen within the functions of our math library). The third and most specialized layer of our hierarchy refines the exception classes even further. The classes popOnEmpty and pushOnFull define two kinds of stackExcp exceptions, whereas the classes zeroOp and divideByZero define two kinds of mathExcp exceptions.

In the following subsections we look at how to throw and handle exceptions with types that are the classes in the hierarchy we just defined.

19.2.2   Throwing an Exception of Class Type

Now that we have seen class types in more detail, let's examine what happens when the iStack member function push() throws an exception:

```
void iStack::push( int value )
{
   if ( full() )
      // value stored in exception object
      throw pushOnFull( value );
   // ...
}
```

Many steps take place as a consequence of executing this throw expression:

1. The throw expression creates a temporary object of class type pushOnFull by calling the class constructor.

2. An exception object of type pushOnFull is created to be passed to the exception handler. The exception object is a copy of the temporary object created by the throw expression in step 1. It is created by calling the class pushOnFull's copy constructor.

3. The temporary object created by the throw expression in step 1 is destroyed before the search for a handler starts.

You may wonder why step 2 is needed; that is, why is an exception object created? The throw expression

```
pushOnFull( value );
```

creates a temporary object that is destroyed at the end of the throw expression. The exception, however, must last until a handler is found, which may be many functions further up the chain of function calls. It is therefore necessary to copy the temporary object into a storage location, called the *exception object*, that is guaranteed to last until the exception has been handled. In some cases it may be possible for the implementation to create the exception object directly, without creating the temporary object in step 1. However, this temporary elimination is not required or always possible.

Because the exception object is created by copying the value of the throw expression, the exception thrown always has the exact type of the expression specified on the throw expression. For example:

```
void iStack::push( int value ) {
   if ( full() ) {
      pushOnFull except( value );
      stackExcp *pse = &except;
      throw *pse; // exception object has type stackExcp
   }
   // ...
}
```

The type of the expression *pse is stackExcp. The type of the exception object created is stackExcp, even though pse refers to an object with the actual type pushOnFull. The actual type of the object referred to by the throw expression is never examined to create the exception object. The exception is therefore not handled by a catch clause of type pushOnFull.

The actions of a throw expression imply some restrictions on the kind of classes that can be used to create exception objects. The throw expression in the iStack member function push() is in error if

1. The class pushOnFull does not have a constructor that accepts an argument of type int or if this constructor is not accessible

2. The class pushOnFull has either a copy constructor or a destructor that is not accessible

3. The class pushOnFull is an abstract base class, because a program cannot create an object of an abstract class type (as mentioned in Section 17.1)

19.2.3   Handling an Exception of Class Type

When exceptions are organized into class hierarchies, an exception of class type may be caught by a catch clause for a public base class of that class type. For example, an exception of type pushOnFull can be handled by a catch clause for exceptions of type stackExcp or Excp.

```
int main( ) {
   try {
      // ...
   }
   catch ( Excp ) {
      // handles popOnEmpty and pushOnFull exceptions
   }
   catch ( pushOnFull ) {
      // handles pushOnFull exceptions
   }
}
```

The order of catch clauses in the previous example is not optimal. Can you see why? Remember that catch clauses are examined in the order in which they appear following the try block. Once a catch clause has been found for an exception, no further catch clause is examined. In the previous example, because the catch clause for Excp exceptions handles exceptions of type pushOnFull, the specialized catch clause for pushOnFull exceptions is never entered! The appropriate order for the catch clauses is the following:

```
catch ( pushOnFull ) {
    // Handles pushOnFull exceptions
}
catch ( Excp ) {
    // Handles other exceptions
}
```

The catch clause for the derived class type must appear first. This ensures that the catch clause for the base class is only entered if no other catch clause applies.

When exceptions are organized in class hierarchies, users of a class library may choose the level of granularity with which their applications will deal with the exceptions thrown from the library. For example, when writing the function main(), we decided that our application would handle exceptions of type pushOnFull in some specific ways and this is why we provided a specialized catch clause for this kind of exception. We also decided that our application would handle all other exceptions in a more general manner. For example:

```
catch ( pushOnFull eObj ) {
    // uses the value() member function of class pushOnFull
    // See Section 11.3
    cerr << "trying to push the value " << eObj.value()
         << " on a full stack\n";
}
catch ( Excp ) {
    // uses the base class member function print()
    Excp::print( "an exception was encountered" );
}
```

As mentioned in Section 11.3, the process of finding a catch clause for an exception thrown does not behave at all like function overload resolution. During function overload resolution, the best viable function is selected by taking into account all of the candidate functions visible at the point of the call. During exception handling, the catch clause for an exception is not necessarily the catch clause that matches the exception best. The catch clause that is selected is the *first match*; that is, the first catch clause encountered that can handle the exception. This is why, in a list of catch clauses, the most specialized catch clause must appear first.

The exception declaration of a catch clause (that is, the declaration in parentheses following the keyword catch) behaves very much like the declaration for a function parameter. In our previous example, the exception declaration resembles a pass-by-value parameter. The object eObj is initialized with a copy of the value of the exception object in the same way that a pass-by-value function parameter is initialized with a copy of the value of the corresponding argument. As it is the case for function parameters, the exception declaration of a catch clause can be changed to a reference declaration. The catch clause then refers directly to the exception object created by the throw expression, instead of creating its own local copy. For the same reasons that parameters of class type should be declared as references to prevent unnecessary copying of large class objects, it is also preferable if exception declarations for exceptions of class type are declared as references. There are differences in the behavior of the catch clause depending on whether the exception declaration is an object or a reference (we look at these throughout the presentation of this section).

Chapter 11 introduces the rethrow expression that is used by a catch clause to pass an exception to another catch clause further up the list of function calls. A rethrow expression has the following form:

```
throw;
```

What is the behavior of such a rethrow expression when it is located in a catch clause for a base class type? For example, what is the type of the exception rethrown if mathFunc() throws an exception of type divideByZero?

```
void calculate( int parm ) {
    try {
        mathFunc( parm ); // throws a divideByZero exception
    }
    catch ( mathExcp mExcp ) {
        // partially handles the exception
        // and rethrows the exception object
        throw;
    }
}
```

Does the exception rethrown have the type of the exception thrown by mathFunc() (that is, divideByZero) or does it have the type of the exception declaration in the catch clause (that is, mathExcp)?

Remember that a throw; expression rethrows the *original* exception object. Since the original exception object has type divideByZero, the exception rethrown has type divideByZero. In the catch clause, the object mExcp is initialized with a copy of the MathExcp base class subobject of the divideByZero exception object. This copy is only accessed within the catch clause and is not the original exception object that is rethrown.

Let's say the class types in our exception hierarchy have destructors. For example:

```
class pushOnFull {
public:
    pushOnFull( int i ) : _value( i ) { }
    int value() { return _value; }
    ~pushOnFull(); // newly declared destructor
private:
    int _value;
};
```

When is this destructor called? To answer this question, we need to examine the catch clause in greater detail:

```
catch ( pushOnFull eObj ) {
   cerr << "trying to push the value " << eObj.value()
        << " on a full stack\n";
}
```

Because the exception declaration declares eObj as a local object to the catch clause, and because the class pushOnFull has a destructor, eObj is destroyed when the catch clause exits. But when is the destructor called for the exception object created when the exception was thrown?

You can probably take a few guesses. One possibility is when the catch clause is entered. Another possibility is when the catch clause exits. However, if the exception is destroyed at either of these two points, it may be destroyed too early. Can you see why? If the catch clause rethrows the exception, passing the exception object to a catch clause higher up in the chain of function calls, the exception object cannot be destroyed before the last catch clause handling the exception has been reached. For this reason, the exception object is not destroyed until the final catch clause for this exception exits.

19.2.4   Exception Objects and Virtual Functions

If the exception object thrown is of derived class type and it is handled by a catch clause for a base class type, the catch clause cannot generally use the features of the derived class type. For example, the member function value() declared in the exception class pushOnFull cannot be used in the catch clause that handles exceptions of type Excp:

```
catch ( Excp &eObj ) {
   // error: Excp does not have a member function value()
   cerr << "trying to push the value " << eObj.value()
        << " on a full stack\n";
}
```

We can redesign our exception class hierarchy to define virtual functions that can be used in the catch clause for the base class Excp to invoke the more specialized member functions in the derived class types. For example:

```
// new class definitions defining virtual functions
class Excp {
public:
   virtual void print() {
      cerr << "An exception has occurred"
           << endl;
   }
};

class stackExcp : public Excp { };
```

```
class pushOnFull : public stackExcp {
public:
   virtual void print() {
      cerr << "trying to push the value " << _value
           << " on a full stack\n";
   }
   // ...
};
```

The `print()` function can then be used in the catch clause as follows:

```
int main( ) {
   try {
      // iStack::push() throws a pushOnFull exception
   }  catch ( Excp eObj ) {
      eobj.print(); // calls virtual function
                    // oops, base class instance invoked
   }
}
```

Even though the exception thrown is of type pushOnFull, and even though the function `print()` is a virtual function, the statement `eObj.print()` prints the following line:

```
An exception has occurred
```

The `print()` function that is called is the member function of the base class Excp, not the overriding function for the derived class pushOnFull. Why isn't the `print()` function for the derived class called?

Remember that the catch clause's exception declaration behaves very much like a parameter declaration. When the catch clause is entered, because the exception declaration declares an object, eObj is initialized with a copy of the base class subobject Excp of the exception object. eObj is an object of type Excp, not an object of type pushOnFull. To call the virtual functions of the derived class objects, the exception declaration must declare a pointer or a reference. For example:

```
int main( ) {
   try {
      // iStack::push() throws a pushOnFull exception
   }
   catch ( Excp &eObj ) {
      eobj.print(); // calls virtual function
                    // pushOnFull::print()
   }
}
```

The exception declaration of the catch clause in this example is also of the base class type Excp, but because eObj is a reference, and because eObj refers to the exception object of type pushOnFull, eObj can be used to invoke virtual functions defined for the pushOnFull class type. When the catch clause calls the `print()` virtual function, the print() function for the derived class pushOnFull is called, and the program prints the following line:

```
trying to push the value 879 on a full stack
```

Therefore, another good reason to declare the exception declaration of the catch clause as a reference is to ensure that the virtual functions associated with the type of the exception object are properly invoked.

19.2.5 Stack Unwinding and Destructor Calls

When an exception is thrown, the search for a catch clause that can handle the exception takes place, starting within the function throwing the exception and proceeding up through the chain of nested function calls, until a catch clause for the exception is found. This process of searching for a catch clause up through the chain of function calls is called *stack unwinding*. Stack unwinding is first introduced in Section 11.3.

During stack unwinding, as the functions in the chain of function calls exit during the search for a catch clause, the actions each function performs are ended abruptly. This may not be so good if a function acquires a resource (for example, if it opens a file or allocates some memory on the free store) and this resource is never released.

There is a programming technique that allows programmers to work around this limitation. During stack unwinding, each time a compound statement or a block exits because the stack is unwound in the search for a catch clause, if the block that exits has some local object that is of class type, the destructor for this object is called automatically by the stack unwinding process before the compound statement or function exits. (Local objects are described in Section 8.1.)

For example, the following class encapsulates the acquisition of the free store memory for an array of ints in its constructor, and encapsulates the release of this memory in its destructor:

```
class PTR {
public:
   PTR()  { ptr = new int[ chunk ]; }
   ~PTR() { delete[] ptr; }
private:
   int *ptr;
};
```

A local object of this type is created in the function manip(), before the function mathFunc() is called:

```
void manip( int parm ) {
   PTR localPtr;
   // ...
   mathFunc( parm ); // throws a divideByZero exception
   // ...
}
```

If mathFunc() throws an exception of type divideByZero, stack unwinding proceeds up the chain of function calls to find a catch clause for the thrown exception. The function manip() is examined as the stack unwinding process proceeds. Because the call to the function mathFunc() is not placed within a try block, manip() is not searched for a catch clause for this exception. Stack unwinding proceeds further up the chain of function calls to the function invoking the function manip(). However, before manip() exits with this unhandled exception, stack unwinding destroys any object of class type local to the function manip() and created before the function mathFunc() is called. The local object localPtr is destroyed before stack unwinding proceeds further up in the chain of function calls, releasing the free store memory referred to by localPtr and preventing a memory leak.

This is why we say that the C++ exception handling process respects the programming technique known as "resource acquisition is initialization; resource release is destruction." If a resource is implemented as a class, and the actions to acquire the resource are encapsulated in the class constructor, and the actions to release the resource are encapsulated in the class destructor, as in our PTR class, an object of such a class type that is local to a function is destroyed automatically if the function exits with an unhandled exception. Any actions that must take place to release acquired resources therefore are not skipped by stack unwinding when these actions are encapsulated in a class destructor called for local objects.

You may remember the auto_ptr facility introduced in Section 8.4 and defined in the C++ standard library. This facility behaves very much like our PTR class. It is a facility that encapsulates the acquisition of the free store memory within its constructors and the release of this memory within its destructor. Using auto_ptr when allocating a single object on the free store guarantees that the free store memory is properly released when a compound statement or a function exits with an unhandled exception during stack unwinding.

19.2.6   Exception Specifications

Using an exception specification, a function declaration may specify the set of exceptions the function may throw directly or indirectly. An exception specification is a guarantee that the function will not throw any exception not listed in the exception specification. Exception specifications are first introduced in Section 11.4. There are a few things that we need to mention regarding exception specifications and class types.

First, exception specifications can be specified on class member functions just as they can for nonmember functions. As with nonmember functions, an exception specification on a member function declaration follows the function parameter list. For example, the class bad_alloc from the C++ standard library is defined such that its

member functions have an empty exception specification `throw()`. This indicates that
its member functions are guaranteed not to throw any exception:

```
class bad_alloc : public exception {
    // ...
public:
    bad_alloc() throw();
    bad_alloc( const bad_alloc & ) throw();
    bad_alloc & operator=( const bad_alloc & ) throw();
    virtual ~bad_alloc() throw();
    virtual const char* what() const throw();
};
```

Notice that if the member function is declared as a `const` or `volatile` member function, such as `what()` in the previous example, the exception specification follows the
`const` or `volatile` qualifier of the function declaration.

The exception specification on all the declarations of a function must specify the
same types. For member functions, if the function is defined outside the class definition, the definition must specify the same exception specification as the declaration of
the member function within the class definition. For example:

```
#include <stdexcept>
// <stdexcept> defines class overflow_error

class transport {
    // ...
public:
    double cost( double, double ) throw ( overflow_error );
    // ....
};

// error: exception specification differs from
//        the declaration in the class member list
double transport::cost( double rate, double distance ) { }
```

A virtual function in a base class may have an exception specification that differs
from the exception specification of the member function that overrides it in a derived
class. However, the exception specification of the derived class virtual function must
be either equally or more restrictive than the exception specification of the base class
virtual function. For example:

```
class Base {
public:
    virtual double f1( double ) throw ();
    virtual int f2( int ) throw ( int );
    virtual string f3( ) throw ( int, string );
    // ...
};
```

```
class Derived : public Base {
public:
    // error: exception specification is less restrictive
    //         than base::f1()'s
    double f1( double ) throw ( string );

    // ok: same exception specification as base::f2()
    int f2( int ) throw ( int );

    // ok: derived f3() is more restrictive
    string f3( ) throw ( int );
    // ...
};
```

Why must the exception specification of the derived class member function be as restrictive or more restrictive than the base class function? This ensures that when the derived virtual function is called through a pointer to a base class type, the call is guaranteed not to violate the exception specification of the base class member function. For example:

```
// guarantees not to throw exceptions
void compute( Base *pb ) throw()
{
    try {
        pb->f3( ); // may throw exception of type int or string
    }
    // handles exceptions from Base::f3()
    catch ( const string & ) { }
    catch ( int ) { }
}
```

The declaration of f3() in class Base guarantees that the function may only throw exceptions of type string or of type int. The function compute() is programmed to take advantage of this guarantee and only defines catch clauses to handle these exceptions. Because f3() in Derived is more restrictive than f3() in Base, our expectations when programming to the Base class interface are never violated.

Finally, in Chapter 11 we mention that no type conversion is allowed between the type of the exception thrown and a type specified in the exception specification. There is a small exception to this rule: when the exception specification specifies a class type or a pointer to a class type. If an exception specification specifies a class, then the function may throw exception objects of a class publicly derived from the class type in the exception specification. (Similarly for pointers, if an exception specification specifies a pointer to a class, the function may throw exception objects that are pointers to a class publicly derived from this class type.) For example:

```
class stackExcp : public Excp { };
class popOnEmpty : public stackExcp { };
```

```
class pushOnFull : public stackExcp { };

void stackManip() throw( stackExcp )
{
    // ...
}
```

The exception specification not only indicates that stackManip() may throw an exception of type stackExcp, but that it may also throw an exception of type popOnEmpty or pushOnFull. Recall that a class publicly derived from a base class reflects an *is-a* relationship and provides a specialization of its more general base class. Because the popOnEmpty and pushOnFull exceptions are a kind of stackExcp, these exceptions do not violate the exception specification of stackManip().

19.2.7   Constructors and Function try Blocks

It is possible to declare a function such that the entire body of the function is contained within a try block. Such a try block is called a *function try block* (we first discuss function try blocks in Section 11.2). For example:

```
int main()
try {
    // main()'s function body
}
catch ( pushOnFull ) {
    // ...
}
catch ( popOnEmpty ) {
    // ...
}
```

A function try block associates a group of catch clauses with a function body. If a statement within the function body throws an exception, the handlers that follow the function body are considered to handle the exception.

A function try block becomes necessary with class constructors. Let's examine why. A constructor definition has the following form:

```
class_name( parameter_list )
// member initialization list:
:   member1( expression1 ) , // initialization for member1
    member2( expression2 )   // initialization for member2
// function body:
{ /* ... */ }
```

expression1 and expression2 may be any kind of expression. In particular, these expressions may call functions that throw exceptions.

Let's reuse the class Account defined in Chapter 14 to show a more concrete example. The constructor for Account can be redefined as follows:

```
inline Account::
Account( const char* name, double opening_bal )
        : _balance( opening_bal - ServiceCharge() )
{
   _name = new char[ strlen(name)+1 ];
   strcpy( _name, name );

   _acct_nmbr = get_unique_acct_nmbr();
}
```

The function ServiceCharge() called by the member initialization for the member _balance may throw an exception. How should we implement this constructor if we want to handle all exceptions thrown by functions called during the construction of an object of type Account?

Placing the try block inside the function body does not work. For example:

```
inline Account::
Account( const char* name, double opening_bal )
        : _balance( opening_bal - serviceCharge() )
{
   try {
      _name = new char[ strlen(name)+1 ];
      strcpy( _name, name );

      _acct_nmbr = get_unique_acct_nmbr();
   }
   catch ( ...) {
      // special handling
      // does not catch exceptions
      // from member initialization list
   }
}
```

Because the try block does not enclose the member initialization list, the catch clause at the end of the constructor body is not considered for exceptions thrown by the function serviceCharge() in the member initialization list.

Using a function try block is the only solution that guarantees that all exceptions thrown during the construction of an object are caught within the constructor. A function try block can be defined for the constructor of class Account as follows:

```
inline Account::
Account( const char* name, double opening_bal )
try
        : _balance( opening_bal - serviceCharge() )
{
   _name = new char[ strlen(name)+1 ];
   strcpy( _name, name );
   _acct_nmbr = get_unique_acct_nmbr();
}
```

```
catch ( ... )
{
    // special handling
    // now catches exception from ServiceCharge()
}
```

Notice that the keyword try *precedes* the member initialization list, and the compound statement of the try block encompasses the constructor function body. The catch clause catch(...) is now considered to handle exceptions thrown either from within the member initialization list or from within the constructor body.

19.2.8   Exception Class Hierarchy in the C++ Standard Library

At the beginning of this section we introduced a hierarchy of exception classes used by our program to report program anomalies. The C++ standard library also provides an exception class hierarchy. The exception classes are used to report program anomalies encountered during the execution of the functions in the C++ standard library. These exception classes can also be used in the programs we write or can be further derived to describe the exceptions in the programs we write.

The root class in the C++ standard library exception hierarchy is called exception. This class is defined in the standard header <exception> and is the base class for every exception thrown by the C++ standard library functions. The class exception's interface is the following:

```
namespace std {
    class exception {
    public:
        exception() throw();
        exception( const exception & ) throw();
        exception& operator=( const exception& ) throw();
        virtual ~exception() throw();
        virtual const char* what() const throw();
    };
}
```

As with every class defined in the C++ standard library, the class exception is placed within the namespace std to prevent the pollution of the global name space in our programs.

The first four functions in the class definition are the default constructor, copy constructor, copy assignment operator, and destructor. Because these member functions are public member functions, any program can freely create, copy, and assign exception objects. The destructor is a virtual function to facilitate the definition of classes further derived from the class exception.

The most interesting function in this list is the function what(), which returns a C-style character string. The purpose of this C-style character string is to provide some sort of textual description of the exception thrown. The function what() is a virtual function. The classes that derive from the exception class may override the function what() with their own version to describe better the derived exception object.

Notice that all the functions in the definition of the class exception have an empty exception specification throw(). This indicates that the member functions of the class exception do not throw any exceptions. A program can manipulate exception objects, (within catch clause for exceptions of type exception, for example) without worrying that the functions creating, copying, and destroying exception objects will throw exceptions.

In addition to the root exception class, the C++ standard library also provides classes that can be used in the programs we write to report program anomalies. In the error model reflected in these predefined classes, errors are divided into two broad categories: *logic errors* and *run-time errors*.

A logic error is an error due to the internal logic of our programs. Logic errors are presumably preventable errors that are detectable before the program starts executing. For example, violations of logical preconditions or class invariants are logic errors. The logic errors defined in the C++ standard library are the following:

```
namespace std {
   class logic_error : public exception {
   public:
      explicit logic_error( const string &what_arg );
   };
   class invalid_argument : public logic_error {
   public:
      explicit invalid_argument( const string &what_arg );
   };
   class out_of_range : public logic_error {
   public:
      explicit out_of_range( const string &what_arg );
   };
   class length_error : public logic_error {        .
   public:
      explicit length_error( const string &what_arg );
   };
   class domain_error : public logic_error {
   public:
      explicit domain_error( const string &what_arg );
   };
}
```

A function might throw an invalid_argument exception if it receives an argument with an invalid value; whereas a function might throw an out_of_range exception if it receives an argument that is not in the expected range of values. A function might throw a length_error exception to report an attempt to produce an object with a length that exceeds its maximal allowable size. An implementation might throw a domain_error exception to report domain errors.

By contrast, a run-time error is due to an event beyond the scope of the program. A run-time error is presumably detectable only while the program is executing. The run-time errors defined in the C++ standard library are the following:

```
namespace std {
    class runtime_error : public exception {
    public:
        explicit runtime_error( const string &what_arg );
    };
    class range_error : public runtime_error {
    public:
        explicit range_error( const string &what_arg );
    };
    class overflow_error : public runtime_error {
    public:
        explicit overflow_error( const string &what_arg );
    };
    class underflow_error : public runtime_error {
    public:
        explicit underflow_error( const string &what_arg );
    };
}
```

A function might throw a range_error exception to report range errors in internal computations. A function might throw an overflow_error exception to report an arithmetic overflow error, whereas it might throw an underflow_error exception to report an arithmetic underflow error.

The class exception is also the base class of the bad_alloc exception thrown by operator new() when it fails to allocate the requested storage (as mentioned in Section 8.4), and the base class of the bad_cast exception thrown when a reference dynamic_cast fails (as mentioned in Section 19.1).

Let's redefine the operator[]() defined for the class template Array presented in Section 16.12 to throw an exception of type out_of_range if the index into the Array is out of bounds:

```
#include <stdexcept>
#include <string>

template <class elemType>
class Array {
public:
    // ...
```

```
        elemType& operator[]( int ix ) const
        {
            if ( ix < 0 || ix >= _size )
            {
                string eObj =
                "out_of_range error in Array<elemType>::operator[]()";

                throw out_of_range( eObj );
            }
            return _ia[ix];
        }

        // ...
    private:
        int _size;
        elemType *_ia;
    };
```

To use the predefined exception classes, our programs must include the header <stdexcept>. The string object eObj passed to the out_of_range constructor describes the exception thrown. This information can be retrieved when the exception is caught using the what() member function of class exception, as follows:

```
    int main()
    {
        try {
            // main() function as defined in 16.2
        }
        catch ( const out_of_range &excp ) {
            // prints:
            // out_of_range error in Array<elemType>::operator[]()
            cerr << excp.what() << "\n";
            return -1;
        }
    }
```

With this implementation, an out-of-bounds index in the function try_array() causes the Array operator[]() to throw an exception of type out_of_range caught in main().

Exercise 19.5

Which exceptions might the following functions throw?

```
        #include <stdexcept>

    (a) void operate() throw( logic_error );
    (b) int mathOper( int ) throw( underflow_error, overflow_error );
    (c) char manip( string ) throw( );
```

Exercise 19.6

Explain how C++ exception handling supports the programming technique known as "resource acquisition is initialization; resource release is destruction."

Exercise 19.7

Why is the list of catch clauses following the try block incorrect? How would you fix it?

```
#include <stdexcept>

int main() {
    try {
        // use of the C++ standard library
    }
    catch( exception ) {
    }
    catch( const runtime_error &re ) {
    }
    catch( overflow_error eobj ) {
    }
}
```

Exercise 19.8

Given a basic C++ program,

```
int main() {
    // use of the C++ standard library
}
```

modify main() to catch any exception thrown by functions in the C++ standard library. The handlers should print the error message associated with the exception before calling abort() (defined in the header <cstdlib>) to terminate main().

19.3   Overload Resolution and Inheritance ◆

All aspects of function overload resolution are influenced by class inheritance. Recall that the three steps of function overload resolution are the following:

1. Select the candidate functions.
2. Select the viable functions.
3. Select the best match function.

(See Section 9.2 for a full discussion.)

   The selection of the candidate functions is influenced by inheritance because the functions associated with the base classes, either their member functions or the functions declared in the namespaces where the base classes are defined, are considered when selecting the candidate functions. The selection of viable functions is influenced by inheritance because a greater set of user-defined conversions are considered for the conversions of the arguments to the types of a viable function parameter. The selection of best viable function is influenced by inheritance because it impacts the rank of the conversion sequences that can apply to an argument to convert it to the type of a function parameter. In this section we examine the influence of inheritance on the three steps of function overload resolution in more detail.

19.3.1 Candidate Functions

Inheritance impacts the first step of function overload resolution — that of establishing the set of candidate functions for a call. The influence of inheritance on this first step varies depending on whether the call is an ordinary function call of the form

```
func( args );
```

or whether the call is to a member function using the member access operators dot and arrow:

```
object.memfunc( args );
pointer->memfunc( args );
```

In this subsection we look at how inheritance influences each situation in turn.

When an argument in an ordinary function call is of class type, a reference to class type, or a pointer to class type, and the class type is defined within a namespace, the functions declared in that namespace with the same name as the function called are candidate functions, even though these functions are not visible at the point of the call (this was presented in more detail in Section 15.10). With inheritance, if the argument is of class type, a reference to class type, or a pointer to class type, and the class has base classes, the functions declared within the namespaces where the base classes are defined, and with the same name as the function called, are also added to the set of candidate functions. For example:

```
namespace NS {
   class ZooAnimal { /* ... */ };
   void display( const ZooAnimal& );
}

// Bear's base class is declared in namespace NS
class Bear : public NS::ZooAnimal { };

int main() {
   Bear baloo;

   display( baloo );
   return 0;
}
```

The argument baloo has class type Bear. The candidate functions for the call to display() are not only the functions with declarations that are visible where the function display() is called, but also the functions in the namespace where the class Bear and its base class ZooAnimal are declared. The function display(const ZooAnimal&) declared in namespace NS is added to the set of candidate functions.

If an argument is of class type and the class definition declares friend functions with the same name as the function that is called, these friend functions are candidate functions, even if the declarations for these friend functions are not visible at the point of the call (as presented in Section 15.10). With inheritance, if the argument type is a class with base classes, the friend functions with the same name as the function that is called and declared within the base class definitions are also added to the set of candidate functions. For example, let's instead declare the function display() shown previously as a friend function within the class ZooAnimal:

```
namespace NS {
   class ZooAnimal {
      friend void display( const ZooAnimal& );
   };
}

// Bear's base class is declared in namespace NS
class Bear : public NS::ZooAnimal { };

int main() {
   Bear baloo;

   display( baloo );
   return 0;
}
```

The function argument baloo has type Bear. Its base class ZooAnimal declares display() as a friend function. display() is a member of namespace NS even though it is never declared in namespace NS directly. A normal lookup in namespace NS does not find the friend function. However, because the call to the function display() has an argument of type Bear, the friend function declared in Bear's base class ZooAnimal is added to the set of candidate functions.

Hence, if an ordinary function call has an argument that is either an object of class type, a pointer to a class type, or a reference to a class type, the candidate functions are the union of

1. The functions visible at the point of the call
2. The functions declared within the namespace where the class type is defined or within the namespaces where the class' base classes are defined
3. The functions that are friends of the class or friends of the class' base classes

Inheritance also influences the set of candidate functions built for a member function call that uses the dot or arrow member access operators. As we saw in Section 18.4, a member function declaration in a derived class does not overload member functions with the same name declared in base classes. Rather, a member function in a derived class hides the declarations of the member functions with the same name in base classes, even though the function parameter lists are different. For example:

```
class ZooAnimal {
public:
    Time feeding_time( string );
    // ...
};
class Bear : public ZooAnimal {
public:
    // hides ZooAnimal::feeding_time( string )
    Time feeding_time( int );
    // ....
};

Bear Winnie;

// error: ZooAnimal::feeding_time( string ) hidden
Winnie.feeding_time( "Winnie" );
```

The member function feeding_time(int) declared in class Bear hides the member function feeding_time(string) declared in Bear's base class ZooAnimal. Because the member function call is through the object Winnie of type Bear, only the scope of class Bear is searched to find candidate functions for the member function call. The only declaration visible in the scope of Bear is feeding_time(int). feeding_time(int) is therefore the only function in the set of candidate functions for the member function call, and the call is in error.

To correct this situation and have member functions from a base class overload member functions from the derived class, the designer of the derived class can introduce the base class member functions into the scope of the derived class with using declarations. For example:

```
class Bear : public ZooAnimal {
public:
    // feeding_time( int ) is overloaded with ZooAnimal's
    using ZooAnimal::feeding_time;
    Time feeding_time( int );
    // ...
};
```

Now two functions feeding_time() are in the scope of the derived class Bear. Both functions are now part of the set of candidate functions for the call

```
// ok: ZooAnimal::feeding_time( string ) called
Winnie.feeding_time( "Winnie" );
```

and the base class member function feeding_time(string) is selected for the call.

With multiple inheritance, when establishing the set of candidate member functions, the declarations for the member functions must be found in the same base class or the call is in error. For example:

```
class Endangered {
public:
   ostream& print( ostream& );
   // ...
};

class Bear : public ZooAnimal {
public:
   void print( );
   using ZooAnimal::feeding_time;
   Time feeding_time( int );
   // ...
};

class Panda : public Bear, public Endangered {
public:
   // ...
};

int main()
{
   Panda yin_yang;

   // error: ambiguous: one of
   //         Bear::print()
   //         Endangered::print( ostream& )
   yin_yang.print( cout );

   // ok: calls Bear::feeding_time()
   yin_yang.feeding_time( 56 );
}
```

When looking up a declaration for the member function print() in the scope of Panda, both Bear::print() and Endangered::print() are found. Because both declarations for print() are not found in the same base class, and even though both functions print() have different parameter lists, the set of candidate functions for the call is empty and the member function call is in error. To fix this error, class Panda must introduce its own print() function. When looking up a declaration for the member function feeding_time() in the scope of Panda, both ZooAnimal::feeding_time() and Bear::feeding_time() are found in the scope of class Bear. Because both declarations are found in the same base class, the set of candidate functions for the call contains both functions, and the member function `Bear::feeding_time()` is selected for the call.

19.3.2   Viable Functions and User-Defined Conversion Sequences

Inheritance also impacts the second step of function overload resolution, that of selecting the viable functions that can be called from the set of candidate functions. A viable function is a function for which there exists type conversions to convert each function call argument to the type of a corresponding, viable function parameter.

In Section 15.9, we describe how the designer of a class can provide a set of user-defined conversions for objects of class type. These user-defined conversions are invoked implicitly by the compiler to convert the argument of a function call to a corresponding, viable function parameter. A user-defined conversion is either a conversion function or a nonexplicit constructor taking one argument. With inheritance, a greater set of user-defined conversions is considered during the second step of function overload resolution.

Conversion functions are inherited like any other class member functions. For example, we may decide to define a conversion function for the class ZooAnimal as follows:

```
class ZooAnimal {
public:

    // conversion: ZooAnimal ==> const char*
    operator const char*();

    // ...
};
```

The derived class Bear inherits this conversion function from its base class ZooAnimal. Whenever a value of type Bear is used where an operand of type `const char*` is expected, the conversion function is called to convert the Bear value implicitly to the type `const char*`. For example:

```
extern void display( const char* );

Bear yogi;

// ok: yogi ==> const char*
display( yogi );
```

Nonexplicit constructors taking one argument define another set of implicit conversions. A constructor can convert a value of its parameter type to its class type. For example, we may decide to define a constructor for the class ZooAnimal as follows:

```
class ZooAnimal {
public:
```

```
// conversion: int ==> ZooAnimal
ZooAnimal( int );

// ...
};
```

This constructor can be used to convert an integer value to a value of type Zoo-Animal. Constructors are not inherited however. The ZooAnimal constructor cannot be used to convert an object when a class type derived from ZooAnimal is needed. For example:

```
const int cageNumber = 8788;

void mumble( const Bear & );

// error: ZooAnimal( int ) is not used
mumble( cageNumber );
```

Because the class type that is the target of the conversion is class Bear, the type of mumble()'s parameter, only the constructors within the class Bear are considered.

19.3.3   Best Viable Function

Inheritance also impacts the third step of the function overload resolution, that of selecting the best viable function. To select the best viable function, the type conversions that can convert the arguments to the type of the corresponding function parameters are ranked. What is the rank of the following implicit conversions?

1. Converting an argument of a derived class type to a parameter of any of its base class types

2. Converting a pointer to a derived class type to a pointer to any of its base class types

3. Initializing a reference to a base class type with an lvalue of a derived class type

When ranking the conversions applied to function arguments, these conversions have the rank of a standard conversion. (The other standard conversions are described in Section 9.3.) These conversions are not user-defined conversions because they do not depend on the conversion functions and constructors defined by the class designer. For example:

```
extern void release( const ZooAnimal& );
Panda yinYang;

// standard conversion: Panda -> ZooAnimal
release( yinYang );
```

Because the argument yinYang of type Panda initializes a reference to a base class type, the conversion has the rank of a standard conversion.

In Section 15.10, we saw that a standard conversion sequence is better than a user-defined conversion sequence when ranking type conversions to select the best viable function. For example:

```
class Panda : public Bear,
              public Endangered
{
    // inherits ZooAnimal::operator const char *()
};

Panda yinYang;

extern void release( const ZooAnimal& );
extern void release( const char * );

// standard conversion: Panda -> ZooAnimal
// selects: release( const ZooAnimal& )
release( yinYang );
```

Both `release(const char*)` and `release(const ZooAnimal&)` are viable functions. The function `release(const ZooAnimal&)` is a viable function because the argument can initialize the reference parameter through a standard conversion. The function `release(const char*)` is a viable function because a user-defined conversion using the conversion function `ZooAnimal::operator const char*()` can convert the argument to the type `const char*`. Because a standard conversion sequence is better than a user-defined conversion sequence, the function `release(const ZooAnimal&)` is selected as the best viable function.

When ranking different standard conversions from a derived class type to different base class types, a conversion to a base class that is less removed from the derived class type is considered a better standard conversion than a conversion to a base class that is further removed from the derived class type. For example, the following call is not ambiguous, although a standard conversion is required in both cases. The conversion to the base class Bear is considered better than the conversion to the base class ZooAnimal because the base class Bear is less removed from the derived class Panda. The best viable function for the call is therefore `release(const Bear&)`:

```
extern void release( const ZooAnimal& );
extern void release( const Bear& );

// ok: release( const Bear& );
release( yinYang );
```

A similar rule also applies to pointers. When ranking different standard conversions from a pointer to a derived class type to pointers to different base class types, the conversion to the base class that is less removed from the derived class type is considered a better standard conversion. A similar rule also extends to the handling of `void*`.

A standard conversion to a pointer to a base class type is better than a conversion to
void*. For example, given the following pair of overloaded functions,

```
void receive( void* );
void receive( ZooAnimal* );
```

the function `receive(ZooAnimal*)` is the best viable function for an argument of
type Panda*.

Multiple inheritance may cause two standard conversions from a derived class
type to different base class types to be equally good if both base classes are equally removed from the derived class type. For example, Panda is derived from both Bear and
Endangered. These base classes are equally removed from the derived class Panda,
and conversions of a Panda class object to either of these base classes are equally good.
Since both conversions are equally good, no best viable function can be selected for the
following call and the call is an error:

```
extern void mumble( const Bear& );
extern void mumble( const Endangered& );

/* error: ambiguous call:
 * choice of mumble()s:
 * void mumble( const Bear & );
 * void mumble( const Endangered & );
 */
mumble( yinYang );
```

To resolve the call, the programmer must supply an explicit cast:

```
mumble( static_cast< Bear >( yinYang ) ); // ok
```

The initialization of a derived class object with an object of base class type, the initialization of a reference of a derived class type with an object of base class type, or the
conversion of a pointer to a base class type to a pointer to a derived class type is never
applied as an implicit conversion. (Such conversions can, however, be performed using an explicit dynamic_cast, as seen in Section 19.1.) No viable function exists for the
following call because no implicit conversion exits to convert the argument of type
ZooAnimal to a derived class type:

```
extern void release( const Bear& );
extern void release( const Panda& );

ZooAnimal za;

// error: no match
release( za );
```

In the following example, the best viable function for the call is release(const
char*). This may seem surprising because the rank of the conversion sequence applied
to the argument to convert it to the type of the function parameter is a user-defined

conversion sequence that uses the ZooAnimal conversion function const char*().
However, because there is no implicit conversion from a base class type to a derived
class type, the function release(const Bear&) is not a viable function and re-
lease(const char*) is the only viable function for the call:

```
class ZooAnimal {
public:
    // conversion: ZooAnimal ==> const char*
    operator const char*();

    // ...
};

extern void release( const char* );
extern void release( const Bear& );

ZooAnimal za;

// za ==> const char*
// ok: release( const char* )
release( za );
```

Exercise 19.9

Given the following class hierarchy, with the following collection of member functions,

```
class Base1 {
public:
    ostream& print();
    void debug();
    void writeOn();
    void log( string );
    void reset( void *);
    // ...
};

class Base2 {
public:
    void debug();
    void readOn();
    void log( double );
    // ...
};

class MI : public Base1, public Base2 {
public:
    ostream& print();
    using Base1::reset;
    void reset( char * );
    using Base2::log;
```

```
         using Base1::log;
         // ...
     };
```

which functions are in the set of candidate member functions for the following calls?

```
     MI *pi = new MI;
     (a) pi->print();   (c) pi->readOn();   (e) pi->log( num );
     (b) pi->debug();   (d) pi->reset(0);   (f) pi->writeOn();
```

Exercise 19.10

Given the following class hierarchy, with the following collection of conversion functions,

```
     class Base {
     public:
        operator int();
        operator const char *();
        // ...
     };
     class Derived : public Base {
     public:
        operator double();
        // ...
     };
```

which function, if any, is selected as the best viable function for the following calls? List the candidate functions, the viable functions, and the type conversions on the argument for each viable function.

```
     (a) void operate( double );
         void operate( string );
         void operate( const Base & );

         Derived *pd = new Derived;
         operate( *pd );

     (b) void calc( int );
         void calc( double );
         void calc( const Derived & );

         Base *pb = new Derived;
         operate( *pb );
```

20

The iostream Library

Input/output facilities are provided through the *iostream library,* an object-oriented class hierarchy that makes use of both multiple and virtual inheritance, and are provided as a component of the C++ standard library. It provides support for the input and output of the built-in data types as well as support for file input and output. In addition, class designers can extend the iostream library to read and write new class types.

To use the iostream library within our programs, we must include its associated header file, as follows:

```
#include <iostream>
```

Input and output operations are provided by the *istream* (input stream) and *ostream* (output stream) classes (a third class, the *iostream* class, is derived from both istream and ostream and allows for bidirectional input/output). For convenience, the library defines the following three standard stream objects:

1. cin, pronounced *see-in,* an istream class object representing *standard input.* In general, cin allows us to read data from the user's terminal.

2. cout, pronounced *see-out,* an ostream class object representing *standard output.* In general, cout allows us to write data to the user's terminal.

3. cerr, pronounced *see-err,* an ostream class object representing *standard error.* cerr is where we direct our program's error messages.

Output is primarily accomplished by the overloaded left shift operator (<<). Similarly, input is primarily accomplished by the overloaded right shift operator (>>). For example:

```
#include <iostream>
#include <string>

int main()
{
```

```
        string in_string;

        // write literal string to user's terminal
        cout << "Please enter your name: ";

        // read user's input into in_string
        cin >> in_string;

        if ( in_string.empty() )
            // generate an error message to user's terminal
            cerr << "error: input string is empty!\n";
        else cout << "hello, " << in_string << "!\n";
    }
```

A useful way of thinking about the two operators is that each "points" in the direction of its data movement. For example,

```
        >> x
```

puts data *into* x, whereas

```
        << x
```

gets data *out from* x. Section 20.1 looks at the support the iostream library provides for data input. Section 20.5 looks at how we can extend the iostream library to allow the data input of new class types. Similarly, Section 20.2 looks at the support the iostream library provides for data output, and Section 20.4 looks at how we can extend the library to allow the data output of new class types.

As well as reading from and writing to the user's terminal, the iostream library supports reading from and writing to files. The following three class types provide file support:

1. ifstream, derived from istream, ties a file to the program for input.

2. ofstream, derived from ostream, ties a file to the program for output.

3. fstream, derived from iostream, ties a file to the program for both input and output.

To use the file stream component of the iostream library, we must include its associated header file:

```
        #include <fstream>
```

(The fstream header file includes the iostream header file and so we do not need to include both.) The same input and output operators are supported for file input/ output. For example:

```
        #include <fstream>
        #include <string>
        #include <vector>
        #include <algorithm>
```

```
int main()
{
    string ifile;

    cout << "Please enter file to sort: ";
    cin >> ifile;

    // construct an ifstream input file object
    ifstream infile( ifile.c_str() );

    if ( ! infile ) {
        cerr << "error: unable to open input file: "
            << ifile << endl;
        return -1;
    }

    string ofile = ifile + ".sort";

    // construct an ofstream output file object
    ofstream outfile( ofile.c_str() );
    if ( ! outfile) {
        cerr << "error: unable to open output file: "
            << ofile << endl;
        return -2;
    }

    string buffer;
    vector< string, allocator > text;

    int cnt = 1;
    while ( infile >> buffer ) {
            text.push_back( buffer );
            cout << buffer << ( cnt++ % 8 ? " " : "\n" );
    }

    sort( text.begin(), text.end() );

    // ok: print out sorted words into outfile
    vector<string,allocator>::iterator iter = text.begin();
    for ( cnt = 1; iter != text.end(); ++iter, ++cnt )
            outfile << *iter
                    << (cnt%8 ? " " : "\n" );

    return 0;
}
```

Here is a sample session of running the program: We are asked to enter a file to sort. We type alice_emma (our input is displayed in bold in the sample output). The program then echoes each word as it is read onto standard output:

```
Please enter file to sort: alice_emma
Alice Emma has long flowing red hair. Her
Daddy says when the wind blows through her
hair, it looks almost alive, like a fiery
bird in flight. A beautiful fiery bird, he
tells her, magical but untamed. "Daddy, shush, there
is no such thing," she tells him, at
the same time wanting him to tell her
more. Shyly, she asks, "I mean, Daddy, is
there?"
```

The program then writes to outfile the sorted sequence of strings. Of course, the punctuation affects the ordering of the words (we'll fix that at the end of the next section):

```
"Daddy, "I A Alice Daddy Daddy, Emma Her
Shyly, a alive, almost asks, at beautiful bird
bird, blows but fiery fiery flight. flowing hair,
hair. has he her her her, him him,
in is is it like long looks magical
mean, more. no red same says she she
shush, such tell tells tells the the there
there?" thing," through time to untamed. wanting when
wind
```

Section 20.6 looks at file input/output in detail.

The iostream library also supports *in-memory input/output,* in which a stream is attached to a string within the program's memory. It can then be written to and read from using the iostream input and output operators. We can define an iostream string object by defining an instance of one of the following three class types:

1. istringstream, derived from istream, reads from a string.

2. ostringstream, derived from ostream, writes into a string.

3. stringstream, derived from iostream, both reads from and writes into a string.

To use any of these classes, we must include its associated header file:

```
#include <sstream>
```

(The sstream header file includes the iostream header file and so we do not need to include both.) In the following code fragment, an ostringstream is used to format an error message. The underlying string is then returned:

```
#include <sstream>

string program_name( "our_program" );
string version( "0.01" );

// ...

string mumble( int *array, int size )
{
```

```
        if ( ! array ) {
            ostringstream out_message;

            out_message << "error: "
                        << program_name << "--" << version
                        << ": " << __FILE__ << ": " << __LINE__
                        << " -- ptr is set to 0; "
                        << " must address some array.\n";

            // returns the underlying string object
            return out_message.str();
        }
        // ...
    }
```

Section 20.8 looks at iostream string objects in detail.

In practice, iostreams support two predefined character types: char and wchar_t. The iostream classes we've described thus far (and which we'll focus on for the rest of the chapter) read and write streams composed of type char. Complementing these are a set of iostream objects and classes supporting the wchar_t type. Each class and class object is distinguished from its char counterpart by the "w" prefix. Thus, the wchar_t standard input object is named wcin; standard output, wcout; and standard error, wcerr. The necessary header files, however, are the same for both char and wchar_t stream classes and class objects.

The wchar_t input and output classes are wostream, wistream, and wiostream. The file input and output classes are wifstream, wofstream, and wfstream. The ostream string input and output classes are wistringstream, wostringstream, and wstringstream.

20.1   The Output Operator<<

The most commonly used output method is to apply the left shift operator (<<) to cout. For example,

```
        #include <iostream>

        int main() {
            cout << "gossipaceous Anna Livia\n";
        }
```

prints as follows on the user's terminal:

```
        gossipaceous Anna Livia
```

Output operators are provided that accept arguments of any of the built-in data types, including const char*, as well as the standard library string and complex class types. Any expression, including a function call, can be made an argument to the output operator provided that the expression evaluates to a data type accepted by an instance of the output operator. For example,

```
#include <iostream>
#include <string.h>

int main()
{
    cout << "The length of "ulysses" is:\t";
    cout << strlen( "ulysses" );
    cout << '\n';

    cout << "The size of "ulysses" is:\t";
    cout << sizeof( "ulysses" );
    cout << endl;
}
```

prints as follows on the user's terminal:

```
The length of "ulysses" is:7
The size of "ulysses" is:8
```

(endl is an ostream *manipulator*, inserting a newline into the output stream, then flushing the ostream buffer. We look at buffering in Section 20.9.)

It's often more convenient to concatenate the output operator into a single statement. For example, the preceding program can be rewritten as follows:

```
#include <iostream>
#include <string.h>

int main()
{
    // output operators can be concatenated

    cout << "The length of "ulysses" is:\t"
         << strlen( "ulysses" ) << 'n';

    cout << "The size of "ulysses" is:\t"
         << sizeof( "ulysses" ) << endl;
}
```

The reason we can concatenate a sequence of output operators (and a sequence of input operators as well) is that the expression

```
cout << "some string"
```

evaluates to the left-hand ostream operator; that is, the result of the expression is the cout object itself, which is then reapplied to the next output operator and so on through the sequence (we say that operator<< associates left to right).

A predefined output operator for pointer types is also provided, allowing for the display of an object's address. By default, these values are displayed in hexadecimal notation. For example,

```
#include <iostream>

int main()
{
    int i = 1024;
    int *pi = &i;

    cout << "i:    " << i
         << "\t&i:\t" << &i << '\n';

    cout << "*pi: " << *pi
         << "\tpi:\t"     << pi  << endl
         << "\t\t&pi:\t" << &pi << endl;
}
```

prints as follows on our terminal:

```
i:    1024  &i: 0x7ffff0b4
*pi: 1024  pi: 0x7ffff0b4
            &pi: 0x7ffff0b0
```

Later we'll see how to print the addresses using decimal notation.

The following program presents something of a puzzle. Our intention is to print out the address value `pstr` contains:

```
#include <iostream>

const char *str = "vermeer";
int main()
{
    const char *pstr = str;
    cout << "The address of pstr is: "
         << pstr << endl;
}
```

When compiled and executed, however, the program unexpectedly generates the following output:

```
The address of pstr is: vermeer
```

The problem is that the type `const char*` is interpreted not as an address value but as a C-style character string. To print out the address value that `pstr` contains, we must override the default handling of `const char*`. We do this in two steps: first cast the const away, then cast `pstr` to type `void*`:

```
<< static_cast<void*>(const_cast<char*>(pstr))
```

When compiled and executed, the program now generates the expected output:

```
The address of pstr is: 0x116e8
```

Here is another puzzle. Our intention is to display the larger of two values:

```
#include <iostream>

inline void
max_out( int val1, int val2 ) {
    cout << ( val1 > val2 ) ? val1 : val2;
}

int main()
{
    int ix = 10, jx = 20;

    cout << "The larger of " << ix;
    cout << ", " << jx << " is ";

    max_out( ix, jx );

    cout << endl;
}
```

When compiled and executed, however, the program generates the following incorrect results:

```
The larger of 10, 20 is 0
```

The problem is that the output operator has a higher precedence than the conditional operator and therefore outputs the true/false value of the comparison of val1 and val2. That is, the expression

```
cout << ( val1 > val2 ) ? val1 : val2;
```

evaluates as

```
(cout << ( val1 > val2 )) ? val1 : val2;
```

Because val1 is not greater than val2, the result of the evaluation is false, which is output as 0. To override the predefined order of operator precedence, the full conditional operator expression must be placed within parentheses:

```
cout << (val1 > val2 ? val1 : val2);
```

This yields the correct output:

```
The larger of 10, 20 is 20
```

The invalid output would probably have been a good deal easier to debug if the literal bool values true and false were output as strings rather than as the values 0 or 1 — that is, if the output had read:

```
The larger of 10, 20 is false
```

By default, the false literal value is output as 0, true as 1. We can override the default by applying the `boolalpha` manipulator. The following program does just that:

```
int main()
{
    cout << "default bool values: "
         << true << " " << false
         << "\nalpha bool values: "
         << boolalpha
         << true << " " << false
         << endl;
}
```

When executed, the program generates the following:

```
default bool values: 1 0
alpha bool values: true false
```

Output of the built-in array type as well as the container types, such as a vector or map, require that we iterate through and output each individual element. For example:

```
#include <iostream>
#include <vector>
#include <string>

string pooh_pals[] = {
        "Tigger", "Piglet", "Eeyore", "Rabbit"
};

int main()
{
    vector<string> ppals( pooh_pals, pooh_pals+4 );

    vector<string>::iterator iter = ppals.begin();
    vector<string>::iterator iter_end = ppals.end();

    cout << "These are Pooh's pals: ";
    for ( ; iter != iter_end; iter++ )
            cout << *iter << " ";

    cout << endl;
}
```

Rather than iterating explicitly through the elements of a container, printing each element in turn, an ostream_iterator can be used to effect the same behavior. For example, here is a equivalent program making use of an ostream_iterator (see Section 12.4 for a full discussion of the ostream_iterator):

```
#include <iostream>
#include <algorithm>
#include <vector>
#include <string>
```

```
string pooh_pals[] = {
      "Tigger", "Piglet", "Eeyore", "Rabbit"
};

int main()
{
    vector<string> ppals( pooh_pals, pooh_pals+4 );

    vector<string>::iterator iter     = ppals.begin();
    vector<string>::iterator iter_end = ppals.end();

    cout << "These are Pooh's pals: ";

    // copies each element to cout ...
    ostream_iterator< string > output( cout, " " );
    copy( iter, iter_end, output );

    cout << endl;
}
```

When compiled and executed, the program generates the following output:

```
These are Pooh's pals: Tigger Piglet Eeyore Rabbit
```

Exercise 20.1

Given the following object definitions,

```
string sa[4] = { "pooh", "tigger", "piglet", "eeyore" };
vector< string > svec( sa, sa+4 );
string robin( "christopher robin" );
const char *pc = robin.c_str();
int ival = 1024;
char blank = ' ';
double dval = 3.14159;
complex purei( 0, 7 );
```

(a) Print out the value of each object on standard output.

(b) Print out the address value of pc.

(c) Print out the minimum value of ival and dval using the result of the conditional operator:

```
ival < dval ? ival : dval
```

20.2 Input

Input is primarily supported by the right shift operator (>>). In the following program, for example, a sequence of values of type int are read from standard input and placed within a vector:

```
#include <iostream>
#include <vector>

int main()
{
    vector<int> ivec;
    int ival;

    while ( cin >> ival )
            ivec.push_back( ival );

    // ...
}
```

The subexpression
```
cin >> ival
```
reads an integer value from standard input and, if successful, copies the value into
ival. The result of the subexpression is the left-hand istream object — in this case, cin
itself. (As we'll see, this permits the concatenation of input operators.)

The expression
```
while ( cin >> ival )
```
reads a sequence of values from standard input until cin evaluates to false. There are
two general conditions under which an istream evaluates to false: either the end-of-
file is read (in which case we have read correctly all the values contained within the
file) or an invalid value has been encountered, such as 3.14159 (the decimal point is
illegal), 1e-1 (the character literal e is illegal), or in general any string literal. In the
case of reading an invalid value, the istream object is placed in an error state and all
reading of values ceases. (In Section 20.7, we look at error conditions in detail.)

A predefined set of input operators are provided that accept arguments of any of
the built-in data types, including the C-style character string as well as the standard
library string and complex class types. For example:

```
#include <iostream>
#include <string>

int main()
{
    int item_number;
    string item_name;
    double item_price;

    cout << "Please enter the item_number, item_name, and price: "
        << endl;

    cin >> item_number;
    cin >> item_name;
```

```
cin >> item_price;

cout << "The values entered are: item# "
     << item_number << " "
     << item_name << " @$"
     << item_price << endl;
}
```

The following is a sample execution of our program:

```
Please enter the item_number, item_name, and price:
10247 widget 19.99
The values entered are: item# 10247 widget @$19.99
```

What if we enter each item on a separate line? This is not a problem. By default, the input operator discards any intervening white space (blank, tab, newline, formfeed, and carriage return, see Section 20.9 for a discussion of how to override the default behavior):

```
Please enter the item_number, item_name, and price:
10247
widget
19.99
The values entered are: item# 10247 widget @$19.99
```

The reading of values is more likely to result in an iostream error than that of writing values. For example, if the sequence of items entered is

```
// error: item_name should come second
BuzzLightyear 10009 8.99
```

the statement

```
cin >> item_number;
```

results in an input error since BuzzLightyear is clearly not a value of type int. When an input error occurs, the istream object, if tested, evaluates as false. For example, a more robust implementation might write the following:

```
cin >> item_number;
if ( ! cin )
    cerr << "error: invalid item_number type entered!\n";
```

The concatenation of read operations, while supported, does not allow for the testing of individual read operations for possible error, and so should be used only when there is no chance of error. Here is our previous program using read operation concatenation:

```
#include <iostream>
#include <string>

int main()
{
    int item_number;
    string item_name;
```

```
        double item_price;

        cout << "Please enter the item_number, item_name, and price: "
             << endl;

        // ok: but more error prone
        cin >> item_number >> item_name >> item_price;

        cout << "The values entered are: item# "
             << item_number << " "
             << item_name << " @$"
             << item_price << endl;
    }
```

The character sequence

```
    ab c
    d    e
```

is composed of the following nine characters: `'a'`, `'b'`, `' '` (space), `'c'`, `'\n'` (newline), `'d'`, `'\t'` (tab), `'e'`, and `'\n'`. The following program, however, using the input operator, only reads the five alphabet characters:

```
    #include <iostream>

    int main()
    {
        char ch;

        // read in, then output each character.
        while ( cin >> ch )
                cout << ch;
        cout << endl;

        // ...
    }
```

When executed, this program outputs the following:

```
    abcde
```

By default, all the white space characters are discarded. If we wish to read the white space as well, either to preserve the format of the original input or to process the white space (such as keeping a count of each newline), one alternative is to make use of the istream `get()` member function (the ostream `put()` member function is generally used in conjunction with `get()` — we'll look at both these functions in more detail later in the text). For example:

```
    #include <iostream>

    int main()
```

```
    {
        char ch;

        // get each character, including white space.
        while ( cin.get( ch ))
                cout.put( ch );
        // ...
    }
```

(A second alternative is to use the `noskipws` manipulator.)

Both of the following sequences are treated as consisting of five strings separated by white space if read by either the `const char*` or string input operators:

```
A fine and private place
"A fine and private place"
```

The presence of quotation marks does not cause embedded white space to be handled as part of an extended string. Rather, the two quotation marks become the first character of the first word and the last character of the last word respectively.

Rather than reading in each individual element explicitly in turn from standard input, an istream_iterator can be used to effect the same behavior. For example:

```
#include <algorithm>
#include <string>
#include <vector>
#include <iostream>

int main()
{
    istream_iterator< string > in( cin ), eos ;
    vector< string > text ;

    // copy the values read from standard input into text
    copy( in , eos , back_inserter( text ) ) ;

    sort( text.begin() , text.end() ) ;

    // remove all duplicate values
    vector< string >::iterator it ;
    it = unique( text.begin() , text.end() ) ;
    text.erase( it , text.end() ) ;

    // display the resulting vector
    int line_cnt = 1 ;
    for ( vector< string >::iterator iter = text.begin();
          iter != text.end() ; ++iter , ++line_cnt )
            cout << *iter
                    << ( line_cnt % 9 ? " " : "\n" ) ;
    cout << endl;
}
```

The input to the program is the text of the program itself. The text is stored in a file we've named istream_iter.C. Under the UNIX system, we can redirect a file to standard input as follows (istream_iter is the name of the program):

```
istream_iter < istream_iter.C
```

(For a non-UNIX system, refer to your Programmer's Guide for assistance.) When executed, the program generates the following output:

```
!= " "\n" #include % ( ) *iter ++iter
++line_cnt , 1 9 : ; << <algorithm> <iostream.h>
<string> <vector> = > >::difference_type >::iterator ? allocator
back_inserter(
cin copy( cout diff_type eos for in in( int
istream_iterator< it iter line_cnt main() sort( string text text.begin()
text.end() text.erase( typedef unique( vector< { }
```

(The iostream iterators are discussed in Section 12.4.)

In addition to the predefined input operators, overloaded instances of the input operator can be introduced to support the reading in of user-defined class types. Section 20.5 looks at this in detail.

20.2.1   String Input

Strings can be read in as either a C-style character array or a string class type. Our recommendation is that you use the string class type. The primary benefit is the automatic management of the storage associated with the string. For example, to read a string in as a C-style character array, we must determine a size for the array — a size large enough to accommodate each potential string. Typically we read each string into this array buffer, then allocate the appropriate memory to hold the string exactly from the free store and copy from the buffer into this made-to-order memory chunk. For example:

```
#include <iostream>
#include <string.h>

char inBuf[ 1024 ];
try
{
  while ( cin >> inBuf ) {
          char *str = new char[ strlen( inBuf )+1 ];
          strcpy( str, inBuf );
          // ... do something to str
          delete [] str;
      }
}
catch( ... ) { delete [] str; throw; }
```

The string type is considerably simpler to manage:

```
#include <iostream>
#include <string>

string str;
while ( cin >> str )
        // ... do something to string
```

In the remainder of this subsection, we look at reading strings in using both the C-style character array and class string input operators. As our input text, we'll return to our young Alice Emma:

```
Alice Emma has long flowing red hair. Her Daddy says
when the wind blows through her hair, it looks almost
alive, like a fiery bird in flight. A beautiful fiery
bird, he tells her, magical but untamed. "Daddy, shush,
there is no such creature," she tells him, at the same time
wanting him to tell her more. Shyly, she asks, "I mean,
Daddy, is there?"
```

We'll type it into a text file named alice_emma and then redirect it to the standard input of our programs. Later, when we introduce file input, we'll open and read it directly. The following program extracts a sequence of strings as C-style character arrays from standard input and determines which of the strings read is largest.

```
#include <iostream>
#include <string.h>

int main()
{
    const int bufSize = 24;
    char buf[ bufSize ], largest[ bufSize ];

    // hold statistics;
    int curLen, max = -1, cnt = 0;
    while ( cin >> buf )
    {
        curLen = strlen( buf );
        ++cnt;

        // new longest word? save it.
        if ( curLen > max ) {
            max = curLen;
            strcpy( largest, buf );
        }
    }

    cout << "The number of words read is "
         << cnt << endl;

    cout << "The longest word has a length of "
```

```
                    << max << endl;

            cout << "The longest word is "
                    << largest << endl;
    }
```

When compiled and executed, the program generates the following output:

```
    The number of words read is 65
    The longest word has a length of 10
    The longest word is creature,"
```

Actually, the result is incorrect. beautiful is the largest word in the text and is nine characters in length. creature is selected, however, because it has the comma and quotation mark attached to it. To have our program interpret the strings as our users expect, we will need to filter out the nonalphabetical elements.

Before we do that, however, let's look at the program a bit closer. In the program, each string is stored in buf, declared to be an array of length 24. If a string were read that equaled or exceeded 24 characters, buf would overflow. The program would likely fail during execution. The setw() iostream manipulator can be used to prevent the overflow of an input array. For example, the previous program might be modified as follows:

```
    while ( cin >> setw( bufSize ) >> buf )
```

where bufSize is the dimension of the character array buf. setw() breaks a string equal to or larger than bufSize into two or more strings of a maximal length of

```
    bufSize - 1
```

A null character is placed at the end of each new string. Use of setw() requires that the program include the iomanip header file:

```
    #include <iomanip>
```

If the visible declarations of buf do not specify a dimension,

```
    char buf[] = "An unrealistic example";
```

the programmer can apply the sizeof operator — provided that the identifier is the name of an array and in a scope visible to the expression:

```
    while ( cin >> setw(sizeof( buf )) >> buf );
```

Use of the sizeof operator in the following example results in unexpected program behavior:

```
    #include <iostream>
    #include <iomanip>

    main()
    {
        const int bufSize = 24;
        char buf[ bufSize ];
```

```
        char *pbuf = buf;

        // each string greater than sizeof(char*)
        // is broken into two or more strings
        while ( cin >> setw(sizeof(pbuf)) >> pbuf )
              cout << pbuf << endl;
}
```

When compiled and executed, the program generates the following unexpected results:

```
$ a.out
The winter of our discontent

The
win
ter
of
our
dis
con
ten
t
```

The problem is that setw() is passed the size of the character pointer rather than the size of the character array to which it points. On this particular machine, a character pointer is four bytes, and so the input is broken into a sequence of strings three characters in length.

The following attempt to correct the mistake is an even more serious error:

```
while ( cin >> setw(sizeof(*pbuf)) >> pbuf )
```

The intention is to pass setw() the size of the array to which pbuf points. The notation

```
*pbuf
```

however, yields only a single char. setw(), in this case, is passed a value of 1. Each execution of the while loop will place a null character into the array to which pbuf points. Standard input is never read; the loop executes, as Buzz Lightyear would say, "To infinity and beyond!"

Using the string class type, all of these allocation problems go away, managed automatically by the string class itself. Here is our same program written using strings:

```
#include <iostream>
#include <string>

int main()
{
    string buf, largest;

    // hold statistics;
    int curLen, max = -1, cnt = 0;
```

```
        while ( cin >> buf ) {
                curLen = buf.size();
                ++cnt;

                // new longest word? save it.
                if ( curLen > max ) {
                        max = curLen;
                        largest = buf;
                }
        }

        // ... rest the same
}
```

The output is still contrary to expectation due to the comma and quotation mark being interpreted as part of the string. Let's write a function to filter those elements from the string:

```
#include <string>
void filter_string( string &str )
{
        // elements to filter out
        string filt_elems( "\",?." );
        string::size_type pos = 0;

        while (( pos = str.find_first_of( filt_elems, pos ))
                        != string::npos )
                        str.erase( pos, 1 );
}
```

This works fine, but hard codes the set of elements that we wish to remove. A better strategy is to allow the user to pass in a string containing the elements. If the user wishes to use the default elements, they can pass in an empty string.

```
#include <string>

void filter_string( string &str,
                    string filt_elems = string("\",?."))
{
        string::size_type pos = 0;

        while (( pos = str.find_first_of( filt_elems, pos ))
                        != string::npos )
                        str.erase( pos, 1 );
}
```

The following more general version of filter_string() accepts a pair of iterators marking off the range of elements to filter:

```
template <class InputIterator>
void filter_string( InputIterator first, InputIterator last,
                    string filt_elems = string("\",?."))
{
    for ( ; first != last; first++ )
    {
            string::size_type pos = 0;
            while (( pos = (*first).find_first_of( filt_elems, pos ))
                        != string::npos )
                    (*first).erase( pos, 1 );
    }
}
```

Our program to make use of this might look like this:

```
#include <string>
#include <algorithm>
#include <iterator>
#include <vector>
#include <iostream>

bool length_less( string s1, string s2 )
        { return s1.size() < s2.size(); }

int main()
{
    istream_iterator< string > input( cin ), eos;

    vector< string > text;
    // copy is a generic algorithm
    copy(   input, eos, back_inserter( text ));

    string filt_elems( "\",.?;:");
    filter_string( text.begin(), text.end(), filt_elems );

    int cnt = text.size();
    // max_element is a generic algorithm
    string *max = max_element( text.begin(), text.end(),
                               length_less );
    int len = max->size();

    cout << "The number of words read is "
        << cnt << endl;

    cout << "The longest word has a length of "
        << len << endl;

    cout << "The longest word is "
        << *max << endl;
}
```

When we used the default less than string operator with `max_element()`, we were surprised by the program's output:

```
The number of words read is 65
The longest word has a length of 4
The longest word is wind
```

`wind` is certainly not the maximal element in terms of length. After puzzling over the results for a moment, we realize that the string less than operator does not evaluate a string's length but its lexicographic relationship. In that sense, `wind` is the maximal string in our text file. To find the maximal length string, we need to provide an alternative less than operator: `length_less()`:

```
The number of words read is 65
The longest word has a length of 9
The longest word is beautiful
```

Exercise 20.2

Read from standard input a sequence of types: string, `double`, string, `int`, string. Check whether an input error occurs.

Exercise 20.3

Read from standard input an unknown number of strings. Store them in a list. Determine both the shortest and longest strings.

20.3   Additional Input/Output Operators

On some occasions, it is necessary to read the input stream as a sequence of uninterpreted bytes rather than as a sequence of data types, such as char, int, string, and so on. The istream member function get() reads the input stream one byte at a time. getline() reads a chunk of bytes marked off either by a newline or some user-specified termination character. There are three forms of the member function get().

1. get(char& ch) extracts a single character from the input stream, including white space, and stores it in ch. It returns the iostream object to which it is applied. For example, the following program gathers various statistics on the input stream, then copies it to the output stream exactly:

```cpp
#include <iostream>

int main()
{
    char ch;
    int  tab_cnt = 0, nl_cnt = 0, space_cnt = 0,
         period_cnt = 0, comma_cnt = 0;
```

```
while ( cin.get( ch )) {
        switch( ch ) {
                case ' ':  space_cnt++;  break;
                case '\t': tab_cnt++;    break;
                case '\n': nl_cnt++;     break;
                case '.':  period_cnt++; break;
                case ',':  comma_cnt++;  break;
        }
        cout.put( ch );
}

cout << "\nour statistics:\n\t"
     << "spaces: "     << space_cnt  << '\t'
     << "new lines: " << nl_cnt      << '\t'
     << "tabs: "       << tab_cnt    << "\n\t"
     << "periods: "    << period_cnt << '\t'
     << "commas: "     << comma_cnt  << endl;
}
```

The put() ostream member function provides an alternative method of out-putting a character into the output stream. put() accepts an argument of type char and returns the ostream class object on which it is invoked.

When compiled and executed, the program generates the following output:

```
Alice Emma has long flowing red hair. Her Daddy says
when the wind blows through her hair, it looks almost alive,
like a fiery bird in flight. A beautiful fiery bird, he tells her,
magical but untamed. "Daddy, shush, there is no such creature,"
she tells him, at the same time wanting him to tell her more.
Shyly, she asks, "I mean, Daddy, is there?"

our statistics:
        spaces: 59       new lines: 6     tabs: 0
        periods: 4       commas: 12
```

2. The second version of get() also reads a single character from the input stream. The difference is that it returns that value rather the istream to which it is applied. It returns an int type rather than char because it also returns the end-of-file representation, which is often represented as -1 to distinguish it from the character set values. To test if the value returned is end-of-file, we compare it against the constant EOF defined in the iostream header. The variable assigned to hold the return value of get() should be declared to be of type int to contain both character values and EOF. Here is a simple example:

```
#include <iostream>

int main()
{
```

```
    int ch;

    // alternatively:
    // while (( ch = cin.get()) && ch != EOF )
    while (( ch = cin.get()) != EOF )
            cout.put(ch);
    return 0;

}
```

Using either of these two get() functions, it requires seven iterations to read the following sequence of characters:

```
a b c
d
```

Seven characters are read ('a', blank, 'b', blank, 'c', newline, 'd'). The eighth iteration encounters EOF. The input operator (>>), because it skips over white space by default, reads the character sequence in four iterations, returning in turn, 'a', 'b', 'c', 'd'. The next form of the get() function could read the character sequence in two iterations.

3. The third version of get() has the following general signature:

```
get(char *sink, streamsize size, char delimiter='\n')
```

sink represents a character array into which the characters read are placed. size represents the maximal number of characters to read from the istream. delimiter indicates a character that, if encountered, should terminate the reading of characters. The delimiter itself is not read, but is left as the next character of the istream. Failure to remove the delimiter before performing a second get() is a common error. In the following program example we use the istream ignore() member function to toss away the delimiter. By default, the newline character serves as the delimiter.

Characters are read until one of the following conditions occurs. Following any of these conditions, a null character is placed in the next open position within the array.

*   size-1 characters are read

*   end-of-file is encountered

*   the delimiter character is encountered (Again, that character is not placed within the array, but is left as the next character of the istream.)

The return value of get() is the istream object through which it is invoked. (gcount() provides a count of the characters read.) Here is a simple example of its use:

```
#include <iostream>

int main()
{
    const int max_line = 1024;
    char line[ max_line ];

    while ( cin.get( line, max_line ))
    {
        // maximum read is max_line - 1 to allow for null
        int get_count = cin.gcount();
        cout << "characters actually read: "
            << get_count << endl;

        // do something with line

        // if we encountered a newline,
        // discard it before we read next line
        if ( get_count < max_line-1 )
            cin.ignore();
    }
}
```

When executed against our young Alice Emma, the program generates the following output:

```
characters actually read: 52
characters actually read: 60
characters actually read: 66
characters actually read: 63
characters actually read: 61
characters actually read: 43
```

To better test its behavior, we created a line longer than max_line characters, placing it at the front of the file containing the Alice Emma's text:

```
characters actually read: 1023
characters actually read: 528
characters actually read: 52
characters actually read: 60
characters actually read: 66
characters actually read: 63
characters actually read: 61
characters actually read: 43
```

By default, ignore() reads and discards a single character from the istream object to which it is applied, but an explicit length and delimiter can be specified. Its general signature is the following:

```
ignore( streamsize length = 1, int delim = traits::eof )
```

`ignore()` reads and discards length characters from the istream, or all characters up to and including the delimiter, or until the end-of-file is encountered. It returns the istream object against which it is applied.

Because programmers often forget to discard the delimiter before reapplying `get()`, use of the `getline()` member function is preferred over `get()` because it discards the delimiter rather than leaving it as the next istream character. The signature of `getline()` is the same as the three-argument form of `get()` (it also returns the istream object through which it is invoked):

```
getline(char *sink, streamsize size, char delimiter='\n')
```

Because both `getline()` and the three-argument form of `get()` might read size characters or less, it is often necessary to query the istream to determine how many characters were actually read. The istream member function gcount() provides just that information; it returns the number of characters actually extracted by the last call of `get()` or `getline()`.

The ostream `write()` member function provides an alternative method of outputting a character array. Rather than outputting characters until a terminating null character is found, it outputs some length of characters, including embedded null characters, if any. It has the following function signature:

```
write( const char *sink, streamsize length )
```

length specifies the number of characters to display. `write()` returns the ostream class object through which it is invoked.

The inverse of the ostream `write()` function is the istream `read()` function, with a signature that is defined as follows:

```
read( char* addr, streamsize size )
```

`read()` extracts size contiguous bytes from the input stream and places them beginning at addr. gcount() returns the number of bytes extracted by the last read() invocation. `read()` returns the istream class object that invokes it. Here is an example of using getline(), gcount(), and write():

```
#include <iostream>

int main()
{
    const lineSize = 1024;
    int lcnt = 0; // how many lines are read
    int max = -1; // size of longest line
    char inBuf[ lineSize ];

    // reads 1024 characters or up to newline
    while (cin.getline( inBuf, lineSize ))
    {
        // how many characters actually read
```

```
        int readin = cin.gcount();

        // statistics: line count, longest line
        ++lcnt;
        if ( readin > max )
            max = readin;

        cout << "Line #" << lcnt
            << "\tChars read: " << readin << endl;

        cout.write( inBuf, readin).put('\n').put('\n');
    }

    cout << "Total lines read: " << lcnt << endl;
    cout << "Longest line read: " << max << endl;
}
```

When run against the first few sentences of Moby Dick, the program generates the following output:

```
Line #1 Chars read: 45
Call me Ishmael.  Some years ago, never mind

Line #2 Chars read: 46
how long precisely, having little or no money

Line #3 Chars read: 48
in my purse, and nothing particular to interest

Line #4 Chars read: 51
me on shore, I thought I would sail about a little

Line #5 Chars read: 47
and see the watery part of the world.  It is a

Line #6 Chars read: 43
way I have of driving off the spleen, and

Line #7 Chars read: 28
regulating the circulation.

Total lines read: 7
Longest line read: 51
```

The istream getline() function only supports input into a character array. The standard library, however, provides a nonmember getline() instance that inputs into a string object, with the following general signature:

```
getline( istream &is, string str, char delimiter );
```

The behavior of this instance of getline() is as follows: A maximum of str::max_size()-1 characters are read. If the input sequence exceeds this limit, the read operation fails and the istream object is placed in an error state. Otherwise, input ceases when either the delimiter is read (it is discarded from the istream, but not inserted into the string) or end-of-file is encountered.

There are three other istream operators of general interest:

```
// push character back into the iostream
putback( char c );

// resets pointer to 'next' istream item backward by one
unget();

// returns next character (or EOF)
// but does not extract it
peek();
```

The following code fragment illustrates how some of these operators might be used:

```
char ch, next, lookahead;

while ( cin.get( ch ))
{
    switch (ch) {
    case '/':
        // is it a line comment? use peek() to see:
        // yes? ignore() rest of line
        next = cin.peek();
        if ( next == '/' )
             cin.ignore( lineSize, '\n' );
        break;
    case '>':
        // look for >>=
        next = cin.peek();
        if ( next == '>' ) {
            lookahead = cin.get();
            next = cin.peek();
            if ( next != '=' )
                cin.putback( lookahead );
        }
        // ...
}
```

Exercise 20.4

Read in the following character sequence from standard input, including all white space, echoing each character back in turn to standard output:

```
a   b  c
d      e
f
```

Exercise 20.5

Read the sentence "riverrun, from bend of bay to swerve of shore" as (a) a sequence of nine strings and (b) a single string.

Exercise 20.6

Using getline() and gcount(), read in a sequence of lines from standard input. Determine the largest line read (make sure a line requiring multiple applications of get-line() is counted as one line).

20.4 Overloading the Output Operator <<

When we implement a class type, we must provide an overloaded instance of both the input and output operator if we wish our class to support those operations. In this section we look at how to overload the output operator. The overloading of the input operator is the subject of the next section. Here is an overloaded instance of the output operator for a WordCount class:

```cpp
#include <iostream>

class WordCount {
    friend ostream&
            operator<<(ostream&, const WordCount&);
public:
    WordCount( string word, int cnt=1 );
    // ...
private:
    string word;
    int occurs;
};

ostream&
operator <<( ostream& os, const WordCount& wd )
{    // format: <occurs> word
    os << "< " << wd.occurs << " > "
       << wd.word;
    return os;
}
```

A design question is whether or not the output operator of the class should generate a trailing newline. The issue is that the output operators for the built-in types do not, and so users do not generally expect the class instance to provide one. The pre-

ferred design choice is for the class instance of the output operator not to generate a
trailing newline.

Once defined, the WordCount instance of the output operator can now be intermixed freely with the other output operators. For example,

```
#include <iostream>
#include "WordCount.h"

int main()
{
    WordCount wd( "sadness", 12 );
    cout << "wd:\n" << wd << endl;
    return 0;
}
```

prints as follows on the user's terminal:

```
wd:
< 12 > sadness
```

The output operator is a binary operator that returns an ostream reference. The
general skeleton of an overloaded definition looks as follows:

```
// general skeleton of the overloaded output operator
ostream&
operator <<( ostream& os, const ClassType &object )
{
    // any special logic to prepare object

    // actual output of members
    os << // ...

    // return ostream object
    return os;
}
```

Its first argument is a reference to an ostream object. The second is generally a
const reference to a particular class type. The return type is an ostream reference. Its
value is always the ostream object against which the output operator is applied.

Because the first argument is an ostream reference, the output operator must be defined as a nonmember function. (Section 15.1 discusses this in detail.) When the operator requires access to nonpublic members, it must be declared as a friend to the class.
(Friends are discussed in Section 15.2.)

Location is a class that holds the line and column number of each occurrence of a
word. Here is its definition:

```
#include <iostream>

class Location {
    friend ostream& operator<<( ostream&, const Location& );
```

```
public:
    Location( int line=0, int col=0 )
            : _line( line ), _col( col ) {}
private:
    short _line;
    short _col;
};

ostream& operator <<( ostream& os, const Location& lc )
{
    // output of a Location object:   < 10,37 >
    os << "<" << lc._line
       << "," << lc._col << "> ";

    return os;
}
```

Let's redefine WordCount to contain both a vector of Location class objects, occur-List, and a string class object word:

```
#include <vector>
#include <string>
#include <iostream>
#include "Location.h"

class WordCount {
    friend ostream& operator<<(ostream&, const WordCount&);

public:
    WordCount(){}
    WordCount( const string &word ) : _word(word){}
    WordCount( const string &word, int ln, int col )
            : _word( word ){ insert_location( ln, col ); }

    string word()    const { return _word; }
    int    occurs() const { return _occurList.size(); }
    void   found( int ln, int col )
              { insert_location( ln, col ); }

private:
    void insert_location( int ln, int col )
        { _occurList.push_back( Location( ln, col )); }

    string              _word;
    vector< Location > _occurList;
};
```

Both the string class and the Location class define an instance of an operator<<(). Here is the new definition of the WordCount output operator:

```
ostream&
operator <<( ostream& os, const WordCount& wd )
{
        os  << "<" << wd._occurList.size() << "> "
            << wd._word << endl;

        int cnt = 0, onLine = 6;
        vector< Location >::const_iterator first =
                wd._occurList.begin();

        vector< Location >::const_iterator last =
                wd._occurList.end();

        for ( ; first != last, ++first )
        {
            // os << Location
            os << *first << " ";

            // formatting: 6 to a line
            if ( ++cnt == onLine )
                { os << "\n"; cnt = 0;  }

        }
        return os;
}
```

Here is a program that utilizes the new definition of WordCount. For simplicity, the occurrences are hand-coded.

```
#include <iostream>
#include "WordCount.h"

int main()
{
    WordCount search( "rosebud" );

    // for simplicity, hand-code occurrences
    search.found(11,3);   search.found(11,8);
    search.found(14,2);   search.found(34,6);
    search.found(49,7);   search.found(67,5);
    search.found(81,2);   search.found(82,3);
    search.found(91,4);   search.found(97,8);

    cout << "Occurrences: " << "\n"
        << search << endl;

    return 0;
}
```

When compiled and executed, it generates the following output:

```
Occurrences:
<10> rosebud
<11,3>   <11,8>   <14,2>   <34,6>   <49,7>   <67,5>
<81,2>   <82,3>   <91,4>   <97,8>
```

The output of this program is stored in a file named output. Our next effort will be to define an input operator to read it back in.

Exercise 20.7

Given the following class Date definition,

```
class Date {
public:
    // ...
private:
    int month, day, year;
};
```

provide an overloaded instance of the output operator (a) generating the format

```
// spell the month out
September 8th, 1997
```

(b) generating the format

```
9 / 8 / 97
```

(c) Which, if either, is preferrable? Why?
(d) Should the Date output operator be a friend function? Why? Why not?

Exercise 20.8

Define the output operator for the following CheckoutRecord class,

```
class CheckoutRecord {
public:
    // ...
private:
    double book_id;
    string title;
    Date date_borrowed;
    Date date_due;
    pair<string,string> borrower;
    vector< pair<string,string>* > wait_list;
};
```

20.5   Overloading the Input Operator >>

Overloading the input operator (>>) is similar to overloading the output operator, except that the possibility of error is considerably greater. For example, here is an implementation of the WordCount input operator:

```
#include <iostream>
#include "WordCount.h"

/* must modify WordCount to specify input operator as friend:
   class WordCount {
       friend ostream& operator<<( ostream&, const WordCount& );
       friend istream& operator>>( istream&, WordCount& );
 */

istream&
operator>>( istream &is, WordCount &wd )
{
    /* format of WordCount object to be read:
     * <2> string
     *     <7,3> <12,36>
     */

    int ch;

    /* read in less-than token. if not present
     * place istream in a fail state and exit
     */
    if ((ch = is.get()) != '<' )
    {
        is.setstate( ios_base::failbit );
        return is;
    }

    // read in size value.
    int occurs;
    is >> occurs;

    // grab >; not checking for error
    while ( is && (ch = is.get()) != '>' ) ;

    is >> wd._word;

    // read in the locations;
    // format of each location: < line, col >
    for ( int ix = 0; ix < occurs; ++ix )
    {
        int line, col;
```

```
        // extract values
        while (is && (ch = is.get())!= '<' ) ;
        is >> line;

        while (is && (ch = is.get())!= ',' ) ;
        is >> col;

        while (is && (ch = is.get())!= '>' ) ;

        wd.occurList.push_back( Location( line, col ));
    }
    return is;
}
```

This example illustrates a number of issues with regard to possible iostream error states:

1. An istream that fails because of a incorrect format should mark the state of istream as fail:

   ```
   is.setstate( ios_base::failbit )
   ```

2. The insertion and extraction operations of an iostream in an error state have no effect. For example,

   ```
   while (( ch = is.get() ) != lbrace)
   ```

   loops forever if the istream object is is in an error state. This is why the condition of is is tested before each call of get():

   ```
   // test whether "is" is in a good state
   while ( is && (ch = is.get()) != lbrace)
   ```

The istream object that is not in a good state evaluates to false. (We look at the condition states of iostream objects in more detail in Section 20.7.)

The following program reads in the WordCount class object written previously by the overloaded output operator defined in the previous section.

```
#include <iostream>
#include "WordCount.h"

int main()
{
    WordCount readIn;

    // operator>>( cin, readIn )
    cin >> readIn;

    if ( !cin ) {
        cerr << "WordCount input error" << endl;
        return -1;
    }
```

```
            // operator<<( cout, readIn )
            cout << readIn << endl;
    }
```

When compiled and executed, the program generates the following output:

```
<10> rosebud
<11,3>  <11,8>  <14,2>  <34,6>  <49,7>  <67,5>
<81,2>  <82,3>  <91,4>  <97,8>
```

Exercise 20.9

The WordCount input operator handles directly the input of individual Location items. Factor this code into a separate Location input operator.

Exercise 20.10

Provide an input operator for the class Date defined in Exercise 20.7 of Section 20.4.

Exercise 20.11

Provide an input operator for the class CheckoutRecord defined in Exercise 20.8 of Section 20.4.

20.6   File Input and Output

A user wishing to connect a file to the program for input or output must include the fstream header file (which in turn includes the iostream header file):

```
#include <fstream>
```

To open a file for output only, we define an ofstream (output file stream) class object. For example:

```
ofstream outfile( "copy.out", ios_base::out );
```

The arguments passed to ofstream's constructor specify, in turn, the name of the file to be opened and the mode under which to open it. An ofstream file can be opened in either output (ios_base::out) or append (ios_base::app) mode. (An ostream file by default is opened in output mode.) The definition of outfile2 is equivalent to that of outfile:

```
// opened in output mode by default
ofstream outfile2( "copy.out" );
```

If an existing file is opened in output mode, all data stored in that file is discarded. If we wish to add to rather than replace the data within an existing file, we should open the file in append mode. The additional data written to the file is then added at its end. In either mode, if the file does not exist, it will be created.

Before attempting to read or write to a file, it is always a good idea to verify that it has been opened successfully. We can test outFile as follows:

```
if ( ! outFile ) { // opened failed
     cerr << "cannot open "copy.out" for output\n";
     exit( -1 );
}
```

The ofstream class is derived from the ostream class. All the ostream operations can be applied to an ofstream class object. For example,

```
char ch = ' ';
outFile.put( '1' ).put( ')' ).put( ch );
outFile << "1 + 1 = " << (1 + 1) << endl;
```

inserts

```
1) 1 + 1 = 2
```

into outfile.

The following program gets characters from standard input and puts them into the file copy.out:

```
#include <fstream>

int main()
{
    // open a file copy.out for output
    ofstream outFile( "copy.out" );

    if ( ! outFile ) {
        cerr << "Cannot open "copy.out" for output\n";
        return -1 ;
    }

    char ch;
    while ( cin.get( ch ) )
            outFile.put( ch );
}
```

User-defined instances of the output operator can also be applied to an ofstream class object. The following program invokes the WordCount output operator defined in the previous section:

```
#include <fstream>
#include "WordCount.h"

int main()
{
    // open a file word.out for output
    ofstream oFile( "word.out" );
```

```
    // test for successful open goes here ...

    // create and set manually
    WordCount artist( "Renoir" );
    artist.found( 7, 12 ); artist.found( 34, 18 );

    // invokes operator <<(ostream&, const WordCount&);
    oFile << artist;
}
```

To open a file for input only, an ifstream class object is used. The ifstream class is derived from istream. The following program reads a file specified by the user and writes its contents to standard output:

```
#include <fstream>

int main()
{
    cout << "filename: ";
    string file_name;

    cin >> file_name;

    // open a file copy.out for input
    ifstream inFile( file_name.c_str() );

    if ( !inFile ) {
        cerr << "unable to open input file: "
             << file_name << " -- bailing out!\n";
        return -1;
    }

    char ch;
    while ( inFile.get( ch ))
           cout.put( ch );
}
```

The following program reads our Alice Emma text file, filters it using the filter_string() function (see Section 20.2.1 both for the Alice Emma text and the definition of filter_string()), sorts the strings, removes duplicate words, then writes the resulting text to an output file.

```
#include <fstream>
#include <iterator>
#include <vector>
#include <algorithm>

template <class InputIterator>
void filter_string( InputIterator first, InputIterator last,
                    string filt_elems = string("\",?."))
```

```
{
    for ( ; first != last; first++ )
    {
        string::size_type pos = 0;
        while ((pos=(*first).find_first_of(filt_elems,pos))
                    != string::npos )
                        (*first).erase( pos, 1 );
    }
}

int main()
{
    ifstream infile( "alice_emma" );

    istream_iterator<string> ifile( infile );
    istream_iterator<string> eos;

    vector< string > text;
    copy( ifile, eos, inserter( text, text.begin() ));

    string filt_elems( "\",.?;:" );
    filter_string( text.begin(), text.end(), filt_elems );

    vector<string>::iterator iter;

    sort( text.begin(), text.end() );
    iter = unique( text.begin(), text.end() );
    text.erase( iter, text.end() );

    ofstream outfile( "alice_emma_sort" );

    iter = text.begin();
    for ( int line_cnt = 1; iter != text.end();
        ++iter, ++line_cnt )
    {
        outfile << *iter << " ";
        if ( ! ( line_cnt % 8 ))
            outfile << '\n';
    }
    outfile << endl;
}
```

When compiled and executed, the program generates the following output:

```
A Alice Daddy Emma Her I Shyly a
alive almost asks at beautiful bird blows but
creature fiery flight flowing hair has he her
him in is it like long looks magical
mean more no red same says she shush
```

```
such tell tells the there through time to
untamed wanting when wind
```

Both an ifstream and an ofstream class object can be defined without specifying a file. A file can be later connected explicitly to a class object through the member function open(). For example:

```
ifstream curFile;
// ...
curFile.open( filename.c_str() );
if ( ! curFile ) // open failed?
      // ...
```

A file can be disconnected from the program by invoking the member function close(). For example:

```
curFile.close();
```

In the following program, five files are opened and closed in turn using the same ifstream class object:

```
#include <fstream>

const int fileCnt = 5;
string fileTabl[ fileCnt ] = {
        "Melville","Joyce","Musil","Proust","Kafka"
};

int main()
{
    ifstream inFile; // not attached to any file

    for ( int ix = 0; ix < fileCnt; ++ix )
    {
            inFile.open( fileTabl[ix].c_str() );
            // ... verify successful open
            // ... process file
            inFile.close();
    }
}
```

An fstream class object can open a file for either input *or* output. The fstream class is derived from the iostream class. In the following example, word.out is first read then written using the fstream class object file. The file word.out, created earlier in this section, contains a WordCount object.

```
#include <fstream>
#include "WordCount.h"

int main()
{
```

```
WordCount wd;
fstream file;

file.open( "word.out", ios_base::in );
file >> wd;
file.close();

cout << "Read in: " << wd << endl;

// ios_base::out would discard current data
file.open( "word.out", ios_base::app );
file << endl << wd << endl;
file.close();
}
```

An fstream class object can also open a file for *both* input and output. For example, the following definition opens word.out in both input and append mode:

```
fstream io( "word.out", ios_base::in|ios_base::app );
```

The bitwise OR operator is used to specify more than one mode. An fstream class object can be repositioned using either the seekg() or seekp() member functions (the g indicates positioning for *getting* characters [used with an ifstream class object] whereas the p indicates positioning for *putting* characters [used with an ifstream class object]). These functions move to an "absolute" address within the file or move a byte offset from a particular position. Both seekg() and seekp() take the following two forms:

```
// set a fixed position within a file
seekg( pos_type current_position );

// offset some amount from current position in some direction
seekg( off_type offset_position, ios_base::seekdir dir );
```

In the first version, the current position is set to some fixed location within the file specified by current_position, where 0 is the beginning of the file. For example, were a file to consist of the characters

```
abc def ghi jkl
```

the following invocation

```
io.seekg( 6 );
```

repositions io to character position 6; in our example, to the character f. The second form repositions the file using an offset either from its current position, to the beginning of the file, or backward from the end of the file, as indicated by the second argument. dir can be set to one of the following:

1. ios_base::beg, the beginning of the file
2. ios_base::cur, the current position of the file
3. ios_base::end, the end of the file

In the following example, each invocation of `seekg()` positions the file at the *i*th record entry for each iteration:

```
for ( int i = 0; i < recordCnt; ++i )
        readFile.seekg( i * sizeof(Record), ios_base::beg );
```

A negative value can also be specified for the first argument. For example, the following moves backward 10 bytes from the current position:

```
readFile.seekg( -10, ios_base::cur );
```

The current read position in an fstream file is returned by either of the two member functions `tellg()` or `tellp()` (again, the 'p' indicates *putting* — and serves an ofstream object; the 'g' indicates *getting* — and serves an ifstream object). For example:

```
// mark current position
ios_base::pos_type mark = writeFile.tellp();

// ...
if ( cancelEntry )
        // return to marked position
        writeFile.seekp( mark );
```

A programmer wishing to advance one Record from the current file position might write either of the following:

```
// equivalent repositioning seek invocations
readFile.seekg( readFile.tellg() + sizeof(Record) );

// this is considered the more efficient
readFile.seekg( sizeof(Record), ios_base::cur );
```

Let's go through an actual programming example in some detail. Here is the problem. We are given a text file to read. We are to compute the byte size of the file and store it at the end of the file. In addition, each time we encounter a newline character, we are to store the current byte size, including the newline, at the end of the file. For example, given the following text file,

```
abcd
efg
hi
j
```

the program should produce the following modified text file:

```
abcd
efg
hi
j
5 9 12 14 24
```

Here is our initial implementation:

```
#include <iostream>
#include <fstream>

main()
{
    // open in both input and append mode
    fstream inOut( "copy.out", ios_base::in|ios_base::app );
    int cnt = 0;    // byte count
    char ch;

    while ( inOut.get( ch ) )
    {
        cout.put( ch ); // echo on terminal
        ++cnt;
        if ( ch == '\n' ) {
            inOut << cnt ;
            inOut.put( ' ' ); // blank space
        }
    }

    // write out final byte count
    inOut << cnt << endl;
    cout << "[ " << cnt << " ]" << endl;
    return 0;
}
```

inOut is an fstream class object attached to the file copy.out, which is opened in both input and append mode. A file opened in append mode will write all data to the end of the file.

Each time we read a character, including white space but not end-of-file, we increment cnt and echo the character on the user's terminal. The purpose of echoing the input is so that we have something to look at and measure if our program does not work as expected.

Each time we encounter a newline, we write the current value of cnt to inOut. Reading the end-of-file terminates the loop. We write the final value of cnt to inOut and also to the screen.

The program compiles. It seems correct. The file contains the first few sentences of *Moby Dick*, the nineteenth-century American novel written by Herman Melville:

```
Call me Ishmael.  Some years ago, never mind
how long precisely, having little or no money
in my purse, and nothing particular to interest
me on shore, I thought I would sail about a little
and see the watery part of the world.  It is a
way I have of driving off the spleen, and
regulating the circulation.
```

When we execute the program, the output generated is the following:

```
[ 0 ]
```

No characters are displayed and the program believes the text file is empty. Obviously, that's incorrect. We've somehow misunderstood something fundamental. Rather than fretting, or becoming unduly discouraged, the thing to do now is think. The problem is that the file is opened in append mode and is therefore positioned at its end. When

```
inOut.get( ch )
```

is executed, end-of-file is encountered and the `while` loop terminates, leaving `cnt` with a value of 0.

While the result of the program is a serious foul-up, the solution is quite trivial once we understand the problem. All we need to do is reposition the file back to the beginning before we begin to read. The statement

```
inOut.seekg( 0 );
```

accomplishes just that. The program is recompiled and rerun. This time, the following output is generated:

```
Call me Ishmael.   Some years ago, never mind
[ 45 ]
```

The display and byte count are generated for only the first line of the text file. The remaining six lines are ignored. Gosh, who ever said that programming is easy? This is part of what it means to be a programmer, particularly when we are learning something new. (Sometimes it is useful to keep a record of the things we misunderstand or do wrong — particularly later when we become impatient with those less experienced than ourselves.) At this point we need to take a deep breath and think about what it is we are trying to do versus what we apparently are doing. Can you see the problem?

The problem is that the file is opened in append mode. The first time `cnt` is written, the file becomes repositioned at its end. The subsequent `get()` encounters end-of-file and once more terminates the `while` loop prematurely.

The solution this time is to reposition the file to where it was prior to the writing of `cnt`. This can be accomplished with the following two additional statements:

```
// mark current position
ios_base::pos_type mark = inOut.tellg();
inOut << cnt << sp;
inOut.seekg( mark ); // restore position
```

When the program is recompiled and executed, the output to the terminal is correct. Examining the output file, however, we discover it is still not quite right: The final byte count, although being written to the terminal, is *not* being written to the file. The output operator following the `while` loop is not being executed.

The problem this time is that `inOut` is in the "state" of having encountered end-of-file. As long as `inOut` remains in this state, input and output operations are *not* performed. The solution is to clear() the state of the file. This is accomplished with the following statement:

```
inOut.clear(); // zero out state flags
```

The complete program looks as follows:

```
#include <iostream>
#include <fstream>

int main()
{
    fstream inOut( "copy.out", ios_base::in|ios_base::app );
    int cnt=0;
    char ch;

    inOut.seekg(0);
    while ( inOut.get( ch ) )
    {
        cout.put( ch );
        cnt++;
        if ( ch == '\n' )
        {
            // mark current position
            ios_base::pos_type mark = inOut.tellg();
            inOut << cnt << ' ';
            inOut.seekg( mark ); // restore position
        }
    }
    inOut.clear();
    inOut << cnt << endl;

    cout << "[ " << cnt << " ]\n";
    return 0;
}
```

When the program is recompiled and executed, it generates the expected output — at last! One of our mistakes in implementing the program was in not providing an explicit statement of the behavior that it needed to support. Each subsequent solution was a response to a problem that manifested itself rather than an analysis of the entire problem that required solution. We got to the same end as we would have with more thought up front, but with considerable more pain and expense of energy.

Exercise 20.12

Using the output operation defined for the Date class of Exercise 20.10 or the CheckoutRecord class of Exercise 20.11 (both in Section 20.5), write a program to create and write to an output file.

Exercise 20.13

Write a program to open and read the file created in Exercise 20.12. Display the contents of the file to standard output.

Exercise 20.14

Write a program to open the file created in Exercise 20.12 for both input and output. Output an instance of either the Date class or the CheckoutRecord class (a) at the beginning of the file, (b) after the second existing object, and (c) at the end of the file.

20.7 Condition States

In general, as users of the iostream library our primary concern is whether or not a stream is in a nonerror state. For example, if we write

```
int ival;
cin >> ival;
```

and type in "Borges", cin is placed in an error state following the unsuccessful attempt to assign a string literal to an integer value. If we typed in 1024, the read is successful and cin remains in a good state. A read operation is only carried out by an input stream in a good state.

To determine if a stream object is in a good state, we generally simply test its truth value:

```
if ( !cin )
        // read operation failed or end of file encountered.
```

To read an unknown number of elements, we generally write the following while loop:

```
while ( cin >> word )
        // ok: read operation successful ...
```

The condition test of the while loop evaluates to false on either reaching end-of-file or on an error condition during a read operation. For most situations, this form of true/false evaluation of a stream object is sufficient. However, in implementing our Word input operator back in Section 20.5, we needed a more fine-grained access of the stream condition state.

A stream object maintains a set of condition flags through which the ongoing state of the stream can be monitored. The following four predicate member functions can be invoked:

1. eof() returns true if the stream has encountered end-of-file. For example:

```
if ( inOut.eof() )
        // ok, everything read in ...
```

2. bad() returns true if an invalid operation, such as "seeking" past end-of-file, has been attempted. Generally, it indicates that a stream is corrupted in some undefined way.

3. fail() returns true if an operation has been unsuccessful, such as failing to open a file stream object or encountering an invalid input format. For example:

```
ifstream iFile( filename, ios_base::in );

if ( iFile.fail() ) // unable to open
        error_message( ... );
```

4. good() returns true if none of the other conditions are true. For example:

```
if ( inOut.good() )
```

There are two methods for modifying explicitly the condition state of an iostream object. Using the clear() member function, we reset the condition state to an explicit value. Using the setstate() member function, rather than reset the condition we simply add a condition to the existing condition of the object. For example, in the input operator for our WordCount class, when we encounter an invalid format, we use setstate() to add the fail condition to the istream object:

```
if ((ch = is.get()) != '<' )
 {
        is.setstate( ios_base::failbit );
        return is;
}
```

The set of condition values available are the following:

```
ios_base::badbit
ios_base::eofbit
ios_base::failbit
ios_base::goodbit
```

To set multiple states, we use the bitwise OR operator, as follows:

```
is.setstate( ios_base::badbit | ios_base::failbit );
```

In our test of the WordCount input operator in Section 20.5 we wrote

```
if ( !( cin >> readIn ))
{
        cerr << "WordCount input error" << endl;
        exit( -1 );
}
```

Alternatively, we might have wished to continue with our program, perhaps alerting our user to an input error and soliciting additional input. To read additional input from cin, however, we must restore it to a good state. We can do this using the clear() member function:

```
cin.clear(); // resets cin to good
```

More generally, `clear()` is used to clear the existing condition state of the object and set zero or more new condition states. For example,

```
cin.clear( ios_base::goodbit );
```

restores `cin` explicitly to a good state. (These two invocations are equivalent because the default value for an invocation of `clear()` is the `goodbit` value.)

The `rdstate()` member function allows us to access explicitly the state of an iostream class object. For example:

```
ios_base::iostate old_state = cin.rdstate();

cin.clear();
process_input();

// now reset cin to old state
cin.clear( old_state );
```

Exercise 20.15

Revise either (or both) input operator for the Date class of Exercise 20.7 and/or the CheckoutRecord class of Exercise 20.8 (both in Section 20.4) to set the condition state of the istream object. Modify the programs used to exercise the operator to check for the explicitly set conditions and, once reported, to reset the condition state of the istream object. Exercise the revised program by providing both good and bad formats.

20.8 String Streams

The iostream library supports in-memory operations on string objects. The ostringstream class inserts characters into a string. The istringstream class reads characters from a string object, and the stringstream class can be used to support both reading and writing. To use a string stream, the associated header file must be included:

```
#include <sstream>
```

For example, the following function reads the entire file alice_emma into an ostringstream class object buf. buf is grown as necessary to accommodate the characters input:

```
#include <string>
#include <fstream>
#include <sstream>

string read_file_into_string()
{
    ifstream ifile( "alice_emma" );
    ostringstream buf;

    char ch;
```

```
        while ( buf && ifile.get( ch ))
                buf.put( ch );

        return buf.str();
    }
```

The `str()` member function returns the string object associated with the ostring-stream class object. This string can now be manipulated the same way as any "ordinary" string object. For example, in the following program, text is memberwise initialized with the string object associated with buf:

```
    int main()
    {
        string text = read_file_into_string();

        // marks the position of each newline within text
        vector< string::size_type > lines_of_text;
        string::size_type pos = 0;

        while ( pos != string::npos )
        {
                pos = text.find( '\n', pos );
                lines_of_text.push_back( pos );
        }

        // ...
    }
```

An ostringstream object can also be used to support the automatic formatting of a compound string; that is, a string consisting of multiple data types. For example, the output operator converts automatically any arithmetic type into a corresponding string representation without our needing to worry about the amount of storage necessary:

```
    #include <iostream>
    #include <sstream>

    int main()
    {
        int ival    = 1024;    int *pival    = &ival;
        double dval = 3.14159; double *pdval = &dval;

        ostringstream format_message;

        // ok: converts values to a string representation
        format_message << "ival: " << ival
            << " ival's address: " << pival << '\n'
            << "dval: " << dval
            << " dval's address: " << pdval << endl;

        string msg = format_message.str();
```

```
cout << " size of message string: " << msg.size()
     << " message: " << msg << endl;
```

```
}
```

In some circumstances it is preferable to collect the set of nonfatal diagnostic errors and warnings rather than to display them as they are encountered. A simple way of accomplishing this is to provide an overloaded set of format functions of the general form

```
string
format( string msg, int expected, int received )
{
     ostringstream message;
     message << msg << " expected: " << expected
             << " received: " << received << "\n";
     return message.str();
}
```

```
string format( string msg, vector<int> *values );
// ... and so on
```

The application can then store the strings for later display, perhaps cataloging them by severity. This can be generalized into a Notify, Log, or Error class.

An istringstream reads from a string object with which it is constructed. One use of an istringstream is to convert a numeric string representation into an arithmetic value. For example:

```
#include <iostream>
#include <sstream>
#include <string>

int main()
{
        int ival    = 1024;    int *pival    = &ival;
        double dval = 3.14159; double *pdval = &dval;

        // creates a string in which each value
        // is stored separated by a space
        ostringstream format_string;
        format_string << ival << " " << pival << " "
                      << dval << " " << pdval << endl;

        // extracts the stored ascii values, placing
        // them in turn in the four objects
        istringstream input_istring( format_string.str() );
        input_istring >> ival >> pival
                      >> dval >> pdval;
}
```

Exercise 20.16

In C, the formatting of an output message is accomplished using the standard C `printf()` family of routines. For example, the following program fragment,

```
int    ival = 1024;
double dval = 3.14159;
char   cval = 'a';
char  *sval = "the end";

printf( "ival: %d\tdval: %g\tcval: %c\tsval: %s",
        ival, dval, cval, sval );
```

generates

```
ival: 1024dval: 3.14159cval: asval: the end
```

The first argument to `printf()` is a format string. Each % character indicates that an argument value is to be substituted; the character following indicates its type. Here are some possible types of values supported:

```
%d        integer
%g        floating point
%c        char
%s        C-style string
```

(See KERNIGHAN88] for a complete discussion.)

The additional arguments to `printf()` are matched positionally to each occurrence of the % format pair. The other characters of the format string are treated as literals and are written directly.

The two primary weaknesses of the `printf()` family of routines are (1) the format string is not extensible to recognize user-defined types and (2) if the type or number of arguments do not match the format string, the error is undetected and the output is badly malformed. The primary appeal of the `printf()` family of routines is the compactness of the format string strategy.

(a) Generate the equivalent formatted output using an ostringstream object.

(b) Contrast the benefits and drawbacks of the two approaches.

20.9   Format State

Each iostream library class object maintains a *format state* that controls the details of formatting operations, such as the notational base for an integral value or the precision of a floating point value. A predefined set of manipulators is available to the programmer for modifying the format state of an object.[1]

---

1. In addition, the programmer can set and unset format state flags directly using the `setf()` and `unsetf()` member functions. We do not cover these operations. For a discussion of this approach, see [STROUSTRUP97].

A manipulator is applied to the stream object the same as if it were data. Rather than causing data to be read or written, however, a manipulator modifies the internal state of the stream object. For example, by default a bool object with a value of true (and the literal constant true) are written as the integer value 1:

```
#include <iostream>

int main()
{
    bool illustrate = true;;
    cout << "bool object illustrate set to true: "
        << illustrate << '\n';
}
```

To modify cout to display illustrate as the word true, we apply the boolalpha manipulator:

```
#include <iostream>

int main()
{
    bool illustrate = true;;
    cout << "bool object illustrate set to true: ";

    // changes state of cout to print bool values
    // using the strings true and false.
    cout << boolalpha;
    cout << illustrate << '\n';
}
```

Because the application of a manipulator returns the stream object to which it is applied, we can concatenate its application with that of data (and other manipulators as well). Here is our small program rewritten to intermix data and manipulators:

```
#include <iostream>

int main()
{
    bool illustrate = true;
    cout << "bool object illustrate: "
        << illustrate
        << "\nwith boolalpha applied: "
        << boolalpha << illustrate << '\n';

    // ...
}
```

Intermixing a manipulator with data, as we do here, is slightly misleading. Applying the manipulator does not just change the representation of the value subsequently output. Rather, the internal format state of the ostream object is modified. In our example, all `bool` values throughout the rest of our program are also displayed as either true or false.

To unset our modification of cout, we must apply the `noboolalpha` manipulator:

```
cout << boolalpha // sets internal state of cout
     << illustrate
     << noboolalpha // unsets internal state of cout
```

As we'll see, many of the manipulators come in similar set/unset pairs.

By default, arithmetic values are written and read in decimal notation. The programmer may change the notational base of integral values to octal or hexadecimal or back to decimal (the representation of floating point values is unaffected) by using the manipulators hex, oct, and dec. For example:

```
#include <iostream>
int main()
{
        int ival = 16;
        double dval = 16.0;

        cout << "ival: " << ival
             << " oct set: " << oct << ival << "\n";

        cout << "dval: " << dval
             << " hex set: " << hex << dval << "\n";

        cout << "ival: " << ival
             << " dec set: " << dec << ival << "\n";
}
```

When compiled and executed, the program generates the following output:

```
ival: 16 oct set: 20
dval: 16 hex set: 16
ival: 10 dec set: 16
```

One problem with our program is that we cannot look at the value and be sure of its notational base. Is 20, for example, really 20, or an octal representation of 16? The manipulator showbase causes an integral value's output to indicate its base by the following conventions:

1. A leading 0x indicates hexadecimal (if we wish to have the X display in upper-case as X, we can apply the uppercase manipulator; to revert back to the lowercase x, we apply the nouppercase manipulator).

2. A leading 0 indicates octal.

3. The absence of either indicates decimal.

Here is our revised program with showbase applied:

```
#include <iostream>
int main()
{
        int ival = 16;
        double dval = 16.0;

        cout << showbase;

        cout << "ival: " << ival
             << " oct set: " << oct << ival << "\n";

        cout << "dval: " << dval
             << " hex set: " << hex << dval << "\n";

        cout << "ival: " << ival  << " dec set: "
             << dec << ival << "\n";

        cout << noshowbase;
}
```

Here is the revised output:

```
ival: 16 oct set: 020
dval: 16 hex set: 16
ival: 0x10 dec set: 16
```

The noshowbase manipulator resets cout not to display the notational base of the integral values.

By default, a floating point value has a precision value of 6. This value may be modified by using either the precision(int) member function or the setprecision() stream manipulator (to use the latter, the iomanip header file must be included). precision() returns the current precision value. For example:

```
#include <iostream>
#include <iomanip>
#include <math.h>

int main()
{
    cout  << "Precision: "
          << cout.precision() << endl
```

```
                    << sqrt(2.0) << endl;

      cout.precision(12);
      cout   << "\nPrecision: "
             << cout.precision() << endl
             << sqrt(2.0) << endl;

      cout   << "\nPrecision: " << setprecision(3)
             << cout.precision() << endl
             << sqrt(2.0) << endl;

      return 0;
   }
```

When compiled and executed, the program generates the following output:

```
Precision: 6
1.41421

Precision: 12
1.41421356237

Precision: 3
1.41
```

Manipulators that take an argument, such as setprecision() and setw() that we looked at earlier, require that we include the iomanip header file:

```
#include <iomanip>
```

Our example does not illustrate two further aspects of setprecision(): (1) integral values are unaffected and (2) floating point values are rounded, not truncated. Thus, 3.14159 becomes 3.142 with precision set to 4, and 3.14 with precision set to 3.

By default, the decimal point is not displayed when the fractional part of the value is 0. For example,

```
cout << 10.00
```

prints as

```
10
```

To force the display of the decimal point, we use the showpoint manipulator:

```
cout << showpoint
     << 10.0
     << noshowpoint << '\n';
```

The noshowpoint manipulator reinstates the default behavior.

Again, by default, floating point values are displayed in fixed decimal notation. To change the display to scientific notation, we use the scientific manipulator. To change it back to fixed decimal, we use the fixed manipulator:

```
cout << "scientific: " << scientific
     << 10.0
     << "fixed decimal: " << fixed
     << 10.0 << '\n';
```

This generates

```
scientific: 1.0e+01
fixed decimal: 10
```

If we should wish to have the 'e' of the scientific notation output display as 'E', we use the uppercase manipulator. To revert back to lowercase, we use the nouppercase manipulator. (The uppercase manipulator does not cause all alpha characters to be displayed in uppercase!)

By default, the overloaded input operators skip white space (blank, tab, newline, formfeed, and carriage return). Given the sequence

```
a bc
d
```

the loop

```
char ch;
while ( cin >> ch )
        // ...
```

executes four times to read the characters a through d, skipping the intervening blanks, possible tabs, and newline characters. The manipulator noskipws causes the input operator not to skip white space:

```
char ch;
cin >> noskipws;
while ( cin >> ch )
        // ...
cin >> skipws;
```

The while loop now requires seven iterations to read the characters a through d. To return to the default behavior, the skipws manipulator is applied to cin.

When we write

```
cout << "please enter a value: ";
```

the literal string is stored in a buffer associated with cout. There are a number of conditions that cause the buffer to be flushed — that is, emptied — in our example by writing it to standard output:

1. The buffer can become full. In this case, it must be flushed to read the next value.

2. We can flush the buffer explicitly using either the flush, ends, or endl manipulator:

```
// flushes the buffer
cout << "hi!" << flush;
```

```
// inserts a null then flushes the buffer
char ch[2]; ch[0] = 'a'; ch[1] = 'b';
cout << ch << ends;

// inserts a newline then flushes the buffer
cout << "hi!" << endl;
```

3. unitbuf, an internal stream state variable, can be set to empty the buffer after each output operation.

4. The ostream object can be *tied* to an istream, in which case the ostream buffer is flushed whenever the istream reads from the input stream. cout is pre-defined to be tied to cin:

```
cin.tie( &cout );
```

The statement

```
cin >> ival;
```

causes the buffer associated associated with cout to be flushed.

An ostream object can be tied to only one istream object at a time. To break an existing tie, we pass in an argument of 0. For example:

```
istream is;
ostream new_os;

// ...

// tie() returns existing tie
ostream *old_tie = is.tie();

is.tie( 0 ); // break existing tie
is.tie( &new_os ); // set new tie

// ...

is.tie( 0 ); // break existing tie
is.tie( old_tie ); // reestablish old tie
```

We can control the width of a numeric or string value that is output with the setw() manipulator. For example, the program

```
#include <iostream>
#include <iomanip>

int main()
{
    int ival = 16;
    double dval = 3.14159;

    cout << "ival: " << setw(12) << ival << '\n'
```

```
            << "dval: " << setw(12) << dval << '\n';
    }
```

generates the following output:

```
    ival:          16
    dval:      3.14159
```

The second `setw()` is necessary because unlike the other manipulators, `setw()` does not modify the format state of the ostream object.

To have the value left justified, we apply the `left` manipulator (the `right` manipulator resets it to the default). If we wish to generate

```
        16
    -    3
```

we apply the `internal` manipulator, which left justifies the sign and right justifies the value, padding the intervening space with blanks. If we wish to fill the blank spaces with an alternative character, we apply the `setfill()` manipulator.

```
    cout << setw(6) << setfill('%') << 100 << endl;
```

generates

```
    %%%100
```

The full set of predefined manipulators is listed in Table 20.1.

Table 20.1 Manipulators

Manipulator	Meaning
boolalpha	represent true and false as strings
*noboolalpha	represent true and false as 0, 1
showbase	generate prefix indicating numeric base
*noshowbase	do not generate notational base prefix
showpoint	always display decimal point
*noshowpoint	only display decimal point with fraction
showpos	display + in non-negative numbers
*noshowpos	do not display + in non-negative numbers
	Continued

Table 20.1 Manipulators (Continued)

Manipulator	Meaning
*skipws	skip white space with input operators
noskipws	do not skip white space with input operators
uppercase	print 0X in hexadecimal, E in scientific
*nouppercase	print 0x in hexadecimal, e in scientific
*dec	display in decimal numeric base
hex	display in hexadecimal numeric base
oct	display in octal numeric base
left	add fill characters to right of value
right	add fill characters to left of value
internal	add fill characters between sign & value
*fixed	display floating point in decimal notation
scientific	display floating point in scientific notation
flush	flush ostream buffer
ends	insert null then flush ostream buffer
endl	insert newline then flush ostream buffer
ws	"eat" white space
`// these require #include <iomanip>`	
`setfill( ch )`	fill white space with ch
`setprecision( n )`	set floating point precision to n
`setw( w )`	read or write value to w characters
`setbase( b )`	output integers in base b
* indicates default stream state	

20.10 A Strongly Typed Library

The iostream library is strongly typed. The attempt, for example, to read from an ostream, or to assign an ostream to an istream, is both caught at compile-time and flagged as a type violation. For example, given the following set of declarations,

```
#include <iostream>
#include <fstream>
class Screen;

extern istream& operator>>( istream&, const Screen& );
extern void print( ostream& );
ifstream inFile;
```

the following two statements result in compile-time type violations:

```
int main()
{
    Screen myScreen;

    // error: expects an ostream&
    print( cin >> myScreen );

    // error: expects >> operator
    inFile << "error: output operator";
}
```

Input/output facilities are provided as a component of the C++ standard library. Chapter 20 does not describe the entire iostream library — in particular, the creation of user-defined manipulators and buffer classes are beyond the scope of a primer. Instead, we have focused on the portion of the iostream library fundamental to providing program input/output.

Appendix

The Generic Algorithms Alphabetically

In this appendix we look at the individual algorithms in turn. We have chosen to present them alphabetically (with minor exceptions) so that they are easier to refer to. The general form of presenting the algorithms is to (1) list the function prototype; (2) provide a paragraph or two describing the algorithm, pointing out in particular any nonintuitive behavior or expectations; and most importantly, (3) provide a program example to illustrate how we might use the algorithm.

The first two arguments to all the generic algorithms (with the necessary fistful of exceptions that make the rule) are a pair of iterators, generally referred to as first and last, marking off the range of elements within the container or built-in array over which to operate. The element range notation (sometimes called a *left-inclusive interval*) is usually written as

```
// to be read as: includes first and
// each element up to but not including last
[ first, last )
```

indicating that the range begins with first and ends with but does *not* include last. When

```
first == last
```

the range is said to be empty.

A requirement of the iterator pair is that it must be possible to reach last beginning with first through repeated application of the increment operator. The compiler cannot itself enforce this, however. Failure to meet this requirement results in undefined run-time behavior — usually an eventual core dump of the program.

Each algorithm's declaration indicates the minimum category of iterator support it requires (see Section 12.4 for a brief discussion of the five iterator categories). find(), for example, which implements a one-pass, read-only traversal over a container, minimally requires an InputIterator. It can also be passed a Forward-, Bidirectional-, or

RandomAccessIterator as well. Passing it an OutputIterator results in an error. Errors in passing an invalid category of iterator to an algorithm are not guaranteed to be caught at compile-time because the iterator categories are not actual types, but type parameters passed to the function template.

Some algorithms support multiple versions, one making use of a built-in operator while a second accepts either a function object or pointer to function providing an alternative implementation of that operator. `unique()`, for example, by default compares two adjacent elements using the equality operator of the underlying element type of the container. If, however, the underlying element type does not provide an equality operator, or if we wish to define element equality differently, we can pass in either a function object or pointer to a function providing the intended semantics. Other algorithms, however, are separated into two uniquely named instances, the predicate instance in each case ending with the suffix `_if`, as in `find_if()`. For example, there is a `replace()` instance using the built-in equality operator and a `replace_if()` instance taking a predicate function object or pointer to function.

For those algorithms that modify the container over which they operate, there are generally two versions: an in-place version that changes the container against which it is applied, and a version that returns a copy of the container with the changes applied. There are, for example, both a `replace()` and a `replace_copy()` algorithm. The copy version always contains `_copy` in its name. A copy version, however, is not provided for every algorithm that transforms its associated container. The `sort()` algorithms, for example, do not provide a copy instance. In this case, if we wish the algorithm to operate on a copy, we need to make and pass in the copy ourselves.

To use any the generic algorithms, we must include the associated header file:

```
#include <algorithm>
```

To use any of the four numeric algorithms: `adjacent_difference()`, `accumulate()`, `inner_product()`, and `partial_sum()`, we must include

```
#include <numeric>
```

The code implementing the algorithms and the associated container types on which they operate in this Appendix reflects the implementations currently available. The iostream library reflects a prestandard implementation, for example — including the use of an `iostream.h` header file. Templates do not support default arguments for template parameters. To have the program run on your current system, you may need to modify one or another declaration.

An excellent, more detailed discussion of the generic algorithms can be found in [MUSSER96], although it is somewhat out of date with the final C++ standard library.

accumulate()

```
template < class InputIterator, class Type >
Type accumulate(
    InputIterator first, InputIterator last,
    Type init );

template < class InputIterator, class Type,
           class BinaryOperation >
Type accumulate(
    InputIterator first, InputIterator last,
    Type init, BinaryOperation op );
```

The first version of accumulate() adds the sum of the values of the elements in the sequence marked off by the iterator pair [first,last) to an initial value specified by init. For example, given the sequence {1,1,2,3,5,8} and an initial value of 0, the result is 20. In the second version, rather than addition, the binary operation passed in is applied to the elements. For example, if we passed the function object times<int> to accumulate(), the result is 240, provided the initial value is 1, not 0, of course. accumulate() is one of the numeric algorithms. To use it, we must include the <numeric> header file.

```
#include <numeric>
#include <list>
#include <functional>
#include <iostream.h>

/*
 * output:
   accumulate()
          operating on values {1,2,3,4}
          result with default addition: 10
          result with plus<int> function object: 10
 */

int main()
{
    int ia[] = { 1, 2, 3, 4 };
    list<int,allocator> ilist( ia, ia+4 );

    int ia_result = accumulate(&ia[0], &ia[4], 0);
    int ilist_res = accumulate(
        ilist.begin(), ilist.end(), 0, plus<int>() );

    cout << "accumulate()\n\t"
         << "operating on values {1,2,3,4}\n\t"
         << "result with default addition: "
         << ia_result << "\n\t"
         << "result with plus<int> function object: "
```

```
            << ilist_res
            << endl;
    }
```

adjacent_difference()

```
    template < class InputIterator, class OutputIterator >
    OutputIterator adjacent_difference(
        InputIterator first, InputIterator last,
        OutputIterator result );

    template < class InputIterator, class OutputIterator,
               class BinaryOperation >
    OutputIterator adjacent_difference(
        InputIterator first, InputIterator last,
        OutputIterator result, BinaryOperation op );
```

The first version of adjacent_difference() creates a new sequence in which the value of each new element other than the first represents the difference of the current and previous element. For example, given the sequence {0,1,1,2,3,5,8}, the first element of the new sequence is simply a copy of the first element of the original sequence: 0. The second element is the difference between the first two elements: 1. The third element is the difference between the second and third element, or 1 −1, or 0, and so on. The new sequence is {0,1,0,1,1,2,3}.

The second version computes the adjacent difference using the specified binary operation. For example, using the same sequence, let's pass in the times<int> function object. Again, the first element of the new sequence is simply a copy of the first element of the original sequence: 0. The second element is the product of the first and second element, also 0. The third element is the product of the second and third element, or 1 * 1, or 1, and so on. The new sequence is {0,0,1,2,6,15,40}.

In both versions the OutputIterator points one past the last element of the new sequence. adjacent_difference() is one of the numeric algorithms. To use either version we must include the <numeric> header file.

```
    #include <numeric>
    #include <list>
    #include <functional>
    #include <iterator>
    #include <iostream.h>

    int main()
    {
        int ia[] = { 1, 1, 2, 3, 5, 8 };

        list<int,allocator> ilist(ia, ia+6);
        list<int,allocator> ilist_result(ilist.size());
```

```
        adjacent_difference(ilist.begin(), ilist.end(),
                            ilist_result.begin() );

        // generates output:
        // 1 0 1 1 2 3

        copy( ilist_result.begin(), ilist_result.end(),
              ostream_iterator<int>(cout," "));
        cout << endl;

        adjacent_difference( ilist.begin(), ilist.end(),
                             ilist_result.begin(), times<int>() );

        // generates output:
        // 1 1 2 6 15 40
        copy( ilist_result.begin(), ilist_result.end(),
              ostream_iterator<int>(cout," "));
        cout << endl;
    }
```

adjacent_find()

```
        template< class ForwardIterator >
        ForwardIterator
        adjacent_find( ForwardIterator first, ForwardIterator last );

        template< class ForwardIterator, class BinaryPredicate >
        ForwardIterator
        adjacent_find( ForwardIterator first,
                       ForwardIterator last, Predicate pred );
```

adjacent_find() looks for the first adjacent pair of duplicate elements within the range marked off by [first,last). It returns a ForwardIterator to the first element of the pair, if found; otherwise, it returns last. For example, given the sequence {0,1,1,2,2,4}, the pair {1,1} is identified and an iterator addressing the first 1 is returned.

```
        #include <algorithm>
        #include <vector>
        #include <iostream.h>
        #include <assert.h>

        class TwiceOver {
        public:
            bool operator() ( int val1, int val2 )
                { return val1 == val2/2 ? true : false; }
        };

        int main()
        {
```

```
        int ia[] = { 1, 4, 4, 8 };
        vector< int, allocator > vec( ia, ia+4 );

        int *piter;
        vector< int, allocator >::iterator iter;

        // piter points to ia[1]
        piter = adjacent_find( ia, ia+4 );
        assert( *piter == ia[ 1 ] );

        // iter points to vec[2]
        iter = adjacent_find( vec.begin(), vec.end(), TwiceOver() );
        assert( *iter == vec[ 2 ] );

        // reach here: everything ok
        cout << "ok: adjacent-find() succeeded!\n";
    }
```

binary_search()

```
        template< class ForwardIterator, class Type >
        bool
        binary_search( ForwardIterator first,
                       ForwardIterator last, const Type &value );

        bool
        binary_search( ForwardIterator first,
                       ForwardIterator last, const Type &value,
                       Compare comp );
```

binary_search() looks for value within the sorted sequence marked off by [first,last). If the value is found, true is returned, otherwise false is returned. The first version presumes that the container is sorted using the less than operator of the underlying type. In the second version we are indicating that the container is sorted using the specified function object.

```
        #include <algorithm>
        #include <vector>
        #include <assert.h>

        int main()
        {
            int ia[] = {29,23,20,22,17,15,26,51,19,12,35,40};

            sort( &ia[0], &ia[12] );
            bool found_it = binary_search( &ia[0], &ia[12], 18 );
            assert( found_it == false );

            vector< int > vec( ia, ia+12 );
            sort( vec.begin(), vec.end(), greater<int>() );
```

```
        found_it = binary_search( vec.begin(), vec.end(),
                                   26, greater<int>() );
        assert( found_it == true );
    }
```

copy()

```
    template < class InputIterator, class OutputIterator >
    OutputIterator
    copy( InputIterator first1, InputIterator last,
          OutputIterator first2 );
```

copy() copies the element sequence marked off by [first, last) into a container beginning at the position marked by first2. It returns first2 advanced one past the last element inserted. For example, given the sequence {0,1,2,3,4,5}, we can shift the elements left by one with the following invocation:

```
    int ia[] = { 0, 1, 2, 3, 4, 5 };

    // shift left by one, resulting in {1,2,3,4,5,5}
    copy( ia+1, ia+6, ia );
```

copy() begins at the second element of ia, copying 1 into the first slot, and so on until each element is copied to the slot on its left.

```
    #include <algorithm>
    #include <vector>
    #include <iterator>
    #include <iostream.h>

    /* generates:
       0 1 1 3 5 8 13
       shifting array sequence left by 1:
       1 1 3 5 8 13 13
       shifting vector sequence left by 2:
       1 3 5 8 13 8 13
    */

    int main()
    {
        int ia[] = { 0, 1, 1, 3, 5, 8, 13 };
        vector< int, allocator > vec( ia, ia+7 );
        ostream_iterator< int >  ofile( cout, " " );

        cout << "original element sequence:\n";
        copy( vec.begin(), vec.end(), ofile ); cout << '\n';

        // shift left by one
        copy( ia+1, ia+7, ia );
```

```
        cout << "shifting array sequence left by 1:\n";
        copy( ia, ia+7, ofile ); cout << '\n';

        // shift left by two
        copy( vec.begin()+2, vec.end(), vec.begin() );

        cout << "shifting vector sequence left by 2:\n";
        copy( vec.begin(), vec.end(), ofile ); cout << '\n';
    }
```

copy_backward()

```
        template < class BidirectionalIterator1,
                   class BidirectionalIterator2 >
        BidirectionalIterator2
        copy_backward( BidirectionalIterator1 first,
                       BidirectionalIterator1 last1,
                       BidirectionalIterator2 last2 );
```

copy_backward() behaves the same as copy() except that the elements are copied in the reverse order. That is, copying begins at last1-1 and proceeds to first. The elements are also copied into the target container backward, beginning with last2-1 and proceeding backward for last1-first elements.

For example, given the sequence {0,1,2,3,4,5}, we can copy the last three elements (3,4,5) into the first three (0,1,2) by setting first to the address of value 0, last1 to the address of value 3, and last2 to the address one past the value 5. Element value 5 is assigned to the previous element value 2, then element 4 to the previous element 1, and finally element 3 to the previous element 0. The resulting sequence is {3,4,5,3,4,5}.

```
        #include <algorithm>
        #include <vector>
        #include <iterator>
        #include <iostream.h>

        class print_elements {
        public:
           void operator()( string elem ) {
              cout << elem
                   << ( _line_cnt++%8 ? " " : "\n\t" );
           }
           static void reset_line_cnt() { _line_cnt = 1; }

        private:
           static int _line_cnt;
        };

        int print_elements::_line_cnt = 1;

        /* generates:
```

```
     original list of strings:
     The light untonsured hair grained and hued like
     pale oak

     sequence after copy_backward( begin+1, end-3, end ):
     The light untonsured hair light untonsured hair grained
     and hued
*/

int main()
{
    string sa[] = {
        "The", "light", "untonsured", "hair",
        "grained", "and", "hued", "like", "pale", "oak" };

    vector< string, allocator > svec( sa, sa+10 );

    cout << "original list of strings:\n\t";
    for_each( svec.begin(), svec.end(), print_elements() );
    cout << "\n\n";

    copy_backward( svec.begin()+1, svec.end()-3, svec.end() );

    print_elements::reset_line_cnt();

    cout << "sequence after "
         << "copy_backward( begin+1, end-3, end ):\n";
    for_each( svec.begin(), svec.end(), print_elements() );
    cout << "\n";
}
```

count()

```
template< class InputIterator, class Type >
iterator_traits<InputIterator>::distance_type
count( InputIterator first,
       InputIterator last, const Type& value );
```

count() compares each element against value using the equality operator within the range marked off by [first,last). It returns a count of the number of elements within the container equal to value. (Note that our implementation of the standard library supports an earlier specification of count().)

```
#include <algorithm>
#include <string>
#include <list>
#include <iterator>

#include <assert.h>
#include <iostream.h>
```

```
#include <fstream.h>

/*****************************************************************
 * text read:
Alice Emma has long flowing red hair. Her Daddy says
when the wind blows through her hair, it looks almost alive,
like a fiery bird in flight. A beautiful fiery bird, he tells her,
magical but untamed. "Daddy, shush, there is no such thing,"
she tells him, at the same time wanting him to tell her more.
Shyly, she asks, "I mean, Daddy, is there?"
 *****************************************************************
  * output of program:
  * count(): fiery occurs 2 times
 *****************************************************************
*/

int main()
{
    ifstream infile( "alice_emma" );
    assert ( infile != 0 );

    list<string,allocator> textlines;

    typedef list<string,allocator>::difference_type diff_type;
    istream_iterator< string, diff_type > instream( infile ),
                      eos;

    copy( instream, eos, back_inserter( textlines ));
    string search_item( "fiery" );

    /*************************************************************
     * note: this is the Standard C++ interface for using count()
     *       however, the current RogueWave implementation
     *       supports the earlier version in which distance_type
     *       had not been developed, and so count() returned its
     *       value via a final argument to itself.
     *
     * this is how the invocation should occur:
     *
     * typedef iterator_traits<InputIterator>::
     * distance_type dis_type;
     *
     * dis_type elem_count;
     * elem_count = count( textlines.begin(), textlines.end(),
     *           search_item );
     *************************************************************/

    int elem_count = 0;
    list<string,allocator>::iterator
```

```
        ibegin = textlines.begin(),
        iend   = textlines.end();

    // obsolete form of count()
    count( ibegin, iend, search_item, elem_count );

    cout << "count(): " << search_item
         << " occurs "  << elem_count << " times\n";
}
```

count_if()

```
template< class InputIterator, class Predicate >
iterator_traits<InputIterator>::distance_type
count_if( InputIterator first,
          InputIterator last, Predicate pred );
```

count_if() applies pred against each element within the range marked off by [first,last). It returns a count of the number of times pred evaluated as true.

```
#include <algorithm>
#include <list>
#include <iostream.h>

class Even {
public:
    bool operator()( int val )
        { return val%2 ? false : true; }
};

int main()
{
    int ia[] = {0,1,1,2,3,5,8,13,21,34};
    list< int,allocator > ilist( ia, ia+10 );

/*
 * unsupported in current implementation
 ********************************************************
    typedef
        iterator_traits<InputIterator>::distance_type
        distance_type;

    distance_type ia_count, list_count;

    // count even elements: 4
    ia_count = count_if( &ia[0], &ia[10], Even() );
    list_count = count_if( ilist.begin(), ilist_end(),
                           bind2nd(less<int>(),10) );
 ********************************************************
 */
```

```
int ia_count = 0;
count_if( &ia[0], &ia[10], Even(), ia_count );

// generates:
//   count_if(): there are 4 elements that are even.

cout << "count_if(): there are "
     << ia_count << " elements that are even.\n";

int list_count = 0;
count_if( ilist.begin(), ilist.end(),
          bind2nd(less<int>(),10), list_count );

// generates:
// count_if(): there are 7 elements that are less than 10.

cout << "count_if(): there are "
     << list_count
     << " elements that are less than 10.\n";
}
```

equal()

```
template< class InputIterator1, class InputIterator2 >
bool
equal( InputIterator1 first1,
       InputIterator1 last, InputIterator2 first2 );

template< class InputIterator1, class InputIterator2,
          class BinaryPredicate >
bool
equal( InputIterator1 first1, InputIterator1 last,
       InputIterator2 first2, BinaryPredicate pred );
```

equal() returns true if the two sequences are equal for the number of elements contained within the range [first,last). If the second sequence contains additional elements, those are not considered. If we wish to guarantee that both sequences are equivalent, we need to write

```
if ( vec1.size() == vec2.size() &&
     equal( vec1.begin(), vec1.end(), vec2.begin() );
```

or use the container equality operator, as in vec1==vec2. If the second container holds less elements than the first, and the algorithm should iterate past its end, the run-time behavior is undefined. By default, the equality operator of the underlying element type is used for comparison; the second version applies pred.

```
#include <algorithm>
#include <list>
```

```
#include <iostream.h>

class equal_and_odd{
public:
    bool
    operator()( int val1, int val2 )
    {
        return ( val1 == val2 &&
                ( val1 == 0 || val1 % 2 ));
    }
};

int main()
{
    int ia[] =  { 0,1,1,2,3,5,8,13 };
    int ia2[] = { 0,1,1,2,3,5,8,13,21,34 };

    bool res;

    // true: both are equal to the length of ia.
    // generates: int ia[7] equal to int ia2[9]? true.

    res = equal( &ia[0], &ia[7], &ia2[0] );
    cout << "int ia[7] equal to int ia2[9]? "
        << ( res ? "true" : "false" ) << ".\n";

    list< int, allocator > ilist( ia,  ia+7 );
    list< int, allocator > ilist2( ia2, ia2+9 );

    // generates: list ilist equal to ilist2? true.

    res = equal( ilist.begin(), ilist.end(), ilist2.begin() );
    cout << "list ilist equal to ilist2? "
        << ( res ? "true" : "false" ) << ".\n";

    // false: 0, 2, 8 are not equal and odd
    // generates: list ilist equal_and_odd() to ilist2? false.

    res = equal( ilist.begin(), ilist.end(),
                ilist2.begin(), equal_and_odd() );

    cout << "list ilist equal_and_odd() to ilist2? "
        << ( res ? "true" : "false" ) << ".\n";

    return 0;
}
```

equal_range()

```
template< class ForwardIterator, class Type >
pair< ForwardIterator, ForwardIterator >
equal_range( ForwardIterator first,
             ForwardIterator last, const Type &value );

template< class ForwardIterator, class Type, class Compare >
pair< ForwardIterator, ForwardIterator >
equal_range( ForwardIterator first,
             ForwardIterator last, const Type &value,
             Compare comp );
```

equal_range() returns a pair of iterators. The first iterator represents the iterator value returned by lower_bound(); the second iterator represents the iterator value returned by upper_bound(); see the respective algorithms for a description of their semantics. For example, given the following sequence:

```
int ia[] = {12,15,17,19,20,22,23,26,29,35,40,51};
```

A call of equal_range() with a value of 21 returns an iterator pair in which both iterators address the value 22. A call of equal_range() with a value of 22 returns an iterator pair in which first addresses the value 22 and second addresses the value 23. The first version uses the less than operator of the underlying type; the second version orders the elements based on pred.

```
#include <algorithm>
#include <vector>
#include <utility>
#include <iostream.h>

/* generates:
   array element sequence after sort:
   12 15 17 19 20 22 23 26 29 35 40 51

   equal_range result of search for value 23:
          *ia_iter.first: 23      *ia_iter.second: 26

   equal_range result of search for absent value 21:
          *ia_iter.first: 22      *ia_iter.second: 22

   vector element sequence after sort:
   51 40 35 29 26 23 22 20 19 17 15 12

   equal_range result of search for value 26:
          *ivec_iter.first: 26    *ivec_iter.second: 23

   equal_range result of search for absent value 21:
          *ivec_iter.first: 20    *ivec_iter.second: 20
*/
```

```
int main()
{
    int ia[] = { 29,23,20,22,17,15,26,51,19,12,35,40 };
    vector< int, allocator > ivec( ia, ia+12 );
    ostream_iterator< int >  ofile( cout, " " );

    sort( &ia[0], &ia[12] );

    cout << "array element sequence after sort:\n";
    copy( ia, ia+12, ofile ); cout << "\n\n";

    pair< int*,int* > ia_iter;
    ia_iter = equal_range( &ia[0], &ia[12], 23 );

    cout << "equal_range result of search for value 23:\n\t"
         << "*ia_iter.first: "  << *ia_iter.first << "\t"
         << "*ia_iter.second: " << *ia_iter.second << "\n\n";

    ia_iter = equal_range( &ia[0], &ia[12], 21 );

    cout << "equal_range result of search for "
         << "absent value 21:\n\t"
         << "*ia_iter.first: "  << *ia_iter.first << "\t"
         << "*ia_iter.second: " << *ia_iter.second << "\n\n";

    sort( ivec.begin(), ivec.end(), greater<int>() );

    cout << "vector element sequence after sort:\n";
    copy( ivec.begin(), ivec.end(), ofile ); cout << "\n\n";

    typedef vector< int, allocator >::iterator iter_ivec;
    pair< iter_ivec, iter_ivec > ivec_iter;

    ivec_iter = equal_range( ivec.begin(), ivec.end(), 26,
                greater<int>() );

    cout << "equal_range result of search for value 26:\n\t"
         << "*ivec_iter.first: "  << *ivec_iter.first << "\t"
         << "*ivec_iter.second: " << *ivec_iter.second
         << "\n\n";

    ivec_iter = equal_range( ivec.begin(), ivec.end(), 21,
                greater<int>() );

    cout << "equal_range result of search for "
         << "absent value 21:\n\t"
         << "*ivec_iter.first: "  << *ivec_iter.first << "\t"
         << "*ivec_iter.second: " << *ivec_iter.second
```

```
                    << "\n\n";
          }
```

fill()

```
          template< class ForwardIterator, class Type >
          void
          fill( ForwardIterator first,
              ForwardIterator last, const Type& value );
```

fill() assigns a copy of value to each element within the range marked off by [first, last).

```
          #include <algorithm>
          #include <list>
          #include <string>
          #include <iostream.h>

          /* generates:
             original array element sequence:
             0 1 1 2 3 5 8

             array after fill(ia+1,ia+6):
             0 9 9 9 9 9 8

             original list element sequence:
             c eiffel java ada perl

             list after fill(++ibegin,--iend):
             c c++ c++ c++ perl
          */

          int main()
          {
             const int value = 9;
             int ia[]  = { 0, 1, 1, 2, 3, 5, 8 };
             ostream_iterator< int > ofile( cout, " " );

             cout << "original array element sequence:\n";
             copy( ia, ia+7, ofile ); cout << "\n\n";

             fill( ia+1, ia+6, value );

             cout << "array after fill(ia+1,ia+6):\n";
             copy( ia, ia+7, ofile ); cout << "\n\n";

             string the_lang( "c++" );
             string langs[5] = { "c", "eiffel", "java", "ada", "perl" };

             list< string, allocator > il( langs, langs+5 );
```

```
        ostream_iterator< string > sofile( cout, " " );

        cout << "original list element sequence:\n";
        copy( il.begin(), il.end(), sofile ); cout << "\n\n";

        typedef list<string,allocator>::iterator iterator;

        iterator ibegin = il.begin(), iend = il.end();
        fill( ++ibegin, --iend, the_lang );

        cout << "list after fill(++ibegin,--iend):\n";
        copy( il.begin(), il.end(), sofile ); cout << "\n\n";
    }
```

fill_n()

```
        template< class ForwardIterator, class Size, class Type >
        void
        fill_n( ForwardIterator first,
                Size n, const Type& value );
```

fill_n() assigns a copy of value to count elements within the range [first, first+count).

```
        #include <algorithm>
        #include <vector>
        #include <string>
        #include <iostream.h>

        class print_elements {
        public:
           void operator()( string elem ) {
              cout << elem
                   << ( _line_cnt++%8 ? " " : "\n\t" );
           }
           static void reset_line_cnt() { _line_cnt = 1; }

        private:
           static int _line_cnt;
        };

        int print_elements::_line_cnt = 1;

        /* generates:
        original element sequence of array container:
        0 1 1 2 3 5 8

        array after fill_n( ia+2, 3, 9 ):
        0 1 9 9 9 5 8
```

```
    original sequence of strings:
            Stephen closed his eyes to hear his boots
            crush crackling wrack and shells

    sequence after fill_n() applied:
            Stephen closed his xxxxx xxxxx xxxxx xxxxx xxxxx
            xxxxx crackling wrack and shells
*/

int main()
{
    int value = 9; int count = 3;
    int ia[]  = { 0, 1, 1, 2, 3, 5, 8 };
    ostream_iterator< int > iofile( cout, " " );

    cout << "original element sequence of array container:\n";
    copy( ia, ia+7, iofile ); cout << "\n\n";

    fill_n( ia+2, count, value );

    cout << "array after fill_n( ia+2, 3, 9 ):\n";
    copy( ia, ia+7, iofile ); cout << "\n\n";

    string replacement( "xxxxx" );
    string sa[] = { "Stephen", "closed", "his", "eyes", "to",
          "hear", "his", "boots", "crush", "crackling",
          "wrack", "and", "shells" };

    vector< string, allocator > svec( sa, sa+13 );

    cout << "original sequence of strings:\n\t";
    for_each( svec.begin(), svec.end(), print_elements() );
    cout << "\n\n";

    fill_n( svec.begin()+3, count*2, replacement );

    print_elements::reset_line_cnt();

    cout << "sequence after fill_n() applied:\n\t";
    for_each( svec.begin(), svec.end(), print_elements() );
    cout << "\n";
}
```

find()

```
template< class InputIterator, class T >
InputIterator
find( InputIterator first,
      InputIterator last, const T &value );
```

The elements in the range marked off by [first,last) are compared for equality with value using the equality operator of the underlying type. If a match is found, the search ends. find() returns an InputIterator to the element. If no match is found, last is returned.

```cpp
#include <algorithm>
#include <iostream.h>
#include <list>
#include <string>

int main()
{
    int array[ 17 ] = { 7,3,3,7,6,5,8,7,2,1,3,8,7,3,8,4,3 };

    int elem = array[ 9 ];
    int *found_it;

    found_it = find( &array[0], &array[17], elem );

    // generates: find the first occurrence of 1 found!
    cout << "find the first occurrence of "
         << elem << "\t"
         << ( found_it ? "found!\n" : "not found!\n" );

    string beethoven[] = {
        "Sonata31", "Sonata32", "Quartet14", "Quartet15",
        "Archduke", "Symphony7" };

    string s_elem( beethoven[ 1 ] );

    list< string, allocator > slist( beethoven, beethoven+6 );
    list< string, allocator >::iterator iter;

    iter = find( slist.begin(), slist.end(), s_elem );

    // generates: find the first occurrence of Sonata32  found!

    cout << "find the first occurrence of "
         << s_elem << "\t"
         << ( iter != slist.end() ? "found!\n" : "not found!\n" );
}
```

find_if()

```cpp
template< class InputIterator, class Predicate >
InputIterator
find_if( InputIterator first,
         InputIterator last, Predicate pred );
```

The elements in the range marked off by [first,last) are examined in turn, and pred is applied to each. If pred evaluates to true, the search ends. find_if() returns an InputIterator to the element. If no match is found, last is returned.

```cpp
#include <algorithm>
#include <list>
#include <set>
#include <string>
#include <iostream.h>

// provides an alternative equality operator
// returns true if string is contained with the
// member object friend set
class OurFriends {
public:
    bool operator()( const string& str ) {
        return ( friendset.count( str ));
    }

    static void
    FriendSet( const string *fs, int count ) {
        copy( fs, fs+count,
                inserter( friendset, friendset.end() ));
    }

private:
    static set< string, less<string>, allocator > friendset;
};

set< string, less<string>, allocator > OurFriends::friendset;

int main()
{
    string Pooh_friends[] = { "Piglet", "Tigger", "Eyeore"  };
    string more_friends[] = { "Quasimodo", "Chip", "Piglet" };
    list<string,allocator> lf( more_friends, more_friends+3 );

    // populate a list of pooh friends
    OurFriends::FriendSet( Pooh_friends, 3 );

    list<string,allocator>::iterator our_mutual_friend;
    our_mutual_friend =
                find_if( lf.begin(), lf.end(), OurFriends());

    // generates:
    //   Ah, imagine our friend Piglet is also a friend of Pooh.
    if ( our_mutual_friend != lf.end() )
        cout << "Ah, imagine our friend "
            << *our_mutual_friend
```

```
          << " is also a friend of Pooh.\n";

     return 0;
}
```

find_end()

```
template< class ForwardIterator1, class ForwardIterator2 >
ForwardIterator1
find_end( ForwardIterator1 first1, ForwardIterator1 last1,
          ForwardIterator2 first2, ForwardIterator2 last2 );

template< class ForwardIterator1, class ForwardIterator2,
          class BinaryPredicate >
ForwardIterator1
find_end( ForwardIterator1 first1, ForwardIterator1 last1,
          ForwardIterator2 first2, ForwardIterator2 last2,
          BinaryPredicate pred );
```

The sequence marked off by [first1,last1) is searched for the last occurrence of a second sequence marked off by the iterator pair [first2,last2). For example, given the character sequence Mississippi and a second sequence ss, find_end() returns a ForwardIterator to the first s of the second ss sequence. If the second sequence is not found within the first, last1 is returned. In the first version, the equality operator of the underlying type is used. In the second version, a binary predicate operation passed in by the user is applied.

```
#include <algorithm>
#include <vector>
#include <iostream.h>
#include <assert.h>

int main()
{
    int array[ 17 ]   = { 7,3,3,7,6,5,8,7,2,1,3,7,6,3,8,4,3 };
    int subarray[ 3 ] = { 3, 7, 6 };

    int *found_it;

    // find the last occurrence of the sequence 3,7,6
    // in array, and return address of first element ...

    found_it = find_end( &array[0], &array[17],
                         &subarray[0], &subarray[3] );

    assert( found_it == &array[10] );

    vector< int, allocator > ivec( array, array+17 );
    vector< int, allocator > subvec( subarray, subarray+3 );
```

```
        vector< int, allocator >::iterator found_it2;
        found_it2 = find_end( ivec.begin(), ivec.end(),
                              subvec.begin(), subvec.end(),
                              equal_to<int>() );

        assert( found_it2 == ivec.begin()+10 );

        cout << "ok: find_end correctly returned beginning of "
             << "last matching sequence: 3,7,6!\n";
    }
```

find_first_of()

```
        template< class ForwardIterator1, class ForwardIterator2 >
        ForwardIterator1
        find_first_of( ForwardIterator1 first1, ForwardIterator1 last1,
                   ForwardIterator2 first2, ForwardIterator2 last2 );

        template< class ForwardIterator1, class ForwardIterator2,
                  class BinaryPredicate >
        ForwardIterator1
        find_first_of( ForwardIterator1 first1, ForwardIterator1 last1,
                   ForwardIterator2 first2, ForwardIterator2 last2,
                   BinaryPredicate pred );
```

The sequence marked off by [first2,last2) holds a collection of elements for which
to search within the sequence with a range that is marked by [first1,last1). For example, imagine that we wish to find the first vowel in the character sequence synesthesia.
To do this, we define our second sequence as aeiou. find_first_of() returns a ForwardIterator to the first instance of an element of the sequence of vowels, in this case
pointing to the first e. If the first sequence does not contain any of the elements of the
second sequence, last1 is returned. In the first version, the equality operator of the underlying type is used. In the second version, a binary operation pred is applied.

```
        #include <algorithm>
        #include <vector>
        #include <string>
        #include <iostream.h>

        int main()
        {
            string s_array[] = { "Ee", "eE", "ee", "Oo", "oo", "ee" };
            string to_find[] = { "oo", "gg", "ee" };

            // returns first occurrence of "ee" -- &s_array[2]
            string *found_it =
                find_first_of( s_array, s_array+6,
                               to_find, to_find+3 );
```

```
// generates:
// found it: ee
//          &s_array[2]:    0x7fff2dac
//          &found_it:      0x7fff2dac

if ( found_it != &s_array[6] )
     cout << "found it: "      << *found_it   << "\n\t"
          << "&s_array[2]:\t" << &s_array[2] << "\n\t"
          << "&found_it:\t"    << found_it    << "\n\n";

vector< string, allocator > svec( s_array, s_array+6);
vector< string, allocator > svec_find( to_find, to_find+3 );

// returns occurrence of "oo" -- svec.end()-2
vector< string, allocator >::iterator found_it2;

found_it2 = find_first_of(
                svec.begin(), svec.end(),
                svec_find.begin(), svec_find.end(),
                equal_to<string>() );

// generates:
// found it, too: oo
//          &svec.end()-2:  0x100067b0
//          &found_it2:     0x100067b0

if ( found_it2 != svec.end() )
     cout << "found it, too: "  << *found_it2   << "\n\t"
          << "&svec.end()-2:\t" << svec.end()-2 << "\n\t"
          << "&found_it2:\t"     << found_it2    << "\n";
}
```

for_each()

```
template< class InputIterator, class Function >
Function
for_each( InputIterator first,
          InputIterator last, Function func );
```

for_each() applies the function func to each element in turn in the range [first,last). func cannot write to the elements (they are InputIterators and so they cannot be guaranteed to support assignment). If we wish to modify the elements, we should use the transform() algorithm. func may return a value, but that value is ignored.

```
#include <algorithm>
#include <vector>
#include <iostream.h>

template <class Type>
void print_elements( Type elem ) { cout << elem << " "; }
```

```
int main()
{
    vector< int, allocator > ivec;

    for ( int ix = 0; ix < 10; ix++ )
        ivec.push_back( ix );

    void (*pfi)( int ) = print_elements;
    for_each( ivec.begin(), ivec.end(), pfi );

    return 0;
}
```

generate()

```
template< class ForwardIterator, class Generator >
void
generate( ForwardIterator first,
          ForwardIterator last, Generator gen );
```

generate() fills a sequence in the range marked off by [first,last) through successive invocations of gen, which can be either a function object or pointer to function.

```
#include <algorithm>
#include <list>
#include <iostream.h>

int odd_by_twos() {
    static int seed = -1;
    return seed += 2;
}

template <class Type>
void print_elements( Type elem ) { cout << elem << " "; }

int main()
{
    list< int, allocator > ilist( 10 );
    void (*pfi)( int ) = print_elements;

    generate( ilist.begin(), ilist.end(), odd_by_twos );

    // generates:
    // elements within list the first invocation:
    // 1 3 5 7 9 11 13 15 17 19

    cout << "elements within list the first invocation:\n";
    for_each( ilist.begin(), ilist.end(), pfi );
```

```
        generate( ilist.begin(), ilist.end(), odd_by_twos );

        // generates:
        // elements within list the second iteration:
        // 21 23 25 27 29 31 33 35 37 39
        cout << "\n\nelements within list the second iteration:\n";
        for_each( ilist.begin(), ilist.end(), pfi );

        return 0;
    }
```

generate_n()

```
        template< class ForwardIterator,
                class Size, class Generator >
        void
        generate_n( OutputIterator first, Size n, Generator gen );
```

generate_n() fills a sequence beginning with first with n successive invocations of gen, which can be either a function object or pointer to function.

```
        #include <algorithm>
        #include <iostream.h>
        #include <list>

        class even_by_twos {
        public:
            even_by_twos( int seed = 0 ) : _seed( seed ){}
            int operator()() { return _seed += 2; }
        private:
            int _seed;
        };

        template <class Type>
        void print_elements( Type elem ) { cout << elem << " "; }

        int main()
        {
            list< int, allocator > ilist( 10 );
            void (*pfi)( int ) = print_elements;

            generate_n( ilist.begin(), ilist.size(), even_by_twos() );

            // generates:
            // generate_n with even_by_twos():
            // 2 4 6 8 10 12 14 16 18 20

            cout << "generate_n with even_by_twos():\n";
            for_each( ilist.begin(), ilist.end(), pfi ); cout << "\n";
```

```
        generate_n(ilist.begin(),ilist.size(),even_by_twos(100));

        // generates:
        // generate_n with even_by_twos( 100 ):
        // 102 104 106 108 110 112 114 116 118 120

        cout << "generate_n with even_by_twos( 100 ):\n";
        for_each( ilist.begin(), ilist.end(), pfi );
    }
```

includes()

```
        template< class InputIterator1, class InputIterator2 >
        bool
        includes( InputIterator1 first1, InputIterator1 last1,
                  InputIterator2 first2, InputIterator2 last2 );

        template< class InputIterator1, class InputIterator2,
                  class Compare >
        bool
        includes( InputIterator1 first1, InputIterator1 last1,
                  InputIterator2 first2, InputIterator2 last2,
                  Compare comp );
```

includes() determines if every element of the sequence [first1,last1) is contained in the sequence [first2,last2). The first version presumes that the sequences are sorted using the less than operator of the underlying element type; the second version uses comp to determine element ordering.

```
        #include <algorithm>
        #include <vector>
        #include <iostream.h>

        int main()
        {
            int ia1[] = { 13, 1, 21, 2, 0, 34, 5, 1, 8, 3, 21, 34 };
            int ia2[] = { 21, 2, 8, 3, 5, 1 };

            // includes must be passed sorted containers
            sort( ia1, ia1+12 ); sort( ia2, ia2+6 );

            // generates: every element of ia2 contained in ia1? true

            bool res = includes( ia1, ia1+12, ia2, ia2+6 );
            cout << "every element of ia2 contained in ia1? "
                 << (res ? "true" : "false") << endl;

            vector< int, allocator > ivect1( ia1, ia1+12 );
            vector< int, allocator > ivect2( ia2, ia2+6 );
```

```
                    // sort in descending order
                    sort( ivect1.begin(), ivect1.end(), greater<int>() );
                    sort( ivect2.begin(), ivect2.end(), greater<int>() );

                    res = includes( ivect1.begin(), ivect1.end(),
                                    ivect2.begin(), ivect2.end(),
                                    greater<int>() );

                    // generates:
                    // every element of ivect2 contained in ivect1? true

                    cout << "every element of ivect2 contained in ivect1? "
                         << (res ? "true" : "false") << endl;
                }
```

inner_product()

```
            template < class InputIterator1, class InputIterator2,
                       class Type >
            Type
            inner_product(
                InputIterator1 first1, InputIterator1 last,
                InputIterator2 first2, Type init );

            template < class InputIterator1, class InputIterator2,
                       class Type,
                       class BinaryOperation1, class BinaryOperation2 >
            Type
            inner_product(
                InputIterator1 first1, InputIterator1 last,
                InputIterator2 first2, Type init,
                BinaryOperation1 op1, BinaryOperation2 op2 );
```

The first version of inner_product() accumulates the product of two sequences of values, adding them in turn to an initial value specified by init. The first sequence is marked off by [first1,last). The second sequence begins at first2 and is incremented in step with the first sequence. For example, given the two sequences {2,3,5,8} and {1,2,3,4}, the result is the sum of the following product pairs:

```
            2*1 + 3*2 + 5*3 + 8*4
```

If we provide an initial value of 0, then the result is 55.

The second version uses the binary operation op1 in place of the default addition operation, and the binary operation op2 in place of the default multiply operation. For example, if we use the same sequence used previously, specifying subtraction for op1 and addition for op2, then the result is the difference of the following addition pairs:

```
            (2+1) - (3+2) - (5+3) - (8+4)
```

inner_product() is one of the numeric algorithms. To use it, we must include the
<numeric> header file.

```cpp
#include <numeric>
#include <vector>
#include <iostream.h>

int main()
{
    int ia[] =  { 2, 3, 5, 8 };
    int ia2[] = { 1, 2, 3, 4 };

    // multiply the element pair from the two arrays
    // then add to the initial value: 0

    int res = inner_product( &ia[0], &ia[4], &ia2[0], 0);

    // generates: inner product of arrays: 55
    cout << "inner product of arrays: "
         << res << endl;

    vector<int, allocator> vec(  ia,  ia+4 );
    vector<int, allocator> vec2( ia2, ia2+4 );

    // add the element pair from the two vectors
    // then subtract from the initial value: 0

    res = inner_product( vec.begin(), vec.end(),
                         vec2.begin(), 0,
                         minus<int>(), plus<int>() );

    // generates: inner product of vectors: -28
    cout << "inner product of vectors: "
         << res << endl;

    return 0;
}
```

inplace_merge()

```cpp
template< class BidirectionalIterator >
void
inplace_merge( BidirectionalIterator first,
               BidirectionalIterator middle,
               BidirectionalIterator last );

template< class BidirectionalIterator, class Compare >
void
inplace_merge( BidirectionalIterator first,
```

```
                    BidirectionalIterator middle,
                    BidirectionalIterator last, Compare comp );
```

inplace_merge() combines the two sorted consecutive input sequences marked off by [first,middle) and [middle,last). The resulting sequence overwrites the two ranges beginning at first. The first version uses the less than operator of the underlying type for element ordering. The second version orders the elements based on a binary comparison operation passed in by the programmer.

```
#include <algorithm>
#include <vector>
#include <iostream.h>

template <class Type>
void print_elements( Type elem ) { cout << elem << " "; }

/*
 * generates:
ia sorted into two subarrays:
12 15 17 20 23 26 29 35 40 51 10 16 21 41 44 54 62 65 71 74

ia inplace_merge:
10 12 15 16 17 20 21 23 26 29 35 40 41 44 51 54 62 65 71 74

ivec sorted into two subvectors:
51 40 35 29 26 23 20 17 15 12 74 71 65 62 54 44 41 21 16 10

ivec inplace_merge:
74 71 65 62 54 51 44 41 40 35 29 26 23 21 20 17 16 15 12 10
*/

int main()
{
    int ia[] = { 29,23,20,17,15,26,51,12,35,40,
                 74,16,54,21,44,62,10,41,65,71 };

    vector< int, allocator > ivec( ia, ia+20 );
    void (*pfi)( int ) = print_elements;

    // place the two subsequences in sorted order
    sort( &ia[0], &ia[10] );
    sort( &ia[10], &ia[20] );

    cout << "ia sorted into two sub-arrays: \n";
    for_each( ia, ia+20, pfi ); cout << "\n\n";

    inplace_merge( ia, ia+10, ia+20 );

    cout << "ia inplace_merge:\n";
```

```
        for_each( ia, ia+20, pfi ); cout << "\n\n";

        sort( ivec.begin(),    ivec.begin()+10, greater<int>() );
        sort( ivec.begin()+10, ivec.end(),         greater<int>() );

        cout << "ivec sorted into two sub-vectors: \n";
        for_each( ivec.begin(), ivec.end(), pfi ); cout << "\n\n";

        inplace_merge( ivec.begin(), ivec.begin()+10,
                       ivec.end(),   greater<int>() );

        cout << "ivec inplace_merge:\n";
        for_each( ivec.begin(), ivec.end(), pfi ); cout << endl;
    }
```

iter_swap ()

```
        template <class ForwardIterator1, class ForwardIterator2>
        void
        iter_swap ( ForwardIterator1 a, ForwardIterator2 b );
```

iter_swap() swaps the values contained within the elements addressed by the two
ForwardIterators a and b.

```
        #include <algorithm>
        #include <list>
        #include <iostream.h>

        int main()
        {
            int ia[]  = { 5, 4, 3, 2, 1, 0 };
            list< int,allocator > ilist( ia, ia+6 );

            typedef list< int, allocator >::iterator iterator;
            iterator iter1 = ilist.begin(), iter2,
                iter_end = ilist.end();

            // bubble sort the list ...
            for ( ; iter1 != iter_end; ++iter1 )
                for ( iter2 = iter1; iter2 != iter_end; ++iter2 )
                    if ( *iter2 < *iter1 )
                        iter_swap( iter1, iter2 );

            // output generated:
            // ilist after bubble sort using iter_swap():
            // { 0 1 2 3 4 5 }

            cout << "ilist afer bubble sort using iter_swap(): { ";
            for ( iter1 = ilist.begin(); iter1 != iter_end; ++iter1 )
                cout << *iter1 << " ";
```

```
        cout << "}\n";
    }
```

lexicographical_compare()

```
        template <class InputIterator1, class InputIterator2 >
        bool
        lexicographical_compare(
           InputIterator1 first1, InputIterator1 last1,
           InputIterator2 first2, InputIterator2 last2 );

        template < class InputIterator1, class InputIterator2,
                   class Compare >
        bool
        lexicographical_compare(
           InputIterator1 first1, InputIterator1 last1,
           InputIterator2 first2, InputIterator2 last2,
           Compare comp );
```

lexicographical_compare() compares the corresponding pair of elements of the two sequences identified by [first1,last1) and [first2,last2). The comparison continues until either the element pair does not match, the pair [last1,last2] is reached, or either last1 or last2 is reached (if the sequences are not of equal size). For the first pair of elements that do not match, the following occurs:

- If the element of the first sequence is less, return true; otherwise, return false.

- If last1 is reached, but last2 is not, return true.

- If last2 is reached, but last1 is not, return false.

- If both last1 and last2 are reached (all the elements match), return false; that is, the first sequence is not lexicographically less than the second sequence.

For example, given the following two sequences

```
        string arr1[] = { "Piglet", "Pooh", "Tigger" };
        string arr2[] = { "Piglet", "Pooch", "Eeyore" };
```

the algorithm matches on the first element pair, but does not match on the second. Pooh evaluates as greater than Pooch because the c is lexicographically less than h (think of the comparison as the ordering done of words listed within a dictionary). The algorithm stops at this point (the third elements are never compared). The result of the comparison is false.

The second version of the algorithm takes a predicate comparison object rather than using the less than operator of the underlying element type.

```
        #include <algorithm>
        #include <list>
        #include <string>
        #include <assert.h>
```

```
#include <iostream.h>

class size_compare {
public:
   bool operator()( const string &a, const string &b ) {
       return a.length() <= b.length();
   }
};

int main()
{
   string arr1[] = { "Piglet", "Pooh", "Tigger" };
   string arr2[] = { "Piglet", "Pooch", "Eeyore" };

   bool res;

   // evaluates to false at second element
   // Pooch is less than Pooh
   // would also evaluate false at third element

   res = lexicographical_compare( arr1, arr1+3,
                                  arr2, arr2+3 );

   assert( res == false );

   // evaluates to true: each element of ilist2
   // has a length less than or equal to the
   // associated ilist1 element

   list< string, allocator > ilist1( arr1, arr1+3 );
   list< string, allocator > ilist2( arr2, arr2+3 );

   res = lexicographical_compare(
           ilist1.begin(), ilist1.end(),
           ilist2.begin(), ilist2.end(), size_compare() );

   assert( res == true );

   cout << "ok: lexicographical_compare succeeded!\n";
}
```

lower_bound()

```
template< class ForwardIterator, class Type >
ForwardIterator
lower_bound( ForwardIterator first,
           ForwardIterator last, const Type &value );

template< class ForwardIterator, class Type, class Compare >
ForwardIterator
```

```
lower_bound( ForwardIterator first,
             ForwardIterator last, const Type &value,
             Compare comp );
```

lower_bound() returns an iterator addressing the first position within the sorted sequence marked off by [first,last) into which value may be inserted without violating the sorted ordering of the container. This position will mark off a value either greater than or equal to value. For example, given the following sequence,

```
int ia[] = {12,15,17,19,20,22,23,26,29,35,40,51};
```

A call of lower_bound() with a value of 21 returns an iterator addressing the value 22. A call of lower_bound() with a value of 22 also returns an iterator addressing the value 22. The first version uses the less than operator of the underlying type; the second version orders the elements based on comp.

```
#include <algorithm>
#include <vector>
#include <iostream.h>

int main()
{
    int ia[] = {29,23,20,22,17,15,26,51,19,12,35,40};
    sort( &ia[0], &ia[12] );

    int search_value = 18;
    int *ptr = lower_bound( ia, ia+12, search_value );

    // generates:
    // The first element 18 can be inserted in front of is 19
    // The previous value is 17

    cout << "The first element "
         << search_value
         << " can be inserted in front of is "
         << *ptr << endl
         << "The previous value is "
         << *(ptr-1) << endl;

    vector< int, allocator > ivec( ia, ia+12 );

    // sort in descending order ...
    sort( ivec.begin(), ivec.end(), greater<int>() );

    search_value = 26;
    vector< int, allocator >::iterator iter;

    // have to tell it appropriate ordering
    // relationship to use in this case ...
```

```
                iter = lower_bound( ivec.begin(), ivec.end(),
                                    search_value, greater<int>() );

                // generates:
                // The first element 26 can be inserted in front of is 26
                // The previous value is 29

                cout << "The first element "
                     << search_value
                     << " can be inserted in front of is "
                     << *iter << endl
                     << "The previous value is "
                     << *(iter-1) << endl;
        }
```

max()

```
        template< class Type >
        const Type&
        max( const Type &aval, const Type &bval );

        template< class Type, class Compare >
        const Type&
        max( const Type &aval, const Type &bval, Compare comp );
```

max() returns the larger of the two elements aval and bval. The first version uses the associated greater than operator of Type; the second version uses the comparison operation comp.

max_element()

```
        template< class ForwardIterator >
        ForwardIterator
        max_element( ForwardIterator first,
                     ForwardIterator last );

        template< class ForwardIterator, class Compare >
        ForwardIterator
        max_element( ForwardIterator first,
                     ForwardIterator last, Compare comp );
```

max_element() returns an iterator pointing to the element containing the largest value within the sequence marked off by [first,last). The first version uses the greater-than operator of the underlying element type; the second version uses the comparison operation comp.

min()

```
        template< class Type >
        const Type&
```

```
min( const Type &aval, const Type &bval );

template< class Type, class Compare >
const Type&
min( const Type &aval, const Type &bval, Compare comp );
```

min() returns the smaller of the two elements aval and bval. The first version uses the associated less than operator of Type; the second version uses the comparison operation comp.

min_element()

```
template< class ForwardIterator >
ForwardIterator
min_element( ForwardIterator first,
             ForwardIterator last );
template< class ForwardIterator, class Compare >
ForwardIterator
min_element( ForwardIterator first,
             ForwardIterator last, Compare comp );
```

min_element() returns an iterator pointing to the element containing the minimum value within the sequence marked off by [first,last). The first version uses the less than operator of the underlying element type; the second version uses the comparison operation comp.

```
// illustrates max(), min(), max_element(), min_element()

#include <algorithm>
#include <vector>
#include <iostream.h>

int main()
{
    int ia[] = { 7, 5, 2, 4, 3 };
    const vector< int, allocator > ivec( ia, ia+5 );

    int mval = max( max( max( max( ivec[4], ivec[3]),
                                   ivec[2]),ivec[1]),ivec[0]);

    // output: the result of nested invocations of max() is: 7
    cout << "the result of nested invocations of max() is: "
         << mval << endl;

    mval = min( min( min( min( ivec[4], ivec[3]),
                               ivec[2]),ivec[1]),ivec[0]);

    // output: the result of nested invocations of min() is: 2
    cout << "the result of nested invocations of min() is: "
         << mval << endl;
```

```
        vector< int, allocator >::const_iterator iter;
        iter = max_element( ivec.begin(), ivec.end() );

        // output: the result of invoking max_element() is also: 7
        cout << "the result of invoking max_element() is also: "
            << *iter << endl;

        iter = min_element( ivec.begin(), ivec.end() );

        // output: the result of invoking min_element() is also: 2
        cout << "the result of invoking min_element() is also: "
            << *iter << endl;
    }
```

merge()

```
    template< class InputIterator1, class InputIterator2,
            class OutputIterator >
    OutputIterator
    merge( InputIterator1 first1, InputIterator1 last1,
            InputIterator2 first2, InputIterator2 last2,
            OutputIterator result );

    template< class InputIterator1, class InputIterator2,
            class OutputIterator, class Compare >
    OutputIterator
    merge( InputIterator1 first1, InputIterator1 last1,
            InputIterator2 first2, InputIterator2 last2,
            OutputIterator result, Compare comp );
```

merge() combines the two sorted sequences marked off by [first1,last1) and
[first2,last2) into a single sorted sequence beginning at result. The OutputIterator
returned points one past the last element copied into the new sequence. The first version uses the less than operator of the underlying type for ordering the elements; the
second version orders the elements based on comp.

```
    #include <algorithm>
    #include <vector>
    #include <list>
    #include <deque>
    #include <iostream.h>

    template <class Type>
    void print_elements( Type elem ) { cout << elem << " "; }

    void (*pfi)( int ) = print_elements;

    int main()
    {
```

```
int ia[]  =  {29,23,20,22,17,15,26,51,19,12,35,40};
int ia2[] = {74,16,39,54,21,44,62,10,27,41,65,71};

vector< int, allocator > vec1( ia,  ia +12 ),
                         vec2( ia2, ia2+12 );
int ia_result[24];
vector<int,allocator> vec_result(vec1.size()+vec2.size());

sort( ia,  ia +12 );
sort( ia2, ia2+12 );

// generates:
// 10 12 15 16 17 19 20 21 22 23 26 27 29 35
//              39 40 41 44 51 54 62 65 71 74

merge( ia, ia+12, ia2, ia2+12, ia_result );
for_each( ia_result, ia_result+24, pfi ); cout << "\n\n";

sort( vec1.begin(), vec1.end(), greater<int>() );
sort( vec2.begin(), vec2.end(), greater<int>() );

merge( vec1.begin(), vec1.end(),
       vec2.begin(), vec2.end(),
       vec_result.begin(), greater<int>() );

// generates:
// 74 71 65 62 54 51 44 41 40 39 35 29 27 26 23 22
//                      21 20 19 17 16 15 12 10
for_each( vec_result.begin(), vec_result.end(), pfi );
cout << "\n\n";
}
```

mismatch()

```
template< class InputIterator1, class InputIterator2 >
pair<InputIterator1, InputIterator2>
mismatch( InputIterator1 first1,
          InputIterator1 last, InputIterator2 first2 );

template< class InputIterator1, class InputIterator2,
          class BinaryPredicate >
pair<InputIterator1, InputIterator2>
mismatch( InputIterator1 first1, InputIterator1 last,
          InputIterator2 first2, BinaryPredicate pred );
```

mismatch() compares two sequences in parallel and identifies the first position in which the elements do not match. A pair of iterators is returned identifying the first position in which the elements do not match. If all the elements match, then an iterator to the last element of each container is returned. For example, given the sequences meet and meat, the two iterators addressing the third element are returned. By default, the equality operator is used for element comparison; the second version allows the user to specify an alternative comparison operation. If the second sequence contains more elements than the first, those elements are ignored. If the second sequence contains less elements than the first, the run-time behavior is undefined.

```cpp
#include <algorithm>
#include <list>
#include <utility>
#include <iostream.h>

class equal_and_odd{
public:
    bool operator()( int ival1, int ival2 )
    {
        // are the two values equal, and either
        // both zero, or both odd?
        return ( ival1 == ival2 &&
                 ( ival1 == 0 || ival1%2 ));
    }
};

int main()
{
    int ia[] =  { 0,1,1,2,3,5,8,13 };
    int ia2[] = { 0,1,1,2,4,6,10   };

    pair<int*,int*> pair_ia = mismatch( ia, ia+7, ia2 );

    // generates: first mismatched pair: ia: 3 and ia2: 4
    cout << "first mismatched pair: ia: "
         << *pair_ia.first << " and ia2: "
         << *pair_ia.second << endl;

    list<int,allocator> ilist( ia,  ia+7 );
    list<int,allocator> ilist2( ia2, ia2+7 );

    typedef list<int,allocator>::iterator iter;
    pair< iter,iter > pair_ilist =
          mismatch( ilist.begin(),  ilist.end(),
                    ilist2.begin(), equal_and_odd() );

    // generates:
    // first mismatched pair either not equal or not odd:
    //                   ilist: 2 and ilist2: 2

    cout << "first mismatched pair either not equal "
         << "or not odd: \n\tilist: "
         << *pair_ilist.first << " and ilist2: "
```

```
                    << *pair_ilist.second << endl;
        }
```

next_permutation()

```
        template< class BidirectionalIterator >
        bool
        next_permutation( BidirectionalIterator first,
                          BidirectionalIterator last );

        template< class BidirectionalIterator, class Compare >
        bool
        next_permutation( BidirectionalIterator first,
                          BidirectionalIterator last, Compare comp );
```

next_permutation() takes the permutation marked off by [first,last) and reorders it into its next permutation (see Section 12.5 for a discussion of how the previous permutation is determined). If no next permutation exists, it returns false; otherwise, it returns true. The first version uses the less than operator of the underlying type for determining the next permutation; the second version orders the elements based on comp. Successive invocations of next_permutation() generate the entire permutation set only if the original string is sorted. For example, in the following program, if we failed to sort musil into ilmsu, we would not generate the full set of permutations.

```
        #include <algorithm>
        #include <vector>
        #include <iostream.h>

        void print_char( char elem ) { cout << elem ; }
        void (*ppc)( char ) = print_char;

        /* generates:
        ilmsu   ilmus   ilsmu   ilsum   ilums   ilusm   imlsu   imlus
        imslu   imsul   imuls   imusl   islmu   islum   ismlu   ismul
        isulm   isuml   iulms   iulsm   iumls   iumsl   iuslm   iusml
        limsu   limus   lismu   lisum   liums   liusm   lmisu   lmius
        lmsiu   lmsui   lmuis   lmusi   lsimu   lsium   lsmiu   lsmui
        lsuim   lsumi   luims   luism   lumis   lumsi   lusim   lusmi
        milsu   milus   mislu   misul   miuls   miusl   mlisu   mlius
        mlsiu   mlsui   mluis   mlusi   msilu   msiul   msliu   mslui
        msuil   msuli   muils   muisl   mulis   mulsi   musil   musli
        silmu   silum   simlu   simul   siulm   siuml   slimu   slium
        slmiu   slmui   sluim   slumi   smilu   smiul   smliu   smlui
        smuil   smuli   suilm   suiml   sulim   sulmi   sumil   sumli
        uilms   uilsm   uimls   uimsl   uislm   uisml   ulims   ulism
        ulmis   ulmsi   ulsim   ulsmi   umils   umisl   umlis   umlsi
        umsil   umsli   usilm   usiml   uslim   uslmi   usmil   usmli
        */
```

```
int main()
{
    vector<char,allocator> vec(5);

    // the character sequence: musil
    vec[0] = 'm'; vec[1] = 'u'; vec[2] = 's';
    vec[3] = 'i'; vec[4] = 'l';

    int cnt = 2;
    sort( vec.begin(), vec.end() );
    for_each( vec.begin(), vec.end(), ppc ); cout << "\t";

    // generate all the permutations of "musil"
    while( next_permutation( vec.begin(), vec.end()))
    {
        for_each( vec.begin(), vec.end(), ppc );
        cout << "\t";

        if ( ! ( cnt++ % 8 )) {
            cout << "\n";
            cnt = 1;
        }
    }

    cout << "\n\n";
    return 0;
}
```

nth_element()

```
template< class RandomAccessIterator >
void
nth_element( RandomAccessIterator first,
             RandomAccessIterator nth,
             RandomAccessIterator last );

template< class RandomAccessIterator, class Compare >
void
nth_element( RandomAccessIterator first,
             RandomAccessIterator nth,
             RandomAccessIterator last, Compare comp );
```

nth_element() reorders the sequence marked off by [first,last) such that all elements less than the nth element occur before it and all elements that are greater occur after. For example, given the array

```
int ia[] = {29,23,20,22,17,15,26,51,19,12,35,40 };
```

an invocation of nth_element() marking the seventh element as nth (it has a value of 26),

```
nth_element( &ia[0], &ia[6], &ia[12] );
```

yields a sequence in which the seven elements less than 26 are to its left, and the four elements greater than 26 are to its right: {23,20,22,17,15,19,12,26,51,35,40,29}, although the elements on either side of the nth element are not guaranteed to be in any particular order. The first version uses the less than operator of the underlying type for comparison; the second version orders the elements based on a binary comparison operation passed by the programmer.

```
#include <algorithm>
#include <vector>
#include <iostream.h>

/*
 * generates:
original order of the vector: 29 23 20 22 17 15 26 51 19 12 35 40
sorting vector based on element 26
12 15 17 19 20 22 23 26 51 29 35 40
sorting vector in descending order based on element 23
40 35 29 51 26 23 22 20 19 17 15 12
*/

int main()
{
    int ia[] = {29,23,20,22,17,15,26,51,19,12,35,40};
    vector< int,allocator > vec( ia, ia+12 );
    ostream_iterator<int> out( cout," " );

    cout << "original order of the vector: ";
    copy( vec.begin(), vec.end(), out ); cout << endl;

    cout << "sorting vector based on element "
         << *( vec.begin()+6 ) << endl;

    nth_element( vec.begin(), vec.begin()+6, vec.end() );
    copy( vec.begin(), vec.end(), out ); cout << endl;

    cout << "sorting vector in descending order "
         << "based on element "
         << *( vec.begin()+6 ) << endl;

    nth_element( vec.begin(), vec.begin()+6,
                 vec.end(),   greater<int>() );

    copy( vec.begin(), vec.end(), out ); cout << endl;
}
```

partial_sort()

```
template< class RandomAccessIterator >
void
```

```
partial_sort( RandomAccessIterator first,
              RandomAccessIterator middle,
              RandomAccessIterator last );

template< class RandomAccessIterator, class Compare >
void
partial_sort( RandomAccessIterator first,
              RandomAccessIterator middle,
              RandomAccessIterator last, Compare comp );
```

partial_sort() sorts the number of elements that can be placed within the range [first,middle). The elements stored within the range [middle,last) are unsorted but fall outside the sequence actually sorted. For example, given the array

```
int ia[] = {29,23,20,22,17,15,26,51,19,12,35,40 };
```

an invocation of partial_sort() marking the sixth element as middle,

```
stable_sort( &ia[0], &ia[5], &ia[12] );
```

yields the sequence in which the five smallest elements are sorted (that is, middle-first elements): {12,15,17,19,20,29,23,22,26,51,35,40}. The elements from middle through last-1 are not placed in any particular order, although their values all fall outside the sequence actually sorted. The first version uses the less than operator of the underlying type; the second version orders the elements based on comp.

partial_sort_copy()

```
template< class InputIterator, class RandomAccessIterator >
RandomAccessIterator
partial_sort_copy( InputIterator first, InputIterator last,
                   RandomAccessIterator result_first,
                   RandomAccessIterator result_last );

template< class InputIterator, class RandomAccessIterator,
          class Compare >
RandomAccessIterator
partial_sort_copy( InputIterator first, InputIterator last,
                   RandomAccessIterator result_first,
                   RandomAccessIterator result_last,
                   Compare comp );
```

partial_sort_copy() behaves the same as partial_sort() except that it copies its partially ordered sequence into the container marked off by the range [result_first,result_last) (so the result is a fully sorted sequence provided that we indicate a separate container into which to be copied). For example, given the two arrays

```
int ia[] = {29,23,20,22,17,15,26,51,19,12,35,40 };
int ia2[5];
```

an invocation of partial_sort_copy() marking the eighth element as middle,

```
        stable_sort( &ia[0],   &ia[7], &ia[12],
                     &ia2[0], &ia[5] );
```

fills ia2 with five sorted elements: {12,15,17,19,20}. The two additional sorted elements are unused.

```
        #include <algorithm>
        #include <vector>
        #include <iostream.h>
        /*
         * generates:
           original order of vector: 69 23 80 42 17 15 26 51 19 12 35 8
           partial sort of vector: seven elements
           8 12 15 17 19 23 26 80 69 51 42 35
           partial_sort_copy() of first seven elements
           of vector in descending order
           26 23 19 17 15 12 8
         */

        int main()
        {
            int ia[] = {69,23,80,42,17,15,26,51,19,12,35,8 };
            vector< int,allocator > vec( ia, ia+12 );
            ostream_iterator<int> out( cout," " );

            cout << "original order of vector: ";
            copy( vec.begin(), vec.end(), out ); cout << endl;

            cout << "partial sort of vector: seven elements\n";
            partial_sort( vec.begin(), vec.begin()+7, vec.end() );
            copy( vec.begin(), vec.end(), out ); cout << endl;

            vector< int, allocator > res(7);
            cout << "partial_sort_copy() of first seven elements\n\t"
                 << "of vector in descending order\n";

            partial_sort_copy( vec.begin(), vec.begin()+7, res.begin(),
                               res.end(), greater<int>() );
            copy( res.begin(), res.end(), out ); cout << endl;
        }
```

partial_sum()

```
        template < class InputIterator, Class OutputIterator >
        OutputIterator
        partial_sum(
            InputIterator first, InputIterator last,
            OutputIterator result );

        template < class InputIterator, Class OutputIterator,
                   class BinaryOperation >
```

```
OutputIterator
partial_sum(
      InputIterator first, InputIterator last,
      OutputIterator result, BinaryOperation op );
```

The first version of `partial_sum()` creates a new sequence of elements in which the value of each new element represents the sum of all the previous elements up to its position within the sequence marked off by [first,last). For example, given the sequence {0,1,1,2,3,5,8} the new sequence is {0,1,2,4,7,12,20}. The fourth element, for example, is the partial sum of the three previous values (0,1,1) plus its own (2), yielding a value of 4.

The second version uses the binary operation passed by the programmer. For example, given the sequence {1,2,3,4}, let's pass in the `times<int>` function object. The resulting sequence is {1,2,6,24}. In both versions the OutputIterator points one past the last element of the new sequence.

`partial_sum()` is one of the numeric algorithms and must include the `<numeric>` standard header file.

```cpp
#include <numeric>
#include <vector>
#include <iostream.h>

/*
 * generates:
   elements: 1 3 4 5 7 8 9
   partial sum of elements:
   1 4 8 13 20 28 37
   partial sum of elements using times<int>():
   1 3 12 60 420 3360 30240
*/

int main()
{
    const int ia_size = 7;
    int ia[ ia_size ] = { 1, 3, 4, 5, 7, 8, 9 };
    int ia_res[ ia_size ];

    ostream_iterator< int  > outfile( cout, " "  );
    vector< int, allocator > vec( ia, ia+ia_size );
    vector< int, allocator > vec_res( vec.size() );

    cout << "elements: ";
    copy( ia, ia+ia_size, outfile ); cout << endl;

    cout << "partial sum of elements:\n";
    partial_sum( ia, ia+ia_size, ia_res );
    copy( ia_res, ia_res+ia_size, outfile ); cout << endl;
```

```
        cout << "partial sum of elements using times<int>():\n";
        partial_sum( vec.begin(), vec.end(), vec_res.begin(),
                   times<int>() );

        copy( vec_res.begin(), vec_res.end(), outfile );
        cout << endl;
    }
```

partition()

```
        template < class BidirectionalIterator, class UnaryPredicate >
        BidirectionalIterator
        partition( BidirectionalIterator first,
                   BidirectionalIterator last, UnaryPredicate pred );
```

partition() reorders the elements in the range marked off by [first,last). All the elements that evaluate as true when passed to the unary predicate, pred, are placed before the elements that evaluate as false. For example, given the sequence {0,1,2,3,4,5,6}, and a predicate testing for elements that are even, the true and false element ranges are {0,2,4,6} and {1,3,5}. Although all the even elements are guaranteed to be placed before any of the odd elements, the relative position of the elements within the reordering are not guaranteed to be preserved. That is, 4 could be placed before 2, or 5 before 3. stable_partition(), discussed later, guarantees to preserve the relative order of the elements within the container.

```
        #include <algorithm>
        #include <vector>
        #include <iostream.h>

        class even_elem {
        public:
            bool operator()( int elem )
                { return elem%2 ? false : true; }
        };

        /*
         * generates:
           original order of elements:
           29 23 20 22 17 15 26 51 19 12 35 40
           partition based on whether element is even:
           40 12 20 22 26 15 17 51 19 23 35 29
           partition based on whether element is less than 25:
           12 23 20 22 17 15 19 51 26 29 35 40
         */

        int main()
        {
            const int ia_size = 12;
            int ia[ia_size]   = { 29,23,20,22,17,15,26,51,19,12,35,40 };
```

```
    vector< int, allocator > vec( ia, ia+ia_size );
    ostream_iterator< int >  outfile( cout, " "  );

    cout << "original order of elements: \n";
    copy( vec.begin(), vec.end(), outfile ); cout << endl;

    cout << "partition based on whether element is even:\n";
    partition( &ia[0], &ia[ia_size], even_elem() );
    copy( ia, ia+ia_size, outfile ); cout << endl;

    cout << "partition based on whether element "
         << "is less than 25:\n";

    partition( vec.begin(), vec.end(), bind2nd(less<int>(),25) );
    copy( vec.begin(), vec.end(), outfile ); cout << endl;
}
```

prev_permutation()

```
template < class BidirectionalIterator >
bool
prev_permutation( BidirectionalIterator first,
                  BidirectionalIterator last );

template < class BidirectionalIterator, class Compare >
bool
prev_permutation( BidirectionalIterator first,
                  BidirectionalIterator last, Compare comp );
```

prev_permutation() takes the permutation marked off by [first,last) and reorders it into its previous permutation (see Section 12.5 for a discussion of how the previous permutation is determined). If no previous permutation exists, it returns false; otherwise, it returns true. The first version uses the less than operator of the underlying type for determining the previous permutation; the second version orders the elements based on a binary comparison operation passed by the programmer.

```
#include <algorithm>
#include <vector>
#include <iostream.h>

// generates:
//    n d a   n a d   d n a   d a n   a n d   a d n

int main()
{
    vector< char, allocator > vec( 3 );
    ostream_iterator< char > out_stream( cout, " " );

    vec[0] = 'n'; vec[1] = 'd'; vec[2] = 'a';
```

```
copy( vec.begin(), vec.end(), out_stream ); cout << "\t";

// generate all the permutations of "dan"
while( prev_permutation( vec.begin(), vec.end() )) {
        copy( vec.begin(), vec.end(), out_stream );
        cout << "\t";
}

cout << "\n\n";
}
```

random_shuffle()

```
template< class RandomAccessIterator >
void
random_shuffle( RandomAccessIterator first,
                RandomAccessIterator last );

template< class RandomAccessIterator,
          class RandomNumberGenerator >
void
random_shuffle( RandomAccessIterator first,
                RandomAccessIterator last,
                RandomNumberGenerator rand );
```

random_shuffle() reorders the elements randomly in the range marked off by [first,last). The second version takes a random number-generating function object or pointer to function. rand is expected to return a value of type double within the interval [0,1].

```
#include <algorithm>
#include <vector>
#include <iostream.h>

int main()
{
   vector< int, allocator > vec;
   for ( int ix = 0; ix < 20; ix++ )
         vec.push_back( ix );

   random_shuffle( vec.begin(), vec.end() );

   // generates:
   // random_shuffle of sequence of values 1 .. 20:
   // 6 11 9 2 18 12 17 7 0 15 4 8 10 5 1 19 13 3 14 16
   cout << "random_shuffle of sequence of values 1 .. 20:\n";
   copy( vec.begin(), vec.end(),
         ostream_iterator< int >( cout," " ));
}
```

remove()

```
template< class ForwardIterator, class Type >
ForwardIterator
remove( ForwardIterator first,
        ForwardIterator last, const Type &value );
```

remove() removes all instances of value within the range specified by [first,last). remove() (as well as remove_if()) does not actually erase the matched elements from the container (that is, the container's size is preserved). Rather, each nonmatching element is assigned in turn to the next free slot beginning with first. The returned ForwardIterator marks one past the new range of elements. For example, consider the sequence {0,1,0,2,0,3,0,4}. Let's say that we wish to remove all 0 values. The resulting sequence is {1,2,3,4,0,3,0,4}. The 1 is copied into the first slot, the 2 into the second slot, the 3 into the third slot, and the 4 into the fourth slot. The 0 at the fifth slot represents the *leftover* of the algorithm. The returned ForwardIterator addresses the 0 of slot 5. Typically, this iterator is then passed to erase() to delete the invalid elements. (The built-in array is not suited to the remove() and remove_if() algorithm because it cannot be resized easily. For this reason, the remove_copy() and remove_copy_if() are the preferred algorithms for use with an array.)

remove_copy()

```
template< class InputIterator, class OutputIterator,
          class Type >
OutputIterator
remove_copy( InputIterator first, InputIterator last,
             OutputIterator result, const Type &value );
```

remove_copy() copies all the nonmatching elements to the container specified by result. The returned OutputIterator marks one past the last element copied. The original container is unchanged.

```
#include <algorithm>
#include <vector>
#include <iostream.h>

/* generates:
   original vector sequence:
   0 1 0 2 0 3 0 4 0 5
   vector after remove, without applying erase():
   1 2 3 4 5 3 0 4 0 5
   vector after erase():
   1 2 3 4 5
   array after remove_copy():
   1 2 3 4 5
*/
```

```
int main()
{
    int value = 0;
    int ia[] = { 0, 1, 0, 2, 0, 3, 0, 4, 0, 5 };

    vector< int, allocator > vec( ia, ia+10 );
    ostream_iterator< int >  ofile( cout," " );
    vector< int, allocator >::iterator vec_iter;

    cout << "original vector sequence:\n";
    copy( vec.begin(), vec.end(), ofile ); cout << '\n';

    vec_iter = remove( vec.begin(), vec.end(), value );

    cout << "vector after remove, without applying erase():\n";
    copy( vec.begin(), vec.end(), ofile ); cout << '\n';

    // erase the invalid elements from container
    vec.erase( vec_iter, vec.end() );

    cout << "vector after erase():\n";
    copy( vec.begin(), vec.end(), ofile ); cout << '\n';

    int ia2[5];
    vector< int, allocator > vec2( ia, ia+10 );
    remove_copy( vec2.begin(), vec2.end(), ia2, value );

    cout << "array after remove_copy():\n";
    copy( ia2, ia2+5 ofile ); cout << endl;
}
```

remove_if()

```
template< class ForwardIterator, class Predicate >
ForwardIterator
remove_if( ForwardIterator first,
           ForwardIterator last, Predicate pred );
```

remove_if() removes all elements within the range specified by [first, last) for which pred evaluates as true. remove_if() (as well as remove()) does not actually erase the matched elements from the container. Rather, each nonmatching element is assigned in turn to the next free slot beginning with first. The returned ForwardIterator marks one past the new range of elements. Typically this iterator is then passed to erase() to actually delete the invalid elements. (The remove_copy_if() is better suited for use with a built-in array.)

remove_copy_if()

```
template< class InputIterator, class OutputIterator,
          class Predicate >
OutputIterator
remove_copy_if( InputIterator first, InputIterator last,
                OutputIterator result, Predicate pred );
```

remove_copy_if() copies all the nonmatching elements to the container specified by result. The returned OutputIterator marks one past the last element copied. The original container is unchanged.

```
#include <algorithm>
#include <vector>
#include <iostream.h>

/* generates:
   original element sequence:
   0 1 1 2 3 5 8 13 21 34
   sequence after applying remove_if < 10:
   13 21 34
   sequence after applying remove_copy_if even:
   1 1 3 5 13 21
*/

class EvenValue {
public:
   bool operator()( int value ) {
        return value % 2 ? false : true; }
};

int main()
{
   int ia[] = { 0, 1, 1, 2, 3, 5, 8, 13, 21, 34 };

   vector< int, allocator >::iterator iter;
   vector< int, allocator >  vec( ia, ia+10 );
   ostream_iterator< int >   ofile( cout, " " );

   cout << "original element sequence:\n";
   copy( vec.begin(), vec.end(), ofile ); cout << '\n';

   iter = remove_if( vec.begin(), vec.end(),
                     bind2nd(less<int>(),10) );
   vec.erase( iter, vec.end() );

   cout << "sequence after applying remove_if < 10:\n";
   copy( vec.begin(), vec.end(), ofile ); cout << '\n';

   vector< int, allocator > vec_res( 10 );
```

```
            iter = remove_copy_if( ia, ia+10,
                               vec_res.begin(), EvenValue() );

            cout << "sequence after applying remove_copy_if even:\n";
            copy( vec_res.begin(), iter, ofile ); cout << '\n';
        }
```

replace()

```
        template< class ForwardIterator, class Type >
        void
        replace( ForwardIterator first, ForwardIterator last,
                 const Type& old_value, const Type& new_value );
```

replace() replaces all instances of old_value with new_value within the range specified by the iterator pair [first, last).

replace_copy()

```
        template< class InputIterator, class OutputIterator,
                  class Type >
        OutputIterator
        replace_copy( InputIterator first, InputIterator last,
                      OutputIterator result,
                      const Type& old_value, const Type& new_value );
```

replace_copy() exhibits the same behavior as replace() except that the new sequence is copied into the container beginning at result. The returned OutputIterator
points one past the last value copied. The original sequence is unchanged.

```
        #include <algorithm>
        #include <vector>
        #include <iostream.h>

        /* generates:
           original element sequence:
           Christopher Robin Mr. Winnie the Pooh Piglet Tigger Eeyore
           sequence after applying replace():
           Christopher Robin Pooh Piglet Tigger Eeyore
           sequence after applying replace_copy():
           Christopher Robin Mr. Winnie the Pooh Piglet Tigger Eeyore
        */

        int main()
        {
            string oldval( "Mr. Winnie the Pooh" );
            string newval( "Pooh" );

            ostream_iterator< string >  ofile( cout, " " );
            string sa[] = {
```

```
            "Christopher Robin", "Mr. Winnie the Pooh",
            "Piglet", "Tigger", "Eeyore"
        };

        vector< string, allocator > vec( sa, sa+5 );

        cout << "original element sequence:\n";
        copy( vec.begin(), vec.end(), ofile ); cout << '\n';

        replace( vec.begin(), vec.end(), oldval, newval );

        cout << "sequence after applying replace():\n";
        copy( vec.begin(), vec.end(), ofile ); cout << '\n';

        vector< string, allocator > vec2;
        replace_copy( vec.begin(), vec.end(),
                      inserter( vec2, vec2.begin() ),
                      newval, oldval );

        cout << "sequence after applying replace_copy():\n";
        copy( vec2.begin(), vec2.end(), ofile ); cout << '\n';
    }
```

replace_if()

```
        template< class ForwardIterator, class Predicate, class Type >
        void
        replace_if( ForwardIterator first, ForwardIterator last,
                    Predicate pred, const Type& new_value );
```

replace_if() replaces all elements within the range specified by [first, last) with new_value, for which pred evaluates as true.

replace_copy_if()

```
        template< class ForwardIterator, class OutputIterator,
                  class Predicate, class Type >
        OutputIterator
        replace_copy_if( ForwardIterator first, ForwardIterator last,
                         OutputIterator result,
                         Predicate pred, const Type& new_value );
```

replace_copy_if() exhibits the same behavior as replace_if() except that the new sequence is copied into the container beginning at result. The returned OutputIterator points one past the last value copied. The original sequence is unchanged.

```
        #include <algorithm>
        #include <vector>
        #include <iostream.h>
```

```
/*
 * generates:
   original element sequence:
   0 1 1 2 3 5 8 13 21 34
   sequence after applying replace_if < 10 with 0:
   0 0 0 0 0 0 0 13 21 34
   sequence after applying replace_if even with 0:
   0 1 1 0 3 5 0 13 21 0
 */

class EvenValue {
public:
    bool operator()( int value ) {
        return value % 2 ? false : true; }
};

int main()
{
    int new_value = 0;

    int ia[] = { 0, 1, 1, 2, 3, 5, 8, 13, 21, 34 };
    vector< int, allocator > vec( ia, ia+10 );
    ostream_iterator< int >  ofile( cout, " " );

    cout << "original element sequence:\n";
    copy( ia, ia+10, ofile ); cout << '\n';

    replace_if( &ia[0], &ia[10],
                bind2nd(less<int>(),10), new_value );

    cout << "sequence after applying replace_if < 10 with 0:\n";
    copy( ia, ia+10, ofile ); cout << '\n';

    replace_if( vec.begin(), vec.end(),
                EvenValue(), new_value );

    cout << "sequence after applying replace_if even with 0:\n";
    copy( vec.begin(), vec.end(), ofile ); cout << '\n';
}
```

reverse()

```
template< class BidirectionalIterator >
void
reverse( BidirectionalIterator first,
         BidirectionalIterator last );
```

reverse() reverses the order of elements in a container within the range marked off by [first,last). For example, given the sequence {0,1,1,2,3}, the reverse sequence is {3,2,1,1,0}.

reverse_copy()

```
template< class BidirectionalIterator, class OutputIterator >
OutputIterator
reverse_copy( BidirectionalIterator first,
              BidirectionalIterator last, OutputIterator result );
```

reverse_copy() exhibits the same behavior as reverse() except that the new sequence is copied into the container beginning at result. The returned OutputIterator points one past the last value copied. The original sequence is unchanged.

```
#include <algorithm>
#include <list>
#include <string>
#include <iostream.h>

/*
 * generates:
   Original sequence of strings:
        Signature of all things I am here to
        read seaspawn and seawrack that rusty boot

   Sequence after reverse() applied:
        boot rusty that seawrack and seaspawn read to
        here am I things all of Signature
 */

class print_elements {
public:
   void operator()( string elem ) {
      cout << elem
           << ( _line_cnt++%8 ? " " : "\n\t" );
   }

   static void reset_line_cnt() { _line_cnt = 1; }

private:
   static int _line_cnt;
};

int print_elements::_line_cnt = 1;

int main()
{
   string sa[] = { "Signature", "of", "all", "things",
        "I", "am", "here", "to", "read",
        "seaspawn", "and", "seawrack", "that",
        "rusty", "boot"
   };
```

```
            list< string, allocator > slist( sa, sa+15 );

            cout << "Original sequence of strings:\n\t";
            for_each( slist.begin(), slist.end(), print_elements() );
            cout << "\n\n";

            reverse( slist.begin(), slist.end() );

            print_elements::reset_line_cnt();

            cout << "Sequence after reverse() applied:\n\t";
            for_each( slist.begin(), slist.end(), print_elements() );
            cout << "\n";

            list< string, allocator > slist_copy( slist.size() );
            reverse_copy( slist.begin(), slist.end(),
                          slist_copy.begin() );
        }
```

rotate()

```
        template< class ForwardIterator >
        void
        rotate( ForwardIterator first,
                ForwardIterator middle, ForwardIterator last );
```

rotate() moves the elements marked by the range [first,middle) to the end of the container. The element addressed by middle becomes the first element of the container. For example, given the word "hissboo", a rotation around the element 'b' would turn the word into "boohiss".

rotate_copy()

```
        template< class ForwardIterator, class OutputIterator >
        OutputIterator
        rotate_copy( ForwardIterator first, ForwardIterator middle,
                     ForwardIterator last,  OutputIterator result );
```

rotate_copy() behaves the same as rotate(), except that the rotated sequence is copied to the container marked off by result. The returned OutputIterator points one past the last element copied. The original sequence is unchanged.

```
        #include <algorithm>
        #include <vector>
        #include <iostream.h>

        /*
         * generates:
           original element sequence:
           1 3 5 7 9 0 2 4 6 8 10
```

```
      rotate on middle element(0) ::
      0 2 4 6 8 10 1 3 5 7 9
      rotate on next to last element(8) ::
      8 10 1 3 5 7 9 0 2 4 6
      rotate_copy on middle element ::
      7 9 0 2 4 6 8 10 1 3 5
 */

int main()
{
   int ia[] = { 1, 3, 5, 7, 9, 0, 2, 4, 6, 8, 10 };

   vector< int, allocator > vec( ia, ia+11 );
   ostream_iterator< int >  ofile( cout, " " );

   cout << "original element sequence:\n";
   copy( vec.begin(), vec.end(), ofile ); cout << '\n';

   rotate( &ia[0], &ia[5], &ia[11] );

   cout << "rotate on middle element(0) ::\n";
   copy( ia, ia+11, ofile ); cout << '\n';

   rotate( vec.begin(), vec.end()-2, vec.end() );

   cout << "rotate on next to last element(8) ::\n";
   copy( vec.begin(), vec.end(), ofile ); cout << '\n';

   vector< int, allocator > vec_res( vec.size() );

   rotate_copy( vec.begin(), vec.begin()+vec.size()/2,
                vec.end(), vec_res.begin() );

   cout << "rotate_copy on middle element ::\n";
   copy( vec_res.begin(), vec_res.end(), ofile );
   cout << '\n';
}
```

search()

```
template< class ForwardIterator1, class ForwardIterator2 >
ForwardIterator
search( ForwardIterator1 first1, ForwardIterator1 last1,
        ForwardIterator2 first2, ForwardIterator2 last2 );

template< class ForwardIterator1, class ForwardIterator2,
          class BinaryPredicate >
ForwardIterator
search( ForwardIterator1 first1, ForwardIterator1 last1,
```

```
         ForwardIterator2 first2, ForwardIterator2 last2,
         BinaryPredicate pred );
```

Given two ranges, search() returns an iterator addressing the first position in the range marked by [first1,last1), in which the second range occurs as a subsequence. If the subsequence does not occur, last1 is returned. For example, within Mississippi, the subsequence iss occurs twice, and search() returns an iterator to the start of the first instance. By default, the equality operator is used for comparison of the elements; the second version allows the user to supply a comparison operation to be used.

```
#include <algorithm>
#include <vector>
#include <iostream.h>

/*
 * generates:
   Expecting to find the substring 'ate': a t e
   Expecting to find the substring 'vat': v a t
 */

int main()
{
    ostream_iterator< char > ofile( cout, " " );

    char str[ 25 ] = "a fine and private place";
    char substr[]  = "ate";

    char *found_str = search(str,str+25,substr,substr+3);

    cout << "Expecting to find the substring 'ate': ";
    copy( found_str, found_str+3, ofile ); cout << '\n';

    vector< char, allocator > vec( str, str+24 );
    vector< char, allocator > subvec(3);

    subvec[0]='v'; subvec[1]='a'; subvec[2]='t';

    vector< char, allocator >::iterator iter;
    iter = search( vec.begin(), vec.end(),
                   subvec.begin(), subvec.end(),
                   equal_to< char >() );

    cout << "Expecting to find the substring 'vat': ";
    copy( iter, iter+3, ofile ); cout << '\n';
}
```

search_n()

```
template< class ForwardIterator, class Size, class Type >
ForwardIterator
search_n( ForwardIterator first, ForwardIterator last,
         Size count, const Type &value );

template< class ForwardIterator, class Size,
         class Type, class BinaryPredicate >
ForwardIterator
search_n( ForwardIterator first, ForwardIterator last,
         Size count, const Type &value, BinaryPredicate pred );
```

search_n() looks for a subsequence of count occurrences of value within the sequence marked by [first,last). If count occurrences of value are not found, last is returned. For example, to find the subsequence ss within the sequence Mississippi, value would be set to 's' and count to 2. Alternatively, to find the two instances of the substring ssi, value would be set to "ssi" and count once again to 2. search_n() returns an iterator to the first element of the found value. By default, the equality operator is used for comparison of the elements; the second version allows the user to supply a comparison operation to be used.

```
#include <algorithm>
#include <vector>
#include <iostream.h>

/*
 * generates:
   Expecting to find two instances of 'o': o o
   Expecting to find the substring 'mou':  m o u
 */

int main()
{
    ostream_iterator< char >  ofile( cout, " " );

    const char blank = ' ';
    const char oh    = 'o';

    char str[ 26 ]  = "oh my a mouse ate a moose";
    char *found_str = search_n( str, str+25, 2, oh );

    cout << "Expecting to find two instances of 'o': ";
    copy( found_str, found_str+2, ofile ); cout << '\n';

    vector< char, allocator > vec( str, str+25 );

    // find the first sequence in which three characters
    // do not equal a blank space: mou of mouse
```

```
        vector< char, allocator >::iterator iter;
        iter = search_n( vec.begin(), vec.end(), 3,
                        blank, not_equal_to< char >() );

        cout << "Expecting to find the substring 'mou':  ";
        copy( iter, iter+3, ofile ); cout << '\n';
    }
```

set_difference()

```
        template < class InputIterator1, class InputIterator2,
                   class OutputIterator >
        OutputIterator
        set_difference( InputIterator1 first1, InputIterator1 last1,
                        InputIterator2 first2, InputIterator2 last2,
                        OutputIterator result );

        template < class InputIterator1, class InputIterator2,
                   class OutputIterator, class Compare >
        OutputIterator
        set_difference( InputIterator1 first1, InputIterator1 last1,
                        InputIterator2 first2, InputIterator2 last2,
                        OutputIterator result, Compare comp );
```

set_difference() constructs a sorted sequence of the elements found in the first sequence (marked off by [first1,last1)) but not contained in the second (marked off by [first2,last2)). For example, given the two sequences {0,1,2,3} and {0,2,4,6}, the set difference is {1,3}. The returned OutputIterator addresses one past the last element placed within the container marked off by result. The first version assumes that the sequences were sorted using the less than operator of the underlying type; the second version assumes the sequences were sorted using comp.

set_intersection()

```
        template < class InputIterator1, class InputIterator2,
                   class OutputIterator >
        OutputIterator
        set_intersection( InputIterator1 first1, InputIterator1 last1,
                          InputIterator2 first2, InputIterator2 last2,
                          OutputIterator result );

        template < class InputIterator1, class InputIterator2,
                   class OutputIterator, class Compare >
        OutputIterator
        set_intersection( InputIterator1 first1, InputIterator1 last1,
                          InputIterator2 first2, InputIterator2 last2,
                          OutputIterator result, Compare comp );
```

set_intersection() constructs a sorted sequence of the elements present in both sequences marked off by [first1,last1) and [first2,last2). For example, given the two sequences {0,1,2,3} and {0,2,4,6}, the set intersection is {0,2}. The element is copied from the first sequence. The returned OutputIterator addresses one past the last element placed within the container marked off by result. The first version assumes that the sequences were sorted using the less than operator of the underlying type; the second version assumes the sequences were sorted using comp.

set_symmetric_difference()

```
template < class InputIterator1, class InputIterator2,
          class OutputIterator >
OutputIterator
set_symmetric_difference(
     InputIterator1 first1, InputIterator1 last1,
     InputIterator2 first2, InputIterator2 last2,
     OutputIterator result );

template < class InputIterator1, class InputIterator2,
          class OutputIterator, class Compare >
OutputIterator
set_symmetric_difference(
     InputIterator1 first1, InputIterator1 last1,
     InputIterator2 first2, InputIterator2 last2,
     OutputIterator result, Compare comp );
```

set_symmetric_difference() constructs a sorted sequence of the elements that are present in the first container but not present in the second, and those elements present in the second container but not in the first. For example, given the two sequences {0,1,2,3} and {0,2,4,6}, the set symmetric difference is {1,3,4,6}. The returned OutputIterator addresses one past the last element placed within the container marked off by result. The first version assumes that the sequences were sorted using the less than operator of the underlying type; the second version assumes the sequences were sorted using comp.

set_union()

```
template < class InputIterator1, class InputIterator2,
          class OutputIterator >
OutputIterator
set_union( InputIterator1 first1, InputIterator1 last1,
           InputIterator2 first2, InputIterator2 last2,
           OutputIterator result );

template < class InputIterator1, class InputIterator2,
          class OutputIterator, class Compare >
OutputIterator
set_union( InputIterator1 first1, InputIterator1 last1,
```

```
                    InputIterator2 first2, InputIterator2 last2,
                    OutputIterator result, Compare comp );
```

set_union() constructs a sorted sequence of the element values contained within
the two ranges marked off by [first1,last1) and [first2,last2). For example, given
the two sequences {0,1,2,3} and {0,2,4,6}, the set union is {0,1,2,3,4,6}. If the element is
present in both containers, such as 0 and 2 in our example, the element of the first container is copied. The returned OutputIterator addresses one past the last element
placed within the container marked off by result. The first version assumes that the
sequences were sorted using the less than operator of the underlying type; the second
version assumes the sequences were sorted using comp.

```
            #include <algorithm>
            #include <set>
            #include <string>
            #include <iostream.h>

            /*
             * generates:
               set #1 elements:
                   Eeyore Piglet Pooh Tigger

               set #2 elements:
                   Heffalump Pooh Woozles

               set_union() elements:
                   Eeyore Heffalump Piglet Pooh Tigger Woozles

               set_intersection() elements:
                   Pooh

               set_difference() elements:
                   Eeyore Piglet Tigger

               set_symmetric_difference() elements:
                   Eeyore Heffalump Piglet Tigger Woozles
             */

            int main()
            {
                string str1[] = { "Pooh", "Piglet", "Tigger", "Eeyore" };
                string str2[] = { "Pooh", "Heffalump", "Woozles" };
                ostream_iterator< string >  ofile( cout, " " );

                set<string,less<string>,allocator> set1( str1, str1+4 );
                set<string,less<string>,allocator> set2( str2, str2+3 );

                cout << "set #1 elements:\n\t";
                copy( set1.begin(), set1.end(), ofile ); cout << "\n\n";
```

```
        cout << "set #2 elements:\n\t";
        copy( set2.begin(), set2.end(), ofile ); cout << "\n\n";

        set<string,less<string>,allocator> res;
        set_union( set1.begin(), set1.end(),
                   set2.begin(), set2.end(),
                   inserter( res, res.begin() ));

        cout << "set_union() elements:\n\t";
        copy( res.begin(), res.end(), ofile ); cout << "\n\n";

        res.clear();
        set_intersection( set1.begin(), set1.end(),
                          set2.begin(), set2.end(),
                          inserter( res, res.begin() ));

        cout << "set_intersection() elements:\n\t";
        copy( res.begin(), res.end(), ofile ); cout << "\n\n";

        res.clear();
        set_difference( set1.begin(), set1.end(),
                        set2.begin(), set2.end(),
                        inserter( res, res.begin() ));

        cout << "set_difference() elements:\n\t";
        copy( res.begin(), res.end(), ofile ); cout << "\n\n";

        res.clear();
        set_symmetric_difference( set1.begin(), set1.end(),
                                  set2.begin(), set2.end(),
                                  inserter( res, res.begin() ));

        cout << "set_symmetric_difference() elements:\n\t";
        copy( res.begin(), res.end(), ofile ); cout << "\n\n";
}
```

sort()

```
template< class RandomAccessIterator >
void
sort( RandomAccessIterator first,
      RandomAccessIterator last );

template< class RandomAccessIterator, class Compare >
void
sort( RandomAccessIterator first,
      RandomAccessIterator last, Compare comp );
```

sort() reorders the elements in the range marked off by [first,last) in ascending order using the less than operator of the underlying type. The second version orders the elements based on comp. (To preserve the order of equal elements, use stable_sort() rather than sort().) We do not provide an explicit program illustrating sort() since it is used in many of the other program examples, such as binary_search(), equal_range(), and inplace_merge().

stable_partition()

```
template< class BidirectionalIterator, class Predicate >
BidirectionalIterator
stable_partition( BidirectionalIterator first,
                  BidirectionalIterator last,
                  Predicate pred );
```

stable_partition() behaves exactly the same as partition() except that stable_partition() guarantees to preserve the relative order of the elements within the container. Here is the same program as executed for partition(), modified to invoke stable_partition():

```
#include <algorithm>
#include <vector>
#include <iostream.h>

/*
 * generates:
   original element sequence:
   29 23 20 22 17 15 26 51 19 12 35 40
   stable_partition on even element:
   20 22 26 12 40 29 23 17 15 51 19
   stable_partition of less than 25:
   23 20 22 17 15 19 12 29 26 51 35 40
 */

class even_elem {
public:
    bool operator()( int elem ) {
        return elem%2 ? false : true;
    }
};

int main()
{
    int ia[] = { 29,23,20,22,17,15,26,51,19,12,35,40 };
    vector< int, allocator > vec( ia, ia+12 );
    ostream_iterator< int >  ofile( cout, " " );

    cout << "original element sequence:\n";
```

```
        copy( vec.begin(), vec.end(), ofile ); cout << '\n';

        stable_partition( &ia[0], &ia[12], even_elem() );

        cout << "stable_partition on even element:\n";
        copy( ia, ia+11, ofile ); cout << '\n';

        stable_partition( vec.begin(), vec.end(),
                          bind2nd(less<int>(),25)  );

        cout << "stable_partition of less than 25:\n";
        copy( vec.begin(), vec.end(), ofile ); cout << '\n';
    }
```

stable_sort()

```
        template< class RandomAccessIterator >
        void
        stable_sort( RandomAccessIterator first,
                     RandomAccessIterator last );

        template< class RandomAccessIterator, class Compare >
        void
        stable_sort( RandomAccessIterator first,
                     RandomAccessIterator last, Compare comp );
```

stable_sort() preserves the order of equal elements within the container as it re-orders the elements in the range marked off by [first,last) in ascending order using the less than operator of the underlying type. The second version orders the elements based on comp.

```
        #include <algorithm>
        #include <vector>
        #include <iostream.h>

        /*
         * generates:
           original element sequence:
           29 23 20 22 12 17 15 26 51 19 12 23 35 40
           stable sort -- default ascending order:
           12 12 15 17 19 20 22 23 23 26 29 35 40 51
           stable sort: descending order:
           51 40 35 29 26 23 23 22 20 19 17 15 12 12
         */

        int main()
        {
            int ia[] = { 29,23,20,22,12,17,15,26,51,19,12,23,35,40 };
            vector< int, allocator > vec( ia, ia+14 );
            ostream_iterator< int >  ofile( cout, " " );
```

```
        cout << "original element sequence:\n";
        copy( vec.begin(), vec.end(), ofile ); cout << '\n';

        stable_sort( &ia[0], &ia[14] );

        cout << "stable sort -- default ascending order:\n";
        copy( ia, ia+14, ofile ); cout << '\n';

        stable_sort( vec.begin(), vec.end(), greater<int>() );

        cout << "stable sort: descending order:\n";
        copy( vec.begin(), vec.end(), ofile ); cout << '\n';
    }
```

swap()

```
        template< class Type >
        void
        swap ( Type &ob1, Type &ob2 );
```

swap() exchange the values stored in objects ob1 and ob2.

```
        #include <algorithm>
        #include <vector>
        #include <iostream.h>

        /*
         * generates:
           original element sequence:
           3 4 5 0 1 2
           sequence applying swap() to support bubble sort:
           0 1 2 3 4 5
         */

        int main()
        {
            int ia[]  = { 3, 4, 5, 0, 1, 2 };
            vector< int, allocator > vec( ia, ia+6 );

            for ( int ix = 0; ix < 6; ++ix )
            for ( int iy = ix; iy < 6; ++iy ) {
            if ( vec[iy] < vec[ ix ] )
            swap( vec[iy], vec[ix] );
            }

            ostream_iterator< int >  ofile( cout, " " );

            cout << "original element sequence:\n";
            copy( ia, ia+6, ofile ); cout << '\n';
```

```
        cout << "sequence applying swap() "
             << "to support bubble sort:\n";

        copy( vec.begin(), vec.end(), ofile ); cout << '\n';
}
```

swap_range()

```
        template <class ForwardIterator1, class ForwardIterator2 >
        ForwardIterator2
        swap_range( ForwardIterator1 first1, ForwardIterator1 last,
                ForwardIterator2 first2 );
```

swap_range() exchanges the element values marked off by [first1,last) with the values beginning at first2. The two sequences can either be disjointed sequences within the same container or within two separate containers. The run-time behavior is undefined if the sequence beginning at first2 is less than that marked off by [first1,last) or if the two sequences overlap within the same container. swap_range() returns the iterator of the second sequence, pointing one past the last value swapped.

```
        #include <algorithm>
        #include <vector>
        #include <iostream.h>

        /*
         * generates:
           original element sequence of first container:
           0 1 2 3 4 5 6 7 8 9
           original element sequence of second container:
           5 6 7 8 9
           array after swap_ranges() in middle of array:
           5 6 7 8 9 0 1 2 3 4
           first container after swap_ranges() of two vectors:
           5 6 7 8 9 5 6 7 8 9
           second container after swap_ranges() of two vectors:
           0 1 2 3 4
         */

        int main()
        {
            int ia[]  = { 0, 1, 2, 3, 4, 5, 6, 7, 8, 9 };
            int ia2[] = { 5, 6, 7, 8, 9 };

            vector< int, allocator > vec( ia, ia+10 );
            vector< int, allocator > vec2( ia2, ia2+5 );

            ostream_iterator< int >  ofile( cout, " " );

            cout << "original element sequence of first container:\n";
```

```
copy( vec.begin(), vec.end(), ofile ); cout << '\n';

cout << "original element sequence of second container:\n";
copy( vec2.begin(), vec2.end(), ofile ); cout << '\n';

// swap within the same sequence
swap_ranges( &ia[0], &ia[5], &ia[5] );

cout << "array after swap_ranges() in middle of array:\n";
copy( ia, ia+10, ofile ); cout << '\n';

// swap across containers
vector< int, allocator >::iterator last =
        find( vec.begin(), vec.end(), 5 );

swap_ranges( vec.begin(), last, vec2.begin() );

cout << "first container after "
     << "swap_ranges() of two vectors:\n";

copy( vec.begin(), vec.end(), ofile ); cout << '\n';

cout << "second container after "
     << "swap_ranges() of two vectors:\n";

copy( vec2.begin(), vec2.end(), ofile ); cout << '\n';
}
```

transform()

```
template< class InputIterator, class OutputIterator,
          class UnaryOperation >
OutputIterator
transform( InputIterator first, InputIterator last,
           OutputIterator result, UnaryOperation op );

template< class InputIterator1, class InputIterator2,
          class OutputIterator, class BinaryOperation >
OutputIterator
transform( InputIterator1 first1, InputIterator1 last,
           InputIterator2 first2, OutputIterator result,
           BinaryOperation bop );
```

The first version of tranform() generates a sequence of elements by invoking op on each element in the range marked off by [first,last). For example, given a sequence {0,1,1,2,3,5} and a function object Double, which doubles each element, the resulting sequence is {0,2,2,4,6,10}.

The second version generates a sequence of elements by invoking bop to a pair of elements, one from the sequence marked off by [first1,last) and the second from the

sequence with the beginning that is marked by first2. The run-time behavior is undefined if the second sequence contains less elements than the first sequence. For example,
given the sequences {1,3,5,9} and {2,4,6,8}, and a function object AddAndDouble that
adds the two elements then doubles their sum, the resulting sequence is {6,14,22,34}.

Both versions of transform() place the resulting sequence in the container marked
off by result. result can address one of the input containers, in effect replacing the
current elements with the elements returned by transform(). The returned OutputIterator points to one-past the last element assigned to result.

```
#include <algorithm>
#include <vector>
#include <math.h>
#include <iostream.h>

/*
 * generates:
   original array values: 3 5 8 13 21
   transform each element by doubling: 6 10 16 26 42
   transform each element by difference: 3 5 8 13 21
 */

int double_val( int val ) { return val + val; }
int difference( int val1, int val2 ) {
    return abs( val1 - val2 ); }

int main()
{
   int ia[]  = { 3, 5, 8, 13, 21 };
   vector<int, allocator> vec( 5 );
   ostream_iterator<int> outfile( cout, " " );

   cout << "original array values: ";
   copy( ia, ia+5, outfile ); cout << endl;

   cout << "transform each element by doubling: ";
   transform( ia, ia+5, vec.begin(), double_val );
   copy( vec.begin(), vec.end(), outfile ); cout << endl;

   cout << "transform each element by difference: ";
   transform( ia, ia+5, vec.begin(), outfile, difference );
   cout << endl;
}
```

unique()

```
template< class ForwardIterator >
ForwardIterator
unique( ForwardIterator first,
        ForwardIterator last );
```

```
template< class ForwardIterator, class BinaryPredicate >
ForwardIterator
unique( ForwardIterator first,
        ForwardIterator last, BinaryPredicate pred );
```

All consecutive groups of elements containing either the same value (using the equality operator of the underlying type) or evaluating as true when passed to pred are collapsed into a single element. Thus, for example, in the word mississippi, the *semantic* result is "misisipi." Notice that since the three i's are not consecutive, they are not collapsed. Similarly, the two pairs of s's, since they are not consecutive, are not collapsed into a single instance. To guarantee all duplicated elements are collapsed, we would first sort the container.

Actually, unique() behaves slightly nonintuitively, similar to the remove() algorithm. In both cases the container's actual size is not changed. Each unique element is assigned in turn to the next free slot beginning with first.

In our example, therefore, the *physical* result is misisipippi, where the character sequence ppi represents, so to speak, the *leftover* piece of the algorithm. The returned ForwardIterator marks the beginning of the leftover. Typically this iterator is then passed to erase() to delete the invalid elements. (Since the built-in array does not support the erase() operation, unique() is less suitable for arrays; unique_copy() is more appropriate.)

unique_copy()

```
template< class InputIterator, class OutputIterator >
OutputIterator
unique_copy( InputIterator first, InputIterator last,
             OutputIterator result );

template< class InputIterator, class OutputIterator,
          class BinaryPredicate >
OutputIterator
unique_copy( InputIterator first,  InputIterator last,
             OutputIterator result, BinaryPredicate pred );
```

unique_copy() copies a single instance of each consecutive group of elements containing either the same value (using the equality operator of the underlying type) or evaluating as true when passed to pred (see unique() for a description). To guarantee all duplicated elements are eliminated, we would first sort the container. The returned OutputIterator addresses the end of the target container.

```
#include <algorithm>
#include <vector>
#include <string>
#include <iterator>
#include <iostream.h>

template <class Type>
```

```
void print_elements( Type elem ) { cout << elem << " "; }

void (*pfi)( int ) = print_elements;
void (*pfs)( string ) = print_elements;

int main()
{
    int ia[] = { 0, 1, 0, 2, 0, 3, 0, 4, 0, 5 };

    vector<int,allocator> vec( ia, ia+10 );
    vector<int,allocator>::iterator vec_iter;

    // results in unchanged sequence: 0s are not consecutive
    // generates: 0 1 0 2 0 3 0 4 0 5
    vec_iter = unique( vec.begin(), vec.end() );
    for_each( vec.begin(), vec.end(), pfi ); cout << "\n\n";

    // sort vector: 0 0 0 0 0 1 2 3 4 5
    // then apply unique:
    // generates: 0 1 2 3 4 5 2 3 4 5

    sort( vec.begin(), vec.end() );
    vec_iter = unique( vec.begin(), vec.end() );
    for_each( vec.begin(), vec.end(), pfi ); cout << "\n\n";

    // erase the invalid elements from container
    // generates: 0 1 2 3 4 5

    vec.erase( vec_iter, vec.end() );
    for_each( vec.begin(), vec.end(), pfi ); cout << "\n\n";

    string sa[] = { "enough", "is", "enough",
                    "enough", "is", "good"
    };

    vector<string,allocator> svec( sa, sa+6 );
    vector<string,allocator> vec_result( svec.size() );
    vector<string,allocator>::iterator svec_iter;

    sort( svec.begin(), svec.end() );
    svec_iter = unique_copy( svec.begin(), svec.end(),
                             vec_result.begin() );

    // generates: enough good is
    for_each( vec_result.begin(), svec_iter, pfs );
    cout << "\n\n";
}
```

upper_bound()

```
template< class ForwardIterator, class Type >
ForwardIterator
upper_bound( ForwardIterator first,
             ForwardIterator last, const Type &value );

template< class ForwardIterator, class Type, class Compare >
ForwardIterator
upper_bound( ForwardIterator first,
             ForwardIterator last, const Type &value,
             Compare comp );
```

upper_bound() returns an iterator addressing the last position within the sorted sequence marked off by the iterator pair [first,last) into which value may be inserted without violating the sorted ordering of the container. This position will mark off a value that is greater than value. For example, given the following sequence,

```
int ia[] = {12,15,17,19,20,22,23,26,29,35,40,51};
```

a call of upper_bound() with a value of 21 returns an iterator addressing the value 22. A call of upper_bound() with a value of 22 returns an iterator addressing the value 23. The first version uses the less than operator of the underlying type; the second version orders the elements based on comp.

```
#include <algorithm>
#include <vector>
#include <assert.h>
#include <iostream.h>

template <class Type>
void print_elements( Type elem ) { cout << elem << " "; }

void (*pfi)( int ) = print_elements;

int main()
{
    int ia[] = {29,23,20,22,17,15,26,51,19,12,35,40};
    vector<int,allocator> vec(ia,ia+12);

    sort(ia,ia+12);
    int *iter = upper_bound(ia,ia+12,19);
    assert( *iter == 20 );

    sort( vec.begin(), vec.end(), greater<int>() );
    vector<int,allocator>::iterator iter_vec;

    iter_vec = upper_bound( vec.begin(), vec.end(),
                            27, greater<int>() );

    assert( *iter_vec == 26 );
```

```
    // generates: 51 40 35 29 27 26 23 22 20 19 17 15 12
    vec.insert( iter_vec, 27 );
    for_each( vec.begin(), vec.end(), pfi ); cout << "\n\n";
}
```

Heap Algorithms

The standard library heap is a *max-heap*. A max-heap is a form of binary tree represented as an array in which the key value in each node is either larger than or equal to the key value of its children (see [SEDGEWICK88] for a full discussion). (An alternative representation is a *min-heap*, in which the key value at any node is less than or equal to that of its children.) In the standard library representation, the largest key value (think of it as the root of the tree) is always at the start of the array. The following sequence of letters, for example, fulfills the requirements of a heap:

```
sequence of letters meeting heap requirements
X   T   O   G   S   M   N   A   E   R   A   I
```

In this example, X is the root node, with the left child T and right child O. Notice that the children are not required to be in sorted order (that is, the left child does not need to be less than the right). G and S are the children of T, while M and N are the children of O. Similarly, A and E are the children of G, R and A are the children of S, I is the left child of M, and N is a leaf node without children.

The four generic heap algorithms provide support for the creation and manipulation of a heap: make_heap(), pop_heap(), push_heap(), and sort_heap(). The latter three algorithms presume that the sequence marked off by the iterator pair represents an actual heap (if the sequence is not, then the run-time behavior of the algorithms is undefined). Note that a list container, because it does not support random access, cannot be used for a heap. While a built-in array can be used to support a heap, the pop_heap() and push_heap() algorithms are difficult to use with arrays since the two algorithms require the resizing of the array. We briefly introduce each of the four algorithms, then illustrate their use with a small program.

make_heap()

```
template< class RandomAccessIterator >
void
make_heap( RandomAccessIterator first,
           RandomAccessIterator last );

template< class RandomAccessIterator, class Compare >
void
make_heap( RandomAccessIterator first,
           RandomAccessIterator last, Compare comp );
```

make_heap() makes into a heap the elements within the range marked off by
[first,last). The two-argument version uses the less than operator of the underlying
type for ordering; the second version orders the elements based on comp.

pop_heap()

```
template< class RandomAccessIterator >
void
pop_heap( RandomAccessIterator first,
        RandomAccessIterator last );

template< class RandomAccessIterator, class Compare >
void
pop_heap( RandomAccessIterator first,
        RandomAccessIterator last, Compare comp );
```

pop_heap() does not actually pop the largest element from the heap, but rather reorders the heap. It swaps first with last-1, then remakes the sequence into a heap using the range [first,last-1). We can then either access the "popped" element using
the container member operation back(), or really remove it using pop_back(). The two-
argument version uses the less than operator of the underlying type for ordering; the
second version orders the elements based on comp.

push_heap()

```
template< class RandomAccessIterator >
void
push_heap( RandomAccessIterator first,
        RandomAccessIterator last );
template< class RandomAccessIterator, class Compare >
void
push_heap( RandomAccessIterator first,
        RandomAccessIterator last, Compare comp );
```

push_heap() presumes that the sequence marked off by the range [first,last-1)
is already a valid heap, and that the new element to be added to the heap is in position
last-1. It remakes the sequence into a heap using the range [first,last). Prior to invoking push_heap(), we must insert the element to the back of the container, perhaps
using the push_back() operator (this is illustrated in the following program example).
The two-argument version uses the less than operator of the underlying type for ordering; the second version orders the elements based on comp.

sort_heap()

```
template< class RandomAccessIterator >
void
sort_heap( RandomAccessIterator first,
        RandomAccessIterator last );
```

```
template< class RandomAccessIterator, class Compare >
void
sort_heap( RandomAccessIterator first,
           RandomAccessIterator last, Compare comp );
```

sort_heap() sorts the sequence in the range [first,last). It presumes the sequence is a valid heap (its behavior is otherwise undefined). (Of course, the sorted heap is no longer a valid heap!) The two-argument version uses the less than operator of the underlying type for ordering; the second version orders the elements based on comp.

```cpp
#include <algorithm>
#include <vector>
#include <iostream.h>

template <class Type>
void print_elements( Type elem ) { cout << elem << " "; }

int main()
{
   int ia[] = {29,23,20,22,17,15,26,51,19,12,35,40 };
   vector< int, allocator > vec( ia, ia+12 );


   // generates: 51 35 40 23 29 20 26 22 19 12 17 15
   make_heap( &ia[0], &ia[12] );
   void (*pfi)( int ) = print_elements;
   for_each( ia, ia+12, pfi ); cout << "\n\n";

   // generates: 12 17 15 19 23 20 26 51 22 29 35 40
   // a min-heap: root is smallest element

   make_heap( vec.begin(), vec.end(), greater<int>() );
   for_each( vec.begin(), vec.end(), pfi ); cout << "\n\n";

   // generates: 12 15 17 19 20 22 23 26 29 35 40 51
   sort_heap( ia, ia+12 );
   for_each(  ia, ia+12, pfi ); cout << "\n\n";

   // add an additional, new smallest element:
   vec.push_back( 8 );

   // generates: 8 17 12 19 23 15 26 51 22 29 35 40 20
   // should place newest smallest element at root

   push_heap( vec.begin(), vec.end(), greater<int>() );
   for_each(  vec.begin(), vec.end(), pfi ); cout << "\n\n";
```

```
        // generates: 12 17 15 19 23 20 26 51 22 29 35 40 8
        // should replace smallest element with second smallest

        pop_heap( vec.begin(), vec.end(), greater<int>() );
        for_each( vec.begin(), vec.end(), pfi ); cout << "\n\n";
}
```

Index